1984

Treasury of
WORLD LITERATURE

Treasury of
WORLD
LITERATURE

Edited by

DAGOBERT D. RUNES

GREENWOOD PRESS, PUBLISHERS
NEW YORK

SIBI ET AMICIS

FOREWORD

A TREASURY of literature is a personal matter. It represents one man's choice of creative writing taken from the vast reservoir at his disposal. Thus, what is inspiring to one may seem dull to another, and quite frequently shallow waters appear to have profound depths to one who is distant.

Our libraries abound with anthologies and symposia, housing in their various abodes segments of one or another literary activity. Their scope differs as widely as their taste. It is not my place to sit in judgment upon their failings or their merits. In the last analysis there are no absolutely valid criteria by which we may adjudicate with finality a piece of writing as being creative. Those who have wandered through the ways and bypaths of the world of books know only too well that the same piece which is placed upon a pedestal by some as being the ultimate in beauty and conception, is thrown away by others as just so much trash.

I say in sincere humility that my judgment is biased—as it must be by my background and my experience—and that in all likelihood I have as far as this volume is concerned muted the voices of many who are truly outstanding, and perhaps made some speak who had better remained silent. As I have worked in three continents, my selections must necessarily reflect them all. I should like to remark at this point that in my opinion the Western world, in its books, has not given Asia an appropriate place on the dais.

It may be that some readers will think I have given in this anthology more space to the Asians than they deserve. It is my own opinion that I have given them not enough. But some of our Eastern friends write with a decidedly Oriental mannerism, so that in spite of its enchantment I was afraid I would not help their cause by presenting the available.

The literature before us is of the written word. The literature of the spoken word, which undoubtedly lived for many thousands of years before that, reverberates in some of the early writings. Some of the renowned fabulists of India and China, for instance, wove their stories from legends and tales that had lived with their people for millennia. In later years, the Greeks and the Romans, and in our era the French and the Germans, varied these fables to suit the taste and the milieu of their people. We shall never know some of the great men or women who originated these charming tales that have ever since bewitched young and old.

For the poetry of old in its purest form, we must turn to Israel, where three thousand and more years ago we find such gems as the Psalter brightening the life of a desert people. Whether all or only some of this was written by the Shepherd King, or by his scholarly son Solomon, is not important, but in their gracefulness and the ardor of their appeal to yearning mankind, nothing else of that era can compare to the songs ringing from King David's harp.

China, India, Persia and Japan spread open a glittering wealth of poetry at the beginning of our medieval era, when the Western world had little literature to give its people aside from some imitations of the Hellenic and Roman epochs long gone by. The riches of Asia's literary treasures are still to be explored.

In the choice of my selections I took pains to omit the products of the professional court writers and palace versifiers whether they were stationed in Bagdad, Rome or the Kremlin. Eulogies to Nero are as painful to listen to as those fabricated for the Queen of England or comrade Stalin.

I have given comparatively little space to the novel, for this literary form is a rather recent one, sometimes compounded of little more than journalistic plots and intricate sex situations. Occasionally these novels, though they frantically hoist the flag of some social cause, do little more than wallow in the sordid mudbanks of cruelty, perversion, criminality, and all types of social abuse. The diaries of a slum dweller or the memoirs of a bus driver do not necessarily make literature.

Wherever possible I have used existing translations with only minor adjustments. It is, of course, frequently difficult to translate works of creative literature, especially when cast in the form of poetry.

I should like to thank Mrs. Rose Morse and Mr. Richard Passmore for their assistance in preparing the manuscript.

D. D. R.

NOTE: Western translators have rendered the names of Oriental authors in a bewildering variety of spellings and styles—family name first, family name last, and so on. In this book such names are given in the form which seems to be most frequently encountered and which therefore will be most easily recognized by English-speaking readers.

Treasury of
WORLD LITERATURE

CONTENTS

xiii

A

AESCHYLUS

AESCHYLUS (Greek, 525-456 B.C.). One of the most prolific and original of
the ancient dramatists. Believed to have written some 90 plays, of which only
7 remain—including *Prometheus Bound*, the *Oresteia* trilogy, and *Seven
Against Thebes*. Using Greek myths to convey philosophic ideas, his tragedies
have a moral grandeur unsurpassed to this day.

THE COMPLAINT OF PROMETHEUS

PROMETHEUS (alone)

O Holy Æther, and swift-winged Winds,
   And River-wells, and laughter innumerous
   Of yon Sea-waves! Earth, mother of us all,
And all-viewing cyclic Sun, I cry on you,—
Behold me a god, what I endure from gods!
   Behold, with throe on throe,
   How, wasted by this woe,
I wrestle down the myriad years of Time!
   Behold, how fast around me
The new King of the happy ones sublime
Has flung the chain he forged, has shamed and bound me!
Woe, woe! to-day's woe and coming morrow's
   I cover with one groan. And where is found me
     A limit to these sorrows?
And yet what word do I say? I have foreknown
Clearly all things that should be; nothing done
Comes sudden to my soul—and I must bear
What is ordained with patience, being aware
Necessity doth front the universe
With an invincible gesture. Yet this curse

1

Which strikes me now, I find it hard to brave
  In silence or in speech. Because I gave
Honor to mortals, I have yoked my soul
To this compelling fate. Because I stole
The secret fount of fire, whose bubbles went
Over the ferrule's brim, and manward sent
Art's mighty means and perfect rudiment,
That sin I expiate in this agony,
  Hung here in fetters, 'neath the blanching sky.
    Ah, ah me! what a sound,
What a fragrance sweeps up from a pinion unseen
Of a god, or a mortal, or nature between,
Sweeping up to this rock where the earth has her bound,
To have sight of my pangs, or some guerdon obtain—
Lo, a god in the anguish, a god in the chain!
    The god Zeus hateth sore,
    And his gods hate again,
As many as tread on his glorified floor,
Because I loved mortals too much evermore.
Alas me! what a murmur and motion I hear,
    As of birds flying near!
    And the air undersings
    The light stroke of their wings—
And all life that approaches I wait for in fear.

A PRAYER TO ARTEMIS

Strophe IV

  Though Zeus plan all things right,
Yet is his heart's desire full hard to trace;
    Nathless in every place
  Brightly it gleameth, e'en in darkest night,
Fraught with black fate to man's speech-gifted race.

Antistrophe IV

  Steadfast, ne'er thrown in fight,
The deed in brow of Zeus to ripeness brought;
    For wrapt in shadowy night,
    Tangled, unscanned by mortal sight,
Extend the pathways of his secret thought.

2

Strophe V

From towering hopes mortals he hurleth prone
    To utter doom: but for their fall
    No force arrayeth he; for all
   That gods devise is without effort wrought.
A mindful Spirit aloft on holy throne
   By inborn energy achieves his thought.

Antistrophe V

But let him mortal insolence behold:—
    How with proud contumacy rife.
    Wantons the stem in lusty life
My marriage craving;—frenzy over-bold,
Spur ever-pricking, goads them on to fate,
By ruin taught their folly all too late.

Strophe VI

Thus I complain, in piteous strain,
    Grief-laden, tear-evoking, shrill;
      Ah woe is me! woe! woe!
    Dirge-like it sounds; mine own death-trill
I pour, yet breathing vital air.
Hear, hill-crowned Apia, hear my prayer!
      Full well, O land,
My voice barbaric thou canst understand;
   While oft with rendings I assail
My byssine vesture and Sidonian veil.

Antistrophe VI

My nuptial right in Heaven's pure sight
    Pollution were, death-laden, rude;
      Ah woe is me! woe! woe!
    Alas for sorrow's murky brood!
Where will this billow hurl me? Where?
Hear, hill-crowned Apia, hear my prayer?
      Full well, O land,
My voice barbaric thou canst understand;
   While oft with rendings I assail
My byssine vesture and Sidonian veil.

3

The oar indeed and home with sails
Flax-tissued, swelled with favoring gales,
Stanch to the wave, from spear-storm free,
Have to this shore escorted me,
Not so far blame I destiny.
But may the all-seeing Father send
In fitting time propitious end;
So our dread Mother's mighty brood
The lordly couch may 'scape, ah me.
　　Unwedded, unsubdued!

Antistrophe VII

Meeting my will with will divine,
Daughter of Zeus, who here dost hold
　　Steadfast thy sacred shrine—
Me, Artemis unstained, behold.
Do thou, who sovereign might dost wield,
Virgin thyself, a virgin shield;
So our dread Mother's mighty brood
The lordly couch may 'scape, ah me,
　　Unwedded, unsubdued!

THE VISION OF CASSANDRA

Cassandra

Phœbus Apollo!

Chorus

Hark!
The lips at last unlocking.

Cassandra

Phœbus! Phœbus!

Chorus

Well, what of Phœbus, maiden? though a name
'Tis but disparagement to call upon
In misery

Cassandra

　Apollo! Apollo! Again!
Oh, the burning arrow through the brain!
　Phœbus Apollo! Apollo!

4

Chorus

Seemingly
Possessed indeed—whether by—

Cassandra

Phœbus! Phœbus!
Through trampled ashes, blood, and fiery rain,
Over water seething, and behind the breathing
War-horse in the darkness—till you rose again,
Took the helm—took the rein—

Chorus

As one that half asleep at dawn recalls
A night of Horror!

Cassandra

Hither, whither, Phœbus? And with whom,
Leading me, lighting me—

Chorus

I can answer that—

Cassandra

Down to what slaughter-house!
Foh! the smell of carnage through the door
Scares me from it—drags me toward it—
    Phœbus Apollo! Apollo!

Chorus

One of the dismal prophet-pack, it seems,
That hunt the trail of blood. But here at fault—
This is no den of slaughter, but the house
Of Agamemnon.

Cassandra

Down upon the towers,
Phantoms of two mangled children hover—and a famished man,
At an empty table glaring, seizes and devours!

Chorus

Thyestes and his children! Strange enough
For any maiden from abroad to know,
Or, knowing—

Cassandra

And look! in the chamber below
The terrible Woman, listening, watching,
Under a mask, preparing the blow
In the fold of her robe—

5

Chorus

Nay, but again at fault:
For in the tragic story of this House—
Unless, indeed the fatal Helen—
No woman—

Cassandra

No Woman—Tisiphone! Daughter
Of Tartarus—love-grinning Woman above,
Dragon-tailed under—honey-tongued, Harpy-clawed,
Into the glittering meshes of slaughter
She wheedles, entices him into the poisonous
Fold of the serpent—

Chorus

Peace, mad woman, peace!
Whose stony lips once open vomit out
Such uncouth horrors.

Cassandra

I tell you the lioness
Slaughters the Lion asleep; and lifting
Her blood-dripping fangs buried deep in his mane,
Glaring about her insatiable, bellowing,
Bounds hither—Phœbus Apollo, Apollo, Apollo!
Whither have you led me, under night alive with fire,
Through the trampled ashes of the city of my sire,
From my slaughtered kinsmen, fallen throne, insulted shrine,
Slave-like to be butchered, the daughter of a royal line!

AESOP

AESOP (Greek, 6th Century B.C.). According to tradition, a foreign slave having great familiarity with the fables of India. Creator of the Animal Fable, a brief tale told to point a simple moral. Believed to have been put to death at Delphi. Later mentioned by Aristophanes and Socrates. Many later collections, in Greek and Latin, freely attributed to him.

THE DOG AND THE SHADOW

A Dog, with a piece of stolen meat between his teeth, was one day crossing a river by means of a plank, when he caught sight of another dog in the water carrying a far larger piece of meat. He opened his jaws to snap at the greater morsel, when the meat dropped in the stream and was lost even in the reflection.

THE DYING LION

A LION, brought to the extremity of weakness by old age and disease, lay dying in the sunlight. Those whom he had oppressed in his strength now came round about him to revenge themselves for past injuries. The Boar ripped the flank of the King of Beasts with his tusks. The Bull came and gored the Lion's sides with his horns. Finally, the Ass drew near, and after carefully seeing that there was no danger, let fly with his heels in the Lion's face. Then, with a dying groan, the mighty creature exclaimed: "How much worse it is than a thousand deaths to be spurned by so base a creature!"

THE MOUNTAIN IN LABOUR

A MOUNTAIN was heard to produce dreadful sounds, as though it were labouring to bring forth something enormous. The people came and stood about waiting to see what wonderful thing would be produced from this labour. After they had waited till they were tired, out crept a Mouse.

HERCULES AND THE WAGGONER

A WAGGONER was driving his team through a muddy lane when the wheels stuck fast in the clay, and the Horses could get no farther. The Man immediately dropped on his knees, and, crying bitterly, besought Hercules to come and help him. "Get up and stir thyself, thou lazy fellow!" replied Hercules. "Whip thy Horses, and put thy shoulder to the wheel. If thou art in need of my help, when thou thyself hast laboured, then shalt thou have it."

THE FROGS THAT ASKED FOR A KING

THE FROGS, who lived an easy, happy life in the ponds, once prayed to Jupiter that he should give them a King. Jupiter was amused by this prayer, and cast a log into the water saying: "There, then, is a King for you." The Frogs, frightened by the great splash, regarded their King with alarm, until at last, seeing that he did not stir, some of them jumped upon his back and began to be merry there, amused

7

ideas for very long, and so once again they petitioned Jupiter to send them a King, a real King who would rule over them, and not lie helpless in the water. Then Jupiter sent the Frogs a Stork, who caught them by their legs, tossed them in the air, and gobbled them up whenever he was hungry. All in a hurry the Frogs besought Jupiter to take away King Stork and restore them to their former happy condition. "No, no," answered Jupiter; "a King that did you no hurt did not please you; make the best of him you now have, lest a worse come in his place!"

THE GNAT AND THE LION

A LIVELY and insolent Gnat was bold enough to attack a Lion, which he so maddened by stinging the most sensitive parts of his nose, eyes and ears that the beast roared with anguish and tore himself with his claws. In vain were the Lion's efforts to rid himself at such a foolish King. However, King Log did not satisfy their of his insignificant tormentor; again and again the insect returned and stung the furious King of Beasts till at last the Lion fell exhausted on the ground. The triumphant Gnat, sounding his tiny trumpet, hovered over the spot exulting in his victory. But it happened that in his circling flight he got himself caught in the web of a Spider, which, fine and delicate as it was, yet had power enough to hold the tiny insect a prisoner. All the Gnat's efforts to escape only held him the more tightly and firmly a prisoner, and he who had conquered the Lion became in his turn the prey of the Spider.

THE WOLF AND THE STORK

A WOLF ate his food so greedily that a bone stuck in his throat. This caused him such great pain that he ran hither and thither, promising to reward handsomely anyone who would remove the cause of his torture. A Stork, moved with pity by the Wolf's cry of pain, and tempted also by the reward, undertook the dangerous operation. When he had removed the bone, the Wolf moved away, but the Stork called out and reminded him of the promised reward. "Reward!" exclaimed the Wolf. "Pray, you greedy fellow, what reward can you expect? You dared to put your head in my mouth, and instead of biting it off, I let you take it out again unharmed. Get away with you! And do not again place yourself in my power."

THE FROG WHO WANTED TO BE AS BIG AS AN OX

A VAIN Frog, surrounded by her children, looked up and saw an Ox grazing near by. "I can be as big as the Ox," she said, and began to blow herself out. "Am I as big now?" she inquired. "Oh, no; not nearly so big!" said the little frogs. "Now?" she asked, blowing herself out still more. "No, not nearly so big!" answered her children. "But now?" she inquired eagerly, and blew herself out still more. "No, not even now," they said; "and if you try till you burst yourself you will never be so big." But the Frog would not listen, and attempting to make herself bigger still, burst her skin and died.

THE DOG IN THE MANGER

A DOG lay in a manger which was full of hay. An Ox, being hungry, came near, and was about to eat when the Dog started up, and, with angry snarls, would not let the Ox approach. "Surely, brute," said the Ox; "you cannot eat the hay yourself, and you will let no one else have any."

THE BUNDLE OF FAGGOTS

AN HONEST Man had the unhappiness to have a quarrelsome family of children. One day he called them before him, and bade them try and break a bundle of faggots. All tried, and all failed. "Now," said he, "unbind the bundle and take every stick by itself, and see if you cannot break them." They did his bidding, and snapped all the sticks one by one with the greatest possible ease. "This, my children," said the Father at last, "is a true emblem of your condition. Keep together and you are safe, divide and you are undone."

THE FOX WITHOUT A TAIL

A FOX was once caught in a trap by his tail, and in order to get free was obliged to leave it behind. He knew that his fellows would make fun of his tailless condition, so he made up his mind to induce them all to part with their tails. At the next assemblage of Foxes he made a speech on the uselessness of tails in general, and the inconvenience of a Fox's tail in particular, declaring that never in his whole life had he felt so comfortable as now in his tailless freedom. When he sat down, a sly old Fox rose, and, waving his brush, said, with a sneer, that if he had lost his tail, he would be convinced by the last speaker's arguments, but until such an accident occurred he fully intended to vote in favour of tails.

9

THE BLIND MAN AND THE PARALYTIC

A BLIND Man finding himself stopped in a rough and difficult road, met with a paralytic and begged his assistance. "How can I help you," replied the paralytic, "when I can scarcely move myself along?" But, regarding the blind man, he added: "However, you appear to have good legs and a broad back, and, if you will lift me and carry me, I will guide you safely through this difficulty, which is more than each one can surmount for himself. You shall walk for me, and I will see you you." "With all my heart," rejoined the blind man; and, taking the paralytic on his shoulders, the two went cheerfully forward in a wise partnership which triumphed over all difficulties.

RYUNOSUKE AKUTAGAWA

RYUNOSUKE AKUTAGAWA (Japanese, 1892-1927). Sophisticated story-teller, essayist and poet. A follower of the novelist, Natsume Soseki. Wrote more than 100 stories, highly imaginative, with fantastic, symbolic plots. Best-known works: *Rashomon, Hana, Jigokuhen*. Was teacher and newspaper-man before committing suicide at 35.

RASHOMON

IT WAS a chilly evening. A servant of a samurai stood under the Rashomon, waiting for a break in the rain.

No one else was under the wide gate. On the thick column, its crimson lacquer rubbed off here and there, perched a cricket. Since the Rashomon stands on Sujaku Avenue, a few other people at least, in sedge hat or nobleman's headgear, might have been expected to be waiting there for a break in the rain storm. But no one was near except this man.

For the past few years the city of Kyoto had been visited by a series of calamities, earthquakes, whirlwinds, and fires, and Kyoto had been greatly devastated. Old chronicles say that broken pieces of Buddhist images and other Buddhist objects, with their lacquer, gold, or silver leaf worn off, were heaped up on roadsides to be sold as firewood. Such being the state of affairs in Kyoto, the repair of the Rashomon was out of the question. Taking advantage of the devastation, foxes and other wild animals made their dens in the

10

ruins of the gate, and thieves and robbers found a home there too. Eventually it became customary to bring unclaimed corpses to this gate and abandon them. After dark it was so ghostly that no one dared approach.

Flocks of crows flew in from somewhere. During the daytime these cawing birds circled round the ridgepole of the gate. When the sky overhead turned red in the afterlight of the departed sun, they looked like so many grains of sesame flung across the gate. But on that day not a crow was to be seen, perhaps because of the lateness of the hour. Here and there the stone steps, beginning to crumble, and with rank grass growing in their crevices, were dotted with the white droppings of crows. The servant, in a worn blue kimono, sat on the seventh and highest step, vacantly watching the rain. His attention was drawn to a large pimple irritating his right cheek.

As has been said, the servant was waiting for a break in the rain. But he had no particular idea of what to do after the rain stopped. Ordinarily, of course, he would have returned to his master's house, but he had been discharged just before. The prosperity of the city of Kyoto had been rapidly declining, and he had been dismissed by his master, whom he had served many years, because of the effects of this decline. Thus, confined by the rain, he was at a loss to know where to go. And the weather had not a little to do with his depressed mood. The rain seemed unlikely to stop. He was lost in thoughts of how to make his living tomorrow, helpless incoherent thoughts protesting an inexorable fate. Aimlessly he had been listening to the pattering of the rain on the Sujaku Avenue.

The rain, enveloping the Rashomon, gathered strength and came down with a pelting sound that could be heard far away. Looking up, he saw a fat black cloud impale itself on the tips of the tiles jutting out from the roof of the gate.

He had little choice of means, whether fair or foul, because of his helpless circumstances. If he chose honest means, he would undoubtedly starve to death beside the wall or in the Sujaku gutter. He would be brought to this gate and thrown away like a stray dog. If he decided to steal . . . His mind, after making the same detour time and again, came finally to the conclusion that he would be a thief.

But doubts returned many times. Though determined that he had no choice, he was still unable to muster enough courage to justify the conclusion that he must become a thief.

11

After a loud fit of sneezing he got up slowly. The evening chill of Kyoto made him long for the warmth of a brazier. The wind in the evening dusk howled through the columns of the gate. The cricket which had been perched on the crimson-lacquered column was already gone.

Ducking his neck, he looked around the gate, and drew up the shoulders of the blue kimono which he wore over his thin underwear. He decided to spend the night there, if he could find a secluded corner sheltered from wind and rain. He found a broad lacquered stairway leading to the tower over the gate. No one would be there, except the dead, if there were any. So, taking care that the sword at his side did not slip out of the scabbard, he set foot on the lowest step of the stairs.

A few seconds later, halfway up the stairs, he saw a movement above. Holding his breath and huddling cat-like in the middle of the broad stairs leading to the tower, he watched and waited. A light coming from the upper part of the tower shone faintly upon his right cheek. It was the cheek with the red, festering pimple visible under his stubby whiskers. He had expected only dead people inside the tower, but he had only gone up a few steps before he noticed a fire above, about which someone was moving. He saw a dull, yellow, flickering light which made the cobwebs hanging from the ceiling glow in a ghostly way. What sort of person would be making a light in the Rashomon . . . and in a storm? The unknown, the evil terrified him.

As quickly as a lizard, the servant crept up to the top of the steep stairs. Crouching on all fours, and stretching his neck as far as possible, he timidly peeped into the tower.

As rumor had said, he found several corpses strewn carelessly about the floor. Since the glow of the light was feeble, he could not count the number. He could only see that some were naked and others clothed. Some of them were women, and all were lolling on the floor with their mouths open or their arms outstretched showing no more signs of life than so many clay dolls. One would doubt that they had ever been alive, so eternally silent they were. Their shoulders, breasts, and torsos stood out in the dim light; other parts vanished in shadow. The offensive smell of these decomposed corpses brought his hand to his nose.

The next moment his hand dropped and he stared. He caught sight of a ghoulish form bent over a corpse. It seemed to be an old woman, gaunt, gray-haired, and nunnish in appearance. With a pine torch in her right hand, she was peeping into the face of a corpse which had long black hair.

Seized more with horror than curiosity, he even forgot to breathe for a time. He felt the hair of his head and body stand on end. As he watched, terrified, she wedged the torch between two floor boards and, laying hands on the head of the corpse, began to pull out the long hairs one by one, as a monkey kills the lice of her young. The hair came out smoothly with the movement of her hands.

As the hair came out, fear faded from his heart, and his hatred toward the old woman mounted. It grew beyond hatred, becoming a consuming antipathy against all evil. At this instant if anyone had brought up the question of whether he would starve to death or become a thief—the question which had occurred to him a little while ago—he would not have hesitated to choose death. His hatred toward evil flared up like the piece of pine wood which the old woman had stuck in the floor.

He did not know why she pulled out the hair of the dead. Accordingly, he did not know whether her case was to be put down as good or bad. But in his eyes, pulling out the hair of the dead in the Rashomon on this stormy night was an unpardonable crime. Of course it never entered his mind that a little while ago he had thought of becoming a thief.

Then, summoning strength into his legs, he rose from the stairs and strode, hand on sword, right in front of the old creature. The hag turned, terror in her eyes, and sprang up from the floor, trembling. For a small moment she paused, poised there, then lunged for the stairs with a shriek.

"Wretch! Where are you going?" he shouted, barring the way of the trembling hag who tried to scurry past him. Still she attempted to claw her way by. He pushed her back to prevent her . . . they struggled, fell among the corpses, and grappled there. The issue was never in doubt. In a moment he had her by the arm, twisted it, and forced her down to the floor. Her arms were all skin and bones, and there was no more flesh on them than on the shanks of a chicken. No sooner was she on the floor than he drew his sword and thrust the silver-white blade before her very nose. She was silent. She trembled as if in a fit, and her eyes were open so wide that they were almost out of their sockets, and her breath came in hoarse gasps. The life of this wretch was his now. This thought cooled his boiling anger and brought a calm pride and satisfaction. He looked down at her, and said in a somewhat calmer voice:

"Look here, I'm not an officer of the High Police Commissioner. I'm a stranger who happened to pass by this gate. I won't bind you or do anything against you, but you must tell me what you're doing up here."

Then the old woman opened her eyes still wider, and gazed at his face intently with the sharp red eyes of a bird of prey. She moved her lips, which were wrinkled into her nose, as though she were chewing something. Her pointed Adam's apple moved in her thin throat. Then a panting sound like the cawing of a crow came from her throat:

"I pull the hair . . . I pull out the hair . . . to make a wig."

Her answer banished all unknown from their encounter and brought disappointment. Suddenly she was only a trembling old woman there at his feet. A ghoul no longer: only a hag who makes wigs from the hair of the dead—to sell, for scraps of food. A cold contempt seized him. Fear left his heart, and his former hatred entered. These feelings must have been sensed by the other. The old creature, still clutching the hair she had pulled off the corpse, mumbled out these words in her harsh broken voice:

"Indeed, making wigs out of the hair of the dead may seem a great evil to you, but these that are here deserve no better. This woman, whose beautiful black hair I was pulling, used to sell cut and dried snake flesh at the guard barracks, saying that it was dried fish. If she hadn't died of the plague, she'd be selling it now. The guards liked to buy from her, and used to say her fish was tasty. What she did couldn't be wrong, because if she hadn't, she would have starved to death. There was no other choice. If she knew I had to do this in order to live, she probably wouldn't care."

He sheathed his sword, and, with his left hand on its hilt, he listened to her meditatively. His right hand touched the big pimple on his cheek. As he listened, a certain courage was born in his heart—the courage which he had not had when he sat under the gate a little while ago. A strange power was driving him in the opposite direction of the courage which he had had when he seized the old woman. No longer did he wonder whether he should starve to death or become a thief. Starvation was so far from his mind that it was the last thing that would have entered it.

"Are you sure?" he asked in a mocking tone, when she finished

14

talking. He took his right hand from his pimple, and, bending forward, seized her by the neck and said sharply:

"Then it's right if I rob you. I'd starve if I didn't."

He tore her clothes from her body and kicked her roughly down on the corpses as she struggled and tried to clutch his leg. Five steps, and he was at the top of the stairs. The yellow clothes he had wrested off were under his arm, and in a twinkling he had rushed down the steep stairs into the abyss of night. The thunder of his descending steps pounded in the hollow tower, and then it was quiet.

Shortly after that the hag raised up her body from the corpses. Grumbling and groaning, she crawled to the top stair by the still flickering torchlight, and through the grey hair which hung over her face, she peered down to the last stair in the torch light.

Beyond this was only darkness . . . unknowing and unknown.

SHOLEM ALEIKHEM

SHOLEM ALEIKHEM (Sholem Rabinovitch, Yiddish, 1859-1916). The tragi-comedian of Jewish literature. Folk-lore style, mingling pathos and humor. Born in Russia, left for Switzerland in 1904, came to America in 1914. Most famous works: *Menakhem Mendel, Tevye der Milkhiker, Motel dem Khazans, Funem Yarid.* Many tales dramatized for stage and films.

THE PASSOVER GUEST

"I HAVE a Passover guest for you, Reb Yoneh, such a guest as you never had since you became a householder."

"What sort is he?"

"A real Oriental citron!"

"What does that mean?"

"It means a 'silken Jew,' a personage of distinction. The only thing against him is—he doesn't speak our language."

"What does he speak, then?"

"Hebrew."

"Is he from Jerusalem?"

"I don't know where he comes from, but his words are full of a's."

Such was the conversation that took place between my father and the beadle, a day before Passover, and I was wild with curiosity to

15

see the "guest" who didn't understand Yiddish, and who talked with a's. I had already noticed, in synagogue, a strange-looking individual, in a fur cap, and a Turkish robe striped blue, red, and yellow. We boys crowded round him on all sides, and stared, and then caught it hot from the beadle, who said children had no business "to creep into a stranger's face" like that. Prayers over, every one greeted the stranger, and wished him a happy Passover, and he, with a sweet smile on his red cheeks set in a round gray beard, replied to each one, "Shalom! Shalom!" instead of our Sholom. This "Shalom! Shalom!" of his sent us boys into fits of laughter. The beadle grew very angry, and pursued us with slaps. We eluded him, and stole deviously back to the stranger, listened to his "Shalom! Shalom!" exploded with laughter, and escaped anew from the hands of the beadle.

I am puffed up with pride as I follow my father and his guest to our house, and feel how all my comrades envy me. They stand looking after us, and every now and then I turn my head, and put out my tongue at them. The walk home is silent. When we arrive, my father greets my mother with "a happy Passover!" and the guest nods his head so that his fur cap shakes. "Shalom! Shalom!" he says. I think of my comrades, and hide my head under the table, not to burst out laughing. But I shoot continual glances at the guest, and his appearance pleases me; I like his Turkish robe, striped yellow, red, and blue, his fresh red cheeks set in a curly gray beard, his beautiful black eyes that look out so pleasantly from beneath his bushy eyebrows. And I see that my father is pleased with him, too, that he is delighted with him. My mother looks at him as though he were something more than a man, and no one speaks to him but my father, who offers him the cushioned reclining-seat at table.

Mother is taken up with the preparations for the Passover meal, and Rikel the maid is helping her. It is only when the time comes for saying Kiddush that my father and the guest hold a Hebrew conversation. I am proud to find that I understand nearly every word of it. Here it is in full.

My father: "Nu?" (That means, "Won't you please say Kiddush?")

The guest: "Nu-nu!" (meaning, "Say it rather yourself!")

My father: "Nu-O?" ("Why not you?")

The guest: "O-nu?" ("Why should I?")

My father: "I-O!" ("You first!")

The guest: "O-ai!" ("*You* first!")
My father: "È-o-i!" ("I beg of you to say it!")
The guest: "Ai-o-ê!" (I beg of you!")
My father: "Ai-e-o-nu?" ("Why should you refuse?")
The guest: "Oi-o-e-nu-nu!" ("If you insist, then I must.")

And the guest took the cup of wine from my father's hand, and recited a Kiddush. But what a Kiddush! A Kiddush such as we had never heard before, and shall never hear again. First, the Hebrew—all a's. Secondly, the voice, which seemed to come, not out of his beard, but out of the striped Turkish robe. I thought of my comrades, how they would have laughed, what slaps would have rained down, had they been present at that Kiddush.

Being alone, I was able to contain myself. I asked my father the Four Questions, and we all recited the Haggadah together. And I was elated to think that such a guest was ours, and no one else's.

Our sage who wrote that one should not talk at meals (may he forgive me for saying so!) did not know Jewish life. When shall a Jew find time to talk, if not during a meal? Especially at Passover, when there is so much to say before the meal and after it. Rikel the maid handed the water, we washed our hands, repeated the Benediction, mother helped us to fish, and my father turned up his sleeves, and started a long Hebrew talk with the guest. He began with the first question one Jew asks another:

"What is your name?"

To which the guest replied all in a's and all in one breath:

"Ayak Bakar Gashal Damas Hanoch Vassam Za'an Chafaf Tatzatz."

My father remained with his fork in the air, staring in amazement at the possessor of so long a name. I coughed and looked under the table, and my mother said, "Favele, you should be careful eating fish, or you might be choked with a bone," while she gazed at our guest with awe. She appeared overcome by his name, although unable to understand it. My father, who understood, thought it necessary to explain it to her.

"You see, Ayak Bakar, that is our Alef-Bes inverted. It is apparently their custom to name people after the alphabet."

"Alef-Bes! Alef-Bes!" repeated the guest with the sweet smile on his red cheeks, and his beautiful black eyes rested on us all, including Rikel the maid, in the most friendly fashion.

Having learned his name, my father was anxious to know whence, from what land, he came. I understand this from the names of

17

countries and towns which I caught, and from what my father translated for my mother, giving her a Yiddish version of nearly every phrase. And my mother was quite overcome by every single thing she heard, and Rikel the maid was overcome likewise. And no wonder! It is not every day that a person comes from perhaps, two thousand miles away, from a land only to be reached across seven seas and a desert, the desert journey alone requiring forty days and nights. And when you get near to the land, you have to climb a mountain of which the top reaches into the clouds, and this is covered with ice, and dreadful winds blow there, so that there is peril of death! But once the mountain is safely climbed, and the land is reached, one beholds a terrestrial Eden. Spices, cloves, herbs, and every kind of fruit—apples, pears, and oranges, grapes, dates, and olives, nuts and quantities of figs. And the houses there are all built of deal, and roofed with silver, the furniture is gold (here the guest cast a look at our silver cups, spoons, forks, and knives), and brilliants, pearls, and diamonds bestrew the roads, and no one cares to take the trouble of picking them up, they are of no value there. (He was looking at my mother's diamond earrings, and at the pearls round her white neck.)

"You hear that?" my father asked her, with a happy face.

"I hear," she answered, and added: "Why don't they bring some over here? They could make money by it. Ask him that, Yoneh!"

My father did so, and translated the answer for my mother's benefit:

"You see, when you arrive there, you may take what you like, but when you leave the country, you must leave everything in it behind, too, and if they shake out of you no matter what, you are done for."

"What do you mean?" questioned my mother, terrified.

"I mean, they either hang you on a tree, or they stone you with stones."

The more tales our guest told us, the more thrilling they became, and just as we were finishing the dumplings and taking another sip or two of wine, my father inquired to whom the country belonged. Was there a king there? And he was soon translating, with great delight, the following reply:

"The country belongs to the Jews who live there, and who are called Sefardîm. And they have a king, also a Jew, and a very pious one, who wears a fur cap, and who is called Joseph ben Joseph. He is the high priest of the Sefardîm, and drives out in a gilded carriage, drawn by six fiery horses. And when he enters the synagogue, the Levites meet him with songs."

"There are Levites who sing in your synagogue?" asked my father, wondering, and the answer caused his face to shine with joy.

"What do you think?" he said to my mother. "Our guest tells me that in his country there is a temple, with priests and Levites and an organ."

"Well, and an altar?" questioned my mother, and my father told her:

"He says they have an altar, and sacrifices, he says, and golden vessels—everything just as we used to have it in Jerusalem."

And with these words my father sighs deeply, and my mother, as she looks at him, sighs also, and I cannot understand the reason. Surely we should be proud and glad to think we have such a land, ruled over by a Jewish king and high priest, a land with Levites and an organ, with an altar and sacrifices—and bright, sweet thoughts enfold me, and carry me away as on wings to that happy Jewish land where the houses are of pine-wood and roofed with silver, where the furniture is gold, and diamonds and pearls lie scattered in the street. And I feel sure, were I really there, I should know what to do—I should know how to hide things—they would shake nothing out of *me*. I should certainly bring home a lovely present for my mother, diamond ear-rings and several pearl necklaces. I look at the one mother is wearing, at her ear-rings, and I feel a great desire to be in that country. And it occurs to me, that after Passover I will travel there with our guest, open my heart to him, tell him the whole truth, and beg him to take me there, if only for a little while. He will certainly do so, he is a very kind and approachable person, he looks at every one, even at Rikel the maid, in such a friendly, such a very friendly way!

So I think, and it seems to me, as I watch our guest, that he has read my thoughts, and that his beautiful black eyes say to me:

"Keep it dark, little friend, wait till after Passover, then we shall manage it!"

I dreamt all night long. I dreamt of a desert, a temple, a high priest, and a tall mountain. I climb the mountain. Diamonds and pearls grow on the trees, and my comrades sit on the boughs, and shake the jewels down onto the ground, whole showers of them, and I stand and gather them, and stuff them into my pockets, and, strange to say, however many I stuff in, there is still room! I stuff and stuff, and still there is room! I put my hand into my pocket,

19

and draw out—not pearls and brilliants, but fruits of all kinds—apples, pears, oranges, olives, dates, nuts, and figs. This makes me very unhappy, and I toss from side to side. Then I dream of the temple, I hear the priests chant, and the Levites sing, and the organ play. I want to go inside and I cannot—Rikel the maid has hold of me, and will not let me go. I beg of her and scream and cry, and again I am very unhappy, and toss from side to side. I wake —and see my father and mother standing there, half dressed, both pale, my father hanging his head, and my mother wringing her hands, and with her soft eyes full of tears. I feel at once that something has gone very wrong, very wrong indeed, but my childish head is incapable of imagining the greatness of the disaster.

The fact is this: our guest from beyond the desert and the seven seas has disappeared, and a lot of things have disappeared with him: all the silver wine-cups, all the silver spoons, knives, and forks; all my mother's ornaments, all the money that happened to be in the house, and also Rikel the maid!

A pang goes through my heart. Not on account of the silver cups, the silver spoons, knives, and forks that have vanished; not on account of mother's ornaments or of the money, still less on account of Rikel the maid, a good riddance! But because of the happy, happy land whose roads were strewn with brilliants, pearls, and diamonds; because of the temple with the priests, the Levites, and the organ; because of the altar and the sacrifices; because of all the other beautiful things that have been taken from me, taken, taken, taken!

I turn my face to the wall, and cry quietly to myself.

VITTORIO ALFIERI

VITTORIO ALFIERI (Italian, 1749-1803). The greatest tragedian of the Italian drama. Of noble birth, began writing at 25, and was an instant success. Plays notable for their intense patriotism and attacks on tyrants and tyranny. Among his 19 tragedies, best are: *Saul, Filippo, Virginia, Mirra.* Wrote in classical style. Called the Shakespeare of Italy.

DAVID SOOTHES SAUL'S MADNESS

Jonathan. Ah come, beloved father; to thy thoughts
Allow a little respite: the pure air

Will bring thee some refreshment; come and sit
A little while among thy children now.
    Saul. What are those words I hear?
    Michal. Beloved father!
    Saul. Who, who are ye? Who speaks of pure air here?
This? 'tis a thick impenetrable gloom;
A land of darkness and the shades of death—
O see! Come nearer me; dost thou observe it?
A fatal wreath of blood surrounds the sun.
Heardst thou the singing of ill-omen'd birds?
The vocal air resounds with loud laments
That smite my ears, compelling me to weep.—
But what? Ye, ye weep also.
    Jon. Mighty God
Of Israel, dost Thou thus Thy face avert
From Saul the king? Is he, Thy servant once,
Abandoned to the adversary thus?
    Michal. Father, thy much-loved daughter is beside thee:
If thou art cheerful, she is also cheerful;
She, if thou weepest, weeps. But, wherefore now
Should we shed tears? For joy hath reappeared.
    Saul. David thou meanest. Ah! Why doth not David
Also embrace me with my other children?
    David. O father! I have been restrained by fear
Of importuning thee. Ah! why canst thou
Not read my heart? I evermore am thine.
    Saul. Thou lovest then—the house of Saul?
    David. I love it?
O Heavens! Dear as the apple of mine eye
To me is Jonathan; I neither know
Nor heed a peril in the world for thee;
Let my wife, if she can, say with what love,
And how much love, I love her.
    Saul. Yet thyself
Thou mightily dost prize.
    David. I prize myself?
No despicable soldier in the camp,
In court thy son-in-law, I deem myself;
And nothing, nothing in the sight of God.
    Saul. Incessantly to me of God thou speakest;
Yet thou well knowest that the crafty rage,

Cruel, tremendous, of perfidious priests,
Has for a long time severed me from God.
Dost thou thus name Him to insult me?
    David. I
Name Him, to give Him glory. Why dost thou
Believe that He no longer is with thee?
He doth not dwell with him who loves Him not:
But doth He ever fail to succor him
Who doth invoke Him, and who hath reposed
In Him implicit trust? He to the throne
Appointed thee; and on that throne He keeps thee:
And if in Him, in Him exclusively
Thou dost confide, He's thine, and thou art His.
    Saul. Who speaks of Heaven? Is he in snowy vest
Enrobed who thus his sacred lip unseals?
Let's see him—No: thou art a warrior: thou
Graspest the sword: approach; and let me see,
If David thus or Samuel doth accost me.—
What sword is this? 'Tis not the same, methinks,
Which I, with my own hands, on thee bestow'd.
    David. This is the sword that my poor sling acquired.
The sword that over me in Elah hung
Threatening my life; in fierce Goliath's hands
I saw it flash a horrid glare of death
Before my eyes: he grasped it: but it bears
Not mine, but his coagulated blood.
    Saul. Was not that sword, a consecrated thing,
In Nob, within the tabernacle hung?
Was it not wrapped within the mystic ephod,
And thus from all unhallowed eyes concealed?
Devoted to the Lord of hosts forever?
    David. 'Tis true; but—
    Saul. Whence didst thou obtain it then?
Who dared to give it? who?
    David. I will explain.
Powerless and fugitive to Nob I came:
Wherefore I fled, thou knowest. Every path
Was crowded with unhappy wretches; I,
Defenceless, found myself at every step
Within the jaws of death. With humble brow
I kneel'd within the tabernacle, where

God's Spirit doth descend: and there, these arms
(Which if a living man might to his side
Refit them, David surely was that man)
Myself demanded of the priest.

    Saul. And he?

    David. Gave them to me.

    Saul. He was?

    David. Ahimelech.

    Saul. Perfidious traitor! Vile!—Where is the altar?
O rage! Ah, all are miscreants! traitors all!
The foes of God; are ye his ministers?
Black souls in vestments white—Where is the axe?
Where is the altar? let him be destroyed.
Where is the victim? I will slay him.

    Michal. Father!

    Jon. O Heav'ns! What mean these words? Where dost thou fly?
Be pacified, I pray thee: there are not
Or altars here, or victims: in the priests
Respect that God who hears thee evermore.

    Saul. Who thus restrains me? Who resists me thus?
Who forces me to sit?

    Jon. My father—

    David. Thou,
Great God of Israel, do Thou succor him!
Thy servant kneels to Thee, and this implores.

    Saul. I am bereft of peace; the sun, my kingdom,
My children, and my power of thought, all, all
Are taken from me! Ah, unhappy Saul!
Who doth console thee? who is now the guide,
The prop of thy bewildered feebleness?
Thy children all are mute, are harsh and cruel.
And of the doting and infirm old man
They only wish the death: and nought attracts
My children, but the fatal diadem,
Which now is twined around thy hoary head.
Wrest it at once: and at the same time sever
From this now tremulous decaying form
Your father's palsied head.—Ah, wretched state!
Better were death. I wish for death.

    Michal. O father!
We all desire thy life: we each of us

Would die ourselves, to rescue thee from death.

Jon. Now, since in tears his fury is dissolved,
Brother, do thou, to recompose his soul,
Exert thy voice. So many times already
Hast thou enthralled him with celestial songs
To calm oblivion.

    Michal. Yes; thou seest now,
The breathing in his panting breast subsides;
His looks, just now so savage, swim in tears:
Now is the time to lend him thy assistance.

    David. May God in mercy speak to him through me.—

Omnipotent, eternal, infinite,
    Thou, who dost govern each created thing;
Thou, who from nothing mad'st me by Thy might,
    Blest with a soul that dares to Thee take wing;
Thou, who canst pierce the abyss of endless night,
    And all its mysteries into daylight bring;
The universe doth tremble at Thy nod,
And sinners prostrate own the outstretched arm of God.

Oft on the gorgeous blazing wings ere now
    Of thousand cherubim wert Thou revealed;
Oft did Thy pure divinity endow
    Thy people's shepherd in the martial field:
To him a stream of eloquence wert Thou;
    Thou wert his sword, his wisdom and his shield:
From Thy bright throne, O God, bestow one ray
To cleave the gathering clouds that intercept the day.

In tears of darkness we——

    Saul. Hear I the voice
Of David? From a mortal lethargy
It seems to wake me, and displays to me
The cheering radiance of my early years.

    David. Who comes, who comes, unseen, yet heard?
A sable cloud of dust appeared,
    Chased by the eastern blast.—
But it has burst; and from its womb
A thousand brandished swords illume
    The track through which it passed.

Saul, as a tower, his forehead rears,
His head a flaming circlet wears.
    The earth beneath his feet
Echoes with tramp of horse and men:
The sea, the sky, the hills, the plain,
    The warlike sounds repeat.

In awful majesty doth Saul appear;
    Horsemen and chariots from before him fly:
Chilled by his presence is each heart with fear;
    And god-like terrors lighten in his eye.

Ye sons of Ammon, late so proud,
Where now the scorn, the insults loud,
    Ye raised against our host?
Your corpses more than fill the plain;
The ample harvest of your slain
    Invalidates your boast.
See what it is thus to depend
On gods unable to defend.—
    But wherefore from afar
Hear I another trumpet sound?
'Tis Saul's:—he levels with the ground
    All Edom's sons of war.

Thus Moab, Zobah, by his arms laid low,
    With impious Amalek, united fall:
Saul, like a stream fed by dissolving snow,
    Defeats, disperses, overwhelms them all.

    Saul. This is the voice of my departed years,
That from the tomb to glory now recalls me.
I live again in my victorious youth,
When I hear this—What do I say? Alas!
Should cries of war be now addressed to me?
Oblivion, indolence, and peace, invite
The old man to themselves.
    David. Let peace be sung.—

Weary and thirsty, see he lies
    Beside his native stream;
God's champion, whose past victories
    Wake many a glorious dream.

25

The sighed-for laurel's evergreen
  Doth screen his head from heat;
His children, all around him seen,
  His sighs and smiles repeat.

They weep and smile, then smile and weep,
  With sympathy endued;
And still a strict accordance keep
  To every varying mood.

One daughter's gentle hand unfits
  His crested helm and sword;
His consort fond beside him sits,
  Embracing her loved lord.

The other doth clear water bring
  From the pure ambient flood,
To cleanse his stately brows, where cling
  Commingled dust and blood.

A cloud of odorous flowers she spreads,
  Which breathe their perfumes near;
And on his honor'd hand she sheds
  The duteous filial tear.

But why sits one apart reclined,
  In pensive mood alone?
Alas, she mourns that others find
  A task, while she has none.

But diff'rent thoughts, with eager haste,
  Attract the band of boys;
Till his turn comes to be embraced,
  One son himself employs

To make the blood-encrusted blade
  From spot and blemish clear:
With envy fired, another said:
  "When shall I poise that spear?

"That pond'rous lance when shall I wield,
  That now defies my strength?"
Another grasps the blazoned shield,
  And stalks behind its length.

Then tears of sweet surprise,
From forth the swimming eyes
   Of Saul are seen to roll:
For of his blooming race,
So full of royal grace,
   He knows that he's the soul.

The pleasure how entire,
How happy is the sire,
Whose waking thoughts inspire
   Affections so sincere!
But now the day is o'er;
The zephyrs breathe no more;
And sleep's soft powers restore
   The monarch we revere.

   Saul. Happy the father of a race like this!
O peace of mind, how precious are thy gifts!
Through all my veins balsamic sweetness flows.

THE DEATH OF SAUL

   Abner. O hapless king! Now whither dost thou **fly?**
This is a dreadful night.
   Saul. But, why this battle?
   Abner. The foe assailed us unawares: we
Wholly discomfited.
   Saul. Discomfited?
And liv'st thou, traitor!
   Abner. I? I live to save thee.
Hither perchance Philistia's hordes are streaming:
We are compelled to shun the first attack:
Meanwhile the day will dawn. Thee will I lead,
With my few followers, to yonder slopes.
   Saul. Shall I then live, while all my people fall?
   Abner. Ah, come! Alas! the tumult grows: approaches.
   Saul. My children—Jonathan—do they too fly?
Do they abandon me?
   Abner. O Heavens! Thy children,—
No, no; they fled not—ill-starred progeny!
   Saul. I understand thee: they are all destroyed.
   Michal. Alas! My brothers!

27

Abner. Thou no more hast sons.

Saul. What now remains for me?—Thou, thou **alone,**
But not for me, remainest.—In my heart
Have I been long time finally resolved:
And now the hour is come. This, Abner, is
The last of my commands. My daughter now
Guide to some place of safety.

Michal. Father, no;
Around thee will I twine myself: the foe
Will never aim a sword against a woman.

Saul. O daughter! say no more: compel me not
To weep. A conquered king should never weep.
Save her, O Abner, go: but, if she fall
Within the foeman's hands, say not, O no,
That she's the child of Saul; but rather tell them
That she is David's wife; they will respect her.
Go; fly.

Abner. She shall, I swear to thee, be safe,
If I can aught avail; but thou meantime.

Michal. My father—ah!—I will not, will not leave **thee.**

Saul. I will it: and I yet am king. But see,
The armed bands approach. Fly, Abner, fly:
Drag her by force with thee, if it be needful.

Michal. O father!—and forever?

Saul (alone). O my children!
I was a father. See thyself alone,
O king; of thy so many friends and servants,
Not one remains. Inexorable God,
Is Thy retributory wrath appeased?—
But, thou remain'st to me, O sword: now come,
My faithful servant in extremity.—
Hark, hark! the howlings of the haughty victors:
The flashing of their burning torches glare
Before my eyes already, and I see
Their swords by thousands.—O thou vile Philistia,
Me thou shalt find, but like a king, here—dead!

HANS CHRISTIAN ANDERSEN

HANS CHRISTIAN ANDERSEN (Danish, 1805-1875). One of the truly great modern storytellers. Childhood and youth of grinding poverty. After failing to achieve theatrical career, finally found success as a writer. Experimented in every field of literature, but universal fame rests on 168 fairy tales and stories, such as "The Ugly Duckling," "The Red Shoes," and "The Emperor's New Clothes."

THE LOVERS

A WHIP Top and a little Ball were together in a drawer among some other toys; and the Top said to the Ball, "Shall we not be bridegroom and bride, as we live together in the same box?"

But the Ball, which had a coat of morocco leather, and was just as conceited as any fine lady, would make no answer to such a proposal.

Next day the little boy came to whom the toys belonged; he painted the Top red and yellow, and hammered a brass nail into it; and it looked splendid when the Top turned round!

"Look at me!" he cried to the Ball. "What do you say now? Shall we not be engaged to each other? We suit one another so well! You jump and I dance! No one could be happier than we two should be."

"Indeed! Do you think so?" replied the little Ball. "Perhaps you do not know my papa and mamma were morocco slippers, and that I have a Spanish cork inside me?"

"Yes, but I am made of mahogany," said the Top; "and the mayor himself turned me. He has a turning lathe of his own and it amuses him greatly."

"Can I depend upon that?" asked the little Ball.

"May I never be whipped again if it is not true!" replied the Top.

"You can speak well for yourself," observed the Ball, "but I cannot grant your request. I am as good as engaged to a swallow; every time I leap up into the air she puts her head out of her nest and says, 'Will you?' And now I have silently said 'Yes,' and that is as good as half engaged; but I promise I will never forget you."

"Yes, that will be much good!" said the Top.

And they spoke no more to each other.

The next day the Ball was taken out by the boy. The Top saw how high it flew into the air, like a bird; at last one could no longer see it. Each time it came back again, but gave a high leap when it touched the earth, and that was done either from its longing to mount up again, or because it had a Spanish cork in its body. But the ninth time the little Ball remained absent, and did not come back again; and the boy sought and sought, but it was gone.

29

"I know very well where it is!" sighed the Top. "It is in the swallow's nest, and has married the swallow."

The more the Top thought of this, the more it longed for the Ball. Just because it could not get the Ball, its love increased; and the fact that the Ball had chosen another formed a peculiar feature in the case. So the Top danced round and hummed, but always thought of the little Ball, which became more and more beautiful in his fancy. Thus several years went by, and now it was an old love.

And the Top was no longer young! But one day he was gilt all over; never had he looked so handsome; he was now a golden Top, and sprang till he hummed again. Yes, that was something worth seeing! But all at once he sprang up too high, and—he was gone.

They looked and looked, even in the cellar, but he was not to be found. Where could he be?

He had jumped into the dust box, where all kinds of things were lying: cabbage stalks, sweepings, and dust that had fallen down from the roof.

"Here's a nice place to lie in! The gilding will soon leave me here. Among what a rabble have I alighted."

And then he looked sideways at a long, leafless cabbage stump, and at a curious round thing that looked like an old apple; but it was not an apple—it was an old Ball, which had lain for years in the gutter on the roof, and was quite saturated with water.

"Thank goodness, here comes one of us, with whom one can talk!" said the little Ball, and looked at the gilt Top. "I am really morocco, worked by maiden's hands, and have a Spanish cork within me; but no one would think it, to look at me. I was very nearly marrying a swallow, but I fell into the gutter on the roof, and have lain there full five years, and become quite wet through. You may believe me; that's a long time for a young girl."

But the Top said nothing. He thought of his old love; and the more he heard, the clearer it became to him that this was she.

Then came the servant girl, and wanted to turn out the dust box.

"Aha! there's a gilt Top!" she cried.

And so the Top was brought again to notice and honor, but nothing was heard of the little Ball. And the Top spoke no more of his old love; for that dies away when the beloved object has lain for five years in a gutter and got wet through; yes, one does not know her again when he meets her in the dust box.

LEONID NICOLAYEVIC ANDREYEV

LEONID NIKOLAYEVIC ANDREYEV (Russian, 1871-1919). Dramatist and novelist of Russian realistic school, following Chekhov. Later developed his own pessimistic philosophy of nihilism. Bitterly opposed Bolshevik regime, and died in exile. Best-known works: *He Who Gets Slapped, The Black Maskers, The Seven Who Were Hanged.* His writing sometimes journalistic, but always worth while.

VALIA

VALIA was reading a huge, very huge book, almost half as large as himself, with very black letters and pictures occupying the entire page. To see the top line Valia had to stretch out his neck, lean far over the table, kneeling in his chair, and putting his short chubby finger on the letters for fear they would be lost among the other ones like it, in which case it was a difficult task to find them again. Owing to these circumstances, unforeseen by the publishers, the reading advanced very slowly, notwithstanding the breath-catching interest of the book.

It was a story about a very strong boy whose name was Prince Bova, and who could, by merely grasping the legs or arms of other boys, wrench them away from the body.

But Valia was suddenly interrupted in his reading; his mother entered with some other woman.

"Here he is," said his mother, her eyes red with weeping. The tears had evidently been shed very recently as she was still crushing a white lace handkerchief in her hand.

"Valichka, darling!" exclaimed the other woman, and putting her arms about his head, she began to kiss his face and eyes, pressing her thin, hard lips to them. She did not fondle him as did his mother, whose kisses were soft and melting; this one seemed loath to let go of him. Valia accepted her pricking caresses with a frown and silence; he was very much displeased at being interrupted, and he did not at all like this strange woman, tall, with bony, long fingers upon which there was not even one ring. And she smelled so bad: a damp, moldly smell, while his mother always exhaled a fresh, exquisite perfume.

At last the woman left him in peace, and while he was wiping his lips she looked him over with that quick sort of glance which seemed to photograph one. His short nose with its indication of a future little hump, his thick, unchildish brows over dark eyes, and the general appearance of stern seriousness, recalled some one to her, and she began to cry. Even her weeping was unlike mama's: the face remained immovable while the tears quickly rolled down one after the other—before one had time to fall another was already chasing after it. Her tears ceased as suddenly as they had commenced, and she asked: "Valichka, do you know me?"—"No."

"I called to see you. Twice I called to see you."

Perhaps she had called upon him, perhaps she had called twice, but how should Valia know of it? With her questions she only hindered him from reading.

"I am your mama, Valia!" said the woman.

Valia looked around in astonishment to find his mama, but she was no longer in the room.

"Why, can there be two mamas?" he asked. "What nonsense you are telling me."

The woman laughed, but this laugh did not please Valia; it was evident that the woman did not wish to laugh at all, and did it purposely to fool him. For some moments they were both silent.

"And what book is it you are reading?"

"About Prince Bova," Valia informed her with serious self-esteem and an evident respect for the big book.

"Ach, it must be very interesting! Tell me, please!" the woman asked with an ingratiating smile.

And once more something unnatural and false sounded in this voice, which tried to be soft and round like the voice of his mother, but remained sharp and prickly. The same insincerity appeared also in all the movements of the woman; she turned on her chair and even stretched out her neck with a manner as if preparing for a long and attentive listening; and when Valia reluctantly began the story, she immediately retired within herself, like a dark-lantern on which the cover is suddenly thrown. Valia felt the offense toward himself and Prince Bova, but, wishing to be polite, he quickly finished the story and added: "That is all."

"Well, good-by, my dear, my dove!" said the strange woman, and once more pressed her lips to Valia's face. "I shall soon call again. Will you be glad?"

"Yes, come please," politely replied Valia, and to get rid of her more quickly he added: "I will be very glad."

The visitor left him, but hardly had Valia found in the book again the word at which he had been interrupted, when mama entered, looked at him, and she also began to weep. He could easily understand why the other woman should have wept; she must have been sorry that she was so unpleasant and tiresome—but why should his mama weep?

"Listen, mama," he said musingly, "how that woman bored me! She says that she is my mama. Why, could there be two mamas to one boy?"

"No, baby, there could not; but she speaks the truth; she is your mother."

"And what are you, then?"

"I am your auntie."

This was a very unexpected discovery, but Valia received it with unshakable indifference; auntie, well, let it be auntie—was it not just the same? A word did not, as yet, have the same meaning for him as it would for a grown person. But his former mother did not understand it, and began to explain why it had so happened that she had been a mother and had become an aunt. Once, long ago, when Valia was very little—

"How little? So?" Valia raised his hand about a quarter of a yard from the table. "Like Kiska?" Valia exclaimed, joyfully surprised, with mouth opened and brow lifted. He spoke of his kitten that had been presented to him.

"Yes."

Valia broke into a happy laugh, but immediately resumed his usual earnestness, and with the condescension of a grown person recalling the mistakes of his youth, he remarked: "How funny I must have been!"

When he was so very little and funny, like Kiska, he had been brought by that woman and given away forever, also like Kiska. And now, when he had become so big and clever, the woman wanted him.

"Do you wish to go to her?" asked his former mother and reddened with joy when Valia resolutely and sternly said: "No, she does not please me!" and once more took up his book.

Valia considered the affair closed, but he was mistaken. This strange woman, with a face as devoid of life as if all the blood had been drained out of it, who had appeared from no one knew where, and vanished without leaving a trace, seemed to have set the whole house in turmoil and filled it with a dull alarm. Mama-auntie often cried and repeatedly asked Valia if he wished to leave her; uncle-papa grumbled, patted his bald pate so that the sparse, gray hair

33

on it stood up, and when auntie-mama was absent from the room he also asked Valia if he would like to go to that woman. Once, in the evening, when Valia was already in his little bed but was not yet sleeping, he heard his uncle and auntie speaking of him and the woman. The uncle spoke in an angry basso at which the crystal pendants of the chandelier gently trembled and sparkled with bluish and reddish lights.

"You speak nonsense, Nastasia Philippovna. We have no right to give the child away."

"She loves him, Grisha."

"And we! Do we not love him? You are arguing very strangely, Nastasia Philippovna. It seems as if you would be glad to get rid of the child—"

"Are you not ashamed of yourself?"

"Well, well, how quick you are to take offense. Just consider this matter cold-bloodedly and reasonably. Some frivolous thing or other gives birth to children, light-heartedly disposes of them by placing them on your threshold, and afterward says: 'Kindly give me my child, because, on account of my lover having abandoned me, I feel lonesome. For theatres and concerts I have no money, so give me the child to serve as a toy to play with.' No, madam, be easy, we shall see who wins in this case!"

"You are unjust to her, Grisha. You know well how ill and lonely she is—"

"You, Nastasia Philippovna, can make even a saint lose patience, by God! And the child you seem to have forgotten? For you is it wholly immaterial whether he is brought up an honest man or a scoundrel? And I could bet my head that he would be brought up by her a scoundrel, rascal, and—scoundrel."

"Grisha!"

"I ask you, for God's sake, not to irritate me! And where did you get this devilish habit of contradicting? 'She is so lonely.' And are *we* not lonely? The heartless woman that you are, Nastasia Philippovna! And why did I marry you!"

The heartless woman broke into tears, and her husband immediately begged her pardon, declaring that only a born fool could pay any attention to the words of such an old ass as he was. Gradually she became calmer and asked: "What does Talonsky say?"

"And what makes you think that he is such a clever fellow?" Gregory Aristarchovich again flew into a passion. "He says that everything depends on how the court will look at it. . . Something

new, is it not, as if we did not know without his telling that everything depends on how the court will look at it! Of course it matters
little to him—what does he care?—he will have his bark and then
safely go his way. If I had *my* way, it would go ill with all these
empty talkers—"

But here Nastasia Philippovna shut the dining-room door and
Valia did not hear the end of the conversation. But he lay for a
long time with open eyes, trying to understand what sort of woman
it was who wished to take him away from his home and ruin him.

On the next day he waited from early morning expecting his
auntie to ask him if he wished to go to his mother; but auntie did
not ask. Neither did his uncle. Instead of this, they both gazed at
Valia as if he were dangerously ill and would soon die; they caressed
him and brought him large books with colored pictures. The woman
did not call any more, but it seemed to Valia that she must be lurking outside the door watching for him, and that as soon as he would
pass the threshold she would seize him and carry him out into a
black and dismal distance where cruel monsters were wriggling and
breathing fire.

In the evenings while his uncle Gregory Aristarchovich was occupied in his study and Nastasia Philippovna was knitting something,
or playing a game of solitaire, Valia read his books, in which the
lines would grow gradually thicker and the letters smaller. Everything in the room was quiet, so quiet that the only thing to be heard
was the rustling of the pages he turned, and occasionally the uncle's
loud cough from the study, or the striking of the abacus counters.
The lamp, with its blue shade, threw a bright light on the blue
plush table-cover, but the corners of the room were full of a quiet,
mysterious gloom. There stood large plants with curious leaves and
roots crawling out upon the surface and looking very much like
fighting serpents, and it seemed as if something large and dark was
moving amidst them. Valia read, and before his wide-open eyes
passed terrible, beautiful and sad images which awakened in him
pity and love, but more often fear. Valia was sorry for the poor
water-nymph who so dearly loved the handsome prince that for
him she had given up her sisters and the deep, peaceful ocean; and
the prince knew nothing of this love, because the poor water-nymph
was dumb, and so he married a gay princess; and while great
festivities in honor of the wedding were in full swing on board the
ship, and music was playing and all were enjoying themselves, the
poor water-nymph threw herself into the dark waves to die. Poor,

sweet little water-nymph, so quiet and sad, and modest! But often terrible, cruel, human monsters appeared before Valia. In the dark nights they flew somewhere on their prickly wings, and the air whistled over their heads, and their eyes burned like red-hot coals. And afterward, they were surrounded by other monsters like themselves while a mysterious and terrible something was happening there. Laughter as sharp as a knife, long and pitiful wailing; strange weird dances in the purplish light of torches, their slanty, fiery tongues wrapped in the red clouds of smoke; and dead men with long, black beards— All this was the manifestation of a single enigmatic and cruel power, wishing to destroy man. Angry and mysterious spectres filled the air, hid among the plants, whispered something, and pointed their bony fingers at Valia; they gazed at him from behind the door of the adjoining unlit room, giggled and waited till he would go to bed, when they would silently dart around over his head; they peeped at him from out of the garden through the large, dark windows, and wailed sorrowfully with the wind.

In and out among all this vicious and terrible throng appeared the image of that woman who had come for Valia. Many people came and went in the house of Gregory Aristarchovich, and Valia did not remember their faces, but this face lived in his memory. It was such an elongated, thin, yellow face, and smiled with a sly, dissembling smile, from which two deep lines appeared at the two corners of the mouth. If this woman took Valia he would die.

"Listen," Valia once said to his aunt, tearing himself away from his book for a moment. "Listen," he repeated with his usual earnestness, and with a glance that gazed straight into the eyes of the person with whom he spoke: "I shall call you mama, not auntie. You talk nonsense when you say that the woman—is mama. You are mama, not she."

"Why?" asked Nastasia Philippovna, blushing like a young girl who had just received a compliment. But along with her joy there could also be heard in her voice the sound of fear for Valia. He had become so strange of late, and timid; feared to sleep alone, as he used to do, raved in his sleep and cried.

"But, Valichka, it is true, she is your mother."

"I really wonder where you get this habit of contradicting!" Valia said after some musing, imitating the tone of Gregory Aristarchovich.

Nastasia Philippovna laughed, but while preparing for bed that night she spoke for a considerable time with her husband, wh

36

boomed like a Turkish drum, abused the empty talkers, and frivolous, hare-brained women, and afterward went with his wife to see Valia.

They gazed long and silently into the face of the sleeping child. The flame of the candle swayed in the trembling hand of Gregory Aristarchovich and lent a fantastic, death-like coloring to the face of the boy, which was as white as the pillows on which it rested. It seemed as if a pair of stern, black eyes looked at them from the dark hollows, demanding a reply and threatening them with misfortune and unknown sorrow, and the lips twitched into a strange, ironic smile as if upon his helpless child-head lay a vague reflection of those cruel and mysterious spectre monsters that silently hovered over it.

"Valia!" whispered the frightened Nastasia. The boy sighed deeply but did not move, as if enchained in the sleep of death.

"Valia! Valia!" the deep, trembling voice of her husband was added to that of Nastasia Philippovna.

Valia opened his eyes, shaded by thick eyelashes; the light of the candle made him wink, and he sprang to his knees, pale and frightened. His uncovered, thin little arms, like a pearl necklace encircled his auntie's full, rosy neck, and hiding his little head upon her breast and screwing up his eyes tight as if fearing that they would open of themselves, he whispered: "I am afraid, mama, I am afraid! Do not go!"

That was a bad night for the whole household; when Valia at last fell asleep, Gregory Aristarchovich got an attack of asthma. He choked, and his full, white breast rose and fell spasmodically under the ice compresses. Toward morning he grew more tranquil, and the worn Nastasia fell asleep with the thought that her husband would not survive the loss of the child.

After a family council at which it was decided that Valia ought to read less and to see more of children of his own age, little girls and boys were brought to the house to play with him. But Valia from the first conceived a dislike for these foolish children who, in his eyes, were too noisy, loud and indecorous. They pulled flowers, tore books, jumped over chairs, and fought like little monkeys; and he, serious and thoughtful, looked on at their pranks with amazement and displeasure, and, going up to Nastasia Philippovna, said: "They tire me! I would rather sit by you." And in the evenings he once more took up his book, and when Gregory Aristarchovich, grumbling at all the deviltry the child read about, and by which he was losing his senses, gently tried to take the book from Valia's hands, the child silently and irresolutely pressed it to himself. And the improvised pedagogue beat a confused retreat and angrily scolded his wife:

"Is this what you call bringing up! No, Nastasia Philippovna, I see you are more fit to take care of kittens than to bring up children. The boy is so spoiled that one can not even take a book away from him."

One morning while Valia was sitting at breakfast with Nastasia Philippovna, Gregory Aristarchovich suddenly came rushing into the dining-room. His hat was tilted on the back of his head, his face was covered with perspiration; while still at the other side of the door he shouted joyfully into the room:

"Refused! The court has refused!"

The diamond earrings in Nastasia Philippovna's ears began to sparkle, and the little knife she held in her hand dropped to the plate.

"Is it true?" she asked, breathlessly.

Gregory Aristarchovich made a serious face, just to show that he had spoken the truth, but immediately forgetting his intention, his face became covered with a whole network of merry wrinkles. Then once more remembering that he lacked that earnestness of demeanor with which important news is usually imparted, he frowned, pushed a chair up to the table, placed his hat upon it, forgot that it was his hat, and thinking the chair to be already occupied by some one, threw a stern look at Nastasia Philippovna, then on Valia, winked his eye at Valia; and only after all these solemn preliminaries did he declare:

"I always said that Talonsky was a devilish clever fellow; can't fool him easily, Nastasia Philippovna."

"So it is true?"

"You are always ready with your eternal doubts. I said the case of Mme. Akimova is dismissed. Clever, is it not, little brother?" he turned to Valia and added in a stern, official tone: "And that said Akimova is to pay the costs."

"That woman will not take me, then?"

"I guess she won't, brother mine! Ach, I have entirely forgotten, I brought you some books!"

Gregory Aristarchovich rushed into the corridor, but halted on hearing Nastasia Philippovna's scream. Valia had fallen back on his chair in a faint.

38

A happy time began for the family. It was as if some one who had lain dangerously ill in the house had suddenly recovered and all began to breathe more easily and freely. Valia lost his fear of the terrible monsters and no longer suffered from nightmares. When the little monkeys, as he called the children, came to see him again, he was the most inventive of the lot. But even into the most fantastic plays he introduced his habitual earnestness and staidness, and when they played Indians. he found it indispensable to divest himself of almost all his clothing and cover his body with red paint.

In view of the businesslike manner in which these games were conducted, Gregory Aristarchovich now found it possible to participate in them, as far as his abilities allowed. In the rôle of a bear he did not appear to great advantage, but he had a great and well deserved success in his rôle of elephant. And when Valia, silent and earnest as a true son of the Goddess Kali, sat upon his father's shoulders and gently tapped upon his rosy bald pate with a tiny toy hammer, he really reminded one of a little Eastern prince who despotically reigns over people and animals.

The lawyer Talonsky tried to convey a hint to Gregory Aristarchovich that all was not safe yet, but the former could not comprehend how three judges could reverse the decision of three other judges, when the laws are the same here and everywhere. And when the lawyer insisted, Gregory Aristarchovich grew angry, and to prove that there was nothing to be feared from the higher court, he brought forward that same Talonsky on whom he now implicitly relied:

"Why, are you not going to be present when the case is brought before the court? Well, then what is there to be talked about. I wish you, Nastasia Philippovna, would make him ashamed of himself."

Talonsky smiled, and Nastasia Philippovna gently chided him for his purposeless doubts. They also spoke of the woman who had caused all the trouble, but now that she could menace them no more, and the court had decided that she must bear all the costs of the trial, they often dubbed her "poor woman."

Since the day Valia had heard that the woman had no longer any power to take him, she had lost in his eyes the halo of mysterious fear, which enveloped her like a mist and distorted the features of her thin face, and Valia began to think of her as he did of all other people. He now repeatedly heard that she was unhappy and could not understand why; but this pale bloodless face grew more simple, natural and near to him, the "poor woman," as they called her, began to interest him, and recalling other poor women of whom he had read, he felt a growing pity and a timid tenderness for her.

He imagined that she must sit alone in some dark room, fearing something and weeping, always weeping, as she had wept then when she had come to see him. And he felt sorry that he had not told her the story of Prince Bova better than he had at the time.

. . . .

It appeared that three judges could, after all, disagree with the decision of three other judges. The higher court had reversed the decision of the district court, the child was adjudged to his real mother. And the appeal was not considered by the senate.

When the woman came to take Valia away with her, Gregory Aristarchovich was not at home, he was at Talonsky's house and was lying in Talonsky's bedroom, and only the bald, rosy pate was visible above the snow-white pillows.

Nastasia Philippovna did not leave her room, and the maid led Valia forth from it already dressed for the road. He wore a fur coat and tall overshoes in which he moved his feet with difficulty. From under his fur cap looked out a pale little face with a frank and serious expression in the dark eyes. Under his arm Valia carried a book in which was the story of a poor water-nymph.

The tall, gaunt woman pressed the boy to her shabby coat and sobbed out: "How you have grown, Valichka! You are unrecognizable," she said, trying to joke, but Valia adjusted his cap and, contrary to habit, did not look into the eyes of the one who from this day on was to be his mother, but into her mouth. It was large, but with beautiful, small teeth; the two wrinkles on the corners of the mouth were still on the same place where Valia had seen them first, only now they were deeper.

"You are not angry with me?" asked mama; but Valia, not replying to her question, said: "Let us be gone."

"Valichka!" came a pitiful scream from Nastasia Philippovna's room, and she appeared on the threshold with eyes swollen from weeping, and clasping her hands she rushed toward the child, sank on her knees, and put her head on his shoulder. She did not utter a sound, only the diamonds in her ears trembled.

"Come, Valia," sternly said the tall woman, taking his hand. "We must not remain any longer among people who have subjected your mother to such torture—such torture!"

40

Her dry voice was full of hatred and she longed to strike the kneeling woman with her foot.

"Ugh! heartless wretches! You would be glad to take even my only child from me!" she wrathfully whispered, and pulled Valia away by his hand. "Come! Don't be like your father, who abandoned me."

"Ta-ke ca-re of him," Nastasia called after them.

The hired sleigh which stood waiting for them flew softly and lightly over the snow and noiselessly carried Valia away from the quiet house with its wonderful plants and flowers, its mysterious fairy-tale world, immeasurable and deep as the sea, with its windows gently screened by the boughs of the tall trees of the garden. Soon the house was lost in the mass of other houses, as similar to each other as the letters in Valia's book, and vanished forever from Valia.

It seemed to him as if they were swimming in a river, the banks of which were constituted of rows of lanterns as close to each other as beads on a string, but when they approached nearer, the beads were scattered, forming large, dark spaces and merging behind into just such a line of light. And then Valia thought that they were standing motionless on the very same spot; and everything began to be like a fairy tale—he himself and the tall woman who was pressing him to her, and everything around him.

The hand in which he carried his book was getting stiff with cold, but he would not ask his mother to take the book from him.

The small room into which Valia's mother had taken him was untidy and hot; in a corner near the large bed stood a little curtained bed such as Valia had not slept in for a long, long time.

"You are frozen! Well, wait, we shall soon have some tea! Well, now you are with your mama. Are you glad?" his mother asked with the hard, unpleasant look of one who has been forced to smile beneath blows all her life long.

"No," Valia replied shyly, frightened at his own frankness.

"No? And I had bought some toys for you. Just look, there they are on the window.

Valia approached the window and examined the toys. They were wretched paper horses with straight, thick legs, Punch with a red cap on, with an idiotically grinning face and a large nose, and little tin soldiers with one foot raised in the air.

Valia had long ago given up playing with toys and did not like them, but from politeness he did not show it to his mother. "Yes, they are nice toys," he said.

41

She noticed the glance he threw at the window, and said with that unpleasant, ingratiating smile:

"I did not know what you liked, darling, and I bought them for you a long time ago."

Valia was silent, not knowing what to reply.

"You must know that I am all alone, Valia, all alone in the wide world; I have no one whose advice I could ask; I thought they would please you." Valia was silent.

Suddenly the muscles of the woman's face relaxed and the tears began to drop from her eyes, quickly, quickly, one after the other, and she threw herself on the bed which gave a pitiful squeak under the weight of her body, and with one hand pressed to her breast, the other to her temples, she looked vacantly through the wall with her pale, faded eyes, and whispered:

"He was not pleased! Not pleased!—"

Valia promptly approached the bed, put his little hand, still red with the cold, on the head of his mother, and spoke with the same serious staidness which distinguished this boy's speech:

"Do not cry, mama. I will love you very much. I do not care to play with toys, but I will love you ever so much. If you wish, I will read to you the story of the poor water-nymph."

GUILLAUME APOLLINAIRE

GUILLAUME APOLLINAIRE (French, 1880-1918). The ancestor of poetic surrealism. Born in Italy, became French citizen in 1914. Died of wounds received in World War I. Fought for new movements in painting and literature: impressionism, cubism, surrealism. Chief works: *Alcools, Calligrammes, Les Mamelles de Tirésias*. The leader of his generation, influenced modern poetry.

FAREWELL

I have culled this twig of heather
Remember the autumn now too late
We shall meet no more in any weather
Odor of the season twig of heather
And remember that I wait.

HUNTING HORNS

Our story is noble and tragic
As a tyrant's mask;
No dangerous drama or magic;
No detail unpoetic
Makes our love-dream pathetic.

And Thomas De Quincey drinking
His opiate hippocras
Of his poor Ann wandered thinking
Let us pass, since all things pass
I shall return at my ease.

Memories are hunting horns
Whose sound dies on the breeze.

SALOME

So that John the Baptist might once more seem glad
Sire I'd dance to the Seraphim's pride
Mother tell me why it is you are so sad
In your robe of a countess at the Dauphin's side

My heart beat beat more loudly at his word
While I danced in the fennel hearkening
And I broidered lilies for a pennon-bird
At the end of his lance for to swing

Now for whom do you want me to broider this thing
His lance buds again on the Jordan banks
And the lilies by your soldiers O Herod king
When they bore him away drooped dead in their ranks

Come all of you with me below the quincunce
Weep not pretty royal jester steady
Take this head dance with it for your motley dunce
Don't touch his brow mother dear is cold already

Sire march before your troops will follow arter
We'll dig a ditch and lay him underground
We'll plant some flowers and we'll dance a round
Till I have lost my garter
The king his sneeze-starter
The child his prayer-charter
The priest his soul-barter

43

MEADOW-SAFFRON

The meadow is pretty but poisonous in the fall.
The cows at pasture there
Slowly absorb the venom;
The meadow-saffron, lilac, ringed,
Flourishes there your eyes are like that flower
Violet as its dark ring and as the fall
And from your eyes my days seep in slow poison.

With a clamor the children pour out of school
With their jackets on, playing harmonicas.
They gather the meadow-saffrons, which are like mothers there
Daughters of their daughters and color of your eyelids

Waving as flowers wave in the wild wind

The shepherd of the flock sings sweetly
While slowly lowing the cows leave once for all
This great field ill-flowered by the fall.

THE LORELEI

At Bacharach was a sorceress with flaxen locks
For love of whom the men around died in flocks

She was called to the tribunal at the bishop's manse
But because of her beauty he absolved her in advance

O beauteous Lorelei with eyes of jeweled smiles
From what magician have you learned your wiles

I am tired of living and mine eyes are accurst
Those who have beheld them, bishop, died of lusting thirst

Mine eyes are flames they are not sparkling jewels
Throw throw to the flames these devil's fuels

I flare in the flames O beauteous Lorelei
Let another condemn you you have bewitched me I

Bishop you jest pray I find the Virgin's breast
Send me to die with the Lord may you rest

My love has gone to a far-off coast
Send me to die for my love is lost

My heart is sore stricken indeed I must die
If I could behold myself it would glaze my eye

My heart is sore stricken since he went away
My heart is sore stricken from his parting day

The bishop summoned three lance-tall cavaliers
Take her to the convent with her insane tears

Go crazy Lora go Lora with trembling sight
You will be a sister robed in black and white

Then off they started all four on the way
The Lorelei besought them and her eyes were like the day

Cavaliers let me mount that distant height
Once more to glimpse my castle ere it pass fore'er from sight

Once more to behold myself mirrored in the flood
Then to the convent of maid- and widowhood

There her loosened locks in the wind waved high
And the cavaliers shouted Lorelei Lorelei

Below on the Rhine a slow skiff crawls
And my lover guides it he has seen me and he calls

My heart becomes calm again 'tis my lover mine
Then she leaned over and she fell into the Rhine

For seeing in the water the beauteous Lorelei
With hair of the sunlight and with eyes of the sky.

LUDOVICO ARIOSTO

LUDOVICO ARIOSTO (Italian, 1474-1533). The outstanding poet of the
Cinquecento. Held political posts at the court of Ferrara, and was governor
of Garfagnana. Wrote first in Latin, later in Italian. His masterpiece is the
epic poem, *Orlando Furioso*, though he wrote numerous comedies and satires.
He added romantic imagination and humor to the traditional Latin epic.

ALCINA THE ENCHANTRESS

Not so much does the palace, fair to see,
    In riches other princely domes excel,
    As that the gentlest, fairest company
    Which the whole world contains, within it dwell:
    Of either sex, with small variety
    Between, in youth and beauty matched as well:
    The fay alone exceeds the rest as far
    As the bright sun outshines each lesser star.

Her shape is of such perfect symmetry,
    As best to feign the industrious painter knows,
    With long and knotted tresses; to the eye
    Not yellow gold with brighter luster glows.
    Upon her tender cheek the mingled dye
    Is scattered, of the lily and the rose.
    Like ivory smooth, the forehead gay and round
    Fills up the space, and forms a fitting bound.

Two black and slender arches rise above
    Two clear black eyes, say suns of radiant light;
    Which ever softly beam and slowly move;
    Round these appears to sport in frolic flight,
    Hence scattering all his shafts, the little Love,
    And seems to plunder hearts in open sight.
    Thence, through mid visage, does the nose descend,
    Where Envy finds not blemish to amend.

As if between two vales, which softly curl,
    The mouth with vermeil tint is seen to glow:
    Within are strung two rows of orient pearl,
    Which her delicious lips shut up or show.
    Of force to melt the heart of any churl,
    However rude, hence courteous accents flow;
    And here that gentle smile receives its birth,
    Which opes at will a paradise on earth.

Like milk the bosom, and the neck of snow;
    Round is the neck, and full and large the breast;
    Where, fresh and firm, two ivory apples grow,
    Which rise and fall, as, to the margin pressed
    By pleasant breeze, the billows come and go.
    Not prying Argus could discern the rest.
    Yet might the observing eye of things concealed
    Conjecture safely, from the charms revealed.

To all her arms a just proportion bear,
    And a white hand is oftentimes descried,
    Which narrow is, and somedeal long; and where
    No knot appears, nor vein is signified.

For finish of that stately shape and rare,
A foot, neat, short, and round, beneath is spied.
Angelic visions, creatures of the sky,
Concealed beneath no covering veil can lie.

A springe is planted in Rogero's way,
  On all sides did she speak, smile, sing, or move;
No wonder then the stripling was her prey,
  Who in the fairy saw uch show of love,
With him the guilt and falsehood little weigh,
  Of which the offended myrtle told above.
Nor will he think that perfidy and guile
Can be united with so sweet a smile.

No! he could now believe, by magic art,
  Astolpho well transformed upon the plain,
For punishment of foul ungrateful heart,
  And haply meriting severer pain.
And, as for all he heard him late impart,
  'Twas prompted by revenge, 'twas false and vain.
By hate and malice was the sufferer stung,
To blame and wound the fay with slanderous tongue.

The beauteous lady whom he loved so well
  Is newly banished from his altered breast;
For (such the magic of Alcina's spell)
  She every ancient passion dispossessed:
And in his bosom, there alone to dwell,
  The image of her love and self impressed.
So witched, Rogero sure some grace deserves,
If from his faith his frail affection swerves.

At board lyre, lute, and harp of tuneful string,
  And other sounds, in mixed diversity,
Made, round about, the joyous palace ring,
  With glorious concert and sweet harmony.
Nor lacked there well-accorded voice to sing
  Of love, its passion and its ecstasy;
Nor who, with rare inventions, choicely versed,
Delightful fiction to the guests rehearsed.

47

What table. spread by whatsoever heir
  Of Ninus, though triumphant were the board,
  Or what more famous and more costly. where
  Cleopatra feasted with the Latian lord.
  Could with this banquet's matchless joys compare,
  By the fond fairy for Rogero stored?
  I think not such a feast is spread above.
  Where Ganymede presents the cup to Jove.

They form a ring, the board and festive cheer
  Removed, and sitting, play a merry game:
  Each asks, still whispering in a neighbor's ear,
  What secret pleases best; to knight and dame
  A fair occasion, without let or fear,
  Their love, unheard of any, to proclaim.
  And in conclusion the two lovers plight
  Their word, to meet together on that night.

Soon, and much sooner than their wont, was ended
  The game at which the palace inmates play:
  When pages on the troop with torches tended.
  And with their radiance chased the night away.
  To seek his bed the paladin ascended,
  Girt with that goodly squadron, in a gay
  And airy bower, appointed for his rest,
  'Mid all the others chosen as the best.

And when of comfits and of cordial wine
  A fitting proffer has been made anew,
  The guests their bodies reverently incline.
  And to their bowers depart the courtly crew.
  He upon perfumed sheets, whose texture fine
  Seemed of Arachne's loom, his body threw:
  Hearkening the while with still attentive ears,
  If he the coming of the lady hears.

At every movement heard on distant floor,
  Hoping 'twas she. Rogero raised his head:
  He thinks he hears; but it is heard no more.
  Then sighs at his mistake: ofttimes from bed

He issued, and undid his chamber door,
   And peeped abroad, but still no better sped:
   And cursed a thousand times the hour that she
   So long retarded his felicity.

"Yes, now she comes," the stripling often said,
   And reckoned up the paces, as he lay,
   Which from her bower were haply to be made
   To that where he was waiting for the fay.
   These thoughts, and other thoughts as vain, he weighed
   Before she came, and, restless at her stay,
   Often believed some hindrance, yet unscanned,
   Might interpose between the fruit and hand.

At length, when dropping sweets the costly fay
   Had put some end to her perfumery,
   The time now come she need no more delay,
   Since all was hushed within the palace, she
   Stole from her bower alone, through secret way,
   And passed towards the chamber silently,
   Where on his couch the youthful cavalier
   Lay, with a heart long torn by Hope and Fear.

When the successor of Astolpho spies
   Those smiling stars above him, at the sight
   A flame, like that of kindled sulphur, flies
   Through his full veins, as ravished by delight
   Out of himself; and now up to the eyes
   Plunged in a sea of bliss, he swims outright.
   He leaps from bed and folds her to his breast,
   Nor waits until the lady be undressed;

Though but in a light sendal clad, that she
   Wore in the place of farthingale or gown;
   Which o'er a shift of finest quality,
   And white, about her limbs the fay had thrown:
   The mantle yielded at his touch, as he
   Embraced her, and that veil remained alone,
   Which upon every side the damsel shows,
   More than clear glass the lily or the rose.

49

The plant no closer does the ivy clip,
　　With whose green boughs its stem is interlaced,
　Than those fond lovers, each from either's lip
　The balmy breath collecting, lie embraced:
　Rich perfume this, whose like no seed or slip
　Bears in sweet Indian or Sabæan waste;
　　While so to speak their joys is either fixed,
　　That oftentimes those meeting lips are mixed.

These things were carried closely by the dame
　　And youth, or if surmised, were never bruited;
　For silence seldom was a cause for blame,
　But oftener as a virtue well reputed.
　By those shrewd courtiers, conscious of his claim,
　Rogero is with proffers fair saluted:
　　Worshiped of all those inmates, who fulfill
　　In this the enamored fay, Alcina's will.

No pleasure is omitted there; since they
　　Alike are prisoners in Love's magic hall.
　They change their raiment twice or thrice a day,
　Now for this use, and now at other call.
　'Tis wrestling, tourney, pageant, bath, and ball;
　Now underneath a hill by fountain cast,
　　They read the amorous lays of ages past;

Now by glad hill, or through the shady dale,
　　They hunt the fearful hare, and now they flush
　With busy dog, sagacious of the trail,
　Wild pheasant from the stubble field or bush.
　Now where green junipers perfume the gale,
　Suspend the snare, or lime the fluttering thrush;
　　And casting now for fish, with net or hook,
　　Disturb their secret haunts in pleasant brook.

Rogero revels there, in like delight,
　　While Charles and Agramant are troubled sore.
　But not for him their story will I slight,
　Nor Bradamant forget; who evermore,
　'Mid toilsome pain and care, her cherished knight,
　Ravished from her, did many a day deplore;

Whom by unwonted ways, transported through
Mid air, the damsel saw, nor whither knew.

Of her I speak before the royal pair,
    Who many days pursued her search in vain;
    By shadowy wood, or over champaign bare,
    By farm and city, and by hill and plain;
    But seeks her cherished friend with fruitless care,
    Divided by such space of land and main:
    Often she goes among the Paynim spears,
    Yet never aught of her Rogero hears.

Of hundreds questioned, upon every side,
    Each day, no answer ever gives content.
    She roams from post to post, and far and wide
    Searches pavilion, lodging, booth, or tent,
    And this, 'mid foot or horseman, unespied,
    May safely do, without impediment,
    Thanks to the ring, whose more than mortal aid,
    When in her mouth, conceals the vanished maid.

She cannot, will not, think that he is dead;
    Because the wreck of such a noble knight
    Would from Hydaspes' distant waves have spread,
    To where the sun descends with westering light.
    She knows not what to think, nor whither sped,
    He roams in earth or air; yet, hapless wight,
    Him ever seeks, and for attendant train
    Has sobs and sighs, and every bitter pain.

At length to find the wondrous cave she thought,
    Where the prophetic bones of Merlin lie,
    And there lament herself until she wrought
    Upon the pitying marble to reply;
    For thence, if yet he lived, would she be taught,
    Or this glad life to hard necessity
    Had yielded up: and, when she was possessed
    Of the seer's counsels, would pursue the best.

With this intention. Bradamant her way
    Directed thither, where in Poictier's wood

The vocal tomb, containing Merlin's clay,
  Concealed in Alpine place and savage, stood.
  But that enchantress sage, who night and day
  Thought of the damsel, watchful for her good,
  She, I repeat, who taught her what should be
  In that fair grotto her posterity;

She who preserved her with protecting care,
  That same enchantress, still benign and wise,
  Who, knowing she a matchless race should bear
  Of men, or rather semi-deities,
  Spies daily what her thoughts and actions are,
  And lots for her each day, divining, tries:—
  She all Rogero's fortune knew, how freed;
  Then borne to India by the griffin steed:

Him on that courser plainly she had eyed,
  Who would not the controlling rein obey;
  When, severed by such interval, he hied,
  Borne through the perilous, unwonted way,
  And knew that he sport, dance, and banquet plied,
  And lapt in idleness and pleasure lay;
  Nor memory of his lord nor of the dame,
  Once loved so well, preserved, nor of his fame.

And thus such gentle knight ingloriously
  Would have consumed his fairest years and best
  In long inaction, afterwards to be,
  Body and soul, destroyed; and *that*, posessed
  Alone by us in perpetuity,
  That flower, whose sweets outlive the fragile rest
  Which quickens man when he in earth is laid,
  Would have been plucked or severed in the blade,

But that enchantress kind, who with more care
  Than for himself he watched, still kept the knight,
  Designed to drag him, by rough road and bare,
  Towards true virtue, in his own despite;
  As often cunning leech will burn and pare
  The flesh, and poisonous drug employ aright:
  Who, though at first his cruel art offend,
  Is thanked, since he preserves us, in the end.

She, not like old Atlantes, rendered blind
  By the great love she to the stripling bore,
  Set not on gifting him with life her mind,
  As was the scope of that enchanter hoar:
  Who, reckless all of fame and praise declined,
  Wished length of days to his Rogero more
  Than that, to win a world's applause, the peer
  Should of his joyous life forego one year.

By him he to Alcina's isle had been
  Dispatched, that in her palace he might dwell,
  Forgetting arms; and, as enchanter seen
  In magic and the use of every spell,
  The heart had fastened of that fairy queen.
  Enamored of the gentle youth, so well,
  That she the knot would never disengage.
  Though he should live to more than Nestor's age.

ARISTOPHANES

ARISTOPHANES (Greek, *ca.* 450-385 B.C.). The great satirical dramatist of his time. Used comedy as vehicle for political, literary, and social criticism. Of possibly 44 plays, 11 survive complete. Best-known: *The Birds, The Frogs, The Clouds, Lysistrata.* Humor is often Rabelaisian, but is motivated by serious moral purpose. His plays are good theater rather than great drama.

GRAND CHORUS OF BIRDS

Come on then, ye dwellers by nature in darkness, and like to the
  leaves' generations,
That are little of might, that are molded of mire, unenduring and
  shadowlike nations,
Poor plumeless ephemerals, comfortless mortals, as visions of
  shadows fast fleeing,
Lift up your mind unto us that are deathless, and dateless the
  date of our being:
Us, children of heaven, us, angels of aye, us, all of whose thoughts
  are eternal:
That ye may from henceforth, having heard of us all things aright
  as to matters supernal.

53

Of the being of birds, and beginning of gods, and of streams, and
the dark beyond reaching,
Trustfully knowing aright, in my name bid Prodicus pack with
his preaching!
It was Chaos and Night at the first, and the blackness of darkness,
and Hell's broad border,
Earth was not, nor air, neither heaven: when in depths of the womb
of the dark without order
First thing, first-born of the black-plumed Night, was a wind-egg
hatched in her bosom,
Gold wings glittering forth of his back, like whirlwinds gustily
turning.
He, after his wedlock with Chaos, whose wings are of darkness,
in Hell broad-burning,
For his nestlings begat him the race of us first, and upraised us
to light new-lighted.
And before this was not the race of the gods, until all things by
Love were united:
And of kind united in kind with communion of nature the sky
and the sea are
Brought forth, and the earth, and the race of the gods everlasting
and blest. So that we are
Far away the most ancient of all things blest. And that we are
of Love's generation
There are manifest manifold signs. We have wings, and with us
have the Love's habitation;
And manifold fair young folk that forswore love once, ere the
bloom of them ended,
Have the men that pursued and desired them subdued by the help
of us only befriended,
With such baits as a quail, a flamingo, a goose, or a cock's comb
staring and splendid.
All best good things that befall men come from us birds, as is
plain to all reason:
For first we proclaim and make known to them spring, and the
winter and autumn in season;
Bid sow, when the crane starts clanging for Afric in shrill-voiced
emigrant number,
And calls to the pilot to hang up his rudder again for the season
and slumber;

And then weave a cloak for Orestes the thief, lest he strip men of
theirs if it freezes.

And again thereafter the kite reappearing announces a change in
the breezes,

And that here is the season for shearing your sheep of their spring
wool. Then does the swallow

Give you notice to sell your great-coat, and provide something
light for the heat that's to follow.

Thus are we as Ammon or Delphi unto you, Dodona, nay, Phœbus
Apollo.

For, as first ye come all to get auguries of birds, even such is in
all things your carriage,

Be the matter a matter of trade, or of earning your bread, or of
any one's marriage.

And all things ye lay to the charge of a bird that belong to discerning prediction:

Winged fame is a bird, as you reckon; you sneeze, and the sign's
as a bird for conviction;

All tokens are "birds" with you—sounds, too, and lackeys and
donkeys. Then must it not follow

That we are to you all as the manifest godhead that speaks in
prophetic Apollo?

SHOLEM ASCH

SHOLEM ASCH (Yiddish, 1880-   ). Versatile novelist and playwright. Foremost exponent of Yiddish literature in contemporary world. Born in Poland,
settled in America in 1910. Early plays produced by Max Reinhardt, and
throughout Europe and America. Later novels conceived on epic scale, idealistic
in concept, realistic in treatment. Major works: *Three Cities, Moses, The
Nazarene, The Apostle.*

A JEWISH CHILD

THE mother came out of the bride's chamber, and cast a piercing
look at her husband, who was sitting beside a finished meal, and
was making pellets of bread crumbs previous to saying grace.

"You go and talk to her! I haven't a bit of strength left!"

"So, Rochel-Leon has brought up children, has she, and can't manage them! Why! People will be pointing at you and laughing —a ruin to your years!"

"To my years! A ruin to *yours! My* children, are they? Are they not yours, too? Couldn't you stay at home sometimes to care for them and help me to bring them up, instead of trapesing round —the black year knows where and with whom?"

"Rochel, Rochel, what has possessed you to start a quarrel with me now? The bridegroom's family will be arriving directly."

"And what do you expect me to do, Moishehle, eh?! For God's sake! Go in to her, we shall be made a laughing-stock."

The man rose from the table, and went into the next room to his daughter. The mother followed.

On the little sofa that stood by the window sat a girl about eighteen, her face hidden in her hands, her arms covered by her loose, thick, black hair. She was evidently crying, for her bosom rose and fell like a stormy sea. On the bed opposite lay the white silk wedding-dress, the Chuppeh-Kleid, with the black, silk Shool-Kleid, and the black stuff morning-dress, which the tailor who had undertaken the outfit had brought not long ago. By the door stood a woman with a black scarf round her head and holding boxes with wigs.

"Channehle! You are never going to do me this dishonour? to make me the talk of the town?" exclaimed the father. The bride was silent.

"Look at me, daughter of Moisheh Groiss! It's all very well for Genendel Freindel's daughter to wear a wig, but not the daughter of Moisheh Groiss? Is that it?"

"And yet Genendel Freindel might very well think more of herself than you: she is more educated than you are, and has a larger dowry," put in the mother.

The bride made no reply.

"Daughter, think how much blood and treasure it has cost to help us to a bit of pleasure, and now you want to spoil it for us? Remember, for God's sake, what you are doing with yourself! We shall be excommunicated, the young man will run away home on foot!"

"Don't be foolish," said the mother who took a wig out of a box from the woman by the door, and approached her daughter.

56

"Let us try on the wig, the hair is just the colour of yours," and she laid the strange hair on the girl's head.

The girl felt the weight, put up her fingers to her head, met among her own soft, cool, living locks, the strange, dead hair of the wig, stiff and cold, and it flashed through her, Who knows where the head to which this hair belonged is now? A shuddering enveloped her, and as though she had come in contact with something unclean, she snatched off the wig, threw it onto the floor and hastily left the room.

Father and mother stood and looked at each other in dismay.

The day after the marriage ceremony, the bridegroom's mother rose early, and, bearing large scissors, and the wig and a hood which she had brought from her home as a present for the bride, she went to dress the latter for the "breakfast."

But the groom's mother remained outside the room, because the bride had locked herself in, and would open her door to no one.

The groom's mother ran calling aloud for help to her husband, who, together with a dozen uncles and brothers-in-law, was still sleeping soundly after the evening's festivity. She then sought out the bridegroom, an eighteen-year-old boy with his mother's milk still on his lips, who, in a silk caftan and a fur cap, was moving about the room in bewildered fashion, his eyes on the ground, ashamed to look anyone in the face. In the end she fell back on the mother of the bride, and these two went in to her together, having forced open the door between them.

"Why did you lock yourself in, dear daughter. There is no need to be ashamed."

"Marriage is a Jewish institution!" said the groom's mother, and kissed her future daughter-in-law on both cheeks.

The girl made no reply.

"Your mother-in-law has brought you a wig and a hood for the procession to the Shool," said her own mother.

The band had already struck up the "Good Morning" in the next room.

"Come now, Kallehshi, Kalleh-leben, the guests are beginning to assemble."

The groom's mother took hold of the plaits in order to loosen them.

The bride bent her head away from her, and fell on her own mother's neck.

57

"I can't, Mame-leben! My heart won't let me, Mame-krön!"

She held her hair with both hands, to protect it from the other's scissors.

"For God's sake, my daughter, my life," begged the mother.

"In the other world you will be plunged for this into rivers of fire. The apostate who wears her own hair after marriage will have her locks torn out with red hot pincers," said the other with the scissors.

A cold shiver went through the girl at these words.

"Mother-life, mother-crown!" she pleaded.

Her hands sought her hair, and the black silky tresses fell through them in waves. Her hair, the hair which had grown with her growth, and lived with her life, was to be cut off, and she was never, never to have it again—she was to wear strange hair, hair that had grown on another person's head, and no one knows whether that other person was alive or lying in the earth this long time, and whether she might not come any night to one's bedside, and whine in a dead voice:

"Give me back my hair, give me back my hair!"

A frost seized the girl to the marrow, she shivered and shook.

Then she heard the squeak of scissors over her head, tore herself out of her mother's arms, made one snatch at the scissors, flung them across the room, and said in a scarcely human voice:

"My own hair! May God Himself punish me!"

That day the bridegroom's mother took herself off home again, together with the sweet-cakes and the geese which she had brought for the wedding breakfast for her own guests. She wanted to take the bridegroom as well, but the bride's mother said: "I will not give him back to you! He belongs to me already!"

The following Sabbath they led the bride in procession to the Shool wearing her own hair in the face of all the town, covered only by a large hood.

But may all the names she was called by the way find their only echo in some uninhabited wilderness.

A summer evening, a few weeks after the wedding: The young man had just returned from the Stübel, and went to his room. The wife was already asleep, and the soft light of the lamp fell on her pale face, showing here and there among the wealth of silky-black hair that bathed it. Her slender arms were flung round her head, as though she feared that someone might come by night to shear them off while she slept. He had come home excited and irritable: this was the fourth week of his married life, and they had not yet called him up to the Reading of the Law, the Chassidim pursued him, and to-day Chayyim Moisheh had blamed him in the presence of the whole congregation, and had shamed him, because *she*, his wife, went about in her own hair. "You're no better than a clay image," Reb Chayyim Moisheh had told him. "What do you mean by a woman's saying she won't. It is written: 'And he shall rule over thee.'"

And he had come home intending to go to her and say: "Woman, it is a precept in the Torah! If you persist in wearing your own hair, I may divorce you without returning the dowry," after which he would pack up his things and go home. But when he saw his little wife asleep in bed, and her pale face peeping out of the glory of her hair, he felt a great pity for her. He went up to the bed, and stood a long while looking at her, after which he called softly:

"Channehle . . . Channehle . . . Channehle. . . ."

She opened her eyes with a frightened start, and looked round in sleepy wonder:

"Nosson, did you call? What do you want?"

"Nothing, your cap has slipped off," he said, lifting up the white nightcap, which had fallen from her head.

She flung it on again, and wanted to turn towards the wall.

"Channehle, Channehle, I want to talk to you."

The words went to her heart. The whole time since their marriage he had, so to say, not spoken to her. During the day she saw nothing of him, for he spent it in the house-of-study or in the Stübel. When he came home to dinner, he sat down to the table in silence. When he wanted anything, he asked for it speaking into the air, and when really obliged to exchange a word with her, he did so with his eyes fixed on the ground, too shy to look her in the face. And now he said he wanted to talk to her, and in such a gentle voice, and they two alone together in their room!

"What do you want to say to me?" she asked softly.

"Channehle," he began, "please don't make a fool of me, and don't make a fool of yourself in people's eyes. Has not God decreed that we should belong together? You are my wife and I am your husband, and is it proper, and what does it look like, a married woman wearing her own hair?"

Sleep still half dimmed her eyes, and had altogether clouded her thought and will. She felt helpless, and her head fell lighty towards his breast.

"Child," he went on still more gently, "I know you are not so depraved as they say. I know you are a pious Jewish daughter, and His Blessed Name will help us, and we shall have pious Jewish children. Put away this nonsense! Why should the whole world be talking about you? Are we not man and wife? Is not your shame mine?"

It seemed to her as though *someone*, at once far away and very near, had come and was talking to her. Nobody had ever yet spoken to her so gently and confidingly. And he was her husband, with whom she would live so long, so long, and there would be children, and she would look after the house!

She leant her head lightly against him.

"I know you are very sorry to lose your hair, the ornament of your girlhood. I saw you with it when I was a guest in your home. I knew that God gave you grace and loveliness, I know. It cuts me to the heart that your hair must be shorn off, but what is to be done? It is a rule, a law of our religion, and after all we are Jews. We might even, God forbid, have a child conceived to us in sin, may Heaven watch over and defend us."

She said nothing, but remained resting lightly in his arm, and his face lay in the stream of her silky-black hair with its cool odour. In that hair dwelt a soul, and he was conscious of it. He looked at her long and earnestly, and in his look was a prayer, a pleading with her for her own happiness, for her happiness and his.

"Shall I?" . . . he asked, more with his eyes than with his lips.

She said nothing, she only bent her head over his lap

He went quickly to the drawer, and took out a pair of scissors.

She laid her head in his lap, and gave her hair as a ransom for their happiness, still half-asleep and dreaming. The scissors squeaked over her head, shearing off one lock after the other, and Channehle lay and dreamt through the night.

On waking next morning, she threw a look into the glass which hung opposite the bed. A shock went through her, she thought she had gone mad, and was in the asylum! On the table beside her lay her shorn hair, dead!

She hid her face in her hands, and the little room was filled with the sound of weeping!

ATTAR

ATTAR (Farid ud-Din, Persian, 1119-1230). One of the three main Persian mystic poets (with Sanai and Rumi). A physician who traveled widely in the East. Said to have been killed during Mongol invasion. His copious works, devoted to teachings of the Sufis, generally written in couplets, include: *Pand-Namah, Mantiq ut-Tayr, Elahi-Namah.*

THE BIRD PARLIAMENT

Once on a time from all the Circles seven
Between the steadfast Earth and rolling Heaven,
The Birds, of all Note, Plumage, and Degree,
That float in Air, and roost upon the Tree;
And they that from the Waters snatch their Meat,
And they that scour the Desert with long Feet:
Birds of all Natures, known or not to Man,
Flock'd from all Quarters into full Divan,
On no less solemn business than to find
Or choose, a Sultan Khalif of their kind,
For whom, if never theirs, or lost, they pin'd.
The Snake had his, 'twas said; and so the Beast
His Lion-lord: and Man had his, at least:
And that the Birds, who nearest were the Skies,
And went apparel'd in its Angel Dyes,
Should be without—under no better Law
Than that which lost all others in the Maw—
Disperst without a Bond of Union—nay,
Or meeting to make each the other's Prey—
This was the Grievance—this the solemn Thing
On which the scatter'd Commonwealth of Wing.
From all the four Winds, flying like to Cloud
That met and blacken'd Heav'n, and Thunder-loud
With sound of whirring Wings and Beaks that clash'd
Down like a Torrent on the Desert dash'd:
Till by Degrees, the Hubbub and Pellmell
Into some Order and Precedence fell,
And, Proclamation made of Silence, each
In special Accent, but in general Speech
That all should understand, as seem'd him best,
The Congregation of all Wings Addrest.

61

And first, with Heart so full as from his Eyes
Ran Weeping, up rose Tajidar the Wise;
The mystic Mark upon whose Bosom show'd
That He alone of all the Birds THE ROAD
Had travel'd: and the Crown upon his head
Had reach'd the Goal; and He stood forth and said:—
"Oh Birds, by what Authority divine
I speak, you know, by His authentic Sign,
And Name, emblazon'd on my Breast and Bill:
Whose Counsel I assist at, and fulfill:
At his Behest I measured as he plann'd
The Spaces of the Air and Sea and Land;
I gaug'd the secret sources of the Springs
From Cloud to Fish: the Shadow of my wings
Dream'd over sleeping Deluge: piloted
The Blast that bore Sulayman's Throne: and led
The Cloud of Birds that canopied his Head;
Whose Word I brought to Balkis: and I shar'd
The Counsel that with Ásaf he prepar'd.
And now You want a Khalif: and I know
Him, and his whereabout, and How to go:
And go alone I could, and plead your cause
Alone for all: but, by the eternal laws,
Yourselves by Toil and Travel of your own
Must for your old Delinquency atone.
Were you indeed not blinded by the Curse
Of Self-exile, that still grows worse and worse,
Yourselves would know that, though *you* see him not,
He is with you this Moment, on this Spot,
Your Lord through all Forgetfulness and Crime,
Here, There, and Everywhere, and through all Time.
But as a Father, whom some wayward Child
By sinful Self-will has unreconcil'd,
Waits till the sullen Reprobate at cost
Of long Repentance should regain the Lost;
Therefore, yourselves to see as you are seen,
Yourselves must bridge the Gulf you made between
By such a Search and Travel to be gone
Up to the mighty mountain Káf, whereon
Hinges the World, and round about whose Knees
Into one Ocean mingle the Sev'n Seas;

In whose impenetrable Forest-folds
Of Light and Dark 'Symurgh' his presence holds;
Not to be reach'd, if to be reach'd at all
But by a Road the stoutest might appall;
Of Travel not of Days or Months, but Years—
Lifelong perhaps: of Dangers, Doubts, and Fears
As yet unheard of: Sweet of Blood and Brain
Interminable—often all in vain—
And, if successful, no Return again:
A Road whose very Preparation scar'd
The Traveler who yet must be prepar'd.
Who then this Travel to Result would bring
Needs both a lion's Heart beneath the Wing,
And even more, a Spirit purified
Of Worldly Passion, Malice, Lust, and Pride:
Yea, ev'n of *Worldly* Wisdom, which grows dim
And dark, the nearer it approaches *Him*,
Who to the Spirit's Eye alone reveal'd;
By sacrifice of Wisdom's self unseal'd;
Without which none who reach the Place could bear
To look upon the Glory dwelling there."

SRI AUROBINDO

SRI AUROBINDO (Sri Aurobindo Ghose, Indian, 1872-1950). Philosopher-poet of modern India. Son of Bengalese physician, educated in England. Anticipatated Gandhi in organizing passive resistance as a political weapon in Bengal. After imprisonment by British, went to live in French Pondicherry. Author of 3 volumes of poetry and 2 major philosophic works: *The Life Divine* and *The Synthesis of Yoga.*

MUSA SPIRITUS

O word concealed in the upper fire,
  Thou who has lingered through centuries,
Descend from thy rapt white desire,
  Plunging through gold eternities.

Into the gulfs of our nature leap,
  Voice of the spaces, call of the Light!

Break the seals of Matter's sleep,
  Break the trance of the unseen height.

In the uncertain glow of human mind,
  Its waste of unharmonied thronging thoughts,
Carve thy epic mountain-lined
  Crowded with deep prophetic grots.

Let thy hue-winged lyrics hover like birds
  Over the swirl of the heart's sea.
Touch into sight with thy fire-words
  The blind indwelling deity.

O Muse of the Silence, the wideness make
  In the unplumbed stillness that hears thy voice,
In the vast mute heavens of the spirit awake
  Where thy eagles of Power flame and rejoice.

Out, out with the mind and its candle flares,
  Light, light the suns that never die.
For my ear the cry of the seraph stars
  And the forms of the Gods for my naked eye!

Let the little troubled life-god within
  Cast his veils from the still soul,
His tiger-stripes of virtue and sin,
  His clamour and glamour and thole and dole;

All make tranquil, all make free.
  Let my heart-beats measure the footsteps of God
As He comes from His timeless infinity
  To build in their rapture His burning abode.

Weave from my life His poem of days,
  His calm pure dawns and His noons of force.
My acts for the grooves of His chariot-race,
  My thoughts for the tramp of His great steeds' course!

BRIDE OF THE FIRE

Bride of the Fire, clasp me now close,—
  Bride of the Fire!
I have shed the bloom of the earthly rose,
  I have slain desire.

Beauty of the Light, surround my life,—
　　Beauty of the Light!
I have sacrificed longing and parted from grief,
　　I can bear thy delight.

Image of ecstasy, thrill and enlace,—
　　Image of bliss!
I would see only thy marvellous face,
　　Feel only thy kiss.

Voice of Infinity, sound in my heart,—
　　Call of the One!
Stamp there thy radiance, never to part,
　　O living Sun.

THE BLUE BIRD

I am the bird of God in His blue;
　　Divinely high and clear
I sing the notes of the sweet and the true
　　For the god's and the seraph's ear.

I rise like a fire from the mortal's earth
　　Into a griefless sky
And drop in the suffering soil of his birth
　　Fire-seeds of ecstasy.

My pinions soar beyond Time and Space
　　Into unfading Light;
I bring the bliss of the Eternal's face
　　And the boon of the Spirit's sight.

I measure the worlds with my ruby eyes;
　　I have perched on Wisdom's tree
Thronged with the blossoms of Paradise
　　By the streams of Eternity.

Nothing is hid from my burning heart;
　　My mind is shoreless and still;
My song is rapture's mystic art,
　　My flight immortal will.

MARY AUSTIN

MARY AUSTIN (American, 1868-1934). A spirited student of anthropological and social problems. Investigated American Indian and early Spanish cultures in the Southwest. Her novels and plays also dealt with social injustices and problems of machine age. Important works: *The Land of Little Rain, A Woman of Genius, No. 26 Jayne Street.*

PAPAGO WEDDING

THERE was a Papago woman out of Panták who had a marriage paper from a white man after she had borne him five children, and the man himself was in love with another woman. This Shuler was the first to raise cotton for selling in the Gila Valley—but the Pimas and Papagoes had raised it long before that—and the girl went with him willingly. As to the writing of marriage, it was not then understood that the white man is not master of his heart, but is mastered by it, so that if it is not fixed in writing it becomes unstable like water and is puddled in the lowest place. The Sisters at San Xavier del Bac had taught her to clean and cook. Shuler called her Susie, which was nearest to her Papago name, and was fond of the children. He sent them to school as they came along, and had carpets in the house.

In all things Susie was a good wife to him, though she had no writing of marriage and she never wore a hat. This was a mistake which she learned from the sisters. They, being holy women, had no notion of the *brujeria* which is worked in the heart of the white man by a hat. Into the presence of their God also, without that which passes for a hat, they do not go. Even after her children were old enough to notice, Susie went about the country with a handkerchief tied over her hair, which was long and smooth on either side of her face, like the shut wings of a raven.

By the time Susie's children were as tall as their mother, there were many white ranchers in the Gila country, with their white wives, who are like Papago women in this, that if they see a man upstanding and prosperous, they think only that he might make some woman happy, and if they have a cousin or a friend, that she should be the woman. Also the white ones think it so shameful for a man to take a woman to his house without a writing that they have no scruple to take him away from her. At Rinconada there was a woman with large breasts, surpassing well looking, and with many hats. She had no husband and was new to the country, and when Shuler drove her about to look at it, she wore each time a different hat.

This the Papagoes observed, and, not having visited Susie when she was happy with her man, they went now in numbers, and by this Susie understood that it was in their hearts that she might have need of them. For it was well known that the white woman had told Shuler that it was a shame for him to have his children going about with a Papago woman who had only a handkerchief to cover her head. She said it was keeping Shuler back from being the principal man among the cotton growers of Gila Valley, to have in his house a woman who would come there without a writing. And when the other white women heard that she had said that, they said the same thing. Shuler said, "My God, this is the truth, I know it," and the woman said that she would go to Susie and tell her that she ought to go back to her own people and not be a shame to her children and Shuler. There was a man from Panták on the road, who saw them go, and turned in his tracks and went back, in case Susie should need him, for the Papagoes, when it is their kin against whom there is *brujeria* made, have inknowing hearts. Susie sat in the best room with the woman and was polite. "If you want Shuler," she said, "you can have him, but I stay with my children." The white woman grew red in the face and went out to Shuler in the field where he was pretending to look after something, and they went away together.

After that Shuler would not go to the ranch except of necessity. He went around talking to his white friends. "My God," he kept saying, "what can I do, with my children in the hands of that Papago?" Then he sent a lawyer to Susie to say that if she would go away and not shame his children with a mother who had no marriage writing and no hat, he would give her money, so much every month. But the children all came in the room and stood by her, and Susie said, "What I want with money when I got my children and this good ranch?" Then Shuler said "My God!" again, and "What can I do?"

The lawyer said he could tell the Judge that Susie was not a proper person to have care of his children, and the Judge would take them away from Susie and give them to Shuler. But when the day came for Susie to come into court, it was seen that though she had a handkerchief on her hair, her dress was good, and the fringe of her shawl was long and fine. All the five children came also, with new clothes, well looking. "My God!" said Shuler, "I must get those kids away from that Papago and into the hands of a white woman." But the white people who had come to see the children taken away saw that although the five looked like Shuler, they had their mouths shut like Papagoes; so they waited to see how things turned out.

Shuler's lawyer makes a long speech about how Shuler loves his children, and how sorry he is in his heart to see them growing up like Papagoes, and water is coming out of Shuler's eyes. Then the Judge asks Susie if she has anything to say why her children shall not be taken away.

"You want to take these children away and giff them to Shuler?" Susie asks him. "What for you giff them to Shuler?" says Susie, and the white people are listening. She says, "Shuler's not the father of them. Thees children all got different fathers," says Susie "Shuler——"

Then she makes a sign with her hand. I tell you if a woman makes that sign to a Papago he could laugh himself dead but he would not laugh off that. Some of the white people who have been in the country a long time know that sign and they begin to laugh.

Shuler's lawyer jumps up. . . . "Your Honour, I object——"

The Judge waves his hand. "I warn you the Court cannot go behind the testimony of the mother in such a case. . . ."

By this time everybody is laughing, so that they do not hear what the lawyer says. Shuler is trying to get out of the side door, and the Judge is shaking hands with Susie.

"You tell Shuler," she says, "if he wants people to think hees the father of thees children he better giff me a writing. Then maybe I think so myself."

"I *will*," said the Judge, and maybe two, three days after that he takes Shuler out to the ranch and makes the marriage writing. Then all the children come around Susie and say, "Now, Mother, you will have to wear a hat." Susie, she says, "Go, children, and ask your father." But it is not known to the Papagoes what happened after that.

B

ISAAK EMMANUILOVICH BABEL

ISAAK EMMANUILOVICH BABEL (Russian, 1894-193?). Classical **story** writer of Communist era. *Konarmiya*, his masterpiece, a collection of powerful tales based on experiences in Red Army. *Benia Creak*, a novel about a famous Jewish bandit. Disappeared around 1935; is presumed, like many of his **race,** to have died in Soviet concentration camp.

THE BIRTH OF A KING

I WAS the one to begin.

"Reb Arie-Leib." I said to the old man, "let us talk about Benia Creak. Let us talk about his lightning beginnings and his terrible end. Three black shadows stand in the way of my imagination. The first is the one-eyed Froim Grach. The rusted steel of his exploits —can it stand comparison with the new power of the King? The second is Kolka Paskovsky. The simple-minded audacity of that man should have been sufficient for successful domination. And as for Haim Drong—couldn't he recognize the brilliance of the new star? Why then was Benia Creak the only one to climb to the top of the rope ladder, while all the others were left hanging below on its wobbly rungs?"

Reb Arie-Leib remained silent, perched on the wall of the cemetery. Before us spread the green quietude of the graves. A man who thirsts for knowldge must learn to be patient. Gravity befits the man who possesses knowledge. That is why Arie-Leib remained silent as he sat on the cemetery wall. At last he spoke:

"Why he? Why not they, you want to know? Now listen—forget for a moment that you have spectacles on your nose and autumn in your heart. Stop making rows at your writing-table and stammering when you have to face an audience. Imagine for a moment that you are making rows in public squares and stammer only on

69

paper. You're a tiger, a lion, a tom-cat. You can spend the night with a Russian woman, and the Russian woman will be satisfied with you. You are twenty-five. If the sky and the earth had a couple of rings attached to them, you would seize these rings and draw the sky and the earth together. And you have for a father a carter, Mendel Creak. What does such a father think of? He thinks of having a good drink of vodka, he thinks of swiping some one across the face, he thinks of his horses—that's all. You want to live, and he makes you die twenty times a day. What would you have done if you were Benia Creak? You would have done nothing. But he did. That's why he's King, and you haven't got a brass farthing in your pocket.

"He, little Benia, went to see Froim Grach, who then was already looking at the world with one eye only, and was what he is now. He said to Froim:

'Take me, Froim. I want to be washed up on your shore. The shore on which I'm washed up will gain by it.'

"Grach asked him:

'Who are you, where do you come from, and what do you live by?'

'Try me, Froim,' said Benia, 'and let us stop smearing the clean table with porridge.'

'All right, let us stop smearing porridge about,' said Grach. 'I will try you.'

"Then the gangsters called a meeting to think over Benia Creak. I was not present at that meeting. But I was told that they held a council. The late Levka Byk was then the elder.

'What's happening under his hat—the hat of this little Benia?' asked the late Byk.

"The one-eyed Grach then gave his opinion:

'Benia talks little but his talk is full of meat. He says little, but you wish he would say more.'

'If that is so,' cried the late Levka, 'then let us try him on Tartakovsky,' decided the council, and all in whom a little conscience was still alive, blushed when they heard this decision. Why did they blush? You'll know why if you follow me where I shall lead you.

"Tartakovsky was nicknamed in Odessa 'Jew-and-a-half' or 'Nine Raids.' He was nicknamed 'Jew-and-a-half' because no one Jew could contain in himself so much insolence and money as possessed Tartakovsky. In height he was taller than the tallest policeman in Odessa, and in weight—heavier than the fattest Jewess. As for

70

'Nine Raids', he was so-called because the gang of Levka Byk and Co. made neither eight nor ten raids on his office, but exactly nine. It was Benia's lot—and he wasn't yet King then—to make the tenth raid on the 'Jew-and-a-half.' When Froim passed this on to him, Benia said: 'Yes,' and walked out, slamming the door. Why did he slam the door? You will find out if you follow me where I shall lead you.

"Tartakovsky has the soul of a murderer, but he belongs to us. He came from our midst. He's our flesh, as if one mother had born us. Half Odessa works in his shops. And he has suffered through his own people of Moldavanka. Twice they kidnapped him in order to get a ransom, and once during a pogrom they staged his funeral with a choir. It was when the hooligans from Sloboda were beating up the Jews. Tartakovsky escaped them, and met a funeral procession with a choir in the Sophia Square.

'Who's being buried with a choir?' he asked.

"Passers-by told him it was Tartakovsky. The procession got as far as the cemetery in Sloboda. Then our people, who had staged the procession, took a machine-gun out of the coffin and opened fire on the hooligans of Sloboda. But the 'Jew-and-a-half' had not foreseen that. He was scared to death. And what fellow would not have been scared in his position?

"A tenth raid on a man who had already been buried once—you must agree, it was downright rudeness. Benia, who was not yet King then, understood that better than any other. But he had said 'yes' to Grach, and on the same day he wrote Tartakovsky a letter, re-sembling all the letters of that sort:

'HIGHLY-RESPECTED ROOVIM OSIPOVICH,

'Be so kind as to put under the tank of rain-water by next Satur-day' . . . and so on. 'In case of refusal, as you have presumed to do on the last few occasions, a very serious disappointment in your family life will await you.

'I sign respectfully, as some one well known to you,

BENCION CREAK'

"Tartakovsky was not a lazy man and answered this letter with-out delay.

'Benia! If you were an idiot, I would have written to you as to an idiot. But I don't know you as such, and the Lord forbid that I should ever know you as such. You must be pretending that you're a baby. Don't you know that there has been a bumper crop of wheat in Argentina this year, and that we cannot even begin selling ours? And I will tell you, with my hand on my heart, that I'm tired of eating such a bitter crust of bread in my old age and to experience all these upsets, after I've been working like a cart-horse all my life. And what have I got after all these years of hard forced labour? Ulcers, sores, worries, and sleeplessness. Drop this nonsense, Benia. Your friend, much more so than you think,

ROOVIM TARTAKOVSKY'

"The 'Jew-and-a-half' did his part. He wrote the letter. But the post-office failed to deliver it. Having received no answer, Benia got angry. On the following day he arrived with three friends at Tartakovsky's office. Four young men, wearing masks and armed with revolvers, burst into the room.

'Hands up!' they shouted, and began to brandish their revolvers in the air.

'Work more calmly, Solomon,' Benia told the one who was shouting louder than the others, 'don't get into such nervous habits when you work.' And turning to the assistant, who was as white as death and as yellow as parchment, he asked:

'Is the "Jew-and-a-half" at the works?'

'He's not at the works,' answered the assistant, whose surname was Mughinstein, and who was called Joseph. He was an unmarried son of Aunt Pessia, a woman who sold chickens in Seredinsky Square.

'But who's in charge here?' they questioned the unfortunate Mughinstein.

'I'm in charge here,' answered the assistant, as green as green grass.

'Then open the cash-box with God's help,' Benia ordered him.

"And in this way an opera in three acts began.

"The highly strung Solomon was packing bank-notes, papers, watches, and monograms into a suit-case, while the late Joseph stood in front of him with his hands raised, and Benia was telling stories from the past of the Hebrew people.

'If he likes to believe he's a Rothschild,' Benia was saying of Tartakovsky, 'then let him burn like a bonfire. Explain it to me, Mughinstein, like a friend: he got a business letter from me, didn't he? Why didn't he get on a tram for five copecks, and drive up to my flat, and have a glass of vodka with my family and a bite of

72

something, whatever God has given us? It would have cost him nothing to have a heart-to-heart talk with me. If he had simply told me: Benia, here's my bank balance, wait a couple of days, let me have a breather. . . . What would I have answered? Swine wouldn't meet swine, but man can meet man. Mughinstein, you understand me?'

'Yes, I understand you,' Mughinstein answered, untruthfully, because he did not see at all why the 'Jew-and-a-half', a respectable wealthy man and the first tradesman in the town, should have gone on a tram to drink vodka with the family of the carter Mendel Creak.

"But meanwhile, misfortune was roaming outside the door like a beggar at sunrise. Misfortune burst into the office with a great noise. It burst in under the image of a Jew called Savka Butzis, and it was as drunk as a water-carrier.

'Ho-ho-ho,' shouted the Jew Savka, 'forgive me, Benchik, I'm late,' and he began to stamp his feet and brandish his arms. Then he fired his revolver, and the bullet hit Mughinstein in the stomach.

"Are words needed? There had been a man, and he ceased to be. There lived an innocent bachelor, like a bird on a branch—and he perished through silliness, through nothing. . . . A Jew came, a Jew who looked like a sailor, and fired not at some bottle with a bangle inside it, but at a live man. Are words needed?

'Leave the office at once,' shouted Benia, and ran out after the others. But before leaving, he had time to tell Butzis:

'I swear by my mother's grave, Savka, you'll lie beside him! . . .'

"Now tell me, young man, who cuts the coupons off other people's shares, what would you have done if you had been in Benia Creak's place? You don't know what you would have done. But he did know. That's why he's King, while you and I sit on the wall of the Jewish cemetery and hold our hands against our faces to protect them from the sun.

"The unfortunate son of Aunt Pessia did not die at once. An hour after he had been brought to the hospital, Benia put in an appearance. He demanded to see the Chief Surgeon and the Matron, and told them, without taking his hands out of the pockets of his cream-coloured trousers:

'I have an interest,' he said, 'in that your patient Joseph Mughinstein should recover. I might just as well introduce myself—Bencion Creak. Camphor, bags of oxygen, a private ward—he must have all that. If not, then remember that no doctor, be he even a doctor of philosophy, needs more than three yards of soil. . . ."

"Still, Mughinstein died the same night. And only then the 'Jew-and-a-half' started such a row that the whole of Odessa could hear him.

'Where do the police begin and where does Benia end?' he screamed.

'The police end where Benia begins,' reasonable people told him, but Tartakovsky wouldn't calm down, and he finished by getting what he asked for. A red motor-car with a musical box played the first march from the opera *Pagliacci* in the Seredinsky Square. In broad daylight the car flew up to the little house where Aunt Pessia lived.

"The car spat out smoke, back-fired, shone with its metal parts, stank of petrol, and played arias on its horn. A man jumped out of it, went into the house and through to the kitchen where little Aunt Pessia was having a fit on the earthen floor. The 'Jew-and-a-half' was sitting on a chair and gesticulating violently.

'A hooligan's snout!' he cried when he saw the visitor. 'Bandit! I wish the earth would spit you out. You're doing fine—killing live men!'

'Monsieur Tartakovsky,' Benia Creak answered him in a quiet voice, 'it's the second day that I've been grieving about the deceased as if he were my own brother. But I know you don't care a damn for my young tears. Shame, Monsieur Tartakovsky—in what safe have you locked up your shame? You had the heart to send the mother of our late Joseph a miserable hundred roubles! My brain rose in my head together with my hair when I heard the news.'

"Here Benia paused for a moment. He had on a chocolate-coloured jacket, cream-white trousers, and magenta shoes.

'Ten thousand at once,' he roared, 'ten thousand at once, and a pension for the rest of her life, even if she lives a hundred and twenty years. If not, then we shall go out of this apartment, Monsieur Tartakovsky, and get into my motor-car.'

"Then they argued and quarrelled with each other. The 'Jew-and-a-half' argued with Benia. I wasn't present at that quarrel. But those, who were there, remember. They compromised on five thousand roubles to be paid on the spot and on fifty roubles to be paid monthly.

'Aunt Pessia,' Benia then said to the dishevelled little woman, who was still rolling on the floor, 'if you need my life, you can have it, but every one makes mistakes, even God. Listen to me with

74

your ears, Aunt Pessia. You have five thousand roubles in ready money and fifty roubles a month until your death. I hope you will live to be a hundred and twenty. Joseph's funeral will be first-rate: six horses like six lions, two hearses with wreaths, a choir from the Brodskaia synagogue, the singer Minkovsky himself will come to sing at your son's funeral.'

"The funeral took place on the following morning. You ask the beggars who sit beside the cemetery about this funeral. Ask the servants from the synagogue about it, ask the tradesmen who sell cosher poultry, or the old women from alms-houses. Odessa had never seen such a funeral. The world will never see another such. Policemen put on their string gloves that day. Inside the synagogues, decorated with garlands of green, their doors wide open, electric lights were blazing. On the heads of white horses which drew the hearse, swung bunches of black ostrich feathers. A choir of sixty persons walked at the head of the procession. The singers were boys, but they sang with the voices of women. The elders of the synagogue, which was endowed by the dealers in cosher poultry, led Aunt Pessia, supporting her under the arms. The elders were followed by members of the Society of Jewish shop-assistants, and following them, came lawyers and barristers, doctors of medicine and trained midwives. On one side of Aunt Pessia walked the women who sold poultry in the Old Market, and on the other side the highly honoured women who sell milk on the Bugaevka, wrapped in their orange-coloured shawls. They stamped their feet like gendarmes on parade, and from their wide hips spread the smell of milk and of the sea. Behind every one slouched along the employees of Roovim Tartakovsky. There were a hundred of them, or five hundred, or two thousand, perhaps. All wore long black coats with satin revers, and new boots which squeaked like sucking-pigs in sacks.

"I will speak now as Jehovah spoke from the burning bush on the Mount of Sinai. Put my words into your ears. All I saw I saw with my own eyes, sitting here on the wall of the Second Jewish Cemetery, beside the stutterer Moiseika and Shimson from the funeral office. I saw all of it, I, Arie-Leib, the proud Jew who lives near the dead.

"The hearse drove up to the cemetery synagogue. The coffin was placed upon the steps. Aunt Pessia trembled like a little bird. The cantor climbed out of his carriage and began the funeral service. The voices of sixty choir-boys accompanied him. And at that moment the red motor-car flew out from round a corner. It played

'Laugh, Pagliaccio,' and stopped. The people were as silent as if they were dead. The trees were silent, so were the choir-boys, so were the beggars. Four men came out of the red car and, walking slowly, carried to the coffin a wreath of undreamed-of roses. And when the funeral service ended, four men propped the coffin with their steel-like shoulders, and with their eyes burning and their chests stuck out, strode along beside the members of the Society of Jewish shop-assistants.

"In front walked Benia Creak whom no one yet called King. He was the first to reach the grave. He mounted the pile of earth and stretched out his hand.

"An employee of the funeral company ran up to him.

'What do you wish to do, young man?'

'I want to make a speech.' Every one who wanted to hear, heard it. I, too, heard it, I, Arie-Leib, and the stutterer Moiseika, who sat on the wall beside me.

'Gentlemen and ladies,' said Benia Creak, 'gentlemen and ladies.' he said, and the sun stood above his head like a sentinel with a rifle. 'You came here to pay your last duties to an honest wage-earner, who perished for a brass farthing. In my own name and in the name of all those who aren't present here, I thank you. gentlemen and ladies. What has our dear Joseph seen in his life? He's seen a couple of trifles. What did he do in life? He counted money which belonged to another. What did he die for? He died for all the wage-earning class. There are people who are already doomed to die, and there are people who haven't yet begun to live. And a bullet which should have pierced a doomed breast, went and pierced our Joseph, who has seen nothing in his life except a couple of trifles. There are people who know how to drink vodka, and there are others who don't know how to drink it. yet drink it all the same. The former get their pleasure, both from grief and from joy, while the latter suffer for all those who drink vodka without knowing how to do it. For that reason, gentlemen and ladies, after we have prayed for the soul of our poor Joseph. I will beg you to accompany to his grave the unknown to you and now dead Savka Butzis.'

"Having made this speech, Benia came off the mound. The men. the trees, and the beggars were all silent. Two grave-diggers carried a coffin of unpainted deal to the neighbouring grave. The cantor finished his prayers, stammering. Benia threw the first spadeful of earth upon the body of Joseph, then walked over to Savka's. All the barristers and ladies with brooches followed him like sheep. He ordered the cantor to read a complete funeral service over Savka, and sixty choir-boys accompanied the cantor. Savka never dreamed of such a funeral service—believe the word of Arie-Leib, a very old man.

"They say that on that day the 'Jew-and-a-half' decided to close down his business. I wasn't there when he decided it. But that neither the cantor, nor the choir, nor the funeral company asked to be paid for their services—that I saw with the eyes of Arie-Leib. Arie-Leib is my name. And I could see nothing more, because the people who left Savka's grave at a quiet pace, started to run as if from a fire. They rushed off in their carriages. in carts, and on foot. And only those four, who had come in a red car, went away in it. The musical box played its march, the machine quivered and flew away.

'A King,' said the stutterer Moiseika, the same who always pinches from me the best seat on the wall.

"Now you know everything. You know who was the first to say the word 'King.' It was Moiseika. You know why he did not call thus either the one-eyed Grach or ·the madman Kolka. You know everything. But what is the use of it to you if you still have spectacles on your nose and autumn in your heart?"

HONORE DE BALZAC

HONORÉ DE BALZAC (French, 1799-1850). One of France's greatest and most prolific novelists, and founder of the French realistic school. Under general title of *La Comédie Humaine*, his novels give an exhaustive picture of his time. Best-known single works: *Le Père Goriot, Eugénie Grandet, Lost Illusions*. His life noteworthy for its poverty, emotional crises, and phenomenal productivity, including 85 novels.

DOOMED TO LIVE

THE clock of the little town of Menda had just struck midnight. At this moment a young French officer was leaning on the parapet of a long terrace which bounded the gardens of the castle. He seemed plunged in the deepest thought—a circumstance unusual amid the thoughtlessness of military life; but it must be owned that never were the hour, the night, and the place more propitious to meditation. The beautiful Spanish sky stretched out its azure dome above his head. The glittering stars and the soft moonlight lit up a charming valley that unfolded all its beauties at his feet. Leaning against a blossoming orange tree he could see, a hundred feet below him, the town of Menda, which seemed to have been placed for shelter from the north winds at the foot of the rock on which the castle was built. As he turned his head he could see the sea, framing the landscape with a broad silver sheet of glistening water. The castle was a blaze of light. The mirth and movement of a ball, the music of the orchestra, the laughter of the officers and their partners in the dance, were borne to him mingled with the distant murmur of the waves. The freshness of the night imparted a sort of energy to his limbs, weary with the heat of the day. Above all, the gardens were planted with trees so aromatic, and flowers so fragrant, that the young man stood plunged, as it were, in a bath of perfumes.

The castle of Menda belonged to a Spanish grandee, then living there with his family. During the whole of the evening his eldest daughter had looked at the officer with an interest so tinged with sadness that the sentiment of compassion thus expressed by the Spaniard might well call up a reverie in the Frenchman's mind.

Clara was beautiful, and although she had three brothers and a sister, the wealth of the Marques de Leganes seemed great enough for Victor Marchand to believe that the young lady would have a rich dowry. But how dare he hope that the most bigoted old hidalgo in all Spain would ever give his daughter to the son of a Parisian grocer? Besides, the French were hated. The Marques was suspected by General Gautier, who governed the province, of planning a revolt in favor of Ferdinand VII. For this reason the battalion commanded by Victor Marchand had been cantoned in the little town of Menda, to hold the neighboring hamlets, which were dependent on the Marques, in check. Recent dispatches from Marshal Ney had given ground for fear that the English would shortly land on the coast, and had indicated the Marques as a man who carried on communication with the cabinet of London.

In spite, therefore, of the welcome which the Spaniard had given him and his soldiers, the young officer Victor Marchand remained constantly on his guard. As he was directing his steps towards the terrace whither he had come to examine the state of the town and

the country districts intrusted to his care, he debated how he ought
to interpret the friendliness which the Marques had unceasingly
shown him, and how the tranquillity of the country could be reconciled with his General's uneasiness. But in one moment these thoughts
were driven from his mind by a feeling of caution and well-grounded
curiosity. He had just perceived a considerable number of lights in
the town. In spite of the day being the Feast of St. James, he had
given orders, that very morning, that all lights should be extinguished
at the hour prescribed by his regulations; the castle alone being
excepted from his order. He could plainly see, here and there, the
gleam of his soldiers' bayonets at their accustomed posts; but there
was a solemnity in the silence, and nothing to suggest that the
Spaniards were a prey to the excitement of a festival. After having
sought to explain the offense of which the inhabitants were guilty,
the mystery appeared all the more unaccountable to him because
he had left officers in charge of the night police and the rounds.
With all the impetuosity of youth, he was just about to leap through
a breach and descend the rocks in haste, and thus arrive more
quickly than by the ordinary road at a small outpost placed at
the entrance of the town nearest to the castle, when a faint sound
stopped him. He thought he heard the light footfall of a woman
upon the gravel walk. He turned his head and saw nothing; but
his gaze was arrested by the extraordinary brightness of the sea.
All of a sudden he beheld a sight so portentous that he stood dumfounded; he thought that his senses deceived him. In the far
distance he could distinguish sails gleaming white in the moonlight.
He trembled and tried to convince himself that this vision was an
optical illusion, merely the fantastic effect of the moon on the
waves. At this moment a hoarse voice pronounced his name. He
looked towards the breach, and saw slowly rising above it the head
of the soldier whom he had ordered to accompany him to the castle.

"Is that you, Commandant?"

"Yes; what do you want?" replied the young man, in a low
voice. A sort of presentiment warned him to be cautious.

"Those rascals down there are stirring like worms. I have
hurried, with your leave, to tell you my own little observations."

"Go on," said Victor Marchand.

"I have just followed a man from the castle who came in this
direction with a lantern in his hand. A lantern's a frightfully suspicious thing. I don't fancy it was tapers my fine Catholic was

going to light at this time of night. 'They want to eat us body and bones!' says I to myself; so I went on his track to reconnoiter. There, on a ledge of rock, not three paces from here, I discovered a great heap of fagots."

Suddenly a terrible shriek rang through the town, and cut the soldier short. At the same instant a gleam of light flashed before the Commandant. The poor grenadier received a ball in the head and fell. A fire of straw and dry wood burst into flame like a house on fire, not ten paces from the young man. The sound of the instruments and the laughter ceased in the ballroom. The silence of death, broken only by groans, had suddenly succeeded to the noises and music of the feast. The fire of a cannon roared over the surface of the sea. Cold sweat trickled down the young officer's forehead; he had no sword. He understood that his men had been slaughtered, and the English were about to disembark. If he lived he saw himself dishonored, summoned before a council of war. Then he measured with his eyes the depth of the valley. He sprang forward, when just at that moment his hand was seized by the hand of Clara.

"Fly!" said she; "my brothers are following to kill you. Down yonder at the foot of the rock you will find Juanito's Andalusian. Quick!"

The young man looked at her for a moment, stupefied. She pushed him on; then, obeying the instinct of self-preservation which never forsakes even the bravest man, he rushed down the park in the direction she had indicated. He leapt from rock to rock, where only the goats had ever trod before; he heard Clara crying out to her brothers to pursue him; he heard the footsteps of the assassins; he heard the balls of several discharges whistle about his ears; but he reached the valley, he found the horse. mounted, and disappeared swift as lightning. In a few hours he arrived at the quarters occupied by General Gautier. He found him at dinner with his staff.

"I bring you my life in my hand!" cried the Commandant, his face pale and haggard.

He sat down and related the horrible disaster. A dreadful silence greeted his story.

"You appear to me to be more unfortunate than criminal." said the terrible General at last. "You are not accountable for the crime of the Spaniards. and unless the Marshal decides otherwise. I acquit you."

These words could give the unfortunate officer but slight consolation.

"But when the Emperor hears of it!" he exclaimed.

"He will want to have you shot," said the General. "However——
But we will talk no more about it," he added severely, "except
how we are to take such a revenge as will strike wholesome fear
upon this country, where they carry on war like savages."

One hour afterwards, a whole regiment, a detachment of cavalry,
and a convoy of artillery were on the road. The General and Victor
marched at the head of the column. The soldiers, informed of the
massacre of their comrades, were filled with extraordinary fury. The
distance which separated the town of Menda from the general quarters
was passed with marvelous rapidity. On the road the General found
whole villages under arms. Each of these wretched townships was
surrounded and their inhabitants decimated.

By some inexplicable fatality, the English ships stood off instead
of advancing. It was known afterwards that these vessels had out-
stript the rest of the transports and only carried artillery. Thus the
town of Menda, deprived of the defenders she was expecting, and
which the sight of the English vessels had seemed to assure, was
surrounded by the French troops almost without striking a blow.
The inhabitants, seized with terror, offered to surrender at discre-
tion. Then followed one of those instances of devotion not rare in
the peninsula. The assassins of the French, foreseeing, from the
cruelty of the General, that Menda would probably be given over
to the flames and the whole population put to the sword, offered to
denounce themselves. The General accepted this offer, inserting as
a condition that the inhabitants of the castle, from the lowest valet
to the Marques himself, should be placed in his hands. This capitula-
tion agreed upon, the General promised to pardon the rest of the
population and to prevent his soldiers from pillaging or setting
fire to the town. An enormous contribution was exacted, and the
richest inhabitants gave themselves up as hostages to guarantee the
payment, which was to be accomplished within twenty-four hours.

The General took all precautions necessary for the safety of his
troops, provided for the defense of the country, and refused to
lodge his men in the houses. After having formed a camp, he went
up and took military possession of the castle. The members of the
family of Leganes and the servants were gagged, and shut up in
the great hall where the ball had taken place, and closely watched.
The windows of the apartment afforded a full view of the terrace

81

which commanded the town. The staff was established in a neighboring gallery, and the General procceded at once to hold a council of war on the measures to be taken for opposing the debarkation. After having dispatched an aid-de-camp to Marshal Ney, with orders to plant batteries along the coast, the General and his staff turned their attention to the prisoners. Two hundred Spaniards, whom the inhabitants had surrendered, were shot down then and there upon the terrace. After this military execution, the General ordered as many gallows to be erected on the terrace as there were prisoners in the hall of the castle, and the town executioner to be brought. Victor Marchand made use of the time from then until dinner to go and visit the prisoners. He soon returned to the General.

"I have come," said he, in a voice broken with emotion, "to ask you a favor."

"You?" said the General, in a tone of bitter irony.

"Alas!" replied Victor, "it is but a melancholy errand that I am come on. The Marques has seen the gallows being erected, and expresses a hope that you will change the mode of execution for his family; he entreats you to have the nobles beheaded."

"So be it!" said the General.

"They further ask you to allow them the last consolations of religion, and to take off their bonds; they promise not to attempt to escape."

"I consent," said the General; "but you must be answerable for them."

"The old man also offers you the whole of his fortune if you will pardon his young son."

"Really!" said the General. "His goods already belong to King Joseph; he is under arrest." His brow contracted scornfully, then he added: "I will go beyond what they ask. I understand now the importance of the last request. Well, let him buy the eternity of his name, but Spain shall remember forever his treachery and its punishment. I give up the fortune and ·his life to whichever of his sons will fulfill the office of executioner. Go, and do not speak to me of it again."

Dinner was ready, and the officers sat down to table to satisfy appetites sharpened by fatigue.

One of them only, Victor Marchand, was not present at the banquet. He hesitated for a long time before he entered the room. The haughty family of Leganes were in their agony. He glanced sadly at the scene before him; in this very room, only the night before, he had watched the fair heads of those two young girls and those three youths as they circled in the excitement of the dance. He shuddered when he thought how soon they must fall, struck off by the sword of the headsman. Fastened to their gilded chairs, the father and mother, their three sons, and their two young daughters, sat absolutely motionless. Eight serving men stood upright before them, their hands bound behind their backs. These fifteen persons looked at each other gravely, their eyes scarcely betraying the thoughts that surged within them. Only profound resignation and regret for the failure of their enterprise left any mark upon the features of some of them. The soldiers stood likewise motionless, looking at them, and respecting the affliction of their cruel enemies. An expression of curiosity lit up their faces when Victor appeared. He gave the order to unbind the condemned, and went himself to loose the cords which fastened Clara to her chair. She smiled sadly. He could not refrain from touching her arm, and looking with admiring eyes at her black locks and graceful figure. She was a true Spaniard; she had the Spanish complexion and the Spanish eyes, with their long curled lashes and pupils blacker than the raven's wing.

"Have you been successful?" she said, smiling upon him mournfully with somewhat of the charm of girlhood still lingering in her eyes.

Victor could not suppress a groan. He looked one after the other at Clara and her three brothers. One, the eldest, was aged thirty; he was small, even somewhat ill made, with a proud disdainful look, but there was a certain nobleness in his bearing; he seemed no stranger to that delicacy of feeling which elsewhere has rendered the chivalry of Spain so famous. His name was Juanito. The second, Felipe, was aged about twenty; he was like Clara. The youngest was eight, Manuel; a painter would have found in his features a trace of that Roman steadfastness which David has given to children's faces in his episodes of the Republic. The old Marques, his head still covered with white locks, seemed to have come forth from a picture of Murillo. The young officer shook his head. When he looked at them, he was hopeless that he would ever see the bargain proposed by the General accepted by either of the four; nevertheless he ventured to impart it to Clara. At first she shuddered, Spaniard though she was; then, immediately recovering her calm demeanor, she went and knelt down before her father.

83

"Father," she said, "make Juanito swear to obey faithfully any orders that you give him, and we shall be content."

The Marquesa trembled with hope; but when she leant towards her husband, and heard—she who was a mother—the horrible confidence whispered by Clara, she swooned away. Juanito understood all; he leapt up like a lion in its cage. After obtaining an assurance of perfect submission from the Marques, Victor took upon himself to send away the soldiers. The servants were led out, handed over to the executioner, and hanged. When the family had no guard but Victor to watch them, the old father rose and said, "Juanito."

Juanito made no answer, except by a movement of the head, equivalent to a refusal; then he fell back in his seat, and stared at his parents with eyes dry and terrible to look upon. Clara went and sat on his knee, put her arm round his neck, and kissed his eyelids.

"My dear Juanito," she said gayly, "if thou didst only know how sweet death would be to me if it were given by thee, I should not have to endure the odious touch of the headsman's hands. Thou wilt cure me of the woes that were in store for me—and, dear Juanito, thou couldst not bear to see me belong to another, well——" Her soft eyes cast one look of fire at Victor, as if to awaken in Juanito's heart his horror of the French.

"Have courage," said his brother Felipe, "or else our race, that has almost given kings to Spain, will be extinct."

Suddenly Clara rose, the group which had formed round Juanito separated, and this son, dutiful in his disobedience, saw his aged father standing before him, and heard him cry in a solemn voice, "Juanito, I command thee."

The young Count remained motionless. His father fell on his knees before him; Clara, Manuel, and Felipe did the same instinctively. They all stretched out their hands to him as to one who was to save their family from oblivion: they seemed to repeat their father's words.—"My son, hast thou lost the energy, the true chivalry of Spain? How long wilt thou leave thy father on his knees? What right hast thou to think of thine own life and its suffering? Madam, is this a son of mine?" continued the old man, turning to his wife.

"He consents," cried she in despair. She saw a movement in Juanito's eyelids, and she alone understood its meaning.

Mariquita, the second daughter, still knelt on her knees, and clasped her mother in her fragile arms; her little brother Manuel, seeing her weeping hot tears, began to chide her. At this moment the almoner of the castle came in; he was immediately surrounded by the rest of the family and brought to Juanito. Victor could bear this scene no longer; he made a sign to Clara, and hastened away to make one last effort with the General. He found him in high good humor in the middle of the banquet, drinking with his officers; they were beginning to make merry.

An hour later a hundred of the principal inhabitants of Menda came up to the terrace, in obedience to the General's orders, to witness the execution of the family of Leganes. A detachment of soldiers was drawn up to keep back these Spanish burghers who were ranged under the gallows on which the servants of the Marques still hung. The feet of these martyrs almost touched their heads. Thirty yards from them a block had been set up, and by it gleamed a scimiter. The headsman also was present, in case of Juanito's refusal. Presently, in the midst of the profoundest silence, the Spaniards heard the footsteps of several persons approaching, the measured tread of a company of soldiers, and the faint clinking of their muskets. These diverse sounds were mingled with the merriment of the officers' banquet,—just as before it was the music of the dance which had concealed preparations for a treacherous massacre. All eyes were turned towards the castle; the noble family was seen advancing with incredible dignity. Every face was calm and serene; one man only leant, pale and haggard, on the arm of the Priest. Upon this man he lavished all the consolations of religion —upon the only one of them doomed to live. The executioner understood, as did all the rest, that for that day Juanito had undertaken the office himself. The aged Marques and his wife, Clara, Mariquita, and their two brothers, came and knelt down a few steps from the fatal spot. Juanito was led thither by the Priest. As he approached the block the executioner touched him by the sleeve and drew him aside, probably to give him certain instructions.

The Confessor placed the victims in such a position that they could not see the executioner; but like true Spaniards, they knelt erect without a sign of emotion.

Clara was the first to spring forward to her brother. "Juanito," she said, "have pity on my faint-heartedness; begin with me."

At that moment they heard the footsteps of a man running at full speed, and Victor arrived on the tragic scene. Clara was already on her knees, already her white neck seemed to invite the edge of the scimiter. A deadly pallor fell upon the officer, but he still found strength to run on.

"The General grants thee thy life if thou wilt marry me." he said to her in a low voice.

The Spaniard cast a look of proud disdain on the officer. "Strike, Juanito," she said, in a voice of profound meaning.

Her head rolled at Victor's feet. When the Marquesa heard the sound a convulsive start escaped her; this was the only sign of her affliction.

"Am I placed right so, dear Juanito?" little Manuel asked his brother.

"Ah, thou weepest, Mariquita!" said Juanito to his sister.

"Yes," answered the girl; "I was thinking of thee, my poor Juanito; thou wilt be so unhappy without us."

At length the noble figure of the Marques appeared. He looked at the blood of his children; then he turned to the spectators, who stood mute and motionless before him. He stretched out his hands to Juanito, and said in a firm voice: "Spaniards, I give my son a father's blessing. Now, *Marques*, strike without fear, as thou art without fault."

But when Juanito saw his mother approach, supported by the Confessor, he groaned aloud, "She fed me at her own breast." His cry seemed to tear a shout of horror from the lips of the crowd. At this terrible sound the noise of the banquet and the laughter and merrymaking of the officers died away. The Marquesa comprehended that Juanito's courage was exhausted. With one leap she had thrown herself over the balustrade, and her head was dashed to pieces against the rocks below. A shout of admiration burst forth. Juanito fell to the ground in a swoon.

"Marchand has just been telling me something about this execution," said a half-drunken officer. "I'll warrant, General, it wasn't by your orders that——"

"Have you forgotten, Messieurs," cried General Gautier, "that during the next month there will be five hundred French families in tears, and that we are in Spain? Do you wish to leave your bones here?"

After this speech there was not a man, not even a sublieutenant, who dared to empty his glass.

In spite of the respect with which he is surrounded—in spite of the title of El Verdugo (the executioner), bestowed upon him as a title of nobility by the King of Spain—the Marques de Leganes is a prey to melancholy. He lives in solitude, and is rarely seen. Overwhelmed with the load of his glorious crime, he seems only to await the birth of a second son, impatient to seek again the company of those Shades who are about his path continually.

JAMES MATTHEW BARRIE

JAMES MATTHEW BARRIE (English, 1860-1937). Scottish-born playwright and novelist, admired today for such plays as *The Admirable Crichton* and *What Every Woman Knows,* and the children's classic, *Peter Pan.* A consummate master of stagecraft, though works sometimes marred by sentimentality. At his unrivaled best in fantasy, combining humor, pathos and whimsey.

COURTSHIPS

WITH the severe Auld Lichts the Sabbath began at six o'clock on Saturday evening. By that time the gleaming shuttle was at rest, Davie Haggart had strolled into the village from his pile of stones on the Whunny road; Hendry Robb, the "dummy," had sold his last barrowful of "rozetty (resiny) roots" for firewood; and the people, having tranquilly supped and soused their faces in their water pails, slowly donned their Sunday clothes. This ceremony was common to all; but here divergence set in. The gray Auld Licht, to whom love was not even a name, sat in his high-backed armchair by the hearth, Bible or "Pilgrim's Progress" in hand, occasionally lapsing into slumber. But—though, when they got the chance, they went willingly three times to the kirk—there were young men in the community so flighty that, instead of dozing at home on Saturday night, they dandered casually into the square, and, forming into knots at the corners, talked solemnly and mysteriously of women.

Not even on the night preceding his wedding was an Auld Licht ever known to stay out after ten o'clock. So weekly conclaves at street corners came to an end at a comparatively early hour, one Coelebs after another shuffling silently from the square until it echoed, deserted, to the townhouse clock. The last of the gallants, gradually discovering that he was alone, would look around him musingly, and, taking in the situation, slowly wend his way home. On no other night of the week was frivolous talk about the softer sex indulged in, the Auld Lichts being creatures of habit who never thought of smiling on a Monday. Long before they reached their teens they were earning their keep as herds in the surrounding glens or filling "pirns" for their parents; but they were generally on the brink of twenty before they thought seriously of matrimony. Up to that time they only trifled with the other sex's affections at a distance—filling a maid's water pails, perhaps, when no one was looking or carrying her wob; at the recollection of which they would slap their knees almost jovially on Saturday night. A wife was expected to assist at the loom as well as to be cunning in the making of marmalade and the firing of bannocks, and there was consequently some heartburning among the lads for maids of skill and muscle. The Auld Licht, however, who meant marriage seldom loitered in the streets. By and by there came a time when the clock looked down through its cracked glass upon the hemmed-in square and saw him not. His companions, gazing at each other's boots, felt that something was going on, but made no remark.

A month ago, passing through the shabby familiar square, I brushed against a withered old man tottering down the street under a load of yarn. It was piled on a wheelbarrow, which his feeble hands could not have raised but for the rope of yarn that supported it from his shoulders; and though Auld Licht was written on his patient eyes, I did not immediately recognize Jamie Whamond. Years ago Jamie was a sturdy weaver and fervent lover whom I had the right to call my friend. Turn back the century a few decades, and we are together on a moonlight night, taking a short cut through the fields from the farm of Craigiebuckle. Buxom were Craigiebuckle's "dochters," and Jamie was Janet's accepted suitor. It was a muddy road through damp grass, and we picked our way silently over its ruts and pools. "I'm thinkin'," Jamie said at last, a little wistfully, " that I micht hae been as weel wi' Christy."

Christy was Janet's sister, and Jamie had first thought of her. Craigiebuckle, however, strongly advised him to take Janet instead, and he consented. Alack! heavy wobs have taken all the grace from Janet's shoulders this many a year, though she and Jamie go bravely down the hill together. Unless they pass the allotted span of life, the "poors-house" will never know them. As for bonny Christy, she proved a flighty thing, and married a deacon in the Established Church. The Auld Licht groaned over her fall, Craigiebuckle hung his head, and the minister told her sternly to go her way. But a few weeks afterwards Lang Tammas, the chief elder, was observed talking with her for an hour in Gowrie's close; and the very next

Sabbath Christy pushed her husband in triumph into her father's pew. The minister, though completely taken by surprise, at once referred to the stranger, in a prayer of great length, as a brand that might yet be plucked from the burning. Changing his text, he preached at him; Lang Tammas, the precentor, and the whole congregation (Christy included), sang at him; and before he exactly realized his position he had become an Auld Licht for life. Christy's triumph was complete when, next week, in broad daylight, too, the minister's wife called, and (in the presence of Betsy Munn, who vouches for the truth of the story) graciously asked her to come up to the manse on Thursday, at 4 P.M., and drink a dish of tea. Christy, who knew her position, of course begged modestly to be excused; but a coolness arose over the invitation between her and Janet—who felt slighted—that was only made up at the laying-out of Christy's father-in-law, to which Janet was pleasantly invited.

When they had red up the house, the Auld Licht lassies sat in the gloaming at their doors on three-legged stools, patiently knitting stockings. To them came stiff-limbed youths who, with a "Blawy nicht, Jeanie" (to which the inevitable answer was, "It is so Charles"), rested their shoulders on the door-post and silently followed with their eyes the flashing needles. Thus the courtship began—often to ripen promptly into marriage, at other times to go no further. The smooth-haired maids, neat in their simple wrappers, knew they were on their trial and that it behooved them to be wary. They had not compassed twenty winters without knowing that Marget Todd lost Davie Haggart because she "fittit" a black stocking with brown worsted, and that Finny's grieve turned from Bell Whamond on account of the frivolous flowers in her bonnet; and yet Bell's prospects, as I happen to know, at one time looked bright and promising. Sitting over her father's peat fire one night gossiping with him about fishing flies and tackle, I noticed the grieve, who had dropped in by appointment with some ducks' eggs on which Bell's clockin hen was to sit, performing some slight-of-hand trick with his coat sleeve. Craftily he jerked and twisted it, till his own photograph (a black smudge on white) gradually appeared to view. This he gravely slipped into the hands of the maid of his choice, and then took his departure, apparently much relieved. Had not Bell's light-headedness driven him away, the grieve would have soon followed up his gift with an offer of his hand. Some night Bell would have "seen him to the door," and they would have stared sheepishly at each other before saying good night. The parting salutation given, the grieve would still have stood his ground, and Bell would have waited with him. At last "Will ye hae 's Bell?" would have dropped from his half-reluctant lips; and Bell would have mumbled, "Ay," with her thumb in her mouth. "Guid nicht to ye, Bell," would be the next remark— "Guid nicht to ye, Jeames," the answer; the humble door would close softly, and Bell and her lad would have been engaged. But, as it was, their attachment never got beyond the silhouette stage, from which, in the ethics of the Auld Lichts, a man can draw back in certain circumstances without loss of honor. The only really tender thing I ever heard an Auld Licht lover say to his sweetheart was when Gowrie's brother looked softly into Easie Tamson's eyes and whispered, "Dou you swite (sweat)?" Even then the effect was produced more by the loving cast in Gowrie's eye that by the tenderness of the words themselves.

The courtships were sometimes of long duration, but as soon as the young man realized that he was courting he proposed. Cases were not wanting in which he realized this for himself, but as a rule he had to be told of it.

There were a few instances of weddings among the Auld Lichts that did not take place on Friday. Betsy Munn's brother thought to assert his two coal carts, about which he was sinfully puffed up, by getting married early in the week; but he was a pragmatical feckless body, Jamie. The foreigner from York that Finny's grieve after disappointing Jinny Whamond, took, sought to sow the seeds of strife by urging that Friday was an unlucky day; and I remember how the minister, who was always great in a crisis, nipped the bickering in the bud by adducing the conclusive fact that he had been married on the sixth day of the week himself. It was a judicious policy on Mr. Dishart's part to take vigorous action at once and insist on the solemnization of the marriage on a Friday or not at all, for he best kept superstition out of the congregation by branding it as heresy. Perhaps the Auld Lichts were only ignorant of the grieve's lass' theory because they had not thought of it. Friday's claims, too, were incontrovertible; for the Saturday's being a slack day gave the couple an opportunity to put their but and ben in order, and on Sabbath they had a gay day of it. three times at the kirk. The honeymoon over, the racket of the loom began again on the Monday.

The natural politeness of the Allardice family gave me my invitation to Tibbie's wedding. I was taking tea and cheese early one wintry afternoon with the smith and his wife, when little Joey Todd in his Sabbath clothes peered in at the passage, and then knocked primly at the door. Andra forgot himself, and called out to him to come in by; but Jess frowned him into silence, and hastily donning her black mutch, received Willie on the threshold. Both halves of the door were open, and the visitor had looked us over carefully before knocking; but he had come with the compliments of Tibbie's mother, requesting the pleasure of Jess and her man that evening to the lassie's marriage with Sam'l Todd, and the knocking at the door was part of the ceremony. Five minutes afterward Joey returned to beg a moment of me in the passage; when I, too, got my invitation. The lad had just received, with an expression of polite surprise, though he knew he could claim it as his right, a slice of crumbling shortbread, and taken his staid departure, when Jess cleared the tea things off the table, remarking simply that it was a mercy we had not got beyond the first cup. We then retired to dress.

About six o'clock, the time announced for the ceremony, I elbowed my way through the expectant throng of men, women and children that already besieged the smith's door. Shrill demands of "toss, toss!" rent the air every time Jess' head showed on the window blind, and Andra hoped, as I pushed open the door, "that I hadna forgotten my bawbees." Weddings were celebrated among the Auld Lichts by showers of ha-pence, and the guests on their way to the bride's house had to scatter to the hungry rabble like housewives feeding poultry. Willie Todd, the best man, who had never come out so strong in his life before, slipped through the back window, while the crowd, led on by Kitty McQueen, seethed in front, and making a bolt for it to the "Sosh," was back in a moment with a handful of small change. "Dinna toss ower lavishly at first," the smith whispered to me nervously, as we followed Jess and Willie into the darkening yard.

The guests were packed hot and solemn in Johnny Allardice' "room": the men anxious to surrender their seat to the ladies who happened to be standing but too bashful to propose it, the ham and the fish frizzling noisily side by side and hissing out every now and then to let all whom it might concern know that Janet Craik was adding more water to the gravy. A better woman never lived; but oh! the hypocrisy of the face that beamed greeting to the guests as if it had nothing to do but politely show them in, and gasped next moment with upraised arms, over what was nearly a fall in crockery. When Janet sped to the door her "spleet new" merion dress fell, to the pulling of a string, over her home-made petticoat, like the drop scene in a theater, and rose as promptly when she returned to slice the bacon. The murmur of admiration that filled the room when she entered with the minister was an involuntary tribute to the spotlessness of her wrapper, and a great triumph for Janet. If there is an impression that the dress of the Auld Lichts was on all occasions as somber as their faces, let it be known that the bride was but one of several in "whites," and that Mag Munn had only at the last moment been dissuaded from wearing flowers. The minister, the Auld Lichts congratulated themselves, disapproved of all such decking of the person and bowing of the head to idols; but on such an occasion he was not expected to observe it. Bell Whamond, however, has reason for knowing that, marriages or no marriages, he drew the line at curls.

By and by Sam'l Todd, looking a little dazed, was pushed into the middle of the room to Tibbie's side, and the minister raised his voice in prayer. All eyes closed reverently, except perhaps the bridegroom's, which seemed glazed and vacant. It was an open question in the community whether Mr. Dishart did not mis his chance at weddings, the men shaking their heads over the comparative brevity of the ceremony, the women worshipping him (though he never hesitated to rebuke them when they showed it too openly) for the urbanity of his manners. At that time, however, only a minister of such experience as Mr. Dishart's predecessor could lead up to a marriage in prayer without inadvertently joining the couple; and the catechizing was mercifully brief. Another prayer followed the union; the minister waived his right to kiss the bride; every one looked at every other one, as if he had for the moment forgotten what he was on the point of saying and found it very annoying; and Janet signed frantically to Willie Todd, who nodded intelligently in reply, but evidently had no idea what she meant. In time Johnny Allardice, our host, who became more and more doited as the night proceeded, remembered his instructions, and led the way to the kitchen, where the guests, having politely informed their hostess that they were not hungry, partook of a hearty tea. Mr. Dishart presided, with the bride and bridegroom near him; but though he tried to give an agreeable turn to the conversation by describing the extensions at the cemetery, his personality oppressed us, and we only breathed freely when he rose to go. Yet we marvelled at his versatility. In shaking hands with the newly married couple the minister reminded them that it was leap year, and wished them "three hundred and sixty-six happy and God-fearing days."

Sam'l' station being too high for it, Tibbie did not have a penny wedding, which her thrifty mother bewailed, penny weddings starting a couple in life. I can recall nothing more characteristic of the nation from which the Auld Lichts sprung than the penny wedding, where the only revellers that were not out of pocket by it were the couple who gave the entertainment. The more the guests ate and drank the better, pecuniarily, for their hosts. The charge for admission to the penny wedding (practically to the feast that followed it) varied in different districts, but with us it was generally a shilling. Perhaps the penny extra to the fiddler accounts for the name penny wedding. The ceremony having been gone through in the bride's house, there was an adjournment to a barn or other convenient place of meeting, where was held the nuptial feast. Long white boards from Rob Angus' sawmill, supported on trestles, stood in lieu of tables; and those of the company who could not find a seat waited patiently against the wall for a vacancy. The shilling gave every guest the free run of the groaning board; but though fowls were plentiful, and even white bread, too, little had been spent on them. The farmers of the neighborhood, who looked forward to providing the young couple with drills of potatoes for the coming winter, made a bid for their custom by sending them a fowl gratis for the marriage supper. It was popularly understood to be the oldest cock of the farmyard, but for all that it made a brave appearance in a shallow sea of soup. The fowls were always boiled —without exception, so far as my memory carries me—the guidwife never having the heart to roast them, and so lose the broth. One round of whisky and water was all the drink to which his shilling entitled the guest. If he wanted more he had to pay for it. There was much revelry, with song and dance, that no stranger could have thought those stiff-limbed weavers capable of; and the more they shouted and whirled through the barn, the more their host smiled and rubbed his hands. He presided at the bar improvised for the occasion, and if the thing was conducted with spirit, his bride flung an apron over her gown and helped him. I remember one elderly bride-groom, who, having married a blind woman, had to do double work at his penny wedding. It was a sight to see him flitting about the torch-lit barn, with a kettle of hot water in one hand and a besom to sweep up crumbs in the other.

Though Sam'l had no penny wedding, however, we made a night of it at his marriage.

Wedding chariots were not in those days, though I know of Auld Lichts being conveyed to marriages nowadays by horses with white ears. The tea over, we formed in couples, and—the best man with the bride, the bridegroom with the best maid, leading the way —marched in slow procession in the moonlight night to Tibbie's new home, between lines of hoarse and eager onlookers. An attempt was made by an itinerant musician to head the company with his fiddle; but instrumental music, even in the streets, was abhorrent to sound Auld Lichts, and the minister had spoken privately to Willie Todd on the subject. As a consequence, Peter was driven from the ranks. The last thing I saw that night, as we filed, bare-headed and solemn, into the newly married couple's house, was Kitty McQueen's vigorous arm, in a dishevelled sleeve, pounding a pair of urchins who had got between her and a muddy ha'penny.

That night there was revelry and boisterous mirth (or what the Auld Lichts took for such) in Tibbie's kitchen. At eleven o'clock Davit Lunan cracked a joke. Davie Haggart, in reply to Bell Dundas' request, gave a song of distinctly secular tendencies. The bride (who had carefully taken off her wedding gown on getting home and donned a wrapper) coquettishly let the bridegroom's father hold her hand. In Auld Licht circles, when one of the company was offered whisky and refused it, the others, as if pained at the offer, pushed it from them as a thing abhorred. But Davie Haggart set another example on this occasion, and no one had the courage to refuse to follow it. We sat late round the dying fire, and it was only Willie Todd's scandalous assertion (he was but a boy) about his being able to dance that induced us to think of moving. In the community, I understand, this marriage is still memorable as the occasion on which Bell Whamond laughed in the minister's face.

BASHO

BASHO (Matsuo Munefusa, Japanese, 1644-1694). Master of the *Hokku* School of Japanese poetry (the *hokku:* a poem of seventeen syllables in three lines). Of samurai family, left feudal service to travel extensively and become a hermit, taking up Zen Buddhism. Works: *Fuyu no hi* and *Haru no hi* (anthologies) ; *Nozarashi kikō* and *Oku no hosomichi* (travel diaries).

NEW YEAR'S DAY

Ah, the New Year's Day reminds me
  Of a lonely autumn evening.

CROWS ON A SNOWY MORNING

The usually hateful crow—
How lovely on the morn of snow!

THE RUINS OF TAKADACHI FORT

The summer grass!
'Tis all that's left
Of ancient warriors' dreams.

VIOLETS

Beside a mountain path,
A graceful find
Is a tiny violet!

A CROW ON A BARE BRANCH

The autumn gloaming deepens into night;
Black 'gainst the slowly-fading orange light,
On withered bough a lonely crow is sitting.

THE OLD POND

A lonely pond in age-old stillness sleeps....
  Apart unstirred by sound or motion . . . . till
Suddenly into it a lithe frog leaps.

A VERSE COMPOSED ON HORSEBACK

The roadside thistle, eager
To see the travellers pass
Was eaten by the passing ass.

THE MILKY WAY

O rough sea! Waves on waves do darkling rise,
The galaxy reaching down where Sado lies.

THE FIREFLY SEEN BY DAYLIGHT

Alas! the firefly seen by daylight
Is nothing but a red-necked insect.

THE FIRST SNOW

The first snow—just enough
To bend the jonquil leaves.

THE MOGAMI RIVER

Behold! the Mogami has sunk
The burning sun into the sea.

CHARLES BAUDELAIRE

CHARLES BAUDELAIRE (French, 1821-1867). Highly original 19th century poet, whose masterpiece, *Les Fleurs du Mal*, created scandal on publication. exerted greatest single influence on French modernists. Work falters between blasphemy and bigotry. Travels to Africa and the East developed exotic taste. Other major accomplishment was translation of Poe into French.

From SAD MADRIGAL

What care I that you be wise?
Be beautiful! Be sad! For tears
Add a charm unto your eyes,
As streams to meadows where they rise;
With the storm the bloom appears.

CORRESPONDENCES

Nature is a temple whose living spires
Send mingled words at times upon the air:
Man journeys through a wood of symbols there
That kindle, as he goes, with friendly fires.

As long-drawn echoes in a far-off bond
Blend in a deep and shadowed unity,
Vast as the night and as vast clarity,
Color and sound and fragrance correspond.

Some perfumes are as fresh as the cheek of a child,
Sweet as the hautboy, as the meadow green,
Others are triumphant, rich, defiled,

With all the expansion of infinite things,
Of amber, incense, musk, and benzoin,
Where the transport of the soul and the senses sings.

THE ALBATROSS

Often, in idle hours, men of the crew
Capture an albatross, great bird of the sea
That follows the vessel gliding through
The briny gulfs in indolent company.

No sooner are these sky-bound kings
Placed on the deck than dumb shame soars;
Piteously they droop their great white wings
To drag on either side of them like oars.

The winged adventurer, how dull and weak!
This handsome fellow wears a clownish guise!
One takes his stubby pipe to poke its beak,
One, limping, mimics how the cripple flies!

The poet resembles this prince of the clouds
Who soars with the tempest and mocks the bow:
Exiled on earth amid roaring crowds
His giant wings are weights to keep him low.

STEPHEN VINCENT BENET

STEPHEN VINCENT BENÉT (American, 1898-1943). Modern American
poet, who combined folksy wholesomeness with new classicism. Most famous
work, *John Brown's Body*, epic narrative of Civil War, won Pulitzer Prize in
1929. Also wrote five novels, two short operas (including *The Devil and Daniel
Webster*), many short stories. Benét celebrated exclusively the folk or epic
aspects of American life.

FREEDOM'S A HARD-BOUGHT THING

A LONG time ago, in times gone by, in slavery times, there was a
man named Cue. I want you to think about him. I've got a reason.
He got born like the cotton in the boll or the rabbit in the pea
patch. There wasn't any fine doings when he got born, but his

mammy was glad to have him. Yes. He didn't get born in the Big House, or the overseer's house, or anyplace where the bearing was easy or the work light. No, Lord. He came out of his mammy in a field hand's cabin one sharp winter, and about the first thing he remembered was his mammy's face and the taste of a piece of bacon rind and the light and shine of the pitch-pine fire up the chimney. Well, now, he got born and there he was.

His daddy worked in the fields and his mammy worked in the fields when she wasn't bearing. They were slaves; they chopped the cotton and hoed the corn. They heard the horn blow before the light came and the horn blow that meant the day's work was done. His daddy was a strong man—strong in his back and his arms. The white folks called him Cuffee. His mammy was a good woman, yes, Lord. The white folks called her Sarah, and she was gentle with her hands and gentle with her voice. She had a voice like the river going by in the night, and at night when she wasn't too tired she'd sing songs to little Cue. Some had foreign words in them—African words. She couldn't remember what some of them meant, but they'd come to her down out of time.

Now, how am I going to describe and explain about that time when that time's gone? The white folks lived in the Big House and they had many to tend on them. Old Marster, he lived there like Pharaoh and Solomon, mighty splendid and fine. He had his flocks and his herds, his butler and his baker; his fields ran from the river to the woods and back again. He'd ride around the fields each day on his big horse, Black Billy, just like thunder and lightning, and evenings he'd sit at his table and drink his wine. Man, that was a sight to see, with all the silver knives and the silver forks, the glass decanters, and the gentlemen and ladies from all over. It was a sight to see. When Cue was young, it seemed to him that Old Master must own the whole world, right up to the edge of the sky. You can't blame him for thinking that.

There were things that changed on the plantation, but it didn't change. There were bad times and good times. There was the time young Marse Edward got bit by the snake, and the time Big Rambo ran away and they caught him with the dogs and brought him back. There was a swivel-eyed overseer that beat folks too much, and then there was Mr. Wade, and he wasn't so bad. There was hog-killing time and Christmas and springtime and summertime. Cue didn't wonder about it or why things happened that way; he didn't expect it to be different. A bee in a hive don't ask you how there come to be a hive in the beginning. Cue grew up strong; he grew up smart with his hands. They put him in the blacksmith shop to help Daddy Jake; he didn't like it, at first, because Daddy Jake was mighty cross-tempered. Then he got to like the work; he learned to forge iron and shape it; he learned to shoe a horse and tire a wagon wheel, and everything a blacksmith does. One time they let him shoe Black Billy, and he shod him light and tight and Old Marster praised him in front of Mr. Wade. He was strong; he was black as night; he was proud of his back and his arms.

Now, he might have stayed that way—yes, he might. He heard freedom talk, now and then, but he didn't pay much mind to it. He wasn't a talker or a preacher; he was Cue and he worked in the blacksmith shop. He didn't want to be a field hand, but he didn't want to be a house servant either. He'd rather be Cue than poor white trash or owned by poor white trash. That's the way he felt; I'm obliged to tell the truth about that way.

Then there was a sickness came and his mammy and his daddy died of it. Old Miss got the doctor for them, but they died just the same. After that, Cue felt lonesome.

He felt lonesome and troubled in his mind. He'd seen his daddy and his mammy put in the ground and new slaves come to take their cabin. He didn't repine about that, because he knew things had to be that way. But when he went to bed at night, in the loft over the blacksmith shop, he'd keep thinking about his mammy and his daddy—how strong his daddy was and the songs that his mammy sang. They'd worked all their lives and had children. though he was the only one left, but the only place of their own they had was the place in the burying ground. And yet they'd been good and faithful servants, because Old Marster said so, with his hat off, when he buried them. The Big House stayed, and the cotton and the corn, but Cue's mammy and daddy were gone like last year's crop. It made Cue wonder and trouble.

He began to take notice of things he'd never noticed. When the horn blew in the morning for the hands to go to the fields, he'd wonder who started blowing that horn, in the first place. It wasn't like thunder and lightning; somebody had started it. When he heard Old Marster say, when he was talking to a friend, "This damned epidemic! It's cost me eight prime field hands and the best-trained butler in the state. I'd rather have lost the Flyaway colt than Old Isaac," Cue put that down in his mind and pondered it. Old Marster didn't mean it mean, and he'd sat up with Old Isaac all night before he died. But Isaac and Cue and the Flyaway colt, they all belonged to Old Marster and he owned them, hide and hair. He owned them, like money in his pockets. Well, Cue had known that all his life, but because he was troubled now, it gave him a queer feeling.

Well, now, he was shoeing a horse for young Marster Shepley one day, and he shod it light and tight. And when he was through, he made a stirrup for young Marster Shepley, and young Marster Shepley mounted and threw him a silver bit, with a laughing word. That shouldn't have bothered Cue, because gentlemen sometimes did that. And Old Marster wasn't mean; he didn't object. But all night Cue kept feeling the print of young Marster Shepley's heel in his hands. And yet he liked young Marster Shepley. He couldn't explain it at all.

Finally, Cue decided he must be conjured. He didn't know who had done it or why they'd done it. But he knew what he had to do. He had to go see Aunt Rachel.

Aunt Rachel was an old, old woman, and she lived in a cabin by herself, with her granddaughter, Sukey. She'd seen Old Marster's father and his father, and the tale went she'd seen George Washington with his hair all white, and General Lafayette in his gold-plated suit of clothes that the King of France gave him to fight in. Some folks said she was a conjure and some folks said she wasn't but everybody on the plantation treated her mighty respectful, because, if she put her eye on you, she mightn't take it off. Well, his mammy had been friends with Aunt Rachel, so Cue went to see her.

She was sitting alone in her cabin by the low light of a fire. There was a pot on the fire, and now and then you could hear it bubble and chunk, like a bullfrog chunking in the swamp, but that was the only sound. Cue made his obleegances to her and asked her about the misery in her back. Then he gave her a chicken he happened to bring along. It was a black rooster, and she seemed pleased to get it. She took it in her thin black hands and it fluttered and clucked a minute. So she drew a chalk line along a board and then it stayed still and frozen. Well, Cue had seen that trick before. But it was different, seeing it done in Aunt Rachel's cabin, with the big pot chunking on the fire. It made him feel uneasy and he jingled the bit in his pocket for company.

After a while the old woman spoke. "Well, Son Cue," said she. "that's a fine young rooster you've brought me. What else did you bring me, Son Cue?"

100

"I brought you trouble," said Cue, in a husky voice, because that was all he could think of to say.

She nodded her head as if she'd expected that. "They mostly brings me trouble," she said. "They mostly brings trouble to Aunt Rachel. What kind of trouble, Son Cue? Man trouble or woman trouble?"

"It's my trouble," said Cue, and he told her the best way he could. When he'd finished, the pot on the fire gave a bubble and a croak, and the old woman took a long spoon and stirred it.

"Well, Son Cue, son of Cuffee, son of Shango," she said, "you've got a big trouble, for sure."

"Is it going to kill me dead?" said Cue.

"I can't tell you right about that," said Aunt Rachel. "I could give you lies and prescriptions. Maybe I would, to some folks. But your Grandaddy Shango was a powerful man. It took three men to put irons on him, and I saw the irons break his heart. I won't lie to you, Son Cue. You've got a sickness."

"Is it a bad sickness?" said Cue.

"It's a sickness in your blood," said Aunt Rachel. "It's a sickness in your liver and your veins. Your daddy never had it that I knows of—he took after his mammy's side. But his daddy was a Corromantee, and they is bold and free, and you takes after him. It's the freedom sickness, Son Cue."

"The freedom sickness?" said Cue.

"The freedom sickness," said the old woman, and her little eyes glittered like sparks. "Some they break and some they tame down," she said, "and some is neither to be tamed or broken. Don't I know the signs and the sorrow—me, that come through the middle passage on the slavery ship and seen my folks scattered like sand? Ain't I seen it coming, Lord—O Lord, ain't I seen it coming?"

"What's coming?" said Cue.

"A darkness in the sky and a cloud with a sword in it," said the old woman, stirring the pot, "because they hold our people and they hold our people."

Cue began to tremble. "I don't want to get whipped," he said. "I never been whipped—not hard."

"They whipped your Grandaddy Shango till the blood ran twinkling down his back," said the old woman, "but some you can't break or tame."

"I don't want to be chased by dogs," said Cue. "I don't want to hear the dogs belling and the paterollers after me."

101

The old woman stirred the pot.

"Old Marster, he's a good marster," said Cue. "I don't want to do him no harm. I don't want no trouble or projecting to get me into trouble."

The old woman stirred the pot and stirred the pot.

"O God, I want to be free," said Cue. "I just ache and hone to be free. How am I going to be free, Aunt Rachel?"

"There's a road that runs underground," said the old woman. "I never seen it, but I knows of it. There's a railroad train that runs, sparking and snorting, underground through the earth. At least that's what they tell me. But I wouldn't know for sure," and she looked at Cue.

Cue looked back at her bold enough, for he'd heard about the Underground Railroad himself—just mentions and whispers. But he knew there wasn't any use asking the old woman what she wouldn't tell.

"How I going to find that road, Aunt Rachel?" he said.

"You look at the rabbit in the briar and you see what he do," said the old woman. "You look at the owl in the woods and you see what he do. You look at the star in the sky and you see what she do. Then you come back and talk to me. Now I'm going to eat, because I'm hungry."

That was all the words she'd say to him that night; but when Cue went back to his loft, her words kept boiling around in his mind. All night he could hear that train of railroad cars, snorting and sparking underground through the earth. So, next morning, he ran away.

He didn't run far or fast. How could he? He'd never been more than twenty miles from the plantation in his life; he didn't know the roads or the ways. He ran off before the horn, and Mr. Wade caught him before sundown. Now, wasn't he a stupid man, that Cue?

When they brought him back, Mr. Wade let him off light, because he was a good boy and never ran away before. All the same, he got ten, and ten laid over the ten. Yellow Joe, the head driver, laid them on. The first time the whip cut into him, it was just like a fire on Cue's skin, and he didn't see how he could stand it. Then he got to a place where he could.

After it was over, Aunt Rachel crope up to his loft and had her granddaughter, Sukey, put salve on his back. Sukey, she was sixteen, and golden-skinned and pretty as a peach on a peach tree. She worked in the Big House and he never expected her to do a thing like that.

"I'm mighty obliged," he said, though he kept thinking it was Aunt Rachel got him into trouble and he didn't feel as obliged as he might.

"Is that all you've got to say to me, Son Cue?" said Aunt Rachel, looking down on him. "I told you to watch three things. Did you watch them?"

"No'm," said Cue. "I run off in the woods just like I was a wild turkey. I won't never do that no more."

"You're right, Son Cue," said the old woman. "Freedom's a hard-bought thing. So, now you've been whipped, I reckon you'll give it up."

"I been whipped," said Cue, "but there's a road running underground. You told me so. I been whipped, but I ain't beaten."

"Now you're learning a thing to remember," said Aunt Rachel, and went away. But Sukey stayed behind for a while and cooked Cue's supper. He never expected her to do a thing like that, but he liked it when she did.

When his back got healed, they put him back with the field gang for a while. But then there was blacksmith work that needed to be done and they put him back in the blacksmith shop. And things went on for a long time just the way they had before. But there was a difference in Cue. It was like he'd lived up till now with his ears and his eyes sealed over. And now he began to open his eyes and his ears.

He looked at the rabbit in the briar and he saw it could hide. He looked at the owl in the woods and he saw it went soft through the night. He looked at the star in the sky and he saw she pointed north. Then he began to figure.

He couldn't figure things fast, so he had to figure things slow. He figure the owl and the rabbit got wisdom the white folks don't know about. But he figure the white folks got wisdom he don't know about. They got reading and writing wisdom, and it seem mighty powerful. He ask Aunt Rachel if that's so, and she say it's so.

That's how come he learned to read and write. He ain't supposed to. But Sukey, she learned some of that wisdom, along with the young misses, and she teach him out of a little book she tote from the Big House. The little book, it's all about bats and rats and cats, and Cue figure whoever wrote it must be sort of touched in the head not to write about things folk would want to know, instead of all those trifling animals. But he put himself to it and he learn. It almost bust his head, but he learn. It's a proud day for him when he write his name, "Cue," in the dust with the end of a stick and Sukey tell him that's right.

Now he began to hear the first rumblings of that train running underground—that train that's the Underground Railroad. Oh, Children, remember the names of Levi Coffin and John Hansen! Remember the Quaker saints that hid the fugitive! Remember the names of all those that helped set our people free!

There's a word dropped here and a word dropped there and a word that's passed around. Nobody know where the word come from or where it goes, but it's there. There's many a word spoken in the quarters that the Big House never hears about. There's a heap said in front of the fire that never flies up the chimney. There's a name you tell to the grapevine that the grapevine don't tell back.

There was a white man, one day came by, selling maps and pictures. The quality folks, they looked at his maps and pictures and he talked with them mighty pleasant and respectful. But while Cue was tightening a bolt on his wagon, he dropped a word and a word. The word he said made that underground train come nearer.

Cue meet that man one night, all alone, in the woods. He's a quiet man with a thin face. He hold his life in his hands every day he walk about, but he don't make nothing of that. Cue's seen bold folks and bodacious folks, but it's the first time he's seen a man bold that way. It made him proud to be a man. The man ask Cue questions and Cue give him answers. While he's seeing that man, Cue don't just think about himself any more. He think about all his people that's in trouble.

The man say something to him; he say, "No man own the earth. It's too big for one man." He say, "No man own another man: that's too big a thing too." Cue think about those words and ponder them. But when he gets back to his loft, the courage drains out of him and he sits on his straw tick, staring at the wall. That's the time the darkness comes to him and the shadow falls on him.

He aches and he hones for freedom, but he aches and he hones for Sukey too. And Long Ti's cabin is empty, and it's a good cabin. All he's got to do is to go to Old Marster and take Sukey with him. Old Marster don't approve to mix the field hand with the house servant, but Cue's different: Cue's a blacksmith. He can

104

see the way Sukey would look, coming back to her in the evening. He can see all that. It ain't freedom, but it's what he's used to. And the other way's long and hard and lonesome and strange.

"O Lord, why you put this burden on a man like me?" say Cue. Then he listen a long time for the Lord to tell him, and it seem to him, at last, that he get an answer. The answer ain't in any words, but it's a feeling in his heart.

So when the time come and the plan ripe and they get to the boat on the river and they see there's one too many for the boat, Cue know the answer. He don't have to hear the quiet white man say, "There's one too many for the boat." He just pitch Sukey into it before he can think too hard. He don't say a word or a groan. He know it's that way and there's bound to be a reason for it. He stand on the bank in the dark and see the boat pull away, like Israel's children. Then he hear the shouts and the shot. He know what he's bound to do then, and the reason for it. He knows it's the paterollers, and he show himself. When he get back to the plantation, he's worn and tired. But the paterollers, they've chased him, instead of the boat.

He creep by Aunt Rachel's cabin and he see the fire at her window. So he scratch at the door and go in. And there she is, sitting by the fire, all hunched up and little.

"You looks poorly, Son Cue," she say, when he come in, though she don't take her eye off the pot.

"I'm poorly, Aunt Rachel," he say. "I'm sick and sorry and distressed."

"What's the mud on your jeans, Son Cue?" she say, and the pot, it bubble and croak.

"That's the mud of the swamp where I hid from the paterollers," he say.

"What's the hole in your leg, Son Cue?" she say, and the pot, it croak and bubble.

"That's the hole from the shot they shot at me," say Cue. "The blood most nearly dried, but it make me lame. But Israel's children, they's safe."

"They's across the river?" say the old woman.

"They's across the river," say Cue. "They ain't room for no more in the boat. But Sukey, she's across."

"And what will you do now, Son Cue?" say the old woman. "For that was your chance and your time, and you give it up for another. And tomorrow morning, Mr. Wade, he'll see that hole in your leg and he'll ask questions. It's a heavy burden you've laid on yourself, Son Cue."

"It's a heavy burden," say Cue, "and I wish I was shut of it. I never asked to take no such burden. But freedom's a hard-bought thing."

The old woman stand up sudden, and for once she look straight and tall. "Now bless the Lord!" she say. "Bless the Lord and praise him! I come with my mammy in the slavery ship—I come through the middle passage. There ain't many that remember that, these days, or care about it. There ain't many that remember the red flag that witched us on board or how we used to be free. Many thousands gone, and the thousands of many thousands that lived and died in slavery. But I remember. I remember them all. Then they took me into the Big House—me that was a Mandingo and a witch woman—and the way I live in the Big House, that's between me and my Lord. If I done wrong, I done paid for it—I paid for it with weeping and sorrow. That's before Old Miss' time and I help raise up Old Miss. They sell my daughter to the South and my son to the West, but I raise up Old Miss and tend on her. I ain't going to repine of that. I count the hairs on Old Miss' head when she's young, and she turn to me, weak and helpless. And for that there'll be a kindness between me and the Big House—a kindness that folks will remember. But my children's children shall be free."

"You do this to me," say Cue, and he look at her, and he look at her, and he look dangerous. "You do this to me, old woman," he say, and his breath come harsh in his throat, and his hands twitch.

"Yes," she say, and look him straight in the eyes. "I do to you what I never even do for my own. I do it for your Grandaddy Shango, that never turn to me in the light of the fire. He turn to that soft Eboe woman, and I have to see it. He roar like a lion in the chains, and I have to see that. So, when you come, I try you and test you, to see if you fit to follow after him. And because you fit to follow after him, I put freedom in your heart, Son Cue."

"I never going to be free," say Cue, and look at his hands. "I done broke all the rules. They bound to sell me now."

"You'll be sold and sold again," say the old woman. "You'll know the chains and the whip. I can't help that. You'll suffer for your people and with your people. But while one man's got freedom in his heart, his children bound to know the tale."

She put the lid on the pot and it stop bubbling.

106

"Now I come to the end of my road," she say, "but the tale don't stop there. The tale go backward to Africa and it go forward, like clouds and fire. It go, laughing and grieving forever, through the earth and the air and the waters—my people's tale."

Then she drop her hands in her lap and Cue creep out of the cabin. He know then he's bound to be a witness, and it make him feel cold and hot. He know then he's bound to be a witness and tell that tale. O Lord, it's hard to be a witness, and Cue know that. But it help him in the days to come.

Now, when he get sold, that's when Cue feel the iron in his heart. Before that, and all his life, he despise bad servants and bad masters. He live where the marster's good; he don't take much mind of other places. He's a slave, but he's Cue, the blacksmith, and Old Marster and Old Miss, they tend to him. Now he know the iron in his heart and what it's like to be a slave.

He know that on the rice fields in the hot sun. He know that, working all day for a handful of corn. He know the bad marsters and the cruel overseers. He know the bite of the whip and the gall of the iron on the ankle. Yes, Lord, he know tribulation. He know his own tribulation and the tribulation of his people. But all the time, somehow, he keep freedom in his heart. Freedom mighty hard to root out when it's in the heart.

He don't know the day or the year, and he forget, half the time. there ever was a gal named Sukey. All he don't forget is the noise of the train in his ears, the train snorting and sparking underground. He think about it at nights till he dream it carry him away. Then he wake up with the horn. He feel ready to die then, but he don't die. He live through the whip and the chain; he live through the iron and the fire. And finally he get away.

When he get away, he ain't like the Cue he used to be—not even back at Old Marster's place. He hide in the woods like a rabbit, he slip through the night like an owl. He go cold and hungry, but the star keep shining over him and he keep his eyes on the star. They set the dogs after him and he hear the dogs belling and yipping through the woods.

He's scared when he hear the dogs, but he ain't scared like he used to be. He ain't more scared than any man. He kill the big dog in the clearing—the big dog with the big voice—and he do it with his naked hands. He cross water three times after that to kill the scent, and he go on.

He got nothing to help him—no, Lord—but he got a star. The

107

star shine in the sky and the star shine—the star point north with its shining. You put that star in the sky, O Lord; you put it for the prisoned and the humble. You put it there—you ain't never going to blink it out.

He hungry and he eat green corn and cowpeas. He thirsty and he drink swamp water. One time he lie two days in the swamp, too puny to get up on his feet, and he know they hunting around him. He think that's the end of Cue. But after two days he lift his head and his hand. He kill a snake with a stone, and after he's cut out the poison bag, he eat the snake to strengthen him, and go on

He don't know what the day is when he come to the wide, cold river. The river yellow and foaming, and Cue can't swim. But he hide like a crawdad on the bank; he make himself a little raft with two logs. He know this time's the last time and he's obliged to drown. But he put out on the raft and it drift him to the freedom side. He mighty weak by then.

He mighty weak, but he careful. He know tales of Billy Shea, the slave catcher; he remember those tales. He slide into the town by night, like a shadow, like a ghost. He beg broken victuals at a door; the woman give them to him, but she look at him suspicious. He make up a tale to tell her, but he don't think she believe the tale. In the gutter he find a newspaper; he pick it up and look at the notices. There's a notice about a runaway man named Cue. He look at it and it make the heart beat in his breast.

He patient; he mighty careful. He leave that town behind. He got the name of another town, Cincinnati, and a man's name in that town. He don't know where it is, he have to ask his way, but he do it mighty careful. One time he ask a yellow man directions: he don't like the look on the yellow man's face. He remember Aunt Rachel; he tell the yellow man he conjure his liver out if the yellow man tell him wrong. The yellow man scared and tell him right. He don't hurt the yellow man; he don't blame him for not wanting trouble. But he made the yellow man change pants with him, because his pants mighty ragged.

He patient; he very careful. When he get to the place he been told about, he look all about that place. It's a big house; it don't look right. He creep around to the back—he creep and he crawl. He look in a window; he see white folks eating their supper. They just look like any white folks. He expect them to look different. He feel mighty bad. All the same, he rap at the window the way he been told. They don't nobody pay attention and he just about to go away. Then the white man get up from the table and open the back door a crack. Cue breathe in the darkness.

"God bless the stranger the Lord sends us," say the white man in a low, clear voice, and Cue run to him and stumble, and the white man catch him. He look up and it's a white man, but he ain't like thunder and lightning.

He take Cue and wash his wounds and bind them up. He feed him and hide him under the floor of the house. He ask him his name and where he's from. Then he send him on. O Lord, remember thy tried servant, Asaph Brown! Remember his name!

They send him from there in a wagon and he's hidden in the straw at the bottom. They send him from the next place in a closed cart with six others, and they can't say a word all night. One time a tollkeeper ask them what's in the wagon, and the driver say, "Southern calico," and the tollkeeper laugh. Cue always recollect that.

One time they get to big water—so big it look like the ocean. They cross that water in a boat; they get to the other side. When they get to the other side, they sing and pray, and white folks look on, curious. But Cue don't even feel happy; he just feel he want to sleep.

He sleep like he never sleep before—not for days and years. When he awake up, he wonder; he hardly recollects where he is. He lying in the loft of a barn. Ain't nobody around him. He get up and go out in the air. It's a fine sunny day.

He get up and go out. He say to himself, *I'm free*, but it don't take hold yet. He say to himself, *This is Canada and I'm free*, but it don't take hold. Then he start to walk down the street.

The first white man he meet on the street he scrunch up in himself and start to run across the street. But the white man don't pay him any mind. Then he know.

He say to himself in his mind, *I'm free. My name's Cue—John H. Cue. I got a strong back and strong arms. I got freedom in my heart. I got a first name and a last name and a middle name. I never had them all before.*

He say to himself, *My name's Cue—John H. Cue. I got a name to tell. I got a hammer to swing. I got a tale to tell my people. I got recollection. I call my first son "John Freedom Cue." I call my first daughter "Come-Out-of-the-Lion's-Mouth."*

Then he walk down the street, and he pass a blacksmith shop.
The blacksmith, he's an old man and he lift the hammer heavy. Cue
look in that shop and smile.

He pass on; he go his way. And soon enough he see a girl like
a peach tree—a girl named Sukey—walking free down the street.

PIERRE JEAN DE BERANGER

PIERRE JEAN DE BÉRANGER (French, 1780-1857). Songwriter and poet,
who was the great bohemian of early 19th century. A clerk who broke with
his father and began writing in a garret. Two imprisonments for his poetry
helped make him idol of Parisian working and middle classes. Several collections of poems and an autobiography published during lifetime. His work,
sometimes sentimental, sometimes licentious, still moving.

FIFTY YEARS

(Cinquante Ans)

Wherefore these flowers? floral applause?
  Ah, no, these blossoms came to say
That I am growing old, because
  I number fifty years to-day.
O rapid, ever-fleeting day!
  O moments lost, I know not how!
O wrinkled cheek and hair grown gray!
  Alas, for I am fifty now!

Sad age, when we pursue no more—
  Fruit dies upon the withering tree:
Hark! some one rapped upon my door.
  Nay, open not. 'Tis not for me—
Or else the doctor calls. Not yet
  Must I expect his studious bow.
Once I'd have called, "Come in, Lizzette"—
  Alas, for I am fifty now!

110

In age what aches and pains abound:
    The torturing gout racks us awhile;
Blindness, a prison dark, profound;
    Or deafness that provokes a smile.
Then Reason's lamp grows faint and dim
    With flickering ray. Children, allow
Old Age the honor due to him—
    Alas, for I am fifty now!

Ah, heaven! the voice of Death I know,
    Who rubs his hands in joyous mood;
The sexton knocks and I must go,—
    Farewell, my friends the human brood!
Below are famine, plague, and strife;
    Above, new heavens my soul endow:
Since God remains, begin, new life!
    Alas, for I am fifty now!

But no, 'tis you, sweetheart, whose youth,
    Tempting my soul with dainty ways,
Shall hide from it the somber truth,
    This incubus of evil days.
Springtime is yours, and flowers; come then,
    Scatter your roses on my brow,
And let me dream of youth again—
    Alas, for I am fifty now!

THE OLD TRAMP
(*Le Vieux Vagabond*)

Here in this gutter let me die;
    Weary and sick and old, I've done.
"He's drunk," will say the passers-by;
    All right, I want no pity,—none.
I see the heads that turn away,
    While others glance and toss me sous.
"Off to your junket! go," I say:
Old tramp—to die I need no help from you.

111

Yes, of old age I'm dying now—
  Of hunger people never die.
I hoped some almshouse might allow
  A refuge when the end was nigh;
But all retreats are overflowed,
  Such crowds are suffering and forlorn.
My nurse, alas! has been the road:
Old tramp—let me die here where I was born.

When young, it used to be my prayer
  To craftsmen, "Let me learn your trade:"
"Clear out—we've got no work to spare;
  Go beg," was all reply they made.
You rich, who bade me work, I've fed
  With relish on the bones you threw;
Made of your straw an easy bed:
Old tramp—I have no curse to vent on you.

Poor wretch, how easy 'twas to steal!
  But no, I'd rather beg my bread.
At most I've thieved a wayside meal
  Of apples ripening overhead.
Yet twenty times have I been thrown
  In prison,—'twas the King's decree;
Robbed of the only thing I own:
Old tramp—at least the sun belongs to me.

The poor—is any country his?
  What are to me your grain, your wine,
Your glory and your industries,
  Your orators? They are not mine.
And when a foreign foe waxed fat
  Within your undefended walls,
I shed my tears, poor fool, at that:
Old tramp—his hand was open to my calls.

Why, like the venomous bug you kill,
  Did you not crush me when you could?
Or, better yet, have taught me skill
  To labor for the common good?

The grub a useful ant may end
   If sheltered from the blast and fed;
And so might I have been your friend:
Old tramp—I die your enemy instead.

THE PEOPLE'S REMINISCENCES

(Les Souvenirs du Peuple)

Ah, many a day the straw-thatched cot
   Shall echo with his glory!
The humblest shed, these fifty years,
   Shall know no other story.
There shall the idle villagers
   To some old dame resort,
And beg her with those good old tales
   To make their evenings short.
"What though they say he did us harm?
   Our love this cannot dim:
Come, granny, talk of him to us;
   Come, granny, talk of him."

"Well, children—with a train of kings
   Once he passed by this spot;
'Twas long ago; I had but just
   Begun to boil the pot.
On foot he climbed the hill, whereon
   I watched him on his way;
He wore a small three-cornered hat;
   His overcoat was gray.
I was half frightened till he said
   'Good-day, my dear!' to me."——
"O granny, granny! did he speak?
   What, granny! you and he?"

"Next year, as I, poor soul, by chance
   Through Paris strolled one day,
I saw him taking, with his Court,
   To Notre Dame his way.

113

The crowd were charmed with such a show;
   Their hearts were filled with pride;
'What splendid weather for the fête!
   Heaven favors him!' they cried.
Softly he smiled, for God had given
   To his fond arms a boy."——
"Oh, how much joy you must have felt!
   O granny, how much joy!"

"But when at length our poor Champagne
   By foes was overrun,
He seemed alone to hold his ground;
   Nor dangers would he shun.
One night—as might be now—I heard
   A knock—the door unbarred—
And saw—good God!—'twas he, himself,
   With but a scanty guard.
'Oh, what a war is this!' he cried,
   Talking this very chair"——
"What! granny, granny, there he sat?
   What! granny, he sat there?"

" 'I'm hungry,' said he: quick I served
   Thin wine and hard brown bread;
He dried his clothes, and by the fire
   In sleep dropped down his head.
Waking, he saw my tears—'Cheer up,
   Good dame,' says he, 'I go
'Neath Paris' walls to strike for France
   One last avenging blow.'
He went; but on the cup he used,
   Such value did I set
It has been treasured——" "What! till now?
   You have it, granny, yet?"

"Here 'tis; but 'twas the hero's fate
   To ruin to be led;
He whom a Pope had crowned, alas!
   In a lone isle lies dead.

'Twas long denied: 'No, no,' said they,
  'Soon shall he reappear!
O'er ocean comes he, and the foe
  Shall find his master here.'
Ah, what a bitter pang I felt,
  When forced to own 'twas true!"——
"Poor granny! Heaven for this will look—
  Will kindly look on you."

BHARTRIHARI

BHARTRIHARI (Sanskrit, —— -651). Distinguished Sanskrit grammarian and lyric poet, compared with Horace. His three *satakas* or "centuries" of verse are *Sringāra Sataka* (*Century of Love*), *Niti Sataka* (*Century of Worldly Life*), and *Vairāgyra Sataka* (*Century of Renunciation*).

LOVE, THE FISHER

Love, the fisher, casts his woman-hook
  Into the sea of lust and fond desire,
And just as soon as greedy men-fish look
  And snap the red bait, lips so sweet, so dire:
Then he is quick to catch them and to cook
  The hungry wretches over passion's fire.

STRUGGLING FANCIES

It is my body leaves my love, not I;
  My body moves away, but not my mind;
For back to her my struggling fancies fly
  Like silken banners borne against the wind.

THE WISE MISOGYNIST

The wise misogynist, poor soul,
  To self-deceit is given;
For heaven rewards his self-control,
  And women swarm in heaven.

115

DIGNITY

The dog will roll, and wag his tail, and fawn,
   Show mouth and belly, just to get some meat;
The majestic elephant gazes gravely on;
   Till coaxed a hundred times, he will not eat.

FLAMING BANNERS

Learning and dignity,
   Wisdom and manners
Last till the god of love
   Plants flaming banners.

BETTER IN THE WILD

Better to dwell in mountains wild
   With beasts of prey
Than in the palaces of gods
   With fools to stay.

THE BETTER PART

Is there no splendid Himalayan height,
   Cooled by the spray from Ganges' holy springs
With rocks where fairies now and then alight,
   That men should fawn upon contemptuous kings?

ARROWS OF LOVE

Where are you going, winsome maid,
Through deepest, darkest night? (he said.)
I go to him whom love has made
Dearer to me than life (she said.)
Ah, girl, and are you not afraid,
For you are all alone? (he said.)
The god of love shall be mine aid,
Arrows of love fly true (she said).

LOVE GROWS BY WHAT IT FEEDS ON

When she is far, I only want to see her;
   When she is seen, I only want to kiss her;
When she is kissed, I never want to flee her;
   I know that I could never bear to miss her.

WHEN I KNEW A LITTLE BIT

When I knew a little bit,
Then my silly, blinded wit,
Mad as elephants in rut,
Thought it was omniscient; but
When I learned a little more
From the scholar's hoarded store,
Madness' fever soon grew cool,
And I knew I was a fool.

SWEET AND BITTER

Sweet are the moonbeams, sweet the grass-grown wood,
Sweet is the peaceful converse of the good,
The poet's song is sweet, the maiden's face
When angry tear-drops lend a sudden grace:
All would be sweet if human fate were fitter;
The thought of death turns all the sweet to bitter.

WHY MY POEMS DIED

The critics all were jealous,
    The patrons full of pride,
The public had no judgment;
    And so my poems died.

WOMEN'S EYES

The world is full of women's eyes,
Defiant, filled with shy surprise,
Demure, a little overfree,
Or simply sparkling roguishly;
It seems a gorgeous lily-bed,
Whichever way I turn my head.

117

BHASA

BHĀSA (Sanskrit, *ca.* A.D. 350). Legendary dramatist, author of thirteen Sanskrit plays discovered in Malabar in 1912. The most important is *Svapnavāsavadatta (The Dream af Vāsavadattā).*

TRUE LOVE

[Scene where the King and his friend, the Court Jester, meet and talk. Padmavati, the newly espoused princess, hears the conversation from behind. Vasavadatta, the former Queen of the King, reported as dead, is in disguise in Padmavati's place and acts as her companion. A maid-servant also attends on them.]

Vidusaka:	Friend, there is none here in the garden. Let me crave of you an answer to a question of mine.
King:	As you please.
Vidusaka:	Whom do you love the more of the two, Vasavadatta, who is no more, or Padmavati, who is alive?
King:	Why do you place me in a dilemma?
Padmavati:	(From her hiding-place) Dear friend! What a mischievous fellow he is for causing this perplexing situation for the King!
Vasavadatta:	(To herself) Indeed, I am equally in a fix.
Vidusaka:	Reveal yourself to me without fear. For the one is no longer alive and the other nowhere within our hearing.
King:	I cannot, I cannot give it out. You are a regular chatterbox.
Padmavati:	Why, the King by this vacillation has almost said it.
Vidusaka:	Upon my honour, I will tell none. See, I have already closed my mouth so tightly that the teeth have bitten off the tip of my tongue.
King:	No, I dare not say it out.
Padmavati:	Look at the Court Jester! Still he is dense and understands not the King's meaning.
Vidusaka:	Please do tell me. I swear upon our lasting friendship that I shall never communicate it to any one else.
King:	Well, you are obstinate and I feel no escape. Please listen.

	However worthy of me Padmavati may be by her beauty, her character and her sweet amiability,
	My love for Vasavadatta remains unshaken and refuses to be lured away by her.
Vasavadatta:	(To herself) I have at last my reward for waiting. Indeed, my presence here *incognito* has its own advantages.
Maid-servant:	Madam, the King lacks grace.
Padmavati:	Why girl, do not say so. The King is gracious enough; for he cherishes still his old love, Vasavadatta.

SERENITY

[Scene: Rama in the company of Sita in his palace. He is informed of Dasaratha's unconscious state in Kaikeyi's palace.]

(*Enter Chamberlain.*)

Chamberlain:	Help, Oh help, Prince!
Rama:	Who wants help?
Chamberlain:	The great King, thy sire.
Rama:	What my father? Well, it is like saying the entire world asks for help. Who is the cause of this sudden mishap?
Chamberlain:	From his nearest the King has received this blow.
Rama:	What! from his own near and dear? Alas, then how can there be consolation.
	The enemy aims his blow only at the body; but relatives aim at the heart.
	Well, Oh! who can be that whose claim to kinship with me thus makes me so much ashamed?
Chamberlain:	Who else but Queen Kaikeyi herself?
Rama:	Ah! Do you mouth Kaikeyi's name? She cannot labour but for ultimate good, I know.
Chamberlain:	How, Prince?
Rama:	Listen to me,
	What could be there for her to covet for which she should perpetrate a wrong?
	How can she require wants when she has for a husband one equal to Indra and for a son one like me?

119

Chamberlain:	Ah, do not expect the same sense of fairness in women, who cannot be trusted. Know, it was she who prevented your anointment as king.
Rama:	Am I not then lucky?
Chamberlain:	How could you justify her for demanding Bharata's coronation unasked? Is it not avaricious?
Rama:	Your partiality towards me makes you blind to the good that is concealed within that prayer.

BHAVABHUTI

BHAVABHUTI (Sanskrit, ca. A.D. 730). Leading Sanskrit dramatist, of the 8th century. Author of three dramas: *Mālatī Mādhava (Stolen Marriage)*, *Mahāvīracharita (Story of the Great Hero)*, and *Uttara Rāmacharita (Later Story of Rama)*.

THE RESCUE OF MALATI

Persons: Madhava, *the lover;* Malati, *the heroine;* Kapala-Kundala, *priestess of the fearful goddess* Chamunda; Aghoraghanta, *priest of the same.*

SCENE: *Inside of the Temple of* Chamunda.—Aghoraghanta, *dancing and invoking the goddess, is about to sacrifice Malati.*

Malati [*dressed as a victim*]—
Unpitying sire, thy hapless daughter dies!
Mother beloved, remorseless fate consigns
Thy gentle heart to agony. Revered
And holy dame, who lived but for thy Malati,
Whose every thought was for her happiness,
Thy love will teach thee long and bitter anguish.
Ah, my dear friend, Lavangika, to thee
But in thy dreams I henceforth shall appear!
Madhava [*enters behind*]—
My fears were true—'tis she! but still she lives.
    [*Listens to Aghoraghanta's invocation.*
What luckless chance is this, that such a maid,

120

With crimson garb and garland like a victim
Adorned for sacrifice, should be the captive
Of impious wretches, like a timid fawn
Begirt by ravenous wolves: that she, the child
Of the all-powerful minister, should lie
Thus in the jaws of death? Ah, cruel destiny,
How ruthless are thy purposes!

Kapala-Kundala—
    Fair maid,
Think upon him whom thou in life hast loved,
For pitiless death is near thee.

Malati—
    Ah, Madhava,
Lord of my heart! Oh may I after death
Live in thy memory! They do not die,
Whom love embalms in long and fond embrace.

Kapala-Kundala—
Poor child, her heart is Madhava's.

Aghoraghanta [*raising his sword*]—
    No matter—
Come what come may, we must delay no longer.
This offering vowed to thee, divine Chamunda,
Deign to accept.

Madhava [*rushing forward and snatching Malati up in his arms*]
    Vile wretch, forbear!

Kapala-Kundala—
The term profane is thine.

Malati—
    Oh, save me, save me! [*Embraces Madhave.*]

Madhava—
    Princess, do not fear.
A faithful friend, who in the hour of death
Finds courage to declare his love, is near thee.
Be of good courage—on this impious wretch
The retribution of his crimes descends.

Aghoraghanta—
What sinful youth is this that interrupts
Our solemn rite?

Kapala-Kundala—
The lover of the maiden.
The pupil of Kamandaki. who treads

These precincts for unholy purposes,
And vends the flesh of man.

Madhava—

    Inform me, princess,
How has this chanced?

Malati—

    I know not. I reposed
At eve upon the terrace. When I woke
I found myself a prisoner.—But what led
Your steps to this retreat?

Madhava [*ashamed*]—

    By passion urged,
Incited by the hope my life might be
Yet blest by this fair hand, I hither came
To invoke the unclean spirits of the dead.
Your cries I heard, and instant hurried here.

Malati—

    And wert thou thus regardless of thyself,
And wandering here for me?

Madhava—

    Blest was the chance
That snatched my love from the uplifted swords
Like the pale moon from Rahu's ravenous jaws.
My mind is yet with various passions tossed,
And terror, pity, wonder, joy, and rage,
By turns possess my soul.

Aghoraghanta—

    Rash Brahman boy,
Thou seek'st thy fate. The pitying stag defies
The tiger in the rescue of his doe,
And both are made the forest monarch's prey.
So shalt thou perish, who darest hope to save
The victim of my sacrifice. Thy blood,
As flies the severed head before my scymetar,
Shall stream an offering to the mighty mother
Of all created beings.

Madhava—

    Wretch accursed,
Impious and vile! Couldst thou raise thy sword
Against this delicate frame, that timid shrunk
Even from the flowers her fond companions cast

122

In sportive mood upon her—but my arm
Like Yama's mace now falls upon thy head.

Malati—

Lord of my life, refrain from violence:
His crime is baffled, let him be. Avoid
All needless peril.

Kapala-Kundala—

Holy sir, be firm;
Destroy the culprit.

*Madhava and Aghoraghanta [to the women, each concerning the
other]*—

Banish your alarms:
The villain dies. What other chance should wait
The issue of the conflict, when the lion,
Whose talons light upon the elephant's brow,
As falls the thunderbolt upon the mountain,
Raises their might against the feeble deer.

[*Noise behind.*]

What, ho! Ye who are now in search of **Malati**,
The venerable priestess whose commands
Are ever wise, enjoins ye to surround
The temple of Karala. This can be
The act of none but him who ministers
To the terrific goddess, and the princess
Can be an offering for no other shrine.

Kapala-Kundala—

We are surrounded!

Aghoraghanta—

Greater is the need
Of manly resolution.

Malati—

My dear father!
My venerable mistress!

Madhava—

I will place
The princess out of peril with her friends,
Then swift return for vengeance.

[*He carries Malati off and returns confronting Aghoraghanta.*]

Now let the falchion piecemeal hew thy form,
Ring on thy bones, and cleave thy sinewy joints,
Sport in the yielding marrow, and divide,

123

Resistless in its fury, limb from limb.
[*Exeunt fighting.*

THE STORY OF THE RAMAYANA

[Rama meeting his twin sons Lava and Kusa without knowing
their identity.]

Lava: Sir! What is this? Thy face so full of benediction for
mankind is so suddenly transformed, sorrow-laden
with tears even as a white lotus bloom bathed in dew.

Kusa: How can Raghupati remain unaffected by grief without
his own Sita? The world to one bereft of one's own
dearest will be a wilderness enough. Such is his love
for his Queen; and his grief is unending. Why then
this question of yours, as if you were not aware of
the story of the *Ramayana*?

Rama: (To himself) Indeed, a most impartial opinion! (Aloud)
Boys, we hear of the *Ramayana* often and are told
that poetry flowed from Valmiki's lips and that the
glory of the Solar race is sung. Let me hear it from
you.

Kusa: We know the entire *Ramayana*. But we can just now
recollect for you two verses only from the earlier portion of it.

Rama: Do sing for me, please.

Kusa: (Singing):

Sita was naturally drawn to the great Rama. His love
grew more even as Sita's looks and qualities increased
with his knowledge of her.

Similarly Rama became dearer to Sita than her own life.
Indeed their hearts alone can plumb the depths of true
love between them.

Rama: Alas! these words pierce me more to the heart.

The many recollections of Sita have awakened me to a
procession of emotions.

My unbearable grief has become alive again.

Lava: Another verse, let me sing, which brings out Rama's
words to Sita on the Citra-kuta, encircled by the
Mandakini River.

(Sings):

This slab of a seat looking as one arranged for you
Has been covered all over with flowers from the over-
hanging Kesara branches.
Rama: (With shame, pleasure, sorrow and love in his feelings)
These boys are innocent to a fault, especially because
they are forest-bred.
Ha, Love! Do you remember those delightful incidents?

HAYYIM NAHMAN BIALIK

HAYYIM NAHMAN BIALIK (Hebrew, 1873-1934). Outstanding Hebrew
poet. Born in Russia, died in Israel, where he was leader of cultural life and
shaper of Zionism. The poet of both the vanishing ghetto and the new
nationalism. In Israel, wrote stories, fairy tales and essays, and last great
poem, *Yatmut.* Also collected legends of the Talmud and Midrash in
Sefer Ha'agada.

WHERE ARE YOU?

Out of your hiding place, heart of my being,
Come forth, come quickly to my side.
If I may find salvation, come and save me;
Come, be my master and my guide.
Bring back for but a day the stolen boy;
Let me perish in the springtide of my joy.
At your lips let my soul succumb,
Between your breasts let me bury my hours,
As a butterfly droops when night has come,
Among the scented flowers.

Where are you?

Before I had known you, heart of my being,
Your name was atremble on my lips.
At night I tossed sleepless, crushed my pillow,
My flesh dissolved, my heart was in eclipse.
And all day long, in the Talmud scroll,
In a ray of light, in the form of a white cloud,
When thoughts concern me, or when prayers console,
Lifted on joyous visions, in deepest sorrow bowed,
My soul sought one end, one desire knew,
You, you, you.

HER EYES

She walked like a fawn unafraid among the trees;
She came upon my sight.
The last rays of the sun spangled the rustling leaves,
Strewing ducats of light.
She walked alone. . . Light splashed upon her face,
Fell pattering to the ground.
Two circles of sunlight caught and held her eyes.
She stood, with never a sound.
Two glittering coals flamed fiercely in the dark:
Lord, hearken to my prayer!
Two adders darted forth and found my heart
And poured their poison there.
Two dragons of fire devoured my flaming heart:
Lord, I am Lilith's prize!
I watched her turn, watched her twinkling heels depart. . .
But I lie drowned in her eyes.

*

The dark is a shroud over living.
Stars die after the spark.
Look! Everywhere—and within me,
Dark, my friend, dark.

Dreams are a shadow that lengthens.
Hearts blossom, and blow.
Look! Everywhere—and within me,
Woe, my friend, woe.

"Light!" is the prayer all are breathing;
A prayer that will not be heard.
Long is the murmur, and weary
The word, the only word.

The night is too worn to pass swiftly.
The moon is pallid and gray,
And yawns, overspent and weary
For day, for the sleep of day.

*

Tuck me in under your wing.
Be a mother and sister to me.
Let your bosom my refuge be,
Where my lorn prayers cling.

126

Hearken, and hear my grief,
At dusk, in an hour of truth:
They say there is youth in the world;
Where is my youth?

Bear one more mystery
I am burned in the fire of:
They say there is love in the world;
What—what is love?

I dreamed, and the stars betrayed
My eager call;
And now there is naught for me in the world,
Nothing at all.

Tuck me in under your wing,
Be a mother and sister to me.
Let your bosom my refuge be,
Where my lorn prayers cling.

BILHANA

BILHANA (Kashmiri, *ca.* A.D. 1100). Kashmir historian and poet. His works: *Vikramānkadeva Charita* (*The History of King Vikramānka*), and *Saurīsuratapanchāsikā* (*Fifty Poems of Stolen Love*).

AN INDIAN LOVE-LAMENT

I

I am to die! yet I remember, dying,
　My Soul's delight—my sweet unequalled, love,
Like a fresh champak's golden blossom lying,
　Her smile its opening leaves; and, bright above,
Over her sleepful brow those lustrous tresses
Dark-winding down, tangled with love's caresses.

II

I die, but I remember! How it thrilled me
　The first glad seeing of her glorious face
Clear-carven like the moon; and how it filled me
　With tremors, drinking in the tender grace

127

Which, like a fine air, clothed her; and the rise
Of her twinned breast-hills, and the strange surprise

III

Of love's new rapture! Dying I recall
    Each marvel of her beauty in its blossom;
The large deep lotos-eyes, whence dew did fall
    Of jewelled tears; the swelling maiden bosom—
Heavy to bear—the long smooth arms; the lips
Where, like the Bee, Desire still clings and sips:

IV

I die, yet well I mind, after embracing,
    When hands relaxed, and gentle strife relented,
And—loosened from the gem-strings interlacing
    Their night-black threads—some wandering locks, rich-scented,
Strayed o'er her chin and cheek, how she would hide
Delicious flush of love, with arms close-tied

V

Over her happy eyes. Dear eyes! I see you
    Shining like stars out of the shade made so,
Tearful for joy. Bright stars of morning be you
    For ever to this heart! Then would she go—
Her sweet head somewhat drooping—to her bath,
With such royal glory as the Queen-swan hath.

VI

Ah, dying—dying—I remember! Let me
    But once again behold her so—behold
Those jet brows, like black crescent-moons, once get me
    So close that love might soothe with comforts cold
The fever of her burning breast—that minute
Would have a changeless, endless Heaven in it.

VII

Yet now, this but abides, to picture surely
    How in the palace-dance foremost she paced;
Her glancing feet and light limbs swayed demurely
    Moonlike, amid their cloudy robes; moon-faced,
With hips majestic under slender waist,
And hair with gold and blooms banded and laced.

128

'Tis to mock Death to think how, where she lay,
  What tender odours drifted from the sheets—
Sandal and musk—such as when pilgrims pray
  Rise for the Gods to savour—subtle sweets
Of her rose-flesh; and, gazing in her eyes,
The love-sick *chakur* had the same deep dyes.

XI

And sometimes, I remember, when we dipped
  Our joys in wine, how her fine blood would flush
Ruddier, to mouth and limb; and how she tripped
  With livelier steps, while saffron-flower's blush
And Kashmir gums, and hill-deer's bag, made sweeting
For breath too sweet, and pearl-teeth—idly eating

X

Honies and betel. How the spell re-grows
  Strong in my soul of that dear face divine,
Hooded in scarlet silk, which, opening, shews
  The brow dew-pearled from haste, dark orbs that shine
With tremulous light of love; as when the Moon
Escapes from Rahu, round and splendent soon.

IX

Ah, my pale Moon eclipsed! How may I bear
  To think on that ill hour of severing
When, in the ear of the King's Daughter dear,
  (So close my mouth touched its warm gems that swing)
I murmured "jivit mangal"—"Fairest! be
Healthful and happy! I will fare to thee!"

BJORNSTJERNE BJORNSON

BJÖRNSTJERNE BJÖRNSON (Norwegian, 1832-1910). One of founders of
modern Norwegian literature. As dramatist, poet, novelist, orator, was political
mentor of his country. Wrote national anthem, was great traveler, and edited
many newspapers and periodicals. His peasant stories outstanding. Best-
known works: *Sigurd Slembe, A Bankruptcy, Beyond Human Power, Paul
Lange and Tora Parsberg.* Nobel Prize, 1903.

THE man whose story is here to be told was the wealthiest and most influential person in his parish; his name was Thord Overaas. He appeared in the priest's study one day, tall and earnest.

"I have gotten a son," said he, "and I wish to present him for baptism."

"What shall his name be?"

"Finn—after my father."

"And the sponsors?"

They were mentioned, and proved to be the best men and women of Thord's relations in the parish.

"Is there anything else?" inquired the priest, and looked up.

The peasant hesitated a little.

"I should like very much to have him baptized by himself," said he, finally.

"That is to say on a week-day?"

"Next Saturday, at twelve o'clock noon."

"Is there anything else?" inquired the priest.

"There is nothing else;" and the peasant twirled his cap, as though he were about to go.

Then the priest rose. "There is yet this, however," said he, and walking toward Thord, he took him by the hand and looked gravely into his eyes: "God grant that the child may become a blessing to you!"

One day sixteen years later, Thord stood once more in the priest's study.

"Really, you carry your age astonishingly well, Thord," said the priest; for he saw no change whatever in the man.

"That is because I have no troubles," replied Thord.

To this the priest said nothing, but after a while he asked: "What is your pleasure this evening?"

"I have come this evening about that son of mine who is to be confirmed to-morrow."

"He is a bright boy."

"I did not wish to pay the priest until I heard what number the boy would have when he takes his place in church to-morrow."

"He will stand number one."

"So I have heard; and here are ten dollars for the priest."

"Is there anything else I can do for you?" inquired the priest, fixing his eyes on Thord.

"There is nothing else."

Thord went out.

Eight years more rolled by, and then one day a noise was heard outside of the priest's study, for many men were approaching, and at their head was Thord, who entered first.

The priest looked up and recognized him.

"You come well attended this evening, Thord," said he.

"I am here to request that the banns may be published for my son; he is about to marry Karen Storliden, daughter of Gudmund, who stands here beside me."

"Why, that is the richest girl in the parish."

"So they say," replied the peasant, stroking back his hair with one hand.

The priest sat a while as if in deep thought, then entered the names in his book, without making any comments, and the men wrote their signatures underneath. Thord laid three dollars on the table.

"One is all I am to have," said the priest.

"I know that very well; but he is my only child, I want to do it handsomely."

The priest took the money.

"This is now the third time, Thord, that you have come here on your son's account."

"But now I am through with him," said Thord, and folding up his pocket-book he said farewell and walked away.

The men slowly followed him.

A fortnight later, the father and son were rowing across the lake, one calm, still day, to Storliden to make arrangements for the wedding.

"This thwart is not secure," said the son, and stood up to straighten the seat on which he was sitting.

At the same moment the board he was standing on slipped from under him; he threw out his arms, uttered a shriek, and fell overboard.

"Take hold of the oar!" shouted the father, springing to his feet and holding out the oar.

But when the son had made a couple of efforts he grew stiff.

"Wait a moment!" cried the father, and began to row toward his son. Then the son rolled over on his back, gave his father one long look, and sank.

Thord could scarcely believe it; he held the boat still, and stared

131

at the spot where his son had gone down, as though he must surely come to the surface again. There rose some bubbles, then some more, and finally one large one that burst; and the lake lay there as smooth and bright as a mirror again.

For three days and three nights people saw the father rowing round and round the spot, without taking either food or sleep: he was dragging the lake for the body of his son. And toward morning of the third day he found it, and carried it in his arms up over the hills to his gard.

It might have been about a year from that day, when the priest, late one autumn evening, heard someone in the passage outside of the door carefully trying to find the latch. The priest opened the door, and in walked a tall, thin man, with bowed form and white hair. The priest looked long at him before he recognized him. It was Thord.

"Are you out walking so late?" said the priest, and stood still in front of him.

"Ah yes! it is late," said Thord, and took a seat.

The priest sat down also, as though waiting. A long, long silence followed. At last Thord said:

"I have something with me that I should like to give to the poor; I want it to be invested as a legacy in my son's name."

He rose, laid some money on the table, and sat down again. The priest counted it.

"It is a great deal of money," said he.

"It is half the price of my gard. I sold it to-day."

The priest sat long in silence. At last he asked, but gently:

"What do you propose to do now, Thord?"

"Something better."

They sat there for a while, Thord with downcast eyes, the priest with his eyes fixed on Thord. Presently the priest said, slowly and softly:

"I think your son has at last brought you a true blessing."

"Yes, I think so myself," said Thord, looking up, while two big tears coursed slowly down his cheeks.

132

GIOVANNI BOCCACCIO

GIOVANNI BOCCACCIO (Italian, 1313-1375). Earliest prose writer in Italian, thus called "father of Italian prose." Most celebrated work, the *Decameron,* a collection of 100 novelle—witty, realistic licentious, often imitated. Author of lesser-known novels (*Fiammetta*), poems (*Il Filostrato*), and biographies (*Life of Dante*). A precursor of the Renaissance, profound influence on later literature.

GRISELDA

IT is a long time ago, that, amongst the marquisses of Saluzzo the principal or head of the family was a youth, called Gualtieri, who, as he was a bachelor, spent his whole time in hawking and hunting, without any thought of ever being encumbered ¹with a wife and children; in which respect, no doubt, he was very wise. But this being disagreeable to his subjects, they often pressed him to marry, to the end that he might neither die without an heir, nor they be left without a lord; offering themselves to provide such a lady for him, and of such a family, that they should have great hopes from her, and he reason enough to be satisfied. "Worthy friends," he replied, "you urge me to do a thing which I was fully resolved against, considering what a difficult matter it is to find a person of suitable temper, with the great abundance everywhere of such as are otherwise, and how miserable also the man's life must be who is tied to a disagreeable woman. As to your getting at a woman's temper from her family, and so choosing one to please me, that seems quite a ridiculous fancy; for, besides the uncertainty with regard to their true fathers, how many daughters do we see resembling neither father nor mother? Nevertheless, as you are so fond of having me noosed, I will agree to be so. Therefore, that I may have no body to blame but myself, should it happen amiss, I will make my own choice; and I protest, let me marry who I will, that, unless you show her the respect that is due to her as my lady, you shall know, to your cost, how grievous it is to me to have taken a wife at your request, contrary to my own inclination." The honest men replied, that they were well satisfied, provided he would but make the trial. Now, he had taken a fancy some time before to the behaviour of a poor country girl, who lived in a village not far from his palace; and thinking that he might live comfortably enough with her, he determined. without seeking any farther, to marry her. Accordingly, he sent for her father, who was a very poor man, and acquainted him with it. Afterwards he summoned all his subjects together, and said to them, "Gentlemen, it was and is your desire that I take a wife; I do it rather to please you, than out of any liking I have to matrimony. You know that you promised me to be satisfied, and to pay her due honour, whoever she is that I shall make choice of. The time is now come when I shall fulfil my promise to you, and I expect you to do the like to me: I have found a young woman in the neighbourhood after my own heart, whom I intend to espouse and bring home in a very few days. Let it be your care, then, to do honour to my nuptials, and to respect her as your sovereign lady: so that I may be satisfied with the performance of your promise, even as you are with that of mine." The people all declared themselves pleased, and promised to regard her in all things as their mistress. Afterwards they made preparations for a most noble feast, and the like did the prince, inviting all his relations, and the great lords in all parts and provinces about him: he had also most rich and costly robes made shaped by a person that seemed to be of the same size with his intended spouse; and provided a girdle, ring, and fine coronet, with everything requisite for a bride. And when the day appointed was come, about the third hour he mounted his horse, attended by all his friends and vassals; and having everything in readiness, he said, "My lords and gentlemen, it is now time to go for my new spouse." So on they rode to the village, and when he was come near the father's house, he saw her carrying some water from the well, in great haste, to go afterwards with some of her acquaintance to see the new marchioness; when he called her by name, which was Griselda, and inquired where her father was. She modestly replied, "My gracious lord, he is in the house." He then alighted from his horse, commanding them all to wait for him, and went alone into the cottage, where he found the father, who was called Giannucolo, and said to him, "Honest man, I am come to espouse thy daughter, but would first ask her some questions before thee." He then inquired, whether she would make it her study to please him, and not be uneasy at any time, whatever he should do or say; and whether she would always be obedient; with more to that purpose. To which she answered, "Yes." He then led her out by the hand, and made her strip before them all; and, ordering the rich apparel to be brought which he had provided, he had her clothed completely, and a coronet set upon her head, all disordered as her hair was;

after which, every one being in amaze, he said, "Behold, this is the person whom I intend for my wife, provided she will accept of me for her husband." Then, turning towards her, who stood quite abashed, "Will you," said he, "have me for your husband?" She replied, "Yes, if it so please your lordship."—"Well," he replied; "and I take you for my wife." So he espoused her in that public manner, and, mounting her on a palfrey, conducted her honourably to his palace, celebrating the nuptials with as much pomp and grandeur as though he had been married to the daughter of the king of France; and the young bride showed apparently that with her garments she had changed both her mind and behaviour. She had a most agreeable person, and was so amiable, and so good-natured withal, that she seemed rather a lord's daughter than that of a poor shepherd; at which every one that knew her before was greatly surprised. She was, too, so obedient to her husband, and so obliging in all respects, that he thought himself the happiest man in the world; and to her subjects likewise so gracious and condescending, that they all honoured and loved her as their own lives, praying for her health and prosperity, and declaring, contrary to their former opinion, that Gualtieri was the most prudent and sharp-sighted prince in the whole world; for that no one could have discerned such virtues under a mean habit, and a country disguise, but himself. In a very short time her discreet behaviour and good works were the common subject of discourse, not in the country only, but everywhere else; and what had been objected to the prince, with regard to his marrying her, now took a contrary turn. They had not lived long together before she proved with child, and at length brought forth a daughter, for which he made great rejoicings. But soon afterwards a new fancy came into his head, and that was, to make trial of her patience by long and intolerable sufferings: so he began wtih harsh words, and an appearance of great uneasiness; telling her, that his subjects were greatly displeased with her for her mean parentage, especially as they saw she bore children; and that they did nothing but murmur at the daughter already born. Which, when she heard, without changing countenance, or her resolution, in any respect, she replied, "My lord, pray dispose of me as you think most for your honour and happiness: I shall entirely acquiesce, knowing myself to be meaner than the meanest of the people, and that I was altogether unworthy of that dignity to which your favour was pleased to advance me." This was very agreeable to the prince, seeing that she was no way elevated with

135

the honour he had conferred upon her. Afterwards, having often told her, in general terms, that his subjects could not bear with the daughter that was born of her, he sent one of his servants, whom he had instructed what to do, who, with a very sorrowful countenance, said to her, "Madam, I must either lose my own life, or obey my lord's commands; now he has ordered me take your daughter, and"—without saying anything more. She, hearing these words, and noting the fellow's looks, remembering also what she had heard before from her lord, concluded that he had orders to destroy the child. So she took it out of the cradle, kissed it, and gave it her blessing; when, without changing countenance, though her heart throbbed with maternal affection, she tenderly laid it in the servant's arms, and said, "Take it, and do what thy lord and mine has commanded; but prythee leave it not to be devoured by the fowls, or wild beasts, unless that be his will." Taking the child, he acquainted the prince with what she said, who was greatly surprised at her constancy, and he sent the same person with it to a relation at Bologna, desiring her, without revealing whose child it was, to see it carefully brought up and educated. Afterwards the lady became with child a second time, and was delivered of a son, at which he was extremely pleased. But, not satisfied with what he had already done, he began to grieve and persecute her still more; saying one day to her, seemingly much out of temper, "Since thou hast brought me this son, I am able to live no longer with my people; for they mutiny to that degree, that, unless I would run the risk of being driven out of my dominions, I must be obliged to dispose of this child as I did the other; and then to send thee away, in order to take a wife more suitable to me." She heard this with a great deal of resignation, making only this reply: "My lord, study only your own ease and happiness, without the least care for me; for nothing is agreeable to me but what is pleasing to yourself." Not many days after, he sent for the son in the same manner as he had done for the daughter; and, seeming also as if he had procured him to be destroyed, had him conveyed to Bologna, to be taken care of with the daughter. This she bore with the same resolution as before, at which the prince wondered greatly, declaring to himself, that no other woman was capable of doing the like. And, were it not that he had observed her extremely fond of her children, whilst that was agreeable to him, he should have thought it want of affection in her: but he saw it was only her entire obedience and condescension. The people, imagining the children were both put to death, blamed him to the last degree, thinking him the most cruel and worst of men, and showing great compassion for the lady; who, whenever she was in company with the ladies of her acquaintance, and they condoled with her for her loss, she would only say, "It was not my will, but his who begot them." But more years being now passed, and he resolving to make the last trial of her patience, declared, before many people, that he could no longer bear to keep Griselda as his wife, owning that he had done very foolishly and like a young man in marrying her, and that he meant to solicit the Pope for a dispensation to take another, and send her away; for which he was much blamed by many worthy persons: but he said nothing in return, only that it should be so. She, hearing this, and expecting to go home to her father, and possibly tend the cattle as she had done before, whilst she saw some other lady possessed of him whom she dearly loved and honoured, was perhaps secretly grieved; but, as she had withstood other strokes of fortune, so she determined resolutely to do now. Soon afterwards Gualtieri had counterfeit letters come to him, as from Rome, acquainting all his people that his holiness thereby dispensed with his marrying another, and turning away Griselda. He had her brought before them, when he said, "Woman, by the Pope's leave I may dispose of thee, and take another wife. As my ancestors, then, have been all sovereign princes of this country, and thine only peasants, I intend to keep thee no longer, but to send thee back to thy father's cottage, with the same portion that thou broughtest me, and afterwards to make choice of one more suitable in quality to myself." It was with the utmost difficulty she could now refrain from tears; and she replied, "My lord, I was always sensible that my servile condition would no way accord with your high rank and descent. For what I have been I own myself indebted to Providence and you; I considered it as a favour lent me: you are now pleased to demand it back; I therefore willingly restore it. Behold the ring with which you espoused me: I deliver it to you. You bid me take the dowry back which I brought you: you will have no need for a teller to count it, nor I for a purse to put it in, much less a sumpter-horse to carry it away; for I have not forgotten that you took me naked: and if you think it decent to expose that body, which has borne you two children, in that manner, I am contented; but I would entreat you, as recompense for my virginity, which I brought you and do not carry away, that you would please to let me have one shift over and above my dowry." He, though ready to weep, yet put on a stern

137

countenance, and said, "Thou shalt have one only then." And, notwithstanding the people all desired that she might have an old gown, to keep her body from shame who had been his wife thirteen years and upwards, yet it was all in vain; so she left his palace in that manner, and returned weeping to her father's, to the great grief of all who saw her. The poor man, never supposing that the prince would keep her long as his wife, and expecting this thing to happen every day, had safely laid up the garments of which she had been despoiled the day he espoused her. He now brought them to her, and she put them on, and went as usual about her father's little household affairs, bearing this fierce trial of adverse fortune with the greatest courage imaginable. The prince then gave it out that he was to espouse a daughter of one of the counts of Panago; and, seeming as if he had made great preparations for his nuptials, he sent for Griselda to come to him, and said to her, "I am going to bring this lady home whom I have just married, and intend to show her all possible respect at her first coming: thou knowest that I have no women with me able to set out the rooms, and do many things which are requisite on so solemn an occasion. As, therefore, thou art best acquainted with the state of the house, I would have thee make such provision as thou shalt judge proper, and invite what ladies thou wilt, even as though thou wert mistress of the house, and, when the marriage is ended, return thee home to thy father's again." Though these words pierced like daggers to the heart of Griselda, who was unable to part with her love for the prince so easily as she had done her great fortune, yet she replied, "My lord, I am ready to fulfil all your commands." She then went into the palace, in her coarse attire, from whence she had just departed in her shift, and with her own hands did she begin to sweep, and set all the rooms to rights, cleaning the stools and benches in the hall like the meanest servant, and directing what was to be done in the kitchen, never giving over till everything was in order and as it ought to be. After this was done, she invited, in the prince's name, all the ladies in the country to come to the feast. And on the day appointed for the marriage, meanly clad as she was, she received them in the most genteel and cheerful mannr imaginable. Now Gualtieri, who had his children carefully brought up at Bologna, (the girl being about twelve years old, and one of the prettiest creatures that ever was seen, and the boy six,) had sent to his kinswoman there, to desire she would bring them, with an honourable retinue, to Saluzzo, giving it out, all the way she came, that she was bringing the young lady to be married to him, without letting any one know to the contrary. Accordingly they all three set forwards, attended by a goodly train of gentry, and, after some day's travelling, reached Saluzzo about dinner-time, when they found the whole country assembled, waiting to see their new lady. The young lady was most graciously received by all the women present, and being come into the hall where the tables were all covered, Griselda, meanly dressed as she was, went cheerfully to meet her, saying, "Your ladyship is most kindly welcome." The ladies, who had greatly importuned the prince, though to no purpose, to let Griselda be in a room by herself, or else that she might have some of her own clothes, and not appear before strangers in that manner, were now seated, and going to be served round, whilst the young lady was universally admired, and every one said that the prince had made a good change; but Griselda in particular highly commended both her and her brother. The marquis now thinking that he had seen enough with regard to his wife's patience, and perceiving that in all her trials she was still the same, being persuaded likewise that this proceeded from no want of understanding in her, because he knew her to be singularly prudent, he thought it time to take her from that anguish which he supposed she might conceal under her firm and constant deportment. So, making her come before all the company, he said, with a smile, "What thinkest thou, Griselda, of my bride?"—"My lord," she replied, "I like her extremely well; and if she be as prudent as she is fair, you may be the happiest man in the world with her; but I most humbly beg you would not take those heart-breaking measures with this lady as you did with your last wife, because she is young, and has been tenderly educated, whereas the other was inured to hardships from a child."

Gualtieri perceiving, that though Griselda thought that person was to be his wife, that she nevertheless answered him with great humility and sweetness of temper, he made her sit down by him, and said, "Griselda, it is now time for you to reap the fruit of your long patience, and that they who have reputed me to be cruel, unjust, and a monster in nature, may know that what I have done has been all along with a view to teach you how to behave as a wife; and, lastly, to secure my own ease and quiet as long as we live together, which I was apprehensive might have been endangered by my marrying. Therefore I had a mind to prove you by harsh and injurious treatment; and not being sensible that you have ever

139

transgressed my will, either in word or deed, I now seem to have met with that happiness I desired. I intend, then, to restore in one hour what I have taken away from you in many, and to make you the sweetest recompense for the many bitter pangs I have caused you to suffer. Accept, therefore, this young lady, whom you thought my spouse, and her brother, as your children and mine. They are the same which you and many others believed that I had been the means of cruelly murdering: and I am your husband, who love and value you above all things; assuring myself that no person in the world can be happier in a wife than I am." With this he embraced her most affectionately, when, rising up together, she weeping for joy, they went where their daughter was sitting, quite astonished with these things, and tenderly saluted both her and her brother, undeceiving them and the whole company. At this the women all arose, overjoyed, from the tables, and taking Griselda into the chamber, they clothed her with her own noble apparel, and as a marchioness, resembling such an one even in rags, and brought her into the hall. And being extremely rejoiced with her son and daughter, and every one expressing the utmost satisfaction at what had come to pass, the feasting was prolonged many days. The marquis was judged a very wise man, though abundantly too severe, and the trial of his lady most intolerable; but as for Griselda, she was beyond compare. In a few days the Count de Panago returned to Bologna, and the marquis took Giannucolo from his drudgery and maintained him as his father-in-law, and so he lived very comfortably to a good old age. Gualtieri afterwards married his daughter to one of equal nobility, continuing the rest of his life with Griselda, and showing her all the respect and honour that was possible. What can we say, then, but that divine spirits may descend from heaven into the meanest cottages, while royal palaces shall produce such as seem rather adapted to have the care of hogs than the government of men?

CHARLOTTE BRONTË

CHARLOTTE BRONTE (English, 1816-1855). Eldest of three talented literary sisters, who lived entire lives in Yorkshire parsonage, died of tuberculosis. Charlotte worked for time as governess. *Jane Eyre*, published under pseudonym of Currer Bell, became Victorian classic. Other novels: *Shirley*, *Villette*, *The Professor*. All her books reflect life of sorrow, struggle and gloom.

From *JANE EYRE*

SOPHIE came at seven to dress me; she was very long indeed in accomplishing her task, so long that Mr. Rochester, grown, I suppose, impatient of my delay, sent up to ask why I did not come. She was just fastening my veil (the plain square of blonde after all) to my hair with a brooch; I hurried from under her hands as soon as I could.

"Stop!" she cried in French. "Look at yourself in the mirror; you have not taken one peep."

So I turned at the door: I saw a robed and veiled figure, so unlike my usual self that it seemed almost the image of a stranger.

"Jane!" called a voice, and I hastened down. I was received at the foot of the stairs by Mr. Rochester.

"Lingerer," he said, "my brain is on fire with impatience, and you tarry so long!"

He took me into the dining-room, surveyed me keenly all over, pronounced me "fair as a lily, and not only the pride of his life, but the desire of his eyes," and then telling me he would give me but ten minutes to eat some breakfast, he rung the bell. One of his lately hired servants, a footman, answered it.

"Is John getting the carriage ready?"

"Yes, sir."

"Is the luggage brought down?"

"They are bringing it down now, sir."

"Go you to the church: see if Mr. Wood (the clergyman) and the clerk are there; return and tell me."

The church, as the reader knows, was just beyond the gates. The footman soon returned.

"Mr. Wood is in the vestry, sir, putting on his surplice."

"And the carriage?"

"The horses are harnessing."

"We shall not want it to go to church, but it must be ready the moment we return; all the boxes and luggage arranged and strapped on, and the coachman in his seat."

"Yes, sir."

"Jane, are you ready?"

I rose. There were no groomsmen, no bridesmaids, no relatives to wait for or marshal; none but Mr. Rochester and I. Mrs. Fairfax stood in the hall as we passed. I would fain have spoken to her, but my hand was held by a grasp of iron; I was hurried along by a

141

stride I could hardly follow; and to look at Mr. Rochester's face was to feel that not a second of delay would be tolerated for any purpose. I wonder what other bridegroom ever looked as he did— so bent up to a purpose, so grimly resolute; or who, under such steadfast brows, ever revealed such flaming and flashing eyes.

I know not whether the day was fair or foul; in descending the drive I gazed neither on sky nor earth: my heart was with my eyes, and both seemed migrated into Mr. Rochester's frame. I wanted to see the invisible thing on which, as we went along, he appeared to fasten a glance fierce and fell. I wanted to feel the thoughts whose force he seemed breasting and resisting.

At the churchyard wicket he stopped; he discovered I was quite out of breath. "Am I cruel in my love?" he said. "Delay an instant; lean on me, Jane."

And now I can recall the picture of the gray old house of God rising calm before me, of a rook wheeling round the steeple, of a ruddy morning sky beyond. I remember something, too, of the green grave-mounds; and I have not forgotten, either, two figures of strangers, straying among the low hillocks, and reading the mementos graven on the few mossy headstones. I noticed them because, as they saw us, they passed round to the back of the church; and I doubted not they were going to enter by the side-aisle door, and witness the ceremony. By Mr. Rochester they were not observed; he was earnestly looking at my face, from which the blood had, I dare say, momentarily fled; for I felt my forehead dewy, and my cheeks and lips cold. When I rallied, which I soon did, he walked gently with me up the path to the porch.

We entered the quiet and humble temple; the priest waited in his white surplice at the lowly altar, the clerk beside him. All was still; two shadows only moved in a remote corner. My conjecture had been correct; the strangers had slipped in before us, and they now stood by the vault of the Rochesters, their backs toward us, viewing through the rails the old, time-stained, marble tomb, where a kneeling angel guarded the remains of Damon de Rochester, slain at Marston Moor, in the time of the civil wars, and of Elizabeth, his wife.

Our place was taken at the communion-rails. Hearing a cautious step behind me, I glanced over my shoulder; one of the strangers —a gentleman, evidently—was advancing up the chancel. The service began. The explanation of the intent of matrimony was gone through;

and then the clergyman came a step further forward, and, bending slightly toward Mr. Rochester, went on.

"I require and charge you both (as ye will answer at the dreadful day of judgment, when the secrets of all hearts shall be disclosed) that if either of you know any impediment why ye may not be lawfully joined together in matrimony, ye do now confess it; for be ye well assured that so many as are coupled together otherwise than God's Word doth allow, are not joined together by God, neither is their matrimony lawful."

He paused, as the custom is. When is the pause after that sentence ever broken by reply? Not, perhaps, once in a hundred years. And the clergyman, who had not lifted his eyes from his book, and had held his breath but for a moment, was proceeding, his hand was already stretched toward Mr. Rochester, as his lips unclosed to ask, "Wilt thou have this woman for thy wedded wife?" when a distinct and near voice said,—

"The marriage cannot go on; I declare the existence of an impediment."

The clergyman looked up at the speaker, and stood mute; the clerk did the same; Mr. Rochester moved slightly, as if an earthquake had rolled under his feet: taking a firmer footing, and not turning his head or eyes, he said, "Proceed."

Profound silence fell when he had uttered that word, with deep but low intonation. Presently Mr. Wood said:

"I cannot proceed without some investigation into what has been asserted, and evidence of its truth or falsehood."

"The ceremony is quite broken off," subjoined the voice behind us. "I am in a condition to prove my allegation; an insuperable impediment to this marriage exists."

Mr. Rochester heard, but heeded not; he stood stubborn and rigid, making no movement but to possess himself of my hand. What a hot and strong grasp he had!—and how like quarried marble was his pale, firm, massive front at this moment! How his eyes shone, still watchful, and yet mild beneath!

Mr. Wood seemed at a loss. "What is the nature of the impediment?" he asked. "Perhaps it may be got over—explained away?"

"Hardly," was the answer. "I have called it insuperable, and I speak advisedly."

The speaker came forward, and leaned on the rails. He continued, uttering each word distinctly, calmly, steadily, but not loudly,—

143

"It simply consists in the existence of a previous marriage; Mr. Rochester has a wife now living."

READER, I married him. A quiet wedding we had; he and I, the parson and clerk, were alone present. When we got back from church, I went into the kitchen of the manor-house, where Mary was cooking the dinner, and John cleaning the knives, and I said,— "Mary, I have been married to Mr. Rochester this morning." The housekeeper and her husband were both of that decent phlegmatic order of people, to whom one may at any time safely communicate a remarkable piece of news without incurring the danger of having one's ears pierced by some shrill ejaculation, and subsequently stunned by a torrent of wordy wonderment. Mary did look up, and she did stare at me; the ladle with which she was basting a pair of chickens roasting at the fire, did for some three minutes hang suspended in air: and for the same space of time John's knives also had rested from the polishing process; but Mary, bending again over the roast, said only,—

"Have you, miss? Well, for sure!"

ELIZABETH BARRETT BROWNING

ELIZABETH BARRETT BROWNING (English, 1806-1861). Wife of Robert Browning, excellent poet in own right. A semi-invalid, lived in Wimpole Street with clergyman father. Her flight to Italy with Browning became famous romantic episode. Most moving work: *Sonnets from the Portuguese*. Others: *The Cry of the Children, Aurora Leigh.*

THE SLEEP
"He giveth His beloved sleep."—Psalm cxxvii, 2

Of all the thoughts of God that are
  Borne inward unto souls afar
  Along the Psalmist's music deep,
Now tell me if that any is
For gift or grace surpassing this,—
"He giveth His beloved sleep"?

144

What would we give to our beloved?
The hero's heart to be unmoved,
    The poet's star-tuned harp to sweep,
The patriot's voice to teach and rouse,
The monarch's crown to light the brows?
    "He giveth *His* beloved sleep."

What do we give to our beloved?
A little faith all undisproved,
    A little dust to overweep,
And bitter memories to make
The whole earth blasted for our sake.
    "He giveth *His* beloved sleep."

"Sleep soft, beloved!" we sometimes say,
But have no tune to charm away
    Sad dreams that through the eyelids creep.
But never doleful dream again
Shall break the happy slumber when
    "He giveth *His* beloved sleep."

O earth, so full of dreary noises!
O men, with wailing in your voices!
    O delvèd gold, the wailers heap!
O strife, O curse, that o'er it fall!
God strikes a silence through you all,
    And "giveth His beloved sleep."

His dews drop mutely on the hill,
His cloud above it saileth still,
    Though on its slope men sow and reap.
More softly than the dew is shed,
Or cloud is floated overhead,
    "He giveth His beloved sleep."

Ay, men may wonder while they scan
A living, thinking, feeling man,
    Confirm'd in such a rest to keep;
But angels say—and through the word
I think their happy smile is *heard*—
    "He giveth His beloved sleep."

145

For me, my heart, that erst did go
Most like a tired child at a show,
    That sees through tears the mummers leap,
Would now its weary vision close,
Would childlike on His love repose
    Who "giveth His beloved sleep!"

And, friends, dear friends, when it shall be
That this low breath is gone from me,
    And round my bier ye come to weep,
Let one, most loving of you all,
Say, "Not a tear must o'er her fall,—
    He giveth His beloved sleep."

MY HEART AND I

I

Enough! we're tired, my heart and I.
    We sit beside the headstone thus,
    And wish that name were carved for us.
The moss reprints more tenderly
    The hard types of the mason's knife.
    As heaven's sweet life renews earth's life
With which we're tired, my heart and I.

II

You see we're tired, my heart and I.
    We dealt with books, we trusted men.
    And in our own blood drenched the pen,
As if such colors could not fly.
    We walked too straight for fortune's end,
    We loved too true to keep a friend;
At last we're tired, my heart and I.

III

How tired we feel, my heart and I!
    We seem of no use in the world;
    Our fancies hang gray and uncurled
About men's eyes indifferently;
    Our voice which thrilled you so, will let
    You sleep; our tears are only wet:
What do we hear, my heart and I?

IV

So tired, so tired, my heart and I!
   It was not thus in that old time
   When Ralph sat with me neath the lime
To watch the sunset from the sky.
   "Dear love, you're looking tired," he said;
   I, smiling at him, shook my head:
'Tis now we're tired, my heart and I.

V

So tired, so tired, my heart and I!
   Though now none takes me on his arm
   To fold me close and kiss me warm
Till each quick breath end in a sigh
   Of happy languor. Now, alone,
   We lean upon this graveyard stone,
Uncheered, unkissed, my heart and I.

VI

Tired out we are, my heart and I.
   Suppose the world brought diadems
   To tempt us, crusted with loose gems
Of powers and pleasures? Let it try.
   We scarcely care to look at even
   A pretty child, or God's blue heaven,
We feel so tired, my heart and I.

VII

Yet who complains? My heart and I?
   In this abundant earth no doubt
   Is little room for things worn out:
Disdain them, break them, throw them by!
   And if before the days grew rough
   We once were loved, used,—well enough,
I think, we've fared, my heart and I.

THE PET-NAME

I

I have a name, a little name,
   Uncadenced for the ear,
Unhonored by ancestral claim,
Unsanctified by prayer and psalm
   The solemn font anear.

147

II

It never did to pages wove
    For gay romance, belong.
It never dedicate did move
As "Sacharissa." unto love—
    "Orinda," unto song.

III

Though I write books, it will be read
    Upon the leaves of none,
And afterwards, when I am dead,
Will ne'er be graved for sight or tread
    Across my funeral stone.

IV

This name, whoever chance to call,
    Perhaps your smile may win.
Nay, do not smile! mine eyelids fall
Over mine eyes, and feel withal
    The sudden tears within.

V

Is there a leaf that greenly grows
    Where summer meadows bloom
But gathereth the winter snows,
And changeth to the hue of those,
    If lasting till they come?

VI

Is there a word, or jest, or game,
    But time encrusteth round
With sad associate thought the same?
And so to me my very name
    Assumes a mournful sound.

VII

My brother gave that name to me
    When we were children twain;
When names acquired baptismally
Were hard to utter as to see
    That life had any pain.

VIII

No shade was on us then, save one
  Of chestnuts from the hill—
And through the word our laugh did run
As part thereof. The mirth being done,
  He calls me by it still.

IX

Nay, do not smile! I hear in it
  What none of you can hear!
The talk upon the willow seat,
The bird and wind that did repeat
  Around, our human cheer.

X

I hear the birthday's noisy bliss,
  My sister's woodland glee,—
My father's praise, I did not miss,
When stooping down he cared to kiss
  The poet at his knees;—

XI

And voices, which to name me, aye
  Their tenderest tones were keeping!—
To some I never more can say
An answer, till God wipes away
  In heaven those drops of weeping.

XII

My name to me a sadness wears;
  No murmurs cross my mind;
Now God be thanked for these thick tears,
Which show, of those departed years,
  Sweet memories left behind!

XIII

Now God be thanked for years enwrought
  With love which softens yet!
Now God be thanked for every thought
Which is so tender it has caught
  Earth's guerdon of regret!

XIV

Earth saddens, never shall remove,
  Affections purely given;
And e'en that mortal grief shall prove
The immortality of love,
  And brighten it with Heaven.

A FALSE STEP

I

Sweet, thou hast trod on a heart.
  Pass! there's a world full of men;
And women as fair as thou art
  Must do such things now and then.

II

Thou only hast stepped unaware,—
  Malice, not one can impute;
And why should a heart have been there
  In the way of a fair woman's foot?

III

It was not a stone that could trip,
  Nor was it a thorn that could rend:
Put up thy proud underlip!
  'Twas merely the heart of a friend.

IV

And yet peradventure one day
  Thou, sitting alone at the glass,
Remarking the bloom gone away,
  Where the smile in its dimplement was,

V

And seeking around thee in vain
  From hundreds who flattered before,
Such a word as, "Oh, not in the main
  Do I hold thee less precious, but more!"
Thou'lt sigh, very like, on thy part,
  "Of all I have known or can know.
I wish I had only that Heart
  I trod upon ages ago!"

ROBERT BROWNING

ROBERT BROWNING (English, 1812-1889). One of major Victorian poets. A dramatist of thought and emotion rather than of action. Metaphysical content of later poems gave him reputation for obscurity. Most admired for dramatic monologues and the long narrative, *The Ring and the Book*, based on actual 17th century murder case. All his work marked by high moral tone of the Victorians.

THE LOST LEADER

Just for a handful of silver he left us,
   Just for a riband to stick in his coat—
Found the one gift of which fortune bereft us,
   Lost all the others she lets us devote;
They, with the gold to give, doled him out silver,
   So much was theirs who so little allowed:
How all our copper had gone for his service!
   Rags—were they purple, his heart had been proud!
We that had loved him so, followed him, honoured him,
   Lived in his mild and magnificent eye,
Learned his great language, caught his clear accents,
   Made him our pattern to live and to die!
Shakespeare was of us, Milton was for us,
   Burns, Shelley, were with us,—they watch from their
      graves!
He alone breaks from the van and the freemen,
   —He alone sinks to the rear and the slaves!
We shall march prospering,—not through his presence;
   Songs may inspirit us,—not from his lyre;
Deeds will be done,—while he boasts his quiescence,
   Still bidding crouch whom the rest bade aspire:
Blot out his name, then, record one lost soul more,
   One task more declined, one more footpath untrod,
One more devils'-triumph and sorrow for angels,
   One wrong more to man, one more insult to God!
Life's night begins: let him never come back to us!
   There would be doubt, hesitation and pain,
Forced praise on our part—the glimmer of twilight,
   Never glad confident morning again!

Best fight on well, for we taught him—strike gallantly,
  Menace our heart ere we master his own;
Then let him receive the new knowledge and wait us,
  Pardoned in heaven, the first by the throne!

INSTANS TYRANNUS

I

Of the million or two, more or less,
I rule and possess,
One man, for some cause undefined,
Was least to my mind.

II

I struck him, he grovelled of course—
For, what was his force?
I pinned him to earth with my weight
And persistence of hate:
And he lay, would not moan, would not curse,
As his lot might be worse.

III

"Were the object less mean, would he stand
At the swing of my hand!
For obscurity helps him and blots
The hole where he squats."
So, I set my five wits on the stretch
To inveigle the wretch.
All in vain! Gold and jewels I threw,
Still he couched there perdue;
I tempted his blood and his flesh,
Hid in roses my mesh,
Choicest cates and the flagon's best spilth:
Still he kept to his filth.
At the thought of his face,
The droop, the low cares of the mouth,
The trouble uncouth

To put out of its pain.
And, "no!" I admonished myself,
"Is one mocked by an elf,

152

Had he kith now or kin, were access
To his heart, did I press:
Just a son or a mother to seize!
No such booty as these!
Were it simply a friend to pursue
'Mid my million or two,
Who could pay me in person or pelf
What he owes me himself!
No: I could not but smile through my chafe:
For the fellow lay safe
As his mates do, the midge and the nit,
—Through minuteness, to wit.

V

Then a humour more great took its place
At the thought of his face,
The droop, the low cares of the mouth,
The trouble uncouth
'Twixt the brows, all that air one is fain
To put out of its pain.
And, "no!" I admonished myself,
Is one baffled by toad or by rat?
The gravamen's in that!
How the lion, who crouches to suit
His back to my foot,
Would admire that I stand in debate!
But the Small turns the Great
If it vexes you,—that is the thing!
Toad or rat vex the King?
Though I waste half my realm to unearth
Toad or rat, 'tis well worth!

So, I soberly laid my last plan
To extinguish the man.
Round his creep-hole, with never a break
Ran my fires for his sake;
Over-head, did my thunder combine
Till I looked from my labour content
To enjoy the event.

VII

When sudden . . . how think ye, the end?
Did I say "without friend"?
Say rather, from marge to blue marge
The whole sky grew his targe
With the sun's self for visible boss,
While an Arm ran across
Which the earth heaved beneath like a breast
Where the wretch was safe prest!
Did you see? Just my vengeance complete.
The man sprang to his feet,
Stood erect, caught at God's skirts, and prayed!
—So, *I* was afraid!

KARL GEORG BÜCHNER

KARL GEORG BÜCHNER (German, 1813-1837). Forerunner of the modern drama. His reputation not established until a century after death. Student of medicine, went underground after writing revolutionary pamphlet. Author of three pessimistic plays: *Dantons Tod, Leonce und Lena,* and *Woyzeck* (the source of Alban Berg's opera). His psychology and realism are uncannily modern.

WOYZECK

The action apparently takes place in Leipzig, 1824.

1 AT THE CAPTAIN'S

The CAPTAIN *in a chair;* WOYZECK *shaving him.*

CAPTAIN. Easy, Woyzeck, take it easy. One thing after the other! You're making me dizzy. You'll finish up early and what'll I do with ten minutes on my hands? Use your head, Woyzeck. You've got thirty years to live. Thirty! That's three hundred sixty months. And days! Hours! Minutes! What are you going to do with that horrible stretch of time? Figure it out for yourself, Woyzeck!

WOYZECK. Yes sir, Captain.

CAPTAIN. *Touched, but condescending.*
Woyzeck, you're a good man, but
With dignity
you have no morals. Morals! That's what a man's got who
behaves morally! Understand? It's a good word. You went and
got yourself a child without the blessing of the Church, as our
right reverend chaplain put it. "Without the blessing of the
Church." Now, I didn't invent the phrase.

WOYZECK. Captain, the Good Lord's not going to be hard on the
little worm, just because no one said Amen before they made
him. The Lord said, "Suffer little children to come unto me."
You see, Captain—with us poor people—it's money, money!
If you don't have money . . . Well, you just can't have morals
when you're bringing someone like yourself into the world.
We're only flesh and blood. People like us can't be holy in
this world—or the next. If we ever did get into heaven, they'd
put us to work on the thunder.

CAPTAIN. Woyzeck, you have no virtue. You are not a virtuous
man.

WOYZECK. Yes, Captain. Virtue. I don't have much of that. But
you see, what happens to us ordinary people—that's just nature.
Now, if I was a gentleman and wore a hat and a watch and a
cane, and could talk smooth—well, I'd like to be virtuous too.
It must be fine to be virtuous, Captain, but I'm just ordinary.

CAPTAIN. You're good, Woyzeck. You're a good man. But you
think too much. It wears you out. You're always so moody.
Well, this conversation has exhausted me too. You can go. But
don't run. Take it easy, nice and easy, out into the street.

3 THE TOWN

MARIE *with her child at the window,* MARGRET. *The Retreat
passes, the Drum-Major in front.*

MARIE, *dandling her child.* Hey, boy! Ta-ra-ra-ra! Hear them?
Here they come!

MARGRET. What a man! Built like a tree.

MARIE. He handles himself like a lion.
The Drum Major salutes her.

MARGRET. Ooh, he's giving you the glad eye, neighbor. I hardly
expected it of *you*.

MARIE, *singing.*
Oh, soldiers are such handsome guys.

155

MARGRET. Your eyes are still shining.

MARIE. Who cares? If you took yours to the pawnbroker's and had them polished up, maybe they'd shine enough to be sold for a couple of buttons.

MARGRET. What's that? Why, you! Listen, Mrs. Virginity, I'm at least respectable. But you, everyone knows you could stare your way through seven pairs of leather pants.

MARIE. You bitch!

Slams the window.

Come on, little fellow. What do people want, anyhow? Maybe you are just a poor whore's kid, but your illegitimate little face still brings joy to your mother. Da, da, dum.

A knock at the window.

Who's there? That you, Franz? Come on in.

WOYZECK. Can't. Got roll call.

MARIE. Get the wood cut for the Captain?

WOYZECK. Yes. Marie.

MARIE. What's the matter, Franz? You look upset.

WOYZECK. It followed me all the way into town. Something we can't understand, that drives you out of your senses. What's going to happen?

MARIE. Franz!

WOYZECK. I've got to go. See you tonight at the fair grounds. I saved something up.

MARIE. That man! He's seeing things. Didn't even notice his own child. He'll crack up with these ideas of his. Why so quiet, little fellow? Are you scared? It's getting so dark it's like going blind. Only that street light shining in. It gives me the creeps.

8   MARIE'S ROOM

MARIE, *the* DRUM-MAJOR.

DRUM-MAJOR. Marie!

MARIE. *Looking at him intently.* Stand·up there!—A chest like a bull and a beard like a lion. In a class by himself—no woman is prouder than I am.

DRUM-MAJOR. But Sunday, when I'm wearing my white gloves and the hat with the plume in it, hot damn! The Prince always says, "By God, there's a real man!"

MARIE, *mockingly.* Does he?

Steps up before him.

A real man!

DRUM-MAJOR. And you're a real piece of woman, too. Hell's bells, let's raise a race of Drum-majors. Eh?

He embraces her.

MARIE, *moody*. Let me go!

DRUM-MAJOR. You wildcat!

MARIE, *violently*. Just touch me!

DRUM-MAJOR. You've got the devil in your eyes.

MARIE. What's the difference?

10 MARIE'S ROOM

MARIE, WOYZECK.

WOYZECK, *staring straight at her and shaking his head*. Hm! I can't see it. I can't see it. You should be able to. You should be able to hold it in your fist.

MARIE, *frightened*. What is it, Franz? You're raving, Franz.

WOYZECK. A sin, so big, and so wide. It should stink, until the angels are smoked out of heaven. You have a red mouth, Marie. No blisters on it? Marie, you're as beautiful as sin—but can mortal sin be so beautiful?

MARIE. Franz, you're talking like you had a fever.

WOYZECK. Hell! Did he stand there? Like this? Like this?

MARIE. The world is old and the day is long, so lots of people can stand in the same place, one after the other.

WOYZECK. I saw him!

MARIE. There's a lot you can see if you have two eyes, you're not blind, and the sun is shining.

WOYZECK. You whore!

He goes for her.

MARIE. Just touch me, Franz! I'd rather have a knife in my ribs than your hands on me. At ten, my father didn't dare touch me. I only had to look at him.

WOYZECK. Bitch! No, it should show on you. Each one of us is a precipice. You get dizzy when you look down.— There should be! She's innocence itself. All right, innocence. You bear the mark on you. Do I know it though? Do I know it? Who does?

12 AN INN

The windows open. Dancing. WOYZECK *posts himself by the window. Marie and the* DRUM-MAJOR *dance by, without noticing him.*

WOYZECK. Him and her! Damn it to hell!

MARIE, *dancing by.* Don't stop! Don't stop!

WOYZECK, *choking.* Don't stop!

He jumps up and falls back on the bench.

Don't stop! Don't stop!

Pounding his hands.

Turn around! Roll on! Why doesn't God blow out the sun so they can all roll on top of each other in filth? Male and Female! Man and Beast! They'll do it in broad daylight! They'll do it on your hands, like flies! Women! That woman is hot, hot! Don't stop!

That bastard! Look how he's feeling her up—all over her body! He's, he's got her—like I did at first.

He slumps down, bewildered.

FOOL. It smells.

WOYZECK. Yes, it smells! She had a red, red mouth. Is that what you smell?

FOOL. I smell blood.

WOYZECK. Blood! Everything's going red before my eyes. Like they were all rolling on top of each other in a sea of it!

14 A ROOM IN THE BARRACKS

Night. ANDRES *and* WOYZECK *in one bed.*

WOYZECK, *softly.* Andres!

ANDRES, *murmurs in his sleep.*

WOYZECK, *shaking* ANDRES. Hey, Andres! Andres!

ANDRES. What do you want?

WOYZECK. I can't sleep. When I close my eyes, everything turns around and I hear the fiddles saying: Don't stop! Don't stop! Then it comes out of the wall, too. Don't you hear anything?

ANDRES. Sure. Let them dance. A man gets tired. God bless us all. Amen.

WOYZECK. It keeps saying: Stab! Stab! And it pulls my eyes open, like a knife. A big, thick knife, lying on a counter in a dark narrow street, with an old man sitting behind it. That's the knife I keep seeing in front of my eyes.

ANDRES. You ought to drink some schnapps with a powder in it. That cuts the fever.

WOYZECK. Don't stop! Don't stop!

ANDRES. Go to sleep, you fool!

He goes to sleep.

158

WOYZECK, *the* JEW.

WOYZECK. The pistol's too much.

JEW. So, are you buying or not buying? Make up your mind!

WOYZECK. How much was the knife?

JEW. It's good and sharp. Going to cut your throat with it? Make up your mind. I'm giving it to you cheap as anybody. You can die cheap, but not for nothing.

WOYZECK. It'll cut more than bread . . .

JEW. Two groschen.

WOYZECK. Here!

Goes out.

JEW. Here! Like it was nothing. And it's good money! The pig!

19 MARIE'S ROOM

MARIE, *leafing through the bible.* "And no guile is found in his mouth." Lord God, Lord God, don't look at me!

Leafs again.

"And the scribes and the Pharisees brought unto him a woman taken in adultery, and set her in the midst . . . And Jesus said unto her, 'Neither do I condemn thee; go, and sin no more.'" Lord God, Lord God, I can't—Lord God, give me the strength to pray!

The child cuddles up to her.

The child stabs me to the heart.

Franz hasn't been here yesterday or today. It's getting hot in here.

She opens the window.

"And stood at his feet weeping, and began to wash his feet with tears, and did wipe them with the hairs of her head, and kissed his feet, and annointed them with ointment."

Beats her breast.

Everything's dead. Saviour, Saviour! If only I could annoint Thy feet!

22 A WOODLAND PATH BY A POND

MARIE *and* WOYZECK.

MARIE. The town's that way. It's dark.

WOYZECK. You're not going. Come on, sit down.

MARIE. But I have to go.

WOYZECK. Your feet will get sore running.

MARIE. You're so changed.

WOYZECK. Do you know how long it's been, Marie?

MARIE. Two years, Pentecost.

WOYZECK. Do you know how long it will last?

MARIE. I have to go and get supper.

WOYZECK. You're not freezing. Marie? No, you're warm. You've got hot lips. Hot! A hot whore's breath! And I'd still give heaven to kiss them again. Are you freezing? When your bones are cold, you don't freeze anymore. You won't freeze in the morning dew.

MARIE. What are you saying?

WOYZECK. Nothing.

Silence.

MARIE. The moon's rising. It's red.

WOYZECK. Like a sword with blood on it!

MARIE. What are you going to do, Franz? You're so pale.

He raises the knife.

Franz, stop! For Heaven's sake! Help! Help!

WOYZECK, *stabbing madly.* Take that, and that! Why can't you die? There! There! Ha! She's still twitching. Still can't? Still twitching?

Stabs again.

Now are you dead? Dead! Dead!

He drops the knife and runs away.

23 THE INN

WOYZECK. Dance, everyone dance! Don't stop! Sweat and stink! He'll get all of you in the end.

He dances.

Whew, Kathe! Sit down. I'm hot, hot!

He takes off his coat.

KATHE. But what's that on your hand?

WOYZECK. On me? Me?

KATHE. Red! Blood!

People gather round.

WOYZECK. Blood? Blood?

INNKEEPER. Ugh! Blood!

WOYZECK. I think, I cut myself. There, on my right hand.

INNEEPER. How come it's on your elbow?

WOYZECK. I wiped it off.

INNKEEPER. Wiped your right hand on your right elbow? You have talent!

FOOL. And the Giant said: I smell, I smell. What do I smell? A man, a man who's bound for Hell! Pah! it stinks already!

WOYZECK. What the devil do you all want? What business is it of yours? Out of my way, or the first one who . . . Hell, do you think I did away with someone? Am I a murderer? What are you gaping at? Gawk at yourselves! Get out of my way! *He runs off.*

24 AT THE POND

WOYZECK *alone.*

WOYZECK. The knife? Where's the knife? I left it here. It'll give me away. Nearer. Nearer yet. What place is this? What's that I hear? Something moving! No, it's quiet. Over there. Marie? Ha, Marie! You're quiet. Everything's quiet! What are you so white for, Marie? What's that red string around your neck? Who did your sins earn that necklace from? You were black with them, black! Did I bleach you white again? Why is your black hair hanging so wild? Didn't you braid your long braids today? Here's something! Cold and wet, and still. The knife! the knife! Got it? Get rid of it!
He runs into the water.
There! Down it goes.
He throws the knife in.
It dives down into the water like a stone. The moon's like a sword with blood on it! Is the whole world going to gab about it? No, it's lying too close. When they're swimming. . . .
He goes into the pond and throws it further.
There, that's it! But, in the summer, when they're diving for mussels? Bah! it'll be rusty. Who'd recognize it—I should have broken it. Am I still bloody? I better wash up. There's a spot and there's another.
Goes deeper into the water.
Time passes. People come.

FIRST PERSON. Wait up!

SECOND PERSON. You hear? Shh! Over there!

FIRST PERSON. Ugh! Over there. What a sound!

SECOND PERSON. It's the water, calling. It's been a long time since anyone was drowned. Let's go, it's not a pleasant thing to hear.

FIRST PERSON. Ugh! There it is again! Like a man, dying.

SECOND. It's eerie. So foggy, that gray mist everywhere, and the bugs humming like broken bells. Let's go!

FIRST. Wait! It's too clear, too loud. It's up there. Come on!

161

CHILDREN.

FIRST CHILD. Let's go look at Marie!

SECOND CHILD. What for?

FIRST CHILD. Don't you know? Everybody's gone out there.

To Marie's Child.

Hey, your mother's dead.

MARIE'S CHILD, *playing horsey.* Giddyap, giddyap!

FIRST CHILD. On the path to the pond.

SECOND CHILD. Hurry up! Let's get there before they bring her back.

MARIE'S CHILD. Giddyap, giddyap!

IVAN BUNIN

IVAN BUNIN (Russian, 1870-1953). Russian poet and noted translator from the English. Lived in exile after 1919. His poetry, largely descriptive, based on experience and travels. Author of famous novel, *The Village,* and short stories, *The Gentleman from San Francisco,* which won him Nobel Prize in 1933. High technical skill has given him reputation as a "writers' writer."

SUNSTROKE

LEAVING the hot, brightly lighted dining saloon after dinner, they went on deck and stood near the rail. She closed her eyes, leant her cheek on the back of her hand, and laughed—a clear charming laugh—everything about this little woman was charming.

"I am quite drunk," she said. "In fact I have gone mad. Where did you come from? Three hours ago I did not know of your existence. I don't even know where you got on the boat. Was it Samara? But it doesn't matter, you're a dear. Am I dizzy, or is the boat really turning round?"

In front of them lay darkness and the light of lamps. A soft wind blew strongly against their faces and carried the light to one side. With the smartness characteristic of the Volga boats, the steamer was making a wide curve towards the small wharf.

The lieutenant took her hand and raised it to his lips. The firm little fragrant hand was tanned. His heart became faint with fear and ecstasy as he thought how strong and bronzed must be the body under the light linen dress after having basked in the South-

162

ern sun on the hot beach for a whole month. (She had told him that she was on her way from Anapi.)

"Let's get off," he murmured.

"Where?" she asked in surprise.

"At this wharf."

"What for?"

He was silent. She raised her hand to her hot cheek again.

"You are mad."

"Let's get off," he repeated stubbornly. "I implore you——"

"Oh, do as you like," she said, turning from him.

With its final impetus, the steamer bumped gently against the dimly lit wharf, and they nearly fell over each other. The end of a rope flew over their heads, the boat heaved back, there was a foam of churning waters, the gangways clattered. The lieutenant rushed away to collect their things.

A moment later they passed through the sleepy ticket office into the ankle-deep sand of the road, and silently got into a dusty open cab. The soft, sandy road sloping gradually uphill, lit by crooked lamp-posts at long intervals on either side, seemed unending, but they reached its top and clattered along a high-road until they came to a sort of square with municipal buildings and a watch-tower. It was all full of warmth and the smells peculiar to a hot night in a small provincial town. The cab drew up at a lighted portico, behind the door of which a steep old wooden stairway was visible, and an old unshaven waiter, in a pink shirt and black coat, reluctantly took their luggage, and led the way in his down-at-heel slippers. They entered a large room stuffy from the hot sun which had beaten on it all day, its white curtains drawn. On the toilet table were two unlit candles.

The instant the door closed on the waiter, the lieutenant sprang towards her with such impetuosity, and they were carried away by a breathless kiss of such passion, that they remembered it for many, many years. Neither of them had ever before experienced anything like it.

At ten o'clock next morning the little, nameless woman left. She never told him her name, and referred to herself jokingly as "the fair stranger." It was a hot, sunny morning. Church bells were ringing, and a market was in full swing in the square in front of the hotel. There were scents of hay and tar and all the odours characteristic of a Russian provincial town.

They had not slept much, but when she emerged from behind

163

the screen, where she had washed and dressed in five minutes, she was as fresh as a girl of seventeen. Was she embarrassed? Very little, if at all. She was as simple and gay as before, and —already rational. "No, no, dear," she said in reply to his request that they should continue the journey together. "No, you must wait for the next boat. If we go together, it will spoil it all. It would be very unpleasant for me. I give you my word of honour that I am not in the least what you may think I am. Nothing at all like this has ever happened to me before or will ever happen again. I seem to have been under a spell. Or, rather, we both seem to have had something like sunstroke."

The lieutenant readily agreed with her. In a bright, happy mood he drove her to the wharf—just before the pink steamer of the Samolet Line started. He kissed her openly on the deck, and had barely time to get ashore before the gangway was lowered. He returned to the hotel in the same care-free, easy mood. But something had changed. The room without her seemed quite different from what it had been with her. He was still full of her; he did not mind, but it was strange. The room still held the scent of her excellent English lavender water, her unfinished cup of tea still stood on the tray, but she was gone. . . . The lieutenant's heart was suddenly filled with such a rush of tenderness that he hurriedly lit a cigarette and began to pace the room, switching his topboots with his cane.

"A strange adventure," he said aloud, laughing and feeling tears well up in his eyes. " 'I give you my word of honour that I am not in the least what you think I am,' and she's gone. Absurd woman!"

The screen had been moved—the bed had not been made. He felt that he had not the strength to look at that bed. He put the screen in front of it, closed the window to shut out the creaking of the wheels and the noisy chatter of the market, drew the white billowing curtains, and sat down on the sofa. Yes, the roadside adventure was over. She was gone, and now, far away, she was probably sitting in the windowed saloon, or on the deck, gazing at the enormous river glittering in the sun, at the barges drifting down-stream, at the yellow shoals, at the shining horizon of sky and water. at the immeasurable sweep of the Volga. And it was good-bye for ever and ever. For where could they possibly meet again? "For," he thought, "I can hardly appear on the scene without any excuse, in the town where she lives her everyday life with her huband, her three-year-old daughter and all her family."

The town seemed to him a special, a forbidden town. He was aggravated and stunned by the thought that she would live her lonely life there, often perhaps remembering him, recalling their brief encounter, that he would never see her again. No, it was impossible. It would be too mad, too unnatural, too fantastic. He suffered and was overwhelmed by horror and despair in feeling that without her his whole life would be futile. "Damn it all!" he thought, as he got up and began to pace the room again, trying not to look at the bed behind the screen. "What in the world's the matter with me? It's not the first time, is it? And yet— Was there anything very special about her, or did anything very special happen? It really is like sunstroke. And how on earth am I to spend a whole day in this hole without her?"

He still remembered all of her, down to the minutest detail: her sunburn, her linen frock, her strong body, her unaffected, bright, gay voice. . . . The sense of ecstatic joy which her feminine charm had given him was still extraordinarily strong, but now a second feeling rose uppermost in his mind—a new, strange, incomprehensible feeling, which had not been there while they had been together, and of which he would not, the day before, have believed himself capable when he had started what he had thought to be the amusement of a passing acquaintance. And now there was no one, no one, whom he could tell. "And the point is," he thought, "that I never shall be able to tell anyone! And how am I to get through this endless day with these memories, this inexplicable agony, in this god-forsaken town on the banks of that same Volga along which the steamer is carrying her away?" He must do something to save himself, something to distract him, he must go somewhere. He put on his hat with an air of determination, took his stick and walked along the corridor with his spurs jingling, ran down the stairs and out on to the porch. But where should he go? A cab was drawn up in front of the hotel. A young, smartly-dressed driver sat on the box calmly smoking a cigar. He was obviously waiting for someone. The lieutenant stared at him, bewildered and astonished: How could anyone sit calmly on a box and smoke and in general be unmoved and indifferent? "I suppose that in the whole town there is no one so miserably unhappy as I am," he thought, as he went towards the market.

It was already breaking up. For some unknown reason he found himself making his way over fresh droppings, among carts, loads of cucumbers, stacks of pots and pans, and women seated on the

165

ground who outdid each other in their efforts to attract his attention. They lifted basins and tapped them that he might hear how sound they were, while the men deafened him with cries of "First-class cucumbers, your honour." It was all so stupid, so ridiculous that he fled from the square. He went into the cathedral, where the choir was singing loudly, resolutely, as though conscious of fulfilling a duty; then he strolled aimlessly about a small, hot, unkempt garden on the edge of a cliff overhanging the silvery steel breadth of the river.

The epaulettes and buttons of his linen uniform were unbearably hot to the touch. The inside of his hat was wet, his face was burning. He returned to the hotel and was delighted to get into the large, empy, cool dining-room, delighted to take off his hat and seat himself at a small table near the open window. The heat penetrated from outside, but it was airy. He ordered iced soup.

Everything was all right in this unknown town, happiness and joy emanated from everything, from the heat and the market smells. Even this old provincial hotel seemed full of gladness, and yet his heart was being torn to pieces. He drank several glasses of vodka and ate a salted cucumber with parsley. He felt that he would unhesitatingly die tomorrow if, by some miracle, he could achieve her return and spend to-day, only this one day, with her, solely, solely in order that he might tell her and prove to her and convince her somehow of his agonising and exalted love for her. "Why prove? Why convince?" He did not know why, but it was more essential than life.

"My nerves have all gone to pieces," he said, pouring out his fifth glass of vodka. He drank the entire contents of the small decanter, hoping to stupefy, to benumb himself, hoping to get rid at last of this agonising and exalted feeling. But, instead, it increased. He pushed away the soup, ordered black coffee, and began to smoke and to think with intensity. What was he to do now, how was he to free himself from this sudden and unexpected love? To free himself—but he felt only too clearly that that was impossible. He rose abruptly, quickly, took his hat and his stick, asked the way to the post office and hurried off, the text of the telegram already composed in his mind: "Henceforth all my life, for all time till death, is yours, in your power." But on reaching the thick-walled old building which housed the post and telegraph, he stopped in dismay. He knew the name of her town, he knew that she had a husband and a child of three, but he knew neither her first name nor her surname. Last night, while they were dining at the hotel, he had asked her several times, and each time she had answered with a laugh: "Why do you want to know who I am? I am Marie Marevna, the mysterious princess of the fairy story; or the fair stranger; isn't that enough for you?"

At the corner of the street, near the post office, was a photographer's window. He stared for a long time at the portrait of an officer in braided epaulettes, with protruding eyes, a low forehead, unusually luxuriant whiskers, and a very broad chest entirely covered with orders. How mad, how ridiculous, how terrifyingly ordinary, everyday things appear when the heart is struck—yes, *struck*, he understood it now, by the "sunstroke" of a love too great, a joy too immense. He looked at the picture of a bridal couple— a young man in a frock-coat and white tie, with closely-cropped hair, very erect, arm-in-arm with a girl in white tulle. His gaze wandered to a pretty piquant girl wearing a student's cap on the back of her head.

Then, filled with envy of all these unknown people who were not suffering, he stared fixedly down the street. "Where shall I go? What shall I do?" The difficult, unanswerable questions occupied both mind and soul.

The street was completely empty. All the houses were alike, middle-class, two-storied white houses with large gardens, but they were lifeless; the pavement was covered with thick white dust; it was all blinding, all bathed in hot, flaming, joyful sun which now somehow seemed futile. In the distance the street rose, humped and ran into the clear, cloudless, grey-mauve horizon. There was something southern about it; it reminded one of Sebastopol, Kerch— Anapi. This was more than he could bear. With eyes half closed and head bowed from the light, staring intently at the pavement, staggering, stumbling, catching one spur in the other, the lieutenant retraced his steps.

He returned to the hotel worn out with fatigue, as though he had done a long day's march in Turkestan or the Sahara. With a final effort he got to his large empty room. It had been "done." The last traces of her were gone except for one hairpin forgotten by her on the table. He took off his coat and looked at himself in the mirror. He saw reflected, skin bronzed and moustache bleached by the sun, the bluish whites of the eyes looking so much whiter on account of the tan, an ordinary enough officer's face, but now wild and excited. And about the whole figure standing there in the thin

167

white shirt and stiff collar there was something pathetically young and terribly unhappy. He lay down on the bed, on his back, resting his dusty boots on the footrail. The windows were open, the blinds were lowered. From time to time a slight wind billowed them out, letting in the heat, the smell of hot roofs and of all the radiant, but now empty, silent, deserted Volga country-side. He lay there, his hands under his head, and stared into space. In his mind he had a vague picture of the far-away south: sun and sea, Anapi. Then arose something fantastic, a town unlike any other town—the town in which she lived, which she had probably already reached. The thought of suicide stubbornly persisted. He closed his eyes and felt hot, smarting tears well up under his eyelids. Then at last he fell asleep, and when he woke he could see by the reddish-yellow light of the sun that it was evening. The wind had died down, the room was as hot and dry as an oven. Yesterday and this morning both seemed ten years ago. Unhurriedly he rose, unhurriedly he washed, drew up the blinds and rang for a samovar and his bill, and for a long time sat there drinking tea with lemon. Then he ordered a cab to be called and his things to be carried down. As he got into the cab with its faded red seat, he gave the waiter five roubles. "I believe I brought you here last night, your honour," said the driver gaily as he gathered up the reins.

By the time they reached the wharf, the Volga was roofed by the blue of the summer night. Multitudes of many-tinted lights were dotted along the river, and bright lamps shone from the masts of the ships.

"I got you here in the nick of time," said the cabdriver ingratiatingly.

The lieutenant gave five roubles to him also, took his ticket and went to the landing-place. Just as it had done yesterday, the boat bumped gently as it touched the wharf, there was the same slight dizziness from the unsteadiness underfoot, the end of a rope was thrown, there was a sound of foaming and rushing water under the paddles as the steamer backed a little. . . .

The brightly lighted, crowded steamer, smelling of food, seemed unusually friendly and agreeable, and in a few minutes it was speeding forward up the river, whither in the morning she had been carried.

The last glimmer of summer twilight gradually faded on the far horizon; capriciously, lazily reflecting their varied hues in the river, making here and there bright patches on the rippling surface under the dim dome of blue, the gleaming lights everywhere sprinkled in the darkness seemed to be swimming, swimming back.

Under an awning on deck sat the lieutenant. He felt older by ten years.

JOHN BUNYAN

JOHN BUNYAN (English, 1628-1688). Uneducated, a tinker by trade, thrown into jail for Baptist preaching. In prison began his great allegory, *The Pilgrim's Progress*, portraying man's journey through this world to the next. Simple, graphic prose has made it, next to Bible, most widely read book in English. Other works: *Grace Abounding, The Holy City*.

THE GOLDEN CITY

Now I saw in my dream that by this time the pilgrims were got over the Enchanted Ground, and entering into the country of Beulah, whose air was very sweet and pleasant, the way lying directly through it, they solaced them there for the season. Yea, here they heard continually the singing of birds, and saw every day the flowers appear in the earth, and heard the voice of the turtle in the land. In this country the sun shineth night and day; wherefore it was beyond the Valley of the Shadow of Death, and also out of the reach of Giant Despair; neither could they from this place so much as see Doubting Castle. Here they were within sight of the city they were going to; also here met them some of the inhabitants thereof; for in this land the shining ones commonly walked, because it was upon the borders of Heaven. In this land, also, the contract between the bride and bridegroom was renewed; yea, here, "as the bridegroom rejoiceth over the bride, so did their God rejoice over them." Here they had no want of corn and wine; for in this place they met abundance of what they had sought for in all their pilgrimage. Here they heard voices from out of the city—loud voices—saying: "Say ye to the daughter of Zion, behold, thy salvation cometh! Behold, his reward is with him!" Here all the inhabitants of the country called them "the holy people, the redeemed of the Lord, sought out," &c.

Now, as they walked in this land, they had more rejoicing than in parts more remote from the kingdom to which they were bound; and drawing nearer to the city yet, they had a more perfect view thereof: it was built of pearls and precious stones, also the streets thereof were paved with gold; so that, by reason of the natural glory of the city, and the reflection of the sunbeams upon it, Christian with desire fell sick; Hopeful also had a fit or two of the same disease: wherefore here they lay by it a while, crying out, because of their pangs: "If you see my Beloved, tell him that I am sick of love."

But being a little strengthened, and better able to bear their sickness, they walked on their way, and came yet nearer and nearer, where were orchards, vineyards and gardens, and their gates opened into the highway. Now, as they came up to these places, behold the gardener stood in the way, to whom the pilgrims said: "Whose goodly vineyards and gardens are these?" He answered:

"They are the King's, and are planted here for his own delight, and also for the solace of pilgrims."

So the gardener had them into the vineyards, and bid them refresh themselves with dainties; he also showed them there the King's walks and arbors, where he delighted to be; and here they tarried and slept.

Now, I beheld in my dream that they talked more in their sleep at this time than ever they did in all their journey; and being in a muse thereabout, the gardener said even to me: "Wherefore musest thou at the matter?" It is the nature of the fruit of the grapes of these vineyards to go down so sweetly as to cause the lips of them that are asleep to speak.

So I saw that when they awoke, they addressed themselves to go up to the city. But, as I said, the reflection of the sun upon the city—for the city was pure gold—was so extremely glorious that they could not as yet with open face behold it, but through an instrument made for that purpose. So I saw that, as they went on, there met them two men in raiment that shone like gold; also their faces shone as the light.

These men asked the pilgrims whence they came; and they told them. They also asked them where they had lodged, what difficulties and dangers, what comforts and pleasures, they had met with in their way; and they told them. Then said the men that met them: "You have but two difficulties more to meet with, and then you are in the city."

Christian and his companion then asked the men to go along

with them; so they told them that they would. But, said they, you must obtain it by your own faith. So I saw in my dream that they went on together till they came in sight of the gate.

Now, I further saw that betwixt them and the gate was a river, but there was no bridge to go over, and the river was very deep. At the sight, therefore, of this river, the pilgrims were much stunned; but the men that went with them said: "You must go through, or you cannot come to the gate."

The pilgrims then began to inquire if there was no other way to the gate; to which they answered: "Yes; but there hath not any, save two—to wit, Enoch and Elijah—been permitted to tread that path since the foundation of the world, nor shall, until the last trumpet shall sound. The pilgrims then—especially Christian—began to despond in their minds, and looked this way and that; but no way could be found by them by which they might escape the river. Then they asked the men if the waters were all of a depth. They said: "No; yet they could not help them in that case; for, said they, you shall find it deeper or shallower, as you believe in the King of the place."

They then addressed themselves to the water, and entering, Christian began to sink, and crying out to his good friend Hopeful, he said:

"I sink in deep waters: the billows go over my head; all the waters go over me. Selah."

Then said the other: "Be of good cheer, my brother; I feel the bottom, and it is good."

Then said Christian: "Ah! my friend, the sorrow of death hath encompassed me about: I shall not see the land that flows with milk and honey."

Then I saw in my dream that Christian was in a muse a while. To whom also, Hopeful added these words: "Be of good cheer; Jesus Christ maketh thee whole;" and with that Christian brake out with a loud voice—"Oh! I see him again; and he tells me: 'When thou passest through the waters, I will be with thee; and through the rivers, they shall not overflow thee.'" Then they both took courage, and the enemy was after that as still as a stone, until they were gone over. Christian, therefore, presently found ground to stand upon, and so it followed that the rest of the river was but shallow. Thus they got over. Now, upon the bank of the river on the other side, they saw the two shining men again, who there waited for them; wherefore, being come out of the river, they saluted them, saying: "We are ministering spirits, sent forth to minister to those that shall be heirs of salvation." Thus they went along toward the gate. Now, you must note that the city stood upon a mighty hill; but the pilgrims went up that hill with ease, because they had these two men to lead them up by the arms; they had likewise left their mortal garments behind them in the river; for though they went in with them, they came out without them. They therefore went up here with much agility and speed, though th; foundation upon which the city was framed was higher than the clouds; they therefore went up through the region of the air, sweetly talking as they went, being comforted because they got safely over the river, and had such glorious companions to attend them.

Now, while they were thus drawing towards the gate, behold a company of the heavenly host came out to meet them; to whom it was said by the other two shining ones:

"These are the men who loved our Lord when they were in the world, and have left all for his holy name; and he hath sent us to fetch them, and we have brought them thus far on their desired journey, that they may go in and look their Redeemer in the face with joy." Then the heavenly host gave a great shout, saying: "Blessed are they that are called to the marriage-supper of the Lamb." There came also out at this time to meet them several of the King's trumpeters, clothed in white and shining raiment, who, with melodious and loud noises, made even the heavens to echo with their sound. These trumpeters saluted Christian and his fellow with ten thousand welcomes from the world; and this they did with shouting and sound of trumpet.

This done, they compassed them round about on every side; some went before, some behind, and some on the right hand, some on the left—as it were to guard them through the upper regions —continually sounding as they went, with melodious noise, in notes on high; so that the very sight was to them that could behold it as if heaven itself was come down to meet them. Thus, therefore, they walked on together; and as they walked, ever and anon these trumpeters, even with joyful sound, would, by mixing their music with looks and gestures, still signify to Christian and his brother how welcome they were into their company, and with what gladness they came to meet them; and now were these two men, as it were, in heaven before they came at it, being swallowed up with the sight of angels, and with hearing their melodious notes. Here, also, they had the city itself in view, and thought they heard all

172

the bells therein to ring, to welcome thereto. But, above all, the warm and joyful thoughts that they had about their own dwelling here with such company, and that for ever and ever. Oh! by what tongue or pen can their glorious joy be expressed! Thus they came up to the gate.

Now, when they were come up to the gate, there were written over in letters of gold: "Blessed are they that do his commandments, that they may have a right to the tree of life, and may enter in through the gates into the city."

Then I saw in my dream that the shining men bid them call at the gate; the which, when they did, some from above looked over the gate, to wit: Enoch, Moses, Elijah, &c.: to whom it was said: These pilgrims are come from the City of Destruction, for the love that they bear to the King of this place; and then the pilgrims gave in unto them each man his certificate, which they had received in the beginning: those, therefore, were carried in to the King, who, when he had read them, said: "Where are the men?" To whom it was answered: They are standing without the gate. The King then commanded to open the gate, "That the righteous nation," said he, "that keepeth truth may enter in."

Now, I saw in my dream that these two men went in at the gate; and lo! as they entered, they were transfigured, and they had raiment put on that shone like gold. There were also that met them with harps to praise withal, and the crowns in token of honor. Then I heard in my dream that all the bells in the city rang again for joy, and that it was said unto them: "Enter ye into the joy of your Lord." I also heard the men themselves, that they sank with a loud voice, saying: "Blessing, honor, and glory, and power be to Him that sitteth upon the throne, and to the Lamb, for ever and ever."

Now, just as the gates were opened to let in the men, I looked in after them, and behold the city shone like the sun; the streets, also, were paved with gold, and in them walked many men with crowns on their heads, palms in their hands, and golden harps, to sing praises withal.

ROBERT BURNS

ROBERT BURNS (Scottish, 1759-1796). Leading Scottish poet of his day. An uneducated natural singer and dialect poet. Learned his trade from popular traditional poetry and balladry. Most notable for love lyrics and satires. Celebrates nature, robust humor, natural passions. Tumultuous private life.

THE TWA DOGS

In that fair part of Scotland's Isle
That bears the name of Old King Coil,
Upon a bonnie day in June,
And latish in the afternoon,
Two dogs, with naught to do at home,
Forgathered once upon a time.

The first I'll name; they called him Caesar,
Kept by his Honour for his pleasure;
His coat, his ears, his mouth, his girth
Showed he was not of Scottish birth
But whelped in some place far abroad,
Where sailors go to fish for cod.
His locked and lettered, fine brass collar
Proved him a gentleman and scholar;
But though he was of high degree
No trace of snobbish ways had he,
But would spend hours in field or ditch
With any gipsy's mongrel bitch.
At church or market, mill or smithy,
No matted cur, however nitty,
But he would hail, right glad to view him,
And wet a post in greeting to him.
The other was a ploughman's collie,
A rhyming, ranting, silly billy
Who for his friend and comrade held him
And in a joke had Luath called him,
After some dog in Highland song
Made centuries since—Lord knows how long.

174

He was a shrewd and faithful tyke
As ever leapt a gate or dyke;
His honest, jolly, brindled face
Won him good friends in every place.
His breast was white, his shaggy back
Well clad with coat of glossy black;
His bushy tail, with upward curl,
Hung o'er his haunches in a swirl.

No doubt but each was fond of t'other
And warmly intimate together;
With social nose they ran and snuffed
For moles or mice at mound and tuft;
At times scoured off on long excursion,
Or rolled each other for diversion;
Until, with larking weary grown,
Upon a knoll they sat them down,
And there began a long digression
About the lords of the creation.

CAESAR

I've often wondered, honest Luath,
What sort of life poor dogs like you have;
And when the gentry's life I mark,
How fare the poor who live by work.
Our Laird gets in his rents and sums,
His coal, his produce, all his claims;
He rises when he thinks he will;
His flunkeys answer to his bell:
He calls his coach; he calls his horse;
He draws a well-filled silken purse
Long as my tail, where, through the stitches
I see his golden guinea riches.
From morn to night it's nought but toiling
At baking, roasting, frying, boiling,
And though the gentry cram and swill
Yet all the servants take their fill
Of sauce, ragouts and spicy hash
That's nothing more than wasteful trash.
Our lap-dog, that small withered wonder,
Eats bigger dinners, yes, by thunder!

Than any honest tenant eats
In all his Honour's wide estates.
What the poor cotters fill their paunch on
I own is past my comprehension.

Caesar, you're right; they're tried enough;
A labourer digging hard and rough
In sodden ditch and stony dyke,
Laying bare quarries and suchlike;
He and his wife he just sustains,
Besides a troop of ragged bairns,
And nought but his strong hands to keep
Them right and tight in food and sleep.
   And when they meet with black disaster,
Like loss of health, or lack of masters,
You'd almost think, a little longer
And they must starve of cold and hunger;
But yet—I never understand it!—
They're mostly wonderful contented;
And strapping lads and clever hussies
Are bred just such a way as this is.

But look, my friend, how you're neglected,
How huffed and cuffed and disrespected!
Lord, man! our gentry care so little
For ploughmen, ditchers and such cattle;
They go as scornful past a hedger
As I would by a stinking badger.
   I've noticed, on our Laird's court-day,
And many a time with sore dismay,
Poor tenants, late with rents and dues,
Taking the factor's harsh abuse;
He'll stamp and threaten, curse and swear
He'll jail them and distrain their gear;
While they must stand with aspect humble,
And hear it all, and fear and tremble!
I see how folk live that have riches;
But surely poor folk must be wretches!

They're not so wretched as you'd think,
Though always on privation's brink:
They're so accustomed to the sight,
The view it gives them little fright.

   Then chance and fortune are so guided
They're always more or less provided;
And though fatigued with close employment,
A spell of rest's a sweet enjoyment.

   The dearest comfort of their lives,
Their thriving brood and faithful wives;
The prattling things are just their pride,
That sweeten board and fireside.

   And then, twelvepenny-worth of ale
Will always over care prevail;
They lay aside their private cares
To canvass Church and State affairs:
They'll talk of patronage and priests
With kindling fury in their breasts;
Or tell what new taxation's coming,
And hear the news from London humming.

   As bleak-faced Hallowmass returns
They hear the jolly rattling churns,
When rural life of every station
Unite in common recreation;
Love smiles, Wit sparkles, social Mirth
Forgets there's trouble on the earth.

   That merry day the year begins
They bar the door on frosty winds;
The strong ale wreathes with mantling cream
And gives a heart-inspiring steam;
The treasured pipe and snuffbox full
Are handed round with right goodwill;
The cheerful elders talk and browse,
The young go romping through the house—
My heart has been so glad to see them
That I for joy ran barking with them.

   Still, it's too true what you have said:
That game is far too often played.
There's many a creditable stock
Of decent, honest, kindly folk,

Are bundled out both root and branch,
Some rascal's greedy pride to quench,
Who thinks to knit himself the faster
In favour with his absent master,
Who, maybe, is a-parliamenting,
For Britain's good his soul indenting—

CAESAR

Faith, lad, you little know about it;
For Britain's good!—good faith! I doubt it!
Say rather, going as premiers lead him,
With Aye or No just as they bid him!
At operas and plays parading,
Mortgaging, gambling, masquerading.
Or maybe, in a frolic daft,
For Hague or Calais boards a craft.
To make a tour, by pleasure swirled,
To learn *bon ton* and see the world.
    There, at Vienna or Versailles,
He breaks his father's old entails,
Or to Madrid diverts his route
To strum guitars or fight with nought;
Or down Italian vistas hurtles,
Whore-hunting among groves of myrtles;
Then boozes muddy German water
To make himself look fair and fatter
And clear the consequential sorrows—
Love-gifts of carnival signoras.
For Britain's good!—for her destruction!
With dissipation, feud and faction!

LUATH

Well, well! dear sirs! is that the way
So many great estates decay?
Are we so goaded, cramped and pressed
For wealth to go that way at last?
    O, if they'd stay away from courts
And please themselves with country sports,
It would for everyone be better,
The laird, the tenant and the cotter!

For these wild, noisy, rambling sparks,
They're not ill-natured in their larks:
Except for stripping ancient glades,
Or speaking lightly of their jades,
Or shooting of a hare or moorcock,
They little harm the simple poor folk.
  But will you tell me, Master Caesar,
Sure, great folks live a life of pleasure?
No cold nor hunger's grip can press them,
The very thought need not distress them.

CAESAR

Lord, man, you'd never envy them
If you were sometimes where I am.
  It's true, they needn't starve or sweat
Through winter's cold or summer's heat;
They've no hard work to cramp their bones
And fill old age with aches and groans:
But human beings are such fools,
For all their colleges and schools,
That when no present ills perplex them
They make enough themselves to vex them;
The less they have to disconcert them
In like proportion less will hurt them.
A country fellow at the plough,
His acres tilled, his heart's aglow;
A country lassie at her wheel,
Her dozens done, she's fine and well;
But gentlemen, and ladies worst,
At dusk with idleness are cursed.
They loiter, lounging, lank and lazy;
Though nothing ails them, yet uneasy;
Their days insipid, dull and tasteless;
Their nights unquiet, long and restless.
And even sports, their balls and races,
Their galloping through public places,
Are such parades of pomp and art,
The joy can scarcely reach the heart.
The men fall out in party matches,
Then make it up in wild debauches:

179

One night they're mad with drink and whoring,
Next day their life is past enduring.
The ladies arm-in-arm, in clusters,
Are great and gracious all as sisters;
But hear their thoughts of one another,
They're downright devils all together.
And then, with eggshell cup and platie,
They sip the scandal-brew so pretty,
Or through long nights, with acid looks,
Pore on the devil's picture books;
Stake on a chance a farmer's stackyard,
And cheat like any unhanged blackguard.

   There are exceptions, man and woman;
But this is gentry's life in common.

By this the sun was out of sight
And twilight darkening brought the night;
A beetle hummed with lazy drone,
The cows stood lowing in the lane;
When up they got with friendly shrugs,
Rejoiced they were not men but dogs;
And each took off his homeward way,
Resolved to meet some other day.

GEORGE GORDON BYRON

GEORGE GORDON BYRON (English, 1788-1824). The most gifted showman
of English Romanticism. Suffered handicap of clubfoot. *Childe Harold's
Pilgrimage* brought early fame and acclaim of English society, despite scandalous private life. Settled in Italy, where he wrote greatest work, the
satirical *Don Juan.* Joined Greek rebels in 1823, died of fever a year later.
   Poetry expresses the essence of romantic melancholy and pessimism.

SHE WALKS IN BEAUTY

SHE walks in beauty, like the night
   Of cloudless climes and starry skies;
And all that's best of dark and bright
   Meet in her aspect and her eyes:
Thus mellowed to that tender light
   Which heaven to gaudy day denies.

One shade the more, one ray the less,
    Had half impaired the nameless grace
Which waves in every raven tress,
    Or softly lightens o'er her face;
Where thoughts serenely sweet express
    How pure, how dear their dwelling-place

And on that cheek, and o'er that brow,
    So soft, so calm, yet eloquent,
The smiles that win, the tints that glow,
    But tell of days in goodness spent,
A mind at peace with all below,
    A heart whose love is innocent!

SO, WE'LL GO NO MORE A-ROVING

So, we'll go no more a-roving
    So late into the night,
Though the heart be still as loving,
    And the moon be still as bright.

For the sword outwears its sheath,
    And the soul wears out the breast,
And the heart must pause to breathe,
    And Love itself have rest.

Though the night was made for loving,
    And the day returns too soon,
Yet we'll go no more a-roving
    By the light of the moon.

THE ISLES OF GREECE

The isles of Greece! the isles of Greece
    Where burning Sappho loved and sung,
Where grew the arts of war and peace,
    Where Delos rose, and Phœbus sprung!
Eternal summer gilds them yet,
But all, except their sun, is set.

The Scian and the Teian muse,
   The hero's harp, the lover's lute,
Have found the fame your shores refuse;
   Their place of birth alone is mute
To sounds which echo further west
Than your sires' "Islands of the Blest."

The mountains look on Marathon—
   And Marathon looks on the sea;
And musing there an hour alone,
   I dreamed that Greece might still be free;
For standing on the Persians' grave,
I could not deem myself a slave.

A king sate on the rocky brow
   Which looks o'er sea-born Salamis;
And ships, by thousands, lay below,
   And men in nations—all were his!
He counted them at break of day—
And when the sun set, where were they?

And where are they? and where art thou,
   My country? On thy voiceless shore
The heroic lay is tuneless now—
   The heroic bosom beats no more!
And must thy lyre, so long divine,
Degenerate into hands like mine?

'Tis something in the dearth of fame,
   Though linked among a fettered race,
To feel at least a patriot's shame,
   Even as I sing, suffuse my face;
For what is left the poet here?
For Greeks a blush—for Greece a tear.

Must *we* but weep o'er days more blest?
   Must *we* but blush?—Our fathers bled.
Earth! render back from out thy breast
   A remnant of our Spartan dead!
Of the three hundred grant but three,
To make a new Thermopylae!

What, silent still? and silent all?
    Ah! no— the voices of the dead
Sound like a distant torrent's fall,
    And answer, "Let one living head,
But one, arise—we come, we come!"
'Tis but the living who are dumb.

In vain—in vain; strike other chords;
    Fill high the cup with Samian wine!
Leave battles to the Turkish hordes,
    And shed the blood of Scio's vine!
Hark! rising to the ignoble call—
How answers each bold Bacchanal!

You have the Pyrric dance as yet;
    Where is the Pyrric phalanx gone?
Of two such lessons, why forget
    The nobler and the manlier one?
You have the letters Cadmus gave—
Think ye he meant them for a slave?

Fill high the bowl with Samian wine!
    We will not think of themes like these!
It made Anacreon's song divine.
    He served—but served Polycrates—
A tyrant; but our masters then
Were still, at least, our countrymen.

The tyrant of the Chersonese
    Was freedom's best and bravest friend;
That tyrant was Miltiades!
    O that the present hour would lend
Another despot of the kind!
Such chains as his were sure to bind.

Fill high the bowl with Samian wine!
    On Suli's rock, and Parga's shore,
Exists the remnant of a line
    Such as the Doric mothers bore;
And there, perhaps, some seed is sown,
The Heracleidan blood might own.

Trust not for freedom to the Franks—
   They have a king who buys and sells;
In native swords and native ranks
   The only hope of courage dwells.
But Turkish force and Latin fraud
Would break your shield, however broad.

Fill high the bowl with Samian wine!
   Our virgins dance beneath the shade—
I see their glorious black eyes shine;
   But gazing on each glowing maid,
My own the burning teardrop laves,
To think such breasts must suckle slaves.

Place me on Sunium's marbled steep,
   Where nothing, save the waves and I,
May hear our mutual murmurs sweep;
   There, swan-like, let me sing and die.
A land of slaves shall ne'er be mine—
Dash down yon cup of Samian wine!

WHEN WE TWO PARTED

When we two parted
   In silence and tears,
Half broken-hearted,
   To sever for years,
Pale grew thy cheek and cold,
   Colder thy kiss;
Truly that hour foretold
   Sorrow to this!

The dew of the morning
   Sunk chill on my brow;
It felt like the waning
   Of what I feel now.
Thy vows are all broken,
   And light is thy fame:
I hear thy name spoken
   And share in its shame.

They name thee before me,
    A knell to mine ear;
A shudder comes o'er me—
    Why wert thou so dear?
They knew not I knew thee
    Who knew thee too well:
Long, long shall I rue thee
    Too deeply to tell.

In secret we met:
    In silence I grieve
That thy heart could forget,
    Thy spirit deceive.
If I should meet thee
    After long years,
How should I greet thee?
    With silence and tears.

ELEGY ON THYRZA

And thou art dead, as young and fair
    As aught of mortal birth;
And form so soft and charms so rare
    Too soon return'd to Earth!
Though Earth received them in her bed,
And o'er the spot the crowd may tread
    In carelessness or mirth,
There is an eye which could not brook
A moment on that grave to look.

I will not ask where thou liest low,
    Nor gaze upon the spot;
There flowers or weeds at will may grow,
    So I behold them not:
It is enough for me to prove
That what I loved and long must love
    Like common earth can rot;
To me there needs no stone to tell
'Tis Nothing that I loved so well.

Yet did I love thee to the last,
    As fervently as thou,
Who didst not change through all the past
    And canst not alter now.
The love where Death has set his seal
Nor age can chill, nor rival steal,
    Nor falsehood disavow:
And, what were worse, thou canst not see
Or wrong, or change, or fault in me.

The better days of life were ours;
    The worst can be but mine:
The sun that cheers, the storm that lours,
    Shall never more be thine.
The silence of that dreamless sleep
I envy now too much to weep;
    Nor need I to repine
That all those charms have pass'd away
I might have watch'd through long decay.

The flower in ripen'd bloom unmatch'd
    Must fall the earliest prey;
Though by no hand untimely snatch'd,
    The leaves must drop away.
And yet it were a greater grief
To watch it withering, leaf by leaf,
    Than see it pluck'd to-day;
Since earthly eye but ill can bear
To trace the change to foul from fair.

I know not if I could have borne
    To see thy beauties fade;
The night that follow'd such a morn
    Had worn a deeper shade:
Thy day without a cloud hath past,
    And thou wert lovely to the last,
    Extinguish'd, not decay'd:
As stars that shoot along the sky
Shine brightest as they fall from high.

186

As once I wept, if I could weep,
  My tears might well be shed,
To think I was not near, to keep
  One vigil o'er thy bed:
To gaze, how fondly! on thy face,
To fold thee in a faint embrace,
  Uphold thy drooping head;
And show that love, however vain,
Nor thou nor I can feel again.

Yet how much less it were to gain,
  Though thou hast left me free,
The loveliest things that still remain
  Than thus remember thee!
The all of thine that cannot die
Through dark and dread Eternity
  Returns again to me,
And more thy buried love endears
Than aught except its living years.

C

PEDRO CALDERON DE LA BARCA

PEDRO CALDERON DE LA BARCA (Spanish, 1600-1681). Baroque and Catholic playwright and poet. Won early fame as dramatist. After service in Spanish army, became priest at 50. Wrote 120 plays, notable for elaborate construction and philosophic content, and many *autos* (religious mysteries). Among them: *La vida es sueño, El alcalde de Zalamea, El médico de Su Honra.*

SEGISMUND'S DREAM

(The King of Poland, frightened by an omen at his son's birth, which the soothsayers have interpreted to mean that the boy will grow up a mere wild beast, bringing fire and slaughter on the country if he succeeds to power, has imprisoned him in a tower till he shall come of age, with a faithful officer for guard. He then has him released—to see if the oracle has been mistaken!—and told that all this confinement and misery has been a dream—as in the "Induction" to the "Taming of the Shrew.")

Segismund (within)—
Forbear! I stifle with your perfume! cease
Your crazy salutations! peace, I say—
Begone, or let me go, ere I go mad
With all this babble, mummery, and glare,
For I am growing dangerous—Air! room! air!—
   (*He rushes in. Music ceases.*)
Oh but to save the reeling brain from wreck
With its bewildered senses!—
   (*He covers his eyes for a while.*)
   (*After looking in the mirror.*)
What, this fantastic Segismund the same

188

Who last night, as for all his nights before,
Lay down to sleep in wolfskin on the ground
In a black turret which the wolf howled round.
And woke again upon a golden bed,
Round which as clouds about a rising sun,
In scarce less glittering caparison,
Gathered gay shapes that, underneath a breeze
Of music, handed him upon their knees
The wine of heaven in a cup of gold,
And still in soft melodious undersong
Hailing me Prince of Poland!—"Segismund,"
They said, "Our Prince! The Prince of Poland!" and
Again, "Oh, welcome, welcome, to his own
Our own Prince Segismund—"

If reason, sense, and self-identity
Obliterated from a worn-out brain,
Art thou not maddest striving to be sane,
And catching at that Self of yesterday
That, like a leper's rags, best flung away!
Or if not mad, then dreaming—dreaming?—well—
Dreaming then—Or, if self to self be true,
Not mocked by that, but as poor souls have been
By those who wronged them, to give wrong new relish?
Or have those stars indeed they told me of
As masters of my wretched life of old,
Into some happier constellation rolled,
And brought my better fortune out on earth
Clear as themselves in heav'n!—

(The great officers of state crowd around him with protestations of
fidelity; Clotaldo, his old warder, comes, and after attempts at
explaining and justifying the situation, Segismund in a fury attempts
to strike his head off; the Princess Estrella, betrothed to the Duke
of Muscovy, enters, and Segismund claims her for his own and
attempts to throttle the Duke; the King is called in, and after a
storm of reproaches which the King parries on the ground of good
intentions, Segismund closes as follows:)

Be assured your Savage, once let loose,
Will not be caged again so quickly; not
By threat or adulation to be tamed.

189

Till he have had his quarrel out with those
Who made him what he is.

King—

Beware! Beware!
Subdue the kindled Tiger in your eye,
Nor dream that it was sheer necessity
Made me thus far relax the bond of fate,
And, with far more of terror than of hope
Threaten myself, my people, and the State.
Know that, if old, I yet have vigor left
To wield the sword as well as wear the crown;
And if my more immediate issue fail,
Not wanting scions of collateral blood.
Whose wholesome growth shall more than compensate
For all the loss of a distorted stem.

Segismund—

That will I straightway bring to trial—Oh,
After a revelation such as this,
The Last Day shall have little left to show
Of righted wrong and villainy requited!
Nay, Judgment now beginning upon earth,
Myself, methinks, in right of all my wrongs,
Appointed heav'n's avenging minister,
Accuser, judge, and executioner,
Sword in hand, cite the guilty—First, as worst,
The usurper of his son's inheritance;
Him and his old accomplice, time and crime
Inveterate, and unable to repay
The golden years of life they stole away.
What, does he yet maintain his state, and keep
The throne he should be judged from? Down with him,
That I may trample on the false white head
So long has worn my crown! Where are my soldiers?
Of all my subjects and my vassals here
Not one to do my bidding? Hark! A trumpet!

The trumpet—

(*He pauses as the trumpet sounds as in Act I., and masked Soldiers
gradually fill in behind the throne.*)

King (*rising before his throne*) —

Aye, indeed, the trumpet blows

A memorable note, to summon those
Who, if forthwith you fall not at the feet
Of him whose head you threaten with the dust,
Forthwith shall draw the curtain of the Past
About you; and this momentary gleam
Of glory, that you think to hold life-fast,
So coming, so shall vanish, as a dream.

 Segismund—
He prophesies; the old man prophesies;
And, at his trumpet's summons, from the tower
The leash-bound shadows loosened after me
My rising glory reach and overlour—
But, reach not I my height, he shall not hold,
But with me back to his own darkness!

 (*He dashes toward the throne and is inclosed by the soldiers.*)
Traitors!
Hold off! Unhand me! Am not I your king?
And you would strangle him!
But I am breaking with an inward Fire
Shall scorch you off, and wrap me on the wings
Of conflagration from a kindled pyre
Of lying prophecies and prophet kings
Above the extinguished stars—Reach me the sword
He flung me—Fill me such a bowl of wine
As that you woke the day with—

 King—
And shall close,—
But of the vintage that Clotaldo knows.

(He is drugged, returned to the tower, and on waking assured that
the recent taste of freedom and kingship was all a dream, and his
former life in the tower the reality.)

 Segismund—
You know
'Tis nothing but a dream?
 Clotaldo—
Nay, you yourself
Know best how lately you awoke from that
You know you went to sleep on?
Why, have you never dreamt the like before?

Segismund—
Never, to such reality.
    Clotaldo—
Such dreams
Are oftentimes the sleeping exhalations
Of that ambition that lies smoldering
Under the ashes of the lowest fortune;
By which, when reason slumbers, or has lost
The reins of sensible comparison,
We fly at something higher than we are—
Scarce ever dive to lower—to be kings,
Or conquerors, crowned with laurel or with gold,
Nay, mounting heav'n itself on eagle wings.
Which, by the way, now that I think of it,
May furnish us the key to this high flight—
That royal Eagle we were watching, and
Talking of as you went to sleep last night.
    Segismund—
Last night? Last night?
    Clotaldo—
Aye, do you not remember
Envying his immunity of flight,
As, rising from his throne of rock, he sailed
Above the mountains far into the West
That burned about him, while with poising wings
He darkled in it as a burning brand
Is seen to smolder in the fire it feeds?
    Segismund—
Last night—last night—Oh, what a day was that
Between that last night and this sad To-day!
    Clotaldo—
And yet, perhaps,
Only some few dark moments, into which
Imagination, once lit up within
And unconditional of time and space,
Can pour infinities.
    Segismund—
And I remember
How the old man they called the King, who wore
The crown of gold about his silver hair,
And a mysterious girdle round his waist,

Just when my rage was roaring at its height,
And after which it was all dark again,
Bid me beware lest all should be a dream.
    Clotaldo—
Aye, there another specialty of dreams,
That once the dreamer 'gins to dream he dreams.
His foot is on the very verge of waking.
    Segismund—
Would it had been upon the verge of death
That knows no waking—
Lifting me up to glory, to fall back,
Stunned, crippled—wretcheder than ev'n before.
    Clotaldo—
Yet not so glorious, Segismund, if you
Your visionary honor wore so ill
As to work murder and revenge on those
Who meant you well.
    Segismund—
Who meant me!—me! their Prince
Chained like a felon—
    Clotaldo—
Stay, stay—Not so fast,
You dreamed the Prince, remember.
    Segismund—
Then in dream
Revenged it only.
True. But as they say
Dreams are rough copies of the waking soul
Yet uncorrected of the higher Will,
So that men sometimes in their dreams confess
An unsuspected, or forgotten, self;
One must beware to check—aye, if one may,
Stifle ere born, such passion in ourselves
As makes, we see, such havoc with our sleep,
And ill reacts upon the waking day.
And, by the bye, for one test, Segismund,
Between such swearable realities—
Since Dreaming, Madness, Passion, are akin
In missing each that salutary rein
Of reason, and the guiding will of man:
One test, I think, of waking sanity

193

Shall be that conscious power of self-control,
To curb all passion, but much most of all
That evil and vindictive, that ill squares
With human, and with holy canon less,
Which bids us pardon ev'n our enemies,
And much more those who, out of no ill will,
Mistakenly have taken up the rod
Which heav'n, they think, has put into their hands.
  Segismund—
I think I soon shall have to try again—
Sleep has not yet done with me.
  Clotaldo—
Such a sleep.
Take my advice—'tis early yet—the sun
Scarce up above the mountain; go within,
And if the night deceived you, try anew
With morning; morning dreams they say come true.
  Segismund—
Oh, rather pray for me a sleep so fast
As shall obliterate dream and waking too.
  (*Exit into the tower.*)
  Clotaldo—
So sleep; sleep fast: and sleep away those two
Night potions, and the waking dream between
Which dream thou must believe; and, if to see
Again, poor Segismund! that dream must be.
And yet, and yet, in these our ghostly lives,
Half night, half day, half sleeping, half awake,
How if our working life, like that of sleep,
Be all a dream in that eternal life
To which we wake not till we sleep in death?
How if, I say, the senses we now trust
For date of sensible comparison,—
Aye, ev'n the Reason's self that dates with them,
Should be in essence or intensity
Hereafter so transcended, and awoke
To a perceptive subtlety so keen
As to confess themselves befooled before,
In all that now they will avouch for most?
One man—like this—but only so much longer
As life is longer than a summer's day,

Believed himself a king upon his throne,
And played at hazard with his fellows' lives,
Who cheaply dreamed away their lives to him.
The sailor dreamed of tossing on the flood:
The soldier of his laurels grown in blood:
The lover of the beauty that he knew
Must yet dissolve to dusty residue:
The merchant and the miser of his bags
Of fingered gold; the beggar of his rags:
And all this stage of earth on which we seem
Such busy actors, and the parts we played,
Substantial as the shadow of a shade,
And Dreaming but a dream within a dream.
    Fife—
Was it not said, sir,
By some philosopher as yet unborn
That any chimney sweep who for twelve hours
Dreams himself king is happy as the king
Who dreams himself twelve hours a chimney-sweep?
    Clotaldo—
A theme indeed for wiser heads than yours
To moralize. upon.

(An insurrection breaking out to reinstate Segismund, a band of
soldiers bring him, asleep, from the tower.)

    Captain—
O Royal Segismund, our Prince and King,
Look on us—listen to us—answer us,
Your faithful soldiery and subjects, now
About you kneeling, but on fire to rise
And cleave a passage through your enemies,
Until we seat you on your lawful throne.
For though your father, King Basilio,
Now King of Poland, jealous of the stars
That prophesy his setting with your rise,
Here holds you ignominiously eclipsed,
And would Astolfo, Duke of Muscovy,
Mount to the throne of Poland after him;
So will not we, your loyal soldiery

195

And subjects; neither those of us now first
Apprised of your existence and your right:
Nor those that hitherto deluded by
Allegiance false, their vizors now fling down,
And craving pardon on their knees with us
For that unconscious disloyalty,
Offer with us the service of their blood;
Not only we and they; but at our heels
The heart, if not the bulk, of Poland follows
To join their voices and their arms with ours,
In vindicating with our lives our own
Prince Segismund to Poland and her throne.

Soldiers—

Segismund, Segismund, Prince Segismund!
Our own King Segismund, etc.

(*They all arise.*)

Segismund—

Again? So soon?—What, not yet done with me?
The sun is little higher up, I think,
Than when I last lay down,
To bury in the depth of your own sea
You that infest its shallows.

Captain—

Sir!

Segismund—

And now,
Not in a palace, not in the fine clothes
We all were in; but here, in the old place,
And in your old accounterment—
Only your vizors off, and lips unlockt
To mock me with that idle title—

Captain—

Nay,
Indeed no idle title, but your own,
Then, now, and now forever. For, behold,
Ev'n as I speak. the mountain passes fill
And bristle with the advancing soldiery
That glitters in your rising glory, sir;
And, at our signal, echo to our cry,
"Segismund, King of Poland!"

(*Shouts, trumpets, etc.*)

Segismund—
Oh, how cheap
The muster of a countless host of shadows,
As impotent to do with as to keep!
All this they said before—to softer music.
    Captain—
Soft music, sir, to what indeed were shadows,
That, following the sunshine of a Court,
Shall back be brought with it—if shadows still,
Yet to substantial reckoning.
    Segismund—
They shall?
The white-haired and white-wandel chamberlain,
So busy with his wand too—the old King
That I was somewhat hard on—he had been
Hard upon me—and the fine feathered Prince
Who crowed so loud—my cousin,—and another,
Another cousin, we will not bear hard on—
And—but Clotaldo?
    Captain—
Fled, my Lord, but close
Pursued; and then—
    Segismund—
Then, as he fled before,
And after he had sworn it on his knees,
Came back to take me—where I am!—No more,
No more of this! Away with you! Begone!
Whether but visions of ambitious night
That morning ought to scatter, or grown out
Of night's proportions you invade the day
To scare me from my little wits yet left,
Begone! I know I must be near awake,
Knowing I dream; or, if not at my voice,
Then vanish at the clapping of my hands,
Or take this foolish fellow for your sport:
Dressing me up in visionary glories,
Which the first air of waking consciousness
Scatters as fast as from the alamander—
That, waking one fine morning in full flower,
One rougher insurrection of the breeze
Of all her sudden honor disadorns

To the last blossom, and she stands again
The winter-naked scarecrow that she was!
   (*Shouts, trumpets, etc.*)
   A Soldier—
Challenging King Basilio's now in sight,
And bearing down upon us.
   Captain—
Sir, you hear;
A little hesitation and delay,
And all is lost—your own right, and the lives
Of those who now maintain it at that cost;
With you all saved and won; without, all lost.
That former recognition of your right
Grant but a dream, if you will have it so;
Great things forecast themselves by shadows great:
Or will you have it, this like that dream too,
People, and place, and time itself, all dream—
Yet, being in't, and as the shadows come
Quicker and thicker than you can escape,
Adopt your visionary soldiery,
Who, having struck a solid chain away,
Now put an airy sword into your hand,
And harnessing you piecemeal till you stand
Amidst us all complete in glittering,
If unsubstantial, steel—

(A battle is fought, in which Segismund is victorious; taught by his
former experience, he resolves to be wise and temperate, and closes
with the following moralizing:)

   You stare upon me all, amazed to hear
The word of civil justice from such lips
As never yet seemed tuned to such discourse.
But listen—In that same enchanted tower,
Not long ago, I learned it from a dream
Expounded by this ancient prophet here;
And which he told me, should it come again,
How I should bear myself beneath it; not
As then with angry passion all on fire,
Arguing and making a distempered soul;
But ev'n with justice, mercy, self-control,

As if the dream I walked in were no dream,
And conscience one day to account for it.
A dream it was in which I thought myself,
And you that hailed me now then hailed me King,
In a brave palace that was all my own,
Within, and all without it, mine; until,
Drunk with excess of majesty and pride,
Methought I towered so high and swelled so wide,
That of myself I burst the glittering bubble,
That my ambition had about me blown,
And all again was darkness. Such a dream
As this in which I may be walking now;
Dispensing solemn justice to you shadows,
Who make believe to listen; but anon,
With all your glittering arms and equipage,
Kings, princes, captains, warriors, plume and steel,
Aye, ev'n with all your airy theater,
May flit into air you seem to rend
With acclamation, leaving me to wake
In the dark tower; or dreaming that I wake
From this that waking is; or this and that
Both waking or both dreaming; such a doubt
Confounds and clouds our mortal life about.
And, whether wake or dreaming; this I know,
How dream-wise human glories come and go;
Whose momentary tenure not to break,
Walking as one who knows he soon may wake
So fairly carry the full cup, so well
Disordered insolence and passion quell,
That there be nothing after to upbraid
Dreamer or doer in the part he played,
Whether To-morrow's dawn shall break the spell,
Or the Last Trumpet of the eternal Day,
When Dreaming with the Night shall pass away.
    (*Exeunt.*)

KAREL CAPEK

KAREL CAPEK (Czech, 1890-1938). Most widely known Czech writer, through plays, *R.U.R.* and *The Life of the Insects*. Also author of six novels, short story collections, travel books. Ardent humanitarian, fond of utopian themes. Like his friend Masaryk, strongly under influence of American ideas. Said to have died "of the death of his country."

THE ISLAND

AT one time there lived in Lisbon a certain Dom Luiz de Faria who later sailed away in order to see the world, and having visited the greater part of it, died on an island as remote as one's imagination can picture. During his life in Lisbon he was a man full of wisdom and judgment. He lived as such men usually do, in a way to gratify his own desires without doing harm to others, and he occupied a position in affairs commensurate with his innate pride. But even that life eventually bored him and became a burden to him. Therefore he exchanged his property for money and sailed away on the first ship out into the world.

On this ship he sailed first to Cadiz and then to Palermo, Constantinople and Beiruth, to Palestine, Egypt and around Arabia clear up to Ceylon. Then they sailed around lower India and the islands including Java whence they struck for the open sea again heading towards the east and south. Sometimes they met fellow countrymen who were homeward bound and who wept with joy when they asked questions about their native land.

In all the countries they visited Dom Luiz saw so many things that were extraordinary and well-nigh marvellous, that he felt as if he had forgotten all his former life.

While they sailed thus over the wide sea, the stormy season overtook them and their boat tossed on the waves like a cork which has neither a goal nor anchor. For three days the storm increased in violence. The third night the ship struck a coral reef.

Dom Luiz during the terrific crash felt himself lifted to a great height and then plunged down into the water. But the water hurled him back and pitched him unconscious on a broken timber.

When he recovered consciousness, he realised that it was bright noon and that he was drifting on a pile of shattered beams wholly alone on a calm sea. At that instant he felt for the first time a real joy in being alive.

He floated thus until evening and throughout the night and the entire succeeding day, but not a glimpse of land did he have. Besides, the pile of rafters on which he floated was becoming loosened by the action of the water, and piece after piece detached itself, Dom Luiz vainly trying to tie them together with strips of his own clothing. At last only three weak timbers remained to him and he sank back in weariness. With a feeling of being utterly forsaken, Dom Luiz made his adieu to life and resigned himself to the will of God.

The third day at dawn he saw that the waves were bearing him to a beautiful island of charming groves and green thickets which seemed to be floating on the bosom of the ocean.

Finally, covered with salt and foam he stepped out on the land. At that instant several savages emerged from the forest, but Dom Luiz gave utterance to an unfriendly shout for he was afraid of them. Then he knelt down to pray, sank to the earth and fell asleep on the shore of the ocean.

When the sun was setting, he was awakened by a great hunger. The sand all around him was marked by the prints of bare flat feet. Dom Luiz was much rejoiced for he realised that around him had walked and sat many savages who had discussed and wondered about him but had done him no injury. Forthwith he went to seek food but it had already grown dark. When he had passed to the other side of the cliff, he beheld the savages sitting in a circle eating their supper. He saw men, women and children in that circle, but he took a position at some distance, not being bold enough to go closer, as if he were a beggar from some far-off province.

A young female of the savage group arose from her place and brought him a flat basket full of fruit. Luiz flung himself upon the basket and devoured bananas, figs, both dried and fresh, other fruits and fresh clams, meat dried in the sun and sweet bread of a very different sort from ours. The girl also brought him a pitcher of spring water and, seating herself in a squat position, she watched him eat and drink. When Luiz had had his fill, he felt a great relief in his whole body and began to thank the girl aloud for her gifts and for the water, for her kind-heartedness and for the mercifulness of all the others. As he spoke thus, a deep gratitude like the sweet anguish of an overflowing heart grew in him and poured itself out in beautiful words which he had never before been able to utter so well. The savage girl sat in front of him and listened.

The following day he continued his inspection, encircling the

Dom Luiz felt that he must repeat his gratitude in a way to make her understand and so he thanked her as fervently as if he were praying. In the meantime the savages had all gone away into the forest and Luiz was afraid that he would remain alone in the unfamiliar place with this great joy in his heart. So he began to relate things to the girl to detain her—telling her where he came from, how the ship was wrecked and what sufferings he had endured on the sea. All the while the savage maid lay before him flat on her stomach and listened silently. Then Luiz observed that she had fallen asleep with her face on the earth. Seating himself at some distance, he gazed at the heavenly stars and listened to the murmur of the sea until sleep overcame him.

When he awoke in the morning, he looked for the maid but she had vanished. Only the impression of her entire body—straight and long like a green twig—remained in the sand. And when Luiz stepped into the hollow, it was warm and sun-heated. Then he followed the shoreline to inspect the island. Sometimes he had to go through forests or underbrush; often he had to skirt swamps and climb over boulders. At times he met groups of savages but he was not afraid of them. He noted that the ocean was a more beautiful blue than anywhere else in the world and that there were blossoming trees and unusual loveliness of vegetation. Thus he journeyed all day long enjoying the beauty of the island which was the most pleasing of any he had ever seen. Even the natives, he observed, were far more handsome than other savage tribes.

The following day he continued his inspection, encircling the entire island which was of an undulating surface blessed with streams and flowering verdure, just as one would picture paradise. By evening he reached the spot on the shore where he had landed from the sea and there sat the young savage girl all alone braiding her hair. At her feet lay the timbers on which he had floated hither. The waves of the impassable sea splashed up as far as the rafters so that he could advance no farther. Here Dom Luiz seated himself beside her and gazed at the sweep of the water bearing off his thoughts wave on wave. After many hundreds of waves had thus come and gone, his heart overflowed with an immeasurable sorrow and he began to pour out his grief, telling how he had journeyed for two days making a complete circumference of the island but that nowhere had he found a city or a harbour or a human being resembling himself. He told how all his comrades had perished at sea and that he had been cast up on an island from which there was no return; that he was left alone among low savage beings who spoke another language in which it was impossible to distinguish words or sense. Thus he complained bitterly and the savage maid listened to him lying on the sand until she fell asleep as if rocked to slumber by the grievous lullaby of his tribulations. Then Luiz became silent and breathed softly.

In the morning they sat together on the rock overlooking the sea giving a view of the entire horizon. There Dom Luiz reviewed his whole life, the elegance and splendour of Lisbon, his love affairs, his voyages and all that he had seen in the world and he closed his eyes to vision more clearly the beautiful scenes in his own life. When he again opened his eyes, he saw the savage girl sitting on her heels and looking before her with a somewhat unintelligent gaze. He saw that she was lovely, with a small body and slender limbs, as brown as the earth, and finely erect.

After that he sat often on the rock looking out for a possible passing ship. He saw the sun rise up from the ocean and sink in its depths and he became accustomed to this just as he did to all else. He learned day by day more of the pleasant sweetness of the island and its climate. It was like an isle of love. Sometimes the savages came to him and gazed on him with respect as they squatted in a circle about him like penguins. Among them were tattooed men and venerable ancients and these brought him portions of food that he might live.

When the rainy season came, Dom Luiz took up his abode in the young savage girl's hut. Thus he lived among the wild natives and went naked just as they did but he felt scorn for them and did not learn a single word of their language. He did not know what name they gave to the island on which he lived, to the roof which covered his head or to the woman who in the eyes of God was his only mate. Whenever he returned to the hut, he found there food prepared for him, a couch and the quiet embrace of his brown wife. Although he regarded her as not really or wholly a human being, but rather more nearly like other animals, nevertheless he treated her as if she understood him, telling her everything in his own language and feeling fully satisfied because she listened to him attentively. He narrated to her everything that occupied his mind—events of his former life in Lisbon, things about his home, details of his travels. At first it grieved him that the savage maiden neither understood his words nor the significance of what he was saying but he became accustomed even to that and continued to recount everything in the

203

same phrases and also with variations and always afterward he took her into his arms.

But in the course of time his narrations grew shorter and more interrupted. The adventures he had had slipped the memory of Dom Luiz just as if they hadn't happened or as if nothing had ever happened. For whole days he would lie on his couch lost in thought and silence. He became accustomed to his new life and continued to sit on his rock but he no longer kept a lookout for passing ships. Thus many years passed and Luiz forgot about returning, forgot the past, even his own native speech, and his mind was as mute as his tongue. Always at night he returned to his hut but he never learned to know the natives any more intimately than he had the day he arrived on the island.

Once in the summer he was deep in the forest when such a strange unrest overwhelmed him suddenly that he ran out of the wood to behold out on the ocean a beautiful ship at anchor. With violently beating heart he rushed to the shore to mount his boulder and when he reached it, he saw on the beach a group of sailors and officers. He concealed himself behind the rock like a savage and listened. Their words touched the margin of his memory and he then realised that the newcomers were speaking his native tongue. He rose then and tried to address them but he only gave utterance to a loud shout. The new arrivals were frightened and he gave a second outcry. They raised their carbines but in that instant his tongue became untangled and he cried out, "Seignors,—have mercy!" All of them cried out in joy and hastened forward to him. But Luiz was seized by a savage instinct to flee before them. They, however, had completely surrounded him and one after another embraced him and overwhelmed him with questions. Thus he stood in the midst of the group—naked and full of anguish, looking in every direction for a loophole of escape.

"Don't be afraid," an elderly officer said to him. "Just recall that you are a human being. Bring him meat and wine for he looks thin and miserable. And you—sit down here among us and rest while you get accustomed again to the speech of human beings instead of to screeches which no doubt apes employ as speech."

They brought Dom Luiz sweet wine, prepared meats and biscuits. He sat among them as if in a dream and ate and gradually began to feel his memory returning. The others also ate and drank and conversed merrily rejoicing that they had found a fellow countryman. When Luiz had partaken of some of the food, a delicious feeling of gratitude filled him just as that time when the savage maiden had fed him but in addition he now felt a joy in the beautiful speech which he heard and understood and in the companionable people who addressed him as a brother. The words now came to his tongue of themselves and he expressed his thanks to them as best he could.

"Rest a little longer," the old officer said to him, "and then you can tell us who you are and how you got here. Then the precious gift of language will return to you for there is nothing more beautiful than the power of speech which permits a man to talk, to relate his adventures and to pour out his feelings."

While he was speaking a young sailor tuned up and began softly to sing a song about a man who went away beyond the sea while his sweetheart implores the sea and the winds and the sky to restore him to her, the pleading grief of the maiden being expressed in the most touching words one could find anywhere. After him others sang or recited other poems of similar content, each of them a little sadder in strain. All the songs gave voice to the longing for a loved one; they told of ships sailing to far distant lands and of the ever changeful sea. At the last everyone was filled with memories of home and of all whom they had left behind. Dom Luiz wept copious tears, painfully happy in the afflictions he had suffered and in their joyous solution, when after having become unused to civilized speech he now heard the beautiful music of poetry. He wept because it was all like a dream which he feared could not be real.

Finally the old officer arose and said, "Children, now we will inspect the island which we found here in the ocean and before the sun sets we will gather here to row back to the ship. At night we will lift anchor and under God's protection, we will sail back. You, my friend," he turned to Luiz, "if you have anything that is yours and that you want to take with you as a souvenir, bring it here and wait for us till just before sunset."

The sailors scattered over the island shore and Dom Luiz betook himself to the savage woman's hut. The farther he advanced the more he loitered, turning over in his mind just how he should tell the savage that he must go away and forsake her. He sat down on a stone and debated with himself for he could not run away without any show of gratitude when he had lived with her for ten years. He recalled all the things she had done for him, how she had provided his food and shelter and had served him with her body and by her labours. Then he entered her hut, sat down beside her and talked a great deal and very hurriedly as if thus he could the better convince her. He told her that they had come for him and that he must now sail away to attend to very necessary affairs of which he conjured up a great quantity. Then he took her in his arms and thanked her for everything that she had done for him and he promised her that he would soon return, accompanying his promises with solemn vows and protestations. When he had talked a long time, he noticed that she was listening to him without the faintest understanding or comprehension. This angered him and, losing his patience, he repeated all his arguments as emphatically as possible and he stamped his feet in his irritability. It suddenly occurred to him that the sailors were probably pushing off, not waiting for him, and he rushed out from the hut in the middle of his speech and hastened to the shore.

But as yet no one was there so he sat down to wait. But the thought worried him that in all likelihood the savage woman had not thoroughly understood what he had said to her about being compelled to go away. That seemed such a terrible thing to him that he suddenly started back on a run to explain everything to her once more. However, he did not step into her hut but looked through a crack to see what she was doing. He saw that she had gathered fresh grass to make a soft bed for him for the night; he saw her placing fruit for him to eat and he noted for the first time that she herself ate only the poorer specimens—those that were dwarfed or spotted and for him she selected the most beautiful—all the large and perfect samples of fruit. Then she sat down as immovable as a statue and waited for him. Of a sudden Dom Luis comprehended clearly that he must yet eat the fruit set out for him and lie down on the couch prepared so carefully and complete her expectations before he could depart.

Meanwhile the sun was setting and the sailors gathered on the shore to push off to the ship. Only Dom Luiz was missing and so they called out to him, "Seignor! Seignor!" When he did not come, they scattered in various directions on the edge of the forest to seek him, all the time continuing to call out to him. Two of the seamen ran quite close to him, calling him all the while but he hid among the shrubbery, his heart pounding in his breast for fear they would find him. Then all the voices died down, and the darkness came. Splashing the oars, the seamen rowed to the vessel loudly lamenting the lost survivor of the wreck. Then absolute quiet ensued and Dom Luiz emerged from the underbrush and returned to the hut. The savage woman sat there unmoved and patient. Dom Luiz ate the fruit, lay down on the freshly made couch with her beside him.

206

When dawn was breaking Dom Luiz lay sleepless and gazed out through the door of the hut where beyond the trees of the forest could be seen the sunlit sea—that sea on which the beautiful ship was just sailing away from the island. The savage woman lay beside him asleep but she was no longer attractive as in former years but ugly and terrible to look upon. Tear after tear rolled down on her bosom while Dom Luiz, in a whisper, lest she might hear, repeated beautiful words, wonderful poems describing the sorrow of longing and of vain eternal yearning.

Then the ship disappeared beyond the horizon and Dom Luiz remained on the island but he never uttered a single word from that day during all the years that preceded his death.

GIOSUE CARDUCCI

GIOSUÈ CARDUCCI (Italian, 1835-1907). Protagonist of the Italian classics in post-Risorgimento literature. Favored return to early literary forms, Roman paganism and imperialism. Opposed to Romanticism and Christianity. Poetry preoccupied with history and landscape of Italy: *Iams and Epodes, Barbarian Odes*. Critical works created great stir in their time.

SONNET

Alone my vessel passes, mid the cry
Of halycons, on the stormy waters borne,
Swept on, by thunder of the billows torn,
Beneath the clamours of the lightening sky.
All Memories turn to that far shore gone by
Their faces wet with tears and sorrow-worn,
And all fair Hopes o'erthrown their glances forlorn
Cast on the splintered oars that broken lie.

Yet at the stern still doth my Genius stand,
While to the creaking masts he hearkeneth,
And cries o'er sea and sky his loud command:
'Row on! row on! O guides of desperate breath,
Toward cloudy ports of the forgetful land,
Toward whitening breakers of the reefs of death.'

PANTHEISM

I told it not, O vigilant stars, to you;
To thee, all-seeing sun, I made no moan;
Her name, the flower of all things fair and true,
Was echoed in my silent heart alone.

Yet now my secret star tells unto star,
Through the brown night, to some vague sphery tune;
The great sun smiles at it, when, sinking far,
He whispers love to the white and rising moon.

On shadowy hills, on shores where life is gay,
Each bush repeats it to each flower that blows;
The flitting birds sing, 'Poet grim and grey,
At last Love's honeyed dreams thy spirit knows.'

I told it not, yet heaven and earth repeat
The name beloved in sounds divine that swell,
And mid the acacia-blossom's perfume sweet
Murmurs the Spirit of All—'She loves thee well.'

SNOWFALL

Slowly flutters the snow from ash-coloured heavens in silence;
Sound or tumult of life rises not up from the town;

Not of herbseller the cry, nor rumorous rattle of wagons,
Not love's passionate song joyous in musical youth.

But, from the belfry swaying, hoarsely the hours thro' the evening
Moan like sighs from a world far from the light of our day.

Wandering song-birds beat at my tarnished window panes; friendly
Spirits returning are they, seeking and calling for me.

Soon, O belovèd ones, soon—be calm, heart ever undaunted—
Soon to the silence I come, soon in the shades to repose.

MIGUEL DE CERVANTES Y SAAVEDRA

MIGUEL DE CERVANTES Y SAAVEDRA (Spanish, 1547-1616). Spain's greatest writer and one of foremost in world literature. Wrote poetry and plays, but greatest triumph was novel, *Don Quixote*. Like *Hamlet* and *Faust*, *Quixote* reveals the many contradictions in man's nature. Imbued with deep humanism and gentle humor, Cervantes died same day as his great contemporary, Shakespeare.

SANCHO PANZA IN HIS ISLAND

SANCHO, with all his attendants, came to a town that had about a thousand inhabitants, and was one of the best where the duke had any power. They gave him to understand that the name of the place was the Island of Barataria, either because the town was called Barataria, or because the government cost him so cheap. As soon as he came to the gates (for it was walled) the chief officers and inhabitants, in their formalities, came out to receive him, the bells rung, and all the people gave general demonstrations of their joy. The new governor was then carried in mighty pomp to the great church, to give Heaven thanks: and, after some ridiculous ceremonies, they delivered him the keys of the gates, and received him as perpetual governor of the Island of Barataria. In the meantime, the garb, the port, the huge beard, and the short and thick shape of the new governor, made everyone who knew nothing of the jest wonder: and even those who were privy to the plot, who were many, were not a little surprised.

In short, from the church they carried him to the court of justice; where, when they had placed him in his seat, "My lord governor," said the duke's steward to him, "it is an ancient custom here, that he who takes possession of this famous island must answer to some difficult and intricate question that is propounded to him; and by the return he makes the people feel the pulse of his understanding, and by an estimate of his abilities, judge whether they ought to rejoice or to be sorry for his coming."

All the while the steward was speaking, Sancho was staring on an inscription in large characters on the wall over against his seat; and, as he could not read, he asked what was the meaning of that which he saw painted there upon the wall. "Sir," said they, "it is an account of the day when your lordship took possession of this island; and the inscription runs thus: 'This day, being such a day of this month, in such a year, the Lord Don Sancho Panza took possession of this island, which may he long enjoy.' " "And who is he?" asked Sancho. "Your lordship," answered the steward; "for we know of no other Panza in the island but yourself, who now sit in this chair." "Well, friend," said Sancho, "pray take notice that Don does not belong to me, nor was it borne by any of my family before me. Plain Sancho Panza is my name; my father was called Sancho, my grandfather Sancho, and all of us have been Panzas, without any Don or Donna added to our name. Now do I already guess your Dons are as thick as stones in this island. But it is enough that Heaven knows my meaning; if my government happens to last but four days to an end, it shall go hard but I will clear the island of these swarms of Dons, that must needs be as troublesome as so many flesh-flies. Come, now for your question, good Mr. Steward, and I will answer it as well as I can, whether the town be sorry or pleased."

At the same instant two men came into the court, the one dressed like a country fellow, the other looked like a tailor, with a pair of shears in his hand. "If it please you, my lord," cried the tailor, "I and this farmer here are come before your worship. This honest man came to my shop yesterday, for, saving your presence, I am a tailor, and, Heaven be praised, free of my company; so, my lord, he showed me a piece of cloth. 'Sir,' quoth he, 'is there enough of this to make a cap?' Whereupon I measured the stuff, and answered him, 'Yes,' if it like your worship. Now, as I imagined, do you see, he could not but imagine (and perhaps he imagined right enough) that I had a mind to cabbage some of his cloth, judging hard of us honest tailors. 'Pr'ythee,' quoth he, 'look there be not enough for two caps?' Now I smelt him out, and told him there was. Whereupon the old knave, (if it like your worship,) going on to the tune, bid me look again, and see whether it would not make three. And at last, if it would not make five. I was resolved to humour my customer, and said it might: so we struck a bargain.

"Just now the man is come for his caps, which I gave him; but when I asked him for my money he will have me give him his cloth again, or pay him for it."—"Is this true, honest man?" said Sancho to the farmer. "Yes, if it please you," answered the fellow; "but pray let him show the five caps he has made me." "With all my heart," cried the tailor; and with that, pulling his hand from under his cloak, he held up five little tiny caps, hanging upon his four fingers and thumb, as upon so many pins. "There," quoth he, "you see the five caps this good gaffer asks for; and may I never whip a stitch more if I have wronged him of the least snip of his cloth, and let any workman be judge." The sight of the caps, and the oddness of the cause, set the whole court a laughing. Only Sancho sat gravely considering a while, and then, "Methinks," said he, "this suit here needs not be long depending, but may be decided without any more ado, with a great deal of equity; and, therefore, the judgment of the court is, that the tailor shall lose his making, and the countryman his cloth, and that the caps be given to the poor prisoners, and so let there be an end of the business."

If this sentence provoked the laughter of the whole court, the next no less raised their admiration. For, after the governor's order was executed, two old men appeared before him, one of them with a large cane in his hand, which he used as a staff. "My lord," said the other, who had none, "some time ago I lent this man ten gold crowns to do him a kindness, which money he was to repay me on demand. I did not ask him for it again in a good while, lest it should prove a greater inconvenience to him to repay me than he laboured under when he borrowed it. However, perceiving that he took no care to pay me, I have asked him for my due; nay, I have been forced to dun him hard for it. But still he did not only refuse to pay me again, but denied he owed me anything, and said, that if I lent him so much money he certainly returned it. Now, because I have no witnesses of the loan, nor he of the pretended payment, I beseech your lordship to put him to his oath, and if he will swear he has paid me, I will freely forgive him before God and the world." "What say you to this, old gentleman with the staff?" asked Sancho. "Sir," answered the old man, "I own he lent me the gold; and since he requires my oath, I beg you will be pleased to hold down your rod of justice, that I may swear upon it how I have honestly and truly returned him his money." Thereupon the governor held down his rod, and in the meantime the defendant gave his cane to the plaintiff to hold, as if it hindered him, while he was to make a cross and swear over the judge's rod: this done, he declared that it was true the other had lent him ten crowns, but that he had really returned him the same sum into his own hands; and that, because he supposed the plaintiff had forgotten it, he was continually asking him for it. The great governor, hearing this, asked the creditor what he had to reply. He made answer, that since his adversary had sworn it he was satisfied; for he believed him to be a better Christian than to offer to forswear himself, and that perhaps he had forgotten he had

211

been repaid. Then the defendant took his cane again, and, having made a low obeisance to the judge, was immediately leaving the court; which, when Sancho perceived, reflecting on the passage of the cane, and admiring the creditor's patience, after he had studied a while with his head leaning over his stomach, and his forefinger on his nose, on a sudden he ordered the old man with the staff to be called back. When he was returned, "Honest man," said Sancho, "let me see that cane a little, I have a use for it." "With all my heart," answered the other; "sir, here it is," and with that he gave it him. Sancho took it, and giving it to the other old man, "There," said he, "go your ways, and Heaven be with you, for now you are paid." "How so, my lord?" cried the old man; "do you judge this cane to be worth ten gold crowns?" "Certainly," said the governor, "or else I am the greatest dunce in the world. And now you shall see whether I have not a headpiece fit to govern a whole kingdom upon a shift." This said, he ordered the cane to be broken in open court, which was no sooner done, than out dropped the ten crowns. All the spectators were amazed, and began to look on their governor as a second Solomon. They asked him how he could conjecture that the ten crowns were in the cane? He told them that having observed how the defendant gave it to the plaintiff to hold while he took his oath, and then swore that he had truly returned him the money into his own hands, after which he took his cane again from the plaintiff —this considered, it came into his head that the money was lodged within the reed; from whence may be learned, that though sometimes those that govern are destitute of sense, yet it often pleases God to direct them in their judgment. Besides, he had heard the curate of his parish tell of such another business, and he had so special a memory, that were it not that he was so unlucky as to forget all he had a mind to remember, there could not have been a better in the whole island. At last the two old men went away, the one to his satisfaction, the other with eternal shame and disgrace: and the beholders were astonished; insomuch, that the person who was commissioned to register Sancho's words and actions, and observe his behaviour, was not able to determine whether he should not give him the character of a wise man, instead of that of a fool, which he had been thought to deserve.

*   *   *   *

The history informs us that Sancho was conducted from the court of justice to a sumptuous palace, where, in a spacious room,

212

he found the cloth laid, and a most neat and magnificent entertainment prepared. As soon as he entered, the wind-music played, and four pages waited on him, in order to the washing his hands, which he did with a great deal of gravity. And now, the instruments ceasing, Sancho sat down at the upper end of the table, for there was no seat but there, and the cloth was only laid for one. A certain personage, who afterwards appeared to be a physician, came and stood at his elbow, with a whalebone wand in his hand. Then they took off a curious white cloth that lay over the dishes on the table, and discovered great variety of fruit and other eatables. One that looked like a student said grace: a page put a laced bib under Sancho's chin, and another, who did the office of sewer, set a dish of fruit before him. But he had hardly put one bit into his mouth, before the physician touched the dish with his wand, and then it was taken away by a page in an instant. Immediately another, with meat, was clapped in the place; but Sancho no sooner offered to taste it, than the doctor, with the wand, conjured it away as fast as the fruit. Sancho was annoyed at this sudden removal, and, looking about him on the company, asked them whether they used to tantalise people at that rate, feeding their eyes, and starving their bellies? "My lord governor," answered the physician, "you are to eat here no otherwise than according to the use and custom of other islands where there are governors. I am a doctor of physic, my lord, and have a salary allowed me in this island for taking charge of the governor's health, and I am more careful of it than of my own, studying night and day his constitution, that I may know what to prescribe when he falls sick. Now, the chief thing I do is to attend him always at his meals, to let him eat what I think convenient for him, and to prevent his eating what I imagine to be prejudicial to his health and offensive to his stomach. Therefore, I now ordered the fruit to be taken away because it was too cold and moist: and the other dish, because it is as much too hot, and over seasoned with spices, which are apt to increase thirst, and he that drinks much destroys and consumes the radical moisture, which is the fuel of life." "So, then," quoth Sancho, "this dish of roasted partridges here can do me no manner of harm." "Hold," said the physician, "the lord governor shall not eat of them while I live to prevent it." "Why so?" cried Sancho. "Because," answered the doctor, "our great master, Hippocrates, the north star and luminary of physic, says in one of his aphorisms, *Omnis saturatio mala, perdricis autem pessima*; that is, 'All repletion is bad, but that of partridges is worst of all!' " "If it be so," said Sancho, "let Mr. Doctor see which of all these dishes on the table will do me the most good, and least harm, and let me eat my bellyful of that, without having it whisked away with his wand. For, by my hopes, and the pleasures of government, as I live, I am ready to die with hunger; and, not to allow me to eat any victuals, (let Mr. Doctor say what he will,) is the way to shorten my life, and not to lengthen it." "Very true, my lord," replied the physician; "however, I am of opinion you ought not to eat of these rabbits, as being a hairy, furry sort of food; nor would I have you taste that veal. Indeed, if it were neither roasted nor par boiled, something might be said; but, as it is, it must not be." "Well, then," said Sancho, "what think you of that huge dish yonder that smokes so? I take it to be an olla podrida, and, that being a hodge-podge of so many sorts of victuals, sure I cannot but light upon something there that will nick me, and be both wholesome and toothsome." "*Absit*," cried the doctor, "far be such an ill thought from us; no diet in the world yields worse nutriment than those wish-washes do. No, leave that luxurious compound to your rich monks and prebendaries, your masters of colleges, and lusty feeders at country weddings; but let them not encumber the tables of governors, where nothing but delicate unmixed viands, in their prime, ought to make their appearance. The reason is, that simple medicines are generally allowed to be better than compounds; for, in a composition, there may happen a mistake by an unequal proportion of the ingredients; but simples are not subject to that accident. Therefore, what I would advise at present, as a fit diet for the governor, for the preservation and support of his health, is a hundred of small wafers, and a few thin slices of marmalade, to strengthen his stomach and help digestion." Sancho, hearing this, leaned back upon his chair, and, looking earnestly in the doctor's face, very seriously asked him what his name was, and where he had studied. "My lord," answered he, "I am called Doctor Pedro Rezio de Augero. The name of the place where I was born is Tirteafuera, and lies between Caraquel and Almodabar del Campo, on the right hand; and I took my degree of Doctor in the University of Ossuna." "Hark you," said Sancho, in a mighty chafe, "Mr. Doctor Pedro Rezio de Augero, born at Tirteafuera, that lies between Caraquel and Almodabar del Campo, on the right hand, and who took your degree of Doctor at the University of Ossuna, and so forth, take yourself away! Avoid the room this moment, or, by the sun's light, I'll get me a good cudgel, and, beginning with your carcase, will so belabour and rib-roast all the physicmongers in the island, that I will not leave therein one of the tribe, of those, I mean, that are ignorant quacks; for, as for learned and wise physicians, I will make much of them, and honour them like so many angels. Once more, Pedro Rezio, I say, get out of my presence. Avaunt! or I will take the chair I sit upon, and comb your head with it to some purpose, and let me be called to an account about it when I give up my office; I do not care, I will clear myself by saying I did the world good service in ridding it of a bad physician, the plague of the commonwealth. Body of me! let me eat, or let them take their government again; for an office that will not afford a man victuals is not worth two horsebeans."

ADALBERT VON CHAMISSO

ADALBERT VON CHAMISSO (German, 1781-1838). French-born, fled the Revolution with his parents and became page to Queen of Prussia at age of nine. Botanist on round-the-world scientific voyage. Author of romantic poems and the tale of Peter Schlemihl, so widely read it has become an international legend.

PETER SCHLEMIHL, THE SHADOWLESS MAN

I. THE GREY MAN

HAVING safely landed after a fatiguing journey, I took my modest belongings to the nearest cheap inn, engaged a garret room, washed, put on my newly-turned black coat, and proceeded to find Mr. Thomas John's mansion. After a severe cross-examination on the part of the hall-porter, I had the honour of being shown into the park where Mr. John was entertaining a party. He graciously took my letter of introduction, continuing the while to talk to his guests. Then he broke the seal, still joining in the conversation, which turned upon wealth. "Anyone," he remarked, "who has not at least a million is, pardon the word, a rogue." "How true," I exclaimed; which pleased him, for he asked me to stay. Then, offering his arm to a fair lady, he led the party to the rose-clad hill. Everybody was very jolly; and I followed behind, so as not to make myself a nuisance.

The beautiful Fanny, who seemed to be the queen of the day, in trying to pick a rose, had scratched her finger, which caused much commotion. She asked for some plaster, and a quiet, lean, tall, elderly man, dressed in grey, who walked by my side, put his hand in his coat pocket, pulled out a pocket-book, and, with a deep bow, handed the lady what she wanted. She took it without thanks, and we all continued to ascend the hill.

Arrived at the top, Mr. John, espying a light spot on the horizon, called for a telescope. Before the servants had time to move, the grey man, bowing modestly, had put his hand in his pocket and pulled out a beautiful telescope, which passed from hand to hand without being returned to its owner. Nobody seemed surprised at the huge instrument issuing from a tiny pocket, and nobody took any more notice of the grey man than of myself.

The ground was damp, and somebody suggested how fine it would be to spread some Turkey carpets. Scarcely had the wish been expressed, when the grey man again put his hand into his pocket, and, with a modest, humble gesture, pulled out a rich Turkey carpet, some twenty yards by ten, which was spread out by the servants without anybody appearing to be surprised. I asked a young gentleman who the obliging man might be. He did not know.

The sun began to get troublesome, and Fanny casually asked the grey man if he might happen to have a tent by him. He bowed deeply, and began to pull out of his pocket canvas, and bars, and ropes, and everything needed for the tent, which was promptly put up. Again nobody seemed surprised. I felt uncanny; especially when, at the next expressed desire, I saw him pull out of his pocket three fine large horses with saddles and trappings! You would not believe it if I did not tell you that I saw it with my own eyes.

It was gruesome. I sneaked away, and had already reached the foot of the hill, when, to my horror, I noticed the grey man approaching. He took off his hat, bowed humbly, and addressed me.

"Forgive my impertinence, sir, but during the short time I have had the happiness to be near you I have been able to look with indescribable admiration upon that beautiful shadow of yours, which you throw from you contemptuously, as it were. Pardon me, but would you feel inclined to sell it?"

I thought he was mad. "Is your own shadow not enough for you? What a strange bargain!"

"No price is too high for this invaluable shadow. I have many a precious thing in my pocket, which you may choose—a mandrake, the dish-cloth of Roland's page, Fortunati's purse——"

"What! Fortunati's purse?"

"Will you condescend to try it?" he said, handing me a money-bag of moderate size, from which I drew ten gold pieces, and another ten, and yet another ten.

I extended my hand, and exclaimed, "A bargain! For this purse you can have my shadow." He seized my hand, knelt down, cleverly detached my shadow from the lawn, rolled it up, folded it, and put it in his pocket. Then he bowed and retired behind the rose-hedge, chuckling gently.

I hurried back to my inn, after having tied the bag around my neck, under my waistcoat. As I went along the sunny street, I heard an old woman's voice, "Heigh, young man, you have lost your shadow!"

"Thank you," I said, threw her a gold piece, and sought the shade of the trees. But I had to cross a broad street again, just as a group of boys were leaving school. They shouted at me, jeered, and threw mud at me. To keep them away I threw a handful of gold among them, and jumped into a carriage. Now I began to feel what I had sacrificed. What was to become of me?

At the inn I sent for my things, and then made the driver take me to the best hotel, where I engaged the state rooms and locked myself up. And what, my dear Chamisso, do you think I did then? I pulled masses of gold out of the bag, covered the floor of the room with ducats, threw myself upon them, made them tinkle, rolled over them, buried my hands in them, until I was exhausted and fell to sleep. Next morning I had to cart all these coins into a cupboard, leaving only just a few handfuls. Then, with the help of the host, I engaged some servants, a certain Bendel, a good, faithful soul, being specially recommended to me as a valet. I spent the whole day with tailors, bootmakers, jewellers, merchants, and bought a heap of precious things, just to get rid of the heaps of gold.

I never ventured out in daytime; and even at night when I happened to step out into the moonlight, I had to suffer untold anguish from the contemptuous sneers of men, the deep pity of women, the shuddering fear of fair maidens. Then I sent Bendel to search for the grey man, giving him every possible indication. He came back late, and told me that none of Mr. John's servants or guests remembered the stranger, and that he could find no trace of him. "By the way," he concluded, "a gentleman whom I met just as I went out, bid me tell you that he was on the point of leaving the country, and that in a year and a day he would call on you to propose new business. He said you would know who he was."

"How did he look?" Bendel described the man in the grey coat! He was in despair when I told him that this was the very person I wanted. But it was too late; he had gone without leaving a trace.

A famous artist for whom I sent to ask him whether he could paint me a shadow, told me that he might, but I should be bound to lose it again at the slightest movement.

"How did you manage to lose yours?" he asked. I had to lie. "When I was travelling in Russia it froze so firmly to the ground that I could not get it off again."

"The best thing you can do is not to walk in the sun," the artist retorted with a piercing look, and walked out.

I confessed my misfortune to Bendel, and the sympathetic lad, after a terrible struggle with his conscience, decided to remain in my service. From that day he was always with me, ever trying to throw his broad shadow over me to conceal my affliction from the world. Nevertheless, the fair Fanny, whom I often met in the hours of dusk and evening, and who had begun to show me marked favour, discovered my terrible secret one night, as the moon suddenly rose from behind a cloud, and fainted with terror.

There was nothing left for me but to leave the town. I sent for horses, took only Bendel and another servant, a rogue named Gauner, with me, and covered thirty miles during the night. Then we continued our journey across the mountains to a little-frequented watering-place, where I was anxious to seek rest from my troubles.

II. A SOUL FOR A SHADOW

Bendel preceded me to prepare a house for my reception, and spent money so lavishly that the rumour spread the King of Prussia was coming incognito. A grand reception was prepared by the townsfolk, with music and flowers and a chorus of maidens in white, led by a girl of wonderful beauty. And all this in broad sunlight! I did not move in my carriage, and Bendel tried to explain that there must be a mistake, which made the good folk believe that I wanted to remain incognito. Bendel handed a diamond tiara to the beautiful maiden, and we drove on amid cheering and firing of guns.

I became known as Count Peter, and when it was found out that the King of Prussia was elsewhere, they all thought I must be some other king. I gave a grand fête, Bendel taking good care to have such lavish illuminations all round that no one should notice the absence of my shadow. I had masses of gold coins thrown among the people in the street, and gave Mina, the beautiful girl who headed the chorus at my arrival, all the jewels I had brought with me, for distribution among her friends. She was the daughter of the verdurer, and I lost no time in making friends with her parents, and succeeded in gaining Mina's affection.

Continuing to spend money with regal lavishness, I myself led a simple and retired life, never leaving my rooms in daylight. Bendel warned me of Gauner's extensive thefts; but I did not mind. Why should I grudge him the money, of which I had an inexhaustible store? In the evenings I used to meet Mina in her garden, and always found her loving, though awed by my wealth and supposed rank. Yet, conscious of my dreadful secret, I dared not ask for her hand. But the year was nearly up since I had made the fateful bargain, and I look forward to the promised visit of the grey man, whom I hoped to persuade to take back his bag for my shadow. In fact, I told the verdurer that on the first of the next month I should ask him for his daughter's hand.

The anniversary arrived—midday, evening, midnight. I waited through the long hours, heard the clock strike twelve; but the grey man did not come! Towards morning I fell into a fitful slumber. I was awakened by angry voices. Gauner forced his way into my room, which was defended by the faithful Bendel.

"What do you want, you rogue?"

"Only to see your shadow, with your lordship's permission."

"How dare you——"

"I am not going to serve a man without a shadow. Either you show it to me, or I go."

I wanted to offer him money; but he, who had stolen millions, refused to accept money from a man without a shadow. He put on his hat, and left the room whistling.

When at dark I went, with a heavy heart, to Mina's bower, I found her, pale and beautiful, and her father with a letter in his hand. He looked at the letter, then scrutinised me, and said, "Do you happen to know, my lord, a certain Peter Schlemihl, who lost his shadow?"

"Oh, my foreboding!" cried Mina. "I knew it; he has no shadow!"

"And you dared," continued the verdurer, "to deceive us? See how she sobs! Confess now how you lost your shadow."

Again I was forced to lie. "Some time ago a man stepped so clumsily into my shadow that he made a big hole. I sent it to be mended, and was promised to have it back yesterday."

"Very well. Either you present yourself within three days with a well-fitting shadow, or, on the next day, my daughter will be another man's wife."

I rushed away, half conscious, groaning and raving. I do not know how long and how far I ran, but I found myself on a sunny heath, when somebody suddenly pulled my sleeve. I turned round. It was the man in the grey coat!

"I announced my visit for to-day. You made a mistake in your impatience. All is well. You buy your shadow back and you will be welcomed by your bride. As for Gauner, who has betrayed you and has asked for Mina's hand—he is ripe for me."

I groped for the bag but the stranger stopped me.

"No, my lord, you keep this; I only want a little souvenir. Be good enough and sign this scrap." On the parchment was written: "I herewith assign to bearer my soul after its natural separation from my body."

I sternly refused. "I am not inclined to stake my soul for my shadow."

He continued to urge, giving the most plausible reasons why I should sign. But I was firm. He even tried to tempt me by unrolling my shadow on the heath. "A line of your pen, and you save your Mina from that rogue's clutches."

At that moment Bendel arrived on the scene, saw me in tears, my shadow on the ground apparently in the stranger's power, and set upon the man with his stick. The grey man walked away, and Bendel followed him, raining blows upon his shoulders, till they disappeared from sight.

I was left with my despair, and spent the day and night on the heath. I was resolved not to return among men, and wandered about for three days, feeding on wild fruit and spring-water. On the morning of the fourth day I suddenly heard a sound, but could see nobody—only a shadow, not unlike my own, but without body. I determined to seize it, and rushed after it. Gradually I gained on it; with a final rush I made for it—and met unexpectedly bodily resistance. We fell on the ground, and a man became visible under me. I understood at once. The man must have had the invisible bird's nest, which he dropped in the struggle, thus becoming visible himself.

The nest being invisible, I looked for its shadow, found it, seized it quickly, and, of course, disappeared from the man's sight. I left him tearing his hair in despair; and I rejoiced at being able to go again among men. Quickly I proceeded to Mina's garden, which was still empty, although I imagined I heard steps following me. I sat down on a bench, and watched the verdurer leaving the house. Then a fog seemed to pass over my head. I looked around, and— oh, horror!—beheld the grey man sitting by my side. He had pulled his magic cap over my head, at his feet was his shadow and my own, and his hand played with the parchment.

"So we are both under the same cap," he began; "now please give me back my bird's nest. Thanks! You see, sometimes we are forced to do what we refuse when asked kindly. I think you had better buy that shadow back. I'll throw in the magic cap."

Meanwhile, Mina's mother had joined the verdurer, and they began to discuss Mina's approaching marriage and Gauner's wealth, which amounted to ten millions. Then Mina joined them. She was urged to consent, and finally said, sobbingly, "I have no further wish on earth. Do with me as you please." At this moment Gauner approached, and Mina fainted.

"Can you endure this?" asked my companion. "Have you no blood in your veins?" He rapidly scratched a slight wound in my hand, and dipped a pen in the blood. "To be sure, red blood! Then sign." And I took the pen and parchment.

I had scarcely touched food for days, and the excitement of this last hour had completely exhausted my strength. Before I had time to sign I swooned away. When I awoke it was dark. My hateful companion was in a towering rage. The sound of festive music came from the brightly illuminated house; groups of people strolled through the garden, talking of Mina's marriage with the wealthy Mr. Gauner, which had taken place this morning.

Disengaging myself from the magic cap, which act made my companion disappear from my view, I made for the garden gate. But the invisible wretch followed me with his taunts. He only left me at the door of my house, with a mocking *"au revoir."* The place had been wrecked by the mob and was deserted. Only the faithful Bendel was there to receive me with tears of mingled grief and joy. I pressed him to my heart, and bid him leave me to my misery. I told him to keep a few boxes filled with gold, that were still in the house, made him saddle my horse, and departed, leaving the choice of the road to the animal, for I had neither aim, nor wish, nor hope.

A pedestrian joined me on the sad journey. After tramping along for a while, he asked permission to put his cloak on my horse. I consented; he thanked me, and then, in a kind of soliloquy, began to praise the power of wealth, and to speak cleverly of metaphysics. Meanwhile, day was dawning; the sun was about to rise, the shadows to spread their splendour—and I was not alone! I looked at my companion—it was the man with the grey coat!

He smiled at my surprise, and continued to converse amiably. In fact, he not only offered to replace for the time being my former servant Bendel, but actually lent me my shadow for the journey. The temptation was great. I suddenly gave my horse the spurs and galloped off at full speed; but, alas! my shadow remained behind and I had to turn back shamefacedly.

"You can't escape me," said my compainion, "I hold you by your shadow." And all the time, hour by hour, day by day, he continued his urging. At last we quarrelled seriously, and he decided to leave me. "If ever you want me, you have only to shake your bag. You hold me by my gold. You know I can be useful, especially to the wealthy; and you have seen it."

I thought of the past and asked him quickly, "Did you get Mr. John's signature?" He smiled. "With so good a friend, the formality was not necessary."

"Where is he? I want to know."

He hesitated, then put his hand into his pocket, and pulled out Mr. John's livid body; the blue lips of the corpse moved, and uttered painfully the words: *"Justo judico Dei judicatus sum; justo judicio Dei condemnatus sum."*

Seized with horror, I threw the inexhaustible moneybag into the abyss, and then spoke the final words. "You fiend, I exorcise you in the name of God! Be off, and never show yourself before mine eyes again!"

He glared at me furiously and disappeared instantly.

III. THE WANDERER

Left now without shadow and without money, save for the few gold pieces still in my pocket, I could almost have been happy, had it not been for the loss of my love. My horse was down below at the inn; I decided to leave it there and to wander on on foot. In the forest I encountered a peasant, from whom I obtained information about the district and its inhabitants. He was an intelligent man, and I quite enjoyed the talk. When we approached the wide bed of a mountain stream, I made him walk in front, but he turned round to speak to me. Suddenly he broke off—"But how is that? You have no shadow!"

Unfortunately!" I said, with a sigh. "During an illness I lost my hair, nails, and shadow. The hair and nails have grown again, but the shadow won't."

"That must have been a bad illness," said the peasant, and walked on in silence till we reached the nearest side-road, when he turned off without saying another word. I wept bitter tears, and my good spirits had vanished. And so I wandered on sadly, avoiding all villages till nightfall, and often waiting for hours to pass a sunny patch unobserved. I wanted to find work in a mine to save me from my thoughts.

My boots began to be worn out. My slender means made me decide to buy a strong pair that had already been used; new ones were too dear. I put them on at once, and walked out of the village, scarcely noticing the way, since I was thinking deeply of the mine I hoped to reach the same night, and of the manner in which I was to obtain employment. I had scarcely walked two hundred steps, when I noticed that I had lost the road. I was in a wild virginal forest. Another few steps and I was on an endless ice-field. The cold was unbearable, and I had to hasten my steps. I ran for a few minutes, and found myself in rice-fields where Chinese labourers were working. There could be no doubt; I had seven-league boots on my feet!

I fell on my knees, shedding tears of gratitude. Now my future was clear. Excluded from society, study and science were to be my future strength and hope. I wandered through the whole world from east to west, from north to south, comparing the fauna and flora of the different regions. To reduce the speed of my progress, I found I had only to pull a pair of slippers over my boots. When I wanted money, I just took an ivory tusk to sell in London. And finally I made a home in the ancient caves of the desert near Thebes.

Once in the far north I encountered a polar bear. Throwing off my slippers, I wanted to step upon an island facing me. I firmly placed my foot on it, but on the other side I fell into the sea, as the slipper had not come off my boot. I saved my life and hurried to

223

the Libyan desert to cure my cold in the sun; but the heat made me ill. I lost consciousness, and when I awoke again I was in a comfortable bed among other beds, and on the wall facing me I saw inscribed in golden letters my own name.

To cut things short—the institution which had received me had been founded by Bendel and the widowed Mina with my money, and in my honour had been called the Schlemihlium. As soon as I felt strong enough, I returned to my desert cave, and thus I live to this day.

You, my dear Chamisso, are to be the keeper of my strange history, which may contain useful advice for many. You, if you will live among men, honour first the shadow, then the money. But, if you live only for your better self, you will need no advice.

FRANCOIS-RENE DE CHATEAUBRIAND

FRANÇOIS-RENÉ DE CHATEAUBRIAND (French, 1768-1848). Father of the Romantic Movement in France. Had active, stormy career, both as writer and statesman. Travels in America reflected in *Atala* and *René*, epic romances of "the noble savage." Other major works: *Genius of Christianity* and *The Martyrs*, pleas for Catholicism, and colorful autobiography, *Mémoires d'Outre-Tombe.*

CHACTAS RELATES THE DEATH OF ATALA

The heroine of "Atala" is the daughter of a white man and a Christianized Indian. By her mother's command she took a vow of virginity, but later fell in love with Chactas, a young Indian. When she was tempted by this passion to break her vow she took poison.

As the last rays of light calm the winds and restore serenity to the sky, so the tender words of the hermit appeased the troubles that agitated the breast of my beloved. Her thoughts now rested only upon my grief, which she endeavored to alleviate; and, to fortify my mind to bear the loss, sometimes she told me that she should die happy, if I would dry up my tears; sometimes she talked of my mother, or my native country; seeking to distract my mind from my present sorrow, by awaking other remembrances, she exhorted me to patience and virtue. "Thou wilt not always be unhappy," said she; "if Heaven sends you this severe trial now, it is only to render you more compassionate to the misfortunes of others. The heart, O Chactas, resembles those trees, which yield a balm to heal the wounds of man only when they are wounded by a knife." When she had thus spoken she turned towards the missionary for that comfort which she had administered unto me; and alternately consoling and consoled, she gave and received the word of life upon the couch of death.

The hermit's zeal seemed to increase; his aged limbs were reanimated by the ardor of his charity. He was constantly preparing drugs, re-kindling the fire, attending the couch, and making pious exhortations on God and the happiness of the just. With the torch of religion in his hand, he showed the way to future regions. The humble cell was filled with the splendor of her Christian death; and the celestial spirits, no doubt, attended the edifying scene, where religion struggled with love, youth, and death.

Divine religion triumphed; and the pious melancholy that succeeded in our hearts, to the transports of passion, was the trophy of her victory. Towards the middle of the night, Atala seemed sufficiently revived to repeat the prayers of the holy priest; rising from the side of her couch a short time after, she extended her hand toward me, and in a trembling voice said, "O son of Outalissi, dost thou remember the first night when thou didst take me for the virgin of the last love! Oh! wonderful omen of our future fate." She then stopped, then resumed, "When I think that I am about to leave thee for ever, my heart makes such efforts to revive, that love seems almost to render me immortal; but God, thy will be done." After a short pause, she added, "It now only remains for me to ask your forgiveness for all the uneasiness that I have caused you. I have made you unhappy by my pride and my caprices. Chactas, a little earth will soon separate us, and deliver you from all my misfortunes." "Forgive you," replied I, bathed in tears; "is it not I who have caused your misfortunes?" "Beloved friend," said she, interrupting me, "you have rendered me very happy, and had I to begin life again, I should prefer the happiness of our short love in exile, to a life of tranquillity in my native country."

Here Atala's voice faltered; the films of death covered her glassy eyes and mouth; her wandering hands seemed to seek the shroud, and she whispered to the invisible spirits; then making an effort, she endeavored, but in vain, to untie the golden crucifix that was suspended around her neck; she begged of me to take it off. and in a low voice said, "When I spoke to thee the first time, near the pile,

225

thou observedst this cross by the light of the fire: it is the only property which Atala possesses. Lopez, thy father and mine, sent it to my mother at my birth. Receive it from me as thine inheritance, preserve it as a memorial of our misfortunes: thou wilt doubtless implore the God of the unfortunate, as thou goest through this life of trouble. O Chactas, I have one last request to make to thee: O my dearest friend, our union on this earth could have been but short, but there is a future state which will be more durable; it is everlasting; and how dreadful to be separated forever. I only precede and wait thy arrival in the celestial regions: if thou lovest me, embrace the Christian religion, which will procure for us an eternal reunion. That divine religion performs a great miracle, since it enables me to quit thee without despair. O Chactas! I only wish to exact one single promise from thee. I know too well the consequence of a rash vow. It might deprive thee of some other woman more happy than myself. O my mother! forgive thy distracted child; O Virgin, take pity on me! I fall again into my former weakness, I avert my thoughts from Thee, O God! when they should all be applied in imploring Thy mercy."

Overwhelmed with grief and sobbing, my heart was ready to burst. I promised Atala that one day I would embrace the Christian religion. At these words, the priest rising as if inspired, extended his arms towards the vault of the cell, and exclaimed, "It is time to call here the presence of the Omnipotent."

As he spoke, methought an invisible hand forced me to prostrate myself at the side of Atala's couch. The priest then opened a secret recess, where a golden urn was concealed, covered by a silk veil; he fell on his knees in devout adoration; the whole cell seemed suddenly illuminated by it. Methought I heard the voices of angels, and the sounds of celestial harps. When the hallowed hermit took the sacred urn from the tabernacle, to me it seemed as if I saw the Great Spirit emerging from the rock.

The priest uncovered the chalice, took a wafer as white as snow between his fingers, and approached Atala, pronouncing mysterious words. She raised her eyes towards Heaven, and was in rapture: all her pains subsided: departing life seemed as if collecting on her faded lips; and her mouth, half opened, received the God concealed under the mystic bread: the holy divine then dipped some cotton in consecrated oil, and anointed her forehead, and after looking a few minutes upon Atala, he suddenly uttered these solemn words: "Depart, Christian soul; go and rejoin thy Creator." Then raising my drooping head, and steadfastly looking at the vase which contained the consecrated oil, I exclaimed, "Will that remedy restore life to Atala?" "Yes, my son," said the pious anchoret, falling in my arms, "to life eternal." Atala had just expired.——

Here Chactas was again obliged to interrupt his narration; his tears fell; sobs stifled his utterance. The blind sachem uncovered his bosom, and taking out Atala's crucifix, "Here," said he, "this is the pledge of love and misery; René, my son, thou canst behold it—but I,—no more; tell me after so many years is not the gold changed; have not my tears left some traces on it? Couldst thou perceive a place where a saint pressed it to her lips? Why is not old Chactas a Christian? What frivolous reasons of policy could make me still adhere to the idolatry of my forefathers? No! I will delay it no longer: the earth cries to me aloud, When wilt thou descend to the grave? and what do you wait for to embrace this divine religion? O earth, thou wilt not wait long. As soon as a priest shall have renovated by the baptismal flood a head grown white with age and sorrow, I hope to be united to Atala."—But to continue our narration.

I cannot now, O René, describe the despair that seized my soul when Atala had breathed her last; such a description would require more warmth than remains to my grief-worn spirits. Yes, the moon that spreads her silvery rays around our heads, and over the vast plains of Kentucky shall cease to shine, and the rivers to flow, before my tears for Atala shall be dried up. For two days I was insensible to the advice of the hermit. In endeavoring to calm my distress, this holy man did not use vain and worldly arguments; he only said, "My son, the will of God be done;" and clasped me in his arms. Had I not felt, I never should have thought there could have been so much comfort in those few words of a resigned Christian. The tenderness, compassion, and unalterable affection, of the pious servant of the Most High, conquered my obstinate grief. Ashamed of the tears he had shed on my account, "O father," said I, "let not the passions of a miserable youth disturb thy aged breast; let me take the sad remains of my beloved; I will bury them in some remote corner of the desert, and if I am condemned to live, I shall endeavor to render myself worthy of those eternal nuptials promised by Atala."

The hermit was delighted with my returning fortitude, and enthusiastically exclaimed, "May the blood of Jesus Christ, our divine master, which was shed in compassion to our miséries, have

227

mercy upon this young man; increase his courage, and restore peace to his troubled mind, and only leave in it a useful and humble recollection of his misfortunes."

The holy priest refused to give up the corpse of the daughter of Lopez, but he offered to assemble the inhabitants of the village and to inter her with all Christian pomp, but I refused, saying, "The misfortunes and virtues of Atala are unknown to the rest of mankind; let a solitary grave be dug by our hands to share their obscurity." We agreed to set out the next day by sunrise to inter Atala, at the foot of the natural bridge, and in the entrance to the groves of death.

Towards night we carried the precious remains of this pious saint to the entrance of the cell on the north side. The hermit had enveloped her in a piece of linen cloth of his mother's spinning —the only thing that he had preserved from Europe, and which he intended for his own shroud. Atala lay stretched on a couch of sensitive plants; her feet, head, and shoulders were uncovered, and her hair was adorned with a flower of a magnolia; it was the sensitive flower which I had placed upon the maiden's head. Her lips, that were like a withered rose, seemed endeavoring to smile: dark blue veins appeared upon her marble cheeks, her beauteous eyelids were closed, her feet were joined, and her alabaster hands pressed an ebony crucifix to her heart; the fatal scapulary was suspended on her bosom; she looked as if enchanted by the spirit of melancholy, and resting in the double sleep of innocence and death. Her appearance was quite celestial, and had any one seen her, and been ignorant that she had possessed animation, he would have supposed her the statue of virginity.

The pious anchoret ceased not to pray during the whole night. I sat in silence at the top of Atala's funeral couch: how often had I supported her sleeping head upon my knees, and how often had I bent over her beauteous form listening to her and inhaling her perfumed breath; but now no soft murmur issued from her motionless bosom, and it was in vain that I waited for my beloved to awake. The moon supplied her pale light to the funeral eve: she rose at midnight, as a fair virgin that weeps over the bier of a departed friend: it covered the whole scene with a deep melancholy, displaying the aged oaks and flowing rivers. From time to time the cenobite plunged a bunch of flowers into consecrated water, and bathed the couch of death with the heavenly dew, repeating in a solemn voice some verses from the ancient poet Job.

"Man cometh forth like a flower, and is cut down; he fleeth also as a shadow, and continueth not.

"Wherefore is light given to him that is in misery? and life unto the bitter in soul?"

Thus did the venerable missionary sing; his grave and tremulous voice was re-echoed in the silent woods, and the name of God and the grave was resounded by the neighboring torrents and mountains: the sad warbling of the Virginia dove, the roaring of the waves, and the bell that called travelers, mixed with these funeral chants, and methought I heard in the groves of death the departed spirits join the hermit's voice in mournful chorus. The eastern horizon was now fringed with gold: sparrow-hawks shrieked on the cliffs, and the squirrels hastened into the crevices of old elms: it was the time appointed for Atala's funeral. I carried the corpse upon my shoulders, the hermit preceding me with a spade in his hand. We descended from one mountain to another: old age and death equally retarded our steps. At the sight of the dog which had discovered us in the forest, and who now leaping with joy followed us another road, I could not refrain from tears. Often did the golden tresses of Atala, fanned by the morning gale obscure my eyes, and often was I obliged to deposit my sacred load upon the grass to recover my strength. At last we arrived at the sad spot: we descended under the bridge. O my dear son, what a melancholy sight to see a young savage and an old hermit kneeling opposite each other busily engaged in digging a grave for an innocent virgin, whose corpse lay stretched in a dried ravine.

When we had finished our dismal task we placed the beauteous virgin in her earthly bed: alas! I had hoped to have prepared another couch for her. Then taking a little dust in my hand, and maintaining the most profound silence I scattered it, and for the last time looked at the remains of my beloved; then I spread the earth on a face of eighteen years. I saw the lovely features and graceful form of my sister gradually disappear behind the curtain of eternity. Her snowy bosom appeared rising under the black clay as a lily that lifts its fair head from the dark mold. "Lopez!" I exclaimed, "behold thy son, burying his sister!" and I entirely covered Atala with the earth of sleep. We returned to the cell, when I informed the priest of the project that I had formed of settling near him. The saint, who was thoroughly acquainted with the heart of man, discovered that my thoughts were the effects of sorrow. He said, "O, Chactas, son of Outalissi, whilst Atala lived, I entreated you to remain here, but now that your destiny is altered, you owe yourself to your native land; believe me, my dear son, grief is not eternal; it will sooner or later forsake the heart of man. Return to Meschacébé [Mississippi], and console your mother, who daily weeps and wants your support.

"Be instructed in the religion of your beloved Atala, and never forget the promise you made her to follow the paths of virtue, and to embrace the Christian religion: I will guard the tomb of your sister. Depart my son; God, the soul of Atala, and the heart of your old friend, will follow you."

Such were the words of the hermit of the rock. His authority was so great, and his wisdom so profound, that it was impossible to disobey him. The next day I quitted my venerable host, who, as he clasped me to his arms, gave me his last counsel and benediction, accompanied with tears. I went to the grave of my Atala, I was surprised to see upon it a little cross, that looked like the top-mast of a wrecked ship seen at a distance. I guessed that the priest had come to pray at the tomb, during the night; this mark of friendship and religion filled my eyes with tears, I felt almost tempted to open the grave, that I might once more behold my beloved Atala; I sat on the earth newly turned, my elbows resting upon my knees, my head supported by my hands; I remained buried in deep and sorrowful meditation. Then for the first time I made the most serious reflections upon the vanity of mankind, and the still greater vanity of human projects.

BANKIM CHANDRA CHATTERJEE

BANKIM CHANDRA CHATTERJEE (Indian, 1838-1894). Leading Bengali novelist and literary pioneer. Historical romances, strongly influenced by Walter Scott: *Ananda Math, Sitārām, Mrinālinī*. His goal was revival of national pride in protest against foreign rule. Also wrote contemporary social novels and *Krishna Charita*, exposition of religious views.

THE BRIDE'S ARRIVAL

No SOONER had Prafulla's boat put in at Bhutnath landing than the news spread through the village that Brajeswar had again brought home a wife; it was whispered she was full-grown, even old. People came running from all directions to see the bride, the young, the old, the blind, the lame, everybody. The cook left her pots and ran; the cutter of fish turned her basket upside down over her fish and ran; the bather came running in wet clothes. The diner went half-hungry. The disputer suddenly agreed with her opponent. The woman spanking her child spared him for once. Off he went in his mother's arms to see the old bride. When the news came a husband was eating. The curry and dhal had been served but not the fish; he had to do without fish that day. An old woman complained to her granddaughter, "How can I go to the pond unless you take me?" At the news of the bride's coming the girl abandoned the old woman and dashed off. The old woman managed somehow to get there too. A young woman, having just been scolded by her mother, was promising not to leave the house again when she heard the news. Her promise was at once forgotten; away she went towards the bride's house. A mother left her baby and ran; the baby toddled after her, crying. A young wife veiled her face and passed shamelessly in front of her seated husband and his elder brother. Running loosened the young women's clothes but they had no time to set them right. Their hair fell down but they did not stop to twist it up again. In their excitement they did not notice what they pulled where. There was an uproar. The goddess of modesty fled in shame.

The bride and bridegroom were standing on a low stool while his mother went through the formalities of reception. People leaned forward to get a look at the bride. She did not relax proprieties and kept her veil three-fourths of a.yard long. No one could see her face. During the ceremony her mother-in-law raised the veil once to look at her. She started a little but said nothing, merely murmuring, "The bride is nice." There were tears in her eyes.

The reception over, her mother-in-law took the bride to her room and then addressed the assembled neighbours: "Mothers! My son's wife has come a long way. She is hungry and thirsty. I am going to give them their food immediately. Our daughter-in-law will stay here in our house. You will see her all the time. Go home now and take your own meals."

Disappointed, the village women went away finding fault. The offence was the mother-in-law's but the bride got most of the blame because no one had seen her face. They all expressed their disgust at an old bride. Again they all opined that such were to be found in Kulin families. Then whoever had seen an old bride in a Kulin home began to tell about it. Govinda Mukerjee had married a woman fifty-five years old. Hari Chatterjee had brought a seventy-year-old maiden wife home. Manu Banerjee married an old woman after she had been brought down to the bank of the Ganges to die. All such tales with embellishments grew familiar on the way. Venting itself in this fashion, the village gradually grew quiet.

GEOFFREY CHAUCER

GEOFFREY CHAUCER (English, *ca.* 1340-1400). The Father of English poetry, whose choice of London dialect determined standard speech. Had full, rich life and sound, practical philosophy. *The Canterbury Tales* shows influence of Boccaccio, Petrarch, and others. Remarkable storyteller, creator of character, humorist. Other works: *Troilus and Criseyde, The Legend of Good Women.*

THE PARDONER'S TALE

THERE dwelt one time in Flanders a company of young folk who followed such folly as riotous living and gaming in stews and taverns, where with harps, lutes and citerns they danced and played at dice both day and night, and ate and drank without restraint. Thus they served the Devil in cursed fashion within those Devil's temples by abominable superfluity.

These rioters, three, of whom I speak, long ere any bell had rung for prime had sat down in a tavern to drink. And as they sat, they heard the tinkle of a bell that was carried before a corpse to his grave. One of them called to his boy. 'Be off with you, and ask straightway what corpse is passing by; and mind you report his name aright.'

'Sir,' quoth the boy, 'that needs not be. It was told me two hours before you came here; he was an old fellow of yours, by God, and he was suddenly slain tonight, as he sat very drunk on his bench. There came a privy thief men call death, that slays all people in this countryside, and with his spear he smote his heart in two, and went his way without a word. A thousand he has slain in this pestilence; and master, ere you come into his presence, methinks it were best to be warned of such an adversary. Be ready to meet him ever; thus my mother taught me, I say no more.'

'By St. Mary,' said the taverner, 'the child speaks truth, for over a mile hence, in a large village, he has slain both woman, child, servant and knave. I trow his habitation be there. It were great wisdom to be advised ere he do injure a man.'

'Yea, God's arms!' quoth this rioter, 'is it such peril to meet with him? I will seek him in the highways and byways, I vow by God's bones. Hearken, fellows, we three be like; let each hold up his hand to the other and become the other's brother, and we will slay this false traitor, Death. He that slays so many shall be slain ere night, by God's Dignity!'

Together these three plighted their troth each to live and die for the rest as though he were their sworn brother, and up they then started in this drunken rage, and forth they went toward that village of which the taverner had spoken; and many a grisly oath they swore, and rent Christ's blessed body. —'Death shall be dead if they can but catch him.'

When they had gone not quite a mile just as they were about to go over a stile, an old man and poor met them and greeted them full meekly, and said, 'Lordings, God be with you!'

The proudest of the three rioters answered, 'What, churl, bad luck to you! Why are you all wrapped up save your face? Why live you so long to so great an age?'

This old man began to peer into his visage, and said, 'Because I cannot find a man, though I walked to India, neither in hamlet nor in city, who will change his youth for mine age. And therefore must I keep mine old age as long as it is God's will. Death, alas will not have me! Thus I walk like a restless caitiff, and early and late I knock with my staff upon the ground which is my mother's gate, and say, "Beloved Mother, let me in. Lo, how I wane away, flesh and blood and skin! Alas when shall my bones be at rest? Mother, with you I would exchange my chest, that has been long time in my chamber, yea for an hair-cloth to wrap me in!" But yet she will not do me that favour; wherefore my face is full pale and withered.—But sirs, it is not courteous to speak churlishly to an old man, unless he trespass in word or deed. You may yourselves read in Holy Writ, "Before an old hoary-head man ye shall arise;" wherefore I counsel you, do no harm now to an old man, no more than you would that men did to you in your old age if it be that

233

you abide so long. And God be with you, wherever you go or be; I must go whither I have to go.'

'Nay old churl, you shall not go, by God,' said the second gamester straightway. 'You part not so lightly by St. John! You spoke right now of that traitor Death who slays all our friends in this country side. By my troth, you are his spy! Tell where he is, or by God and the Holy Sacrament you shall die. Truly you are of his consent to slay us young folk, false thief!'

'Now, sirs,' quoth he, 'If you be so lief to find Death, turn up this crooked way; for by my faith I left him in that grove under a tree, and there he will abide, nor for all your boasting will he hide him. See you that oak? Right here you shall find him. May God, Who redeemed mankind, save you and amend you!' Thus said this old man.

And each of these rioters ran till he came to the tree, and there they found florins coined of fine round gold well nigh seven bushels, as they thought. No longer sought they then after Death, but each was so glad at the sight that they sat them down by the precious hoard. The worst of them spoke the first word. 'Brethren,' he said, 'heed what I say; my wit is great, though I jest oft and play. This treasure has been given us by Fortune that we may live our lives in mirth and jollity, and lightly as it comes, so we will spend it. Eh! God's precious dignity! Who would have weened today that we should have so fair a grace! But could this gold be carried to my house or else to yours,—for you know well all this gold is ours,—then were we in high felicity! But truly by day it may not be done. Men would say we were sturdy thieves and hang us for our treasure. This treasure must be carried by night, as wisely and as slyly as may be. Wherefore I advise that we draw cuts amongst us all, and he that draws the shortest shall run with a blithe heart to the town and that full swift and privily bring us bread and wine. And two of us shall cunningly guard this treasure, and at night, if he will not tarry, we will carry it where we all agree is safest.'

One of them brought the cuts in his fist and bade them draw and look where the lot should fall. It fell to the youngest of them and he went forth toward the town at once. So soon as he was gone one said to the other, 'You well know you are my sworn brother, and you will profit by what I tell you. Here is gold and plenty of it, to be divided amongst us three. You know well our fellow is gone. If I can shape it so that it be divided betwixt us two, had I not done you a friendly turn?'

The other answered, 'I wot not how that may be. He knows well the gold is with us two. What shall we do? What shall we say?'

'Shall it be a secret?' said the first wicked fellow. 'I shall tell you in a few words what we shall do to bring it about.'

'I agree,' quoth the other, 'not to betray you, by my troth.'

'Now,' quoth the first, 'you know well we be two and that two should be stronger than one. Look when he is set down; do you arise as though you would play with him, and I will rive him through the two sides while you struggle with him as in sport; and look that you do the same with your dagger. And then shall all this gold be shared, dear friend, betwixt you and me. Then may we both fulfil all our lusts, and play at dice at our will.' And thus, as you heard me say, were these two villains accorded to slay the third.

The youngest, who went to town, revolved full often in his heart the beauty of those bright new florins. 'Oh Lord,' quoth he, 'if so be I could have all this gold to myself, no man living under God's throne should live so merry as I!' And at last the fiend, our enemy, put it into his thought to buy poison with which he might slay his two fellows; for the fiend found him in such a way of life that he had leave to bring him to sorrow, for this was his full intention namely to slay them both and never to repent. And forth he went without tarrying into the town to an apothecary, and prayed him to sell him some poison that he might kill his rats; and there was also a pole-cat in his yard, which he said, had killed his capons and he would fain wreak him upon the vermin that destroyed him by night. The apothecary answered, 'And you shall have such a thing, that, so may God save my soul, no creature in all this world can eat or drink of this composition the amount of a grain of wheat, but he shall at once forfeit his life. Yea, die he shall, and that in less time than you can walk a mile, this poison is so strong and violent.'

This cursed man clutched the box of poison in his hand and then ran into the next street to a man and borrowed of him three large bottles. Into two of them he poured his poison, but the third he kept clean for his drink, for all night long he planned to labour in carrying away his gold. And when this rioter, the Devil take him! had filled his three great bottles with wine, he repaired again to his fellows.

What need to speak about it more? for just as they had planned his death, even so they slew him, and that anon. And when this was done, one spake thus, 'Now let us sit and drink and make merry, and then we will bury his body.' And then by chance, he took one of the bottles where the poison was, and he drank and gave his fellow to drink also. Wherefore anon they both died. And certes, Avicenna wrote never in any canon or any chapter more wondrous sufferings of empoisoning than these two wretches showed ere they died. Thus ended these two murderers as well as the poisoner.

ANTON CHEKHOV

ANTON CHEKHOV (Russian, 1860-1904). Great master of Russian short story, whose style heavily influenced modern writing. Meticulously wrought tales, concerned with introspective, inarticulate emotions rather than with outward events. Grandson of a serf, became the artist of twilight Czarist Russia. His great plays, *The Cherry Orchard, The Sea Gull, Three Sisters, Uncle Vanya*, left indelible mark on modern theater, but never successfully imitated.

THE SLANDERER

SERGEY KAPITONICH AKHINEYEV, the teacher of calligraphy, gave his daughter Natalya in marriage to the teacher of history and geography, Ivan Petrovich Loshadinikh. The wedding feast went on swimmingly. They sang, played, and danced in the parlor. Waiters, hired for the occasion from the club, bustled about hither and thither like madmen, in black frock coats and soiled white neckties. A loud noise of voices smote the air. From the outside people looked in at the windows—their social standing gave them no right to enter.

Just at midnight the host, Akhineyev, made his way to the kitchen to see whether everything was ready for the supper. The kitchen was filled with smoke from the floor to the ceiling; the smoke reeked with the odors of geese, ducks, and many other things. Victuals and beverages were scattered about on two tables in artistic disorder. Marfa, the cook, a stout, red-faced woman, was busying herself near the loaded tables.

"Show me the sturgeon, dear," said Akhineyev, rubbing his hands and licking his lips. "What a fine odor! I could just devour the whole kitchen! Well, let me see the sturgeon!"

Marfa walked up to one of the benches and carefully lifted a greasy newspaper. Beneath that paper, in a huge dish, lay a big fat sturgeon, amid capers, olives, and carrots. Akhineyev glanced at the sturgeon and heaved a sigh of relief. His face became radiant, his eyes rolled. He bent down, and, smacking his lips, gave vent to a sound like a creaking wheel. He stood a while, then snapped his fingers for pleasure, and smacked his lips once more.

"Bah! The sound of a hearty kiss. Whom have you been kissing there, Marfusha?" some one's voice was heard from the adjoining room, and soon the closely cropped head of Vankin, the assistant school instructor, appeared in the doorway. "Whom have you been kissing here? A-a-ah! Very good! Sergey Kapitonich! A fine old man indeed! With the female sex tête-à-tête!"

"I wasn't kissing at all," said Akhineyev, confused; "who told you, you fool? I only—smacked my lips on account of—in consideration of my pleasure—at the sight of the fish."

"Tell that to some one else, not to me!" exclaimed Vankin, whose face expanded into a broad smile as he disappeared behind the door. Akhineyev blushed.

"The devil knows what may be the outcome of this!" he thought. "He'll go about tale-bearing now, the rascal. He'll disgrace me before the whole town, the brute!"

Akhineyev entered the parlor timidly and cast furtive glances to see what Vankin was doing. Vankin stood near the piano and, deftly bending down, whispered something to the inspector's sister-in-law, who was laughing.

"That's about me!" thought Akhineyev. "About me, the devil take him! She believes him, she's laughing. My God! No, that mustn't be left like that. No. I'll have to fix it so that no one shall believe him. I'll speak to all of them, and he'll remain a foolish gossip in the end."

Akhineyev scratched his head, and, still confused, walked up to Padekoi.

"I was in the kitchen a little while ago, arranging things there for the supper," he said to the Frenchman. "You like fish, I know, and I have a sturgeon just so big. About two yards. Ha, ha, ha! Yes, by the way, I have almost forgotten. There was a real anecdote about that sturgeon in the kitchen. I entered the kitchen a little while ago and wanted to examine the food. I glanced at the sturgeon and for pleasure, I smacked my lips—it was so piquant! And just at that moment the fool Vankin entered and says—ha, ha, ha—and says: 'A-a! A-a-ah! You have been kissing here?'—with Marfa;

just think of it—with the cook! What a piece of invention, that blockhead. The woman is ugly, she looks like a monkey, and he says we were kissing. What a queer fellow!"

"Who's a queer fellow?" asked Tarantulov, as he approached them.

"I refer to Vankin. I went out into the kitchen—"

The story of Marfa and the sturgeon was repeated.

"That makes me laugh. What a queer fellow he is. In my opinion it is more pleasant to kiss the dog than to kiss Marfa," added Akhineyev, and, turning around, he noticed Mzda.

"We have been speaking about Vankin," he said to him. "What a queer fellow. He entered the kitchen and noticed me standing beside Marfa, and immediately he began to invent different stories. 'What?' he says, 'you have been kissing each other!' He was drunk, so he must have been dreaming. 'And I,' I said, 'I would rather kiss a duck than kiss Marfa. And I have a wife,' said I, 'you fool.' He made me appear ridiculous."

"Who made you appear ridiculous?" inquired the teacher of religion, addressing Akhineyev.

"Vankin. I was standing in the kitchen, you know, and looking at the sturgeon—" And so forth. In about half an hour all the guests knew the story about Vankin and the sturgeon.

"Now let him tell," thought Akhineyev, rubbing his hands. "Let him do it. He'll start to tell them, and they'll cut him short: 'Don't talk nonsense, you fool! We know all about it.' "

And Akhineyev felt so much appeased that, for joy, he drank four glasses of brandy over and above his fill. Having escorted his daughter to her room, he went to his own and soon slept the sleep of an innocent child, and on the following day he no longer remembered the story of the sturgeon. But, alas! Man proposes and God disposes. The evil tongue does its wicked work, and even Akhineyev's cunning did not do him any good. One week later, on a Wednesday, after the third lesson, when Akhineyev stood in the teachers' room and discussed the vicious inclinations of the pupil Visyekin, the director approached him, and, beckoning to him, called him aside.

"See here, Sergey Kapitonich," said the director. "Pardon me. It isn't my affair, yet I must make it clear to you, nevertheless. It is my duty— You see, rumors are on foot that you are on intimate terms with that woman—with your cook— It isn't my affair, but— You may be on intimate terms with her, you may kiss her— You may do whatever you like, but, please, don't do it so openly! I beg of you. Don't forget that you are a pedagogue."

Akhineyev stood as though frozen and petrified. Like one stung by a swarm of bees and scalded with boiling water, he went home. On his way it seemed to him as though the whole town stared at him as at one besmeared with tar— At home new troubles awaited him.

"Why don't you eat anything?" asked his wife at their dinner. "What are you thinking about? Are you thinking about Cupid, eh? You are longing for Marfushka. I know everything already, you Mahomet. Kind people have opened my eyes, you barbarian!"

And she slapped him on the cheek.

He rose from the table, and staggering, without cap or coat, directed his footsteps toward Vankin. The latter was at home.

"You rascal!" he said to Vankin. "Why have you covered me with mud before the whole world? Why have you slandered me?"

"How; what slander? What are you inventing?"

"And who told everybody that I was kissing Marfa? Not you, perhaps? Not you, you murderer?"

Vankin began to blink his eyes, and all the fibres of his face began to quiver. He lifted his eyes toward the image and ejaculated:

"May God punish me, may I lose my eyesight and die, if I said even a single word about you to any one! May I have neither house nor home!"

Vankin's sincerity admitted of no doubt. It was evident that it was not he who had gossiped.

"But who was it? Who?" Akhineyev asked himself, going over in his mind all his acquaintances, and striking his chest. "Who was it?"

CHIKAMATSU MONZAEMON

CHIKAMATSU MONZAEMON (Japanese, 1653-1725). The Shakespeare of Japan. Wrote for Kabuki theater, also for puppet theater. Author of numerous plays, mostly historical or domestic dramas. Due to conventions of puppet theater, and allusiveness of writing, plays extremely difficult to translate. Most popular: *Battles of Kokusenya, The Double Suicide of Sonezaki.*

ADVENTURES OF THE HAKATA DAMSEL

Four days after leaving the capital Soshichi and Kojoro found themselves at Seki, a post-town in the province of Isé. There the

239

foot-worn travellers halted before a stone image of Jizo, a guardian god of children. Fervently were they praying to the deity that he might soften Sozaémon toward them when palanquin bearers accosted them.

"Cannot we serve you, sir?"

"That may be. We are going to the province of Owari. How much will you charge to carry us to the next stage?"

"It is five miles to Ishivakushi, the next stage, so we ask you for *korori*."

Soshichi was startled.

"I don't know how much *korori* is."

"A hundred *mon*, sir."

"Too much. Come down to seventy."

"Very good, sir."

With the care-worn fugitives within their palanquins the bearers presently began a rapid march, keeping in time in their steps to the cries: *"Sokosei!"—"Katasei!"—"Makkasei!"* Mile succeeded mile, until Oiwaki was reached, where it was customary to change palanquins and bearers. The carriers therefore stopped. Kojoro stepped out promptly, but Soshichi would not get down, so great was his fear lest the bearers' sign *"korori"* should prove a bad omen. His mind might be said to be fettered with apprehension ere his body was tied to the detective's cord.

"Well, Kojoro," said Soshichi, "you had better change palanquins and go ahead of me."

"I will."

"And wait for me at a place called Yokkaichi."

"I will, my husband."

Kojoro, all unaware of Soshichi's fears, changed palanquins and let herself be carried ahead. A few minutes later a palanquin arrived from the next stage. The newcomers addressed Soshichi's bearers.

"Isn't your passenger the companion of the young woman who's just gone on? Let us exchange passengers."

"That'll suit us nicely. Now, sir, we're going to do an exchange. Please descend."

The bearers lifted the blind of the palanquin for Soshichi. The passenger of the other palanquin had already stepped out. He was lightly dressed in drawers and leggings, carried a packet in his hand and a *hayanawa* in his belt. Soshochi but glimpsed at him

240

and shuddered. He turned his face away and covered his head with a *tenugui*. Hurriedly he descended and with a brief "Thank you, bearers", stepped into the other palanquin and quickly pulled down the blind.

"I'm in a hurry," he said in a tremulous voice. "I'll give you extra; start quickly."

He had hardly uttered these words when a shrill voice cried, "We arrest Komachiya Soshichi!"

The next moment a strong hempen cord had been wound round his palanquin. The terror-stricken captive struggled in the palanquin but to no purpose; and he could but cry like a caged bird. Armed detectives, lying in ambush, emerged and surrounded him.

"Prisoner, you know what charge we arrest you on. The official information asserts that there are eight in your gang. We have come to arrest you. Do you permit yourself to be arrested, or shall we have to bind you by force?"

To this the prisoner made no reply, but was heard to address a plaintive prayer to Amida Buddha.

"No," said the first detective, "let us take him as he is to the next stage and bind him when we get there. That's more convenient. Now, bearers, move off."

"Certainly, sir, but inasmuch as he can't escape death, why don't you bind him here?"

So murmuring, the bearers approached the palanquin and lifted it, when, to their amazement, blood dribbled down *gaba-gaba* from it, instantaneously forming a scarlet patch upon the ground. The occupant uttered a groan of pain. The affrighted coolies cried, "The prisoner has killed himself in the palanquin! Come and look!"

The palanquin was hastily set to earth. The bearers drew apart. The detectives unwound the cord from the palanquin and raised its blind. Soshichi, with fixed eyes, was gasping after a mortal fashion. The long blade plunged in his right side was buried to the hilt. Its point protruded from his left. The detectives were speechless with terror and dismay.

Kojoro, bound, was brought back. Seeing her husband's plight she was struck with unspeakable grief. She trod the tide of blood. She thrust her face into the palanquin.

"I am here, Soshichi San. Kojoro is here, Soshichi. I was bound a few minutes ago. Till last night we slept together. We had a vow to die in the same hour. And now, despite our vows, you have

241

died alone, leaving me behind to suffer by myself. That is selfish of you. But never mind that now. You must be in pain; I see you are in great pain."

With these words she wept and, sinking down, placed her face in the dying man's lap. Intelligence returned to the eyes of Soshichi.

"Ah, Kojoro," he gasped, "are you bound? I am a wicked man who has broken the national laws and disobeyed my father. I have so narrowed the compass of the wide world that my own home could no longer be a home to me and have wandered to this place till at last I am caught in a heavenly net—quite naturally and justly. Were I brought to my home and there executed I should bring disgrace on all my relatives and prove doubly undutiful to my father. With this thought in my mind I have done the deed you see. This is just retribution I now receive for having joined Kezori Kuémon's gang of smugglers and having lived above my station. And since in the eye of the law a wife cannot escape connection with her husband's crime, you are bound, undergo dishonour and are made to suffer—all of which is caused by my own wicked nature. But for Soshichi you would not have suffered thus. Poor girl? How great must be your grief! You have to sacrifice your life on account of the man with whom you have lived for but a short space of time. Pray forgive me, Kojoro."

Soshichi breathed with difficulty. Death second by second drew nearer. The stern detectives, taking pity upon the sorrowful pair, spoke gently. "When you reach prison you will not be suffered to see each other. Man must help man. Take your fill of speech now."

The more Kojoro listened to Soshichi's kind words the more sorrowful she grew.

"Soshichi San, my dear, you are not to blame. For whose sake is it you have done what you have done? Out of eagerness to prevent Kojoro passing into another's hands you joined Kuémon and forsook even your father. At the risk of your life you became my husband, so dearly have you loved me. So overcome am I at your goodness to me that I cannot find even in Chinese or Hindoo, still less in Japanese, fit words to express my gratitude. Were my hands but unbound I would prostrate myself before you ere I die."

Anguish took her. She wept so bitterly that she seemed almost to lose consciousness.

"Now," gasped Soshichi, "now comes the last moment we behold each other in this life. In the next world, remember, we shall be husband and wife. Namu Amida Buddha."

The voice that prayed was faint. Then he drew the sword from his side and almost in the same moment ceased to breathe. Piteous was Kojoro's cry. "Husband, stay for me a moment! I would accompany you! Sooner or later I shall be slain. Officers, have mercy! Slay me here—slay me, I entreat you!"

She wailed and rushed hither and thither in the frenzy of madness. At this moment a police superintendent and his underlings arrived, convoying Kezori Kuémon, his followers and their respective courtesans. All were bound. All had been captured in one place or another. The leader of the party unrolled a scroll and read as follows:

"Prisoners, I read you an Imperial mandate. Listen to it with gratitude. Forasmuch as you have committed the crime of smuggling in connection with great ships in the offing in defiance of the national laws, you richly deserve capital punishment. But in honour of his coronation, His Majesty the Emperor is graciously pleased to pardon you and to release you from such a penalty."

The gratitude of the prisoners knew no bounds. They cried out for joy. The police superintendent addressed the courtesans.

"Forasmuch as your profession compelled you to become the companions of these men you are guilty of no crime. Henceforward you can go whither you choose. Now, men, set these women free."

The constables released the women. The courtesans caressed the abrasions the cords had caused.

"The power of His Majesty the Emperor," they exclaimed, "is great indeed! Our hands are freed from the cords. We feel like birds escaped from their cages."

But Kojoro, albeit set at freedom like her companions, continued to weep. At length she lifted her head.

"Sorrow it is that my husband Soshichi has forsaken me and his soul winged its way to the other world or ever the compassion of this edict could be made known to him. This life is not now worth while the living for this 'Kojoro of Hakata', who is just like a bird which has lost its mate by death. Officers, have mercy! Slay me!"

The bitter tears fell.

"Your grief is natural," said the sympathetic superintendent. "Though your husband was one of a gang of ruffians, he joined them out of youthful folly and infatuation. It follows therefore that his offence was small. We regret that his impetuosity should have led to his suicide. We grieve on your behalf, but nothing is to be done. Your best course will be to serve your father-in-law in

243

Soshichi's place and busy yourself in prayers for the peace of the departed soul. Now, my men, treat the prisoners as the Imperial edict commands."

Of the smugglers who had escaped death, some were branded or tattooed upon the face, others had their ears or noses cut off that they might not repeat their offences. Then they were set free.

The rumour of the adventures of the hapless Hakata damsel did not take long to spread far and wide. It remained a topic of conversation for generations afterwards.

CH'U YUAN

CH'U YUAN (Chinese, *ca.* 343-277 B.C.). Greatest poet of ancient China. According to legend, a loyal minister who drowned self when he lost emperor's favor. Poems, though personal, are still close to ritual song. The *Li Sao* one of most famous long poems in Chinese.

STRAY THOUGHTS

My Heart with Grief is heavy,
   I sigh with Head down hung.
My Thoughts are like a tangled Skein,
   And yet the Night is young.

In Autumn all Things wither,
   The World is full of Hate,
My Prince is easily enraged,
   And my Affliction great.

The People's Suff'rings move my Heart,
   Our Land I cannot leave.
Here for my Loved One my stray Thoughts
   Into a Song I weave.
Oh, once you gave your Promise,
   At Dusk we two should meet;
But then you went back on your Word,
   For such was your Deceit.

You praise another's Beauty,
  Admire another's Grace,
Forswear your former Pledge to me,
  And turn an angry Face.
I longed for Reconcilement,
  But kept by Fear apart,
I dare no more draw near to you,
  So Grief besets my Heart.

I put my Thought in Verses
  My Prince disdains to hear,
I know true Worth no Favour wins,
  And Enemies will sneer.

All that I said was truthful,
  How could the Prince forget?
By honest Counsel I would make
  Him more illustrious yet.

I take a Sage as Model,
  And in his Steps would tread.
I strive for Excellence so that
  My Prince's Fame may spread.

Virtue is not outside us,
  Fame springs from noble Deeds,
All Reputations must be won,
  As Fruit must grow from Seeds.

Interlude
So I plead before my Love,
But his Heart I cannot move.
He approves another's Grace.
In his Heart I have no Place.

Chorus
A Bird flies from the South once more
To the great Stream's northern Shore.
In fair Splendour see him stand,
All alone in a far-off Land;

None to befriend him beneath the Sun,
For Mediators here are none.
Departed Long and in Disgrace,
I have no Way to plead my Case.
Beside the Northern Hill I sigh,
My Tears drop where the Stream flows by,
The short Midsummer Nights are here,
Yet each seems long as one whole Year.
The Capital is far away,
But there each Night in Thought I stray.
By narrow winding Track or wide,
Southward, with Moon and Stars my Guide,
Forward I press, but all in Vain:
My Soul is weary of such Pain!
Yet still my Nature is too Proud
To change or flatter like the Crowd!
For me no one will mediate,
None knows or cares for my sad Fate.

Refrain

Long the Bay and strong the Tide,
  As up the Stream I go.
I make my Journey southward still,
  In Hope to ease my Woe.
The Journey here is hard when Cliffs
  Reach steeply to the Sky,
And hard it is to climb or cross
  The Mountain Paths so high.
Brought to a Halt I hesitate,
  And rest here for the Night.
My Mind is clouded, and there seems
  To be no End in Sight.
My Thoughts have travelled far afield,
  In Grief I heave a Sigh,
This Place is strange and desolate,
  No Go-between have I!
My Thoughts in Verses I have set,
  Some Ease of Mind to seek;
But still my Grief is unassuaged,
  For who will hear me speak?

THOUGHTS BEFORE DROWNING

In balmy early Summer Days,
  When Trees and Grasses teem,
With lonely and dejected Heart
  I reach the southern Stream.

Now all around appears forlorn,
  So silent and so still,
While sad and melancholy Thoughts
  Upon me cast a Chill.

Once more I recollect the Past,
  And Wrongs of former Days.
Let Others stoop some Gain to win,
  But I'll not change my Ways.

Such Men as change for selfish Gain
  I always have despised;
But hold the Principles of Old,
  The former Rules have prized.

With Sternness and Benevolence
  An upright Man is filled.
If Craftsmen will not ply the Axe,
  Men doubt that they are skilled.

You see a Picture in the Night,
  And black the Colours find.
If skillful Craftsmen squint to see,
  You need not think them blind.

Now Darkness is construed as Light,
  And Fair to Foul is turned,
Now Hens and Geese can fly on high,
  While Phoenixes are spurned.

Now Good and Bad are thought the same,
  And Jade confused with Stone.
To Men made blind by Prejudice,
  My Virtues are unknown.

I feel my Task too hard for me;
    Despairing of Success,
I do not know to whom to show
    The Jewels I possess.

The country Dogs bark savagely
    At One they do not know.
And Fools suspect all Men of Worth,
    And slavish Envy show.

They will not see my Dignity,
    My Learning or my Grace,
And all my subtle Scholarship
    Endeavour to abase.

I double my Benevolence,
    To Honesty I hold;
But who can understand my Worth,
    Since dead the Sage of Old?

How is it that for such long Years
    The Good remain apart?
The ancient Kings are too long gone
    To hold them in our Heart.

I curb my Indignation now,
    My Anger I repress;
I shall not change or hesitate
    In Danger or Distress.

I journey on and take no Rest
    Till darkly sinks the Sun.
But now I ease my heavy Heart—
    My Race will soon be done.

Refrain
On and on the Rivers slow
Down their several Courses flow.
Dark the Way and overgrown,
And the Future all unknown.

All my Time in Anguish spent,
No End set to my Lament,
By the World misunderstood,
With no Friend or Kinsman good.

Though my Conscience is quite clear,
I can find no Witness here.
Gone the Charioteer so prized,
The swift Horses are despised.

Sad or happy, each Man's Fate
Overtakes him soon or late.
If I keep a steadfast Heart,
Fear in me can have no Part.

Death, I know, must come to All,
Nor for Mercy would I call.
Saints, I follow in your Wake!
Your Example shall I take!

CONFUCIUS

CONFUCIUS (Chinese, *ca.* 551-479 B.C.). Great poet and philosopher, source
of Chinese wisdom for twenty centuries. His *Shih Ching (Book of Odes)*
laid foundation of Chinese literature. Authorship of other extensive collections
is disputed, probably legendary. His work glorifies the moral virtues: loyalty,
brotherhood, truth, justice, tolerance, etc.

A CHALLENGE

If, boy, thy thoughts of me were kind,
    I'd lift my skirts and wade the Tsin;
But if thou be of other mind,
    Is there none else my love would win?
        O craziest of crazy boys!

Ay, if thy thoughts of me were kind,
    I'd lift my skirts and wade the Wei;
But if thy thoughts are else inclined,
    Is there none other gallant nigh?
        O craziest of crazy boys!

THE ABSENT HUSBAND

I picked and picked the mouse ears,
  Nor gained one basket load;
My heart was with my husband:
  I flung them on the road.

I climbed yon rugged mountain,
  My ponies all broke down;
I filled my golden goblet
  Long anxious thought to drown.

l climbed yon lofty ridges,
  With my ponies black and bay;
I filled for me my horn cup
  Long torture to allay.

I climbed yon craggy uplands,
  My steeds grew weak and ill;
My footmen were exhausted;—
  And here I sorrow still!

LAMENT OF A DISCARDED WIFE

When east winds blow unceasingly,
  They bring but gloominess and rain.
Strive, strive to live unitedly,
  And every angry thought restrain.
Some plants we gather for their leaves,
  But leave the roots untouched beneath;
So, while unsullied was my name,
  I should have lived with you till death.

With slow, slow step I took the road,
  My inmost heart rebelling sore,
You came not far with me, indeed,
  You only saw me to the door.
Who calls the lettuce bitter fare,
  The cress is not a whit more sweet.
Ay, feast there with your new-found bride,
  Well pleased, as when fond brothers meet.

250

The Wei, made turbid by the king,
  Grows limpid by the islets there.
There, feasting with your new-found bride
  For me no longer now you care.
Yet leave to me my fishing dam;
  My wicker nets, remove them not.
My person spurned—some vacant hour
  May bring compassion for my lot.

Where ran the river full and deep,
  With raft or boat I paddled o'er;
And where it flowed in shallower stream,
  I dived or swam from shore to shore.
And what we had, or what we lost,
  For that I strained my every nerve;
When other folks had loss, I'd crawl
  Upon my knees, if aught 'twould serve.

And you can show me no kind care,
  Nay, treated like a foe am I!
My virtue stood but in your way,
  Like traders' goods that none will buy.
Once it was feared we could not live;
  In your reverses then I shared:
And now, when fortune smiles on you,
  To very poison I'm compared.

I have laid by a goodly store,—
  For winter's use it was to be;—
Feast on there with your new-found bride,—
  I was for use in poverty!
Rude fits of anger you have shown,
  Now left me to be sorely tried.
Ah, you forget those days gone by,
  When you came nestling to my side!

COMRADES IN WAR TIME

How say we have no clothes?
  One plaid for both will do.
Let but the king, in raising men,
  Our spears and pikes renew,—
  We'll fight as one, we two!

How say we have no clothes?
   One skirt our limbs shall hide.
Let but the king, in raising men,
   Halberd and lance provide,—
   We'll do it, side by side!

How say we have no clothes?
   My kirtle thou shalt wear.
Let but the king, in raising men,
   Armor and arms prepare,
   The toils of war we'll share.

TRUST THY LAST FRIEND AGAINST THE WORLD

   A babbling current fails
To float a load of thorns away,—
Of brothers, few are left us now,
Yet we remain, myself and thou:
   Believe not others' tales,
Others will lead thee far astray.

   The babbling current fails
To float the firewood fagots far.—
Of brothers there are left but few,
Yet I and thou remain, we two:
   Believe not others' tales,
For verily untrue they are!

JOSEPH CONRAD

JOSEPH CONRAD (English, 1857-1924). Polish-born novelist, who went early to sea on English ships. Retiring from navy, became British subject, taught self to write English, and became greatest writer of sea stories in the language. Most-praised novel: *Lord Jim.* Others: *Nostromo, Victory, Youth, The Secret Agent, The Nigger of the Narcissus.*

THE LAGOON

THE white man, leaning with both arms over the roof of the little house in the stern of the boat, said to the steersman—
   "We will pass the night in Arsat's clearing. It is late."

The Malay only grunted, and went on looking fixedly at the river. The white man rested his chin on his crossed arms and gazed at the wake of the boat. At the end of the straight avenue of forests cut by the intense glitter of the river, the sun appeared unclouded and dazzling, poised low over the water that shone smoothly like a band of metal. The forests, somber and dull, stood motionless and silent on each side of the broad stream. At the foot of big, towering trees, trunkless nipa palms rose from the mud of the bank, in bunches of leaves enormous and heavy, that hung unstirring over the brown swirl of eddies. In the stillness of the air every tree, every leaf, every bough, every tendril of creeper and every petal of minute blossoms seemed to have been bewitched into an immobility perfect and final. Nothing moved on the river but the eight paddles that rose flashing regularly, dipped together with a single splash; while the steersman swept right and left with a periodic and sudden flourish of his blade describing a glinting semicircle above his head. The churned-up water frothed alongside with a confused murmer. And the white man's canoe, advancing upstream in the short-lived disturbance of its own making, seemed to enter the portals of a land from which the very memory of motion had forever departed.

The white man, turning his back upon the setting sun, looked along the empty and broad expanse of the sea-reach. For the last three miles of its course the wandering, hesitating river, as if enticed irresistibly by the freedom of an open horizon, flows straight into the sea, flows straight to the east—to the east that harbors both light and darkness. Astern of the boat the repeated call of some bird, a cry discordant and feeble, skipped along over the smooth water and lost itself, before it could reach the other shore, in the breathless silence of the world.

The steersman dug his paddle into the stream, and held hard with stiffened arms, his body thrown forward. The water gurgled aloud; and suddenly the long straight reach seemed to pivot on its center, the forests swung in a semicircle, and the slanting beams of sunset touched the broadside of the canoe with a fiery glow, throwing the slender and distorted shadows of its crew upon the streaked glitter of the river. The white man turned to look ahead. The course of the boat had been altered at right angles to the stream, and the carved dragon-head of its prow was pointing now at a gap in the fringing bushes of the bank. It glided through, brushing the overhanging twigs, and disappeared from the river like some slim and amphibious creature leaving the water for its lair in the forests.

253

The narrow creek was like a ditch: tortuous, fabulously deep; filled with gloom under the thin strip of pure and shining blue of the heaven. Immense trees soared up, invisible behind the festooned draperies of creepers. Here and there, near the glistening blackness of the water, a twisted root of some tall tree showed amongst the tracery of small ferns, black and dull, writhing and motionless, like an arrested snake. The short words of the paddlers reverberated, loudly between the thick and somber walls of vegetation. Darkness oozed out from between the trees, through the tangled maze of the creepers, from behind the great fantastic and unstirring leaves; the darkness, mysterious and invincible; the darkness scented and poisonous of impenetrable forests.

The men poled in the shoaling water. The creek broadened, opening out into a wide sweep of a stagnant lagoon. The forests receded from the marshy bank, leaving a level strip of bright green, reedy grass to frame the reflected blueness of the sky. A fleecy pink cloud drifted high above, trailing the delicate coloring of its image under the floating leaves and the silvery blossoms of the lotus. A little house, perched on high piles, appeared black in the distance. Near it, two tall nibong palms, that seemed to have come out of the forests in the background, leaned slightly over the ragged roof, with a suggestion of sad tenderness and care in the droop of their leafy and soaring heads.

The steersman, pointing with his paddle, said, "Arsat is there. I see his canoe fast between the piles."

The polers ran along the sides of the boat glancing over their shoulders at the end of the day's journey. They would have preferred to spend the night somewhere else than on this lagoon of weird aspect and ghostly reputation. Moreover, they disliked Arsat, first as a stranger, and also because he who repairs a ruined house, and dwells in it, proclaims that he is not afraid to live amongst the spirits that haunt the places abandoned by mankind. Such a man can disturb the course of fate by glances or words; while his familiar ghosts are not easy to propitiate by casual wayfarers upon whom they long to wreak the malice of their human master. White men care not for such things, being unbelievers and in league with the Father of Evil, who leads them unharmed through the invisible dangers of this world. To the warnings of the righteous they oppose an offensive pretense of disbelief. What is there to be done?

So they thought, throwing their weight on the end of their long poles. The big canoe glided on swiftly, noiselessly, and smoothly, towards Arsat's clearing, till, in a great rattling of poles thrown down, and the loud murmurs of "Allah be praised!" it came with a gentle knock against the crooked piles below the house.

The boatmen with uplifted faces shouted discordantly, "Arsat! O Arsat!" Nobody came. The white man began to climb the rude ladder giving access to the bamboo platform before the house. The juragan of the boat said sulkily, "We will cook in the sampan, and sleep on the water."

"Pass my blankets and the basket," said the white man, curtly.

He knelt on the edge of the platform to receive the bundle. Then the boat shoved off, and the white man, standing up, confronted Arsat, who had come out through the low door of his hut. He was a man young, powerful, with broad chest and muscular arms. He had nothing on but his sarong. His head was bare. His big, soft eyes stared eagerly at the white man, but his voice and demeanor were composed as he asked, without any words of greeting—

"Have you medicine, Tuan?"

"No," said the visitor in a startled tone. "No. Why? Is there sickness in the house?"

"Enter and see," replied Arsat, in the same calm manner, and turning short round, passed again through the small doorway. The white man, dropping his bundles, followed.

In the dim light of the dwelling he made out on a couch of bamboos a woman stretched on her back under a broad sheet of red cotton cloth. She lay still, as if dead; but her big eyes, wide open, glittered in the gloom, staring upwards at the slender rafters, motionless and unseeing. She was in a high fever, and evidently unconscious. Her cheeks were sunk slightly, her lips were partly open, and on the young face there was the ominous and fixed expression—the absorbed, contemplating expression of the unconscious who are going to die. The two men stood looking down at her in silence.

"Has she been long ill?" asked the traveler.

"I have not slept for five nights," answered the Malay, in a deliberate tone. "At first she heard voices calling her from the water and struggled against me who held her. But since the sun of today rose she hears nothing—she hears not me. She sees nothing. She sees not me—me!"

He remained silent for a minute, then asked softly—

"Tuan, will she die?"

"I fear so," said the white man, sorrowfully. He had known Arsat

255

years ago, in a far country in times of trouble and danger, when no friendship is to be despised. And since his Malay friend had come unexpectedly to dwell in the hut on the lagoon with a strange woman, he had slept many times there, in his journeys up and down the river. He liked the man who knew how to keep faith in council and how to fight without fear by the side of his white friend. He liked him—not so much perhaps as a man likes his favorite dog—but still he liked him well enough to help and ask no questions, to think sometimes vaguely and hazily in the midst of his own pursuits, about the lonely man and the long-haired woman with audacious face and triumphant eyes, who lived together hidden by the forests—alone and feared.

The white man came out of the hut in time to see the enormous conflagration of sunset put out by the swift and stealthy shadows that, rising like a black and impalpable vapor above the tree-tops, spread over the heaven, extinguishing the crimson glow of floating clouds and the red brilliance of departing daylight. In a few moments all the stars came out above the intense blackness of the earth and the great lagoon gleaming suddenly with reflected lights resembled an oval patch of night sky flung down into the hopeless and abysmal night of the wilderness. The white man had some supper out of the basket, then collecting a few sticks that lay about the platform, made up a small fire, not for warmth, but for the sake of the smoke, which would keep off the mosquitos. He wrapped himself in the blankets and sat with his back against the reed wall of the house, smoking thoughtfully.

Arsat came through the doorway with noiseless steps and squatted down by the fire. The white man moved his outstretched legs a little.

"She breathes," said Arsat in a low voice, anticipating the expected question. "She breathes and burns as if with a great fire. She speaks not; she hears not—and burns!"

He paused for a moment, then asked in a quiet, incurious tone—

"Tuan . . . will she die?"

The white man moved his shoulders uneasily and muttered in a hesitating manner—

"If such is her fate."

"No, Tuan," said Arsat, calmly. "If such is my fate. I hear, I see, I wait. I remember . . . Tuan, do you remember the old days? Do you remember my brother?"

"Yes," said the white man. The Malay rose suddenly and went in.

The other, sitting still outside, could hear the voice in the hut. Arsat said: "Hear me! Speak!" His words were succeeded by a complete silence. "O Diamelen!" he cried, suddenly. After that cry there was a deep sigh. Arsat came out and sank down again in his old place.

They sat in silence before the fire. There was no sound within the house, there was no sound near them; but far away on the lagoon they could hear the voices of the boatmen ringing fitful and distinct on the calm water. The fire in the bows of the sampan shone faintly in the distance with a hazy red glow. Then it died out. The voices ceased. The land and the water slept invisible, unstirring and mute. It was as though there had been nothing left in the world but the glitter of stars streaming, ceaseless and vain, through the black stillness of the night.

The white man gazed straight before him into the darkness with wide-open eyes. The fear and fascination, the inspiration and the wonder of death—of death near, unavoidable, and unseen, soothed the unrest of his race and stirred the most indistinct, the most intimate of his thoughts. The ever-ready suspicion of evil, the gnawing suspicion that lurks in our hearts, flowed out into the stillness round him—into the stillness profound and dumb, and made it appear untrustworthy and infamous, like the placid and impenetrable mask of an unjustifiable violence. In that fleeting and powerful disturbance of his being the earth enfolded in the starlight peace became a shadowy country of inhuman strife, a battle-field of phantoms terrible and charming, august or ignoble, struggling ardently for the possession of our helpless hearts. An unquiet and mysterious country of inextinguishable desires and fears.

A plaintive murmur rose in the night; a murmur saddening and startling, as if the great solitudes of surrounding woods had tried to whisper into his ear the wisdom of their immense and lofty indifference. Sounds hesitating and vague floated in the air round him, shaped themselves slowly into words; and at last flowed on gently in a murmuring stream of soft and monotonous sentences. He stirred like a man waking up and changed his position slightly. Arsat, motionless and shadowy, sitting with bowed head under the stars, was speaking in a low and dreamy tone—

". . . for where can we lay down the heaviness of our trouble but in a friend's heart? A man must speak of war and of love. You, Tuan, know what war is, and you have seen me in time of danger seek death as other men seek life! A writing may be lost; a lie may be written; but what the eye has seen is truth and remains in the mind!"

"I remember," said the white man, quietly. Arsat went on with mournful composure—

"Therefore I shall speak to you of love. Speak in the night. Speak before both night and love are gone—and the eye of day looks upon my sorrow and my shame; upon my blackened face; upon my burnt-up heart."

A sigh, short and faint, marked an almost imperceptible pause, and then his words flowed on, without a stir, without a gesture.

"After the time of trouble and war was over and you went away from my country in the pursuit of your desires, which we, men of the islands, cannot understand, I and my brother became again, as we had been before, the sword-bearers of the Ruler. You know we were men of family, belonging to a ruling race, and more fit than any to carry on our right shoulder the emblem of power. And in the time of prosperity Si Dendring showed us favor, as we, in time of sorrow, had showed to him the faithfulness of our courage. It was a time of peace. A time of deer-hunts and cock-fights; of idle talks and foolish squabbles between men whose bellies are full and weapons are rusty. But the sower watched the young rice-shoots grow up without fear, and the traders came and went, departed lean and returned fat into the river of peace. They brought news, too. Brought lies and truth mixed together, so that no man knew when to rejoice and when to be sorry. We heard from them about you also. They had seen you here and had seen you there. And I was glad to hear, for I remembered the stirring times, and I always remembered you, Tuan, till the time came when my eyes could see nothing in the past, because they had looked upon the one who is dying there—in the house."

He stopped to exclaim in an intense whisper, "O Mara bahia! O Calamity!" then went on speaking a little louder:

"There's no worse enemy and no better friend than a brother, Tuan, for one brother knows another, and in perfect knowledge is strength for good or evil. I loved my brother. I went to him and told him that I could see nothing but one face, hear nothing but one voice. He told me: 'Open your heart so that she can see what is in it—and wait. Patience is wisdom. Inchi Midah may die or our Ruler may throw off his fear of a woman!' . . . I waited! . . . You remember the lady with the veiled face, Tuan, and the fear of our

258

Ruler before her cunning and temper. And if she wanted her servant, what could I do? But I fed the hunger of my heart on short glances and stealthy words. I loitered on the path to the bath-houses in the daytime, and when the sun had fallen behind the forest I crept along the jasmine hedges of the women's courtyard. Unseeing, we spoke to one another through the scent of flowers, through the veil of leaves, through the blades of long grass that stood still before our lips; so great was our prudence, so faint was the murmur of our great longing. The time passed swiftly . . . and there were whispers amongst women—and our enemies watched—my brother was gloomy, and I began to think of killing and of a fierce death. . . . We are of a people who take what they want—like you whites. There is a time when a man should forget loyalty and respect. Might and authority are given to rulers, but to all men is given love and strength and courage. My brother said, 'You shall take her from their midst. We are two who are like one.' And I answered, 'Let it be soon, for I find no warmth in sunlight that does not shine upon her.' Our time came when the Ruler and all the great people went to the mouth of the river to fish by torchlight. There were hundreds of boats, and on the white sand, between the water and the forests, dwellings of leaves were built for the households of the Rajahs. The smoke of cooking-fires was like a blue mist of the evening, and many voices rang in it joyfully. While they were making the boats ready to beat up the fish, my brother came to me and said, 'Tonight!' I looked to my weapons, and when the time came our canoe took its place in the circle of boats carrying the torches. The lights blazed on the water, but behind the boats there was darkness. When the shouting began and the excitement made them like mad we dropped out. The water swallowed our fire, and we floated back to the shore that was dark with only here and there the glimmer of embers. We could hear the talk of slave-girls amongst the sheds. Then we found a place deserted and silent. We waited there. She came. She came running along the shore, rapid and leaving no trace, like a leaf driven by the wind into the sea. My brother said gloomily, 'Go and take her; carry her into our boat.' I lifted her in my arms. She panted. Her heart was beating against my breast. I said, 'I take you from those people. You came to the cry of my heart, but my arms take you into my boat against the will of the great!' 'It is right,' said my brother. 'We are men who take what we want and can hold it against many. We should have taken her

259

in daylight.' I said, 'Let us be off'; for since she was in my boat I began to think of our Ruler's many men. 'Yes. Let us be off,' said my brother. 'We are cast out and this boat is our country now—and the sea is our refuge.' He lingered with his foot on the shore, and I entreated him to hasten, for I remembered the strokes of her heart against my breast and thought that two men cannot withstand a hundred. We left, paddling downstream close to the bank; and as we passed by the creek where they were fishing, the great shouting had ceased, but the murmur of voices was loud like the humming of insects flying at noonday. The boats floated, clustered together, in the red light of torches, under a black roof of smoke; and men talked of their sport. Men that boasted, and praised, and jeered—men that would have been our friends in the morning, but on that night were already our enemies. We paddled swiftly past. We had no more friends in the country of our birth. She sat in the middle of the canoe with covered face; silent as she is now; unseeing as she is now—and I had no regret at what I was leaving because I could hear her breathing close to me—as I can hear her now."

He paused, listened with his ear turned to the doorway, then shook his head and went on:

"My brother wanted to shout the cry of challenge—one cry only —to let the people know we were freeborn robbers who trusted our arms and the great sea. And again I begged him in the name of our love to be silent. Could I not hear her breathing close to me? I knew the pursuit would come quick enough. My brother loved me. He dipped his paddle without a splash. He only said, 'There is a half a man in you now—the other half is in that woman. I can wait. When you are a whole man again, you will come back with me here to shout defiance. We are sons of the same mother.' I made no answer. All my strength and all my spirit were in my hands that held the paddle—for I longed to be with her in a safe place beyond the reach of men's anger and of women's spite. My love was so great, that I thought it could guide me to a country where death was unknown, if I could only escape from Inchi Midah's fury and from our Ruler's sword. We paddled with haste, breathing through our teeth. The blades bit deep into the smooth water. We passed out of the river; we flew in clear channels amongst the shallows. We skirted the black coast; we skirted the sand beaches where the sea speaks in whispers to the land; and the gleam of white sand flashed back past our boat, so swiftly she ran upon the water. We spoke not. Only once I said, 'Sleep, Diamelen, for soon you may want all your strength.' I heard the sweetness of her voice, but I never turned my head. The sun rose and still we went on. Water fell from my face like rain from a cloud. We flew in the light and heat. I never looked back, but I knew that my brother's eyes, behind me, were looking steadily ahead, for the boat went as straight as a bushman's dart, when it leaves the end of the sumpitan. There was no better paddler, no better steersman than my brother. Many times, together, we had won races in that canoe. But we never had put out our strength as we did then—then, when for the last time we paddled together! There was no braver or stronger man in our country than my brother. I could not spare the strength to turn my head and look at him, but every moment I heard the hiss of his breath getting louder behind me. Still he did not speak. The sun was high. The heat clung to my back like a flame of fire. My ribs were ready to burst, but I could no longer get enough air into my chest. And then I felt I must cry out with my last breath, 'Let us rest!' . . . 'Good!' he answered; and his voice was firm. He was strong. He was brave. He knew not fear and no fatigue . . . My brother!"

A murmur powerful and gentle, a murmur vast and faint; the murmur of trembling leaves, of stirring boughs, ran through the tangled depths of the forests, ran over the starry smoothness of the lagoon, and the water between the piles lapped the slimy timber once with a sudden splash. A breath of warm air touched the two men's faces and passed on with a mournful sound—a breath loud and short like an uneasy sigh of the dreaming earth.

Arsat went on in an even, low voice.

"We ran our canoe on the white beach of a little bay close to a long tongue of land that seemed to bar our road; a long wooded cape going far into the sea. My brother knew that place. Beyond the cape a river has its entrance, and through the jungle of that land there is a narrow path. We made a fire and cooked rice. Then we lay down to sleep on the soft sand in the shade of our canoe, while she watched. No sooner had I closed my eyes than I heard her cry of alarm. We leaped up. The sun was halfway down the sky already, and coming in sight in the opening of the bay we saw a prau manned by many paddlers. We knew it at once; it was one of our Rajah's praus. They were watching the shore, and saw us. They beat the gong, and turned the head of the prau into the bay.

I felt my heart become weak within my breast. Diamelen sat on the sand and covered her face. There was no escape by sea. My brother laughed. He had the gun you had given him, Tuan, before you went away, but there was only a handful of powder. He spoke to me quickly: 'Run with her along the path. I shall keep them back, for they have no firearms, and landing in the face of a man with a gun is certain death for some. Run with her. On the other side of that wood there is a fisherman's house—and a canoe. When I have fired all the shots I will follow. I am a great runner, and before they can come up we shall be gone. I will hold out as long as I can, for she is but a woman—that can neither run nor fight, but she has your heart in her weak hands.' He dropped behind the canoe. The prau was coming. She and I ran, and as we rushed along the path I heard shots. My brother fired—once—twice—and the booming of the gong ceased. There was silence behind us. That neck of land is narrow. Before I heard my brother fire the third shot I saw the shelving shore, and I saw the water again; the mouth of a broad river. We crossed a grassy glade. We ran down to the water. I saw a low hut above the black mud, and a small canoe hauled up. I heard another shot behind me. I thought, 'That is his last charge.' We rushed down to the canoe; a man came running from the hut, but I leaped on him, and we rolled together in the mud. Then I got up, and he lay still at my feet. I don't know whether I had killed him or not. I and Diamelen pushed the canoe afloat. I heard yells behind me, and I saw my brother run across the glade. Many men were bounding after him. I took her in my arms and threw her into the boat, then leaped in myself. When I looked back I saw that my brother had fallen. He fell and was up again, but the men were closing round him. He shouted, 'I am coming!' The men were close to him. I looked. Many men. Then I looked at her. Tuan, I pushed the canoe! I pushed it into deep water. She was kneeling forward looking at me, and I said, "Take your paddle,' while I struck the water with mine. Tuan, I heard him cry. I heard him cry my name twice; and I heard voices shouting, 'Kill! Strike!' I never turned back. I heard him calling my name again with a great shriek, as when life is going out together with the voice—and I never turned my head. My own name! . . . My brother; Three times he called—but I was not afraid of life. Was she not there in that canoe? And could I not with her find a country where death is forgotten—where death is unknown!"

The white man sat up. Arsat rose and stood, an indistinct and silent figure above the dying embers of the fire. Over the lagoon a mist drifting and low had crept, erasing slowly the glittering images of the stars. And now a great expanse of white vapor covered the land: it flowed cold and gray in the darkness, eddied in noiseless whirls round the tree-trunks and about the platform of the house, which seemed to float upon a restless and impalpable illusion of a sea. Only far away the tops of the trees stood outlined on the twinkle of heaven, like a somber and forbidding shore—a coast deceptive, pitiless and black.

Arsat's voice vibrated loudly in the profound peace.

"I had her there! I had her! To get her I would have faced all mankind. But I had her—and—"

His words went out ringing into the empty distances. He paused, and seemed to listen to them dying away very far—beyond help and beyond recall. Then he said quietly—

"Tuan, I loved my brother."

A breath of wind made him shiver. High above his head, high above the silent sea of mist the drooping leaves of the palms rattled together with a mournful and expiring sound. The white man stretched his legs. His chin rested on his chest, and he murmured sadly without lifting his head—

"We all love our brothers."

Arsat burst out with an intense whispering violence—

"What did I care who died? I wanted peace in my own heart."

He seemed to hear a stir in the house—listened—then stepped in noiselessly. The white man stood up. A breeze was coming in fitful puffs. The stars shone paler as if they had retreated into the frozen depths of immense space. After a chill gust of wind there were a few seconds of perfect calm and absolute silence. Then from behind the black and wavy line of the forest a column of golden light shot up into the heavens and spread over the semicircle of the eastern horizon. The sun had risen. The mist lifted, broke into drifting patches, vanished into thin flying wreaths; and the unveiled lagoon lay, polished and black, in the heavy shadows at the foot of the wall of trees. A white eagle rose over it with a slanting and ponderous flight, reached the clear sunshine and appeared dazzlingly brilliant for a moment, then soaring higher, became a dark and motionless speck before it vanished into the blue as if it had left the earth forever. The white man, standing gazing upwards before the doorway, heard in the hut a confused and broken murmur of distracted words ending with a loud groan. Suddenly Arsat stumbled out with outstretched hands, shivered, and stood still for some time with fixed eyes. Then he said—

"She burns no more."

Before his face the sun showed its edge above the tree-tops rising steadily. The breeze freshened; a great brilliance burst upon the lagoon, sparkled on the rippling water. The forests came out of the clear shadows of the morning, became distinct, as if they had rushed nearer—to stop short in a great stir of leaves, of nodding boughs, of swaying branches. In the merciless sunshine the whisper of unconscious life grew louder, speaking in an incomprehensible voice round the dumb darkness of that human sorrow. Arsat's eyes wandered slowly, then stared at the rising sun.

"I can see nothing," he said half aloud to himself.

"There is nothing," said the white man, moving to the edge of the platform and waving his hand to his boat. A shout came faintly over the lagoon and the sampan began to glide towards the abode of the friend of ghosts.

"If you want to come with me, I will wait all the morning," said the white man, looking away upon the water.

"No, Tuan," said Arsat, softly. "I shall not eat or sleep in this house, but I must first see my road. Now I can see nothing—see nothing! There is no light and no peace in the world; but there is death—death for many. We are sons of the same mother—and I left him in the midst of enemies; but I am going back now."

He drew a long breath and went on in a dreamy tone:

"In a little while I shall see clear enough to strike—to strike. But she has died, and . . . now . . . darkness."

He flung his arms wide open, let them fall along his body, then stood still with unmoved face and stony eyes, staring at the sun. The white man got down into his canoe. The poles ran smartly along the sides of the boat, looking over their shoulders at the beginning of a weary journey. High in the stern, his head muffled up in white rags, the juragan sat moody, letting his paddle trail in the water. The white man, leaning with both arms over the grass roof of the little cabin, looked back at the shining ripple of the boat's wake. Before the sampan passed out of the lagoon into the creek he lifted his eyes. Arsat had not moved. He stood lonely in the searching sunshine; and he looked beyond the great light of a cloudless day into the darkness of a world of illusions.

264

JAMES FENIMORE COOPER

JAMES FENIMORE COOPER (American, 1789-1851). The great romancer of the American frontier. Produced more than 50 books: novels, travel sketches, social criticism. Popular reputation rests on sea stories (*The Pilot*), and Leatherstocking tales (*The Last of the Mohicans, The Pathfinder, The Deerslayer*). Labored zealously in 19th century to further international understanding of American democracy.

THE ARIEL ON THE SHOALS

THE SEA was becoming more agitated, and the violence of the wind was gradually increasing. The latter no longer whistled amid the cordage of the vessel, but it seemed to howl surlily as it passed the complicated machinery that the frigate obtruded on its path. An endless succession of white surges rose above the heavy billows, and the very air was glittering with the light that was disengaged from the ocean. The ship yielded each moment more and more before the storm, and, in less than half an hour from the time that she had lifted her anchor, she was driven along with tremendous fury by the full power of a gale of wind. Still, the hardy and experienced mariners who directed her movements, held her to the course that was necessary to their preservation, and still Griffith gave forth, when directed by their unknown pilot, those orders that turned her in the narrow channel where safety was alone to be found.

So far the performance of his duty appeared easy to the stranger, and he gave the required directions in those still, calm tones that formed so remarkable a contrast to the responsibility of his situation. But when the land was becoming dim, in distance as well as darkness, and the agitated sea was only to be discovered as it swept by them in foam, he broke in upon the monotonous roaring of the tempest with the sounds of his voice, seeming to shake off his apathy and rouse himself to the occasion.

"Now is the time to watch her closely, Mr. Griffith," he cried; "here we get the true tide and the real danger. Place the best quarter-master of your ship in those chains, and let an officer stand by him and see that he gives us the right water."

"I will take that office on myself," said the captain; "pass a light into the weather main-chains."

"Stand by your braces!" exclaimed the pilot with startling quickness. "Heave away that lead!"

These preparations taught the crew to expect the crisis, and every officer and man stood in fearful silence at his assigned station awaiting the issue of the trial. Even the quarter-master at the cun gave out his orders to the men at the wheel in deeper and hoarsen tones than usual, as if anxious not to disturb the quiet and orden of the vessel.

While this deep expectation pervaded the frigate, the piercing cry of the leadsman, as he called, "By the mark seven!" rose above the tempest, crossed over the decks, and appeared to pass away to leeward, borne on the blast like the warnings of some water-spirit.

" 'Tis well," returned the pilot, calmly; "try it again."

The short pause was succeeded by another cry, "and a half-five!'

"She shoals! she shoals!" exclaimed Griffith; "keep her a good full."

"Ay! you must hold the vessel in command, now," said the pilot, with those cool tones that are most appalling in critical moments, because they seem to denote most preparation and care.

The third call of "By the deep four!" was followed by a prompt direction from the stranger to tack.

Griffith seemed to emulate the coolness of the pilot, in issuing the necessary orders to execute this manœuvre.

The vessel rose slowly from the inclined position into which she had been forced by the tempest, and the sails were shaking violently, as if to release themselves from their confinement while the ship stemmed the billows, when the well-known voice of the sailing-master was heard shouting from the forecastle—"Breakers! breakers, dead ahead!"

This appalling sound seemed yet to be lingering about the ship, when a second voice cried—"Breakers on our lee-bow!"

"We are in a bight of the shoals, Mr. Gray," said the commander. "She loses her way; perhaps an anchor might hold her."

"Clear away that best-bower!" shouted Griffith through his trumpet.

"Hold on!" cried the pilot, in a voice that reached the very hearts of all who heard him; "hold on every thing."

The young man turned fiercely to the daring stranger who thus defied the discipline of his vessel, and at once demanded—"Who is it that dares to countermand my orders?—is it not enough that you run the ship into danger, but you must interfere to keep her there? If another word—"

266

"Peace, Mr. Griffith," interrupted the captain, bending from the rigging, his gray locks blowing about in the wind, and adding a look of wildness to the haggard face that he exhibited by the light of his lantern; "yield the trumpet to Mr. Gray; he alone can save us."

Griffith threw his speaking-trumpet on the deck, and as he walked proudly away, muttered in bitterness of feeling—"Then all is lost, indeed, and, among the rest, the foolish hopes with which I visited this coast."

There was, however, no time for reply; the ship had been rapidly running into the wind, and, as the efforts of the crew were paralyzed by the contradictory orders they had heard, she gradually lost her way, and in a few seconds all her sails were taken aback.

Before the crew understood their situation, the pilot had applied the trumpet to his mouth, and, in a voice that rose above the tempest, he thundered forth his orders. Each command was given distinctly, and with a precision that showed him to be master of his profession. The helm was kept fast, the head yards swung up heavily against the wind, and the vessel was soon whirling round on her heel with a retrograde movement.

Griffith was too much of a seaman not to perceive that the pilot had seized, with a perception almost intuitive, the only method that promised to extricate the vessel from her situation. He was young, impetuous and proud, but he was also generous. Forgetting his resentment and his mortification, he rushed forward among the men, and, by his presence and example, added certainty to the experiment. The ship fell off slowly before the gale, and bowed her yards nearly to the water, as she felt the blast pouring its fury on her broadsides while the surly waves beat violently against her stern, as if in reproach at departing from her usual manner of moving.

The voice of the pilot, however, was still heard, steady and calm, and yet so clear and high as to reach every ear; and the obedient seamen whirled the yards at his bidding in despite of the tempest, as if they handled the toys of their childhood. When the ship had fallen off dead before the wind, her head sails were shaken, her aft-yards trimmed, and her helm shifted before she had time to run upon the danger that had threatened, as well to leeward as to windward. The beautiful fabric, obedient to her government, threw her bows up gracefully toward the wind again, and, as her sails were trimmed, moved out from amongst the dangerous shoals in which she had been embayed, as steadily and swiftly as she had approached them.

A moment of breathless astonishment succeeded the accomplishment of this nice manœuvre, but there was no time for the usual expressions of surprise. The stranger still held the trumpet, and continued to lift his voice amid the howlings of the blast, whenever prudence or skill directed any change in the management of the ship. For an hour longer there was a fearful struggle for their preservation, the channel becoming at each step more complicated, and the shoals thickening around the mariners on every side. The lead was cast rapidly, and the quick eye of the pilot seemed to pierce the darkness with a keenness of vision that exceeded human power. It was apparent to all in the vessel, that they were under the guidance of one who understood the navigation thoroughly, and their exertions kept pace with their reviving confidence. Again and again the frigate appeared to be rushing blindly on shoals, where the sea was covered with foam, and where destruction would have been as sudden as it was certain, when the clear voice of the stranger was heard warning them of the danger and inciting them to their duty. The vessel was implicitly yielding to his government, and during those anxious moments, when she was dashing the waters aside, throwing the spray over her enormous yards, each ear would listen eagerly for those sounds that had obtained a command over the crew that can only be acquired, under such circumstances, by great steadiness and consummate skill. The ship was recovering from the inaction of changing her course in one of those critical tacks that she had made so often when the pilot for the first time addressed the commander of the frigate, who still continued to superintend the all-important duty of the leadsman.

"Now is the pinch," he said; "and if the ship behaves well, we are safe—but if otherwise, all we have yet done will be useless."

The veteran seaman whom he addressed left the chains at this portentous notice, and, calling to his first lieutenant, required of the stranger an explanation of his warning.

"See you yon light on the southern headland?" returned the pilot; "you may know it from the star near it by its sinking, at times, in the ocean. Now observe the hummock a little north of it, looking like a shadow on the horizon—'tis a hill far inland. If we keep that light open from the hill, we shall do well—but if not, we surely go to pieces."

"Let us tack again!" exclaimed the lieutenant.

The pilot shook his head, as he replied—"There is no more tacking or box-hauling to be done to-night. We have barely room to pass out of the shoals on this course, and if we can weather the 'Devil's Grip,' we clear their outermost point—but if not, as I said before, there is but an alternative."

"If we had beaten out the way we entered," exclaimed Griffith, "we should have done well."

"Say, also, if the tide would have let us do so," returned the pilot calmly. "Gentlemen, we must be prompt; we have but a mile to go, and the ship appears to fly. That topsail is not enough to keep her up to the wind; we want both jib and mainsail."

" 'Tis a perilous thing to loosen canvas in such a tempest!" observed the doubtful captain.

"It must be done," returned the collected stranger; "we perish without—see! the light already touches the edge of the hummock; the sea casts us to leeward!"

"It shall be done!" cried Griffith, seizing the trumpet from the hand of the pilot.

The orders of the lieutenant were executed almost as soon as issued, and, every thing being ready, the enormous folds of the mainsail were trusted loose to the blast. There was an instant when the result was doubtful; the tremendous threshing of the heavy sails seeming to bid defiance to all restraint, shaking the ship to her centre; but art and strength prevailed, and gradually the canvas was distended, and, bellying as it filled, was drawn down to its usual place by the power of a hundred men. The vessel yielded to this immense addition of force, and bowed before it like a reed bending to a breeze. But the success of the measure was announced by a joyful cry from the stranger that seemed to burst from his inmost soul.

"She feels it! she springs her luff! observe," he said, "the light opens from the hummock already; if she will only bear her canvas, we shall go clear!"

A report like that of a cannon interrupted his exclamation, and something resembling a white cloud was seen drifting before the wind from the head of the ship, till it was driven into the gloom far to leeward.

" 'Tis the jib blown from the bolt-ropes," said the commander of the frigate. "This is no time to spread light duck—but the mainsail may stand it yet."

"The sail would laugh at a tornado," returned the lieutenant; "but that mast springs like a piece of steel."

"Silence all!" cried the pilot. "Now, gentlemen, we shall soon know our fate. Let her luff—luff you can!"

This warning effectually closed all discourse, and the hardy mariners, knowing that they had already done all in the power of man to insure their safety, stood in breathless anxiety awaiting the result. At a short distance ahead of them, the whole ocean was white with foam, and the waves, instead of rolling on in regular succession, appeared to be tossing about in mad gambols. A single streak of dark billows, not half a cable's length in width, could be discerned running into this chaos of water; but it was soon lost to the eye amid the confusion of the disturbed element. Along this narrow path the vessel moved more heavily than before, being brought so near the wind as to keep her sails touching. The pilot silently proceeded to the wheel, and with his own hands he undertook the steerage of the ship. No noise proceeded from the frigate to interrupt the horrid tumult of the ocean, and she entered the channel among the breakers with the silence of a desperate calmness. Twenty times, as the foam rolled away to leeward, the crew were on the eve of uttering their joy, as they supposed the vessel past the danger; but breaker after breaker would still rise before them, following each other into the general mass to check their exultation. Occasionally the fluttering of the sails would be heard; and when the looks of the startled seamen were turned to the wheel, they beheld the stranger grasping its spokes, with his quick eye glancing from the water to the canvas. At length the ship reached a point where she appeared to be rushing directly into the jaws of destruction, when suddenly her course was changed, and her head receded rapidly from the wind. At the same instant the voice of the pilot was heard shouting—"Square away the yards!—in mainsail!"

A general burst from the crew echoed, "Square away the yards!" and quick as thought the frigate was seen gliding along the channel before the wind. The eye had hardly time to dwell on the foam, which seemed like clouds driving in the heavens, and directly the gallant vessel issued from her perils, and rose and fell on the heavy waves of the open sea.

STEPHEN CRANE

STEPHEN CRANE (American, 1871-1900). Great realistic writer, who died
of tuberculosis at 28, after writing greatest Civil War novel—*The Red Badge
of Courage*. Brief life filled with illness and trouble; he was much maligned
as journalist and foreign correspondent. Other masterpieces of realism:
The Open Boat and *Maggie: A Girl of the Streets*, works far in advance of
their time.

THE BRIDE COMES TO YELLOW SKY

I

THE great pullman was whirling onward with such dignity of
motion that a glance from the window seemed simply to prove
that the plains of Texas were pouring eastward. Vast flats of green
grass, dull-hued spaces of mesquit and cactus, little groups of frame
houses, woods of light and tender trees, all were sweeping into
the east, sweeping over the horizon, a precipice.

A newly married pair had boarded this coach at San Antonio.
The man's face was reddened from many days in the wind and
sun, and a direct result of his new black clothes was that his brick-
coloured hands were constantly performing in a most conscious
fashion. From time to time he looked down respectfully at his attire.
He sat with a hand on each knee, like a man waiting in a barber's
shop. The glances he devoted to other passengers were furtive and
shy.

The bride was not pretty, nor was she very young. She wore a
dress of blue cashmere, with small reservations of velvet here and
there, and with steel buttons abounding. She continually twisted
her head to regard her puff sleeves, very stiff, straight, and high.
They embarrassed her. It was quite apparent that she had cooked,
and that she expected to cook, dutifully. The blushes caused by the
careless scrutiny of some passengers as she had entered the car
were strange to see upon this plain, under-class countenance, which
was drawn in placid, almost emotionless lines.

They were evidently very happy. "Ever been in a parlour-car
before?" he asked, smiling with delight.

"No," she answered; "I never was. It's fine, ain't it?"

"Great! And then after a while we'll go forward to the diner,
and get a big lay-out. Finest meal in the world. Charge a dollar."

"Oh, do they?" cried the bride. "Charge a dollar? Why, that's
too much—for us—ain't it, Jack?"

"Not this trip, anyhow," he answered bravely. "We're going to go the whole thing."

Later he explained to her about the trains. "You see, it's a thousand miles from one end of Texas to the other; and this train runs right across it, and never stops but four times." He had the pride of an owner. He pointed out to her the dazzling fittings of the coach; and in truth her eyes opened wider as she contemplated the sea-green figured velvet, the shining brass, silver, and glass, the wood that gleamed as darkly brilliant as the surface of a pool of oil. At one end a bronze figure sturdily held a support for a separated chamber, and at convenient places on the ceiling were frescos in olive and silver.

To the minds of the pair, their surroundings reflected the glory of their marriage that morning in San Antonio; this was the environment of their new estate; and the man's face in particular beamed with an elation that made him appear ridiculous to the negro porter. This individual at times surveyed them from afar with an amused and superior grin. On other occasions he bullied them with skill in ways that did not make it exactly plain to them that they were being bullied. He subtly used all the manners of the most unconquerable kind of snobbery. He oppressed them; but of this oppression they had small knowledge, and they speedily forgot that infrequently a number of travellers covered them with stares of derisive enjoyment. Historically there was supposed to be something infinitely humorous in their situation.

"We are due in Yellow Sky at 3:42," he said, looking tenderly into her eyes.

"Oh, are we?" she said, as if she had not been aware of it. To evince surprise at her husband's statement was part of her wifely amiability. She took from a pocket a little silver watch; and as she held it before her, and stared at it with a frown of attention, the new husband's face shone.

"I bought it in San Anton' from a friend of mine," he told her gleefully.

"It's seventeen minutes past twelve," she said, looking up at him with a kind of shy and clumsy coquetry. A passenger, noting this play, grew excessively sardonic, and winked at himself in one of the numerous mirrors.

At last they went to the dining-car. Two rows of negro waiters, in glowing white suits, surveyed their entrance with the interest, and also the equanimity, of men who had been forewarned. The

272

pair fell to the lot of a waiter who happened to feel pleasure in steering them through their meal. He viewed them with the manner of a fatherly pilot, his countenance radiant with benevolence. The patronage, entwined with the ordinary deference, was not plain to them. And yet, as they returned to their coach, they showed in their faces a sense of escape.

To the left, miles down a long purple slope, was a little ribbon of mist where moved the keening Rio Grande. The train was approaching it at an angle, and the apex was Yellow Sky. Presently it was apparent that, as the distance from Yellow Sky grew shorter, the husband became commensurately restless. His brick-red hands were more insistent in their prominence. Occasionally he was even rather absent-minded and far-away when the bride leaned forward and addressed him.

As a matter of truth, Jack Potter was beginning to find the shadow of a deed weigh upon him like a leaden slab. He, the town marshal of Yellow Sky, a man known, liked, and feared in his corner, a prominent person, had gone to San Antonio to meet a girl he believed he loved, and there, after the usual prayers, had actually induced her to marry him, without consulting Yellow Sky for any part of the transaction. He was now bringing his bride before an innocent and unsuspecting community.

Of course people in Yellow Sky married as it pleased them, in accordance with a general custom; but such was Potter's thought of his duty to his friends, or of their idea of his duty, or of an unspoken form which does not control men in these matters, that he felt he was heinous. He had committed an extraordinary crime. Face to face with this girl in San Antonio, and spurred by his sharp impulse, he had gone headlong over all the social hedges. At San Antonio he was like a man hidden in the dark. A knife to sever any friendly duty, any form, was easy to his hand in that remote city. But the hour of Yellow Sky—the hour of daylight—was approaching.

He knew full well that his marriage was an important thing to his town. It could only be exceeded by the burning of the new hotel. His friends could not forgive him. Frequently he had reflected on the advisability of telling them by telegraph, but a new cowardice had been upon him. He feared to do it. And now the train was hurrying him toward a scene of amazement, glee, and reproach. He glanced out of the window at the line of haze swinging slowly in toward the train.

Yellow Sky had a kind of brass band, which played painfully, to the delight of the populace. He laughed without heart as he thought of it. If the citizens could dream of his prospective arrival with his bride, they would parade the band at the station and escort them, amid cheers and laughing congratulations, to his adobe home.

He resolved that he would use all the devices of speed and plains-craft in making the journey from the station to his house. Once within that safe citadel, he could issue some sort of vocal bulletin, and then not go among the citizens until they had time to wear off a little of their enthusiasm.

The bride looked anxiously at him. "What's worrying you, Jack?"

He laughed again. "I'm not worrying, girl; I'm only thinking of Yellow Sky."

She flushed in comprehension.

A sense of mutual guilt invaded their minds and developed a finer tenderness. They looked at each other with eyes softly aglow. But Potter often laughed the same nervous laugh; the flush upon the bride's face seemed quite permanent.

The traitor to the feelings of Yellow Sky narrowly watched the speeding landscape. "We're nearly there," he said.

Presently the porter came and announced the proximity of Potter's home. He held a brush in his hand, and, with all his airy superiority gone, he brushed Potter's new clothes as the latter slowly turned this way and that way. Potter fumbled out a coin and gave it to the porter, as he had seen others do. It was a heavy and muscle-bound business, as that of a man shoeing his first horse.

The porter took their bag, and as the train began to slow they moved forward to the hooded platform of the car. Presently the two engines and their long string of coaches rushed into the station of Yellow Sky.

"They have to take water here," said Potter, from a constricted throat and in mournful cadence, as one announcing death. Before the train stopped his eye had swept the length of the platform, and he was glad and astonished to see there was none upon it but the station-agent, who, with a slightly hurried and anxious air, was walking toward the water-tanks. When the train had halted, the porter alighted first, and placed in position a little temporary step.

"Come on, girl," said Potter, hoarsely. As he helped her down they each laughed on a false note. He took the bag from the negro, and bade his wife cling to his arm. As they slunk rapidly away, his hang-dog glance perceived that they were unloading the two trunks, and also that the station-agent, far ahead near the baggage-car, had turned and was running toward him, making gestures. He laughed, and groaned as he laughed, when he noted the first effect of his marital bliss upon Yellow Sky. He gripped his wife's arm firmly to his side, and they fled. Behind them the porter stood, chuckling fatuously.

II

The California express on the Southern Railway was due at Yellow Sky in twenty-one minutes. There were six men at the bar of the Weary Gentleman saloon. One was a drummer who talked a great deal and rapidly; three were Texans who did not care to talk at that time; and two were Mexican sheep-herders, who did not talk as a general practice in the Weary Gentleman saloon. The barkeeper's dog lay on the board walk that crossed in front of the door. His head was on his paws, and he glanced drowsily here and there with the constant vigilance of a dog that is kicked on occasion. Across the sandy street were some vivid green grass-plots, so wonderful in appearance, amid the sands that burned near them in a blazing sun, that they caused a doubt in the mind. They exactly resembled the grass mats used to represent lawns on the stage. At the cooler end of the railway station, a man without a coat sat in a tilted chair and smoked his pipe. The fresh-cut bank of the Rio Grande circled near the town, and there could be seen beyond it a great plum-coloured plain of mesquit.

Save for the busy drummer and his companions in the saloon, Yellow Sky was dozing. The new-comer leaned gracefully upon the bar, and recited many tales with the confidence of a bard who has come upon a new field.

"—and at the moment that the old man fell downstairs with the bureau in his arms, the old woman was coming up with two scuttles of coal, and of course—"

The drummer's tale was interrupted by a young man who suddenly appeared in the open door. He cried: "Scratchy Wilson's drunk, and has turned loose with both hands." The two Mexicans at once set down their glasses and faded out of the rear entrance of the saloon.

The drummer, innocent and jocular, answered: "All right, old man. S'pose he has? Come in and have a drink, anyhow."

But the information had made such an obvious cleft in every skull in the room that the drummer was obliged to see its importance. All had become instantly solemn. "Say," said he, mystified, "what is this?" His three companions made the introductory gesture of eloquent speech; but the young man at the door forestalled them.

"It means, my friend," he answered, as he came into the saloon, "that for the next two hours this town won't be a health resort."

The barkeeper went to the door, and locked and barred it; reaching out of the window, he pulled in heavy wooden shutters, and barred them. Immediately a solemn, chapellike gloom was upon the place. The drummer was looking from one to another.

"But say," he cried, "what is this, anyhow? You don't mean there is going to be a gun-fight?"

"Don't know whether there'll be a fight or not," answered one man, grimly; "but there'll be some shootin'—some good shootin'."

The young man who had warned them waved his hand. "Oh, there'll be a fight fast enough, if any one wants it. Anybody can get a fight out there in the street. There's a fight just waiting."

The drummer seemed to be swayed between the interest of a foreigner and a perception of personal danger.

"What did you say his name was?" he asked.

"Scratchy Wilson," they answered in chorus.

"And will he kill anybody? What are you going to do? Does this happen often? Does he rampage around like this once a week or so? Can he break in that door?"

"No; he can't break down that door," replied the barkeeper. "He's tried it three times. But when he comes you'd better lay down on the floor, stranger. He's dead sure to shoot at it, and a bullet may come through."

Thereafter the drummer kept a strict eye upon the door. The time had not yet been called for him to hug the floor, but, as a minor precaution, he sidled near to the wall. "Will he kill anybody?" he said again.

The men laughed low and scornfully at the question.

"He's out to shoot, and he's out for trouble. Don't see any good in experimentin' with him."

"But what do you do in a case like this? What do you do?"

A man responded: "Why, he and Jack Potter—"

"But," in chorus the other men interrupted, "Jack Potter's in San Anton'."

"Well, who is he? What's he got to do with it?"

"Oh, he's the town marshal. He goes out and fights Scratchy when he gets on one of these tears."

"Wow!" said the drummer, mopping his brow. "Nice job he's got."

The voices had toned away to mere whisperings. The drummer wished to ask further questions, which were born of an increasing anxiety and bewilderment; but when he attempted them, the men merely looked at him in irritation and motioned him to remain silent. A tense waiting hush was upon them. In the deep shadows of the room their eyes shone as they listened for sounds from the street. One man made three gestures at the barkeeper; and the latter, moving like a ghost, handed him a glass and a bottle. The man poured a full glass of whisky in a swallow, and turned again toward the door in immovable silence. The drummer saw that the barkeeper, without a sound, had taken a Winchester from beneath the bar. Later he saw this individual beckoning to him, so he tiptoed across the room.

"You better come with me back of the bar."

"No, thanks," said the drummer, perspiring; "I'd rather be where I can make a break for the back door."

Whereupon the man of bottles made a kindly but peremptory gesture. The drummer obeyed it, and, finding himself seated on a box with his head below the level of the bar, balm was laid upon his soul at sight of various zinc and copper fittings that bore a resemblance to armour-plate. The barkeeper took a seat comfortably upon an adjacent box.

"You see," he whispered, "this here Scratchy Wilson is a wonder with a gun—a perfect wonder; and when he goes on the war-trail, we hunt our holes—naturally. He's about the last one of the old gang that used to hang out along the river here. He's a terror when he's drunk. When he's sober he's all right—kind of simple—wouldn't hurt a fly—nicest fellow in town. But when he's drunk—whoo!"

There were periods of stillness. "I wish Jack Potter was back from San Anton'," said the barkeeper. "He shot Wilson up once —in the leg—and he would sail in and pull out the kinks in this thing."

Presently they heard from a distance the sound of a shot, followed by three wild yowls. It instantly removed a bond from the men in the darkened saloon. There was a shuffling of feet. They looked at each other. "Here he comes," they said.

III

A man in a maroon-coloured flannel shirt, which had been purchased for purposes of decoration, and made principally by some Jewish women on the East Side of New York, rounded a corner and walked into the middle of the main street of Yellow Sky. In either hand the man held a long, heavy, blue-black revolver. Often he yelled, and these cries rang through a semblance of a deserted village, shrilly flying over the roofs in a volume that seemed to have no relation to the ordinary vocal strength of a man. It was as if the surrounding stillness formed the arch of a tomb over him. These cries of ferocious challenge rang against walls of silence. And his boots had red tops with gilded imprints, of the kind beloved in winter by little sledding boys on the hillsides of New England.

The man's face flamed in a rage begot of whisky. His eyes, rolling, and yet keen for ambush, hunted the still doorways and windows. He walked with the creeping movement of the midnight cat. As it occurred to him, he roared menacing information. The long revolvers in his hands were as easy as straws; they were moved with an electric swiftness. The little fingers of each hand played sometimes in a musician's way. Plain from the low collar of the shirt, the cords of his neck straightened and sank, straightened and sank, as passion moved him. The only sounds were his terrible invitations. The calm adobes preserved their demeanour at the passing of this small thing in the middle of the street.

There was no offer of fight—no offer of fight. The man called to the sky. There were no attractions. He bellowed and fumed and swayed his revolvers here and everywhere.

The dog of the barkeeper of the Weary Gentleman saloon had not appreciated the advance of events. He yet lay dozing in front of his master's door. At sight of the dog, the man paused and raised his revolver humorously. At sight of the man, the dog sprang up and walked diagonally away, with a sullen head, and growling. The man yelled, and the dog broke into a gallop. As it was about to enter an alley, there was a loud noise, a whistling, and something spat the ground directly before it. The dog screamed, and, wheeling in terror, galloped headlong in a new direction. Again there was

278

a noise, a whistling, and sand was kicked viciously before it. Fear-stricken, the dog turned and flurried like an animal in a pen. The man stood laughing, his weapons at his hips.

Ultimately the man was attracted by the closed door of the Weary Gentleman saloon. He went to it and, hammering with a revolver, demanded drink.

The door remaining imperturbable, he picked a bit of paper from the walk, and nailed it to the framework with a knife. He then turned his back contemptuously upon this popular resort and, walking to the opposite side of the street and spinning there on his heel quickly and lithely, fired at the bit of paper. He missed it by a half-inch. He swore at himself, and went away. Later he comfortably fusilladed the windows of his most intimate friend. The man was playing with this town; it was a toy for him.

But still there was no offer of fight. The name of Jack Potter, his ancient antagonist, entered his mind, and he concluded that it would be a glad thing if he should go to Potter's house, and by bombardment induce him to come out and fight. He moved in the direction of his desire, chanting Apache scalp-music.

When he arrived at it, Potter's house presented the same still front as had the other adobes. Taking up a strategic position, the man howled a challenge. But this house regarded him as might a great stone god. It gave no sign. After a decent wait, the man howled further challenges, mingling with them wonderful epithets.

Presently there came the spectacle of a man churning himself into deepest rage over the immobility of a house. He fumed at it as the winter wind attacks a prairie cabin in the North. To the distance there should have gone the sound of a tumult like the fighting of two hundred Mexicans. As necessity bade him, he paused for breath or to reload his revolvers.

IV

Potter and his bride walked sheepishly and with speed. Sometimes they laughed together shamefacedly and low.

"Next corner, dear," he said finally.

They put forth the efforts of a pair walking bowed against a strong wind. Potter was about to raise a finger to point the first appearance of the new home when, as they circled the corner, they came face to face with a man in a maroon-coloured shirt, who was feverishly pushing cartridges into a large revolver. Upon the instant the man dropped his revolver to the ground and, like lightning,

279

whipped another from its holster. The second weapon was aimed at the bridegroom's chest.

There was a silence. Potter's mouth seemed to be merely a grave for his tongue. He exhibited an instinct to at once loosen his arm from the woman's grip, and he dropped the bag to the sand. As for the bride. her face had gone as yellow as old cloth. She was a slave to hideous rites, gazing at the apparitional snake.

The two men faced each other at a distance of three paces. He of the revolver smiled with a new and quiet ferocity.

"Tried to sneak up on me," he said. "Tried to sneak up on me!" His eyes grew more baleful. As Potter made a slight movement, the man thrust his revolver venomously forward. "No; don't you do it, Jack Potter. Don't you move a finger toward a gun just yet. Don't you move an eyelash. The time has come for me to settle with you, and I'm goin' to do it my own way, and loaf along with no interferin'. So if you don't want a gun bent on you, just mind what I tell you."

Potter looked at his enemy, "I ain't got a gun on me, Scratchy," he said. "Honest, I ain't." He was stiffening and steadying, but yet somewhere at the back of his mind a vision of the Pullman floated: the sea-green figured velvet, the shining brass, silver, and glass, the wood that gleamed as darkly brilliant as the surface of a pool of oil—all the glory of the marriage, the environment of the new estate. "You know I fight when it comes to fighting, Scratchy Wilson; but I ain't got a gun on me. You'll have to do all the shootin' yourself."

His enemy's face went livid. He stepped forward, and lashed his weapon to and fro before Potter's chest. "Don't you tell me you ain't got no gun on you, you whelp. Don't tell me no lie like that. There ain't a man in Texas ever seen you without no gun. Don't take me for no kid." His eyes blazed with light, and his throat worked like a pump.

"I ain't takin' you for no kid," answered Potter. His heels had not moved an inch backward. "I'm takin' you for a damn fool. I tell you I ain't got a gun, and I ain't. If you're goin' to shoot me up, you better begin' now; you'll never get a chance like this again."

So much enforced reasoning had told on Wilson's rage; he was calmer. "If you ain't got a gun, why ain't you got a gun?" he sneered. "Been to Sunday-school?"

"I ain't got a gun because I've just come from San Anton' with my wife. I'm married," said Potter. "And if I'd thought there was going to be any galoots like you prowling around when I brought my wife home, I'd had a gun, and don't you forget it."

"Married!" said Scratchy, not at all comprehending.

"Yes, married. I'm married," said Potter, distinctly.

"Married?" said Scratchy. Seemingly for the first time, he saw the drooping, drowning woman at the other man's side. "No!" he said. He was like a creature allowed a glimpse of another world. He moved a pace backward, and his arm, with the revolver, dropped to his side. "Is this the lady?" he asked.

"Yes; this is the lady," answered Potter.

There was another period of silence.

"Well," said Wilson at last, slowly, "I s'pose it's all off now."

"It's all off if you say so, Scratchy. You know I didn't make the trouble." Potter lifted his valise.

"Well, I 'low it's off, Jack," said Wilson. He was looking at the ground. "Married!" He was not a student of chivalry; it was merely that in the presence of this foreign condition he was a simple child of the earlier plains. He picked up his starboard revolver, and, placing both weapons in their holsters, he went away. His feet made funnel-shaped tracks in the heavy sand.

D

DANDIN

DANDIN (Sanskrit, *ca.* 7th century A.D.). Colorful and picturesque Sanskrit author of a picaresque novel, *Dasakumāracharita (The Adventures of the Ten Princes)*. The play *Mricchakatika* is attributed to him by some.

THE COURTESAN'S MOTHER

THESE are the aspects on which a courtesan's mother has to concentrate her attention in rearing up her child, namely, to apply perfumed cosmetics to the limbs of the girl even from her childhood; to put her on such nutritious diet as would supply her with enough bodily radiance, strength, complexion and wits as well as her normal appetite and digestion; to keep even the man who gave her life from visiting her frequently after her fifth year of life; to celebrate her birthdays and other events of her life in adequate style; to initiate her into the arts of love-making with all their accessory aids; to familiarise her with the secrets of the arts of dancing, music, instrumental play, histrionics, painting and the culinary art; to teach her how to prepare sandal paste and flower pigments as well as to gain efficiency in calligraphy and conversational graces; to supply her with that amount of acquaintance of the Sastras such as grammar, logic and philosophy so as to enable her to carry on discussions without showing want of information; to guide her in the science of living; to teach her knowledge of games and dice-throwing as well as equip her with the necessary zest for watching cock- and bull-fights; to induce her to learn from adept and experienced gallants the trick of amorous wooing; to decorate her person attractively on occasions of festival and public carnival and to send her out attended upon by a proper retinue; to make her ingratiate herself in the favour of men of influence and rank in order to suc-

282

ceed in her performances before audiences; to propitiate the virtuosos in the various arts in order to gain a favourable atmosphere for her own excursions into them; to make astrologers and palmists spread her prospective fame from a reading of her chart; to gather from that group who visit dancing girls enough of appreciation for her good looks, qualities, wit and figure; to give her away to anyone blindly in love with her in case he is rich and independent also; otherwise, to yield her up to one who has high intellectual attainments though poorly equipped with worldly materials; to persuade her to live with one by Gandharva wedding but later on to extort money from him and finally, if need be, to resort to courts of law for recovering her money claims.

GABRIELE D'ANNUNZIO

GABRIELE D'ANNUNZIO (Italian, 1863-1938). Flamboyant, romantic poet and dramatist. Influential in early 20th century Italy. Pushed anti-religious, anti-democratic ideas of Carducci to grotesque extremes. Attracted by themes of violence, illness, erotic decadence. Most widely read novel: *The Triumph of Death*. Plays include *La Gioconda, Francesca da Rimini*.

FOUR SONNETS

I

He was a love-child. In his gloomy eye
  Burned flames of desperate hatred, prompt to glow,
  Like lurid gleams of sunset from the sky
  Fallen in foul waters of a ditch below;
  Pale, lean he was: his red hair stood up high
  Over his head deformed and marked with woe,
  And his misshapen body made awry
  As if from stone hewn by an axe's blow.

And yet—! None knew his heart-beats in the night,
  None saw his burning tears, none heard him weep
  Tears breaking his poor heart, in youth's despite,
  When o'er the deck broke from the odorous deep
  Vast waves of perfume 'neath the full moonlight,
  And nought was heard save long-drawn breaths of sleep.

II

Ah, none! She passes o'er the sands of gold,
   Singing a song, and with the sunlight crowned;
   Given to the Loves her ample breasts unfold,
   Given to the winds her tresses flow unbound.
Joyous with youth her honest eyes and bold,
   Blue like the tropic skies, seek all around
Fancies and dreams, while to the heavens out-rolled
   O'er the opal sea her joyous songs resound.

He breathless, quivering with passions vain,
   Crouched in the boat along the swaying keel,
Holds in his hands his temples filled with pain—
   'See to the nets!' the skipper's orders peal,
As he kicks him where he lies. And o'er the main
   Her jocund songs arise, rebound and wheel.

III

The song said: 'Sea-weeds! flowers o' the ample sea!
   Down in the waters green the mermaids dwell
   In gardens coralline, where mansions be,
Built for fair maids who love their sweethearts well.'
The song said: 'Flower of may on the hawthorn tree!
   There is a grotto made of many a shell,
   Deep in the waters blue, a home of glee
Built for fair maids who love's sweet story tell.'

And Rufus thought to himelf: 'I am a cur!
   For me there is no smile for dear love's sake,
And never a kiss for me! I am a cur!
   Up! draw the bridle tight! I work and ache;
My blood I sell for bread, while none demur:
   Yet—if one day the worn-out cord should break?'

IV

The murderer climbed the cliff with hurrying feet,
   With pale and anxious face, with aching head,
Like a wild beast struck mad in the summer heat,
   Grasping the guilty knife still dripping red.

The angry sea-gulls in battalions fleet
Raised o'er the crags their clamorous shout, and fled;
And the death-cry shook far off a lugger's sheet
As he hurled himself to the wave that onward sped.

Far echoed o'er the golden sands the sound
Of human labour: mournful and unblest,
Voices of women surged along the ground;
And tossed upon the sea's sublime unrest,
On emerald deeps with zones of glory crowned,
A corpse turned to the sun its shattered breast.

DANTE ALIGHIERI

DANTE ALIGHIERI (Italian, 1265-1321). One of world's great poets, and
Italy's supreme literary figure. Dabbled in politics, banished from Florence,
lived in bitter exile. Love for Beatrice de' Portinari glorified in *The Divine
Comedy*, philosophical-political allegory of 100 cantos, and in *La Vita Nuovo*,
collection of 31 love poems. His writing important in shaping Italian into a
literary language.

THE DIVINE COMEDY

"Through me ye enter the abode of woe:
    Through me to endless sorrow are ye brought:
    Through me amid the souls accurst ye go.
Justice did first my lofty Maker move;
    By power Almighty was my fabric wrought,
    By highest Wisdom, and by Primal Love.
Ere I was form'd, no things created were,
    Save those eternal—I eternal last:
    All hope abandon—ye who enter here."
These words, inscribed in colour dark, I saw
    High on the summit of a portal vast;
    Whereat I cried: "O master! with deep awe
Their sense I mark." Like one prepared, he said,
    "Here from thy soul must doubt be cast away;
    Here must each thought of cowardice be dead.—
Now, at that place I told thee of, arrived,
    The melancholy shades shalt thou survey,
    Of God—the mind's supremest good—deprived."

Then, as he clasp'd my hand with joyful mien,
  That comfort gave, and bade me cease to fear,
  He led me down into the world unseen.
There sobs, and wailings, and heart-rending cries,
  Resounded through the starless atmosphere,
  Whence tears began to gather in mine eyes.
Harsh tongues discordant—horrible discourse—
  Words of despair—fierce accents of despite—
  Striking of hands—with curses deep and hoarse,
Raised a loud tumult, which unceasing whirl'd
  Throughout that gloom of everlasting night,
  Like to the sand in circling eddies hurl'd.
Then (horror compassing my head around)
  I cried: "O master, what is this I hear?
  And who are these so plunged in grief profound?"
He answered me: "The groans which thou hast heard
  Proceed from those, who, when on earth they were,
  Nor praise deserved, nor infamy incurr'd.
Here with those caitiff angels they abide,
  Who stood aloof in heaven—to God untrue,
  Yet wanting courage with His foes to side.
Heaven drove them forth, its beauty not to stain:
  And Hell refuses to receive them too:—
  From them no glory could the damn'd obtain."
"O master, what infliction do they bear,"
  I said, "which makes them raise such shrieks of woe?
  He answer'd: "That I will in brief declare.
No hope of death have this unhappy crew;
  And their degraded life is sunk so low,
  With envy every other state they view.
No record hath the world of this vile class,
  Alike by Justice and by Pity spurn'd:
  Speak we no more of them—but look—and pass."
And as I look'd, a banner I beheld,
  That seemed incapable of rest, and turn'd,
  In one unvaried round for aye impell'd;
While shades were following in so long a train,
  I ne'er forsooth could have believed it true
  That Death such myriads of mankind had slain

And when I had examined many a shade,
    Behold! that abject one appear'd in view,
      Who, mean of soul, the grand refusal made.
Straight I perceived, and distant recognised,
    In that vast concourse the assembly vile
      Of those by God and by His foes despised.
These wretched ones, who never were alive,
    All naked stood, for sorely stung the while
      By wasps and hornets that around them drive.
The cruel swarm bedew'd their cheeks with blood
    Which trickled to their feet with many a tear,
      While worms disgusting drank the mingled flood.
Then, onward as I stretch'd mine eye, I saw
    A mighty stream, with numbers standing near;
      Whereat I said: "O master! by what law
Do these sad souls, whose state I fain would learn,
    So eagerly to cross the river haste,
      As by the doubtful twilight I discern?"
"These things," he answer'd me, "shall all be told
    Soon as our feet upon the bank are placed
      Of Acheron, that mournful river old."
Mine eyes cast down, my looks o'erwhelm'd with shame
    Fearing my questions had oppress'd the sage,
      I spake not till beside the stream we came.
Lo! in a vessel o'er the gloomy tide
    An old man comes—his locks all white with age:—
      "Woe, woe to you, ye guilty souls!" he cried;
"Hope not that heaven shall ever bless your sight;
    I come to bear you to the other shore,—
      To ice, and fire, in realms of endless night:
And thou—who breathest still the vital air—
    Begone—nor stay with these who live no more."
      But when he saw that yet I linger'd there—
"By other port," he said, "by other way,
    And not by this, a passage must thou find;
      Thee a far lighter vessel shall convey."
"Charon," my guide return'd, "thy wrath restrain,
    Thus is it will'd where will and power are join'd;
      Therefore submit, nor question us again."

The dark lake's pilot heard;—and at the sound
    Fell instant his rough cheeks, while flashing raged
    His angry eyes in flaming circles round.
But they—soon as these threatenings met their ear—
    Poor, naked, weary souls—their colour changed;
    And their teeth chatter'd through excess of fear.
God they blasphemed, their parents, man's whole race,
    The hour, the spot,—and e'en the very seed
    To which their miserable life they trace:
Then, while full bitterly their sorrows flow'd,
    They gather'd to that evil strand, decreed
    To all who live not in the fear of God.
Charon, the fiend, with eyes of living coal,
    Beckoning the mournful troop, collects them there,
    And with his oar strikes each reluctant soul.
As leaves in Autumn, borne before the wind,
    Drop one by one, until the branch, laid bare.
    Sees all its honours to the earth consign'd:
So cast them downward at his summons all
    The guilty race of Adam from that strand,—
    Each, as a falcon, answering to the call,
Thus pass they slowly o'er the water brown;
    And ere on the opposing bank they land,
    Fresh numbers to this shore come crowding down.
"All those, my son," exclaim'd the courteous guide,
    "Who in the wrath of the Almighty die,
    Are gather'd here from every region wide:
Goaded by Heavenly Justice in its ire,
    To pass the stream they rush thus hastily;
    So that their fear is turn'd into desire.
By virtuous soul this wave is never cross'd;
    Wherefore, if Charon warn thee to depart,
    The meaning of his words will not be lost."
This converse closed—the dusky region dread
    Trembled so awfully, that o'er my heart
    Doth terror still a chilly moisture shed.
Sent forth a blast that melancholy realm,
    Which flashing a vermilion light around,
    At once did all my senses overwhelm;
And down I sank like one in slumber bound.

ALPHONSE DAUDET

ALPHONSE DAUDET (French, 1840-1897). Associated with French natural-
ists, but essentially a romanticist. Creator of gentle satires and sentimental
stories. Gave up teaching to write, gained early fame and popularity. Best-
known stories in *Lettres de mon Moulin*. Best-known novel: *Sapho*.

THE DEATH OF THE DAUPHIN

THE little Dauphin is ill; the little Dauphin is dying. In all the
churches of the kingdom the Holy Sacrament remains exposed night
and day, and great tapers burn, for the recovery of the royal child.
The streets of the old capital are sad and silent, the bells ring no
more, the carriages slacken their pace. In the neighborhood of the
palace the curious towns-people gaze through the railings upon the
beadles with gilded paunches, who converse in the courts and put
on important airs.

All the castle is in a flutter. Chamberlains and major-domos run
up and down the marble stair-ways. The galleries are full of pages
and of courtiers in silken apparel, who hurry from one group to
another, begging in low tones for news. Upon the wide perrons the
maids of honor, in tears, exchange low courtesies and wipe their
eyes with daintily embroidered handkerchiefs.

A large assemblage of robed physicians has gathered in the Or-
angery. They can be seen through the panes waving their long black
sleeves and inclining their periwigs with professional gestures. The
governor and the equerry of the little Dauphin walk up and down
before the door awaiting the decision of the Faculty. Scullions pass
by without saluting them. The equerry swears like a pagan; the
governor quotes verses from Horace.

And meanwhile, over there, in the direction of the stables, is
heard a long and plaintive neighing; it is the little Dauphin's sorrel,
forgotten by the hostlers, and calling sadly before his empty manger.

And the King? Where is his Highness the King? The King has
locked himself up in a room at the other end of the castle. Majesties
do not like to be seen weeping. For the Queen it is different. Sitting
by the bedside of the little Dauphin, she bows her fair face, bathed
in tears, and sobs very loudly before everybody, like a mere draper's
wife.

On the bed embroidered with lace the little Dauphin, whiter than
the pillows on which he is extended, lies with closed eyes. They think

289

that he is asleep; but no, the little Dauphin is not asleep. He turns towards his mother, and seeing her tears, he asks:

"Madame la Reine, why do you weep? Do you really believe that I am going to die?"

The Queen tries to answer. Sobs prevent her from speaking.

"Do not weep, Madame la Reine. You forget that I am the Dauphin, and that Dauphins cannot die thus."

The Queen sobs more violently, and the little Dauphin begins to feel frightened.

"Holloa!" says he, "I do not want Death to come and take me away, and I know how to prevent him from coming here. Order up on the spot forty of the strongest lansquenets to keep guard around our bed! Have a hundred big cannons watch day and night, with lighted fuses, under our windows! And woe to Death if he dares to come near us!"

In order to humor the royal child, the Queen makes a sign. On the spot the great cannons are heard rolling in the courts, and forty tall lansquenets, with halberds in their fists, draw up around the room. They are all veterans, with grizzly mustaches. The little Dauphin claps his hands on seeing them. He recognizes one, and calls,

"Lorrain! Lorrain!"

The veteran makes a step towards the bed.

"I love you well, my old Lorrain. Let me see your big sword. If Death wants to fetch me, you will kill him, won't you?"

Lorrain answers:

"Yes, Monseigneur."

And two great tears roll down his tanned cheeks.

At that moment the chaplain approaches the little Dauphin. and pointing to the crucifix, talks to him in low tones. The little Dauphin listens with astonished air; then, suddenly interrupting him,

"I understand well what you are saying, Monsieur l'Abbé; but still, couldn't my little friend Beppo die in my place, if I gave him plenty of money?"

The chaplain continues to talk to him in low tones, and the little Dauphin looks more and more astonished.

When the chaplain has finished, the little Dauphin resumes, with a heavy sigh:

"What you have said is all very sad, Monsieur l'Abbé; but one thing consoles me, and that is that up there, in the Paradise of the stars, I shall still be the Dauphin. I know that the good God is my cousin, and cannot fail to treat me according to my rank."

Then he adds, turning towards his mother:

"Bring me my fairest clothes, my doublet of white ermine, and my pumps of velvet! I wish to look brave to the angels, and to enter Paradise in the dress of a Dauphin."

A third time the chaplain bends over the little Dauphin, and talks to him in low tones. In the midst of his discourse the royal child interrupts him angrily.

"Why, then," he cries, "to be Dauphin is nothing at all!"

And refusing to listen to anything more, the little Dauphin turns towards the wall and weeps bitterly.

DAVID

DAVID (Hebrew, ca. 1000 B.C.). The kingly harpist. King of Judea and Israel. Famous as a poet and warrior.

PSALM XXXVII

FRET not thyself because of evil doers, neither be thou envious against the workers of iniquity.

For they shall soon be cut down like the grass, and wither as the green herb.

Trust in the Lord, and do good; so shall thou dwell in the land, and verily thou shalt be fed.

Delight thyself also in the Lord; and he shall give thee the desires of thy heart.

Commit thy way unto the Lord; trust also in him; and he shall bring it to pass.

And he shall bring forth thy righteousness as the light, and thy judgement as the noon-day.

Rest in the Lord, and wait patiently for him: fret not thyself because of him who prospereth in his way, because of the man who bringeth wicked devices to pass.

Cease from anger, and forsake wrath: fret not thyself in any wise to do evil.

For evil doers shall be cut off: but those that wait upon the Lord, they shall inherit the earth.

For yet a little while, and the wicked shall not be: yea, thou shalt diligently consider his place, and it shall not be.

But the meek shall inherit the earth; and shall delight themselves in the abundance of peace.

The wicked plotteth against the just, and gnasheth upon him with his teeth.

The Lord shall laugh at him: for he seeth that his day is coming.

The wicked have drawn out the sword, and have bent their bow, to cast down the poor and needy, *and* to slay such as be of upright conversation.

Their sword shall enter into their own heart, and their bows shall be broken.

A little that a righteous man hath *is* better than the riches of many wicked.

For the arms of the wicked shall be broken: but the Lord upholdeth the righteous.

The Lord knoweth the days of the upright: and their inheritance shall be forever.

They shall not be ashamed in the evil time: and in the days of famine they shall be satisfied.

But the wicked shall perish, and the enemies of the Lord *shall be* as the fat of lambs: they shall consume; into smoke shall they consume away.

The wicked borroweth, and payeth not again: but the righteous showeth mercy, and giveth.

For *such as be* blessed of him shall inherit the earth; and *they that be* cursed of him shall be cut off.

The steps of a *good* man are ordered by the Lord: and he delighteth in his way.

Though he fall, he shall not be utterly cast down: for the Lord upholdeth *him with* his hand.

I have been young, and *now* am old; yet have I not seen the righteous forsaken, nor his seed begging bread.

He is ever merciful, and lendeth; and his seed *is* blessed.

Depart from evil, and do good; and dwell for evermore.

For the Lord loveth judgement, and forsaketh not his saints; they are preserved for ever: but the seed of the wicked shall be cut off.

The righteous shall inherit the land and dwell therein for ever.

The mouth of the righteous speaketh wisdom, and his tongue talketh of judgement.

The law of his God *is* in his heart; none of his steps shall slide.

The wicked watcheth the righteous, and seeketh to slay him.

The Lord will not leave him in his hand, nor condemn him when he is judged.

Wait on the Lord, and keep his way, and he shall exalt thee to inherit the land: when the wicked are cut off, thou shalt see *it*.

I have seen the wicked in great power, and spreading himself like a green bay-tree.

Yet he passed away, and lo, he *was* not: yea, I sought him, but he could not be found.

Mark the perfect *man*, and behold the upright: for the end of *that* man *is* peace.

But the transgressors shall be destroyed together: the end of the wicked shall be cut off.

But the salvation of the righteous *is* of the Lord: *he is* their strength in the time of trouble.

And the Lord shall help them, and deliver them: he shall deliver them from the wicked, and save them, because they trust in him.

DANIEL DEFOE

DANIEL DEFOE (English, *ca.* 1660-1731). Most celebrated for *The Surprising Adventures of Robinson Crusoe,* now a children's classic, but primarily a journalist and politician. Served two years in jail for political dissent. Forerunners of the early novel and modern realism: *Moll Flanders, Journal of the Plague Year, Roxana.*

IN DEFENCE OF HIS RIGHT

A GENTLEMAN of a very good estate married a lady of also a good fortune, and had one son by her, and one daughter, and no more, and after a few years his lady died. He soon married a second venter; and his second wife, though of an inferior quality and fortune to the former, took upon her to discourage and discountenance his children by his first lady, and made the family very uncomfortable, both to the children and to their father also.

The first thing of consequence which this conduct of the mother-in-law produced in the family, was that the son, who began to be a man, asked the father's leave to go abroad to travel. The mother-in-law, though willing enough to be rid of the young man, yet because it would require something considerable to support his expenses abroad, violently opposed it, and brought his father also to refuse him after he had freely given him his consent.

This so affected the young gentleman, that after using all the dutiful applications to his father that he could possibly do, as well by himself as by some other relations, but to no purpose; and being a little encouraged by an uncle, who was brother to his mother, his father's first lady, he resolved to go abroad without leave, and accordingly did so.

What part of the world he travelled into I do not remember; it seems his father had constantly intelligence from him for some time, and was prevailed with to make him a reasonable allowance for his subsistence, which the young gentleman always drew bills for, and they were honourably paid; but after some time, the mother-in-law prevailing at home, one of his bills of exchange was refused, and being protested, was sent back without acceptance; upon which he drew no more, nor did he write any more letters, or his father hear anything from him for upwards of four years, or thereabout.

Upon this long silence, the mother-in-law made her advantage several ways; she first intimated to his father that he must needs be dead; and consequently, his estate should be settled upon her eldest son (for she had several children). His father withstood the motion very firmly, but the wife harassed him with her importunities; and she argued upon two points against him, I mean the son.

First, if he was dead, then there was no room to object, her son being heir at law.

Secondly, if he was not dead, his behaviour to his father in not writing for so long a time was inexcusable, and he ought to resent it, and settle the estate as if he were dead; that nothing could be more disobliging, and his father ought to depend upon it that he was dead, and treat him as if he was so; for he that would use a father so, should be taken for one dead, as to his filial relation, and be treated accordingly.

His father, however, stood out a long time, and told her that he could not answer it to his conscience; that there might happen many things in the world, which might render his son unable to write; that he might be taken by the Turks, and carried into slavery; or he might be among the Persians or Arabians (which it seems was the case), and so could not get any letters conveyed; and that he could not be satisfied to disinherit him, till he knew whether he had reason for it or no, or whether his son had offended him or no.

These answers, however just, were far from stopping her impor-tunities, which she carried on so far, that she gave him no rest, and it made an unquiet family; she carried it very ill to him, and in a word, made her children do so too; and the gentleman was so wearied out with it, that once or twice he came to a kind of consent to do it, but his heart failed him, and then he fell back again and refused.

However, her having brought him so near it, was an encourage-ment to her to go on with her restless solicitations, till at last he came thus far to a provisional agreement, that if he did not hear from his son by such a time, or before it, he would consent to a re-settling the estate.

She was not well satisfied with the conditional agreement, but being able to obtain no other, she was obliged to accept of it as it was; though, as she often told him, she was far from being satisfied with it as to the time, for he had fixed it for four years, as above.

He grew angry at her telling him so, and answered, that she ought to be very well satisfied with it, for that it was time little enough, as his son's circumstances might be.

Well, she teased him however so continually, that at last she brought him down to one year: but before she brought him to that, she told him one day in heat, that she hoped his ghost would one time or other appear to him, and tell him that he was dead, and that he ought to do justice to his other children, for he should never come to claim the estate.

When he came, so much against his will, to consent to shorten the time to one year, he told her that he hoped his son's ghost, though he was not dead, would come to her, and tell her he was alive, before the time expired. "For why," says he, "may not in-jured souls walk while embodied, as well as afterwards?"

It happened one evening after this, that they had a most violent family quarrel upon this subject, when on a sudden a hand ap-peared at a casement, endeavouring to open it; but as all the iron casements used in former times opened outward, but hasped and fastened themselves in the inside, so the hand seemed to try to open the casement, but could not. The gentleman did not see it, but his wife did, and she presently started up, as if she was frightened, and, forgetting the quarrel they had upon their hands: "Lord bless me!" says she, "there are thieves in the garden." Her husband ran im-mediately to the door of the room they sat in, and opening it, looked out.

"There's nobody in the garden," says he; so he clapped the door to again, and came back.

"I am sure," says she, "I saw a man there."

"It must be the devil then," says he, "for I'm sure there's nobody in the garden."

"I'll swear," says she, "I saw a man put his hand up to open the casement; but finding it fast, and I suppose," adds she, "seeing us in the room, he walked off."

"It is impossible he could be gone," says he; "did not I run to the door immediately? and you know the garden walls on both sides hinder him going."

"Pry'thee," says she angrily, "I an't drunk nor in a dream, I know a man when I see him, and 'tis not dark, the sun is not quite down."

"You're only frighted with shadows," says he (very full of ill-nature): "folks generally are so that are haunted with an evil conscience: it may be 'twas the devil."

"No, no, I'm not soon frightened," says she; "if 'twas the devil, 'twas the ghost of your son: it may be come to tell you he was gone to the devil, and you might give your estate to your eldest bastard, since you won't settle it on the lawful heir."

"If it was my son," says he, "he's come to tell us he's alive, I warrant you, and to ask how you can be so much a devil to desire me to disinherit him;" and with these words: "Alexander," says he aloud, repeating it twice, starting up out of his chair, "if you are alive, show yourself, and don't let me be insulted thus every day with your being dead."

At those very words, the casement which the hand had been seen at by the mother, opened of itself, and his son Alexander looked in with a full face and staring directly upon the mother with an angry countenance, cried "Here," and then vanished in a moment.

The woman that was so stout before, shrieked out in a most dismal manner, so that the whole house was alarmed; her maid ran into the parlour, to see what was the matter, but her mistress was fainted away in her chair.

She was not fallen upon the ground, because it being a great easy chair, she sunk a little back against the side of the chair, and help coming immediately in, they kept her up; but it was not till a great while after, that she recovered enough to be sensible of anything.

Her husband ran immediately to the parlour door, and opening

296

it, went into the garden, but there was nothing; and after that he ran to another door that opened from the house into the garden, and then to two other doors which opened out of his garden, one into the stable-yard, and another into the field beyond the garden, but found them all fast shut and barred; but on one side was his gardener, and a boy, drawing the rolling-stone: he asked them if anybody else had been in the garden, but they both constantly affirmed nobody had been there; and they were both rolling a gravel-walk near the house.

Upon this he comes back into the room, sits him down again, and said not one word for a good while; the woman and servants being busy all the while, and in a hurry, endeavouring to recover his wife.

After some time she recovered so far as to speak, and the first words she said, were:

"L—d bless me! what was it?"

"Nay," says her husband, "it was Alexander, to be sure."

With that she fell into a fit, and screamed and shrieked out again most terribly.

Her husband not thinking that would have affected her, did what he could to persuade her out of it again; but that would not do, and they were obliged to carry her to bed, and get some help to her; but she continued ill for several days after.

However, this put an end for some considerable time to her solicitations about his disinheriting her son-in-law.

But time, that hardens the mind in cases of a worse nature, wore this off also by degrees, and she began to revive the old cause again, though not at first so eagerly as before.

Nay, he used her a little hardly upon it too, and if ever they had any words about it he would bid her hold her tongue, or that if she talked any more upon that subject, he would call Alexander again to open the casement.

This aggravated things much; and though it terrified her a great while, yet at length she was so exasperated, that she told him she believed he dealt with the devil, and that he had sold himself to the devil only to be able to fright his wife.

He jested with her, and told her any man would be beholden to the devil to hush a noisy woman, and that he was very glad he had found the way to do it, whatever it cost him.

She was so exasperated at this, that she threatened him if he played any more of his hellish arts with her she would have him indicted for a wizard, and having a familiar; and she could prove it, she said, plain enough, for that he had raised the devil on purpose to fright his wife.

The fray parted that night with ill words and ill nature enough, but he little thought she intended as she said, and the next day he had forgot it all, and was as good-humoured as if nothing had happened.

But he found his wife chagrined and disturbed very much, full of resentment, and threatening him with what she resolved to do.

However, he little thought she intended him the mischief she had in her head, offering to talk friendly to her; but she rejected it with scorn, and told him she would be as good as her word, for she would not live with a man that should bring the devil into the room as often as he thought fit, to murder his wife.

He strove to pacify her by fair words, but she told him she was in earnest with him: and, in a word, she was in earnest; for she goes away to a justce, and making an affidavit that her husband had a familiar spirit, and that she went in danger of her life, she obtained a warrant for him to be apprehended.

In short, she brought home the warrant, showed it to him, and told him she had not given it into the hands of an officer, because he should have the liberty to go voluntarily before the justice of the peace, and if he thought fit to let her know when he would be ready, she would be so too, and would get some of her own friends to go along with her.

He was surprised at this, for he little thought she had been in earnest with him, and endeavoured to pacify her by all the ways possible; but she found she had frightened him heartily, and so indeed she had, for though the thing had nothing in it of guilt, yet he found it might expose him very much, and being loath to have such a thing brought upon the stage against him, he used all the entreaties with her that he was able, and begged her not to do it.

But the more he humbled himself the more she triumphed over him; and carrying things to an unsufferable height of insolence, she told him at last, she would make him do justice, as she called it; that she was sure she could have him punished if he continued obstinate, and she would not be exposed to witchcraft and sorcery; for she did not know to what length he might carry it.

To bring the story to a conclusion; she got the better of him to such a degree, that he offered to refer the thing to indifferent persons, friends on both sides; and they met several times, but could bring it to no conclusion. His friends said there was nothing in it, and they would not have him comply with anything upon the pretence of it; that he called for his son, and somebody opened the casement and cried, "Here"; that there was not the least evidence of witchcraft in that, and insisted that she could make nothing of it.

Her friends carried it high, instructed by her: she offered to swear that he had threatened her before with his son's ghost; that now he visibly raised a spectre; for that calling upon his son, who was dead to be sure, the ghost immediately appeared; that he could not have called up the devil thus to personate his son, if he had not dealt with the devil himself, and had a familiar spirit, and that this was of dangerous consequence to her.

Upon the whole, the man wanted courage to stand it, and was afraid of being exposed; so that he was grievously perplexed, and knew not what to do.

When she found him humbled as much as she could desire, she told him, if he would do her justice, as she called it (that is to say, settle his estate upon her son), she would put it up, on condition that he should promise to fright her no more with raising the devil.

That part of her proposal exasperated him again, and he upbraided her with the slander of it, and told her he defied her, and she might do her worst.

Thus it broke off all treaty, and she began to threaten him again; however, at length she brought him to comply, and he gives a writing under his hand to her, some of her friends being by, promising that he would comply if his son did not arrive, or send an account of himself, within four months.

She was satisfied with this, and they were all made friends again, and accordingly he gave the writing; but when he delivered it to her in presence of her two arbitrators, he took the liberty to say to her, with a grave and solemn kind of speech:

"Look you," says he, "you have worried me into this agreement by your fiery temper, and I have signed it against justice, conscience, and reason; but depend upon it, I shall never perform it."

One of the arbitrators said, "Why, sir, this is doing nothing; for if you resolve not to perform it, what signifies the writing? why do you promise what you do not intend shall be done? This will but kindle a new flame to begin with, when the time fixed expires."

"Why," says he, "I am satisfied in my mind that my son is alive."

"Come, come," says his wife, speaking to the gentleman that had argued with her husband, "let him sign the agreement, and let me alone to make him perform the conditions."

"Well," says her husband, "you shall have the writing, and you shall be let alone; but I am satisfied you will never ask me to perform it; and yet I am no wizard," adds he, "as you have wickedly suggested."

She replied, that she would prove that he dealt with the devil, for that he raised an evil spirit by only calling his son by name; and so began to tell the story of the hand and the casement.

"Come," says the man to the gentleman that was her friend, "give me the pen; I never dealt with but one devil in my life, and there it sits," turning to his wife; "and now I have made an agreement with her that none but the devil would desire any man to sign, and I will sign it; I say, give me the pen, but she nor all the devils in hell will ever be able to get it executed; remember I say so."

She began to open at him, and so a new flame would have been kindled, but the gentlemen moderated between them, and her husband setting his hand to the writing put an end to the fray at that time.

At the end of four months she challenged the performance, and a day was appointed, and her two friends that had been the arbitrators were invited to dinner upon this occasion, believing that her husband would have executed the deeds; and accordingly the writings were brought all forth, engrossed, and read over; and some old writings, which at her marriage were signed by her trustees, in order to her quitting some part of the estate to her son, were also brought to be cancelled: the husband being brought over, by fair means or foul, I know not whether, to be in a humour, for peace' sake, to execute the deeds, and disinherit his son; alleging that, indeed, if he was dead it was no wrong to him, and if he was alive, he was very unkind and undutiful to his father, in not letting him hear from him in all that time.

Besides, it was urged that if he should at any time afterwards appear to be alive, his father (who had very much increased, it seems, in his wealth) was able to give him another fortune, and to make him a just satisfaction for the loss he should sustain by the paternal estate.

Upon these considerations, I say, they had brought over the poor low-spirited husband to be almost willing to comply; or, at least, willing or unwilling, it was done, and, as above, they met accordingly.

When they had discoursed upon all the particulars, and, as above, the new deeds were read over, she or her husband took the old writings up to cancel them; I think the story says it was the wife, not her husband, that was just going to tear off the seal, when on a sudden they heard a rushing noise in the parlour where they sat, as if somebody had come in at the door of the room which opened from the hall, and went through the room towards the garden door, which was shut.

They were all surprised at it, for it was very distinct, but they saw nothing. The woman turned pale, and was in a terrible fright; however, as nothing was seen, she recovered a little, but began to ruffle her husband again.

"What," says she, "have you laid your plot to bring up more devils again?"

The man sat composed, though he was under no little surprise too.

One of her gentlemen said to him, "What is the meaning of all this?"

"I protest, sir," says he, "I know no more of it than you do."

"What can it be then?" said the other gentleman.

"I cannot conceive," says he, "for I am utterly unacquainted with such things."

"Have you heard nothing from your son?" says the gentleman.

"Not one word," says the father; "no, not the least word these five years."

"Have you wrote nothing to him," says the gentleman, "about this transaction?"

"Not a word," says he; "for I know not where to direct a letter to him."

"Sir," says the gentleman, "I have heard much of apparitions, but I never saw them in my life, nor did I ever believe there was anything of reality in them; and, indeed, I saw nothing now; but the passing of some body, or spirit, or something, across the room just now is plain; I heard it distinctly. I believe there is some unseen thing in the room, as much as if I saw it."

"Nay," says the other arbitrator, "I felt the wind of it as it passed by me. Pray," adds he, turning to the husband, "do you see nothing yourself?"

"No, upon my word," says he, "not the least appearance in the world."

"I have been told," says the first arbitrator, "and have read, that an apparition may be seen by some people and be invisible to others, though all in the same room together."

However, the husband solemnly protested to them all that he saw nothing.

"Pray, sir," says the first arbitrator, "have you seen anything at any other time, or heard any voices or noises, or had any dreams about this matter?"

"Indeed," says he, "I have several times dreamed my son is alive, and that I had spoken with him; and once that I asked him why he was so undutiful, and slighted me so, as not to let me hear of him in so many years, seeing he knew it was in my power to disinherit him."

"Well, sir, and what answer did he give?"

"I never dreamed so far on as to have him answer; it always waked me."

"And what do you think of it yourself," says the arbitrator; "do you think he's dead?"

"No, indeed," says the father, "I do believe in my conscience he's alive, as much as I believe I am alive myself; and I am going to do as wicked a thing of its kind as ever any man did."

"Truly," says the second arbitrator, "it begins to shock me, I don't know what to say to it; I don't care to meddle any more with it, I don't like driving men to act against their consciences."

With this the wife, who, as I said, having a little recovered her spirits, and especially encouraged because she saw nothing, started up: "What's all this discourse to the purpose," says she; "is it not all agreed already? what do we come here for?"

"Nay," says the first arbitrator, "I think we meet now not to inquire into why it is done, but to execute things according to agreement, and what are we frighted at?"

"I'm not frighted," says the wife, "not I; come," says she to her husband, haughtily, "sign the deed; I'll cancel the old writings if forty devils were in the room;" and with that she takes up one of the deeds, and went to tear off the seal.

That moment the same casement flew open again, though it was fast in the inside, just as it was before; and the shadow of a body was seen, as standing in the garden without, and the head reaching up to the casement, the face looking into the room, and staring directly at the woman with a stern and an angry countenance: "Hold," said the spectre, as if speaking to the woman, and immediately clapped the casement to again, and vanished.

It is impossible to describe here the consternation this second apparition put the whole company into; the wife, who was so bold just before, that she would do it though forty devils were in the room, screamed out like a woman in fits, and let the writing fall out of her hands: the two arbitrators were exceedingly terrified, but not so much as the rest; but one of them took up the award which they had signed, in which they. awarded the husband to execute the deed to dispose of the estate from the son.

"I dare say," said he, "be the spirit a good spirit or a bad, it will not be against cancelling this;" so he tore his name out of the award, and so did the other, by his example, and both of them got up from their seats, and said they would have no more to do in it.

But that which was most unexpected of all was that the man himself was so frighted, that he fainted away; notwithstanding it was, as it might be said, in his favour.

This put an end to the whole affair at that time; and, as I understand by the sequel, it did so for ever.

The story has many particulars more in it, too long to trouble you with: but two particulars, which are to the purpose, I must not omit, viz.:

1. That in about four or five months more after this second apparition, the man's son arrived from the East Indies, whither he had gone four years before in a Portuguese ship from Lisbon.

2. That upon being particularly inquired of about these things, and especially whether he had any knowledge of them, or any apparition to him, or voices, or other intimation as to what was doing in England, relating to him; he affirmed constantly that he had not, except that once he dreamed his father had written him an angry letter, threatening him that if he did not come home he would disinherit him and leave him not one shilling. But he added, that he never did receive any such letter from his father in his life, or from any one else.

RICHARD DEHMEL

RICHARD DEHMEL (German, 1863-1920). Ardent anti-traditionalist, who went to extremes opposing prejudice and convention. A virtuoso in poetry (*Zwei Menschen*), theater (*Die Menschenfreunde*), and the essay (*Gott und die Welt*).

THE SILENT TOWN

A town lies in the valley,
A pale day fades and dies;
And it will not be long before
Neither moon nor starlight,
Night only fills the skies.

From all the mountain ridges
Creeps mist, and swathes the town;
No farm, no house, no wet red roof
Can pierce the thickly woven woof,
And scarce even spires and bridges.

But as the wanderer shudders,
Deep down a streak of light rejoices
His heart; and, through the smoke and haze,
Children's voices
Begin a gentle hymn of praise.

HELPLESSNESS

But when thou hadst departed,
I grew so lonely-hearted,
    I longed for thee so sore.
I stood with fingers aching,
As though I should lose thee shaking
    The handle of thy barred and bolted door.

And through the panes between us
I begged with eyes as keen as
    A beggar's in the South;
But up the steps thou wentest,
No backward look thou bentest,
    Thou didst not call me back unto thy mouth.

With senses stunned I hearkened,
Heard but in the passage darkened
   The rattling of thy keys;
And then the shadows caught me,
That in the park had sought me,
   When we two saw the moon sink o'er the trees.

ANGRY SEA

Thus once again! Through fog and howling squall:
   The sails shook, and the sailors shouted loudly;
At the bowsprit stood the water like a tall
   Tower: I felt your fear in my knees: and proudly
Your unknown face beside me gloomed.

Yet once again your eye upon me frowned,
   Your hair was like a flame behind you sweeping,
While wrestled in the waves a sound
   As of a little child that will be weeping—
You warded me no more.

You let my arms around your shoulder lie,
   Your wild wet hair my greedy mouth was lashing,
Our kiss was wonderfully sweetened by
   The foam of great salt waves about us crashing—
Then I in joy cried out.

Thus once again! What shadow chills thy brow?
   Or does the open ocean make thee craven?
The sea will whip thee warm! Come soon, come now!
   The ferry is dancing in the foggy haven—
Out! To the heights!

FROM A SAD BREAST

The roses still are like a flame,
   The dark leaves gently shake;
   I in the grass am grown awake,
O that you came,
   For the deep midnight's sake.

305

The moon is hid by the garden door,
  O'er which its light is shed
On the lake with willow-shadowed shore,
  In the moist clover I bury my head;
I never loved you so before!

As now I know I have not known,
  For all that ever I caressed
  Your neck, and blind your secretest
Being enjoyed, why you would groan,
  When I o'erflowed, from your sad breast.

Had you but seen yon glowworms glide,
  Two glowworms and their light the same!
Never again will I leave your side!
  O that you came!
  The roses still are like a flame.

KNOW'ST THOU YET?

Know'st thou yet, how pale, how white,
When I lay in eves of Maytime,
After kisses of the daytime,
Poured out at thy feet before thee,
Daffodillies trembled o'er me?

Then in deep June's azure night,
Know'st thou yet, how soft and seething,
When we, tired of wild caresses,
Wove around us thy wild tresses,
Daffodillies scents were breathing?

At thy feet again are gleaming,
When the silvery gloamings shimmer,
When the nights of azure glimmer,
Daffodillies scents are streaming.
Know'st thou yet, how hot? how white?

A GRAVE

These are the evenings prematurely pale.
  The dahlias that in the sunlight shone
Like last frail roses, now are standing stale,
  Rosettes of stone whose colour has grown wan.
The swaths of mist across the churchyard trail.

Come, sister. Yonder hedge of brass you see
   Rails round a lady withered in her spring.
   She loved me well. Come home, I am shivering.
Life gave her nothing but her own heart: she
Did good in silence, suffering silently.

THE LABORER

We have a bed, and a baby too,
My wife!
We have work besides, we have work for two,
And we have the sun, and the wind, and the rain,
And we only need one little thing more,
To be as free as the birds that soar:
Only time.

When we go through the fields on the Sunday morn,
My child,
And far and away o'er the bending corn,
We see the swarming swallows flash,
Then we only need a bit of a dress,
To have the birds' bright loveliness:
Only time.

The storm is gathering black as jet,
Feel the poor.
Only a little eternity yet;
We need nothing else, my wife, my child,
Except all things through us that thrive,
To be bold as the birds through the air that drive:
Only time!

HARVEST SONG

There stands a field of golden sheaves,
To the very edge of the world it heaves.
   Grind, mill, grind!

The wind falls in the wide land,
Many mills at the sky-edge stand.
   Grind, mill, grind!

There comes a sunset dark and red,
Many poor people are crying for bread.
    Grind, mill, grind!

The night holds in its lap the storm,
To-morrow the men to work will swarm.
    Grind, mill, grind!

Clean are the fields swept, never again
A man shall cry in hunger-pain.
    Grind, mill, grind!

THREATENING PROSPECT

The sky is whirling, the land flies fast;
  And while, by the express shocked and shaken,
Furrow on furrow whizzes past,
  Thee thy shivering limbs awaken:
    The sun of morning comes.

Through the hung mist with toiling wings
  Break herded crows that autumn is thinning,
While thick upon the dunged field clings
  The smoke of workshops just beginning;
    The sun of morning comes.

Under the trailing gray crape lies
  A chain of slag-heaps filling acres,
Chimney on chimney scales the skies,
  Standing by coffins fearsome wakers;
    The sun of morning comes.

Along the rapid landscape rolls
  A pair of road-dikes from the horizon,
Framed in by gnarled and weathered boles
  Of apple-trees a pale sheen lies on;
    The sun of morning comes.

Now sweeps thy gaze the opposite verge,
  Where boughs, of fruit despoiled, are showing,
And suddenly tree on tree they surge,
  With crumpled leafage fire-red glowing:
    The day is there.

GRAZIA DELEDDA

GRAZIA DELEDDA (Italian, 1875-1936). Considered by many Italy's greatest woman novelist. Nobel Prize winner, 1926. Regionalist of the island of Sardinia. A woman of great sympathy and understanding for the psychology of the little people. Has been compared with Thomas Hardy. Novels: *Elias Portolu, Cenere, Nostalgie.*

THE OPEN DOOR

ON holy Wednesday Simon Barca went to confession. He was desperate, and a desperate man is glad to remember God, as an ill man the doctor.

So Simon went to the Basilica, a national monument which still lends a richness to the once prosperous countryside, and where at that hour of the morning, only a few monks from the nearby monastery were celebrating Mass, in chapels where the damp had spread a green film over the ancient frescoes. The peasant women, with hoods over their heads and coarse skirts swathed tightly round them and laced up with thin silver chains, were singing the Rosary in their Latin dialect: their voices faded away in the airy depths of the Basilica as amongst the ruins of a temple; through the wide open doors a wild fragrance of spurge and budding alder trees wafted in from the valley. Simon went to confess himself to the prior, who filled the little confessional with his huge body, snoring and puffing away in there like a bear in a cage.

"Father, I'm a lost man: I want to kill some fellow Christian, I feel so desperate. I have committed the worst sins. Until a little time ago I was the dutiful son of a family, the only son, Father. At twenty I still slept with my mother; but she was hardly dead when bad companions gathered round me like flies round a raisin pip; and my uncle, priest though he is, turned me out of the house instead of helping me, and now when he sees me he looks the other way. Yes, I have committed the very worst sins: I have gambled, drunk, gone with bad women, consulted witches, blasphemed, wished my neighbour ill, coveted others' belongings, committed . . . yes, Father . . . I forged a signature, and the bill of exchange falls due in a few days . . . and I shall have to go to prison and I shall be dishonoured. . . . It is all the fault of bad companions, and they have deserted me now: and every door is closed against me . . there is not one open door, now, for me! But I'm repentant,

Father, and will go to prison and atone, but give me the good Lord's absolution, so that I may fulfil the Easter duties and suffer innocent like Christ our Saviour."

The prior wheezed on and made no answer. Simon, his thin, dark rogue's face in his hands, breathed hard too, and thought:

"Perhaps he's scandalised: perhaps he is pleased to hear that the real cause of my ruin is my uncle Barca the priest. Monks and priests can't bear the sight of each other. Perhaps, to spite my uncle, he'll give me the money to pay the bill."

But the prior snored and said nothing: his warm breath blew on Simon's face. Tired of waiting, the penitent roused himself from his dream of expiation and his malicious thoughts; his big eyes, dark and childish, contracted, and a bitter smile deepened the hallows in his shaven cheeks. The prior was asleep. Ah, even God is deaf to the cries of a despairing sinner.

*   *   *

Simon stole away very quietly, his heart sad, his mind a ferment of ugly thoughts. The proceedings of the day were starting round the great altar, and the priest Barca's mobile voice could already be heard chanting with trills and shakes. People were coming and going: now men were arriving too; they were tall, with long square beards as in Moses' time, dressed in leather jackets and short serge trousers, full like skirts. Some seemed like prophets, they were so solemn, calm and unaffected; others were small, lean as our Simon, hardened by the wind and by evil thoughts.

The women, too, recalled those in the Bible. Simon met one in the court of the Basilica, a tall dry widow, with an olive face and huge greenish eyes, swathed in her almost priestly clothes as in a black sheath, and she only wanted a bunch of ears of corn to be a second mother-in-law of Boaz. Simon shuddered when he saw her; he shuddered with hatred, for the woman was a kind of housekeeper for Barca, and he shuddered at the sudden thought that at that moment there was no one in his uncle's house: and as if night had suddenly fallen, he began to see things and people in a mist, and he stalked along by the walls, stumbling against the stones which lay about the rough roads. So he found himself before his house, like a surviving bit of a tower, and only then the light seemed to flood back all around him.

He went in, and soon after, at the little window of the first and only storey, his face appeared, pensive as that of a general forming a plan of battle from the height of a fortress. Simon's field of battle was the limited picture spread beneath him: it consisted of the country road crossed by a stream, where rushes and grass grew as in open country; the widow's little house opposite his; the big, dark house of his uncle the priest, and its yard, beside the widow's, shut in by a little chapel with a kitchen garden so overgrown with weeds and shaded by cypress trees that it seemed the corner of a cemetery. Simon thought how he had spent his childhood and his youth jumping the wall between his uncle's yard and the chapel's garden; he wondered if the time had come for repeating the feat, only the other way about, from the church garden into his uncle's yard. No one else was so familiar with the hidden corners, the passages, the twistings and turnings.

He shut his eyes, and saw the jutting out piece of the ground floor wall where the priest Barca used to put the big key of his room before going out; he opened them again, and, agitated, remembered that vast, rather mysterious room, lighted by a tiny lamp, filled with sacred images and bound books. Here, as a child, he had more than once surprised his uncle, in shirt and skull-cap, counting over gold pieces like a wizard, or skilfully piercing his name on bank-notes with a pin. One day, crawling on the floor, crouching down to imitate a wild-boar, Simon had moved one of the floor blocks, and under it had found a box full of money. Now he recalled those times as a prisoner remembers his days of freedom . . . . .

For three days he remained almost continually at the window, only leaving it to eat a mouthful of rye bread and some goat's cheese. Yes, while his uncle stored his money under the floor-blocks, he had to live like a poor shepherd; his house was empty, deserted, without furniture (he had sold it), even without doors (sold as well), and the spiders spun their webs over the rough boar's skin trunk in which he kept his poor mother's wedding dress and widow's weeds.

To console himself he would drink a small glass of brandy and go back to the window.

From below he smelt the fragrance of the cakes the women were getting ready for Easter, and he saw the smoke rise from wood or tiled roofs. Already a nightingale was singing in the valley, and the fluffy April clouds floated by over the chapel garden, white as bits of girls' clothing blown off some hedge by the wind.

On Holy Thursday the widow left his uncle's house and opened

311

the chapel, usually closed. Helped by the other women of the neighbourhood she pulled down the Christ, laid it on the ground between four lights and four dishes of sprouting corn, and so formed the Sepulchre. But everyone was going to the Basilica, where they were celebrating the Passion and two real thieves (at least they had once been condemned for theft) were tied to the cross beside Christ. From his window Simon saw his uncle himself, short, fat, prancing, and the tall widow, dry and stiff, walk one after the other towards the Basilica. He went down, but once in the street he leant his shoulder against the wall and stood for a long time motionless and pensive, listening to the far-off chanting of the procession. It was dusk; the new moon was sinking behind the violet tinted hills, in a greenish sky, and the evening star was rising, and seemed as if it would come along the streets of the village like Mary and Christ.

"In a few moments the procession will be here," thought Simon, and moved; but he walked close by the wall; he was afraid of going past the dead Christ stretched on the floor between the lights and the corn shoots.

Suddenly, coming to his uncle's door, he shivered. The door was open; someone must be in the house and it was useless to go on. He turned back and once more leant against the wall. But who could be in his uncle's house? The servants, peasants and shepherds, only came back on Saturday evening; the priest and the widow were in the procession. He went forward again to the door, knocked, called: "Basila! Basila!"

His voice lost itself inside the already dark house as in a cave. He went in, closed the door, flung himself up the stairs, traversed the narrow passages, found the jutting-out wall, found the key, opened, and was in his uncle's room. He seemed to be in a dream. The window was shut; a light like those round the dead Christ was burning before the picture of the Holy Martyrs. There was a crowd of them, men, women. old people. children, but all looking up with gentle faces, and Simon was not afraid of them. By the greenish glow of the light he bent and began to feel the floor blocks one by one, like a bricklayer with the job of mending the floor; but not one of the bricks moved, and he stood up and passed his hand across his forehead, wet with cold sweat.

The chanting of the procession reached his ears, and he shivered all over. He leant against his uncle's old bed, and the bed moved aside. creaking and shaking as if seized by the robber's own terror and perturbation. Then Simon looked at the block under the foot of the bed, and it seemed to him that it moved: he bent and pulled it up with his nails, and in the space beneath, buried in the dust, he found an iron box with two thousand lire notes in it.

* * *

On Easter Day Barca the priest discharged the widow Basila, and immediately scandalous tales spread over the whole country. It was common knowledge that Barca had lost many thousand lire, some said two, some three, some twenty; and that Basila had forgotten and left his house door open on Good Friday. The police officer went to the priest's house; but the priest tried to appear unconcerned, clapped his hands and said:

"Trifles! miserable trifles!"

On Tuesday the widow's little house was searched with care, and she was arrested and set free again the next day. There was no evidence against her; but the inhabitants or rather the families in the district split into two parties; the men defended Basila saying that perhaps she had really forgotten the open door, so making it easy for any thief to go in; the women sneered: "And in a few short minutes the robber made himself at home and helped himself?"

Finally people stopped this talk; but the widow was looked down on by everyone. She was given no more work; she stopped going to church and lived in poverty in her wretched house. Simon used to see her, always upright on the threshold, her face pale and sad, but her great greenish eyes turned upwards like those of the Holy Martyrs.

* * *

Simon paid the false bill of exchange and bought back his doors and his cloak. No one was surprised, for like every gambler, he often had these ups and downs of fortune, and only his creditor knew about the bill. What astonished everyone was to see him suddenly change his way of living. He stopped going with bad women and gave up his disreputable companions, he went to church and nodded to his uncle. But his uncle persisted in turning away when he saw him, and one day when Simon went up to him determined to stop him and kiss his hand, he not only ignored his greeting but literally turned his back on him.

Simon stood petrified. He leant against the wall and remained fixed there, overcome by a terrible thought.

"He knows!"

Then he went to the widow Basila and said to her:

"Do you think you could bake, and wash, and mend my clothes for me? Fix your own wage."

The widow was standing up before a dead fire combing her hair; it was thick and very long, of a golden chestnut colour, and made a halo of martyrdom round her olive face; but when she saw Simon she covered her cheeks and breast with it like a veil, and shook her head in a threatening way, whilst her greenish eyes flashed beneath her knitted eyebrows, thick and black.

"You have someone already to bake and wash for you! Get out of here!"

He went like a whipped dog and leant against his wall again.

"She knows!"

He spent the days in this way, leaning against the wall, often whittling with a little knife at his walnut stick. or some plug of straw. but more often doing nothing at all. Never before, even at his worst times, had he lived so aimlessly. He was haunted by the widow's threatening eyes, and felt an almost physical ill when he thought that Basila had fallen into poverty and ill-repute through his fault; some nights he had fearsome dreams; the trunk with his mother's clothes in it seemed a live boar, and fixed staring eyes on the doors bought back with that money.

The summer passed, and in the autumn he moved his seat along the wall, seeking the sun. From the new place he saw the widow Basila more clearly, seated too in the sun spinning or sewing, barefooted, and sad as a slave.

The winter was long and severe. The poor people suffered much from hunger, and Barca and a lady who lived in the neighbourhood sent bread and vegetables to all the needy except the widow. For Christmas a lady with whom Simon had often wandered about, sent him a present of a ram's leg. He already had a little pig and a lamb: and thinking that Basila had nothing but potatoes, sent her the ram's leg, and to his astonishment found that she did not refuse the gift. Then all the rest of the winter, seized by a mania for expiation, he went on sending her gifts, often depriving himself of some real necessity.

Spring came again: once more the women put bowls of corn to sprout in cupboards, to adorn the sepulchres. Holy Friday evening Simon went to the procession and afterwards stood for some time in the usual spot, beside the wall, in the warm. whisper-filled evening. A yellowish glow was coming from the crack of Basila's door, and Simon stared with queer eyes at that light which seemed mysterious to him. Suddenly he went and knocked and asked the woman if she would marry him.

*   *   *

People talked, then stopped talking. After all, Basila was only ten years older than Simon, and a good housewife: indeed, before long the young man's house was transformed, clean, with the stove always alight and the little yard swarming with fowls. Simon was seen on a horse again, as in the time when his mother was alive; they all said that he had married Basila to spite his uncle.

He was not in love with his wife, but he followed her advice and was glad at having lifted a weight off his conscience, and married a wise woman. The latter went to church again and talked in a brief manner, and it seemed to Simon that he had gone back to the happy times with his mother when he, still innocent at twenty, went to bed with her and repeated the prayers she suggested to him.

One day, several months after his marriage, the woman who had sent him the ram's leg called him as he was passing by her door, and asked him to lend her a hundred crowns.

He began to laugh: "If I had a hundred crowns I should set out to go round the world."

"I'll pay you the interest, Simon Barca! I can pay; I'll give you twenty per cent, like the others."

"You are going mad, Mallena Porceu!"

"What, mad? Tell me you don't trust me, Simon Barca, but don't insult me. You and your wife have lent money for interest, at twenty per cent., to certain people. Why can't you give me some too? Or is it true what your uncle Barca says? That your wife gives the money without you knowing?"

Simon grew pale, but answered:

"My uncle's in his second childhood, and you're what you are!"

The following days he was seen again leaning against the wall, as in his dark times. He was asking himself ceaselessly: "Why was the door open?" and his brain was toiling and toiling, digging down deep into a black chasm, seeking the truth as the miner seeks gold in the bowels of the earth.

"She must have taken a good part of the money, and left the door open to make people think some robber had gone in. Oh, the sly old cat! . . ." he thought furiously. But before believing his own idea he wanted to make sure with his eyes themselves.

Again it was Good Friday evening, and Basila had gone to

315

church. Simon waited for that time so as to be free to search the whole house; but hunt as he might, in drawers, in lockers, in the mattresses, he found nothing.

He looked round, tired of searching and in the half-light the trunk which still contained his mother's clothes seemed again like a live boar. He tried to open it, but could not. Then he remembered that Basilà always kept the key with her. He went down to the kitchen, came back with an axe and began to strike at the trunk as if it were really a fierce boar. The lid came open. Simon knelt down and began to search; he found Basila's widow's clothes, and out of her black hood fluttered, silently, two, three, many bank-notes red, green, yellowish, like withered walnut leaves. Amongst the others was one of a thousand: he took it up, held it against the candle light and read Barca's name pierced on it with a pin. Then he began to curse and batter his head.

"But why did it happen to me? why me of all people?" he cried aloud.

Suddenly a sad, sweet song like a murmuring wood floated in from the road. Simon grew quiet and stood listening, his head bent and his eyes wide open, and as the procession approached, he shook and sweated as when he had leant against his uncle's old bed.

CHARLES DICKENS

CHARLES DICKENS (English, 1812-1870). Sentimental-realistic novelist, one of the great Victorians. Despised greed and injustice, chose his material from lower classes, usually with some object of reform. Prejudiced but influential. Most prolific, his characters famous in English-speaking world. *David Copperfield, A Tale of Two Cities, Great Expectations, Oliver Twist, Pickwick Papers, A Christmas Carol.*

THE CONVICT IN THE MARSHES

MY FATHER's family name being Pirrip and my Christian name Philip, my infant tongue could make of both names nothing longer or more explicit than Pip. So I called myself Pip, and came to be called Pip.

I give Pirrip as my father's family name, on the authority of his tombstone and my sister—Mrs. Joe Gargery, who married the black-smith. As I never saw my father or my mother, and never saw any likeness of either of them (for their days were long before the days of photographs), my first fancies regarding what they were like were unreasonably derived from their tombstones. The shape of the letters on my father's gave me an odd idea that he was a square, stout, dark man, with curly black hair. From the character and turn of the inscription, *"Also Georgiana, Wife of the Above,"* I drew a childish conclusion that my mother was freckled and sickly. To five little stone lozenges, each about a foot and a half long, which were arranged in a neat row beside their grave, and were sacred to the memory of five little brothers of mine—who gave up trying to get a living exceedingly early in that universal struggle—I am indebted for a belief I religiously entertained that they had all been born on their backs with their hands in their trousers pockets, and had never taken them out in this state of existence.

Ours was the marsh country, down by the river, within, as the river wound, twenty miles of the sea. My first most vivid and broad impression of the identity of things seems to me to have been gained on a memorable raw afternoon towards evening. At such a time I found out for certain that this bleak place overgrown with nettles was the churchyard; and that Philip Pirrip, late of this parish, and also Georgiana, wife of the above, were dead and buried; and that Alexander, Bartholomew, Abraham, Tobias, and Roger, infant children of the aforesaid, were also dead and buried; and that the dark flat wilderness beyond the churchyard, intersected with dikes and mounds and gates, with scattered cattle feeding on it, was the marshes; and that the low leaden line beyond was the river; and that the distant savage lair from which the wind was rushing was the sea; and that the small bundle of shivers growing afraid of it all and beginning to cry was Pip.

"Hold your noise!" cried a terrible voice, as a man started up from among the graves at the side of the church porch. "Keep still, you little devil, or I'll cut your throat!"

A fearful man, all in coarse gray, with a great iron on his leg. A man with no hat, and with broken shoes, and with an old rag tied round his head. A man who had been soaked in water, and smoth-ered in mud, and lamed by stones, and cut by flints, and stung by nettles and torn by briers; who limped, and shivered, and glared, and growled; and whose teeth chattered in his head as he seized me by the chin.

317

"Oh! Don't cut my throat, sir," I pleaded in terror. "Pray don't do it, sir."

"Tell us your name!" said the man. "Quick!"

"Pip, sir."

"Once more," said the man, staring at me. "Give it mouth!"

"Pip. Pip, sir."

"Show us where you live," said the man. "Pint out the place!"

I pointed to where our village lay, on the flat inshore among the alder trees and pollards, a mile or more from the church.

The man, after looking at me for a moment, turned me upside down and emptied my pockets. There was nothing in them but a piece of bread. When the church came to itself—for he was so sudden and strong that he made it go head over heels before me, and I saw the steeple under my feet—when the church came to itself, I say, I was seated on a high tombstone, trembling, while he ate the bread ravenously.

"You young dog," said the man, licking his lips, "what fat cheeks you ha' got."

I believed they were fat, though I was at that time undersized for my years, and not strong.

"Darn me if I couldn't eat 'em," said the man, with a threatening shake of his head, "and if I han't half a mind to't!"

I earnestly expressed my hope that he wouldn't, and held tighter to the tombstone on which he had put me; partly to keep myself upon it; partly to keep myself from crying.

"Now lookee here!" said the man. "Where's your mother?"

"There, sir!" said I.

He started, made a short run, and stopped and looked over his shoulder.

"There, sir!" I timidly explained. "Also Georgiana. That's my mother."

"Oh!" said he, coming back. "And is that your father alonger your mother?"

"Yes, sir," said I; "him too; late of this parish."

"Ha!" he muttered then, considering. "Who d'ye live with—supposing you're kindly let to live, which I han't made up my mind about?"

"My sister, sir — Mrs. Joe Gargery — wife of Joe Gargery, ᠅, blacksmith, sir."

"Blacksmith, eh?" said he. And looked down at his leg.

After darkly looking at his leg and at me several times, he ᠅

closer to my tombstone, took me by both arms, and tilted me back as far as he could hold me; so that his eyes looked most powerfully down into mine, and mine looked most helplessly up into his.

"Now lookee here," he said, "the question being whether you're to be let to live. You know what a file is?"

"Yes, sir."

"And you know what wittles is?"

"Yes, sir."

After each question he tilted me over a little more, so as to give me a greater sense of helplessness and danger.

"You get me a file." He tilted me again. "And you get me wittles." He tilted me again. "You bring 'em both to me." He tilted me again. "Or I'll have your heart and liver out." He tilted me again.

I was dreadfully frightened, and so giddy that I clung to him with both hands, and said, "If you would kindly please to let me keep upright, sir, perhaps I shouldn't be sick, and perhaps I could attend more."

He gave me a most tremendous dip and roll, so that the church jumped over its own weathercock. Then, he held me by the arms in an upright position on the top of the stone, and went on in these fearful terms:—

"You bring me, to-morrow morning early, that file and them wittles. You bring the lot to me, at that old Battery over yonder. You do it, and you never dare to say a word or dare to make a sign concerning your having seen such a person as me, or any person sumever, and you shall be let to live. You fail, or you go from my words in any partickler, no matter how small it is, and your heart and your liver shall be tore out, roasted and ate. Now, I ain't alone, as you may think I am. There's a young man hid with me, in comparison with which young man I am a Angel. That young man hears the words I speak. That young man has a secret way pecooliar to himself of getting at a boy, and at his heart, and at his liver. It is in wain for a boy to attempt to hide himself from that young man. A boy may lock his door, may be warm in bed, may tuck himself up, may draw the clothes over his head, may think himself comfortable and safe, but that young man will softly creep and creep his way to him and tear him open. I am a keeping that young man from harming of you at the present moment, with great difficulty. I find it wery hard to hold that young man off of your inside. Now what do you say?"

319

I said that I would get him the file, and I would get him what broken bits of food I could, and I would come to him at the Battery, early in the morning.

"Say, Lord strike you dead if you don't!" said the man.

I said so, and he took me down.

"Now," he pursued, "you remember what you've undertook, and you remember that young man, and you get home!"

"Goo-good night, sir," I faltered.

"Much of that!" said he, glancing about him over the cold, wet flat. "I wish I was a frog. Or a eel!"

At the same time he hugged his shuddering body in both his arms—clasping himself, as if to hold himself together—and limped towards the low church wall. As I saw him go, picking his way among the nettles, and among the brambles that bound the green mounds, he looked in my young eyes as if he were eluding the hands of the dead people, stretching up cautiously out of their graves, to get a twist upon his ankle and pull him in.

When he came to the low church wall, he got over it, like a man whose legs were numbed and stiff, and then turned round to look for me. When I saw him turning, I set my face towards home, and made the best use of my legs. But presently I looked over my shoulder, and saw him going on again towards the river, still hugging himself in both arms, and picking his way with his sore feet among the great stones dropped into the marshes here and there for stepping places when the rains were heavy, or the tide was in.

The marshes were just a long black horizontal line then, as I stopped to look after him; and the river was just another horizontal line, not nearly so broad nor yet so black; and the sky was just a row of long angry red lines and dense black lines intermixed. On the edge of the river I could faintly make out the only two black things in all the prospect that seemed to be standing upright: one of these was the beacon by which the sailors steered,—like an unhooped cask upon a pole,—an ugly thing when you were near it; the other a gibbet, with some chains hanging to it which had once held a pirate. The man was limping on towards this latter, as if he were the pirate come to life, and come down, and going back to hook himself up again. It gave me a terrible turn when I thought so; and as I saw the cattle lifting their heads to gaze after him, I wondered whether they thought so too. I looked all round for the horrible young man, and could see no signs of him. But now I was frightened again, and ran home without stopping.

EMILY DICKINSON

EMILY DICKINSON (American, 1830-1886). The greatest American woman poet, whose reputation emerged 40 years after her death. During life, a gentle recluse intimate with nature and private tragedy. Her poetry remarkable for its economy of means, whimsey of imagery, intensity of feeling.

THE SOUL SELECTS

The soul selects her own society,
Then shuts the door;
On her divine majority
Obtrude no more.

Unmoved, she notes the chariots pausing
At her low gate;
Unmoved, an emperor is kneeling
Upon her mat.

I've known her from an ample nation
Choose one;
Then close the valves of her attention
Like stone.

MY LIFE CLOSED TWICE

My life closed twice before its close;
It yet remains to see
If Immortality unveil
A third event to me,

So huge, so hopeless to conceive,
As these that twice befell.
Parting is all we know of heaven,
And all we need of hell.

OF ALL THE SOULS THAT STAND CREATE

Of all the souls that stand create
I have elected one.
When sense from spirit files away,
And subterfuge is done;

When that which is and that which was
Apart, intrinsic, stand,
And this brief tragedy of flesh
Is shifted like a sand;

When figures show their royal front
And mists are carved away—
Behold the atom I preferred
To all the lists of clay!

THE MOUNTAINS GROW UNNOTICED

The mountains grow unnoticed,
Their purple figures rise
Without attempt, exhaustion,
Assistance or applause.

In their eternal faces
The sun with broad delight
Looks long—and last—and golden,
For fellowship at night.

I NEVER SAW A MOOR

I never saw a moor,
I never saw the sea;
Yet know I how the heather looks,
And what a wave must be.

I never spoke with God,
Nor visited in Heaven;
Yet certain am I of the spot
As if the chart were given.

APPARENTLY WITH NO SURPRISE

Apparently with no surprise
To any happy flower,
The frost beheads it at its play
In accidental power.

The blond assassin passes on;
The sun proceeds unmoved
To measure off another day
For an approving God.

THE HEART ASKS PLEASURE FIRST

The heart asks pleasure first;
And then, excuse from pain;
And then, those little anodynes
That deaden suffering;

And then, to go to sleep;
And then, if it should be
The will of its Inquisitor,
The liberty to die.

THERE IS NO FRIGATE LIKE A BOOK

There is no frigate like a book
    To take us lands away,
Nor any courses like a page
    Of prancing poetry.

This traverse may the poorest take
    Without oppress of toll;
How frugal is the chariot
    That bears a human soul!

THE CHARIOT

Because I could not stop for Death,
He kindly stopped for me;
The carriage held but just ourselves,
And Immortality.

We slowly drove, he knew no haste,
And I had put away
My labor and my leisure, too,
For his civility.

We passed the school where children played,
Their lessons scarcely done;
We passed the fields of gazing grain,
We passed the setting sun.

323

We paused before a house that seemed
A swelling of the ground:
The roof was scarcely visible,
The cornice but a mound.

Since then, 'tis centuries; but each
Feels shorter than the day
I first surmised the horses' heads
Were toward eternity.

DEATH

Death is a dialogue between
The spirit and the dust.
"Dissolve," says Death; the spirit, "Sir,
I have another trust."
Death doubts it, argues from the ground.
The spirit turns away,
Just laying off, for evidence,
An overcoat of clay.

DEATH

The bustle in the house
The morning after death
Is solemnest of industries
Enacted upon earth;—

The sweeping up the heart
And putting love away
We shall not want to use again
Until eternity.

RESURGAM

At last to be identified!
At last, the lamps upon thy side
The rest of life to see!
Past midnight, past the morning star!
Past sunrise! Ah! what leagues there are
Between our feet and day!

THIRST

We thirst at first,—'tis nature's act;
    And, later, when we die
A little water supplicate
    Of fingers going by.

It intimates the finer wants
    Whose adequate supply
Is that great water in the West,
    Termed Immortality.

JOHN DONNE

JOHN DONNE (English, 1572-1631). Famed as preacher and metaphysical poet. Left Catholic Church for Church of England, became Dean of St. Paul's. Turned the English lyric to new subtleties of expression. Early love poems frankly sensuous. Later religious verse sometimes obscure but always noble. One of the idols of modern poets.

SONG

Go, and catch a falling star,
    Get with child a mandrake root,
Tell me, where all past years are,
    Or who cleft the Devil's foot,
Teach me to hear Mermaids singing,
    Or to keep off envy's stinging,
        And find
        What wind
Serves to advance an honest mind.

If thou be'st born to strange sights,
    Things invisible to see,
Ride ten thousand days and nights,
    Till age snow white hairs on thee,
Thou, when thou return'st, wilt tell me
All strange wonders that befell thee,
        And swear
        No where
Lives a woman true, and fair.

If thou find'st one, let me know,
　Such a Pilgrimage were sweet;
Yet do not, I would not go,
　Though at next door we might meet,
Though she were true, when you met her,
And last, till you write your letter,
　　　　Yet she
　　　　Will be
False, ere I come, to two, or three.

THE SUN RISING

　　Busy old fool, unruly sun,
　　　Why dost thou thus
Through windows and through curtains call on us?
Must to thy motions lovers' seasons run?
　　　Saucy pedantic wretch, go chide
　　　Late schoolboys and sour prentices,
　　Go tell court-huntsmen that the King will ride,
　　Call country ants to harvest offices;
Love, all alike, no season knows, nor clime,
Nor hours, days, months, which are the rags of time.

　　　Thy beams, so reverend and strong
　　　Why shouldst thou think?
I could eclipse and cloud them with a wink,
But that I would not lose her sight so long;
　　　If her eyes have not blinded thine,
　　　Look, and tomorrow late tell me
　　Whether both the Indias of spice and mine
　　Be where thou left'st them, or lie here with me.
Ask for those kings whom thou saw'st yesterday,
And thou shalt hear, all here in one bed lay.

　　　She is all states, and all princes I;
　　　Nothing else is.
Princes do but play us; compared to this,
All honour's mimic, all wealth alchemy.
　　　Thou, sun, art half as happy as we,
　　　In that the world's contracted thus;

326

Thine age asks ease, and since thy duties be
To warm the world, that's done in warming us.
Shine here to us, and thou art everywhere;
This bed thy center is, these walls thy sphere.

THE ECSTASY

Where, like a pillow on a bed,
  A pregnant bank swelled up to rest
The violet's reclining head,
  Sat we two, one another's best.
Our hands were firmly cemented
  With a fast balm, which thence did spring;
Our eye-beams twisted, and did thread
  Our eyes upon one double string;
So to entergraft our hands, as yet
  Was all the means to make us one,
And pictures in our eyes to get
  Was all our propagation.

SEND BACK MY LONG-STRAY'D EYES
TO ME

Send back my long-stray'd eyes to me,
Which, O! too long have dwelt on thee:
But if from you they've learnt such ill,
  To sweetly smile,
  And then beguile,
Keep the deceivers, keep them still.

Send home my harmless heart again,
Which no unworthy thought could stain;
But if it has been taught by thine
  To forfeit both
  Its word and oath,
Keep it, for then 'tis none of mine.

Yet send me back my heart and eyes,
For I'll know all thy falsities;
That I one day may laugh, when thou
  Shalt grieve and mourn—
  Of one the scorn,
Who proves as false as thou art now.

327

THE GOOD MORROW

I wonder, by my troth, what thou and I
Did, till we loved? were we not weaned till then?
But sucked on country pleasures, childishly?
Or snorted we in the Seven Sleepers' den?
'Twas so; but this, all pleasures fancies be;
If ever any beauty I did see,
Which I desired, and got, 'twas but a dream of thee.

And now good morrow to our waking souls,
Which watch not one another out of fear;
For love all love of other sights controls,
And makes one little room an everywhere.
Let sea-discoverers to new worlds have gone;
Let maps to other, worlds on worlds have shown;
Let us possess one world; each hath one, and is one.

My face in thine eye, thine in mine appears,
And true plain hearts do in the faces rest;
Where can we find two better hemispheres
Without sharp north, without declining west?
Whatever dies, was not mix'd equally;
If our two loves be one, or thou and I
Love so alike that none can slacken, none can die.

THE LEGACY

When last I died, and, dear, I die
    As often as from thee I go,
    Though it be but an hour ago
—And lovers' hours be full eternity—
I can remember yet, that I
    Something did say, and something did bestow;
Though I be dead, which sent me, I might be
Mine own executor, and legacy.

I heard me say, "Tell her anon,
    That myself," that is you, not I,
    "Did kill me," and when I felt me die,
I bid me send my heart, when I was gone;

But I alas! could there find none;
     When I had ripp'd, and search'd where hearts should lie,
It kill'd me again, that I who still was true
In life, in my last will should cozen you.

Yet I found something like a heart,
     But colors it and corners had;
     It was not good, it was not bad,
It was entire to none, and few had part;
As good as could be made by art
     It seemed, and therefore for our loss be sad.
I meant to send that heart instead of mine,
But O! no man could hold it, for 'twas thine.

FEODOR MIKHAYLOVICH DOSTOYEVSKY

FEODOR MIKHAYLOVICH DOSTOYEVSKY (Russian, 1821-1881). Master
of the psychological novel. Spokesman for the downtrodden little people of
Czarist Russia. Important factors in life: epilepsy, penal servitude in Siberia,
passion for gambling. Novels concerned with mystery of human personality,
good and evil, God and immortality. Character analysis foreshadows modern
psychology. His four masterpieces: *The Brothers Karamazov, Crime and
Punishment, The Idiot, The Possessed.*

THE MURDERER'S CONFESSION TO SONIA

RASKOLNIKOFF wished to smile, but, do what he would, his countenance retained its sorrow-stricken look. He lowered his head, covering his face with his hands. All at once, he fancied that he was
beginning to hate Sonia. Surprised, frightened even, at so strange
a discovery, he suddenly raised his head and attentively considered
the girl, who, in her turn, fixed on him a look of anxious love.
Hatred fled from Raskolnikoff's heart. It was not that; he had only
mistaken the nature of the sentiment he had experienced. It signified that the fatal moment had come. Once more he hid his face in
his hands and bowed his head. Suddenly he grew pale, rose, and,
after looking at Sonia, he mechanically went and sat on her bed,
without uttering a single word. Raskolnikoff's impression was the
very same he had experienced when standing behind the old wo-

man—he had loosened the hatchet from the loop, and said to himself: "There is not a moment to be lost!"

"What is the matter?" asked Sonia, in bewilderment.

No reply. Raskolnikoff had relied on making explanations under quite different conditions, and did not himself understand what was now at work within him. She gently approached him, sat on the bed by his side, and waited, without taking her eyes from his face. Her heart beat as if it would break. The situation was becoming unbearable; he turned towards the girl his lividly-pale face, his lips twitched with an effort to speak. Fear had seized upon Sonia.

"What is the matter with you?" she repeated, moving slightly away from him.

"Nothing, Sonia; don't be afraid. It is not worth while; it is all nonsense!" he murmured, like a man absent in mind. "Only, why can I have come to torment you?" added he all at once, looking at his interlocutress. "Yes, why? I keep on asking myself this question, Sonia."

Perhaps he had done so a quarter of an hour before, but at this moment his weakness was such that he scarcely retained consciousness; a continued trembling shook his whole frame.

"Oh! how you suffer!" said she, in a voice full of emotion, whilst looking at him.

"It is nothing! But this is the matter in question, Sonia." (For a moment or so, a pale smile hovered on his lips.) "You remember what I wished to tell you yesterday?" Sonia waited anxiously. "I told you, on parting, that I was, perhaps, bidding you farewell for ever, but that if I should come to-day, I would tell you who it was that killed Elizabeth." She began to tremble in every limb. "Well, then, that is why I have come."

"I know you told me that yesterday," she went on in a shaky voice. "How do you know that?" she added vivaciously. Sonia breathed with an effort. Her face grew more and more pale.

"I know it."

"Has *he* been discovered?" she asked, timidly, after a moment's silence.

"No, *he* has not been discovered."

For another moment she remained silent. "Then how do you know it?" she at length asked, in an almost unintelligible voice.

He turned towards the girl. and looked at her with a singular rigidity, whilst a feeble smile fluttered on his lips. "Guess!" he said.

Sonia felt on the point of being seized with convulsions. "But

330

you—why frighten me like this?" she asked, with a childlike smile.

"I know it, because I am very intimate with *him!*" went on Raskolnikoff, whose look remained fixed on her, as if he had not strength to turn his eyes aside. "Elizabeth—he had no wish to murder her—he killed her without premeditation. He only intended to kill the old woman, when he should find her alone. He went to her house —but at the very moment Elizabeth came in—he was there—and he killed her."

A painful silence followed upon these words. For a moment both continued to look at one another. "And so you can't guess?" he asked abruptly, feeling like a man on the point of throwing himself from the top of a steeple.

"No," stammered Sonia, in a scarcely audible voice.

"Try again."

At the moment he pronounced these words, Raskolnikoff experienced afresh, in his heart-of-hearts, that feeling of chilliness he knew so well. He looked at Sonia, and suddenly read on her face the same expression as on that of Elizabeth, when the wretched woman recoiled from the murderer advancing towards he, hatchet in hand. In that supreme moment Elizabeth had raised her arm, as children do when they begin to be afraid, and ready to weep, fix a glaring immovable glance on the object which frightens them. In the same way Sonia's face expressed indescribable fear. She also raised her arm, and gently pushed Raskolnikoff aside, whilst touching his breast with her hand, and then gradually drew back without ceasing to look hard at him. Her fear affected the young man, who, for his part, began to gaze on her with a scared expression.

"Have you guessed?" he murmured at last.

"My God!" exclaimed Sonia.

Then she sank exhausted on the bed, and buried her face in the pillows; a moment after, however, she rose with a rapid movement, approached him, and, seizing him by both hands, which her slender fingers clutched like nippers, she fixed on him a long look. Had he made a mistake? She hoped so, but she had no sooner cast a look on Raskolnikoff's face than the suspicion which had flashed on her mind became certainty.

"Enough, Sonia! enough! Spare me!" he implored in a plaintive voice. The event upset all his calculations, for it certainly was not *thus* that he had intended to confess his crime.

Sonia seemed beside herself; she jumped from her bed, went to the middle of the room wringing her hands, she then quickly returned in the same way, sat once more by the young man's side, almost touching him with her shoulder. Suddenly she shivered, uttered a cry, and, without knowing why, fell on her knees before Raskolnikoff. "You are lost!" she exclaimed, with an accent of despair. And, rising suddenly, she threw herself on his neck, and kissed him, whilst lavishing on him tokens of tenderness.

Raskolnikoff broke away, and, with a sad smile, looked at the girl: "I do not understand you, Sonia. You kiss me after I told you *that*—. You cannot be conscious of what you are doing."

She did not hear the remark. "No, at this moment there cannot be a more wretched man on earth than you are!" she exclaimed with a transport of passion, whilst bursting into sobs.

Raskolnikoff felt his heart grow soft under the influence of a sentiment which for some time past he had not felt. He did not try to fight against the feeling; two tears spurted from his eyes and remained on the lashes. "Then you will not forsake me, Sonia?" said he with an almost suppliant look.

"No, no; never, nowhere!" she cried, "I shall follow you, shall follow you everywhere! Heaven! Wretch that I am! And why have I not known you sooner? Why did you not come before? Heaven!"

"You see I have come."

"Now? What is to be done now? Together, together," she went on, with a kind of exaltation, and once more she kissed the young man. "Yes, I will go with you to the galleys!"

These words caused Raskolnikoff a painful feeling; a bitter and almost haughty smile appeared on his lips. "Perhaps I may not yet wish to go to the galleys, Sonia," said he.

The girl rapidly turned her eyes on him. She had up to the present experienced no more than immense pity for an unhappy man. This statement, and the tone of voice in which it was pronounced, suddenly recalled to the girl that the wretched man was an assassin. She cast on him an astonished look. As yet, she did not know how nor why he had become a criminal. At this moment, these questions suggested themselves to her, and, once more doubting, she asked herself: "He, he a murderer? Is such a thing possible? But no, it cannot be true! Where am I?" she asked herself, as if she could have believed herself the sport of a dream. "How is it possible that you, being what you are, can have thought of such a thing? Oh! why?"

"To steal, if you wish to know. Cease, Sonia!" he replied in wearied and rather vexed accents.

Sonia remained stupefied; suddenly a cry escaped her: "Were you hungry? Did you do so to help your mother? Speak!"

"No, Sonia! no!" he stammered, drooping his head. "I was not so poor as all that. It is true I wanted to help my mother, but that was not the real reason.—Do not torment me, Sonia!"

The girl beat her hands together. "Is it possible that such a thing can be real? Heaven! is it possible? How can I believe such a thing? You say you killed to rob; you, who deprive yourself of all for the sake of others! Ah!" she cried suddenly. "That money you gave to Catherine Ivanovna! — that money! Heavens! can it be that?"

"No, Sonia!" he interrupted somewhat sharply. "This money comes from another source, I assure you. It was my mother who sent it to me during my sickness, through the intervention of a merchant, and I had just received it when I gave it. Razoumikin saw it himself, he even went so far as to receive it for me. The money was really my own property." Sonia listened in perplexity, and strove to understand. "As for the old woman's money, to tell the truth, I really do not know whether there was any money at all," he went on hesitatingly. "I took from her neck a well-filled chamois-leather purse. But I never examined the contents, probably because I had no time to do so. I took different things, sleeve-links, watch-chains. These things I hid, in the same way as the purse, on the following day, under a large stone in a yard which looks out on the V—— Prospect. Everything is still there."

Sonia listened with avidity. "But why did you take nothing, since, as you tell me, you committed murder to steal?" she went on, clinging to a last and very vague hope.

"I don't know—as yet I am undecided whether to take this money or not," replied Raskolnikoff in the same hesitating voice; then he smiled. "What silly tale have I been telling you?"

"Can he be mad?" Sonia asked herself, but she soon dispelled such an idea; no, it was something else, which she most certainly did not understand.

"Do you know what I am going to tell you, Sonia?" he went on in a convinced tone: "If nothing but need had urged me to commit a murder," laying stress on every word, and his look, although frank was more or less puzzling, "I should now be *happy!* Let me tell you that! And what can the motive be to you, since I told you just now that I had acted badly?" he cried despairingly, a moment afterwards. "What was the good of this foolish triumph over myself? Ah! Sonia, was it for that I came to you?" She once more wished to speak, but remained silent. "Yesterday, I made a proposal to you that we should both of us depart together, because you are all that is left to me."

"Why did you wish me to accompany you?" asked the girl timidly.

"Not to rob or to kill, I assure you," answered Raskolnikoff, with a caustic smile. "We are not of the same way of thinking. And—do you know, Sonia?—it is only of late that I have known why I asked you yesterday to accompany me. When I asked you to do so, I did not as yet know what it would lead to. I see it now. I have but one wish—it is that you should not leave me. You will not do so, will you, Sonia?" She clasped his hand. "And why have I told her this? Why make such a confession?" he exclaimed, a moment afterwards. He looked at her with infinite compassion, whilst his voice expressed the most profound despair. "I see, Sonia, that you are waiting for some kind of explanation, but what am I to say? You understand nothing about the matter, and I should only be causing you additional pain. I see you are once more commencing to weep and embrace me. Why do so at all? Because, failing in courage to bear my own burden, I have imposed it on another—because I seek in the anguish of others some mitigation for my own. And you can love a coward like that?"

"But you are likewise suffering!" exclaimed Sonia.

For a moment he experienced a new feeling of tenderness. "Sonia, my disposition is a bad one, and that can explain much. I have come because I am bad. Some would not have done so. But I am an infamous coward. Why, once more, have I come? I shall never forgive myself for that!"

"No, no!—on the contrary, you have done well to come," cried Sonia; "it is better, much better, I should know all!"

Raskolnikoff looked at her with sorrowful eye. "I was ambitious to become another Napoleon; that was why I committed a murder. Can you understand it now?"

"No," answered Sonia, naïvely and in a timid voice. "But speak! speak! I shall understand it all!"

"You will, say you? God! we shall see!" For some time Raskolnikoff collected his ideas. "That fact is that, one day, I asked myself the following question: 'Supposing Napoleon to have been in my place, supposing that to commence his career he had neither had Toulon, nor Egypt, nor the crossing of Mont Blanc, but, in lieu of all these brilliant exploits, he was on the point of committing a murder with a view to secure his future, would he have recoiled at the idea of killing an old woman, and of robbing her of three thousand roubles? Would he have agreed that such a deed was too much wanting in prestige and much too—criminal a one?' For a long time I have split my head on that question, and could not help experiencing a feeling of shame when I finally came to the conclusion that he not only would not have hesitated, but that he would not have understood the possibility of such a thing. Every other expedient being out of his reach, he would not have flinched, he would have done so without the smallest scruple. Hence, I ought not to hesitate—being justified on the authority of Napoleon!"

JOHN DRYDEN

JOHN DRYDEN (English, 1631-1700). Dominant literary figure of the Restoration. Dramatist, poet, essayist, critic. Influential in establishing heroic couplet, which dominated English poetry for a century. Best-known poem: "Alexander's Feast." Drama: *All for Love.* Prose: *An Essay of Dramatic Poesy.*

ZEGRI AND ABENCERRAGE

Scene: *Granada, and the Christian Camp besieging it.   Present:* Boabdelin, Abenamar, Abdelmelech, *and* Guards.

Boabdelin—
     The alarm-bell rings from our Alhambra walls,
     And from the streets sound drums and atabals.
                         (Within, a bell, drums, and trumpets.)
          Enter a Messenger.
     How now? from whence proceed these new alarms?
Messenger—
     The two fierce factions are again in arms;
     And changing into blood the day's delight,
     The Zegrys with the the Abencerrages fight;
     On each side their allies and friends appear;
     The Macas here, the Alabezes there;
     The Gazuls with the Bencerrages join,
     And, with the Zegrys, all great Gomel's line.

335

Boabdelin—
Draw up behind the Vivarambla place;
Double my guards,—these factions I will face;
And try if all the fury they can bring
Be proof against the presence of their king.
    (Exit Boabdelin.)
The Factions appear: At the head of the Abencerrages, Ozmyn; *at
the head of the Zegrys,* Zulema, Hamet, Gomel, *and* Selin; Aben-
amar *and* Abdelmelech *join with the Abencerrages.*
Zulema—
The faint Abencerrages quit their ground:
Press them; put home your thrusts to every wound.
Abdelmelech—
Zegry, on manly force our line relies;
Thine poorly takes the advantage of surprise:
Unarmed and much outnumbered we retreat;
You gain no fame, when basely you defeat.
If thou art brave, seek nobler victory;
Save Moorish blood; and, while our bands stand by,
Let two and two an equal combat try.
Hamet—
'Tis not for fear the combat we refuse.
But we our gained advantage will not lose.
Zulema—
In combating, but two of you will fall;
And we resolve we will despatch you all.
Ozmyn—
We'll double yet the exchange before we die,
And each of ours two lives of yours shall buy.
    Almanzor *enters betwixt them, as they stand ready to engage.*
Almanzor—
I cannot stay to ask which cause is best:
But this is so to me, because opprest.
                        (Goes to the Abencerrages.)
    To them Boabdelin *and his* Guards, *going betwixt them.*
Boabdelin—
On your allegiance, I command you stay;
Who passes here, through me must make his way;
My life's the Isthmus; through this narrow line
You first must cut, before those seas can join.
What fury, Zegrys, has possessed your minds?

What rage the brave Abencerrages blinds?
If of your courage you new proofs would show,
Without much travel you may find a foe.
Those foes are neither so remote nor few
That you should need each other to pursue.
Lean times and foreign wars should minds unite;
When poor men mutter, but they seldom fight.
O holy Allah! that I live to see
Thy Granadines assist their enemy!
You fight the Christians' battles; every life
You lavish thus, in this intestine strife,
Does from our weak foundations take one prop,
Which helped to hold our sinking country up.

Ozmyn—
'Tis fit our private enmity should cease;
Though injured first, yet I will first seek peace.

Zulema—
No, murderer, no; I never will be won
To peace with him, whose hand has slain my son.

Ozmyn—
Our phrophet's curse
On me and all the Abencerrages light,
If unprovoked I with your son did fight.

Abdelmelech—
A band of Zegrys ran within the place,
Matched with a troop of thirty of our race.
Your son and Ozmyn the first squadrons led,
Which, ten by ten, like Parthians, charged and fled,
The ground was strowed with canes where we did meet,
Which crackled underneath our coursers' feet;
When Tarifa (I saw him ride apart)
Changed his blunt cane for a steel-pointed dart,
And, meeting Ozmyn next—
Who wanted time for treason to provide,—
He basely threw it at him, undefied.

Ozmyn (showing his arms)—
Witness this blood—which when by treason sought,
That followed, sir, which to myself I ought.

Zulema—
His hate to thee was grounded on a grudge,
Which all our generous Zegrys just did judge:

337

Thy villain-blood thou openly didst place
Above the purple of our kingly race.
Boabdelin—
From equal stems their blood both houses draw,
They from Morocco, you from Cordova.
Hamet—
Their mongrel race is mixed with Christian breed;
Hence 'tis that they those dogs in prisons feed.
Abdelmelech—
Our holy prophet wills, that charity
Should even to birds and beast extended be:
None knows what fate is for himself designed;
The thought of human chance should make us kind.
Gomel—
We waste that time we to revenge should give:
Fall on; let no Abencerrage live.
Advances before the rest of his party. Almanzor *advances on the
other side, and describes a line with his sword.*
Almanzor—
Upon thy life pass not this middle space;
Sure death stands guarding the forbidden place.
Gomel—
To dare that death, I will approach yet nigher;
Thus,—wert thou compassed in with circling fire.
(*They fight.*)
Boabdelin—
Disarm them both; if they resist you, kill.
Almanzor, *in the midst of the guards, kills* Gomel, *and then is
disarmed.*
Almanzor—
Now you have but the leavings of my will.
Boabdelin—
Kill him! this insolent unknown shall fall,
And be the victim to atone you all.
Ozmyn—
If he must die, not one of us will live:
That life he gave for us, for him we give.
Boabdelin—
It was a traitor's voice that spoke those words;
So are you all, who do not sheathe your swords.

Zulema—
  Outrage unpunished, when a prince is by,
  Forfeits to scorn the rights of majesty:
  No subject his protection can expect,
  Who what he owes himself does first neglect.
Abenamar—
  This stranger, sir, is he,
  Who lately in the Vivarambla place
  Did, with so loud applause, your triumphs grace
Boabdelin—
  The word which I have given, I'll not revoke;
  If he be brave, he's ready for the stroke.
Almanzor—
  No man has more contempt than I of breath,
  But whence hast thou the right to give me death?
  Obeyed as sovereign by thy subjects be,
  But know, that I alone am king of me.
  I am as free as nature first made man,
  Ere the base laws of servitude began,
  When wild in woods the noble savage ran.
Boabdelin—
  Since, then, no power above your own you know,
  Mankind should use you like a common foe;
  You should be hunted like a beast of prey:
  By your own law I take your life away.
Almanzor—
  My laws are made but only for my sake;
  No king against himself a law can make.
  If thou pretend'st to be a prince like me,
  Blame not an act which should thy pattern be.
  I saw the oppressed, and thought it did belong
  To a king's office to redress the wrong:
  I brought that succor which thou ought'st to bring,
  And so, in nature, am thy subjects' king.
Boabdelin—
  I do not want your counsel to direct,
  Or aid to help me punish or protect.
Almanzor—
  Thou want'st them both, or better thou wouldst know,
  Than to let factions in thy kingdoms grow.

339

Divided interests, while thou think'st to sway,
Draw, like two brooks, thy middle stream away:
For though they band and jar, yet both combine
To make their greatness by the fall of thine.
Thus, like a buckler, thou art held in sight,
While they behind thee with each other fight.
Boabdelin—
Away, and execute him instantly! (*To his Guards.*)
Almanzor—
Stand off; I have not leisure yet to die.
    To them, enter Abdalla *hastily.*
Abdalla—
Hold, sir! for heaven's sake hold!
Defer this noble stranger's punishment,
Or your rash orders you will soon repent.
Boabdelin—
Brother, you know not yet his insolence.
Abdalla—
Upon yourself you punish his offense:
If we treat gallant strangers in this sort,
Mankind will shun the inhospitable court;
And who, henceforth, to our defense will come,
If death must be the brave Almanzor's doom?
From Africa I drew him to your aid,
And for his succor have his life betrayed.
Boabdelin—
Is this the Almanzor whom at Fez you knew,
When first their swords the Xeriff brothers drew?
Abdalla—
This, sir, is he, who for the elder fought,
And to the juster cause the conquest brought;
Till the proud Santo, seated on the throne,
Disdained the service he had done to own:
Then to the vanquished part his fate he led;
The vanquished triumphed, and the victor fled.
Vast is his courage, boundless is his mind,
Rough as a storm, and humorous as wind:
Honor's the only idol of his eyes;
The charms of beauty like a pest he flies;
And, raised by valor from a birth unknown,
Acknowledges no power above his own.

Boabdelin (*coming to Almanzor*)—
    Impute your danger to our ignorance;
    The bravest men are subject most to chance:
    Granada much does to your kindness owe;
    But towns, expecting sieges, cannot show
    More honor than to invite you to a foe.
Almanzor—
    I do not doubt but I have been to blame:
    But, to pursue the end for which I came,
    Unite your subjects first; then let us go,
    And pour their common rage upon the foe.
Boabdelin (*to the factions*)—
    Lay down your arms, and let me beg you cease
    Your enmities.
Zulema—
            We will not hear of peace,
    Till we by force have first revenged our slain.
Abdelmelech—
    The action we have done we will maintain.
Selin—
    Then let the king depart, and we will try
    Our cause by arms.
Zulema—
            For us and victory.
Boabdelin—A king entreats you.
Almanzor—
    What subjects will precarious kings regard?
    A beggar speaks too softly to be heard:
    Lay down your arms! 'tis I command you now.
    Do it—or, by our prophet's soul I vow,
    My hands shall right your king on him I seize.
    Now let me see whose look but disobeys.
All—
    Long live king Mahomet Boabdelin!
Almanzor—
    No more; but hushed as midnight silence go:
    He will not have your acclamations now.
    Hence, you unthinking crowd!—
            (*The Common People go off in both parties.*)
    Empire, thou poor and despicable thing,
    When such as these make or unmake a king!

ALEXANDRE DUMAS

ALEXANDRE DUMAS (1802-1870). Prolific romantic novelist. *The Three Musketeers, The Count of Monte Cristo, The Man in the Iron Mask,* still read for their vitality and narrative ingenuity. With team of collaborators, produced 300 such romances. Also wrote melodramas for stage, and was active in political affairs.

MARGUERITE DE VALOIS

1. *Henry of Navarre and Marguerite*

ON Monday, August 18, 1572, a great festival was held in the palace of the Louvre. It was to celebrate the marriage of Henry of Navarre and Marguerite de Valois, a marriage that perplexed a good many people, and alarmed others.

For Henry de Bourbon, King of Navarre, was the leader of the Huguenot party, and Marguerite was the daughter of Catherine de Medici, and the sister of the king, Charles IX., and this alliance between a Protestant and a Catholic, it seemed, was to end the strife that rent the nation. The king, too, had set his heart on this marriage, and the Huguenots were somewhat reassured by the king's declaration that Catholic and Huguenot alike were now his subjects, and were equally beloved by him. Still, there were many on both sides who feared and distrusted the alliance.

At midnight, six days later, on August 24, the tocsin sounded, and the massacre of St. Bartholomew began.

The marriage, indeed, was in no sense a love match; but Henry succeeded at once in making Marguerite his friend, for he was alive to the dangers that surrounded him.

"Madame," he said, presenting himself at Marguerite's rooms on the night of the wedding festival, "whatever many persons may have said, I think our marriage is a good marriage. I stand well with you—you stand well with me. Therefore, we ought to act towards each other like good allies, since to-day we have been allied in the sight of God! Don't you think so?"

"Without question, sir!"

"I know, madame, that the ground at court is full of dangerous abysses; and I know that, though I am young and have never injured any person, I have many enemies. The king hates me, his brothers, the Duke of Anjou and the Duke d' Alençon, hate me. Catherine de Medici hated my mother too much not to hate me.

342

Well, against these menaces, which must soon become attacks, I can only defend myself by your aid, for you are beloved by all those who hate me!"

"I?" said Marguerite.

"Yes, you!" replied Henry. "And if you will—I do not say love me—but if you will be my ally I can brave anything; while, if you become my enemy, I am lost."

"Your enemy! Never, sir!" exclaimed Marguerite.

"And my ally?"

"Most decidedly!"

And Marguerite turned round and presented her hand to the king. "It is agreed," she said.

"Political alliance, frank and loyal?" asked Henry.

"Frank and loyal," was the answer.

At the door Henry turned and said softly, "Thanks, Marguerite; thanks! You are a true daughter of France. Lacking your love, your friendship will not fail me. I rely on you, as you, for your part, may rely on me. Adieu, madame."

He kissed his wife's hand; and then, with a quick step, the king went down the corridor to his own apartment. "I have more need of fidelity in politics than in love," he said to himself.

If on both sides there was little attempt at fidelity in love, there was an honourable alliance, which was maintained unbroken and saved the life of Henry of Navarre from his enemies on more than one occasion.

On the day of the St. Bartholomew massacre, while the Huguenots were being murdered throughout Paris, Charles IX., instigated by his mother, summoned Henry of Navarre to the royal armoury, and called upon him to turn Catholic or die.

"Will you kill me, sire—me, your brother-in-law?" exclaimed Henry.

Charles IX turned away to the open window. "I must kill someone," he cried, and firing his arquebuse, struck a man who was passing.

Then, animated by a murderous fury, Charles loaded and fired his arquebuse without stopping, shouting with joy when his aim was successful.

"It's all over with me!" said Henry to himself. "When he sees no one else to kill, he will kill me!"

Catherine de Medici entered as the king fired his last shot. "Is it done?" she said, anxiously.

"No," the king exclaimed, throwing his arquebuse on the floor. "No; the obstinate blockhead will not consent!"

Catherine gave a glance at Henry which Charles understood perfectly, and which said, "Why, then, is he alive?"

"He lives," said the king, "because he is my relative."

Henry felt that it was with Catherine he had to contend.

"Madame," he said, addressing her, "I can see quite clearly that all this comes from you and not from brother-in-law Charles. It was you who planned this massacre to ensnare me into a trap which was to destroy us all. It was you who made your daughter the bait. It has been you who have separated me now from my wife, that she might not see me killed before her eyes!"

"Yes; but that shall not be!" cried another voice; and Marguerite, breathless and impassioned, burst into the room.

"Sir," said Marguerite to Henry, "your last words were an accusation, and were both right and wrong. They have made me the means for attempting to destroy you, but I was ignorant that in marrying me you were going to destruction. I myself owe my life to chance, for this very night they all but killed me in seeking you. Directly I knew of your danger I sought you. If you are exiled, sir, I will be exiled too; if they imprison you they shall imprison me also; if they kill you, I will also die!"

She gave her hand to her husband, and he seized it eagerly.

"Brother," cried Marguerite to Charles IX., "remember, you made him my husband!"

"Faith, Margot is right, and Henry is my brother-in-law," said the king.

II

THE BOAR HUNT

As time went on, if Catherine's hatred of Henry of Navarre did not diminish, Charles IX. certainly became more friendly.

Catherine was for ever intriguing and plotting for the fortunes of her sons and the downfall of her son-in-law, but Henry always managed to evade the webs she wove. At a certain boar-hunt Charles was indebted to Henry for his life.

It was at the time when the king's brother, D'Anjou, had accepted the crown of Poland, and the second brother, D'Alençon, a weak-minded, ambitious man, was secretly hoping for a crown somewhere, that Henry paid his debt for the king's mercy to him on the night of St. Bartholomew.

Charles was an intrepid hunter, but the boar had swerved as the king's spear was aimed at him, and, maddened with rage, the animal had rushed at him. Charles tried to draw his hunting-knife, but the sheath was so tight it was impossible.

"The boar! the boar!" shouted the king. "Help, D'Alençon, help!"

D'Alençon was ghastly white as he placed his arquebuse to his shoulder and fired. The ball, instead of hitting the boar, felled the king's horse.

"I think," D'Alençon murmured to himself, "that D'Anjou is King of France, and I King of Poland."

The boar's tusk had indeed grazed the king's thigh when a hand in an iron glove dashed itself against the mouth of the beast, and a knife was plunged into its shoulder.

Charles rose with difficulty, and seemed for a moment as if about to fall by the dead boar. Then he looked at Henry of Navarre, and for the first time in four-and-twenty years his heart was touched.

"Thanks, Harry!" he said. "D'Alençon, for a first-rate marksman you made a most curious shot."

On Marguerite coming up to congratulate the king and thank her husband, Charles added, "Margot, you may well thank him. But for him Henry III. would be King of France."

"Alas, madame," returned Henry, "M. D'Anjou, who is always my enemy, will now hate me more than ever; but everyone has to do what he can."

Had Charles IX. been killed, the Duke d'Anjou would have been King of France, and D'Alençon most probably King of Poland. Henry of Navarre would have gained nothing by this change of affairs.

Instead of Charles IX., who tolerated him, he would have had the Duke d'Anjou on the throne, who, being absolutely at one with his mother, Catherine, had sworn his death, and would have kept his oath.

These ideas were in his brain when the wild boar rushed on Charles, and like lightning he saw that his own existence was bound up with the life of Charles IX. But the king knew nothing of the spring and motive of the devotion which had saved his life, and on the following day he showed his gratitude to Henry by carrying him off from his apartments, and out of the Louvre. Catherine, in her fear lest Henry of Navarre should some day be King of France, had arranged the assassination of her son-in-law; and Charles, getting wind of this, warned him that the air of the

Louvre was not good for him that night, and kept him in his company. Instead of Henry, it was one of his followers who was killed.

III

THE POISONED BOOK

Once more Catherine resolved to destroy Henry. The Huguenots had plotted with D'Alençon that he should be King of Navarre, since Henry not only abjured Protestantism but remained in Paris, being kept there indeed by the will of Charles IX.

Catherine, aware of D'Alençon's scheme, assured her son that Henry was suffering from an incurable disease, and must be taken away from Paris when D'Alencon started for Navarre.

"Are you sure that Henry will die?" asked D'Alencon.

"The physician who gave me a certain book assured me of it."

"And where is this book? What is it?"

Catherine brought the book from her cabinet.

"Here it is. It is a treatise on the art of rearing and training falcons by an Italian. Give it to Henry, who is going hawking with the king to-day, and will not fail to read it."

"I dare not!" said D'Alençon shuddering.

"Nonsense!" replied Catherine. "It is a book like any other, only the leaves have a way of sticking together. Don't attempt to read it yourself, for you will have to wet the finger in turning over each leaf, which takes up so much time."

"Oh," said D'Alençon, "Henry is with the court! Give me the book, and while he is away I will put it in his room."

D'Alençon's hand was trembling as he took the book from the queen-mother, and with some hesitation and fear he entered Henry's apartment and placed the volume, open at the title page.

But it was not Henry, but Charles, seeking his brother-in-law, who found the book and carried it off to his own room. D'Alençon found the king reading.

"By heavens, this is an admirable book!" cried Charles. "Only it seems as if they had stuck the leaves together on purpose to conceal the wonders it contains."

D'Alençon's first thought was to snatch the book from his brother, but he hesitated.

The king again moistened his finger and turned over a page.

"Let me finish this chapter," he said, "and then tell me what you please. I have already read fifty pages."

"He must have tasted the poison five-and-twenty times," thought D'Alençon. "He is a dead man!"

The poison did its deadly work. Charles was taken ill while out hunting, and returned to find his dog dead, and in its mouth pieces of paper from the precious book on falconry. The king turned pale. The book was poisoned! Many things flashed across his memory, and he knew his life was doomed.

Charles summoned René, a Florentine, the court perfumer to Catherine de Medici, to his presence, and bade him examine the dog.

"Sire," said René, after a close investigation, "the dog has been poisoned by arsenic."

"He has eaten a leaf of this book," said Charles; "and if you do not tell me whose book it is I will have your flesh torn from your bones by red-hot pincers."

"Sire," stammered the Florentine, "this book belongs to me!"

"And how did it leave your hands?"

"Her majesty the queen-mother took it from my house."

"Why did she do that?"

"I believe she intended sending it to the King of Navarre, who had asked for a book on hawking."

"Ah," said Charles, "I understand it all! The book was in Harry's room. It is destiny; I must yield to it. Tell me," he went on, turning to René, "this poison does not always kill at once?"

"No, sire; but it kills surely. It is a matter of time."

"Is there no remedy?"

"None, sire, unless it be instantly administered."

Charles compelled the wretched man to write in the fatal volume, "This book was given by me to the queen-mother, Catherine de Medici.—René," and then dismissed him.

Henry, at his own prayer and for his personal safety, was confined in the prison of Vincennes by the king's order. Charles grew worse, and the physicians discussed his malady without daring to guess at the truth.

Then Catherine came one day and explained to the king the cause of his disease.

"Listen, my son; you believe in magic?"

"Oh, fully," said Charles, repressing his smile of incredulity.

"Well," continued Catherine, "all your sufferings proceed from magic. An enemy afraid to attack you openly has done so in secret; a terrible conspiracy has been directed against your majesty. You doubt it, perhaps, but I know it for a certainty."

"I never doubt what you tell me," replied the king sarcastically. "I am curious to know how they have sought to kill me."

"By magic. Look here." The queen drew from under her mantle a figure of yellow wax about ten inches high, wearing a robe covered with golden stars, and over this a royal mantle.

"See, it has on its head a crown," said Catherine, "and there is a needle in its heart. Now do you recognise yourself?"

"Myself?"

"Yes, in your royal robes, with the crown on your head."

"And who made this figure?" asked the king, weary of the wretched farce. "The King of Navarre, of course!"

"No, sire; he did not actually make it, but it was found in the rooms of M. de la Mole, who serves the King of Navarre."

"So, then, the person who seeks to kill me is M. de la Mole?" said Charles.

"He is only the instrument, and behind the instrument is the hand that directs it," replied Catherine.

"This, then, is the cause of my illness. And now what must I do —for I know nothing of sorcery?"

"The death of the conspirator destroys the charm. Its power ends with his life. You are convinced now, are you not, of the cause of your illness?"

"Oh, certainly," Charles answered ironically. "And I am to punish M. de la Mole, as you say he is the guilty party?"

"I say he is the instrument, and," muttered Catherine, "we have infallible means for making him confess the name of his principal."

Catherine left hurriedly without understanding the sardonic laughter of the king, and as she went out Marguerite appeared.

"Oh, sire—sire," cried Marguerite, "you know what *she* says is false. It is terrible to accuse one's own mother, but she only lives to persecute the man who is devoted to you, Henry—your Henry— and I swear to you that what she says is false!"

"I think so, too, Margot. But Henry is safe. Safer in disgrace in Vincennes than in favour at the Louvre."

"Oh, thanks, thanks! But there is another person in whose welfare I am interested, whom I hardly dare mention to my brother, much less to my king."

"M. de la Mole, is it not? But do you know that a figure dressed in royal robes and pierced to the heart was found in his rooms?"

"I know it; but it was the figure of a woman, not of a man."

"And the needle?"

"Was a charm not to kill a man, but to make a woman love him."

"What was the name of this woman?"

"Marguerite!" cried the queen, throwing herself down and bathing the king's hand in her tears.

"Margot, what if I know the real author of the crime? For a crime has been committed, and I have not three months to live. I am poisoned, but it must be thought I die by magic."

"You know who is guilty?"

"Yes; but it must be kept from the world, and so it must be believed I die of magic, and by the agency of him they accuse."

"But it is monstrous!" exclaimed Marguerite. "You know he is innocent. Pardon him—pardon him!"

"I know it, but the world must believe him guilty. Let your friend die. His death alone can save the honour of our family. I am dying that the secret may be preserved."

M. de la Mole, after enduring excruciating tortures at the hands of Catherine, without making any admissions, died on the scaffold.

IV

"THE BOURBON SHALL NOT REIGN!"

Before he died Charles showed Catherine the poisoned book, which he had kept under lock and key.

"And now burn it, madame. I read this book too much, so fond was I of the chase. And the world must not know the weaknesses of kings. When it is burnt, please summon my brother Henry. I wish to speak to him about the regency."

Catherine brought Henry of Navarre to the king, and warned him that if he accepted the regency he was a dead man.

Charles, however, though on his deathbed, declared Henry should be regent.

"Madame," he said, addressing his mother, "if I had a son he would be king, and you would be regent. In your stead, did you decline, the King of Poland would be regent; and in his stead, D'Alencon. But I have no son, and therefore the throne belongs to D'Anjou, who is absent. To make D'Alencon regent is to invite civil war. I have therefore chosen the fittest person for regent. Salute him, madame; salute him, D'Alençon. It is the King of Navarre!"

"Never," cried Catherine, "shall my race yield to a foreign one! Never shall a Bourbon reign while a Valois lives!"

She left the room, followed by D'Alençon.

"Henry," said Charles, "after my death you will be great and powerful. D'Anjou will not leave Poland—they will not let him. D'Alençon is a traitor. You alone are capable of governing. It is not the regency only, but the throne I give you."

A stream of blood choked his speech.

"The fatal moment is come," said Henry. "Am I to reign, or to live?"

"Live, sire!" a voice answered, and René appeared. "The queen has sent me to ruin you, but I have faith in your star. It is foretold that you shall be king. Do you know that the King of Poland will be here very soon? He has been summoned by the queen. A messenger has come from Warsaw. You shall be king, but not yet."

"What shall I do, then?"

"Fly instantly to where your friends wait for you."

Henry stooped and kissed his brother's forehead, then disappeared down a secret passage, passed through the postern, and, springing on his horse, galloped off.

"He flies! The King of Navarre flies!" cried the sentinels.

"Fire on him! Fire!" said the queen.

The sentinels levelled their pieces, but the king was out of reach.

"He flies!" muttered D'Alençon. "I am king, then!"

At the same moment the drawbridge was hastily lowered, and Henry D'Anjou galloped into the court, followed by four knights, crying, "France! France!"

"My son!" cried Catherine joyfully.

"Am I too late?" said D'Anjou.

"No. You are just in time. Listen!"

The captain of the king's guards appeared at the balcony of the king's apartment. He broke the wand he held in two pieces, and holding a piece in either hand, called out three times, "King Charles the Ninth is dead! King Charles the Ninth is dead! King Charles the Ninth is dead!"

"Charles the Ninth is dead!" said Catherine, crossing herself. "God save Henry the Third!"

All repeated the cry.

"I have conquered," said Catherine, "and the odious Bourbon shall not reign!"

E

JOSEPH VON EICHENDORFF

JOSEPH VON EICHENDORFF (German, 1788-1857). The latter-day poet of German medievalism. Characterized by typical Romantic themes: love of nature, wanderlust, romantic longings. Wrote in many forms, but most characteristic work, a novella, *Aus dem Leben eines Taugenichts (From the Life of a Good-for-Nothing)*, is combination of poetry and prose.

Poems from
"FROM THE LIFE OF A GOOD-FOR-NOTHING"

The favoured ones, the loved of Heaven,
   God sends to roam the world at will;
His wonders to their gaze are given
   By field and forest, stream and hill.

The dullards who at home are staying
   Are not refreshed by morning's ray;
They grovel, earth-born calls obeying,
   And petty cares beset their day.

The little brooks o'er rocks are springing,
   The lark's gay carol fills the air:
Why should not I with them be singing
   A joyous anthem free from care?

I wander on, in God confiding,
   For all are His, wood, field, and fell;
O'er earth and skies He still presiding,
   For me will order all things well.

             *   *   *

I gaze around me, going
   By forest, dale, and lea,
O'er heights where streams are flowing,
My every thought bestowing,
   Ah, Lady fair, on thee.

And in my garden, finding
   Bright flowers fresh and rare,
While many a wreath I'm binding,
Sweet thoughts therein I'm winding
   Of thee, my Lady fair.

For me 'twould be too daring
   To lay them at her feet.
They'll soon away be wearing,
But love beyond comparing
   Is thine, my Lady sweet.

In early morning waking,
   I toil with ready smile,
And though my heart be breaking,
I'll sing to hide its aching,
   And dig my grave the while.

* * *

When the earliest morning ray
Through the valley finds its way,
Hill and forest fair awaking,
All who can their flight are taking.

And the lad who's free from care
Shouts, with cap flung high in air,
'Song its flight can aye be winging;
Let me, then, be ever singing.'

THE BROKEN RING

Adown in yon cool valley
   I hear a mill-wheel go:
Alas! my love has left me,
   Who once dwelt there below.

A ring of gold she gave me,
   And vowed she would be true;
The vow long since was broken,
   The gold ring snapped in two.

I would I were a minstrel,
  To rove the wide world o'er,
And sing afar my measures,
  And rove from door to door;

Or else a soldier, flying
  Deep into furious flight,
By silent camp-fires lying
  A-field in gloomy night.

Hear I the mill-wheel going:
  I know not what I will;
'Twere best if I were dying—
  Then all were calm and still.

MORNING PRAYER

O silence, wondrous and profound!
  O'er earth doth solitude still reign;
The woods alone incline their heads,
  As if the Lord walked o'er the plain.

I feel new life within me glow;
  Where now is my distress and care?
Here in the blush of waking morn,
  I blush at yesterday's despair.

To me, a pilgrim, shall the world,
  With all its joy and sorrows, be
But as a bridge that leads, O Lord,
  Across the stream of time to Thee.

And should my song woo worldly gifts,
  The base rewards of vanity—
Dash down my lyre! I'll hold my peace
  Before thee to eternity.

GEORGE ELIOT

GEORGE ELIOT (Mary Ann Evans, English 1819-1880). Leading author of the Victorian novel. Was assistant editor of *Westminster Review*, knew many intellectuals of her day. Novels marked by deep humanity, subtle psychology, concern for philosophical issues. *Middlemarch*, her masterpiece, a detailed study of Victorian Era. Others: *Adam Bede, The Mill on the Floss, Silas Marner, Romola.*

SILAS MARNER

I. *Why Silas Came to Raveloe*

IN the early years of the nineteenth century a linen-weaver named Silas Marner worked at his vocation in a stone cottage that stood among the nutty hedgerows near the village of Raveloe, and not far from the edge of a deserted stone-pit.

It was fifteen years since Silas Marner had first come to Raveloe; he was then simply a pallid young man with prominent, short-sighted brown eyes. To the villagers among whom he had to settle he seemed to have mysterious peculiarities, chiefly owing to his advent from an unknown region called "Northard." He invited no comer to step across his door-sill, and he never strolled into the village to drink a pint at the Rainbow, or to gossip at the wheel-wrights'; he sought no man or woman, save for the purposes of his calling, or in order to supply himself with necessaries.

At the end of fifteen years the Raveloe men said just the same things about Silas Marner as at the beginning. There was only one important addition which the years had brought; it was that Master Marner had laid by a fine sight of money somewhere, and that he could buy up "bigger men than himself."

But while his daily habits presented scarcely any visible change, Marner's inward life had been a history and a metamorphosis as that of every fervid nature must be when it has been condemned to solitude. His life, before he came to Raveloe, had been filled with the close fellowship of a narrow religious sect, where the poorest layman had the chance of distinguishing himself by gifts of speech; and Marner was highly thought of in that little hidden world, known to itself as the church assembling in Lantern Yard. He was believed to be a young man of exemplary life and ardent faith, and a peculiar interest had been centred in him ever since he had fallen at a prayer-meeting into a trance or cataleptic fit, which lasted for an hour.

Among the members of his church there was one young man, named William Dane, with whom he lived in close friendship; and it seemed to the unsuspecting Silas that the friendship suffered no chill, even after he had formed a closer attachment, and had become engaged to a young servant-woman.

At this time the senior deacon was taken dangerously ill, and Silas and William, with others of the brethren, took turns at night-watching. On the night the old man died, Silas fell into one of his trances, and when he awoke at four o'clock in the morning death had come, and further, a little bag of money had been . stolen from the deacon's bureau, and Silas's pocket-knife was found inside the bureau. For some time Silas was mute with astonishment, then he said, "God will clear me; I know nothing about the knife being there, or the money being gone. Search me and my dwelling."

The search was made, and it ended in William Dane finding the deacon's bag, empty, tucked behind the chest of drawers in Silas's chamber.

According to the principles of the church in Lantern Yard prosecution was forbidden to Christians. But the members were bound to take other measures for finding out the truth, and they resolved on praying and drawing lots; there was nothing unusual about such proceedings a hundred years ago. Silas knelt with his brethren, relying on his own innocence being certified by immediate Divine interference. *The lots declared that Silas Marner was guilty*. He was solemnly suspended from church-membership, and called upon to render up the stolen money; only on confession and repentance could he be received once more within the fold of the church. Marner listened in silence. At last, when everyone rose to depart, he went towards William Dane and said, in a voice shaken by agitation, "The last time I remember using my knife was when I took it to cut a strap for you. I don't remember putting it in my pocket again. *You* stole the money, and you have woven a plot to lay the sin at my door. But you may prosper for all that; there is no just God, but a God of lies, that bears witness against the innocent!"

There was a general shudder at this blasphemy. Poor Marner went out with that despair in his soul—that shaken trust in God and man which is little short of madness to a loving nature. In the bitterness of his wounded spirit, he said to himself, "*She* will cast me off, too!" and for a whole day he sat alone, stunned by despair.

355

The second day he took refuge from benumbing unbelief by getting into his loom and working away as usual, and before many hours were past, the minister and one of the deacons came to him with a message from Sarah, the young woman to whom he had been engaged, that she held her engagement at an end. In little more than a month from that time Sarah was married to William Dane, and not long afterwards it was known to the brethren in Lantern Yard that Silas Marner had departed from the town.

II. *The Second Blow*

When Silas Marner first came to Raveloe he seemed to weave like a spider, from pure impulse, without reflection. Then there were the calls of hunger, and Silas, in his solitude, had to provide his own breakfast, dinner, and supper, to fetch his own water from the well, and put his own kettle on the fire; and all these immediate promptings helped to reduce his life to the unquestioning activity of a spinning insect. He hated the thought of the past; there was nothing that called out his love and fellowship towards the strangers he had come amongst; and the future was all dark, for there was no Unseen Love that cared for him.

It was then, when all purpose of life was gone, that Silas got into the habit of looking towards the money he received for his weaving, and grasping it with a sense of fulfilled effort. Gradually, the guineas, the crowns, and the half-crowns, grew to a heap, and Marner drew less and less for his own wants, trying to solve the problem of keeping himself strong enough to work sixteen hours a day on as small an outlay as possible. He handled his coins, he counted them, till their form and colour were like the satisfaction of a thirst to him; but it was only in the night, when his work was done, that he drew them out, to enjoy their companionship. He had taken up some bricks in his floor underneath his loom, and here he had made a hole in which he set the iron pot that contained his guineas and silver coins, covering the bricks with sand whenever he replaced them.

So, year after year, Silas Marner lived in this solitude, his guineas rising in the iron pot, and his life narrowing and hardening itself more and more as it became reduced to the functions of weaving and hoarding.

This is the history of Silas Marner until the fifteenth year after he came to Raveloe. Then, about the Christmas of that year, a second great change came over his life.

It was a raw, foggy night, with rain, and Silas was returning from the village, plodding along, with a sack thrown round his shoulders, and with a horn lantern in his hand. His legs were weary, but his mind was at ease with the sense of security that springs from habit. Supper was his favorite meal, because it was his time of revelry, when his heart warmed over his gold.

He reached his door in much satisfaction that his errand was done; he opened it, and to his short-sighted eyes everything remained as he had left it, except that the fire sent out a welcome increase of heat.

As soon as he was warm he began to think it would be a long while to wait till after supper before he drew out his guineas, and it would be pleasant to see them on the table before him as he ate his food.

He rose and placed his candle unsuspectingly on the floor near his loom, swept away the sand, without noticing any change, and removed the bricks. The sight of the empty hole made his heart leap violently, but the belief that his gold was gone could not come at once—only terror, and the eager effort to put an end to the terror. He passed his trembling hand all about the hole, then he held the candle and examined it curiously, trembling more and more. He searched in every corner, he turned his bed over, and shook it, and kneaded it; he looked in the brick oven; and when there was no other place to be searched, he felt once more all round the hole.

He could see every object in his cottage, and his gold was not there. He put his trembling hands to his head, and gave a wild, ringing scream—the cry of desolation. Then the idea of a thief began to present itself, and he entertained it eagerly, because a thief might be caught and made to release the gold. The robber must be laid hold of. Marner's ideas of legal authority were confused, but he felt that he must go and proclaim his loss; and the great people in the village — the clergyman, the constable, and Squire Cass — would make the thief deliver up the stolen money.

It was to the village inn Silas Marner went, where the parish clerk and a select company were assembled, and told the story of his loss—£272 12s. 6d. in all. The machinery of the law was set in motion, but no thief was ever captured, nor could grounds be found for suspicion against any persons.

What had really happened was that Dunsey Cass, Squire Cass's second son — a mean, boastful rascal — on his way home on foot from hunting, saw the light in the weaver's cottage, and knocked, hoping to borrow a lantern, for the lane was unpleasantly slippery, and the night dark. But all was silence in the cottage, for the weaver at that moment had not yet reached home. For a minute Dunsey thought that old Marner might be dead, fallen over the stone pits. And from that came the decision that he must be dead. If so, the question arose, what would become of the money that everybody said the old miser had put by?

Dunstan Cass was in difficulties for want of money, and he had killed his brother's horse that day on the hunting-field. Who would know, if Marner was dead, that anybody had come to take his hoard of money away?

There were only three hiding-places where he had heard of cottagers' hoards being found: the thatch, the bed, and a hole in the floor. His eyes traveling eagerly over the floor, noted a spot where the sand had been more carefully spread.

Dunstan found the hole and the money, now hidden in two leathern bags. From their weight he judged they must be filled with guineas. Quickly he hastened out into the darkness with the bags, and Dunstan Cass was seen no more alive.

At the very moment when he turned his back on the cottage Silas Marner was not more than a hundred yards away.

III. *Silas Marner's Visitor*

It was New Year's Eve, and Squire Cass was giving a dance to the neighbouring gentry of Raveloe. There had been snow in the afternoon, but at seven o'clock it had ceased, and a freezing wind had sprung up.

A woman, shabbily dressed, with a child in her arms, was making her way towards Raveloe, seeking the Red House, where Squire Cass lived. It was not the squire she wanted, but his eldest son, Godfrey, to whom she was secretly married. The marriage—the result of rash impulse—had been an unhappy one from the first, for Godfrey's wife was the slave of opium. The squire had long desired that his son should marry Miss Nancy Lammeter, and would have turned him out of house and home had he known of the unfortunate marriage already contracted. Cold and weariness drove the woman, even while she walked, to the only comfort she knew. She raised the black remnant to her lips, and then flung the empty phial away. Now she walked, always more and more drowsily, and clutched more and more automatically the sleeping child at her bosom. Soon she felt nothing but a supreme longing to lie down and sleep; and so sank down against a straggling furze-bush, an easy pillow enough; and the bed of snow, too, was soft. The cold was no longer felt, but her arms did not at once relax their instinctive clutch, and the little one slumbered on.

The complete torpor came at last; the fingers lost their tension, the arms unbent; then the little head fell away from the bosom, and the blue eyes of the child opened wide on the cold starlight. At first there was a little peevish cry of "Mammy," as the child rolled downward; and then, suddenly, its eyes were caught by a bright gleaming light on the white ground, and with the ready transition of infancy it decided the light must be caught.

In an instant the child had slipped on all fours, and, after making out that the cunning gleam came from a very bright place, the little one, rising on its legs, toddled through the snow—toddled on to the open door of Silas Marner's cottage, and right up to the warm hearth where was a bright fire.

The little one, accustomed to be left to itself for long hours without notice, squatted down on the old sack spread out before the fire, in perfect contentment. Presently the little golden head sank down, and the blue eyes were veiled by their delicate half-transparent lids.

But where was Silas Marner while this strange visitor had come to his hearth? He was in the cottage, but he did not see the child. Since he had lost his money he had contracted the habit of opening his door, and looking out from time to time, as if he thought that his money might, somehow, be coming back to him.

That morning he had been told by some of his neighbours that it was New Year's Eve, and that he must sit up and hear the old year rung out, and the new rung in, because that was good luck, and might bring his money back again. Perhaps this friendly Raveloe way of jesting had helped to throw Silas into a more than usually excited state. Certainly he opened his door again and again that night, and the last time, just as he put out his hand to close it, the invisible wand of catalepsy arrested him, and there he stood like a graven image, powerless to resist either the good or evil that might enter.

When Marner's sensibility returned he was unaware of the break in his consciousness, and only noticed that he was chilled and faint.

Turning towards the hearth it seemed to his blurred vision as if there was a heap of gold on the floor; but instead of hard coin his fingers encountered soft, warm curls. In utter amazement, Silas fell on his knees to examine the marvel: it was a sleeping child, a round, fair thing, with soft, yellow rings all over its head. Could this be the little sister come back to him in a dream—his little sister whom he had carried about in his arms for a year before she died? That was the first thought. *Was* it a dream? It was very much like his little sister. How and when had the child come in without his knowledge?

But there was a cry on the hearth; the child had awakened, and Marner stooped to lift it on to his knee. He had plenty to do through the next hour. The porridge, sweetened with some dry brown sugar, stopped the cries of the little one for "mammy." Then it occurred to Silas's dull bachelor mind that the child wanted its wet boots off, and this having been done, the wet boots suggested that the child had been walking on the snow.

He made out the marks of the little feet in the snow, and, holding the child in his arms, followed their track to the furze-bush. Then he became aware that there was a human body, half covered with the shifting snow.

With the child in his arms, Silas at once went for the doctor, who was spending the evening at the Red House. And Godfrey Cass recognised that it was his own child he saw in Marner's arms.

The woman was dead—had been dead for some hours, the doctor said: and Godfrey, who had accompanied him to Marner's cottage, understood that he was free to marry Nancy Lammeter.

"You'll take the child to the parish to-morrow?" Godfrey asked, speaking as indifferently as he could.

"Who says so?" said Marner sharply. "Will they make me take her? I shall keep her till anybody shows they've a right to take her away from me. The mother's dead, and I reckon it's got no father. It's a lone thing, and I'm a lone thing. My money's gone—I don't know where, and this is come from I don't know where."

Godfrey returned to the Red House with a sense of relief and gladness, and Silas kept the child. There had been a softening of feeling to him in the village since the day of his robbery, and now an active sympathy was aroused amongst the women. The child was christened Hephzibah, after Marner's mother, and was called Eppie for short.

IV. *Eppie's Decision*

Eppie had come to link Silas Marner once more with the whole world. The disposition to hoard had utterly gone, and there was no longer any repulsion around to him.

As the child grew up, one person watched with keener, though more hidden interest than any other the prosperous growth of Eppie under the weaver's care. The squire was dead, and Godfrey Cass was married to Nancy Lammeter. He had no child of his own save the one that knew him not. No Dunsey had ever turned up, and people had ceased to think of him.

Sixteen years had passed, and now Aaron Winthrop, a well-behaved young gardener, is wanting to marry Eppie, and Eppie is willing to have him "some time."

" 'Everybody's married some time,' Aaron says," said Eppie. "But I told him that wasn't true, for I said look at father—he's never been married."

"No, child," said Silas, "your father was a lone man till you was sent to him."

"But you'll never be lone again, father," said Eppie tenderly. "That was what Aaron said—'I could never think o' taking you away from Master Marner, Eppie.' And I said, 'It 'ud be no use if you did, Aaron.' And he wants us all to live together, so as you needn't work a bit, father, only what's for your own pleasure, and he'd be as good as a son to you—that was what he said."

The proposal to separate Eppie from her foster-father came from Godfrey Cass.

When the old stone-pit by Marner's cottage went dry, owing to drainage operations, the skeleton of Dunstan Cass was found, wedged between two great stones. The watch and seals were recognised, and all the weaver's money was at the bottom of the pit. The shock of this discovery moved Godfrey to tell Nancy the secret of his earlier marriage.

"Everything comes to light, Nancy, sooner or later," he said. "That woman Marner found dead in the snow—Eppie's mother—was my wife. Eppie is my child. I oughtn't to have left the child unowned. I oughtn't to have kept it from you."

"It's but little wrong to me, Godfrey," Nancy answered sadly. "You've made it up to me—you've been good to me for fifteen years. It'll be a different coming to us, now she's grown up."

They were childless, and it hadn't occurred to them as they approached Silas Marner's cottage that Godfrey's offer might be declined. At first Godfrey explained that he and his wife wanted to adopt Eppie in place of a daughter.

"Eppie, my child, speak," said old Marner faintly. "I won't stand in your way. Thank Mr. and Mrs. Cass."

"Thank you, ma'am—thank you, sir," said Eppie dropping a curtsy; "but I can't leave my father, nor own anybody nearer than him."

Godfrey Cass was irritated at this obstacle.

"But I've a claim on you, Eppie," he returned. "It's my duty, Marner, to own Eppie as my child, and provide for her. She's my own child. Her mother was my wife. I've a natural claim on her."

"Then, sir, why didn't you say so sixteen years ago, and claim her before I'd come to love her, i'stead o' coming to take her from me now, when you might as well take the heart out o' my body? When a man turns a blessing from his door, it falls to them as take it in. But let it be as you will. Speak to the child. I'll hinder nothing."

"Eppie, my dear," said Godfrey, looking at his daughter not without some embarrassment, "it'll always be our wish that you should show your love and gratitude to one who's been a father to you so many years; but we hope you'll come to love us as well, and though I haven't been what a father should ha' been to you all these years, I wish to do the utmost in my power for you now, and provide for you as my only child. And you'll have the best of mothers in my wife."

Eppie did not come forward and curtsy as she had done before, but she held Silas's hand in hers and grasped it firmly.

"Thank you, ma'am—thank you, sir, for your offers—they're very great and far above my wish. For I should have no delight in life any more if I was forced to go away from my father."

In vain Nancy expostulated mildly.

"I can't feel as I've got any father but one," said Eppie. "I've always thought of a little home where he'd sit i' the corner, and I should fend and do everything for him. I can't think o' no other home. I wasn't brought up to be a lady, and," she ended passionately, "I'm promised to marry a working man, as'll live with father and help me to take care of him."

Godfrey Cass and his wife went out.

A year later Eppie was married, and Mrs. Godfrey Cass provided the wedding dress, and Mr. Cass made some necessary alterations to suit Silas's larger family.

"Oh, father," said Eppie, when the bridal party returned from the church, "what a pretty home ours is! I think nobody could be happier than we are!"

MIHAIL EMINESCU

MIHAIL EMINESCU (Rumanian, 1850-1889). Outstanding Rumanian poet. Highly sensitive and romantic, unable to adjust to everyday life. Killed by another inmate in insane asylum. Wrote 60 poems, a novel, fairy tales, and articles on wide range of subjects. His pessimism reflected in later Rumanian writers.

SONNET

How many stars in lofty heaven ascending;
How many billows seam the ocean's flowing,
With serried lights and scintillations glowing,
And endless movement—is our thought transcending.
Choose as thou wilt, the road of Life's bestowing;
Rising to greatness, or to crime descending;
Dust and the darkness Fate for each is sending;
To mute oblivion, like the rest, art going.
I saw me dying; 'mid the shadowed porches
They did appear in lonely earth would lay me;
I heard the requiem chants, and saw the torches.
O dulcet shadow; pray thee, draw more nigh me,
That I may feel Death's hovering shade approaches,
With weeping lids and dark wings, pausing by me.

O'ER THE TREES

O'er the trees the moon is showing;
  Stir the leaves in forest brake,
And the alder branches shake,
  Whilst the wistful horn is blowing.

Further wending, further wending;
  Heard more faint, and yet more faint;
To my soul with sorrow blent,
  Healing hope of Death thou'rt sending.

Why art silent, when, becalmèd,
  Turns my sad heart to thy strain?
Gentle horn, wilt sound again,
  Sound for me thy notes encharmèd?

WHY COMEST NOT? WHY COMEST NOT?

Behold the swallows quit the eaves,
And fall the yellowed walnut leaves,
The hoar frost doth the vineyard rot;
Why comest not? Why comest not?

Unto mine arms, O love, return;
Mine eager eyes to thee shall yearn;
My weary head find gentle rest
Upon thy breast; upon thy breast.

Dost thou remember? Oft indeed
We twain did hie o'er vale and mead;
And oft I raised thee, sweetheart mine;
Ah, many a time! Ah, many a time!

On earth full many women dwell
Whose eyes the sparkling stars excel;
But how so bright their eyes may be,
They're not like thee! They're not like thee!

Since thy dear bounty sweet affords
My life the joys of love's accords,
For me thou dost the stars outshine;
Beloved mine! Beloved mine!

Now speed the last of Autumn days,
The dead leaves scatter on the ways,
The lonely fields are dank and drear—
Why art not here? Why art not here?

364

EURIPIDES

EURIPIDES (Greek, 485-406 B.C.). The most influential and popular of the
Greek tragedians. The dramatist of great human passions, as opposed to more
philosophic conceptions of Aeschylus and Sophocles. Wrote over 80 plays, of
which 19 survive—including *Alcestis, Medea, Electra, Orestes*. These seem
almost modern in portrayal of strong personalities in grip of warring emotions.

MEDEA'S WRONGS

Nurse of Medea. All is variance now
And hate: for Jason, to his children false,
False to my mistress, for a royal bride
Hath left her couch, and wedded Creon's daughter,
Lord of this land. Ill doth Medea brook
This base dishonor; on his oath she calls,
Recalls their plighted hands, the firmest pledge
Of mutual faith, and calls the gods to witness
What a requital she from Jason finds.
Of food regardless, and in sorrow sunk
She lies, and melts in tears each tedious hour
Since first she knew her lord had injured her;
Nor lifts her eye, nor lifts her face from the earth
Deaf to her friends' entreaties as a rock,
Or billow of the sea; save when she turns
Her snowy neck, and to herself bewails
Her father, and her country, and her house,
Which she betray'd to follow this base man,
Who treats her now with such indignity.
Affliction now hath taught her what it is
Not to forsake a parent and his house.
She hates her children, nor with pleasure sees them.
I fear her, lest she form some strange design;
For violent her temper, and of wrongs
Impatient: well I know her, and I fear her,
Lest, in the dead of night, when all are laid
In deep repose, she steal into the house,
And plunge into their breast the piercing sword;
Or murder ev'n the monarch of the land,
Or the new-married Jason, on herself
Drawing severer ills: for like a storm
Her passions swell, and he that dares enrage her
Will have small cause to boast his victory.

But see, her sons from the gymnastic ring
Returning, heedless of their mother's ills;
For youth holds no society with grief.

Enter Tutor, with the Sons of Medea.

Tut.   Thou old domestic servant of my mistress,
Why dost thou take thy station at the gates,
And ruminate in silence on thy griefs?
How hath Medea wish'd to be alone?

Nur.   Thou good old man, attendant on the sons
Of Jason, faithful servants with their lords
Suffer in their afflictions, and their hearts
Are touch'd with social sorrow; and my griefs
Swell, for Medea's sufferings, to such height,
That strong desire impell'd me to come forth,
And tell them to the earth and to the skies.

Tut.   Admits she yet no respite to her groans?

Nur.   I wonder at thee: no, these ills but now
Are rising, to their height not yet advanced.

Tut.   I heard one say, not seeming to attend,
But passing on to where they play with dice,
Among the grave old men, who then by chance
Were sitting near Pirene's hallow'd stream,
That Creon, lord of this fair land, will drive
These children and their mother from the state
Of Corinth: whether this report be true
I know not, but I wish it otherwise.

Nur.   Will Jason bear to see his sons thus wrong'd,
Though he regards their mother now no more?

Tut.   To new alliances the old gives place,
And to this house he is no more a friend.

Nur.   Ruin would follow, to the former ill
If this were added ere the first subsides.

Tut.   Be cautious then; it were unseasonable
Our queen knew this; in silence close thy lips.

Nur.   Go in, my children, go: all will be well;
And take thou heed, keep them aloof, nor let them
Come near their mother while her griefs are fresh:
Cruel her eye, and wild; I mark'd it late,
Expressive of some dark design on these:

Nor will she check her fury, well I know,
Till the storm bursts on some one: may its stroke
Fall on some hostile head, not on a friend.

    Medea (within.) Wretch that I am, what anguish rends my
        heart!
Wretched Medea, how art thou undone!

    Nur. Ay, thus it is. Your mother, my dear children,
Swells with resentment, swells with rage. Go in,
Go quickly in; but come not in her eye,
Approach her not, but keep you from the wild
And dreadful fury of her violent temper.
Go now, go quickly in; this rising cloud
Of grief forebodes a storm, which soon will fall
With greater rage: inflamed with injuries,
What will not her tempestuous spirit dare?

    Med. Ah me! ah me! what mighty wrongs I bear,
Wrongs that demand my tears and loud laments!
Ye sons accursed of a detested mother,
Perish, together with your father perish,
And in one general ruin sink your house!

    Nur. Ah me unhappy! in their father's fault
Why make thy sons associates? Why on them
Rises thy hatred? Oh, I fear, I fear,
My children, lest some evil threatens you.
Kings have a fiery quality of soul,
Accustom'd to command; if once they feel
Control, though small, their anger blazes out,
Not easily extinguish'd; hence I deem
An equal mediocrity of life
More to be wish'd; if not in gorgeous state,
Yet without danger glides it on to age.
There's a protection in its very name,
And happiness dwells with it: but the height
Of towering greatness long to mortal man
Remains not fix'd, and, when misfortune comes
Enraged, in deeper ruin sinks the house.

    Chorus. I heard the voice, I heard the loud laments
Of the unhappy Colchian: do her griefs
(Say, reverend matron), find no respite yet?
From the door's opening valve I heard her voice.
No pleasure in the sorrows of your home

I take; for deeds are done not grateful to me.

Nur. This is no more a home; all here is vanish'd,
Nor leaves a trace behind. The monarch's house
He makes his own; while my unhappy mistress
In her lone chamber melts her life away
In tears, unmoved by all the arguments
Urged by her friends to soothe her sorrowing soul.

Med. O that the ethereal lightning on this head
Would fall! Why longer should I wish to live?
Unhappy me! Death would be welcome now,
And kindly free me from this hated life.

Cho. Dost thou hear this, O Jove, O Earth, O Light,
The mournful voice of this unhappy dame?
Why thus indulge this unabated force
Of nuptial love, self-rigorous, hastening death?
Let it not be thy wish: if a new bed
Now charms thy husband, be not his offence
Engraved too deep: Jove will avenge thy wrongs;
Let not thy sorrows prey upon thy heart.

Med. O powerful Themis, O revered Diana,
See what I suffer, though with sacred oaths
This vile, accursed husband I had bound!
Oh, might I one day see him and his bride
Rent piecemeal in their house, who unprovoked
Have dared to wrong me thus! Alas, my father!
Alas, my country! whom my shameful flight
Abandon'd, having first my brother slain!

Cho. I hear her lamentations mixed with groans,
Which in the anguish of her heart she vents;
And on her faithless husband, who betray'd
Her bed, she calls aloud; upon the gods,
Thus basely wrong'd, she calls, attesting Themis,
Daughter of Jove, the arbitress of oaths,
Who led her to the shores of Greece, across
The rolling ocean, when the shades of night
Darken'd its waves, and steer'd her through the straits.

MEDEA'S LAST WORDS TO HER CHILDREN

O children, children! you have still a city,
A home, where, lost to me and all my woe,
You will live out your lives without a mother!

But I—lo! I am for another land,
Leaving the joy of you. To see you happy,
To deck your marriage-bed, to greet your bride,
To light your wedding torch shall not be mine!
O me, thrice wretched in my own self-will!
In vain then, dear my children! did I rear you;
In vain I travailed, and with wearing sorrow
Bore bitter anguish in the hour of childbirth!
Yea, of a sooth, I had great hope of you,
That you should cherish my old age, and deck
My corpse with loving hands, and make me blessed
'Mid women in my death. But now, ah me!
Hath perished that sweet dream. For long without you
I shall drag out a dreary, doleful age.
And you shall never see your mother more
With your dear eyes: for all your life is changed.
Woe, woe!
Why gaze you at me with your eyes, my children?
Why smile your last sweet smile? Ah me! ah me!
What shall I do? My heart dissolves within me,
Friends, when I see the glad eyes of my sons!
I cannot. No: my will that was so steady,
Farewell to it. They too shall go with me:
Why should I wound their sire with what wounds them,
Heaping tenfold his woes on my own head?
No. no, I shall not. Perish my proud will.
Yet whence this weakness? Do I wish to reap
The scorn that springs from enemies unpunished?
Dare it I must. What craven fool am I,
To let soft thoughts flow trickling from my soul!
Go, boys, into the house: and he who may not
Be present at my solemn sacrifice—
Let him see to it. My hand shall not falter.
Ah! ah!
Nay, do not, O my heart! do not this thing!
Suffer them, O poor fool; yea, spare thy children!
There in thy exile they will gladden thee.
Not so: by all the plagues of nethermost Hell,
It shall not be that I, that I should suffer
My foes to triumph and insult my sons!
Die must they: this must be, and since it must,

I, I myself will slay them, I who bore them.
So it is fixed, and there is no escape.
Even as I speak, the crown is on her head,
The bride is dying in her robes, I know it.
But since this path most piteous I tread,
Sending them forth on paths more piteous far,
I will embrace my children. O my sons,
Give, give your mother your dear hands to kiss!
O dearest hands, and mouths most dear to me,
And forms and noble faces of my sons!
Be happy even there: what here was yours,
Your father robs you of. O loved embrace!
O tender touch and sweet breath of my boys!
Go, go, go, leave me! Lo, I cannot bear
To look on you, my woes have overwhelmed me!
Now know I all the ill I have to do:
But rage is stronger than my better mind;
Rage, cause of greatest crimes and griefs to mortals.

ABRAHAM IBN EZRA

ABRAHAM IBN EZRA (Spanish-Hebrew, 1092-1167). Wandering hymnist and philosopher. Traveled through many non-Moslem lands, so became first Hebrew-Spaniard to write entirely in Hebrew. Wrote many liturgical poems, philosophic works, and an Arabic study of Spanish-Hebrew poetry.

I. SONGS

I

The shadow of the houses leave behind,
In the cool boscage of the grove reclined,
The wine of friendship from love's goblet drink,
And entertain with cheerful speech the mind.

Drink, friend! behold, the dreary winter's gone,
The mantle of old age has time withdrawn.
The sunbeam glitters in the morning dew,
O'er hill and vale youth's bloom is surging on.

Cup-bearer! quench with snow the goblet's fire,
Even as the wise man cools and stills his ire.
Look, when the jar is drained, upon the brim
The light foam melteth with the heart's desire.

Cup-bearer! bring anear the silver bowl,
And with the glowing gold fulfil the whole,
Unto the weak new vigor it imparts,
And without lance subdues the hero's soul.

My love sways, dancing, like the myrtle-tree,
The masses of her curls disheveled, see!
She kills me with her darts, intoxicates
My burning blood, and will not set me free.

Within the aromatic garden come,
And slowly in its shadows let us roam,
The foliage be the turban for our brows,
And the green branches o'er our heads a dome.

All pain thou with the goblet shalt assuage,
The wine-cup heals the sharpest pangs that rage,
Let others crave inheritance of wealth,
Joy be our portion and our heritage.

Drink in the garden, friend, anigh the rose,
Richer than spice's breath the soft air blows.
If it should cease a little traitor then,
A zephyr light its secret would disclose.

II

Thou who art clothed in silk, who drawest on
Proudly thy raiment of fine linen spun,
Bethink thee of the day when thou alone
Shalt dwell at last beneath the marble stone.

Anigh the nests of adders thine abode,
With the earth-crawling serpent and the toad.
Trust in the Lord, He will sustain thee there,
And without fear thy soul shall rest with God.

If the world flatter thee with soft-voiced art,
Know 'tis a cunning witch who charms thy heart,
Whose habit is to wed man's soul with grief,
And those who are close-bound in love to part.

He who bestows his wealth upon the poor,
Has only lent it to the Lord, be sure—
Of what avail to clasp it with clenched hand?
It goes not with us to the grave obscure.

The voice of those who dwell within the tomb,
Who in corruption's house have made their home;
"O ye who wander o'er us still today,
When will ye come to share with us the gloom?"

How can'st thou ever of the world complain,
And murmuring, burden it with all thy pain?
Silence! thou art a traveller at an inn,
A guest, who may but over night remain.

Be thou not wroth against the proud, but show
How he who yesterday great joy did know,
Today is begging for his very bread,
And painfully upon a crutch must go.

How foolish they whose faith is fixed upon
The treasures of their worldly wealth alone,
Far wiser were it to obey the Lord,
And only say, "The will of God be done!"

Has Fortune smiled on thee? Oh, do not trust
Her reckless joy, she still deceives and must.
Perpetual snares she spreads about thy feet,
Thou shalt not rest till thou art mixed with dust.

Man is a weaver on the earth. 'tis said,
Who weaves and weaves—his own days are the thread,
And when the length allotted he hath spun,
All life is over, and all hope is dead.

II. IN THE NIGHT

Unto the house of prayer my spirit yearns,
Unto the sources of her being turns,
To where the sacred light of heaven burns,
She struggles thitherward by day and night.

The splendor of God's glory blinds her eyes,
Up without wings she soareth to the skies,
With silent aspiration seeks to rise,
In dusky evening and in darksome night.

To her the wonders of God's works appear,
She longs with fervor Him to draw anear,
The tidings of His glory reach her ear,
From morn to even, and from night to night.

The banner of thy grace did o'er me rest,
Yet was thy worship banished from my breast.
Almighty, thou didst seek me out and test
To try and to instruct me in the night.

Infatuate I trifled youth away,
In nothingness dreamed through my manhood's day.
Therefore my streaming tears I may not stay,
They are my meat and drink by day and night.

In flesh imprisoned is the son of light,
This life is but a bridge when seen aright.
Rise in the silent hour and pray with might,
Awake and call upon the God by night!

Hasten to cleanse thyself of sin, arise!
Follow Truth's path that leads unto the skies,
As swift as yesterday existence flies,
Brief even as a watch within the night.

Man enters life for trouble: all he has,
And all that he beholds, is pain, alas!
Like to a flower does he bloom and pass,
He fadeth like a vision of the night.

The surging floods of life around him roar,
Death feeds upon him, pity is no more,
To others all his riches he gives o'er,
And dieth in the middle hour of night.

Crushed by the burden of my sins I pray,
Oh, wherefore shunned I not the evil way?
Deep are my sighs, I weep the livelong day,
And wet my couch with tears night after night.

My spirit stirs, my streaming tears still run,
Like to the wild birds' notes my sorrows' tone,
In the hushed silence loud resounds my groan,
My soul arises moaning in the night.

Within her narrow soul oppressed with dread,
Bare of adornment and with grief-bowed head
Lamenting, many a tear her sad eyes shed,
She weeps with anguish in the gloomy night.

For tears my burden seem to lighten best,
Could I but weep my heart's blood, I might rest.
My spirit bows with mighty grief oppressed,
I utter forth my prayer within the night.

Youth's charm has like a fleeting shadow gone,
With eagle wings the hours of life have flown.
Alas! the time when pleasure I have known,
I may not now recall by day or night.

The haughty scorn pursues me of my foe,
Evil his thought, yet soft his speech and low.
Forget it not, but bear his purpose so
Forever in thy mind by day and night.

Observe a pious fast, be whole again,
Hasten to purge thy heart of every stain.
No more from prayer and penitence refrain,
But turn unto thy God by day and night.

He speaks: "My son, yea, I will send thee aid,
Bend thou thy steps to me, be not afraid.
No nearer friend than I am, hast thou made,
Possess thy soul in patience one more night."

III. ELEGY

My thoughts impelled me to the resting-place
Where sleep my parents, many a friend and brother.
I asked them (no one heard and none replied):
"Do ye forsake me, too, oh father, mother?"
Then from the grave, without a tongue, these cried,
And showed my own place waiting by their side.

F

WILLIAM FAULKNER

WILLIAM FAULKNER (American, 1897-   ). Considered by some the most important American novelist, but until recently more admired abroad than in this country. Nobel Prize winner, 1949. Novels describe decay of a Southern county and its major families. Major works: *The Sound and the Fury, As I Lay Dying, Light in August, Intruder in the Dust, A Fable.*

A ROSE FOR EMILY

WHEN Miss Emily Grierson died, our whole town went to her funeral: the men through a sort of respectful affection for a fallen monument, the women mostly out of curiosity to see the inside of her house, which no one save an old man-servant—a combined gardener and cook—had seen in at least ten years.

It was a big, squarish frame house that had once been white, decorated with cupolas and spires and scrolled balconies in the heavily lightsome style of the Seventies, set on what had once been our most select street. But garages and cotton gins had encroached and obliterated even the august names of that neighborhood; only Miss Emily's house was left, lifting its stubborn and coquettish decay above the cotton wagons and the gasoline pumps—an eyesore among eyesores. And now Miss Emily had gone to join the representatives of those august names where they lay in the cedar-bemused cemetery among the ranked and anonymous graves of Union and Confederate soldiers who fell at the battle of Jefferson.

Alive, Miss Emily had been a tradition, a duty, and a care; a sort of hereditary obligation upon the town, dating from that day in 1894 when Colonel Sartoris, the mayor—he who fathered the edict that no Negro woman should appear on the streets without an apron —remitted her taxes, the dispensation dating from the death of her father on into perpetuity. Not that Miss Emily would have accepted charity. Colonel Sartoris invented an involved tale to the effect that Miss Emily's father had loaned money to the town, which the town, as a matter of business, preferred this way of repaying. Only a man of Colonel Sartoris' generation and thought could have invented it, and only a woman could have believed it.

When the next generation, with its more modern ideas, became mayors and aldermen, this arrangement created some little dissatisfaction. On the first of the year they mailed her a tax notice. February came, and there was no reply. They wrote her a formal letter, asking her to call at the sheriff's office at her convenience. A week later the mayor wrote her himself, offering to call or send his car for her, and received in reply a note on paper of an archaic shape, in a thin, flowing calligraphy in faded ink, to the effect that she no longer went out at all. The tax notice was also enclosed, without comment.

They called a special meeting of the Board of Aldermen. A deputation waited upon her, knocked at the door through which no visitor had passed since she ceased giving china-painting lessons eight or ten years earlier. They were admitted by the old Negro into a dim hall from which a stairway mounted into still more shadow. It smelled of dust and disuse—a close, dank smell. The Negro led them into the parlor. It was furnished in heavy, leather-covered furniture. When the Negro opened the blinds of one window, they could see that the leather was cracked; and when they sat down, a faint dust rose sluggishly about their thighs, spinning with slow motes in the single sun-ray. On a tarnished gilt easel before the fireplace stood a crayon portrait of Miss Emily's father.

They rose when she entered—a small, fat woman in black, with a thin gold chain descending to her waist and vanishing into her belt, leaning on an ebony cane with a tarnished gold head. Her skeleton was small and spare; perhaps that was why what would have been merely plumpness in another was obesity in her. She looked bloated, like a body long submerged in motionless water, and of that pallid hue. Her eyes, lost in the fatty ridges of her face, looked like two small pieces of coal pressed into a lump of dough as they moved from one face to another while the visitors stated their errand.

She did not ask them to sit. She just stood in the door and listened quietly until the spokesman came to a stumbling halt. Then they could hear the invisible watch ticking at the end of the gold chain. Her voice was dry and cold. "I have no taxes in Jefferson. Colonel

Sartoris explained it to me. Perhaps one of you can gain access to the city records and satisfy yourselves."

"But we have. We are the city authorities, Miss Emily. Didn't you get a notice from the sheriff, signed by him?"

"I received a paper, yes," Miss Emily said. "Perhaps he considers himself the sheriff . . . I have no taxes in Jefferson."

"But there is nothing on the books to show that, you see. We must go by the—"

"See Colonel Sartoris. I have no taxes in Jefferson."

"But, Miss Emily—"

"See Colonel Sartoris." (Colonel Sartoris had been dead almost ten years.) "I have no taxes in Jefferson. Tobe!" The Negro appeared. "Show these gentlemen out."

II

So she vanquished them, horse and foot, just as she had vanquished their fathers thirty years before about the smell. That was two years after her father's death and a short time after her sweetheart—the one we believed would marry her—had deserted her. After her father's death she went out very little; after her sweetheart went away, people hardly saw her at all. A few of the ladies had the temerity to call, but were not received, and the only sign of life about the place was the Negro man—a young man then—going in and out with a market basket.

"Just as if a man—any man—could keep a kitchen properly," the ladies said; so they were not surprised when the smell developed. It was another link between the gross, teeming world and the high and mighty Griersons.

A neighbor, a woman, complained to the mayor, Judge Stevens, eighty years old.

"But what will you have me do about it, madam?" he said.

"Why, send her word to stop it," the woman said. "Isn't there a law?"

"I'm sure that won't be necessary," Judge Stevens said. "It's probably a snake or a rat that nigger of hers killed in the yard. I'll speak to him about it."

The next day he received two more complaints, one from a man who came in diffident deprecation. "We really must do something about it, Judge. I'd be the last one in the world to bother Miss

378

Emily, but we've got to do something." That night the Board of Aldermen met—three gray-beards and one younger man, a member of the rising generation.

"It's simple enough," he said. "Send her word to have her place cleaned up. Give her a certain time to do it in, and if she don't . . ."

"Dammit, sir," Judge Stevens said, "will you accuse a lady to her face of smelling bad?"

So the next night, after midnight, four men crossed Miss Emily's lawn and slunk about the house like burglars, sniffing along the base of the brickwork and at the cellar openings while one of them performed a regular sowing motion with his hand out of a sack slung from his shoulder. They broke open the cellar door and sprinkled lime there, and in all the outbuildings. As they recrossed the lawn, a window that had been dark was lighted and Miss Emily sat in it, the light behind her, and her upright torso motionless as that of an idol. They crept quietly across the lawn and into the shadow of the locusts that lined the street. After a week or two the smell went away.

That was when people had begun to feel really sorry for her. People in our town, remembering how Old Lady Wyatt, her great-aunt, had gone completely crazy at last, believed that the Griersons held themselves a little too high for what they really were. None of the young men was quite good enough to Miss Emily and such. We had long thought of them as a tableau: Miss Emily a slender figure in white in the background, her father a spraddled silhouette in the foreground, his back to her and clutching a horse-whip, the two of them framed by the back-flung front door. So when she got to be thirty and was still single, we were not pleased exactly, but vindicated; even with insanity in the family she wouldn't have turned down all of her chances if they had really materialized.

When her father died, it got about that the house was all that was left to her; and in a way, people were glad. At last they could pity Miss Emily. Being left alone, and a pauper, she had become humanized. Now she too would know the old thrill and the old despair of a penny more or less.

The day after his death all the ladies prepared to call at the house and offer condolence and aid, as is our custom. Miss Emily met them at the door, dressed as usual and with no trace of grief on her face. She told them that her father was not dead. She did that for three days, with the ministers calling on her, and the doctors, trying to persuade her to let them dispose of the body. Just as they were about to resort to law and force, she broke down, and they buried her father quickly.

We did not say she was crazy then. We believed she had to do that. We remembered all the young men her father had driven away, and we knew that with nothing left, she would have to cling to that which had robbed her, as people will.

III

She was sick for a long time. When we saw her again, her hair was cut short, making her look like a girl, with a vague resemblance to those angels in colored church windows—sort of tragic and serene.

The town had just let the contracts for paving the sidewalks, and in the summer after her father's death they began the work. The construction company came with niggers and mules and machinery, singing in time to the rise and fall of picks. Pretty soon he knew everybody in town. Whenever you heard a lot of laughing anyman, with a big voice and eyes lighter than his face. The little boys would follow in groups to hear him cuss the niggers, and the niggers and a foreman named Homer Barron, a Yankee—a big, dark, ready where about the square, Homer Barron would be in the center of the group. Presently we began to see him and Miss Emily on Sunday afternoons driving in the yellow-wheeled buggy and the matched team of bays from the livery stable.

At first we were glad that Miss Emily would have an interest because the ladies all said, "Of course a Grierson would not think seriously of a Northerner, a day laborer." But there were still others, older people, who said that even grief could not cause a real lady to forget *noblesse oblige*—without calling it *noblesse oblige*. They just said, "Poor Emily. Her kinsfolk should come to her." She had some kin in Alabama; but years ago her father had fallen out with them over the estate of Old Lady Wyatt, the crazy woman, and there was no communication between the two families. They had not even been represented at the funeral.

And as soon as the old people said, "Poor Emily," the whispering began. "Do you suppose it's really so?" they said to one another. "Of course it is. What else could . . ." This behind their hands; rustling of craned silk and satin behind jalousies closed upon the sun of Sunday afternoon as the thin, swift clop-clop-clop of the matched team passed: "Poor Emily."

She carried her head high enough—even when we believed that she was fallen. It was as if she demanded more than ever the recognition of her dignity as the last Grierson; as if it had wanted that touch of earthiness to reaffirm her imperviousness. Like when she bought the rat poison, the arsenic. That was over a year after they had begun to say "Poor Emily," and while the two female cousins were visiting her.

"I want some poison," she said to the druggist. She was over thirty then, still a slight woman, though thinner than usual, with cold, haughty black eyes in a face the flesh of which was strained across the temples and about the eye-sockets as you imagine a light-house-keeper's face ought to look. "I want some poison," she said.

"Yes, Miss Emily. What kind? For rats and such? I'd recom—"

"I want the best you have. I don't care what kind."

The druggist named several. "They'll kill anything up to an elephant. But what you want is—"

"Arsenic," Miss Emily said. "Is that a good one?"

"Is . . . arsenic? Yes, ma'am. But what you want—"

"I want arsenic."

The druggist looked down at her. She looked back at him, erect, her face like a strained flag. "Why, of course," the druggist said. "If that's what you want. But the law requires you to tell what you are going to use it for."

Miss Emily just stared at him, her head tilted back in order to look him eye for eye, until he looked away and went and got the arsenic and wrapped it up. The Negro delivery boy brought her the package; the druggist didn't come back. When she opened the package at home there was written on the box, under the skull and bones: "For rats."

IV

So the next day we all said, "She will kill herself"; and we said it would be the best thing. When she had first begun to be seen with Homer Barron, we had said, "She will marry him." Then we said, "She will persuade him yet," because Homer himself had remarked—he liked men, and it was known that he drank with the younger men in the Elk's Club—that he was not a marrying man. Later we said, "Poor Emily" behind the jalousies as they passed on Sunday afternoon in the glittering buggy, Miss Emily with her head high and Homer Barron with his hat cocked and a cigar in his teeth, reins and whip in a yellow glove.

Then some of the ladies began to say that it was a disgrace to the town and a bad example to the young people. The men did not want to interfere, but at last the ladies forced the Baptist minister—Miss Emily's people were Episcopal—to call upon her. He would never divulge what happened during that interview, but he refused to go back again. The next Sunday they again drove about the streets, and the following day the minister's wife wrote to Miss Emily's relations in Alabama.

So she had blood-kin under her roof again and we sat back to watch developments. At first nothing happened. Then we were sure that they were to be married. We learned that Miss Emily had been to the jeweler's and ordered a man's toilet set in silver, with the letter H. B. on each piece. Two days later we learned that she had bought a complete outfit of men's clothing, including a nightshirt, and we said, "They are married." We were really glad. We were glad because the two female cousins were even more Grierson than Miss Emily had ever been.

So we were not surprised when Homer Barron—the streets had been finished some time since—was gone. We were a little disappointed that there was not a public blowing-off, but we believed that he had gone on to prepare for Miss Emily's coming, or to give her a chance to get rid of the cousins. (By that time it was a cabal, and we were all Miss Emily's allies to help circumvent the cousins.) Sure enough, after another week they departed. And, as we had expected all along, within three days Homer Barron was back in town. A neighbor saw the Negro man admit him at the kitchen door at dusk one evening.

And that was the last we saw of Homer Barron. And of Miss Emily for some time. The Negro man went in and out with the market basket, but the front door remained closed. Now and then we would see her at a window for a moment, as the men did that night when they sprinkled the lime, but for almost six months she did not appear on the streets. Then we knew that this was to be expected too; as if that quality of her father which had thwarted her woman's life so many times had been too virulent and too furious to die.

When we next saw Miss Emily, she had grown fat and her hair was turning gray. During the next few years it grew grayer and grayer until it attained an even pepper-and-salt iron-gray, when it ceased turning. Up to the day of her death at seventy-four it was still that vigorous iron-gray, like the hair of an active man.

From that time on her front door remained closed, save for a period of six or seven years, when she was about forty, during which she gave lessons in china-painting. She fitted up a studio in one of the downstairs rooms, where the daughters and granddaughters of Colonel Sartoris' contemporaries were sent to her with the same regularity and in the same spirit that they were sent to church on Sundays with a twenty-five-cent piece for the collection plate. Meanwhile her taxes had been remitted.

Then the newer generation became the backbone and the spirit of the town, and the painting pupils grew up and fell away and did not send their children to her with boxes of color and tedious brushes and pictures cut from the ladies' magazines. The front door closed upon the last one and remained closed for good. When the town got free postal delivery, Miss Emily alone refused to let them fasten the metal numbers above her door and attach a mailbox to it. She would not listen to them.

Daily, monthly, yearly we watched the Negro grow grayer and more stooped, going in and out with the market basket. Each December we sent her a tax notice, which would be returned by the post office a week later, unclaimed. Now and then we would see her in one of the downstairs windows—she had evidently shut up the top floor of the house—like the carven torso of an idol in a niche, looking or not looking at us, we could never tell which. Thus she passed from generation to generation—dear, inescapable, impervious, tranquil, and perverse.

And so she died. Fell ill in the house filled with dust and shadows, with only a doddering Negro man to wait on her. We did not even know she was sick; we had long since given up trying to get any information from the Negro. He talked to no one, probably not even to her,· for his voice had grown harsh and rusty, as if from disuse.

She died in one of the downstairs rooms, in a heavy walnut bed with a curtain, her gray head propped on a pillow yellow and moldy with age and lack of sunlight.

V

The Negro met the first of the ladies at the front door and let them in, with their hushed, sibilant voices and their quick, curious glances, and then he disappeared. He walked right through the house and out the back and was not seen again.

The two female cousins came at once. They held the funeral on the second day, with the town coming to look at Miss Emily beneath a mass of bought flowers, with the crayon face of her father musing profoundly above the bier and the ladies sibilant and macabre; and the very old men—some in their brushed Confederate uniforms—on the porch and the lawn, talking of Miss Emily as if she had been a contemporary of theirs, believing that they had danced with her and courted her perhaps, confusing time with its mathematical progression, as the old do, to whom all the past is not a diminishing road but, instead, a huge meadow which no winter ever quite touches, divided from them now by the narrow bottle-neck of the most recent decade of years.

Already we knew that there was one room in that region above stairs which no one had seen in forty years, and which would have to be forced. They waited until Miss Emily was decently in the ground before they opened it.

The violence of breaking down the door seemed to fill this room with pervading dust. A thin, acrid pall as of the tomb seemed to lie everywhere upon this room decked and furnished as for a bridal; upon the valence curtains of faded rose color, upon the rose-shaded lights, upon the dressing table, upon the delicate array of crystal and the man's toilet things backed with tarnished silver, silver so tarnished that the monogram was obscured. Among them lay a collar and tie, as if they had just been removed, which, lifted, left upon the surface a pale crescent in the dust. Upon a chair hung the suit, carefully folded; beneath it the two mute shoes and the discarded socks.

The man himself lay in the bed.

For a long while we just stood there, looking down at the profound and fleshless grin. The body had apparently once lain in the attitude of an embrace, but now the long sleep that outlasts love, that conquers even the grimace of love, had cuckolded him. What was left of him, rotted beneath what was left of the nightshirt, had become inextricable from the bed in which he lay; and upon him and upon the pillow beside him lay that even coating of the patient and biding dust.

Then we noticed that in the second pillow was the indentation of a head. One of us lifted something from it, and leaning forward, that faint and invisible dust dry and acrid in the nostrils, we saw a long strand of iron-gray hair.

FIRDAUSI

FIRDAUSI (Abul Kasim Mansur, Persian, *ca.* 941-1025). The Persian Homer. The *Shah-namah*, commissioned by Persia's ruler, recounts in 60,000 couplets Iran's legends and history from prehistoric times to Arab conquest. Spent most of life on this, one of world's great epics. Influenced all later Persian poets.

RUSTAM AND AKWAN DEV

Kai Khosrau sat in a garden bright
   With all the beauties of balmy Spring;
And many a warrior armor-dight
With a stout kamand and an arm of might
   Supported Persia's King.

With trembling mien and a pallid cheek,
   A breathless hind to the presence ran;
And on bended knee, in posture meek,
With faltering tongue that scarce could speak,
   His story thus began:—

"Alackaday! for the news I bear
   Will like to the follies of Fancy sound;
Thy steeds were stabled and stalled with care,
When a Wild Ass sprang from its forest lair
   With a swift resistless bound,—

"A monster fell, of a dusky hue,
   And eyes that flashed with a hellish glow;
Many it maimed and some it slew,
Then back to the forest again it flew,
   As an arrow leaves the bow."

Kai Khosrau's rage was a sight to see:
   "Now curses light on the foul fiend's head!
Full rich and rare shall his guerdon be
Whose stalwart arm shall bring to me
   The monster, alive or dead!"

But the mail-clad warriors kept their ground,
    And their bronzèd cheeks were blanched with fear;
With scorn the Shah on the cowards frowned,—
"One champion bold may yet be found
    While Rustam wields a spear!"

No tarrying made the son of Zal,
    Small reck had he of the fiercest fray;
But promptly came at the monarch's call,
And swore that the monster fiend should fall
    Ere closed the coming day.

The swift Rakush's sides he spurred,
    And speedily gained the darksome wood;
Nor was the trial for long deferred,—
But soon a hideous roar was heard,
    Had chilled a baser blood.

Then darting out like a flashing flame,
    Traverse his path the Wild Ass fled;
And the hero then with unerring aim
Hurled his stout kamand, but as erst it came,
    Unscathed the monster fled.

"Now Khuda in heaven!" bold Rustam cried,—
    "Thy chosen champion deign to save!
Not all in vain shall my steel be tried,
Though he who my powers has thus defied
    Be none but Akwan Dev."

Then steadily chasing his fiendish foe,
    He thrust with hanger, he smote with brand:
But ever avoiding the deadly blow
It vanished away like the scenes that show
    On Balkh's delusive sand.

For full three wearisome nights and days
    Stoutly he battled with warlike skill;
But the Demon such magical shifts essays
That leaving his courser at large to graze,
    He rests him on a hill.

But scare can slumber his eyelids close,
　　Ere Akwan Dev from afar espies;
And never disturbing his foe's repose
The earth from under the mound he throws,
　　And off with the summit flies.

"Now, daring mortal!" the Demon cried,—
　　"Whither wouldst have me carry thee?
Shall I cast thee forth on the mountain side,
Where the lions roar and the reptiles glide,
　　Or hurl thee into the sea?"

"O bear me off to the mountain side,
　　Where the lions roar and the serpents creep!
For I fear not the creatures that spring or glide;
But where is the arm that can stem the tide,
　　Or still the raging deep?"

Loud laughed the fiend as his load he threw
　　Far plunging into the roaring flood;
And louder laughed Rustam as out he flew,
For he fain had chosen the sea, but knew
　　The fiend's malignant mood.

Soon all the monsters that float or swim,
　　With ravening jaws down on him bore;
But he hewed and hacked them limb from limb,
And the wave pellucid grew thick and dim
　　With streaks of crimson gore.

With thankful bosom he gains the strand,
　　And seeketh his courser near and far,
Till he hears him neigh, and he sees him stand
Among the herds of a Tartar band,
　　The steeds of Isfendiyar.

But Rustam's name was a sound of dread,
　　And the Tartar heart it had caused to quake;
The herd was there, but the hinds had fled,—
So all the horses he captive led
　　For good Kai Khosrau's sake.

387

Then loud again through the forest rings
  The fiendish laugh and the taunting cry;
But his kamand quickly the hero flings,
And around the Demon it coils and clings,
  As a cobweb wraps a fly.

Kai Khosrau sat in his garden fair,
  Mourning his Champion lost and dead,
When a shout of victory rent the air,
And Rustam placed before his chair
  A Demon Giant's head.

GUSTAVE FLAUBERT

GUSTAVE FLAUBERT (French, 1821-1880). One of the great French stylists. Recluse because of epilepsy, devoted self to cult of classical art. *Salammbô* and *The Temptation of Saint Anthony*, masterpieces of romanticism; *Madame Bovary*, the great novel of French realism. Other works: *The Sentimental Education, Bouvard and Pécuchet*. Flaubert's struggle for objectivity defeated itself, but he remains one of greatest novelists.

SALAMMBÔ AND HER LOVER

MATHO was bound on the elephant's back, his four limbs crosswise and all the unwounded escorted him, hurrying with a great commotion back to Carthage.

The water-clock of Khamoûn marked the fifth hour of the night when they reached Malqua. Here Matho reopened his eyes. There were such vast numbers of lights on the houses that the city seemed to be all in flames.

A mighty clamor came confusedly to him, and lying on his back he gazed at the stars. Then a door closed upon him, and darkness enveloped him. . . .

There were rejoicings at Carthage — rejoicings deep, universal, extravagant, frantic; the holes of the ruins had been stopped up, the statues of the Gods had been repainted, the streets were strewn with myrtle branches, incense smoked at the corners of the crossways, and the throng on the terraces looked, in their variegated garments, like heaps of flowers blooming in the air.

The people accosted one another, and embraced one another with tears;—the Tyrian towns were taken, the Nomads dispersed, and all the Barbarians annihilated. The Acropolis was hidden beneath colored velaria; the beaks of the triremes, drawn up in line outside the mole, shone like a dike of diamonds; everywhere there was a sense of the restoration of order, the beginning of a new existence, and the diffusion of vast happiness: it was the day of Salammbô's marriage with the king of the Numidians.

On the terrace of the temple of Khamon there were three long tables laden with gigantic plates, at which the Priests, Ancients and Rich were going to sit, and there was a fourth and higher one for Hamilcar, Narr' Havas, and Salammbô; for as she saved her country by the restoration of the zaïmph, the people turned her wedding into a national rejoicing, and were waiting in the square below till she should appear.

But their impatience was excited by another and more acrid longing: Matho's death had been promised for the ceremony.

It had been proposed at first to flay him alive, to pour lead into his entrails, to kill him with hunger; he should be tied to a tree, and an ape behind him should strike him on the head with a stone; he had offended Tanith, and the cynocephaluses of Tanith should avenge her. Others were of the opinion that he should be led about on a dromedary after linen wicks, dipped in oil, had been inserted in his body in several places—and they took pleasure in the thought of the large animal wandering through the streets with this man writhing beneath the fires like a candelabrum blown about by the wind.

But what citizens should be charged with his torture, and why disappoint the rest? They would have liked a kind of death in which the whole town might take part, in which every hand, every weapon, everything Carthaginian, to the very paving stones in the streets and the waves in the gulf, could rend him, and crush him, and annihilate him. Accordingly the Ancients decided that he should go from his prison to the square of Khamon without any escort, and with his arms fastened to his back; it was forbidden to strike him to the heart, in order that he might live the longer; to put out his eyes, so that he might see his torture through; to hurl anything against his person, or to lay more than three fingers upon him at a time.

Although he was not to appear until the end of the day, the people sometimes fancied that he could be seen, and the crowd would rush

toward the Acropolis, and empty the streets, to return with lengthened murmurings. Some people had remained standing in the same
place since the day before, and they would call on one another from
a distance and show their nails, which they had allowed to grow,
the better to bury them in his flesh. Others walked restlessly up and
down; some were as pale as though they were awaiting their own
execution.

Suddenly lofty feather fans rose above the heads, behind the Map-
palian district. It was Salammbô leaving her palace; a sigh of relief
found vent.

But the procession was long in coming; it marched with deliberation.

First there filed past the priests of the Pataec Gods, then those of
Eschmoun, of Melkarth, and all the other colleges in succession, with
the same insignia, and in the same order as had been observed at
the time of the sacrifice. The pontiffs of Moloch passed with heads
bent, and the multitude stood aside from them in a kind of remorse.
But the priests of Rabbetna advanced with a proud step, and with
lyres in their hands; the priestesses followed them in transparent
robes of yellow or black, uttering cries like birds and writhing like
vipers, or else whirling round to the sound of flutes to imitate the
dance of the stars, while their light garments wafted puffs of delicate scents through the streets.

The Kedeschim, with painted eyelids, who symbolized the her-
maphroditism of the Divinity, received applause among these women, and, being perfumed and dressed like them, they resembled
them in spite of their flat breasts and narrower hips. Moreover, on
this day the female principle dominated and confused all things; a
mystic lasciviousness moved in the heavy air; the torches were already lighted in the depths of the sacred woods; there was to be a
great prostitution there during the night; three vessels had brought
courtesans from Sicily, and others had come from the desert.

As the colleges arrived they ranged themselves in the courts of the
temples, on the outer galleries, and along double staircases which
rose against the walls, and drew together at the top. Files of white
robes appeared between the colonnades, and the architecture was
peopled with human statues, motionless as statues of stone.

Then came the masters of the exchequer, the governors of the provinces, and all the Rich. A great tumult prevailed below. Adjacent
streets were discharging the crowd, hierodules were driving it back
with blows of sticks; and then Salammbô appeared in a litter sur-

mounted by a purple canopy, and surrounded by the Ancients crowned with their golden tiaras.

Thereupon an immense shout arose; the cymbols and crotala sounded more loudly, the tambourines thundered, and the great purple canopy sank between the two pylons.

It appeared again on the first landing. Salammbô was walking slowly beneath it; then she crossed the terrace to take her seat behind on a kind of throne cut out of the carapace of a tortoise. An ivory stool with three steps was pushed beneath her feet; two negro children knelt on the edge of the first step, and sometimes she would rest both arms, which were laden with rings of excessive weight, upon their heads.

From ankle to hip she was covered with a network of narrow meshes which were in imitation of fish scales, and shone like mother-of-pearl; her waist was clasped by a blue zone, which allowed her breasts to be seen through two crescent-shaped slashings; the nipples were hidden by carbuncle pendants. She had a headdress made of peacock's feathers studded with gems; an ample cloak, as white as snow, fell behind her—and with her elbows at her sides, her knees pressed together, and circles of diamonds on the upper part of her arms, she remained perfectly upright in a hieratic attitude.

Her father and her husband were on two lower seats, Narr' Havas dressed in a light simar and wearing his crown of rock salt, from which there strayed two tresses of hair as twisted as the horns of Ammon; and Hamilcar in a violet tunic figured with gold vine branches, and with a battle sword at his side.

The python of the temple of Eschmoun lay on the ground amid pools of pink oil in the space inclosed by the tables, and, biting its tail, described a large, black circle. In the middle of the circle there was a copper pillar bearing a crystal egg; and, as the sun shone upon it, rays were emitted on every side.

Behind Salammbô, stretched the priests of Tanith in linen robes; on her right the Ancients, in their tiaras, formed a great gold line, and on the other side the Rich, with their emerald scepters, a great green line—while quite in the background, where the priests of Moloch were ranged, the cloaks looked like a wall of purple. The other colleges occupied the lower terraces. The multitude obstructed the streets. It reached to the house tops, and extended in long files to the summit of the Acropolis. Having thus the people at her feet, the firmament above her head, and around her the immensity of the sea, the gulf, the mountains, and the distant provinces, Salammbô in her splendor was blended with Tanith, and seemed the very Genius of Carthage, and its embodied soul.

The feast was to last all night, and lamps with several branches were planted like trees on the painted woolen cloths which covered the low tables. Large electrum flagons, blue glass amphoras, tortoiseshell spoons, and small round loaves were crowded between the double row of pearl-bordered plates; bunches of grapes with their leaves had been rolled round ivory vine stocks after the fashion of the thyrsus; blocks of snow were melting on ebony trays, and lemons, pomegranates, gourds, and watermelons formed hillocks beneath the lofty silver plate; boars with open jaws were wallowing in the dust of spices; hares, covered with their fur, appeared to be bounding amid the flowers; there were shells filled with forcemeat; the pastry had symbolic shapes; when the covers of the dishes were removed doves flew out.

The slaves, meanwhile, with tunics tucked up, were going about on tiptoe; from time to time a hymn sounded on the lyres, or a choir of voices rose. The clamor of the people, continuous as the noise of the sea, floated vaguely around the feast, and seemed to lull it in a broader harmony; some recalled the banquet of the Mercenaries; they gave themselves up to dreams of happiness; the sun was beginning to go down, and the crescent of the moon was already rising in another part of the sky.

But Salammbô turned her head as though some one had called her; the people, who were watching her, followed the direction of her eyes.

The door of the dungeon, hewn in the rock at the foot of the temple, on the summit of the Acropolis, had just opened; and a man was standing on the threshold of this black hole.

He came forth bent double, with the scared look of fallow deer when suddenly enlarged.

The light dazzled him, he stood motionless awhile. All had recognized him and they held their breath.

In their eyes the body of this victim was something peculiarly theirs, and was adorned with almost religious splendor. They bent forward to see him, especially the women. They burned to gaze upon him who had caused the deaths of their children and husbands; and from the bottom of their souls there sprang up in spite of themselves an infamous curiosity, a desire to know him completely, a wish mingled with remorse which turned to increased execration.

At last he advanced; then the stupefaction of surprise disappeared. Numbers of arms were raised, and he was lost to sight.

The staircase of the Acropolis had sixty steps. He descended them as though he were rolled down in a torrent from the top of a mountan; three times he was seen to leap, and then he alighted below on his feet.

His shoulders were bleeding, his breast was panting with great shocks; and he made such efforts to burst his bonds that his arms, which were crossed on his naked loins, swelled like pieces of a serpent.

Several streets began in front of him, leading from the spot at which he found himself. In each of them a triple row of bronze chains fastened to the navels of the Pataec Gods extended in parallel lines from one end to the other; the crowd was massed against the houses, and servants, belonging to the Ancients, walked in the middle brandishing thongs.

One of them drove him forward with a great blow; Matho began to move.

They thrust their arms over the chains, shouting out that the road had been left too wide for him; and he passed along, felt, pricked, and slashed by all those fingers; when he reached the end of one street another appeared; several times he flung himself to one side to bite them; they speedily dispersed, the chains held him back, and the crowd burst out laughing.

A child rent his ear; a young girl, hiding the point of a spindle in her sleeve, split his cheek; they tore handfuls of hair from him and strips of flesh; others smeared his face with sponges steeped in filth and fastened upon their sticks. A stream of blood started from the right side of his neck; frenzy immediately set in. This last Barbarian was to them a representative of all the Barbarians, and all the army; they were taking vengeance on him for their disasters, their terrors, and their shame. The rage of the mob developed with its gratification; the curving chains were overstrained, and were on the point of breaking; the people did not feel the blows of the slaves who struck at them to drive them back; some clung to the projections of the houses; all the openings in the walls were stopped up with heads; and they howled at him the mischief that they could not inflict upon him.

It was atrocious, filthy abuse, mingled with ironical encouragements and with imprecations; and, his present tortures not being enough for them, they foretold to him others that should be still more terrible in eternity.

This vast baying filled Carthage with stupid continuity. Frequently a single syllable—a hoarse, deep, and frantic intonation—would be repeated for several minutes by the entire people. The walls would vibrate with it from top to bottom, and both sides of the street would seem to Matho to be coming against him, and carrying him off the ground, like two immense arms stifling him in the air.

Nevertheless he remembered that he had experienced something like it before. The same crowd was on the terraces, there were the same looks and the same wrath; but then he had walked free, all had then dispersed, for a God covered him—and the recollection of this, gaining precision by degrees, brought a crushing sadness upon him. Shadows passed before his eyes; the town whirled round his head, his blood streamed from a wound in his hip, he felt that he was dying; his hams bent, and he sank quite gently upon the pavement.

Some one went to the peristyle of the temple of Melkarth, took thence the bar of a tripod, heated red hot in the coals, and, slipping it beneath the first chain, pressed it against his wound. The flesh was seen to smoke; the hootings of the people drowned his voice; he was standing again.

Six paces further on, and he fell a third and again a fourth time; but some new torture always made him rise. They discharged little drops of boiling oil through tubes at him; they strewed pieces of broken glass beneath his feet; still he walked on. At the corner of the street of Satheb he leaned his back against the wall beneath the penthouse of a shop, and advanced no further.

The slaves of the Council struck him with their whips of hippopotamus leather, so furiously and long that the fringes of their tunics were drenched with sweat. Matho appeared insensible; suddenly he started off and began to run at random, making noise with his lips like one shivering with severe cold. He threaded the streets of Boudes, and the street of Sœpo, crossed the Green Market, and reached the square of Khamon.

He now belonged to the priests; the slaves had just dispersed the crowd, and there was more room. Matho gazed round him and his eyes encountered Salammbô.

At the first step that he had taken she had risen; then, as he approached, she had involuntarily advanced by degrees to the edge of the terrace; and soon all external things were blotted out, and she saw only Matho. Silence fell in her soul—one of those abysses wherein the whole world disappears beneath the pressure of a single thought, a memory, a look. This man who was walking toward her attracted her.

Excepting his eyes he had no appearance of humanity left; he was a long, perfectly red shape; his broken bonds hung down his thighs, but they could not be distinguished from the tendons of his wrists, which were laid quite bare; his mouth remained wide open; from his eye sockets there darted flames which seemed to rise up to his hair—and the wretch still walked on!

He reached the foot of the terrace. Salammbô was leaning over the balustrade; those frightful eyeballs were scanning her, and there rose within her a consciousness of all that he had suffered for her. Although he was in his death agony, she could see him once more kneeling in his tent, encircling her waist with his arms, and stammering out gentle words; she thirsted to feel them and hear them again; she did not want him to die! At this moment Matho gave a great start; she was on the point of shrieking aloud. He fell backward and did not stir again.

Salammbô was borne back, nearly swooning, to her throne by the priests who flocked about her. They congratulated her; it was her work. All clapped their hands and stamped their feet, howling her name.

A man darted upon the corpse. Although he had no beard he had the cloak of a priest of Moloch on his shoulder, and in his belt that species of knife which they employed for cutting up the sacred meat, and which terminated, at the end of the handle, in a golden spatula. He cleft Matho's breast with a single blow, then snatched out the heart and laid it upon the spoon; and Schahabarim, uplifting his arm, offered it to the sun.

The sun sank behind the waves; his rays fell like long arrows upon the red heart. As the beatings diminished the planet sank into the sea; and at the last palpitation it disappeared.

Then from the gulf to the lagoon, and from the isthmus to the pharos, in all the streets, on all the houses, and on all the temples, there was a single shout; sometimes it paused, to be again renewed; the building shook with it; Carthage was convulsed, as it were, in the spasm of Titanic joy and boundless hope.

Narr' Havas, drunk with pride, passed his left arm beneath Salammbô's waist in token of possession; and taking a gold patera in his right hand, he drank to the Genius of Carthage.

Salammbô rose like her husband, with a cup in her hand, to drink also. She fell down again with her head lying over the back of the throne,—pale, stiff, with parted lips,—and her loosened hair hung to the ground.

FRIEDRICH DE LA MOTTE-FOUQUE

FRIEDRICH DE LA MOTTE-FOUQUÉ (German, 1777-1843). German novelist, given to romantic fantasies. Very popular in his day for medieval and nordic romances. Now remembered chiefly for fairy tale, "Undine."

UNDINE

I. *The Water Sprite*

ABOUT a century ago an aged fisherman sat mending his nets by his cottage door, in front of a lovely lake. Behind his dwelling stretched a sombre forest, reputed to be haunted by goblin creatures. Through this gloomy solitude the pious old fisherman frequently passed, religiously dispelling all terrors by singing hymns as he went with his fish to a town near the border of the forest.

One evening he heard the sound of a horse's hoofs, and presently appeared a knight riding on a splendid steed, and clad in resplendent armour. The stranger stopped, and besought shelter for the night, and the good old fisherman accorded him a most cheery welcome, taking him into the cottage, where sat his aged wife by a scanty fire. Soon the three were freely conversing. The knight told of his travels and revealed that he was Sir Huldbrand of Ringstetten, where he had a castle by the Rhine.

A splash against the window surprising the guest he was informed by his host, with some little show of vexation, that little tricks were often played by a foster-child of the old couple, named Undine, a girl of eighteen.

The door flew open, and a lovely girl glided, laughing, into the room. Without the slightest token of shyness she gazed at the knight for a few moments, then asked why he had come to the poor cottage.

"Have you come through the wild forest?"

He confessed that he had, and she instantly demanded a recital of his adventures. With a slight shudder at his own recollections of the strange creatures he had encountered, Huldbrand consented, but a reproof from the fisherman at her obtrusiveness angered Undine. The girl sprang up and rushed forth into the night, exclaiming, "Sleep alone in your smoky old hut!"

In great alarm, the fisherman and Huldbrand rose to follow the girl, but she had vanished in the darkness. Remarking that she had acted so before, the old fisherman invited Huldbrand to sit by the fire and talk awhile, and began to relate how Undine had come to live with them.

The couple had lost their only child, a wonderfully beautiful little girl. At the age of three, when sitting in her mother's lap at the edge of the lake, she seemed to be attracted by some lovely apparition in the water, for, suddenly stretching out her hands and laughing, she had in a moment sprung into the lake. No trace of the child could ever be found. But the same evening a lovely little girl, three or four years old, with water streaming from her golden tresses, suddenly entered the cottage, smiling sweetly at the fisherman and his wife. They hastily undressed the little stranger and put her to bed. She uttered not a word, but simply smiled. In the morning she talked a little, confusedly telling how she had been in a boat on the lake with her mother, and had fallen in, and could recollect nothing more. She could say nothing as to who she was or whence she came. But she talked often of golden castles and crystal domes.

While the fisherman was talking thus to the knight, he was suddenly interrupted by the noise of rushing water. Floods seemed to be bursting forth, and he and his guest, going hastily to the door, saw by the moonlight that the brook which issued from the forest was surging in a wild torrent over its margin, while a roaring wind was lashing the lake. In great alarm both shouted, "Undine! Undine!" But there was no response, and the two ran off in different directions in search of the fugitive.

It was Huldbrand who discovered the girl. Clambering down some rocks at the edge of the stream, thinking Undine might have fallen there, he was hailed by the sweet voice of the girl herself.

"Venture not," she cried. "The old man of the stream is full of tricks."

Looking across at a tiny isle in the stream, the knight saw her nestling in the grass, smiling, and in an instant he had crossed.

"The fisherman is distressed at your absence," said he. "Let us go back."

Looking at him with her beautiful blue eyes, the girl replied, "If you think so, well; whatever you think is right to me."

Taking Undine in his arms, Huldbrand bore her over the stream to the cottage, where she was received with joy. Dawn was breaking, and breakfast was prepared under the trees. Undine flung herself on the grass at Huldbrand's feet, and at her renewed request the knight told the story of his forest adventures.

"It is now about eight days since I rode into the city on the other side of the forest to join in a great tournament. In one of the intervals between the jousts I noticed a lovely lady among the spectators. I learned that she was Bertalda, foster-daughter of a great duke, and each evening I became her partner in the dances.

"This Bertalda was a wayward girl, and each day pleased me less and less; but I continued in her company, and asked her jestingly to give me a glove. She said she would do so if I would explore alone the haunted forest. As an honorable knight I could not decline the challenge, and yesterday I set out on the enterprise. Before I had penetrated very far within the glades, I saw what looked like a bear in the branches of an oak; but the creature, in a harsh, human voice, growled that it was getting branches with which to roast me at night. My horse was scared at this, and other grim apparitions, but at last I emerged from the forest, and saw the lake and this cottage."

When he had finished, the fisherman spoke of the best way by which the visitor could return to the city; but, with sly laughter, Undine declared that the knight could not depart, for if he attempted now to cross the deluged wood, he would be overwhelmed.

II. *"I Have No Soul!"*

HULDBRAND, detained at the cottage by the increasing overflow of the stream, enjoyed the most perfect satisfaction with his sojourn.

The old folks with pleasure regarded the two young people as betrothed, and Huldbrand assumed that he was accepted by the girl, whom he had come to look upon as not being in reality one of this poor household, but one of some illustrious family, and when, one evening, an aged priest appeared at the cottage, driven in by the storm, Huldbrand addressed to him a request that he should on the spot at once unite him and the maiden, as they were pledged to each other. A discussion arose, but matters were at length settled, and

393

the old wife produced two consecrated tapers. Lighting these, the priest, with brief, solemn ceremony, celebrated the nuptials.

Undine had been quiet and grave during these proceedings, but a singular change took place in her demeanour as soon as the rite had been performed. She began at intervals to indulge in wild freaks, teasing the priest, and indulging in a variety of silly tricks. At length the priest gently expostulated with Undine, exhorting her so to attune her soul that it might always be in concord with that of her husband.

Her reply amazed the listeners, for she said, "If one has no soul, as I have none, what is there to harmonise?" Then she burst into a fit of passionate weeping, to the consternation of all the little company. As she again and again wept, the priest, fearing that she was possessed by some evil spirit, sought to exorcise it. The priest turned to the bridegroom with the assurance that he could discover nothing evil in the bride, mysterious though her behaviour was, and he commended him to be loving and true to her.

The next morning Undine, when she and her husband made their appearance, responded gracefully to the paternal greeting of the priest, beseeching his pardon for her folly of the previous evening, and begging him to pray for the good of her soul. Through the whole day Undine behaved angelically. She was kind, quiet, and gentle. At eventide she led her husband out to the edge of the stream, which, to the wonder of Huldbrand, had subsided into gentle, rippling waves.

She whispered, "Carry me across to that little isle, and we will decide there."

Wondering, he carried her across, and, laying her on the turf, listened as she began.

"My loved one, know that there are strange beings which, though seeming almost like mortals, are rarely visible to human eyes—salamanders in the flames, gnomes down in the earth, spirits in the air. And in the water are myriads of spirits dwelling in crystal domes, in the coral-trees, and in the lovely shells. These are far more beautiful than the fairest of human beings, and sometimes a fisherman has seen a tender mermaid, and has listened to her song. Such wonderful creatures are called Undines, and one of these you see now before you!

"We should be far superior to other beings—for we consider ourselves human—but for one defect. We have no souls, and nothing remains of us after this mortal life is over. Yet every being aspires to rise higher, and so my father, who is a great water prince in the Mediterranean Sea, desired that his only daughter should become possessed of a soul. But this can only come to pass with loving union with one of your race. Now, O my dearly beloved, I have to thank you that I am gifted with a soul, and it will be due to you should all my life be made wretched. For what will become of me if you forsake me? If you would do so, do it now! Then I will plunge into the stream—which is my uncle—and as he brought me here, so will he take me back to my parents, a loving, suffering woman with a soul."

Undine would have said yet more, but Huldbrand, astonishing though the recital was, with tears and kisses vowed he would never leave his lovely wife; and with her leaning in loving trustfulness on his arm, they returned to the hut.

The next day, at Undine's strange urgency, farewell was said with bitter tears and lamentations.

Undine was placed on the beautiful horse, and Huldbrand and the priest walked on either side as the three passed through the solemn glades of the wood. A fourth soon joined them. He was dressed in a white robe, like that of the priest, and presently attempted to speak to Undine. But she shrank from him, declaring she wished to have nothing to do with him.

"Oh, oh!" cried the stranger, with a laugh. "What kind of a marriage is this you have made, that you must not speak to your relative? Do you not know I am your uncle Kühleborn, who brought you to this region, and that I am here to protect you from goblins and sprites? So let me quietly accompany you."

"We are near the end of the forest, and shall not need you further," was her rejoinder. But he grinned at her so frightfully that she shrieked for help, and the knight aimed at his head a blow from his sword. Instantly Kühleborn was transformed into a gushing waterfall, foaming over them from a rock near by and drenching all three.

III. *"Woe! Woe!"*

THE sudden disappearance of the young knight had caused a sensation in the city, for the duke and duchess, and the friends and servants of Huldbrand, feared he had perished in the forest during the terrible tempest. When he suddenly reappeared, all rejoiced except Bertalda, who was profoundly vexed at seeing with him a beautiful bride. She so far reconciled herself to the conditions that a warm friendship sprang up between Undine and herself.

It was agreed that Bertalda should accompany the wedded pair to Ringstetten, and with the consent of the noble foster-parents of Bertalda the three appointed a day for the departure. One beautiful evening, as they walked about the market-place round the great fountain, suddenly a tall man emerged from among the people and stopped in front of Undine. He quickly whispered something in her ear, and though at first she seemed vexed at the intrusion, presently she clapped her hands and laughed joyously. Then the stranger mysteriously vanished, and seemed to disappear in the fountain.

Huldbrand had suspected that he had seen this man before, and now felt assured that he was Kühleborn. Undine admitted the fact, and said that her uncle had told her a secret, which she was to reveal on the third day afterwards, which would be the anniversary of Bertalda's nameday.

The anniversary came, and strange incidents happened. After the banquet given by the duke and duchess, Undine suddenly gave a signal, and from among the retainers at the door came forth the old fisherman and his wife, and Undine declared that in these Bertalda saw her real parents. The proud maiden instantly flew into a violent rage, weeping passionately, and utterly refused to acknowledge the old couple as her father and mother. She declared that Undine was an enchantress and a witch, sustaining intercourse with evil spirits.

Undine, with great dignity, indignantly denied the accusation, while Bertalda's violent conduct created a feeling of disgust in the minds of all in the assembly. The matter was settled in a simple manner, for the duke commanded Bertalda to withdraw to a private apartment with the duchess and the two old folks from the hut, that an investigation might be made. It was soon over, for the noble lady was able presently to inform the company that Undine's story was absolutely true. The guests silently departed, and Undine sank sobbing into her husband's arms.

Next day Bertalda, humbled by these events, sought pardon of Undine for her evil behaviour, and was instantly welcomed with loving assurances of forgiveness. Moreover, she was cordially invited to go with the pair to Ringstetten.

"We will share all things there as sisters," said Undine.

The three journeyed to the distant castle, and took up their abode together. Soon Kühleborn appeared on the scene, but Undine at once repulsed him. Next, when her husband was one day hunting, she ordered the great well in the courtyard to be covered with a big stone, on which she cut some curious characters.

Bertalda waywardly complained that this proceeding deprived her of water that was good for her complexion, but Undine privately explained to Huldbrand that she had caused the servants to seal up this spring because only by that way of access could her uncle Kühleborn come to disturb their peace.

As time passed on, Huldbrand gradually cooled towards his wife and turned affectionately towards Bertalda. Undine bore patiently and silently the sorrow thus inflicted on her. But when her husband was impatient and angry she would plead with him never to speak to her in accents of unkindness when they happened to be on the water, for the water spirits had her completely in their power on their element, and would seek to protect her and even seize her and take her down for ever to dwell in the crystal castles of the deep.

After some estrangements, Undine and Bertalda had again become loving friends, and Huldbrand's affection for his wife had revived with its old and welcome warmth, while the attachment between him and Bertalda seemed forgotten.

One day the three were enjoying a delightful excursion on the glorious Danube. Bertalda had taken off a beautiful coral necklace which Huldbrand had given her. She leaned over and drew the coral beads across the surface, enjoying the glitter thus caused, when suddenly a great hand from beneath seized the necklace and snatched it down. The maiden's scream of terror was answered by mocking laughter from the water.

In an outburst of passion, Huldbrand started up and poured forth curses on the river and its denizens, whether spirits or sirens. With tears in her eyes, Undine besought him softly not to scold her there, and she took from her neck a beautiful necklace and offered it to Bertalda as a compensation.

But the angry knight snatched it away, and hurled it into the river, exclaiming, "Are you still connected with them? In the name of all the witches, remain among them with your presents, and leave us mortals in peace, you sorceress!"

Bitterly weeping and crying, "Woe! Woe!" she vanished over the side of the vessel. Her last words were, "Remain true! Woe! Woe!" Huldbrand lay swooning on the deck, and little waves seemed to be sobbing on the surface of the Danube, "Woe! Woe! Remain true!"

IV. The White Stranger

FOR a time deep sorrow fell on the lord of Ringstetten and Bertalda. They lived long in the castle quietly, often weeping for Undine, tenderly cherishing her memory. Undine often visited Huldbrand in his dreams, caressing him and weeping silently so that his cheeks were wet when he awoke. But these visions grew less frequent, and the knight's grief diminished by degrees. At length he and Bertalda were married, but it was in spite of a grave warning from Father Heilmann, who declared that Undine had appeared to him in visions, beseeching him to warn Huldbrand and Bertalda to leave each other. They were too infatuated to heed the admonition, and a priest from a neighbouring monastery promised to perform the ceremony in a few days.

Meantime, when lying between sleeping and waking, the knight seemed fanned by the wings of a swan, and, as he fell asleep, seemed borne along on the wings of swans which sang their sweetest music. All at once he seemed to be hovering over the Mediterranean Sea. Its waters were so crystalline that he could see through them to the bottom, and there, under a crystal arch, sat Undine, weeping bitterly. She seemed not to perceive him. Kühleborn approached her, and told her that Huldbrand was to be wedded again, and that it would be her duty, from which nothing could release her, to end his life.

"That I cannot do," said she. "I have sealed up the fountain against me and my race."

Huldbrand felt as if he were soaring back again over the sea, and at length he seemed to reach his castle. He awoke on his couch, but he could not bring himself to break off the arrangements that had been made.

The marriage feast at Ringstetten was not as bright and happy as such occasions usually are, for a veil of gloom seemed to rest over the company. Even the bride affected a happy and thoughtless demeanour which she did not really feel. The company dispersed early, Bertalda retiring with her maidens, and Huldbrand with his attendants.

In her apartment Bertalda, with a sigh, noticed how freckled was her neck, and a remark she made to her maidens as she gazed in the mirror excited the eager attention of one of them. She heard her fair mistress say, "Oh, that I had a flask of the purifying water from the closed fountain!" Presently the officious waiting-woman was seen leading men to the fountain. With levers they quickly lifted the stone, for some mysterious force seemed to aid them.

Then from the fountain solemnly rose a white column of water. It was presently perceived that it was a pale female figure, veiled in white. She was weeping bitterly as she walked slowly to the building, while Bertalda and her attendants, pale with terror, watched from the window. The figure passed on, and at the door of Huldbrand's room, where the knight was partly undressed, was heard a gentle tap. The white figure slowly entered. It was Undine, who softly said, "They have opened the spring, and now I am here and you must die." Said the knight, "It must be so! But let me die in your embrace."

"Most gladly, my beloved one," said she, throwing back her veil and disclosing her face divinely smiling. Imprinting on his lips a sacred kiss, Undine clasped the knight in her arms, weeping as if she would weep her very soul away. Huldbrand fell softly back on the pillows of his couch, a corpse.

At the funeral of Huldbrand the veiled figure appeared when the procession formed a circle round the grave. All knelt in mute devotion at a signal from Father Heilmann. When they rose again the white stranger had vanished, and on the spot where she had knelt a silvery little fountain gushed forth, which almost encircled the grave and then ran on till it reached a lake near by. And to this day the inhabitants cherish the tradition that thus the poor rejected Undine still lovingly embraces her husband.

ANATOLE FRANCE

ANATOLE FRANCE (Jacques Anatole François Thibault, French, 1844-1924). The poet of irony and pity, with his heart in the Middle Ages. Novelist, historian, short story writer: *Thaïs, Penguin Island, The Crime of Sylvestre Bonnard, Life of Joan of Arc.* Nobel Prize, 1921. Though his work dates, its survival seems ensured because of its wit and stylistic talent.

A ROMAN SENATOR

Cæsar, on the stones of the deserted hall,
Under the folds of his toga, lay in majesty.
The green-lipped bronze of Pompey, proud and tall,
Smiled at the white corpse bloodily.

The spirit just fled through a road made clear
By the steel of Brutus and of Liberty,
Hovered sadly over the lifeless, dear
Flesh fond death made pale yet fair to see.

On a bare marble bench near by, at rest,
The even movements of his mighty chest
Marking his snores, a Senator took his leisure.

The silence woke him and, disturbed, he cried
Across the silent horror at his side:
"I vote to give the imperial crown to Cæsar!"

EVE'S BLOOD

Love hides many treasures in its deeps.
Nature's primordial hardihoods,
That mingled nude thighs in woodland quest,
Still modestly surge in the bride's breast·
Watchful of our conventions, she keeps
The blood of that Eve of the early woods.

THE BAD WORKMAN

Master Laurent Coster, with poetry in his heart,
Left his companions who, from morn to night,
Born vintners, made the boards of the wine-press start—
And Coster dreaming followed his fancy's flight.

For he loved the demon Aspasia with all his soul.
Sometimes he'd sit upon his bench at church
And see in the fumes above the incense bowl
The Woman of Hell who was his only search.

Or else alone at the brink of a mossy well,
Clasping the hands no labor could impel,
He'd hark forever to her siren song. . . .

And I, as well, can neither work nor pray;
I am like Coster, a laborer astray
Through looking in your dark eyes overlong.

"I have burned my garments of gold, and my violin.
While the brazier of repentance shines on me
I shall seek the Pope to wash away my sin.

"O Holy Father, hear with clemency
By what rare sins and demon joy thereof,
Remote from Jesus, I was blind to his decree.

"In the enchanted city, all other peaks above,
With beauteous Venus I dwelt seven years.
Absolve me now, by Jesus whom we love."

The cross of the Holy Father, as he hears,
Trembles: "Your frightful sins the Lord will pardon
When leaf or flower on his cross appears!"

Tears do the gallant's heavy spirit harden.
"Since, Madame Virgin, I no more may yearn
To tend the flowers of your heavenly garden,

"Nor as a shining taper for you burn,
The tender Lady Venus will comfort me:
Never to leave her more, I now return!"

"In truth I'm glad, yes, glad, to see
Thee, Knight; sit down and drink, I pray.
A long time, Tannhäuser, I have longed for thee."

The cross having blossomed on the third day,
The Holy Father sent a post full speed
To seek Tannhäuser up hill and away.

With Venus, he was drinking mellow mead,—
And there will linger, while marriage songs are played,
Until the Angel's trump to Judgment lead.

Not thus should man's bright soul be overlaid:
If they are damned who love the brave device
Of the clear word and the clear smile of a maid

There'll be no one to sing in Paradise.

FERDINAND FREILIGRATH

FERDINAND FREILIGRATH (German, 1810-1876). German poet whose
revolutionary sentiments forced him frequently abroad. Influenced by Byron
and Victor Hugo, whom he translated.

THE SPECTER CARAVAN

'Twas midnight in the Desert, where we rested on the ground;
There my Beddaweens were sleeping and their steeds were stretched
    around;
In the farness lay the moonlight of the Mountains of the Nile,
And the camel bones that strewed the sands for many an arid mile.

With my saddle for a pillow did I prop my weary head,
And my kaftan cloth unfolded o'er my limbs was lightly spread,
While beside me, as the Kapitan and watchman of my band,
Lay my Bazra sword and pistols twain a shimmering on the sand.

And the stillness was unbroken, save at moments by a cry
From some stray belated vulture sailing blackly down the sky,
Or the snortings of a sleeping steed at waters fancy-seen,
Or the hurried warlike mutterings of some dreaming Beddaween.

When, behold!—a sudden sandquake,—and between the earth and
    moon
Rose a mighty Host of Shadows, as from out some dim lagoon;
Then our coursers gasped with terror, and a thrill shook every man;
And the cry was—"Allah Akbar! 'tis the Specter Caravan!"

On they came, their hueless faces toward Mecca evermore;
On they came, long files of camels, and of women whom they bore,
Guides, and merchants, youthful maidens bearing pitchers in their
    hands,
And behind them troops of horsemen following, sumless as the
    sands!

More and more! the phantom pageant overshadowed all the plains;
Yea! the ghastly camel bones arose, and grew to camel trains;
And the whirling column clouds of sand to forms in dusky garbs,—
Here afoot as Hadjee pilgrims, there as warriors on their barbs!

Whence we knew the Night was come when all whom Death had
    sought and found,
Long ago amid the sands whereon their bones yet bleach around,
Rise by legions from the darkness of their prisons low and lone,
And in dim procession march to kiss the Kaaba's Holy Stone.

And yet more, and more forever!—still they swept in pomp along,
Till I asked me,—Can the Desert hold so vast a muster throng?
Lo! the Dead are here in myriads; the whole World of Hades
    waits,
As with eager wish to press beyond the Babelmandeb Straits!

Then I spake: "Our steeds are frantic: To your saddles, every one!
Never quail before these Shadows! You are children of the Sun!
If their garments rustle past you, if their glances reach you here,
Cry Bismillah! and that mighty Name shall banish every fear.

"Courage, comrades! Even now the moon is waning far a-west,—
Soon the welcome Dawn will mount the skies, in gold and crimson
    vest,—
And in thinnest air will melt away those phantom shapes forlorn,
When again upon your brows you feel the odor winds of Morn!"

THE LION'S RIDE

King of deserts reigns the lion; will he through his realm go
    riding,
Down to the lagoon he paces, in the tall sedge there lies hiding.
Where gazelles and camelopards drink, he crouches by the shore;
Ominous, above the monster, moans the quivering sycamore.

When, at dusk, the ruddy hearth-fires in the Hottentot kraals are
    glowing,
And the motley, changeful signals on the Table Mountain growing
Dim and distant—when the Caffre sweeps along the lone karroo—
When in the bush the antelope slumbers, and beside the stream the
    gnu—

408

Lo! majestically stalking, yonder comes the tall giraffe,
Hot with thirst, the gloomy waters of the dull lagoon to quaff;
O'er the naked waste behold her, with parched tongue, all panting
    hasten—
Now she sucks the cool draught, kneeling, from the stagnant, slimy
    basin.

Hark, a rustling in the sedges! with a roar, the lion springs
On her back now. What a race-horse! Say, in proudest stalls of
    kings,
Saw one ever richer housings than the courser's motley hide,
On whose back the tawny monarch of the beasts tonight will ride?

Fixed his teeth are in the muscles of the nape, with greedy strain;
Round the giant courser's withers waves the rider's yellow mane.
With a hollow cry of anguish, leaps and flies the tortured steed;
See her, how with skin of leopard she combines the camel's speed!

See, with lightly beating footsteps, how she scours the moonlit
    plains!
From their sockets start the eyeballs; from the torn and bleeding
    veins,
Fast the thick, black drops come trickling, o'er the brown and
    dappled neck,
And the flying beast's heart-beatings audible the stillness make.

Like the cloud, that, guiding Israel through the land of Yemen,
    shone,
Like a spirit of the desert, like a phantom, pale and wan,
O'er the desert's sandy ocean, like a waterspout at sea,
Whirls a yellow, cloudy column, tracking them where'er they flee.

On their track the vulture follows, flapping, croaking, through the
    air,
And the terrible hyena, plunderer of tombs, is there;
Follows them the stealthy panther—Cape-town's folds have known
    him well;
Them their monarch's dreadful pathway, blood and sweat full
    plainly tell.

On his living throne, they, quaking, see their ruler sitting there,
With sharp claw the painted cushion of his seat they see him tear.
Restless the giraffe must bear him on, till strength and lifeblood
    fail her;
Mastered by such daring rider, rearing, plunging, naught avail her.

To the desert's verge she staggers—sinks—one groan—and all is
    o'er.
Now the steed shall feast the rider, dead, and smeared with dust
    and gore.
Far across, o'er Madagascar, faintly now the morning breaks;
Thus the king of beasts his journey nightly through his empire
    makes.

ROBERT FROST

ROBERT FROST (American, 1875- .). The poet of the ordinary tongue.
Called the interpreter of New England. Spent much of life as professor at
Amherst College. His supremely simple poems convey universal truths through
homely, country images. Collections: *North of Boston, Mountain Interval,
New Hampshire, West-running Brook, A Further Range, A Masque of Reason.*

The Need of Being Versed in Country Things

The house had gone to bring again
To the midnight sky a sunset glow.
Now the chimney was all of the house that stood,
Like a pistil after the petals go.

The barn opposed across the way,
That would have joined the house in flame
Had it been the will of the wind, was left
To bear forsaken the place's name.

No more it opened with all one end
For teams that came by the stony road
To drum on the floor with scurrying hoofs
And brush the mow with the summer load.

The birds that came to it through the air
At broken windows flew out and in,
Their murmur like the sigh we sigh
From too much dwelling on what has been.

Yet for them the lilac renewed its leaf,
And the aged elm, though touched with fire;
And the dry pump flung up an awkward arm;
And the fence post carried a strand of wire.

For them there was really nothing sad.
But though they rejoiced in the nest they kept,
One had to be versed in country things
Not to believe the phoebes wept.

The Gift Outright

The land was ours before we were the land's.
She was our land more than a hundred years
Before we were her people. She was ours
In Massachusetts, in Virginia,
But we were England's, still colonials,
Possessing what we were still unpossessed by,
Possessed by what we now no more possessed.
Something we were withholding made us weak
Until we found out that it was ourselves
We were withholding from our land of living,
And forthwith found salvation in surrender.
Such as we were we gave ourselves outright
(The deed of gift was many deeds of war)
To the land vaguely realizing westward,
But still unstoried, artless, unenhanced,
Such as she was, such as she would become.

FUZULI

FUZULÎ (Mehmet Suleiman Oglou, Turkish, *ca.* 1494-1572). Leading representative of the classical school of Turkish literature. Wrote also in Arabic and Persian. Led humble, unhappy life, died of plague. Called "the poet of the heart." Chief works: *Divan* (a collection of short odes known as *ghazals* or "gazels") and *Leyla ve Mejnun,* a romance of unhappy lovers.

GAZEL

O breeze, thou'rt kind, of balm to those whom pangs affright, thou
    news hast brought,
To wounded frame of life, to life of life's delight thou news hast
    brought.
Thou'st seen the mourning nightingale's despair in sorrow's autumn
    drear,
Like springtide days, of smiling roseleaf fresh and bright, thou
    news hast brought.
If I should say thy words are heaven-inspired, in truth, blaspheme
    I not;
Of Faith, whilst unbelief doth earth hold fast and tight, thou news
    hast brought.
They say the loved one comes to soothe the hearts of all her lovers
    true;
If that the case, to yon fair maid of lovers' plight thou news hast
    brought.
Of rebel demon thou hast cut the hope Suleyman's throne to gain;
That in the sea secure doth lie his Ring of might, thou news hast
    brought.
Fuzuli, through the parting night, alas, how dark my fortune grew!
Like zephyr of the dawn, of shining sun's fair light thou news hast
    brought.

GAZEL

O thou Perfect Being, Source whence wisdom's mysteries arise;
Things, the issue of thine essence, show wherein thy nature lies.
Manifester of all wisdom, thou art he whose pen of might
Hath with rays of stars illumined yonder gleaming page, the skies.
That a happy star, indeed, the essence clear of whose bright self
Truly knoweth how the blessings from thy word that flow to prize.

But a jewel flawed am faulty I: alas, forever stands
Blank the page of my heart's journal from thought of thy writing
    wise.
In the journal of my actions Evil's lines are black indeed;
When I think of Day of Gathering's terrors, blood flows from my
    eyes.
Gathering of my tears will form a torrent on the Reckoning Day,
If the pearls, my tears, rejecting, he but view them to despise:
Pearls my tears are, O Fuzuli, from the ocean deep of love;
But they're pearls these, oh! most surely, that the Love of Allah
    buys!

GAZEL

Is't strange if beauties' hearts turn blood through envy of thy cheek
    most fair?
For that which stone to ruby turns is but the radiant sunlight's glare.
Or strange is't if thine eyelash conquer all the stony-hearted ones?
For meet an ebon shaft like that a barb of adamant should bear!
Thy cheek's sun-love hath on the hard, hard hearts of fairy beauties
    fall'n,
And many a steely-eyed one hath received thy bright reflection fair.
The casket, thy sweet mouth, doth hold spell-bound the *huri*-faced
    ones all;
The virtue of Suleyman's Ring was that fays thereto fealty sware.
Is't strange if, seeing thee, they rub their faces lowly midst the dust?
That down to Adam bowed the angel throng doth the Qur'an
    declare!
On many and many a heart of stone have fall'n the pangs of love
    for thee!
A fire that lies in stone concealed is thy heart-burning love's dread
    glare!
Within her ward, with garments rent, on all sides rosy-cheeked ones
    stray;
Fuzuli, through those radiant hues, that quarter beams a garden
    fair.

GAZEL

From the turning of the Sphere my luck hath seen reverse and woe;
Blood I've drunk, for from my banquet wine arose and forth did go.
With the flame, my burning sighs, I've lit the wand'ring wildered
    heart;

I'm a fire, doth not all that which turns about me roasted glow?
With thy rubies wine contended—oh! how it hath lost its wits!
Need 'tis yon ill-mannered wretch's company that we forego.
Yonder Moon saw not my burning's flame upon the parting day—
How can e'er the sun about the taper all night burning know?
Every eye that all around tears scatters, thinking of thy shaft,
Is an oyster-shell that causeth rain-drops into pearls to grow.
Forms my sighing's smoke a cloud that veils the bright cheek of
    the moon;
Ah! that yon fair Moon will ne'er the veil from off her beauty
    throw!
Ne'er hath ceased the rival e'en within her ward to vex me sore;
How say they, Fuzuli, "There's in Paradise nor grief nor woe"?

G

SOLOMON IBN GABIROL

SOLOMON IBN GABIROL (Spanish-Hebrew, 1021-1058). The Hebrew poet
of the Golden Period of Moorish Spain. Little is known of his life. One of
the greatest of medieval poets, deeply religious and philosophical. Philosophic
works, written in Arabic, influenced Duns Scotus, Spinoza, Schopenhauer.
Most noted poem: *Kether Meluth (Royal Crown).*

NIGHT

Night, and the heavens beam serene with peace,
Like a pure heart benignly smiles the moon.
Oh, guard thy blessed beauty from mischance,
This I beseech thee in all tender love.
See where the Storm his cloudy mantle spreads,
An ashy curtain covereth the moon.
As if the tempest thirsted for the rain,
The clouds he presses, till they burst in streams.
Heaven wears a dusky raiment, and the moon
Appeareth dead—her tomb is yonder cloud,
And weeping shades come after, like the people
Who mourn with tearful grief a noble queen.
But look! the thunder pierced night's close-linked mail,
His keen-tipped lance of lightning brandishing;
He hovers like a seraph-conqueror.—
Dazed by the flaming splendor of his wings,
In rapid flight as in a whirling dance,
The black cloud-ravens hurry scared away.
So, though the powers of darkness chain my soul,
My heart, a hero, chafes and breaks its bonds.

Will night already spread her wings and weave
Her dusky robe about the day's bright form,
Boldly the sun's fair countenance displacing,
And swathe it with her shadow in broad day?
So a green wreath of mist enrings the moon,
Till envious clouds do quite encompass her.
No wind! and yet the slender stem is stirred,
With faint, slight motion as from inward tremor.
Mine eyes are full of grief—who sees me, asks,
"Oh, wherefore dost thou cling unto the ground?"
My friends discourse with sweet and soothing words;
They all are vain, they glide above my head.
I fain would check my tears; would fain enlarge
Unto infinity, my heart—in vain!
Grief presses hard my breast, therefore my tears
Have scarcely dried, ere they again spring forth.
For these are streams no furnace heat may quench,
Nebuchadnezzar's flames may dry them not.
What is the pleasure of the day for me,
If, in its crucible, I must renew
Incessantly the pangs of purifying?
Up, challenge, wrestle, and o'ercome! Be strong!
The late grapes cover all the vine with fruit.
I am not glad, though even the lion's pride
Content itself upon the field's poor grass.
My spirit sinks beneath the tide, soars not
With fluttering seamews on the moist, soft strand.
I follow Fortune not, where'er she lead.
Lord o'er myself, I banish her, compel,
And though her clouds should rain no blessed dew,
Though she withhold the crown, the heart's desire,
Though all deceive, though honey change to gall,
Still am I lord, and will in freedom strive.

MEDITATIONS

Forget thine anguish,
  Vexed heart, again.
Why shouldst thou languish,
  With earthly pain?

416

The husk shall slumber,
　　Bedded in clay
Silent and sombre,
　　Oblivion's prey!
But, Spirit immortal,
Thou at Death's portal,
　　Tremblest with fear.
　　If he caress thee,
　　Curse thee or bless thee,
　　Thou must draw near,
From him the worth of thy works to hear.

　　Why full of terror,
　　Compassed with error,
　　Trouble thy heart,
　　For thy mortal part?
　　The soul flies home—
　　The corpse is dumb.
　　Of all thou didst have,
Follows naught to the grave.
　　Thou fliest thy nest,
Swift as a bird to thy place of rest.

　　What avail grief and fasting,
　　Where nothing is lasting?
　　Pomp, domination,
　　Become tribulation.
　　In a health-giving draught,
　　A death-dealing shaft.
　　Wealth——an illusion,
　　Power—a lie,
　　Over all, dissolution
　　Creeps silent and sly.
　　Unto others remain
　　The goods thou didst gain
　　With infinite pain.

Life is a vine-branch;
　　A vintager, Death.
He threatens and lowers
　　More near with each breath.

417

Then hasten, arise!
  Seek God, O my soul!
For time quickly flies,
  Still far is the goal.
Vain heart praying dumbly,
  Learn to prize humbly,
  The meanest of fare.
Forget all thy sorrow,
  Behold, Death is there!

  Dove-like lamenting,
  Be full of repenting,
Lift vision supernal
To raptures eternal.
  On ev'ry occasion
  Seek lasting salvation.
Pour thy heart out in weeping,
While others are sleeping.
  Pray to Him when all's still,
  Performing his will.
And so shall the angel of peace be thy warden,
And guide thee at last to the heavenly garden.

JOHN GALSWORTHY

JOHN GALSWORTHY (English, 1867-1933). Novelist and playwright. A gentle critic of our social disorder. Trained for the bar, but turned to literature. His major work, *The Forsyte Saga*, paints detailed picture of late Victorian era. Other novels more superficial. Still performed play, *Justice*, displays a concern over social wrongs.

QUALITY

I KNEW him from the days of my extreme youth, because he made my father's boots; inhabiting with his elder brother two little shops let into one, in a small by-street—now no more, but then most fashionably placed in the West End.

That tenement had a certain quiet distinction; there was no sign upon its face that he made for any of the Royal Family—merely his own German name of Gessler Brothers; and in the window a few pairs of boots. I remember that it always troubled me to account for those unvarying boots in the window, for he made only what was ordered, reaching nothing down, and it seemed so inconceivable that what he made could ever have failed to fit. Had he bought them to put there? That, too, seemed inconceivable. He would never have tolerated in his house leather on which he had not worked himself. Besides, they were too beautiful—the pair of pumps, so inexpressibly slim; the patent leathers with cloth tops, making water come into one's mouth; the tall brown riding boots, with marvellous sooty glow, as if, though new, they had been worn a hundred years. Those pairs could only have been made by one who saw before him the Soul of Boot—so truly were they prototypes incarnating the very spirit of all foot-gear. These thoughts, of course, came to me later, though even when I was promoted to him, at the age of perhaps fourteen, some inkling haunted me of the dignity of himself and brother. For to make boots—such boots as he made—seemed to me then, and still seems to me, mysterious and wonderful.

I remember well my shy remark, one day, while stretching out to to him my youthful foot:

"Isn't it awfully hard to do, Mr. Gessler?"

And his answer, given with a sudden smile from out of the sardonic redness of his beard: "Id is an Ardt!"

Himself, he was as little as if made from leather, with his yellow crinkly reddish hair and beard, and neat folds slanting down his cheeks to the corners of his mouth, and his guttural and one-toned voice; for leather is a sardonic substance, and stiff and slow of purpose. And that was the character of his face, save that his eyes, which were grey-blue, had in them the simple gravity of one secretly possessed by the Ideal. His elder brother was so very like him—though watery, paler in every way, with a great industry—that sometimes in early days I was not quite sure of him until the interview was over. Then I knew that it was he, if the words, "I will ask my brudder," had not been spoken; and that, if they had, it was his elder brother.

When one grew old and wild and ran up bills, one somehow never ran them up with Gessler Brothers. It would not have seemed becoming to go in there and stretch out one's foot to that blue iron-spectacled glance, owing him for more than—say—two pairs, just the comfortable reassurance that one was still his client.

For it was not possible to go to him very often—his boots lasted

419

terribly, having something beyond the temporary—some, as it were, essence of boot stitched into them.

One went in, not as into most shops, in the mood of; "Please serve me, and let me go!" but restfully, as one enters a church; and, sitting on the single wooden chair, waited—for there was never anybody there. Soon, over the top edge of that sort of well—rather dark, as smelling soothingly of leather—which formed the shop, there would be seen his face, or that of his elder brother, peering down. A guttural sound, and the tip-tap of bast slippers beating the narrow wooden stairs, and he would stand before one without coat a little bent, in leather apron, with sleeves turned back, blinking—as if awakened from some dream of boots, or like an owl surprised in daylight and annoyed at his interruption.

And I would say: "How do you do, Mr. Gessler? Could you make me a pair of Russian leather boots?"

Without a word he would leave me, retiring whence he came, or into the other portion of the shop, and I would continue to rest in the wooden chair, inhaling the incense of his trade. Soon he would come back, holding in his thin, veined hand a piece of gold-brown leather. With eyes fixed on it, he would remark: "What a beautiful biece!" When I, too, had admired it, he would speak again. "When do you wand dem?" And I would answer: "Oh! As soon as you conveniently can." And he would say: "To-morrow fordnight?" Or if he were his elder brother: "I will ask my brudder!"

Then I would murmur: "Thank you! Good morning, Mr. Gessler." "Goot morning!" he would reply, still looking at the leather in his hand. And as I moved to the door, I would hear the tip-tap of his bast slippers restoring him, up the stairs, to his dream of boots. But if it were some new kind of foot-gear that he had not yet made me, then indeed he would observe ceremony—divesting me of my boot and holding it long in his hand, looking at it with eyes at once critical and loving, as if recalling the glow with which he had created it, and rebuking the way in which one had disorganised this master-piece. Then, placing my foot on a thin piece of paper, he would two or three times tickle the outer edges with a pencil and pass his nervous fingers over my toes, feeling himself into the heart of my requirements.

I cannot forget that day on which I had occasion to say to him: "Mr. Gessler, that last pair of town walking-boots creaked, you know."

He looked at me for a time without replying, as if expecting me to withdraw or qualify the statement, then said:

"Id shouldn't 'ave greaked."

"It did, I'm afraid."

"You goddem wed before dey found demselves?"

"I don't think so."

At that he lowered his eyes, as if hunting for memory of those boots, and I felt sorry I had mentioned this grave thing.

"Zend dem back!" he said; "I will look at dem."

A feeling of compassion for my creaking boots surged up in me, so well could I imagine the sorrowful long curiosity of regard which he would bend on them.

"Zome boods," he said slowly, "are bad from birdt. If I can do noding wid dem, I dake dem off your bill."

Once (once only) I went absent-mindedly into his shop in a pair of boots bought in an emergency at some large firm's. He took my order without showing me any leather, and I could feel his eyes penetrating the inferior integument of my foot. At last he said:

"Dose are nod my boods."

The tone was not one of anger, nor of sorrow, not even of contempt, but there was in it something quiet that froze the blood. He put his hand down and pressed a finger on the place where the left boot, endeavoring to be fashionable, was not quite comfortable.

"Id 'urds you dere," he said. "Dose big virms 'ave no self-respect. Drash!" And then as if something had given way within him, he spoke long and bitterly. It was the only time I ever heard him discuss the conditions and hardships of the trade.

"Dey get id all," he said, "dey get id by adverdisement, nod by work. Dey dake it way from us, who lofe our boods. Id gomes to his—bresently I haf no work. Every year id gets less—you will see." And looking at his lined face I saw things I had never noticed before, bitter things and bitter struggle—and what a lot of grey hairs there seemed suddenly in his red beard!

As best I could, I explained the circumstances of the purchase of those ill-omened boots. But his face and voice made so deep impression that during the next few minutes I ordered many pairs. Nemesis fell! They lasted more terribly than ever. And I was not able conscientiously to go to him for nearly two years.

When at last I went I was surprised to find that outside one of the two little windows of his shop another name was painted, also that

421

of a boot-maker—making, of course, for the Royal Family. The old familiar boots, no longer in dignified isolation, were huddled in the window. Inside, the now contracted well of the one little shop was more scented and darker than ever. And it was longer than usual, too, before a face peered down, and the tip-tap of the bast slippers began. At last he stood before me, and, gazing through those rusty iron spectacles, said:

"Mr. ——, isn'd id?"

"Ah! Mr. Gessler," I stammered, "but your boots are really *too* good, you know! See, these are quite decent still!" And I stretched out to him my foot. He looked at it.

"Yes," he said, "beople do nod wand good boods, id seems."

To get away from his reproachful eyes and voice I hastily remarked: "What have you done to your shop?"

He answered quietly: "Id was too exbensive. Do you wand some boods?"

I ordered three pairs, though I had only wanted two, and quickly left. I had, I do not know quite what feeling of being part, in his mind, of a conspiracy against him; or not perhaps so much against him as against his idea of boot. One does not, I suppose, care to feel like that; for it was again many months before my next visit to his shop, paid I remember, with the feeling: "Oh, well, I can't leave the old boy—so here goes! Perhaps it will be his elder brother!"

For his elder brother, I knew, had not character enough to reproach me, even dumbly.

And, to my relief, in the shop there did appear to be his elder brother, handling apiece of leather.

"Well, Mr. Gessler," I said, "how are you?"

He came close and peered at me.

"I am breddy well," he said slowly: "but my elder brudder is dead."

And I saw that it was indeed himself—but how aged and wan! And never before had I heard him mention his brother. Much shocked, I murmured: "Oh! I am sorry!"

"Yes," he answered, "he was a good man, he made a good bood; but he is dead." And he touched the top of his head, where the hair had suddenly gone as thin as it had been on that of his poor brother, to indicate, I suppose, the cause of death. "He could nod ged over losing de oder shop. Do you wand any boods?" And he held up the leather in his hand: "Id's a beaudiful biece."

I ordered several pairs. It was very long before they came—but

422

they were better than ever. One simply could not wear them out. And soon after that I went abroad.

It was over a year before I was again in London. And the first shop I went to was my old friend's. I had left a man of sixty, I came back to one of seventy-five, pinched and worn and tremulous, who genuinely, this time, did not at first know me.

"Oh! Mr. Gessler," I said, sick at heart; "how splendid your boots are! See, I've been wearing this pair nearly all the time I've been abroad; and they're not half worn out, are they?"

He looked long at my boots—a pair of Russian leather, and his face seemed to regain steadiness. Putting his hand on my instep, he said:

"Do dey vid you here? I 'ad drouble wid dat bair, I remember."

I assured him that they had fitted beautifully.

"Do you wand any boods? he said. "I can make dem quickly; id is a slack dime."

I answered: "Please, please! I want boots all round—every kind!"

"I will make a vresh model. Your foot must be bigger." And with utter slowness, he traced round my foot, and felt my toes, only once looking up to say:

"Did I tell you my brudder was dead?"

To watch him was painful, so feeble had he grown; I was glad to get away.

I had given those boots up, when one evening they came. Opening the parcel, I set the four pairs out in a row. Then one by one I tried them on. There was no doubt about it. In shape and fit, in finish and quality of leather, they were the best he had ever made me. And in the mouth of one of the Town walking-boots I found his bill. The amount was the same as usual, but it gave me quite a shock. He had never before sent it till quarter day. I flew down-stairs, and wrote a cheque, and posted it at once with my own hand.

A week later, passing the little street, I thought I would go in and tell him how splendidly the new boots fitted. But when I came to where his shop had been, his name was gone. Still there, in the window, were the slim pumps, the patent leathers with cloth tops, the sooty riding boots.

I went in, very much disturbed. In the two little shops—again made into one—was a young man with an English face.

"Mr. Gessler in?" I said.

He gave me a strange, ingratiating look.

"No, sir," he said, "no. But we can attend to anything with

pleasure. We've taken the shop over. You've seen our name, no doubt, next door. We make for some very good people."

"Yes, yes," I said; "but Mr. Gessler?"

"Oh!" he answered; "dead.'

"Dead! But I received these boots from him last Wednesday week."

"Ah!" he said, "a shockin' go. Poor old man starved 'imself."

"Good God!"

"Slow starvation, the doctor called it! You see he went to work in such a way! Would keep the shop on; wouldn't have a soul touch his boots except himself. When he got an order, it took him such a time. People won't wait. He lost everybody. And there he'd sit, goin' on and on—I will say that for him—not a man in London made a better boot! But look at the competition! He never advertised! Would 'ave the best leather, too, and do it all 'imself. Well, there it is. What could you expect with his ideas?"

"But starvation——!"

"That may be a bit flowery, as the sayin' is—but I know myself he was sittin' over his boots day and night, to the very last. You see I used to watch him. Never gave himself time to eat; never had a penny in the house. All went in rent and leather. How he lived so long I don't know. He regular let his fire go out. He was a character. But he made good boots."

"Yes," I said, "he made good boots."

And I turned and went out quickly, for I did not want that youth to know that I could hardly see.

VSEVOLOD GARSHIN

VSEVOLOD GARSHIN (Russian, 1855-1888). Russian writer of novellas. Lived his short adult life in melancholy frustration, suffering from experiences in Serbian and Turkish wars. Committed suicide. Stories permeated with urgent sense of justice and compassion.

THE SIGNAL

SEMYON IVANOV was a track-walker. His hut was ten versts away from a railroad station in one direction and twelve versts away in the other. About four versts away there was a cotton mill that had opened the year before, and its tall chimney rose up darkly from behind the forest. The only dwellings around were the distant huts of the other track-walkers.

Semyon Ivanov's health had been completely shattered. Nine years before he had served right through the war as servant to an officer. The sun had roasted him, the cold frozen him, and hunger famished him on the forced marches of forty and fifty versts a day in the heat and the cold and the rain and the shine. The bullets had whizzed about him, but, thank God! none had struck him.

Semyon's regiment had once been on the firing line. For a whole week there had been skirmishing with the Turks, only a deep ravine separating the two hostile armies; and from morn till eve there had been a steady cross-fire. Thrice daily Semyon carried a steaming samovar and his officer's meals from the camp kitchen to the ravine. The bullets hummed about him and rattled viciously against the rocks. Semyon was terrified and cried sometimes, but still he kept right on. The officers were pleased with him, because he always had hot tea ready for them.

He returned from the campaign with limbs unbroken but crippled with rheumatism. He had experienced no little sorrow since then. He arrived home to find that his father, an old man, and his little four-year-old son had died. Semyon remained alone with his wife. They could not do much. It was difficult to plow with rheumatic arms and legs. They could no longer stay in their village, so they started off to seek their fortune in new places. They stayed for a short time on the line, in Kherson and Donshchina, but nowhere found luck. Then the wife went out to service, and Semyon continued to travel about. Once he happened to ride on an engine, and at one of the stations the face of the station-master seemed familiar to him. Semyon looked at the station-master and the station-master looked at Semyon, and they recognized each other. He had been an officer in Semyon's regiment.

"You are Ivanov?" he said.

"Yes, your Excellency."

"How do you come to be here?"

Semyon told him all.

"Where are you off to?"

"I cannot tell you, sir."

"Idiot! What do you mean by 'cannot tell you'?"

"I mean what I say, your Excellency. There is nowhere for me to go to. I must hunt for work, sir."

The station-master looked at him, thought a bit, and said: "See

425

here, friend, stay a while at the station. You are married, I think. Where is your wife?"

"Yes, your Excellency, I am married. My wife is at Kursk, in service with a merchant."

"Well, write to your wife to come here. I will give you a free pass for her. There is a position as track-walker open. I will speak to the Chief on your behalf."

"I shall be very grateful to you, your Excellency," replied Semyon.

He stayed at the station, helped in the kitchen, cut firewood, kept the yard clean, and swept the platform. In a fortnight's time his wife arrived, and Semyon went on a hand-trolley to his hut. The hut was a new one and warm, with as much wood as he wanted. There was a little vegetable garden, the legacy of a former track-walker, and there was about half a dessiatin of plowed land on either side of the railway embankment. Semyon was rejoiced. He began to think of doing some farming, of purchasing a cow and a horse.

He was given all necessary stores—a green flag, a red flag, lanterns, a horn, hammer, screw-wrench for the nuts, a crow-bar, spade. broom, bolts and nails: they gave him two books of regulations and a time-table of the trains. At first Semyon could not sleep at night, and learned the whole time-table by heart. Two hours before a train was due he would go over his section, sit on the bench at his hut, and look and listen whether the rails were trembling or the rumble of the train could be heard. He even learned the regulations by heart, although he could only read by spelling out each word.

It was summer; the work was not heavy; there was no snow to clear away and the trains on that line were infrequent. Semyon used to go over his verst twice a day, examine and screw up nuts here and there, keep the bed level, look at the water-pipes, and then go home to his own affairs. There was only one drawback—he always had to get the inspector's permission for the least little thing he wanted to do. Semyon and his wife were even beginning to be bored.

Two months passed, and Semyon commenced to make the acquaintance of his neighbors, the track-walkers on either side of him. One was a very old man, whom the authorities were always meaning to relieve. He scarcely moved out of his hut. His wife used to do all his work. The other track-walker, nearer the station, was a young man, thin but muscular. He and Semyon met for the first time on the line midway between the huts. Semyon took off his hat and bowed. "Good health to you, neighbor," he said

The neighbor glanced askance at him. "How do you do?" he replied; then turned around and made off.

Later the wives met. Semyon's wife passed the time of day with her neighbor, but neither did she say much.

On one occasion Semyon said to her: "Young woman, your husband is not very talkative."

The woman said nothing at first, then replied: "But what is there for him to talk about? Every one has his own business. Go your way, and God be with you."

However after another month or so they became acquainted. Semyon would go with Vasily along the line, sit on the edge of a pipe, smoke, and talk of life. Vasily, for the most part, kept silent, but Semyon talked of his village and of the campaign through which he had passed.

"I have had no little sorrow in my day," he would say; "and goodness knows I have not lived long. God has not given me happiness, but what He may give, so will it be. That's so, friend Vasily Stepanych."

Vasily Stepanych knocked the ashes out of his pipe against a rail, stood up and said: "It is not luck which follows us in life, but human beings. There is no crueller beast on this earth than man. Wolf does not eat wolf, but man will readily devour man."

"Come, friend, don't say that; a wolf eats wolf."

"The words came into my mind and I said it. All the same, there is nothing crueller than man. If it were not for his wickedness and greed, it would be possible to live. Everybody tries to sting you to the quick, to bite and eat you up."

Semyon pondered a bit. "I don't know, brother," he said; "perhaps it is as you say, and perhaps it is God's will."

"And perhaps," said Vasily, "it is waste of time for me to talk to you. To put everything unpleasant on God, and sit and suffer, means, brother, being not a man but an animal. That's what I have to say." And he turned and went off without saying good-bye.

Semyon also got up. "Neighbor," he called, "why do you lose your temper?" But his neighbor did not look round, and kept on his way.

Semyon gazed after him until he was lost to sight in the cutting at the turn. He went home and said to his wife: "Arina, our neighbor is a wicked person, not a man."

However, they did not quarrel. They met again and discussed the same topics.

"Ah, friend, if it were not for men we should not be poking in these huts," said Vasily on one occasion.

"And what if we are poking in these huts? It's not so bad. You can live in them."

"Live in them, indeed! Bah, you! . . . You have lived long and learned little, looked at much and seen little. What sort of life is there for a poor man in a hut here or there? The cannibals are devouring you. They are sucking up all your life-blood, and when you become old, they will throw you out just as they do husks to feed the pigs on. What pay do you get?"

"Not much, Vasily Stepanych—twelve rubles."

"And I, thirteen and a half rubles. Why? By the regulations the company should give us fifteen rubles a month with firing and lighting. Who decides that you should have twelve rubles, or I thirteen and a half? Ask yourself! And you say a man can live on that? You understand it is not a question of one and a half rubles or three rubles—even if they paid us each the whole fifteen rubles. I was at the station last month. The director passed through. I saw him. I had that honor. He had a separate coach. He came out and stood on the platform. . . . I shall not stay here long; I shall go somewhere, anywhere, follow my nose."

"But where will you go, Stepanych? Leave well enough alone. Here you have a house, warmth, a little piece of land. Your wife is a worker."

"Land! You should look at my piece of land. Not a twig on it—nothing. I planted some cabbages in the spring, just when the inspector came along. He said: 'What is this? Why have you not reported this? Why have you done this without permission? Dig them up, roots and all.' He was drunk. Another time he would not have said a word, but this time it struck him. Three rubles fine! . . ."

Vasily kept silent for a while, pulling at his pipe, then added quietly: "A little more and I should have done for him."

"You are hot-tempered."

"No, I am not hot-tempered, but I tell the truth and think. Yes, he will still get a bloody nose from me. I will complain to the Chief. We will see then!" And Vasily did complain to the Chief.

Once the Chief came to inspect the line. Three days later important personages were coming from St. Petersburg and would pass over the line. They were conducting an inquiry, so that previous to their journey it was necessary to put everything in order. Ballast was laid down, the bed was leveled, the sleepers carefully examined, spikes driven in a bit, nuts screwed up, posts painted, and orders given for yellow sand to be sprinkled at the level crossings. The woman at the neighboring hut turned her old man out to weed. Semyon worked for a whole week. He put everything in order, mended his kaftan, cleaned and polished his brass plate until it fairly shone. Vasily also worked hard. The Chief arrived on a trolley, four men working the handles and the levers, making the six wheels hum. The trolley traveled at twenty versts an hour, but the wheels squeaked. It reached Semyon's hut, and he ran out and reported in soldierly fashion. All appeared to be in repair.

"Have you been here long?" inquired the Chief.

"Since the second of May, your Excellency."

"All right. Thank you. And who is at hut No. 164?"

The traffic inspector (he was traveling with the Chief on the trolley) replied: "Vasily Spiridov."

"Spiridov, Spiridov. . . . .Ah! is he the man against whom you made a note last year?"

"He is."

"Well, we will see Vasily Spiridov. Go on!" The workmen laid to the handles, and the trolley got under way. Semyon watched it, and thought, "There will be trouble between them and my neighbor."

About two hours later he started on his round. He saw some one coming along the line from the cutting. Something white showed on his head. Semyon began to look more attentively. It was Vasily. He had a stick in his hand, a small bundle on his shoulder, and his cheek was bound up in a handkerchief.

"Where are you off to?" cried Semyon.

Vasily came quite close. He was very pale, white as chalk, and his eyes had a wild look. Almost choking, he muttered: "To town— to Moscow—to the head office."

"Head office? Ah, you are going to complain, I suppose. Give it up! Vasily Stepanych, forget it."

"No, mate, I will not forget. It is too late. See! He struck me in the face, drew blood. So long as I live I will not forget. I will not leave it like this!"

Semyon took his hand. "Give it up, Stepanych. I am giving you good advice. You will not better things. . . ."

"Better things! I know myself I shan't better things. You were right about Fate. It would be better for me not to do it, but one must stand up for the right."

"But tell me, how did it happen?"

"How? He examined everything, got down from the trolley, looked into the hut. I knew beforehand that he would be strict, and so I had put everything into proper order. He was just going when I made my complaint. He immediately cried out: 'Here is a Government inquiry coming, and you make a complaint about a vegetable garden. Here are privy councilors coming, and you annoy me with cabbages!' I lost patience and said something—not very much, but it offended him, and he struck me in the face. I stood still; I did nothing, just as if what he did was perfectly all right. They went off; I came to myself, washed my face, and left."

"And what about the hut?"

"My wife is staying there. She will look after things. Never mind about the roads."

Vasily got up and collected himself. "Good-bye, Ivanov. I do not know whether I shall get any one at the office to listen to me."

"Surely you are not going to walk?"

"At the station I will try to get on a freight train, and to-morrow I shall be in Moscow."

The neighbors bade each other farewell. Vasily was absent for some time. His wife worked for him night and day. She never slept, and wore herself out waiting for her husband. On the third day the commission arrived. An engine, luggage-van, and two first-class saloons; but Vasily was still away. Semyon saw his wife on the fourth day. Her face was swollen from crying and her eyes were red.

"Has your husband returned?" he asked. But the woman only made a gesture with her hands, and without saying a word went her way.

Semyon had learned when still a lad to make flutes out of a kind of reed. He used to burn out the heart of the stalk, make holes where necessary, drill them, fix a mouth-piece at one end, and tune them so well that it was possible to play almost any air on them. He made a number of them in his spare time, and sent them by his friends amongst the freight brakemen to the bazaar in the town. He got two kopeks apiece for them. On the day following the visit of the commission he left his wife at home to meet the six o'clock train, and started off to the forest to cut some sticks. He went to the end of his section—at this point the line made a sharp turn—descended the embankment, and struck into the wood at the foot of the mountain. About half a verst away there was a big marsh, around which splendid reeds for his flutes grew. He cut a whole bundle of stalks and started back home. The sun was already dropping low, and in the dead stillness only the twittering of the birds was audible, and the crackle of the dead wood under his feet. As he walked along rapidly, he fancied he heard the clang of iron striking iron, and he redoubled his pace. There was no repair going on in his section. What did it mean? He emerged from the woods, the railway embankment stood high before him; on the top a man was squatting on the bed of the line busily engaged in something. Semyon commenced quietly to crawl up towards him. He thought it was some one after the nuts which secure the rails. He watched, and the man got up, holding a crow-bar in his hand. He had loosened a rail, so that it would move to one side. A mist swam before Semyon's eyes; he wanted to cry out, but could not. It was Vasily! Semyon scrambled up the bank, as Vasily with crow-bar and wrench slid headlong down the other side.

"Vasily Stepanych! My dear friend, come back! Give me the crow-bar. We will put the rail back; no one will know. Come back! Save your soul from sin!"

Vasily did not look back, but disappeared into the woods.

Semyon stood before the rail which had been torn up. He threw down his bundle of sticks. A train was due; not a freight, but a passenger-train. And he had nothing with which to stop it, no flag. He could not replace the rail and could not drive in the spikes with his bare hands. It was necessary to run, absolutely necessary to run to the hut for some tools. "God help me!" he murmured.

Semyon started running towards his hut. He was out of breath, but still ran, falling every now and then. He had cleared the forest; he was only a few hundred feet from his hut, not more, when he heard the distant hooter of the factory sound—six o'clock! In two minutes' time No 7 train was due. "Oh, Lord! have pity on innocent souls!" In his mind Semyon saw the engine strike against the loosened rail with its left wheel, shiver, careen, tear up and splinter the sleepers—and just there, there was a curve and the embankment seventy feet high, down which the engine would topple — and the third-class carriages would be packed . . . little children. . . . All sitting in the train now, never dreaming of danger. "Oh, Lord! Tell me what to do! . . . No, it is impossible to run to the hut and get back in time."

Semyon did not run on to the hut, but turned back and ran faster

431

than before. He was running almost mechanically, blindly; he did not know himself what was to happen. He ran as far as the rail which had been pulled up; his sticks were lying in a heap. He bent down, seized one without knowing why, and ran on farther. It seemed to him the train was already coming. He heard the distant whistle; he heard the quiet, even tremor of the rails; but his strength was exhausted, he could run no farther, and came to a halt about six hundred feet from the awful spot. Then an idea came into his head, literally like a ray of light. Puilling off his cap, he took out of it a cotton scarf, drew his knife out of the upper part of his boot, and crossed himself, muttering, "God bless me!"

He buried the knife in his left arm above the elbow; the blood spurted out, flowing in a hot stream. In this he soaked his scarf, smoothed it out, tied it to the stick and hung out his red flag.

He stood waving his flag. The train was already in sight. The driver would not see him—would come close up, and a heavy train cannot be pulled up in six hundred feet.

And the blood kept on flowing. Semyon pressed the sides of the wound together so as to close it, but the blood did not diminish. Evidently he had cut his arm very deep. His head commenced to swim, black spots began to dance before his eyes, and then it became dark. There was a ringing in his ears. He could not see the train or hear the noise. Only one thought possessed him. "I shall not be able to keep standing up. I shall fall and drop the flag; the train will pass over me. Help me, O Lord!"

All turned black before him, his mind became a blank, and he dropped the flag; but the blood-stained banner did not fall to the ground. A hand seized it and held it high to meet the approaching train. The engineer saw it, shut the regulator, and reversed steam. The train came to a standstill.

People jumped out of the carriages and collected in a crowd. They saw a man lying senseless on the footway, drenched in blood, and another man standing beside him with a blood-stained rag on a stick.

Vasily looked around at all. Then, lowering his head, he said: "Bind me, I tore up a rail!"

THEOPHILE GAUTIER

THÉOPHILE GAUTIER (French, 1811-1872). One of the prominent founders
of the French Romantic Movement. Painter, newspaperman, extensive traveler.
Wrote art, dramatic and literary criticism, ballets and pantomimes. Both
poetry and prose are highly polished, exotic, objective. Best-known novel:
Mademoiselle de Maupin.

THE MUMMY'S FOOT

I HAD entered, in an idle mood, the shop of one of those curiosity-
vendors, who are called *marchands de bric-à-brac* in that Parisian
argot, which is so perfectly unintelligible elsewhere in France.

You have doubtless glanced occasionally through the windows of
some of these shops, which have become so numerous now that it is
fashionable to buy antiquated furniture, and that every petty stock-
broker thinks he must have his *chambre au moyen âge.*

There is one thing there which clings alike to the shop of the
dealer in old iron, the wareroom of the tapestry-maker, the labora-
tory of the chemist, and the studio of the painter:—in all those
gloomy dens where a furtive daylight filters in through the window-
shutters, the most manifestly ancient thing is dust;—the cobwebs
are more authentic than the guimp laces; and the old pear-tree furniture on exhibition is actually younger than the mahogany which
arrived but yesterday from America.

The warehouse of my *bric-à-brac* dealer was a veritable Caphar-
naum; all ages and all nations seemed to have made their rendezvous
there; an Etruscan lamp of red clay stood upon a Boule cabinet,
with ebony panels, brightly striped by lines of inlaid brass; a duchess of the court of Louis XV nonchalantly extended her fawn-like
feet under a massive table of the time of Louis XIII with heavy spiral
supports of oak, and carven designs of chimeras and foliage intermingled.

Upon the denticulated shelves of several sideboards glittered immense Japanese dishes with red and blue designs relieved by gilded
hatching; side by side with enameled works by Bernard Palissy,
representing serpents, frogs, and lizards in relief.

From disemboweled cabinets escaped cascades of silver-lustrous
Chinese silks and waves of tinsel, which an oblique sunbeam shot
through with luminous beads; while portraits of every era, in

frames more or less tarnished, smiled through their yellow varnish.

The striped breastplate of a damascened suit of Milanese armor glittered in one corner; Loves and Nymphs of porcelain; Chinese Grotesques, vases of *céladon* and crackle-ware; Saxon and old Sèvres cups encumbered the shelves and nooks of the apartment.

The dealer followed me closely through the tortuous way contrived between the piles of furniture; warding off with his hand the hazardous sweep of my coat-skirts; watching my elbows with the uneasy attention of an antiquarian and a usurer.

It was a singular face, that of the merchant:—an immense skull, polished like a knee, and surrounded by a thin aureole of white hair, which brought out the clear salmon tint of his complexion all the more strikingly, lent him a false aspect of patriarchal *bonhomie*, counteracted, however, by the scintillation of two little yellow eyes which trembled in their orbits like two louis-d'or upon quicksilver. The curve of his nose presented an aquiline silhouette, which suggested the Oriental or Jewish type. His hands—thin, slender, full of nerves which projected like strings upon the fingerboard of a violin, and armed with claws like those on the terminations of bats' wings—shook with senile trembling; both those convulsively agitated hands became firmer than steel pincers or lobsters' claws when they lifted any precious article—an •onyx cup, a Venitian glass, or a dish of Bohemian crystal. This strange old man had an aspect so thoroughly rabbinical and cabalistic that he would have been burnt on the mere testimony of his face three hundred centuries ago.

"Will you not buy something from me to-day, sir? Here is a Malay kreese with a blade undulating like flame; look at those grooves contrived for the blood to run along, those teeth set backwards so as to tear out the entrails in withdrawing the weapon—it is a fine character of ferocious arm, and will look well in your collection: this two-handed sword is very beautiful—it is the work of Josepe de la Hera; and this *colichemarde*, with its fenestrated guard—what a superb specimen of handicrâft!"

"No; I have quite enough weapons and instruments of carnage;—I want a small figure, something which will suit me as a paperweight; for I cannot endure those trumpery bronzes which the stationers sell, and which may be found on everybody's desk."

The old gnome foraged among his ancient wares, and finally arranged before me some antique bronzes—so-called, at least; fragments of malachite; little Hindoo or Chinese idols—a kind of pussah toys in jadestone, representing the incarnations of Brahma or Vishnoo, and wonderfully appropriate to the very undivine office of holding papers and letters in place.

I was hesitating between a porcelain dragon, all constellated with warts—its mouth formidable with bristling tusks and ranges of teeth—and an abominable Mexican fetish, representing the god Zitziliputzili *au naturel*, when I caught sight of a charming foot, which I at first took for a fragment of some antique Venus.

It had those beautifully ruddy and tawny tints that lend to Florentine bronze that warm living look so much preferable to the gray-green aspect of common bronzes, which might easily be mistaken for statues in a state of putrefaction: satin gleams played over its rounded forms, doubtless polished by the amorous kiss of twenty centuries; for it seemed a Corinthian bronze, a work of the best era of art—perhaps molded by Lysippus himself.

"That foot will be my choice," I said to the merchant, who regarded me with an ironical and saturnine air, and held out the object desired that I might examine it more fully.

I was surprised at its lightness; it was not a foot of metal, but in sooth a foot of flesh—an embalmed foot—a mumy's foot: on examining it still more closely the very grain of the skin, and the almost imperceptible lines impressed upon it by the texture of the bandages, became perceptible. The toes were slender and delicate, and terminated by perfectly formed nails, pure and transparent as agates; the great toe, slightly separated from the rest, afforded a happy contrast, in the antique style, to the position of the other toes, and lent it an aerial lightness—the grace of a bird's foot,—the sole, scarcely streaked by a few almost imperceptible cross lines, afforded evidence that it had never touched the bare ground, and had only come in contact with the finest matting of Nile rushes, and the softest carpets of panther skin.

"Ha, ha!—you want the foot of the Princess Hermonthis,"—exclaimed the merchant, with a strange giggle, fixing his owlish eyes upon me—"ha, ha ha!—for a paper-weight!—an original idea!—artistic idea! Old Pharaoh would certainly have been surprised had some one told him that the foot of his adored daughter would be used for a paperweight after he had a mountain of granite hollowed out as a receptacle for the triple coffin, painted and gilded—covered with hieroglyphics and beautiful paintings of the Judgment of Souls,"—continued the queer little merchant, half audibly, as though talking to himself!

"How much will you charge me for this mummy fragment?"

"Ah, the highest price I can get; for it is a superb piece: if I had the match of it you could not have it for less than five hundred francs;—the daughter of a Pharaoh! nothing is more rare."

"Assuredly that is not a common article; but, still, how much do you want? In the first place I can buy anything that costs five louis, but nothing dearer;—you might search my vest pockets and most secret drawers without even finding one poor five-franc piece more."

"Five louis for the foot of the Princess Hermonthis! that is very little, very little indeed; 'tis an authentic foot," muttered the merchant, shaking his head, and imparting a peculiar rotary motion to his eyes. "Well, take it, And I will give you the bandages into the bargain," he added, wrapping the foot in an ancient damask rag—"very fine! real damask—Indian damask which has never been redyed; it is strong, and yet it is soft," he mumbled, stroking the frayed tissue with his fingers, through the trade-acquired habit which moved him to praise even an object of so little value that he himself deemed it only worth the giving away.

He poured the gold coins into a sort of medieval alms-purse hanging at his belt, repeating:

"The foot of the Princess Hermonthis, to be used for a paper-weight."

Then turning his phosphorescent eyes upon me, he exclaimed in a voice strident as the crying of a cat which has swallowed a fish-bone:

"Old Pharaoh will not be well pleased; he loved his daughter—the dear man!"

"You speak as if you were a contemporary of his: you are old enough, goodness knows! but you do not date back to the Pyramids of Egypt," I answered, laughingly, from the threshold.

I went home, delighted with my acquisition.

With the idea of putting it to profitable use as soon as possible, I placed the foot of the divine Princess Hermonthis upon a heap of papers scribbled over with verses, in themselves an undecipherable mosaic work of erasures: articles freshly begun; letters forgotten, and posted in the table drawer instead of the letter-box—an error of which absent-minded people are peculiarly liable. The effect was charming, *bizarre*, and romantic.

Well satisfied with this embellishment, I went out with the gravity and pride becoming one who feels that he has the ineffable advantage over all the passers-by whom he elbows, of possessing a piece of the Princess Hermonthis, daughter of Pharaoh.

I looked upon all who did not possess, like myself, a paper-weight so authentically Egyptian, as very ridiculous people; and it seemed to me that the proper occupation of every sensible man should consist in the mere fact of having a mummy's foot upon his desk.

Happily I met some friends, whose presence distracted me in my infatuation with this new acquisition: I went to dinner with them; for I could not very well have dined with myself.

When I came back that evening, with my brain slightly confused by a few glasses of wine, a vague whiff of Oriental perfume delicately titillated my olfatory nerves: the heat of the room had warmed the natron, bitumen, and myrrh in which the *paraschistes, who cut* open the bodies of the dead, had bathed the corpse of the princess;— it was a perfume at once sweet and penetrating—a perfume that four thousand years had not been able to dissipate.

The Dream of Egypt was Eternity: her odors have the solidity of granite, and endure as long.

I soon drank deeply from the black cup of sleep: for a few hours all remained opaque to me; Oblivion and Nothingness inundated me with their somber waves.

Yet light gradually dawned upon the darkness of my mind; dreams commenced to touch me softly in their silent flight.

The eyes of my soul were opened; and I beheld my chamber as it actually was; I might have believed myself awake, but for a vague consciousness which assured me that I slept, and that something fantastic was about to take place.

The odor of the myrrh had augmented in intensity: and I felt a slight headache, which I very naturally attributed to several glasses of champagne that we had drunk to the unknown gods and our future fortunes.

I peered through my room with a feeling of expectation which I saw nothing to justify: every article of furniture was in its proper place; the lamp, softly shaded by its globe of ground crystal, burned upon its bracket; the water-color sketches shone under their Bohemian glass; the curtains hung down languidly; everything wore an aspect of tranquil slumber.

After a few moments, however, all this calm interior appeared to become disturbed; the woodwork cracked stealthily; the ash-covered log suddenl emitted a jet of blue flame; and the disks of the pateras seemed like great metallic eyes, watching, like myself, for the things which were about to happen.

My eyes accidentally fell upon the desk where I had placed the foot of the Princess Hermonthis.

Instead of remaining quiet—as behooved a foot which had been embalmed for four thousand years— it commenced to act in a nervous manner; contracted itself, and leaped over the papers like a startled frog;—one would have imagined that it had suddenly been brought into contact with a galvanic battery: I could distinctly hear the dry sound made by its little heel, hard as the hoof of a gazelle.

I became rather discontented with my acquisition, inasmuch as I wished my paper-weights to be of a sedentary disposition, and thought it very unnatural that feet should walk about without legs; and I commenced to experience a feeling closely akin to fear.

Suddenly I saw the folds of my bed-curtain stir; and heard a bumping sound, like that caused by some person hopping on one foot across the floor. I must confess I became alternately hot and cold; that I felt a strange wind chill my back; and that my suddenly rising hair caused my nightcap to execute a leap of several yards.

The bed-curtains opened and I beheld the strangest figure imaginable before me.

It was a young girl of a very deep coffee-brown complexion, like the bayadere Amani, and possessing the purest Egyptian type of perfect beauty: her eyes were almond-shaped and oblique, with eyebrows so black that they seemed blue; her nose was exquisitely chiseled, almost Greek in its delicacy of outline; and she might indeed have been taken for a Corinthian statue of bronze, but for the prominence of her cheekbones and the slightly African fullness of her lips, which compelled one to recognize her as belonging beyond all doubt to the hieroglyphic race which dwelt upon the banks of the Nile.

Her arms, slender and spindle-shaped, like those of very young girls, were encircled by a peculiar kind of metal bands and bracelets of glass beads; her hair was all twisted into little cords; and she wore upon her bosom a little idol-figure of green paste, bearing a whip with seven lashes, which proved it to be an image of Isis: her brow was adorned with a shining plate of gold; and a few traces of paint relieved the coppery tint of her cheeks.

As for her costume, it was very odd indeed.

Fancy a *pagne* or skirt all formed of little strips of material beuizened with red and black hieroglyphics, stiffened with bitumen, and apparently belonging to a freshly unbandaged mummy.

In one of those sudden flights of thought so common in dreams I heard the hoarse falsetto of the *bric-à-brac* dealer, repeating like a monotonous refrain the phrase he had uttered in his shop with so enigmatic an intonation:

"Old Pharaoh will not be well pleased: he loved his daughter, the dear man!"

One strange circumstance, which was not at all calculated to restore my equanimity, was that the apparition had but one foot; the other was broken off at the ankle!

She approached the table where the foot was starting and fidgeting about more than ever, and there supported herself upon the edge of the desk. I saw her eyes fill with pearly-gleaming tears.

Although she had not as yet spoken, I fully comprehended the thoughts which agitated her: she looked at her foot—for it was indeed her own—with an exquisitely graceful expression of coquettish sadness; but the foot leaped and ran hither and thither as though impelled on steel springs.

Twice or thrice she extended her hand to seize it, but could not succeed.

Then commenced between Princess Hermonthis and her foot—which appeared to be endowed with a special life of its own—a very fantastic dialogue in a most ancient Coptic tongue, such as might have been spoken thirty centuries ago in the syrinxes of the land of Ser: luckily, I understood Coptic perfectly well that night.

The Princess Hermonthis cried, in a voice sweet and vibrant as the tones of a crystal bell:

"Well, my dear little foot, you always flee from me; yet I always took good care of you. I bathed you with perfumed water in a bowl of alabaster; I smoothed your heel with pumice-stone mixed with palm oil; your nails were cut with golden scissors and polished with a hippopotamus tooth; I was careful to select *tatbebs* for you, painted and embroidered and turned up at the toes, which were the envy of all the young girls in Egypt: you wore on your great toe rings bearing the device of the sacred Scarabæus; and you supported one of the lightest bodies that a lazy foot could sustain."

The foot replied, in a pouting and chagrined tone:

"You know well that I do not belong to myself any longer;—I have been bought and paid for; the old merchant knew what he was about; he bore you a grudge for having refused to espouse him;—

this is an ill turn which he has done you. The Arab who violated your royal coffin in the subterranean pits of the necropolis of Thebes was sent thither by him: he desired to prevent you from being present at the reunion of the shadowy nations in the cities below. Have you five pieces of gold for my ransom?"

"Alas, no!—my jewels, my rings, my purses of gold and silver, they were all stolen from me," answered the Princess Hermonthis, with a sob.

"Princess," I then exclaimed, "I never retained anybody's foot unjustly;—even though you have not got the five louis which it cost me, I present it to you gladly: I should feel unutterably wretched to think that I were the cause of so amiable a person as the Princess Hermonthis being lame."

I delivered this discourse in a royally gallant, troubadour tone, which must have astonished the beautiful Egyptian girl.

She turned a look of deepest gratitude upon me; and her eyes shone with bluish gleams of light.

She took her foot—which surrendered itself willingly this time— like a woman about to put on her little shoe, and adjusted it to her leg with much skill.

This operation over, she took a few steps about the room, as though to assure herself that she was really no longer lame.

"Ah, how pleased my father will be!—he who was so unhappy because of my mutilation, and who from the moment of my birth set a whole nation at work to hollow me out a tomb so deep that he might preserve me intact until that last day, when souls must be weighed in the balance of Amenthi! Come with me to my father;— he will receive you kindly; for you have given me back my foot."

I thought this proposition natural enough. I arrayed myself in a dressing-gown of large-flowered pattern, which lent me a very Pharaonic aspect; hurriedly put on a pair of Turkish slippers, and informed the Princess Hermonthis that I was ready to follow her.

Before starting, Hermonthis took from her neck the little idol of green paste, and laid it on the scattered sheets of paper which covered the table.

"It is only fair," she observed smilingly, "that I should replace your paper-weight."

She gave me her hand, which felt soft and cold, like the skin of a serpent; and we departed.

We passed for some time with the velocity of an arrow through a fluid and grayish expanse, in which half-formed silhouettes flitted swiftly by us, to right and left.

For an instant we saw only sky and sea.

A few moments later obelisks commenced to tower in the distance: pylons and vast flights of steps guarded by sphinxes became clearly outlined against the horizon.

We had reached our destination.

The princess conducted me to the mountain of rose-colored granite, in the face of which appeared an opening so narrow and low that it would have been difficult to distinguish it from the fissures in the rock, had not its location been marked by two stelæ wrought with sculptures.

Hermonthis kindled a torch, and led the way before me.

We traversed corridors hewn through the living rock: their walls, covered with hieroglyphics and paintings of allegorical processions, might well have occupied thousands of arms for thousands of years in their formation;—these corridors, of interminable length, opened into square chambers, in the midst of which pits had been contrived, through which we descended by cramp-irons or spiral stairways;—these pits again conducted us into other chambers, opening into other corridors, likewise decorated with painted sparrow-hawks, serpents coiled in circles, the symbols of the *tau* and *pedum*—prodigious works of art which no living eye can ever examine—interminable legends of granite which only the dead have time to read through all eternity.

At last we found ourselves in a hall so vast, so enormous, so immeasurable, that the eye could not reach its limits; files of monstrous columns stretched far out of sight on every side, between which twinkled livid stars of yellowish flame;—points of light which revealed further depths incalculable in the darkness beyond.

The Princess Hermonthis still held my hand, and graciously saluted the mummies of her acquaintance.

My eyes became accustomed to the dim twilight, and objects became discernible.

I beheld the kings of the subterranean races seated upon thrones —grand old men, though dry, withered, wrinkled like parchment, and blackened with naphtha and bitumen—all wearing *pshents* of gold, and breastplates with gorgets glittering with precious stones; their eyes immovably fixed like the eyes of sphinxes, and their long beards whitened by the snow of centuries. Behind them stood their peoples, in the stiff and constrained posture enjoined by Egyptian art, all eternally preserving the attitude prescribed by the hieratic code. Behind these nations, the cats, ibises, and crocodiles contemporary with them—rendered monstrous of aspect by their swathing bands—mewed, flapped their wings, or extended their jaws in a saurian giggle.

All the Pharaohs were there—Cheops, Chephrenes, Psammetichus, Sesostris, Amenotaph—all the dark rulers of the pyramids and syrinxes;—on yet higher thrones sat Chronos and Xixouthros—who was contemporary with the deluge; and Tubal Cain, who reigned before it.

The beard of King Xixouthros had grown seven times around the granite table, upon which he leaned, lost in deep reverie—and buried in dreams.

Further back, through a dusty cloud, I beheld dimly the seventy-two pre-Adamite Kings, with their seventy-two peoples — forever passed away.

After permitting me to gaze upon this bewildering spectacle a few moments, the Princess Hermonthis presented me to her father Pharaoh, who favored me with a most gracious nod.

"I have found my foot again!—I have found my foot!" cried the Princess, clapping her little hands together with every sign of frantic joy: "it was this gentleman who restored it to me."

The races of Kemi, the races of Nahasi—all the black, bronzed, and copper-colored nations repeated in chorus:

"The Princess Hermonthis has found her foot again!"

Even Xixouthros himself was visibly affected.

He raised his heavy eyelids, stroked his mustache with his fingers, and turned upon me a glance weighty with centuries.

"By Oms, the dog of Hell, and Tmei, daughter of the Sun and of Truth! this is a brave and worthy lad!" exclaimed Pharaoh, pointing to me with his scepter, which was terminated with a lotus-flower.

"What recompense do you desire?"

Filled with that daring inspired by dreams in which nothing seems impossible, I asked him for the hand of the Princess Hermonthis;—the hand seemed to me a very proper antithetic recompense for the foot.

Pharaoh opened wide his great eyes of glass in astonishment at my witty request.

"What country do you come from? and what is your age?"

"I am a Frenchman; and I am twenty-seven years old, venerable Pharaoh."

"——Twenty-seven years old! and he wishes to espouse the Princess Hermonthis, who is thirty centuries old!" cried out at once all the Thrones and all the Circles of Nations.

Only Hermonthis herself did not seem to think my request unreasonable.

"If you were even only two thousand years old," replied the ancient King, "I would willingly give you the Princess; but the disproportion is too great; and, besides, we must give our daughters husbands who will last well: you do not know how to preserve yourselves any longer; even those who died only fifteen centuries ago are already no more than a handful of dust;—behold! my flesh is solid as basalt; my bones are bars of steel!

"I shall be present on the last day of the world, with the same body and the same features which I had during my lifetime: my daughter Hermonthis will last longer than a statue of bronze.

"Then the last particles of your dust will have been scattered abroad by the winds; and even Isis herself, who was able to find the atoms of Osiris, would scarce be able to recompose your being.

"See how vigorous I yet remain, and how mighty is my grasp," he added, shaking my hand in the English fashion with a strength that buried my rings in the flesh of my fingers.

He squeezed me so hard that I awoke, and found my friend Alfred shaking me by the arm to make me get up.

"O you everlasting sleeper!—must I have you carried out into the middle of the street, and fireworks exploded in your ears? It is after noon; don't you recollect your promise to take me with you to see M. Aguado's Spanish pictures?"

"God! I forgot all, all about it," I answered, dressing myself hurriedly; "we will go there at once; I have the permit lying on my desk."

I started to find it;—but fancy my astonishment when I beheld, instead of the mummy's foot I had purchased the evening before, the little green paste idol left in its place by the Princess Hermonthis!

KHALIL GIBRAN

KHALIL GIBRAN (Syro-American, 1883-1931). Syro-American writer of inspirational literature. Born in Lebanon, came to America at 11. Studied in Europe, then formed coterie of Syrian writers in New York. Early works in Arabic: *Al-arwāh al-mutamarridat (Spirits Rebellious)*. Later ones in English: *The Prophet*. Taught a religion of love, beauty and redemption.

BEHIND THE GARMENT

RACHEL woke at midnight and gazed intently at something invisible in the sky of her chamber. She heard a voice more soothing than the whispers of Life, and more dismal than the moaning call of the abyss, and softer than the rustling of white wings, and deeper than the message of the waves. . . . It vibrated with hope and with futility, with joy and with misery, and with affection for life, yet with desire for death. Then Rachel closed her eyes and sighed deeply, and gasped, saying, "Dawn has reached the extreme end of the valley; we should go toward the sun and meet him." Her lips were parted, resembling and echoing a deep wound in the soul.

At that moment the priest approached her bed and felt her hand, but found it as cold as the snow; and when he grimly placed his fingers upon her heart, he determined that it was as immobile as the ages, and as silent as the secret of his heart.

The reverend father bowed his head in deep despair. His lips quivered as if wanting to utter a divine word, repeated by the phantoms of the night in the distant and deserted valleys.

After crossing her arms upon her bosom, the priest looked toward a man sitting in an obscured corner of the room, and with a kind and merciful voice he said, "Your beloved has reached the great circle of light. Come, my brother, let us kneel and pray."

The sorrowful husband lifted his head; his eyes stared, gazing at the unseen, and his expression then changed as if he saw understanding in the ghost of an unknown God. He gathered the remnants of himself and walked reverently toward the bed of his wife, and knelt by the side of the clergyman who was praying and lamenting and making the sign of the cross.

Placing his hand upon the shoulder of the grief-stricken husband, the Father said quietly, "Go to the adjoining room, brother, for you are in great need of rest."

He rose obediently, walked to the room and threw his fatigued

444

body upon a narrow bed, and in a few moments he was sailing in the world of sleep like a little child taking refuge in the merciful arms of his loving mother.

*　*　*　*　*

The priest remained standing like a statue in the center of the room, and a strange conflict gripped him. And he looked with tearful eyes at the cold body of the young woman and then through the parted curtain at her husband, who had surrendered himself to the allure of slumber. An hour, longer than an age and more terrible than Death, had already passed, and the priest was still standing between two parted souls. One was dreaming as a field dreams of the coming Spring after the tragedy of Winter, and the other was resting eternally.

Then the priest came close to the body of the young woman and knelt as if worshipping before the altar; he held her cold hand and placed it against his trembling lips, and looked at her face that was adorned with the soft veil of Death. His voice was at the same time calm as the night and deep as the chasm and faltering as with the hopes of man. And in voice he wept, "Oh Rachel, bride of my soul, hear me! At last I am able to talk! Death has opened my lips so that I can now reveal to you a secret deeper than Life itself. Pain has unpinioned my tongue and I can disclose to you my suffering, more painful than pain. Listen to the cry of my soul, Oh Pure Spirit, hovering between the earth and the firmament. Give heed to the youth who waited for you to come from the field, gazing upon you from behind the trees, in fear of your beauty. Hear the priest, who is serving God, calling to you unashamed, after you have reached the City of God. I have proved the strength of my love by concealing it!"

Having thus opened his soul, the Father leaned over and printed three long, warm, and mute kisses upon her forehead, eyes and throat, pouring forth all his heart's secret of love and pain, and the anguish of the years. Then he suddenly withdrew to the dark corner and dropped in agony upon the floor, shaking like an Autumn leaf, as if the touch of her cold face had awakened within him the spirit to repent; whereupon he composed himself and knelt, hiding his face with his cupped hands, and he whispered softly, "God. . . . Forgive my sin; forgive my weakness, Oh Lord. I could no longer resist disclosing that which You knew. Seven years have I kept the deep secrets hidden in my heart from the spoken word, until Death

445

came and tore them from me. Help me, Oh God, to hide this terrible
and beautiful memory which brings sweetness from life and bitterness from You. Forgive me, My Lord, and forgive my weakness."
Without looking at the young woman's corpse, he continued suffering and lamenting until Dawn came and dropped a rosy veil upon
those two still images, revealing the conflict of Love and Religion
to one man; the peace of Life and Death to the other.

ANDRE GIDE

ANDRÉ GIDE (French, 1869-1951). Contemporary French novelist. Sensitive
and sensuous protagonist of egotism. Rebelled against Puritan background
after meeting Oscar Wilde in Algeria. Insisted on doctrine of individual
morality, but became a stylist in classic tradition. Most widely read novel:
The Counterfeiters. Others: *The Immoralist, The Pastoral Symphony, Strait
Is the Gate.* Autobiography: *If It Die . . .*

MY MOTHER

I

WHEN I had finished my first studies, my mother thought it would
be a good thing to introduce me to "society". But aside from some
not too distant cousins and the wives of a few of my father's colleagues at the Faculty of Law, transplanted from Rouen to Paris,
she had never tried to make any acquaintances. Furthermore, the
world in which it seemed I was to be interested, that of men of letters or artists, was not "her" world; she would have felt herself out
of place in it.

I no longer know to what drawing-room she took me that day.
It must have been that of my cousin Saussine, at whose home, on
the rue d'Athènes, I took tiresome dancing lessons twice a week. It
was the day they received. There were numerous introductions, and
the conversation was approximately what all society conversations
are, made up of little nothings and affectations. I turned my attention less to the other ladies than to my mother. I scarcely recognized
her. She, ordinarily so modest, so reserved, and seemingly fearful
of her own opinion, appeared in that social gathering, full of assurance and, without pushing herself forward at all, perfectly at her

446

ease. One would have said that she was playing a role exactly as it should be, without, moreover, attaching any importance to it, but willingly consenting to mingle in the game of the society parade to which one contributes hardly anything but outward appearances. It even seemed to me that, in the twaddle and foolishness all about, a few particularly sensible sentences of hers threw the general conversation into disorder; the ridiculous remarks immediately collapsed and disappeared into thin air, like ghosts at the crowing of the cock. I was amazed, and told her so, as soon as we escaped from that Vanity Fair, and found ourselves alone together.

For my part, I dined that evening with Pierre Louys, I believe. At any rate, I remember that I left her as we turned the corner of rue d'Athènes. But I came back to her almost immediately after dinner. I was in a hurry to see her. We were then living on the rue de Commaille. The windows of our apartment opened on a deep garden that no longer exists to-day. My mother was on the balcony. She had taken off her finery, and I rediscovered her in her simple, drab, everyday clothes. It was the season when the first acacias smell sweet. My mother seemed worried; she did not make confidences easily and doubtless the co-operation of springtime was needed to invite her to speak.

"Is what you said to me as we left our cousin's true?" she began with a great effort. "You really think so? I was . . . well, as good as the others?"

And as I began to exclaim, she continued mournfully:

"If your father had told me so even once . . . I never dared ask him, and I needed so terribly to know, when we went out together, if he was . . . "

She was silent for a moment. I looked at her trying to hold back her tears. She finished in a lower tone of voice, hardly audible:

". . . if he was pleased with me."

I think that those were her exact words which suddenly let me understand how many worries, unasked questions and expectations could, under the appearance of happiness, still dwell in even the most united of couples. And such were my parents in the eyes of everyone and of their son. What my mother had vainly awaited was not a compliment from my father, but only the assurance that she had been able to prove herself worthy of him, that he had not been disappointed in her. But what my father thought, I knew no more than she; and I understood, that evening, that every soul carries to the tomb to hide it there, some secret.

II

Everything that was natural in my mother, I loved. But it happened that her impulses were checked by covention and the bent that a bourgeois education too often leaves behind it. (Not always; thus I remember that she dared brave the disapproval of all her family when she went to care for the farmers of La Roque attacked during a typhus epidemic.) That education, excellent, doubtless, when it is a question of curbing evil instincts, attacks equally, but then very unfortunately, the generous emotions of the heart; then a sort of calculation restrains or directs them. I should like to give an example of this:

My mother announced to me her intention of making a gift of Littré to Anna Shackleton, our poor friend, whom I loved as a son. I was bursting with joy, when she added:

"The one I gave your father is bound in morocco. I thought that, for Anna, a shagreen binding would be sufficient."

I understood at once, what I had not known before, that shagreen costs much less. The joy suddenly left my heart. And without a doubt my mother noticed it, for she went on quickly:

"She won't see the difference."

No, that shabby cheating was not natural to her. To her giving was natural. But I was irritated also by that sort of complicity to which she had invited me.

I have lost the memory of a thousand more important things. Why did those few sentences of my mother's engrave themselves so deeply on my heart? Perhaps because I felt myself capable of thinking and saying them myself, in spite of the violent reprobation they aroused in me. Perhaps because I became conscious of that bent against which I should have to struggle and that I was sadly amazed to discover in my mother. Everything else melted into the harmonious ensemble of her face; and it is perhaps just because I did not recognize her any more by that trait, truly unworthy of her, that my memory took possession of it. What a warning! What strength that educational bent had, then, to triumph in this way from time to time! But my mother remained too surrounded by beings deformed in the same way, to be able to recognize in herself, among all the acquired characteristics, those spontaneous to her nature; above all, she remained too fearful and unsure of herself to give them the upper hand. She remained worried about others and their opinions; always desirous of the best, but a best answering to

448

accepted rules; always tending toward this best, and without even suspecting (and too modest to recognize it) that the best in her was exactly what she obtained with the least effort.

JEAN GIRAUDOUX

JEAN GIRAUDOUX (French, 1882-1944). Influential modern playwright and novelist. Profound and searching in thought. Was diplomat after First World War. Achieved first success as novelist *(Siegfried et le Limousin)*, then as dramatist. Chose fantastic themes to treat serious problems of our time. Plays translated: *Amphitryon 38, Intermezzo, The Madwoman of Chaillot, Ondine, Tiger at the Gates.*

MAY ON LAKE ASQUAM

I AM stretched out in the middle of a great ring of mountains. When I get up onto my feet, I become their very pivot. I have put the sun on my left, as they taught me to do at school, and I am writing to you. The lake below me bears fragile islands on its surface, and pine logs, from the drifts broken up during the winter, wash vagrantly in its bays and coves. Humming-birds thrusting voraciously among the apple-blossoms, wound their swift bills on the hard wood and glance off again. To soothe the sore feet of the farm turkeys—a degenerate race—Mrs. Green is greasing the limbs of the tree where they come to roost. A thrush grazes me, a little breeze begins to stir. As when a bird alights by a dreaming poet and he is moved to see the very thought he was seeking within himself drop then, perfect— so a sweet and tender love, instead of stirring in my heart, lifts this page, fans me with its soft breath. In boat-houses hidden in the reeds the farmers are testing the motors of the boats which will be launched for their masters next month. Mrs. Green is beating a rose-colored puff for me, because my bed ends under the window, and when I wake in the morning I see my sunny feet under the spread—and yet feel cold. In the depths of the creeks where ·the new-cut pines are floating, the lumbermen jump from one log to the next, whistling as they go. I envy them their balance; I feel over-weighted with a lake and a sun on my left, and nothing on my right. Where am I? I am in a land which I instantly recognize to be enormous, because these wasps that are this second buzzing about my head are three times bigger than they are in Europe. I am in the middle of New Hampshire, which is having its first sight of the sky-blue uniform, and, supposing that I have chosen this color myself, imagines me to be sensitive and generous. The Harvard Regiment is having a week of examinations, and I am taking a rest.

The motor left Boston early on Monday, reaching the suburbs at the hour when the typewriters, perched on their high-heeled, pointed shoes, in their low-necked foulard dresses, and bent slant-wise to the wind, climb into the tramcars without touching the rail, anxious only for their hands; the stenographers following them rigidly erect, thinking only of their heads. On the door-steps Irish girls with brown braids looped over their ears passed on to us, through soft blue eyes, the holiest thoughts they had been pondering in the night. We were following the highway bordered with Washington elms, very old trees whose trunks had been repaired with the sort of cement of which they make statues in this country; and immortality —as sap was lacking—had already reached the topmost branches. Lakes that grew clearer and clearer the farther we went held the water of the richer and richer parts of Boston, and we came at last to the very round, very blue lake that supplies Beacon Street.

At noon we were at Portsmouth, where I presided at a meeting the children were holding on the beach to sell their pet animals, for the benefit of their French godchildren. There were at least a hundred of them, all grave, eager, or at least acquiescent, save Grace Henderson, who clung to her white calf and wept. They bought it of her quickly, and in pity gave it back to her; but her brother obliged her to sell it again, and so she had to struggle and suffer three times over. There were Cuban birds, that you bought with their cages; native birds that you bought so as to set them free; turtles which sold badly, as they wore the initials of their first master carved on their backs; goats; and there were animals which were also immolated for the cause—sad dogs, who had no resistance left in them, and sold themselves; a little elephant which clasped his mistress by a belt that gave, by a sleeve that tore, and so did not dare to take her by the pigtail. The governesses, to console their children, quickly bought these other animals, and took turns standing on a platform to read out letters from the godsons: "*Venez chez moi, j'irai chez vous,*" wrote Jean Perrot, "*et si je meurs je veux vous voir.*" Some professors who were there were amazed to discover that all French children use rhythmic prose.

Then came green forests cut by tumbling brooks, where little boys, who were fishing for trout with both hands, hailed us with a wink, as they did not dare to move or call out. Then came the country of the field-mice, where the owls have such fat haunches that they have to perch sideways for fear of tumbling off their twigs head first. Then came Sandwich, where a Lithuanian was waving his national flag, protesting all by himself against conscription. Then came Lake Asquam, and this local hilltop where I have lain stretched out ever since, at the foot of a slim giant birch, which has only one tuft of verdure at its top, and will fall if it puts out a single other leaf.

My hostess is Mrs. Green, the farmer's wife, who wears her gray hair braided down her back, and a big striped shawl, and eyeglasses; but she twists the calves' tails, and fights with the rooster. When a word gets stuck in my fountain pen I shake it out into the lake from my steamer-chair. Sometimes, though, it is inside me that it hesitates, and then I have to get up myself, lean on my elbows, sometimes even stoop all the way over.

Who am I with? With two friends—a forester and an Australian poet. The morning belongs to Carnegie, the forester. By six o'clock he has me up and off on a dash to his district, straight across the islands where every owner keeps a different scheme of hours, according as he likes to see his children get up early or late. Silent beasts are waking in woods that still have their Indian names; the muskrat is taking his bath, the blue heron flies from an isthmus to an island, from an island to an islet, flying ever toward that little round point of noon. We land in haste, to avoid an upset—for a new-cut pine log is already sliding down the toboggan to the lake— and go to the sawmill by a path that was once covered with sawdust, but that my forester has had tarred since he lost his gold chain. He teaches me the secret sign by which one may recognize the red pine, the white pine, and the black pine; he gathers together his group of woodcutters, who are going off to France, and forces me to pronounce our biggest trees in French—the oak, the elm; I saw my favorite beeches with difficulty. In the short cuts we walk through the briars stiffly, as people who do not speak the same tongue always do, and not one of these noble gestures is lost, my dear, for the forest is full of lynxes. In the clearings he shows me the remains of the wood fires he has kindled since his childhood, and twenty years of embers still blacken his fingers. He is moved and sits down, my love, to dream . . . and suddenly four little woodchucks, my sweet, hurry timidly out of the ground; real little woodchucks, my heart.

451

We catch them—they bite us, and try to get away—we pet them, my dear love.

But the night belongs to Rogers, the Australian. The whole world is dark, invisible; only one red point to be seen, Carnegie's cigar—he is noiselessly paddling on the lake. But miles away the chosen tree that announces the moon suddenly twinkles down its whole length. That is because a whole moon is coming. Everything is radiant, everything shines. Rocks begin to show themselves, as white and polished as bleached bones. Far around the lake the reflection of the forest, just now cleft and jutting, becomes an even border. It is the hour when the Indians gave a name to all the things that surround us. The white mountains turn white, the yellow birches yellow, and blue, blue grow the owls. Every separate plane of the lake seems to lie on a different level, and the moon gnaws the water where it falls over the dams. A divine night, this, when the White Mountains are of silver and the birches of gold. At last the hour has come when I can find an epithet for my soul, and a name for my house. The bullfrog groans; the loon, black swan of the lake, utters cries, first piercing, then muffled, for he continuously ducks his head under the water and pulls it out again. The true moon cautiously climbs farther and farther from the false moon. . . .

But Rogers insists on talking. He wants me to talk to him of Seeger, who is dead, of Blakely, who is dead—of all the American poets who were killed before the American war began. He persists in talking French, without allowing me to help him, and circles about the words he no longer knows: about the word "debonair," the word "ladder," the word "serenity." From my refuge in the very heart of the word I wait placidly for him, sometimes in the heart of a proper name, in the heart of Baudelaire—a stuffy place, his statue. Then he reads me his verses, which he wishes to adapt to Europe, because the Australian mouths are so different from our own.

"July has frozen the rivers," he says, "and the useless bridges are collected in the barn."

I shake my head; he understands, and corrects himself:

"Summer has frozen the rivers, and the bridges" . . .

The loon sings on. The lake suddenly bursts into flame, for Carnegie is lighting a second cigar. Rogers grows emotional, takes my hand and circles about a word which expresses both loons and friendships, a word which even we in France, alas, do not know.

When the storm breaks; when, by millions, the owners of the

wooden houses bring their red-striped tents in from the rain: when a flash of lightning allows you to see—through the isinglass of the top of the car in front of you—the shadow of two gray heads; when the black bird with the red wings folds his wings; when the pro-German shuts his window and suddenly feels so lonely and beaten that he bursts into tears; when, in the public parks, the crowds swarm under the tents of the recruiting sergeants, and help them move their posters, and torpedoes, and mortars under shelter; when the mother astride the purple motor-cycle tries in vain to reach out a hand and feel the baby dozing in the side-car; when the golden stags, the dragons and the golden cows whirl madly on the clock-towers of the barns, but always in time; when a Hannan shoe lies on the deserted avenue; when a blast of wind lifts the page of the one-armed accountant, and he holds it down with the point of his pen, calling for help; when one hears nothing on the sidewalks, on on the sea, on the buildings, but the rain . . . then when a sunbeam comes down, and a sharp cloud cuts it, and it falls; when the rain-bow shivers, its left on the solid city cement, its right on the sea; when you gather the sun into a corner of the sky, as if it were your one last match—and it finally burns; when a victorious sunbeam, fall-ing on the terrace beats by the fraction of an inch a rain-drop that has come from thousands of miles less far away; when the baby in the side-car gets the last drop of all, and begins to cry—then when the pond-lilies climb up to the level of the new pond that has formed about them; when the farmer in his rubber boots tramps out to empty his pitch cans and his maple syrup cans of their water; when a child, for no reason at all, wants to burn a joss-stick; when the traveler, at the turn of the Cañon, gets down to pat his mule and all at once remounts quickly for the storm is rumbling again, and he wants to keep his saddle dry; when the rain begins to beat down once more, in a deluge, the very same rain, as you can plainly recognize by its drops: then I think of him, of Seeger, who loved storms, and I shudder.

"How did Seeger die?" asks Rogers.

In a month Rogers will be leaving for the war, and he loses no opportunity of informing himself how the poets, his colleagues, were killed. It would be very odd if two poets were killed in the same way, the same identical way; each one of these deaths is death that fate will deny him. He will not wander, like Rupert Brooke, repeating one Christian name after another, and dying at the first woman's name. He will not have him, as Dollero did, to write me three letters; the first with a splinter and his blood saying good by; the second with his nurse's pencil, hoping to see me; the last with the doctor's fountain pen—confident, happy, unfinished. He will not drop dead like Hesslin, the German poet, on the back of a mystical sergeant who rose slowly with his load, and bore it to the hospital without casting a backward look. He will need a whole grave to himself, since he is not to die like Blakely, whose poor remains fitted into a Palmer's biscuit box. It will not be at dark, as it was with Drouot, or at noon, as it was with Clermont. If Seeger died at dawn, there is no time left for him but night. Bitter night, running under the days like some infernal strawberry vine. Soft night, with its lake, its loons. Night on the Sydney steamers, when the world turns silent, and nothing stands in the way of a poet's thoughts but the mute strain of a vessel. Night near some French spring where you lie, scarcely aware of your wound, and nibble a leaf of water-cress. Somber night, in whose very center, sharp cut against the velvet dark, the sun suddenly appears. Happy he who dies at night!

"How did Seeger die? Did you know him?"

Rogers is astigmatic, wears heavy gold-rimmed spectacles with lenses of different pattern, and always asks you two questions at a time. Yes, I had seen him. Once it was in the Luxembourg, in summer; he was just coming into the unreal garden, with its world of fantastic and tender Parisians—those who felt themselves too heavy could buy little balloons at the gate. Another time it was at the house of a friend whom he had tried to find the two preceding evenings; on the first he left a couplet, on the second a sonnet. My friend allowed himself to be surprised in bed, the third day, and so did not get his poem.

"Did he suffer? Have you seen his last verses?"

For Rogers also collects the last poems of all the poets who have been killed. He even collects their last letters in prose, where sometimes two words clash into each other and rhyme—the same thing happens when a departing warrior is dressing in his apartment, with his friends standing about—and makes them tremble. It may be a last letter written to an aunt between the two last poems, when, in spite of himself, he uses the poetic epithet (as the other does not come)—talks of "steeds," and "blades," and "meads," and feels obliged to be somewhat ironic. Last poems where nearly all of them saw death as it was, in fact, to overtake them, Seeger like a mistress, longing for a rendezvous, Dollero like a storm with three stray birds, Blakely like a headless monster—and when only Brooke foresaw things all wrong. Poor Brooke who told us *"Si je meurs, dites vous que dans une terre ètrangère il y aura toujours un coin de terre anglaise. Une poussière plus riche que la terre y sera contenue, un corps d'Angleterre lavé par les rivières anglaises, brûle par le soleil anglais," "un corps horizontal tendu sur la ligne de tous les corps anglais,"* and in the end died on a boat, and was thrown into the sea with a cannon ball to keep his shroud upright. So that, for all one's pity one is put on one's guard, and when one turns over his other poems one no longer believes exactly what they say; no longer believes that love is *une rue ouverte où se precipite ce qui jamais ne voient, un traître qui livre au destin la citadelle du coeur, un enfant étendu.* One grows obstinate about it, insists on believing that love is a street, if you like, but a street with no outlet; a traitor perhaps, but in that case a friendly traitor; and sometimes one sees the charming fellow standing quite vertical, floating sadly in the air.

"How did Seeger die?"

It is summer. Everything that prevents one from breathing in the summer—his cap, his gas-mask—he throws off. He holds his cigar behind him, because of the smoke; the company thief steals it away from him—thank heaven, for so his hands will not burn up after his death. Then he stretches himself, but without lifting his arms, crosswise. He has just one minute to live. There is your watch before you, with its second hand: one minute and he will be dead. In his pocket is the bottle of heliotrope perfume that he is to break as he falls. Now you have not even time, before he dies, to write that short sentence which he took for his motto, the one that he wrote at the head of every poem—about the poplars. If it is a shell, the cannon is being loaded. If it is a bullet, the German soldier is tapping his charge and slipping it in. Seeger raises his head. The sky is very blue. A poplar, yes, a poplar is outlined on the horizon. Seeger climbs the firing step—a bird, yes, a . . .

So my three days of rest have gone, and now it is noon. I think of you who wrote me every week from Europe, a letter of variable mood —Even the color of the paper is inconstant, and each one, like the flash of a revolving lighthouse, throws a new region into high relief. Love is a restive horse, a saddled antelope, a faithful traitor. The sun is just above me now. I was writing, to spare my eyes, in the shadow of my head; there is no shadow left; adieu, Madame, I write the last word, I write your name, full in the sun.

JOHANN WOLFGANG VON GOETHE

JOHANN WOLFGANG VON GOETHE (German, 1749-1832). Germany's greatest poet and the philosopher of classical poetry. Writer of universal scope—even his recorded conversations are significant. Wielded tremendous influence during life and afterward. Initiated *Sturm und Drang* movement *(Sorrows of Werther)*. Autobiographical novel: *Wilhelm Meister*. Epic: *Hermann and Dorothea*. Drama: *Egmont*. His masterpiece, *Faust*, philosophic-poetic drama, one of Western world's supreme classics.

FAUST

A Tragedy

Faust.   All that philosophy can teach,
The craft of lawyer and of leech,
I've mastered, ah! and sweated through
Theology's dreary deserts, too;
Yet here, poor fool! for all my lore,
I stand no wiser than before.
They call me magister, save the mark!
Doctor, withal! and these ten years I
Have been leading my pupils a dance in the dark,
Up hill, down dale, through wet and through dry—
And yet, that nothing can ever be
By mortals known, too well I see!
This is burning the heart clean out of me.
More brains have I than all the tribe
Of doctor, magister, parson, and scribe.
From doubts and scruples my soul is free;
Nor hell nor devil has terrors for me:
But just for this I am dispossessed
Of all that gives pleasure to life and zest.
I can't even juggle myself to own
There is any one thing to be truly known,
Or aught to be taught in science or arts,
To better mankind and to turn their hearts.
Besides, I have neither land nor pence,
Nor worldly honour nor influence.
A dog in my case would scorn to live!

456

So myself to magic I've vowed to give,
And see, if through spirit's might and tongue
The heart from some mysteries cannot be wrung;
If I cannot escape from the bitter woe
Of babbling of things that I do not know,
And get to the root of those secret powers
Which hold together this world of ours,
The sources and centres of force explore,
And chaffer and dabble in words no more.
Oh, broad bright moon, if this might be
The last of the nights of agony,
The countless midnights, these weary eyes
Have from this desk here watched thee rise!
Then, sad-eyed friend, thy wistful looks
Shone in upon me o'er paper and books;
But oh! might I wander, in thy dear light,
O'er the trackless slopes of some mountain height,
Round mountain caverns with spirits sail,
Or float o'er the meads in thy hazes pale;
And, freed from the fumes of a fruitless lore,
Bathe in thy dews, and be whole once more!

Ah me! am I penned in this dungeon still?
Accursed doghole, clammy and chill!
Where heaven's own blessed light must pass,
Shorn of its rays, through the painted glass,
Narrowed and cumbered by piles of books,
That are gnawed by worms and grimed with dust,
And which, with its smoke-stained paper looks
Swathed to the roof in a dingy rust;
Stuck round with phials, and chests untold,
With instruments littered, and lumbered with old,
Crazy, ancestral household ware—
This is your world! A world most rare!

And yet can you wonder why your soul
Is numbed within your breast, and why
A dead, dull anguish makes your whole
Life's pulses falter, and ebb, and die?

How should it be but so? Instead
Of the living nature, whereinto
God has created man, things dead
And drear alone, encompass you—
Smoke, litter, dust, the skeletons
Of birds and beasts, and dead men's bones!

Up, up! Away to the champaign free!
And this mysterious volume, writ
By Nostradamus' self, is it
Not guide and counsel enough for thee?
Then wilt thou learn by what control
The stars within their orbits roll,
And if thou wilt let boon Nature be
The guide and monitress to thee,
Thy soul shall expand with tenfold force,
As spirit with spirit holds discourse.
Dull poring, think not, that can here
Expound these holy signs to thee!
Ye spirits, ye are hovering near,
If ye can hear me, answer me!

Throws open the book, and discovers the sign of the Macrocosm.

Ha! as it meets my gaze, what rapture, gushing
Through all my senses, mounts into my brain!
Youth's ecstasy divine, I feel it rushing,
Like quickening fire, through every nerve and vein!
Was it a god who chronicled these signs,
Which all the war within me still,
The aching heart with sweetness fill,
And to mine eyes, in clearest lines,
Unveil all Nature's powers as with a mystic thrill?
Am I a god? All grows so bright.
In these pure outlines I behold
Nature at work before my soul unrolled.
Now can I read the sage's saw aright:
"Not barred to man the world of spirits is;
Thy sense is shut, thy heart is dead!
Up, student, lave,—nor dread the bliss,—
Thy earthly breast in the morning red!"

Gazes intently at the sign.

Into one whole how all the things blend,
One in the other working, living!
What powers celestial, lo! ascend, descend,
Each unto each the golden pitchers giving!
And, wafting blessings from their wings,
From heaven through farthest earth career,
While through the universal sphere
One universal concord rings!

Oh, what a show! yet but a show! Ah me!
Where, boundless Nature, shall I clutch at thee?
Ye breasts, where are ye? Ye perennial springs
Of life, whereon hang heaven and earth,
Whereto the blighted bosom clings,
Ye gush, ye slake all thirst, yet I pine on in dearth!

Turns the leaves of the book angrily, and sees the sign of the Earth
Spirit.

How differently I feel before this sign!
Earth Spirit, thou to me art nearer;
My faculties grow loftier, clearer,
Even now I glow as with new wine.
Courage I feel, into the world to roam,
To bid earth's joy and sorrows hail,
'Mid storm and struggle to make my home,
And in the crash of shipwreck not to quail.
Clouds gather o'er my head;
The moon conceals her light,
The lamp's gone out. The air
Grows thick and close! Red flashes play
Around me. From the vaulted roof
A shuddering horror creeps
And on me lays its gripe!
Spirit by me invoked, I feel
Thou'rt hovering near,—thou art, thou art!
Unveil thyself!
Ha! What a tugging at my heart!
Stirred through their depths, my senses reel
With passions new and strange! I feel
My heart is thine, thine wholly! Hear!
Thou must! ay, though it cost my life, thou must **appear!**

459

Seizes the book, and utters the sign of the Spirit mysteriously. A red light flashes, in which the Spirit appears.

Spirit. Who calls on me?
Faust (turning away). Dread vision gaunt!
Spirit. By potent art thou'st dragged me here;
Thou'st long been sucking at my sphere,
And now—
Faust. I loathe thee. Hence, avaunt!
Spirit. To view me were thy prayer and choice,
To see my face, to hear my voice.
Well! by thy potent prayer won o'er,
I come. And thou, that wouldst be more
Than mortal, having thy behest,
Art with a craven fear possessed!
Where is thy pride of soul? Where now the breast
Which in itself a universe created,
Sustained and fostered,—which dilated
With giant throes of rapture, in the hope
As peer with spirits such as me to cope?
Where art thou, Faust, whose summons rang so wide,
Is this thing thou? This, my mere breath doth make
Through every nerve and fibre quake?
A crawling, cowering, timorous worm?
Faust. Thou film of flame, art thou a thing to fear?
I am, I am that Faust! I am thy peer!
Spirit. In the currents of Life, in Action's storm,
I wander and I wave;
Everywhere I be!
Birth and the grave,
An infinite sea,
A web ever growing,
A life ever glowing;
Thus at Time's whizzing loom I spin,
And weave the living vesture that God is mantled in!
Faust. Thou busy Spirit, who dost sweep
From sphere to sphere, from deep to deep,
Ranging the world from end to end,
How near akin I feel to thee!
Spirit. Thou'rt like the Spirit, thou dost comprehend,
But not like me!
                              Vanishes.

460

Faust. O happy he who still can hope
Out of this sea of error to arise!
We long to use what lies beyond our scope,
Yet cannot use even what within it lies.
But let us not, by saddening thoughts like these,
The blessing of this happy hour o'errun.
See, how they gleam, the green-girt cottages,
Fired by the radiance of the evening sun!
It slopes, it sets. Day wanes. On with a bound
It speeds, and lo! a new world is alive!
O God, for wings to lift me from the ground,
Onward, still onward, after it to strive!
Beneath me, I should see, as on I pressed,
The hushed world ever bathed in evening's beams,
Each mountain-top on fire, each vale at rest,
The silver brook flow into golden streams.
Nor peak nor mountain-chasm should then defeat
My onward course, so godlike and so free.
Lo, with its bays all winking in the heat,
Bursts on my wonder-smitten eyes the sea!
But now the god appears about to sink!
Fresh impulse stirs me, not to be confined.
I hurry on, his deathless light to drink,
The day before me, and the night behind,
The heavens above me, and the waves below.
A lovely dream! Meanwhile, the sun his face
Has hid. Ah, with the spirit's wing will no
Corporeal wings so readily keep pace!
Yet is the yearning with us all inborn,
Upwards and onwards to be struggling still,
When over us we hear the lark, at morn,
Lost in the sky, her quivering carol trill;
When o'er the mountains' pine-clad summits drear
The eagle wheels afar on outstretched wing,
When over flat and over mere
The crane is homewards labouring.
   Wagner. I too have often had my whims and moods,
But never was by such an impulse stirred.
A man soon looks his fill at fields and woods;
The wings I ne'er shall envy of a bird.
How differently the spirit's pure delights

Waft us from book to book, from page to page!
They give a beauty to the winter's nights,
A cheerful glow that can its chill assuage.
And some fine manuscript when you unroll,
Ah, then all heaven descends into your soul!
    Faust.   One only aspiration thou hast known,
Oh, never seek to know the other, never!
Two souls, alas! within my bosom throne,
That each from other fiercely longs to sever.
One, with a passionate love that never tires,
Cleaves as with cramps of steel to things of earth,
The other upwards through earth's mists aspires
To kindred regions of a loftier worth.
Oh, in the air if spirits be,
That float 'twixt earth and heaven, and lord it there,
Then from your golden haze descend, and me
Far hence to fields of new existence bear!
Yes, if a magic mantle were but mine,
To stranger lands to waft me at my call,
I'd prize it more than robes of costliest shine,
I would not change it for a monarch's pall

* * *

    Mephistopheles.   These my tiny spirits be.
Hark, with what sagacity
They advise thee to pursue
Action, pleasure ever new!
Out into the world so fair
They would lure and lead thee hence,
From this lonely chamber, where
Stagnate life and soul and sense.
No longer trifle with the wretchedness,
That, like a vulture, gnaws your life away!
The worst society will teach you this,
You are a man 'mongst men, and feel as they.
Yet 'tis not meant, I pray you, see,
To thrust you 'mong the rabble rout;—
I'm done of your great folks, no doubt,
But if, in fellowship with me,
To range through life you are content,
I will most cheerfully consent

To be your own upon the spot.
I am your chum. You'd rather not?
Well! If your scruples it will save,
I am your servant, yea, your slave!

    Faust.   And in return what must I do for you?

    Mephistopheles.   Oh, time enough to talk of that!

    Faust.   Nay, nay!
The devil's selfish—is and was always—
And is not like for mere God's sake to do
A liberal turn to any child of clay.
Out with the terms, and plainly! Such as thou
Are dangerous servants in a house, I trow.

    Mephistopheles.   I bind myself to serve you here,—to **do**
Your bidding promptly, whatsoe'er it be,
And, when we come together yonder, you
Are then to do the same for me.

    Faust.   I prize that yonder at a rush!
Only this world to atoms crush,
And then that other may arise!
From earth my every pleasure flows,
Yon Sun looks down upon my woes;
Let me but part myself from those.
Then come what may, in any guise!
To idle prate I'll close mine ears,
If we hereafter hate or love,
Or if there be in yonder spheres,
As here, an Under and Above!

    Mephistopheles.   You're in the proper mood to venture! **Bind**
Yourself, and pleasure in my sleights you'll find,
While this life lasts. I'll give you more
Than eye of man hath ever seen before.

    Faust.   What wilt thou give, thou sorry devil? **When**
Were the aspiring souls of men
Fathomed by such a thing as thee?
Oh, thou hast food that satisfieth never,
Gold, ruddy gold thou hast, that restlessly
Slips, like quicksilver, through the hand for ever;
A game, where we must losers be;
A girl, that, on my very breast,
My neighbour woos with smile and wink;
Fame's rapturous flash of godlike zest,

That, meteor-like, is doomed to sink.
Show me the fruit that, ere 'tis plucked, doth rot,
And trees that every day grow green anew!

Mephistopheles. Such task as this affrights me not.
I have such treasures at command for you.
But, my good friend, the time draws nigh
When we may banquet on the best in peace!

Faust. If e'er at peace on sluggard's couch I lie,
Then may my life upon the instant cease!
Cheat thou me ever by thy glozing wile,
So that I cease to scorn myself, or e'er
My senses with a perfect joy beguile,
Then be that day my last! I offer fair,
How say'st thou?

Mephistopheles. Done!

Faust. My hand upon it! There!
If to the passing moment e'er I say,
"Oh, linger yet, thou art so fair!"
Then cast me into chains you may,
Then will I die without a care!
Then may the death-bell sound its call,
Then art thou from thy service free,
The clock may stand, the index fall,
And time and tide may cease for me!

Mephistopheles. Think well; we sha'n't forget the terms you
name.

Faust. Your perfect right I must allow.
Not rashly to the pact I came.
I am a slave as I am now;
Yours or another's, 'tis to me the same!

Mephistopheles. Then at the Doctors' feast this very day
Will I my post, as your attendant take.
Just one thing more! To guard against mistake,
Oblige me with a line or two, I pray.

Faust. Pedant, must thou have writing, too?
Hast thou no true man, or man's promise, known?
Is not my word of mouth enough for you,
To pledge my days for all eternity?
Does not the universe go raving on,
In all its ever-eddying currents, free

To pass from change to change and I alone,
Shall a mere promise curb or fetter me?
Yet doth man's heart so hug the dear deceit,
Who would its hold without a pang undo?
Blest he. whose soul is with pure truth replete,
No sacrifice shall ever make him rue.
But, oh, your stamped and scribbled parchment sheet
A spectre is, which all men shrink to view.
The word dies ere it quits the pen,
And wax and sheepskin lord it then.
What would you have, spirit of ill!
Brass, marble, parchment, paper?—Say,
Am I to write with pen, or style, or graver?
I care not—choose whiche'er you will.
    Mephistopheles.   Why, throw your eloquence away,
Or give it such a very pungent savour?
Pshaw! Any scrap will do—'tis quite the same—
With the least drop of blood just sign your name.
    Faust.   If that will make you happy, why, a claim
So very whimsical I'll freely favour.
    Mephistopheles.   Blood is a juice of quite peculiar **kind.**
    Faust.   Fear not that I the compact will evade!
My life's whole struggle, heart and mind,
Chimes with the promise I have made.
Too high I've soared—too proudly dreamt,
I'm only peer for such as thee;
The Mighty Spirit spurns me with contempt,
And Nature veils her face from me.
Thought's chain is snapt;—for many a day
I've loathed all knowledge every way.
So quench we now our passion's fires
In sense and sensual delights,
Unveil all hidden magic sleights,
To minister to our desires!
Let us plunge in the torrent of time, and range
Through the weltering chaos of chance and change,
Then pleasure and pain. disaster and gain,
May course one another adown my brain.
Change and excitement may work as they can,
Rest there is none for the spirit of man.

Forest and Cavern

Faust (alone).   Majestic spirit, thou hast given me all
For which I prayed. Thou not in vain didst turn
   Thy countenance to me in fire and flame.
Thou glorious Nature for my realm hast given,
With power to feel, and to enjoy her. Thou
No mere cold glance of wonder hast vouchsafed,
But let'st me peer deep down into her breast,
Even as into the bosom of a friend.
Before me thou in long procession lead'st
All things that live, and teachest me to know
My kindred in still grove, in air, and stream.
And, when the storm sweeps roaring through the woods,
Upwrenching by the roots the giant pines,
Whose neighbouring trunks, and intertangled boughs,
In crashing ruin tear each other down,
And shake with roar of thunder all the hills,
Then dost thou guide me to some sheltering cave,
There show'st me to myself, and mine own soul
Teems marvels forth I weened not of before.
And when the pure moon, with her mellowing light,
Mounts as I gaze, then from the rocky walls,
And out from the dank underwood, ascend
Forms silvery-clad of ages long ago,
And soften the austere delight of thought.

Oh, now I feel no perfect boon is e'er
Achieved by man. With this ecstatic power,
Which brings me hourly nearer to the gods,
A yokemate thou hast given me, whom even now
I can no more dispense with, though his cold
Insulting scorn degrades me to myself,
And turns my gifts to nothing with a breath.
Within my breast he fans unceasingly
A raging fire for that bewitching form.
So to fruition from desire I reel,
And 'midst fruition languish for desire.

466

NIKOLAI GOGOL

NIKOLAI GOGOL (Russian, 1809-1852). One of the founders of Russian literature. Primarily a realist, wrote comedy with pathetic overtones. Personally an eccentric and hypochondriac. Famous satiric play: *The Inspector General*. Important nationalistic novels: *Dead Souls, Taras Bulba*. Exerted tremendous influence on later Russians, especially Dostoyevsky and the Soviets.

ST. JOHN'S EVE

THOMA GRIGOROVITCH had one very strange eccentricity: to the day of his death he never liked to tell the same thing twice. There were times when, if you asked him to relate a thing afresh, he would interpolate new matter, or alter it so that it was impossible to recognize it. Once upon a time, one of those gentlemen who like every sort of frippery, and issue mean little volumes, no thicker than an A B C book, every month, or even every week, wormed this same story out of Thoma Grigorovitch, and the latter completely forgot about it. But that same young gentleman, in the pea-green caftan, came from Poltava, bringing with him a little book, and, opening it in the middle, showed it to us. Thoma Grigorovitch was on the point of setting his spectacles astride of his nose, but recollected that he had forgotten to wind thread about them and stick them together with wax, so he passed it over to me. As I understand something about reading and writing, and do not wear spectacles, I undertook to read it. I had not turned two leaves when all at once he caught me by the hand and stopped me.

"Stop! tell me first what you are reading."

I confess that I was a trifle stunned by such a question.

"What! what am I reading, Thoma Grigorovitch? Why? your own words."

"Who told you that they were my words?"

"Why, what more would you have? Here it is printed: 'Related by such and such a sacristan.'"

"Spit on the head of the man who printed that! he lies, the dog of a Moscow peddler! Did I say that? ''Twas just the same as though one hadn't his wits about him!' Listen, I'll tell the tale to you on the spot." We moved up to the table, and he began.

My grandfather (the kingdom of heaven be his! may he eat only wheaten rolls and poppy-seed cakes with honey, in the other world!)

could tell a story wonderfully well. When he used to begin a tale you could not stir from the spot all day, but kept on listening. He was not like the story-teller of the present day, when he begins to lie, with a tongue as though he had had nothing to eat for three days, so that you snatch your cap and flee from the house. I remember my old mother was alive then, and in the long winter evenings when the frost was crackling out of doors, and had sealed up hermetically the narrow panes of our cottage, she used to sit at her wheel, drawing out a long thread in her hand, rocking the cradle with her foot, and humming a song, which I seem to hear even now.

The lamp, quivering and flaring up as though in fear of something, lighted up our cottage; the spindle hummed; and all of us children, collected in a cluster, listened to our grandfather, who had not crawled off the stove for more than five years, owing to his great age. But the wondrous tales of the incursions of the Zaporozhian Cossacks and the Poles, the bold deeds of Polkova, of Poltar-Kozhukh, and Sagaidatchnii, did not interest us so much as the stories about some deed of old, which always sent a shiver through our frames and made our hair rise upright on our heads. Sometimes such terror took possession of us in consequence of them, that, from that evening forward, Heaven knows how wonderful everything seemed to us. If one chanced to go out of the cottage after nightfall for anything, one fancied that a visitor from the other world had lain down to sleep in one's bed; and I have often taken my own smock, at a distance, as it lay at the head of the bed, for the Evil One rolled up in a ball! But the chief thing about grandfather's stories was, that he had never lied in all his life; and whatever he said was so was so.

I will now tell you one of his wonderful tales. I know that there are a great many wise people who copy in the courts, and can even read civil documents, but who, if you were to put into their hand a simple prayer-book, could not make out the first letter in it, and would show all their teeth in derision. These people laugh at everything you tell them. Along comes one of them—and doesn't believe in witches! Yes, glory to God that I have lived so long in the world! I have seen heretics to whom it would be easier to lie in confession than it would be to our brothers and equals to take snuff, and these folk would deny the existence of witches! But let them just dream about something and they won't even tell what it was! There, it is no use talking about them!

No one could have recognized the village of ours a little over a hundred years ago; it was a hamlet, the poorest kind of a hamlet. Half a score of miserable farmhouses, unplastered and badly thatched, were scattered here and there about the fields. There was not a yard or a decent shed to shelter animals or wagons. That was the way the wealthy lived; and if you had looked for our brothers, the poor— why, a hole in the ground—that was a cabin for you! Only by the smoke could you tell that a God-created man lived there. You ask why they lived so? It was not entirely through poverty; almost every-one led a raiding Cossack life, and gathered not a little plunder in foreign lands; it was rather because it was little use building up a good wooden house. Many folk were engaged in raids all over the country—Crimeans, Poles, Lithuanians! It was quite possible that their own countrymen might make a descent and plunder everything. Anything was possible.

In this hamlet a man, or rather a devil in human form, often made his appearance. Why he came, and whence, no one knew. He prowled about, got drunk, and suddenly disappeared as if into the air, leaving no trace of his existence. Then, behold, he seemed to have dropped from the sky again, and went flying about the street of the village, of which no trace now remains, and which was not more than a hundred paces from Dikanka. He would collect together all the Cossacks he met; then there were songs, laughter, and cash in plenty, and vodka flowed like water. . . . He would address the pretty girls, and give them ribbons, earrings, strings of beads—more than they knew what to do with. It is true that the pretty girls rather hesitated about accepting his presents: God knows, perhaps, what unclean hands they had passed through. My grandfather's aunt, who kept at that time a tavern, in which Basavriuk (as they called this devil-man) often caroused, said that no consideration on the earth would have induced her to accept a gift from him. But then, again, how avoid accepting? Fear seized on every one when he knit his shaggy brows, and gave a sidelong glance which might send your feet God knows whither: whilst if you did accept, then the next night some fiend from the swamp, with horns on his head, came and began to squeeze your neck, if there was a string of beads upon it, or bite your finger, if there was a ring upon it; or drag you by the hair, if ribbons were braided in it. God have mercy, then, on those who held such gifts! But here was the difficulty: it was impossible to get rid of them; if you threw them into the water, the diabolical ring or necklace would skim along the surface and into your hand.

There was a church in the village—St. Pantelei, if I remember rightly. There lived there a priest, Father Athanasii, of blessed memory. Observing that Basavriuk did not come to church even at Easter, he determined to reprove him and impose penance upon him. Well, he hardly escaped with his life. "Hark ye, sir!" he thundered in reply, "learn to mind your own business instead of meddling in other people's if you don't want that throat of yours stuck together with boiling kutya."

What was to be done with this unrepentant man? Father Athanasii contented himself with announcing that any one who should make the acquaintance of Basavriuk would be counted a Catholic, an enemy of Christ's orthodox church, not a member of the human race.

In this village there was a Cossack named Korzh, who had a laborer whom people called Peter the Orphan—perhaps because no one remembered either his father or mother. The church elder, it is true, said that they had died of the pest in his second year; but my grandfather's aunt would not hear of that, and tried with all her might to furnish him with parents, although poor Peter needed them about as much as we need last year's snow. She said that his father had been in Zaporozhe, and had been taken prisoner by the Turks, amongst whom he underwent God only knows what tortures, until, having by some miracle disguised himself as a eunuch, he made his escape. Little cared the black-browed youths and maidens about Peter's parents. They merely remarked that if he only had a new coat, a red sash, a black lambskin cap with a smart blue crown on his head, a Turkish saber by his side, a whip in one hand and a pipe with handsome mountings in the other, he would surpass all the young men. But the pity was, that the only thing poor Peter had was a gray gaberdine with more holes in it than there are gold pieces in a Jew's pockets. But that was not the worst of it. Korzh had a daughter, such a beauty as I think you can hardly have chanced to see. My grandfather's aunt used to say—and you know that it is easier for a woman to kiss the Evil One than to call any one else a beauty—that this Cossack's maiden's cheeks were as plump and fresh as the pinkest poppy when, bathed in God's dew, it unfolds its petals, and coquets with the rising sun; that her brows were evenly arched over her bright eyes like black cords, such as our maidens buy nowadays, for their crosses and ducats, off the Moscow peddlers who visit the villages with their baskets; that her little mouth, at sight of which the youths smacked their lips, seemed made to warble the songs of nightingales; that her hair, black as the raven's wing, and soft as young flax, fell in curls over her shoulders, for our

470

maidens did not then plait their hair in pigtails interwoven with pretty, bright-hued ribbons. Eh! may I never intone another alleluia in the choir, if I would not have kissed her, in spite of the gray which is making its way through the old wool which covers my pate, and of the old woman beside me, like a thorn in my side! Well, you know what happens when young men and maidens live side by side. In the twilight the heels of red boots were always visible in the place where Pidorka chatted with her Peter. But Korzh would never have suspected anything out of the way, only one day—it is evident that none but the Evil One could have inspired him—Peter took into his head to kiss the maiden's rosy lips with all his heart, without first looking well about him; and that same Evil One—may the son of a dog dream of the holy cross!—caused the old graybeard, like a fool, to open the cottage door at that moment. Korzh was petrified, dropped his jaw, and clutched at the door for support. Those unlucky kisses completely stunned him.

Recovering himself, he took his grandfather's hunting whip from the wall, and was about to belabor Peter's back with it, when Pidorka's little six-year-old brother Ivas rushed up from somewhere or other, and grasping his father's legs with his little hands, screamed out, "Daddy, Daddy! don't beat Peter!" What was to be done? A father's heart is not made of stone. Hanging the whip again upon the wall, he led Peter quietly from the house. "If you ever show yourself in my cottage again, or even under the windows, look out, Peter, for, by heaven, your black mustache will disappear; and your black locks, though wound twice about your ears will take leave of your pate, or my name is not Terentiy Korzh." So saying, he gave him such a taste of his fist in the nape of his neck, that all grew dark before Peter, and he flew headlong out of the place.

So there was an end of their kissing. Sorrow fell upon our turtle doves; and a rumor grew rife in the village that a certain Pole, all embroidered with gold, with mustaches, saber, spurs, and pockets jingling like bells of the bag with which our sacristan Taras goes through the church every day, had begun to frequent Korzh's house. Now, it is well known why a father has visitors when there is a black-browed daughter about. So, one day, Pidorka burst into tears, and caught the hand of her brother Ivas. "Ivas, my dear! Ivas, my love! fly to Peter, my child of gold, like an arrow from a bow. Tell him all: I would have loved his brown eyes, I would have kissed his fair face, but my fate decrees otherwise. More than one handkerchief have I wet with burning tears. I am sad and heavy at heart. And my own father is my enemy. I will not marry the Pole, whom I do not love. Tell him they are making ready for a wedding, but there will be no music at our wedding: priests will sing instead of pipes and viols. I shall not dance with my bridegroom; they will carry me out. Dark, dark will be my dwelling of maple wood; and instead of chimneys, a cross will stand upon the roof."

Peter stood petrified, without moving from the spot, when the innocent child lisped out Pidorka's words to him. "And I, wretched man, had thought to go to the Crimea and Turkey, to win gold and return to thee, my beauty! But it may not be. We have been over-looked by the evil eye. I too shall have a wedding, dear one; but no ecclesiastics will be present at that wedding. The black crow instead of the pope will caw over me; the bare plain will be my dwelling; the dark blue cloud my roof-tree. The eagle will claw out my brown eyes; the rain will wash my Cossack bones, and the whirlwinds will dry them. But what am I? Of what should I complain? 'Tis clear God willed it so. If I am to be lost, then so be it!" and he went straight to the tavern.

My late grandfather's aunt was somewhat surprised at seeing Peter at the tavern, at an hour when good men go to morning mass; and stared at him as though in a dream when he called for a jug of brandy, about half a pailful. But the poor fellow tried in vain to drown his woe. The vodka stung his tongue like nettles, and tasted more bitter than worm-wood. He flung the jug from him upon the ground.

"You have sorrowed enough, Cossack," growled a bass voice be hind him. He looked round—it was Basavriuk! Ugh, what a face! His hair was like a brush, his eyes like those of a bull. "I know what you lack: here it is." As he spoke he jingled a leather purse which hung from his girdle and smiled diabolically. Peter shuddered. "Ha, ha, ha! how it shines!" he roared, shaking out ducats into his hands: "Ha, ha, ha! how it jingles! And I only ask one thing for a whole pile of such shiners."

"It is the Evil One!" exclaimed Peter. "Give me them! I'm ready for anything!"

They struck hands upon it, and Basavriuk said, "You are just in time, Peter: to-morrow is St. John the Baptist's day. Only on this one night in the year does the fern blossom. I will await you at midnight in the Bear's ravine."

I do not believe that chickens await the hour when the housewife brings their corn with as much anxiety as Peter awaited the evening.

He kept looking to see whether the shadows of the trees were not lengthening, whether the sun was not turning red towards setting; and, the longer he watched, the more impatient he grew. How long it was! Evidently God's day had lost its end somewhere. But now the sun has set. The sky is red only on one side, and it is already growing dark. It grows colder in the fields. It gets gloomier and gloomier, and at last quite dark. At last! With heart almost bursting from his bosom, he set out and cautiously made his way down through the thick woods into the deep hollow called the Bear's ravine. Basavriuk was already waiting there. It was so dark that you could not see a yard before you. Hand in hand they entered the ravine, pushing through the luxuriant thorn-bushes and stumbling at almost every step. At last they reached an open spot. Peter looked about him; he had never chanced to come there before. Here Basavriuk halted.

"Do you see before you three hillocks? There are a great many kinds of flowers upon them. May some power keep you from plucking even one of them. But as soon as the fern blossoms, seize it, and look not round, no matter what may seem to be going on behind thee."

Peter wanted to ask some questions, but behold, Basavriuk was no longer there. He approached the three hillocks—where were the flowers? He saw none! The wild steppe-grass grew all around, and hid everything in its luxuriance. But the lightning flashed; and before him was a whole bed of flowers, all wonderful, all strange: whilst amongst them there were also the simple fronds of fern. Peter doubted his senses, and stood thoughtfully before them, arms akimbo.

"What manner of prodigy is this? why, one can see these weeds ten times a day. What is there marvelous about them? Devil's-face must be mocking me!"

But behold! the tiny flower-bud of the fern reddened and moved as though alive. It was a marvel, in truth. It grew larger and larger, and glowed like a burning coal. The tiny stars of light flashed up, something burst softly, and the flower opened before his eyes like a flame, lighting the others about it.

"Now is the time," thought Peter and extended his hand. He saw hundreds of hairy hands reach also for the flower from behind him, and there was a sound of scampering in his rear. He half closed his eyes, and plucked sharply at the stalk, and the flower remained in his hand.

Upon a stump sat Basavriuk, quite blue like a corpse. He did not move so much as a finger. His eyes were immovably fixed on something visible to him alone: his mouth was half open and speechless. Nothing stirred around. Ugh! it was horrible!—But then a whistle was heard, which made Peter's heart grow cold within him; and it seemed to him that the grass whispered, and the flowers began to talk among themselves in delicate voices, like little silver bells, whilst the trees rustled in murmuring contention;—Basavriuk's face suddenly became full of life, and his eyes sparkled. "The witch has just returned," he muttered between his teeth. "Hearken, Peter: a charmer will stand before you in a moment; do whatever she commands; if not—you are lost forever."

Then he parted the thorn-bushes with a knotty stick, and before him stood a tiny farmhouse. Basavriuk smote it with his fist, and the wall transformed itself into a cat and flew straight at his eyes.

"Don't be angry, don't be angry, you old Satan!" said Basavriuk, employing such words as would have made a good man stop his ears. Behold, instead of a cat, an old woman all bent into a bow, with a face wrinkled like a baked apple, and a nose and chin like a pair of nut-crackers.

"A fine charmer!" thought Peter; and cold chills ran down his back. The witch tore the flower from his hand, stooped and muttered over it for a long time, sprinkling it with some kind of water. Sparks flew from her mouth, and foam appeared on her lips.

"Throw it away," she said, giving it back to Peter.

Peter threw it, but what wonder was this? The flower did not fall straight to the earth, but for a long while twinkled like a fiery ball through the darkness, and swam through the air like a boat. At last it began to sink lower and lower, and fell so far away that the little star, hardly larger than a poppy-seed, was barely visible. "There!" croaked the old woman, in a dull voice; and Basavriuk, giving him a spade, said, "Dig here Peter: you will find more gold than you or Korzh ever dreamed of."

Peter spat on his hands, seized the spade, pressed his foot on it. and turned up the earth, a second, a third, a fourth time. The spade clinked against something hard, and would go no farther. Then his eyes began to distinguish a small, iron-bound coffer. He tried to seize it, but the chest began to sink into the earth, deeper, farther and deeper still: whilst behind him he heard a laugh like a serpent's hiss.

"No, you shall not have the gold until you shed human blood." said the witch, and she led up to him a child of six, covered with a white sheet, and indicated by a sign that he was to cut off his head.

Peter was stunned. A trifle, indeed, to cut off a man's, or even an innocent child's, head for no reason whatsoever! In wrath he tore off the sheet enveloping the victim's head, and behold! before him stood Ivas. The poor child crossed his little hands, and hung his head. Peter flew at the witch with the knife like a madman, and was on the point of laying hands on her.

"What did you promise for the girl?" thundered Basavriuk; and like a shot he was on his back. The witch stamped her foot; a blue flame flashed from the earth and illuminated all within it. The earth became transparent as if molded of crystal; and all that was within it became visible as if in the palm of the hand. Ducats, precious stones, in chests and pots, were piled in heaps beneath the very spot they stood on. Peter's eyes flashed, his mind grew troubled. . . . He grasped the knife like a madman, and the innocent blood spurted into his eyes. Diabolical laughter resounded on all sides. Misshapen monsters flew past him in flocks. The witch, fastening her hands in the headless trunk like a wolf, drank its blood. His head whirled. Collecting all his strength, he set out to run. Everything grew red before him. The trees seemed steeped in blood, and burned and groaned. The sky glowed and threatened. Burning points, like lightning, flickered before his eyes. Utterly exhausted, he rushed into his miserable hovel and fell to the ground like a log. A deathlike sleep overpowered him.

Two days and two nights did Peter sleep, without once wakening. When he came to himself, on the third day, he looked long at all the corners of his hut; but in vain did he endeavor to recollect what had taken place; his memory was like a miser's pocket from which you cannot entice a quarter of a kopek. Stretching himself, he heard something clash at his feet. He looked; there were two bags of gold. Then only, as if in a dream, he recollected that he had been seeking for treasure, and that something had frightened him in the woods. But at what price he had obtained it, and how, he could by no means tell.

Korzh saw the sacks—and was mollified. "A fine fellow Peter, quite unequalled! yes, and did I not love him? Was he not to me as my own son?" And the old man repeated this fiction until he wept over it himself. Pidorka began to tell Peter how some passing gipsies had stolen Ivas; but he could not even recall him—to such a degree had the Devil's influence darkened his mind. There was no reason for delay. The Pole was dismissed and the wedding-feast prepared; rolls were baked, towels and handkerchiefs embroidered; the young people were seated at table; the wedding-loaf was cut; guitars, cymbals, pipes, viols sounded, and pleasure was rife.

A wedding in the olden times was not like one of the present day. My grandfather's aunt used to tell how the maidens—in festive head-dresses, of yellow, blue and pink ribbons, above which they bound gold braid; in thin chemisettes embroidered on all the seams with red silk, and strewn with tiny silver flowers; in morocco shoes, with high iron heels—danced the gorlitza as swimmingly as peacocks, and as wildly as the whirlwind; how the youths—with their ship-shaped caps upon their heads, the crowns of gold brocade, and two horns projecting, one in front and another behind, of the very finest black lambskin; in tunics of the finest blue silk with red borders—stepped forward one by one, their arms akimbo in stately form, and executed the hopak; how the lads—in tall Cossack caps, and light cloth gaberdines, girt with silver embroidered belts, their short pipes in their teeth—skipped before them and talked nonsense. Even Korzh as he gazed at the young people could not help getting gay in his old age. Guitar in hand, alternately puffing at his pipe and singing, a brandy-glass upon his head, the graybeard began the national dance amid loud shouts from the merrymakers.

What will not people devise in merry mood? They even began to disguise their faces till they did not look like human beings. On such occasions one would dress himself as a Jew, another as the devil; they would begin by kissing each other, and end by seizing each other by the hair. God be with them! you laughed till you held your sides. They dressed themselves in Turkish and Tatar garments. All upon them glowed like a conflagration, and they began to joke and play pranks. . . .

An amusing thing happened to my grandfather's aunt, who was at this wedding. She was wearing an ample Tatar robe, and, wineglass in hand, was entertaining the company. The Evil One instigated one man to pour vodka over her from behind. Another, at the same moment, evidently not by accident, struck a light, and held it to her. The flame flashed up, and poor aunt, in terror, flung her dress off, before them all. Screams. laughter. jests arose as if at a fair. In a word. the old folks could not recall so merry a wedding.

Pidorka and Peter began to live like a gentleman and lady. There was plenty of everything and everything was fine. . . . But honest folk shook their heads when they marked their way of living. "From the devil no good can come." they unanimously agreed. "Whence. except from the tempter of orthodox people, came this wealth?

Where else could he have got such a lot of gold? Why, on the very day that he got rich, did Basavriuk vanish as if into thin air?"

Say, if you can, that people only imagine things! A month had not passed, and no one would have recognized Peter. He sat in one spot, saying no word to anyone; but continually thinking and seemingly trying to recall something. When Pidorka succeeded in getting him to speak, he appeared to forget himself, and would carry on a conversation, and even grow cheerful; but if he inadvertantly glanced at the sacks, "Stop, stop! I have forgotten," he would cry, and again plunge into reverie and strive to recall something. Sometimes when he sat still a long time in one place, it seemed to him as though it were coming, just coming back to mind, but again all would fade away. It seemed as if he was sitting in the tavern: they brought him vodka; vodka stung him; vodka was repulsive to him. Some one came along and struck him on the shoulder; but beyond that everything was veiled in darkness before him. The perspiration would stream down his face, and he would sit exhausted in the same place.

What did not Pidorka do? She consulted the sorceresses; and they poured out fear, and brewed stomachache—but all to no avail. and so the summer passed. Many a Cossack had mowed and reaped; many a Cossack, more enterprising than the rest, had set off upon an expedition. Flocks of ducks were already crowding the marshes, but there was not even a hint of improvement.

It was red upon the steppes. Ricks of grain, like Cossack's caps, dotted the fields here and there. In the highway were to be encountered wagons loaded with brushwood and logs. The ground had become more solid, and in places was touched with frost. Already had the snow begun to fall and the branches of the trees were covered with rime like rabbitskin. Already on frosty days the robin redbreast hopped about on the snow-heaps like a foppish Polish nobleman, and picked out grains of corn; and children, with huge sticks, played hockey upon the ice; while their fathers lay quietly on the stove, issuing forth at intervals with lighted pipes in their lips, to growl in regular fashion, at the orthodox frost or to take the air, and thresh the grain spread out in the barn. At last the snow began to melt, and the ice slipped away: but Peter remained the same; and, the more time went on, the more morose he grew. He sat in the cottage as though nailed to the spot, with the sacks of gold at his feet. He grew averse to look at Pidorka; and still he thought of but one thing, still he tried to recall something, and got angry and ill-tempered because he could not. Often, rising wildly from his seat, he gesticulated violently and fixed his eyes on something as though desirous of catching it: his lips moved as though desirous of uttering some long-forgotten word, but remained speechless. Fury would take possession of him: he would gnaw and bite his hands like a man half crazy, and in his vexation would tear out his hair by the handful, until, calming down, he would relapse into forgetfulness, as it were, and then would again strive to recall the past and be again seized with fury and fresh tortures. What visitation of God was this?

Pidorka was neither dead nor alive. At first it was horrible to her to remain alone with him in the cottage; but, in course of time, the poor woman grew accustomed to her sorrow. But it was impossible to recognize the Pidorka of former days. No blushes, no smiles: she was thin and worn with grief, and had wept her bright eyes away. Once someone who took pity on her advised her to go to the witch who dwelt in the Bear's ravine, and enjoyed the reputation of being able to cure every disease in the world. She determined to try this last remedy: and finally persuaded the old woman to come to her. This was on St. John's Eve, as it chanced. Peter lay insensible on the bench, and did not observe the newcomer. Slowly he rose, and looked about him. Suddenly he trembled in every limb, as though he were on the scaffold: his hair rose upon his head, and he laughed a laugh that thrilled Pidorka's heart with fear.

"I have remembered, remembered!" he cried, in terrible joy; and, swinging a hatchet round his head, he struck at the old woman with all his might. The hatchet penetrated the oaken door nearly four inches. The old woman disappeared; and a child of seven, covered in a white sheet, stood in the middle of the cottage. . . . The sheet flew off. "Ivas!" cried Pidorka, and ran to him; but the apparition became covered from head to foot with blood, and illumined the whole room with red light.

She ran into the passage in her terror, but, on recovering herself a little, wished to help Peter. In vain! The door had slammed to behind her, so that she could not open it. People ran up, and began to knock: they broke in the door, as though there were but one mind among them. The whole cottage was full of smoke; and just in the middle, where Peter had stood, was a heap of ashes from whence smoke was still rising. They flung themselves upon the sacks: only broken potsherds lay there instead of ducats. The Cossacks stood with staring eyes and open mouths, as if rooted to the earth, not daring to move a hair, such terror did this wonder inspire in them.

I do not remember what happened next. Pidorka made a vow to

478

go upon a pilgrimage, collected the property left her by her father, and in a few days it was as if she had never been in the village. Whither she had gone, no one could tell. Officious old women would have despatched her to the same place whither Peter had gone; but a Cossack from Kief reported that he had seen, in a cloister, a nun withered to a mere skeleton who prayed unceasingly. Her fellow-villagers recognized her as Pidorka by the tokens—that no one heard her utter a word; and that she had come on foot, and had brought a frame for the picture of God's mother, set with such brilliant stones that all were dazzled at the sight.

But this was not the end, if you please. On the same day that the Evil One made away with Peter, Basavriuk appeared again; but all fled from him. They knew what sort of a being he was—none else than Satan, who had assumed human form in order to unearth treasures; and, since treasures do not yield to unclean hands, he seduced the young. That same year, all deserted their earthen huts and collected in a village; but even there there was was no peace on account of that accursed Basavriuk.

My late grandfather's aunt said that he was particularly angry with her because she had abandoned her former tavern, and tried with all his might to revenge himself upon her. Once the village elders were assembled in the tavern, and, as the saying goes, were arranging the precedence at the table, in the middle of which was placed a small roasted lamb, shame to say. They chattered about this, that and the other—among the rest about various marvels and strange things. Well, they saw something; it would have been nothing if only one had seen it, but all saw it, and it was this: the sheep raised his head; his goggling eyes became alive and sparkled; and the black, bristling mustache, which appeared for one instant, made a significant gesture at those present. All at once recognized Basavriuk's countenance in the sheep's head; my grandfather's aunt thought it was on the point of asking her for vodka. The worthy elders seized their hats and hastened home.

Another time, the church elder himself, who was fond of an occasional private interview with my grandfather's brandy-glass, had not succeeded in getting to the bottom twice, when he beheld the glass bowing very low to him. "Satan, take you, let us make the sign of the cross over you!" And the same marvel happened to his better half. She had just begun to mix the dough in a huge kneading-trough when suddenly the trough sprang up. "Stop, stop! where are you go-ing?" Putting its arms akimbo, with dignity, it went skipping all about the cottage. You may laugh, but it was no laughing matter to our grandfathers. And in vain did Father Athanasii go through the village with holy water, and chase the devil through all the streets with his brush. My late grandfather's aunt long complained that, as soon as it was dark, some one came knocking at her door and scratching at the wall.

Well! all appears to be quiet now, in the place where our village stands; but it was not so very long ago—my father was still alive— that I remember how a good man could not pass the ruined tavern which a dishonest race had long managed for their own interest. From the smoke-blackened chimneys smoke poured out in a pillar and, rising high in the air, rolled off like a cap, scattering burning coals over the steppe; and Satan (the son of a dog should not be mentioned) sobbed so pitifully in his lair that the startled ravens rose in flocks from the neighboring oak-wood and flew through the air with wild cries.

CARLO GOLDONI

CARLO GOLDONI (Italian, 1707-1793). Reformed native Italian comedy in 18th century by replacing artificial pantomime with realistic character and situations. Author of some 150 plays—many in French, since he spent last 20 years in France. Influenced by Molière and English writers. Works: *The Clever Widow, The Hostess, Pamela, The Beneficent Bear, The Fan.*

THE BENEFICENT BEAR

(Act II, scene 4)

Angelica (aside). What have I to do with Signor Dorval? I can go away.

Dorval. Mademoiselle Angelica!

Ang. Sir?

Dor. Have you seen your uncle? Has he told you nothing?

Ang. I saw him this morning, sir.

Dor. Before he went out of the house?

Ang. Yes, sir.

Dor. Has he returned?

Ang. No, sir.

Dor. (aside). Good. She knows nothing of it.

Ang. Excuse me, sir. Is there anything new in which I am concerned?

Dor.   Your uncle takes much interest in you.

Ang. (with modesty).   He is very kind.

Dor. (seriously).   He thinks often of you.

Ang.   It is fortunate for me.

Dor.   He thinks of marrying you. *(Angelica blushes.)* What say you to it? Would you like to be married?

Ang.   I depend on my uncle.

Dor.   Shall I say anything more to you on the subject?

Ang. (with a little curiosity).   But—as you please, sir.

Dor.   The choice of a husband is already made.

Ang. (aside).   O heavens! I tremble.

Dor. (aside).   She seems to be pleased.

Ang. (trembling).   Sir, I am curious to know—

Dor.   What, Mademoiselle?

Ang.   Do you know who is intended for me?

Dor.   Yes, and you know him too.

Ang. (with joy).   I know him too?

Dor. . Certainly, you know him.

Ang.   May I, sir, have the boldness—

Dor.   Speak, Mademoiselle.

Ang.   To ask you the name of the young man?

Dor.   The name of the young man?

Ang.   Yes, if you know him.

Dor.   Suppose he were not so young?

Ang. (aside, with agitation).   Good heavens!

Dor.   You are sensible—you depend on your uncle—

Ang. (trembling).   Do you think, sir, my uncle would sacrifice me?

Dor.   What do you mean by sacrificing you?

Ang.   Mean—without the consent of my heart. My uncle is so good—but who could have advised him—who could have proposed this match? *(With temper.)*

Dor. (a little hurt.)   But this match—Mademoiselle—suppose it were I.

Ang. (with joy).   You, sir? Heaven grant it!

Dor. (pleased).   Heaven grant it!

Ang.   Yes, I know you; I know you are reasonable. You are sensible; I can trust you. If you have given my uncle this advice, if you have proposed this match, I hope you will now find some means of making him change his plan.

Dor. (aside). Eh! this is not so bad. *(To Angelica.)* Mademoiselle—

Ang. (distressed). Signor?

Dor. (with feeling). Is your heart engaged?

Ang. Ah, sir—

Dor. I understand you.

Ang. Have pity on me!

Dor. (aside). I said so, I foresaw right; it is fortunate for me I am not in love—yet I began to perceive some little symptoms of it.

Ang. But you do not tell me, sir.

Dor. But, Mademoiselle—

Ang. You have perhaps some particular interest in the person they wish me to marry?

Dor. A little.

Ang. I tell you I shall hate him.

Dor. (aside). Poor girl! I am pleased with her sincerity.

Ang. Come, have compassion; be generous.

Dor. Yes, I will be so, I promise you; I will speak to your uncle in your favor, and will do all I can to make you happy.

Ang. (with joy and transport). Oh, how dear a man you are! You are my benefactor, my father. *(Takes his hand.)*

Dor. My dear girl!

(Enter Geronte.)

Geronte (with animation). Excellent, excellent! Courage, my children, I am delighted with you. *(Angelica retires, mortified; Dorval smiles.)* How! does my presence alarm you? I do not condemn this proper show of affection. You have done well, Dorval, to inform her. Come, my niece, embrace your future husband.

Ang. (in consternation). What do I hear?

Dor. (aside and smiling). Now I am unmasked.

Ger. (to Angelica, with warmth). What scene is this? Your modesty is misplaced. When I am not present, you are near enough to each other; when I come in, you go far apart. Come here. *(To Dorval with anger.)* And do you too come here.

Dor. (laughing). Softly, my friend.

Ger. Why do you laugh? Do you feel your happiness? I am very willing you should laugh, but do not put me in a passion; do you hear, you laughing gentleman? Come here and listen to me.

Dor. But listen yourself.

Ger. (to Angelica, and endeavoring to take her hand). Come near, both of you.

Ang. (weeping). My uncle!

Ger. Weeping! What's the matter, my child? I believe you are making a jest of me. *(Takes her hand, and draws her forward; then turns to Dorval.)* You shall escape me no more.

Dor. At least let me speak.

Ger. No, no!

Ang. My dear uncle—

Ger. (with warmth). No, no. *(He becomes serious.)* I have been to my notary's, and have arranged everything; he has taken a note of it in my presence, and will soon bring the contract here for us to subscribe.

Dor. But will you listen to me?

Ger. No, no. As to her fortune, my brother had the weakness to leave it in the hands of his son; this will no doubt cause some obstacle on his part, but it will not embarrass me. Every one who has transactions with him suffers. The fortune cannot be lost, and in any event I will be responsible for it.

Ang. (aside). I can bear this no longer.

Dor. (embarrassed). All proceeds well, but—

Ger. But what?

Dor. The young lady may have something to say in this matter. *(Looking at Angelica.)*

Ang. (hastily and trembling). I, sir?

Ger. I should like to know if she can say anything against what I do, what I order, and what I wish. My wishes, my orders, and what I do, are all for her good. Do you understand me?

Dor. Then I must speak myself.

Ger. What have you to say?

Dor. That I am very sorry, but this marriage cannot take place.

Ger. Not take place! *(Angelica retreats frightened; Dorval steps back.)* *(To Dorval.)* You have given me your word of honor.

Dor. Yes, on condition—

Ger. (turning to Angelica). It must then be this impertinent. If I could believe it! if I had any reason to suspect it! *(Threatens her.)*

Dor. (seriously). No. sir. you are mistaken.

Ger. (to Dorval. Angelica makes her escape). It is you, then, who refuse? So you abuse my friendship and affection for you!

Dor. (raising his voice). But hear reason—

Ger. What reason? what reason? There is no reason. I am a

483

man of honor, and if you are so, too, it shall be done at once. *(Turning round, he calls)* Angelica!

Dor. What possesses the man? He will resort to violence on the spot. *(Runs off.)*

Ger. (alone). Where is she gone? Angelica! Hallo! who's there? Piccardo! Martuccia! Pietro! Cortese!—But I'll find her. It is you I want. *(Turns round and, not seeing Dorval, remains motionless.)* What! he treat me so! *(Calls.)* Dorval! my friend! Dorval—Dorval! my friend! Oh, shameful—ungrateful! Hallo! Is no one there? Piccardo!

(Enters Piccardo.)

Piccardo. Here, sir.

Ger. You rascal! Why don't you answer?

Pic. Pardon me, sir, here I am.

Ger. Shameful! I called you ten times.

Pic. I am sorry, but—

Ger. Ten times! It is scandalous.

Pic. (aside and angry). He is in a fury now.

Ger. Have you seen Dorval?

Pic. Yes, sir.

Ger. Where is he?

Pic. He is gone.

Ger. How is he gone?

Pic. (roughly). He is gone as other people go.

Ger. Ah, insolent! do you answer your master in this manner? *(Threatens him.)*

Pic. (very angrily). Give me my discharge, sir.

Ger. Your discharge—worthless fellow! *(Makes him retreat. Piccardo falls between the chair and the table. Geronte runs and helps him up.)*

Pic. Oh! *(He shows much pain.)*

Ger. Are you hurt? Are you hurt?

Pic. Very much hurt; you have crippled me.

Ger. Oh, I am sorry! Can you walk?

Pic. (still angry). I believe so, sir. *(He tries, and walks badly.)*

Ger. (sharply). Go on.

Pic. Do you drive me away, sir?

Ger. (warmly). No. Go to your wife's house, that you may be taken care of. *(Pulls out his purse and offers him money.)* Take this to get cured.

Pic. (aside, with tenderness). What a master!

Ger. Take it. *(Giving him money.)*

Pic. (with modesty).   No, sir, I hope it will be nothing.

Ger. Take it, I tell you.

Pic. (Still refusing it).   Sir—

Ger. (very warmly).   What! you refuse my money Do you refuse it from pride, or spite, or hatred? Do you believe I did it on purpose? Take this money. Take it. Come, don't put me in a passion.

Pic. Do not get angry, sir. I thank you for all your kindness. *(Takes the money.)*

Ger. Go quickly.

Pic. Yes, sir. *(Walks badly.)*

Ger. Go slowly.

Pic. Yes, sir.

Ger. Wait, wait; take my cane.

Pic. Sir—

Ger. Take it, I tell you! I wish you to do it.

Pic. (takes the cane).   What goodness!

(Exit.)
(Enter Martuccia.)

Ger. It is the first time in my life that—Plague on my temper! *(Taking long strides.)* It is Dorval who put me in a passion.

Martuccia. Do you wish to dine, sir?

Ger. May the devil take you! *(Runs out and shuts himself in his room.)*

Mar. Well, well! He is in a rage: I can do nothing for Angelica to-day; Valerio can go away.

OLIVER GOLDSMITH

OLIVER GOLDSMITH (English, 1728-1774). Forerunner of the English Romantic School. From wealthy family, tried numerous professions before settling on literature. Produced classics in three fields: *The Deserted Village* (romantic poem), *The Vicar of Wakefield* (sentimental-realistic novel), *She Stoops to Conquer* (comedy drama). Also short stories of merit.

THE DISABLED SOLDIER

No OBSERVATION is more common, and at the same time more true, than that one half of the world are ignorant how the other half lives. The misfortunes of the great are held up to engage our atten-

485

tion; are enlarged upon in tones of declamation; and the world is called upon to gaze at the noble sufferers: the great, under the pressure of calamity, are conscious of several others sympathizing with their distress; and have, at once, the comfort of admiration and pity.

There is nothing magnanimous in bearing misfortunes with fortitude, when the whole world is looking on: men in such circumstances will act bravely even from motives of vanity: but he who, in the vale of obscurity, can brave adversity; who without friends to encourage, acquaintances to pity, or even without hope to alleviate his misfortunes, can behave with tranquillity and indifference, is truly great: whether peasant or courtier, he deserves admiration, and should be held up for our imitation and respect.

While the slightest inconveniences of the great are magnified into calamities; while tragedy mouths out their sufferings in all the strains of eloquence, the miseries of the poor are entirely disregarded; and yet some of the lower ranks of people undergo more real hardships in one day, than those of a more exalted station suffer in their whole lives. It is inconceivable what difficulties the meanest of our common sailors and soldiers endure without murmuring or regret; without passionately declaiming against providence, or calling their fellows to be gazers on their intrepidity. Every day is to them a day of misery, and yet they entertain their hard fate without repining.

With what indignation do I hear an Ovid, a Cicero, or a Rabutin complain of their misfortunes and hardships, whose greatest calamity was that of being unable to visit a certain spot of earth, to which they had foolishly attached an idea of happiness. Their distresses were pleasures, compared to what many of the adventuring poor every day endure without murmuring. They ate, drank, and slept; they had slaves to attend them, and were sure of subsistence for life; while many of their fellow creatures are obliged to wander without a friend to comfort or assist them, and even without shelter from the severity of the season.

I have been led into these reflections from accidentally meeting, some days ago, a poor fellow, whom I knew when a boy, dressed in a sailor's jacket, and begging at one of the outlets of the town, with a wooden leg. I knew him to have been honest and industrious when in the country, and was curious to learn what had reduced him to his present situation. Wherefore, after giving him what I thought proper, I desired to know the history of his life and misfortunes, and the manner in which he was reduced to his present distress. The disabled soldier, for such he was, though dressed in a sailor's habit, scratching his head, and leaning on his crutch, put himself into an attitude to comply with my request, and gave me his history as follows:

"As for my misfortunes, master, I can't pretend to have gone through any more than other folks; for, except the loss of my limb, and my being obliged to beg, I don't know any reason, thank Heaven, that I have to complain. There is Bill Tibbs, of our regiment, he has lost both his legs, and an eye to boot; but, thank Heaven, it is not so bad with me yet.

"I was born in Shropshire; my father was a laborer, and died when I was five years old, so I was put upon the parish. As he had been a wandering sort of a man, the parishioners were not able to tell to what parish I belonged, or where I was born, so they sent me to another parish, and that parish sent me to a third. I thought in my heart, they kept sending me about so long, that they would not let me be born in any parish at all; but at last, however, they fixed me. I had some disposition to be a scholar, and was resolved at least to know my letters: but the master of the workhouse put me to business as soon as I was able to handle a mallet; and here I lived an easy kind of life for five years. I only wrought ten hours in the day, and had my meat and drink provided for my labor. It is true, I was not suffered to stir out of the house, for fear, as they said, I should run away; but what of that? I had the liberty of the whole house, and the yard before the door, and that was enough for me. I was then bound out to a farmer, where I was up both early and late; but I ate and drank well; and liked my business well enough, till he died, when I was obliged to provide for myself; so I resolved to go seek my fortune.

"In this manner I went from town to town, worked when I could get employment, and starved when I could get none; when, happening one day to go through a field belonging to a justice of peace, I spied a hare crossing the path just before me; and I believe the devil put it into my head to fling my stick at it. Well, what will you have on't? I killed the hare, and was bringing it away, when the justice himself met me; he called me a poacher and a villain, and collaring me, desired I would give an account of myself. I fell upon my knees, begged his worship's pardon, and began to give a full account of all that I knew of my breed, seed, and generation; but though I gave a very true account, the justice said I could give no account; so I was indicted at the sessions, found guilty of being

487

poor, and sent up to London to Newgate, in order to be transported as a vagabond.

"People may say this and that of being in jail, for my part, I found Newgate as agreeable a place as ever I was in in all my life. I had my belly full of eat and drink, and did no work at all. This kind of life was too good to last forever; so I was taken out of prison, after five months, put on board of ship, and sent off, with two hundred more, to the plantations. We had but an indifferent passage, for being all confined in the hold, more than a hundred of our people died for want of sweet air; and those that remained were sickly enough, God knows. When we came ashore we were sold to the planters, and I was bound for seven years more. As I was no scholar, for I did not know my letters, I was obliged to work among the negroes; and I served out my time, as in duty bound to do.

"When my time was expired, I worked my passage home, and glad I was to see old England again, because I loved my country. I was afraid, however, that I should be indicted for a vagabond once more, so did not much care to go down into the country, but kept about the town, and did little jobs when I could get them.

"I was very happy in this manner for some time till one evening, coming home from work, two men knocked me down, and then desired me to stand. They belonged to a press-gang. I was carried before the justice, and as I could give no account of myself, I had my choice left, whether to go on board a man-of-war, or list for a soldier. I chose the latter, and in this post of a gentleman, I served two campaigns in Flanders, was at the battles of Val and Fontenoy, and received but one wound through the breast here; but the doctor of our regiment soon made me well again.

"When the peace came on I was discharged; and as I could not work, because my wound was sometimes troublesome, I listed for a landman in the East India Company's service. I have fought the French in six pitched batles; and I verily believe that if I could read or write, our captain would have made me a corporal. But it was not my good fortune to have any promotion, for I soon fell sick, and so got leave to return home again with forty pounds in my pocket. This was at the beginning of the present war, and I hoped to be set on shore, and to have the pleasure of spending my money; but the Government wanted men, and so I was pressed for a sailor, before ever I could set a foot on shore.

"The boatswain found me, as he said, an obstinate fellow: he swore he knew that I understood my business well, but that I shammed Abraham, to be idle; but God knows, I knew nothing of sea-business, and he beat me without considering what he was about. I had still, however, my forty pounds, and that was some comfort to me under every beating; and the money I might have had to this day, but that our ship was taken by the French, and so I lost all.

"Our crew was carried into Brest, and many of them died, because they were not used to live in a jail; but, for my part, it was nothing to me, for I was seasoned. One night, as I was asleep on the bed of boards, with a warm blanket about me, for I always loved to lie well, I was awakened by the boatswain, who had a dark lantern in his hands. 'Jack,' says he to me 'will you knock out the French sentry's brains?' 'I don't care,' says I, striving to keep myself awake, 'if I lend a hand.' 'Then, follow me,' says he, 'and I hope we shall do business.' So up I got, and tied my blanket, which was all the clothes I had, about my middle; and went with him to fight the Frenchman. I hate the French because they are all slaves, and wear wooden shoes.

"Though we had no arms, one Englishman is able to beat five French at any time; so we went down to the door where both the sentries were posted, and rushing upon them, seized their arms in a moment, and knocked them down. From thence nine of us ran together to the quay, and seizing the first boat we met, got out of the harbor and put to sea. We had not been here three days before we were taken up by the Dorset privateer, who were glad of so many good hands; and we consented to run our chance. However, we had not as much luck as we expected. In three days we fell in with the *Pompadour* privateer of forty guns, while we had but twenty-three, so to it we went, yard-arm and yard-arm. The fight lasted three hours, and I verily believe we should have taken the Frenchman, had we but had some men left behind; but unfortunately we lost all our men just as we were going to get the victory.

"I was once more in the power of the French, and I believe it would have gone hard with me had I been brought back to Brest; but by good fortune we were retaken by the *Viper*. I had almost forgotten to tell you that in that engagement I was wounded in two places: I lost four fingers off the left hand, and my leg was shot off. If I had the good fortune to have lost my leg and use of my hand on board a king's ship, and not aboard a privateer, I should have been entitled to clothing and maintenance during the rest of my life; but that was not my chance: one man is born with a silver spoon in his mouth, and another with a wooden ladle. However, blessed be God, I enjoy good health. and **will** forever love liberty and old England. Liberty, property, and old England, forever, huzza!"

Thus saying, he limped off, leaving me in admiration at his intrepidity and content; nor could I avoid acknowledging that an habitual acquaintance with misery serves better than philosophy to teach us to despise it.

IVAN ALEXANDROVICH GONCHAROV

IVAN ALEXANDROVICH GONCHAROV (Russian, 1812-1891). One of foremost of the great roll of Russian novelists of 19th century. Best-known to Western readers for *Oblomof*, a realistic novel about Russia's so-called "superfluous man."

THE EVOLUTION OF OBLOMOF

ILYA ILYICH OBLOMOF, nobleman by birth, college secretary by occupation, was living for the twelfth consecutive year at Petersburg.

At first, during his parents' lifetime, he lived in rather close quarters, occupying two rooms, and contenting himself with the one servant, Zakhar, brought with him from the country. But after the death of his father and mother he became the sole possessor of three hundred and fifty souls, which fell to him as a legacy in one of the remote provinces, almost in Asia. Instead of five thousand he received now from seven to ten thousand paper rubles income, and his living too assumed another and more generous scale. He rented larger apartments, added a cook to his household, and bought a span of horses. At that time he was still young, and if it cannot be said that he was lively, at any rate he was livelier than now. He still had a thousand different aspirations, was always hoping for something, and expecting much of fate as well as of himself. He was preparing himself for a career; above all, of course, for a role in the government service, which was the very object of his coming to Petersburg. Afterwards he thought, too, of a rôle in society. Finally, in a distant perspective, in the turning of youth to mature age, domestic happiness gleamed and smiled in fancy. But day after day passed, and years followed years; the down on his chin turned to a rough beard, the beaming eyes faded to two dull spots, the shape grew stout, the hair began to fall out pitilessly;—it struck thirty, but he had not advanced a step on any career, and still stood at the threshold of his arena where he was ten years before.

Life, to him, was divided into halves: one of which consisted of work and weariness—which with him were synonymous; the other of rest and quiet enjoyment. That is why his principal career, the government service, jarred on him most unpleasantly from the first.

Brought up in a remote provincial corner, amidst the gentle and hearty native manners and customs, passing in the course of twenty years from embrace to embrace of relatives, friends, and acquaintances, he had become so thoroughly imbued with the family principle that even his future service appeared to him a sort of domestic occupation,—like that, for example, of making entries in a book of receipts and expenditures, as his father used to. He imagined that the officials of a place formed a small, harmonious family among themselves, unceasingly solicitous for their mutual repose and contentment; that invariable attendance at the office was not an obligatory custom, which had to be observed every day; and that wetness, heat, or merely indisposition would always serve as sufficient and legitimate excuses for neglect of his work. But how distressed he was when he saw that nothing short of an earthquake would entitle a well man to remain away from his office, and by ill luck, earthquakes are unknown in Petersburg; a flood, it is true, might serve equally well as a hindrance, but floods seldom occur either. Still more was Oblomof startled when packets gleamed before his eyes with the superscription "important" and "very urgent"; when he was required to make various researches and extracts, to rummage among documents, and to write reports two fingers thick, which are humorously called "memoranda." Besides, everything was wanted in a hurry. Everybody was hurrying some way or other, and no one kept still at anything; a man scarcely got one thing out of his hands when he eagerly seized something else, as if his whole existence were in that; this finished, he forgot it and flew at a third—there was never once an end to it. Once or twice he was wakened in the night and obliged to write "memoranda"; sometimes he would be called away from company by a courier—always on account of these "memoranda": all of which alarmed him and wearied him greatly. "When am I to live? *live?*" he repeated sorrowfully.

He had been told at home that the chief was the father of his subordinates, and so he formed the pleasantest and fondest idea of this person. He pictured him somewhat in the light of a second father, who breathed only to recompense his subordinates one after another, deservedly or undeservedly, and to provide for not only their needs but their pleasures. Ilya Ilyich thought that a chief was so much concerned about the welfare of a subordinate that he would anxiously inquire how he had passed the night, why his eyes looked heavy, and didn't his head ache? But he was cruelly undeceived the first day of his service. With the arrival of the chief began scurrying and confusion; all were upset, all hustled each other about; many rearranged their toilet; fearing that as they were they didn't look fine enough to show themselves to the chief. This, as Oblomof noticed later, was because there are some chiefs who read in the faces confronting them, of underlings almost out of their wits, not only respect for them, but zeal as well, and often fitness for the service.

Ilya Ilyich did not need to stand in such fear of his own chief, a kind and chatty man, who never harmed any one; his clerks were as content as could be, and asked no better. No one ever heard him say an unpleasant word, or shout or storm; and he never ordered anything done, but always begged it. Work to do—he begged you; to dine with him—he begged you; to put yourself under arrest —he begged you. He never called any one "thou," but every one "you" whether a single official or all in a body. Yet his subordinates were inexplicably timid in the chief's presence: they answered his friendly questions not with their own voice, but with a strangely different one, which they never used in speaking with others. Ilya Ilyich, too, became suddenly afraid, without himself knowing why, when his superior entered the room, and his voice would fail and give place to an unpleasant falsetto as soon as the chief started to speak with him. Ilya Ilyich suffered from fear and weariness in the service, even under this good, indulgent chief. God knows what would have become of him if he had fallen under a stern, exacting one. Oblomof had to serve two years; possibly he would have held out a third also, till he received a title, but a peculiar accident occasioned his quitting the service earlier.

He once sent some important papers to Archangel instead of to Astrakhan. The matter came to light; the culprit was sought for. All the others waited with curiosity for the chief to call Oblomof and coldly and calmly inquire, "Was it you who sent these papers to Astrakhan?" and all were in doubt with what voice Ilya Ilyich would reply. Some thought he would not answer at all—would not have the power. Glancing at the others, Ilya Ilyich was afraid too, though he knew as well as the rest that the chief would confine himself to a reproof. But his own conscience was far more severe than any reproach. Oblomof did not wait for the deserved punishment; he went home and sent a medical certificate. In this certificate it was recited that "I, the subscriber, testify, over my seal, that the college secretary Ilya Oblomof is attacked by hypertrophy of the heart, with dilitation of the left ventricle" (*hypertrophia cordis cum dilatatione ejus ventriculi sinistri*), "and at the same time by a chronic pain in the liver" (*hepatitis*) "which threatens development dangerous to the health and life of the patient, which ailments forbid his daily attendance at the office. Therefore, to prevent a repetition and aggravation of these painful attacks, I deem it necessary for Mr. Oblomof to discontinue for a time his attendance at the office, and I prescribe generally the abstention from mental occupation and every kind of activity."

But this availed for a short time only: he would have to get well—and there again in perspective was the daily round of duty. Oblomof could not endure it, and tendered his resignation. Thus ended—and never to be resumed—his official employment.

His role in society was more successful. In the first years of his residence in Petersburg, in his fresh youthful days, his calm features were oftener animated, his eyes shone for a long period with a vital fire, and beamed forth rays of light, of hope, and of strength. He had emotions like every one else, hoped, found delight in trivialities, and suffered because of bagatelles. But all that was long ago, at that tender time when man fancies every other man a sincere friend, falls in love with almost every woman, and is prepared to offer each his hand and his heart,—which often results in anguish to others for the rest of their lives. In these happy days there likewise fell to Ilya Ilyich's share, from the host of pretty women, not a few tender, velvety, even passionate glances, an ocean of smiles that promised much, two or three unprivileged kisses, and still more of affectionate hand-pressures actually painful even to tears.

Still, he never fell a victim to the fair sex, never was its slave, nor even a very assiduous adorer, for the very reason that association with women brings great disquietude. Oblomof generally confined himself to adoring them afar at a respectful distance. Seldom did chance bring him to that point in his companionship with a woman where he could glow for some days and think himself beloved. So his love affairs never went the length of a romance; they stopped at the beginning, and from innocence, simplicity, and purity he never yielded to love for some boarding-school girl in her teens. . . .

Immediately after the overseer's first letter, about unpaid rents and bad harvests, he first replaced his friend the cook by a woman cook, then sold his horses, and finally discharged his other "friends." Scarcely anything took him out of doors, and he shut himself up in his lodgings closer and more immovably every day.

From the first he found it hard to remain dressed all day; then he became too lazy to dine out, except with intimate friends—preferably in bachelor households where one could take off his cravat, unbutton his waistcoat, "lop out," or even sleep an hour or so. Soon even these evening calls wearied him; for you had to put on a coat and shave every day. He had read somewhere that only the morning exhalations were wholesome, while those of the evening were injurious; and he began to be afraid of dampness. Despite all these whims, his friend Stoltz succeeded in dragging him out into the world; but Stoltz was often absent from Petersburg, in Moscow, Nijni, the Crimea, even foreign lands, and without him Oblomof sank clean to the ears again in solitude and isolation, out of which only something unusual could bring him, something out of the course of the every-day incidents of life. Nothing of the sort happened, however, nor could be forecast in the future.

Added to all this, there returned to him with age a certain childish timidity, an apprehension of danger and misfortune in whatever lay without the sphere of his daily existence—the result of estrangement from the varieties of external phenomena. He was not frightened, for example, by a crack in the ceiling of his bedroom: he was used to that. No more did it occur to him that the air in a room always closed, and the constant sitting in seclusion, were more injurious to the health than evening damp, and that overfilling the stomach daily is a kind of gradual suicide; but he was wonted to these and did not fear them. He was not accustomed to movement, to life, to throngs and confusion. In a large crowd he was stifled; he got into a boat with but uncertain hope of reaching the other shore; he rode in a carriage expecting a runaway and smash-up. Or else a nervous fear overcame him: he was afraid of the silence around him—or simply, without himself knowing why, chills would run over his body. He often glanced fearfully sidewise at a dark corner, expecting his imagination to play him a trick and conjure up some supernatural vision.

So played itself out his rôle in society. Slothfully he let go all youthful hopes, which disappointed him or which he disappointed;

all those tenderly sad, luminous memories with which many a heart throbs even in declining years.

What then did he do at home? Read, write, study? Yes, if a book or a newspaper fell into his hands, he set out to read it. Did he chance to hear of a notable work, he was seized with a desire to become acquainted with it; he hunted about, asked for the book, and if it were brought soon, threw himself on it, and an idea of the subject began to take shape in his mind—another page and he would have grasped it: but look, he is lying down already, gazing apathetically at the ceiling, the book beside him, unread, uncomprehended. His ardor cooled even quicker than it kindled; and he never returned to the forsaken book. His head was a confused magazine of dead facts, persons, epochs, figures, religions, unrelated political economics or mathematics or other sciences, problems, and the like. It was a library composed solely of odd volumes in all branches of learning.

Study affected Ilya Ilyich curiously. For him, between learning and life there was an absolute gulf, which he made no attempt to cross. For him life was life and science was science. He studied all existent and long non-existent laws, he even went through a course in practical law procedure: then when a theft in his house made it necessary to compose a letter to the police, took a sheet of paper and a pen, thought and thought, and finally sent for the public scrivener. The accounts of the estate were kept by the overseer. "What has science to do with that!" he argued, with dubitation.

He returned to his solitude without sufficient weight of knowledge to give direction to the thoughts that wandered at will in his head or slumbered in idleness. What then did he do? He kept on tracing the pattern of his own life. In it he found, not without reason, more philosophy and poetry than could be exhausted, even without books or learning. Having deserted the service and society, he began to solve the problem of his existence by other means. He reflected upon his destiny, and finally discovered that the sphere of his activity and profession reposed in himself. He realized that the welfare of the family and the care of the property fell to his share. Up to this time he had no systematic knowledge of his own affairs, which Stoltz sometimes attended to in his stead; he did not know his exact receipts and expenditures, struck no balance sheet—nothing.

The senior Oblomof had transmitted the estate to his son just as he received it from his father. Though he spent his whole life in the country, he did not elaborate nor break his head over innovations, as men do nowadays; how to discover new sources of productivity

495

for the soil, or increase and reënforce the old, and so on. As and wherewith the fields had been sown by his grandfather, and such ɛɜ were then the methods of marketing the crops, such they remained under him. The old man was wont to be delighted if a good hɑrvest or advanced prices gave him an income larger than last yeaɾ's: he called that a blessing of God. But he disliked to scheme and ꞩ rivu for a harvest of money. "God gives, let us be satisfied," he said.

Ilya Ilyich pinned his faith nc longer to father or grandfathe꞉. He had studied and lived in the world: it all suggested to hiɾ_ a variety of ideas strange till then. He understood that not onlɟ i gain no sin, but that it is every citizen's duty to contribute by honꬴst work to the general well-being. Thus it was that the largest part ꞏ ꬴ the life-design he traced in his solitude was devoted to a new and fresh plan, in accordance with the needs of the time, for administering his property and managing his peasants. The fundamental idea of the plan, the arrangement, the principal parts—all have long been ready in his head; there remain now only details, estimates, and figures. He has worked untiringly for several years on this plan; hꬴ thinks about it and ponders it, both afoot and in bed, at home as well as in company; now filling out, now changing various portions, now recalling to mind some point conceived yesterday and forgotten during the night; and sometimes, swift as lightning, a new, unexpected idea flashes upon him and begins to seethe in his brain—the work is going on swimmingly. He is not petty executive of others' ready-made notions: himself is the creator and himself the executor of his ideas. As soon as he rises from bed in the morning, after his tea he throws himself at once on the sofa, rests his head in his hands and meditates, without sparing his strength, till his head at length is fatigued by the arduous labor, and his conscience says: "Enough done to-day for the public good."

Free from business cares, Oblomof loved to retire into himself and live in a self-created world. He was accessible to the joy of lofty purpose; he was no stranger to the general interests of humanity. Many a time in the depth of his soul he wept bitterly over the miseries of mankind; he experienced mysterious nameless sufferinᵦ and sorrow, and vague longing for a distant land, probably for that world where his teacher, Stoltz, had often led him;—and sweet tears trickled down his cheeks. Sometimes, too, he is filled with contempt for human vices, for the falsehood, the calumny, the evil that floods the world, and he is inflamed with a desire to show mankind his hurts: suddenly there glow within him ideas that come and g

496

in his mind, like waves on the sea, then grow to purposes, setting all his blood on fire; the purposes are transformed to endeavor; impelled by a moral force, he changes his attitude twice or thrice in a minute; with sparkling eyes he half rises in his bed, stretches forth his hand and casts an inspired look about him. Now, now the endeavor is about to be realized, turn into a fact—and then, great Heaven! what miracles, what beneficial results might not be expected from an effort so sublime!—But see, the morning passes, the day is already inclining to its end, and with it Oblomof's wearied strength inclines to repose; the storms and tempests in his soul abate, his head cools from thought, the blood courses more slowly in his veins. Oblomof, tranquil and pensive, stretches himself on his back, and casting a mournful glance toward the window, with melancholy eyes follows the sun as it sinks majestically behind some four-story house. How many times he has thus followed the setting sun!

In the morning life returns; once more emotions and illusions. He often loves to fancy himself some invincible general, before whom not only Napoleon but Yeruslan Lazarevich are as nothing; he pictures a war and its causes: in his mind, for example, the people of Africa hurl themselves on Europe; or he organizes new crusades, makes war, decides the destinies of nations, destroys cities, spares, puts to death, does deeds of kindness and magnanimity. Or else he chooses the career of the thinker, or the great artist: all do him honor; he reaps laurels; the crowd follows him, crying, "There he is, there he is, there goes Oblomof, our celebrated Ilya Ilyich!"

In bitter moments he is tormented by cares, turns from one side to the other, lies face down, sometimes even completely loses himself; then he rises from bed, falls on his knees, and begins to pray warmly, fervently, beseeching Heaven to avert from him some threatening storm. Then, having shifted the care of his fate on Heaven, he becomes calm and indifferent toward everything in the world, and the storm is wholly forgotten.

Thus he puts his moral strength in play; thus he often agitates himself for entire days, and only awakes with a deep sigh from enchanting visions or painful anxieties when the day is declining, and the great sphere of the sun begins to descend in glory behind the four-story house. Then he follows it again with a dreamy look and a melancholy smile, and rests peacefully from his emotions.

MAXIM GORKY

MAXIM GORKY (Alexei Maximovich Peshkov, Russian, 1868-1936). Pioneer of Russian Revolution in his magnificent, socially-conscious stories. Orphaned when a child, spent years wandering through Russia. Short stories notable for compassionate treatment of outcasts. Famous also for uncompromising realistic drama, *The Lower Depths*. Autobiographical works: *My Childhood, My University Days, My Mother*. Successfully hid bitter disappointment with Stalinist dictatorship, but died under mysterious circumstances.

ONE AUTUMN NIGHT

ONCE in the autumn I happened to be in a very unpleasant and inconvenient position. In the town where I had just arrived and where I knew not a soul, I found myself without a farthing in my pocket and without a night's lodging.

Having sold during the first few days every part of my costume without which it was still possible to go about, I passed from the town into the quarter called "Yste," where were the steamship wharves—a quarter which during the navigation season fermented with boisterous, laborous life, but now was silent and deserted, for we were in the last days of October.

Dragging my feet along the moist sand, and obstinately scrutinizing it with the desire to discover in it any sort of fragment of food, I wandered alone among the deserted buildings and warehouses, and thought how good it would be to get a full meal.

In our present state of culture hunger of the mind is more quickly satisfied than hunger of the body. You wander about the streets, you are surrounded by buildings not bad-looking from the outside and—you may safely say it—not so badly furnished inside, and the sight of them may excite within you. stimulating ideas about architecture, hygiene, and many other wise and high-flying subjects. You may meet warmly and neatly dressed folks—all very polite, and turning away from you tactfully, not wishing offensively to notice the lamentable fact of your existence. Well, well, the mind of a hungry man is always better nourished and healthier that the mind of the well-fed man; and there you have a situation from which you may draw a very ingenious conclusion in favor of the ill fed.

The evening was approaching, the rain was falling, and the wind blew violently from the north. It whistled in the empty booths and shops, blew into the plastered window-panes of the taverns, and whipped into foam the wavelets of the river which splashed noisily on the sandy shore, casting high their white crests, racing one after another into the dim distance, and leaping impetuously over one another's shoulders. It seemed as if the river felt the proximity of winter, and was running at random away from the fetters of ice which the north wind might well have flung upon her that very night. The sky was heavy and dark; down from it swept incessantly scarcely visible drops of rain, and the melancholy elegy in nature all around me was emphasized by a couple of battered and mis-shapen willow-trees and a boat, bottom upwards, that was fastened to their roots.

The overturned canoe with its battered keel and the miserable old trees rifled by the cold wind—everything around me was bankrupt, barren, and dead, and the sky flowed with undryable tears. . . . Everything around was waste and gloomy . . . it seemed as if every-thing were dead, leaving me alone among the living, and for me also a cold death waited.

I was then eighteen years old—a good time!

I walked and walked along the cold wet sand, making my chat-tering teeth warble in honor of cold and hunger, when suddenly, as I was carefully searching for something to eat behind one of the empty crates, I perceived behind it, crouching on the ground, a figure in woman's clothes dank with the rain and clinging fast to her stooping shoulders. Standing above her, I watched to see what she was doing. It appeared that she was digging a trench in the sand with her hands—digging away under one of the crates.

"Why are you doing that?" I asked, crouching down on my heels quite close to her.

She gave a little scream and was quickly on her legs again. Now that she stood there staring at me, with her wide-open gray eyes full of terror, I perceived that it was a girl of my own age, with a very pleasant face embellished unfortunately by three large blue marks. This spoilt her, although these blue marks had been dis-tributed with a remarkable sense of proportion, one at a time, and all were of equal size—two under the eyes, and one a little bigger on the forehead just over the bridge of the nose. This symmetry was evidently the work of an artist well inured to the business of spoiling the human physiognomy.

The girl looked at me, and the terror in her eyes gradually died out. . . . She shook the sand from her hands, adjusted her cotton head-gear, cowered down, and said:

"I suppose you, too, want something to eat? Dig away then! My hands are tired. Over there"—she nodded her head in the direction of a booth—"there is bread for certain . . . and sausages too. . . . That booth is still carrying on business."

I began to dig. She, after waiting a little and looking at me, sat down beside me and began to help me.

We worked in silence. I cannot say now whether I thought at that moment of the criminal code, of morality, of proprietorship, and all the other things about which, in the opinion of many experienced persons, one ought to think every moment of one's life. Wishing to keep as close to the truth as possible, I must confess that apparently I was so deeply engaged in digging under the crate that I completely forgot about everything else except one thing: What could be inside that crate?

The evening drew on. The gray, mouldy, cold fog grew thicker and thicker around us. The waves roared with a hollower sound than before, and the rain pattered down on the boards of that crate more loudly and more frequently. Somewhere or other the night-watchman began springing his rattle.

"Has it got a bottom or not?" softly inquired my assistant. I did not understand what she was talking about, and kept silence.

"I say, has the crate got a bottom? If it has we shall try in vain to break into it. Here we are digging a trench, and we may, after all come upon nothing but solid boards. How shall we take them off? Better smash the lock; it is a wretched lock."

Good ideas rarely visit the heads of women, but as you see, they visit them sometimes. I have always valued good ideas, and have always tried to utilize them as far as possible.

Having found the lock, I tugged at it and wrenched off the whole thing. My accomplice immediately stooped down and wriggled like a serpent into the gaping-open, four-cornered cover of the crate whence she called to me approvingly, in a low tone:

"You're a brick!"

Nowadays a little crumb of praise from a woman is dearer to me than a whole dithyramb from a man, even though he be more eloquent than all the ancient and modern orators put together. Then, however, I was less amiably disposed than I am now, and paying no attention to the compliment of my comrade, I asked her curtly and anxiously:

"Is there anything?"

In a monotonous tone she set about calculating our discoveries.

"A basketful of bottles—thick furs—a sunshade—an iron pail."

All this was uneatable. I felt that my hopes had vanished. . . . But suddenly she exclaimed vivaciously:

"Aha! here it is!"

"What?"

"Bread . . . a loaf . . . it's only wet . . . take it!"

A loaf flew to my feet and after it herself, my valiant comrade. I had already bitten off a morsel, stuffed it in my mouth, and was chewing it. . . .

"Come, give me some too! . . . And we mustn't stay here. . . . Where shall we go?" She looked inquiringly about on all sides. . . . It was dark, wet, and boisterous.

"Look! there's an upset canoe yonder . . . let us go there."

"Let us go then!" And off we set, demolishing our booty as we went, and filling our mouths with large portions of it. . . . The rain grew more violent, the river roared; from somewhere or other resounded a prolonged mocking whistle—just as if someone great who feared nobody was whistling down all earthly institutions and along with them this horrid autumnal wind and us, its heroes. This whistling made my heart throb painfully, in spite of which I greedily went on eating, and in this respect the girl walking on my left, kept even pace with me.

"What do they call you?" I asked her—why I know not.

"Natasha," she answered shortly, munching loudly.

I stared at her. My heart ached within me; and then I stared into the mist before me, and it seemed to me as if the inimical countenance of my Destiny was smiling at me enigmatically and coldly.

The rain scourged the timbers of the skiff incessantly, and its soft patter induced melancholy thoughts, and the wind whistled as it flew down into the boat's battered bottom through a rift, where some loose splinters of wood were rattling together—a disquieting and depressing sound. The waves of the river were splashing on the shore, and sounded so monotonous and hopeless, just as if they were telling something unbearably dull and heavy, which was boring them into utter disgust, something from which they wanted to run away and yet were obliged to talk about all the same. The

501

sound of the rain blended with their splashing, and a long-drawn sigh seemed to be floating above the overturned skiff—the endless, laboring sigh of the earth, injured and exhausted by the eternal changes from the bright and warm summer to the cold, misty and damp autumn. The wind blew continually over the desolate shore and the foaming river—blew and sang its melancholy songs. . . .

Our position beneath the shelter of the skiff was utterly devoid of comfort; it was narrow and damp, tiny cold drops of rain dribbled through the damaged bottom; gusts of wind penetrated it. We sat in silence and shivered with cold. I remembered that I wanted to go to sleep. Natasha leaned her back against the hull of the boat and curled herself up into a tiny ball. Embracing her knees with her hands, and resting her chin upon them, she stared doggedly at the river with wide-open eyes; on the pale patch of her face they seemed immense, because of the blue marks below them. She never moved, and this immobility and silence—I felt it—gradually produced within me a terror of my neighbor. I wanted to talk to her, but I knew not how to begin.

It was she herself who spoke.

"What a cursed thing life is!" she exclaimed plainly, abstractedly, and in a tone of deep conviction.

But this was no complaint. In these words there was too much of indifference for a complaint. This simple soul thought according to her understanding—thought and proceeded to form a certain conclusion which she expressed aloud, and which I could not confute for fear of contradicting myself. Therefore I was silent, and she, as if she had not noticed me, continued to sit there immovable.

"Even if we croaked . . . what then . . .?" Natasha began again, this time quietly and reflectively, and still there was not one note of complaint in her words. It was plain that this person, in the course of her reflections on life, was regarding her own case, and had arrived at the conviction that in order to preserve herself from the mockeries of life, she was not in a position to do anything else but simply "croak"—to use her own expression.

The clearness of this line of thought was inexpressibly sad and painful to me, and I felt that if I kept silence any longer I was really bound to weep. . . . And it would have been shameful to have done this before a woman, especially as she was not weeping herself. I resolved to speak to her.

"Who was it that knocked you about?" I asked. For the moment I could not think of anything more sensible or more delicate.

"Pashka did it all," she answered in a dull and level tone.

"And who is he?"

"My lover. . . . He was a baker."

"Did he beat you often?"

"Whenever he was drunk he beat me. . . . Often!"

And suddenly, turning towards me, she began to talk about herself, Pashka, and their mutual relations. He was a baker with red mustaches and played very well on the banjo. He came to see her and greatly pleased her, for he was a merry chap and wore nice clean clothes. He had a vest which cost fifteen rubles and boots with dress tops. For these reasons she had fallen in love with him, and he became her "creditor." And when he became her creditor, he made it his business to take away from her the money which her other friends gave to her for bonbons, and, getting drunk on this money, he would fall to beating her; but that would have been nothing if he hadn't also begun to "run after" other girls before her very eyes.

"Now wasn't that an insult? I am not worse than the others. Of course that meant that he was laughing at me, the blackguard. The day before yesterday I asked leave of my mistress to go out for a bit, went to him, and here I found Dimka sitting beside him, drunk. And he, too, was half seas over. I said, 'You scoundrel, you!' And he gave me a thorough hiding. He kicked me and dragged me by the hair. But that was nothing to what came after. He spoiled everything I had on—left me just as I am now! How could I appear before my mistress? He spoiled everything . . . my dress and my jacket too—it was quite a new one; I gave a fiver for it . . . and tore my kerchief from my head. . . . Oh, Lord! What will become of me now?" she suddenly whined in a lamentable, overstrained voice.

The wind howled, and became ever colder and more boisterous. . . . Again my teeth began to dance up and down, and she, huddled up to avoid the cold, pressed as closely to me as she could, so that I could see the gleam of her eyes through the darkness.

"What wretches all you men are! I'd burn you all in an oven; I'd cut you in pieces. If any one of you was dying I'd spit in his mouth, and not pity him a bit. Mean skunks! You wheedle and wheedle, you wag your tails like cringing dogs, and we fools give ourselves up to you, and it's all up with us! Immediately you trample us underfoot. . . . Miserable loafers!"

She cursed us up and down, but there was no vigor, no malice,

503

no hatred of these "miserable loafers" in her cursing that I could hear. The tone of her language was by no means corresponded with its subject-matter, for it was calm enough, and the gamut of her voice was terribly poor.

Yet all this made a stronger impression on me than the most eloquent and convincing pessimistic books and speeches, of which I had read a good many and which I still read to this day. And this, you see, was because the agony of a dying person is much more natural and violent than the most minute and picturesque descriptions of death.

I felt really wretched—more from cold than from the words of my neighbor. I groaned softly and ground my teeth.

Almost at the same moment I felt two little arms about me—one of them touched my neck and the other lay upon my face—and at the same time an anxious, gentle, friendly voice uttered the question:

"What ails you?"

I was really to believe that someone else was asking me this and not Natasha, who had just declared that all men were scoundrels, and expressed a wish for their destruction. But she it was, and now she began speaking quickly, hurriedly.

"What ails you, eh? Are you cold? Are you frozen? Ah, what a one you are, sitting there so silent like a little owl! Why, you should have told me long ago that you were cold. Come . . . Lie on the ground . . . stretch yourself out and I will lie . . . there! How's that? Now put your arms round me? . . . tighter! How's that? You shall be warm very soon now. . . . And then we'll lie back to back. . . . The night will pass so quickly, see if it won't. I say . . . have you too been drinking . . . ? Turned out of your place, eh? . . . It doesn't matter."

And she comforted me. . . . She encouraged me.

May I be thrice accursed! What a world of irony was in this single fact for me! Just imagine! Here was I, seriously occupied at this very time with the destiny of humanity, thinking of the reorganization of the social system, of political revolutions, reading all sorts of devilishly wise books whose abysmal profundity was certainly unfathomable by their very authors—at this very time, I say, I was trying with all my might to make of myself "a potent, active social force." It even seemed to me that I had partially accomplished my object; anyhow, at this time, in my ideas about myself, I had got so far as to recognize that I had an exclusive right to exist, that I had the necessary greatness to deserve to live my life, and that I was fully competent to play a great historical part therein. And a woman was now warming me with her body, a wretched, battered, hunted creature, who had no place and no value in life, and whom I had never thought of helping till she helped me herself, and whom I really would not have known how to help in any way even if the thought of it had occurred to me.

Ah! I was ready to think that all this was happening to me in a dream—in a disagreable, an oppressive dream.

But, ugh! it was impossible for me to think that, for cold drops of rain were dripping down upon me, the woman was pressing close to me, her warm breath was fanning my face, and—despite a slight odor of vodka—it did me good. The wind howled and raged, the rain smote upon the skiff, the waves splashed, and both of us, embracing each other convulsively, nevertheless shivered with cold. All this was only too real, and I am certain that nobody ever dreamed such an oppressive and horrid dream as that reality.

But Natasha was talking all the time of something or other, talking kindly and sympathetically, as only women can talk. Beneath the influence of her voice and kindly words, a little fire began to burn up within me, and something inside my heart thawed in consequence.

Then tears poured from my eyes like a hailstorm, washing away from my heart much that was evil, much that was stupid, much sorrow and dirt which had fastened upon it before that night. Natasha comforted me.

"Come, come, that will do, little one! Don't take on! That'll do! God will give you another chance . . . you will right yourself and stand in your proper place again . . . and it will be all right. . . ."

And she kept kissing me . . . many kisses did she give me . . . burning kisses . . . and all for nothing. . . .

Those were the first kisses from a woman that had ever been bestowed upon me, and they were the best kisses too, for all the subsequent kisses cost me frightfully dear, and really gave me nothing at all in exchange.

"Come, don't take on so, funny one! I'll manage for you to-morrow if you cannot find a place." Her quiet, persuasive whispering sounded in my ears as if it came through a dream. . . .

There we lay till dawn. . . .

And when the dawn came, we crept from behind the skiff and went into the town. . . .Then we took friendly leave of each other and never met again, although for half a year I searched in every hole and corner for that kind Natasha with whom I spent the autumn night just described.

If she be already dead—and well for her if it were so—may she rest in peace! And if she be alive . . . still I say "Peace to her soul!" And may the consciousness of her fall never enter her soul . . . for that would be a superfluous and fruitless suffering if life is to be lived. . . .

THOMAS GRAY

THOMAS GRAY (English, 1716-1771). Precursor of English Romanticism. Magnificent craftsman, with classical background. Passed most of life as professor, wrote frequently in Latin. *Elegy Written in a Country Churchyard* one of favorite and most quoted poems in the language. Excellent *Pindaric Odes* less well known.

ELEGY IN A COUNTRY CHURCHYARD

The curfew tolls the knell of parting day,
  The lowing herd winds slowly o'er the lea,
The ploughman homeward plods his weary way,
  And leaves the world to darkness and to me.

Now fades the glimmering landscape on the sight,
  And all the air a solemn stillness holds,
Save where the beetle wheels his droning flight,
  And drowsy tinklings lull the distant folds;

Save that from yonder ivy-mantled tower,
  The moping owl does to the moon complain
Of such as, wandering near her secret bower,
  Molest her ancient solitary reign.

Beneath those rugged elms, that yew-tree's shade,
  Where heaves the turf in many a mouldering heap
Each in his narrow cell forever laid,
  The rude forefathers of the hamlet sleep.

The breezy call of incense breathing-morn,
    The swallow twittering from the straw-built shed,
The cock's shrill clarion, or the echoing horn,
    No more shall rouse them from their lowly bed.

For them no more the blazing hearth shall burn,
    Or busy housewife ply her evening care;
No children run to lisp their sire's return,
    Or climb his knees the envied kiss to share.

Oft did the harvest to their sickle yield;
    Their furrow oft the stubborn glebe has broke;
How jocund did they drive their team afield!
    How bowed the woods beneath their sturdy stroke!

Let not ambition mock their useful toil,
    Their homely joys and destiny obscure;
Nor grandeur hear, with a disdainful smile,
    The short and simple annals of the poor.

The boast of heraldry, the pomp of power,
    And all that beauty, all that wealth e'er gave,
Await alike the inevitable hour—
    The paths of glory lead but to the grave.

Nor you, ye proud, impute to these the fault,
    If memory o'er their tomb no trophies raise,
Where, through the long-drawn aisle and fretted vault,
    The pealing anthem swells the note of praise.

Can storied urn or animated bust
    Back to its mansion call the fleeting breath?
Can honor's voice provoke the silent dust,
    Or flattery soothe the dull cold ear of death?

Perhaps in this neglected spot is laid
    Some heart once pregnant with celestial fire,
Hands that the rod of empire might have swayed
    Or waked to ecstasy the living lyre.

But knowledge to their eyes her ample page,
　　Rich with the spoils of time, did ne'er unroll;
Chill penury repressed their noble rage,
　　And froze the genial current of the soul.

Full many a gem of purest ray serene
　　The dark, unfathomed caves of ocean bear;
Full many a flower is born to blush unseen,
　　And waste its sweetness in the desert air.

Some village Hampden, that, with dauntless breast,
　　The little tyrant of his fields withstood
Some mute inglorious Milton here may rest,
　　Some Cromwell, guiltless of his country's blood.

The applause of listening senates to command,
　　The threats of pain and ruin to despise,
To scatter plenty o'er a smiling land,
　　And read their history in a nation's eyes,—

Their lot forbade; nor circumscribed alone
　　Their growing virtues, but their crimes confined;
Forbade to wade through slaughter to a throne,
　　And shut the gates of mercy on mankind;

The struggling pangs of conscious truth to hide,
　　To quench the blushes of ingenious shame,
Or heap the shrine of luxury and pride
　　With incense kindled at the muse's flame.

Far from the madding crowd's ignoble strife,
　　Their sober wishes never learned to stray;
Along the cool sequestered vale of life
　　They kept the noiseless tenor of their way.

Yet e'en these bones from insult to protect,
　　Some frail memorial still erected nigh,
With uncouth rhymes and shapeless sculpture decked,
　　Implores the passing tribute of a sigh.

Their names, their years, spelled by the unlettered muse,
   The place of fame and eulogy supply;
And many a holy text around she strews,
   That teach the rustic moralist to die.

For who, to dumb forgetfulness a prey,
   This pleasing, anxious being e'er resigned,
Left the warm precincts of the cheerful day,
   Nor cast one longing, lingering look behind?

On some fond breast the parting soul relies,
   Some pious hand the closing eye requires;
Even from the tomb the voice of nature cries,
   Even in our ashes live their wonted fires.

For thee, who, mindful of the unhonored dead,
   Dost in these lines their artless tale relate,
If chance, by lonely contemplation led,
   Some kindred spirit shall inquire thy fate.

Haply some hoary-headed swain may say,
   "Oft have we seen him at the peep of dawn,
Brushing with hasty steps the dews away,
   To meet the sun upon the upland lawn.

"There at the foot of yonder nodding beech,
   That wreathes its old fantastic roots so high,
His listless length at noontide would he stretch,
   And pore upon the brook that bubbles by.

"Hard by yon wood, now smiling as in scorn,
   Muttering his wayward fancies, he would rove,
Now drooping, woeful wan, like one forlorn,
   Or crazed with care, or crossed in hopeless love.

"One morn I missed him on the 'customed hill,
   Along the heath, and near his favorite tree;
Another came; nor yet beside the rill,
   Nor up the lawn, nor at the wood was he;

509

"The next, with dirges due, in sad array,
   Slow through the churchyard path we saw him borne—
Approach and read (for thou canst read) the lay
   'Graved on the stone beneath yon aged thorn."

THE EPITAPH

Here rests his head upon the lap of earth,
   A youth to fortune and to fame unknown;
Fair science frowned not on his humble birth,
   And melancholy marked him for her own.

Large was his bounty, and his soul sincere,
   Heaven did a recompense as largely send;
He gave to misery all he had—a tear;
   He gained from Heaven ('twas all he wished) a friend.

No farther seek his merits to disclose,
   Or draw his frailties from their dread abode
(There they alike in trembling hope repose),
   The bosom of his Father and his God.

FRANZ GRILLPARZER

FRANZ GRILLPARZER (Austrian, 1791-1872). Chief Austrian dramatist.
Developed classical and historical themes in contemporary terms, informing
them with 19th century idealism and psychology. Mood of pessimism prevails.
Suffered from political censorship of his time. Major works: *The Golden
Fleece* (treatment of Medea legend), *The Dream of Life, Woe to Him
That Lies!*

SAPPHO

Act V

Rhamnes—   Her name upon the stars
She has traced with diamond-pointed letters,
And only with the stars 'twill fade away.
In distant lands, among strange men, 'twill

Echo, long after these our mortal frames
Have perished, our graves no more are found.
Then Sappho's soul will speak from out strange lips;
Her songs will live embalmed in unknown tongues,
And thine, thy name will live! Be proud of thy
Undying name! In distant lands, by men
Unknown, when centuries have passed away,
And time has swallowed all, 'twill echo then
From every mouth, "'Twas Sappho sang the song,
And Phaon caused her death."
    Melitta— Forbear! forbear!
    Phaon— A maniac wouldst thou make me? Who'll save me
from this torment?

Eucharis enters.

    Eucharis— Rhamnes, thou art here! come! hasten!
    Rhamnes— Whither?
    Eucharis— To Sappho. I fear she is ill.
    Rhamnes— The gods
Forbid!
    Eucharis— I followed her afar, till gained
The largest hall. Concealed, and with sharp eye,
Her motions all I watched. Leaning, and raised
Upon a pedestal, she looked far o'er
The distant sea, that raged and chafed upon
The rock-bound coast. With pallid cheek and eyes,
Veiled with their lids, all motionless she stood,
Among those marble statues, one of them.
Only she seized upon the altar flowers,
The gold and ornaments within her reach,
And cast them, musing, deep in the raging sea.
Their fall with longing eyes she seemed to follow.
I nearer drew; but now a sound I heard
That shook her inmost soul. Suspended from
On high, the sea breeze touched the lyre,
And pensive played within its untuned strings;
Deep sighing, she looked up, and all her being
Thrilled, shaken invisibly by higher
Powers. Her eyes with a strange fire illumed,
A lovely smile played o'er her mouth.
The firm-closed lips were parted now, and words

Came forth so solemn and profound they seemed
Not Sappho's words, but edicts of the gods!
"O friend!" she said, "thou dost admonish me
Of passing time; O thanks! I understand
Thee well." How the wall she gained, and how
The lyre high-hanging reached, I know not.
Her arm, a beam of light it seemed; and as
I looked she held the lyre and pressed the strings
Upon her storm-moved breast; while audibly
The breathing sounds came forth and passed away.
Suspended as a votive wreath upon
The domestic altar, hung her crown; she took
And wound it round her head; the purple robe,
A glowing veil, o'er her fair shoulders threw.
Who first had seen her now, with lyre in hand,
And look inspired, upraised, the altar steps
Ascending, with her whole light form enwrapped
In light, in prayer had bent his trembling knees,
And hailed her the immortal. Silent
And motionless she stood, yet through my limbs
Crept shuddering fear; I quailed beneath
Her piercing eye, and fled to thee.
    Rhamnes— Left her?
Return! yet see, herself comes near!
*(Sappho enters richly dressed as in the first act: the purple mantle on
    her shoulders, the laurel crown upon her head, and the golden
    lyre in her hand. She is surrounded by her women, and descends
    the steps of the marble colonnade.)*
    Melitta— Sappho! dearest mistress!
    Sappho (calm and earnest)— What wouldst thou, then?
    Melitta— Rent is the bandage from my opened eyes.
Let me again become thy slave. Receive
Again what's thine, and pardon me.
    Sappho— So ill
Advised believe me not. No gift from thee
Will Sappho take. That was my own, thou canst
Not give nor take.
    Phaon (kneeling)— O listen, Sappho!
    Sappho— Beware! kneel not to me; devoted am I to the gods!
    Phaon— With gentle eye thou look'st at me, O Sappho!
Rememberest thou—

Sappho— Thou speakest of things long past,
Thee, Phaon, I sought! and found myself.
Thou understood me not. Farewell! on firmer
Ground my hopes must rest!
    Phaon— Hatest thou me, then?
    Sappho— Hatred! Love! Is there no third? Worthy wert
Thou, and are so still, and ever will to me
Be so; like a dear chance companion
That accident awhile led in my boat. The goal
Once reached, we part, each wandering on
His path alone; yet often from the path,
The widening path, recall the friendly meeting.
                          (Her voice fails.

    Phaon (much moved)— O Sappho!
    Sappho— Forbear! we part in peace!
    (To the others)— You who have Sappho's weakness seen, O
        pardon!
To Sappho's weakness be ye reconciled!
The bow when bent first shows its power.
    (She points to the altar in the background)— The flame
Is lit. To Aphrodite it mounts, clear as
The beam of coming day.
    (To her Servants and Phaon)— And now remove!
Leave me to counsel with mine own—mine own!
    Rhamnes— Obey her will. Let all withdraw   *(They draw back.*
    Sappho (approaches the altar that stands close to the cliff)—
Ye lofty gods! divine! With blessings rich
You've crowned my life. My hand the muses' lyre
Has touched; the poet's cup for me runs o'er.
A heart to feel, a mind to think, and power
    To form my thought to music, you have given.
With rich blessings you have blessed me. I thank you!
With victory you've crowned my feeble brow,
And sowed in distant lands the poet's fame,
Of immortality the seed. Echoes
From strangers' tongues the song I struck upon
My golden lyre, and only with the earth
The fame of Sappho dies.
I thank you!
In life's unmingled cup, crowned high with sweets,
The poet only sips, but does not drink.

Obedient to your highest wish, the sweet,
Unemptied cup I place aside, and drink not.
What you decreed, all-powerful gods,
Has Sappho finished! Deny me not
The last reward within your power to grant—
No weakness, no decay, let Sappho know.
In her full strength, in nature's bloom, O take
Her quickly to yourselves!
Forbid that e'er a priestess of the gods
Should be the theme of god-denying foes!
The sport of fools, in their own folly wise!
You bruised the flower, break now the stem;
Perfect in truth what was begun in love,
And spare the conflict's bleeding struggle. Grant,
O grant the victory! the victor's weakness spare!
The flame is kindling while the sun ascends!
I feel I'm heard! Great gods, I thank you!
Melitta! Phaon! come nearer to me!
   (She kisses Phaon on the forehead)—
A friend from distant worlds salutes thee thus!
   (Embracing Melitta)—
Thy mother, dead, sends thee this kiss! Farewell!
There, on the altar of love's goddess, love
Fulfills, of love, the melancholy fate!
   (She hastens to the altar.)
   Rhamnes— What means she? Inspired is all her being.
The splendor of immortals wraps her round.
*(Sappho, who has gradually approached the edge of the cliff, upon
which the altar stands, stretches both hands over Melitta and
Phaon.)*
   Sappho— To men give love! ambition to the gods!
What for you blooms, enjoy, and think of Sappho!
Of life the last debt I pay! The gods,
To you, grant blessings; and to me—themselves.
   (She springs from the cliff into the sea.)
   Phaon— Hold! Sappho! hold!
   Melitta— Alas, she falls! she dies.
   Phaon (busied with Melitta)—
Quick! quick! She dies! Forth from the shore to save!
   Rhamnes (has climbed upon the rock)—
The gods protect! There on that cliff she falls;

There is she crushed, destroyed! Bears she off?
Impossible! alas! too late!
    Phaon— Why weep
You here? a boat! haste! haste to save her.
    Rhamnes (descending)—
Forbear! it is too late! Grant her the grave
The gods decree. That she, disdaining this
False earth, within the sacred waves has
Chosen for her rest.
    Phaon— Dead!
    Rhamnes— Dead!
    Phaon— Dead! alas!
Impossible! She is not dead! not dead!
    Rhamnes— Withered the laurel! broken are the strings;
Upon the earth there was no home for her;
To heaven has Sappho, to her own, returned!

H

HAFIZ

HÁFIZ (Shams ud-Din Mohammed, Persian, *ca.* 1320-1389). Unequaled master of the *ghazal* (short lyric poem). His *Divan*, containing over 500 *ghazals,* influenced later Persian, Indian and Turkish poets, and Westerners such as Goethe. A subtle mystic and superb satirist.

CHARMS THAT CHARM NOT

Without the loved one's cheek the rose
   Can charm not.
The spring, unless the wine-cup flows,
   Can charm not.
The greenwood's border and the orchard's air,
Unless some tulip cheek be there,
   Can charm not.
The sugar-lipped, the fair of rosy frame,
Whom kisses nor embrace can claim,
   Can charm not.
The dancing cypress, the enrapturing flower,
If no nightingale gladden the bower,
   Can charm not.
The painter's picture, though with genius rife,
Without the picture that has life,
   Can charm not.
Wine, flower, and bower abound in charm, yet they,
Lack we the friend who makes us gay,
   Can charm not.
Thy soul, O Hafiz! is a coin that none prize;
And it, though poured forth largess-wise,
   Can charm not.

THE FEAST OF SPRING

My breast is filled with roses,
    My cup is crowned with wine,
And the veil her face discloses—
    The maid I hail as mine.
The monarch, wheresoe'er he be,
Is but a slave compared to me.

Their glare no torches throwing,
    Shall in our bower be found—
Her eyes, like moonbeams glowing,
    Cast light enough around;
And other odors I can spare
Who scent the perfume of her hair.

The honey-dew thy charm might borrow,
    Thy lip alone to me is sweet;
When thou art absent, faint with sorrow
    I hide me in some lone retreat.
Why talk to me of power or fame?
    What are those idle toys to me?
Why ask the praises of my name,
    My joy, my triumph is in thee.

How blest am I! around me swelling
    The notes of melody arise!
I hold the cup with wine excelling,
    And gaze upon thy radiant eyes.

O Hafiz—never waste thy hours
    Without the cup, the lute, and love,
For 'tis the sweetest time of flowers,
    And none these moments shall reprove.
The nightingales around thee sing;
It is the joyous feast of spring.

THE DRUNKARD'S EXCUSE

Know you the true reason and cause why it is that I drink?
    From pride and from folly I strutted and swelled through the
        town:

517

And now those detestable vices, from which the saints shrink,
  I will in the depths of the ocean of drunkenness drown.

MY BIRD

My soul is as a sacred bird, the highest heaven its nest,
Fretting within its body-bars, it finds on earth its nest;
When rising from its dusty heap this bird of mine shall soar
'Twill find upon the lofty gate the nest it had before.
The Sidrah shall receive my bird, when it has winged its way,
And on the Empyrean's top, my falcon's foot shall stay.
Over the ample field of earth is fortune's shadow cast,
Where upon wings and pennons borne this bird of mine has passed.
No spot in the two worlds it owns, above the sphere its goal,
Its body from the quarry is, from "No Place" is its soul.
'Tis only in the glorious world my bird its splendor shows,
The rosy bowers of Paradise its daily food bestows.

JUDAH HALEVI

JUDAH HALEVI (Spanish-Hebrew, *ca.* 1080-1140).. One of greatest Hebrew
poets of Spanish Golden Period, called the Sweet Singer of Zion. Physician
by profession, emigrated to Palestine to devote rest of life to writing *Songs of
Zion.* Also famous: *Sefer ha-Kuzari,* a dialogue on Jewish religion and history,
in effect an essay on national revival. Religious and liturgical poems still used
in prayer.

I. A LETTER TO HIS FRIEND ISAAC

But yesterday the earth drank like a child
  With eager thirst the autumn rain.
Or like a wistful bride who waits the hour
  Of love's mysterious bliss and pain.
And now the Spring is here with yearning eyes;
  Midst shimmering golden flower-beds,
On meadows carpeted with varied hues,
  In richest raiment clad, she treads.

She weaves a tapestry of bloom o'er all,
    And myriad eyed young plants upspring,
White, green, or red like lips that to the mouth
    Of the beloved one sweetly cling.
Whence come these radiant tints, these blended beams?
    Here's such a dazzle, such a blaze,
As though earth stole the splendor of the stars,
    Fain to eclipse them with her rays.
Come! go we to the garden with our wine,
    Which scatters sparks of hot desire,
Within our hand 't is cold, but in our veins
    It flashes clear, it glows like fire.
It bubbles sunnily in earthen jugs.
We catch it in the crystal glass,
    Then wander through cool, shadowy lanes and breathe
    The spicy freshness of the grass.
Whilst we with happy hearts our circuit keep,
    The gladness of the Earth is shown.
She smileth, though the trickling rain-drops weep
    Silently o'er her, one by one.
She loves to feel the tears upon her cheek,
    Like a rich veil, with pearls inwove.
Joyous she listens when the swallows chirp,
    And warbles to her mate, the dove.
Blithe as a maiden midst the young green leaves,
    A wreath she'll wind, a fragrant treasure;
All living things in graceful motion leap,
    As dancing to some merry measure.
The morning breezes rustle cordially,
    Love's thirst is sated with the balm they send.
Sweet breathes the myrtle in the frolic wind,
    As though remembering a distant friend.
The myrtle branch now proudly lifted high,
    Now whispering to itself drops low again.
The topmost palm-leaves rapturously stir,
    For all at once they hear the birds' soft strain.
So stirs, so yearns all nature, gayly decked,
    To honor *Isaac* with her best array.
Hear'st thou the word? She cries—I beam with joy,
Because with Isaac I am wed today.

II. ADMONITION

Long in the lap of childhood didst thou sleep,
Think how thy youth like chaff did disappear;
Shall life's sweet Spring forever last? Look up,
Old age approaches ominously near.
Oh, shake thou off the world, even as the bird
Shakes off the midnight dew that clogged his wings.
Soar upward, seek redemption from thy guilt
And from the earthly dross that round thee clings.
Draw near to God, His holy angels know,
For whom His bounteous streams of mercy flow.

III. LOVE SONGS

"See'st thou o'er my shoulders falling,
    Snake-like ringlets waving free?
Have no fear, for they are twisted
    To allure thee unto me."

Thus she spake, the gentle dove,
    Listen to thy plighted love:—
"Ah, how long I wait, until
    Sweetheart cometh back (she said)
Laying his caressing hand
    Underneath my burning head."

KNUT HAMSUN

KNUT HAMSUN (Norwegian, 1859-1952). One of great literary figures of
modern Norway. Novelist, playwright and poet. Nobel Prize, 1920. Famous
novel: *Growth of the Soil*. Nature mystic and biting critic of materialist
civilization—yet succumbed to one of its lowest forms, Nazism.

THE CALL OF LIFE

DOWN near the inner harbor in Copenhagen there is a street called
Vestervold, a relatively new, yet desolate, boulevard. There are few
houses to be seen on it, few gas lamps, and almost no people whatever. Even now, in summer, it is rare that one sees people promenading there.

Well, last evening I had something of a surprise in that street.

I had taken a few turns up and down the sidewalk when a lady came towards me from the opposite direction. There were no other people in sight. The gas lamps were lighted, but it was nevertheless dark—so dark that I could not distinguish the lady's face. One of the usual creatures of the night, I thought to myself, and passed her by.

At the end of the boulevard I turned about and walked back. The lady had also turned about, and I met her again. She is waiting for some one, I thought, and I was curious to see whom she could be waiting for. And again I passed her by.

When I met her the third time I tipped my hat and spoke to her. "Good evening! Are you waiting for some one?"

She was startled. No—that is, yes—she was waiting for some one.

Did she object to my keeping her company till the person she was expecting arrived?

No—she did not object in the least, and she thanked me. For that matter, she explained, she was not expecting any one. She was merely taking the air—it was so still here.

We strolled about side by side. We began talking about various things of no great consequence. I offered my arm.

"Thank you, no," she said, and shook her head.

There was no great fun promenading in this way; I could not see her in the dark. I struck a match to see what time it was. I held the match up and looked at her too.

"Nine-thirty," I said.

She shivered as if she were freezing. I seized the opportunity.

"You are freezing?" I asked. "Shan't we drop in some place and get something to drink? At Tivoli? At the National?"

"But, don't you see, I can't go anywhere now," she answered.

And I noticed then for the first time that she wore a very long black veil.

I begged her pardon, and blamed the darkness for my mistake. And the way in which she took my apology at once convinced me that she was not one of the usual night wanderers.

"Won't you take my arm?" I suggested again. "It may warm you a bit."

She took my arm.

We paced up and down a few turns. She asked me to look at the time again.

"It is ten," I said. "Where do you live?"

"On Gamle Kongevei."

I stopped her.

"And may I see you to your door?" I asked.

"Not very well," she answered. "No, I can't let you . . . You live on Bredgade, don't you?"

"How do you know that?" I asked surprised.

"Oh, I know who you are," she answered.

A pause. We walked arm in arm down the lighted streets. She walked rapidly, her long veil streaming behind.

"We had better hurry," she said.

At her door in Gamle Kongevei she turned toward me as if to thank me for my kindness in escorting her. I opened the door for her, and she entered slowly. I thrust my shoulder gently against the door and followed her in. Once inside she seized my hand. Neither of us said anything.

We mounted two flights of stairs and stopped on the third floor. She herself unlocked the door to her apartment, then opened a second door, and took me by the hand and led me in. It was presumably a drawing-room; I could hear a clock ticking on the wall. Once inside the door the lady paused a moment, threw her arms about me suddenly, and kissed me tremblingly, passionately, on the mouth. Right on the mouth.

"Won't you be seated," she suggested. "Here is a sofa. Meanwhile I'll get a light."

And she lit a lamp.

I looked about me, amazed, yet curious. I found myself in a spacious and extremely well furnished drawing-room with other, half open, doors leading into several rooms on the side. I could not for the life of me make out what sort of person it was I had come across.

"What a beautiful room!" I exclaimed. "Do you live here?"

"Yes, this is my home," she answered.

"Is this your home? You live with your parents then?"

"Oh, no," she laughed. "I am an old woman, as you'll see!"

And she removed her veil and her wraps.

"There—see! What did I tell you!" she said, and threw her arms about me once again, abruptly, driven by some uncontrollable urge.

She might have been twenty-two or three, wore a ring on her right hand, and might for that matter really have been a married woman. Beautiful? No, she was freckled, and had scarcely any eyebrows. But there was an effervescent life about her, and her mouth was strangely beautiful.

I wanted to ask her who she was, where her husband was, if she had any, and whose house this was I was in, but she threw herself about me every time I opened my mouth and forbade me to be inquisitive.

"My name is Ellen," she explained. "Would you care for something to drink? It really won't disturb any one if I ring. Perhaps you'd step in here, in the bed-room, meanwhile."

I went into the bed-room. The light from the drawing room illumined it partially. I saw two beds. Ellen rang and ordered wine, and I heard a maid bring in the wine and go out again. A little later Ellen came into the bed-room after me, but she stopped short in the door. I took a step towards her. She uttered a little cry and at the same time came towards me.

This was last evening.

What further happened? Ah, patience! There is much more!

It was beginning to grow light this morning when I awoke. The daylight crept into the room on either side of the curtain. Ellen was also awake and smiled toward me. Her arms were white and velvety, her breast unusually high. I whispered something to her, and she closed my mouth with hers, mute with tenderness. The day grew lighter and lighter.

Two hours later I was on my feet. Ellen was also up, busy dressing herself—she had got her shoes on. Then it was I experienced something which even now strikes me as a gruesome dream. I was at the wash stand. Ellen had some errand or other in the adjoining room, and as she opened the door I turned around and glanced in. A cold draft from the open windows in the room rushed in upon me, and in the center of the room I could just make out a corpse stretched out on a table. A corpse, in a coffin, dressed in white, with a gray beard, the corpse of a man. His bony knees protruded like madly clenched fists underneath the sheet, and his face was sallow and ghastly in the extreme. I could see everything in full daylight. I turned away and said not a word.

When Ellen returned I was dressed and ready to go out. I could scarcely bring myself to respond to her embraces. She put on some additional clothes; she wanted to accompany me down as far as the street door, and I let her come, still saying nothing. At the door she pressed close to the wall so as not to be seen.

"Well, good-bye," she whispered.

"Till to-morrow?" I asked, in part to test her.

"No, not to-morrow."

"Why not to-morrow?"

"Not so many questions, dear. I am going to a funeral to-morrow. a relation of mine is dead. Now there—you know it."

"But the day after to-morrow?"

"Yes, the day after to-morrow, at the door here, I'll meet you Good-bye!"

I went.

Who was she? And the corpse? With its fists clenched and th.; corners of its mouth drooping—how ghastly comic! The day afte, to-morrow she would be expecting me. Ought I to see her again?

I went straight down to the Bernina Café and asked for a directory. I looked up number so and so Gamle Kongevei, and—there— there was the name. I waited some little time till the morning papers were out. Then I turned quickly to the announcements of deaths. And—sure enough—there I found hers too, the very first in the list, in bold type: "My husband, fifty-three years old, died to-day after a long illness." The announcement was dated the day before yesterday.

I sat for a long time and pondered.

A man marries. His wife is thirty years younger than he. He contracts a lingering illness. One fair day he dies.

And the young widow breathes a sigh of relief.

THOMAS HARDY

THOMAS HARDY (English, 1840-1928). Novelist and poet. Realistic observer of village and palace, at his best when writing of native Wessex. Began career as architect. His major novels are tragedies: *The Mayor of Casterbridge, The Return of the Native, Tess of the D'Urbervilles, Jude the Obscure.* Pessimistic epic drama, *The Dynasts,* considered by some his masterpiece.

SQUIRE PETRICK'S LADY

FOLK who are at all acquainted with the traditions of Stapleford Park will not need to be told that in the middle of the last century it was owned by that trump of mortgagees, Timothy Petrick, whose

skill in gaining possession of fair estates by granting sums of money
on their title-deeds has seldom if ever been equaled in our part
of England. Timothy was a lawyer by profession, and agent to
several noblemen, by which means his special line of business became opened to him by a sort of revelation. It is said that a relative
of his, a very deep thinker, who afterwards had the misfortune to
be transported for life for mistaken notions on the signing of a
will, taught him considerable legal lore, which he creditably resolved
never to throw away for the benefit of other people, but to reserve
it entirely for his own.

However, I have nothing in particular to say about his early and
active days, but rather of the time when, an old man, he had become
the owner of vast estates by the means I have signified—among
them the great manor of Stapleford, on which he lived, in the
splendid old mansion now pulled down; likewise estates at Marlott,
estates near Sherton Abbas, nearly all the borough of Millpool, and
many properties near Ivell. Indeed, I can't call to mind half his
landed possessions, and I don't know that it matters much at this
time of day, seeing that he's been dead and gone many years.
It is said that when he bought an estate he would not decide to
pay the price till he had walked over every single acre with his
own two feet, and prodded the soil at every point with his own
spud, to test its quality, which, if we regard the extent of his properties, must have been a stiff business for him.

At the time I am speaking of he was a man over eighty, and his
son was dead; but he had two grandsons, the eldest of whom, his
namesake, was married, and was shortly expecting issue. Just then
the grandfather was taken ill, for death, as it seemed, considering
his age. By his will the old man had created an entail (as I believe
the lawyers call it), devising the whole of the estates to his elder
grandson and his issue male, failing which to his younger grandson and his issue male, failing which, to remoter relatives, who need
not be mentioned now.

While old Timothy Petrick was lying ill, his elder grandson's
wife, Annetta, gave birth to her expected child, who, as fortune
would have it, was a son. Timothy, her husband, though sprung of
a scheming family, was no great schemer himself; he was the single
one of the Petricks then living whose heart had never been greatly
moved by sentiments which did not run in the groove of ambitions;
and on this account he had not married well, as the saying is, his
wife having been the daughter of a family of no better beginnings

than his own; that is to say, her father was a country townsman of the professional class. But she was a very pretty woman, by all accounts, and her husband had seen, courted, and married her in a high tide of infatuation, after a very short acquaintance, and with very little knowledge of her heart's history. He had never found reason to regret his choice as yet, and his anxiety for her recovery was great.

She was supposed to be out of danger, and herself and the child progressing well, when there was a change for the worse, and she sank so rapidly that she was soon given over. When she felt she was about to leave him, Annetta sent for her husband, and, on his speedy entry and assurance that they were alone, she made him solemnly vow to give the child every care in any circumstances that might arise, if it should please Heaven to take her. This, of course, he readily promised. Then after some hesitation she told him that she could not die with a falsehood upon her soul, and dire deceit in her life; she must make a terrible confession to him before her lips were sealed forever. She thereupon related an incident concerning the the baby's parentage which was not as he supposed.

Timothy Petrick, though a quick-feeling man, was not of a sort to show nerves outwardly; and he bore himself as heroically as he possibly could do in this trying moment of his life. That same night his wife died; and while she lay dead, and before her funeral, he hastened to the bedside of his sick grandfather, and revealed to him all that had happened—the baby's birth, his wife's confession, and her death, beseeching the aged man, as he loved him, to bestir himself now, at the eleventh hour, and alter his will so as to dish the intruder. Old Timothy, seeing matters in the same light as his grandson, required no urging against allowing anything to stand in the way of legitimate inheritance; he executed another will, limiting the entail to Timothy, his grandson, for life, and his male heirs thereafter to be born, after them to his other grandson, Edward, and Edward's heirs. Thus the newly born infant, who had been the center of so many hopes, was cut off and scorned as none of the elect.

The old mortgagee lived but a short time after this, the excitement of the discovery having told upon him considerably, and he was gathered to his fathers like the most charitable man in his neighborhood. Both his wife and grandparent being buried, Timothy settled down to his usual life as well as he was able, mentally satis-

526

fied that he had, by prompt action, defeated the consequences of such dire domestic treachery as had been shown towards him, and resolving to marry a second time as soon as he could satisfy himself in the choice of a wife.

But men do not always know themselves. The imbittered state of Timothy Petrick's mind bred in him by degrees such a hatred and mistrust of womankind that, though several specimens of high attractiveness came under his eyes, he could not bring himself to the point of proposing marriage. He dreaded to take up the position of husband a second time, discerning a trap in every petticoat, and a Slough of Despond in possible heirs. "What has happened once, when all seemed so fair, may happen again," he said to himself. "I'll risk my name no more." So he abstained from marriage, and overcame his wish for a lineal descendant to follow him in the ownership of Stapleford.

Timothy had scarcely noticed the unfortunate child that his wife had borne, after arranging for a meager fulfillment of his promise to her to take care of the boy, by having him brought up in his house. Occasionally, remembering his promise, he went and glanced at the child, saw that he was doing well, gave a few special directions, and again went his solitary way. Thus he and the child lived on in the Stapleford mansion-house till two or three years had passed by. One day he was walking in the garden, and by some accident left his snuff-box on a bench. When he came back to find it he saw the little boy standing there; he had escaped his nurse, and was making a plaything of the box, in spite of the convulsive sneezings which the game brought in its train. Then the man with the incrusted heart became interested in the little fellow's persistence in his play under such discomforts; he looked in the child's face, saw there his wife's countenance, though he did not see his own, and fell into thought on the piteousness of childhood—particularly of despised and rejected childhood, like this before him.

From that hour, try as he would to counteract the feeling, the human necessity to love something or other got the better of what he had called his wisdom, and shaped itself in a tender anxiety for the youngster Rupert. This name had been given him by his dying mother when, at her request, the child was baptized in her chamber, lest he should not survive for public baptism; and her husband had never thought of it as a name of any significance till, about this time, he learned by accident that it was the name of the young Marquis of Christminster, son of the Duke of Southwesterland, for whom Annetta had cherished warm feelings before her marriage. Recollecting some wandering phrases in his wife's last words, which he had not understood at the time, he perceived at last that this was the person to whom she had alluded when affording him a clew to little Rupert's history.

He would sit in silence for hours with the child, being no great speaker at the best of times; but the boy, on his part, was too ready with his tongue for any break in discourse to arise because Timothy Petrick had nothing to say. After idling away his mornings in this manner, Petrick would go to his own room and swear in long, loud whispers, and walk up and down, calling himself the most ridiculous dolt that ever lived, and declaring that he would never go near the little fellow again; to which resolve he would adhere for the space, perhaps, of a day. Such cases are happily not new to human nature, but there never was a case in which a man more completely befooled his former self than in this.

As the child grew up, Timothy's attachment to him grew deeper, till Rupert became almost the sole object for which he lived. There had been enough of the family ambition latent in him for Timothy Petrick to feel a little envy when, some time before this date, his brother Edward had been accepted by the Honorable Harriet Mountclere, daughter of the second viscount of that name and title; but having discovered, as I have before stated, the paternity of his boy Rupert to lurk in even a higher stratum of society, those envious feelings speedily dispersed. Indeed, the more he reflected thereon, after his brother's aristocratic marriage, the more content did he become. His late wife took softer outline in his memory, as he thought of the lofty taste she had displayed, though only a plain burgher's daughter, and the justification for this weakness in loving the child—the justification that he had longed for—was afforded now in the knowledge that the boy was by nature, if not by name, a representative of one of the noblest houses in England.

"She was a woman of grand instincts, after all," he said to himself, proudly. "To fix her choice upon the immediate successor in that ducal line—it was finely conceived! Had he been of low blood like myself or my relations she would scarce have deserved the harsh measure that I have dealt out to her and her offspring. How much less, then, when such groveling tastes were farthest from her soul! The man Annetta loved was noble, and my boy is noble in spite of me."

The after-clap was inevitable, and it soon came. "So far," he reasoned, "from cutting off his child from inheritance of my estates, as I have done, I should have rejoiced in the possession of him! He is of pure stock on one side at least, while in the ordinary run of affairs he would have been a commoner to the bone."

Being a man, whatever his faults, of good old beliefs in the divinity of kings and those about 'em, the more he overhauled the case in this light the more strongly did his poor wife's conduct in improving the blood and breed of the Petrick family win his heart. He considered what ugly, idle, hard-drinking scamps many of his own relations had been; the miserable scriveners, usurers, and pawnbrokers that he had numbered among his forefathers, and the probability that some of their bad qualities would have come out in a merely corporeal child, to give him sorrow in his old age, turn his black hairs gray, his gray hairs white, cut down every stick of timber, and Heaven knows what all, had he not, like a skillful gardener, minded his grafting and changed the sort; till at length this right-minded man fell down on his knees every night and morning and thanked God that he was not as other meanly descended fathers in such matters.

It was in the peculiar disposition of the Petrick family that the satisfaction which ultimately settled in Timothy's breast found nourishment. The Petricks had adored the nobility, and plucked them at the same time. That excellent man Izaak Walton's feelings about fish were much akin to those of old Timothy Petrick, and of his descendants in a lesser degree, concerning the landed aristocracy. To torture and to love simultaneously is a proceeding strange to reason, but possible to practise, as these instances show.

Hence, when Timothy's brother Edward said slightingly one day that Timothy's son was well enough, but that he had nothing but shops and offices in his backward perspective, while his own children, should he have any, would be far different, in possessing such a mother as the Honorable Harriet, Timothy felt a bound of triumph within him at the power he possessed of contradicting that statement if he chose.

So much was he interested in his boy in this new aspect that he now began to read up chronicles of the illustrious house ennobled as the Dukes of Southwesterland, from their very beginning in the glories of the Restoration of the blessed Charles till the year of his own time. He mentally noted their gifts from royalty, grants of lands, purchases, intermarriages, plantings, and buildings; more particularly their political and military achievements, which had been great, and their performances in arts and letters, which had been by no means contemptible. He studied prints of the portraits of that family, and then, like a chemist watching a crystallization, began to examine young Rupert's face for the unfolding of those historic curves and shades that the painters Vandyke and Lely had perpetuated on canvas.

When the boy reached the most fascinating age of childhood, and his shouts of laughter rang through Stapleford House from end to end, the remorse that oppressed Timothy Petrick knew no bounds. Of all people in the world this Rupert was the one on whom he could have wished the estates to devolve; yet Rupert, by Timothy's own desperate strategy at the time of his birth, had been ousted from all inheritance of them; and, since he did not mean to remarry, the manors would pass to his brother and his brother's children, who would be nothing to him, whose boasted pedigree on one side would be nothing to his Rupert's.

Had he only left the first will of his grandfather alone!

His mind ran on the wills continually, both of which were in existence, and the first, the canceled one, in his own possession. Night after night, when the servants were all abed, and the click of safety-locks sounded as loud as a crash, he looked at that first will, and wished it had been the second and not the first.

The crisis came at last. One night, after having enjoyed the boy's company for hours, he could no longer bear that his beloved Rupert should be dispossessed, and he committed the felonious deed of altering the date of the earlier will to a fortnight later, which made its execution appear subsequent to the date of the second will already proved. He then boldly propounded the first will as the second.

His brother Edward submitted to what appeared to be not only incontestible fact, but a far more likely disposition of old Timothy's property: for, like many others, he had been much surprised at the limitations defined in the other will, having no clew to their cause. He joined his brother Timothy in setting aside the hitherto accepted document, and matters went on in their usual course, there being no dispositions in the substituted will differing from those in the other, except such as related to a future which had not yet arrived.

The years moved on. Rupert had not yet revealed the anxiously expected historic lineaments which should foreshadow the political abilities of the ducal family aforesaid, when it happened on a certain day that Timothy Petrick made the acquaintance of a well-known physician of Budmouth, who had been the medical adviser and friend of the late Mrs. Petrick's family for many years, though after Annetta's marriage, and consequent removal to Stapleford, he had seen no more of her, the neighboring practitioner who attended the Petricks having then become her doctor as a matter of course. Timothy was impressed by the insight and knowledge disclosed in the conversation of the Budmouth physician, and the acquaintance ripening to intimacy, the physician alluded to a form of hallucination to which Annetta's mother and grandmother had been subject —that of believing in certain dreams as realities. He delicately inquired if Timothy had ever noticed anything of the sort in his wife during her lifetime; he, the physician, had fancied that he discerned germs of the same peculiarity in Annetta when he attended her in her girlhood. One explanation begat another, till the dumbfounded Timothy Petrick was persuaded in his own mind that Annetta's confession to him had been based on a delusion.

"You look down in the mouth!" said the doctor, pausing.

"A bit unmanned. 'Tis unexpected-like," sighed Timothy.

But he could hardly believe it possible; and, thinking it best to be frank with the doctor, told him the whole story which, till now, he had never related to living man, save his dying grandfather. To his surprise, the physician informed him that such a form of delusion was precisely what he would have expected from Annetta's antecedents at such a physical crisis in her life.

Petrick prosecuted his inquiries elsewhere; and the upshot of his labors was, briefly, that a comparison of dates and places showed irrefutably that his poor wife's assertion could not have foundation in fact. The young Marquis of her tender passion—a highly moral and bright-minded nobleman—had gone abroad the year before Annetta's marriage, and had not returned until after her death. The young girl's love for him had been a delicate ideal dream—no more.

Timothy went home, and the boy ran out to meet him; whereupon a strangely dismal feeling of discontent took possession of his soul. After all, then, there was nothing but plebeian blood in the veins of the heir to his name and estates; he was not to be succeeded by a noble-natured line. To be sure, Rupert was his son; but that glory and halo he believed him to have inherited from the ages. outshining that of his brother's children, had departed from Rupert's brow forever; he could no longer read history in the boy's face and centuries of domination in his eyes.

His manner towards his son grew colder and colder from that day forward; and it was with bitterness of heart that he discerned the characteristic features of the Petricks unfolding themselves by degrees. Instead of the elegant knife-edged nose, so typical of the Dukes of Southwesterland, there began to appear on his face the broad nostril and hollow bridge of his grandfather Timothy. No illustrious line of politicians was promised a continuator in that graying blue eye, for it was acquiring the expression of the orb of a particularly objectionable cousin of his own; and, instead of the mouth-curves which had thrilled Parliamentary audiences in speeches now bound in calf in every well-ordered library, there was the bull-lip of that very uncle of his who had had the misfortune with the signature of a gentleman's will, and had been transported for life in consequence.

To think how he himself, too, had sinned in this same matter of a will for this mere fleshly reproduction of a wretched old uncle whose very name he wished to forget! The boy's Christian name, even, was an imposture and an irony, for it implied hereditary force and brilliancy to which he plainly would never attain. The consolation of real sonship was always left him certainly; but he could not help groaning to himself, "Why cannot a son be one's own and somebody else's likewise?"

The Marquis was shortly afterwards in the neighborhood of Stapleford, and Timothy Petrick met him, and eyed his noble countenance admiringly. The next day, when Petrick was in his study, somebody knocked at the door.

"Who's there?"

"Rupert."

"I'll Rupert thee, you young imposter! Say, only a poor commonplace Petrick!" his father grunted. "Why didn't you have a voice like the Marquis I saw yesterday!" he continued, as the lad came in. "Why haven't you his looks, and a way of commanding as if you'd done it for centuries—hey?"

"Why? How can you expect it, father, when I'm not related to him?"

"Ugh! Then you ought to be!" growled his father.

BRET HARTE

BRET HARTE (American, 1836-1902). The sentimental popularizer of the Western tale in America. Born in Albany, New York, went to California in 1854, and worked as teacher, miner, printer, editor. Best-known stories: "The Outcasts of Poker Flat" and "The Luck of Roaring Camp."

THE OUTCASTS OF POKER FLAT

As Mr. John Oakhurst, gambler, stepped into the main street of Poker Flat on the morning of the 23d of November, 1850, he was conscious of a change in its moral atmosphere since the preceding night. Two or three men, conversing earnestly together, ceased as he approached, and exchanged significant glances. There was a Sabbath lull in the air, which, in a settlement unused to Sabbath influences, looked ominous.

Mr. Oakhurst's calm, handsome face betrayed small concern in these indications. Whether he was conscious of any predisposing cause was another question. "I reckon they're after somebody," he reflected: "likely it's me." He returned to his pocket the handkerchief with which he had been wiping away the red dust of Poker Flat from his neat boots, and quietly discharged his mind of any further conjecture.

In point of fact, Poker Flat was "after somebody." It had lately suffered the loss of several thousand dollars, two valuable horses, and a prominent citizen. It was experiencing a spasm of virtuous reaction, quite as lawless and ungovernable as any of the acts that had provoked it. A secret committee had determined to rid the town of all improper persons. This was done permanently in regard to two men who were then hanging from the boughs of a sycamore in the gulch, and temporarily in the banishment of certain ladies. It is but due to the sex, however, to state that their impropriety was professional, and it was only in such easily established standards of evil that Poker Flat ventured to sit in judgment.

Mr. Oakhurst was right in supposing that he was included in this category. A few of the committee had urged hanging him as a possible example and a sure method of reimbursing themselves from his pockets of the sums he had won from them. "It's agin justice," said Jim Wheeler, "to let this yer young man from Roaring Camp—an entire stranger—carry away our money." But a crude sentiment of equity residing in the breasts of those who had been fortunate enough to win from Mr. Oakhurst overruled this narrower local prejudice.

Mr. Oakhurst received his sentence with philosophic calmness, none the less coolly that he was aware of the hesitation of his judges. He was too much of a gambler not to accept his fate. With him life was at best an uncertain game, and he recognized the usual percentage in favor of the dealer.

A body of armed men accompanied the deported wickedness of Poker Flat to the outskirts of the settlement. Besides Mr. Oakhurst, who was known to be a coolly desperate man, and for whose intimidation the armed escort was intended, the expatriated party consisted of a young woman familiarly known as "The Duchess"; another who had won the title of "Mother Shipton"; and "Uncle Billy," a suspected sluice-robber and confirmed drunkard. The cavalcade provoked no comments from the spectators, nor was any word uttered by the escort. Only when the gulch which marked the uttermost limit of Poker Flat was reached, the leader spoke briefly and to the point. The exiles were forbidden to return at the peril of their lives.

As the escort disappeared, their pent-up feelings found vent in a few hysterical tears from the Duchess, some bad language from Mother Shipton, and a Parthian volley of expletives from Uncle Billy. The philosophic Oakhurst alone remained silent. He listened calmly to Mother Shipton's desire to cut somebody's heart out, to the repeated statements of the Duchess that she would die in the road, and to the alarming oaths that seemed to be bumped out of Uncle Billy as he rode forward. With the easy good humor characteristic of his class, he insisted upon exchanging his own riding-horse, "Five-spot," for the sorry mule which the Duchess rode. But even this act did not draw the party into any closer sympathy. The young woman readjusted her somewhat draggled plumes with a feeble, faded coquetry; Mother Shipton eyed the possessor of "Five-spot" with malevolence, and Uncle Billy included the whole party in one sweeping anathema.

The road to Sandy Bar—a camp that, not having as yet experienced the regenerating influences of Poker Flat, consequently seemed to offer some invitation to the emigrants—lay over a steep mountain range. It was distant a day's severe travel. In that advanced season the party soon passed out of the moist, temperate regions of the foothills into the dry, cold bracing air of the Sierras. The trail was narrow and difficult. At noon the Duchess, rolling out of her saddle upon the ground, declared her intention of going no farther, and the party halted.

The spot was singularly wild and impressive. A wooded amphitheater surrounded on three sides by precipitous cliffs of naked granite, sloped gently toward the crest of another precipice that overlooked the valley. It was, undoubtedly, the most suitable spot for a camp, had camping been advisable. But Mr. Oakhurst knew that scarcely half the journey to Sandy Bar was accomplished, and the party was not equipped or provisioned for delay. This fact he pointed out to his companions curtly, with a philosophic commentary on the folly of "throwing up their hand before the game was played out." But they were furnished with liquor, which in this emergency stood them in place of food, fuel, rest and prescience. In spite of his remonstrances, it was not long before they were more or less under its influence. Uncle Billy passed rapidly from a bellicose state into one of stupor, the Duchess became maudlin, and Mother Shipton snored. Mr. Oakhurst alone remained erect, leaning against a rock, calmly surveying them.

Mr. Oakhurst did not drink. It interfered with a profession which required coolness, impassiveness, and presence of mind, and, in his own language, he "couldn't afford it." As he gazed at his recumbent fellow exiles, the loneliness begotten of his pariah trade, his habits of life, his very vices, for the first time seriously oppressed him. He bestirred himself in dusting his black clothes, washing his hands and face, and other acts characteristic of his studiously neat habits, and for a moment forgot his annoyance. The thought of deserting his weaker and more pitiable companions never perhaps occurred to him. Yet he could not help feeling the want of that excitement which, singularly enough, was most conducive to that calm equanimity for which he was notorious. He looked at the gloomy walls that rose a thousand feet sheer above the circling pines around him, at the sky ominously clouded, at the valley below, already deepening into shadow; and, doing so, suddenly he heard his own name called.

A horseman slowly ascended the trail. In the fresh, open face of the newcomer Mr. Oakhurst recognized Tom Simson, otherwise known as "The Innocent," of Sandy Bar. He had met him some months before over a "little game," and had, with perfect equanimity, won the entire fortune—amounting to some forty dollars—of that guileless youth. After the game was finished, Mr. Oakhurst drew the youthful speculator behind the door and thus addressed him:

"Tommy, you're a good little man, but you can't gamble worth a cent. Don't try it ever again." He then handed him his money back, pushed him gently from the room, and so made a devoted slave of Tom Simson.

There was a remembrance of this in his boyish and enthusiastic greeting of Mr. Oakhurst. He had started, he said, to go to Poker Flat to seek his fortune. "Alone?" No, not exactly alone; in fact (a giggle), he had run away with Piney Woods. Didn't Mr Oakhurst remember Piney? She that used to wait on the table at the Temperance House? They had been engaged a long time, but old Jake Woods had objected, and so they had run away, and were going to Poker Flat to be married, and here they were. And they were tired out, and how lucky it was they had found a place to camp, and company. All this the Innocent delivered rapidly, while Piney, a stout, comely damsel of fifteen, emerged from behind the pine tree, where she had been blushing unseen, and rode to the side of her lover.

Mr. Oakhurst seldom troubled himself with sentiment, still less with propriety; but he had a vague idea that the situation was not fortunate. He retained, however, his presence of mind sufficiently to kick Uncle Billy, who was about to say something, and Uncle Billy, was sober enough to recognize in Mr. Oakhurst's kick a superior power that would not bear trifling. He then endeavored to dissuade Tom Simson from delaying further, but in vain. He even pointed out the fact that there was no provision, nor means of making a camp. But, unluckily, the Innocent met this objection by assuring the party that he was provided with an extra mule loaded with provisions, and by the discovery of a rude attempt at a log house near the trail. "Piney can stay with Mrs. Oakhurst," said the Innocent, pointing to the Duchess, "and I can shift for myself."

Nothing but Mr. Oakhurst's admonishing foot saved Uncle Billy from bursting into a roar of laughter. As it was, he felt compelled to retire up the cañon until he could recover his gravity. There he confided the joke to the tall pine trees, with many slaps of his leg, contortions of his face, and the usual profanity. But when he returned to the party, he found them seated by a fire—for the air had grown strangely chill and the sky overcast—in apparently amicable conversation. Piney was actually talking in an impulsive girlish fashion to the Duchess, who was listening with an interest and animation she had not shown for many days. The Innocent was holding forth, apparently with equal effect, to Mr. Oakhurst and Mother

536

Shipton, who was actually relaxing into inward amiability. "Is this yer a d—d picnic?" said Uncle Billy, with inward scorn, as he surveyed the sylvan group, the glancing firelight, and the tethered animals in the foreground. Suddenly an idea mingled with the alcoholic fumes that disturbed his brain. It was apparently of a jocular nature, for he felt impelled to slap his leg again and cram his fist into his mouth.

As the shadows crept slowly up the mountain, a slight breeze rocked the tops of the pine trees and moaned through their long and gloomy aisles. The ruined cabin, patched and covered with pine boughs, was set apart for the ladies. As the lovers parted, they unaffectedly exchanged a kiss, so honest and sincere that it might have been heard above the swaying pines. The frail Duchess and the malevolent Mother Shipton were probably too stunned to remark upon this last evidence of simplicity, and so turned without a word to the hut. The fire was replenished, the men lay down before the door, and in a few minutes were asleep.

Mr. Oakhurst was a light sleeper. Toward morning he awoke benumbed and cold. As he stirred the dying fire, the wind, which was now blowing strongly, brought to his cheek that which caused the blood to leave it—snow!

He started to his feet with the intention of awakening the sleepers, for there was no time to lose. But turning to where Uncle Billy had been lying, he found him gone. A suspicion leaped to his brain, and a curse to his lips. He ran to the spot where the mules had been tethered—they were no longer there. The tracks were already rapidly disappearing in the snow.

The momentary excitement brought Mr. Oakhurst back to the fire with his usual calm. He did not waken the sleepers. The Innocent slumbered peacefully, with a smile on his good-humored, freckled face; the virgin Piney slept beside her frailer sisters as sweetly as though attended by celestial guardians; and Mr. Oakhurst, drawing his blanket over his shoulders, stroked his mustaches and waited for the dawn. It came slowly in a whirling mist of snowflakes that dazzled and confused the eye. What could be seen of the landscape appeared magically changed. He looked over the valley, and summed up the present and future in two words, "Snowed in!"

A careful inventory of the provisions, which, fortunately for the party, had been stored within the hut, and so escaped the felonious fingers of Uncle Billy, disclosed the fact that with care and prudence they might last ten days longer. "That is," said Mr. Oakhurst *sotto voce* to the Innocent, "if you're willing to board us. If you ain't—and perhaps you'd better not—you can wait till Uncle Billy gets back with provisions." For some occult reason, Mr. Oakhurst could not bring himself to disclose Uncle Billy's rascality, and so offered the hypothesis that he had wandered from the camp and had accidentally stampeded the animals. He dropped a warning to the Duchess and Mother Shipton, who, of course, knew the facts of their associate's defection. "They'll find out the truth about us *all* when they find out anything," he added significantly, "and there's no good frightening them now."

Tom Simson not only put all his worldly store at the disposal of Mr. Oakhurst, but seemed to enjoy the prospect of their enforced seclusion. "We'll have a good camp for a week, and then the snow'll melt, and we'll all go back together." The cheerful gayety of the young man and Mr. Oakhurst's calm infected the others. The Innocent, with the aid of pine boughs, extemporized a thatch for the roof less cabin, and the Duchess directed Piney in the rearrangement of the interior with a taste and a tact that opened the blue eyes of that provincial maiden to their fullest extent. "I reckon now you're used to fine things at Poker Flat," said Piney. The Duchess turned away sharply to conceal something that reddened her cheeks through their professional tint, and Mother Shipton requested Piney not to "chatter." But when Mr. Oakhurst returned from a weary search for the trail, he heard the sound of happy laughter echoed from the rocks. He stopped in some alarm, and his thoughts first naturally reverted to the whiskey, which he had prudently cached. "And yet it don't somehow sound like whiskey," said the gambler. It was not until he caught sight of the blazing fire through the still blinding storm, and the group around it, that he settled to the conviction that it was "square fun."

Whether Mr. Oakhurst had cached his cards with the whiskey as something debarred the free access of the community, I cannot say. It was certain that, in Mother Shipton's words, he "didn't say 'cards' once" during that evening. Haply the time was beguiled by an accordian, produced somewhat ostentatiously by Tom Simson from his pack. Notwithstanding some difficulties attending the manipulation of this instrument, Piney Woods managed to pluck several reluctant melodies from its keys, to an accompaniment by the Innocent on a pair of bone castanets. But the crowning festivity of the evening was reached in a rude camp-meeting hymn, which the lovers, joining hands, sang with great earnestness and vociferation. I fear that a certain defiant tone and Covenanter's swing to its chorus, rather than any devotional quality, caused it speedily to infect the others, who at last joined in the refrain:—

> "I'm proud to live in the service of the Lord,
> And I'm bound to die in his army."

The pines rocked, the storm eddied and whirled above the miserable group, and the flames of their altar leaped heavenward, as if in token of the vow.

At midnight the storm abated, the rolling clouds parted, and the stars glittered keenly above the sleeping camp. Mr. Oakhurst, whose professional habits had enabled him to live on the smallest possible amount of sleep, in dividing the watch with Tom Simson somehow managed to take upon himself the greater part of that duty. He excused himself to the Innocent by saying that he had "often been a week without sleep." "Doing what?" asked Tom. "Poker!" replied Oakhurst sententiously. "When a man gets a streak of luck—nigger-luck—he don't get tired. The luck gives in first. Luck," continued the gambler reflectively, "is a mighty queer thing. All you know about it for certain is that it's bound to change. And it's finding out when it's going to change that makes you. We've had a streak of bad luck since we left Poker Flat—you come along, and, slap, you get into it, too. If you can hold your cards right along you're all right. For," added the gambler, with cheerful irrelevance—

> "'I'm proud to live in the service of the Lord,
> And I'm bound to die in his army.'"

The third day came, and the sun, looking through the white-curtained valley, saw the outcasts divide their slowly decreasing store of provisions for the morning meal. It was one of the peculiarities of that mountain climate that its rays diffused a kindly warmth over the wintry landscape, as if in regretful commiseration of the past. But it revealed drift on drift of snow piled high around the hut—a hopeless, uncharted, trackless sea of white lying below the rocky shores to which the castaways still clung. Through the marvelously clear air the smoke of the pastoral village of Poker Flat rose miles away. Mother Shipton saw it, and from a remote pinnacle of her rocky fastness hurled in that direction a final malediction. It was her last vituperative attempt, and perhaps for that reason was invested with a certain degree of sublimity. It did her good, she privately informed the Duchess. "Just you go out there and cuss, and see." She then set herself to the task of amusing "the child," as she and the Duchess were pleased to call Piney. Piney was no chicken, but it was a soothing and original theory of the pair thus to account for the fact that she didn't swear and wasn't improper.

When night crept up again through the gorges, the reedy notes of the accordian rose and fell in fitful spasms and long-drawn gasps by the flickering camp-fire. But music failed to fill entirely the aching void left by insufficient food, and a new diversion was proposed by Piney,—story-telling. Neither Mr. Oakhurst nor his female companions caring to relate their personal experiences, this plan would have failed too, but for the Innocent. Some months before he had chanced upon a stray copy of Mr. Pope's ingenious translation of the Iliad. He now proposed to narrate the principle incidents of that poem—having thoroughly mastered the argument and fairly forgotten the words—in the current vernacular of Sandy Bar. And so for the rest of that night the Homeric demigods again walked the earth. Trojan bully and wily Greek wrestled in the winds, and the great pines in the cañon seemed to bow to the wrath of the son of Peleus. Mr. Oakhurst listened with quiet satisfaction. Most especially was he interested in the fate of "Ash-heels," as the Innocent persisted in denominating the "swift-footed Achilles."

So, with small food and much of Homer and the accordian, a week passed over the heads of the outcasts. The sun again forsook them, and again from leaden skies the snowflakes were sifted over the land. Day by day closer around them drew the snowy circle, until at last they looked from their prison over drifted walls of dazzling white, that towered twenty feet above their heads. It became more and more difficult to replenish their fires, even from the fallen trees beside them, now half hidden in the drifts. And yet no one complained. The lovers turned from the dreary prospect and looked into each other's eyes, and were happy. Mr. Oakhurst settled himself coolly to the losing game before him. The Duchess, more cheerful than she had been, assumed the care of Piney. Only Mother Shipton—once the strongest of the party—seemed to sicken and fade. At midnight on the tenth day she called Oakhurst to her side. "I'm going," she said, in a voice of querulous weakness, "but don't say anything about it. Don't waken the kids. Take the bundle from under my head, and open it." Mr. Oakhurst did so. It contained Mother Shipton's rations for the last week, untouched. "Give 'em to the child," she said, pointing to the sleeping Piney. "You've starved yourself," said the gambler. "That's what they call it," said the woman querulously, as she lay down again, and, turning her face to the wall, passed quietly away.

The accordian and the bones were put aside that day, and Homer was forgotten. When the body of Mother Shipton had been committed to the snow, Mr. Oakhurst took the Innocent aside, and showed him a pair of snow-shoes, which he had fashioned from the old pack-saddle. "There's one chance in a hundred to save her yet," he said, pointing to Piney; "but it's there," he added, pointing toward Poker Flat. "If you can reach there in two days, she's safe." "And you?" asked Tom Simson. "I'll stay here," was the curt reply.

The lovers parted with a long embrace. "You are not going, too?" said the Duchess, as she saw Mr. Oakhurst apparently waiting to accompany him. "As far as the cañon," he replied. He turned suddenly and kissed the Duchess, leaving her pallid face aflame, and her trembling limbs rigid with amazement.

Night came, but not Mr. Oakhurst. It brought the storm again and the whirling snow. Then the Duchess, feeding the fire, found that some one had quietly piled beside the hut enough fuel to last a few days longer. The tears rose to her eyes, but she hid them from Piney.

The women slept but little. In the morning, looking into each other's faces, they read their fate. Neither spoke, but Piney, accepting the position of the stronger, drew near and placed her arm around the Duchess's waist. They kept this attitude for the rest of the day. That night the storm reached its greatest fury, and, rending asunder the protecting vines, invaded the very hut.

Toward morning they found themselves unable to feed the fire, which gradually died away. As the embers slowly blackened, the Duchess crept closer to Piney, and broke the silence of many hours: "Piney, can you pray?" "No, dear," said Piney simply. The Duchess, without knowing exactly why, felt relieved, and, putting her head upon Piney's shoulder, spoke no more. And so reclining, the younger and purer pillowing the head of her soiled sister upon her virgin breast. they fell asleep.

The wind lulled as if it feared to waken them. Feathery drifts of snow, shaken from the long pine boughs, flew like white winged birds, and settled about them as they slept. The moon through the rifted clouds looked down upon what had been the camp. But all human stain, all trace of earthly travail, was hidden beneath the spotless mantle mercifully flung from above.

They slept all that day and the next, nor did they waken when voices and footsteps broke the silence of the camp. And when pitying fingers brushed the snow from their wan faces, you could scarcely have told from the equal peace that dwelt upon them which was she that had sinned. Even the law of Poker Flat recognized this, and turned away, leaving them still locked in each other's arms.

But at the head of the gulch, on one of the largest pine trees, they found the deuce of clubs pinned to the bark with a bowie-knife. It bore the following, written in pencil in a firm hand:—

†

BENEATH THIS TREE
LIES THE BODY
OF
JOHN OAKHURST
WHO STRUCK A STREAK OF BAD LUCK
ON THE 23D OF NOVEMBER 1850,
AND
HANDED IN HIS CHECKS
ON THE 7TH DECEMBER 1850

‡

And pulseless and cold, with a derringer by his side and a bullet in his heart, though still calm as in life, beneath the snow lay he who was at once the strongest and yet the weakest of the outcasts of Poker Flat.

GERHART HAUPTMANN

GERHART HAUPTMANN (German, 1862-1946). Won early, and most lasting, fame as revolutionary naturalist with *The Weavers*, drama of social protest. In later years leaned to classicism and symbolism: *The Fool in Christ* (novel), *Iphegenia in Aulis* (play). Early social consciousness did not prevent his final association with Nazism.

THE WEAVERS

Enter Ansorge, an earthenware pan with soup in one hand, in the other a half-finished quarter-bushel basket.

Ansorge. Glad to see you again, Moritz!

Jaeger. Thank you, Father Ansorge—same to you!

Ansorge (shoving his pan into the oven). Why, lad, you look like a duke!

Old Baumert. Show him your watch, Moritz. An' he's got a new suit of clothes besides them he's on, an' thirty shillings in his purse.

Ansorge (shaking his head). Is that so? Well, well!

Emma (puts the potato-parings into a bag). I must be off; I'll maybe get a drop o' skim milk for these. *(Goes out.)*

Jaeger (the others hanging on his words). You know how you all used to be down on me. It was always: Wait, Moritz, till your soldiering time comes—you'll catch it then. But you see how well I've got on. At the end of the first half-year I had my good-conduct stripes. You've got to be willing—that's where the secret lies. I brushed the sergeant's boots; I groomed his horse; I fetched his beer. I was as sharp as a needle. Always ready, accouterments clean and shining—first at stables, first at roll-call, first in the saddle. And when the bugle sounded to the assault—why, then, blood and thunder, and ride to the devil with you!! I was as keen as a pointer. Says I to myself: There's no help for it now, my boy, it's got to be done; and I set my mind to it and did it. Till at last the major said before the whole squadron: There's a hussar, now, that shows you what a hussar should be!

(Silence. He lights his pipe.)

Ansorge (shaking his head). Well, well, well! You had luck with you, Moritz. *(Sits down on the floor, with his willow twigs beside him, and continues mending the basket, which he holds between his legs.)*

Old Baumert. Let's hope you've brought some of it to us.—Are we to have a drop to drink your health in?

Jaeger. Of course you are, Father Baumert. And when this bottle's done, we'll send for more. *(He flings a coin on the table.)*

Ansorge (open mouthed with amazement). Oh my! Oh my! What goings on, to be sure! Roast meat frizzlin' in the oven! A bottle o' brandy on the table! *(He drinks out of the bottle.)* Here's to you, Moritz!—Well, well, well!

(The bottle circulates freely after this.)

Old Baumert. If we could any way have a bit o' meat on Sundays and holidays. instead of never seein' the sight of it from year's end to year's end! Now we'll have to wait till another poor little dog finds its way into the house like this one did four weeks gone by—an' that's not likely to happen soon again.

Ansorge. Have you killed the little dog?

Old Baumert. We had to do that or starve.

Ansorge. Well, well!

Mother Baumert. A nice, kind little beast he was, too!

Jaeger. Are you as keen as ever on roast dog hereabouts?

Old Baumert. My word, if we could only get enough of it!

Mother Baumert. A nice little bit o' meat like that does you a lot o' good.

Old Baumert. Have you lost the taste for it, Moritz? Stay with us a bit, and it'll soon come back to you.

Ansorge (sniffing). Yes, yes! That will be a tasty bite—what a good smell it has!

Old Baumert (sniffing). Splendid!

Ansorge. Come, then, Moritz, tell us your opinion, you that's been out and seen the world. Are things at all like improving for us weavers, eh?

Jaeger. They would need to.

Ansorge. We're in an awful state here. It's not livin' an' it's not dyin'. A man fights to the bitter end, but he's bound to be beat at last—to be left without a room over his head, you may say without ground under his feet. As long as he can work at the loom he can earn some sort o' poor, miserable livin'. But it's many a day since I've been able to get that sort o' job. Now I tries to put a bite into my mouth with this here basket-makin'. I sits at it late into the night, and by the time I tumbles into bed I've earned three-halfpence. I put it to you if a man can live on that, when everything's so dear? Nine shillin' goes in one lump for house tax, three shillin' for land tax, nine shillin' for mortgage interest—that makes one pound one. I may reckon my year's earnin' at just double that money, and that leaves me twenty-one shillin' for a whole year's food, an' fire, an' clothes, an' shoes; and I've got to keep up some sort of a place to live in. Is it any wonder if I'm behindhand with my interest payments?

Old Baumert. Some one would need to go to Berlin an' tell the King how hard put to it we are.

Jaeger. Little good that would do, Father Baumert. There's been plenty written about it in the newspapers. But the rich people, they can turn and twist things round—as cunning as the devil himself.

Old Baumert (shaking his head). To think they've no more sense than that in Berlin!

Ansorge. And is it really true, Moritz? Is there no law to help us? If a man hasn't been able to scrape together enough to pay his mortgage interest, though he's worked the very skin off his hands, must his house be taken from him? The peasant that's lent the money on it, he wants his rights—what else can you look for from him? But what's to be the end of it all, I don't know. If I'm put out o' the house—*(In a voice choked by tears.)* I was born here, and here my father sat at his loom for more than forty year. Many was the time he said to mother: Mother, when I'm gone. the house'll still be here. I've worked hard for it. Every nail means a night's weaving, every plank a year's dry bread. A man would think that—

Jaeger. They're quite fit to take the last bite out of your mouth—that's what they are.

Ansorge. Well, well, well! I would rather be carried out than have to walk out now in my old days. Who minds dyin'? My father, he was glad to die. At the very end he got frightened, but I crept into bed beside him, an' he quieted down again. I was a lad of thirteen then. I was tired and fell asleep beside him—I knew no better—and when I woke he was quite cold.

Mother Baumert (after a pause). Give Ansorge his soup out o' the oven, Bertha.

Bertha. Here, Father Ansorge, it'll do you good.

Ansorge (eating and shedding tears). Well, well, well!

(Old Baumert has begun to eat meat out of the saucepan.)

Mother Baumert. Father, father, can't you have patience an' let Bertha serve it up properly?

Old Baumert (chewing). It's two years now since I took the sacrament. I went straight after that an' sold my Sunday coat, an' we bought a good bit o' pork, an' since then never a mouthful of meat has passed my lips till to-night.

Jaeger. How should *we* need meat? The manufacturers eat it for us. It's the fat of the land *they* live on. Whoever doesn't believe that has only to go down to Bielau and Peterswaldau. He'll see fine things there—palace upon palace, with towers and iron railings and plate-glass windows. Who do they all belong to? Why, of course, the manufacturers! No signs of bad times there! Baked and boiled and fried—horses and carriages and governesses—they've money to pay for all that and goodness knows how much more. They're swelled out to bursting with pride and good living.

Ansorge. Things was different in my young days. Then the manufacturers let the weaver have his share. Now they keep everything to theirselves. An' would you like to know what's at the bottom of it all? It's that the fine folks nowadays believes neither in God nor devil. What do they care about commandments or punishments? And so they steal our last scrap o' bread, and leave us no chance of earnin' the barest living. For it's their fault. If our manufacturers was good men, there would be no bad times for us.

Jaeger. Listen, then, and I'll read you something that will please you. *(He takes one or two loose papers from his pocket.)* I say, August, run and fetch another quart from the public house. Eh, boy, do you laugh all day long?

Mother Baumert. No one knows why, but our August's always happy—grins an' laughs, come what may. Off with you then, quick! *(Exit August with the empty brandy bottle.)* You've got something good now, eh, father?

Old Baumert (still chewing; spirits rising from the effect of food and drink). Moritz, you're the very man we want. You can read an' write. You understand the weaving trade, and you've a heart to feel for the poor weaver's sufferin's. You should stand up for us here.

Jaeger. I'd do that quick enough! There's nothing I'd like better than to give the manufacturers round here a bit of a fright—dogs that they are! I'm an easy-going fellow, but let me once get worked up into a real rage, and I'll take Dreissiger in the one hand and Dittrich in the other, and knock their heads together till the sparks fly out of their eyes.—If we could only arrange all to join together, we'd soon give the manufacturers a proper lesson—without help from King or Government—all we'd have to do would be to say, We want this and that, and we don't want the other thing. There would be a change of days then. As soon as they see that there's some pluck in us, they'll cave in. I know the rascals; they're a pack of cowardly hounds.

Mother Baumert. There's some truth in what you say. I'm not an ill-natured woman. I've always been the one to say as how there must be rich folks as well as poor. But when things comes to such a pass as this—

Jaeger. The devil may take them all, for what I care. It would be no more than they deserve.

(Old Baumert has quietly gone out.)

Bertha. Where's father?

Mother Baumert. I don't know where he can have gone.

Bertha. Do you think he's not been able to stomach the meat, with not gettin' none for so long?

Mother Baumert (in distress, crying). There now, there! He's not even able to keep it down when he's got it. Up it comes again, the only bite o' good food as he's tasted this many a day.

Reënter Old Baumert, crying with rage.

Old Baumert. It's no good! I'm too far gone! Now that I've at last got hold of somethin' with a taste in it, my stomach won't keep it. *(He sits down on the bench by the stove, crying.)*

Jaeger (with a sudden violent ebullition of rage). And yet there are people not far from here, justices they call themselves too, over-fed brutes, that have nothing to do all the year round but invent new ways of wasting their time. And these people say that the weavers would be quite well off if only they weren't so lazy.

Ansorge. The men as say that are no men at all, they're monsters.

Jaeger. Never mind, Father Ansorge; we're making the place hot for 'em. Becker and I have been and given Dreissiger a piece of our mind, and before we came away we sang him "Bloody Justice."

Ansorge. Good Lord! Is that the song?

Jaeger. Yes; I have it here.

Ansorge. They call it Dreissiger's song, don't they?

Jaeger. I'll read it to you.

Mother Baumert. Who wrote it?

Jaeger. That's what nobody knows. Now listen.

(He reads, hesitating like a schoolboy, with incorrect accentuation, but unmistakably strong feeling. Despair, suffering, rage, hatred, thirst for revenge, all find utterance.

The justice to us weavers dealt
    Is bloody, cruel, and hateful;
Our life's one torture, long drawn out:
    For Lynch law we'd be grateful.

Stretched on the rack day after day,
    Hearts sick and bodies aching,
Our heavy sighs their witness bear
    To spirit slowly breaking.

(The words of the song make a strong impression on Old Baumert. Deeply agitated, he struggles against the temptation to interrupt Jaeger. At last he can keep quiet no longer.)

Old Baumert (to his wife, half laughing, half crying, stammering). Stretched on the rack day after day. Whoever wrote that, mother,

547

wrote the truth. You can bear witness—eh, how does it go? "Our heavy sighs their witness bear"—what's the rest?

Jaeger. "To spirit slowly breaking."

Old Baumert. You know the way we sigh, mother, day and night, sleepin' and wakin'.

(Ansorge has stopped working, and cowers on the floor, strongly agitated. Mother Baumert and Bertha wipe their eyes frequently during the course of the reading.

Jaeger (continues to read)—

The Dreissigers true hangmen are,
  Servants no whit behind them;
Masters and men with one accord
  Set on the poor to grind them.

You villains all, you brood of hell!—

Old Baumert (trembling with rage, stamping on the floor)—
Yes, brood of hell!!!

Jaeger (reads)—
You fiends in fashion human,
A curse will fall on all like you,
  Who prey on man and woman.

Ansorge. Yes, yes, a curse upon them!

Old Baumert (clenching his fist, threateningly). You prey on man and woman.

Jaeger (reads)—

The suppliant knows he asks in vain,
  Vain every word that's spoken.
"If not content, then go and starve—
  Our rules cannot be broken."

Old Baumert. What is it? "The suppliant knows he asks in vain"? Every word of it's true—every word—as true as the Bible. He knows he asks in vain.

Ansorge. Yes, yes! It's all no good.

Jaeger (reads)—

Then think of all our woe and want,
  O ye who hear this ditty!
Our struggle vain for daily bread
  Hard hearts would move to pity.

548

But pity's what *you've* never known,--
   You'd take both skin and clothing,
You cannibals, whose cruel deeds
   Fill all good men with loathing.

Old Baumert (jumps up, beside himself with excitement). Both skin and clothing. It's true, it's all true! Here I stand, Robert Baumert, master-weaver, of Kaschbach. Who can bring up anything against me?—I've been an honest, hard-working man all my life long, an' look at me now! What have I to show for it? Look at me! See what they've made of me! Stretched on the rack day after day. *(He holds out his arms.)* Feel that! Skin and bone! "You villains all, you brood of hell!!" *(He sinks down on a chair, weeping with rage and despair.)*

Ansorge (flings his basket from him into a corner, rises, his whole body trembling with rage, gasps). And the time's come now for a change, I say. We'll stand it no longer! We'll stand it no longer! Come what may!

NATHANIEL HAWTHORNE

NATHANIEL HAWTHORNE (American, 1804-1864). Classic American novelist of New England. Housebound by boyhood leg injury. Worked as adult for port of Salem, became U.S. Consul abroad. Puritan heritage centers his novels about problems of guilt and moral pride. Most famous: *The Scarlet Letter*. Others: *The House of the Seven Gables, The Marble Faun, The Blithedale Romance, Twice-Told Tales*

THE AMBITIOUS GUEST

One September night a family had gathered round their hearth and piled it high with the driftwood of mountain streams, the dry cones of the pine, and the splintered ruins of great trees, that had come crashing down the precipice. Up the chimney roared the fire, and brightened the room with its broad blaze. The faces of the father and mother had a sober gladness; the children laughed. The eldest daughter was the image of Happiness at seventeen, and the aged grandmother, who sat knitting in the warmest place, was the image of Happiness grown old. They had found the "herb heart's-ease" in the bleakest spot of all New England. This family were situated in the Notch of the White Hills, where the wind was sharp throughout the year and piteously cold in the winter, giving their cottage all its fresh inclemency before it descended on the valley of the Saco. They dwelt in a cold spot and a dangerous one, for a mountain towered above their heads so steep that the stones would often rumble down its sides and startle them at midnight.

The daughter had just uttered some simple jest that filled them all with mirth, when the wind came through the Notch and seemed to pause before their cottage, rattling the door with a sound of wailing and lamentation before it passed into the valley. For a moment it saddened them, though there was nothing unusual in the tones. But the family were glad again when they perceived that the latch was lifted by some traveler whose footsteps had been unheard amid the dreary blast which heralded his approach and wailed as he was entering, and went moaning away from the door.

Though they dwelt in such a solitude, these people held daily converse with the world. The romantic pass of the Notch is a great artery through which the life-blood of internal commerce is continually throbbing between Maine on one side and the Green Mountains and the shores of the St. Lawrence on the other. The stage coach always drew up before the door of the cottage. The wayfarer with no companion but his staff paused here to exchange a word, that the sense of loneliness might not utterly overcome him ere he could pass through the cleft of the mountain or reach the first house in the valley. And here the teamster on his way to Portland market would put up for the night, and, if a bachelor, might sit an hour beyond the usual bedtime and steal a kiss from the mountain maid at parting. It was one of those primitive taverns where the traveler pays only for food and lodging, but meets with a homely kindness beyond all price. When the footsteps were heard, therefore, between the outer door and the inner one, the whole family rose up, grandmother, children, and all as if about to welcome someone who belonged to them, and whose fate was linked with theirs.

The door was opened by a young man. His face at first wore the melancholy expression, almost despondency, of one who travels a wild and bleak road at nightfall and alone, but soon brightened up when he saw the kindly warmth of his reception. He felt his heart spring forward to meet them all, from the old woman who wiped the chair with her apron to the little child that held out its arms to him. One glance and smile placed the stranger on a footing of innocent familiarity with the oldest daughter.

"Ah! this fire is the right thing," cried he, "especially when there is such a pleasant circle around it. I am quite benumbed, for the Notch is just like the pipe of a great pair of bellows; it has blown a terrible blast in my face all the way from Bartlett."

"Then you are going toward Vermont?" said the master of the house as he helped to take a light knapsack off the young man's shoulders.

"Yes, to Burlington, and far enough beyond," replied he. "I meant to have been at Ethan Crawford's tonight, but a pedestrian lingers along such a road as this. It is no matter; for when I saw this good fire and all your cheerful faces, I felt as if you had kindled it on purpose for me and were waiting my arrival. So I shall sit down among you and make myself at home."

The frank-hearted stranger had just drawn his chair to the fire when something like a heavy footstep was heard without, rushing down the steep side of the mountain as with long and rapid strides, and taking such a leap in passing the cottage as to strike the opposite precipice. The family held their breath, because they knew the sound, and their guest held his by instinct.

"The old mountain has thrown a stone at us for fear we should forget him," said the landlord, recovering himself. "He sometimes nods his head and threatens to come down, but we are old neighbors, and agree together pretty well upon the whole. Besides, we have a sure place of refuge hard by if he should be coming in good earnest."

Let us now suppose the stranger to have finished his supper of bear's meat, and by his natural felicity of manner to have placed himself on a footing of kindness with the whole family; so that they talked as freely together as if he belonged to their mountain brood. He was of a proud yet gentle spirit, haughty and reserved among the rich and great, but ever ready to stoop his head to the lowly cottage door and be like a brother or a son at the poor man's fireside. In the household of the Notch he found warmth and simplicity of feeling, the pervading intelligence of New England, and a poetry of native growth which they had gathered when they little thought of it from the mountain-peaks and chasms, and at the very threshold of their romantic and dangerous abode. He had traveled far and alone; his whole life, indeed, had been a solitary path, for, with the lofty caution of his nature, he had kept himself apart from

551

those who might otherwise have been his companions. The family, too, though so kind and hospitable, had that consciousness of unity among themselves and separation from the world at large which in every domestic circle should still keep a holy place where no stranger may intrude. But this evening a prophetic sympathy impelled the refined and educated youth to pour out his heart before the simple mountaineers, and constrained them to answer him with the same free confidence. And thus it should have been. Is not the kindred of a common fate a closer tie than that of birth?

The secret of the young man's character was a high and abstracted ambition. He could have borne to live an undistinguished life, but not to be forgotten in the grave. Yearning desire had been transformed to hope, and hope, long cherished, had become like certainty that, obscurely as he journeyed now, a glory was to beam on all his pathway, though not, perhaps, while he was treading it. But when present, they would trace the brightness of his footsteps, brightening as meaner glories faded, and confess that a gifted one had passed from his cradle to his tomb with none to recognize him.

"As yet," cried the stranger, his cheek glowing and his eye flashing with enthusiasm— "as yet I have done nothing. Were I to vanish from the earth tomorrow, none would know so much of me as you—that a nameless youth came up at nightfall from the valley of the Saco, and opened his heart to you in the evening, and passed through the Notch by sunrise, and was seen no more. Not a soul would ask, 'Who was he? Whither did the wanderer go?' But I cannot die till I have achieved my destiny. Then let Death come; I shall have built my monument."

There was a continual flow of natural emotion gushing forth amid abstracted reverie which enabled the family to understand this young man's sentiments, though so foreign from their own. With quick sensibility of the ludicrous, he blushed at the ardor into which he had been betrayed.

"You laugh at me," said he, taking the eldest daughter's hana and laughing himself. "You think my ambition as nonsensical as if I were to freeze myself to death on the top of Mount Washington only that people might spy at me from the country roundabout. And truly that would be a noble pedestal for a man's statue."

"It is better to sit here by this fire," answered the girl, blushing, "and be comfortable and contented, though nobody thinks about us."

"I suppose," said her father, after a fit of musing, "there is something natural in what the young man says; and if my mind had been turned that way, I might have felt just the same. It is strange, wife, how his talk has set my head running on things that are pretty certain never to come to pass."

"Perhaps they may," observed the wife. "Is the man thinking what he will do when he is a widower?"

"No, no!" cried he, repelling the idea with reproachful kindness. "When I think of your death, Esther, I think of mine, too. But I was wishing we had a good farm in Bartlett or Bethlehem or Littleton, or some other township round the White Mountains, but not where they could tumble on our heads. I should want to stand well with my neighbors and be called squire and sent to General Court for a term or two; for a plain, honest man may do as much good there as a lawyer. And when I should be grown quite an old man, and you an old woman, so as not to be long apart, I might die happy enough in my bed, and leave you all crying around me. A slate gravestone would suit me as well as a marble one, with just my name and age, and a verse of a hymn, and something to let people know that I lived an honest man and died a Christian."

"There, now!" exclaimed the stranger; "it is our nature to desire a monument, be it slate or marble, or a pillar of granite, or a glorious memory in the universal heart of man."

"We're in a strange way tonight," said the wife, with tears in her eyes. "They say it's a sign of something when folks' minds go a-wandering so. Hark to the children!"

They listened accordingly. The younger children had been put to bed in another room, but with an open door between; so that they could be heard talking busily among themselves. One and all seemed to have caught the infection from the fireside circle, and were outvying each other in wild wishes and childish projects of what they would do when they came to be men and women. At length a little boy, instead of addressing his brothers and sisters, called out to his mother:

"I'll tell you what I wish, mother," cried he: "I want you and father and grandma'm, and all of us, and the stranger, too, to start right away and go and take a drink out of the basin of the Flume."

Nobody could help laughing at the child's notion of leaving a warm bed and dragging them from a cheerful fire to visit the basin of the Flume—a brook which tumbles over the precipe deep within the Notch.

553

The boy had hardly spoken, when a wagon rattled along the road and stopped a moment before the door. It appeared to contain two or three men who were cheering their hearts with the rough chorus of a song which resounded in broken notes between the cliffs, while the singers hesitated whether to continue their journey or put up here for the night.

"Father," said the girl, "they are calling you by name."

But the good man doubted whether they had really called him, and was unwilling to show himself too solicitous of gain by inviting people to patronize his house. He therefore did not hurry to the door, and, the lash being soon applied, the travelers plunged into the Notch, still singing and laughing, though their music and mirth came back drearily from the heart of the mountain.

"There, mother!" cried the boy again; "they'd have given us a ride to the Flume."

Again they laughed at the child's pertinacious fancy for a night ramble. But it happened that a light cloud passed over the daughter's spirit; she looked gravely into the fire and drew a breath that was almost a sigh. It forced its way, in spite of a little struggle to repress it. Then, starting and blushing, she looked quickly around the circle, as if they had caught a glimpse into her bosom. The stranger asked what she had been thinking of.

"Nothing," answered she, with a downcast smile; "only I felt lonesome just then."

"Oh, I have always had a gift of feeling what is in other people's hearts," said he, half seriously. "Shall I tell the secrets of yours? For I know what to think when a young girl shivers by a warm hearth and complains of lonesomeness at her mother's side. Shall I put these feelings into words?"

"They would not be a girl's feelings any longer if they could be put into words," replied the mountain nymph, laughing, but avoiding his eye.

All this was said apart. Perhaps a germ of love was springing in their hearts so pure that it might blossom in Paradise, since it could not be matured on earth; for women worship such gentle dignity as his, and the proud, contemplative, yet kindly, soul is oftenest captivated by simplicity like hers. But while they spoke softly, and he was watching the happy sadness, the lightsome shadows, the shy yearnings of a maiden's nature, the wind through the Notch took a deeper and drearier sound. It seemed, as the fanciful stranger said, like the choral strain of the spirits of the blast who in old Indian times had their dwelling among these mountains, and made their heights and recesses a sacred region. There was a wail along the road as if a funeral were passing. To chase away the gloom, the family threw pine-branches on their fire till the dry leaves crackled and the flame arose, discovering once again a scene of peace and humble happiness. The light hovered about them fondly and caressed them all. There were the little faces of the children peeping from their bed apart, and here the father's frame of strength, the mother's subdued and careful mien, the high-browed youth, the budding girl, and the good old grandam still knitting in the warmest place.

The aged woman looked up from her task, and with fingers ever busy was the next to speak.

"Old folks have their notions," said she, "as well as young ones. You've been wishing and planning and letting your heads run on one thing and another till you've set my mind a-wandering too. Now, what should an old woman wish for when she can go but a step or two before she comes to her grave? Children, it will haunt me night and day till I tell you."

"What is it, mother?" cried the husband and wife, at once.

Then the old woman, with an air of mystery which drew the circle closer round the fire, informed them that she had provided her grave-clothes some years before—a nice linen shroud, a cap with a muslin ruff, and everything of a finer sort than she had worn since her wedding day. But this evening an old superstition had strangely recurred to her. It used to be said in her younger days that if anything were amiss with a corpse, if only the ruff were not smooth or the cap did not set right, the corpse, in the coffin and beneath the clods, would strive to put up its cold hands and arrange it. The bare thought made her nervous.

"Don't talk so, grandmother," said the girl, shuddering.

"Now," continued the old woman with singular earnestness, yet smiling strangely at her own folly, "I want one of you, my children, when your mother is dressed and in the coffin,—I want one of you to hold a looking-glass over my face. Who knows but I may take a glimpse at myself, and see whether all's right."

"Old and young, we dream of graves and monuments," murmured the stranger youth. "I wonder how mariners feel when the ship is sinking and they, unknown and undistinguished, are to be buried together in the ocean, that wide and nameless sepulcher?"

For a moment the old woman's ghastly conception so engrossed the minds of her hearers that a sound abroad in the night, rising like the roar of a blast, had grown broad, deep and terrible before the fated group were conscious of it. The house and all within it trembled; the foundations of the earth seemed to be shaken, as if this awful sound were the peal of the last trump. Young and old exchanged one wild glance and remained an instant pale, affrighted, without utterance or power to move. Then the same shriek burst simultaneously from all their lips:

"The slide! The slide!"

The simplest words must intimate, but not portray, the unutterable horror of the catastrophe. The victims rushed from their cottage, and sought refuge in what they deemed a safer spot, where, in contemplation of such an emergency, a sort of barrier had been reared. Alas! they had quitted their security and fled right into the pathway of destruction. Down came the whole side of the mountain in a cataract of ruin. Just before it reached the house the stream broke into two branches, shivered not a window there, but overwhelmed the whole vicinity, blocked up the road and and annihilated everything in its dreadful course. Long ere the thunder of that great slide had ceased to roar among the mountains the mortal agony had been endured and the victims were at peace. Their bodies were never found.

The next morning the light smoke was seen stealing from the cottage chimney, up the mountain-side. Within, the fire was yet smoldering on the hearth, and the chairs in a circle round it, as if the inhabitants had but gone forth to view the devastation of the slide, and would shortly return to thank Heaven for their miraculous escape. All had left separate tokens by which those who had known the family were made to shed a tear for each. Who has not heard their name? The story has been told far and wide, and will forever be a legend of these mountains. Poets have sung their fate.

There were circumstances which led some to suppose that a stranger had been received into the cottage on this awful night, and had shared the catastrophe of all its inmates; others denied that there were sufficient grounds for such a conjecture. Woe for the high souled youth with his dream of earthly immortality! His name and person utterly unknown, his history, his way of life, his plans, a mystery never to be solved, his death and his existence equally a doubt,—whose was the agony of that death moment?

556

JOHANN PETER HEBEL

JOHANN PETER HEBEL (German, 1760-1826). German poet and storyteller. Son of a servant, became teacher and prelate. Goethe considered him among greatest dialect poets. Published annual almanac of stories and anecdotes *(Schatzkästlein des Rheinischen Hausfreundes)*, from which he collected the volume that established his fame.

KANNITVERSTAN

IN EMMENDINGEN and Gundelfingen, as well as in Amsterdam, a man has the opportunity every day, I dare say, to reflect on the inconstancy of all earthly things—if he wants to—and to learn how to be satisfied with his lot even though life is no bed of roses. But it was by the oddest roundabout route that a German journeyman in Amsterdam came, through error, to the perception of this truth.

After he had come to that great and prosperous city of commerce, full of splendid houses, heaving ships, and busy people, his eye fell upon a house larger and more beautiful than any he had ever seen on all his travels from Tuttlingen to Amsterdam. For a long time he gazed in wonder at this costly building, at the six chimneys on its roof, at its beautiful cornices, and at the high windows, each larger than the front door to his father's house.

Finally, yielding to an impulse, he addressed a passer-by. "My good friend," he asked, "can you tell me the name of the gentleman who owns this marvelous house with the windows full of tulips, asters, and gilliflowers?" But the man, who probably had something more important to attend to and, unfortunately, understood just as much German as his questioner did Dutch—to wit, nothing—growled: *"Kannitverstan,"* and whisked by. This is a Dutch word—or three of them, if one looks at it properly—and means no more than "I cannot understand you."

But the good stranger thought it to be the name of the gentleman he'd asked about. "That must be a mighty rich man, that Mr. Kannitverstan," he said to himself, and walked on.

Making his way through the narrow streets, he came at length to the estuary that is called Het Ey, meaning "the Y." There stood ship after ship and mast after mast, and he was beginning to wonder how he could ever manage to take in all of these marvels with his own two eyes, when his glance fell upon a large merchantman that

557

recently had put in from the East Indies and was being unloaded. Whole rows of piled crates and bales stood side by side on the wharf, and more were being rolled out: casks full of sugar and coffee, full of rice and pepper, and with them—pardon—mouse droppings too.

After he had watched for a long time, he asked a fellow who was carrying a crate on his shoulders the name of the fortunate man to whom the sea had brought all these wares. *"Kannitverstan,"* was the answer.

Then he thought: "Aha, so that's how it is! If the sea floats him such riches, no wonder he can put up houses with gilt-potted tulips in the windows." So he went away, sorrowfully reflecting how poor a man he was among so many rich people in this world. But just as he was thinking: "I wish I, too, would be as well off some day as this Mr. Kannitverstan," he turned a corner and saw a great funeral procession. Four black-draped horses were pulling a black-covered hearse slowly and lugubriously, as though they were aware they were carrying a dead man to his peace. A long cortege of friends and acquaintances of the departed followed behind, pair after pair, muffled in black cloaks, and mute. A solitary bell sounded in the distance. Our stranger was seized by the melancholy feeling that no good man can suppress at the sight of a funeral, and he remained standing reverently, with his hat in his hands, until all was over. Then he attached himself to the last mourner (who was just figuring how much he would make on his cotton if the bale price should rise ten florins), tugged at his coat, guilelessly begged his pardon, and said: "He must indeed have been a good friend of yours, the gentleman for whom the bell is tolling, that you follow his coffin so grieved and pensive."

"Kannitverstan," was the answer.

A few large tears descended from the eyes of our good journeyman from Tuttlingen, and he felt sad and relieved at once. "Poor Kannitverstan," he exclaimed, "what have you now of all your riches? Exactly what I shall get one day from my poverty: a linen shroud! And of all your beautiful flowers, you have, perhaps, a rosemary on your cold breast, or some rue." With these thoughts he accompanied the funeral procession to the grave as though he belonged with it, and saw the supposed Mr. Kannitverstan sink down to his final resting-place, and was more moved by the Dutch funeral oration, of which he understood not a word, than by many a German one to which he had paid no attention.

558

He left with the others and went away with a light heart, and at an inn where German was understood, he ate, with relish, a piece of Limburg cheese. And whenever afterward his heart became heavy because so many people in this world were so rich and he was so poor, he only thought of Mr. Kannitverstan of Amsterdam—of his big house, his opulent ship, and his narrow grave.

HEINRICH HEINE

HEINRICH HEINE (German, 1797-1856). Greatest lyricist in the German tongue. Regarded as leader of Young Germany. Settled in Paris, and interpreted French and Germans to each other. A hasty convert who remained a tender admirer of Judaism and acid critic of Christianity all his life. Noted for his irony, wit, mercurial intelligence. Famous poems: *"Die Lorelei,"* *"Du Bist Wie eine Blume."*

SONGS

Thou Who Art So Fair and Pure

Thou, so fair, so pure of guile,
Maiden of the sunny smile
Would to thee it were my fate
All my life to dedicate!

Like the moonbeams' tender shine
Gleam these gentle eyes of thine;
Thy soft cheeks so ruddy bright
Scatter rays of rosy light.

Thy dear little mouth doth show
Pearls within, a shining row;
But the gem of gems the best
Is enshrined within thy breast.

It was love divinely deep,
That into my heart did leap,
When I looked on thee erewhile,
Maiden of the sunny smile!

Alone with the anguish that tore me
    'Neath the forest boughs I stept;
Anon came the old dream o'er me,
    And into my heart it crept.

Who taught ye this word, not to fear it,
    Little birds, singing up there so free?
Oh, hush! if my heart should hear it,
    Very sad it again would be.

"This way came a fair girl, she taught it;
    As she sang it, it was all we heard;
And up we little birds caught it,
    The dainty-sweet golden word."

Never think with such fables to wile me!
    Little birds, ye are wondrously sly;
You wish of my grief to beguile me,
    But I trust nothing living, not I.

The Two Grenadiers

For France two grenadiers held their way,
    Had prisoners been in Russia;
And sorrowful men they were, when they
    The frontier reached of Prussia.

For there they heard of a dire event,—
    How the world 'gainst France had risen, her
Grande armée had shattered and shent,
    And taken her Emperor prisoner.

They mingled their tears, these two grenadiers,
    To the sad tale ever returning;
"Oh would," said one, "that my days were done!
My old wounds, how they're burning!"

"All's up!" said the other; "and sooner than not
    I would die like you, never doubt me;
But a wife and child at home I've got,
    And they must be starved without me!"

"Hang wife and child! It is something more,
    And better far, that I pant for;
My Emperor prisoner! My Emperor!
    Let them go beg what they want for!

"If I die just now, as 'tis like I may,
    Then, comrade, this boon grant me,
Take my body with you to France away,
    And in France's dear earth plant me.

"The *Croix d'Honneur*, with its crimson band,
    On my heart see that you place it;
Then give me my rifle in my hand,
    And my sword, around me to brace it.

"So will I lie, and listen all ear,
    Like a sentinel, low in my bed there,
Till the roar of the cannon some day I hear,
    And the chargers' neigh and their tread there.

"Then I'll know 'tis my Emperor riding by;
    The sabres flash high that attend him,
And out from my grave full-armed spring I
    The Emperor! to shield and defend him!"

Whene'er I Look into Thine Eyes

Whene'er I look into thine eyes,
Then every fear that haunts me flies;
But when I kiss thy mouth, oh then
I feel a giant's strength again.

Whene'er I couch me on thy breast,
I know what heaven is to the blest;
But when thou sayest, "I love thee!"
Then must I weep, and bitterly.

Thou Lovest Me Not

My love you cannot, cannot brook!
    I don't let that distress me;
So I but on thy face may look,
    In that's enough to bless me.

561

You hate, you hate, you hate me! is
  Your rosy-red mouth's greeting:
But let me have that mouth to kiss,
  And I'm content, my sweeting!

A Pine-Tree Stands Alone

A pine-tree stands alone on
  A bare bleak northern height;
The ice and snow they swathe it,
  As it sleeps there, all in white.

'Tis dreaming of a palm-tree,
  In a far-off Eastern land,
That mourns, alone and silent,
  On a ledge of burning sand.

My Songs Are Poisoned!

My songs, they are poisoned—poisoned!
  How otherwise could it be?
Over the flowers of my life's fresh hours
  Has poison been poured by thee.

My songs, they are poisoned—poisoned!
  How otherwise could it be?
Many serpents I bear in my heart, and there
  I bear with them, thee, love, thee.

In Dreams, Oh, I Have Wept, Love!

In dreams, oh, I have wept, love!
  I dreamed in the grave you were laid;
I awoke, and my cheek was wet, love,
  And tears still adown it strayed.

In dreams, oh, I have wept, love!
  I dreamt you were false to me;
I awoke, and I went on weeping
  Long, long and bitterly.

562

In dreams, oh, I have wept, love!
  I dreamed you still held me dear;
I awoke, and unto this hour, love,
  Weep many a scalding tear.

The Loreley

I cannot tell what's coming o'er me,
  That makes me so eerie and low:
An old-world legend before me,
  Keeps rising, and will not go.

The air chills, day is declining,
  And smoothly Rhine's waters run,
And the peaks of the mountains are shining
  Aloft in the setting sun.

A maiden of wondrous seeming,
  Most beautiful, sits up there;
Her jewels in gold are gleaming,
  She combs out her golden hair.

With a comb of red gold she parts it,
  And still as she combs it, she sings;
Her song pierces home to our hearts, it
  Has tones of a sweetness that stings.

The boatman, he thrills as he hears it
  Out there in his little skiff:
He sees not the reef as he nears it,
  He only looks up to the cliff.

The waters will sweep, I am thinking,
  O'er skiff, and o'er boatman ere long;
And this is, when daylight is sinking,
  What Loreley did with her song.

Thou Lovely Fisher-Maiden

My bonnie blithe fisher-maiden,
  Row in your boat to the strand;
Come here and sit down beside me,
  And chat with me hand in hand.

563

Rest your dear little head on my bosom,
    And be not so frightened, child;
Every day you trust without thinking
    Yourself to the ocean wild.

My heart is quite like the ocean,
    It has tempests, and ebb, and flow;
And fine pearls lie there a-many,
    Down, down in its depths below.

Thou Art Even as a Flower Is

Thou art even as a flower is,
    So gentle, and pure, and fair;
I gaze on thee, and sadness
    Comes over my heart unaware.

I feel as though I should lay, sweet,
    My hands on thy head, with a prayer
That God may keep thee alway, sweet,
    As gentle, and pure, and fair!

Oh, the Sweet Lies Lurk in Kisses!

Oh, the sweet lies lurk in kisses!
    Oh, the charm of make-believe!
Oh, to be deceived sweet bliss is,
    Bliss still sweeter to deceive!

What thou'lt grant, I know, my fairest,
    Vowing, "Nay, I never must!"
I will trust whate'er thou swearest,
    I will swear what thou wilt trust.

The Shades of the Summer Evening

The shades of the summer evening lie
    On forest and meadows green;
The golden moon shines in the azure sky
    Through balm-breathing air serene.

The cricket is chirping, the brooklet near,
   In the water a something stirs,
And the wanderer can in the stillness hear
   A plash and a sigh through the furze.

There all by herself the fairy bright
   Is bathing down in the stream;
Her arms and throat, betwitching and white,
   In the moonshine glance and gleam.

There Was an Aged King

There was an aged king,
   His heart was heavy, his locks were grey;
This poor old king, he wedded
   A maiden young and gay.

There was a pretty foot-page,
   His looks were fair, and his heart was light;
The sammet train he carried
   Of that queen so young and bright.

Dost know the old, old story?
   So sweet in the telling, so sad to tell!
They had both to die, oh the pity!
   They had loved each other too well.

MEMOIRS

Little Veronica

   Whether it be because of the rhythmic beat of the oars, or the
swaying of the boat, or the fragrance of the hills of the river bank,
where joy doth grow, it always comes to pass that the most troubled
spirit finds peace in floating lightly in a little boat on the bosom of
the dear, clear river Rhine. In truth, kind old Father Rhine cannot
endure his children weeping; to stay their tears he takes them in
his trusty arms and rocks them and tells them his most lovely tales

565

and promises them his most golden treasures, perhaps even the hoard of the Niblungs sunk there in the dim distant past. . . .

O! it is a fair country full of loveliness and sunshine. The hills of the river bank are mirrored in the blue stream with their ruined castles and woods and ancient towns. There on their thresholds sit the townsfolk in the summer evenings and drink out of great mugs, and gossip, how the vines flourish, thank God, and how trials must be held in public, and how Marie Antoinette had been guillotined without more ado, and how the tobacco monopoly had raised the price of tobacco, and how all men are equal, and what a capital fellow Görres is.

For my part I never bothered about such conversations, but much preferred to sit with the girls in the arched window and laugh as they laughed, and have flowers thrown in my face and pretend to be angry, until they told me their secrets or some other vastly important story. The fair Gertrude could scarcely contain her delight when I sat with her; she was like a flaming rose, and when she fell upon my neck I used to think she would burst into flame and go off in smoke in my arms. The fair Catherine used to melt away in tender melody, when she talked to me, and her eyes were of a blue pure and sweet such as I have never found in human beings or beasts and only very rarely in flowers; it was lovely to look upon them, and so many sweet thoughts would come into my head as I gazed. But the fair Hedwig loved me; for when I came to her she bowed her head so that her black tresses fell over her blushing face, and her bright eyes shone like stars in the dark sky. Never a word came from her modest lips, and I, too, had nothing to say to her. I coughed, and she trembled. Often she would beg me through her sisters not to climb the rocks so fast, and not to bathe in the Rhine when I was hot with running or had been drinking. I used to listen sometimes when she prayed devoutly before the little picture of the Virgin Mary, which, spangled with gold, and lit up by a little flickering lamp, stood in a niche of the hall of the house. I heard clearly how she prayed the Mother of God to forbid Him to climb and drink and bathe. I might have loved her if she had been indifferent to me; and I was indifferent to her because I knew that she loved me.

The fair Johanna was a cousin of the three sisters; I liked much to be with her. She knew the most beautiful stories, and when she reached out of the window with her white hand towards the hills, where all the happenings of the story had been, a spell was cast over me and I could see the old knights coming out of the ruined castles and hacking away at each other's armour, and the Lorelei stood once more on the hill-top and sang her sweet, seductive song, and the Rhine lapped so peacefully, so wisely, and yet with such dreadful mocking—and the fair Johanna looked at me strangely, as warily, and as mysteriously brooding as though she herself belonged to the fairy world of which she told. She was a slim, pale girl; she was consumptive and had long, long thoughts; her eyes were clear as truth; her lips pious and arched; in her features was a great story, but a sacred story—perhaps a legend of love? I know not, and I never had the courage to ask her. When I gazed for long upon her, I became peaceful and glad, and it was as though there were Sunday in my breast, and the angels were holding divine service in it.

At such times I used to tell her stories of my childhood, and she always listened gravely, and, strange, when I could not remember the names, she used to call them to mind for me. When I asked her in my astonishment how she knew the names, she used to smile and tell me by way of answer that the birds had told her who had made their nest in the eaves of her window; and she would have me believe that they were the very same birds which, as a boy, I had once bought from the cruel peasant children with my pocket-money to let them fly away. But I believe that she knew everything, because she was so pale and died so young. She knew also when she was to die, and wished me to leave Andenach the day before. When I left her, she gave me both her hands—they were clear, white hands and pure as the Host—and said: "You are very kind, and when you are angry, think of little Veronica, who is no more."

First Impressions in Paris

I had done and suffered much, and when the sun of the July Revolution rose in France I was very weary and stood in need of some relaxation. The air of my own country was every day more unwholesome for me, and I had seriously to think of a change of climate, and I had visions; the clouds oppressed me and cut all sorts of terrible capers before me. Often I thought the sun was a Prussian cockade; at night I dreamed of an ugly black vulture that ate my liver, and I was very melancholy. I also made the acquaintance of an old judge of Berlin who had passed many years in the fortress of Spandau, and he told me how unpleasant it is to have to wear irons in winter. It seemed to me very unchristian not to warm the irons a little. If our chains were warmed a little they would not make so unpleasant an impression, and even men of a chilly nature could then bear them well; care should also be taken to scent fetters with roses and laurel as they do here in this country. I asked my old judge if he had often been given oysters to eat at Spandau. He said, "No," and that Spandau was far from the sea. Meat, too, he said, was rare there, and there was no other winged creature than the flies that fell in the soup. At the same time I made the acquaintance of a French *commis voyageur*, who travelled in wine and could not praise enough the jolly life in Paris, saying, how the sky is hung with fiddles, and how they sing from morning to night the Marseillaise and *"En avant, marchons!"* and *"Lafayette aux cheveux blancs,"* and how liberty, equality, and fraternity are written up at all the street corners; incidentally he praised the champagne of his firm, of whose cards he gave me a great number, and he promised me letters of introduction to the best Parisian restaurants, in case I should ever visit the capital in search of pleasure. And now as some sort of recreation is necessary, and Spandau is too far from the sea to eat oysters there, and the fly soup of Spandau did not attract me much, and also the Prussian chains are very cold in winter and would not be good for my health, I made up my mind to go to Paris and in the fatherland of champagne and the Marseillaise to drink the one and to hear the other, together with *"En avant, marchons!"* and *"Lafayette aux cheveux blancs."*

On May 1, 1831, I crossed the Rhine. I did not see the old river god, Father Rhine; I contented myself with throwing my visiting card into the water. I only saw the cathedral of Strassburg from a distance; he wagged his head like good Old Eckart when he sees a youngster going to the Venusberg.

At Saint Denis I awoke from a sweet morning sleep and heard for the first time the cry of the driver—"Paris! Paris!"—and the handbells of the cocoa-sellers. Here already you breathe the air of the capital which is visible on the horizon. An old rascal of a tout tried to persuade me to visit the tombs of the kings, but I had not come to France to see the kings; I contented myself with letting the guide tell me the legends of the place, how, for instance, the wicked Pagan king had Saint Denis' head cut off, and the Saint ran from Paris to Saint Denis with his head in his hand to be buried there, and to have the place called after him. "If you think," said my

568

guide, "if you think of the distance you cannot but be amazed at the miracle that any one could go so far on foot without a head"— and he added with a strange smile: "*Dans des cas pareils il n'y a que le premier pas qui coûte.*" It was worth two francs and I gave them to him *pour l'amour de Voltaire,* whose mocking smile I had already met in him. In twenty minutes I was in Paris, and entered through the triumphal arch of the Boulevard Saint Denis, which was originally erected in honour of Louis XIV, but now served to glorify my entry into Paris. I was really surprised by the crowd of gay people. dressed very tastefully like fashion plates. Then I was impressed by them all speaking French, which is with us the mark of the polite world; but everybody is as polite here as the aristocracy in my country. The men were all so courteous, and the lovely ladies all so smiling. If any one jostled me without at once begging my pardon, then I could wager that he was a fellow countryman; and if ever a pretty woman looked sourly, then she had either been eating Sauerkraut or could read Klopstock in the original. I found everything so amazing, and the sky was so blue, and the air so sweet, so generous, and the beams of the July sun flickered hither and thither; the cheeks of the fair Lutetia were touched with the flaming kisses of that sun, and in her bosom her bridal nosegay was not yet withered. At the street corners *"Liberté, égalité, fraternité"* had in places been erased.

I sought at once the restaurants for which I had my letters of introduction; the proprietors assured me that they would have received me without letters of introduction, that I had such an honest and distinguished appearance as to be a recommendation in itself. Never did a German cookshop-keeper say the like to me, even if he thought it; such a fellow thinks that he must say nothing pleasant, and that his German frankness compels him only to say to one's face disagreeable things. In the manners and speech of the French there is so much of that precious flattery that costs so little and yet is so kindly and refreshing. My poor sensitive soul, that often recoiled in shyness from German coarseness, opened out to the flattering sounds of French urbanity. God gave us our tongues so that we might say pleasant things to our fellow men.

There was a hitch in my French when I arrived; but after half an hour's conversation with a little flower-seller in the Passage de l'Opéra, my French, which had grown rusty since the Battle of Waterloo, became fluent again and I stumbled about in the most gallant conjugations and explained to my little friend the Linnaean system, by which flowers are classified according to the filaments; she herself followed another method and divided the flowers into those which smelled sweet and those which smelled offensive. I believed that she applied the same method of classification to men. She was astonished that I was so learned, in spite of my youth, and she trumpeted the fame of my learning through all the Passage de l'Opéra. I drank in delightedly the sweet scents of flattery and was much amused. I walked on flowers, and many a roast pigeon flew into my open gaping maw. What amusing things I saw on my arrival! All the notabilities of public pleasure and official absurdity.

Paris delighted me much with the cheeriness which appears in everything, and influences even the most doleful disposition. Strange! Paris is the scene of the greatest tragedies of the history of the world, tragedies at the memory of which hearts in the most distant lands tremble, eyes grow wet; but it is with the spectator of these great tragedies as it was once with me when I saw the *Tour de Nesle* at the Porte St. Martin. I was sitting behind a lady who was wearing a hat of rose-red gauze, and this hat was so wide that it cut off altogether my view of the stage, so that I could see the tragedy enacted through the red gauze of the hat, so that all the horrors of the *Tour de Nesle* appeared in the rosiest light. Yes, there is such a rosy light in Paris, which makes bright every tragedy for the spectator, so that it does not touch his enjoyment of life, and so the terrors which we bring to Paris lose their most bitter sting. Sorrows are strangely softened. In the air of Paris wounds are healed quicker than anywhere else; there is something so noble, so gentle, so sweet in the air, as in the people themselves.

ERNEST HEMINGWAY

ERNEST HEMINGWAY (American, 1898-   ). Influential novelist, brought to modern fiction new techniques of clipped dialogue and excessive scenes of violence. Experience in First World War produced *A Farewell to Arms.* Postwar "lost generation" classic: *The Sun Also Rises.* Covered Spanish Civil War as journalist, and wrote *For Whom the Bell Tolls.* Also addicted to hunting *(The Green Hills of Africa)* and bullfighting *(Death in the Afternoon)*—both nonfiction. Nobel Prize, 1954.

TEN INDIANS

AFTER one Fourth of July, Nick, driving home late from town in the big wagon with Joe Garner and his family, passed nine drunken Indians along the road. He remembered there were nine because Joe Garner, driving along in the dusk, pulled up the horses, jumped down into the road and dragged an Indian out of the wheel rut. The Indian had been asleep, face down in the sand. Joe dragged him into the bushes and got back up on the wagon-box.

"That makes nine of them," Joe said, "just between here and the edge of town."

"Them Indians," said Mrs. Garner.

Nick was on the back seat with the two Garner boys. He was looking out from the back seat to see the Indian where Joe had dragged him alongside of the road.

"Was it Billy Tabeshaw?" Carl asked.

"No."

"His pants looked mighty like Billy."

"All Indians wear the same kind of pants."

"I didn't see him at all," Frank said. "Pa was down into the road and back up again before I seen a thing. I thought he was killing a snake."

"Plenty of Indians'll kill snakes tonight, I guess," Joe Garner said.

"Them Indians," said Mrs. Garner.

They drove along. The road turned off from the main highway and went up into the hills. It was hard pulling for the horses and the boys got down and walked. The road was sandy. Nick looked back from the top of the hill by the schoolhouse. He saw the lights of Petoskey and, off across Little Traverse Bay, the lights of Harbour Springs. They climbed back in the wagon again.

"They ought to put some gravel on that stretch," Joe Garner said. The wagon went along the road through the woods. Joe and Mrs. Garner sat close together on the front seat. Nick sat between the two boys. The road came out into a clearing.

"Right here was where Pa ran over the skunk."

"It was further on."

"Where?"

"Down by the lake. They were looking for dead fish along the beach."

"They were coons probably," Carl said.

"They were skunks. I guess I know skunks."

"You ought to," Carl said. "You got an Indian girl."

"Stop talking that way, Carl," said Mrs. Garner.

"Well, they smell about the same."

571

Joe Garner laughed.

"You stop laughing, Joe," Mrs. Garner said. "I won't have Carl talk that way."

"Have you got an Indian girl, Nickie?" Joe asked.

"No."

"He has too, Pa," Frank said. "Prudence Mitchell's his girl."

"She's not."

"He goes to see her every day."

"I don't." Nick, sitting between the two boys in the dark, felt hollow and happy inside himself to be teased about Prudence Mitchell. "'She ain't my girl," he said.

"Listen to him," said Carl. "I see them together every day."

"Carl can't get a girl," his mother said, "not even a squaw."

Carl was quiet.

"Carl ain't no good with girls," Frank said.

"You shut up."

"You're all right, Carl," Joe Garner said. "Girls never got a man anywhere. Look at your pa."

"Yes, that's what you would say," Mrs. Garner moved close to Joe as the wagon jolted. "Well, you had plenty of girls in your time."

"I'll bet Pa wouldn't ever have had a squaw for a girl."

"Don't you think it," Joe said. "You better watch out to keep Prudie, Nick."

His wife whispered to him and Joe laughed.

"What you laughing at?" asked Frank

"Don't you say it, Garner," his wife warned. Joe laughed again.

"Nickie can have Prudence," Joe Garner said. "I got a good girl."

"That's the way to talk," Mrs. Garner said.

The horses were pulling heavily in the sand. Joe reached out in the dark with the whip.

"Come on, pull into it. You'll have to pull harder than this tomorrow."

They trotted down the long hill, the wagon jolting. At the farm-house everybody got down. Mrs. Garner unlocked the door, went inside, and came out with a lamp in her hand. Carl and Nick unloaded the things from the back of the wagon. Frank sat on the front seat to drive to the barn and put up the horses. Nick went up the steps and opened the kitchen door. Mrs. Garner was building a fire in the stove. She turned from pouring kerosene on the wood.

"Good-by, Mrs. Garner," Nick said. "Thanks for taking me."

"Oh shucks, Nickie."

"I had a wonderful time."

"We like to have you. Won't you stay and eat some supper?"

"I better go. I think Dad probably waited for me."

"Well, get along then. Send Carl up to the house, will you?"

"All right."

"Good night, Nickie."

"Good night, Mrs. Garner."

Nick went out the farmyard and down to the barn. Joe and Frank were milking.

"Good night," Nick said. "I had a swell time."

"Good night, Nick," Joe Garner called. "Aren't you going to stay and eat?"

"No, I can't. Will you tell Carl his mother wants him?"

"All right. Good night, Nickie."

Nick walked barefoot along the path through the meadow below the barn. The path was smooth and the dew was cool on his bare feet. He climbed a fence at the end of the meadow, went down through a ravine, his feet wet in the swamp mud, and then climbed up through the dry beech woods until he saw the lights of the cottage. He climbed over the fence and walked around to the front porch. Through the window he saw his father sitting by the table, reading in the light from the big lamp. Nick opened the door and went in.

"Well, Nickie," his father said, "was it a good day?"

"I had a swell time, Dad. It was a swell Fourth of July."

"Are you hungry?"

"You bet."

"What did you do with your shoes?"

"I left them in the wagon at Garner's."

"Come on out to the kitchen."

Nick's father went ahead with the lamp. He stopped and lifted the lid of the ice-box. Nick went on into the kitchen. His father brought in a piece of old chicken on a plate and a pitcher of milk and put them on the table before Nick. He put down the lamp.

"There's some pie too," he said. "Will that hold you?"

"It's grand."

His father sat down in a chair beside the oil-cloth-covered table. He made a big shadow on the kitchen wall.

"Who won the ball game?"

"Petoskey. Five to three."

His father sat watching him eat and filled his glass from the milk-pitcher. Nick drank and wiped his mouth on his napkin. His father reached over to the shelf for the pie. He cut Nick a big piece. It was huckleberry pie.

"What did you do, Dad?"

"I went out fishing in the morning."

"What did you get?"

"Only perch."

His father sat watching Nick eat the pie.

"What did you do this afternoon?" Nick asked.

"I went for a walk up by the Indian camp."

"Did you see anybody?"

"The Indians were all in town getting drunk."

"Didn't you see anybody at all?"

"I saw your friend, Prudie."

"Where was she?"

"She was in the woods with Frank Washburn. I ran onto them. They were having quite a time."

His father was not looking at him.

"What were they doing?"

"I didn't stay to find out."

"Tell me what they were doing."

"I don't know," his father said. "I just heard them threshing around."

"How did you know it was them?"

"I saw them."

"I thought you said you didn't see them."

"Oh, yes, I saw them."

"Who was it with her?" Nick asked.

"Frank Washburn."

"Were they—were they——"

"Were they what?"

"Were they happy?"

"I guess so."

His father got up from the table and went out the kitchen screen door. When he came back Nick was looking at his plate. He had been crying.

"Have some more?" His father picked up the knife to cut the pie.

"No," said Nick.

"You better have another piece."

"No, I don't want any."

His father cleared off the table.

"Where were they in the woods?" Nick asked.

"Up back of the camp." Nick looked at his plate. His father said, "You better go to bed, Nick."

"All right."

Nick went into his room, undressed, and got into bed. He heard his father moving around in the living room. Nick lay in the bed with his face in the pillow.

"My heart's broken," he thought. "If I feel this way my heart must be broken."

After a while he heard his father blow out the lamp and go into his own room. He heard a wind come up in the trees outside and felt it come in cool through the screen. He lay for a long time with his face in the pillow, and after a while he forgot to think about Prudence and finally he went to sleep. When he awoke in the night he heard the wind in the hemlock trees outside the cottage and the waves of the lake coming in on the shore, and he went back to sleep. In the morning there was a big wind blowing and the waves were running high up on the beach and he was awake a long time before he remembered that his heart was broken.

O. HENRY

O. HENRY (William Sydney Porter, American, 1862-1910). Imaginative, ironic storyteller, famous for surprise endings. At one time America's most widely read story writer. Author of some 600 tales. Characters drawn from everyday life, with sympathy for the underdog. Titles of collections: *Cabbages and Kings, The Four Million, Heart of the West.*

THE WHIRLIGIG OF LIFE

JUSTICE-OF-THE-PEACE BENAJA WIDDUP sat in the door of his office smoking his elder-stem pipe. Halfway to the zenith the Cumberland range rose blue-gray in the afternoon haze. A speckled hen swaggered down the main street of the "settlement," cackling foolishly.

Up the road came a sound of creaking axles, and then a slow cloud of dust, and then a bull-cart bearing Ransie Bilbro and his wife. The cart stopped at the Justice's door, and the two climbed down. Ransie was a narrow six feet of sallow brown skin and yellow hair.

The imperturbability of the mountains hung upon him like a suit of armor. The woman was calicoed, angled, snuff-brushed, and weary with unknown desires. Through it all gleamed a faint protest of cheated youth unconscious of its loss.

The Justice of the Peace slipped his feet into his shoes, for the sake of dignity, and moved to let them enter.

"We-all," said the woman, in a voice like the wind blowing through pine boughs, "wants a divo'ce." She looked at Ransie to see if he noted any flaw or ambiguity or evasion or partiality or self-partisanship in her statement of their business.

"A divo'ce," repeated Ransie, with a solemn nod. "We-all can't git along together nohow. It's lonesome enough fur to live in the mount'ins when a man and a woman keers fur one another. But when she's a-spittin' like a wildcat or a-sullenin' like a hoot-owl in the cabin, a man ain't got no call to live with her."

"When he's a no-'count varmint," said the woman, without any especial warmth, "a-traipsin' along of scalawags and moonshiners and a-layin' on his back pizen 'ith co'n whiskey, and a-pesterin' folks with a pack o' hungry, triflin' houn's to feed!"

"When she keeps a-throwin' skillet lids," came Ransie's antiphony, "slings b'ilin' water on the best coon-dog in the Cumberlands, and sets herself agin' cookin' a man's victuals, and keeps him awake o' nights accusin' him of a sight of doin's!"

"When he's al'ays a-fightin' the revenues, and gits a hard name in the mount'ins fur a mean man, who's gwine to be able fur to sleep o' nights?"

The Justice of the Peace stirred deliberately to his duties. He placed his one chair and a wooden stool for his petitioners. He opened his book of statutes on the table and scanned the index. Presently he wiped his spectacles and shifted his inkstand.

"The law and the statutes," said he, "air silent on the subjeck of divo'ce as fur as the jurisdiction of this co't air concerned. But, accordin' to equity and the Constitution and the golden rule, it's a bad barg'in that can't run both ways. If a justice of the peace can marry a couple, it's plain that he is bound to be able to divo'ce 'em. This here office will issue a decree of divo'ce and abide by the decision of the Supreme Co't to hold it good."

Ransie Bilbro drew a small tobacco-bag from his trousers pocket. Out of this he shook upon the table a five-dollar note. "Sold a b'erskin and two foxes fur that," he remarked. "It's all the money we got."

"The regular price of a divo'ce in this co't," said the Justice, "air five dollars." He stuffed the bill into the pocket of his homespun vest with a deceptive air of indifference. With much bodily toil and mental travail he wrote the decree upon half a sheet of foolscap, and then copied it upon the other. Ransie Bilbro and his wife listened to his reading of the document that was to give them freedom:

"Know all men by these presents that Ransie Bilbro and his wife, Ariela Bilbro, this day personally appeared before me and promised that hereinafter they will neither love, honor, nor obey each other, neither for better nor worse, being of sound mind and body, and accept summons for divorce according to the peace and dignity of the State. Herein fail not, so help you God. Benaja Widdup, justice of the peace in and for the county of Piedmont, State of Tennessee."

The Justice was about to hand one of the documents to Ransie. The voice of Ariela delayed the transfer. Both men looked at her. Their dull masculinity was confronted by something sudden and unexpected in the woman.

"Judge, don't you give him that air paper yit. 'Tain't all settled, nohow. I got to have my rights first. I got to have my ali-money. 'Tain't no kind of a way to do fur a man to divo'ce his wife 'thout her havin' a cent fur to do with. I'm a-layin' off to be a-goin' up to brother Ed's up on Hogback Mount'in. I'm bound fur to hev a pa'r of shoes and some snuff and things besides. Ef Rance kin affo'd a divo'ce, let him pay me ali-money."

Ransie Bilbro was stricken to dumb perplexity. There had been no previous hint of alimony. Women were always bringing up startling and unlooked-for issues.

Justice Benaja Widdup felt that the point demanded judicial decision. The authorities were also silent on the subject of alimony. But the woman's feet were bare. The trail to Hogback Mountain was steep and flinty.

"Ariela Bilbro," he asked, in official tones, "how much did you 'low would be good and sufficient ali-money in the case befo' the co't."

"I 'lowed," she answered, "fur the shoes and all, to say five dollars. That ain't much fur ali-money, but I reckon that'll git me up to brother Ed's."

"The amount," said the Justice, "air not onreasonable. Ransie Bilbro, you air ordered by the co't to pay the plaintiff the sum of five dollars befo' the decree of divo'ce air issued."

"I hain't no mo' money," breathed Ransie, heavily. "I done paid you all I had."

"Otherwise," said the Justice, looking severely over his spectacles, "you air in contempt of co't."

"I reckon if you gimme till to-morrow," pleaded the husband, "I mout be able to rake or scrape it up somewhars. I never looked for to be a-payin' no ali-money."

"The case air adjourned," said Benaja Widdup "till to-morrow, you-all will present yo'selves and obey the order of the co't. Followin' of which the decrees of divo'ce will be delivered." He sat down in the door and began to loosen a shoestring.

"We mout as well go down to Uncle Ziah's," decided Ransie, "and spend the night." He climbed into the cart on one side, and Ariela climbed in on the other. Obeying the flap of his rope the little red bull slowly came around on a tack, and the cart crawled away in the nimbus arising from its wheels.

Justice-of-the-peace Benaja Widdup smoked his elder-stem pipe. Late in the afternoon he got his weekly paper, and read it until the twilight dimmed its lines. Then he lit the tallow candle on his table, and read until the moon rose, marking the time for supper. He lived in the double log cabin on the slope near the girdled poplar. Going home to supper he crossed a little branch darkened by a laurel thicket. The dark figure of a man stepped from the laurels and pointed a rifle at his breast. His hat was pulled down low, and something covered most of his face.

"I want yo' money," said the figure, "'thout any talk. I'm gettin' nervous, and my finger's a-wabblin on this here trigger."

"I've only got f-f-five dollars," said the Justice, producing it from his vest pocket.

"Roll it up," came the order, "and stick it in the end of this here gun-bar'l."

The bill was crisp and new. Even fingers that were clumsy and trembling found little difficulty in making a spill of it and inserting it (this with less ease) into the muzzle of the rifle.

"Now I reckon you kin be goin' along," said the robber.

The Justice lingered not on his way.

The next day came the little red bull, drawing the cart to the office door. Justice Benaja Widdup had his shoes on, for he was expecting the visit. In his presence Ransie Bilbro handed to his wife a five-dollar bill. The official's eye sharply viewed it. It seemed to curl up as though it had been rolled and inserted into the end of a gun-barrel. But the Justice refrained from comment. It is true that other bills might be inclined to curl. He handed each one a decree of divorce. Each stood awkwardly silent, slowly folding the guarantee of freedom. The woman cast a shy glance full of constraint at Ransie.

"I reckon you'll be goin' back up to the cabin," she said, "along 'ith the bull-cart. There's bread in the tin box settin' on the shelf. I put the bacon in the b'ilin'-pot to keep the hounds from gittin' it. Don't forget to wind the clock to-night."

"You air a-goin' to your brother Ed's?" asked Ransie, with fine unconcern.

"I was 'lowin' to get along up thar afore night. I ain't sayin' as they'll pester theyselves any to make me welcome, but I hain't no-whar else fur to go. It's a right smart ways, and I reckon I better be goin'. I'll be a-sayin' good-bye, Ranse—that is, if you keer fur to say so."

"I don't know as anybody's a hound dog," said Ransie, in a martyr's voice, "fur to not want to say good-bye—'less you air so anxious to git away that you don't want me to say it."

Ariela was silent. She folded the five-dollar bill and her decree carefully, and placed them in the bosom of her dress. Benaja Widdup watched the money disappear with mournful eyes behind his spectacles.

And then with his next words he achieved rank (as his thoughts ran) with either the great crowd of the world's sympathizers or the little crowd of its great financiers.

"Be kind o' lonesome in the old cabin to-night, Ranse," he said.

Ransie Bilbro stared out at the Cumberlands, clear blue now in the sunlight. He did not look at Ariela.

"I 'low it might be lonesome," he said; "but when folks git mad and wants a divo'ce, you can't make folks to stay."

"Nobody never said they didn't."

"Nobody never said they did. I reckon I better start on now to brother Ed's."

"Nobody can't wind that old clock."

"Want me to go back along 'ith you in the cart and wind it fur you, Ranse?"

The mountaineer's countenance was proof against emotion. But he reached out a big hand and enclosed Ariela's thin brown one. Her soul peeped out once through her impassive face, hallowing it.

"Them hounds shan't pester you no more," said Ransie. "I reckon I been mean and low down. You wind that clock, Ariela."

"My heart, hit's in that cabin, Ranse," she whispered, "along 'ith you. I ain't a-goin' to git mad no more. Le's be startin', Ranse, so's we kin git home by sundown.'

Justice-of-the-peace Benaja Widdup interposed as they started for the door, forgetting his presence.

"In the name of the State of Tennessee," he said, "I forbid you-all to be a-defyin' of its laws and statutes. This co't is mo' than willin' and full of joy to see the clouds of discord and misunderstandin' rollin' away from two lovin' hearts, but it air the duty of the co't to p'eserve the morals and integrity of the State. The co't reminds you that you air no longer man and wife, but air divo'ced by regular decree, and as such air not entitled to the benefits and 'purtenances of the mattermonal estate."

Ariela caught Ransie's arm. Did those words mean that she must lose him now when they had just learned the lesson of life?

"But the co't air prepared," went on the Justice, "fur to remove the disabilities set up by the decree of divo'ce. The co't air on hand to perform the solemn ceremony of mari'ge, thus fixin' things up and enablin' the parties in the case to resume the honor'ble and elevatin' state of mattermony which they desires. The fee fur performin' said ceremony will be, in this case, to wit, five dollars."

Ariela caught the gleam of promise in his words. Swiftly her hand went to her bosom. Freely as an alighting dove the bill fluttered to the Justice's table. Her sallow cheek colored as she stood hand in hand with Ransie and listened to the reuniting words.

Ransie helped her into the cart, and climbed in beside her. The little red bull turned once more, and they set out, hand-clasped, for the mountains.

Justice-of-the-peace Benaja Widdup sat in his door and took off his shoes. Once again he fingered the bill tucked down in his vest pocket. Once again he smoked his elder-stem pipe. Once again the speckled hen swaggered down the main street of the "settlement," cackling foolishly.

JOHANN GOTTFRIED VON HERDER

JOHANN GOTTFRIED VON HERDER (German, 1744-1803). A sage among
the poets. Disciple of Kant, friend of Goethe. Wrote many essays on literature
(On German Life and Art), translated folk songs *(Voices of the Nations in
Song)*. A brilliant critic, important in shaping 18th and 19th century literature.

SIR OLAF

Sir Olaf he rideth west and east
To bid the folk to his bridal feast.

On the wold are dancing an elvish band,
And Erl-king's daughter proffers her hand.

"Now welcome, Sir Olaf: what haste's with thee?
Step into our circle and dance with me."

"To dance I neither will nor may,
To-morrow's dawn is my bridal-day."

"Nay, stay, Sir Olaf, and dance with me,
And golden spurs will I give to thee."

"To dance I neither will nor may,
To-morrow's dawn is my bridal-day."

"Nay, stay, Sir Olaf, and dance with me,
A heap of gold will I give to thee."

"For all thy gold I will not stay,
And dance I neither will nor may."

"If thou wilt not dance, Sir Olaf, with me,
Then Pest and Sickness shall follow thee."

She touched Sir Olaf upon the heart—
Ne'er in his life had he felt such smart.

She lifted him up on his steed that tide,
"Ride home! ride fast to thy troth-plight bride!"

And when he came to his castle-door,
His mother stood there, and trembled sore.

"Now say, sweet son, right speedilie
Why art thou wan, and white of blee?"

"Well may my face be wan and white.
I was in Erl-king's realm last night."

"Now tell me, my son so true and tried,
What thing shall I say to thy plighted bride?"

"Say that I hunt in the good greenwood,
With hound and horse as a good knight should."

When scarce the dawn in heaven shone red,
Came the train with the bride Sir Olaf should wed.

They sat at meat, they sat at wine;
"Now where is Sir Olaf, bridegroom of mine?"

"Sir Olaf rode out to the greenwood free,
With horse and hound to the hunt rode he."

The bride she lifted a cloth of red:
Beneath, Sir Olaf was lying dead.

ESTHONIAN BRIDAL SONG

Deck thyself, maiden,
With the hood of thy mother;
Put on the ribands
Which thy mother once wore:
On thy head the band of duty,
On thy forehead the band of care.
Sit in the seat of thy mother,
And walk in thy mother's footsteps.
And weep not, weep not, maiden:
If thou weepest in thy bridal attire,
Thou wilt weep all thy life.

HERMANN HESSE

HERMANN HESSE (German, 1877-   ). Swiss glorifier of nature and child-hood. After school, became locksmith and bookseller. Moved from Germany to Switzerland in 1912 to escape German militarism. Nobel Prize, 1946. *Peter Camenzind.* first successful novel. *Steppenwolf,* celebrated psychoanalytic novel. Others: *Demian, Death and the Lover, Magister Ludi.*

TALK IN A GONDOLA

What I dream, you ask? That yesterday
We had died, we two. In fair array—
Clad in white, our hair with flowers wound,
In our gondola we're seaward bound;
Bells from yonder campanile peal,
But the water gurgles round the keel,
Drowns the distant toll that's gently failing.
Onward, onward to the sea we're sailing,
Where the ships with masts that tower high,
Sombre shadows, rest against the sky,
Where on fishing-boats there gleam the moist
Deep-stained red and yellow sails they hoist,
Where the roaring mighty waves are swelling,
Where the sailors lurid tales are telling.
Through a gate of bluest water, deeply
Downward now our boat is gliding steeply.
In the depths we find a wid'ning range
Filled with many trees of coral strange,
Where in lustrous shells that hidden gleam
Pale gigantic pearls with beauty beam.
Silvery fishes pass us, glist'ning, shy,
Leaving tinted trails as they flit by,
In whose furrows other fish instead
Gleam with slender tails of golden red.
At the bottom, fathoms deep, we dream;
As if bells were calling it will seem,
Now and then, as if a wind that fanned
Sang us songs we cannot understand,
Songs of narrow streets we long ago
Left behind, of things we used to know,

Songs so far, far off about the ways
That we trod in long forgotten days.
And with wonder we'll remember slowly
Now a street, now some cathedral holy,
Or the shouting of a gondolier,
Many names that once we used to hear.
Smiling then as children smile in sleep,
Moving still our silent lips we keep,
And the word will, ere it spoken seems,
Fall into oblivion, death in dreams.
Over us the mighty vessels float,
Sails are bright on many a sombre boat,
Snow-white birds in gleaming sunshine fly,
Glistening nets upon the water lie,
Spanning all, with arches high and true
Glows the heavens' vault of sunlit blue.

IN THE FOG

In the fog to wander, how queer!
Lonely is every bush and stone,
No tree sees the other near,
Each is alone.

Once my world was full of friends,
When my life still had light;
Now that the fog descends,
Not one is in sight.

Only he is wise who knows
The steady gloom to fall
That slowly round him grows,
Severed from all.

In the fog to wander, how queer!
Solitude is life's own.
No man sees the other near,
Each is alone.

HITOMARO KAKINOMOTO

HITOMARO KAKINOMOTO (Japanese, *ca.* 655-710). Greatest of the Japanese Manyō poets. Nothing known of his life. Surviving work collected in the *Manyōshū*—scores of long poems and several hundred *tanka*, vigorous epics and delicate lyrics.

Poems from
THE MANYOSHU

In the sea of Iwami,
By the cape of Kara,
There amid the stones under sea
Grows the deep-sea *miru* weed;
There along the rocky strand
Grows the sleek sea-tangle.

Like the swaying sea-tangle,
Unresisting would she lie beside me—
My wife whom I love with a love
Deep as the *miru*-growing ocean.
But few are the nights
We two have lain together.

Away I have come, parting from her
Even as the creeping vines do part.
My heart aches within me;
I turn back to gaze—
But because of the yellow leaves
Of Watari Hill,
Flying and fluttering in the air,

I cannot see plainly
My wife waving her sleeve to me.
Now as the moon, sailing through the cloud rift
Above the mountain of Yakami,
Disappears, leaving me full of regret,
So vanishes my love out of sight;
Now sinks at last the sun,
Coursing down the western sky.

I thought myself a strong man,
But the sleeves of my garment
Are wetted through with tears.

ENVOYS

My black steed
Galloping fast,
Away have I come,
Leaving under distant skies
The dwelling-place of my love.

Oh, yellow leaves
Falling on the autumn hill,
Cease a while
To fly and flutter in the air
That I may see my love's dwelling-place!

AFTER THE DEATH OF HIS WIFE

Since in Karu lived my wife,
I wished to be with her to my heart's content;
But I could not visit her constantly
Because of the many watching eyes—
Men would know of our troth,
Had I sought her too often
So our love remained secret like a rock-pent pool;
I cherished her in my heart,
Looking to after-time when we should be together,
And lived secure in my trust
As one riding a great ship.
Suddenly there came a messenger
Who told me she was dead—
Was gone like a yellow leaf of autumn.
Dead as the day dies with the setting sun,
Lost as the bright moon is lost behind the cloud,
Alas, she is no more, whose soul
Was bent to mine like the bending seaweed!

When the word was brought to me
I knew not what to do nor what to say;
But restless at the mere news,
And hoping to heal my grief
Even a thousandth part,
I journed to Karu and searched the market-place
Where my wife was wont to go!

There I stood and listened,
But no voice of her I heard,
Though the birds sang in the Unebi Mountain;
None passed by, who even looked like my wife.
I could only call her name and wave my sleeve.

ENVOYS

In the autumn mountains
The yellow leaves are so thick.
Alas, how shall I seek my love
Who has wandered away?—
I know not the mountain track.

I see the messenger come
As the yellow leaves are falling.
Oh, well I remember
How on such a day we used to meet—
My wife and I!

In the days when my wife lived,
We went out to the embankment near by—
We two, hand in hand—
To view the elm-trees standing there
With their outspreading branches
Thick with spring leaves. Abundant as their
    greenery
Was my love. On her leaned my soul.
But who evades mortality?—
One morning she was gone, flown like an early bird.
Clad in a heavenly scarf of white,
To the wide fields where the shimmering *kagero* rises
She went and vanished like the setting sun.

The little babe—the keepsake
My wife has left me—
Cries and clamours.
I have nothing to give; I pick up the child
And clasp it in my arms.

In her chamber, where our two pillows lie,
Where we two used to sleep together,
Days I spend alone, broken-hearted:
Nights I pass, sighing till dawn.

Though I grieve, there is no help;
Vainly I long to see her.
Men tell me that my wife is
In the mountains of Hagai—
Thither I go,
Toiling along the stony path;
But it avails me not,
For of my wife, as she lived in this world,
I find not the faintest shadow.

ENVOYS

To-night the autumn moon shines—
The moon that shone a year ago,
But my wife and I who watched it then together
Are divided by ever-widening wastes of time.

When leaving my love behind
In the Hikité mountains—
Leaving her there in her grave,
I walk down the mountain path,
I feel not like one living.

THE MOUNTAIN TOP

Because the plum trees on the peak
  Are up so high,
The buzz of bees about their bloom
  Comes from the sky!

MY LOVE WHO LOVES ME NOT
*But who must at least come with the
rest of the village to my funeral*

If I die of love, why, let me die,
  For then, since I have died,
She'll cross the threshold where I lie
  And stand—once—by my side.

FRIEDRICH HOLDERLIN

FRIEDRICH HÖLDERLIN (German, 1770-1843). Classical poet of Germany.
A poor tutor, lost his reason as a man of thirty, spent better part of life as a
ward of a carpenter. Most of works published by friends after his madness.
Reputation slight in own day, grew later.

HYPERION'S SONG OF FATE

Ye wander there in the light
On flower-soft fields, ye blest immortal
    Spirits.
Radiant godlike zephyrs
Touch you as gently
As the hand of a master might
Touch the awed lute-string.
Free of fate as the slumbering
Infant, breathe the divine ones.
Guarded well
In the firm-sheathed bud
Blooms eternal
Each happy soul;
And their rapture-lit eyes
Shine with a tranquil
Unchanging lustre.
But we, 'tis our portion,
We never may be at rest.
They stumble, they vanish,
The suffering mortals,
Hurtling from one hard
Hour to another,
Like waves that are driven
From cliff-side to cliff-side,
Endlessly down the uncertain abyss.

EVENING PHANTASIE

Before his hut reposes in restful shade
The ploughman; wreaths of smoke from his hearth ascend.
    And sweet to wand'rers comes the tone of
        Evening bells from the peaceful village.

The sailor too puts into the haven now,
In distant cities cheerily dies away
   The busy tumult; in the arbor
     Gleams the festal repast of friendship.

But whither I? In labor, for slight reward
We mortals live; in alternate rest and toil
   Contentment dwells; but why then sleeps not
     Hid in my bosom the thorn unsparing?

The ev'ning heaven blooms as with springtime's hue;
Uncounted bloom the roses, the golden world
   Seems wrapt in peace; oh, bear me thither,
     Purple-wrought clouds! And may for me there

Both love and grief dissolve in the joyous light!
But see, as if dispelled by the foolish prayer,
   The wonder fades! 'Tis dark, and lonely
     Under the heaven I stand as erstwhile.

Come then to me, soft Sleep. Overmuch requires
The heart; and yet thou too at the last shalt fade,
   Oh youth, thou restless dream-pursuer!
     Peaceful and happy shall age then follow.

HOMER

HOMER (Greek, 9th century B.C.). According to tradition, the blind author
of the *Iliad* and the *Odyssey*, great epics based on the Greek legends. Exact
identity never established. Homer set standard for epic poetry of Western
literature: swift, brilliant narrative, primitive imagery, celebration of exploits
of a whole people through an epic hero.

PRIAM RECLAIMS HECTOR'S BODY

On did the old man pass; and he entered, and found the Peleides
Seated apart from his train: two only of Myrmidons trustful,
Hero Automedon only, and Alkimus, sapling of Ares,
Near to him minist'ring stood; he reposed him but now from the
   meal-time,

Sated with food and with wine, nor removed from him yet was the
  table.
All unobserved of them entered the old man stately, and forthwith
Grasped with his fingers the knees and was kissing the hands of
  Achilles—
Terrible, murderous hands, by which son upon son had been slaugh-
  tered.
As when a man who has fled from his home with the curse of the
  blood-guilt,
Kneels in a far-off land, at the hearth of some opulent stranger,
Begging to shelter his head, there is stupor on them that behold
  him;
So was Achilles dumb at the sight of majestical Priam—
He and his followers all, each gazing on other bewildered.
But he uplifted his voice in their silence, and made supplication:
"Think of thy father at home" (he began), "O godlike Achilles!
Him, my coeval, like me within age's calamitous threshold.
Haply this day there is trouble upon him, some insolent neighbors
Round him in arms, nor a champion at hand to avert the disaster:
Yet even so there is comfort for him, for he hears of thee living;
Day unto day there is hope for his heart amid worst tribulation,
That yet again he shall see his beloved from Troia returning.
Misery only is mine; for of all in the land of my fathers,
Bravest and best were the sons I begat, and not one is remaining.
Fifty were mine in the hour that the host of Achaia descended:
Nineteen granted to me out of one womb, royally mothered,
Stood by my side; but the rest were of handmaids born in my dwell-
  ing.
Soon were the limbs of the many unstrung in the fury of Ares:
But one peerless was left, sole prop of the realm and the people;
And now at last he too, the protector of Ilion, Hector,
Dies by thy hand. For his sake have I come to the ships of Achaia,
Eager to ransom the body with bountiful gifts of redemption.
Thou have respect for the gods, and on me, O Peleides! have pity,
Calling thy father to mind; but more piteous is my desolation,
Mine, who alone of mankind have been humbled to this of en-
  durance
Pressing my mouth to the hand that is red with the blood of my
  children."
  Hereon Achilles, awaked to a yearning remembrance of Peleus,

Rose up, took by the hand, and removed from him gently the old
man.
Sadness possessing the twain—one, mindful of valorous Hector,
Wept with o'erflowing tears, low laid at the feet of Achilles;
He, sometime for his father, anon at the thought of Patroclus,
Wept, and aloft in the dwelling their long lamentation ascended.
But when the bursting of grief had contented the godlike Peleides,
And from his heart and his limbs irresistible yearning departed,
Then from his seat rose he, and with tenderness lifted the old man,
Viewing the hoary head and the hoary beard with compassion;
And he addressed him, and these were the air-winged words that
he uttered:—
"Ah unhappy! thy spirit in truth has been burdened with evils.
How could the daring be thine to come forth to the ships of Achaia
Singly, to stand in the eyes of the man by whose weapon thy chil-
dren,
Many and gallant, have died? full surely thy heart is of iron.
But now seat thee in peace, old man, and let mourning entirely
Pause for a space in our minds, although heavy on both be affliction;
For without profit and vain is the fullness of sad lamentation,
Since it was destined so of the gods for unfortunate mortals
Ever in trouble to live, but they only partake not of sorrow;
For by the threshold of Zeus two urns have their station of old time,
Whereof the one holds dolings of good, but the other of evil;
And to whom mixt are the doles of the thunder-delighting Kronion,
He sometime is of blessing partaker, of misery sometime;
But if he gives him the ill, he has fixed him the mark of disaster,
And over bountiful earth the devouring Necessity drives him,
Wandering ever forlorn, unregarded of gods and of mortals.
Thus of a truth did the gods grant glorious gifts unto Peleus,
Even from the hour of his birth, for above compare was he favored,
Whether in wealth or in power, in the land of the Myrmidons reign-
ing;
And albeit a mortal, his spouse was a goddess appointed.
Yet even to him, of the god there was evil apportioned,—that never
Lineage of sons should be born in his home, to inherit dominion.
One son alone he begat, to untimely calamity foredoomed;
Nor do I cherish his age, since afar from the land of my fathers
Here in the Troas I sit, to the torment of thee and thy children.
And we have heard, old man, of thine ancient prosperity also,

Lord of whatever is held between Lesbos the seat of the Macar,
Up to the Phrygian bound and the measureless Hellespontos;
Ruling and blest above all, nor in wealth nor in progeny equaled:
Yet from the hour that the gods brought this visitation upon thee,
Day unto day is thy city surrounded with battles and bloodshed.
Howso, bear what is sent, nor be grieved in thy soul without ceas-
    ing.
Nothing avails it, O king! to lament for the son that has fallen;
Him thou canst raise up no more, but thyself may have new tribu-
    lation."
    So having said, he was answered by Priam the aged and god-
    like:—
'Seat not me on the chair, O beloved of Olympus! while Hector
Lies in the tent uninterred; but I pray thee deliver him swiftly,
That I may see with mine eyes; and, accepting the gifts of redemp-
    tion,
Therein have joy to thy heart; and return thou homeward in safety,
Since of thy mercy I live and shall look on the light of the morning."
    Darkly regarding the king, thus answered the rapid Achilles:—
"Stir me to anger no more, old man: of myself I am minded
To the release of the dead; for a messenger came from Kronion
Hither, the mother that bore me, the child of the Ancient of Ocean.
Thee, too, I know in my mind, nor has aught of thy passage escaped
    me;
How that some god was the guide of thy steps to the ships of Achaia.
For never mortal had dared to advance, were he blooming in man-
    hood,
Here to the host by himself; nor could sentinels all be avoided;
Nor by an imbecile push might the bar be dislodged at my bulwark.
Therefore excite me no more, old man, when my soul is in sorrow,
Lest to thyself peradventure forebearance continue not alway,
Suppliant all that thou art—but I break the behest of the godhead."
    So did he speak; but the old man feared, and obeyed his com-
    mandment.
Forth of the door of his dwelling then leapt like a lion Peleides;
But not alone: of his household were twain that attended his going,
Hero Automedon first, and young Alkimus, he that was honored
Chief of the comrades around since the death of belovèd Patroclus.
These from the yoke straightway unharnessed the mules and the
    horses,

593

And they conducted within the coeval attendant of Priam,
Bidding him sit in the tent; then swiftly their hands from the mule-
    wain,
Raise the uncountable wealth of the king's Hectorean head-gifts.
But two mantles they leave, and a tunic of beautiful texture,
Seemly for wrapping the dead as the ransomer carries him home-
    ward.
Then were the handmaidens called, and commanded to wash and
    anoint him,
Privately lifted aside, lest the son should be seen of the father,
Lest in the grief of his soul he restrain not his anger within him,
Seeing the corse of his son, but enkindle the heart of Achilles,
And he smite him to death, and transgress the command of Kronion.
But when the dead had been washed and anointed with oil by the
    maidens,
And in the tunic arrayed and enwrapt in the beautiful mantle,
Then by Peleides himself was he raised and composed on the hand-
    bier;
Which when the comrades had lifted and borne to its place in the
    mule-wain,
Then groaned he; and he called on the name of his friend, the
    beloved:—
"Be not wroth with me now, O Patroclus, if haply thou hearest,
Though within Hades obscure, that I yield the illustrious Hector
Back to his father dear. Not unworthy the gifts of redemption;
And unto thee will I render thereof whatsoever is seemly."

HORACE

HORACE (Roman, 65-8 B.C.). Latin poet, subtle, elegant, cheerful, profoundly
influential. One of notable group whose patron was the wealthy Maecenas.
Friend of Virgil. First work: *Satires*. Later: *Epistles, Odes*. His *Ars Poetica*,
written toward end of life, had permanent influence on all European criticism.

ODES

BOOK III, ODE 1

I scorn and shun the rabble's noise.
    Abstain from idle talk. A thing
    That ear hath not yet heard, I sing,
The Muses' priest, to maids and boys.

To Jove the flocks which great kings sway,
    To Jove great kings allegiance owe.
    Praise him: he laid the giants low:
All things that are, his nod obey.

This man may plant in broader lines
    His fruit trees: that, the pride of race
    Enlists a candidate for place:
In worth, in fame, a third outshines

His mates; or, thronged with clients, claims
    Precedence. Even-handed Fate
    Hath but one law for small and great:
That ample urn holds all men's names.

He o'er whose doomed neck hangs the sword
    Unsheathed, the dainties of the South
    Shall lack their sweetness in his mouth:
No note of bird or harpsichord

Shall bring him Sleep. Yet Sleep is kind,
    Nor scorns the huts of laboring men;
    The bank where shadows play, the glen
Of Temple dancing in the wind.

He, who but asks "Enough," defies
    Wild waves to rob him of his ease;
    He fears no rude shocks, when he sees
Arcturus set or Hædus rise:

When hailstones lash his vines, or fails
    His farm its promise, now of rains
    And now of stars that parch the plains
Complaining, unkindly gales.

—In straitened seas the fish are pent;
    For dams are sunk into the deep:
    Pile upon pile the builders heap,
And he, whom earth could not content,

The Master. Yet shall Fear and Hate
    Climb where the Master climbs: nor e'er
    From the armed trireme parts black Care;
He sits behind, the horseman's mate.

And if red marble shall not ease
    The heartache; nor the shell that shines
    Star-bright; nor all Falernum's vines,
All scents that charmed Achæmenes:

Why should I rear me halls of rare
    Design, on proud shafts mounting high?
    Why bid my Sabine vale good-by
For doubled wealth and doubled care?

EPODE 2

Alphius

Happy the man, in busy schemes unskilled,
    Who, living simply, like our sires of old,
Tills the few acres which his father tilled,
    Vexed by no thoughts of usury or gold;

The shrilling clarion ne'er his slumber mars,
    Nor quails he at the howl of angry seas;
He shuns the forum, with its wordy jars,
    Nor at a great man's door consents to freeze.

The tender vine-shoots, budding into life,
    He with the stately poplar tree doth wed,
Lopping the fruitless branches with his knife,
    And grafting shoots of promise in their stead;

Or in some valley, up among the hills,
    Watches his wandering herds of lowing kine,
Or fragrant jars with liquid honey fills,
    Or shears his silly sheep in sunny shine;

Or when Autumnus o'er the smiling land
    Lifts up his head with rosy apples crowned,
Joyful he plucks the pears, which erst his hand
    Graffed on the stem they're weighing to the ground;

Plucks grapes in noble clusters purple-dyed,
    A gift for thee, Priapus, and for thee,
Father Sylvanus, where thou dost preside,
    Warding his bounds beneath thy sacred tree.

Now he may stretch his careless limbs to rest,
    Where some old ilex spreads its sacred roof;
Now in the sunshine lie, as likes him best,
    On grassy turf of close elastic woof.

And streams the while glide on with murmurs low,
    And birds are singing 'mong the thickets deep,
And fountains babble, sparkling as they flow,
    And with their noise invite to gentle sleep.

But when grim winter comes, and o'er his grounds
    Scatters its biting snows with angry roar,
He takes the field, and with a cry of hounds
    Hunts down into the toils the foaming boar;

Or seeks the thrush, poor starveling, to ensnare,
    In filmy net with bait delusive stored,
Entraps the traveled crane, and timorous hare,
    Rare dainties these to glad his frugal board.

Who amid joys like these would not forget
    The pangs which love to all its victims bears,
The fever of the brain, the ceaseless fret,
    And all the heart's lamentings and despairs?

But if a chaste and blooming wife, beside,
    The cheerful home with sweet young blossoms fills,
Like some stout Sabine, or the sunburnt bride
    Of the lithe peasant of the Apulian hills

597

Who piles the hearth with logs well dried and old
　　Against the coming of her wearied lord,
And, when at eve the cattle seek the fold,
　　Drains their full udders of the milky hoard;

And bringing forth from her well-tended store
　　A jar of wine, the vintage of the year,
Spreads an unpurchased feast,—oh then, not more
　　Could choicest Lucrine oysters give me cheer,

Or the rich turbot, or the dainty char,
　　If ever to our bays the winter's blast
Should drive them in its fury from afar;
　　Nor were to me a welcomer repast

The Afric hen or the Ionic snipe,
　　Than olives newly gathered from the tree,
That hangs abroad its clusters rich and ripe,
　　Or sorrel, that doth love the pleasant lea,

Or mallows wholesome for the body's need,
　　Or lamb foredoomed upon some festal day
In offering to the guardian gods to bleed,
　　Or kidling which the wolf hath marked for prey.

What joy, amidst such feasts, to see the sheep,
　　Full of the pasture, hurrying homewards come;
To see the wearied oxen, as they creep,
　　Dragging the upturned plowshare slowly home!

Or, ranged around the bright and blazing hearth,
　　To see the hinds, a house's surest wealth,
Beguile the evening with their simple mirth,
　　And all the cheerfulness of rosy health!

Thus spake the miser Alphius; and, bent
　　Upon a country life, called in amain
The money he at usury had lent;—
　　But ere the month was out, 'twas lent again.

598

RICARDA HUCH

RICARDA HUCH (German, 1864-1947). Neo-romantic lyricist. Outstanding woman poet in modern German literature. Also wrote novels, including remarkable detective story, *The Deruga Trial*. Verse traditional in form, but rich in imagination and intuition.

MIDNIGHT

To this grave of mine
Come not in the morning,
Come on ways of darkness,
Dearest, by the dim moonshine.

For when through the skies
Bells are tolling midnight,
From my earthly prison
To the lovely air I rise.

In my death-dress white
On my grave I linger,
Watch the stars and measure
Time's placid tread at night.

Come and have no fear!
Can you still give kisses?
I forgot them never
While I slept the winters drear.

Kiss me hard and long.
In the east already
Sings the morning sunlight
—Lack-a-day!—its joyful song.

You were mine again!
Go and taste life's sweetness!—
I in deep, deep darkness
Sleep once more with pain.

VICTOR HUGO

VICTOR HUGO (French, 1802-1885). Chief exponent of the Romantic School of the drama; turned later to the novel. Among his main works: *The Punishments, Contemplation, The Legend of the Centuries, Les Misérables, The Hunchback of Notre Dame.* Also wrote poetry, somewhat stilted. Incurred displeasure of Napoleon III, was banished to the Channel Isles. The most widely known author of 19th century France.

LES MISERABLES

I.

Jean Valjean, Galley Slave

EARLY in October 1815, at the close of the afternoon, a man came into the little town of D——. He was on foot, and the few people about looked at him suspiciously. The traveller was of wretched appearance, though stout and robust, and in the full vigour of life. He was evidently a stranger, and tired, dusty, and wearied with a long day's tramp.

But neither of the two inns in the town would give him food or shelter though he offered good money for payment.

He was an ex-convict—that was enough to exclude him.

In despair he went to the prison, and asked humbly for a night's lodging, but the jailer told him that was impossible unless he got arrested first.

It was a cold night and the wind was blowing from the Alps; it seemed there was no refuge open to him.

Then, as he sat down on a stone bench in the market-place and tried to sleep, a lady coming out of the cathedral noticed him, and, learning his homeless state, bade him knock at the bishop's house, for the good bishop's charity and compassion were known in all the neighborhood.

At the man's knock the bishop, who lived alone with his sister, Madame Magloire, and an old housekeepes, said "Come in"; and the ex-convict entered.

He told them at once that his name was Jean Valjean, that he was a galley-slave, who had spent nineteen years at the hulks, and that he had been walking for four days since his release. "It is the same wherever I go," the man went on. "They all say to me, 'Be off!'

600

I am very tired and hungry. Will you let me stay here? I will pay."

"Madame Magloire," said the bishop, "please lay another knife and fork. Sit down, monsieur, and warm yourself. We shall have supper directly, and your bed will be got ready while you are supping."

Joy and amazement were on the man's face; he stammered his thanks as though beside himself.

The bishop, in honour of his guest, had silver forks and spoons placed on the table.

The man took his food with frightful voracity, and paid no attention to anyone till the meal was over. Then the bishop showed him his bed in an alcove, and an hour later the whole household was asleep.

Jean Valjean soon woke up again.

For nineteen years he had been at the galleys. Originally a pruner of trees, he had broken a baker's window and stolen a loaf one hard winter when there was no work to be had, and for this the sentence was five years. Time after time he had tried to escape, and had always been recaptured; and for each offence a fresh sentence was imposed.

Nineteen years for breaking a window and stealing a loaf! He had gone into prison sobbing and shuddering. He came out full of hatred and bitterness.

That night, at the bishop's house, for the first time in nineteen years, Jean Valjean had received kindness. He was moved and shaken. It seemed inexplicable.

He got up from his bed. Everyone was asleep, the house was perfectly still.

Jean Valjean seized the silver plate-basket which stood in the bishop's room, put the silver into his knapsack, and fled out of the house.

In the morning, while the bishop was breakfasting, the gendarmes brought in Jean Valjean. The sergeant explained that they had met him running away, and had arrested him, because of the silver they found on him.

"I gave you the candlesticks, too!" said the bishop; "they are silver. Why did not you take them with the rest of the plate?" Then, turning to the gendarmes, "It is a mistake."

"We are to let him go?" said the sergeant.

"Certainly," said the bishop.

601

The gendarmes retired.

"My friend," said the bishop to Jean Valjean, "here are your candlesticks. Take them with you." He added in a low voice, "Never forget that you have promised me to use this silver to become an honest man. My brother, you belong no longer to evil, but to good."

Jean Valjean never remembered having promised anything. He left the bishop's house and the town dazed and stupefied. It was a new world he had come into.

He walked on for miles, and then sat down by the roadside to think.

Presently a small Savoyard boy passed him, and as he passed dropped a two-franc piece on the ground.

Jean Valjean placed his foot upon it. In vain the boy prayed him for the coin. Jean Valjean sat motionless, deep in thought.

Only when the boy had gone on, in despair, did Jean Valjean wake from his reverie.

He shouted out, "Little Gervais, little Gervais!" for the boy had told him his name. The lad was out of sight and hearing, and no answer came.

The enormity of his crime came home to him, and Jean Valjean fell on the ground, and for the first time in nineteen years he wept.

II

Father Madeleine

On a certain December night in 1815 a stranger entered the town of M——, at the very time when a great fire had just broken out in the town hall.

This man at once rushed into the flames, and at the risk of his own life saved the two children of the captain of gendarmes. In consequence no one thought of asking for his passport.

The stranger settled in the town; by a happy invention he improved the manufacture of the black beads, the chief industry of M——, and in three years, from a very small capital, he became a rich man, and brought prosperity to the place.

In 1820, Father Madeleine, for so the stranger was called, was made Mayor of M—— by unanimous request, an honour he had declined the previous year. Before he came everything was languishing in the town, and now, a few years later, there was healthy life for all.

Father Madeleine employed everybody who came to him. The only condition he made was—honesty. From the men he expected good-will, from the women, purity.

Prosperity did not make Father Madeleine change his habits. He performed his duties as mayor, but lived a solitary and simple life, avoiding society. His strength, although he was a man of fifty, was enormous. It was noticed that he read more as his leisure increased, and that as the years went by his speech became gentler and more polite.

One person only in all the district looked doubtfully at the mayor, and that was Javert, inspector of police.

Javert, born in prison, was the incarnation of police duty—implacable, resolute, fanatical. He arrived in M—— when Father Madeleine was already a rich man, and he felt sure he had seen him before.

One day in 1823 the mayor interfered to prevent Javert sending a poor woman, named Fantine, to prison. Fantine had been dismissed from the factory without the knowledge of M. Madeleine; and her one hope in life was her little girl, whom she called Cosette. Now, Cosette was boarded out at the village of Montfermeil, some leagues distance from M——, with a family grasping and dishonest, and to raise money for Cosette's keep had brought Fantine to misery and sickness.

The mayor could save Fantine from prison, he could not save her life; but before the unhappy woman died she had delivered a paper to M. Madeleine authorising him to take her child, and M. Madeleine had accepted the trust.

It was when Fantine lay dying in the hospital that Javert, who had quite decided in his own mind who M. Madeleine was, came to the mayor and asked to be dismissed from the service.

"I have denounced you, M. le Maire, to the prefect of police at Paris, as Jean Valjean, an ex-convict, who has been wanted for the robbery of a little Savoyard more than five years ago."

"And what answer did you receive?"

"That I was mad, for the real Jean Valjean has been found."

"Ah!"

Javert explained that an old man had been arrested for breaking into an orchard; that on being taken to the prison he had been recognised by several people as Jean Valjean, and that he, Javert, himself recognised him. To-morrow he was to be tried at Arras, and, as he was an ex-convict, his sentence would be for life.

Terrible was the anguish of M. Madeleine that night. He had

done all that man could do to obliterate the past, and now it seemed another was to be taken in his place. The torture and torment ended. In the morning M. Madeleine set out for Arras.

M. Madeleine arrived before the orchard-breaker was condemned. He proved to the court's astonishment that he, the revered and philanthropic Mayor of M——, was Jean Valjean, and that the prisoner had merely committed a trivial theft. Then he left the court, returned to M——, removed what money he had, buried it, and arranged his affairs.

A few days later Jean Valjean was sent back to the galleys at Toulon, and with his removal the prosperity of M—— speedily collapsed. This was in July 1823. In November of that year the following paragraph appeared in the Toulon paper.

"Yesterday, a convict, on his return from rescuing a sailor, fell into the sea and was drowned. His body has not been found. His name was registered as Jean Valjean."

III

A Hunted Man

At Christmas in the year 1823, an old man came to the village of Montfermeil, called at the inn, paid money to the rascally innkeeper, Thénardier, and carried off little Cosette to Paris.

The old man rented a large garret in an old house, and Cosette became inexpressibly happy with her doll and the good man who loved her so tenderly.

Till then Jean Valjean had never loved anything. He had never been a father, lover, husband, or friend. When he saw Cosette, and had rescued her, he felt his heart strangely moved. All the affection he had was aroused, and went out towards this child. Jean Valjean was fifty-five and Cosette eight, and all the love of his life, hitherto untouched, melted into a benevolent devotion.

Cosette, too, changed. She had been separated from her mother at such an early age that she could not remember her. And the Thénardiers had treated her harshly. In Jean Valjean she found a father, just as he found a daughter in Cosette.

Weeks passed away. These two beings led a wonderfully happy life in the old garret; Cosette would chatter, laugh, and sing all day.

Jean Valjean was careful never to go out in the daytime, but he began to be known in the district as "the mendicant who gives away money." There was one old man who sat by some church steps, and who generally seemed to be praying, whom Jean Valjean always liked to relieve. One night when Jean Valjean had dropped a piece of money into his hand as usual, the beggar suddenly raised his eyes, stared hard at him, and then quickly dropped his head. The movement was like a flash. Jean Valjean started, and went home greatly troubled. The face which he fancied he had seen was that of Javert.

A few nights later Jean Valjean found that Javert had taken lodgings in the same house where he and Cosette lived. Taking the child by the hand, he at once set out for fresh quarters. They passed through silent and empty streets, and crossed the river, and it seemed to Jean Valjean that no one was in pursuit. But soon he noticed four men plainly shadowing him, and a shudder went over him. He turned from street to street, trying to escape from the city, and at last found himself entrapped in a *cul-de sac*. What was to be done?

There was no time to turn back. Javert had undoubtedly picketed every outlet. Fortunately for Jean Valjean, there was a deep shadow in the street, so that his own movements were unseen.

While he stood hesitating, a patrol of soldiers entered the street, with Javert at their head. They frequently halted. It was evident that they were exploring every hole and corner, and one might judge they would take a quarter of an hour before they reached the spot where Jean Valjean was. It was a frightful moment. Capture meant the galleys, and Cosette lost for ever. There was only one thing possible—to scale the wall which ran along a wide portion of the street. But the difficulty was Cosette; there was no thought of abandoning her.

First, Jean Valjean procured a rope from the lamp-post, for the lamps had not been lit that night owing to the moonlight. This he fastened round the child, taking the other end between his teeth. Half a minute later he was on his knees on top of the wall. Cosette watched him in silence. All at once she heard Jean Valjean saying in a very low voice. "Lean against the wall. Don't speak, and don't be afraid."

She felt herself lifted from the ground, and before she had time to think where she was she found herself on top of the wall.

Jean Valjean grasped her, put the child on his back, and crawled along the wall till he came to a sloping roof. He could hear the thundering voice of Javert giving orders to the patrol to search the *cul-de-sac* to the end.

Jean Valjean slipped down the roof, still carrying Cosette, and leaped on the ground. It was a convent garden he had entered.

On the other side of the wall the clatter of muskets and the imprecations of Javert resounded; from the convent came a hymn.

Cosette and Jean Valjean fell on their knees. Presently Jean Valjean discovered that the gardener was an old man whose life he had saved at M——, and who, in his gratitude, was prepared to do anything for M. Madeleine.

It ended in Cosette entering the convent school as a pupil, and Jean Valjean being accepted as the gardener's brother. The good nuns never left the precincts of their convent, and cared nothing for the world beyond their gates.

As for Javert, he had delayed attempting an arrest, even when his suspicions had been aroused, because, after all, the papers said the convict was dead. But once convinced, he hesitated no longer.

His disappointment when Jean Valjean escaped him was midway between despair and fury. All night the search went on; but it never occurred to Javert that a steep wall of fourteen feet could be climbed by an old man with a child.

Several years passed at the convent.

Jean Valjean worked daily in the garden, and shared the hut and the name of the old gardener, M. Fauchelevent. Cosette was allowed to see him for an hour every day.

The peaceful garden, the fragrant flowers, the merry cries of the children, the grave and simple women, gradually brought happiness to Jean Valjean; and his heart melted into gratitude for the security he had found.

IV

Something Higher Than Duty

For six years Cosette and Jean Valjean stayed at the convent; and then, on the death of the old gardener, Jean Valjean, now bearing the name of Fauchelevent, decided that as Cosette was not going to be a nun, and as recognition was no longer to be feared, it would be well to remove into the city.

So a house was taken in the Rue Plumet, and here, with a faithful servant, the old man dwelt with his adopted child. But Jean Valjean took other rooms in Paris, in case of accidents.

Cosette was growing up. She was conscious of her good looks, and she was in love with a well-connected youth named Marius, the son of Baron Pontmercy.

606

Jean Valjean learnt of this secret lovemaking with dismay. The idea of parting from Cosette was intolerable to him.

Then, in June, 1832, came desperate street fighting in Paris, and Marius was in command of one of the revolutionary barricades.

At this barricade Javert had been captured as a spy, and Jean Valjean, who was known to the revolutionaries, found his old, implacable enemy tied to a post, waiting to be shot. Jean Valjean requested to be allowed to blow out Javert's brain himself, and permission was given.

Holding a pistol in his hand, Jean Valjean led Javert, who was still bound, to a lane out of sight of the barricade, and there with his knife cut the ropes from the wrists and feet of his prisoner.

"You are free," he said. "Go; and if by any chance I leave this place alive, I am to be found under the name of Fauchelevent, in the Rue de l'Homme-Armé, No. 7."

Javert walked a few steps, and then turned back, and cried, "You worry me. I would rather you killed me!"

"Go!" was the only answer from Jean Valjean.

Javert moved slowly away; and when he had disappeared Jean Valjean discharged his pistol in the air.

Soon the last stand of the insurgents was at an end, and the barricade destroyed. Jean Valjean, who had taken no part in the struggle, beyond exposing himself to the bullets of the soldiers, was unhurt; but Marius lay wounded and insensible in his arms.

The soldiers were shooting down all who tried to escape. The situation was terrible.

There was only one chance for life—underground. An iron grating, which led to the sewers, was at his feet. Jean Valjean tore it open, and disappeared with Marius on his shoulders.

He emerged, after a horrible passage through a grating by the bank of the river, only to find there the implacable Javert!

Jean Valjean was quite calm.

"Inspector Javert," he said, "help me to carry this man home; then do with me what you please."

A cab was waiting for the inspector. He ordered the man to drive to the address Jean Valjean gave him. Marius, still unconscious, was taken to his grandfather's house.

"Inspector Javert," said Jean Valjean, "grant me one thing more. Let me go home for a minute; then you may take me where you will."

Javert told the driver to go to Rue de l'Homme-Armé, No. 7.

When they reached the house, Javert said, "Go up; I will wait here for you!"

But before Jean Valjean reached his rooms Javert had gone, and the street was empty.

Javert had not been at ease since his life had been spared. He was now in horrible uncertainty. To owe his life to an ex-convict, to accept this debt, and then to repay him by sending him back to the galleys was impossible. To let a malefactor go free while he, Inspector Javert, took his pay from the government was equally impossible. It seemed there was something higher and above his code of duty, something he had not come into collision with before. The uncertainty of the right thing to be done destroyed Javert, to whom life had hitherto been perfectly plain. He could not live recognising Jean Valjean as his saviour, and he could not bring himself to arrest Jean Valjean.

Inspector Javert made his last report at the police-station, and then, unable to face the new conditions of life, walked slowly to the river and plunged into the Seine, where the water rolls round and round in an endless whirlpool.

Marius recovered, and married Cosette; and Jean Valjean lived alone. He had told Marius who he was—Jean Valjean, an escaped convict; and Marius and Cosette gradually saw less and less of the old man.

But before Jean Valjean died Marius learnt the whole truth of the heroic life of the old man who had rescued him from the lost barricade. For the first time he realised that Jean Valjean had come to the barricade only to save him, knowing him to be in love with Cosette.

He hastened with Cosette to Jean Valjean's room; but the old man's last hour had come.

"Come closer, come closer, both of you," he cried. "I love you so much. It is good to die like this! You love me too, my Cosette. I know you've always had a fondness for the poor old man. And you, M. Pontmercy, will always make Cosette happy. There were several things I wanted to say, but they don't matter now. Come nearer, my children, I am happy in dying!"

Cosette and Marius fell on their knees, and covered his hands with kisses.

Jean Valjean was dead!

I

HENRIK IBSEN

HENRIK IBSEN (Norwegian, 1828-1906). From poor family. Was apprenticed
to an apothecary. Decided to devote himself to poetry and playwrighting.
Became theater director. Among major works: *Brand, Peer Gynt, A Doll's
House, Ghosts, The Wild Duck, Hedda Gabler.* One of the great antagonists
of social shams and pretenses.

PEER GYNT

Scene IX

Peer Gynt. (Throwing turban away)
There goes the Turk and Prophet—I'm Peer once more.
Those heathen customs I cannot endure.
I'm lucky that it's only a matter of clothes,
And not bred in the bone, as the old saw goes.
It behooves a man to live like a Christian,
To shun the gaudy peacock dress of a Pagan,
To fear God, walk in His steps, break no laws,
Be yourself and keep out of the devil's claws.
These folks will some day say kind words, revere
Your name, and place a wreath upon your bier.
                    (taking a few steps)
Why, that ornery rascal, that little faker!
She surely took me, hook, line and sinker.
She was on the verge of turning my head.
Well, that's over, thank heaven! The less said
The better. But it's some comfort, I was off guard
In a weak moment. Soothsaying's a hazard—
That's not my forte. After all, I'm still a man—

In courting the little goose, I was only human.
Ha! There's no fool like an old fool, they say.

(Bursts out laughing)

Sir Peter Gynt singing, dancing, so blithe and gay;
Strumming the lute, crowing like a rooster.
Ha! Then plucked by a hen of every feather.
Yes, plucked, plucked clean to the bone—
I have only a trifle I can call my own.

(feeling in his pockets)

A little cash in hand, in America some holdings—
Not quite broke, not enough to hobnob with kings.
I feel better foot-loose, with no trappings—
Horses, coachmen, servants and the like.
No! I'm not washed up yet. I'll soon strike
Something good; of course, as a merchantman
And lover, I'm finished. However, I don't plan
To retrace my steps. No, I'll turn over a new leaf.
I must find some noble task. I'll find relief—
Say in my autobiography. No, 'twould be too long,
I'll just write a history of the world—a song
Of humanity, with all its joy and grief.
Like a feather, I'll float down history's stream,
And make it live again, as in a dream.

(With quiet emotion)

See brave men battle for truth and right,
Of course, I'll keep safely out of sight;
See saints and sages sacrificed for spite:
See war, the trade of Kings, wax and wane;
See the conquering heroes come and go—
In short, I'll skim off the cream of history,
I'll give them something different and new,
I can always fall back on my lying.
Aye, I'll bury myself in antiquity
And forsake the beaten paths of the living.
The present's not worth a pair of shoe-strings.
Here, I think, I may find myself again.
Proud and vain are the ways of men and kings—
Their souls have no wings, their deeds no salt.

(Shrugs his shoulders)

And woman—ah, that's the Maker's fault!

Scene X

A summer day, far up North. A hut in the woods. A door, with a large wooden bar, stands open. Above the door a pair of large antlers. A small herd of goats grazes by the side of the hut. Solveig, now middle-aged but fair and comely, sits and spins outside in the sunlight.

Solveig. *(Looks down the path and sings)*
The seasons slowly come and go;
 I know you will return some day;
 Here I abide, lad, and spin and pray
As I promised, lad, long, long ago.
   (calls the goats, and spins and sings again)
God guard you, wherever you are;
 God bless you when you kneel in prayer;
 I'll abide in thee, lad, forever;
If above, lad, I'll meet you there.

Scene XI

In Egypt, Dawn at the foot of the Statue of Memnon.

Peer Gynt. *(Comes on, stops and looks around.)*
Just the right place for Gynt, the Historian
To begin. For the present I'm an Egyptian,
And, of course, with the emphasis on I.
Next, I'll take ancient Assyria on high.
To begin right back at the world's creation
Would lead only to trouble and confusion.
Anyhow, Bible lore's not popular to-day—
I'll just take a bird's-eye view, as they say.
I'll abridge or elaborate here and there,
Pick out the high spots in true Gynt flair—
When you describe a horse you don't enumerate
All the hairs in his tail.

611

MUHAMMAD IQBAL

MUHAMMAD IQBAL (Indian, 1876-1938). Foremost poet of Moslem India in
20th century. Uneventful life, educated at Lahore and in England, earned
living as lawyer. Wrote in several languages, most of poetry in Urdu or
Persian. Persian works are more philosophical, the Urdu more lyrical and
popular. Strong social consciousness.

COMMUNITY

Upon what manner man is bound to man:
That tale's a thread, the end whereof is lost
Beyond unravelling. We can descry
The Individual within the Mass,
And we can pluck him as a flower is plucked
Out of the garden. All his nature is
Entranced with individuality,
Yet only in Society he finds
Security and preservation. On
The road of life, the furnace of life's fire,
That roaring battle-field, sets him aflame.
Men grow habituated each to each,
Like jewels threaded on a single cord;
Succour each other in the war of life
In mutual bond, like workmen bent upon
A common task. Through such polarity
The constellations congregate, each star
In several attraction keeping each
Poised firmly and unshaken. Caravans
May pitch their tents on mountain or on hill,
Broad meadow, fringe of desert, sandy mound.
Yet slack and lifeless hangs the warp and woof
Of the Group's labour, unresolved the bud
Of its deep meditation, still unplayed
The flickering levin of its instrument,
Its music hushed within its muted strings,
Unsmitten by the pounding of the quest,
The plectrum of desire; disordered still
Its new-born concourse, and so thin its wine
As to be blotted up with cotton flock;

New-sprung the verdure of its soil, and cold
The blood in its vine's veins; a habitat
Of demons and of fairy sprites its thoughts,
So that it leaps in terror from the shapes
Conjured by its own surmise; shrunk the scope
Of its crude life, its narrow thoughts confined
Beneath the rim of its constricting roof;
Fear for its life the meagre stock-in-trade
Of its constituent elements; its heart
Trembling before the whistle of the wind;
Its spirit shies away from arduous toil,
Little disposed to pluck at Nature's skirt,
But whatsoever springs of its own self
Or falls from heaven, that it gathers up.
Till God discovers a man pure of heart
In His good time, who in a single word
A volume shall rehearse; a minstrel he
Whose piercing music gives new life to dust.
Through him the unsubstantial atom glows
Radiant with life, the meanest merchandise
Takes on new worth. Out of his single breath
Two hundred bodies quicken; with one glass
He livens an assembly. His bright glance
Slays, but forthwith his single uttered word
Bestows new life, that so Duality
Expiring, Unity may come to birth.
His thread, whose end is knotted to the skies,
Weaves all together life's dissevered parts.
Revealing a new vista to the gaze,
He can convert broad desert and bare vale
Into a garden. At his fiery breath
A people leap like rue upon a fire
In sudden tumult, in their heart one spark
Caught from his kindling, and their sullen clay
Breaks instantly aflame. Where'er he treads
The earth receiving vision, every mote
May wink the eye at Moses' Sinai.
The naked understanding he adorns,
With wealth abundant fills its indigence,
Fans with his skirts its embers, purifies
Its gold of every particle of dross.

He strikes the shackles from the fettered slave,
Redeems him from his masters, and declares:
'No other's slave thou art, nor any less
Than those mute idols.' So unto one goal
Drawing each on, he circumscribes the feet
Of all within the circle of one Law,
Reschools them in God's wondrous Unity,
And teaches them the habit and the use
Of self-surrender to the Will Divine.

WASHINGTON IRVING

WASHINGTON IRVING (American, 1783-1859). First American man of letters, supporting self by writing. Traveled widely abroad, first American literary ambassador. Fame established with *The Sketch Book*, containing "Rip Van Winkle" and "The Legend of Sleepy Hollow." Interest in Spain created *The Alhambra*. Later became ambassador to Spain. Charm lies in his urbane style, genial temperament.

THE LEGEND OF THE ENCHANTED SOLDIER

EVERYBODY has heard of the Cave of St. Cyprian at Salamanca, where in old times judicial astronomy, necromancy, chiromancy, and other dark and damnable arts were secretly taught by an ancient sacristan; or, some will have it, by the devil himself in that disguise. The cave has long been shut up and the very site of it forgotten; though, according to tradition, the entrance was somewhere about where the stone cross stands in the small square of the seminary of Carvajal, and this tradition appears in some degree corroborated by the circumstances of the following story:—

There was at one time a student of Salamanca, Don Vicente by name, of that merry but mendicant class who set out on the road to learning without a penny in pouch for the journey, and who during college vacations beg from town to town and village to village to raise funds to enable them to pursue their studies through the ensuing term. He was now about to set forth on his wanderings, and, being somewhat musical, slung on his back a guitar with which to amuse the villagers and pay for a meal or a night's lodging.

As he passed by the stone cross in the seminary square he pulled off his hat and made a short invocation to St. Cyprian for good luck, when casting his eyes upon the earth he perceived something glitter at the foot of the cross. On picking it up, it proved to be a seal ring of mixed metal, in which gold and silver appeared to be blended. The seal bore as a device two triangles crossing each other so as to form a star. This device is said to be a cabalistic sign invented by King Solomon the Wise, and of mighty power in all cases of enchantment; but the honest student, being neither sage or conjurer, knew nothing of the matter. He took the ring as a present from St. Cyprian in reward of his prayer, slipped it on his finger, made a bow to the cross, and strumming his guitar set off merrily on his wandering.

The life of a mendicant student in Spain is not the most miserable in the world, especially if he has any talent at making himself agreeable. He rambles at large from village to village and city to city wherever curiosity or caprice may conduct him. The country curates, who, for the most part, have been mendicant students in their time, give him shelter for the night and a comfortable meal, and often enrich him with several quartos or halfpence in the morning. As he presents himself from door to door in the streets of the cities he meets with no harsh rebuff, no chilling contempt, for there is no disgrace attending his mendicity. Many of the most learned men in Spain have commenced their career in this manner; but if, like the student in question, he is a good-looking varlet and a merry companion, and, above all, if he can play the guitar, he is sure of a hearty welcome among the peasants, and smiles and favors from their wives and daughters.

In this way, then, did our ragged and musical son of learning make his way over half the kingdom, with the fixed determination to visit the famous city of Granada before his return. Sometimes he was gathered for the night into the fold of some village pastor; sometimes he was sheltered under the humble but hospitable roof of the peasant. Seated at the cottage door with his guitar he delighted the simple folk with his ditties; or striking up a fandango or bolero, set the brown country lads and lasses dancing in the mellow twilight. In the morning he departed with kind words from host and hostess.

At length he arrived at the great object of his musical vagabondizing, the far-famed city of Granada, and hailed with wonder and delight its Moorish towers, its lovely Vega, and its snowy

615

mountains glistening through a summer atmosphere. It is needless to say with what eager curiosity he entered its gates and wandered through its streets, and gazed upon its Oriental monuments. Every female face peering through a window or beaming from a balcony was to him a Zorayda or a Zelinda, nor could he meet a stately dame on the Alameda, but he was ready to fancy her a Moorish princess and to spread his student's robe beneath her feet.

His musical talent, his happy humor, his youth, and his good looks won him a universal welcome in spite of his ragged robes, and for several days he led a gay life in the old Moorish capital and its environs. One of his occasional haunts was the fountain of Avellanos, in the valley of the Darro. It is one of the popular resorts of Granada, and has been so since the days of the Moors; and here the student had an opportunity of pursuing his studies of female beauty, a branch of study to which he was a little prone.

Here he would take his seat with his guitar, improvise love ditties to admiring groups, or prompt with his music the ever ready dance. He was thus engaged one evening, when he beheld a padre of the Church advancing, at whose approach every one touched the hat. He was evidently a man of consequence; he certainly was a mirror of good, if not of holy, living; robust and rosy-faced, and breathing at every pore, with the warmth of the weather and the exercise of the walk. As he passed along he would every now and then draw a maravedi out of his pocket, and bestow it on a beggar, with an air of signal beneficence. "Ah, the blessed father!" would be the cry. "Long life to him, and may he soon be a bishop!"

To aid his steps in ascending the hill, he leaned gently now and then on the arm of a handmaid.

The good padre looked benignantly on the company about the fountain, and took his seat with some emphasis on a stone bench, while the handmaid hastened to bring him a glass of sparkling water. He sipped it deliberately, and with relish, tempering it with one of those spongy pieces of frosted eggs and sugar so dear to Spanish epicures, and on returning the glass to the hand of the damsel pinched her cheek with infinite loving-kindness.

"Ah, the good pastor!" whispered the student to himself. "What a happiness would it be to be gathered into his fold with such a damsel for a companion!"

But no such good fare was likely to befall him. In vain he essayed those powers of pleasing which he had found so irresistible with country curates and country lasses. Never had he touched his guitar with such skill; never had he poured forth more soul-moving ditties; but he had no longer a country curate or country lass to deal with. The worthy priest evidently did not relish music, and the modest damsel never raised her eyes from the ground. They remained but a short time at the fountain. The good padre hastened their return to Granada. The damsel gave the student one shy glance in retiring, but it plucked the heart out of his bosom!

He inquired about them after they had gone. Padre Thomas was one of the saints of Granada, a model of regularity—punctual in his hour of rising; his hour of taking a paseo for an appetite; his hour of playing his game of tresillo, of an evening, with some of the dames of the cathedral circle; his hour of supping; and his hour of retiring to rest, to gather fresh strength for another day's round of similar duties. He had an easy, sleek mule for his riding; a matronly housekeeper, skilled in preparing titbits for his table.

Adieu now to the gay, thoughtless life of the student; the side glance of a bright eye had been the undoing of him. Day and night he could not get the image of this most modest damsel out of his mind. He sought the mansion of the padre. Alas! it was above the class of houses accessible to a strolling student like himself. The worthy padre had no sympathy with him; he had never been obliged to sing for his supper. He blockaded the house by day, catching a glance of the damsel now and then as she appeared at a casement; but these glances only fed his flame without encouraging his hope. He serenaded her balcony at night, and at one time was flattered by the appearance of something white at a window. Alas, it was only the nightcap of the padre.

Never was lover more devoted; never damsel more shy; the poor student was reduced to despair. At length arrived the eve of St. John, when the lower classes of Granada swarm into the country, dance away the afternoon, and pass midsummer's night on the banks of the Darro and the Xenil. Happy are they who, on this eventful night, can wash their faces in those waters just as the cathedral bell tells midnight; for at that precise moment they have a beautifying power. The student, having nothing to do, suffered himself to be carried away by the holiday-seeking throng until he found himself in the narrow valley of the Darro, below the lofty hill and ruddy towers of the Alhambra. The dry bed of the river, the rocks which border it, the terraced gardens which overhang it, were alive with variegated groups, dancing under the vines and fig trees to the sound of the guitar and castanets.

The student remained for some time in doleful dumps, leaning against one of the huge misshapen stone pomegranates which adorn the ends of the little bridge over the Darro. He cast a wistful glance upon the merry scene, where every cavalier had his dame; or, to speak more appropriately, every Jack his Jill; sighed at his own solitary state, a victim to the black eye of the most unapproachable of damsels, and repined at his ragged garb, which seemed to shut the gate of hope against him.

By degrees his attention was attracted to a neighbor equally solitary with himself. This was a tall soldier, of a stern aspect and grizzled beard, who seemed posted as a sentry at the opposite pomegranate. His face was bronzed by time; he was arrayed in ancient Spanish armor, with buckler and lance, and stood immovable as a statue. What surprised the student was, that though thus strangely equipped, he was totally unnoticed by the passing throng, albeit that many almost brushed against him.

"This is a city of old-time peculiarities," thought the student, "and doubtless this is one of them with which the inhabitants are too famliar to be surprised." His own curiosity, however, was awakened; and, being of a social disposition, he accosted the soldier.

"A rare old suit of armor that which you wear, comrade. May I ask what corps you belong to?"

The soldier gasped out a reply from a pair of jaws which seemed to have rusted on their hinges.

"The royal guard of Ferdinand and Isabella."

"Santa Maria! Why, it is three centuries since that corps was in service."

"And for three centuries have I been mounting guard. Now I trust my tour of duty draws to a close. Dost thou desire fortune?"

The student held up his tattered cloak in reply.

"I understand thee. If thou hast faith and courage, follow me, and thy fortune is made."

"Softly, comrade. To follow thee would require small courage in one who has nothing to lose but life and an old guitar, neither of much value; but my faith is of a different matter, and not to be put in temptation. If it be any criminal act by which I am to mend my fortune, think not my ragged cloak will make me undertake it."

The soldier turned on him a look of high displeasure. "My sword," said he, "has never been drawn but in the cause of the faith and the throne. I am an old Christian; trust in me and fear no evil."

The student followed him, wondering. He observed that no one heeded their conversation, and that the soldier made his way through the various groups of idlers unnoticed, as if invisible.

Crossing the bridge, the soldier led the way by a narrow and steep path past a Moorish mill and aqueduct, and up the ravine which separates the domains of the Generalife from those of the Alhambra. The last ray of the sun shone upon the red battlements of the latter, which beetled far above; and the convent bells were proclaiming the festival of the ensuing day. The ravine was overshadowed by fig trees, vines, and myrtles, and the outer towers and walls of the fortress. It was dark and lonely, and the twilight-loving bats began to flit about. At length the soldier halted at a remote and ruined tower, apparently intended to guard a Moorish aqueduct. He struck the foundation with the butt end of his spear. A rumbling sound was heard, and the solid stones yawned apart, leaving an opening as wide as a door.

"Enter in the name of the Holy Trinity," said the soldier, "and fear nothing." The student's heart quaked, but he made the sign of the cross, muttered his Ave Maria, and followed his mysterious guide into a deep vault cut out the solid rock under the tower, and covered with Arabic inscriptions. The soldier pointed to a stone seat hewn along one side of the vault. "Behold," said he, "my couch for three hundred years." The bewildered student tried to force a joke. "By the blessed St Anthony," said he, "but you must have slept soundly, considering the hardness of your couch."

"On the contrary, sleep has been a stranger to these eyes; incessant watchfulness has been my doom. Listen to my lot. I was one of the royal guards of Ferdinand and Isabella, but was taken prisoner by the Moors in one of their sorties, and confined a captive in this tower. When preparations were made to surrender the fortress to the Christian sovereigns, I was prevailed upon by an alfaqui, a Moorish priest, to aid him in secreting some of the treasures of Boabdil in this vault. I was justly punished for my fault. The alfaqui was an African necromancer, and by his infernal arts cast a spell upon me to guard his treasures. Something must have happened to him, for he never returned, and here I have remained ever since, buried alive. Years and years have rolled away; earthquakes have shaken this hill; I have heard stone by stone of the tower above tumbling to the ground in the natural operation of time; but the spellbound walls of the vault have set both time and earthquakes at defiance.

"Once every hundred years, on the festival of St. John, the enchantment ceases to have thorough sway. I am permitted to go forth and post myself upon the bridge of the Darro, where you met me, waiting until some one shall arrive who may have power to break this magic spell. I have hitherto mounted guard there in vain. I walk as in a cloud, concealed from mortal sight. You are the first to accost me for now three hundred years. I behold the reason. I see on your finger the seal ring of Solomon the Wise, which is proof against all enchantment. With you it remains to deliver me from this awful dungeon, or to leave me to keep guard here for another hundred years."

The student listened to this tale in mute wonderment. He had heard many tales of treasure shut up under strong enchantment in the vaults of the Alhambra, but had treated them as fables. He now felt the value of the seal ring, which had, in a manner, been given to him by St. Cyprian. Still, though armed by so potent a talisman, it was an awful thing to find himself tête-à-tête in such a place with an enchanted soldier, who, according to the laws of nature, ought to have been quietly in his grave for nearly three centuries.

A personage of this kind, however, was quite out of the ordinary run, and not to be trifled with, and he assured him he might rely upon his friendship and good will to do everything in his power for his deliverance.

"I trust to a motive more powerful than friendship," said the soldier.

He pointed to a ponderous iron coffer, secured by locks inscribed with Arabic characters. "That coffer," said he, "contains countless treasure in gold and jewels and precious stones. Break the magic spell by which I am enthralled, and one-half of this treasure shall be thine."

"But how am I to do it?"

"The aid of a Christian priest and a Christian maid is necessary; the priest to exorcise the powers of darkness, the damsel to touch this chest with the seal of Solomon. This must be done at night. But have a care. This is solemn work, and not to be effected by the carnal-minded. The priest must be an old Christian, a model of sanctity; and must mortify the flesh, before he comes here, by a rigorous fast of four-and-twenty hours; and as to the maiden, she must be above reproach, and proof against temptation. Linger not in finding such aid. In three days my furlough is at an end; if not delivered before midnight of the third, I shall have to mount guard for another century."

"Fear not," said the student, "I have in my eye the very priest and damsel you describe; but how am I to regain admission to this tower?"

"The seal of Solomon will open the way for thee."

The student issued forth from the tower much more gaily than he had entered. The wall closed behind him, and remained solid as before.

The next morning he repaired boldly to the mansion of the priest, no longer a poor, strolling student, thrumming his way with a guitar; but an ambassador from the shadowy world, with enchanted treasures to bestow. No particulars are told of his negotiation, excepting that the zeal of the worthy priest was easily kindled at the idea of rescuing an old soldier of the faith and a strong box of King Chico from the very clutches of Satan; and then what alms might be dispensed, what churches built, and how many poor relatives enriched with the Moorish treasure!

As to the handmaid, she was ready to lend her hand, which was all that was required, to the pious work; and if a shy glance now and then might be believed, the ambassador began to find favor in her modest eyes.

The greatest difficulty, however, was the fast to which the good padrè had to subject himself. Twice he attempted it, and twice the flesh was too strong for the spirit. It was only on the third day that he was enabled to withstand the temptations of the cupboard; but it was still a question whether he would hold out until the spell was broken.

At a late hour of the night the party groped their way up the ravine, by the light of a lantern, and bearing a basket with provisions for exorcising the demon of hunger so soon as the other demons should be laid in the Red Sea.

The seal of Solomon opened their way into the tower. They found the soldier, seated on the enchanted strong box, awaiting their arrival. The exorcism was performed in due style. The damsel advanced, and touched the locks of the coffer with the seal of

621

Solomon. The lid flew open, and such treasures of gold and jewels and precious stones as flashed upon the eye!

"Here's cut, and come again!" cried the student, exultingly, as he proceeded to cram his pockets.

"Fairly and softly," exclaimed the soldier. "Let us get the coffer out entire, and then divide."

They accordingly went to work with might and main, but it was a difficult task; the chest was enormously heavy, and had been embedded there for centuries. While they were thus employed, the good dominie drew on one side, and made a vigorous onslaught on the basket, by way of exorcising the demon of hunger which was raging within him. In a little while a fat capon was devoured, and washed down by a deep potation; and, by way of grace after meat, he gave a kind-hearted kiss to the damsel who waited on him. It was quietly done in a corner, but the tell-tale walls babbled it forth as if in triumph. Never was chaste salute more awful in its effects. At the sound the soldier gave a great cry of despair; the coffer, which was half raised, fell back in its place and was locked once more. Priest, student, and damsel found themselves outside of the tower, the wall of which closed with a thundering jar. Alas! the good padre had broken his fast too soon.

When recovered from his surprise, the student would have re-entered the tower, but learnt to his dismay that the damsel, in her fright, had let fall the seal of Solomon; it remained within the vault.

In a word, the cathedral bell tolled midnight; the spell was renewed; the soldier was doomed to mount guard for another hundred years; and there he and the treasure remain to this day, and all because the kind-hearted padre kissed his handmaid.

Thus ends the legend as far as it has been authenticated. There is a tradition, however, that the student had brought off treasure enough in his pocket to set him up in the world; that he prospered in his affairs, that the worthy padre gave him the damsel in marriage, by way of amends for the blunder in the vault; and she proved a pattern for wives.

The story of the enchanted soldier remains one of the popular traditions of Granada, though told in a variety of ways; the common people affirm that he still mounts guard on midsummer eve, beside the gigantic stone pomegranate on the bridge of the Darro, but remains invisible excepting to such lucky mortal as may possess the seal of Solomon.

J

JENS PETER JACOBSEN

JENS PETER JACOBSEN (Danish, 1847-1885). Danish realistic novelist and poet. Sought to find the laws of nature in the realm of literature. Disciple of great Danish critic Brandes. Worked with such care that he produced only two novels *(Fru Marie Grubbe, Niels Lyhne),* a volume of tales *(Mogens and Other Stories),* and a few poems.

THE PLAGUE AT BERGAMO

OLD Bergamo lay up there at the top of a squatty mountain encircled by walls and towers. New Bergamo lay below at the foot of the mountain, exposed to every wind that blows.

In the new town the plague broke out and wrought havoc indescribable. Many died, and the rest fled across the plains to every point of the compass. The men of Old Bergamo set fire to the deserted town, to disinfect the air. In vain. Men began to die on the mountain, also; at first one a day, then five, then ten, then a dozen.

There were many who sought to escape, but they could not flee as those in the new town had done; they lived like hunted beasts, hiding in tombs, under bridges, behind hedges, and in the tall grass of the green fields. For the peasants stoned all strangers from their hearths, or beat them as they would mad dogs, cruelly, pitilessly—in self-protection, as they thought, for the first fugitives had brought with them the pestilence into their houses.

So the people of Old Bergamo were as prisoners in their own town. Day by day the sun blazed hotter, and day by day the terrible infection carried off more victims.

In the very beginning, when the plague came among them, they bound themselves together in unity and peace, and had taken care to decently bury the dead, and had kindled great fires in the mar-

623

kets and open places, so that the purging fumes might be blown through the streets. Juniper and vinegar had been given to the poor. Above all they had gone to church, early and late, singly and in processions; each day they lifted their voices in prayer. As the sun sank behind the mountains the church bells tolled their dirge from a hundred hanging mouths. Days were set aside for fasting, and the relics were placed upon the altars.

At last, in their extremity, amid the blare of trumpets and tubas, they proclaimed the Holy Virgin forevermore Podesta of the city.

All this was of no help. And when the people saw that nothing could aid them, that Heaven either would not or could not send them relief, they did not fold their hands together and say, "God's will be done." It was as if sin, growing by a secret, stealthy sickness, had flared into an evil, open, raging pestilence, stalking hand in hand with the body's disease, the one to kill their souls, even as the other defiled their flesh—so incredible were their deeds, so monstrous their cruelty.

"Let us eat to-day, for to-morrow we die!" It was as if this theme, set to music, were played in an endless, devilish symphony on instruments without number. The most unnatural vices flourished among them. Even such rare arts as necromancy, sorcery, and devil worship became familiar to them; for there were many who sought from the powers of hell that protection which Providence had not been willing to accord them. Everything that suggested charity and sympathy had vanished; each thought only of himself. If a beggar, faint with the first delirium of the plague, fell in the street, he was driven from door to door with sharp weapons and with stones. From the dead that lay rotting in the houses, and from the bodies hastily buried in the earth, arose a sickening stench that mingled with the heavy air of the streets, and drew ravens and crows hither in swarms and in clouds, so that the walls and housetops were black with them. And about the town walls great strange birds perched here and there—birds that came from afar, with rapacious beaks and talons expectantly curved; and they sat and stared with their quiet, hungry eyes as if awaiting the moment when the doomed town would be reduced to a heap of carrion.

Eleven weeks had passed since the plague had first broken out. Then the tower watchman and others who chanced to be on high ground perceived a singular procession winding from the plains into the narrow streets of the new town, between the smoke-blackened stone walls and the charred frames of houses. A great throng! Assuredly six hundred and more, men and women, young and old. Some among them bore large, black crosses, and some held above their heads broad banners, red as blood and fire. They sang as they marched, and strange, despairingly plaintive melodies rose in the still, oppressively hot air.

Brown, gray, black, were the colors these people wore. Yet all had a red sign on their breasts. As they came nearer and nearer this was seen to be the sign of the cross. They crowded up the steep, stone-girt space that led to the old town. Their faces were as waves of white sea; they bore scourges in their hands; a rain of fire was painted on their banners. And in the surging mass the black crosses swung from side to side. Face after face plunged into the gloom of the tower gate and emerged into the light on the other side with blinking eyes.

Then the chant was taken up anew—a *miserere*. They grasped their scourges and marched even more sturdily than if their chant had been a battle song. Their aspect was that of a people who had come from a starving town. Their cheeks were sunken; their cheekbones protruded; their lips were bloodless, and dark rings encircled their eyes. All the scourges were stained with blood.

With astonishment and uneasiness all Bergamo flocked together to gaze upon them. Red, bloated faces stood out against those that were pale; heavy, lust-weary eyes were lowered before the keen, flashing glances of the pilgrims; grinning, blasphemous mouths were struck dumb by these chants. The townspeople were spellbound.

But it was not long before the pall was shaken off. Some recognized among the cross-bearers a half-crazed cobbler of Brescia, and in a moment the procession became a butt of ridicule. Moreover, this was something new, a diversion from the monotony of everyday life, and as the strangers marched on to the cathedral, they were followed as a band of jugglers might be or as a tame bear is followed.

But soon anger seized the jostling crowd. It was clear that these cobblers and tailors had come to convert them, to pray, and to speak words that none wished to hear. Two gaunt, grizzled philosophers who had formulated blasphemy into a system incited the populace out of sheer wickedness of heart, so that the mob grew more threatening as the procession marched to the church, and more fiercely enraged. Bergamo was about to lay hands on these singular, scourge-bearing tailors. Not a hundred paces from the portal of the church a tavern opened its doors and a whole band of

625

roisterers poured out, one on the shoulders of another. And they took their places at the head of the procession, singing and howling, assuming a mock-religious mien—all save one, who jerked his thumbs contemptuously toward the grass-grown steps of the church. Rough laughter then arose, and pilgrims and blasphemers entered the sanctuary in peace.

It was strange to be in that place again, to roam through the great cool nave, in air heavy with the stale fumes of snuffed wax tapers, over sunken flagstones so familiar to the foot, and over stones with their worn ornaments and polished inscriptions, in contemplation of which the mind had often grown so weary. And while the eye, half curiously, half involuntarily rested in the dim half-light of the vaults or strayed over the mellow gaudiness of dusty gold and grimy colors, or began to lose itself in the grotesque shadows of the apse, a kind of longing arose, not to be suppressed.

Meanwhile the tavern roisterers played their pranks on the main altar itself. A tall, strong young butcher removed his white apron and wound it about his neck so that it hung at his back like a cloak. Thus arrayed, he celebrated mass, with the wildest and most shocking words of sacrilege. A small, elderly, round-bellied fellow, lively and agile in spite of his fat, with the face of a peeled pumpkin, played sexton and responded with ribald songs; he made his genuflexions and turned his back upon the altar, and rang his bell like a clown; and the other tipplers, as they made their genuflexions, threw themselves flat on the ground and roared with laughter, hiccuping drunkenly.

All within the church laughed, hooted, and jeered at the strangers, and bade them notice how God was esteemed in Old Bergamo. Yet they wished not so much to mock God as to rack the souls of these penitents with their impiety.

In the centre of the nave the pilgrims halted and groaned, such was their anguish. Their blood boiled with hate, and they thirsted for vengeance. They prayed to God, with hands and eyes uplifted, that He might smite His blasphemers for·the mockery offered Him in His house. Gladly would they perish with the presumptuous infidels, if He would but show His might; blissfully would they be crushed beneath His feet, if He would but triumph, and if these godless throats might be made to shriek in agony and despair.

They lifted up their voices in a *miserere*, each note of which rang like a prayer for that rain of fire that once swept over Sodom, for the strength that was Samson's when he grasped the pillars of the

626

Philistine temple. They prayed with words and with song; they bared their shoulders and prayed with their scourges. Kneeling, row on row, stripped to the waist they whirled stinging, knotted cords over their backs.

Frantically they scourged, until the blood spurted under their hissing lashes. Each stroke was an offering to God. Stroke on stroke came down, until arms sank or were cramped into knots. Thus they lay, row on row, with frenzied look and foaming mouth, blood dripping from their bodies.

And those that saw this of a sudden felt their hearts beat, felt the blood mount to their temples, their breathing grow hard. Their knees shook. To be the slave of a powerful, stern divinity, to fling one's self at the feet of the Lord, to be His own, not in mute devotion, not in the mild inefficacy of prayer, but in a fury of passion, in the intoxication of self-humiliation, in blood and lamentation, and smitten with the moist, glistening tongues of scourges—this they could understand. Even the butcher held his peace; and the toothless philosophers bowed their grizzled heads.

Silence reigned in the church; only a gentle breathing passed through the multitude.

Then one of the strangers, a young friar, rose and spoke. His was the pallor of bloodless flesh; his black eyes glowed; and the sad lines of his mouth were as if cut with a knife in wood, and not mere furrows in a human face.

He lifted up his thin, suffering hands in prayer to Heaven, and the black sleeves of his gown slipped back from his lean arms.

Then he spoke—of hell, of its eternity, of the eternity of Heaven, of the solitary world of pain which each of the damned must suffer and must fill with his cries of agony. In that world were seas of sulphur, meadows of wasps, flames to be wrapped about them like a cloak, and hard flames that would pierce them like a probe twisting in a wound.

Breathlessly all listened to his words; for he spoke as if he had seen these things with his own eyes. And they asked themselves: "Is this man not one of the damned, sent to us from the mouth of hell, to testify?"

Then he preached long of the commandments and their rigor, of the need of obeying them to the very letter, and of the dire punishment that awaited him who sinned against them. " 'But Christ died for our sins,' ye say. 'We are no longer bound by the Word.' But I say that hell will not be cheated of one of you, and not one of the iron teeth of hell's wheel will your flesh escape. Ye build upon Calvary's cross? Come! Come and see it! I will lead you to its foot. It was on a Friday, as ye know, when they cast Him from their gates and laid the heavier end of a cross upon His shoulders and suffered Him to bear it to a barren and naked hill without the city; and they walked beside Him and stirred up the dust with their feet, so that it rested over them like a red cloud. And they tore His garments from Him, even as the lords of justice strip a criminal before all eyes, that all might see His body. And they threw Him down upon His cross, and stretched Him upon it, and drove an iron nail through each of His unresistant hands and a nail through His crossed feet. And they raised the cross in a hole dug in the earth; but it would stand neither firm nor upright. So they shook it and drove wedges and blocks around it. And those that did this turned down the brims of their hats so that the blood of His hands might not drip into their eyes.

"And He from on high looked down upon the soldiers casting dice for His seamless coat, and down upon all the howling mob for whose salvation He suffered. Not one tearful eye was there in all the multitude. And those who were below looked up at Him, hanging from the cross, suffering, and faint. They read the inscription above His head: 'King of the Jews,' and they mocked Him and called up to Him: 'Thou that destroyest the temple, and buildest it in three days, save Thyself. If Thou be the Son of God, come down from the cross.'

"Then God's noble Son waxed wroth and saw that these were unworthy of salvation, this mob that swarmed over the earth; and He wrenched His feet from the nail, and He clenched His fingers and tore His hands away, so that the arms of the cross bent as a bow. And He leaped to the earth and caught up His garment, so that the dice rolled over the precipice of Golgotha, and threw it about His person with the righteous wrath of a king, and ascended into heaven. And the cross stood bare; and the great work of atonement remained unfulfilled. No mediator stands between us and God. No Jesus died for us on the cross! No Jesus died for us on the cross!"

He ceased.

As he uttered the last words he bent toward the multitude and with his lips and hands flung his words, as it were, upon their heads. A groan of fear ran through the church. Sobs could be heard.

Then the butcher with uplifted, threatening hands, pallid as a corpse, stepped forward and commanded:

"Monk, nail Him to the cross again, nail Him—!"

And from all lips, pleadingly, threateningly, a storm of voices rolled to the vault above: "Crucify Him!"

But the monk looked down upon these fluttering, uplifted hands, upon these distorted faces with the dark openings of their screaming mouths, from which the teeth flashed like those of tormented beasts of prey; and in the ecstasy of the moment he extended his arms toward Heaven, and laughed. Then he descended; and his people raised the banners of the fiery rain and their plain, black crosses and pushed out of the church. Once more they marched, singing, across the marketplace, and once more they passed through the mouth of the tower gate.

And the people of Old Bergamo stared after them, as they proceeded down the mountain. The steep, wall-girt road was obscured in the uncertain light of the setting sun, and the procession could be only half seen in the glare. Their huge crosses, swaying in the crowd from side to side, cast sharp, black shadows on the glowing walls of the town.

In the distance a chant could be heard. A banner or two gleamed red from the charred site of the new town, and the pilgrims vanished into the bright plain.

HENRY JAMES

HENRY JAMES (American, 1843-1916). Novelist and critic, noted as precise stylist. Educated in Europe, led cosmopolitan life, eventually became British citizen. Favorite theme: contrast between naïve Americans and sophisticated Europeans. Later writing became more and more subtle, overrefined, idiosyncratic. Some of novels: *The American, The Portrait of a Lady, The Wings of the Dove, Washington Square, The Ambassadors, The Golden Bowl.*

CONFIDENCE

CHAPTER I

IT WAS in the early days of April; Bernard Longueville had been spending the winter in Rome. He had travelled northward with the consciousness of several social duties that appealed to him from the further side of the Alps, but he was under the charm of the Italian

629

spring, and he made a pretext for lingering. He had spent five days at Siena, where he had intended to spend but two, and still it was impossible to continue his journey. He was a young man of a contemplative and speculative turn, and this was his first visit to Italy, so that if he dallied by the way he should not be harshly judged. He had a fancy for sketching, and it was on his conscience to take a few pictorial notes. There were two old inns at Siena, both of them very shabby and very dirty. The one at which Longueville had taken up his abode was entered by a dark, pestiferous archway, surmounted by a sign which at a distance might have been read by the travellers as the Dantean injunction to renounce all hope. The other was not far off, and the day after his arrival, as he passed it, he saw two ladies going in who evidently belonged to the large fraternity of Anglo-Saxon tourists, and one of whom was young and carried herself very well. Longueville had his share—or more than his share—of gallantry, and this incident awakened a regret. If he had gone to the other inn he might have had charming company: at his own establishment there was no one but an æsthetic German who smoked bad tobacco in the dining-room. He remarked to himself that this was always his luck, and the remark was characteristic of the man; it was charged with the feeling of the moment, but it was not absolutely just; it was the result of an acute impression made by the particular occasion; but it failed in appreciation of a providence which had sprinkled Longueville's career with happy accidents—accidents, especially, in which his characteristic gallantry was not allowed to rust for want of exercise. He lounged, however, contentedly enough through these bright, still days of a Tuscan April, drawing much entertainment from the high picturesqueness of the things about him. Siena, a few years since, was a flawless gift of the Middle Ages to the modern imagination. No other Italian city could have been more interesting to an observer fond of reconstructing obsolete manners. This was a taste of Bernard Longueville's, who had a relish for serious literature, and at one time had made several lively excursions into mediæval history. His friends thought him very clever, and at the same time had an easy feeling about him which was a tribute to his freedom from pedantry. He was clever, indeed, and an excellent companion; but the real measure of his brilliancy was in the success with which he entertained himself. He was much addicted to conversing with his own wit, and he greatly enjoyed his own society. Clever as he often was in talking with his friends, I am not sure that his best things, as the phrase is, were not for his own ears. And this was not on account of any cynical contempt for the understanding of his fellow-creatures: it was simply because what I have called his own society was more of a stimulus than that of most other people. And yet he was not for this reason fond of solitude; he was, on the contrary, a very sociable animal. It must be admitted at the outset that he had a nature which seemed at several points to contradict itself, as will probably be perceived in the course of this narration.

He entertained himself greatly with his reflections and meditations upon Sienese architecture and early Tuscan art, upon Italian street-life and the geological idiosyncrasies of the Apennines. If he had only gone to the other inn, that nice-looking girl whom he had seen passing under the dusky portal with her face turned away from him might have broken bread with him at this intellectual banquet. There came a day, however, when it seemed for a moment that if she were disposed she might gather up the crumbs of the feast. Longueville, every morning after breakfast, took a turn in the great square of Siena—the vast *piazza*, shaped like a horse-shoe, where the market is held beneath the windows of that crenellated palace from whose overhanging cornice a tall, straight tower springs up with a movement as light as that of a single plume in the bonnet of a captain. Here he strolled about, watching a brown *contadino* disembarrass his donkey, noting the progress of half an hour's chaffer over a bundle of carrots, wishing a young girl with eyes like animated agates would let him sketch her, and gazing up at intervals at the beautiful, slim tower, as it played at contrasts with the large blue air. After he had spent the greater part of a week in these grave considerations, he made up his mind to leave Siena. But he was not content with what he had done for his portfolio. Siena was eminently sketchable, but he had not been industrious. On the last morning of his visit, as he stood staring about him in the crowded piazza, and feeling that, in spite of its picturesqueness, this was an awkward place for setting up an easel, he bethought himself, by contrast, of a quiet corner in another part of the town, which he had chanced upon in one of his first walks—an angle of a lonely terrace that abutted upon the city-wall, where three or four super-annuated objects seemed to slumber in the sunshine—the open door of an empty church, with a faded fresco exposed to the air in the arch above it, and an ancient beggar woman sitting beside it on a three-legged stool. The little terrace had an old polished parapet, about as high as a man's breast, above which was a view of strange, sad-colored hills. Outside, to the left, the wall of the town made an outward bend, and exposed its rugged and rusty complexion. There was a smooth stone bench set into the wall of the church, on which Longueville had rested for an hour, observing the composition of the little picture of which I have indicated the elements, and of which the parapet of the terrace would form the foreground. The thing was what painters call a subject, and he had promised himself to come back with his utensils. This morning he returned to the inn and took possession of them, and then he made his way through a labyrinth of empty streets, lying on the edge of the town, within the wall, like the superfluous folds of a garment whose wearer has shrunken with old age. He reached his little grass-grown terrace, and found it as sunny and as private as before. The old mendicant was mumbling petitions, sacred and profane, at the church door; but save for this the stillness was unbroken. The yellow sunshine warmed the brown surface of the city-wall, and lighted the hollows of the Etruscan hills. Longueville settled himself on the empty bench, and, arranging his little portable apparatus, began to ply his brushes. He worked for some time smoothly and rapidly, with an agreeable sense of the absence of obstacles. It seemed almost an interruption when, in the silent air, he heard a distant bell in the town strike noon. Shortly after this, there was another interruption. The sound of a soft footstep caused him to look up; whereupon he saw a young woman standing there and bending her eyes upon the graceful artist. A second glance assured him that she was that nice girl whom he had seen going into the other inn with her mother, and suggested that she had just emerged from the little church. He suspected, however—I hardly know why—that she had been looking at him for some moments before he perceived her. It would perhaps be impertinent to inquire what she thought of him; but Longueville, in the space of an instant, made two or three reflections upon the young lady. One of them was to the effect that she was a handsome creature, but that she looked rather bold; the burden of the other was that—yes, decidedly—she was a compatriot. She turned away almost as soon as she met his eyes; he had hardly time to raise his hat, as, after a moment's hesitation, he proceeded to do. She herself appeared to feel a certain hesitation; she glanced back at the church door, as if under the impulse to retrace her steps. She stood there a moment longer—long enough to let him see that she was a person of easy attitudes—and then she walked away slowly to the parapet of the terrace. Here she stationed her-

632

self, leaning her arms upon the high stone ledge, presenting her back to Longueville, and gazing at rural Italy. Longueville went on with his sketch, but less attentively than before. He wondered what this young lady was doing there alone, and then it occurred to him that her companion—her mother, presumably—was in the church. The two ladies had been in the church when he arrived; women liked to sit in churches; they had been there more than half an hour, and the mother had not enough of it even yet. The young lady, however, at present preferred the view that Longueville was painting; he became aware that she had placed herself in the very centre of his foreground. His first feeling was that she would spoil it; his second was that she would improve it. Little by little she turned more into profile, leaning only one arm upon the parapet, while the other hand, holding her folded parasol, hung down at her side. She was motionless; it was almost as if she were standing there on purpose to be drawn. Yes, certainly she improved the picture. Her profile, delicate and thin, defined itself against the sky, in the clear shadow of a coquettish hat; her figure was light; she bent and leaned easily; she wore a gray dress, fastened up as was then the fashion, and displaying the broad edge of a crimson petticoat. She kept her position; she seemed absorbed in the view. "Is she *posing*—is she attitudinizing for my benefit?" Longueville asked of himself. And then it seemed to him that this was a needless assumption, for the prospect was quite beautiful enough to be looked at for itself, and there was nothing impossible in a pretty girl having a love of fine landscape. "But posing or not," he went on, "I will put her into my sketch. She has simply put herself in. It will give it a human interest. There is nothing like having a human interest." So, with the ready skill that he possessed, he introduced the young girl's figure into his foreground, and at the end of ten minutes he had almost made something that had the form of a likeness. "If she will only be quiet for another ten minutes," he said, "the thing will really be a picture." Unfortunately, the young lady was not quiet; she had apparently had enough of her attitude and her view. She turned away, facing Longueville again, and slowly came back, as if to re-enter the church. To do so she had to pass near him, and as she approached he instinctively got up, holding his drawing in one hand. She looked at him again, with that expression that he had mentally characterized as "bold" a few minutes before—with dark, intelligent eyes. Her hair was dark and dense; she was a strikingly handsome girl.

"I am so sorry you moved," he said, confidently, in English. "You were so—so beautiful."

She stopped, looking at him more directly than ever; and she looked at his sketch, which he held out toward her. At the sketch, however, she only glanced, whereas there was observation in the eye that she bent upon Longueville. He never knew whether she had blushed; he afterward thought she might have been frightened. Nevertheless, it was not exactly terror that appeared to dictate her answer to Longueville's speech.

"I am much obliged to you. Don't you think you have looked at me enough?"

"By no means. I should like so much to finish my drawing."

"I am not a professional model," said the young lady.

"No. That's my difficulty," Longueville answered, laughing. "I can't propose to remunerate you."

The young lady seemed to think this joke in indifferent taste. She turned away in silence; but something in her expression, in his feeling at the time, in the situation, incited Longueville to higher play. He felt a lively need of carrying his point.

"You see it will be pure kindness," he went on,—"a simple act of charity. Five minutes will be enough. Treat me as an Italian beggar."

He had laid down his sketch and had stepped forward. He stood there, obsequious, clasping his hands and smiling.

His interruptress stopped and looked at him again, as if she thought him a very odd person; but she seemed amused. Now, at any rate, she was not frightened. She seemed even disposed to provoke him a little.

"I wish to go to my mother," she said.

"Where is your mother?" the young man asked.

"In the church, of course. I didn't come here alone!"

"Of course not; but you may be sure that your mother is very contented. I have been in that little church. It is charming. She is just resting there; she is probably tired. If you will kindly give me five minutes more, she will come out to you."

"Five minutes?" the young girl asked.

"Five minutes will do. I shall be eternally grateful." Longueville was amused at himself as he said this. He cared infinitely less for his sketch than the words appeared to imply; but, somehow, he cared greatly that this graceful stranger should do what he had proposed.

634

The graceful stranger dropped an eye on the sketch again.

"Is your picture so good as that?" she asked.

"I have a great deal of talent," he answered, laughing. "You shall see for yourself, when it is finished."

She turned slowly toward the terrace again.

"You certainly have a great deal of talent, to induce me to do what you ask." And she walked to where she had stood before. Longueville made a movement to go with her, as if to show her the attitude he meant; but, pointing with decision to his easel, she said—

"You have only five minutes." He immediately went back to his work, and she made a vague attempt to take up her position. "You must tell me if this will do," she added, in a moment.

"It will do beautifully," Longueville answered, in a happy tone, looking at her and plying his brush. "It is immensely good of you to take so much trouble."

For a moment she made no rejoinder, but presently she said—

"Of course if I pose at all I wish to pose well."

"You pose admirably," said Longueville.

After this she said nothing, and for several minutes he painted rapidly and in silence. He felt a certain excitement, and the movement of his thoughts kept pace with that of his brush. It was very true that she posed admirably; she was a fine creature to paint. Her prettiness inspired him, and also her audacity, as he was content to regard it for the moment. He wondered about her—who she was, and what she was—perceiving that the so-called audacity was not vulgar boldness, but the play of an original and probably interesting character. It was obvious that she was a perfect lady, but it was equally obvious that she was irregularly clever. Longueville's little figure was a success—a charming success, he thought, as he put on the last touches. While he was doing this, his model's companion came into view. She came out of the church, pausing a moment as she looked from her daughter to the young man in the corner of the terrace; then she walked straight over to the young girl. She was a delicate little gentlewoman, with a light, quick step.

Longueville's five minutes were up; so, leaving his place, he approached the two ladies, sketch in hand. The elder one, who had passed her hand into her daughter's arm, looked up at him with clear, surprised eyes; she was a charming old woman. Her eyes were very pretty, and on either side of them, above a pair of fine dark brows, was a band of silvery hair, rather coquettishly arranged.

"It is my portrait," said her daughter, as Longueville drew near. "This gentleman has been sketching me."

"Sketching you, dearest?" murmured her mother. "Wasn't it rather sudden?"

"Very sudden—very abrupt!" exclaimed the young girl with a laugh.

"Considering all that, it's very good," said Longueville, offering his picture to the elder lady, who took it and began to examine it. "I can't tell you how much I thank you," he said to his model.

"It's very well for you to thank me now," she replied. "You really had no right to begin."

"The temptation was so great."

"We should resist temptation. And you should have asked my leave."

"I was afraid you would refuse it; and you stood there, just in my line of vision."

"You should have asked me to get out of it."

"I should have been very sorry. Besides, it would have been extremely rude."

The young girl looked at him a moment.

"Yes, I think it would. But what you have done is ruder."

"It is a hard case!" said Longueville. "What could I have done, then, decently?"

"It's a beautiful drawing," murmured the elder lady, handing the thing back to Longueville. Her daughter, meanwhile, had not even glanced at it.

"You might have waited till I should go away," this argumentative young person continued.

Longueville shook his head.

"I never lose opportunities!"

"You might have sketched me afterwards, from memory."

Longueville looked at her, smiling.

"Judge how much better my memory will be now!"

She also smiled a little, but instantly became serious.

"For myself, it is an episode I shall try to forget. I don't like the part I have played in it."

"May you never play a less becoming one!" cried Longueville. "I hope that your mother, at least, will accept a memento of the occasion." And he turned again with the sketch to her companion, who had been listening to the girl's conversation with this enterprising stranger, and looking from one to the other with an air of earnest confusion. "Won't you do me the honor of keeping my sketch?" he said. "I think it really looks like your daughter."

"Oh, thank you, thank you; I hardly dare," murmured the lady, with a deprecating gesture.

"It will serve as a kind of amends for the liberty I have taken," Longueville added; and he began to remove the drawing from its paper block.

"It makes it worse for you to give it to us," said the young girl.

"Oh, my dear, I am sure it's lovely!" exclaimed her mother. "It's wonderfully like you."

"I think that also makes it worse!"

Longueville was at last nettled. The young lady's perversity was perhaps not exactly malignant; but it was certainly ungracious. She seemed to desire to present herself as a beautiful tormentress.

"How does it make it worse?" he asked, with a frown.

He believed she was clever, and she was certainly ready. Now, however, she reflected a moment before answering.

"That you should give us your sketch," she said at last.

"It was to your mother I offered it," Longueville observed.

But this observation, the fruit of his irritation, appeared to have no effect upon the young girl.

"Isn't it what painters call a study?" she went on. "A study is of use to the painter himself. Your justification would be that you should keep your sketch, and that it might be of use to you."

"My daughter is a study, sir, you will say," said the elder lady in a little, light, conciliating voice, and graciously accepting the drawing again.

"I will admit," said Longueville, "that I am very inconsistent. Set it down to my esteem, madam," he added, looking at the mother.

"That's for you, mamma," said his model, disengaging her arm from her mother's hand and turning away.

The mamma stood looking at the sketch with a smile which seemed to express a tender desire to reconcile all accidents.

"It's extremely beautiful," she murmured, "and if you insist on my taking it——"

"I shall regard it as a great honor."

"Very well, then; with many thanks, I will keep it." She looked at the young man a moment, while her daughter walked away.

Longueville thought her a delightful little person; she struck him as a sort of transfigured Quakeress—a mystic with a practical side. "I am sure you think she is a strange girl," she said.

"She is extremely pretty."

"She is very clever," said the mother.

"She is wonderfully graceful."

"Ah, but she's good!" cried the old lady.

"I am sure she comes honestly by that," said Longueville, expressively, while his companion, returning his salutation with a certain scrupulous grace of her own, hurried after her daughter.

Longueville remained there staring at the view, but not especially seeing it. He felt as if he had at once enjoyed and lost an opportunity. After a while he tried to make a sketch of the old beggar-woman who sat there in a sort of palsied immobility, like a rickety statue at a church-door. But his attempt to reproduce her features was not gratifying, and he suddenly laid down his brush. She was not pretty enough—she had a bad profile.

JAMI

JAMI (Persian, 1414-1492). The last great classical poet of Persia. Mystic and scholar, devoted to Sufism. Highly honored by the Ottoman sultans. Wrote three *Divans* of lyric poetry, seven long *Masnavis*, and great variety of prose works.

ZULAIKHA

... There was a King in the West. His name
Taimùs, was spread wide by the drum of Fame.
Of royal power and wealth possessed,
No wish unanswered remained in his breast.
His brow gave luster to Glory's crown,
And his foot gave the thrones of the Mighty renown.
With Orion from heaven his host to aid,
Conquest was his when he bared his blade.
His child Zulaikha was passing fair:
None in his heart might with her compare,—

638

Of his royal house the most brilliant star,
A gem from the chest where the treasures are.
Praise cannot equal her beauty; no!
But its faint, faint shadow my pen may show.
Like her own bright hair falling loosely down,
I will touch each charm to her feet from her crown.
May the soft reflection of that bright cheek
Lend light to my spirit and bid me speak!
And that flashing ruby, her mouth, bestow
The power to tell of the things I know!
  Her stature was like to a palm tree grown
In the Garden of Grace, where no sin is known;
Bedewed by the love of her father the King,
She mocked the cypress that rose by the spring.
Sweet with the odor of musk, a snare
For the heart of the Wise, was the maiden's hair;
Tangled at night, in the morning through
Her long thick tresses a comb she drew,
And cleft the heart of the musk deer in twain
As for that rare odor he sighed in vain.
A dark shade fell from her loose hair sweet
As jasmine over the rose of her feet.
A broad silver tablet her forehead displayed
For the heaven-set lessons of beauty made;
Under its edge two inverted Núns
Showed black as musk their splendid half-moons,
And beneath them lively and bright were placed
Two Sáds by the pen of her Maker traced.
From Nún to the ring of the Mim there rose
Pure as silver, like Alif, her nose.
To the cipher, her mouth, add Alif: then
She had ten strong spells for the conquest of men.
That laughing ruby to view exposed
A Sín when the knot of her lips unclosed
At the touch of her pure white teeth, and between
The lines of crimson their flash was seen.
Her face was the garden of Iram, where
Roses of every hue are fair.
The dusky moles that enhanced the red
Were like Moorish boys playing in each rose bed.

Of silver that paid no tithe, her chin
Had a well with the Water of Life therein.
If a sage in his thirst came near to drink,
He would feel the spray ere he reached the brink;
But lost were his soul if he nearer drew,
For it was a well and a whirlpool too.
Her neck was of ivory. Thither drawn,
Came with her tribute to beauty the fawn;
And the rose hung her head at the gleam of the skin
Of the shoulders fairer than jessamine.
Her breasts were orbs of a light most pure,
Twin bubbles new risen from Fount Kafúr;
Two young pomegranates grown on one spray,
Where bold hope never a finger might lay.
The touchstone itself was proved false when it tried
Her arms' fine silver thrice purified;
But the pearl-pure amulets fastened there
Were the hearts of the holy absorbed in prayer.
The loveliest gave her their souls for rue;
And round the charm their own heartstrings drew.
Her arms filled her sleeves with silver from them
Whose brows are bound with a diadem.
To labor and care her soft hand lent aid,
And to wounded hearts healing unction laid.
Like reeds were those taper fingers of hers
To write on each heart love's characters.
Each nail on those fingers so long and slim
Showed a new moon laid on a full moon's rim;
And her small closed hand made the moon confess
That she never might rival its loveliness.
Two columns fashioned of silver upheld
That beauty which never was paralleled;
And, to make the tale of her charms complete,
They were matched by the shape of her exquisite feet,—
Feet so light and elastic no maid might show,
So perfectly fashioned from heel to toe,—
If on the eye of a lover she stepped,
Her foot would float on the tear he wept.

THE JATAKA

THE JATAKA (Pali-Sanskrit, 1st century B.C.). One of the sacred books of Buddhism. A collection of some 550 *jatakas*, or brief tales combining legends and maxims of the Buddha with animal fables and the theme of reincarnation.

THE STRIDER OVER BATTLE-FIELDS

THIS was related by the Teacher while dwelling at Jetavana monastery; and it was concerning Nanda the elder.

For when the Teacher made his visit home to Kapilapura, he induced his youngest brother, Prince Nanda, to join the Order. Then he departed from Kapilapura and, traveling from place to place, he came and dwelt at Savatthi.

Now when the venerable Nanda had taken the Blessed One's bowl, and was leaving home, Belle-of-the-Country heard the report that Prince Nanda was going away in company with the Teacher, and with hair half-braided she looked out of the window, and called out to him: 'Come back quickly, my love!' And her speech remained in the venerable Nanda's mind, so that he became lovesick, and discontented, and pined away until the network of his veins showed on the surface of his body.

When the Teacher heard of all this, he thought: 'What if now I were to establish Nanda in saintship?' And going to the cell which was Nanda's sleeping-room, and taking his seat on the mat that was offered him, he said:

'Nanda, are you contented under this dispensation?'

'Reverend Sir, I am not contented, for I am exceedingly in love with Belle-of-the-Country.'

'Nanda, have you ever taken a trip through the Himalya mountains?'

'Reverend Sir, I never have.'

'Then let us go now.'

'Reverend Sir, I have no magical power. How can I go?'

'I will take you, Nanda,' said the Teacher, 'by my own magical power.'

Then he took the elder by the hand, and sprang into the air. As they passed along he pointed out to him a field that had been burned over, and on a charred stump was seated a she-monkey with her nose and tail destroyed, her hair singed off, her skin fissured and peeled to the quick, and all smeared with blood.

'Nanda, do you see this she-monkey?'

'Yes, Reverend Sir.'

'Take good note of her.'

Then he took him and showed him Manosila table-land, which is sixty leagues in extent, and Anotatta, and the rest of the seven great lakes, and the five great rivers, and the Himalya range containing many hundred pleasant spots, and graced with Gold Mountain, Silver Mountain, and Jewel Mountain.

Then said he: 'Nanda, have you ever seen the Heaven of the Suite of the Thirty-three?'

'Reverend Sir, I never have.'

'Come then, Nanda, and I will show it to you.'

And he took him thither, and sat down on Sakka's marble throne.

And Sakka, the king of the gods, came up with the gods of two heavens, and did obeisance, and sat down respectfully at one side. And his female attendants, twenty-five million in number, and five hundred pink-footed, celestial nymphs came up also, and did obeisance, and sat down respectfully at one side.

The Teacher suffered the venerable Nanda to look upon these five hundred celestial nymphs again and again with passion.

'Nanda,' said he, 'do you see these pink-footed celestial nymphs?'

'Yes, Reverend Sir.'

'Pray, now, are these or Belle-of-the-Country the prettier?'

'Reverend Sir, as is the burned she-monkey compared to Belle-of-the-Country, so is Belle-of-the-Country compared to these.'

'Well, Nanda, what then?'

'Reverend Sir, what does one do to obtain these celestial nymphs?'

'By performing the duties of a monk does one obtain these nymphs.'

'Reverend Sir, if the Blessed One will be my guarantee that if I perform the duties of a monk I shall obtain these nymphs, I will perform the duties of a monk.'

'Do so, Nanda. I am your guarantee.'

Thus did the elder take the Tathagata as a guarantee in the presence of the assembled gods. Then he said:

'Reverend Sir, do not delay. Come, let·us go. I will perform the duties of a monk.'

Then the Teacher returned with him to Jetavana monastery; and the elder began to perform the duties of a monk.

'Sariputta,' said then the Teacher, addressing the Captain of the Doctrine, 'my youngest brother, Nanda, took me as guarantee for some celestial nymphs in the presence of the gods assembled in the Heaven of the Suite of the Thirty-three.'

Thus he told him. And in the same way he told it to Maha-Moggallana the elder, the Maha-Kassapa the elder, to Anuruddha the elder, to Ananda the elder and Treasurer of the Doctrine, and so on to all the eighty great disciples, and also to the greater part of the other priests.

The Captain of the Doctrine, Sariputta the elder, then drew near to Nanda the elder, then said:

'Is it true, as they say, brother Nanda, that in the presence of the gods assembled in the Heaven of the Suite of the Thirty-three you took The One Possessing the Ten Forces as a guarantee for some celestial nymphs, if you performed the duties of a monk? If that be so, is not your chaste religious life all for the sake of women? All for the sake of your passions? What is the difference between your thus doing the duties of a monk for the sake of women, and a laborer who performs his work for hire?'

This speech put the elder to shame, and made him quite dispirited. And in the same way all the eighty great disciples, and the remaining priests also, shamed the venerable Nanda. And realizing that he had behaved in an unworthy manner, in shame and remorse he summoned up his heroism, and attained to insight and to saintship; and coming to the Teacher, he said:

'Reverend Sir, I release the Blessed One from his promise.'

Said the Teacher: 'When you attained to saintship, O Nanda, I became released from my promise.'

When the priests heard of this occurrence, they raised a discussion in the lecture-hall.

'Brethren, how amenable to admonition is Nanda the elder! One admonition was sufficient to arouse in him shame and remorse, so that he performed the duties of a monk, and attained to saintship.'

The Teacher came and inquired: 'Priests, what now is the subject of your discourse?'

And they told him.

'Priests, formerly also, and not now for the first time, was Nanda amenable to admonition.' So saying, he related the bygone occurrence:

Once upon a time, when Brahmadatta was ruling at Benares, the future Buddha was born in the family of an elephant-trainer; and when he had come of age, and become accomplished as an elephant-trainer, he took service under a king who was hostile to the King of Benares. And he trained the State elephant until it was very well trained.

Then the King resolved to conquer the kingdom of Benares, and taking the future Buddha with him, and mounting the State elephant, with a mighty army he went to Benares, and surrounded the place. Then he sent a letter to the King saying, 'Give me the kingdom, or give me battle.'

Brahmadatta resolved to give battle; and having manned the walls, the watchtowers, and the gates, he did so.

His enemy had his State elephant armed with a defensive suit of mail, put on armor himself, and mounted on the elephant's shoulders. 'I will break into the city, kill my enemy, and take possession of the kingdom.' With this thought he seized a sharp goad, and urged the elephant in the direction of the city.

But the elephant, when he saw the hot mud, the stones from the catapults, and the various kinds of missiles thrown by the defenders, did not dare to advance, but retreated in mortal terror.

Then his trainer drew near: 'Old fellow,' said he, 'you are a hero, a strider over battle-fields. Retreat at such a time is not worthy of you.' And thus admonishing the elephant, he pronounced the following stanzas:

'A strider over battle-fields,
A hero, strong one, art thou called.
Why, then, behemoth, dost retreat
On coming near the gateway arch?

'Break down in haste the great crossbar!
The city-pillars take away!
And crashing through the gateway arch,
Enter, behemoth, quickly in!'

This one admonition was sufficient. For when the elephant heard it, he turned back, twisted his trunk round the city-pillars, and pulled them up like so many mushrooms. Then, crashing down the gateway arch, and forcing the cross-bar, he broke his way into the city, captured the kingdom, and gave it to his master.

When the Teacher had given this doctrinal instruction, he identified the characters of the birth-story:

'In that existence the elephant was Nanda, the King was Ananda, while the elephant-trainer was I myself.'

JAYADEVA

JAYADEVA (Sanskrit, *ca.* 1119-1179). Sanskrit poet at the court of the last king of Bengal. Author of celebrated love poem, the *Gītā Govinda (Song of the Cowherd).*

HYMN TO VISHNU

O thou that held'st the blessed Veda dry
    When all things else beneath the floods were hurled;
Strong Fish-God! Ark of Men! *Jai!* Hari, *jai!*
    Hail, Keshav, hail; thou Master of the world!

The round world rested on thy spacious nape;
    Upon thy neck, like a mere mole, it stood:
O thou, that took'st for us the Tortoise-shape,
    Hail, Keshav, Hail! Ruler of wave and wood!

The world upon thy curving tusk sate sure,
    Like the Moon's dark disc in her crescent pale;
O thou who didst for us assume the Boar,
    Immortal Conqueror! hail, Keshav, hail!

When thou thy Giant-Foe didst seize and rend,
    Fierce, fearful, long, and sharp were fang and nail;
Thou who the Lion and the Man didst blend,
    Lord of the Universe, hail, Narsingh, hail!

Wonderful Dwarf!—who with a threefold stride
    Cheated King Bali—where thy footsteps fall
Men's sins, O Wamuna! are set aside:
    O Keshav, hail! thou Help and Hope of all!

The sins of this sad earth thou didst assail,
    The anguish of its creatures thou didst heal;
Freed are we from all terrors by thy toil:
    Hail, Purshuram, hail! Lord of the biting steel!

To thee the fell Ten-Headed yielded life.
    Thou in dread battle laid'st the monster low!
Ah, Rama! dear to Gods and men that strife;
    We praise thee, Master of the matchless bow!

With clouds for garments glorious thou dost fare,
  Veiling thy dazzling majesty and might,
As when Jamuna saw thee with the share,
  A peasant—yet the King of Day and Night.

Merciful-hearted! when thou camest as Boodh—
  Albeit 'twas written in the Scriptures so—
Thou bad'st our altars to be no more imbrued
  With blood of victims: Keshav! bending low—

We praise thee, Wielder of the sweeping sword,
  Brilliant as curving comets in the gloom,
Whose edge shall smite the fierce barbarian horde;
  Hail to thee, Keshav! hail, and hear, and come,

And fill this song of Jayadev with thee,
  And make it wise to teach, strong to redeem,
And sweet to living souls. Thou Mystery!
  Thou Light of Life! Thou Dawn beyond the dream!

Fish! that didst outswim the flood;
Tortoise! whereon earth hath stood;
Boar! who with thy tush held'st high
The world, that mortals might not die;
Lion! who hast giants torn;
Dwarf! who laugh'dst a king to scorn;
Sole Subduer of the Dreaded!
Slayer of the many-headed!
Mighty Ploughman! Teacher tender!
Of thine own the sure Defender!
Under all thy ten disguises
Endless praise to thee arises.

JUAN RAMON JIMENEZ

JUAN RAMON JIMÉNEZ (Spanish, 1881-   ). Influential modern Spanish
poet, leader of Darío-French-Symbolist School. A native of Andalusia, went
into exile at time of Civil War. Now living in America. Highly polished artist,
whose aim is "pure poetry." Important publications: *Baladas de primavera,*
Diario de un poeta recién casado, Poesías escojidas.

FORTUNATE BEING

Singing you go, and laughing through the water,
and through the air you go whistling and laughing,

a round of blue and gold, of green and silver,
so happy passing and repassing ever
amidst the first red blossoming of April,
the distinct form of instantaneous
equalities of light, of life, of color,
with us, kindled like river banks aflame!

What a happy being you are,
with universal and eternal happiness!
Happy, you break through the waves of the air,
you swim contrary to the waves of water!
Do you not have to eat, neither to sleep?
All the springtime, is it yours to enjoy?
All of the green, all of the blue,
the flowering all, is it yours?
There is no fear in your glory;
your fate is to return, return, return,
in rounds of green and silver, blue and gold,
through an eternity of eternities!

You give your hand to us in a moment
of possible affinity, of sudden love,
of radiant concession;
and with your warm contact,
in wild vibration of flesh and of soul,
we are enkindled with sweet harmony,
and we, made new, forget the usual,
we shine for an instant, happy with gold.
It seems that we too are going to be
perennial as you,
that we shall fly from ocean to the mountain,
that we shall leap from heaven to the sea,
and that we shall return, return, return
for an eternity of eternities.
We sing and we laugh through the air,
through the water we laugh and whistle.

But you must not forget yourself,
you are the casual, perpetual presence,
you are the fortunate creature,
the only magic being without shadow,
the one adored for warmth and grace,

the free, enraptured robber
that, in rounds of blue and gold, green and silver,
goes laughing, whistling through the air,
through the water singing and laughing!

THE BEST THAT I HAVE

Green sea and grey sky and blue sky
and loving albatross upon the waves,
and in all, the sun, and thou in the sun,
observing desired and desiring god,
lighting with distinct golden rays my arrival;
the arrival of him that I am today,
of him that even yesterday I doubted
he could be in thee as I am.

What a changed man in me, desiring god,
from the being doubting the legend
of the god of the many glib speakers,
to be the firm believer
in the story I myself have created
all through my life for thee.

Now I come to this termination
of a year of my natural life,
in the depths of the air where I keep thee,
above this sea, these depths of water,
to this beautiful, blinding termination,
where thou art gradually entering me,
content to be thine, to be mine,
through the best that I have, my own expression.

From ELEGIES

The dazzling whiteness of my first love
At the sweet, sad sound of reveille!
What celestial joy was it that opened those oriental gardens
To my youthful soul, that morning?
It was a holiday. All pallid sorrow died out
In the green of false springtime;
Everything was charged with laughter, with flowers.
The ground was rushes, the air was pennons.

648

And that sweet blue night, on that bench,
Under the doubled shadow of the drooping acacia,
While the moon gave its white flax to the world,
She said she had loved me all her life long.

Alas! I would live through all my sorrows again,
Even the darkest, to see such a morning
As that on which the sun purified my brow
At the sweet, sad sound of reveille.

From THE DIARY OF A NEWLY-MARRIED MAN

Remorse
(Between Philadelphia and New York, a rainy night, May 24)

Must you acquiesce, my soul,
In forgetting in the morning?
If four great nails, well nailed,
My soul, right into your entrails,
Were to open four great, pure roses
From those four livid words
That he will hold nailed
In his kind heart
From then on!

Must you acquiesce
Merely in being quite happy,
Soul?

From STONE AND HEAVEN

Dream Nocturne

The earth leads by the earth.
But, sea,
You lead by the heavens.
With what security of gold and silver light
Do the stars mark the road for us!
One would think
That the earth was the road
Of the body,

That the sea was the road
Of the soul.
Yes. It seems
That the soul is the only traveler
Of the sea; that the body, alone,
Remains behind, on the beach,
Without her, saying goodbye,
Heavy, cold, as though dead.
How like
Is a journey by sea
To death,
To eternal life!

MAURUS JOKAI

MAURUS JOKAI (Hungarian, 1825-1904). Most widely read Hungarian novelist. Unusual narrative skill, wrote chiefly to entertain. Author of 100 novels. Most colorful are those celebrating glories of old Hungary; 22 translated into English, including: *Midst the Wild Carpathians, The Baron's Sons, Timar's Two Worlds, The Yellow Rose.*

TIMAR'S TWO WORLDS

1. How Ali Saved His Daughter

A MOUNTAIN-CHAIN, pierced through from base to summit—a gorge four miles in length walled in by lofty precipices; and between these walls flows the Danube in its rocky bed.

At this time there were no steamers on the Danube, but a vessel, called the St. Barbara, approaches, drawn against the stream by thirty-two horses. The fate of the vessel lies in the hands of two men—the pilot and the captain.

The name of the captain is Michael Timar. He is a man of about thirty, with fair hair and dreamy blue eyes.

At the door of the ship's cabin sits a man of fifty, smoking a Turkish chibouque. Euthemio Trikaliss is the name under which he is registered in the way-book, and he is the owner of the cargo. The ship itself belongs to a merchant of Komorn called Athanas Brazovics.

Out of one of the cabin windows looks the face of a young girl,

Timéa, the daughter of Euthemio, and the face is as white as marble. Timéa and her father are the only passengers of the St. Barbara.

When the captain lays aside his speaking-trumpet he has time to chat with Timéa, who understands only modern Greek, which the captain speaks fluently.

It is always a dangerous voyage, for the current is fierce and the rocks are death-traps. To-day, too, the St. Barbara was pursued by a Turkish gunboat. But the vessel makes its way safely, in spite of current and rocks, and the Turkish gunboat gives up the chase.

Three days later the St. Barbara had reached the island of Orsova; the plains of Hungary are to the north of the river, Servia to the south.

Provisions had run short, and Timar decided to go on shore. There were no signs of human habitation at first, but Timar's sharp eyes had discovered a faint smoke rising above the tops of the poplars. He worked his way in a small skiff through the reeds, reached dry land, pushed through hedges and bushes, and then stood transfixed with admiration.

A cultivated orchard of some five or six acres was before him, and beyond that a flower-garden, full of summer bloom.

Timar went up through the orchard and flower garden to a cottage, built partly in the rock, and covered with creepers. A huge, black Newfoundland dog was lying before the door.

A woman's voice answered Timar's "good-morning," and the dog raised no objection to the captain going indoors.

"It never hurts good people," said the woman.

Timar explained his mission. The wind had brought his vessel to a standstill; he was short of provisions, and he had two passengers who would be grateful for shelter on land for the night.

The woman promised him food and a room for his passengers in exchange for grain, and at her word the dog brought him by a better path to the river.

Presently Timar was back again with Euthemio and Timéa, and now a young girl appeared, whom the housewife called Noemi.

Before supper was over, the growling of the dog announced a new arrival, and a man of youthful appearance, who introduced himself as Theodor Krisstyan, an old friend of the lady of the house, whom he called Madame Therese, entered and made himself quickly at home. It was plain that his hostess both feared and disliked Theodor, while Timar, who had met him before, regarded him as a spy in the pay of the Turkish government.

651

In the morning the wind had gone down, Theodor had vanished, and Timar and his passengers prepared to renew their journey.

Therese told Timar her story before he left; how she and her daughter Noemi had lived there for twelve years, and who the objectionable Theodor was. Then she added, in a whisper. "I fancy this man Krisstyan's visit was either on your account, or that of the other gentleman. Be on your guard if either of you dread the discovery of a secret."

Trikaliss looked very gloomy when he heard the stranger had left before sunrise, and the following night he called Timar to his cabin.

"I am dying," he said. "I want to die—I have taken poison. Timéa will not wake till all is over. My true name is not Euthemio Trikaliss, but Ali Tschorbadschi. I was once governor of Candia, and then treasurer in Stamboul. You know there is a revolution proceeding in Turkey; my turn was coming. Not that I was a conspirator, but the treasury wanted my money and the seraglio my daughter. Death is easy for me, but I will not let my daughter go into the harem nor myself be made a beggar. Therefore I hired your vessel, and loaded it with grain. The owner, Athanas Brazovics, is a connection of mine; I have often shown him kindness, he can return it now. By a miracle we got safely through the rocks and whirlpools of the river, and eluded the pursuit of the Turkish brigantine, and now I stumble over a straw into my grave.

"That man who followed us last evening was a spy of the Turkish government. He recognised me, and sealed my fate. The government would not demand me from Austria as a political refugee, but as a thief. This is unjust, for what I took was my own. But I am pursued as a thief, and Austria gives up escaped thieves if Turkish spies can trace them. By dying I can save my daughter and her property. Swear to me by your faith and your honour you will carry out my instructions. Here in this casket is about a thousand ducats. Take Timéa to Athanas Brazovics, and beg him to adopt my daughter. Give him the money, he must spend it on the education of the child, and give him also the cargo, and beg him to be present when the sacks are emptied. You understand!"

The dying man looked in Timar's face, and struggled for breath. "Yes—the Red Crescent!" he stammered. "The Red Crescent!" Then the death-throes closed his lips—one struggle, and he was a corpse.

II. Timar Tempted and Fallen

WHEN the St. Barbara had nearly reached Komorn it struck an uprooted tree, lying in ambush under water, and immediately began to sink. It is absolutely impossible to save a vessel wrecked in this way. The crew all left the sinking craft, and Timar rescued Timéa, and with her the casket with the thousand ducats.

Then the captain drove off with the fatherless girl to the house of Athanas Brazovics in the town of Komorn.

At first Athanas kissed Timéa very heartily, but when he learnt that his vessel was lost, and all Timéa's property, except the thousand ducats, and the wheat sacks—now spoilt by water—he altered his tune.

He and his wife Sophie decided that Timéa should live with them as an adopted child, and at the same time attend on their daughter Athalie as a waiting-maid. Athalie and her mother treated the poor girl with scornful contempt.

As for Timar, Athanas turned on him savagely, as though the captain could have prevented the wreck!

On the advice of his friend, Lieutenant Katschuka, who was betrothed to Athalie, Timar purchased the sunken grain next day when it was put up for auction, buying the whole cargo for 10,000 gulden. "You will do the poor orphan a good turn if you buy it," said the lieutenant. "Otherwise, the value of the cargo will all go in salvage."

Timar at once made arrangements for hauling up the sacks, and for the immediate drying and grinding of the corn, and all day labourers were at work on the wreck.

At nightfall Timar, left alone, noticed one sack differently marked from the rest—marked with a red crescent! Within this sack was a long leathern bag. He broke it open and found it full of diamonds, emeralds, and sapphires richly set in girdles and bracelets and rings. A whole heap of unset diamonds were in an agate box. The whole treasure was worth at least 1,000,000 gulden. The St. Barbara had carried a million on board!

"To whom does this treasure belong?"

So Timar put the question to himself, and answered it.

"Why, whom should it belong to but you? You bought the sunken cargo, just as it is, with the sacks and the grain. If the treasurer stole the jewels from the sultan, the sultan probably stole them in his campaigns."

"And Timéa?"

"Timéa would not know how to use the treasure, and her adopted father would absorb it, and get rid of nine-tenths of it. What would be the result if Timéa gets it? She would be a rich lady, and would not cast a look at you from her height. Now things are the other way—you will be a rich man and she a poor girl. You do not want the treasure for yourself. You will invest it profitably, and when you have earned with the first million a second and a third, you will go to the poor girl and say, 'There, take it—it is all yours; and take me, too.' You only wish to become rich in order to make her happy."

The moon and the waves cried to Timar, "You are rich—you are a made man!"

But when it was dark an inward voice whispered, "You are a thief!"

From that day all Timar's undertakings flourished, and step by step he reached the summit of an ordinary successful business man's ambition—the title of nobility. At the same time Brazovics, who had treated Timar with brutal inconsiderateness because of the wreck of the St. Barbara, went steadily down-hill, borrowing and embezzling trust moneys in his fall.

Lieutenant Katschuka had declared all along that he could not marry Athalie without a dowry, and when the wedding day arrived, Brazovics, unable to face his creditors, and knowing himself bankrupt, penniless, and fraudulent, committed suicide. Katschuka immediately declared the engagement at an end. In his heart he had long wearied of Athalie, and looked with desire on Timéa. The orphan girl from the first had loved the lieutenant with silent, unspoken affection.

When the Brazovics' house was put up for sale Timar bought it outright, furniture and all, and then said to Timéa, "From this day forth you are the mistress of this house. Everything in it belongs to you, all is inscribed in your name. Accept it from me. You are the owner of the house, and if there is a little shelter for me in your heart, and you did not refuse my hand—then I should be only too happy."

Timéa gave her hand to Timar, and said in a low, firm voice, "I accept you as my husband, and will be a faithful and obedient wife."

This man had always been so good to her. He had never made sport of her nor flattered her, and he had saved her life on the

Danube when the St. Barbara was sinking. He had given her all her heart could desire except one thing, and that belonged to another.

III. *The Ownerless Island*

On his betrothal to Timéa a great burden was lifted from the soul of Timar. Since the day when the treasure of Ali Tschorbadschi had enabled him to achieve power and riches, Timar had been haunted by the voice of self-accusation: "This money does not belong to you—it was the property of an orphan. You are a man of gold! You are a thief!"

But now the defrauded orphan had received back her property. Only Timar forgot that he had demanded in exchange the girl's heart.

Timéa promised to be a faithful and obedient wife, but on the wedding-day when Timar said, "Do you love me?" she only opened her eyes, and asked, "What is love?"

Timar found he had married a marble statue; and that all his riches would not buy his wife's love. He became wretched, conscious that his wife was unhappy, that he was the author of their mutual misery.

Then, in the early summer, Timar went off from Komorn to shoot water-fowl. He meant to go to the ownerless island at Ostrova —it was three years since that former visit.

Therese and Noemi welcomed him cordially at the island, and Timar forgot his troubles when he was with them. Therese told him her story; how her husband, ruined by the father of Theodor Krisstyan and by Athanas Brazovics, had committed suicide, and how, forsaken and friendless, she had brought her child to this island, which neither Austria nor Turkey claimed, and where no tax-collector called. With her own hands she had turned the wilderness into a paradise, and the only fear she had was that Theodor Krisstyan, who had discovered her retreat, might reveal it to the Turkish government.

Therese had no money and no use for it, but she exchanged fruit and honey for grain, salt, clothes, and hardware, and the people with whom she bartered were not inclined to gossip about her affairs.

So no news concerning the island ever went to Vienna, Komorn, or Constantinople, and the fact of Timar's great prosperity had not reached the islanders. He was welcomed as a hard-working man, and Therese did not know that Timar had been powerful enough to get a ninety years' lease of the island from both Turkish and Austrian governments; perhaps no very difficult matter, as the existence of the island was unknown, and there were fees to be paid over the concession.

When he told her what he had done, Noemi threw her arms round his neck.

Theodor Krisstyan was furious, but Timar procured him a post in Brazil, and for a long time the disreputable spy was too far off to be troublesome.

And now on this island Timar found health and rest. It became his home, and for the summer months every year he would slip away from Komorn, and no one, not even Timéa, guessed his secret. When he returned Timéa's cold, white face was still an unsolved riddle to her husband. She would greet him kindly, but never was there any token that she loved him. Timar's ever-increasing business operations were excuse for his long absences, but all the same the double life he was leading made him ill. He could not tell Timéa of Therese and Noemi, and he could not tell them on the island that he was married.

Timéa, on her side, devoted herself more and more to her husband's business in his absence, and when Major Katschuka once called and asked her if she could not arrange for a divorce, she answered gently, "My husband is the noblest man in the world. Should I separate from him who has no one but me to love him? Am I to tell him that I hate him, I who owe everything to him, and who brought him no dowry but a loveless heart?"

Timar learnt from Athalie, who lived in Timéa's house, of this reply, and felt more in despair than ever. He wanted Timéa to be happy, she had never been his wife except in name, for he had been waiting for her love.

And he wanted to go away, and leave all his riches behind, and settle on the island. Now more than ever was he wanted on the island, for Therese had died of heart failure, and the years had made Noemi a woman.

IV. "My Name is Nobody"

It was winter, and Timar had gone off alone to a house that belonged to him near a frozen lake. He felt the time had come for flight. but whither?

Theodor Krisstyan had turned up again. In Brazil he had heard a story of Ali Tschorbadschi's jewels from an old criminal from Turkey, and he had returned to blackmail Timar. But he did not find him till Timar was at the frozen lake.

Krisstyan's story was not true. Timar knew that the accusations were false as he listened to the vagabond's indictment. He had not "killed" Timéa's father, nor "stolen" his treasure. But he had played a false game, and his position was a false one. Krisstyan demanded a change of raiment, and Timar let him take clothes and shirts. But at last the blackmailer's demands became too insolent, and Timar drove him out of the house.

And now it seemed to Timar that his own career was finished. This ruffian Krisstyan could expose the foundation of his wealth, and how could he live discredited before the world?

On the frozen water there were great fissures between the blocks of ice. Within the waves of the lake death would come quickly. Timar walked out on the ice, and there before him the head of Theodor Krisstyan rose in the water and then sank. The spy had not known the treachery of the fissures.

Timar fled to the ownerless island, and when the corpse of Krisstyan was recovered, in an advanced stage of decomposition, Timéa declared she recognised her husband's clothes.

So the body of Theodor Krisstyan was buried with great pomp, and a year later Timéa married Major Katschuka, and then, haunted by the doubt whether her first husband was really dead, pined away.

No blessing rested on the wealth Timar left behind him. The only son Timéa bore to the major was a great spendthrift, and in his hands the fabulous wealth vanished as quickly as it had grown.

And what is passing meanwhile on the ownerless island?

Forty years have passed since Timar's disappearance from Komorn, and the island is now a complete model farm. Recently, a friend of mine, an ardent naturalist, took me to the island. I had heard as a child of Timar and his wealth.

Every inch of ground is utilised or serves to beautify the place. The tobacco grown here has the most exquisite aroma, and the beehives look from a distance like a small town with many-shaped roofs.

It is easy to see that the owner of the island understands luxury, and yet that owner never has a farthing to call his own; no money ever enters the island. Those, however, who need the exports know also the requirements of the islanders, and bring them for barter.

657

The whole colony consisted of one family, and each was called only by his Christian name. The six sons of the first settler had married women of the district, and the numbers of grandchildren and great-grandchildren already exceeded forty, but the island maintained them all. Poverty was unknown; they lived in luxury; each knew some trade, and if they had been ten times as many, their labour would have supported them.

When we arrived on the island, the nominal head of the family, a well-built man of forty, received us cordially, and in the evening presented us to his parents.

When my name was mentioned to the old man he looked long at me, and a visible colour rose in his cheeks. I began to tell him of what was going on in the world, that Hungary was now united to Austria, and that the taxes were very heavy.

He blew a cloud from his pipe, and the smoke said, "My island has nothing to do with that, we have no taxes here."

I told him of wars, financial panics, the strife of religion and politics, and the smoke seemed to say, "We wage war with no one here. Thank God, we have no money here and no elections or ministers."

Presently the old man asked me where I was born, and what my profession was? And when I told him that I wrote romances, he said, "Guess my story. There was once a man who left a world in which he was admired and respected, and created a second world in which he was loved."

"May I venture to ask your name?" I said.

The old man seemed to grow a head taller; then, raising his trembling hands, he laid them on my head. And it seemed to me as if once, long, long before those same hands had rested on my head when childish curls covered it, and that I had seen that noble face before.

"My name is Nobody," he replied to my question; and after that night I saw him no more during our stay on the island.

The privileges granted by two governments to the owner of the island will last for fifty years more. And who knows what may happen to the world in fifty years?

BEN JONSON

BEN JONSON (English, 1572-1637). Delightful singer of Shakespeare's time and later. Also actor, dramatist and critic. Wrote masques for noble patrons and popular plays: *Every Man in His Humour, Volpone.* Had large coterie in London and was literary dictator for quarter of century. Loved most for his lyrics, such as "Drink to Me Only with Thine Eyes."

EPITAPH ON ELIZABETH, L. H.

Wouldst thou hear what man can say
   In a little? Reader, stay.
Underneath this stone doth lie
   As much beauty as could die;
Which in life did harbor give
   To more virtue than doth live.
If at all she had a fault,
   Leave it buried in this vault.
One name was Elizabeth,
   Th' other let it sleep with death;
Fitter, where it died to tell,
   Than that it lived at all. Farewell.

WHY I WRITE NOT OF LOVE

Some act of Love's bound to rehearse,
I thought to bind him in my verse;
Which when he felt, Away, quoth he,
Can poets hope to fetter me?
It is enough they once did get
Mars and my mother in their net;
I wear not these my wings in vain.
With which he fled me, and again
Into my rhymes could ne'er be got
By any art. Then wonder not
That since my numbers are so cold,
When Love is fled, and I grow old.

SONG, TO CELIA [1]

Come, my Celia, let us prove
While we may the sports of love;
Time will not be ours forever,
He at length our good will sever.
Spend not then his gifts in vain;
Suns that set may rise again,
But if once we lose this light,
'Tis with us perpetual night.
Why should we defer our joys?
Fame and rumor are but toys.
Cannot we delude the eyes
Of a few poor household spies?
Or his easier ears beguile,
So removed by our wile?
'Tis no sin love's fruit to steal;
But the sweet theft to reveal,
To be taken, to be seen,
These have crimes accounted been.

SONG, TO CELIA [2]

Drink to me only with thine eyes,
　And I will pledge with mine;
Or leave a kiss but in the cup,
　And I'll not look for wine.
The thirst that from the soul doth rise
　Doth ask a drink divine;
But might I of Jove's nectar sup,
　I would not change for thine.

I sent thee late a rosy wreath,
　Not so much honoring thee,
As giving it a hope that there
　It could not withered be.
But thou thereon didst only breathe,
　And sent'st it back to me,
Since when it grows and smells, I swear,
　Not of itself, but thee.

HIS EXCUSE FOR LOVING

Let it not your wonder move,
Less your laughter, that I love.
Though I now write fifty years,
I have had, and have, my peers;
Poets though divine are men,
Some have loved as old again.
And it is not always face,
Clothes, or fortune, gives the grace,
Or the feature, or the youth;
But the language and the truth,
With the ardor and the passion,
Gives the lover weight and fashion.

If you then will read the story,
First prepare you to be sorry
That you never knew till now
Either whom to love, or how;
But be glad, as soon with me,
When you know that this is she
Of whose beauty it was sung:
She shall make the old man young,
Keep the middle age at stay,
And let nothing high decay;
Till she be the reason why
All the world for love may die.

HER TRIUMPH

See the chariot at hand here of love,
    Wherein my lady rideth!
Each that draws is a swan or a dove,
    And well the car love guideth.
As she goes all hearts do duty
        Unto her beauty,
And enamoured do wish so they might
        But enjoy such a sight,
That they still were to run by her side,
Through swords, through seas, whither she would ride.

Do but look on her eyes; they do light
    All that love's world compriseth!
Do but look on her hair; it is bright
    As love's star when it riseth!
Do but mark, her forehead's smoother
        Than words that soothe her;
And from her arched brows, such a grace
        Sheds itself through the face,
As alone there triumphs to the life
All the gain, all the good of the elements' strife.

Have you seen but a bright lily grow
    Before rude hands have touched it?
Ha' you marked but the fall o' the snow
    Before the soil hath smutched it?
Ha' you felt the wool of beaver,
        Or swan's down ever?
Or have smelt o' the bud o' the briar?
        Or the nard in the fire?
Or have tasted the bag of the bee?
O so white! O so soft! O so sweet is she!

THE PLANT AND FLOWER OF LIGHT

It is not growing like a tree
In bulk, doth make man better be;
Or standing long an oak, three hundred year,
To fall a log at last, dry, bald, and sere;
A lily of a day
Is fairer far in May,
Although it fall and die that night,
It was the plant and flower of light.
In small proportions we just beauties see;
And in short measures, life may perfect be.

TO CYNTHIA

Queen and huntress, chaste and fair,
Now the sun is laid to sleep,
Seated in thy silver chair
State in wonted manner keep;

662

Hesperus entreats thy light,
Goddess excellently bright.

Earth, let not thy envious shade
Dare itself to interpose;
Cynthia's shining orb was made
Heaven to clear, when day did close;
  Bless us then with wishèd sight,
  Goddess excellently bright.

Lay thy bow of pearl apart,
And thy crystal shining quiver;
Give unto the flying hart
Space to breathe, how short soever,
  Thou that mak'st a day of night,
  Goddess excellently bright.

JAMES JOYCE

JAMES JOYCE (Irish, 1882-1941). Most controversial innovator of modern letters. Experiments with new techniques influenced "stream-of-consciousness" school. Unhappy youth in Ireland reflected in *A Portrait of the Artist as a Young Man*. In self-imposed exile to Paris, wrote *Ulysses*, description of a day's life in Dublin. Published first in Paris, permitted in America by famous court decision. Last work, *Finnegans Wake*, so difficult only Joyce *aficionados* understand it.

ARABY

NORTH Richmond Street, being blind, was a quiet street except at the hour when the Christian Brothers' School set the boys free. An uninhabited house of two storeys stood at the blind end, detached from its neighbours in a square ground. The other houses of the street, conscious of decent lives within them, gazed at one another with brown imperturbable faces.

The former tenant of our house, a priest, had died in the back drawing-room. Air, musty from having been long enclosed, hung in all the rooms, and the waste room behind the kitchen was littered with old useless papers. Among these I found a few paper-covered books, the pages of which were curled and damp: *The Abbot*, by Walter Scott, *The Devout Communicant* and *The Memoirs of Vidocq*. I liked the last best because its leaves were yellow. The wild garden behind the house contained a central apple-tree and a few straggling bushes under one of which I found the late tenant's rusty bicycle-pump. He had been a very charitable priest; in his will he had left all his money to institutions and the furniture of his house to his sister.

When the short days of winter came, dusk fell before we had well eaten our dinners. When we met in the street the houses had grown somber. The space of sky above us was the color of ever-changing violet and towards it the lamps of the street lifted their feeble lanterns. The cold air stung us and we played till our bodies glowed. Our shouts echoed in the silent street. The career of our play brought us through the dark muddy lanes behind the houses where we ran the gauntlet of the rough tribes from the cottages, to the back doors of the dark dripping gardens where odors arose from the ashpits, to the dark odorous stables where a coachman smoothed and combed the horse or shook music from the buckled harness. When we returned to the street, light from the kitchen windows had filled the areas. If my uncle was seen turning the corner we hid in the shadow until we had seen him safely housed. Or if Mangan's sister came out on the doorstep to call her brother in to his tea we watched her from our shadow peer up and down the street. We waited to see whether she would remain or go in and, if she remained, we left our shadow and walked up to Mangan's steps resignedly. She was waiting for us, her figure defined by the light from the half-opened door. Her brother always teased her before he obeyed and I stood by the railings looking at her. Her dress swung as she moved her body and the soft rope of her hair tossed from side to side.

Every morning I lay on the floor in the front parlor watching her door. The blind was pulled down to within an inch of the sash so that I could not be seen. When she came out on the doorstep my heart leaped. I ran to the hall, seized my books and followed her. I kept her brown figure always in my eye and, when we came near the point at which our ways diverged, I quickened my pace and passed her. This happened morning after morning. I had never spoken to her, except for a few casual words, and yet her name was like a summons to all my foolish blood.

Her image accompanied me even in places the most hostile to

romance. On Saturday evenings when my aunt went marketing I had to go to carry some of the parcels. We walked through the flaring streets, jostled by drunken men and bargaining women, amid the curses of laborers, the shrill litanies of shop-boys who stood on guard by the barrels of pigs' cheeks, the nasal chanting of street-singers, who sang a *come-all-you* about O'Donovan Rossa, or a ballad about the troubles in our native land. These noises converged in a single sensation of life for me: I imagined that I bore my chalice safely through a throng of foes. Her name sprang to my lips at moments in strange prayers and praises which I myself did not understand. My eyes were often full of tears (I could not tell why) and at times a flood from my heart seemed to pour out into my bosom. I thought little of the future. I did not know whether I would ever speak to her or not or, if I spoke to her, how I could tell her of my confused adoration. But my body was like a harp and her words and gestures were like fingers running upon the wires.

One evening I went into the back drawing-room in which the priest had died. It was a dark rainy evening and there was no sound in the house. Through one of the broken panes I heard the rain impinge upon the earth, the fine incessant needles of water playing in the sodden beds. Some distant lamp or lighted window gleamed below me. I was thankful that I could see so little. All my senses seemed to desire to veil themselves and, feeling that I was about to slip from them, I pressed the palms of my hands together until they trembled, murmuring: *"O love! O love!"* many times.

At last she spoke to me. When she addressed the first words to me I was so confused that I did not know what to answer. She asked me was I going to *Araby*. I forgot whether I answered yes or no. It would be a splendid bazaar, she said she would love to go.

"And why can't you?" I asked.

While she spoke she turned a silver bracelet round and round her wrist. She could not go, she said, because there would be a retreat that week in her convent. Her brother and two other boys were fighting for their caps and I was alone at the railings. She held one of the spikes, bowing her head towards me. The light from the lamp opposite our door caught the white curve of her neck, lit up her hair that rested there and, falling, lit up the hand upon the railing. It fell over one side of her dress and caught the white border of a petticoat, just visible as she stood at ease.

"It's well for you," she said.

"If I go," I said, "I will bring you something."

What innumerable follies laid waste my waking and sleeping thoughts after that evening! I wished to annihilate the tedious intervening days. I chafed against the work of school. At night in my bedroom and by day in the classroom her image came between me and the page I strove to read. The syllables of the word *Araby* were called to me through the silence in which my soul luxuriated and cast an Eastern enchantment over me. I asked for leave to go to the bazaar on Saturday night. My aunt was surprised and hoped it was not some Freemason affair. I answered few questions in class. I watched my master's face pass from amiability to sternness; he hoped I was not beginning to idle. I could not call my wandering thoughts together. I had hardly any patience with the serious work of life which, now that it stood between me and my desire, seemed to me child's play, ugly monotonous child's play.

On Saturday morning I reminded my uncle that I wished to go to the bazaar in the evening. He was fussing at the hallstand, looking for the hat-brush, and answered me curtly:

"Yes, boy, I know."

As he was in the hall I could not go into the front parlor and lie at the window. I left the house in bad humor and walked slowly towards the school. The air was pitilessly raw and already my heart misgave me.

When I came home to dinner my uncle had not yet been home. Still it was early. I sat staring at the clock for some time and, when its ticking began to irritate me, I left the room. I mounted the staircase and gained the upper part of the house. The high, cold, empty gloomy rooms liberated me and I went from room to room singing. From the front window I saw my companions playing below in the street. Their cries reached me weakened and indistinct and, leaning my forehead against the cool glass, I looked over at the dark house where she lived. I may have stood there for an hour, seeing nothing but the brown-clad figure cast by my imagination, touched discreetly by the lamplight at the curved neck, at the hand upon the railings and at the border below the dress.

When I came downstairs again I found Mrs. Mercer sitting at the fire. She was an old garrulous woman, a pawnbroker's widow, who collected used stamps for some pious purpose. I had to endure the gossip of the tea-table. The meal was prolonged beyond an hour and still my uncle did not come. Mrs. Mercer stood up to go: she was sorry she couldn't wait any longer, but it was after eight o'clock and she did not like to be out late, as the night air was bad for her. When she had gone I began to walk up and down the room, clenching my fists. My aunt said:

"I'm afraid you may put off your bazaar for this night of Our Lord."

At nine o'clock I heard my uncle's latchkey in the halldoor. I heard him talking to himself and heard the hallstand rocking when it had received the weight of his overcoat. I could interpret these signs. When he was midway through his dinner I asked him to give me the money to go to the bazaar. He had forgotten.

"The people are in bed and after their first sleep now," he said.

I did not smile. My aunt said to him energetically:

"Can't you give him the money and let him go? You've kept him late enough as it is."

My uncle said he was very sorry he had forgotten. He said he believed in the old saying: "All work and no play makes Jack a dull boy." He asked me where I was going and, when I had told him a second time he asked me did I know *The Arab's Farewell to his Steed*. When I left the kitchen he was about to recite the opening lines of the piece to my aunt.

I held a florin tightly in my hand as I strode down Buckingham Street towards the station. The sight of the streets thronged with buyers and glaring with gas recalled to me the purpose of my journey. I took my seat in a third-class carriage of a deserted train. After an intolerable delay the train moved out of the station slowly. It crept onward among ruinous houses and over the twinkling river. At Westland Row Station a crowd of people pressed to the carriage doors; but the porters moved them back, saying that it was a special train for the bazaar. I remained alone in the bare carriage. In a few minutes the train drew up beside an improvised wooden platform. I passed out on to the road and saw by the lighted dial of a clock that it was ten minutes to ten. In front of me was a large building which displayed the magical name.

I could not find any sixpenny entrance and, fearing that the bazaar would be closed, I passed in quickly through a turnstile, handing a shilling to a weary-looking man. I found myself in a big hall girdled at half its height by a gallery. Nearly all the stalls were closed and the greater part of the hall was in darkness. I recognised a silence like that which pervades a church after a service. I walked into the center of the bazaar timidly. A few people were gathered about the stalls which were still open. Before a curtain, over which the words *Café Chantant* were written in colored lamps, two men were counting money on a salver. I listened to the fall of the coins.

Remembering with difficulty why I had come I went over to one of the stalls and examined porcelain vases and flowered tea-sets. At the door of the stall a young lady was talking and laughing with two young gentlemen. I remarked their English accents and listened vaguely to their conversation.

"O, I never said such a thing!"

"O, but you did!"

"O, but I didn't!"

"Didn't she say that?"

"Yes. I heard her."

"O, there's a . . . fib!"

Observing me the young lady came over and asked me did I wish to buy anything. The tone of her voice was not encouraging; she seemed to have spoken to me out of a sense of duty. I looked humbly at the great jars that stood like eastern guards at either side of the dark entrance to the stall and murmured:

"No, thank you."

The young lady changed the position of one of the vases and went back to the two young men. They began to talk of the same subject. Once or twice the young lady glanced at me over her shoulder.

I lingered before her stall, though I knew my stay was useless, to make my interest in her wares seem the more real. Then I turned away slowly and walked down the middle of the bazaar. I allowed the two pennies to fall against the sixpence in my pocket. I heard a voice call from one end of the gallery that the light was out. The upper part of the hall was now completely dark.

Gazing up into the darkness I saw myself as a creature driven and derided by vanity; and my eyes burned with anguish and anger.

K

FRANZ KAFKA

FRANZ KAFKA (German, 1883-1924). Austrian-born novelist, whose influence became international 20 years after death. A lonely, tormented figure, who suffered from tuberculosis. Published only few stories during lifetime. Three posthumous novels—*The Castle, The Trial, Amerika*—notable for atmosphere of paranoia, the individual struggling against anonymous powers. Fantastic motives combined with detailed realism.

A COUNTRY DOCTOR

I WAS in great perplexity; I had to start on an urgent journey; a seriously ill patient was waiting for me in a village ten miles off; a thick blizzard of snow filled all the wide spaces between him and me; I had a gig, a light gig with big wheels, exactly right for our country roads; muffled in furs, my bag of instruments in my hand, I was in the courtyard all ready for the journey; but there was no horse to be had, no horse. My own horse had died in the night, worn out by the fatigues of this icy winter; my servant girl was now running round the village trying to borrow a horse; but it was hopeless, I knew it, and I stood there forlornly, with the snow gathering more and more thickly upon me, more and more unable to move. In the gateway the girl appeared, alone, and waved the lantern; of course, who would lend a horse at this time for such a journey? I strode through the courtyard once more; I could see no way out; in my confused distress I kicked at the dilapidated door of the year-long uninhabited pigsty. It flew open and flapped to and fro on its hinges. A steam and smell as of horses came out from it. A dim stable lantern was swinging inside from a rope. A man, crouching on his hams in that low space, showed an open blue-eyed face. "Shall I yoke up?" he asked, crawling out on all fours. I did not know what to say and merely stooped down to see what else was in the sty. The servant girl was standing beside me. "You never know what you're going to find in your own house," she said, and we both laughed. "Hey there, Brother, hey there, Sister!" called the groom, and two horses, enormous creatures with powerful flanks, one after the other, their legs tucked close to their bodies, each well-shaped head lowered like a camel's, by sheer strength of buttocking squeezed out through the door hole which they filled entirely. But at once they were standing up, their legs long and their bodies steaming thickly. "Give him a hand," I said, and the willing girl hurried to help the groom with the harnessing. Yet hardly was she beside him when the groom clipped hold of her and pushed his face against hers. She screamed and fled back to me; on her cheek stood out in red the marks of two rows of teeth. "You brute," I yelled in fury, "do you want a whipping?" but in the same moment reflected that the man was a stranger; that I did not know where he came from, and that of his own free will he was helping me out when everyone else had failed me. As if he knew my thoughts he took no offense at my threat but, still busied with the horse, only turned round once towards me. "Get in," he said then, and indeed: every-thing was ready. A magnificent pair of horses, I observed, such as I had never sat behind, and I climbed in happily. "But I'll drive, you don't know the way," I said. "Of course," said he, " I'm not coming with you anyway. I am staying with Rose." "No," shrieked Rose, fleeing in the house with a justified presentiment that her fate was inescapable; I heard the key turn in the locks; I could see, moreover, how she put out the lights in the entrance hall and in further flight all through the rooms keep herself from being dis-covered. "You're coming with me," I said to the groom, "or I won't go, urgent as my journey is. I'm not thinking of paying for it by handing the girl over to you." "Gee up!" he said; clapped his hands; the gig whirled off like a log in a freshet; I could just hear the door of my house splitting and bursting as the groom charged at it and then I was deafened and blinded by a storming rush that steadily buffeted all my senses. But this only for a moment, since, as if my patient's farmyard had opened out just before my courtyard gate, I was already there; the horses had come quietly to a stand-still; the blizzard had stopped; moonlight all around; my patient's parents hurried out of the house, his sister behind them; I was almost lifted out of the gig; from their confused ejaculations I gathered not a word; in the sickroom the air was almost unbreath-able; the neglected stove was smoking; I wanted to push open a window; but first I had to look at my patient. Gaunt, without any fever, not cold, not warm, with vacant eyes, without a shirt, the youngster heaved himself up from under the feather bedding, threw his arms around my neck, and whispered in my ear: "Doctor, let me die." I glanced round the room; no one had heard it; the parents were leaning forward in silence waiting for my verdict; the sister had set a chair for my handbag; I opened the bag and hunted among my instruments; the boy kept clutching at me from his bed to remind me of his entreaty; I picked up a pair of tweezers, examined them in the candlelight and laid them down again. "Yes," I thought blasphemously, "in cases like this the gods are helpful, send the missing horse, add to it a second because of the urgency, and to crown everything bestow even a groom—" And only now did I remember Rose again; what was I to do, how could I rescue her, how could I pull her away from under that groom at ten miles' distance, with a team of horses I couldn't control. These horses, now, they had somehow slipped the reins loose, pushed the windows open from outside, I did not know how; each of them had stuck a head in at a window and, quite unmoved by the startled cries of the family, stood eyeing the patient. "Better go back at once," I thought, as if the horses were summoning me to the return journey, yet I permitted the patient's sister, who fancied that I was dazed by the heat, to take my fur coat from me. A glass of rum was poured out for me, the old man clapped me on the shoulder, a familiarity justified by this offer of his treasure. I shook my head; in the narrow confines of the old man's thoughts I felt ill; that was my only reason for refusing the drink. The mother stood by the bedside and cajoled me towards it; I yielded, and, while one of the horses whinnied loudly to the ceiling, laid my head to to the boy's breast, which shivered under my wet beard. I confirmed what I already knew; the boy was quite sound, something a little wrong with his circulation, saturated with coffee by his solicitous mother, but sound and best turned out of bed with one shove. I am no world reformer and so I let him lie. I was the district doctor and did my duty to the uttermost, to the point where it became almost too much. I was badly paid and yet generous and helpful to the poor. I had still to see that Rose was all right, and then the boy might have his way and I wanted to die too. What was I doing there in that endless winter! My horse was dead, and not a single person in the village would lend me another. I had to get my team out of the pigsty; if they hadn't chanced to be horses I should have had to travel with swine. That was how it was. And

671

I nodded to the family. They knew nothing about it, and, had they known, would not have believed it. To write prescriptions is easy, but to come to an understanding with people is hard. Well, this should be the end of my visit, I had once more been called out needlessly. I was used to that, the whole district made my life a torment with my night bell, but that I should have to sacrifice Rose this time as well, the pretty girl who had lived in my house for years almost without noticing her—that sacrifice was too much to ask, and I had somehow to get it reasoned out in my head with the help of what craft I could muster, in order not to let fly at this family, which with the best will in the world could not restore Rose to me. But as I shut my bag and put an arm out for my fur coat, the family meanwhile standing together, the father sniffing at the glass of rum in his hand, the mother, apparently disappointed in me—why, what do people expect?—biting her lips with tears in her eyes, the sister fluttering a blood-soaked towel, I was somehow ready to admit conditionally that the boy might be ill after all. I went towards him, he welcomed me smiling as if I were bringing him the most nourishing invalid broth—ah, now both horses were whinnying together; the noise, I suppose, was ordained by heaven to assist my examination of the patient—and this time, I discovered that the boy was indeed ill. His right side, near the hip, was an open wound as big as the palm of my hand. Rose-red, in many variations of shade, dark in the hollows, lighter at the edges, softly granulated, with irregular clots of blood, open as a surface mine to the daylight. That was how it looked from a distance. But on closer inspection there was another complication. I could not help a low whistle of surprise. Worms, as thick and as long as my little finger, themselves rose-red and blood-spotted as well, were wriggling from their fastness in the interior of the wound towards the light, with small white heads and many little legs. Poor boy, you were past helping. I had discovered your great wound; this blossom in your side was destroying you. The family was pleased; they saw me busying myself; the sister told the mother, the mother the father, the father told several guests who were coming in, through the moonlight at the open door, walking on tiptoe, keeping their balance with outstretched arms. "Will you save me?" whispered the boy with a sob, quite blinded by the life within his wound. That is what people are like in my district. Always expecting the impossible from the doctor. They have lost their ancient beliefs; the parson sits at home and unravels his vestments,

672

one after another; but the doctor is supposed to be omnipotent with his merciful surgeon's hand. Well, as it pleases them; I have not thrust my services on them; if they misuse me for sacred ends, I let that happen to me too; what better do I want, old country doctor that I am, bereft of my servant girl! And so they came, the family and the village elders, and stripped my clothes off me; a scholar choir with the teacher at the head of it stood before the house and sang these words to an utterly simple tune:

> Strip his clothes off, then he'll heal us,
> If he doesn't, kill him dead!
> Only a doctor, only a doctor.

Then my clothes were off and I looked at the people quietly, my fingers in my beard and my head cocked to one side. I was altogether composed and equal to the situation and remained so, although it was no help to me, since they now took me by the head and feet and carried me to the bed. The laid me down in it next to the wall, on the side of the wound. Then they all left the room; the door was shut; the singing stopped; clouds covered the moon; the bedding was warm around me; the horses' heads in the open windows wavered like shadows. "Do you know," said a voice in my ear, "I have very little confidence in you. Why, you were only blown in here, you didn't come on your own feet. Instead of helping me, you're cramping me on my deathbed. What I'd like best is to scratch your eyes out." "Right," I said, " it is a shame. And yet I am a doctor. What am I to do? Belive me, it is not too easy for me either." "Am I supposed to be content with this apology? Oh, I must be, I can't help it. I always have to put up with things. A fine wound is all I brought into the world; that was my sole endowment." "My young friend," said I, "your mistake is: you have not a wide enough view. I have been in all the sickrooms, far and wide, and I tell you: your wound is not so bad. Done in a tight corner with two strokes of the ax. Many a one proffers his side and can hardly hear the ax in the forest, far less that it is coming nearer to him." "Is that really so, or are you deluding me in my fever?" "It is really so, take the word of honor of an official doctor." And he took it and lay still. But now it was time for me to think of escaping. The horses were still standing faithfully in their places. My clothes, my fur coat, my bag were quickly collected; I didn't want to waste time dressing; if the horses raced home as they had come, I should only be springing, as it were, out of this bed into my own. Obediently a horse backed away from the window; I threw my bundle into the gig; the fur coat missed its mark and was caught on a hook only by the sleeve. Good enough. I swung myself on to the horse. With the reins loosely trailing, one horse barely fastened to the other, the gig swaying behind, my fur coat last of all in the snow. "Gee up!" I said, but there was no galloping; slowly, like old men, we crawled through the snowy wastes; a long time echoed behind us the new but faulty song of the children:

O be joyful, all you patients,
The doctor's laid in bed beside you!

Never shall I reach home at this rate; my flourishing practice is done for; my successor is robbing me, but in vain, for he cannot take my place; in my house the disgusting groom is raging; Rose is his victim; I do not want to think about it any more. Naked, exposed to the frost of this most unhappy of ages, with an earthly vehicle, unearthly horses, old man that I am, I wander astray. My fur coat is hanging from the back of the gig, but I cannot reach it and none of my limber pack of patients lifts a finger. Betrayed! Betrayed! A false alarm on the night bell once answered—it cannot be made good, not ever.

NAGAI KAFU

NAGAI KAFU (Japanese, 1879-   ). Modern Japanese fiction writer, strongly influenced by American and French literature. Spent most of youth in China, America and France.

THE BILL-COLLECTING

I

INSTANTLY after she got up from the bed where she was sleeping with Omatsu, her companion, Oyo put on her narrow-sleeved Hanten as usual, and, wrapping her head with a towel in the manner of the "sister's cap," she began to sweep the parlour.

Oyo is the maidservant in Kinugawa, an assignation house.

As they had guests in the inner room of Yojohan, who had been lodging there since the evening before, Oyo wiped up every place with the dust cloth except that room, including the railings and stairways of the first floor. Coming down to the fireplace near the counter she found the mistress, with toothbrush in her mouth, already uncovering the charcoal fire of the previous evening. In contrast to the dark, humid interior where the odour of wine seemed to drift from somewhere, the winter sunshine glittering on the opposite side of the street and through the frosted-glass screen of the front lattice gate, looked quite warm and cheerful. As soon as the mistress saw Oyo, who was bidding her "Good-morning," she said all at once:

"Now, Oyo, I wish you would go directly after breakfast, as the place is far."

Being thus ordered, Oyo took up her chopsticks for breakfast, eating before Omatsu and Otetsu the cook. After having finished her toilet and changed her dress, and listening again to the instructions and messages from the mistress, she started. It was almost seven o'clock when she set out in the new wooden clogs that were given her by the regular geisha girls as a present at the end of the last year, and she heard the voice of the cook-supplier at the kitchen, the man who came to get the plates and bowls.

Oyo went out by the familiar short-cut through the lane between the houses of the geisha girls. Coming out into the open street of Ginza, which was filled with sunshine, she looked around her as though surprised at the new appearance of things. Her bosom pulsated to the sounds of trolleys passing by, and she not only felt that she had forgotten all the messages charged by the mistress, but even the route which she thought she had understood well when she left home. She became confused, so that the way seemed further than she had supposed.

It had been five years since Oyo entered service, in the autumn, at the age of fourteen, at Kinugawa, the assignation house. She had been at Hakone and at Enoshima, she knew Haneda and the shrine of Narita, but it was only as an attendant of the guests and geisha girls in the great carousels of many people that she went to these places. Once, though she was a woman, she had walked alone through the night with two or three hundred yen in cash in her sash. But it was not further than a few blocks where she went to an accustomed bank on behalf of the mistress. It was only once or twice in a year that she rode a really long distance by trolley, to visit her home at Minami-Senju for holiday.

To a woman of down-town who knows nothing about the suburbs of Tokyo, except Fukagawa, Shinagawa, and Asakusa, even to

675

hear the name of Okubo in the uptown district where Oyo was going to-day to collect the bill, caused her to imagine a place where foxes and badgers live. As she also felt fearful that she might not be able to return home that day if she did not catch the trolley as soon as possible, she hurried to the square of Owaricho, not even stopping at the beautiful show windows of Matsuya, and Mikamiya and Tenshodo.

"Good-morning, Maid Oyo!"

Suddenly, being thus addressed from the crowd which was waiting for the trolley, Oyo turned back and saw an unemployed girl of Tamaomiya, who had her hair dressed in Hisashigami and wore the half-coat of Koki silk.

"Kimi chan. Going to temple?"

As is a habit of woman, Oyo looked at the hair and clothing of this geisha girl, which was not particularly unusual.

"No. I have a patient at home," Kimi chan, the employed girl, said apologetically, as though answering the question of the employer. "Where are you going?"

"To the place called Okubo. I was told to take the Shinjuku line. Is this the place to wait for it?"

"Shinjuku. . . . Then it is on the other side. You must take the car from the other side of the street."

"Oh!" Oyo cried, with such a loud voice that she surprised herself. And as if she could not hear the formal salutation of the employed girl, "Please keep me in mind again . . ." she crossed the square to the other side almost in rapture. Though it was a winter morning her forehead perspired. Having heaved a sigh of relief before the glass door of the Café Lion, Oyo turned back with a wonder-stricken look to the other side of the street where was the clock on the roof of the Hattori clock store, thinking that it was a marvellous thing that she was not killed in the midst of the square where so many trolleys are crossing. By that time the employed girl of Tamaomiya, almost crushed among the crowds on the conductor's platform, went away toward the Mihara bridge, and though many almost empty cars followed it, the only thing that passed the tracks where Oyo was waiting was a lumbering horse truck loaded with casks. The sidewalk near to the Café Lion was so filled with persons waiting for transfers that they overflowed on to the street pavement. Unconsciously, Oyo looked at the blue sky of winter, calling to mind the clock on the roof of Hattori's

676

building, which pointed to half-past eleven. She became so impatient that she felt she could not wait any longer. The complaints of the persons who were waiting for transfers, speaking in loud voices, the breaking of the wires or the stoppage of the electric current, disturbed her as though it were the announcement of a fire burning her house. Exhausted by waiting, Oyo, like the others, leaned against the glass door of the Café and hung her head. Suddenly becoming conscious of a commotion, Oyo also ran in order not to be too late for the car, but, being only a helpless woman, she could hardly approach the first car. Even the next one she missed, for a big man of dark complexion, crossing in from the side, had pushed her away when her foot was already on the step. Moreover, her side lock of Ichogaeshi was rubbed up by the sleeve of the double manteau with great force.

"Now I won't mind what becomes of me. I will wait even half a day, or a day, as long as they want me to wait."

Oyo, who had already become desperate, purposely followed behind the crowd, to take the next approaching car.

When they came to Hibiya park, a seat was left, so Oyo could at last rest her tired back. Then the inside of the car was calmer and the streets outside opened out and became more quiet, and in the warmth of the inside of the car, with the sun shining on the back of her neck and shoulders, she nodded involuntarily with the light jolting of the car. The fatigue of the body, which has to work every night until one o'clock at the earliest, pressed on her eyelids all at once. As Oyo is the favourite servant of the mistress, raised by her from childhood, she must help her not only in the parlour of the guests, but also as chambermaid. To be made a companion in the late drinking of the guests in her busy time is bearable, but the most disgusting thing is the troublesome task of washing clean, in a hot-water cup, the whole set of artificial teeth of a guest nearly sixty years of age, every time after his meal.

In a short time there were indications of the stopping of the car and passengers coming and going. Oyo awakened all at once, surprised, and looked out of the window. She saw a leafy tree, a high bank and a low bridge on the waterless moat. The conductors, enough to frighten her, were assembled in front of the new house at the corner. Many empty cars were left as if they were to be given away. With this sight of unfamiliar streets, Oyo felt unutterable helplessness. She became anxious about the thing in her sash, fearing that it had been stolen in her absent-minded moments. Also she doubted whether this was the place to leave the car. Impatiently she moved a bit from the end and said:

"Please, what is this place?"

The high-boned, flat-faced, slant-eyed conductor, who seemed to perceive the embarrassed figure of Oyo by a glance, did not move from the platform. Shrugging his shoulders, as if cold, and turning his head to the other side, he pulled the bell so that Oyo, who had left her seat, was upset by the moving car and thrown with all the weight of her body on the lap of a man looking like a foreman of the labourers, who was sitting near to the entrance. Feeling abashed, Oyo tried to get up quickly; she noticed that a big arm, as heavy as iron, was laid on her back as if to embrace her body; she struggled with all her might.

"Ehe! he! he!"

With the vile, frightful laughter there was a smell of wine.

"How can I stand it when I am held fast by a girl!"

"What good luck to have!" chanted one of the group that was sitting on the other side, and they burst into laughter.

Oyo flushed like fire, and wished even to jump out of the moving car. After that she felt that all the eyes in the car were looking constantly at her. Even then, she had not gained her composure after the fright of the moment when she felt herself closely embraced by a labourer. All at once Oyo became conscious that no one in the car was dressed like her—in Meisen silk, with folds laid somewhat loose, grey Hawori with an embroidered crest on it, and an apron of Itoöri neatly tied. All the other women were in Hisashigami and in close folds, and most of the men passengers were soldiers. Her helplessness riding among these unknown people became more keen. Just at the time when she was about to ask the conductor, who came to inspect the transfer tickets, regarding the station before Shinjuku, her embarrassment and helplessness became all but overwhelming.

"This is the Awoyama line, Miss. If you wish to go to Shinjuku, there is no other way but to transfer at Awoyama Itchome, and again at Shiocho." Throwing the transfer ticket on the lap of Oyo, the conductor hurried to fix the dislocated pole.

As she had understood that she could go all the way without transferring, Oyo, on hearing that she had to transfer not once but twice, felt as if she was thrown at last into the labyrinthine jungle of Yawata.

678

II

After going here and there, Oyo was able at last to realise that Tenmacho Nichome was the station before Shinjuku. How far would the trouble of the unknown route continue? Oyo regretted that she had come, and thought that she would never again go on an errand to an unknown place, no matter how she might be scolded. It is far better to stay at home with the sweeping, and to dry the bed-clothes or to wash the Yukata to offer to the guests. In this broad street, more bustling than she could have expected, she could not tell whether she had to turn to the right or to the left. Nevertheless, as she could not stand in the middle of the street, she was thinking about paying her own money secretly to ride in a Kuruma, when she saw a Kurumaya from the stand, and asked him how much she would have to pay to ride to Okubo.

"Give me fifty sen."

"Don't fool me."

Being much provoked, Oyo did not even turn to the Kurumaya, who called out something to her from her back, and walked aimlessly to a side street. Seeing a little girl with tucks at her shoulders in front of a tobacco shop, she asked in an almost weeping tone:

"Please, my girl, will you kindly let me know how to get to Yochomachi of Okubo?"

"Yochomachi?" said the girl cheerfully. "Go straight this way, and going down a slope you will find a policeman's post. . . . You had better ask at the policeman's post."

Oyo felt revived for the first time.

"Thank you ever so much."

Putting an overwhelming sentiment of thanks into these simple words, Oyo walked away, looking curiously at the sights on both sides of the somewhat narrow street. There was a European building for moving pictures on one side. From the lane near to the building a few geisha girls came out, laughing about something in loud voices. Looking at them, Oyo wondered: "Why are there geisha girls in such a place?" Suddenly she heard a tremendous noise. Before she could think what was the matter, she saw many soldiers on horseback riding from the open street to this narrow side street. There was the gate of a temple at one side of the beginning of the slope, and, taking advantage of an open place, Oyo was fortunate enough to get out of the way. She saw six or seven men employed on the telegraph wires, squatting on the earth, eating

679

their luncheon. A bamboo ladder was leaned against a wire pole on the other side of the street.

"Hello! The beauty!"

Their teasing started Oyo running away in embarrassment.

"We are receiving an extraordinary Benten."

"Hey, my girl! May I offer you a glass?"

Some of them were looking intently at the folds of her skirts. They could not contain themselves any longer, when a sudden wind had brushed aside the skirts of her underclothes. All of them burst in at once.

"Luck to see!"

"It is worth two yen at Sinjuku!"

"The red clothes are said to keep long!" And they continued to say things which were unbearable to hear. But is not the procession of the soldiers endless, stirring up the sand on all sides? And how much Oyo wished to escape!

Oyo finally got away from the place and went down the slope, almost running, when she suddenly stumbled on a stone and hardly kept from falling. In front of it she saw something that looked like a squirming heap of rags, which said:

"Ladies and gentlemen, passing by, please, a penny . . ."

Two or three leper beggars, at whom one could not bear to look a second time, were making bows on the sand of the street. The town at the foot of the slope was visible, with the dirty roofs in confusion, at the bottom of the valley-like lowland. Oyo wondered without any reason whether the town over yonder was the outcasts' quarter.

Going down the slope and turning to the left as she was instructed by the girl of the tobacco shop she easily found a policeman's post. As a policeman who looked good-natured was standing in the middle of the street, she asked him her route.

"What number of Yochomachi is it?"

"It is number sixty-two. The house is Mr. Inuyama's."

"Number sixty-two—then you have to go straight along this way, and go up the slope before a big wine-shop."

"I see."

"And let me see, is it the third side street after you go straight up the slope? . . . You turn there to the left, where you will find number sixty-two."

"Much obliged to you."

Before she had gone less than half a block, she found a wine-shop that looked like the one she was told about, and also a slope, so she thought the rest of the route was quite short. Feeling somewhat proud that she had come this far alone without the Kuruma or without going much out of the way, she forgot a while even the fatigue of her legs, but when she began to go up the slope, she had to meet another unexpected trouble.

Though the down-town district had had such continuous clear weather that it was annoyed by the dust, the up-town quarter of the city seemed to have had rain the night before and the street, which was not broad, was so deep in mud that Oyo could not even find the sidewalk. By the time she discovered that the mud was melting frost, which had not had time to dry, not only the toes of her new wooden clogs, but also her white socks newly washed, were all splashed with mud. On one side of the road was the bank covered with sepiaria and on the other side was a cryptomeria hedge, where, taking advantage of the fact that there were no passers-by, Oyo took out her pocket-papers and wiped, she knew not how often, the mud from the mat lining of her wooden clogs. As she glanced up she thought the third side street to which she had been directed by the policeman might be the corner she sought.

III

The mud of the melting frost became harder and harder. A big, masterless dog was roaming about with a menacing look. The rasping sounds of a violin were heard. The dreary sigh of the wind came from the trees near by. Far at the end of the side street the ground seemed to slope again, and, though the winter sunshine was falling gently on the roofs of the new houses and on the deep forest that covered the rears of all the houses, either side of the road was dark in shade, and all the houses were surrounded with fences of four-inch boards. Each had a small gate containing a slide-door, the faces of which were smeared with mud that had not been washed off, which seemed to have been placed there in mischief by the boys in the neighbourhood.

The number and name of the house, which Oyo found at last, after examining all the labels on the houses on both sides, was on the support of the small gate, where the mud was splashed thickest and dirtiest.

Inuyama Takemasa. . . .

Oyo looked at it again before she entered the gate. The gentleman called Mr. Inuyama was the most captious, unsympathetic and unreasonable among the numerous guests that came to Kinugawa. No matter how busy they were in attendance in the parlours, he would not be satisfied if he could not call up Oyo and all the other maids into his room. If the mistress did not come to salute him every time he came he would be angry and say: "You insult me," or "You treat me coldly." It was said that he gave up his membership in the parliament as it did not suit his dignity. His profession at present was that of a politician. He was fond of geishas as young as babies, and if the girls did not obey his will, he was so furious that nobody could touch him, and Oyo not only despised him more than any of the other guests, but also was afraid, without any reason, of his forbidding appearance and loud voice. He always wore European clothes and used to come in a Kuruma pulled by two drawers, saying that the lower class of people ride in the trolley. Once in a certain conversation, when the mistress had said to him that "in these days not only the expenses of your pleasure and the tips for geisha become dearer, but even your expense for Kuruma must be very considerable," he laughed:

"Mistress, the money is earned to spend. Ha! ha! ha! ha!"

But these prosperous days were no longer. When it was hardly December of that year, Mr. Inuyama suddenly stopped coming, and in spite of many letters he would not respond to the bill of two hundred yen of that month and the fifty-yen balance of the previous month. Kinugawa was obliged to talk it over with a geisha who first brought Mr. Inuyama after their meeting at a certain Matsumotoro, but, it was almost clear that she could not shake her sleeve when she had none, and so January passed in this way, and now it was February. The mistress sent Oyo to the mansion of Mr. Inuyama to reconnoitre.

Oyo had known numerous cases of this kind, not only of men like Mr. Inuyama, but also of many other guests. She thought this nothing more than the bad ways of people. She thought only that they will be enjoying themselves at some other house, if they do not come to hers, then, it will be good of them if they will be more considerate and pay the bill. The reason Oyo looked again at the label on the gate was the fact that the gate of his mansion was so dirty. But, to enter the gate was better than the annoyance of walking around aimlessly any longer in the frost-melting road, so she looked around from the porch with its dirty and broken paper-screen, wondering which was the servants' entrance.

On the right hand, beyond the bamboo fence, was visible the roof of a one-storied house looking cold under the garden trees. She got a glimpse of an old red blanket and a dirty cotton gown hung on a clothes-pole, through the crevices of the bamboo fence. On the left hand, further on, were one-storied houses with lattice gates, and another that looked like a rented house. Beside the wheel-well, where the plum-blossoms showed their buds, a fish-monger was cutting a salted salmon. Two maidservants in careless Hisashigami, who carried babies under quilted gowns and wore European aprons which had become grey, seemed to be at the height of their silly conversation with the fishmonger. As soon as they caught sight of Oyo, whose appearance was quite different, they sharpened their eyes, and, seeming rather to fear her, looked her over attentively from top to toe. The road from the well to the servants' entrance was spread with straw bags of charcoal, and the muddy water of the melting frost ran into the feet of people walking on them. Being in much perplexity Oyo could not move a step, and bending her waist, said:

"I beg your pardon."

Both of the maidservants stood wonder-stricken with open mouths.

"Is this Mr. Inuyama's house?"

Suddenly one of the maidservants began to grow uneasy, and, perceiving her manner, Oyo said:

"I came with a message from Kyobashi. Is the master at home?"

"He is absent."

Then the baby on her back began to cry.

Oyo, as she was ordered by the mistress, remembered how to proceed when she was told the master was absent, namely, to call madam to the servants' entrance and leave the word that she was the messenger from Mizuta, which was the name of her mistress. However, as Oyo was only eighteen or nineteen, she felt somewhat timid and stood on the walk, forgetting even that the water of the melting frost was overflowing on her polished wooden clogs. The baby on the back of the maidservant cried more and more.

"Chiyo! Chiyo!" Suddenly, a voice of woman, close to her ears, aroused her.

Being astonished, Oyo turned and saw at the broken paper-screens of the servants' entrance not farther than six inches, the big face of a woman, like a horse, with the eyes widely separated from each other. The careless Hisashigami could not be beaten by the maidservants. She was a big, clumsy madam in a dirty and creased Higu.

Just then, the fishmonger came to offer three slices of the salted salmon to madam. Madam continued talking with the fishmonger, and Oyo, at last somewhat aroused and feeling at the same time a sense of deep disappointment, went out from the gate as if to escape. For she felt that her troubles in coming so far had been all in vain. She was exceedingly sorry for her mistress, as she had been entirely deceived by this humbug.

When Oyo rode again in the trolley she felt, at first, the fatigue of the vain effort and at the same time the fact that she was unbearably hungry, but being unable to do anything about it, she arrived at Ginza. The sun was already declining. Calling to her mind the clockstand of Hattori, which she saw when she was waiting for the car that morning, she looked up, and lo! was it not already near to four o'clock. Oyo felt her heart sinking with melancholy, picturing in her mind the flash of her mistress' eye, who never would say to her: "How early you are!" when she returned from the far-away errand. The electric lights were already lit in the shops. . . .

KAGAWA KAGEKI

KAGAWA KAGEKI (Japanese, 1768-1843). Leading *tanka* poet of his day. A prodigy who composed verse as a child. Earned living as instructor of poetry. Famous collection of verse: *Keien isshi*. Also prepared important editions of early Japanese texts.

SWALLOWS

Although the swallows are not like
  The friends with whom I freely may
Hold converse, what a joy it is
  To meet these birds from far away!

PINE-TREES AND THE MOON

The forms of all the pine-trees
  Have stood forth into sight;
But yet the moon has not left
  The rim of the mountain height.

WILD GEESE

Far in the distance, across the hazy sky,
  I saw the wild geese flock and fly away;
Yesterday I saw them take their flight,
  Also to-day.

A MAIDEN

The girl of whom in olden days
I once caught glimpses through a hedge,
Making my horse tread on young grass—
Alas! she, too, by now must have grown old!

THE CRICKET

O, cricket, chirruping
  Under my bed,
Do not tell other men
  My whispers with my beloved.

KALIDASA

KĀLIDĀSA (Sanskrit, 5th century A.D.). Legendary, greatest of all Sanskrit dramatists and poets. Nothing known of life, though apparently he was a thorough scholar and wide traveler throughout India. Left three dramas, two epics, two shorter poems. His masterpiece, the play *Sakuntalā*, created sensation when translated in 1789, influenced Goethe, Schiller, Herder.

THE CITY OF UJJAIN

Swerve from thy northern path; for westward rise
The palace balconies thou may'st not slight
  In fair Ujjain; and if bewitching eyes,
That flutter at thy gleams, should not delight
  Thine amorous bosom, useless were thy gift of sight.

The neighbouring mountain-stream that gliding grants
A glimpse of charms in whirling eddies pursed,
  While noisy swans accompany her dance
Like a tinkling zone, will slake thy loving thirst—
A woman always tells her love in gestures first.

Thou only, happy lover! canst repair
The desolation that thine absence made:
   Her shrinking current seems the careless hair
That brides deserted wear in single braid,
And dead leaves falling give her face a paler shade.

   Oh, fair Ujjain! Gem to Avanti given,
Where village ancients tell their tales of mirth
   And old romance! Oh, radiant glimpse of heaven,
Home of a blest celestial band whose worth
Sufficed, though fallen from heaven, to bring down heaven on earth.

   Where the river-breeze at dawn, with fragrant gain
From friendly lotus-blossoms, lengthens out
   The clear, sweet passion-warbling of the crane,
To cure the women's languishing, and flout
With a lover's coaxing all their hesitating doubt.

   Enriched with odours through a window drifting
From perfumed hair, and greeted as a friend
   By peacock pets their wings in dances lifting,
On flower-sweet balconies thy labour end,
Where prints of dear pink feet an added glory lend.

   Black as the neck of Siva, very God,
Dear therefore to his hosts, thou mayest go
   To his dread shrine, round which the gardens nod,
When breezes rich with lotus-pollen blow
And ointments that the gaily bathing maidens know.

   Reaching that temple at another time,
Wait till the sun is lost to human eyes;
   For if thou mayest play the part sublime
Of Siva's drum at evening sacrifice,
Then hast thou in thy thunders grave a priceless prize.

   The women there, whose girdles long have tinkled
In answer to the dance, whose hands yet seize
   And wave their fans with lustrous gems besprinkled,
Will feel thine early drops that soothe and please,
And recompense thee from black eyes like clustering bees.

Clothing thyself in twilight's rose-red glory,
Embrace the dancing Siva's tree-like arm;
    He will prefer thee to his mantle hoary,
And spare his grateful goddess-bride's alarm,
Whose eager gaze will manifest no fear of harm.

JOHN KEATS

JOHN KEATS (English, 1795-1821). A major poet of English Romantic
Period. Exquisite workmanship made him the "poet of the most poetical type."
Short, unhappy life, died in Rome of tuberculosis. Hopeless love for Fanny
Brawne inspired many poems and letters. Shakespeare and Milton his models.
Wrote some of most perfect poems in the language: "La Belle Dame Sans
        Merci," "The Eve of St. Agnes," Odes and Sonnets.

ODE TO A NIGHTINGALE

My heart aches, and a drowsy numbness pains
    My sense, as though of hemlock I had drunk,
Or emptied some dull opiate to the drains
    One minute past, and Lethe-wards had sunk:
'Tis not through envy of thy happy lot,
    But being too happy in thy happiness,
        That thou, light-winged Dryad of the trees,
            In some melodious plot
    Of beechen green, and shadows numberless,
        Singest of summer in full-throated ease.

O for a draught of vintage! that hath been
    Cooled a long age in the deep-delved earth,
Tasting of Flora and the country green,
    Dance, and Provençal song, and sunburnt mirth!
O for a beaker full of the warm South!
    Full of the true, the blushful Hippocrene,
        With beaded bubbles winking at the brim,
            And purple-stained mouth;
    That I might drink, and leave the world unseen,
        And with thee fade away into the forest dim:

Fade far away, dissolve, and quite forget
    What thou among the leaves hast never known,

The weariness, the fever, and the fret
  Here, where men sit and hear each other groan;
Where palsy shakes a few, sad, last grey hairs,
  Where youth grows pale, and spectre-thin, and dies;
    Where but to think is to be full of sorrow
      And leaden-eyed despairs;
  Where beauty cannot keep her lustrous eyes,
    Or new love pine at them beyond tomorrow.

Away! away! for I will fly to thee,
  Not charioted by Bacchus and his pards,
But on the viewless wings of Poesy,
  Though the dull brain perplexes and retards:
Already with thee! tender is the night,
  And haply the Queen-Moon is on her throne,
    Clustered around by all her starry Fays;
      But here there is no light,
  Save what from heaven is with the breezes blown
    Through verdurous glooms and winding mossy ways.

I cannot see what flowers are at my feet,
  Nor what soft incense hangs upon the boughs,
But, in embalmed darkness, guess each sweet
  Wherewith the seasonable month endows
The grass, the thicket, and the fruit-tree wild;
  White hawthorn, and the pastoral eglantine;
    Fast-fading violets covered up in leaves;
      And mid-May's eldest child,
The coming musk-rose, full of dewy wine,
  The murmurous haunt of flies on summer eves.

Darkling I listen; and for many a time
  I have been half in love with easeful Death,
Called him soft names in many a mused rhyme,
  To take into the air my quiet breath;
Now more than ever seems it rich to die,
  To cease upon the midnight with no pain,
    While thou art pouring forth thy soul abroad
      In such an ecstasy!
  Still wouldst thou sing, and I have ears in vain—
    To thy high requiem become a sod.

Thou wast not born for death, immortal Bird!
  No hungry generations tread thee down;
The voice I hear this passing night was heard
  In ancient days by emperor and clown:
Perhaps the self-same song that found a path
  Through the sad heart of Ruth, when, sick for home,
    She stood in tears amid the alien corn;
      The same that ofttimes hath
  Charmed magic casements, opening on the foam
  Of perilous seas, in faery lands forlorn.

Forlorn! the very word is like a bell
  To toll me back from thee to my sole self!
Adieu! the fancy cannot cheat so well
  As she is famed to do, deceiving elf.
Adieu! adieu! thy plaintive anthem fades
  Past the near meadows, over the still stream,
    Up the hill-side; and now 'tis buried deep
      In the next valley-glades:
  Was it a vision, or a waking dream?
  Fled is that music:—do I wake or sleep?

ODE ON A GRECIAN URN

Thou still unravish'd bride of quietness,
  Thou foster-child of silence and slow time,
Sylvian historian, who canst thus express
  A flowery tale more sweetly than our rhyme:
What leaf-fring'd legend haunts about thy shape
  Of deities or mortals, or of both,
    In Tempe or the dales of Arcady?
What men or gods are these? What maidens loth?
  What mad pursuit? What struggle to escape?
    What pipes and timbrels? What wild ecstasy?

Heard melodies are sweet, but those unheard
  Are sweeter; therefore, ye soft pipes, play on;
Not to the sensual ear, but, more endear'd,
  Pipe to the spirit ditties of no tone:

Fair youth, beneath the trees, thou canst not leave
　　Thy song, nor ever can those trees be bare;
　　　Bold Lover, never, never canst thou kiss,
Though winning near the goal—yet, do not grieve;
　　She cannot fade, though thou hast not thy bliss,
　　　For ever wilt thou love, and she be fair!

Ah, happy, happy boughs! that cannot shed
　　Your leaves, nor ever bid the Spring adieu;
And, happy melodist, unwearied,
　　For ever piping songs for ever new;
More happy love! more happy, happy love!
　　For ever warm and still to be enjoy'd,
　　　For ever panting, and for ever young;
All breathing human passion far above,
　　That leaves a heart high-sorrowful and cloy'd,
　　　A burning forehead, and a parching tongue.

Who are these coming to the sacrifice?
　　To what green altar, O mysterious priest,
Lead'st thou that heifer lowing at the skies,
　　And all her silken flanks with garlands drest?
What little town by river or sea shore,
　　Or mountain-built with peaceful citadel,
　　　Is emptied of its folk, this pious morn?
And, little town, thy streets for evermore
　　Will silent be: and not a soul to tell
　　　Why thou art desolate, can e'er return.

O Attic shape! Fair attitude! with brede
　　Of marble men and maidens overwrought,
With forest branches and the trodden weed;
　　Thou, silent form, dost tease us out of thought
As doth eternity: Cold Pastoral!
　　When old age shall this generation waste,
　　　Thou shalt remain, in midst of other woe
Than ours, a friend to man, to whom thou say'st,
　　'Beauty is truth, truth beauty'—that is all
　　　Ye know on earth, and all ye need to know.

TO AUTUMN

Season of mists and mellow fruitfulness,
    Close bosom-friend of the maturing sun;
Conspiring with him how to load and bless
    With fruit the vines that round the thatch-eves run;
To bend with apples the moss'd cottage-trees,
    And fill all fruit with ripeness to the core;
        To swell the gourd, and plump the hazel shells
With a sweet kernel; to set budding more,
    And still more, later flowers for the bees,
    Until they think warm days will never cease,
        For Summer has o'er-brimm'd their clammy cells.

Who hath not seen thee oft amid thy store?
    Sometimes whoever seeks abroad may find
Thee sitting careless on a granary floor,
    Thy hair soft-lifted by the winnowing wind;
Or on a half-reap'd furrow sound asleep,
    Drows'd with the fume of poppies, while thy hook
        Spares the next swath and all its twined flowers:
And sometimes like a gleaner thou dost keep
    Steady thy laden head across a brook;
    Or by a cyder-press, with patient look,
        Thou watchest the last oozings hours by hours.

Where are the songs of Spring? Ay, where are they?
    Think not of them, thou hast thy music too,—
While barred clouds bloom the soft-dying day,
    And touch the stubble-plains with rosy hue;
Then in a wailful choir the small gnats mourn
    Among the river sallows, borne aloft
        Or sinking as the light wind lives or dies;
And full-grown lambs loud bleat from hilly bourn;
    Hedge-crickets sing; and now with treble soft
    The red-breast whistles from a garden-croft;
        And gathering swallows twitter in the skies.

GOTTFRIED KELLER

GOTTFRIED KELLER (Swiss, 1819-1890). A Swiss writer who wrote some
of best German literature of 19th century. Largely self-educated, became first
a painter, then a writer. Autobiographical novel, *Der Grüne Heinrich*, one of
most praised "educational novels." Short stories skillful, realistic, sensitive.

A LEGEND OF THE DANCE

ACCORDING to Saint Gregory, Musa was the dancer among the
saints. The child of good people, she was a bright young lady, a
diligent servant of the Mother of God, and subject only to one
weakness, such an uncontrollable passion for the dance that when
the child was not praying she was dancing, and that on all imaginable occasions. Musa danced with her playmates, with children, with
the young men, and even by herself. She danced in her own room
and every other room in the house, in the garden, in the meadows.
Even when she went to the altar it was to a gracious measure rather
than a walk, and even on the smooth marble flags before the church
door, she did not scruple to practice a few hasty steps.

In fact, one day when she found herself alone in the church, she
could not refrain from executing some figures before the altar, and,
so to speak, dancing a pretty prayer to the Virgin Mary. She became
so oblivious of all else that she fancied she was merely dreaming
when she saw an oldish but handsome gentleman dancing opposite
her and supplementing her figures so skilfully that the pair got into
the most elaborate dance imaginable. The gentleman had a royal
purple robe, a golden crown on his head, and a glossy black curled
beard, which age had touched as with streaks of starlight. At the
same time music sounded from the choir where half a dozen small
angels stood, or sat with their chubby little legs' hanging over the
screen, and fingered or blew their various instruments. The urchins
were very pleasant and skilful. Each rested his music on one of the
stone angels with which the choir screen was adorned, except the
smallest, a puffy-cheeked piper who sat crosslegged and contrived to
hold his music with his pink toes. He was the most diligent of them
all. The others dangled their feet, kept spreading their pinions, one
or other of them, with a rustle, so that their colors shimmered like
doves' breasts, and they teased each other as they played.

Musa found no time to wonder at all this until the dance, which lasted a pretty long time, was over; for the merry gentleman seemed to enjoy himself as much as the maid, who felt as if she were dancing about in heaven. But when the music ceased and Musa stood there panting, she began to be frightened in good earnest, and looked in astonishment at the ancient, who was neither out of breath nor warm, and who now began to speak. He introduced himself as David, the Virgin Mary's royal ancestor, and her ambassador. He asked if she would like to pass eternal bliss in an unending pleasure dance, compared with which the dance they had just finished could only be called a miserable crawl.

To this she promptly answered that she would like nothing better. Whereupon the blessed King David said again that in that case she had nothing more to do than to renounce all pleasure and all dancing for the rest of her days on earth and devote herself wholly to penance and spiritual exercises, and that without hesitation or relapse. The maiden was taken aback at these conditions, and asked whether she must really give up dancing altogether. She questioned indeed whether there was any dancing in Heaven; for there was a time for everything. This earth looked very fit and proper for dancing; it stood to reason that Heaven must have very different attractions, else death were a superfluity.

But David explained to her that her notions on the subject were erroneous, and proved from many Bible texts, and from his own example that dancing was assuredly a sanctified occupation for the blessed. But what was wanted just now was an immediate decision, Yes or No, whether she wished to enter into eternal joy by way of temporal self-denial, or not. If she did not, then he would go farther on; for they wanted some dancers in Heaven.

Musa stood, still doubtful and undecided, and fumbled anxiously with her finger-tips in her mouth. It seemed too hard never to dance again from that moment, all for the sake of an unknown reward. At that, David gave a signal, and suddenly the musicians struck up some bars of a dance of such unheard-of bliss and unearthliness that the girl's soul leaped in her body, and her limbs twitched; but she could not get one of them to dance, and she noticed that her body was far too heavy and stiff for the tune. Full of longing, she thrust her hand into the King's and made the promise which he demanded.

Forthwith he was no more to be seen, and the angel-musicians whirred and fluttered and crowded out and away through an open window. But, in mischievous childish fashion, before going they dealt the patient stone angels a sounding slap on the cheeks with their rolled-up music.

Musa went home with devout step, carrying that celestial melody in her ears; and having laid all her dainty raiment aside, she got a coarse gown made and put it on. At the same time she built herself a cell at the end of her parents' garden, where the deep shade of the trees lingered, made a scant bed of moss and from that day onward separated herself from all her kindred, and took up her abode there as a penitent and saint. She spent all her time in prayer, and often disciplined herself with a scourge. But her severest penance consisted in holding her limbs stiff and immovable, for whenever she heard a sound, the twitter of a bird or the rustling of the leaves in the wind, her feet twitched as much as to tell her they must dance.

As this involuntary twitching would not forsake her, and often seduced her to a little skip before she was aware, she caused her tender feet to be fastened together by a light chain. Her relatives and friends marveled day and night at the transformation, rejoiced to possess such a saint, and guarded the hermitage under the trees as the apple of their eye. Many came for her counsel and intercession. In particular, they used to bring young girls to her who were rather clumsy on their feet, for it was observed that everyone whom she touched at once became light and graceful in gait.

So she spent three years in her cell, but by the end of the third year Musa had become almost as thin and transparent as a summer cloud. She lay continually on her bed of moss, gazed wistfully into Heaven, and was convinced that she could already see the golden sandals of the blessed, dancing and gliding about through the azure.

At last one harsh autumn day the tidings spread that the saint lay on her death-bed. She had taken off her dark penitential robe, and caused herself to be arrayed in bridal garments of dazzling white. So she lay with folded hands and smilingly awaited the hour of death. The garden was all filled with devout persons, the breezes murmured, and the leaves were falling from the trees on all sides. But suddenly the sighing of the wind changed into music, which appeared to be playing in the tree-tops, and as the people looked up, lo, all the branches were clad in fresh green, the myrtles and pomegranates put out blossom and fragrance, the earth decked itself with flowers, and a rosy glow settled upon the white, frail form of the dying saint.

That same instant she yielded up her spirit. The chain about her feet sprang asunder with a sharp twang, Heaven opened wide all around, full of unbounded radiance so that all could see in. Then they saw many thousands of beautiful young men and maidens in the utmost splendor, dancing circle upon circle farther than the eye could reach. A magnificent King enthroned on a cloud, with a special band of small angels seated on its edge, bore down a little way towards earth, and received the form of the sainted Musa from before the eyes of all the beholders who filled the garden. They saw, too, how she sprang into the open Heaven and immediately danced out of sight among the jubilant radiant circle.

That was a high feast-day in Heaven. Now the custom (to be sure, it is denied by Saint Gregory of Nyssa, but stoutly maintained by his namesake of Nazianza) on feast-days was to invite the nine Muses, who sat for the rest of their time in Hell and to admit them to Heaven that they might be of assistance. They were well entertained, but once the feast was over had to go back to the other place.

When, now, the dances and songs and all the ceremonies had come to an end and the heavenly company sat down, Musa was taken taken to a table where the nine Muses were being served. They sat huddled together half scared, glancing about with their fiery black or dark-blue eyes. The busy Martha of the Gospels was caring for them in person. She had on her finest kitchen-apron and a tiny little smudge on her white chin and was pressing all manner of good things on the Muses in the friendliest possible way, but when Musa and Saint Cecilia and some other artistic women arrived and greeted the shy Pierians cheerfully, and joined their company, they began to thaw, grew confidential, and the feminine circle became quite pleasant and happy. Musa sat beside Terpsichore, and Cecilia between Polyhymnia and Euterpe, and all took one another's hands. Next came the little minstrel urchins and made up to the beautiful women with an eye to the bright fruit which shone on the ambrosial table. King David himself came and brought a golden cup, out of which all drank, so that gracious joy warmed them. He went round the table, not omitting as he passed to chuck pretty Erato under the chin. While things were going on so favorably at the Muses' table, Our Gracious Lady herself appeared in all her beauty and goodness, sat down a few minutes beside the Muses, and kissed the august Urania with the starry coronet tenderly upon the lips, when she took her departure, whispering to her that she would not rest until the Muses could remain in Paradise forever.

But that never came about. To declare their gratitude for the

kindness and friendliness which had been shown them, and to prove
their goodwill, the Muses took counsel together and practised a
hymn of praise in a retired corner of the Underworld. They tried to
give it the form of the solemn chorals which were the fashion in
Heaven. They arranged it in two parts of four voices each, with a
sort of principal part, which Urania took, and they thus produced
a remarkable piece of vocal music.

The next time a feast-day was celebrated in Heaven, and the
Muses again rendered their assistance, they seized what appeared
to be a favorable moment for their purpose, took their places, and
began their song. It began softly, but soon swelled out mightily,
but in those regions it sounded so dismal, almost defiant and harsh,
yet so wistful and mournful that first of all a horrified silence prevailed, and next the whole assembly was seized with a sad longing
for earth and home, and broke into universal weeping.

A sigh without end throbbed throughout Heaven. All the Elders
and Prophets started up in dismay while the Muses, with the best of
intentions, sang louder and more mournfully, and all Paradise, with
the Patriarchs and Elders and Prophets and all who ever walked or
lay in green pastures, lost all command of themselves. Until at last,
the High and Mighty Trinity Himself came to put things right, and
reduced the too zealous Muses to silence with a long reverberating
peal of thunder.

Then quiet and composure were restored to Heaven, but the poor
nine Sisters had to depart and never dared enter it again from that
day onward.

OMAR KHAYYAM

OMAR KHAYYAM (Persian, 1050-1123). Most widely known of the Persian
poets through Edward Fitzgerald's translation of the *Rubaiyat*. Honored in
Iran as astronomer, algebraist and philosopher. Compiled astronomical tables
and first Arabic algebra. Left 280 quatrains, epigrammatic in style, counseling
a temperate hedonism as antidote to the cruelties of fate.

RUBAIYAT OF OMAR KHAYYAM

I

Awake! for Morning in the Bowl of Night
Has flung the Stone that puts the Stars to Flight;
    And Lo! the Hunter of the East has caught
The Sultan's Turret in a Noose of Light.

II

Dreaming when Dawn's Left Hand was in the Sky
I heard a Voice within the Tavern cry,
   "Awake, my Little ones, and fill the Cup
Before Life's Liquor in its Cup be dry."

III

And, as the Cock crew, those who stood before
The Tavern shouted—"Open then the Door!
   You know how little while we have to stay,
And, once departed, may return no more."

IV

Now the New Year reviving old Desires,
The thoughtful Soul to Solitude retires,
   Where the *white hand of Moses* on the Bough
Puts out, and Jesus from the Ground suspires.

V

Iram indeed is gone with all its Rose,
And Jamshyd's Sev'n-ring'd Cup where no one knows;
   But still the Vine her ancient Ruby yields,
And still a Garden by the Water blows.

VI

And David's Lips are lock't; but in divine
High-piping Pehlevi, with "Wine! Wine! Wine!
   Red Wine!"—the Nightingale cries to the Rose
That yellow Cheek of hers to incarnadine.

VII

Come, fill the Cup, and in the Fire of Spring
The Winter Garment of Repentance fling:
   The Bird of Time has but a little way
To fly—and Lo! the Bird is on the Wing.

VIII

And look—a thousand Blossoms with the Day
Woke—and a thousand scatter'd into Clay:
    And this first Summer Month that brings the Rose
Shall take Jamshyd and Kaikobad away.

IX

But come with old Khayyam, and leave the Lot
Of Kaikobad and Kaihosru forgot:
    Let Rustum lay about him as he will,
Or Hatim Tai cry Supper—heed them not.

X

With me along some Strip of Herbage strown
That just divides the desert from the town,
    Where name of Slave and Sultan scarce is known,
And pity Sultan Mahmud on his Throne.

XI

Here with a Loaf of Bread beneath the Bough,
A flask of Wine, a Book of Verse—and Thou
    Beside me singing in the Wilderness—
And Wilderness is Paradise enow.

XII

"How sweet is mortal Sovranty"—think some:
Others—"How blest the Paradise to come!"
    Ah, take the Cash in hand and waive the Rest;
Oh, the brave Music of a *distant* Drum!

XIII

Look to the Rose that blows about us—"Lo,
Laughing," she says, "into the World I blow:
    At once the silken Tassel of my Purse
Tear, and its Treasure on the Garden throw."

698

XIV

The Worldly Hope men set their Hearts upon
Turns Ashes—or it prospers; and anon,
   Like Snow upon the Desert's dusty Face
Lighting a little Hour or two—is gone.

XV

And those who husbanded the Golden Grain,
And those who flung it to the Winds like Rain,
   Alike to no such aureate Earth are turn'd
As, buried once, Men want dug up again.

XVI

Think, in this batter'd Caravanserai
Whose Doorways are alternate Night and Day,
   How Sultan after Sultan with his Pomp
Abode his Hour or two, and went his way.

XVII

They say the Lion and the Lizard keep
The Courts where Jamshyd gloried and drank deep:
   And Bahram, that great Hunter—the Wild Ass
Stamps O'er his Head, and he lies fast asleep.

XVIII

I sometimes think that never blows so red
The Rose as where some buried Cæsar bled;
   That every Hyacinth the Garden wears
Dropt in its Lap from some once lovely Head.

XIX

And this delightful Herb whose tender Green
Fledges the River's Lip on which we lean—
   Ah, lean upon it lightly! for who knows
From what once lovely Lip it springs unseen!

KAN KIKUCHI

KAN KIKUCHI (Japanese, 1888-1948). Contemporary Japanese short story writer, novelist and playwright. Precise, clear-cut stylist. Influenced by West, helped introduce realism into Japanese theater. Plays translated: *The Miracle, Love and Four Other Plays, The Father Returns, The Madman on the Roof, Better Than Revenge.*

THE MADMAN ON THE ROOF

Characters

Yoshitaro Katsushima, *the madman, 24 years of age*
Suejiro Katsushima, *his brother, a 17-year-old high school student*
Gisuke Katsushima, *their father*
Oyoshi Katsushima, *their mother*
Tosaku, *a neighbor*
Kichiji, *a man-servant, 20 years of age*
A Priestess, *about 50 years of age*

Place: *a small island in Sanuki Strait*
Time: *1900*

The stage-setting represents the backyard of the Katsushimas, who are the richest family on the island. A bamboo fence prevents one from seeing more of the house than the high roof, which stands out sharply against the rich greenish sky of the southern island summer. At the left of the stage one can catch a glimpse of the sea shining in the sunlight.

Yoshitaro, the elder son of the family, is sitting astride the ridge of the roof, and is looking out over the sea.

Gisuke (*speaking from within the house*). Yoshi is sitting on the roof again. He will get a sunstroke—the sun is so terribly hot. (*Coming out.*) Kichiji!—Where is Kichiji?

Kichiji (*appearing from the right*). Yes! What do you want?

Gisuke. Bring Yoshitaro down. He has no hat on, up there in the hot sun. He will get a sunstroke. How did he get up there, anyway? (*Coming through the gate to the center of the stage, and looking up to the roof.*) I don't see how he can stand it, sitting on that hot slate roof. (*He calls.*) Yoshitaro! You better come down. If you stay up there you will get a sunstroke, and maybe die. Come

700

on now—hurry! If you don't come down, I'll get after you with a stick.

Yoshitaro (protesting like a spoiled child). No; I don't want to. Something interesting. The priest of the Konpira God is dancing in the clouds. Dancing with an angel in pink robes. They are calling to me to come. *(Crying out ecstatically.)* Wait! I am coming!

Gisuke. If you talk like that you will fall, as you did the other day. You are already crippled and insane. How you worry your parents! Come down, you fool!

Kichiji. Master, don't get so angry. The young master doesn't understand anything. He's under the influence of evil spirits. Why, he climbed the roof of the Honzen Temple without even a ladder; a low roof like this one is the easiest thing in the world for him. I tell you it's the evil spirits that make him climb. Nothing can stop him.

Gisuke. You may be right; but he worries me to death.

Kichiji. Everyone on the island says he is under the influence of the evil fox-spirit, but I don't believe that, for I never heard of a fox climbing trees.

Gisuke (He calls again). Yoshi! Come down! *(Dropping his voice.)* Kichiji, you had better go up and fetch him.

(Kichiji goes out after the ladder. Tosaku, the neighbor, enters.)

Tosaku. Good-day, sir. Your son is on the roof again.

Gisuke. Yes; he is up there as usual. I don't like it, but when I keep him locked in a room he is unhappy as a fish out of water. Then, when I think that is too cruel, and let him out, back he goes up on the roof.

Tosaku. By the way, a Priestess has just come to the island. How would you like to have her pray for your son?—That is really what I came to see you about.

Gisuke. Is that so? Well, we have tried prayers several times before, but it has never done any good.

Tosaku. The Priestess who is here now believes in the Konpira God. She is very miraculous. People say she is inspired by the Konpira God, so that her prayers are quite different from those of a mountain priest. Why don't you try her once?

Gisuke. Suejiro says he doesn't believe in any prayers. . . . But there isn't any harm in letting her try.

(Kichiji enters carrying the ladder, and disappears behind he fence.)

Tosaku. Then I will go Kinkichi's house and bring her here. In the meantime you get your son down off the roof.

Gisuke. All right. Thanks for your trouble. *(After seeing that Tosaku has gone, he calls again.)* Yoshi! Be quiet now and come down.

Yoshitaro (drawing away from Kichiji as a Buddhist might from a heathen). If you touch me the fairies will destroy you!

(Kichiji hurriedly catches Yoshitaro by the shoulder and pulls him to the ladder. Yoshitaro suddenly becomes gentle. He comes down to the center of the stage, followed by Kichiji. Yoshitaro is lame in his right leg.)

Gisuke (calling). Oyoshi! Come out here a minute.

Oyoshi (from within). What do you want?

Gisuke. I have sent for the Priestess.

Oyoshi (appearing at the gate). That may be a good idea. You never can tell what may help him.

(Tosaka enters, leading the Priestess. She has a cunning look.)

Tosaku. This is the lady I spoke to you about.

Gisuke. Ah, good-afternoon! You are welcome.—This boy is a great worry, and causes us much shame.

Priestess (casually). Don't worry about him. I will cure him immediately with the help of the God. *(Looking at Yoshitaro.)* This is the one?

Gisuke. Yes. He is twenty-four years old, and can do nothing but climb up to high places.

Priestess. How long has he been this way?

Gisuke. Ever since he was born. Even when he was a baby, he wanted to be climbing. When he was four or five years old he climbed onto the low shrine, then onto the high shrine of Buddha, and finally onto a very high shelf. When he was seven or eight he began climbing trees. At fifteen or sixteen he climbed to the top of mountains, and stayed there all day long, where he says he talked with fairies and with gods, and such things. What do you think is the matter with him?

Priestess. There's no doubt but that it is the evil fox-spirit. All right, I will pray for him. *(Looking at Yoshitaro.)* Listen now! I am the messenger of the Konpira God of this island. And all that I say comes from the God.

Yoshitaro (uneasily). You say the Konpira God? Did you ever see him?

Priestess (staring at him). Don't say such sacrilegious things! The God cannot be seen.

Yoshitaro (exultantly). Oh, I have seen him many times! He is an old man with white robes and a golden crown. He is my best friend.

Priestess (taken aback at this assertion, and speaking to Gisuke). This is the evil fox-spirit, all right, but a very extreme case. Now then, I will ask the God.

(She chants a prayer in a ridiculous manner. Yoshitaro, held fast by Kichiji, watches the Priestess blankly. She works herself into a frenzy, and falls to the ground in a faint. Presently she rises to her feet and looks about her strangely.)

Priestess (in a changed voice). I am the Konpira God residing in this island!

(All except Yoshitaro fall to their knees with exclamations of reverence.)

Priestess (with affected dignity). The elder son of this family is under the influence of the evil fox-spirit. Hang him up on the branch of a tree and purify him with the smoke of green pine-needles. If you doubt what I say, you are condemned!

(She faints again. There are more exclamations of astonishment.)

Priestess (rising and looking about her as though unconscious of what has taken place). What has happened? Did the God speak?

Gisuke. It was miraculous. The God answered.

Priestess. Whatever the God told you to do, you must do at once, or be condemned. I warn you for your own sake.

Gisuke (hesitating somewhat). Kichiji, you may go and get the green pine-needles.

Yoshitaro. That was not the voice of the Konpira God. He wouldn't listen to a priestess like you!

Priestess (as though insulted). I will get even with you. Just wait! Don't you talk back to the God like that, you wretched fox!

(Kichiji enters with an armful of green pine-needles. Oyoshi becomes frightened. Gisuke and Kichiji rather reluctantly set fire to

the pine-needles, then bring Yoshitaro to the fire. Gisuke and Kichiji attempt to get Yoshitaro's face into the smoke. Suddenly Suejiro appears in the gateway. He wears a high-school uniform, and is a dark-complexioned, active boy. He stands amazed at the scene before him.)

Suejiro. What is the meaning of this smoke?

Yoshitaro (coughing from the smoke, and looking at his brother as at a savior). That you, Sue? Father and Kichiji have been putting me in the smoke.

Suejiro (angrily). Father! What foolish thing are you doing? Haven't I told you time and again about this sort of business?

Gisuke. But the miraculous Priestess, inspired by the God of——

Suejiro (interrupting). Rubbish! You do these foolish things merely because he is so helpless. *(He looks contemptuously at the Priestess and crosses over and stamps the fire out with his feet.)*

Gisuke (more courageously). Suejiro, I have no education, and you have, so I am always willing to listen to you. But this fire was made at the God's command, and you mustn't stamp on it.

Suejiro. Smoke won't cure him. People will laugh at you for talking about the fox-spirit. Why, if all the gods in the country were called upon together, they couldn't cure even a cold. When the doctors can't cure him, no one can. I've told you before that he doesn't suffer. If he did, we would have to do something for him. But as long as he can climb up on the roof, he is happy from morning till night. There is no one in the whole country as happy as he is—perhaps no one in the world. Besides, if you cure him now, what can he do? He is twenty-four years old and knows nothing—not even the alphabet; and he has had no experience. If he were cured, he would be conscious of being crippled, and would be the most miserable man in the country. Is that what you want to see? It's all because you want to make him normal. But isn't it foolish to become normal merely to suffer? *(Looking sidewise at the Priestess.)* Tosaku-san, if you brought her here, you had better take her away.

Tosaku. Well, we'll go home right away. It was my mistake that I brought you here.

Gisuke (giving Tosaku some money). Maybe you will excuse him. He is young and he has such a temper.

(The Priestess and Tosaku go out.)

704

Oyoshi. I suspected her from the very first. If she was inspired by a real god, she wouldn't do such cruel things.

Gisuke (suddenly). But where has Yoshitaro gone, anyway?

Kichiji (pointing at the roof). He is up there.

Gisuke (having to smile). As usual.

(During the preceding excitement, Yoshitaro has slipped away and climbed back up on the roof. The four persons below look at each other and smile.)

Suejiro. A normal person would be angry with you for having put him in the smoke; but you see, he has forgotten everything. *(He calls.)* Brother!

Yoshitaro (as brotherly affection springs from his heart). Suejiro! I asked the Konpira God, and he says he doesn't know her!

Suejiro (smiling). You are right. The God will inspire you instead of a Priestess like her.

(Through a rift in the clouds, the golden light of sunset strikes on the roof.)

Suejiro (exclaiming). What a beautiful sunset!

Yoshitaro (his face lighted by the sun's reflection). Sue, look! Can't you see a golden palace in yonder cloud? There! There! Can't you see? Just look! How beautiful!

Suejiro (as he feels the sorrow of sanity). Yes, I see. I see it, too. Wonderful.

Yoshitaro (filled with joy). There! From within the palace I hear the music of flutes—which I love best of all! Is it not beautiful?

(The parents have gone into the house. The mad brother on the roof, and the sane brother on the ground, remain looking at the golden sunset.)

CURTAIN

705

RUDYARD KIPLING

RUDYARD KIPLING (English, 1865-1936). Poet and novelist of British imperialism. Born in India, he brought to the West the life of English society in the colony. Emphasized patriotism, comradeship, physical courage. Excellent craftsman, phenomenally popular in his day. *Barrack-Room Ballads, Plain Tales from the Hills, Just So Stories, The Light That Failed, The Jungle Books.*

FALSE DAWN

No MAN will ever know the exact truth of this story; though women may sometimes whisper it to one another after a dance, when they are putting up their hair for the night and comparing lists of victims. A man, of course, cannot assist at these functions. So the tale must be told from the outside—in the dark—all wrong.

Never praise a sister to a sister, in the hope of your compliments reaching the proper ears, and so preparing the way for you later on. Sisters are women first, and sisters afterwards; and you will find that you do yourself harm.

Saumarez knew this when he made up his mind to propose to the elder Miss Copleigh. Saumarez was a strange man, with a few merits, so far as men could see, though he was popular with women, and carried enough conceit to stock a Viceroy's Council, and leave a little over for the commander-in-chief's staff. He was a civilian. Very many women took an interest in Saumarez, perhaps because his manner to them was inoffensive. If you hit a pony over the nose at the outset of your acquaintance, he may not love you, but he will take a deep interest in your movements ever afterward. The elder Miss Copleigh was nice, plump, winning and pretty. The younger was not so pretty, and, from men disregarding the hint set forth above, her style was repellent and unattractive. Both girls had, practically, the same figure, and there was a strong likeness between them in look and voice; though no one could doubt for an instant which was the nicer of the two.

Saumarez made up his mind, as soon as they came into the station from Behar, to marry the elder one. At least, we all made sure that he would, which comes to the same thing. She was twenty-two and he was thirty-three, with pay and allowances of nearly fourteen hundred rupees a month. So the match, as we arranged it, was in every way a good one. Saumarez was his name, and summary was his nature, as a man once said. Having drafted his resolution, he formed a select committee of one to sit upon it, and resolved to take his time. In our unpleasant slang, the Copleigh girls "hunted in couples." That is to say, you could do nothing with one without the other. They were very loving sisters; but their mutual affection was sometimes inconvenient. Saumarez held the balance-hair true between them, and none but himself could have said to which side his heart inclined; though every one guessed. He rode with them a good deal, and danced with them, but he never succeeded in detaching them from each other for any length of time.

Women said that the two girls kept together through deep mistrust, each fearing that the other would steal a march on her. But that has nothing to do with a man. Saumarez was silent for good or bad, and as business-likely attentive as he could be, having due regard to his work and his polo. Beyond doubt both girls were fond of him.

As the hot weather drew nearer and Saumarez made no sign, women said that you could see their trouble in the eyes of the girls —that they were looking strained, anxious, and irritable. Men are quite blind in these matters unless they have more of the woman than the man in their composition, in which case it does not matter what they say or think. I maintain it was the hot April days that took the color out of the Copleigh girls' cheeks. They should have been sent to the Hills early. No one—man or woman—feels an angel when the hot weather is approaching. The younger sister grew more cynical—not to say acid—in her ways; and the winningness of the elder wore thin. There was more effort in it.

Now the Station wherein all these things happened was, though not a little one, off the line of rail, and suffered through want of attention. There were no gardens, or bands or amusements worth speaking of, and it was nearly a day's journey to come into Lahore for a dance. People were grateful for small things to interest them.

About the beginning of May, and just before the final exodus of Hill-goers, when the weather was very hot and there were not more than twenty people in the Station, Saumarez gave a moonlight riding picnic at an old tomb, six miles away, near the bed of the river. It was a "Noah's Ark" picnic; and there was to be the usual arrangement of quarter-mile intervals between each couple, on account of the dust. Six couples came altogether, including chap-

707

erones. Moonlight picnics are useful just at the very end of the
season, before all the girls go away to the Hills. They lead to under-
standings, and should be encouraged by chaperones; especially those
whose girls look sweetest in riding habits. I knew a case once. But
that is another story. That picnic was called the "Great Pop Picnic,"
because everyone knew Saumarez would propose then to the eldest
Miss Copleigh; and, besides his affair, there was another which
might possibly come to happiness. The social atmosphere was heavily
charged and wanted clearing.

We met at the parade ground at 10; the night was fearfully hot.
The horses sweated even at walking pace, but anything was better
than sitting still in our own dark houses. When we moved off under
the full moon we were four couples, one triplet, and Mr. Saumarez
rode with the Copleigh girls, and I loitered at the tail of the procession wondering with whom Saumarez would ride home. Every
one was happy and contented; but we all felt that things were going
to happen. We rode slowly; and it was nearly midnight before we
reached the old tomb, facing the ruined tank, in the decayed gardens where we were going to eat and drink. I was late in coming
up; and, before I went in to the garden I saw that the horizon to
the north carried a faint, dun-colored feather. But no one would
have thanked me for spoiling so well-managed an entertainment
as this picnic—and a dust-storm, more or less, does no great harm.

We gathered by the tank, some one had brought out a banjo—
which is a most sentimental instrument—and three or four of us
sang. You must not laugh at this. Our amusements in out-of-the-
way stations are very few indeed. Then we talked in groups, or
together, lying under the trees, with the sun-baked roses dropping
their petals on our feet, until supper was ready. It was a beautiful
supper, as cold and as iced as you could wish; and we stayed long
over it.

I had felt that the air was growing hotter and hotter; but nobody
seemed to notice it until the moon went out and a burning hot wind
began lashing the orange trees with a sound like the noise of the
sea. Before we knew where we were, the dust-storm was on us, and
everything was roaring, whirling darkness. The supper table was
blown bodily into the tank. We were afraid of staying anywhere
near the old tomb for fear it might be blown down. So we felt our
way to the orange trees where the horses were picketed and waited
for the storm to blow over. Then the little light that was left van-

708

ished, and you could not see your hand before your face. The air was heavy with dust and sand from the bed of the river, that filled boots and pockets and drifted down necks and coated eyebrows and mustaches. It was one of the worst dust-storms of the year. We were all huddled together close to the trembling horses, with the thunder chattering overhead, and the lightning spurting like water from a sluice, all ways at once.

There was no danger, of course, unless the horses broke loose. I was standing with my head down wind and my hands over my mouth, hearing the trees thrashing each other. I could not see who was next me till the flashes came. Then I found that I was packed near Saumarez and the eldest Miss Copleigh, with my own horse just in front of me. I recognized the eldest Miss Copleigh, because she had a *pagri* round her helmet and the younger had not. All the electricity in the air had gone into my body and I was quivering and tingling from head to foot—exactly as a corn shoots and tingles before rain. It was a grand storm. The wind seemed to be picking up the earth and pitching it to leeward in great heaps; and the heat beat up from the ground like the heat of the Day of Judgment.

The storm lulled slightly after the first half-hour, and I heard a despairing little voice close to my ear, saying to itself, quietly and softly, as if some lost soul were flying about with the wind: "O my God!" Then the younger Miss Copleigh stumbled into my arms, saying: "Where is my horse? Get my horse. I want to go home. I *want* to go home. Take me home."

I thought that the lightning and the black darkness had frightened her; so I said there was no danger, but she must wait till the storm blew over. She answered: "It is not *that!* It is not *that!* I want to go home! Oh, take me away from here!"

I said that she could not go till the light came; but I felt her brush past me and go away. It was too dark to see where. Then the whole sky was split open with one tremendous flash, as if the end of the world were coming, and all the women shrieked.

Almost directly after this I felt a man's hand on my shoulder and heard Saumarez bellowing in my ear. Through the rattling of the trees and howling of the wind, I did not catch his words at once, but at last I heard him say: "I've proposed to the wrong one! What shall I do?" Saumarez had no occasion to make this confidence to me. I was never a friend of his, nor am I now; but I fancy neither of us were ourselves just then. He was shaking as he stood with excitement, and I was feeling queer all over with the electricity. I could not think of anything to say except: "More fool you for proposing in a dust storm." But I did not see how that would improve the mistake.

Then he shouted: "Where's Edith—Edith Copleigh?" Edith was the younger sister. I answered out of my astonishment: "What do you want with *her?*" Would you believe it, for the next two minutes, he and I were shouting at each other like maniacs—he vowing that it was the younger sister he had meant to propose to all along, and I telling him till my throat was hoarse that he must have made a mistake. I can't account for this except, again, by the fact that we were neither of us ourselves. Everything seemed to me like a bad dream—from the stamping of the horses in the darkness to Saumarez telling me the story of his loving Edith Copleigh since the first. He was still clawing my shoulder and begging me to tell him where Edith Copleigh was, when another lull came and brought light with it, and we saw the dust-cloud forming on the plain in front of us. So we knew the worst was over. The moon was low down, and there was just the glimmer of the false dawn that comes about an hour before the real one. But the light was very faint, and the dun cloud roared like a bull. I wondered where Edith Copleigh had gone; and as I was wandering I saw three things together: First, Maud Copleigh's face come smiling out of the darkness and move toward Saumarez, who was standing by me. I heard the girl whisper, "George," and slide her arm through the arm that was not clawing my shoulder, and I saw that look on her face which only comes once or twice in a lifetime—when a woman is perfectly happy, and the air is full of trumpets and gorgeous-colored fire and the Earth turns into cloud because she loves and is loved. At the same time, I saw Saumarez's face as he heard Maud Copleigh's voice, and fifty yards away from the clump of orange trees I saw a brown holland habit getting upon a horse.

It must have been my state of over-excitement that made me so quick to meddle with what did not concern me. Saumarez was moving off to the habit; but I pushed him back and said: "Stop here and explain. I'll fetch her back!" And I ran out to get at my own horse. I had a perfectly unnecessary notion that everything must be done decently and in order, and that Saumarez's first care was to wipe the happy look out of Maud Copleigh's face. All the time I was linking up the curb-chain I wondered how he would do it.

I cantered after Edith Copleigh, thinking to bring her back slowly on some pretense or another. But she galloped away as soon as she saw me, and I was forced to ride after her in earnest. She called back over her shoulder, "Go away! I'm going home. Oh, go *away!*" two or three times; but my business was to catch her first, and argue later. The ride just fitted in with the rest of the evil dream. The ground was very bad, and now and again we rushed through the whirling, choking "dust-devils" in the skirts of the flying storm. There was a burning hot wind blowing that brought up a stench of stale brick-kilns with it; and through the half light and through the dust-devils, across that desolate plain, flickered the brown holland habit on the gray horse. She headed for the Station at first.

Then she wheeled round and set off for the river through beds of burned-down jungle-grass, bad even to ride a pig over. In cold blood I should never have dreamed of going over such a country at night, but it seemed quite right and natural with the lightning crackling over head, and a reek like the smell of the Pit in my nostrils. I rode and shouted, and she bent forward and lashed her horse, and the aftermath of the dust-storm came up and caught us both, and drove us down wind like pieces of paper.

I don't know how far we rode; but the drumming of the horse-hoofs and the roar of the wind and the race of the faint blood-red moon through the yellow mist seemed to have gone on for years and years, and I was literally drenched with sweat from my helmet to my gaiters when the gray stumbled, recovered himself, and pulled up dead lame. My brute was used up altogether. Edith Copleigh was in a sad state, plastered with dust, her helmet off, and crying bitterly. "Why can't you let me alone?" she said. "I only wanted to get away and go home. Oh, *please* let me go!"

"You have got to come back with me, Miss Copleigh. Saumarez has something to say to you."

It was a foolish way of putting it; but I hardly knew Miss Copleigh, and, though I was playing Providence at the cost of my horse, I could not tell her in as many words what Saumarez had told me. I thought he could do that better himself. All her pretense about being tired and wanting to go home broke down, and she rocked herself to and fro in the saddle as she sobbed, and the hot wind blew her black hair to leeward. I am not going to repeat what she said, because she was utterly unstrung.

This, if you please, was the cynical Miss Copleigh. Here was I, almost an utter stranger to her, trying to tell her that Saumaraz loved her, and she was to come back to hear him say so. I believe I made myself understood, for she gathered the gray together and made him hobble somehow, and we set off for the tomb, while the storm went thundering down to Umballa and a few big drops of warm rain fell. I found out that she had been standing close to Saumarez when he proposed to her sister, and had wanted to go home to cry in peace, as an English girl should. She dabbed her eyes with her pocket handkerchief as we went along, and babbled to me out of sheer lightness of heart and hysteria. That was perfectly unnatural; and yet, it seemed all right at the time and in the place. All the world was only the two Copleigh girls, Saumarez and I, ringed in with the lightning and the dark; and the guidance of this misguided world seemed to lie in my hands.

When we returned to the tomb in the deep, dead stillness that followed the storm, the dawn was just breaking and nobody had gone away. They were waiting for our return. Saumarez most of all. His face was white and drawn. As Miss Copleigh and I limped up, he came forward to meet us, and, when he helped her down from her saddle, he kissed her before all the picnic. It was like a scene in a theater, and the likeness was heightened by all the dust-white, ghostly-looking men and women under the orange trees clapping their hands—as if they were watching a play—at Saumarez' choice. I never knew anything so un-English in my life.

Lastly, Saumarez said we must all go home, or the Station would come out to look for us, and *would* I be good enough to ride home with Maud Copleigh? Nothing would give me greater pleasure, I said.

So we formed up, six couples in all, and went back two by two, Saumarez walking at the side of Edith Copleigh, who was riding his horse.

The air was cleared; and little by little, as the sun rose, I felt we were all dropping back again into ordinary men and women, and that the "Great Pop Picnic" was a thing altogether apart and out of the world—never to happen again. It had gone with the dust-storm and the tingle in the hot air.

JOSEPH KISS

JOSEPH KISS (Hungarian, 1843-1921). Most genuine Hungarian poet. Taught in Hebrew schools.

JEHOVAH

I

I have seen the great world, I have wandered afar,
I have worshipped the southern clime's beauteous star;
From Tisra's bright shore I have wandered far forth,
By my spirit of roving sent south and sent north.
At the foot of the Alps, where the rose grows knee-deep,
And the blue sky of Italy never doth weep,
But sweet odors and colors bright fade into naught,
And fly, like the cloudlets on zephyr's wings caught;
Tossed hither and thither, like chaff o'er the plain,
As to hold it you long, but the longing is vain,
Even thus from my soul, like a dream of the dawn,
Fades this picture so bright, from mem'ry withdrawn.

The years, in their flight, efface as by stealth,
Every trace of its beauty, its splendour and wealth;
Yet sometimes the sight of some tall, barren rock,
The floodgates of memories sad will unlock.
Its crags seem like features that me terrify,
I watch it with dread, reaching up to the sky,
In bleakness so bare, though majestic withal
It stands, and its frowning my soul doth appall,
And concealed at its base, 'neath foliage green,
A part of itself, that broke from it, is seen,
By the force of the storm and by tempest 'twas wrought,
To which once more these storms new life have brought,
They are parts of himself, sweet children, his own,
Yet a different life from his own they have known.

Where saw I that face which haunts, fills my heart?
From marble was't hewn, a creature of art?
The flashing of the eye, and the majestic pose,
The Titanic genius of Angelo shows.

713

On his forehead he beareth the imprint of woe,
From his visage of iron his soul we may know.
Does it live, or did fancy the image create,
While I, 'neath Saint Peter's dome, mighty and great,
Once did stand? No. There I was dreaming again,
A winter morn's dream, which still I retain.

II

I know it now, from home did hail that face,—
How could I see it and not sooner trace,—
In cassock dark, the figure gaunt, erect,
Whose every slow movement commandeth respect.
And the boys, we who romped in the street,
With awe avoided him, afraid to greet;
We gathered then and put our heads together,
As sparrows seek the trees in stormy weather.
An hundred years, it seems, upon his shoulders weigh,
Yet proud he walks, as in his manliest day;
A living legend, covered with a shroud
He movéd thus among the human crowd,
Full of foreboding, yet 'twas never known,
What in his seeming endless life had grown.
This sage, in fame of greatest learning stood,
To tell though, where acquired, no one could;
And yet 'twas whispered e'en, that learned was he
In holy Cabalah's dark secrecy;
That he himself, at his own wish could bring
About, that he could live as lives a king;
That he had vowed to be forever poor,
A straw-thatched hut he did as home secure.
He read his books, to synagogue he went,
To worldly things he no attention lent.
He spoke the tongue of races that are dead,
And Syrian and Chaldaic filled his head;
Late into night, and in the early dawn,
Queer hieroglyphics had his attention drawn.
Wisdom and wine, he thinks the worthier far
When ripened both by passing age they are;
Wisdom is One; and faith its foremost claim,
Wisdom is One; Jehovah is his name . . .

714

Who sends chastisement to the fourth degree,
That God who saith: "Revenge is my decree!"
That is his God, and like a breath upon a glass,
Or like the burning tears shed by a child, alas!
Thus came and went before his aged eyes
Some generations, and dissolved the ties
That he had known, and all was frail that came,
Steadfast but he and great Jehovah's name.

Unspeaking, melancholy and morose,
Beneath his eyelids, it seems in deep repose
A world of thought doth lie, a boundless world,
Which storm and lightning flash had oft-times hurled
And tossed about. His fellow-men he shunned;
Indeed, it seemed as if he lived beyond
His days; but when one was about to die,—
Unbid or bid, he promptly came to try
With hope divine to fill the dying soul,
And sacred hymns then from his lips would roll.
The dying man would ope his shaded eye,
And gather strength and faith wherewith to die.
Full many a night no sleep nor rest he had,
But needs must struggle for his daily bread.
O'er parchment leaves he would for hours bend,
And trace thereon the writ, with iron hand;
The holy writ, the testament of old,
He copied carefully, and strong and bold
His letters were, and day and night he wrote
The name of Him, who in his anger smote
Him, who revered not Him, with iron rod, . . .
The name of Him he loved, Jehovah, God, . . .
Because all day these letters dead he saw,
The letters dead became for him the law.
Fanatically he, the bygone days
Did wish returned, the awful dark, dread ways
And when on earth Jehovah was—the torch,—
And who profaned Him and died by sword or scorch.
The letters dead to him were living law,
To punish swift, the high priest would but draw
His sword; and burned on stake or stoned to death
He who the wrath of God encountereth.

And at this barren rock's stone feet there grew
A beauteous flower, fair and sweet to view.
The brooklet's murmur and the zephyr's sigh
To nourish her, would with each other vie.
The soil was barren, no moisture from above,
Privation, poverty, no parent's love
Her share, and yet, in spite of all, she grows,—
This child of Job,—as lovely as a rose.
So sweet and pure, a fairy queen she is,
There blend in her in charming harmonies.
Those gifts of heaven which heart and mind most please.
Her form divine, her movement queenly grace,
And radiantly beautiful her face.
Melodious her voice, like silver bell
Which holds the rustic listener in spell
When in the eve he hears the distant knell;
And what she says and what she thinks is bright
As wings of gaudy butterflies, which light
On flowers fair, in dewy morn and night.
Above all these, her eyes, ah, me! those eyes!
It matters nothing how my fish-line tries
To hook the proper word, I'll not succeed
The superb beauty of those eyes to read;
But I will tell a tale, do you give heed:
The midnight's depth, the height of mid-day's sun
Each from the other loving glances won;
They longed to meet, and for each other sighed;
They met, each other loved, and ever bide
Each with the other, and until to-day
They live in bliss; the truth of what I've told,
Do Miriam's flaming, darkling eyes enhold.

The fields and gardens gave her needed food,
Her soul grew in its very solitude,
A kindly nursing which in its due course
Matured her feelings and with hidden force
Her fancy rose. From tattered leaves she found,
She learned to read and write; and held her bound

716

Full many a night, when she would read by stealth
Each word, each line, each tale, each song; and wealth
Of thought did gain. Her hungry soul did yearn
In learning's banquet hall to sit and learn;
Her soul with almost holy fire aglow,
To rise above her sphere, so dull and slow,
Aspired; and she did vow to learn, to know;
Her daily life to cast away, not prone
'Fore fate to lie; but make her life her own;
And this she did, more pure her life, more bold
Half dream of hers and half as story told. . . .

And once a book came in her hands, complete,—
Though coverless and gone the title-sheet,
And pity 'twas, the author was unknown.
She read it oft, an hundred times a year,
As if it were a song which to the ear
Melodiously clings, and we repeat,
Because it fills our hearts and souls complete.

She read each play and felt that every role
Had taken hold, and filled her very soul;
Now Juliet, she roamed in love's estate,
To-morrow moaned o'er Desdemona's fate;
Then Lady Macbeth, with her blood-stained hands,
Then Imogen,—Cordelia now she stands,
And when the foolish, simple country swain
Would seek with awkward praise her love to gain,
She would the role of Queen Titania play, . . .
Thus Miriam, Job's daughter, lived her day.

IV

In autumn eve, the poplar tree tops sigh,
The swallow soon will flit, soon homeward fly:
To-morrow's dawn may find unfilled the nest,
Sweet bird, wilt here, thou seek again thy rest?
The window of the straw-thatched hut now brightly shines,
The poplar's trembling crown it illumines.
The poplar's trembling crown seems golden bright,
Its beauteous hue lends glory to the night.

V

His hoary head old Job leans on his hands,
Lost in deep thought, though work his care commands;
Before him lies the yellow parchment leaf,
And quill and ink, and yet, some hidden grief
Keeps him from work; he cannot trace his pen,
The very letters dance when now and then
He tries to work; some cloud bedulls his brain;
But as a lion wakening, his mane
Doth toss, so now old Job doth seem to wake;
Into his hand the quill doth firmly take,
And, dipping deep in ink, begins to write,
And what he writes, brings to his soul delight.
It suits his mood, 'tis Moses' second book
And chapter thirty-two, and he, whose look
At holy writ is frequent, knows how there
'Tis told, the old law-giver was aware,
That while he was with God, on their behalf,
The people made and worshipped the golden calf;
How great his wroth, his sorrow greater still,
And Moses' song men's souls must ever thrill.

Joshua said: "Dost, Master, hear the voice
From yonder camp? O'er victories they rejoice."
The Master said: "It is not so, my son;
'Tis not the joyous voice of victory won
That comes from camp, nor yet defeat's sad wail,
But other voices reach us from the vale." . . .
And marvel: As these things he now indited;
His ravished ears hear song and shout and hail
As once old Moses heard in ancient tale.
And song and shout and shout and song he hears,
Roused are the spirits of those bygone years,
Yet no, no spirit voices these, 'tis plain,
This music earthly is, this noise profane,
A band of strolling players at the inn
Have built a tent, and there their plays begin;
The villagers, or all who could but go,
Are there, enjoying this uncommon show.
They cheer and weep, the play has touched their heart,
The play and players gain the praise of art.

This was the voice old Job had heard, and then
He slowly takes again in hand his pen
To write, but lo! he soon again must cease,
It seems his soul to-night can find no peace.
The music dies away, no noise below,
He sees the wraiths of days of long ago
That torture him, the weary, hoary head—
Why are the days gone by not really dead!

He once three manly boys had called his own;
Life took them all, not death; aye, life alone
Robbed him of them; the one who really died,
Alone, lives in his heart with loving pride.
The strife, the times, the change, the very air
Of the to-day, which dawns ere one's aware,
And which we notice only when their wave
Prevails, and yesterdays are in their grave:
The spirit of the times which ever runs,
Had swallowed, Moloch-like, all his three sons.
No faith, no aim, ideals none, no rite,
The father and the son do now unite;
The holy tie, which with its powers divine
Men in their hearts with loving care enshrine,
The ties of heart and blood, old Job, with scorn
And pride, from his parental heart had torn.

He blessed his son, and for his welfare prayed;
Told him to go. A last farewell him bade!
The boy was only thirteen years of age,
Too young, think you, to enter on life's stage?
But custom and the law demand it so,
And out into the world the lad did go.
For years he seemed as lost, but once there came
A letter from a place of strangest name:
"Dear father,"—wrote the son,—"here in this land,
The victories of steam are truly grand."
The father's answer was one single word:
"Jehovah!"—as the son had often heard.
Another letter came: "Here on the banks
Of the Missouri I, in labor's ranks

719

Toil day and night to fell the ancient trees,
And inch by inch new territories seize;
Lay railroad ties, and oft the Indian chase.
At night, to starlit heaven I often gaze,
And think of home when the hyena's howl
And Indians' shrieks around our camp who prowl
Keep me awake; but then the amulet,
Dear father, which you gave, I have it yet."

And then no further news, and years rolled by, . . .
The young grew old, the old perforce must die.
The eldest son of Job was long forgot, . . .
When to the village came with lively trot
On horse and wheel, as might a king in state,
A train of men; what stir it did create,
The horses, carriages, the lively swarm;
The negro servants in their uniform;
It was a lively, captivating scene,
The like of which the village ne'er had seen.
Before the straw-thatched hut they stopped, behold
Upon the threshold stands erect, though old,
Proud Job; and from a carriage steps a man,—
The southern sun had turned his skin to tan,—
A giant figure, he, a worthy son
Of worthy sire, pleasant to look upon.
A lady, too, alights; a woman fair;
He leads her to his father, standing there.
Old Job outspreads his arms, about to kiss
His long-lost son and daughter, his is bliss!
When suddenly he shrieks and starts aback,
A golden cross hangs on the woman's neck.
"Apostate, thou!" he cries; "thou'rt not my son!
Apostate, thou! No nearer come! begone!
Ne'er shalt thou o'er my threshold step, swear I,
Jehovah, witness! I my son deny!"

VII

His memories are sad. Beneath their weight
His soul doth rise, as even then, too late . . .

The old wound opes and freely bleeds again
As it bled once when first he knew life's bane.
He sobs and weeps, his heart may almost break,
Most painful are the ways his thoughts do take.
He had, yea, it is true, another son,
A splendid boy, who admiration won
By his bright thought and brain and mind.
He, too, went forth,—and onward, but to find
Himself on paths his sires had never trod;
In plant and stone he sought to find his God.
The highest goals of learning he did gain,
Found everything, but sought a God in vain.
His name and fame shine brightly as a star
Among the great men who immortal are.
Savant, philosopher, known o'er the globe,
Alas! no longer he a son of Job!

And silently a sentient, burning tear
Rolls down his face, so strong and yet austere.
God only knows, these tears well from his heart,
The thought for his third, youngest son impart.
He suffered not, that he the world should roam,
He loved this boy the best, kept him at home.
A lively youth, of mischief full and fun,
That kind of boy who's loved by every one,
The picture of himself while he a boy,
This youngest son of his, his greatest joy.
He was not yet fifteen, . . . when lo! the world
Did seem to turn and quake; flags were unfurled,
Thrones shook, and shouts did mark the Bastille's fall.
With martial noise "To arms!" goes forth the call!
Blood-red the very grass, blood-red the dawn . . .
The boy enlists, nor waits till he be drawn.
Beneath a heavy gun he would succumb,
And his the burden was to bear the drum.
And with his drum from field to field he went,
Until at last a bullet his rest sent. . . .

VIII

The taper's burning low, and now to bed
He is about to take his weary head;

And as he rises, 't seems a deeper gloom
Obtains; his own dark shadow fills the room.
"Miriam, my darling child!" he whispers low,
Thou art still mine; the boys, oh, great my woe,
I've lost them all! May angels guard thy sleep,
Gabriel, Raphael, o'er thee watch and keep
From thee the evil spirit of the night,
That naught thy golden dream and slumber blight;
Jehovah, keep my Miriam sweet, secure!"
And then, to still the pain he must endure,
He goes to look upon his child, his own;
And to her room on tip-toe steals; a throne
To him her couch, on which his child inclines!
But, lo! the pale moon only illumines,—
Has he seen right? he stares,—he sees, to-night
An empty couch,—Miriam has taken flight!

IX

And as the stag, who hears the shot and feels
It whistling, grazing past, and knows it deals
A deadly aim: though once that aim was bad,
And suddenly stands still,—with eyes like mad
Looks right and left, and sniffs the air; then he
With sudden leap will fly, but to be free,
Though danger lurks perhaps behind each tree:
Thus acted Job. First stunned, he gasps for breath,
His glaring eyes are shadowed, as by death;
His mind grows blank; he knows not what to do;
The heart is broken of the poor old Jew.
And then in accents slow: "She, too, she, too;
My last and only child is gone from me,
My Miriam is taken by God's decree."
And then he sobs, and freely flow his tears,
He weeps as those who stand before friends' biers;
Not for himself he feels the awful blow,
'Tis for his child his burning tears do flow.
When past the agony of his great woe,
While still convulsed his sturdy, giant frame:
"All gone, all lost, yet I fore'er exclaim:
Steadfast is One! Jehovah is His Name!"

And then his window opes. His eye is dry;
But here and there a star is in the sky;
His eagle eye far into night doth spy.
The heavens, it seems, are overcast with clouds,
As if all nature donned funeral shrouds.
As if to list to him had come in crowds;
As if all heaven and earth had come to know
That he, in spite of awful blow and woe,
His ancient faith in Him did not forego!
Then with a voice, which shakes the very walls
Of his small hut, and by its power appals,
Into the night with trembling voice he calls:
"Lord! God! Thou givest and taketh with thy breath,
Adonai, God, Thine is all life and death!"

HEINRICH VON KLEIST

HEINRICH VON KLEIST (German, 1777-1811). Playwright and journalist.
Impulsive peregrinant. While traveling, once arrested as spy and spent six
months in French jail. His plays slow to gain recognition. When financial
situation became desperate, staged double suicide with a Berlin merchant's
wife. Works: *Penthesilea, The Prince of Homburg, Michael Kolhaas.*

THE BEGGAR-WOMAN OF LOCARNO

At the foot of the Alps, near Locarno in Upper Italy, stood once a
castle, the property of a marquis; of this castle, as one goes southward from the St. Gotthard, one sees now only the ashes and ruins.
In one of its high and spacious rooms there once lay, on a bundle
of straw which had been thrown down for her, an old, sick woman,
who had come begging to the door, and had been taken in and
given shelter out of pity by the mistress of the castle. The Marquis,
returning from the hunt, happened to enter this room, where he
usually kept his guns, while the old woman lay there, and angrily
ordered her to come out of the corner where the bundle of straw had
been placed and to get behind the stove. In rising the old woman
slipped on the polished floor and injured her spine severely; so much
did she hurt herself that only with unspeakable agony could she
manage to cross the room, as she was ordered, to sink moaning
behind the stove and there to die.

723

Some years later the Marquis, owing to war and bad harvests, having lost most of his fortune, decided to sell his estates. One day a nobleman from Florence arrived at the castle which, on account of its beautiful situation, he wished to buy. The Marquis, who was very anxious to bring the business to a successful conclusion, gave instructions to his wife to prepare for their guest the above-mentioned room, which was now very beautifully furnished. But imagine their horror when, in the middle of the night, the nobleman, pale and distracted, entered their room, solemnly assuring them that his room was haunted by something which was not visible, but which sounded as if somebody lying on straw in one corner of the room got up and slowly and feebly but with distinct steps crossed the room to lie down moaning and groaning behind the stove.

The Marquis, horrified, he did not himself know why, laughed with forced merriment at the nobleman and said he would get up at once and keep him company for the rest of the night in the haunted room, and when the morning came he ordered his horses to be brought round, bade farewell, and departed.

This incident, which created a great sensation, unhappily for the Marquis frightened away several would-be buyers; and when amongst his own servants strangely and mysteriously the rumour arose that queer things happened in the room at midnight, he determined to make a definite stand in the matter and to investigate it himself the same night. For that reason he had his bed moved into the room at twilight, and watched there without sleeping until midnight. To his horror, as the clock began to strike midnight, he became aware of the mysterious noise; it sounded as though somebody rose from straw which rustled beneath him, crossed the room and sank down sighing and groaning behind the stove. The next morning when he came downstairs his wife inquired what he had discovered; he looked round with nervous and troubled glances, and after fastening the door assured her that the rumour was true. The Marquise was more terrified than ever in her life, and begged him, before the rumour grew, to make a cold-blooded trial in her company. Accompanied by a loyal servant, they spent the following night in the room and heard the same ghostly noises; and only the pressing need to get rid of the castle at any cost enabled the Marquise in the presence of the servant to smother the terror which she felt, and to put the noise down to some ordinary and casual event which it would be easy to discover. On the evening of the third day, as both of them, with beating hearts, went up the stairs to the guest-room, anxious to get at the cause of the disturbance, they found that the watch-dog, who happened to have been let off his chain, was standing at the door of the room; so that, without giving a definite reason, both perhaps unconsciously wishing to have another living thing in the room besides themselves, they took him into the room with them. About eleven o'clock the two of them, two candles on the table, the Marquise fully dressed, the Marquis with dagger and pistol which he had taken from the cupboard beside him, sat down one on each bed; and while they entertained one another as well as they could by talking, the dog lay down, his head on his paws, in the middle of the room and slept. As the clock began to strike midnight the horrible sound began; somebody whom human eyes could not see raised himself on crutches in the corner of the room; the straw could be heard rustling beneath him; and at the first step the dog woke, pricked up his ears, rose from the ground growling and barking, and, just as though somebody were making straight for him, moved backwards towards the stove. At the sight the Marquise, her hair rising, rushed from the room, and while the Marquis, who had snatched up his dagger, called 'Who is there?' and received no answer, she, like a mad woman, had ordered the coach to be got out, determined to drive away to the town immediately. But before she had packed a few things together and got them out of the door she noticed that all around her the castle was in flames. The Marquis, overcome with horror, and tired of life, had taken a candle and set fire to the wooden panelling on all sides. In vain she sent people in to rescue the wretched man; he had already found his end in the most horrible manner possible; and his white bones, gathered together by his people, still lie in that corner of the room from which he once ordered the beggar-woman of Locarno to rise.

FRIEDRICH GOTTLIEB KLOPSTOCK

FRIEDRICH GOTTLIEB KLOPSTOCK (German, 1724-1803). Main architect of 18th century independent German writing. Author of great biblical epic, *The Messiah*, and *Odes*. Both works influential on contemporaries, bringing deeply felt emotion into classical forms. Late "bardic" poems stimulated German nationalism.

THE CONTEMPLATION OF GOD

Trembling I rejoice,
Nor would believe the Voice,

If that the Eternal were
Not the Greater Promiser!
For, oh! I know, I feel
I am a sinner still—
Should know, should feel the same,
The sorrow and the shame;
Albeit Deity my spot
More clearly shown to me had not,
Unveiling to my wiser view
The wounded soul's condition true.
    With bended knee,
Astonished and intensely praying,
    That I my God shall see!

Oh! meditate the thought divine,
Thou thought-capacious soul of mine,
Who near the body's grave art ever,
Yet art eternal, and shalt perish never!
Not that thou venturest into
The Holiest of all to go—
Much unconsidered, never prized,
Ne'er celebrated, ne'er agonized!—
Celestial graces
Have in the Sanctuary their dwelling places;—
From afar only but one softened glimmer,
    So that therewith I die not suddenly—
One beam, which night of earth for me makes dimmer,
    Of Thy bright glory let me see!

The man how great! who thus his prayer preferred—
    "Grace have I found of Thee!
    Then show Thy glory unto me!"—
Thus dared, and by the Infinite was heard!
That Land of Golgotha he never entered;—
Once, only once, he failed in God to trust—
An early death avenged the doubt he ventured!—
    How great proved him a punishment so just!
Him hid the Father on the clouded Hill;
    The Filial Glory passed the finite o'er;—
God of God spake! the trump the while was still,
    Nor did the thunder's voice on Sinai roar!

Now, in that cloud of seeming night
He sees already, in the light
Of day, no shade makes visibler,
Long centuries—(so we aver)—
Beyond the bounds of time; and, feeling free
    Of moments passed successively,
Thy glory now beholdeth he—
    Holy! Holy! Holy!

Most nameless rapture of my soul!
    Thought of the Vision blest to come!
My great assurance and my goal!
    The Rock whereon I stand, and gaze up to my heavenly home!

When that the terrors both of Sin and Death
Fearfully threat to prostrate me beneath,
Upon this rock, oh! let me stand,
    Thou whom the Dead of God behold!
When grasped in the almighty hand
    Of death, that may not be controlled!
My soul, above mortality
Exalt thyself! Look up and see—
Behold the Father's glory radiant shine
In the human face of Jesus Christ divine!
Hosanna! let the loud Hosanna tell—
    The plenitude of Deity
Doth in the man Christ Jesus dwell—
Yet scarcely sounds the cherub's harp—it shakes!
Scarce sounds the voice—it trembles—trembles! Now wakes!

        Hosanna! Hosanna!
    The plenitude of Deity
    Doth in the humanity
        Of Christ Jesus dwell!

Even then when on our world shone brighter still
A god-beam, and Redemption did fulfill
That prophecy of blood—when he knew scorn
And woe, whereto none else was ever born—
Unseen by mortals, Cherubim beheld
The Father's glory, unexcelled,

727

Shine in the face, where aye it shone,
Of the co-eternal Son!

I see—I see the Witness! Lo!
Seven midnights, sore perplexed, had he
Doubted, and with severest agony
   Adoring, wrestled so!—
Yes, him I see—
To him appears the Risen! His hands explore
The wounds divine; and now perceiveth he
(About him heaven and earth expire!)
In the Son's face the glory of his Sire!—
I hear him! He exclaims—in doubt no more—
(About him heaven and earth expire!)
"Thou art my Lord and God—the God whom I adore!"

HERMAN AND THUSNELDA

"Ha! there comes he, with sweat, with Roman blood,
With battle dust bedecked! Never so fair
   Was Herman—never flamed
   His eye so brightly yet!

Come! for desire I tremble! Reach to me
The eagle, the blood-dropping sword! Come, breathe
   Here—rest in mine embrace
   From the too fearful fight!

Rest here, that I may wipe away the sweat
Off from thy brow, and from thy cheek the blood—
   How glows thy cheek! Thus ne'er
   Thusnelda Herman loved!

Not even then, when in the oak shade first
With thy brown arm thou wilder compassed me;
   Flying, I stayed, and saw
   The' undying fame in thee

Which now is thine. Relate it all in groves,
That timidly Augustus, with his gods,

Drinks nectar now—that more
Immortal Herman is!"

"Why curlest thou my hair? Lies not the dumb
Dead father before us? Oh, had his host
    Augustus led—there he
    Might lie yet bloodier!"

"Herman—nay, let me raise thy sinking hair,
That o'er the garland thread its tresses may;—
    Siegmar is with the gods!—
    Follow—nor weep for him!"

THE TWO MUSES

I saw—oh, tell me, saw I what now is,
Or what shall be?—with Britain's Muse I saw
    The German in the race compete,
    Fly ardent for the crowning goal.

There, where the prospect terminates, two goals
Closed the career. Oaks of the forest one
    Shaded; and near the other waved
    Palms in the glimmering of the eve.

To contest used, the Muse of Albion stept
Into the arena proudly, as when she
    Dared mate the Grecian Muse, and brave
    The heroine of the Capitol.

She saw her young and trembling rival, who
With high emotion trembled; yea, her cheek
    With roses, worthy of victory,
    Glowed, and her golden hair flew wide.

With pain already in her throbbing breast,
She held the breath restrained; hung, forward bent,
    Towards the goal;—the herald raised
    His trump—her eyes swam drunkenly.

729

Proud of thy courage, of herself, thee scanned
The lofty Britoness with noble glance.
 Tuiscone. "Yes, near the bards
 I grew with thee in oaken groves;—

But I was told thou wert no more. O Muse!
Pardon, if that thou art immortal, me
 Pardon, that now I first am taught
 What at the goal I'll better learn!

Yonder it stands;—but mark the further one!
Seest thou its crown? This courage thus suppressed,
 This silence proud, this look of fire
 Fixed on the earth—I knew it well!

Yet, ponder once again, ere sounds to thee
The herald's dangerous signal. Strove not I
 With her of old Thermopylæ,
 And eke with her of the Seven Hills?"

She spake. The solemn, the decisive time
Approaches with the herald. With a look
 Of ardor spake Teutona quick—
 "Thee I, admiring, love, O Muse!

But dearer yet love immortality
And yonder palms! Oh—if thy genius will,—
 Touch them before me;—but, e'en then,
 Will I seize likewise on the crown!

Oh, how I tremble! Ye immortal gods!
I haply may reach first the goal sublime!—
 Then may I feel, O Britoness!
 Thy breath on my loose-flowing locks!" ̇

The herald clanged. With eagle speed they flew,—
Their far career smoked up with dust, like clouds;—
 I looked—beyond the oak the dust,
 Still billowing, hid them from my sight!

VLADIMIR KOROLENKO

VLADIMIR KOROLENKO (Russian, 1853-1921). Half-Ukrainian, half-Polish writer. Spent much of life in Siberian exile, but remained genial and optimistic. Courageous defender of freedom. As story writer, forms link between Turgenev and Chekhov. Best-known novels: *Makar's Dream, The Blind Musician*; stories: "The Frost," "The Old Bell-Ringer."

THE OLD BELL-RINGER

It was growing dark.

The tiny village, nestling by the distant stream, in a pine forest, was merged in that twilight peculiar to starry spring nights, when the fog, rising from the earth, deepens the shadows of the woods and fills the open spaces with a silvery blue mist. . . . Everything was still, pensive and sad. The village quietly slumbered.

The dark outlines of the wretched cabins were barely visible; here and there lights glimmered; now and then you could hear a gate creak; or a dog would suddenly bark and then stop. Occasionally, out of the dark, murmuring forest emerged the figure of a pedestrian, or that of a horseman; or a cart would jolt by. These were the inhabitants of lone forest hamlets going to their church for the great spring holiday.

The church stood on a gentle hill in the center of the village. The ancient belfry, tall and murky, was lost in the blue sky.

The creaking of the staircase could be heard as the old bell-ringer Mikheyich mounted to the belfry, and his little lantern, suspended in mid-air, looked like a star in space.

It was difficult for the old man to climb the staircase. His legs served him badly, and his eyes saw but dimly. . . . An old man like him should have been at rest by now, but God spared him from death. He had buried his sons and his grandsons; he had accompanied old men and young men to their resting place, but he still lived on. 'Twas hard. Many the times he had greeted the spring holiday, and he could not remember how often he had waited in that very belfry the appointed hour. And how God had again willed that . . .

The old man went to the opening in the tower and leaned on the banister. In the darkness below, around the church, he made out the village cemetery in which the old crosses with their outstretched arms seemed to protect the ill-kept graves. Over these bowed here and there a few leafless birch trees. The aromatic odor of young

731

buds, wafted to Mikheyich from below, brought with it a feeling of the melancholy of eternal sleep.

Where would he be a year hence? Would he again climb to this height, beneath the brass bell to awaken the slumbering night with its metallic peal, or would he be lying in a dark corner of the graveyard, under a cross? God knows! . . . He was prepared; in the meantime God granted him the happiness of greeting the holiday once more.

"Glory be to God!" His lips whispered the customary formula as his eyes looked up to the heaven bright with a million twinkling stars and made the sign of the cross.

"Mikheyich, ay, Mikheyich!" called out to him the tremulous voice of an old man. The aged sexton gazed up at the belfry, shading his unsteady, tear-dimmed eyes with his hand, trying to see Mikheyich.

"What do you want? Here I am," replied the bell-ringer, looking down from the belfry. "Can't you see me?"

"No, I can't. It must be time to ring. What do you say?"

Both looked at the stars. Myriads of God's lights twinkled on high. The fiery Wagoner was above them. Mikheyich meditated.

"No, not yet a while. . . . I know when. . . ."

Indeed he knew. He did not need a watch. God's stars would tell him when. . . . Heaven and earth, the white cloud gently floating in the sky, the dark forest with its indistinct murmur and the rippling of the stream enveloped by the darkness—all that was familiar to him, part of him. Not in vain had he spent his life here.

The distant past arose before him. He recalled how for the first time he had mounted to this belfry with his father. Lord! how long ago that was, and yet how recent it seemed! . . . He saw himself a blond lad; his eyes sparkled; the wind—not the wind that raises the dust in the streets, but a strange one, that flaps its noiseless wings, tousled his hair. . . . Way down below, tiny beings walked about, and the village huts looked small; the forest had receded, and the oval clearing on which the village stood seemed enormous, so endless . . .

"And there it is, all of it!" smiled the gray-haired old man, gazing at the little clearing. . . . That was the way of life. As a young man one can not see the end of it. And now, there it was, as if in the palm of one's hand, from the beginning to the grave over there which he had fancied for himself in the corner of the cemetery. . . . Well, glory be to God! it was time to rest. The burden of life he had borne honorably, and the damp earth seemed like his mother. . . . Soon, very soon!

But the hour had come. Mikheyich looked once more at the stars, took off his cap, made the sign of the cross, and grasped the bell-ropes. In a moment, the night air echoed with the resounding stroke. Another, a third, a fourth . . . one after the other, filling the quiescent, holy eve, there poured forth powerful, drawn-out, singing sounds.

The bell stopped. The church service had begun. Mikheyich had formerly been in the habit of going down to stand in the corner by the door in order to pray and hear the singing. This time he remained in the belfry. It was too much to walk the stairs, and, moreover, he felt rather tired. He sat down on the bench and, as he listened to the melting sounds of brass, fell to musing. About what? He would have been unable to say. . . . The tower was dimly lit by the feeble light of his lantern. The still vibrating bells were invisible in the darkness; from time to time a faint murmur of singing in the church below reached him, and the night wind stirred the ropes attached to the iron tongues of the bells.

The old man let his head droop upon his breast, while his mind was confused with fancies. "Now they are singing a hymn," he thought, and imagined himself in church, where he heard the children's voices in the choir, and saw Father Naum, long since dead, leading the congregation in prayer; hundreds of peasants' heads rose and fell, like ripened stalks of grain before the wind. . . . The peasants made the sign of the cross. . . . All of these are familiar, although they are all dead. . . . There he beheld his father's severe face; there was his brother fervently praying. And he also stood there, abloom with health and strength, filled with unconscious hope of happiness. . . . And where was that happiness? . . . For a moment, the old man's thoughts flared up, illuminating various episodes in his past life. . . .

He saw hard work, sorrow, care . . . where was this happiness? A hard lot will trace furrows even in a young face, will bend a powerful back and teach him to sigh as it had taught his older brother.

There on the left, among the village women, with her head humbly bowed, stood his sweetheart. A good woman, may she inherit the kingdom of Heaven! How much she had suffered, poor

733

woman. . . . Constant poverty and work, and the inevitable sorrows of a woman's life will wither her beauty; her eyes will lose their luster, and instead of the customary serenity, dull fear of unexpected calamities will settle perpetually on her face. . . . Well, then, where was her happiness? . . . One son was left to them, their one hope and joy; but he was too weak to withstand temptation.

And there was his rich enemy, kneeling and praying to be forgiven for the many tears he had caused orphans to shed. He crossed himself ardently and struck his forehead against the ground. . . . Mikheyich's heart boiled within him, and the dusky faces of the ikons frowned down upon human sorrow and human wickedness.

All that was past, behind him. For him the whole world was now bounded by this bell-tower, where the wind moaned in the darkness and stirred the ropes. . . . "God be your judge!" muttered the old man, drooping his gray head, while tears rolled gently down his cheeks.

"Mikheyich, ay, Mikheyich! Have you fallen asleep up there?" shouted someone from below.

"What?" the old man answered, rising to his feet. "God! Have I really been sleeping? Such a thing never happened before!"

With quick, experienced hands he grasped the ropes. Below him, the peasant mob moved about like an ant-hill; banners, sparkling with gilt brocade, fluttered in the air. . . . The procession made the circuit of the church, and soon the joyous call reached Mikheyich, "Christ is risen from the dead!"

The old man's heart responded fervently to this call. . . . It seemed to him that the tapers were burning more brightly, and the crowd was more agitated; the banners seemed to be animated, and the wakened wind gathered the billows of sound on its wings, floated them up and blended them with the loud festal pealing of the bells.

Never before had old Mikheyich rung like this!

It seemed as if the old man's heart had passed into the lifeless brass, and the tones of the bells sang and laughed and wept, and, welding in a sublime stream of harmony, rose high and higher into a heaven resplendent with myriad stars, and, trembling, flowed down to earth.

A powerful bass bell proclaimed, "Christ is risen!" And two tenors, trembling with the alternate beats of their iron tongues, repeated joyfully, "Christ is risen!"

And two small sopranos, seemingly hastening so as not to be left behind, crowded in among the more powerful voices and, like little children, sang hurriedly, cheerfully, "Christ is risen!"

The old belfry seemed to tremble and shake, and the wind, flapping its wings in the old bell-ringer's face, repeated, "Christ is risen!"

The old heart forgot its life, full of cares and grief. The old bell-ringer forgot that his life was confined to the narrow limits of the dreary belfry, that he was alone in the world, like an old storm-broken stump. . . . He heard those singing and weeping sounds that rose to heaven and fell again to the sorrowing earth, and it seemed to him that he was surrounded by his sons and grandsons, that he heard their joyful voices; the voices of young and old blend into a chorus and sing to him of happiness and joy which he had never tasted in his life. . . . He pulled the ropes, while tears rolled down his cheeks, and his heart beat violently with the illusion of happiness. . . .

Below, people listened and said to each other that never before had old Mikheyich rung so well.

Suddenly the large bell uttered an uncertain sound, and grew dumb. The smaller ones rang out an unfinished tone, and then stopped, as if abashed, to listen to the lugubrious echo of the prolonged and palpitating note gradually dying away upon the air. . . . The old bell-ringer, utterly exhausted, fell back on the bench, and the last two tears trickled slowly down his pallid cheeks. . . .

"Ho, there! Send up a substitute; the old bell-ringer has rung his final stroke."

ZYGMUNT KRASINSKI

ZYGMUNT KRASINSKI (Polish, 1812-1859). Poet, playwright and novelist. Romanticist with deep philosophical undertone. Embittered by hostile Polish reaction to father's loyalty to Russia, lived most of life abroad. Best-known work: *The Undivine Comedy*, a mystic vision of social revolution. Also ranks high among Polish poets.

A LEGEND

IT seemed to me that precisely during the vigil at the Birth of our Lord I emerged from the gates of Rome and walked along the Campanile. The pagan graves were warming themselves in the rays of the sun—it was early morn—and the sky as clear and the plain as sad as in ages past.

I walked all day long borne by the strength of the soul. The ancient aqueducts ran along beside me but I went on beyond. The ivy, as in the pictured models of the manger of Christ, rustled on the walls of the ancient ruins. Above me swept flocks of white birds—before me on the ground wriggled a glistening snake. The roar of the ocean began to call me!

And when I stood on the highest summit of the earth, when I beheld the sea the sun was already setting—and far out over the water stood a black blot like a living thing, constantly growing larger and flying landward towards me—until it increased to a huge size when the sun had faded completely and twilight had begun to descend.

It was a great black ship, without sails or masts—dashing the waves into foam with its timbers. From the centre of the ship a column of smoke belched forth gliding back into the infinite.

Ever more darkly—like an inky spectre it circled in the expanse with thunderous roar—when two night lights gleamed before it on the ocean and a voice sounded from the deck, "Is this the last night of the vigil of the Birth of our Lord?"

Alarmed in spirit I answered from my height, "It is true, to-day is the vigil." And at once the ship stopped at the very edge, the pale stream enveloped her, and slack and sparks were emitted from her sides. In the ruddy glow rapidly declining—for a moment the deck gleamed brightly. Figures stood there in crimson caps and white cloaks—I heard the jangling of chains.—It seemed to me that a heavy long bridge was lowered from the ship to the shore —and upon it in the darkness the figures came rushing out directing their steps toward me.

And when they were very close, they asked us with one voice, "Which way is the road that leads to Rome?" I answered, "There is no road. This is a wilderness." And they answered, "Then lead us." And when I hesitated, they again spoke in low, sad tones, "We are what is left of the Polish nobility, an angel appeared to us, an angel not unlike those whom our forefathers saw, for he had wings without brilliance and a mourning veil over his brow—but we know he was sent from heaven, and he it was who directed us hither. We have been sailing for a long time, the gales have been terrific and many difficulties have we had at sea but the will of the Lord shall be accomplished if to-day at midnight, we arrive at the basilica of St. Peter."

Thereupon I said to them, "Follow me, thou unhappy people."

736

And I turned to go back from the shore of the ocean toward the city, trembling and praying as if I were crossing a cemetery and as if the dead were rising up and following me.

A wind arose and no more clouds were visible. Everywhere in the deep dark sky the stars were twinkling, while below was a vast black plain! Only now and then we passed dusky mounds or a pile of grey ruins or mayhap the gates of an aqueduct. In the distance one could hear the rustle of tall reeds—above at times sounded the shriek of a night bird, and near by, somewhere among the sunken graves came the murmurings from beneath the earth!

They strode along behind me—I could feel on my back their heavy breathing—I moved on swiftly for they were in haste—I could hear the plumes on their caps flutter in the breeze and the very folds of their capes puff up with the wind!

It seemed to me that I beheld a wandering light in the distance —and immediately a second and a third. When I advanced I beheld a great number of lights on the plain moving rapidly from all sides in one direction. And the sound of many voices began to hum in the wilderness.

When I came nearer I saw a great body of pilgrims passing over the Campanile with torches in their hands. The glow which they cast went with them between two solid walls of blackness but the light glistened on the tall crosses, pictures of saints and on the flags of various nations which fluttered in the breezes.

Into the very centre of the multitudes I led my own group, and at that instant I beheld the melancholy features of those who followed me. A strange ectasy was in their eyes but it was not the lustre of life. They carried swords on which they leaned as did the other pilgrims upon their staffs.

Hardly had I entered with them into the light of the torches when it seemed to me that the masses stood still asking, "Who are you and whence do you come?"

They paused and a strange smile passed over their lips while they answered as one, "Is there no longer anyone on this earth who recognises us?"

A low hum constantly growing in strength filled the air and it seemed to me that all the bands of pilgrims of a sudden cried out, "We know you—you are the last heroes of the earth."

Then they marched forward saying, "We saw an angel with a black band on his brow who commanded us to hasten to Rome. Tell us, did any of you also hear that voice?"

In the multitude a great tumult arose in answer, "Amen,—that same angel bade us leave our homes—his voice increased in the night about our heads and he gave us no peace. In these days, he said, Christ would be born for the last time at the grave of Peter and from that moment nothing shall be born nor nothing shall die on earth."

And the multitude became silent and stood as if startled by its own words.

The Poles were the first to move onward—throwing back their white capes over their shoulders—. From all sides of the Campanile a greater and greater mass of pilgrims crowded forward. Already we saw the battlements of the city—already we heard the harmony of the bells—sounding more clearly the nearer we came.

On the gates, on the towers, festoons of lights appeared and more loudly echoed the bells as one after another awoke to join the rest until soon all the church bells of Rome resounded.

It seemed to me that the night was transformed into white day. I did not in the least recognise the streets from which I had departed in the morning. There where once ruins projected frequented only by owls—baskets of blooming flowers and glowing lamps now swung. The Roman populace came forth in throngs shouting: "Let us rejoice—rejoice ye all, for today Christ is born to us."

And when they beheld the Polish nobles entering the gates and the stream of pilgrims behind them gaily springing forward they cried out: "Why are you so sad, you, our guests? If the long voyage has wearied you, moisten your lips with the juice of the orange. Remove your white caps and your black cloaks—behold, here are clusters of myrtle—here, camelias, we offer them to you to adorn your temples with garlands!"

But in silence and with furrowed brows, the Poles advanced through their midst and marching said to me, "Where is the basilica of Peter? We must hasten and our hearts are downcast. Is the midnight hour close in truth?"

I led them across the Forum. It seemed to me that the Amphitheatre of Flavianus—recently empty, dark and ancient—stood now like a giant of resplendant light from its base to its massive shields gleaming with lamps so that every ivy leaf upon them could be plainly distinguished. Women and children in glistening garments promenaded through various portions of the structure and clapped their hands in welcome to us who approached.

738

Every arch in the Forum and every column glowed and blazed. At the summit a wall of golden flames, the Capitol, shone forth. The very stars in heaven had grown pallid before the great flood of brilliance.

The people continued to shout: "Hosanna, Hosanna!" And the pilgrims sang psalms of penitence. The masses perpetually surged hither and thither, sounding guitars, scattering flaring sparks in the air, and through the centre of all this sea we proceeded in garments of blackness, slowly, in sorrow of soul.

From every balcony, every roof, from the streets, violets and roses descended upon us.

Already the bell of the Capitol boomed far behind us, and before us in the wide space sounded the bell of St. Peter. At last it rang independently, more sonorously than all the rest.

We hastened in the direction of that voice, we crossed the bridge over the Tiber, the houses on its banks standing out like quiet conflagrations, the river like a ribbon of flame. The angel palace bristled with cannon, every instant one of them blazed forth and thundered.

We turned and entered the courtyard of St Peter's. Its dome was hung with thousands of scarlet lamps, the cross at its summit like a diamond, the pillars at either side of the courts as if of twisted fires. In the centre were two fountains like two flowing rainbows, and I beheld a vast mass of people waiting there. The doors of the cathedral stood open and within an infinitude of blazing brightness.

While it was possible the Poles and the other pilgrims advanced but at the steps and at the base of the portico, the throng closed up the way. Pausing therefore, they demanded a passageway, but ever more closely from the front, from the rear and from the sides, the crowds pressed in upon them.

Then the voices of the Romans arose: "Are we not the first, has not this church been our own for ages upon ages?" And among the pilgrims were heard other voices saying: "Up to this time the Polish nobles have led the way for us, shall they be allowed to enter the holy place before us?"

And I looked and saw that the Poles had lifted their swords in token that they would defend themselves. With a pure fire their blades flashed in the clear air!

But at that instant on the battlements of the basilica high above the heads of the people appeared a figure in royal purple which

739

spoke in thunderous tones: "Let pass those who for the Catholic faith ransomed another nation from death and later for that faith perished themselves. Give passageway to the dead, first of all!" And the cardinal extended his hand toward the right and toward the left as if he were dividing the multitude, and down below the masses did indeed separate and make way——which seeing, he turned back into the building.

And together with the Poles I mounted the steps and advanced directly through the portico into the church and on up to the chief altar before the lamps which burn at the tomb of Peter. Here they paused, and removing their crimson caps, they unfastened their white capes and kneeling, worshipped, holding their unsheathed weapons in hand.

The snowy gleam of marble shone in the vast cathedral, the silvery transparent smoke of the incense rose to the arched dome and floated above us. On the mosaic floor lay scattered flowers and palms. From all the chapels echoed choirs of gentle joyful voices and off in the distance around the doors, the space began to fill. The pilgrims marched through that world of song and light just as they did through the city, dark and unrejoicing. A stream of Romans rolled into the basilica, noisily. And when each group had taken its place under its own banner, at its own altar, then the great expanse became silent again, as if it were a vast vacant space. The songs in the chapels were stilled and from the Vatican echoed the sounds of trumpets giving sign that the people were approaching.

Through the centre of the church proceeded all the friars and monks of Rome, the elders one after another, some in white robes, others in grey horse-hair cloth, with crucifixes in their hands. Then came the bishops wearing their mitres and silvery trains and after them the cardinals in splendid crimson, around them priests in dalmatics and troops of children in white garments, carrying wine, incense and wreaths.

And when the procession arrived at the main altar where the crowds separated forming a clear path between walls of living people who now suddenly fell to their knees, an aged grey-haired man walked slowly forward, wearing on his head a triple crown and a white vestment over his golden surplice.

At a great distance behind him remained the soldiers, attendants and the throne borne by priests. He stood alone in the centre of the throng and of the cathedral, alone he ascended the main altar.

740

It semed to me, that each step took an interminable length of time and that he never would come to us.

And as he thus advanced in the centre of those bowing before him touching their foreheads to the ground, he closed his eyes at times as if seeking relief from so many lights. Now and then he essayed to make but tremblingly left unfinished the sign of his blessing, until, pausing, he sighed and lifted up his hands to heaven, but he was unable to hold them upraised—they sank exhaustedly!

At his deep drawn sigh, the people lifted their heads. The sorrow of their father caused all to grow pale and then, I noted, that from the main altar one of the cardinals had turned away, the same one who had ordered that we should be admitted. With grave step, he descended towards the aged eldest of elders and extended his hand, turning shining eyes upon the grave of Peter. The aged man advanced a few steps but with lingering difficulty. The cardinal shook the rings of his long hair with a sidelong motion giving signal to those who had remained in the rear who at once hastened forward carrying the golden throne.

Then the father who is on earth grasped the arm of the throne with his pallid hand and seated himself. Quickly they lifted him up and the trumpets in the church again thundered forth. The cardinal walked along beside the throne. The people lifted themselves from the floor, the bell began to ring and twelve times the arched dome quivered. Around the main altar a cloud of incense arose and from it the pope ascended the steps as the cardinal announced: "Christ is born."

From amid the group of pilgrims at once a voice cried out mournfully: "Will not the words of the angel be borne out in truth that Christ is born for the last time?"

And the Roman people shouted out angrily: "Who dares blaspheme in the church of Peter?"

One of the Polish nobles stepped fortn crying: "They are not blaspheming. We do not fear you—they speak the truth—I myself and my brethren beheld the angel of sorrow."

The cardinal again like a prince of power waved his hand and said, "Peace unto the people of good will, pray ye now for the mass has begun—the time is short and today there must be prayers on earth as in heaven."

We all began to pray awaiting great things. And our holy fath.. sat before us on the throne.

741

From the chapels again rose voices like angels' choirs, full of heavenly rapture. A portion of the night passed and white-robed priests came and offered their hands to our father. He descended from the throne and approached the altar taking the chalice in his hands, for the moment had come for the holy sacrifice. The cardinal poured wine into the chalice.

Just at the moment the chalice was being uplifted, when all had fallen to their knees, a voice from the air was heard which uttered, "I live!" And when, aquiver, we raised our heads, we beheld a large figure with head bent upon the central gate, slowly dissolving —ever becoming more misty—the hands bloody, the feet bleeding, but the figure itself of snowy whiteness—and—melting like snow —it vanished.

Then the cardinal, as the pope holding the chalice in his hands, still hesitated, himself uttered the words: "Ite, missa est!" and then he cried in a powerful voice, "The times are fulfilled!" and rending the purple on his breast, he extended his hand toward the grave of Peter saying, "Awake and speak!"

From every lamp above the tomb a fiery tongue burst forth and a wreath of flames swung over the dark sepulcher. From the depths of that darkness, a body arose with hands upstretched to the dome, and standing buried in the tomb to its breast, it shrieked, "Woe!"

After this outcry it seemed to all of us that the vaulted arch of the dome cracked for the first time.

The cardinal then said, "Peter, do you recognise me?"

And the body answered, "Your head rested on the bosom of the Master at the last supper and you have never perished from the earth."

The cardinal responded, "Now it is commanded to me to linger among human beings and to embrace the earth and hold it to my bosom as the Master held mine that last night of His life on earth."

And the body replied, "Do as you have been commanded."

Then the cardinal again waved his hands as with the authority of a prince, and the body repeated: "Woe be unto me!" and fell with a terrible crash as into an abyss, back into its grave. Above, the vaulted arches began anew to shiver and break.

Horror overwhelmed us all. Only the Polish nobles gazed with dauntless eyes, leaning upon their swords.

The pope in his triple crown had knelt down on the steps of the altar and, as immovable as a statue, continued kneeling.

The cardinal spoke: "Go forth, all of you—you and you and you,—lest some of you perish beneath the ruins of these walls."

The people answered from all sides, "Lead us—you—under whose protection we have this day entered."

A cry of terror arose for the arches ever more thunderously burst into fissures, the pillars and columns all about shook and lamps were shattered and extinguished by a great wind.

Then spoke the cardinal, "Father—mine—do you wish to remain here?"

And the aged man lifting his hands to his crown, answered in a sorrowful voice: "I wish to die here—leave me, my son."

All the people heard these words, and shrieked, "Run—let us run away!"

And the Romans were the first to recover and began to flee.

And each troop or band moved from its altar with its banner and made haste to fly away.

Then the cardinal, kneeling at last, pressed his lips to the old man's brow and made the sign of a blessing around his crown like a garland of livid light in the air, then he descended and walked toward the gate of the church with a marvellous glow encircling his brow. The entire church was twisted and bent as a dying body in the last throes, but he, with·uplifted hand, staved the cracking, tumbling vault above the people and stood watching until the last one of them had gone.

And departing he said to the Polish nobles, "People, follow after me."

But these did not answer.

He turned his head back again and said, "Follow after me."

They did not move.

When he had reached the gate, driving the people before him like a shepherd, he beckoned them for the last time with his hand.

But they only lifted up their swords as if with their edges they would hold up the falling walls and they cried out altogether, "We shall not desert that aged man—it is bitter, indeed, to die all alone —and who should die with him if not we?—Go you, all—we do not know how to run away."

The cardinal stopped on the very threshold and from a distance made to them the sign of his blessing and of the garland of livid light. In his eyes that moment a tear glistened as he said, "Yet a moment more and you perish."

743

But in that moment they were hastening to the main altar to offer a hand to the kneeling and dying. They advanced in their white caps and in the gleaming of their swords—and the four twisted columns of the altar snapped like a split tree and came crashing down—even the metal canopy dropped in ruins—the entire cupola like a sinking world, fell to the ground.

And all the porticoes, even the palace of the Vatican and the colonnade in the court cracked and burst, falling into dust. Both of the fountains like two white doves, fell to the ground perishing. The populace rushed ever farther on like a sea forced from its shores and, it seemed that it was already morn, though the sun had not yet risen. But I seemed to see only the morning star above a pile of ruins, as high, as immense as had formerly been the basilica of Peter.

Upon this gigantic mountain the cardinal ascended and it seemed that I followed after him carried on by strength of soul.

When he had attained the summit, he seated himself there as on a throne and gazed at the world. His purple robes dropped from his body and he was transformed into a figure of white ensilvered by the mild glow. In his hands was a book and over it he bent his head reading attentively.

His face was entranced with an expression of love and fulness of peace.

I approached him and said just as the sun began to rise: "Sir, is it true that Christ was born for the last time yesterday in that church which to-day is no more?"

With a strange smile and without lifting his eyes from his book, he responded, "From the time of Christ none are born and none die on this earth."

Hearing this I lost my great fear and asked, "Sir, and those whom I led thither yesterday, shall they lie forever under those ruins,—all those dead around the aged dead man?"

And the white saint answered me, "Fear not for them. Because they performed the last service for him, God will reward them—for those who pass out of life are like those who are entering upon it, the dead just as the living are of God. Instead of loss—they gain —it will be better for them and for the sons of their sons."

And when I understood, I rejoiced and my soul awakened.

L

SELMA LAGERLOF

SELMA LAGERLÖF (Swedish, 1858-1940). Most important Swedish woman novelist. Deeply imbued with love of the supernatural and wondersome. Decided to write book based on traditions and stories of her province; *Gösta Berlings Saga* became world classic. Also famous: *Jerusalem*, novel of Swedish farmers who emigrated to Palestine; *The Wonderful Adventures of Nils*, children's story. Nobel Prize, 1909.

THE ECLIPSE

THERE were Stina of Ridgecote and Lina of Birdsong and Kajsa of Littlemarsh and Maja of Skypeak and Beda of Finn-darkness and Elin, the new wife on the old soldier's place, and two or three other peasant women besides—all of them lived at the far end of the parish, below Storhöjden, in a region so wild and rocky none of the big farmowners had bothered to lay hands on it.

One had her cabin set up on a shelf of rock, another had hers put up at the edge of a bog, while a third had one that stood at the crest of a hill so steep it was a toilsome climb getting to it. If by chance any of the others had a cottage built on more favorable ground, you may be sure it lay so close to the mountain as to shut out the sun from autumn fair time clear up to Annunciation Day

They each cultivated a little potato patch close by the cabin, though under serious difficulties. To be sure, there were many kinds of soil there at the foot of the mountain, but it was hard work to make the patches of land yield anything. In some places they had to clear away so much stone from their fields, it would have built a cow-house on a manorial estate; in some they had dug ditches as deep as graves, and in others they had brought their earth in sacks and spread it on the bare rocks. Where the soil was not so poor, they were forever fighting the tough thistle and pig-

745

weed which sprang up in such profusion you would have thought the whole potato land had been prepared for their benefit.

All the livelong day the women were alone in their cabins; for even where one had a husband and children, the man went off to his work every morning and the children went to school. A few among the older women had grown sons and daughters, but they had gone to America. And some there were with little children, who were always around, of course; but these could hardly be regarded as company.

Being so much alone, it was really necessary that they should meet sometimes over the coffee cups. Not that they got on so very well together, nor had any great love for each other; but some liked to keep posted on what the others were doing, and some grew despondent living like that, in the shadow of the mountain, unless they met people now and then. And there were those, too, who needed to unburden their hearts, and talk about the last letter from America, and those who were naturally talkative and jocular, and who longed for opportunity to make use of these happy God-given talents.

Nor was it any trouble at all to prepare for a little party. Coffee-pot and coffee cups they all had of course, and cream could be got at the manor, if one had no cow of one's own to milk; fancy biscuits and small cakes one could, at a pinch, get the dairyman's driver to fetch from the municipal bakery, and country merchants who sold coffee and sugar were to be found everywhere. So, to get up a coffee party was the easiest thing imaginable. The difficulty lay in finding an occasion.

For Stina of Ridgecote, Lina of Birdsong, Kajsa of Littlemarsh, Maja of Skypeak, Beda of Finn-darkness, and Elin, the new wife at the old soldier's, were all agreed that it would never do for them to celebrate in the midst of the common everyday life. Were they to be that wasteful of the precious hours which never return, they might get a bad name. And to hold coffee parties on Sundays or great Holy Days was out of the question; for then the married women had husband and children at home, which was quite company enough. As for the rest—some liked to attend church, some wished to visit relatives, while a few preferred to spend the day at home, in perfect peace and stillness, that they might really feel it was a Holy Day.

Therefore they were all the more eager to take advantage of every possible opportunity. Most of them gave parties on their name-days, though some celebrated the great event when the wee little one cut its first tooth, or when it took its first steps. For those who received money-letters from America that was always a convenient excuse, and it was also in order to invite all the women of the neighborhood to come and help tack a quilt or stretch a web just off the loom.

All the same, there were not nearly as many occasions to meet as were needed. One year one of the women was at her wit's end. It was her turn to give a party, and she had no objection to carrying out what was expected of her; but she could not seem to hit upon anything to celebrate. Her own name-day she could not celebrate, being named Beda, as Beda has been stricken out of the almanac. Nor could she celebrate that of any member of her family, for all her dear ones were resting in the churchyard. She was very old, and the quilt she slept under would probably outlast her. She had a cat of which she was very fond. Truth to tell, it drank coffee just as well as she did; but she could hardly bring herself to hold a party for a cat!

Pondering, she searched her almanac again and again, for there she felt she must surely find the solution of her problem.

She began at the beginning, with "The Royal House" and "Signs and Forecasts," and read on, right through to "Markets and Postal Transmittances for 1912," without finding anything.

As she was reading the book for the seventh time, her glance rested on "Eclipses." She noted that that year, which was the year of our Lord nineteen-hundred twelve, on April seventeenth there would be a solar eclipse. It would begin at twenty minutes past high noon and end at 2:40 o'clock, and would cover nine-tenths of the sun's disk.

This she had read before, many times, without attaching any significance to it; but now, all at once, it became dazzling clear to her.

"Now I have it!" she exclaimed.

But it was only for a second or two that she felt confident; and then she put the thought away, fearing that the other women would just laugh at her.

The next few days, however, the idea that had come to her when reading her almanac kept recurring to her mind, until at last she began to wonder whether she hadn't better venture. For when she thought about it, what friend had she in all the world she loved better than the Sun? Where her hut lay not a ray of sunlight penetrated her room the whole winter long. She counted the days until the Sun would come back to her in the spring. The Sun was the only one who was always friendly and gracious to her and of wh m she could never see enough.

She looked her years, and felt them, too. Her hands shook as if she were in a perpetual chill and when she saw herself in the looking-glass, she appeared so pale and washed out, as if she had been lying out to bleach. It was only when she stood in a strong, warm, down-pouring sunshine that she felt like a living human being and not a walking corpse.

The more she thought about it, the more she felt there was no day in the whole year she would rather celebrate than the one when her friend the Sun battled against darkness, and after a glorious conquest, came forth with new splendor and majesty.

The seventeenth of April was not far away, but there was ample time to make ready for a party. So, on the day of the eclipse Stina, Lina, Kajsa, Maja, and the other women all sat drinking coffee with Beda at Finn-darkness. They drank their second and their third cups, and chatted about everything imaginable. For one thing, they said they couldn't for the life of them understand why Beda should be giving a party.

Meanwhile, the eclipse was under way. But they took little notice of it. Only for a moment, when the sky turned blackish gray, when all nature seemed under a leaden pall, and there came driving a howling wind with sounds as of the Trumpet of Doom and the lamentations of Judgment Day—only then did they pause and feel a bit awed. But here they each had a fresh cup of coffee, and the feeling soon passed.

When all was over, and the Sun stood out in the heavens so beamingly happy——it seemed to them it had not shone with such brilliancy and power the whole year—they saw old Beda go over to the window, and stand with folded hands. Looking out toward the sunlit slope, she sang in her quavering voice:

> "Thy shining sun goes up again,
> I thank Thee, O my Lord!
> With new-found courage, strength and hope,
> I raise a song of joy."

Thin and transparent, old Beda stood there in the light of the window, and as she sang the sunbeams danced about her, as if wanting to give her, also, of their life and strength and color.

748

When she had finished the old hymn-verse she turned and looked at her guests, as if in apology.

"You see," she said, "I haven't any better friend than the Sun, and I wanted to give her a party on the day of her eclipse. I felt that we should come together to greet her, when she came out of her darkness."

Now they understood what old Beda meant, and their hearts were touched. They began to speak well of the Sun. "She was kind to rich and poor alike, and when she came peeping into the hut on a winter's day, she was as comforting as a glowing fire on the hearth. Just the sight of her smiling face made life worth living, whatever the troubles one had to bear."

The women went back to their homes after the party, happy and content. They somehow felt richer and more secure in the thought that they had a good, faithful friend in the Sun.

LAO SHE

LAO SHE (Shu Ch'ing-ch'un, Chinese, 1897-   ). Leading writer of satirical fiction. During war with Japan was president of Writer's League, wrote patriotic plays. *Ssu-shih t'ung-t'ang*, novel of occupied Peking, widely acclaimed.

THE LAST TRAIN

THE train started a long while ago, and now the wheels rumbled mournfully along the rails, the passengers sighed and counted the hours: seven o'clock, eight, nine, ten—by ten o'clock the train would arrive, and they would be home around midnight. It might not be too late, for the children might already be put to bed. It was New Year's Day, and they were all in a hurry to get home. They looked at the cans, the fruit and the toys heaped up on the shelves, and already they could hear the children crying 'Papa, papa!', and thinking of all this, they lost themselves in their thoughts; but there were others who were well aware that they would not be home before daybreak.

There were not many passengers in the second-class carriage. There was fat Mr. Chang and thin Mr. Chiao, and they sat in the same compartment opposite one another. Whenever they got up, they spread their blankets over their seats to show that intruders would not be welcomed. When the train started they found to their surprise that there were very few passengers indeed, and somehow this led them more than ever to feel grieved at the thought that they were travelling in a train on New Year's Day. There were other similarities between the two passengers: they were both holding free passes, and both of them had been unable to obtain the pass until the previous day. They were both indignant at this treatment, for in the good old days friends were made of sterner stuff, and so they shook their heads and put the blame on these so-called friends who had prevented them from reaching their home before the New Year's Day.

Old Mr. Chang removed his fox-fur coat and tucked his legs under his body, but he discovered that the seat was too narrow for sitting comfortably in this posture. Meanwhile, the temperature of the carriage rose and beads of perspiration began to roll down his brow. 'Boy, towels!' he shouted, and then to Mr. Chiao he said: 'I wonder why they turn so much heat on nowadays'. He gasped. 'It wouldn't be so hot if we were travelling on an aeroplane.'

Old Mr. Chiao had taken off his coat a long while ago, and now he was wearing a robe lined with white sheep's fur, and over that a sleeveless jacket of shining black satin. He showed no sign of feeling faint. He said: 'One can get a free pass on an aeroplane, too. It isn't difficult'. And he drawled off with a faint smile.

'It's better not to risk travelling by air', old Mr. Chang said, trying hard to keep his crossed legs under him, but succeeding only with great difficulty. 'Boy, towels!'

The 'boy' was over forty, and his neck was as thin as a stick, so thin that one imagined that it was quite easy to pluck off his head and plant it back again. You could see him hurrying backwards and forwards along the passageway, his hands full of steaming towels. He was always eager to serve, but really—the way the management made you work on such a sacred day—it was really inconceivable. Taking advantage of the rocking movement of the train, he swung his body towards a certain Mr. K'ou. 'Like a towel, sir? It's trying to travel at this time of the year.'

Mr. K'ou was dressed with considerable éclat. He wore a dark serge overcoat with a beaver collar, with a brand new black satin, melon-shaped hat. He had removed neither his coat nor his hat, and he sat there as rigid as a chairman on a platform waiting

750

solemnly for the moment when he would address a huge audience. He took the towel, stretching out his arm at full length, and taking care not to fold his elbow he described a semi-circle with the towel until it reached his face. Then he rubbed his face fastidiously and ostentatiously. When his face emerged from the whirling cloud of the towel it dazzled and lent to his person a renewed splendour and dignity. He nodded to the 'boy', without explaining why he was travelling on New Year's Day.

And meanwhile the waiter knew perfectly well that the man was a friend of the manager. The carriage began to rock again, and the movement of the carriage hurled him into the passage way. Steadying himself, he untwisted a towel and holding it delicately by two corners he offered it to Mr. Chang. 'Would you like one, sir?', and the man reached out for it, his thick palm touching the central part of it, which was the hottest. He pressed it to his face, rubbing hard as though he were cleaning a mirror. Then he handed another one to Mr. Chiao, who showed no enthusiasm, but took the towel and with it proceeded to clean his nostrils and fingernails delicately. When he returned it to the waiter, it was all greasy and black.

'The inspectors will soon be coming now', he began. 'When they have gone, you will want to have a rest, and if any of you gentlemen would like a cushion, just let me know.' And he went on a little later: 'There are not many passengers on board, and you'll all be able to have a nap. It's a pity you gentlemen are spending a day like this on a train, but as for us waiters—'. He sighed. He realized that he had been talking too much.

'What's wrong with the heating system?' Mr. Chang asked, as he tossed back the towel.

'I wouldn't advise you to open the window', the waiter answered. 'Nine to ten you'll catch cold. The railway is under a rotten management.' The chance lay wide open for him, and he entered quickly. 'They make you work all the year round, and don't even let you rest on New Year's Day. Well, all talking is vain.'

And so it was, for the train had drawn into a small wayside station. Half a dozen soldiers came into the compartment. Their boots thundered on the floor, their leather belts flashed in the light and their luggage consisted of four large cases of fireworks wrapped in scarlet paper and decorated with characters cut out of gold paper. The boxes were so large that for a long time they were undecided what to do with them. Finally, a man who resembled a battalion commander, said that they should be put on the floor. Boots thundered. A cloud of grey caps, grey uniforms and grey leggings. A moment later someone said: 'Hurry!', and they obediently disappeared. A whistle sounded from the train, rather muffled. Lights and shadows flitted about, and the wheels began to rumble and the train to roll out of the station.

The waiter walked from one end of the carriage to the other, looking as though there was something on his mind. He stole a glance at the two soldiers and then at the heap of fireworks which lay so uncompromisingly on the floor, barring his way; but he dared not say anything. The battalion commander was lying down, tired out, his pistol on the little table at the side of the carriage. The platoon commander had not yet dared to imitate him, but he had removed his cap and was now violently scratching his scalp. The waiter took care not to awaken the senior officer, but he smiled voluminously at the junior. 'What was I going to say?' he said in a half-apologetic tone of voice, hesitantly. 'Oh yes, I was going to suggest that it might be a better idea to put the crackers up on the shelf.'

'Why?' the officer answered, mouth awry with head scratching.

'You know, I was afraid people might step on them', the waiter replied, his head shrinking tortoise-fashion into his shoulders.

'If I have any more trouble from you, what about fighting it out?' the officer suddenly shouted. He had been worn thin by the ill-humour of his senior officer, and he was perfectly prepared to fight.

But the waiter was in no need of a fight, and he abruptly disappeared. As he passed Mr. Chang, he said: 'The inspectors will be here soon, sir'.

Mr. Chang and Mr. Chiao were developing a cordial friendship. The ticket inspection began.

Meanwhile the waiter was taking this opportunity to inform Mr. Chang and Mr. Chiao to get their tickets ready. They gave him their tickets. He was awestruck when he realized that the tickets were free passes, and his reverence for the two gentlemen became even greater than before. He returned Mr. Chang's pass at once, but he ventured to detain Mr. Chiao's for a moment because it was clearly indicated on the pass that the holder was a woman, and there was indisputable evidence that Mr. Chiao was a man. The two inspectors drew apart and began to whisper into each other's

752

ear. A moment later they nodded to one another, and it was clear that they had reached a common understanding that on New Year's Day a man might pass for a woman. The waiter returned Mr. Chiao's ticket with both hands, apologetically.

The battalion commander was now snoring. As soon as he noticed the arrival of the inspectors, the platoon commander put his legs up on the seat and showed every sign of an unwillingness to be disturbed. The inspectors' attention was immediately arrested by the pile of fireworks which littered the passageway. They nodded in admiration, overcome by the length and the solidity of the fireworks. And they passed through the compartment, and it was not until the first inspector reached the door that he turned to the waiter and said: 'You'd better tell them to put the fireworks on the shelves', and in order to save the waiter from further embarrassment the second inspector added quickly: 'Better still if you did it for them'. The waiter nodded his thin neck like a pendulum without saying anything, but all the while he was asking himself: 'You haven't the courage to tell them—that's what it is—so what can I do except nod my head?—and besides, there is a great difference between nodding and doing.' The truth dawned on his mind. The fireworks must *not* be moved.

Go-home-go-home-go-home-go-home. The wheels roared in chorus. But they were very slow. The star-strewn sky undulated. Hills, trees, villages, graves, flashed past in clusters. The train dashed on and on in the darkness. Smoke, soot and sparks shot up furiously, and then disappeared. The train ran on, flying breathlessly, one patch of darkness following on another. The lights were ablaze, the temperature steaming, all the passengers were weary to death, and not one was inclined to sleep. Go-home-go-home-go-home. The farewell rites to the Old Year, the libations to the gods, the offerings to the Ancestors, the writing on the spring scrolls, the firecrackers, the dumplings, the sweetmeats, the dinners and the wine—all these became suddenly very real to them, filling their eyes and their ears, their palates and their nostrils. A smile would light upon their lips and instantly disappear, dying away at the recollection that they were still physically in the train. Go-home-go-home-go-home-go-home.

Mr. Chang took down from the shelf two bottles of distilled wine, and said to Mr. Chiao: 'We're just like old friends now. How about a drop of this? We might as well enjoy New Year's Day

—no reason why we shouldn't enjoy ourselves'. He handed over a cup of the wine. 'Real Yinkow wine. Twenty years old. You can't get it on the market. Bottoms up.'

Mr. Chiao was too polite to refuse.

'Marvellous!' Mr. Chiao wetted his lips. 'Marvellous! Nothing like it anywhere.'

They filled up one another's cups, and slowly and imperceptibly their faces turned crimson. Their tongues were unloosened. They talked of their families, their jobs, their friends, the difficulty of earning money, free passes. Their cups clinked, their hearts clinked, their eyes moistened, they were permeated with warmth.

Mr. Chang looked at his bottle—there was not very much left now. He untied his collar. Beads of perspiration stood out on his brow; his eyes were bloodshot and his tongue was stiff. Though still talkative, his talk was reduced to mere babbling; he had not yet completely lost his self-control, he could still put a curb on the curious inner urge which nearly led him to curse in front of his new-found friend, and the resultant of these forces took the form, not of a quarrel, or incivility, but rather of exultation and gaiety. Mr. Chiao, on the other hand, had been able to stomach only half of the bottle assigned to him, but his face was already turning deathly pale. He produced a packet of cigarettes and threw one at Mr. Chang. Both lit their cigarettes.

Go-home-go-home-go-home-go-home. In Mr. Chang's ears the wheels sounded as though they were going at breakneck speed. His heart beat fast, and suddenly everything began buzzing. His head turned round and round in the air, buzzing like a fly. All objects were dancing and glowing in red circles. When the buzzing ceased, his heart once more began to beat at its accustomed ritual, and he opened his eyes slightly, partially regaining his strength. He pretended nothing had happened, and groping for the matchbox he relit his extinguished cigarette. Then he threw the match away. Suddenly on the table a greenish flame flared up, smelling of alcohol, spinning among the cups and bottles, fluttering, rising, spreading out. Mr. Chiao was startled out of his dreams as the cigarette which he held in his hand suddenly caught fire. He threw it away. He beat the table with both hands to extinguish the fire, and in doing this he knocked down the cups and bottles. Iridescent tongues licked the unopened parcels. Mr. Chang's face was hidden in flames. Mr. Chiao thought of running away. The flames on the table soared up, and the parcels on the shelf above seemed to reach down to catch the rising columns of flames. Flame linked with flame. Mr. Chiao himself was ablaze. The fire reached his eyebrows, charring them, snapping at his hair, which sizzled, lighting up the alcohol on his lips and turning him into a fire-breathing monster.

Suddenly: pop, pop, pop . . . It sounded like machine-gun fire. The platoon commander had hardly opened his eyes when a cracker exploded on his nose and sent sparks and blood flying in fine sprays. He rose, and began frantically running. There were explosions everywhere, under his feet, all round his body. The noise was deafening as though they had stepped on a land mine. The battalion commander was swallowed up in the fire before he could open his eyes. He was trying to open his eyes when the right eye received a direct hit from one of the exploding crackers.

Mr. K'ou started up. He cast a quick glance at his luggage on the shelf. Some of the parcels were already burning, and the fire was closing in from all sides—from above, from below, and even from a long way away. Flames licked at him, and an idea flashed through his mind. He picked up one of his shoes from the floor and smote at the windowpane. He wanted to jump out of the window. The glass was broken, a gale rushed in, the fire turned wild. His collar of beaver-skin, the four bedrolls, the five boxes, his clothes—they were all swallowed up in the flames. The train ran on, the wind was roaring, the firecrackers kept going off. Mr. K'ou ran like a wild animal.

Mr. Chang was dead-drunk, and he lay there like a log. Mr. Chiao, Mr. K'ou and the platoon commander were running about in all directions, stark staring mad. The battalion commander knelt on the bench and wailed. The fire had already penetrated every corner of the carriage; the smell of sulphur was suffocating. The crackers were no longer exploding—they had all been burnt. The noise died away, but the smoke grew thicker. And at last those who were running about no longer ran about, and those who were wailing no longer wailed. The fire began to devour the furniture. The train kept darting forward, the wind kept roaring. Red tongues of flame struggled within the dense clouds of smoke, hoping for an outlet. The smoke turned milky, and the flames began to thrash at the windows. The whole carriage was transparent with light, and tongues of fire streamed away like streamers, a thousand torches burning brightly in the wind.

Brilliant rockets shot out in sprays. The night was dark and the train was a chain of lanterns pouring out licking flames. Of the

755

second-class carriage, only a charred skeleton remained. The flames, having nothing to feed on, moved backwards and forwards, and finally entered the third-class carriage. Smoke came first, sending out a pungent, and slightly sweet smell of charred flesh and furniture. Fire followed. 'Fire! Fire' Fire' Everyone was shouting in fearful panic. They lost their heads. They broke the windows in an attempt to leap out, and then hesitated. Some began to run, and then they would fall against one another and fall down. Some sat transfixed to their seats, unable even to cry. Turbulence. Panic. Every effort proved vain. They howled, folded their arms round their heads, beat off the flames with their clothes, ran, jumped out of the carriage. . . .

The fire had discovered a new colony, with rich resources and a great population. It was mad with joy. Hundreds of flames began dancing in the most fantastic patterns. They rolled themselves up into balls, shot out like meteors, gathered in red-and-green pools of fire. They squeaked and gibbered as they burned human flesh and broiled human hair. The crowd howled, the wind roared, the fire crackled. The whole car was on fire. The smoke was heavy. It was a lovely cremation.

The train arrived at the next station, where it was due to stop. It stopped. Signalmen, ticket-inspectors, guards, the stationmaster and the assistant stationmaster, the clerks and the hangers-on all looked at the burning carriages in amazement, and could do nothing, because there were no fire engines and no implements for putting out fires. The second-class carriage, and the two adjacent third-class carriages in front and behind were silent and still. From them a plume of blue smoke curled up—languidly and leisurely.

It was reported later that fifty-two corpses were found on the train, and the bodies of eleven more who had jumped off and killed themselves, were found along the line.

After the Lantern Festival—that is, fifteen days after the New Year—an inspector arrived.

The guard knew nothing. The first inspector knew nothing. The second inspector knew nothing.

Finally, the waiter was examined. He declared that he knew nothing about the fire, which must have started when he was in the dining-car. The tribunal decided that he was irrevocably wrong, and should be punished for having left his post of duty. And he was duly discharged from the service.

The inspector submitted his report with a detailed account of the tragedy written in the most admirable style.

'I don't care at all', the waiter said to his wife. 'They put you on duty on New Year's Day, and then, when everything goes wrong, they think we will be starved if we leave their wretched railway.'

'What nonsense!' his wife answered. 'I'm not worried about that. What I am worried about is the cabbage that got burnt.'

LAO-TZU

LAO-TZU (Chinese, 6th century B.C.). Legendary sage of China. Author of the celebrated *Tao Te Ching*, 81 chapters of prose and verse. Important in the whole Taoist movement ("Tao," "the Eternal" or "Way of Life" according to reason and virtue).

PARAPHRASE

1

There are ways but the Way is uncharted;
There are names but not nature in words:
Nameless indeed is the source of creation
But things have a mother and she has a name.

The secret waits for the insight
Of eyes unclouded by longing;
Those who are bound by desire
See only the outward container.

These two come paired but distinct
By their names.
Of all things profound,
Say that their pairing is deepest,
The gate to the root of the world.

2

Since the world points up beauty as such,
There is ugliness too.
If goodness is taken as goodness,
Wickedness enters as well.

For is and is-not come together;
Hard and easy are complementary;
Long and short are relative;
High and low are comparative;
Pitch and sound make harmony;
Before and after are a sequence.

Indeed the Wise Man's office
Is to work by being still;
He teaches not by speech
But by accomplishment;
He does for everything,
Neglecting none;
Their life he gives to all,
Possessing none;
And what he brings to pass
Depends on no one else.
As he succeeds,
He takes no credit
And just because he does not take it,
Credit never leaves him.

3

A man of highest virtue
Will not display it as his own;
His virtue then is real.
Low virtue makes one miss no chance
To show his virtue off;
His virtue then is nought.
High virtue is at rest;
It knows no need to act.
Low virtue is a busyness
Pretending to accomplishment.

Compassion at its best
Consists in honest deeds;
Morality at best
Is something done, aforethought;
High etiquette, when acted out
Without response from others,
Constrains a man to bare his arms
And make them do their duty!

Truly, once the Way is lost,
There comes then virtue;
Virtue lost, comes then compassion;
After that morality;
And when that's lost, there's etiquette,
The husk of all good faith,
The rising point of anarchy.

Foreknowledge is, they say,
The Doctrine come to flower;
But better yet, it is
The starting point of silliness.
So once full-grown, a man will take
The meat and not the husk,
The fruit and not the flower.
Rejecting one, he takes the other.

4

These things in ancient times received the One:

The sky obtained it and was clarified;
The earth received it and was settled firm;
The spirits got it and were energized;
The valleys had it, filled to overflow;
All things, as they partook it came alive;
The nobles and the king imbibed the One
In order that the realm might upright be;
Such things were then accomplished by the One.

Without its clarity the sky might break;
Except it were set firm, the earth might shake;
Without their energy the gods would pass;
Unless kept full, the valleys might go dry;
Except for life, all things would pass away;
Unless the One did lift and hold them high,
The nobles and the king might trip and fall.

The humble folk support the mighty ones;
They are base on which the highest rest.
The nobles and the king speak of themselves

As "orphans," "desolate" and "needy ones."
Does this not indicate that they depend
Upon the lowly people for support?

Truly, a cart is more than the sum of its parts.

Better to rumble like rocks
Than to tinkle like jade.

DAVID HERBERT LAWRENCE

DAVID HERBERT LAWRENCE (English, 1885-1930). Controversial English novelist and poet. An enigmatic battler against social prejudice. Son of a coal miner, rebelled bitterly against industrialism. Also concerned with better relations between sexes. *Sons and Lovers,* partly autobiographical novel. *Lady Chatterly's Lover,* banned in England and America because of frankness. Spent last years of life in Mexico and Italy.

DREAMS OLD AND NASCENT

My world is a painted fresco, where coloured shapes
Of old, ineffectual lives linger blurred and warm;
An endless tapestry the past has woven drapes
The halls of my life, compelling my soul to conform.

The surface of dreams is broken,
The picture of the past is shaken and scattered.
Fluent, active figures of men pass along the railway, and I am woken
From the dreams that the distance flattered.

Along the railway, active figures of men.
They have a secret that stirs in their limbs as they move
Out of the distance, nearer, commanding my dreamy world.

Here in the subtle, rounded flesh
Beats the active ectasy.
In the sudden lifting of my eyes, it is clearer,
The fascination of the quick, restless Creator moving through the
    mesh
Of men, vibrating in ecstasy through the rounded flesh.

Oh my boys, bending over your books,
In you is trembling and fusing
The creation of a new-patterned dream, dream of a generation:
And I watch to see the Creator, the power that patterns the dream.

The old dreams are beautiful, beloved, soft-toned, and sure,
But the dream-stuff is molten and moving mysteriously,
Alluring my eyes; for I, am I not also dream-stuff,
Am I not quickening, diffusing myself in the pattern, shaping and
   shapen?

Here in my class is the answer for the great yearning:
Eyes where I can watch the swim of old dreams reflected on the
   molten metal of dreams,
Watch the stir which is rhythmic and moves them all as a heart-beat
   moves the blood,
Here in the swelling flesh the great activity working,
Visible there in the change of eyes and the mobile features.

Oh the great mystery and fascination of the unseen Shaper,
The power of the melting, fusing Force—heat, light, all in one,
Everything great and mysterious in one, swelling and shaping the
   dream in the flesh,
As it swells and shapes a bud into blossom.

Oh the terrible ecstasy of the consciousness that I am life!
Oh the miracle of the whole, the widespread, labouring concentration
Swelling mankind like one bud to bring forth the fruit of a dream,
Oh the terror of lifting the innermost I out of the sweep of the
   impulse of life,
And watching the Great Thing labouring through the whole round
   flesh of the world;
And striving to catch a glimpse of the shape of the coming dream,
As it quickens within the labouring, white-hot metal,
Catch the scent and the colour of the coming dream,
Then to fall back exhausted into the unconscious, molten life!

LEE HOU-CHU

LEE HOU-CHU (Chinese, 937-978). King of the South T'ang Kingdom in the
time of the Ten Kingdoms, and greatest poet of his time. His administration,
more devoted to arts than wars, fell easily to Sung Emperor. Great lover of
music, women and Buddhism. Master of the *tzu*, a song set to a definite tune.

THE FISHERMAN

The vernal breeze an oar;
My skiff a leaf;
A line of fishing string;
A light hook.
An islet full of flowers;
A pitcher full of wine.
Among ten thousand ching of waves
I have my freedom.

The wave-flowers break into a thousand layers of snow.
Peach and plum blossoms from the quiet army of Spring.
A flask of wine;
A fishing rod and line.
Who is as happy as I?

FADING FLOWERS

The morning moon sets;
Last night's smoke is blown away.
Speechless I recline on the pillow.
Returning from my dreams I hanker after the scented grass.

In the far sky, the cry of swans is thin.

The singing orioles scatter;
The fading flowers fall;
Lonely are the painted hall and the deep courtyard.
Do not sweep away the red petals;
Let them await the feet of the returning dancers.

SPRING

To find spring one must walk out in the early Spring.
To love a flower do not wait till the flower is old.
She holds the bluish cup in her supple hand;
The brimming wine is clear.

What harm is there in smiling and laughing?
In the Forbidden Garden spring yet lingers.
Ah, to be drunk together and to converse leisurely!
Poems flow to the sound of the goat-drum
Calling on the flowers to blossom forth.

PALE MOON

In the long night,
I loiter round the bower,
Indolent.
The feast of ching-min is just over;
I already feel the Spring wane.
The sound of falling rain is stifled by the wind.
The blurred moon is pale among the shifting clouds.

Breezes pass lightly through the yearning peach and apricot.
Who is chattering there at the swing with laughter?
My heart is one, but its threads of thoughts are ten thousand.
There is no place on earth for me to smooth them out.

NIKOLAUS LENAU

NIKOLAUS LENAU (Nikolaus Niembsch von Strehlenau, Austrian, 1802-1850). Austrian lyric poet. The bohemian of the Balkans. Lived erratically, died in delusion. Like Leopardi, a poet of despair. An accomplished violinist, with deep feeling for nature.

SONGS BY THE LAKE

I

In the sky the sun is failing,
    And the weary day would sleep.
Here the willow fronds are trailing
    In the water still and deep.

From my darling I must sever:
  Stream, oh tears, stream forth amain!
In the breeze the rushes quiver
  And the willow sighs in pain.

On my soul in silence grieving
  Mild thou gleamest from afar,
As through rushes interweaving
  Gleams the mirrored evening star.

IV

Sunset dull and drear;
  Dark the clouds drive past;
Sultry, full of fear,
  All the winds fly fast.

Through the sky's wild rack
  Shoots the lightning pale;
O'er the waters black
  Burns its flickering trail.

In the vivid glare
  Half I see thy form,
And thy streaming hair
  Flutters in the storm.

V

On the lake as it reposes
  Dwells the moon with glow serene
Interweaving pallid roses
  With the rushes' crown of green.

Stags from out the hillside bushes
  Gaze aloft into the night,
Waterfowl amid the rushes
  Vaguely stir with fluttering light.

Down my tear-dim glance I bend now,
  While through all my soul a rare
Thrill of thought toward thee doth tend now
  Like an ecstasy of prayer.

764

THE POSTILION

Passing lovely was the night,
   Silver clouds flew o'er us,
Spring, methought, with splendor dight
   Led the happy chorus.

Sleep-entranced lay wood and dale,
   Empty now each by-way;
No one but the moonlight pale
   Roamed upon the highway.

Breezes wandering in the gloom
   Soft their footsteps numbered
Through Dame Nature's sleeping-room
   Where her children slumbered.

Timidly the brook stole by,
   While the beds of blossom
Breathed their perfume joyously
   On the still night's bosom.

My postilion, heedless all,
   Cracked his whip most gaily,
And his merry trumpet-call
   Rang o'er hill and valley.

Hoofs beat steadily the while,
   As the horses gamboled,
And along the shady aisle
   Spiritedly rambled.

Grove and meadow gliding past
   Vanished at a glimmer:
Peaceful towns were gone as fast,
   Like to dreams that shimmer.

Midway in the Maytide trance
   Tombs were shining whitely;
'Twas the churchyard met our glance—
   None might view it lightly.

Close against the mountain braced
    Ran the long white wall there,
And the cross, in sorrow placed,
    Silent rose o'er all there.

Jehu straight, his humor spent,
    Left his tuneful courses;
On the cross his gaze he bent
    Then pulled up his horses.

"Here's where horse and coach must wait—
    You may think it odd, sir:—
But up yonder, lies my mate
    Underneath the sod, sir.

"Better lad was never born—
    (Sir, 'twas God's own pity!)
No one else could blow the horn
    Half as shrill and pretty.

"So I stop beside the wall
    Every time I pass here,
And I blow his favorite call
    To him under grass here."

Toward the churchyard then he blew
    One call after other,
That they might go ringing through
    To his sleeping brother.

From the cliff each lively note
    Echoing resounded,
As it were the dead man's throat
    Answering strains had sounded.

On we went through field and hedge,
    Loosened bridles jingling;
Long that echo from the ledge
    In my ear kept tingling.

TO THE BELOVED FROM AFAR

His sweet rose here oversea
    I must gather sadly;
Which, beloved, unto thee
    I would bring how gladly!

But alas! if o'er the foam
    I this flower should carry,
It would fade ere I could come;
    Roses may not tarry.

Farther let no mortal fare
    Who would be a wooer,
Than unwithered he may bear
    Blushing roses to her,

Or than nightingale may fly
    For her nesting grasses,
Or than with the west wind's sigh
    Her soft warbling passes.

THE THREE GIPSIES

Three gipsy men I saw one day
    Stretched out on the grass together,
As wearily o'er the sandy way
    My wagon brushed the heather.

The first of the three was fiddling there
    In the glow of evening pallid,
Playing a wild and passionate air,
    The tune of some gipsy ballad.

From the second's pipe the smoke-wreaths curled,
    He watched them melt at his leisure.
So full of content, it seemed the world
    Had naught to add to his pleasure.

And what of the third?—He was fast asleep,
  His harp to a bough confided;
The breezes across the strings did sweep,
  A dream o'er his heart-strings glided.

The garb of all was worn and frayed,
  With tatters grotesquely mended;
But flouting the world, and undismayed,
  The three with fate contended.

They showed me how, by three-fold scoff,
  When cares of life perplex us,
To smoke, or sleep, or fiddle them off,
  And scorn the ills that vex us.

GIACOMO LEOPARDI

GIACOMO LEOPARDI (Italian, 1798-1837). Italian poet of pessimism and
despair. Unhappy childhood and ill health throughout life. A visionary and
mystic naturalist, who rejected civilization and thought Italy corrupt and
decadent. Intense personal emotion gave his work strength and validity.
Best-known: *To Italy, On the Monument to Dante, The Lone Sparrow, The
Broom Plant.*

THE LAST SONG OF SAPPHO

Thou peaceful night, thou chaste and silver ray
Of the declining Moon; and thou, arising
Amid the quiet forest on the rocks,
Herald of day; O cherished and endeared,
Whilst Fate and Doom were to my knowledge closed,
Objects of sight! No lovely land or sky
Doth longer gladden my despairing mood.
By unaccustomed joy we are revived
When o'er the liquid spaces of the Heavens
And o'er the fields alarmed doth wildly whirl
The tempest of the winds, and when the car,
The ponderous car of Jove, above our heads
Thundering, divides the heavy air obscure.
O'er mountain peaks and o'er abysses deep
We love to float amid the swiftest clouds;

We love the terror of the herds dispersed,
   The streams that flood the plain,
And the victorious, thunderous fury of the main.

   Fair is thy sight, O sky divine, and fair
   Art thou, O dewy Earth! Alas! of all
   This beauty infinite, no slightest part
   To wretched Sappho did the Gods or Fate
   Inexorable give. Unto thy reign
   Superb, O Nature, an unwelcome guest
   And a disprized adorer doth my heart
   And do mine eyes implore thy lovely forms;
   But all in vain. The sunny land around
   Smiles not for me, nor from ethereal gates
   The blush of early dawn; not me the songs
   Of brilliant-feathered birds, not me the trees
   Salute with murmuring leaves; and where in shade
   Of drooping willows doth a liquid stream
   Display its pure and crystal course, from my
   Advancing foot the soft and flowing waves
   Withdrawing with affright,
Disdainfully it takes through flowery dell its flight.

   What fault so great, what guiltiness so dire
   Did blight me ere my birth, that adverse grew
   To me the brow of fortune and the sky?
   How did I sin, a child, when ignorant
   Of wickedness is life, that from that time
   Despoiled of youth and of its fairest flowers,
   The cruel Fates wove with relentless wrath
   The web of my existence? Reckless words
   Rise on thy lips; the events that are to be
   A secret council guides. Secret is all,
   Our agony excepted. We were born,
   Neglected race, for tears; the reason lies
   Amid the Gods on high. O cares and hopes
   Of early years! To beauty did the Sire,
   To glorious beauty an eternal reign
   Give o'er this human kind; for warlike deed,
   For learned lyre or song,
In unadornèd shape, no charms to fame belong.

769

Ah! let us die. The unworthy garb divested,
The naked soul will take to Dis its flight
And expiate the cruel fault of blind
Dispensers of our lot. And thou for whom
Long love in vain, long faith, and fruitless rage
Of unappeased desire assailed my heart,
Live happily, if happily on earth
A mortal yet hath lived. Not me did Jove
Sprinkle with the delightful liquor from
The niggard urn, since of my childhood died
The dreams and fond delusions. The glad days
Of our existence are the first to fly;
And then disease and age approach, and last,
The shade of frigid Death. Behold! of all
The palms I hoped for and the errors sweet,
Hades remains; and the transcendent mind
Sinks to the Stygian shore
Where sable Night doth reign, and silence evermore.

THE VILLAGERS' SATURDAY NIGHT

From copse and glade the maiden takes her way
When in the west the setting sun reposes;
She gathered flowers; her slender fingers bear
A fragrant wealth of violets and roses,
And with their beauty she will deck her hair,
Her lovely bosom with their leaves entwine;
Such is her wont on every festive day.
The aged matron sits upon the steps
And with her neighbors turns the spinning wheel,
Facing the heavens where the rays decline;
And she recalls the years,—
The happy years when on the festive day ·
It was her wont her beauty to array,
And when amidst her lovers and compeers
In youth's effulgent pride
Her rapid feet through mazy dance did glide.

The sky already darkens, and serene
The azure vault its loveliness reveals;

From hill and tower a lengthened shadow steals
In silvery whiteness of the crescent moon.
We hear the distant bell
Of festive morrow tell;
To weary hearts how generous a boon!
The happy children in the open space
In dancing numbers throng
With game and jest and song;
And to his quiet home and simple fare
The laborer doth repair
And whistles as he goes,
Glad of the morrow that shall bring repose.

Then, when no other light around is seen,
No other sound or stir,
We hear the hammer strike,
The grating saw of busy carpenter;
He is about and doing, so unlike
His quiet neighbors; his nocturnal lamp
With helpful light the darkened workshop fills,
And he makes haste his business to complete
Ere break of dawn the heavenly regions greet.

This of the seven is the happiest day,
With hope and joyance gay;
To-morrow grief and care
The unwelcome hours will in their progress bear;
To-morrow one and all
In thought their wonted labors will recall.

O merry youth! Thy time of life so gay
Is like a joyous and delightful day,—
A day clear and serene
That doth the approaching festival precede
Of thy fair life. Rejoice! Divine indeed
Is this fair day, I ween.
I'll say no more; but when it comes to thee,
Thy festival, may it not evil be.

MIKHAIL YURYEVICH LERMONTOV

MIKHAIL YURYEVICH LERMONTOV (Russian, 1814-1841). Russian poet, whose work marked end of era inaugurated by Pushkin. Led wild life, died in duel after brief, rancorous military career. Gloomy cynicism makes him most Byronic of Russian poets. Had great sympathy for the common people. Best work: lyric poems and a novel, *A Hero of Our Time*.

DAGGER

I love you well, my steel-white dagger,
Comrade luminous and cold;
Forged by a Georgian dreaming vengeance,
Whetted by Circassians bold.

A tender hand, in grace of parting,
Gave you to mark a meeting brief;
For blood there glimmered on your metal
A shining tear—the pearl of grief.

And black eyes, clinging to my glances,
Filled deep with liquid sorrow seemed;
Like your clear blade where flame is trembling,
They darkened quickly and they gleamed.

You were to be my long companion.
Give me your counsel to the end!
I will be hard of soul and faithful,
Like you, my iron-hearted friend!

A SAIL

White is the sail and lonely
  On the misty infinite blue;
Flying from what in the homeland?
  Seeking for what in the new?

The waves romp, and the winds whistle,
  And the mast leans and creaks;
Alas! He flies not from fortune,
  And no good fortune he seeks.

Beneath him the stream, luminous, azure,
  Above him the sun's golden breast;
But he, a rebel, invites the storms,
  As though in the storms were rest.

COMPOSED WHILE UNDER ARREST

When waves invade the yellowing wheat,
And the saplings sway with a wind-song brief;
When the raspberry plum in the garden sweet
Hides him under the cool green leaf;

When sprinkled with lights of limpid dew,
At rose of evening or gold of morn,
The lilies-of-the-valley strew
Their silver nodding under the thorn;

When the brook in the valley with cooling breast,
Plunging my soul in a cloudy dream,
Murmurs a legend of lands of rest
At the rise of his happy and rapid stream;

Then humbled is my heart's distress,
And lulled the anguish of my blood;
Then in the earth my happiness,
Then in the heaven my God.

A THOUGHT

I gaze with grief upon our generation.
Its future black or vacant—and to-day,
Bent with a load of doubt and understanding,
In sloth and cold stagnation it grows old.
When scarcely from the cradle we were rich
In follies, in our fathers' tardy wits.
Life wearied us—a road without a goal,
A feast upon a foreign holiday.
Toward good and evil shamefully impassive,
In mid-career we fade without a fight.

773

Before a danger pusillanimous,
Before a power that scorns us we are slaves.
Precocious fruit, untimely ripe, we hang,
Rejoicing neither sight nor touch nor tongue,
A wrinkled orphan runt among the blossoms,
Their beauty's hour the hour of its decay.

The hues of poetry, the shapes of art,
Wake in our minds no lovely ecstasy.
We hoard the dregs of feelings that are dead,
Misers, we dig and hide a debased coin.
We hate by chance, we love by accident;
We make no sacrifice to hate or love.
Within our minds presides a secret chill
Even while the flame is burning in our blood.
A bore to us our fathers' gorgeous sporting,
Their conscientious childish vast debauch.
We hasten tomb-wards without joy or glory,
With but a glance of ridicule thrown back.
A surly-hearted crowd and soon forgotten,
We pass in silence, trackless from the world,
Tossing no fruit of dreaming to the ages,
No deed of genius even half begun.
Our dust the justice of the citizen
In future time will judge in songs of venom. . . .
Will celebrate the weak and squandering father
In bitter mockery the cheated son.

THE MOUNTAIN

A golden cloud slept for her pleasure
All night on the gaunt hill's breast;
Light-heart to her play-ground of azure,
How early she sped from the nest.
But the soft moist trace of her sleeping
Lay in the folds of the hill.
He pondered; his tears are creeping
Down to the desert still.

774

GOTTHOLD EPHRAIM LESSING

GOTTHOLD EPHRAIM LESSING (German, 1729-1781). German critic and dramatist. One of the very distinguished Continental liberals. Gave up clerical career to become playwright. With Moses Mendelssohn and Nicolai, produced critical journal. *Laokoon*, famous treatise defining differences between poetry and other arts. *Nathan the Wise*, important drama pleading religious tolerance.

SALADIN AND NATHAN

Saladin.   Draw nearer, Jew—yet nearer—close to me!
Lay fear aside.
    Nathan.   Fear, Sultan, 's for your foes.
    Saladin.   Your name is Nathan?
    Nathan.   Yes.
    Saladin.   Nathan the Wise.
    Nathan.   No.
    Saladin.   But, at least the people call you so.
    Nathan.   That may be true. The people!
    Saladin.   Do you think
I treat the people's voice contemptuously.
I have been wishing long to know the man
Whom it has called the Wise.
    Nathan.   What if it named
Him so in scorn? If wise means prudent only—
And prudent, one who knows his interest well?
    Saladin.   Who knows his real interest, you mean.
    Nathan.   Then, Sultan, selfish men were the most prudent,
And wise, and prudent, then, would mean the same.
    Saladin.   You're proving what your speeches contradict.
You know the real interests of man:
The people know them not—have never sought
To know them. That alone can make man wise.
    Nathan.   Which every man conceives himself to be.
    Saladin.   A truce to modesty! To meet it ever,
When we are seeking truth is wearisome. (*Springs up.*)
So, let us to the point. Be candid, Jew,
Be frank and honest.
    Nathan.   I will serve you, prince,
And prove that I am worthy of your favor.
    Saladin.   How will you serve me?

Nathan.   You shall have the best
Of all I have, and at the cheapest rate.
   Saladin.   What mean you? Not your wares?—My sister, then,
Shall make the bargain with you. (That's for the listener!)
I am not versed in mercantile affairs,
And with a merchant's craft I've naught to do.
   Nathan.   Doubtless you would inquire if I have marked
Upon my route the movements of the foe?
Whether he's stirring? If I may presume——
   Saladin.   Neither was that my object. On that point
I know enough. But hear me.
   Nathan.   I obey.
   Saladin.   It is another, a far different thing
On which I seek for wisdom; and since you
Are called the Wise, tell me which faith or law
You deem the best.
   Nathan.   Sultan, I am a Jew.
   Saladin.—And I a Mussulman. The Christian stands
Between us. Here are three religions, then,
And of these three one only can be true.
A man like you remains not where his birth
By accident has cast him; or if so,
Conviction, choice, or ground of preference,
Supports him. Let me, Nathan, hear from you,
In confidence, the reasons of your choice.
Which I have lacked the leisure to examine.
It may be, Nathan, that I am the first
Sultan who has indulged this strange caprice,
Which need not, therefore, make a Sultan blush.
Am I first? Nay, speak; or if you seek
A brief delay to shape your scattered thoughts,
I yield it freely. (Has she overheard?
She will inform me if I've acted right.)
Reflect then, Nathan, I shall soon return.
(Exit.)

   Nathan. (*alone*).   Strange! how is this? What can the Sultan
want?
I came prepared for cash—he asks for truth!
Truth! as if truth were cash! A coin disused—
Valued by weight! If so, 'twere well, indeed!
But coin quite new, not coin but for the die,

776

To be flung down and on the counter told—
It is not that. Like gold tied up in bags,
Will truth lie hoarded in the wise man's head,
To be produced at need? Now, in this case,
Which of us plays the Jew? He asks for truth.
Is truth what he requires? his aim, his end?
Or does he use it as a subtle snare?
That were too petty for his noble mind.
Yet what is e'er too petty for the great?
Did he not rush at once into the house,
Whilst, as a friend, he would have paused or knocked?
I must beware. Yet to repel him now,
And act the stubborn Jew, is not the thing;
And wholly to fling off the Jew, still less.
For if no Jew, he might with justice ask,
Why not a Mussulman?—That thought may serve.—
Others than children may be quieted
With tales well told. But see, he comes—he comes.

    Saladin. (*aside*). (The coast is clear)—I am not come too soon?
Have you reflected on this matter, Nathan?
Speak! no one hears.

    Nathan. Would all the world might hear!

    Saladin. And are you of your cause so confident.
'Tis wise, indeed, of you to hide no truth,
For truth to hazard all, even life and goods.

    Nathan. Ay, when necessity and profit bid.

    Saladin. I hope that henceforth I shall rightly bear
One of my names, "Reformer of the world
And of the law!"

    Nathan. A noble title, truly;
But, Sultan, ere I quite explain myself,
Permit me to relate a tale.

    Saladin. Why not?
I ever was a friend of tales well told.

    Nathan. Well told! Ah, Sultan! that's another thing.

    Saladin. What! still so proudly modest? But begin.

    Nathan. In days of yore, there dwelt in Eastern lands
A man, who from a valued hand received
A ring of priceless worth. An opal stone
Shot from within an ever-changing hue,
And held this virtue in its form concealed,

To render him of God and man beloved,
Who wore it in this fixed unchanging faith.
No wonder that its Eastern owner ne'er
Withdrew it from his finger, and resolved
That to his house the ring should be secured.
Therefore he thus bequeathed it: first to him
Who was the most beloved of his sons,
Ordaining then that he should leave the ring
To the most dear among his children; then,
That without heeding birth, the fav'rite son,
In virtue of the ring alone, should still
Be lord of all the house. You hear me, Sultan?
    Saladin. I understand. Proceed.
    Nathan. From son to son,
The ring at length descended to a sire
Who had three sons, alike obedient to him,
And whom he loved with just and equal love.
The first, the second, and the third, in turn,
According as they each apart received
The overflowings of his heart, appeared
Most worthy, as his heir, to take the ring,
Which, with good-natured weakness, he in turn
Had promised privately to each; and thus
Things lasted for a while. But death approached,
The father now embarrassed, could not bear
To disappoint two sons, who trusted him.
What's to be done? In secret he commands
The jeweler to come, that from the form
Of the true ring, he may bespeak two more.
Nor cost nor pains are to be spared, to make
The rings alike—quite like the true one. This
The artist managed. When the rings were brought
The father's eye could not distinguish which
Had been the model. Overjoyed, he calls
His sons, takes leave of each apart—bestows
His blessing and his ring on each—and dies.
You hear me?
    Saladin. (*who has turned away in perplexity*). Ay! I hear. Conclude the tale.
    Nathan. 'Tis ended, Sultan! All that follows next
May well be guessed. Scarce is the father dead,

When with his ring each separate son appears,
And claims to be the lord of all the house.
Question arises, tumult and debate—
But all in vain—the true ring could no more
Be then distinguished than—(*after a pause, in which he awaits the
Sultan's reply*) the true faith now.
    Saladin.   Is that your answer to my question?
    Nathan.   No!
But it may serve as my apology.
I cannot venture to decide between
Rings which the father had expressly made,
To baffle those who would distinguish them.
    Saladin.   Rings, Nathan! Come, a truce to this! **The creeds**
Which I have named have broad, distinctive marks,
Differing in raiment, food, and drink!
    Nathan.   'Tis true!
But then they differ not in their foundation.
Are not all built on history alike,
Traditional or written? History
Must be received on trust. Is it not so?
In whom are we most likely to put trust?
In our own people? in those very men
Whose blood we are? who, from our earliest youth,
Have proved their love for us, have ne'er deceived,
Except in cases where 'twere better so?
Why should I credit my forefathers less
Than you do yours? or can I ask of you
To charge your ancestors with falsehood, that
The praise of truth may be bestowed on mine?
And so of Christians.
    Saladin.   By our Prophet's faith,
The man is right. I have no more to say.
    Nathan.   Now let us to our rings once more **return.**
We said the sons complained; each to the judge
Swore from his father's hand immediately
To have received the ring—as was the case—
In virtue of a promise that he should
One day enjoy the ring's prerogative.
In this they spoke the truth. Then each maintained
It was not possible that to himself
His father had been false. Each could not think

His father guilty of an act so base.
Rather than that, reluctant as he was
To judge his brethren, he must yet declare
Some treach'rous act of falsehood had been done.

 Saladin. Well! and the judge? I'm curious now to hear
What you will make him say. Go on, go on!

 Nathan. The judge said: If the father is not brought
Before my seat, I cannot judge the case.
Am I to judge enigmas? Do you think
That the true ring will here unseal its lips?
But, hold! You tell me that the real ring
Enjoys the secret power to make the man
Who wears it, both by God and man beloved.
Let that decide. Who of the three is loved
Best by his brethren? Is there no reply?
What! do these love-exciting rings alone
Act inwardly? Have they no outward charm?
Does each one love himself alone? You're all
Deceived deceivers. All your rings are false.
The real ring, perchance, has disappeared;
And so your father, to supply the loss,
Has caused three rings to fill the place of one.

 Saladin. O, charming, charming!

 Nathan. And, the judge continued,
If you insist on judgment, and refuse
My counsel, be it so. I recommend
That you consider how the matter stands.
Each from his father has received a ring:
Let each then think the real ring his own.
Your father, possibly, desired to free
His power from one ring's tyrannous control.
He loved you all with an impartial love,
And equally, and had no inward wish
To prove the measure of his love for one ·
By pressing heavily upon the rest.
Therefore, let each one imitate this love;
So, free from prejudice, let each one aim
To emulate his brethren in the strife
To prove the virtues of his several ring,
By offices of kindness and of love,
And trust in God. And if, in years to come,

The virtues of the ring shall reappear
Amongst your children, then, once more
Come to this judgment seat. A greater far
Than I shall sit upon it, and decide.
So spake the modest judge.

Saladin. O God, O God!

Nathan. And if now, Saladin, you think you're he——

Saladin (approaches Nathan *and takes his hand, which he retains
to the end of the scene).* This promised judge— I? Dust! I?
—Naught! O God!

Nathan. What is the matter, Sultan?

Saladin. Dearest Nathan!
That judge's thousand years are not yet past;
His judgment seat is not for me. But go,
And still remain my friend.

Nathan. Has Saladin aught else to say?

Saladin. No.

Nathan. Nothing?

Saladin. Truly nothing.

Nathan. I could have wished
An opportunity to ask a boon.

Saladin. Wait not for opportunity. Speak now.

Nathan. I have been trav'ling, and am just returned
From a long journey, from collecting debts.
Hard cash is troublesome these perilous times,
I know not where I may bestow it safely.
These coming wars need money; and, perchance,
You can employ it for me, Saladin?

Saladin. (fixing his eyes upon Nathan*).* I ask not, Nathan, have
you seen Al-Hafi?
Nor if some shrewd suspicion of your own
Moves you to make this offer.

Nathan. What suspicion?

Saladin. I do not ask—forgive me,—it is just,
For what avails concealment? I confess
I was about——

Nathan. To ask this very thing?

Saladin. Yes!

Nathan. Then our objects are at once fulfilled.

781

SINCLAIR LEWIS

SINCLAIR LEWIS (American, 1885-1951). The satirist of American middle-class life. After six early novels, achieved recognition with *Main Street*, followed by *Babbitt, Arrowsmith, Dodsworth*. Later work less effective, except for *It Can't Happen Here*, exposing perils of Fascism. First American to win Nobel Prize in Literature, 1930.

YOUNG MAN AXELBROD

THE cottonwood is a tree of a slovenly and plebeian habit. Its woolly wisps turn gray the lawns and engender neighborhood hostilities about our town. Yet it is a mighty tree, a refuge and an inspiration; the sun flickers in its towering foliage, whence the tattoo of locusts enlivens our dusty summer afternoons. From the wheat country out to the sagebrush plains between the buttes and the Yellowstone it is the cottonwood that keeps a little grateful shade for sweating homesteaders.

In Joralemon we call Knute Axelbrod "Old Cottonwood." As a matter of fact, the name was derived not so much from the quality of the man as from the wide grove about his gaunt white house and red barn. He made a comely row of trees on each side of the country road, so that a humble, daily sort of a man, driving beneath them in his lumber wagon, might fancy himself lord of a private avenue.

And at sixty-five Knute was like one of his own cottonwoods, his roots deep in the soil, his trunk weathered by rain and blizzard and baking August noons, his crown spread to the wide horizon of day and the enormous sky of a prairie night.

This immigrant was an American even in speech. Save for a weakness about his j's and w's, he spoke the twangy Yankee English of the land. He was the more American because in his native Scandinavia he had dreamed of America as a land of light. Always through disillusion and weariness he beheld America as the world's nursery for justice, for broad, fair towns, and eager talk; and always he kept a young soul that dared to desire beauty.

As a lad Knute Axelbrod had wished to be a famous scholar, to learn the ease of foreign tongues, the romance of history, to unfold in the graciousness of wise books. When he first came to America he worked in a sawmill all day and studied all evening. He mastered enough book-learning to teach district school for two terms; then, when he was only eighteen, a great-hearted pity for faded little Lena Wesselius moved him to marry her. Gay enough, doubtless, was their hike by prairie schooner to new farmlands, but Knute was promptly caught in a net of poverty and family. From eighteen to fifty-eight he was always snatching children away from death or the farm away from mortgages.

He had to be content—and generously content he was—with the second-hand glory of his children's success and, for himself, with pilfered hours of reading—that reading of big, thick, dismal volumes of history and economics which the lone mature learner chooses. Without ever losing his desire for strange cities and the dignity of towers he stuck to his farm. He acquired a half-section, free from debt, fertile, well-stocked, adorned with a cement silo, a chicken-run, a new windmill. He became comfortable, secure, and then he was ready, it seemed, to die; for at sixty-three his work was done, and he was unneeded and alone.

His wife was dead. His sons had scattered afar, one a dentist in Fargo, another a farmer in the Golden Valley. He had turned over his farm to his daughter and son-in-law. They had begged him to live with them, but Knute refused.

"No," he said, "you must learn to stand on your own feet. I vill not give you the farm. You pay me four hundred dollars a year rent, and I live on that and vatch you from my hill."

On a rise beside the lone cottonwood which he loved best of all his trees Knute built a tar-paper shack, and here he "bached it"; cooked his meals, made his bed, sometimes sat in the sun, read many books from the Joralemon library, and began to feel that he was free of the yoke of citizenship which he had borne all his life.

For hours at a time he sat on a backless kitchen chair before the shack, a wide-shouldered man, white-bearded, motionless; a seer despite his grotesquely baggy trousers, his collarless shirt. He looked across the miles of stubble to the steeple of the Jackrabbit Forks church and meditated upon the uses of life. At first he could not break the rigidity of habit. He rose at five, found work in cleaning his cabin and cultivating his garden, had dinner exactly at twelve, and went to bed by afterglow. But little by little he discovered that he could be irregular without being arrested. He stayed abed till seven or even eight. He got a large, deliberate, tortoise-shell cat, and played games with it; let it lap milk upon the table, called it the Princess, and confided to it that he had a "sneaking idee", that men were fools to work so hard. Around this coatless old man, his stained waistcoat flapping about a huge torso, in a shanty of rumpled bed and pine table covered with sheets of food-daubed newspaper, hovered all the passionate aspiration of youth and the dreams of ancient beauty.

He began to take long walks by night. In his necessitous life night had ever been a period of heavy slumber in close rooms. Now he discovered the mystery of the dark; saw the prairies wide-flung and misty beneath the moon, heard the voices of grass and cottonwoods and drowsy birds. He tramped for miles. His boots were dew-soaked, but he did not heed. He stopped upon hillocks, shyly threw wide his arms, and stood worshiping the naked, slumbering land.

These excursions he tried to keep secret, but they were bruited abroad. Neighbors, good, decent fellows with no sense about walking in the dew at night, when they were returning late from town, drunk, lashing their horses and flinging whisky bottles from racing democrat wagons, saw him, and they spread the tidings that Old Cottonwood was "getting nutty since he gave up his farm to that son-in-law of his and retired. Seen the old codger wandering around at midnight. Wish I had his chance to sleep. Wouldn't catch me out in the night air."

Any rural community from Todd Center to Seringapatam is resentful of any person who varies from its standard, and is morbidly fascinated by any hint of madness. The countryside began to spy on Knute Axelbrod, to ask him questions, and to stare from the road at his shack. He was sensitively aware of it, and inclined to be surly to inquisitive acquaintances. Doubtless that was the beginning of his great pilgrimage.

As a part of the general wild license of his new life—really, he once roared at that startled cat, the Princess: "By gollies! I ain't going to brush my teeth tonight. All my life I've brushed 'em, and alvays vanted to skip a time vunce"—Knute took considerable pleasure in degenerating in his taste in scholarship. He wilfully declined to finish *The Conquest of Mexico*, and began to read light novels borrowed from the Joralemon library. So he rediscovered the lands of dancing and light wines, which all his life he had desired. Some economics and history he did read, but every evening he would stretch out in his buffalo-horn chair, his feet on the cot and the Princess in his lap, and invade Zenda or fall in love with Trilby.

Among the novels he chanced upon a highly optimistic story of Yale in which a worthy young man "earned his way through" college, stroked the crew, won Phi Beta Kappa, and had the most entertaining, yet moral, conversations on or adjacent to "the dear old fence."

As a result of this chronicle, at about three o'clock one morning, when Knute Axelbrod was sixty-four years of age, he decided that he would go to college. All his life he had wanted to. Why not do it?

When he awoke he was not so sure about it as when he had gone to sleep. He saw himself as ridiculous, a ponderous, oldish man among clean-limbed youths, like a dusty cottonwood among silver birches. But for months he wrestled and played with that idea of a great pilgrimage to the Mount of Muses; for he really supposed college to be that sort of place. He believed that all college students, except for the wealthy idlers, burned to acquire learning. He pictured Harvard and Yale and Princeton as ancient groves set with marble temples, before which large groups of Grecian youths talked gently about astronomy and good government. In his picture they never cut classes or ate.

With a longing for music and books and graciousness such as the most ambitious boy could never comprehend, this thick-faced farmer dedicated himself to beauty, and defied the unconquerable power of approaching old age. He sent for college catalogues and school books, and diligently began to prepare himself for college.

He found Latin irregular verbs and the whimsicalities of algebra fiendish. They had nothing to do with actual life as he had lived it. But he mastered them; he studied twelve hours a day, as once he had plodded through eighteen hours a day in the hayfield. With history and English he knew much of them from his recreative reading. From German neighbors he had picked up enough Plattdeutsch to make German easy. The trick of study began to come back to him from his small school teaching of forty-five years before. He began to believe that he could really put it through. He kept assuring himself that in college, with rare and sympathetic instructors to help him, there would not be this baffling search, this nervous strain.

But the unreality of the things he studied did disillusion him, and

785

he tired of his new game. He kept it up chiefly because all his life he had kept up onerous labor without any taste for it. Toward the autumn of the second year of his eccentric life he no longer believed that he would ever go to college.

Then a busy little grocer stopped him on the street in Joralemon and quizzed him about his studies, to the delight of the informal club which always loafs at the corner of the hotel.

Knute was silent, but dangerously angry. He remembered just in time how he had once laid wrathful hands upon a hired man, and somehow the man's collar bone had been broken. He turned away and walked home, seven miles, still boiling. He picked up the Princess, and, with her mewing on his shoulder, tramped out again to enjoy the sunset.

He stopped at a reedy slough. He gazed at a hopping plover without seeing it. Suddenly he cried:

"I am going to college. It opens next veek. I t'ink that I can pass the examinations."

Two days later he had moved the Princess and his sticks of furniture to his son-in-law's house, had bought a new slouch hat, a celluloid collar and a solemn suit of black, had wrestled with God in prayer through all of a star-clad night, and had taken the train for Minneapolis, on the way to New Haven.

While he stared out of the car window Knute was warning himself that the millionaires' sons would make fun of him. Perhaps they would haze him. He bade himself avoid all these sons of Belial and cleave to his own people, those who "earned their way through."

At Chicago he was afraid with a great fear of the lightning flashes that the swift crowds made on his retina, the batteries of ranked motor cars that charged at him. He prayed, and ran fo: his train to New York. He came at last to New Haven.

Not with gibing rudeness, but with politely quizzical eyebrows, Yale received him, led him through entrance examinations, which after sweaty plowing with the pen, he barely passed, and found for him a roommate. The roommate was a large-browed soft white grub named Ray Gribble, who had been teaching school in New England and seemed chiefly to desire college training so that he might make more money as a teacher. Ray Gribble was a hustler, he instantly got work tutoring the awkward son of a steel ma: and for board he waited on table.

He was Knute's chief acquaintance. Knute tried to fool him.sft into thinking he liked the grub, but Ray couldn't keep his da:)

hands off the old man's soul. He had the skill of a professional exhorter of young men in finding out Knute's motives, and when he discovered that Knute had a hidden desire to sip at gay, polite literature, Ray said in a shocked way:

"Strikes me a man like you, that's getting old, ought to be thinking more about saving your soul than about all these frills. You leave this poetry and stuff to these foreigners and artists, and you stick to Latin and math. and the Bible. I tell you, I've taught school, and I've learned by experience."

With Ray Gribble, Knute lived grubbily, an existence of torn comforters and smelly lamp, of lexicons and logarithm tables. No leisurely loafing by fireplaces was theirs. They roomed in West Divinity, where gather the theologues, the lesser sort of law students, a whimsical genius or two, and a horde of unplaced freshmen and "scrub seniors."

Knute was shockingly disappointed, but he stuck to his room because outside of it he was afraid. He was a grotesque figure, and he knew it, a white-polled giant squeezed into a small seat in a classroom, listening to instructors younger than his own sons. Once he tried to sit on the fence. No one but "ringers" sat on the fence any more, and at the sight of him trying to look athletic and young, two upper-class men snickered, and he sneaked away.

He came to hate Ray Gribble and his voluble companions of the submerged tenth of the class, the hewers of tutorial wood. It is doubtless safer to mock the flag than to question that best-established tradition of our democracy—that those who "earn their way through" college are necessarily stronger, braver, and more assured of success than the weaklings who talk by the fire. Every college story presents such a moral. But tremblingly the historian submits that Knute discovered that waiting on table did not make lads more heroic than did football or happy loafing. Fine fellows, cheerful and fearless, were many of the boys who "earned their way," and able to talk to richer classmates without fawning; but just as many of them assumed an abject respectability as the most convenient pose. They were pickers up of unconsidered trifles; they toadied to the classmates whom they tutored; they wriggled before the faculty committee on scholarships; they looked pious at Dwight Hall prayer-meetings to make an impression on the serious minded; and they drank one glass of beer at Jake's to show the light minded that they meant nothing offensive by their piety. In revenge for cringing to the insolent athletes whom they tutored, they would, when safe among their own kind, yammer about the "lack of democracy of college today." Not that they were so indiscreet as to do anything about it. They lacked the stuff of really rebellious souls. Knute listened to them and marveled. They sounded like young hired men talking behind his barn at harvest time.

This submerged tenth hated the dilettantes of the class even more than they hated the bloods. Against one Gilbert Washburn, a rich esthete with more manner than any freshman ought to have, they raged righteously. They spoke of seriousness and industry till Knute, who might once have desired to know lads like Washburn, felt ashamed of himself as a wicked, wasteful old man.

Humbly though he sought, he found no inspiration and no comradeship. He was the freak of the class, and aside from the submerged tenth, his classmates were afraid of being "queered" by being seen with him.

As he was still powerful, one who could take up a barrel of pork on his knees, he tried to find friendship among the athletes. He sat at Yale Field, watching the football tryouts, and tried to get acquainted with the candidates. They stared at him and answered his questions grudgingly—beefy youths who in their simple-hearted way showed that they considered him plain crazy.

The place itself began to lose the haze of magic through which he had first seen it. Earth is earth, whether one sees it in Camelot or Joralemon or on the Yale campus—or possibly even in the Harvard yard! The buildings ceased to be temples to Knute; they became structures of brick or stone, filled with young men who lounged at windows and watched him amusedly as he tried to slip by.

The Gargantuan hall of Commons became a tri-daily horror because at the table where he dined were two youths who, having uncommonly penetrating minds, discerned that Knute had a beard, and courageously told the world about it. One of them, named Atchison, was a superior person, very industrious and scholarly, glib in mathematics and manners. He despised Knute's lack of definite purpose in coming to college. The other was a play-boy, a wit and a stealer of street signs, who had a wonderful sense for a subtle jest; and his references to Knute's beard shook the table with jocund mirth three times a day. So these youths of gentle birth drove the shambling, wistful old man away from Commons, and thereafter he ate at the lunch counter at the Black Cat.

788

Lacking the stimulus of friendship, it was the harder for Knute to keep up the strain of studying the long assignments. What had been a week's pleasant reading in his shack was now thrown at him as a day's task. But he would not have minded the toil if he could have found one as young as himself. They were all so dreadfully old, the money-earners, the serious laborers at athletics, the instructors who worried over their life work of putting marks in class-record books.

Then, on a sore, bruised day, Knute did meet one who was young.

Knute had heard that the professor who was the idol of the college had berated the too-earnest lads in his Browning class, and insisted that they read *Alice in Wonderland*. Knute floundered dustily about in a second-hand bookshop till he found an "Alice," and he brought it home to read over his lunch of a hot-dog sandwich. Something in the grave absurdity of the book appealed to him, and he was chuckling over it when Ray Gribble came into the room and glanced at the reader.

"Huh!" said Mr. Gribble.

"That's a fine, funny book," said Knute.

"Huh! *Alice in Wonderland!* I've heard of it. Silly nonsense. Why don't you read something really fine, like Shakespeare or *Paradise Lost?*"

"Vell——" said Knute, all he could find to say.

With Ray Gribble's glassy eye on him, he could no longer roll and roar with the book. He wondered if indeed he ought not to be reading Milton's pompous anthropological misconceptions. He went unhappily out to an early history class, ably conducted by Blevins, Ph.D.

Knute admired Blevins, Ph.D. He was so tubbed and eyeglassed and terribly right. But most of Blevins' lambs did not like Blevins. They said he was a "crank." They read newspapers in his class and covertly kicked one another.

In the smug, plastered classroom, his arm leaning heavily on the board tablet-arm of his chair, Knute tried not to miss one of Blevins' sardonic proofs that the correct date of the second marriage of Themistocles was two years and seven days later than the date assigned by that illiterate ass, Frutari of Padua. Knute admired young Blevins' performance, and he felt virtuous in application to these hard, unnonsensical facts.

He became aware that certain lewd fellows of the lesser sort were playing poker just behind him. His prairie-trained ear caught whispers of "Two to dole," and "Raise you two beans." Knute revolved, and frowned upon these mockers of sound learning. As he turned back he was aware that the offenders were chuckling, and continuing their game. He saw that Blevins, Ph.D., perceived that something was wrong; he frowned, but he said nothing. Knute sat in meditation. He saw Blevins as merely a boy. He was sorry for him. He would do the boy a good turn.

When class was over he hung about Blevins' desk till the other students had clattered out. He rumbled:

"Say, Professor, you're a fine fellow. I do something for you. If any of the boys make themselves a nuisance, you yust call on me, and I spank the son of a guns."

Blevins, Ph.D., spake in a manner of culture and nastiness:

"Thanks so much, Axelbrod, but I don't fancy that will ever be necessary. I am supposed to be a reasonably good disciplinarian. Good day. Oh, one moment. There's something I've been wishing to speak to you about. I do wish you wouldn't try quite so hard to show off whenever I call on you during quizzes. You answer at such needless length, and you smile as though there were something highly amusing about me. I'm quite willing to have you regard me as a humorous figure, privately, but there are certain classroom conventions, you know, certain little conventions."

"Why, Professor!" wailed Knute, "I never make fun of you! I didn't know I smile. If I do, I guess it's yust because I am so glad when my stupid old head gets the lesson good."

"Well, well, that's very gratifying, I'm sure. And if you will be a little more careful——"

Blevins, Ph.D., smiled a toothy, frozen smile, and trotted off to the Graduates' Club, to be witty about old Knute and his way of saying "yust," while in the deserted classroom Knute sat chill, an old man and doomed. Through the windows came the light of Indian summer; clean, boyish cries rose from the campus. But the lover of autumn smoothed his baggy sleeve, stared at the blackboard, and there saw only the gray of October stubble about his distant shack. As he pictured the college watching him, secretly making fun of him and his smile, he was now faint and ashamed, now bull-angry. He was lonely for his cat, his fine chair of buffalo horns, the sunny doorstep of his shack, and the understanding land. He had been in college for about one month.

Before he left the classroom he stepped behind the instructor's desk and looked at an imaginary class.

"I might have stood there as a prof if I could have come earlier," he said softly to himself.

Calmed by the liquid autumn gold that flowed through the streets, he walked out Whitney Avenue toward the butte-like hill of East Rock. He observed the caress of the light upon the scarped rock, heard the delicate music of leaves, breathed in air pregnant with tales of old New England. He exulted: " 'Could write poetry now if yust—if I yust could write poetry!"

He climbed to the top of East Rock, whence he could see the Yale buildings like the towers of Oxford, and see Long Island Sound, and the white glare of Long Island beyond the water. He marveled that Axelbrod of the cottonwood country was looking across an arm of the Atlantic to New York state. He noticed a freshman on a bench at the edge of the rock, and he became irritated. The freshman was Gilbert Washburn, the snob, the dilettante, of whom Ray Gribble had once said: "That guy is the disgrace of the class. He doesn't go out for anything, high stand or Dwight Hall or anything else. Thinks he's so doggone much better than the rest of the fellows that he doesn't associate with anybody. Thinks he's literary, they say, and yet he doesn't even heel the 'Lit,' like the regular literary fellows! Got no time for a loafing, mooning snob like that."

As Knute stared at the unaware Gil, whose profile was fine in outline against the sky, he was terrifically public-spirited and disapproving and that sort of moral thing. Though Gil was much too well dressed, he seemed moodily discontented.

"What he needs is to vork in a threshing crew and sleep in the hay," grumbled Knute almost in the virtuous manner of Gribble. "Then he vould know when he vas vell off, and not look like he had the earache. Pff!" Gil Washburn rose, trailed toward Knute, glanced at him, sat down on Knute's bench.

"Great view!" he said. His smile was eager.

That smile symbolized to Knute all the art of life he had come to college to find. He tumbled out of his moral attitude with ludicrous haste, and every wrinkle of his weathered face creased deep as he answered:

"Yes: I t'ink the Acropolis must be like this here."

"Say, look here, Axelbrod; I've been thinking about you."

"Yas?"

"We ought to know each other. We two are the class scandal. We came here to dream, and these busy little goats like Atchison and Giblets, or whatever your roommate's name is, think we're fools not to go out for marks. You may not agree with me, but I've decided that you and I are precisely alike."

"What makes you t'ink I come here to dream?" bristled Knute.

"Oh, I used to sit near you at Commons and hear you try to quell old Atchison whenever he got busy discussing the reasons for coming to college. That old, moth-eaten topic! I wonder if Cain and Abel didn't discuss it at the Eden Agricultural College. You know, Abel the markgrabber, very pious and high stand, and Cain wanting to read poetry."

"Yes," said Knute, "and I guess Prof. Adam say, 'Cain, don't you read this poetry; it von't help you in algebry.'"

"Of course. Say, wonder if you'd like to look at this volume of Musset I was sentimental enough to lug up here today. Picked it up when I was abroad last year."

From his pocket Gil drew such a book as Knute had never seen before, a slender volume, in a strange language, bound in hand-tooled crushed levant, an effeminate bibelot over which the prairie farmer gasped with luxurious pleasure. The book almost vanished in his big hands. With a timid forefinger he stroked the levant, ran through the leaves.

"I can't read it, but that's the kind of book I alvays t'ought there must be some like it." he sighed.

"Listen!" cried Gil. "Ysaye is playing up at Hartford tonight. Let's go hear him. We'll trolley up. Tried to get some of the fellows to come, but they thought I was a nut."

What an Ysaye was, Knute Axelbrod had no notion; but "Sure!" he boomed.

When they got to Hartford they found that between them they had just enough money to get dinner, hear Ysaye from gallery seats, and return only as far as Meriden. At Meriden Gil suggested:

"Let's walk back to New Haven, then. Can you make it?"

Knute had no knowledge as to whether it was four miles or forty back to the campus, but "Sure!" he said. For the last few months he had been noticing that, despite his bulk, he had to be careful, but tonight he could have flown.

In the music of Ysaye, the first real musician he had ever heard,

Knute had found all the incredible things of which he had slowly been reading in William Morris and "Idylls of the King." Tall cnights he had beheld, and slim princesses in white samite, the misty gates of forlorn towns, and the glory of the chivalry that never was.

They did walk, roaring down the road beneath the October moon, stopping to steal apples and to exclaim over silvered hills, taking a puerile and very natural joy in chasing a profane dog. It was Gil who talked, and Knute who listened, for the most part; but Knute was lured into tales of the pioneer days, of blizzards, of harvesting, and of the first flame of the green wheat. Regarding the Atchisons and Gribbles of the class both of them were youthfully bitter and supercilious. But they were not bitter long, for they were atavisms tonight. They were wandering minstrels, Gilbert the troubadour with his man-at-arms.

They reached the campus at about five in the morning. Fumbling for words that would express hs feeling, Knute stammered:

"Vell, it vas fine. I go to bed now and I dream about——"

"Bed? Rats! Never believe in winding up a party when it's going strong. Too few good parties. Besides, it's only the shank of the evening. Besides, we're hungry. Besides—oh, besides! Wait here a second. I'm going up to my room to get some money, and we'll have some eats. Wait! Please do!"

Knute would have waited all night. He had lived almost seventy years and traveled fifteen hundred miles and endured Ray Gribble to find Gil Washburn.

Policemen wondered to see the celluloid-collared old man and the expensive-looking boy rolling arm in arm down Chapel Street in search of a restaurant suitable to poets. They were all closed.

"The Ghetto will be awake by now," said Gil. "We'll go buy some eats and take 'em up to my room. I've got some tea there."

Knute shouldered through dark streets beside him as naturally as though he had always been a nighthawk, with an aversion to anything as rustic as beds. Down on Oak Street, a place of low shops, smoky lights and alley mouths, they found the slum already astir. Gil contrived to purchase boxed biscuits, cream cheese. chicken-loaf, a bottle of cream. While Gil was chaffering, Knute stared out into the street milkily lighted by wavering gas and the first feebleness of coming day; he gazed upon Kosher signs and advertisements in Russian letters, shawled women and bearded rabbis; and as he looked he gathered contentment which he could never lose. He had traveled abroad tonight.

The room of Gil Washburn was all the useless, pleasant things Knute wanted it to be. There was more of Gil's Paris days in it than of his freshmanhood: Persian rugs, a silver tea service, etchings, and books. Knute Axelbrod of the tar-paper shack and piggy farmyards gazed in satisfaction. Vast, bearded, sunk in an easy chair, he clucked amiably while Gil lighted a fire.

Over supper they spoke of great men and heroic ideals. It was good talk, and not unspiced with lively references to Gribble and Atchison and Blevins, all asleep now in their correct beds. Gil read snatches of Stevenson and Anatole France; then at last he read his own poetry.

It does not matter whether that poetry was good or bad. To Knute it was a miracle to find one who actually wrote it.

The talk grew slow, and they began to yawn. Knute was sensitive to the lowered key of their Indian-summer madness, and he hastily rose. As he said good-by he felt as though he had but to sleep a little while and return to his unending night of romance.

But he came out of the dormitory upon day. It was six-thirty of the morning, with a still, hard light upon red-brick walls.

"I can go to his room plenty times now; I find my friend," Knute said. He held tight the volume of Musset, which Gil had begged him to take.

As he started to walk the few steps to West Divinity Knute felt very tired. By daylight the adventure seemed more and more incredible.

As he entered the dormitory he sighed heavily:

"Age and youth, I guess they can't team together long." As he mounted the stairs he said: "If I saw the boy again, he vould get tired of me. I tell him all I got to say." And as he opened his door, he added: "This is what I come to college for—this one night. I go avay before I spoil it."

He wrote a note to Gil, and began to pack his telescope. He did not even wake Ray Gribble, sonorously sleeping in the stale air.

At five that afternoon, on the day coach of a westbound train, an old man sat smiling. A lasting content was in his eyes, and in his hands a small book in French.

LIN HO-CHING

LIN HO-CHING (Chinese, 967-1028). A rustic word painter of the Sung Period. Received classical Chinese education. Due to delicate health, retired to home in the country. Also a skillful painter, fond of plum trees. Poetry simple, serene, refined.

MAKING A POEM ON MY DEAR PLUM BLOSSOM

All these years I have been the owner of this pretty garden,
And have never written a poem to my beloved plum blossom.
Patiently I wait for your buds to open and bloom.
The moon has shed her light upon you many times.
The lonely scene is always reflected in the moonlight.
Still prettier looks the evening landscape in the falling snow.
Let me only talk about your pure scent, and I never feel lonely
    and sad,
For I am always singing and drinking to keep you company.

WEST LAKE

How wonderful and skillful is the universal spirit!
Though itself shapeless, it has formed the West Lake
Like a beautiful picture painted on a screen.
In Spring its water is purer than the eyes of a monk.
A greenish-blue sheen is spread like a veil over the evening hills.

My hut's white-washed walls reflect the moving shadow of a fish.
A crane's feather drops upon the dewy orchid.
The boat drifts along to the sounds of a flute.
In gentle breeze and slanting rain these are vague and distant.

THE SHADOWS OF SPRING

It looks like rain. This is the time for meditation.
When drunk I enjoy lying in the shadows in Spring.
It is so cold that I pity myself and the swallow.
I fear the pear blossoms cannot endure this cold night breeze.
My thin curtain cannot keep off the chilly wind.

Even a far-playing flute saddens me.
In the garden and fields a bitter wind blows.
And the fragrant flowers seem to sense the danger.

IN RETREAT

Few people pass through my humble door.
My hut lies near by the tree-covered hills.
When I fish at evening a lake breeze refreshes me.
The scent of sun-warmed Spring flowers makes me drowsy.
Little by little the moss becomes like a smooth cloth.
Bolstering the edges of the rock
Why stand so many people by the cave?
Perhaps they wait for an immortal there.

LI PO

LI PO (Chinese, 701-762). Greatest of the Chinese lyricists. A wandering, melancholy troubadour. Occasionally accepted employment—for two years a court poet. Imprisoned briefly for involvement in a rebellion just before death. His lyrics the model for spontaneous romantic verse in China. Poetry gives impression that he lived for the moment, intoxicated by nature, wine or love.

WEEP NOT, YOUNG WOMEN

It is always in sad Autumn that our enemies sweep down from their mountains to invade us.

The trumpets summon the warriors! They will ride on till they reach the Great Wall, and then they will ride beyond it out on the great Kobi desert.

There, only the cold bare moon. Only cold beads of dew on swords and shields. How they shiver!

Weep not, young women . . . this is no time to start your weeping. Who knows how long that you must weep?

THE FISHERMAN

The earth has swallowed the snow. Again we see the plum-trees in blossom.

The new willow-leaves are gold, the waters of the lakes are silver.

Now the butterflies powdered with gold lay velvet heads within the hearts of flowers.

In his still boat the fisherman pulls up his dripping net, rippling the still water.

He thinks of a girl at home, like a dark swallow in the nest. He think of a girl at home, waiting like a swallow for her mate.

BIRDS SINGING AT DUSK

The cool wind of evening blows bird-song to the window where a maiden sits. She is embroidering bright flowers on a piece of silk.

Her head is raised; her work falls through her fingers; her thoughts have flown to him who is away.

"A bird can easily find its mate among the leaves, but all a maiden's tears, falling like rain from Heaven, will not bring back her distant lover."

She bends again to her embroidery: "I will weave a little verse among these flowers of his robe . . . perhaps he will read it and come back again."

PICKING THE LOTUS

My boat is rising and falling underneath the harvest moon. Drifting alone on the Southern Lake, I reach to pick the white flowers of the lotus.

Fierce desire pulls me . . . I yearn to tell them of my passion. Alas, my boat floats away at the mercy of the moving current. My heart looks back in sadness.

SONG OF CHANG-KAN

When you were but a schoolboy
  And I a little lass,
You used to walk on bamboo stilts—
  I peeped to see you pass.
We were such merry children
  In the village of Chang-kan,
But now I am a woman
  And now you are a man.

I'd scarce seen fourteen summers
  When I was made your wife;
I could not raise my eyes to yours,
  Afraid of love and life.
I hid in dusky corners,
  I came not at your call,
But ere the year was ended
  Love overshadowed all.

I thought that you were steadfast
  As the lover by the stream
Who waited in the rising tide
  The lady of his dream;
But now I stand awatching
  On my terrace all alone
Like her who watched and waited
  Until she turned to stone.

You travel to the whirlpools
  And even to Chu-tang
Where chattering monkeys climb the cliff;
  I wait here in Chang-kan.
I watch your fading footprints,
  Now overgrown with green,
And though I sweep and sweep them
  They keep their mossy sheen.

Sere in my western garden
  The autumn leafage lies;
Yellow with August sunshine
  Flit pairing butterflies.

I watch them as they hover
  From bending grass to grass,
And my heart is wrung with weeping
  When I see them pass.

I've sat so long with sorrow
  My red cheeks lose their red.
Send me a letter from afar
  By tireless rider sped:
Let me but know in season
  Your boat is going through
The three grim Gorges of the West,
  And I will come to you.

I'll come as far to meet you
  As ever you may say;
The treacherous sands of the Chang-fang,
  They shall not bar my way.
No danger, toil or trouble
  Shall keep me as I go,
For now I am a woman
  And I love you so.

PASSIONATE GRIEF

A lady weeping in the night

She who rolls up her pearl-hung shade
    Is fair as any,
Yet drawn with grief are her delicate brows,
    Frail moth antennae.

Hot tears course down her cheeks—
    How fast they flow!—
But why, ah, we in the street
    Will never know.

LI SHANG-YIN

LI SHANG-YIN (Chinese, 813-858). Imaginative allegorist, who had undistinguished public career but high literary reputation. Poems formal in style, suffused with personal feeling. Many of them love poems, headed "No Title."

Part I. THE MAN

In how many folds of scented gauze patterned with phoenix tails
  is the round jade top of your awning enclosed for the night?
(Though) you have a fan like a full moon, yet your blushes find
  it hard to hide behind it.
The carts rumble by to a sound like thunder and so many words
  cannot reach you.
Otherwise it is quiet and still and the golden lamp has burnt low.
There is no word that can pass from where you are to where I am,
  where the pomegranate flowers are red.
The dappled horse is tethered to the weeping willow on the bank
Whither in the south west could we go trusting to a favorable wind?

Part II. THE WOMAN

Up here behind fold upon fold of curtains is my Mo-ch'ou Hall
After a long night the early dawn creeps slowly along.
It was in a dream that the fairy girl lived on the banks (of a river).
The small maiden who lived by the bridge after all (managed to)
  live without a husband.
The wind and waves do not realize how weak are the stems of the
  water chestnut.

A POEM WITH NO TITLE

It seems only last night that the stars shone and the wind blew;
Your quarters were at the painted tower in the west,
Mine in the pavilion of the cinnamon tree hall in the east.
Alas, to-day, I am no coloured phoenix that can fly to you with
  double wings,
But my mind is quick to apprehend spiritual affinity and can get
  through to you.
(On that evening) we sat opposite to each other and we amused

800

ourselves with sending across the hook while the spring wine was warm.

Each in our place we played "hitting the cover" to the light of red candles

Until, alas, I had to go, hearing the drum that called for the early morning audience.

Then I rode away home to the orchid tower;

Now I am like the river weed that flows this way and that.

NO TITLE

When we were able to meet it was hard enough and now we are parted for ever it is harder still;

The east wind has died down, and the hundred flowers have faded.

The silkworm of spring spins its silk up to the moment of its death;

The wax candle is burnt down to the end and only then are its tears dry.

In the morning I gaze into my mirror and grieve that my cloudy hair must change;

In the night the bright cold moon calls forth my sad songs,

(Yet after all) it is only a short road from here to paradise.

Will not the blue bird be indulgent and allow me to steal a glance.

THE INLAID ZITHER

The brocade-embroidered zither had fifty strings, no one knows why;

Each string and each support made one think of the years of one's prime.

Chuang Tzu dreamt at morning he was a butterfly.

After death, the soul of the Emperor Wang took up its brief springtime abode in the body of a nightjar,

While in the wide ocean under the bright moon the mermaids drop their tears which become pearls.

Why at Lan-t'ien in the warm sunshine does jade engender mists?

Can we hope for these kinds of portents to come again?

Or are they only things that had form once but have vanished away?

LIU CHI

LIU CHI (Chinese, 1311-1375). Most celebrated poet of the Mongol Period. Court adviser of first Ming Emperor. Prolific poet and author of philosophic dialogues. Poems distinguished by charm and feeling for beauty rather than by depth.

THE CONVENT OF SIANG-FU

So I sprang to horse at cockcrow all a fever to depart,
    Galloped, galloped to the convent, ere the calling bells were still,
Over dimpled lawns a zephyr woke the lily's jewelled heart,
    And the moon's faint crescent faltered down the cleft of wooded hill.
Oh the lonely little convent with its secret haunts of prayer!
    With its shadowed cells for dreaming, where eternities abide.
Down the cedar-scented alley not a footfall stirred the air,
    But the monks' low droning echoed in the green gloom far and wide.

NIGHT, SORROW, AND SONG

The rain's in the air
And the winds arouse,
Shaking the cinnamon boughs,
And the begonias' gay parterre;
Raising dust and wreathing mist,
Whirling all things where they list—
Leaves in many-coloured showers,
Bright petals of innumerable flowers.
Knocking at all doors their hustling
Sets the silken curtains rustling,
Till, as shrunken draughts, they creep
Into the shrouded halls of sleep,
Raise the hair and ruck the skin
Of the startled folk therein.

I am grown weary of my lonely state,
Tired of the tongueless hours that wait,
Dreaming of her whom skies of blue
And twilight æons hid from view.

Swiftly the waters take their flight
Grandly the mountains rise,
Yon birds that taper to the skies
Why have they lost their plumage bright?
Would they might bear my messages of love!
Alas! the trackless heav'ns unroll above;
From west to east the river flows,
But the waves return not to my calling;
Once more the rare magnolia blows,
But hour by hour her flowers are falling.
My jasper lyre is laid apart,
Hushed for a while the lute of jade;
I hear the beating of my heart,
And watch the moon lean down the glade.

Then, ere the shadows wane,
Out of the night's unrest
Ballad and old refrain
Lure me to seek again
The dream-built Isles of the Blest.

JACK LONDON

JACK LONDON (American, 1876-1916). Novelist, adventurer and utopian. An illegitimate child, worked for his living as a boy in California. Joined Klondike gold rush without making fortune. After *The Call of the Wild*, became one of most popular writers of his day. Wrote over 50 books inspired by faith in socialism. Well-known works: *The Sea Wolf, White Fang, Martin Eden*.

TO BUILD A FIRE

DAY HAD broken cold and grey, exceedingly cold and grey, when the man turned aside from the main Yukon trail and climbed the high earth-bank, where a dim and little-travelled trail led eastward through the fat spruce timberland. It was a steep bank, and he paused for breath at the top, excusing the act to himself by looking at his watch. It was nine o'clock. There was no sun nor a hint of sun, though there was not a cloud in the sky. It was a clear day, and yet there seemed an intangible pall over the face of things, a subtle gloom that made the day dark, and that was due to the absence of sun. This fact did not worry the man. He was used to the lack of sun. It had been days since he had seen the sun, and he knew that a few more days must pass before that cheerful orb, due south, would just peep above the sky-line and dip immediately from view.

The man flung a look back along the way he had come. The Yukon lay a mile wide and hidden under three feet of ice. On top of this ice were as many feet of snow. It was all pure white, rolling in gentle undulations where the ice-jams of the freeze-up had formed. North and south, as far as his eye could see, it was unbroken white, save for a dark hair-line that curved and twisted from around the spruce-covered island to the south, and that curved and twisted away into the north, where it disappeared behind another spruce-covered island. This dark hair-line was the trail—the main trail—that led south five hundred miles to the Chilkoot Pass, Dyea, and salt water; and that led north seventy miles to Dawson, and still on to the north a thousand miles to Nulato, and finally to St. Michael on Bering Sea, a thousand miles and a half a thousand more.

But all this—the mysterious, far-reaching hair-line trail, the absence of sun from the sky, the tremendous cold, and the strangeness and weirdness of it all—made no impression on the man. It was not because he was long used to it. He was a newcomer in the land, a *chechaquo*, and this was his first winter. The trouble with him was that he was without imagination. He was quick and alert in the things of life, but only in the things, and not in the significances. Fifty degrees below zero meant eighty-odd degrees of frost. Such fact impressed him as being cold and uncomfortable, and that was all. It did not lead him to meditate upon his frailty as a creature of temperature, and upon man's frailty in general, able only to live within certain narrow limits of heat and cold; and from there on it did not lead him to the conjectural field of immortality and man's place in the universe. Fifty degrees below zero stood for a bite of frost that hurt and that must be guarded against by the use of mittens, ear-flaps, warm moccasins, and thick socks. Fifty degrees below zero was to him just precisely fifty degrees below zero. That there should be anything more to it than that was a thought that never entered his head.

As he turned to go on, he spat speculatively. There was a sharp, explosive crackle that startled him. He spat again. And again, in the air, before it could fall to the snow, the spittle crackled. He knew that at fifty below spittle crackled on the snow, but this spittle had crackled in the air. Undoubtedly it was colder than fifty below—how much colder he did not know. But the temperature did not matter. He was bound for the old claim on the left fork of Henderson Creek, where the boys were already. They had come over across the divide from the Indian Creek country, while he had come the roundabout way to take a look at the possibilities of getting out logs in the spring from the islands in the Yukon. He would be in to camp by six o'clock; a bit after dark, it was true, but the boys would be there, a fire would be going, and a hot supper would be ready. As for lunch, he pressed his hand against the protruding bundle under his jacket. It was also under his shirt, wrapped up in a handkerchief and lying against the naked skin. It was the only way to keep the biscuits from freezing. He smiled agreeably to himself as he thought of those biscuits, each cut open and sopped in bacon grease, and each enclosing a generous slice of fried bacon.

He plunged in among the big spruce trees. The trail was faint. A foot of snow had fallen since the last sled had passed over, and he was glad he was without a sled, travelling light. In fact, he carried nothing but the lunch wrapped in the handkerchief. He was surprised, however, at the cold. It certainly was cold, he concluded, as he rubbed his numb nose and cheek-bones with his mittened hand. He was a warm-whiskered man, but the hair on his face did not protect the high cheek-bones and the eager nose that thrust itself aggressively into the frosty air.

At the man's heels trotted a dog, a big native husky, the proper wolf-dog, grey-coated and without any visible or tempermental difference from its brother, the wild wolf. The animal was depressed by the tremendous cold. It knew that it was no time for travelling. Its instinct told it a truer tale than was told to the man by the man's judgment. In reality, it was not merely colder than fifty below zero; it was colder than sixty below, than seventy below. It was seventy-five below zero. Since the freezing-point is thirty-two above zero, it meant that one hundred and seven degrees of frost obtained. The dog did not know anything about thermometers. Possibly in its brain there was no sharp consciousness of a condition of very cold such as was in the man's brain. But the brute had its instincts. It experienced a vague but menacing apprehension that subdued it and made it slink along at the man's heels, and that made it question eagerly every unwonted movement of the man as if expecting him to go into camp or to seek shelter somewhere and build a fire. The dog had learned fire, and it wanted fire, or else to burrow under the snow and cuddle its warmth away from the air.

The frozen moisture of its breathing had settled on its fur in a fine powder of frost, and especially were its jowls, muzzle, and eyelashes whitened by its crystalled breath. The man's red beard and mustache were likewise frosted, but more solidly, the deposit taking the form of ice and increasing with every warm, moist breath he exhaled. Also, the man was chewing tobacco, and the muzzle of ice held his lips so rigidly that he was unable to clear his chin when he expelled the juice. The result was that a crystal beard of the color and solidity of amber was increasing its length on his chin. If he fell down it would shatter itself, like glass, into brittle fragments. But he did not mind the appendage. It was the penalty all tobacco-chewers paid in that country, and he had been out before in two cold snaps. They had not been so cold as this, he knew, but by the spirit thermometer at Sixty Mile he knew they had been registered at fifty below and at fifty-five.

He held on through the level stretch of woods for several miles, crossed a wide flat of nigger-heads, and dropped down a bank to the frozen bed of a small stream. This was Henderson Creek, and he knew he was ten miles from the forks. He looked at his watch. It was ten o'clock. He was making four miles an hour, and he calculated that he would arrive at the forks at half-past twelve. He decided to celebrate that event by eating his lunch there.

The dog dropped in again at his heels, with a tail drooping discouragement, as the man swung along the creek-bed. The furrow of the old sled-trail was plainly visible, but a dozen inches of snow covered the marks of the last runners. In a month no man had come up or down that silent creek. The man held steadily on. He was not much given to thinking, and just then particularly he had nothing to think about save that he would eat lunch at the forks and that at six o'clock he would be in camp with the boys. There was nobody to talk to; and, had there been, speech would have been impossible because of the ice-muzzle on his mouth. So he continued monotonously to chew tobacco and to increase the length of his amber beard.

Once in a while the thought reiterated itself that it was very cold and that he had never experienced such cold. As he walked along he rubbed his cheek-bones and nose with the back of his mittened hand. He did this automatically, now and again changing hands. But rub as he would, the instant he stopped his cheek-bones went numb, and the following instant the end of his nose went numb. He was sure to frost his cheeks; he knew that, and experienced a pang of regret that he had not devised a nose-strap of the sort Bud wore in cold snaps. Such a strap passed across the cheeks, as well, and saved them. But it didn't matter much, after all. What were frosted cheeks? A bit painful, that was all; they were never serious.

Empty as the man's mind was of thoughts, he was keenly observant, and he noticed the changes in the creek, the curves and bends and timber-jams, and always he sharply noted where he placed his feet. Once, coming around a bend, he shied abruptly, like a startled horse, curved away from the place where he had been walking, and retreated several paces back along the trail. The creek he knew was frozen clear to the bottom,—no creek could contain water in that arctic winter,—but he knew also that there were springs that bubbled out from the hillsides and ran along under the snow and on top the ice of the creek. He knew that the coldest snaps never froze these springs, and he knew likewise their danger. They were traps. They hid pools of water under the snow that might be three inches deep, or three feet. Sometimes a skin of ice half an inch thick covered them, and in turn was covered by the snow. Sometimes there were alternate layers of water and ice-skin, so that when one broke through he kept on breaking through for a while, sometimes wetting himself to the waist.

That was why he had shied in such panic. He had felt the give under his feet and heard the crackle of a snow-hidden ice-skin. And to get his feet wet in such a temperature meant trouble and danger. At the very least it meant delay, for he would be forced to stop and build a fire, and under its protection to bare his feet while he dried his socks and moccasins. He stood and studied the creek-bed and its banks, and decided that the flow of water came from the right. He reflected awhile, rubbing his nose and cheeks, then skirted to the left, stepping gingerly and testing the footing for each step. Once clear of the danger, he took a fresh chew of tobacco and swung along at his four-mile gait.

In the course of the next two hours he came upon several similar traps. Usually the snow above the hidden pools had a sunken, candied appearance that advertised the danger. Once again, however, he had a close call; and once, suspecting danger, he compelled the dog to go on in front. The dog did not want to go. It hung back until the man shoved it forward, and then it went quickly across the white, unbroken surface. Suddenly it broke through, floundered to one side, and got away to firmer footing. It had wet its forefeet and legs, and almost immediately the water that clung to it turned to ice. It made quick efforts to lick the ice off its legs, then dropped down in the snow and began to bite out the ice that had formed between the toes. This was a matter of instinct. To permit the ice to remain would mean sore feet. It did not know this. It merely obeyed the mysterious prompting that arose from the deep crypts of its being. But the man knew, having achieved a judgment on the subject, and he removed the mitten from his right hand and helped tear out the ice-particles. He did not expose his fingers more than a minute, and was astonished at the swift numbness that smote them. It certainly was cold. He pulled on the mitten hastily, and beat the hand savagely across his chest.

At twelve o'clock the day was at its brightest. Yet the sun was too far south on its winter journey to clear the horizon. The bulge of the earth intervened between it and Henderson Creek, where the man walked under a clear sky at noon and cast no shadow. At half-past twelve, to the minute, he arrived at the forks of the creek. He was pleased at the speed he had made. If he kept it up, he would certainly be with the boys by six| He unbuttoned his jacket and shirt and drew forth his lunch. The action consumed no more than a quarter of a minute, yet in that brief moment the numbness laid hold of the exposed fingers. He did not put the mitten on, but, instead, struck the fingers a dozen sharp smashes against his leg. Then he sat down on a snow-covered log to eat. The sting that followed upon the striking of his fingers against his leg ceased so quickly that he was startled. He had had no chance to take a bite of biscuit. He struck the fingers repeatedly and returned them to the mitten, baring the other hand for the purpose of eating. He tried to take a mouthful, but the ice-muzzle prevented. He had forgotten to build a fire and thaw out. He chuckled at his foolishness, and as he chuckled he noted the numbness creeping into the exposed fingers. Also, he noted that the stinging which had first come to his toes when he sat down was already passing away. He wondered whether the toes were warm or numb. He moved them inside the moocasins and decided that they were numb.

He pulled the mitten on hurriedly and stood up. He was a bit frightened. He stamped up and down until the stinging returned into the feet. It certainly was cold, was his thought. That man from Sulphur Creek had spoken the truth when telling how cold it sometimes got in the country. And he had laughed at him at the time!

That showed one must not be too sure of things. There was no mistake about it, it *was* cold. He strode up and down, stamping his feet and threshing his arms, until reassured by the returning warmth. Then he got out matches and proceeded to make a fire. From the undergrowth, where high water of the previous spring had lodged a supply of seasoned twigs, he got his fire-wood. Working carefully from a small beginning, he soon had a roaring fire, over which he thawed the ice from his face and in the protection of which he ate his biscuits. For the moment the cold of space was outwitted. The dog took satisfaction in the fire, stretching out close enough for warmth and far enough away to escape being singed.

When the man had finished, he filled his pipe and took his comfortable time over a smoke. Then he pulled on his mittens, settled the earflaps of his cap firmly about his ears, and took the creek trail up the left fork. The dog was disappointed and yearned back toward the fire. This man did not know cold. Possibly all the generations of his ancestry had been ignorant of cold, of real cold, of cold one hundred and seven degrees below freezing-point. But the dog knew; all its ancestry knew, and it had inherited the knowledge. And it knew that it was not good to walk abroad in such fearful cold. It was the time to lie snug in a hole in the snow and wait for a curtain of cloud to be drawn across the face of outer space whence this cold came. On the other hand, there was no keen intimacy between the dog and the man. The one was the toil-slave of the other, and the only caresses it had ever received were the caresses of the whip-lash and of harsh and menacing throat-sounds that threatened the whiplash. So the dog made no effort to communicate its apprehension to the man. It was not concerned in the welfare of the man; it was for its own sake that it yearned back toward the fire. But the man whistled, and spoke to it with the sound of whip-lashes, and the dog swung in at the man's heels and followed after.

The man took a chew of tobacco and proceeded to start a new amber beard. Also, his moist breath quickly powdered with white his mustache, eyebrows, and lashes. There did not seem to be so many springs on the left fork of the Henderson, and for half an hour the man saw no signs of any. And then it happened. At a place where there were no signs, where the soft, unbroken snow seemed to advertise solidity beneath, the man broke through. It was not deep. He wet himself halfway to the knees before he floundered out to the firm crust.

He was angry, and cursed his luck aloud. He had hoped to get into camp with the boys at six o'clock, and this would delay him an hour, for he would have to build a fire and dry out his foot-gear. This was imperative at that low temperature—he knew that much; and he turned aside to the bank, which he climbed. On top, tangled in the underbrush about the trunks of several small spruce trees, was a high-water deposit of dry fire-wood—sticks and twigs, principally, but also larger portions of seasoned branches and fine, dry, last-year's grasses. He threw down several large pieces on top of the snow. This served for a foundation and prevented the young flame from drowning itself in the snow it otherwise would melt. The flame he got by touching a match to a small shred of birch-bark that he took from his pocket. This burned even more readily than paper. Placing it on the foundation, he fed the young flame with wisps of dry grass and with the tiniest dry twigs.

He worked slowly and carefully, keenly aware of his danger. Gradually, as the flame grew stronger, he increased the size of the twigs with which he fed it. He squatted in the snow, pulling the twigs out from their entanglement in the brush and feeding directly to the flame. He knew there must be no failure. When it is seventy-five below zero, a man must not fail in his first attempt to build a fire—that is, if his feet are wet. If his feet are dry, and he fails, he can run along the trail for half a mile and restore his circulation. But the circulation of wet and freezing feet cannot be restored by running when it is seventy-five below. No matter how fast he runs, the wet feet will freeze the harder.

All this the man knew. The old timer on Sulphur Creek had told him about it the previous fall, and now he was appreciating the advice. Already all sensation had gone out of his feet. To build the fire he had been forced to remove his mittens, and the fingers had quickly gone numb. His pace of four miles an hour had kept his heart pumping blood to the surface of his body and to all the extremities. But the instant he stopped, the action of the pump eased down. The cold of space smote the unprotected tip of the planet, and he, being on that unprotected tip, received the full force of the blow. The blood of his body recoiled before it. The blood was alive, like the dog, and like the dog it wanted to hide away and cover itself up from the fearful cold. So long as he walked four miles an hour, he pumped that blood, willy-nilly, to the surface; but now it ebbed away and sank down into the recesses of his body. The extremities were the first to feel its absence. His wet feet froze the faster, and his exposed fingers numbed the faster, though they had not yet begun to freeze. Nose and cheeks were already freezing, while the skin of all his body chilled as it lost its blood.

But he was safe. Toes and nose and cheeks would be only touched by the frost, for the fire was beginning to burn with strength. He was feeding it with twigs the size of his finger. In another minute he would be able to feed it with branches the size of his wrist, and then he could remove his wet foot-gear, and, while it dried, he could keep his naked feet warm by the fire, rubbing them at first, of course, with snow. The fire was a success. He was safe. He remembered the advice of the old-timer on Sulphur Creek, and smiled. The old-timer had been very serious in laying down the law that no man must travel alone in the Klondike after fifty below. Well, here he was; he had had the accident; he was alone; and he had saved himself. Those old-timers were rather womanish, some of them, he thought. All a man had to do was to keep his head, and he was all right. Any man who was a man could travel alone. But it was surprising, the rapidity with which his cheeks and nose were freezing. And he had not thought his fingers could go lifeless in so short a time. Lifeless they were, for he could scarcely make them move together to grip a twig, and they seemed remote from his body and from him. When he touched a twig, he had to look and see whether or not he had hold of it. The wires were pretty well down between him and his finger-ends.

All of which counted for little. There was the fire, snapping and crackling and promising life with every dancing flame. He started to untie his moccasins. They were coated with ice; the thick German socks were like sheaths of iron halfway to the knees; and the moccasin strings were like rods of steel all twisted and knotted as by some conflagration. For a moment he tugged with his numb fingers, then, realizing the folly of it, he drew his sheath-knife.

But before he could cut the strings, it happened. It was his own fault or, rather, his mistake. He should not have built the fire under the spruce tree. He should have built it in the open. But it had been easier to pull the twigs from the brush and drop them directly on the fire. Now the tree under which he had done this carried a weight of snow on its boughs. No wind had blown for weeks, and each bough was fully freighted. Each time he had pulled a twig he had communicated a slight agitation to the tree—an imperceptible agitation, so far as he was concerned, but an agitation sufficient to bring about the disaster. High up in the tree one bough capsized its load of snow. This fell on the boughs beneath, capsizing them. This process continued, spreading out and involving the whole tree.

It grew like an avalanche, and it descended without warning upon the man and the fire, and the fire was blotted out! Where it had burned was a mantle of fresh and disordered snow.

The man was shocked. It was as though he had just heard his own sentence of death. For a moment he sat and stared at the spot where the fire had been. Then he grew very calm. Perhaps the old-timer on Sulphur Creek was right. If he had only had a trail-mate he would have been in no danger now. The trail-mate could have built the fire. Well, it was up to him to build the fire over again, and this second time there must be no failure. Even if he succeeded, he would most likely lose some toes. His feet must be badly frozen by now, and there would be some time before the second fire was ready.

Such were his thoughts, but he did not sit and think them. He was busy all the time they were passing through his mind. He made a new foundation for a fire, this time in the open, where no treacherous tree could blot it out. Next, he gathered dry grasses and tiny twigs from the high-water flotsam. He could not bring his fingers together to pull them out, but he was able to gather them by the handful. In this way he got many rotten twigs and bits of green moss that were undesirable, but it was the best he could do. He worked methodically, even collecting an armful of the larger branches to be used later when the fire gathered strength. And all the while the dog sat and watched him, a certain yearning wistfulness in its eyes, for it looked upon him as the fire-provider, and the fire was slow in coming.

When all was ready, the man reached in his pocket for a second piece of birch-bark. He knew the bark was there, and, though he could not feel it with his fingers, he could hear its crisp rustling as he fumbled for it. Try as he would, he could not clutch hold of it. And all the time, in his consciousness, was the knowledge that each instant his feet were freezing. This thought tended to put him in a panic, but he fought against it and kept calm. He pulled on his mittens with his teeth, and threshed his arms back and forth, beating his hands with all his might against his sides. He did this sitting down, and he stood up to do it; and all the while the dog sat in the snow, its wolf-brush of a tail curled around warmly over its forefeet, its sharp wolf-ears pricked forward intently as it watched the man. And the man as he beat and threshed with his arms and hands, felt a great surge of envy as he regarded the creature that was warm and secure in its natural covering.

After a time he was aware of the first far-away signals of sensation in his beaten fingers. The faint tingling grew stronger till it evolved into a stinging ache that was excruciating, but which the man hailed with satisfaction. He stripped the mitten from his right hand and fetched forth the birch-bark. The exposed fingers were quickly going numb again. Next he brought out his bunch of sulphur matches. But the tremendous cold had already driven the life out of his fingers. In his effort to separate one match from the others, the whole bunch fell in the snow. He tried to pick it out of the snow, but failed. The dead fingers could neither touch nor clutch. He was very careful. He drove the thought of his freezing feet, and nose, and cheeks, out of his mind, devoting his whole soul to the matches. He watched, using the sense of vision in place of that of touch, and when he saw his fingers on each side the bunch, he closed them—that is, he willed to close them, for the wires were down, and the fingers did not obey. He pulled the mitten on the right hand, and beat it fiercely against his knee. Then, with both mittened hands, he scooped the bunch of matches, along with much snow, into his lap. Yet he was no better off.

After some manipulation he managed to get the bunch between the heels of his mittened hands. In this fashion he carried it to his mouth. The ice crackled and snapped when by a violent effort he opened his mouth. He drew the lower jaw in, curled the upper lip out of the way, and scraped the bunch with his upper teeth in order to separate a match. He succeeded in getting one, which he dropped on his lap. He was no better off. He could not pick it up. Then he devised a way. He picked it up in his teeth and scratched it on his leg. Twenty times he scratched before he succeeded in lighting it. As it flamed he held it with his teeth to the birch-bark. But the burning brimstone went up his nostrils and into his lungs, causing him to cough spasmodically. The match fell into the snow and went out.

The old-timer on Sulphur Creek was right, he thought in the moment of controlled despair that ensued; after fifty below, a man should travel with a partner. He beat his hands, but failed in exciting any sensation. Suddenly he bared both his hands, removing the mittens with his teeth. He caught the whole bunch between the heels of his hands. His arm-muscles not being frozen enabled him to press the hand-heels tightly against the matches. Then he scratched the bunch along his leg. It flared into flame, seventy sulphur matches at once! There was no wind to blow them out. He kept his head to one side to escape the strangling fumes, and held the blazing bunch to the birch-bark. As he so held it, he became aware of sensation in his hand. His flesh was burning. He could smell it. Deep down below the surface he could feel it. The sensation developed into pain that grew acute. And still he endured it, holding the flame of the matches clumsily to the bark that would not light readily because his own burning hands were in the way, absorbing most of the flame.

At last, when he could endure no more, he jerked his hands apart. The blazing matches fell sizzling into the snow, but the birch-bark was alight. He began laying dry grasses and the tiniest twigs on the flame. He could not pick and choose, for he had to lift the fuel between the heels of his hands. Small pieces of rotten wood and green moss clung to the twigs, and he bit them off as well as he could with his teeth. He cherished the flame carefully and awkwardly. It meant life, and it must not perish. The withdrawal of blood from the surface of his body now made him begin to shiver, and he grew more awkward. A large piece of green moss fell squarely on the little fire. He tried to poke it out with his fingers, but his shivering frame made him poke too far, and he disrupted the nucleus of the little fire, the burning grasses and tiny twigs separating and scattering.He tried to poke them together again, but in spite of the tenseness of the effort, his shivering got away with him, and the twigs were hopelessly scattered. Each twig gushed a puff of smoke and went out. The fire-provider had failed. As he looked apathetically about him, his eyes chanced on the dog, sitting across the ruins of the fire from him, in the snow, making restless, hunching movement, slightly lifting one forefoot and then the other, shifting its weight back and forth on them with wistful eagerness.

The sight of the dog put a wild idea into his head. He remembered the tale of the man, caught in a blizzard, who killed a steer and crawled inside the carcass, and so was saved. He would kill the dog and bury his hands in the warm body until the numbness went out of them. Then he could build another fire. He spoke to the dog, calling it to him; but in his voice was a strange note of fear that frightened the animal, who had never known the man to speak in such way before. Something was the matter, and its suspicious nature sensed danger—it knew not what danger, but somewhere, somehow, in its brain arose an apprehension of the man. It flattened its ears down at the sound of the man's voice, and its restless, hunching movements and the liftings and shiftings of its forefeet became more pronounced; but it would not come to the man. He got on his hands and knees and crawled toward the dog. This unusual posture again excited suspicion, and the animal sidled mincingly away.

The man sat up in the snow for a moment and struggled for calmness. Then he pulled on his mittens, by means of his teeth, and got upon his feet. He glanced down at first in order to assure himself that he was really standing up, for the absence of sensation in his feet left him unrelated to the earth. His erect position in itself started to drive the webs of suspicion from the dog's mind; and when he spoke peremptorily, with the sound of whip-lashes in his voice, the dog rendered its customary allegiance and came to him. As it came within reaching distance, the man lost his control. His arms flashed out to the dog, and he experienced genuine surprise when he discovered that his hands could not clutch, that there was neither bend nor feeling in the fingers. He had forgotten for the moment that they were frozen and that they were freezing more and more. All this happened quickly, and before the animal could get away, he encircled its body with his arms. He sat down in the snow, and in this fashion held the dog, while it snarled and whined and struggled.

But it was all he could do, hold its body encircled in his arms and sit there. He realized that he could not kill the dog. There was no way to do it. With his helpless hands he could neither draw nor hold his sheathknife nor throttle the animal. He released it, it plunged wildly away, with tail between its legs, and still snarling. It halted forty feet away and surveyed him curiously, with ears sharply pricked forward. The man looked down at his hands in order to locate them, and found them hanging on the ends of his arms. It struck him as curious that one should have to use his eyes in order to find out where his hands were. He began threshing his arms back and forth, beating the mittened hands against his sides. He did this for five minutes, violently, and his heart pumped enough blood up to the surface to put a stop to his shivering. But no sensation was aroused in the hands. He had an impression that they hung like weights on the ends of his arms, but when he tried to run the impression down, he could not find it.

A certain fear of death, dull and oppressive, came to him. This fear quickly became poignant as he realized that it was no longer a mere matter of freezing his fingers and toes, or of losing his hands and feet, but that it was a matter of life and death with the chances against him. This threw him into a panic, and he turned and ran up the creek-bed along the old dim trail. The dog joined in behind and kept up with him. He ran blindly, without intention, in fear such as he had never known in his life. Slowly, as he ploughed and floundered through the snow, he began to see things again,—the banks of the creek, the old timber-jams, the leafless aspens, and the sky. The running made him feel better. He did not shiver. Maybe, if he ran on, his feet would thaw out; and, anyway, if he ran far enough, he would reach camp and the boys. Without doubt he would lose some fingers and toes and some of his face; but the boys would take care of him, and save the rest of him when he got there. And at the same time there was another thought in his mind that said he would never get to the camp and the boys; that it was too many miles away, that the freezing had too great a start on him, and that he would soon be stiff and dead. This thought he kept in the background and refused to consider. Sometimes it pushed itself forward and demanded to be heard, but he thrust it back and strove to think of other things.

It struck him as curious that he could run at all on feet so frozen that he could not feel them when they struck the earth and took the weight of his body. He seemed to himself to skim along above the surface, and to have no connection with the earth. Somewhere he had once seen a winged Mercury, and he wondered if Mercury felt as he felt when skimming over the earth.

His theory of running until he reached camp and the boys had one flaw in it: he lacked the endurance. Several times he stumbled, and finally he tottered, crumpled up, and fell. When he tried to rise, he failed. He must sit and rest, he decided, and next time he would merely walk and keep on going. As he sat and regained his breath, he noted that he was feeling quite warm and comfortable. He was not shivering, and it even seemed that a warm glow had come to his chest and trunk. And yet, when he touched his nose or cheeks, there was no sensation. Running would not thaw them out. Nor would it thaw out his hands and feet. Then the thought came to him that the frozen portions of his body must be extending. He tried to keep this thought down, to forget it, to think of something else; he was aware of the panicky feeling that it caused, and he was afraid of the panic. But the thought asserted itself, and persisted, until it produced a vision of his body totally frozen. This was too much, and he made another wild run along the trail. Once he slowed down to a walk, but the thought of the freezing extending itself made him run again.

And all the time the dog ran with him, at his heels, When he fell down a second time, it curled its tail over its forefeet and sat in front of him, facing him, curiously eager and intent. The warmth and security of the animal angered him, and he cursed it till it flattened down its ears appeasingly. This time the shivering came more quickly upon the man. He was losing in his battle with the frost. It was creeping into his body from all sides. The thought of it drove him on, but he ran no more than a hundred feet, when he staggered and pitched headlong. It was his last panic. When he had recovered his breath and control, he sat up and entertained in his mind the conception of meeting death with dignity. However, the conception did not come to him in such terms. His idea of it was that he had been making a fool of himself, running around like a chicken with its head cut off—such was the simile that occurred to him. Well he was bound to freeze anyway, and he might as well take it decently. With this new-found peace of mind came the first glimmerings of drowsiness. A good idea, he thought, to sleep off to death. It was like taking an anaesthetic. Freezing was not so bad as people thought. There were lots worse ways to die.

He pictured the boys finding his body next day. Suddenly he found himself with them, coming along the trail and looking for himself. And, still with them, he came around a turn in the trail and found himself lying in the snow. He did not belong with himself any more, for even then he was out of himself, standing with the boys and looking at himself in the snow. It certainly was cold, was his thought. When he got back to the States he could tell the folks what real cold was. He drifted on from this to a vision of the old-timer on Sulphur Creek. He could see him quite clearly, warm and comfortable, and smoking a pipe.

"You were right, old hoss; you were right," the man mumbled to the old timer of Sulphur Creek.

Then the man drowsed off into what seemed to him the most comfortable and satisfying sleep he had ever known. The dog sat facing him and waiting. The brief day drew to a close in a long, slow twilight. There were no signs of a fire to be made, and, besides, never in the dog's experience had it known a man to sit like that in the snow and make no fire. As the twilight drew on, its eager yearning for the fire mastered it, and with a great lifting and shifting of forefeet, it whined softly, then flattened its ears down in anticipation of being chided by the man. But the man remained silent. Later, the dog whined loudly. And still later it crept close to the man and caught the scent of death. This made the animal bristle and back away. A little longer it delayed, howling under the stars that leaped and danced and shone brightly in the cold sky. Then it turned and trotted up the trail in the direction of the camp it knew, where were the other food-providers and fire-providers.

HENRY WADSWORTH LONGFELLOW

HENRY WADSWORTH LONGFELLOW (American, 1807-1882). At one time (possibly still) America's most popular poet. After traveling abroad, took professorship at Harvard. Verses combined the romantic, the sentimental, and the ethical in a proportion that instantly caught popular taste. Famous narrative poems: *Evangeline, The Song of Hiawatha, The Courtship of Miles Standish.* Later critics prefer less-known lyrics, which show true poetic gift.

MY LOST YOUTH

Often I think of the beautiful town
  That is seated by the sea;
Often in thought go up and down
The pleasant streets of that dear old town,
  And my youth comes back to me.
    And a verse of a Lapland song
    Is haunting my memory still:
    "A boy's will is the wind's will,
And the thoughts of youth are long, long thoughts."

I can see the shadowy lines of its trees,
  And catch, in sudden gleams,
The sheen of the far-surrounding seas,
And islands that were the Hesperides
  Of all my boyish dreams.
    And the burden of that old song,
    It murmurs and whispers still:
    "A boy's will is the wind's will,
And the thoughts of youth are long, long thoughts."

I remember the black wharves and the slips,
  And the sea-tides tossing free;

And Spanish sailors with bearded lips,
And the beauty and mystery of the ships,
    And the magic of the sea.
        And the voice of that wayward song
        Is singing and saying still:
        "A boy's will is the wind's will,
And the thoughts of youth are long, long thoughts."

I remember the bulwarks by the shore,
    And the fort upon the hill;
The sunrise gun, with its hollow roar,
The drum-beat repeated o'er and o'er,
    And the bugle wild and shrill.
        And the music of that old song
        Throbs in my memory still:
        "A boy's will is the wind's will,
And the thoughts of youth are long, long thoughts."

I remember the sea-fight far away,
    How it thundered o'er the tide!
And the dead captains, as they lay
In their graves, o'erlooking the tranquil bay
    Where they in battle died.
        And the sound of that mournful song
        Goes through me with a thrill:
        "A boy's will is the wind's will,
And the thoughts of youth are long, long thoughts."

I can see the breezy dome of groves,
    The shadows of Deering's Woods;
And the friendships old and the early loves
Come back with a Sabbath sound, as of doves
    In quiet neighborhoods.
        And the verse of that sweet old song,
        It flutters and murmurs still:
        "A boy's will is the wind's will,
And the thoughts of youth are long, long thoughts."

I remember the gleams and glooms that dart
    Across the school-boy's brain;
The song and the silence in the heart,

That in part are prophecies, and in part
    Are longings wild and vain.
       And the voice of that fitful song
       Sings on, and is never still:
       "A boy's will is the wind's will,
And the thoughts of youth are long, long thoughts."

There are things of which I may not speak;
    There are dreams that cannot die;
There are thoughts that make the strong heart weak,
And bring a pallor into the cheek,
    And a mist before the eye.
       And the words of that fatal song
       Come over me like a chill:
       "A boy's will is the wind's will,
And the thoughts of youth are long, long thoughts."

Strange to me now are the forms I meet
    When I visit the dear old town;
But the native air is pure and sweet,
And the trees that o'ershadow each well-known street,
    As they balance up and down,
       Are singing the beautiful song,
       Are sighing and whispering still:
       "A boy's will is the wind's will,
And the thoughts of youth are long, long thoughts."

And Deering's Woods are fresh and fair,
    And with joy that is almost pain
My heart goes back to wander there,
And among the dreams of the days that were,
    I find my lost youth again.
       And the strange and beautiful song,
       The groves are repeating it still:
       "A boy's will is the wind's will,
And the thoughts of youth are long, long thoughts."

THE SKELETON IN ARMOR

Speak! speak! thou fearful guest!
Who, with thy hollow breast

Still in rude armor drest,
   Comest to daunt me!
Wrapt not in Eastern balms,
But with thy fleshless palms
Stretched, as if asking alms,
   Why dost thou haunt me?

Then, from those cavernous eyes
Pale flashes seemed to rise,
As when the Northern skies
   Gleam in December;
And, like the water's flow
Under December's snow,
Came a dull voice of woe
   From the heart's chamber.

'I was a Viking old!
My deeds, though manifold,
No Skald in song has told,
   No Saga taught thee!
Take heed, that in thy verse
Thou dost the tale rehearse,
Else dread a dead man's curse;
   For this I sought thee.

'Far in the Northern Land,
By the wild Baltic's strand,
I, with my childish hand,
   Tamed the gerfalcon;
And, with my skates fast-bound
Skimmed the half-frozen Sound,
That the poor whimpering hound
   Trembled to walk on.

'Oft to his frozen lair
Tracked I the grisly bear,
While from my path the hare
   Fled like a shadow;
Oft through the forest dark
Followed the were-wolf's bark,
Until the soaring lark
   Sang from the meadow.

'But when I older grew,
Joining a corsair's crew,
O'er the dark sea I flew
    With the marauders.
Wild was the life we led;
Many the souls that sped,
Many the hearts that bled,
    By our stern orders.

'Many a wassail-bout
Wore the long Winter out;
Often our midnight shout
    Set the cocks crowing,
As we the Berserk's tale
Measured in cups of ale,
Draining the oaken pail,
    Filled to o'erflowing.

'Once as I told in glee
Tales of the stormy sea,
Soft eyes did gaze on me,
    Burning yet tender:
And as the white stars shine
On the dark Norway pine,
On that dark heart of mine
    Fell their soft splendor.

'I wooed the blue-eyed maid,
Yielding, yet half afraid,
And in the forest's shade
    Our vows were plighted.
Under its loosened vest
Fluttered her little breast,
Like birds within their nest
    By the hawk frighted.

'Bright in her father's hall
Shields gleamed upon the wall.
Loud sang the minstrels all,

Chanting his glory;
When of old Hildebrand
I asked his daughter's hand,
Mute did the minstrels stand
　To hear my story.

'While the brown ale he quaffed,
Loud then the champion laughed,
And as the wind-gusts waft
　The sea-foam brightly,
So the loud laugh of scorn,
Out of those lips unshorn,
From the deep drinking-horn
　Blew the foam lightly.

'She was a Prince's child,
I but a Viking wild,
And though she blushed and smiled,
　I was discarded!
Should not the dove so white
Follow the sea-mew's flight,
Why did they leave that night
　Her nest unguarded?

'Scarce had I put to sea,
Bearing the maid with me,
Fairest of all was she
　Among the Norsemen!
When on the white sea-strand,
Waving his armed hand,
Saw we old Hildebrand,
　With twenty horsemen.

'Then launched they to the blast,
Bent like a reed each mast,
Yet we were gaining fast,
　When the wind failed us;
And with a sudden flaw
Came round the gusty Skaw,
So that our foe we saw
　Laugh as he hailed us.

'And as to catch the gale
Round veered the flapping sail,
"Death!" was the helmsman's hail,
   "Death without quarter!"
Mid-ships with iron keel
Struck we her ribs of steel;
Down her black hulk did reel
   Through the black water!

'As with his wings aslant,
Sails the fierce cormorant,
Seeking some rocky haunt,
   With his prey laden,—
So toward the open main,
Beating to sea again,
Through the wild hurricane,
   Bore I the maiden.

'Three weeks we westward bore,
And when the storm was o'er,
Cloud-like we saw the shore
   Stretching to leeward;
There for my lady's bower
Built I the lofty tower,
Which, to this very hour,
   Stands looking seaward.

"There lived we many years;
Time dried the maiden's tears;
She had forgot her fears,
   She was a mother;
Death closed her mild blue eyes,
Under that tower she lies;
Ne'er shall the sun arise
   On such another!

'Still grew my bosom then,
Still as a stagnant fen!
Hateful to me were men,
   The sunlight hateful!

In the vast forest here,
Clad in my warlike gear,
Fell I upon my spear,
    Oh, death was grateful!

'Thus, seamed with many scars,
Bursting these prison bars,
Up to its native stars
    My soul ascended!
There from the flowing bowl
Deep drinks the warrior's soul,
Skoal! to the Northland! *skoal!*'
    Thus the tale ended.

FEDERICO GARCIA LORCA

FEDERICO GARCIA LORCA (Spanish, 1899-1936). Best-known contemporary Spanish poet and dramatist. Fiery anti-Fascist, executed during the Spanish Civil War. Folklorist, musician, lecturer, amateur painter. As a dramatist, dealt with primitive passions: trilogy—*Bodas de Sangre, Yerma, La Casa de Bernarda Alba.* Poetry, in translation: *Lament for the Death of a Bullfighter, The Poet in New York, Poems.*

JOURNEY

A hundred riders in mourning,
where will they go
by the lowering sky
of the orange grove?
Neither in Cordova nor in Seville
will they appear;
nor in Granada that longs
for the sea.
Those sleepy horses
will carry them
to the labyrinth of crosses
where song trembles.
With seven piercing cries,
where will they go,
the hundred Andalusian riders
of the orange grove?

AFTER PASSING

The children gaze
at a distant point.

The candles die.
Some blind girls
question the moon,
and spirals of weeping
climb on the wind.

The mountains gaze
at a distant point.

THE SILENCE

Hear the silence, my child.
It is an undulated silence
where valleys and echoes slip,
a silence
that bows heads
to the ground.

VILLAGE

Upon the barren mountain
a Calvary.
Clear water
and centenary olive trees.
Through the narrow streets
cloaked men,
and on the towers
weathercocks turning.
Eternally
turning.
Oh lost village
in the Andalusia of tears!

SURPRISED

Left dead in the street
with a dagger in his chest.
No one knew him.
How the street lamp trembled!

Mother.
How the tiny lamp trembled
in the street!
Early dawn. No one
could face his eyes
open wide in the cruel wind.
Dead he was left in the street
with a dagger in his chest
and no one knew him.

AND THEN

Labyrinths
born of time
vanish.

(Only desert
remains.)

The heart,
fountain of desires,
vanishes.

(Only desert
remains.)

The illusion of dawn
and kisses
vanishes.

Only desert
remains.
Undulating
desert.

AY!

The cry leaves in the wind
a shadow of cypress.

(Leave me in this field,
weeping.)

All has been demolished in the world.
Nothing remains but silence.

(Leave me in this field,
weeping.)

The lightless horizon
is bitten with bonfires.

(I have told you, leave me
in this field,
weeping.)

LUSIN

LUSIN (Chou Shu-jen, Chinese, 1881-1936). Important leader in modern Chinese literary revolution. While a student in Japan, studied Western literature and took European ideals back to China. Forced to leave professorship at Peking National University because of radical ideas. Essays had immediate influence; 26 short stories more likely to endure. *Ah Q and Others* has been translated into many languages.

MEDICINE

It is autumn, and late at night, so that the moon has already gone. The sky is a sheet of darkling blue. Everything still sleeps, except those who wander in the night, and Hua Lao-shuan. He sits up suddenly in his bed; leaning over, he rubs a match and touches it to a lamp which is covered with grease. A pale greenish light flickers and reveals the two rooms of a tea house.

"Father of Hsiao-shuan, are you leaving?" queries the voice of a woman. There is a series of tearing coughs in the small room in the rear.

"M-m." Lao-shuan, listening for a moment, fastens his garment and then stretches forth a hand toward the woman. "Give it," he says.

Hua Ta-ma fumbles beneath her pillow and drags forth a small packet of silver dollars, which she hands to him. Nervously he thrusts it into his pocket, then pats it twice, to reassure himself. He lights a paper lantern and blows out the oil lamp. Carrying the lantern, he goes into the small rear room. There is a rustle and then more coughing. When it is quiet again, Lao-shuan calls out, in an undertone: "Hsiao-shuan—don't bother getting up. The shop—your mother will see to that."

His son does not answer him, and Lao-shuan, thinking he will sleep undisturbed, goes through the low door into the street. In the blackness nothing is at first visible save a gray ribbon of path. The lantern illumines only his two feet, which move rhythmically Dogs appear here and there, then sidle off again. None even barks. Outside, the air is cold, and it refreshes Lao-shuan, so that it seems to him he is all at once a youth, and possesses the miraculous power of touching men into life. He takes longer strides. Gradually the sky brightens, till the road is more clearly marked.

Absorbed in his walking, Lao-shuan is startled when, almost in front of him, he sees a crossroad. He stops, and then withdraws a few steps, to stand under the eaves of a shop, in front of its closed door. After a long wait, his bones are chilled.

"Unh, an old fellow?"

"High-spirited, up so early . . ."

Opening his eyes, Lao-shuan sees several people passing near him. One of them turns back and looks at him intently. He cannot distinguish the features clearly, but the man's eyes are bright with a cold, lusting gleam, eyes of famishment suddenly coming upon something edible. Looking at his lantern, Lao-shuan sees that it has gone out. He feels quickly at his pocket; the hard substance is still there. Then he peers out, and on either side of him are numerous strange people, loitering and looking oddly like ghosts in the dim light. Then he gazes fixedly at them, and gradually they do not seem unusual at all.

He discerns several soldiers among the crowd. On their coats they wear, both in front and behind, the large white circle of cloth of the government troops, which can be seen for some distance. As one draws nearer, the wine-colored border of their uniform is also evident. There is a trampling of many feet, and a large number of people gathers, little groups here and there merging swiftly into one crush that advances like the ocean's tide. Reaching the crossroad, they halt and form a semicircle, with their backs toward Lao-shuan.

Necks stretch forth from collars and incline toward the same point, as if, like so many ducks, they are held by some invisible hand. For a moment all is still. Lao-shuan seems to hear a sound from somewhere beyond the necks. A stir sweeps through the on-lookers. With a sudden movement, they abruptly disperse. People jostle one another hurriedly, and some, pushing past Lao-shuan, almost tumble him to the ground in their haste.

"*Hai!* One hand gives the money, another hand gives the goods!" screams a man clad entirely in black, who halts before Lao-shuan. In his eyes is a metallic glitter. They resemble the bright luster of a pair of swords. They stab into Lao-shuan's soul, and his body seems to shrivel to half its normal size. The dark man thrusts one huge, empty paw at him, while in the other he offers a steamed roll, stained with a fresh and still warm red substance, drops of which trickle to the earth.

Hurriedly, Lao-shuan fumbles for his dollars. He attempts to hand them over to the black-garbed man, from whose hand slowly depend the drops of red, but somehow he cannot embolden himself to re-ceive the saturated roll.

"What's he afraid of? Why not take it?" the fellow demands, brusque and impatient. Lao-shuan continues to hesitate until the other roughly snatches his lantern, tears off its paper shade and uses it to wrap up the roll. Then he thrusts this package into Lao-shaun's hand, and at the same time seizes the silver and gives it a cursory feel. As he turns away he murmurs, "That old fool . . ."

"And to cure what person?" Lao shuan seems to hear someone ask him. He does not reply. His attention is centered upon the pack-age, and he embraces it as if it were the only child descended from a house of ten generations. Nothing else in the world matters, now that he is about to transplant into his own home the robust life which he holds in his hands. He hopes, thereby, to reap much happi-ness.

The sun lifts over the horizon. Before him, the long street leads straight into his tea house. Behind him, the light of day caresses a worn tablet at the crossroad, on which are four characters limned in faint gold: "Ancient—Pavilion—"

Lao-shuan, reaching home, finds the tea house swept clean, with the rows of tables smooth and glistening but as yet serving no cus-tomers. Only Hsiao-shuan sits alone at a table by the wall and eats his food. Large drops of sweat drip down his forehead, and his little lined coat sticks against his sunken spine. His shoulder blades project sharply, from under his coat, so that there appears on his back, as though embossed, the character *pa*. Seeing it causes Lao-shuan to pinch his brow together. He wife emerges hastily from the kitchen, her mouth open, her lips quivering.

"Do you have it?" she asks.

"Yes, I have it."

The pair disappears into the kitchen for a time, where they consult. Then Hua Ta-ma comes hurriedly forth, goes out and in a moment returns with a dried lotus leaf, which she spreads on the table. Lao-shuan unwraps the crimson-stained roll and neatly repacks it in the sheet of lotus. Meanwhile, Hsiao-shuan has finished his meal and his mother warns him: "Sit still, Little Door-latch. Don't come here yet."

When the fire burns briskly in the mud stove, the father thrusts his little green and red parcel into the oven. There is a red and black flame. A strange odor permeates the rooms.

"*Hao.* It smells good, but is it? What are you eating?" demands Camel-Back Fifth, who arrives at this moment and sniffs the air questioningly. He is one of those who pass their days in tea houses, the first to come in the morning, the last to leave at night. Now, tumbling to a table by the lane, he sits down to make idle inquiry.

"Could it be baked rice *congee?*"

Nobody replies. Lao-shuan silently serves him boiled tea.

"Come in, Hsiao-shuan," Hua Ta-ma calls from the inner room, in the center of which she has placed a stool. The Little Door-latch sits, and his mother, saying in a low voice, "Eat it, and your sickness will vanish," hands him a plate on which is a round object, black in color.

Hsiao-shuan picks it up. For a moment he gazes at it curiously, as if he might somehow hold his own life in his hand. His heart is unspeakably moved with wonder. Very carefully, he splits the object. A jet of white vapor gushes forth, and immediately dissolves in the air. Now Hsiao-shuan sees that it is a white flour roll, broken in half. Soon it has entered his stomach, so that even the taste of it cannot be clearly remembered. In front of him there is the empty dish; on one side stands his father and, on the opposite side, his mother. Their eyes are potent with a strange look, as if they desire to pour something into him, yet at the same draw something forth. It is exciting. It is too much for Hsaio-shuan's little heart, which

831

throbs furiously. He presses his hands against his chest and begins to cough.

"Sleep a little; you'll be well."

So Hsiao-shuan coughs himself to sleep, obeying the advice of his mother. Having waited patiently till he is quiet, she drapes over him a lined quilt, which consists mostly of patches.

In the tea house are many customers, and Lao-shaun is kept engaged in his enterprise. He darts from one table to another, pouring hot water and tea, and seemingly intent on his tasks. But under his eyes are dark hollows.

"Lao-shuan," inquires a man with whiskers streaked with white, "are you not a little unwell?"

"No."

"No? But I already see that it's unlikely. Your smile now—" The bearded one contradicts himself.

"Lao-shuan is always busy. Of course if his son were—" begins Camel-Back Fifth. His remarks is interrupted by the arrival of a man whose face is massive, with distorted muscles. He wears a black cotton shirt, unbuttoned and pulled together carelessly around the waist with a broad black cloth girdle [the apparel of an executioner]. As he enters, he shouts to Lao-shuan:

"Eaten, eh? Is he well already? Lao-shuan, luck is with you! Indeed lucky! If it were not that I get news quickly—"

With the kettle in one hand and the other hanging straight beside him in an attitude of respect, Lao-shuan listens and smiles. All the guests listen with deference, and Hua Ta-ma, her eyes dark and sleepless, also comes forth and smiles, serving the new arrival some tea leaves, with the added flourish of a green olive. Lao-shuan himself fills the cup with boiling water.

"It is a guaranteed cure! Different from all others! Think of it, brought back while still warm, eaten while warm!" shouts the gentleman with the coarse face.

"Truly, were it not for Big Uncle Kan's services, how could it be—" Hua Ta-ma thanks him, in deep gratitude.

"Guaranteed cure! Guaranteed cure! Eaten up like that while still warm. A roll with human blood is an absolute cure for any kind of consumption!"

Mention of the word "consumption" seems to disconcert Hua Ta-ma; for her face suddenly turns pallid, though the smile quickly creeps back. She manages to withdraw so inconspicuouly that Big Uncle Kan still shouts with the full vigor of his lungs and does not

832

notice that she is gone till from the inner room, where Hsiao-shuan sleeps, there comes the sound of dry, raucous coughing.

"So, it is true Hsiao-shuan has come upon friendly luck. That sickness will unquestionably be cured utterly. There's no surprise in Lao-shuan's constant smiling." Thus speaks the whiskered old man, who walks toward Big Uncle Kan. "I hear," he says to the latter in a suppressed voice, "that the criminal executed today is a son of the Hsia family. Now, whose son is he? And, in fact, executed for what?"

"Whose?" demands Big Uncle. "Can he be other than the son of the fourth daughter-in-law of the Hsias? That little *tung-hsii!*" Observing that he has an alert audience, Big Uncle expands, his facial muscles become unusually active and he raises his voice to heroic heights, shouting: "The little thing did not want to live! He simply did not want life, that's all."

"And I got what from the execution this time? Not the merest profit! Even the clothes stripped from him were seized by Red Eye Ah Yi, the jailer. Our Uncle Lao-shuan was the luckiest. Second comes the Third Father of the Hsia family. He actually pocketed the reward—twenty-five ounces of silver!—all alone. He gave not so much as a single cash to anyone!"

Hsiao-shuan walks slowly from the little room, his hands pressed to his chest, and coughing without respite. He enters the kitchen, fills a bowl with cold rice and sits down at once to eat. Hua Ta-ma goes to him and inquires softly: "Hsiao-shuan, are you better? Still as hungry as ever?"

"Guaranteed cure, guaranteed!" Big Uncle Kan casts a glance at the lad but quickly turns back to the crowd and declares: "Third Father of Hsia is clever. Had he not been the first to report the matter to the official, his whole house would have been beheaded, and all their property confiscated. But instead? Silver!"

"That little tung-hsi was an altogether rotten egg. He even attempted to induce the head jailer to join the rebellion!"

"*Ai-ya!* If it were actually done, think of it," indignantly comments a youth in his twenties, sitting at a back table.

"You should know that Red Eye Ah Yi was anxious to gather some details; so he entered into conversation. 'The realm of *Ta Ching Dynasty* really belongs to us all,' he told Red Eye. Now, what do you make of that? Is it possible that such talk is actually human?

"Red Eye knew that there was only a mother in his home, but he could not believe that he was so poor that 'not a drop of oil and

833

water' could be squeezed from him. His rage already had burst his abdomen, yet the boy attempted to 'scratch the tiger's head'! Ah Yi gave him several smacks on the face."

"Ah Yi knows his boxing. His blows must have done the wretch good!" exults Camel-Back Fifth, from a corner table.

"No! Would you believe it? His worthless bones were unafraid. The fellow actually said, what is more, that it was a pity!"

Black-and-White Whiskers snorted, "What is it? How could pity be shown in beating a thing like that?"

"You've not listened well," sneers Big Uncle contemptuously. "The little tung-hsi meant to say that Ah Yi hmself was to be pitied!"

The listeners' eyes suddenly dull, and there is a pause in the conversation. Hsiao-shuan perspiring copiously, had finished his rice. His head seems to be steaming.

"So he said Red Eye should be pitied! Now, that is pure insanity!" Black-and-White Whiskers feels proudly that he has logically solved the whole matter. "Obviously, he had gone mad!"

"Gone mad," approvingly echoes the youth who spoke earlier. He too feels like a discoverer.

Equanimity is restored to the other teahouse visitors. They renew their laughing and talking. Hsiao-shuan, under cover of the confusion of sounds, seizes the opportunity to cough hoarsely, with all his emaciated strength.

Big Uncle Kan moves over to pat the child's shoulder, repeating, "Guaranteed cure, Hsiao-shuan. You mustn't cough like that. Guaranteed cure!"

"Gone mad," says Camel-Back Fifth, nodding his head.

Originally, the land adjacent to the city wall beyond the West Gate was public property. The narrow path that now cavorts through it was first made by feet seeking a short cut, which in time came to be a natural boundary line. On the left of it, as one goes out from the gate, are buried those who have been executed or have starved to death in prison. On the right are grouped the graves of the paupers. All of these graves are so numerous and closely arranged that they remind one of the sweet buns laid out in a rich man's home for a birthday celebration.

The Clear and Bright Day, when graves are visited, has dawned unusually cold, and willows have just issued new buds about the size of a half-grain of rice. Hua Ta-ma has laid out four dishes and a bowl of rice in front of a new grave on the right side, has left tears over it and has burned imitation money. Now she sits dazedly on the ground, as if waiting for something, but nothing which she herself could explain. A light breeze sweeps by, and her short hair flutters. It is much grayer than last year.

Down the narrow path comes another woman, gray also, and in torn rags. She carries a worn round basket, lacquered red, with a string of paper ingots hanging from it. Now and then she halts her slow walk. Finally she notices Hua Ta-ma gazing at her, and she hesitates, embarrassed. A look of confused shame crosses her pale, melancholy face. Then, emboldening herself, she walks to a grave on the left of the path and lays down her lacquered basket.

It so happens that the grave is directly opposite Hsiao-shuan's with only the narrow path between them. Hua Ta-ma watches mechanically as the woman lays out four dishes and a bowl of rice; burns paper money and weeps. It occurs to her that in that grave also there is a woman's son. She watches curiously as the woman moves about absently and stares vacantly into space. Suddenly she sees her begin to tremble and stagger backward, as if in stupor.

Hua Ta-ma is touched. "She may be mad with sorrow," she fears. She rises, and, stepping across the path, speaks to her quietly: "Old Mother, don't grieve any more. Let us both go home." The woman nods stupidly, her eyes still staring. Suddenly she utters an exclamation, "Look! What is that?"

Looking along the woman's pointing finger, Hua Ta-ma's eyes take in the grave before them, which is unkempt and has ugly patches of yellow earth on it. Looking more closely she is startled to see, at the top of the little mound, a circlet of scarlet and white flowers.

For many years neither of them has seen clearly, and yet now both see these fresh blossoms. They are not many, but they are neatly arranged; they are not very splendid, but they are comely in an orderly way. Hua Ta-ma looks quickly at her son's grave, and at the others, but only here and there are a few scattered blossoms of blue and white that have braved the cold; there are no others of scarlet. She experiences a nameless emptiness of heart, as if in need, but of what she does not wish to know. The other walks nearer and examines the flowers closely. "What could be the explanation?" she muses.

Tears stream from her face, and she cries out: "Yü, my son! You have been wronged, but you do not forget. Is it that your heart is still full of pain, and you choose this day and this method of telling me?" She gazes around, but, seeing only a black crow brooding in a leafless tree, she continues: "Yü, my son! It was a trap; you were 'buried alive.' Yet Heaven knows! Rest your eyes in peace, but give me a sign. If you are here in the grave, if you are listening to me, cause the crow to fly here and alight on your grave. Let me know!"

There is no more breeze, and everywhere the dry grass stands erect, like bristles of copper. A faint sound hangs in the air and vibrates, growing less and less audible, till finally it ceases entirely. Then everything becomes as quiet as death. The two old women stood motionless in the midst of the dry grass, intently watching the crow. Among the straight limbs of the tree, its head drawn in, the crow sits immobile and as if cast in iron.

Much time passes. Those who come to visit graves begin to increase in numbers. To Hua Ta-ma it seems that gradually a heavy burden lifts from her, and to the other she says, "Come, let us go."

The old woman sighs dejectedly and gathers up her offertory dishes. She lingers for still another moment, then at length walks slowly, murmuring, "What could it have been?"

When they have walked only some thirty paces they suddenly hear a sharp cry from above. "Yah-h-h." Turning round with a shudder they see the crow brace itself on a limb and then push forth, spreading its broad wings and flying like an arrow toward the far horizon.

M

ANTONIO MACHADO

ANTONIO MACHADO (Spanish, 1875-1939). Poet of the inner life. Andalusian Professor of French, who fled to France after the Spanish Civil War. Poetry of great simplicity, bare of adornment, has been compared with that of Yeats. Books: *Soledades, Campos de Castilla, Nuevas canciones.*

PERCHANCE IN DREAMS

Perchance, in dreams, the hand
of the sower of stars
struck the chords of some forgotten music

as a note of the immense lyre,
and the humble wave reached our lips
as a few simple words of truth.

IBERIAN GOD

As the gambler drew his bow
For vengeance in the song,
So the Iberian recklessly let go
A sharp shaft to the Lord of blighting wrong
Who felled his wheat with hail and killed his fruit;
But he praised the Lord who brought his crops to head
Full eared, gold to the root,
The rye and wheat that tomorrow would be his bread.

"Lord of ruin and loss,
I adore because I fear, because I wait,
But my heart is blasphemous:
Bowing to earth, I pray in pride and hate.

"I know Thy power, my chain I recognize,
Lord, for Thee I dig my bread in sweat and sighs;
O master of the flooding clouds that cost
So dear to summer yield,
Of the autumn drought and spring's belated frost,
Of the scorching heat that sears the harvest field.

"Lord of the bow above the tender grass
Where the white ewe grazes,
Lord of the hut undone when tempests pass
And of the fruit where the worm carves its mazes,

"Thy breathing quickens the hearth fire when it
Is low, Thy splendor ripens ruddy grain,
And on Midsummer Eve the olive pit
Forms and hardens where Thy hand has lain.

"O master of fortunes and of poverties,
Good luck and bad, who yet
Giv'st to the rich man favors and soft ease
And to the poor, his hope and bitter sweat,

"Lord, Lord, in the twelve months' whirling round
I have watched my seed with patient labor sown
Run the same risk in the hard and faithless ground
As a gambler's cash on the losing hazard thrown.

"Lord, paternal now, who wert before a God
Cruel, two-faced, Thy love with vengeance dimmed,
To Thee my prayer of blasphemy and laud
Ascends, a gambler's die cast on the wind."

This man who, insulting God, at his altar prayed,
Defiant of all fate's frowning might forbode,
With dreaming tamed the seas and highways laid
Across them, saying, He is the ocean road.

Is it not this man who raised his God to be
Above all war? Beyond
Fate, beyond earth and sea,
Beyond death and dying, free of every bond?

Did not the Iberian tree,
The encina, yield her branch for holy fire
And, burning, find unity
With God in love's pure flame on the sacred pyre?

But now, so quickly day grows into day!
There are new hearths; for these
New roses thrive in field and wooded bay
And fresh green branches on the ancient trees.

The fatherland is still
Waiting to open furrows to the plow;
For the seed of God there is a field to till
Overgrown with burdocks, thorns, and thistles now.

Day merges into day; the past is wide
To the morrow, the morrow to the infinite;
Men of Spain, no yesterday has died,
Future and past have yet no holy writ.

Did ever the Spanish God His face reveal?
My heart awaits the hand
Of an Iberian, vigorous and leal,
To carve in oaken timbers of Castile
The God austere who reigns in this brown land.

AUTUMN DAWN

A highroad's barren scar
Among the grey rock-spires
And humble pastures far
Where strong black bulls are grazing. Brambles, thickets, briars.

The dew has drenched with cold
The landscape in the dark
And the poplars' frieze of gold,
Toward the river's arc.

A hint of dawn half seen
With purple crags for frame.
Beside his greyhounds keen,
His eager gun at rest, a hunter stalking game.

AT THE BURIAL OF A FRIEND

They gave him earth, one horrible afternoon
Of the month of July, under a fiery sun.

At a step from the open sepulchre
There were roses with rotting petals
Amongst geraniums whose scent was keen
And whose flowers were red. The sky

Pure and blue. A breeze
That was strong and dry was blowing.

Suspended from the great cords,
The coffin was let down,
Heavily, to the bottom of the ditch,
By the two gravediggers. . . .

And, as it came to rest, it struck with a loud, solemn noise, in the
   silence.

The thud of a coffin on the earth is a thing
That is, absolutely, serious.

Against the black box broke
The heavy, dusty lumps of earth. . . .

The air drew its whitish breath
From the deep ditch.

—And thou, already shadowless, sleepest and restest.
Long peace to thy bones. . . .

Definitively,
Sleep thou, a quiet, and real, sleep.

POEM

The street in shadow. The high old mansions hide
The dying sun; there are echoes of light in the balconies.

Do you not see, in the charm of that flowered balcony,
The rosy oval of a face you know?

The image, behind the pane, with its equivocal reflection,
Gleams and vanishes, like an old daguerreotype.

In the street only the sound of your step is heard.
Slowly the echoes of its passing die away.

Oh, anguish. The heart grows heavy and hurts. "Is it she?"
It could not be. . . . Go on. . . . The star in the sky.

CHILDISH DREAM

A clear night
Of holiday and moonlight
Night of my dreams
Night of joy

—my soul was brightness
That, to-day, is all fog
My hair
Was not yet black—

The youngest fairy
Took me in her arms
When that joyous holiday
Burned in the square

So, in the crackling
Of the illuminations
Love wove
Its skeins of dances

And in that night
Of holiday and moonlight
Night of my dreams
Night of joy

The youngest fairy
Kissed my forehead. . . .
With her fine hand
Said her goodbyes to me

All the rose trees
Give their perfumes
All the loves
Unfold love

POEM

The loved house
In which she lived
Shows,
On a pile of rubble, ruined
And demolished
A shapeless, wooden skeleton
Black, eaten away.

The moon throws its clear light
In dreams that gleam like silver
On the windows. Ill-dressed, sad,
I walk through the old street.

MAURICE MAETERLINCK

MAURICE MAETERLINCK (Belgian, 1862-1949). Natural scientist and
shadowy symbolist. Poet, dramatist and philosopher. Won first recognition as
playwright: *Pelléas and Mélisande* (set to music by Debussy), *The Bluebird*,
Interior. His theater permeated by sense of doom and death. In *Life of the
Bee* and *Life of the Ant*, he wrote artfully on scientific matters. Nobel Prize,
1911.

THE LIFE OF THE DEAD

LAST night, I had a visit from an uncle who died about fifty years
ago. During his lifetime, he was what we call a "jolly old fellow,"
a positive and practical mind. He told me that the cemetery which
we had chosen as his quarters was cozy and well managed by one
of his friends of the Great Beyond, a remarkable, decent and distinguished gravedigger. My dear uncle was feeling at home and

was very happy. A part of himself, in which he never had been seriously interested, had left him to go he knew not where; but all that was human, solid and well balanced had accompanied him in his new and last abode. The dead had organized, underground, small but very lively friendly, or rather brotherly gatherings, where neighbors met to talk over the happenings of the cemetery, for every day brought new arrivals, two or three dead, sometimes even one or two dozens, in the prosperous days of an epidemic. These unexpected tourists had to be received affectionately if they were relatives or friends, and with every courtesy if they were strangers. These gatherings were highly exclusive, and no one was admitted without serious investigations. A class system had spontaneously been established. The deceased were divided in three classes, that is those who, to speak as you speak up here, did not have as yet an evil smell, that is, the new arrivals whose odorless stage was rather transitory: then the ones who emitted strong exhalations, you judge disagreeable, who constituted the middle class, the most numerous, and finally the superior class, the sepulchral aristocracy, whose members were proclaimed immortal because they had ceased emitting any scent, and consisted only of bleached bones, aseptic and carefully polished.

"But, uncle," I interrupted, "why is it that you do not feel certain emanations that we deem unpleasant? Is it because you do not have a nose?"

"It is not a question of nose anymore, but a purely scientific question. There are no evil smells. It is a regrettable error of the inhabitants on the surface. All odors are chemically pure, whether they come from the lily, the rose, the violet or the gardens of the Great Beyond."

"Uncle, another question, if I may? . . ."

"Go ahead, dear, go ahead. I am here to answer you, for we know almost everything. . . ."

"Uncle, how do you receive those who have been incinerated?"

"We despise them! They are renegades, traitors, deserters. They are ashamed of death. They disavow it. They would like to abolish it; and when they come here begging for a place for their little jars of human preserves, we throw those little jars out of the window, into eternity, for we are eternal . . .

"But do not speak to me about those people. . . . When do you expect to join me?"

"I do not know yet. Do you?"

"I could know, if I wanted to, but I would not tell you. Anyhow, as soon as you arrive, let me know. I shall take you under my wing and facilitate your admission in our circles, for it involves a lot of red tape. The dead are even worse bureaucrats than the Americans, and for the most unimportant formality, such as recuperating a lost nail, a tooth, or a radius one has to go through twenty offices, give sixty signatures, disclose the first and last names of one's parents, grand-parents; produce one's birth certificate, marriage certificate, death certificate of sisters, brothers, first and other cousins. It is a deplorable habit of which we have as yet not been able to rid ourselves. It is true that it takes care of our moments of leisure which are long, although very agreeable. . . ."

"Uncle, I also would like to ask you . . ."

"Go on, go on, my child, I am at your disposal."

"What will you do when there is no more place left in your garden in the Great Beyond? It seems to be rather crowded already."

"We will take the one of the living."

"And if they do not want to give it up to you?"

"We will make dead out of them."

"Does that mean that you have the right to kill?"

"We do not have to kill them. We have only to wait. It is time which kills them."

"But uncle, what happens in case of exhumation? What happens to you? What do you feel?"

"We did not have any exhumation yet; but there has been some talk about it. . . . It is supposed to be more unpleasant than moving. You lose everything and do not find your own friendships and little schemes anymore. Happily, exhumation occurs rather seldom. . . ."

"I can see, uncle, that not even death is free of troubles."

"What do you expect, my child, all lives have their little inconveniences."

"Uncle, I would also like to ask you . . . Uncle, where are you? . . . Are not you going to answer me anymore? . . ."

I insisted in vain, I did not get an answer. He had returned into eternal silence. . . .

844

STEPHANE MALLARME

STÉPHANE MALLARMÉ (French, 1842-1898). Dreamlike symbolist poet. Small output, of wide influence on modern poetry. As youth studied in England, returned to France to teach English. Later celebrated for his literary soirées. His most famous poem, "Afternoon of a Faun," was inspiration for first great piece of impressionist music (by Debussy). His entire work delicate, evasive, often obscure.

THE AFTERNOON OF A FAUN

These nymphs, I would make them eternal.
   So rare,
Their delicate rose, that it drifts on the air,
Drowsy with clustering sleep.
   Did I love a dream?
My doubt, fruit of the ancient night, breaks forth
In many a subtle branch, which, on the swell
Of the true forest,
Proves that I proffer to myself,—alas!
The triumph of an ideal want
Of roses.
   Think:
Perhaps these women of your niceties
Are but the figures of your fabled hope!
Faun, the illusion leaps from the blue, cold eyes
As a spring all of tears, of her most pure:
And she all sighs is a contrast
As a warm day's breath on the fleece!
No! By the weary and motionless swoon
Stifling with summer the fresh lilting morn,
No murmur of water but my flute wafts
To the dew-sprinkled woods of consent.
   The only wind
Hustling its sound through the twin-born pipes
Dispersing its arid rain—
The while the horizon unfrowning—
Is the calm, artificial, evident sigh
Of Inspiration, rising to its source.

O Sicilian shores of a quiet fen
Which my vanity sacks to the jealous suns
Submissive under the flowers of sparks,
Reveal:
"Here was I culling hollow reeds,
Tamed by my talent, when, on the glaucous gold
Of distant verdures yielding to the flood
Their richest vines,
A living whiteness surged to its repose:
At the soft prelude to the birth of song
The flock of swans—no!—naiads, fled or plunged."

Inert and scorched in the tawny hour,
Unnoticing by what collective art
Too many hymens scamper off, desired
By him who seeketh Woman:
Then I shall waken, lone, erect,
Under an ancient surge of light,
At the first fervor:
Lilies! and candor in one of you all.

Else that sweet nothing rumored from their lip,
The kiss, that whispers low of perfidy;
My breast, virgin of evidence. testifies a sting
Mysterious, and of a sacred tooth;
But bah! such a secret elects to confide
In the vast twin-born reed that plays to the clouds:
That, sloughing off the cheek's pale pain,
Dreams, in a lengthy solo, I'll delight
The beauty of the roundabout with it
And false confusions with my credulous song;
Of notes so loud that modulated love
Shrinks from the inconsiderable dream
Of back or pure flank in my closed regard,
A resounding, vain, and endless-dreary line.

Strain then, O instrument of flights, malign Syrinx,
To flower anew by bords where you await me!
I, in my noisy pride, shall sing,
Sing long and longingly of goddesses;
And by the paintings of idolaters
Still in their shadows charm the girdle free:

846

So, when I've sucked the splendor from the grape
To banish regret dispelled by my deceit,
Mocking the summer sky,
I raise the empty cluster, with a puff
Belling the luminous skins, for frenzy flushed,
And watch through them till night fall.
Oh, nymphs, bell them with many memories:
"*My gaze, piercing the rushes,*
Lances each deathless form, that in the wave
Drowns its mad burning, while its passion-cry
Leaps to the forest-heaven;
And the glorious bath of tresses drops below
In lightnings and shudders—O diadems!
I hasten; when, at my ankles (bruised,
Knowing the languor of the ill of being twain)
Are sleepers conjoined, in danger of themselves.
I embrace them, not disentwining,
And bear to this grove, which futile shadows flee,
Roses yielding their fragrance to the sun;
Here our frolic shall linger with the day it burns."

I adore you, O wrath of virgins,
O untamed delight of the holy nude burden
That glides, to escape my lips of drinking fire,
As the lightning leaps! The silent dread of the flesh:
From the head of the cruel to the heart of the weak
From whom their innocence droppeth, moist
With tears of frenzy, or less mournful dew.
"*I sinned, gay at defeating these treacherous terrors,*
In having divided the disheveled cluster
Of kisses the gods had so close intermingled;
For, as my lips moved in the passionate smiling
I plunged in the sensuous joy of one only
(Holding by a single finger
So that the frozen candor of her breast
Her sister's crimson ferment might encolor—
Her sister enkindled—
The little one artless, unblushing)
Out of my arms, weak with uncertain dyings,
The ever thankless prey was gone
Without ruth for the sob of my frenzy."

Shall I grieve? toward pleasure others will draw me on
By their tresses bound to the horns of my brow:
You know, my passion, how, purple and overripe,
Each pomegranate bursts and hums of bees;
And our blood, smitten with what will capture it,
Flows for the eternal swarming of desire.
When these woods are tinted of ashes and gold
A festival exults in the darkened forest:
Etna! it is to you that Venus comes
Setting on your lava her ingenuous heels,
When in sad thundering sleep the fires die.
I hold the queen!
   O sure chastisement!
     No,
But the soul empty of words and the dull form
Slowly succumb to the proud silence of noon:
Now I must sleep and forget the blasphemy,
Outspread on the parched sand—and, as I love,
Open my mouth to the healing star of wine!

Couple, farewell; I shall see the shadow that you are.

THOMAS MANN

THOMAS MANN (German, 1875-1955). One of the most distinguished modern men of letters. Came to America to escape Nazism, preferred to return to Europe after war. Early fiction depicted life in Germany (*Buddenbrooks*) and prewar Europe *(The Magic Mountain)*. In stories *(Death in Venice)* and essays, he was arbiter between the artist and the average man. In later years, preoccupied with social and moral issues (in the *Joseph* cycle and *Doctor Faustus*).

A WEARY HOUR

HE GOT up from the table, his little, fragile writing-desk; got up as though desperate, and with hanging head crossed the room to the tall, thin, pillar-like stove in the opposite corner. He put his hands to it; but the hour was long past midnight and the tiles were nearly stone cold. Not getting even his little comfort that he sought, he leaned back against them and, coughing, drew together the folds of his dressing-gown, between which a draggled lace shirt-frill stuck out; he snuffed hard through his nostrils to get a little air, for as usual he had a cold.

It was a particular, a sinister cold, which scarcely ever quite disappeared. It inflamed his eyelids and made the flanges of his nose all raw; in his head and limbs it lay like a heavy, sombre intoxication. Or was this cursed confinement to his room, to which the doctor had weeks ago condemned him, to blame for all his languor and flabbiness? God knew if it was the right thing—perhaps so, on account of his chronic catarrh and the spasms of his chest and belly. And for weeks on end now, yes, weeks, bad weather had reigned in Jena—hateful, horrible weather, which he felt in every nerve of his body—cold, wild, gloomy. The December wind roared in the stovepipe with a desolate god-forsaken sound—he might have been wandering on a heath, by night and storm, his soul full of unappeasable grief. Yet this close confinement—that was not good either; not good for thought, nor for the rhythm of the blood, where thought was engendered.

The six-sided room was bare and colourless and devoid of cheer: a whitewashed ceiling wreathed in tobacco smoke, walls covered with trellis-patterned paper and hung with silhouettes in oval frames, half a dozen slender-legged pieces of furniture; the whole lighted by two candles burning at the head of the manuscript on the writing-table. Red curtains draped the upper part of the window-frames; mere festooned wisps of cotton they were, but red, a warm, sonorous red, and he loved them and would not have parted from them; they gave a little air of ease and charm to the bald unlovely poverty of his surroundings. He stood by the stove and blinked repeatedly, straining his eyes across at the work from which he had just fled: that load, that weight, that gnawing conscience, that sea which to drink up, that frightful task which to perform, was all his pride and all his misery, at once his heaven and his hell. It dragged, it stuck, it would not budge—and now again . . . ! It must be the weather; or his catarrh, or his fatigue. Or was it the work? Was the thing itself an unfortunate conception, doomed from its beginning to despair?

He had risen in order to put a little space between him and his task, for physical distance would often result in improved perspective, a wider view of his material and a better chance of conspectus.

Yes, the mere feeling of relief on turning away from the battlefield had been known to work like an inspiration. And a more innocent one than that purveyed by alcohol or strong, black coffee.

The little cup stood on the side-table. Perhaps it would help him out of the impasse? No, no, not again! Not the doctor only, but somebody else too, a more important somebody, had cautioned him against that sort of thing—another person, who lived over in Weimar and for whom he felt a love which was a mixture of hostility and yearning. That was a wise man. He knew how to live and create; did not abuse himself, was full of self-regard.

Quiet reigned in the house. There was only the wind, driving down the Schlossgasse and dashing the rain in gusts against the panes. They were all asleep—the landlord and his family, Lotte and the children. And here he stood by the cold stove, awake, alone, tormented; blinking across at the work in which his morbid self-dissatisfaction would not let him believe.

His neck rose long and white out of his stock and his knock-kneed legs showed between the skirts of his dressing-gown. The red hair was smoothed back from a thin, high forehead; it retreated in bays from his veined white temples and hung down in thin locks over the ears. His nose was aquiline, with an abrupt whitish tip; above it the well-marked line of the brows almost met. They were darker than his hair and gave the deep-set, inflamed eyes a tragic, staring look. He could not breathe through his nose; so he opened his thin lips and made the freckled, sickly cheeks look even more sunken thereby.

No, it was a failure, it was all hopelessly wrong. The army ought to have been brought in! The army was the root of the whole thing. But it was impossible to present it before the eyes of the audience —and was art powerful enough thus to enforce the imagination? Besides, his hero was no hero; he was contemptible, he was frigid. The situation was wrong, the language was wrong; it was a dry pedestrian lecture, good for a history class, but as drama absolutely hopeless!

Very good, then, it was over. A defeat. A failure. Bankruptcy. He would write to Körner, the good Körner, who believed in him, who clung with childlike faith to his genius. He would scoff, scold, beseech—this friend of his; would remind him of the *Carlos*, which likewise had issued out of doubts and pains and rewritings and after all the anguish turned out to be something really fine, a genuine masterpiece. But times were changed. Then he had been a man still capable of taking a strong, confident grip on a thing and giving it triumphant shape. Doubts and struggles? Yes. And ill he had been, perhaps more ill than now; a fugitive, oppressed and hungry, at odds with the world; humanly speaking, a beggar. But young, still young! Each time, however low he had sunk, his resilient spirit had leaped up anew; upon the hour of affliction had followed the feeling of triumphant self-confidence. That came no more, or hardly ever, now. There might be one night of glowing exaltation—when the fires of his genius lighted up an impassioned vision of all that he might do if only they burned on; but it had always to be paid for with a week of enervation and gloom. Faith in the future, his guiding star in times of stress, was dead. Here was the despairing truth: the years of need and nothingness, which he had thought of as the painful testing-time, turned out to have been the rich and fruitful ones; and now that a little happiness had fallen to his lot, now that he had ceased to be an intellectual freebooter and occupied a position of civic dignity, with office and honours, wife and children— now he was exhausted, worn out. To give up, to own himself beaten —that was all there was left to do. He groaned; he pressed his hands to his eyes and dashed up and down the room like one possessed. What he had just thought was so frightful that he could not stand still on the spot where he had thought it. He sat down on a chair by the further wall and stared gloomily at the floor, his clasped hands hanging down between his knees.

His conscience . . . how loudly his conscience cried out! He had sinned, sinned against himself all these years, against the delicate instrument that was his body. Those youthful excesses, the nights without sleep, the days spent in close, smoke-laden air, straining his mind and heedless of his body; the narcotics with which he had spurred himself on—all that was now taking its revenge.

And if it did—then he would defy the gods, who decreed the guilt and then imposed the penalties. He had lived as he had to live, he had not had time to be wise, not time to be careful. Here in this place in his chest, when he breathed, coughed, yawned, always in the same spot came this pain, this piercing, stabbing, diabolical little warning; it never left him, since that time in Erfurt five years ago when he had catarrhal fever and inflammation of the lungs. What was it warning him of? Ah, he knew only too well what it meant—no matter how the doctor chose to put him off. He had no time to be wise and spare himself, no time to save his strength by submission to moral laws. What he wanted to do he must do soon, quickly, do today.

And the moral laws? . . . Why was it that precisely sin, surrender to the harmful and the consuming, actually seemed to him more moral than any amount of wisdom and frigid self-discipline? Not that constituted morality: not the contemptible knack of keeping a good conscience—rather the struggle and compulsion, the passion and pain.

Pain . . . how his breast swelled at the word! He drew himself up and folded his arms; his gaze, beneath the close-set auburn brows, was kindled by the nobility of his suffering. No man was utterly wretched so long as he could still speak of his misery in high-sounding and noble words. One thing only was indispensable: the courage to call his life by large and fine names. Not to ascribe his sufferings to bad air and constipation; to be well enough to cherish emotions, to scorn and ignore the material. Just on this one point to be naïve, though in all else sophisticated. To believe, to have strength to believe, in suffering. . . . But he *did* believe in it; so profoundly, so ardently, that nothing which came to pass with suffering could seem to him either useless or evil. His glance sought the manuscript, and his arms tightened across his chest. Talent itself— was that not suffering? And if the manuscript over there, his unhappy effort, made him suffer, was not that quite as it should be—a good sign, so to speak? His talents had never been of the copious. ebullient sort; were they to become so he would feel mistrustful. That only happened with beginners and bunglers, with the ignorant and easily satisfied, whose life was not shaped and disciplined by the possession of a gift. For a gift, my friends down there in the audience, a gift is not anything simple, not anything to play with: it is not mere ability. At bottom it is a compulsion; a critical knowledge of the ideal, a permanent dissatisfaction, which rises only through suffering to the height of its powers. And it is to the greatest, the most unsatisfied, that their gift is the sharpest scourge. Not to complain, not to boast; to think modestly, patiently of one's pain: and if not a day in the week, not even an hour, be free from it— what then? To make light and little of . it all, of suffering and achievement alike—that was what made a man great.

He stood up, pulled out his snuff-box and sniffed eagerly, then suddenly clasped his hands behind his back and strode so briskly through the room that the flames of the candles flickered in the draught. Greatness, distinction, world conquest and an imperishable name! To be happy and unknown, what was that by comparison? To be known—known and loved by all the world—ah, they might call that egotism, those who knew naught of the urge, naught of the sweetness of this dream! Everything out of the ordinary is egotistic, in proportion to its suffering. "Speak for yourselves," it says, "ye without mission on this earth, ye whose life is so much easier than mine!" And Ambition says: "Shall my sufferings be vain? No, they must make me great!"

The nostrils of his great nose dilated, his gaze darted fiercely about the room. His right hand was thrust hard and far into the opening of his dressing-gown, his left arm hung down, the fist clenched. A fugitive red played in the gaunt cheeks—a glow thrown up from the fire of his artistic egoism; that passion for his own ego, which burnt unquenchably in his being's depths. Well he knew it, the secret intoxication of this love! Sometimes he needed only to contemplate his own hand, to be filled with the liveliest tenderness towards himself, in whose service he was bent on spending all the talent, all the art that he owned. And he was right so to do, there was nothing base about it. For deeper still than his egoism lay the knowledge that he was freely consuming and sacrificing himself in the service of a high ideal, not as a virtue, of course, but rather out of sheer necessity. And this was his ambition: that no one should be greater than he who had not also suffered more for the sake of the high ideal. No one. He stood still, his hand over his eyes, his body turned aside in a posture of shrinking and avoidance. For already the inevitable thought had stabbed him: the thought of that other man, that radiant being, so sense-endowed, so divinely unconscious, that man over there in Weimar, whom he loved and hated. And once more, as always, in deep disquiet, in feverish haste, there began working within him the inevitable sequence of his thoughts: he must assert and define his own nature, his own art, against that other's. Was the other greater? Wherein, then, and why? If he won, would he have sweated blood to do so? If he lost, would his downfall be a tragic sight? He was no hero, no; a god, perhaps. But it was easier to be a god than a hero. Yes, things were easier for him. He was wise, he was deft, he knew how to distinguish between knowing and creating; perhaps that was why he was so blithe and carefree, such an effortless and gushing spring! But if creation was divine, knowledge was heroic, and he who created in knowledge was hero as well as god.

The will to face difficulties. . . . Did anyone realize what discipline and self-control it cost him to shape a sentence or follow out a hard train of thought? For after all he was ignorant, undisciplined, a slow, dreamy enthusiast. One of Cæsar's letters was harder to write than the most effective scene—and was it not almost for that very reason higher? From the first rhythmical urge of the inward creative force towards matter, towards the material, towards casting in shape and form—from that to the thought, the image, the word, the line—what a struggle, what a Gethsemane! Everything that he wrote was a marvel of yearning after form, shape, line, body; of yearning after the sunlit world of that other man who had only to open his godlike lips and straightway call the bright unshadowed things he saw by name!

And yet—and despite that other man. Where was there an artist, a poet, like himself? Who like him created out of nothing, out of his own breast? A poem was born as music in his soul, as pure, primitive essence, long before it put on a garment of metaphor from the visible world. History, philosophy, passion were no more than pretexts and vehicles for something which had little to do with them, but was at home in orphic depths. Words and conceptions were keys upon which his art played and made vibrate the hidden strings. No one realized. The good souls praised him, indeed, for the power of feeling with which he struck one note or another. And his favourite note, his final emotional appeal, the great bell upon which he sounded his summons to the highest feasts of the soul—many there were who responded to its sound. Freedom! But in all their exaltation, certainly he meant by the word both more and less than they did. Freedom—what was it? A self-respecting middle-class attitude towards thrones and princes? Surely not that. When one thinks of all that the spirit of man has dared to put into the word! Freedom from what? After all, from what? Perhaps, indeed, even from happiness, from human happiness, that silken bond, that tender, sacred tie. . . .

From happiness. His lips quivered. It was as though his glance turned inward upon himself; slowly his face sank into his hands. . . . He stood by the bed in the next room, where the flowered curtains hung in motionless folds across the window, and the lamp shed a bluish light. He bent over the sweet head on the pillow . . . a ringlet of dark hair lay across her cheek, that had the paleness of pearl; the childlike lips were open in slumber. "My wife! Beloved, didst thou yield to my yearning and come to me to be my joy? And that thou art. . . . Lie still and sleep; nay, lift not those sweet shadowy lashes and gaze up at me, as sometimes with thy great, dark, questioning, searching eyes. I love thee so! By God I swear it. It is only that sometimes I am tired out, struggling at my self-imposed task, and my feelings will not respond. And I must not be too utterly thine, never utterly happy in thee, for the sake of my mission."

He kissed her, drew away from her pleasant, slumbrous warmth, looked about him, turned back to the outer room. The clock struck; it warned him that the night was already far spent; but likewise it seemed to be mildly marking the end of a weary hour. He drew a deep breath, his lips closed firmly; he went back and took up his pen. No, he must not brood, he was too far down for that. He must not descend into chaos; or at least he must not stop there. Rather out of chaos, which is fullness, he must draw up to the light whatever he found there fit and ripe for form. No brooding! Work! Define, eliminate, fashion, complete!

And complete it he did, that effort of a labouring hour. He brought it to an end, perhaps not to a good end, but in any case to an end. And being once finished, lo, it was also good. And from his soul, from music and idea, new works struggled upward to birth and, taking shape, gave out light and sound, ringing and shimmering, and giving hint of their infinite origin—as in a shell we hear the sighing of the sea whence it came.

ALESSANDRO MANZONI

ALESSANDRO MANZONI (Italian, 1785-1873). Profound historical romanticist. Founder of the Romantic School in Italy. His novel, *I Promessi Sposi* (*The Betrothed*), Italians sometimes rank next to the *Divine Comedy*. Influenced by Sir Walter Scott, but probes more deeply into historical issues. Also wrote poems and verse plays.

THE INTERRUPTED WEDDING

DON ABBONDIO (the priest) was sitting in an old armchair, wrapped in a dilapidated dressing-gown, with an ancient cap on his head, which made a frame all round his face. By the faint light of a small lamp the two thick white tufts of hair which projected from under the cap, his bushy white eyebrows, moustache, and pointed beard all seemed, on his brown and wrinkled face, like bushes covered with snow on a rocky hillside seen by moonlight.

"Ah! ah!" was his salutation, as he took off his spectacles and put them into the book he was reading.

"Your Reverence will say we are late in coming," said Tonio, bowing, as did Gervaso, but more awkwardly.

"Certainly it is late—late in every way. Do you know that I am ill?"

"Oh! I am very sorry, sir!"

"You surely must have heard that I am ill, and don't know when I can see anyone. . . . But why have you brought that—that fellow with you?"

"Oh! just for company, like, sir!"

"Very good—now let us see."

"There are twenty-five new *berlinghe*, sir— those with Saint Ambrose on horseback on them," said Tonio, drawing a folded paper from his pocket.

"Let us see," returned Abbondio, and taking the paper, he put on his spectacles, unfolded it, took out the silver pieces, turned them over and over, counted them and found them correct.

"Now, your Reverence, will you kindly give me my Teckla's necklace?"

"Quite right," replied Don Abbondio; and going to a cupboard, he unlocked it, and having first looked round, as if to keep away any spectators, opened one side, stood in front of the open door, so that no one could see in, put in his head to look for the pledge, and his arm to take it out, and, having extracted it, locked the cupboard, unwrapped the paper, said interrogatively, "All right?" wrapped it up again and handed it over to Tonio.

"Now," said the latter, "would you please let me have a little black and white, sir?"

"This, too!" exclaimed Don Abbondio; "they are up to every trick! Eh! how suspicious the world has grown! Can't you trust me?"

"How, your Reverence, not trust you? You do me wrong! But as my name is down on your book, on the debtor side, . . . and you have already had the trouble of writing it once, so . . . in case anything were to happen, you know . . ."

"All right, all right," interrupted Don Abbondio, and, grumbling to himself, he opened the table drawer, took out pen, paper and inkstand, and began to write, repeating the words out loud as he set them down. Meanwhile, Tonio, and, at a sign from him, Gervaso, placed themselves in front of the table, so as to prevent the writer from seeing the door, and, as if in mere idleness, began to move

856

their feet about noisily on the floor, in order to serve as a signal to those outside, and, at the same time, to deaden the sound of their footsteps. Don Abbondio, intent on his work, noticed nothing. Renzo and Lucia, hearing the signal, entered on tiptoe, holding their breath, and stood close behind the two brothers. Meanwhile, Don Abbondio, who had finished writing, read over the document attentively, without raising his eyes from the paper, folded it and saying, "Will you be satisfied now?" took off his spectacles with one hand, and held out the sheet to Tonio with the other. Tonio, while stretching out his hand to take it, stepped back on one side, and Gervaso, at a sign from him, on the other, and between the two appeared Renzo and Lucia. Don Abbondio saw them, started, was dumfounded, became furious, thought it over, and came to a resolution, all in the time that Renzo took in uttering these words: "Your Reverence, in the presence of these witnesses, this is my wife!" His lips had not yet ceased moving when Don Abbondio let fall the receipt, which he was holding in his left hand, raised the lamp and seizing the table-cloth with his right hand, dragged it violently towards him, throwing book, papers and inkstand to the ground, and, springing between the chair and table, approached Lucia. The poor girl, with her sweet voice all trembling, had only just been able to say "This is . . ." when Don Abbondio rudely flung the table-cloth over her head, and immediately dropping the lamp which he held in his other hand, used the latter to wrap it tightly round her face, nearly suffocating her, while he roared at the top of his voice, like a wounded bull, "Perpetua! Perpetua! treason! help!" When the light was out the priest let go his hold of the girl, went groping about for the door leading into an inner room, and, having found it, entered and locked himself in, still shouting, "Perpetua! treason! help! get out of this house! get out of this house!" In the other room all was confusion; Renzo, trying to catch the priest, and waving his hands about as though he had been playing at blindman's buff, had reached the door and kept knocking, crying out, "Open! open! don't make a noise!" Lucia called Renzo in a feeble voice, and said supplicatingly, "Let us go! do let us go!" Tonio was down on his hands and knees, feeling about the floor to find his receipt, while Gervaso jumped about and yelled like one possessed, trying to get out by the door leading to the stairs.

In the midst of this confusion we cannot refrain from a momentary reflection. Renzo, raising a noise by night in another man's house, which he had surreptitiously entered, and keeping its ownei besieged in an inner room, has every appearance of being an oppressor,—yet, after all, when you come to look at it, he was the oppressed. Don Abbondio, surprised, put to flight. frightened out of his wits while quietly attending to his own business, would seem to be the victim; and yet in reality, it was he who did the wrong. So goes the world, as it often happens; at least, so it used to go in the seventeenth century.

CHRISTOPHER MARLOWE

CHRISTOPHER MARLOWE (English, 1564-1593). Precursor of Shakespeare in English drama. After brief diplomatic career, settled in London, to become one of "University Wits." Killed, under questionable circumstances, in a tavern brawl, at 29. Greatest plays: *Tamburlaine the Great, The Tragicall History of Dr. Faustus, The Jew of Malta.*

THE PASSIONATE SHEPHERD TO HIS LOVE

Come live with me and be my Love,
And we will all the pleasures prove
That hills and valleys, dale and field,
And all the craggy mountains yield.

There will we sit upon the rocks
And see the shepherds feed their flocks,
By shallow rivers, to whose falls
Melodious birds sing madrigals.

There will I make thee beds of roses
And a thousand fragrant posies,
A cap of flowers and a kirtle
Embroider'd all with leaves of myrtle.

A gown made of the finest wool,
Which from our pretty lambs we pull,
Fair linéd slippers for the cold.
With buckles of the purest gold.

A belt of straw and ivy buds
With coral clasps and amber studs:
And if these pleasures may thee move,
Come live with me and be my Love.

Thy silver dishes for thy meat
As precious as the gods do eat.
Shall on an ivory table be
Prepared each day for thee and me.

The shepherd swains shall dance and sing
For thy delights each May morning:
If these delights thy mind may move,
Then live with me and be my Love.

JOHN MASEFIELD

JOHN MASEFIELD (English, 1878-   ). Exultant poet of the ordinary man.
British Poet Laureate from 1930. Ran away to sea at 14. Worked for a time
in New York. In his poetry, influenced by Kipling; in novels, by Conrad. Best-
known volumes of verse: *Salt-Water Ballads, The Everlasting Mercy, Reynard
the Fox.*

THE WESTERN ISLANDS

ONCE there were two sailors; and one of them was Joe, and the
other one was Jerry, and they were fishermen. And they'd a young
apprentice-feller, and his name was Jim. And he was a great one for
his pot, and Jerry was a wonder at his pipe; and Jim did all the
work, and both of them banged him. So one time Joe and Jerry
were in the beer-house, and there was a young parson there, telling
the folks about foreign things, about plants and that. 'A,' he says,
'what wonders there are in the west.'

" 'What sort of wonders, begging your pardon, sir,' says Joe.
'What sort of wonders might them be?'

" 'Why, all sorts of wonders,' says the parson. 'Why in the west,'
he says, 'there's things you wouldn't believe. No, you wouldn't be-

lieve; not till you'd seen them,' he says. 'There's diamonds growing on the trees. And great, golden, glittering pearls as common as pea-straw. And there's islands in the west. Ah, I could tell you of them. Islands? I rather guess there's islands. None of your Isles of Man. None of your Alderney and Sark. Not in them seas.'

" 'What sort of islands might they be, begging your pardon, sir?' says Jerry.

" 'Why," he says (the parson feller says), 'ISLANDS. Islands as big as Spain. Islands with rivers of rum and streams of sarsaparilla. And none of your roses. Rubies and ame-thynes is all the roses grows in them parts. With golden stalks to them, and big diamond sticks to them, and the taste of pork-crackling if you eat them. They're the sort of roses to have in your area,' he says.

" 'And what else might there be in them parts, begging your pardon, sir?' says Joe.

" 'Why,' he says, this parson says, 'there's wonders. There's not only wonders but miracles. And not only miracles, but sperrits.'

" 'What sort of sperrits might they be, begging your pardon?' says Jerry, 'Are they rum and that?'

" 'When I says sperrits,' says the parson feller, 'I mean ghosts.'

" 'Of course ye do," says Joe.

" 'Yes, ghosts' says the parson, 'And by ghosts I mean sperrits. And by sperrits I mean white things. And by white things I mean things as turn your hair white. And there's red devils there, and blue devils there, and a great gold queen a-waiting for a man to kiss her. And the first man as dares to kiss that queen, why he becomes king, and all her sacks of gold become his.'

" 'Begging your pardon, sir,' said Jerry, 'but whereabouts might these here islands be?'

" 'Why, in the west,' says the parson. 'In the west, where the sun sets.'

" 'Ah,' said Joe and Jerry. 'What wonders there are in the world.'

"Now, after that, neither one of them could think of anything but these here western islands. So at last they take their smack, and off they go in search of them. And Joe had a barrel of beer in the bows, and Jerry had a box of twist in the waist, and pore little Jim stood and steered abaft all. And in the evenings Jerry and Joe would bang their pannikins together, and sing of the great times they meant to have when they were married to the queen. Then they would clump pore little Jim across the head, and tell him to watch out, and keep her to her course, or they'd ride him down like you would a main

860

tack. And he'd better mind his eye, they told him, or they'd make him long to be boiled and salted. And he'd better put more sugar in the tea, they said, or they'd cut him up for cod-bait. And who was he, they asked, to be wanting meat for dinner, when there was that much weevilly biscuit in the bread-barge? And boys was going to the dogs, they said, when limbs the like of him had the heaven-born insolence to want to sleep. And a nice pass things was coming to, they said, when a lad as they'd done everything for, and saved, so to speak, from the workhouse, should go for to snivel when they hit him a clip. If they'd said a word, when they was hit, when they was boys, they told him, they'd have had their bloods drawed, and been stood in the wind to cool. But let him take heed, they said, and be a good lad, and do the work of five, and they wouldn't half wonder, they used to say, as he'd be a man before his mother. So the sun shone, and the stars came out golden, and all the sea was a sparkle of gold with them. Blue was the sea, and the wind blew, too, and it blew Joe and Jerry west as fast as a cat can eat sardines.

"And one fine morning the wind fell calm, and a pleasant smell came over the water, like nutmegs on a rum-milk-punch. Presently the dawn broke. And, lo, and behold, a rousing great wonderful island, all scarlet with coral and with rubies. The surf that was beating on her sands went shattering into silver coins, into dimes; and pesetas, and francs, and fourpenny bits. And the flowers on the cliffs was all one gleam and glitter. And the beauty of that island was a beauty beyond the beauty of Sally Brown, the lady as kept the beer-house. And on the beach of that island, on a golden throne, like, sat a women so lovely that to look at her was as good as a church-service for one.

" 'That's the party I got to kiss,' said Jerry. 'Steady, and beach her, Jim, boy,' he says. 'Run her ashore, lad. That's the party is to be my queen.'

" 'You've got a neck on you, all of a sudden,' said Joe. 'You ain't the admiral of this fleet. Not by a wide road you ain't. I'll do all the kissing as there's any call for. You keep clear, my son.'

" 'Keep clear, is it?' said Jerry. 'You tell me to keep clear? You tell me again, and I'll put a head on you—'ll make you sing like a kettle. Who are you to tell me to keep clear?'

" 'I tell you who I am,' said Joe. 'I'm a better man than you are. That's what I am. I'm Joe the Tank, from Limehouse Basin, and there's no tinker's donkey-boy'll make me stand from under. Who are you to go kissing queens? Who are you that talk so proud and so mighty? You've a face on you would make a Dago tired. You look like a sea-sick Kanaka that's boxed seven rounds with a buzz-saw. You've no more manners than a hog, and you've a lip on you would fetch the enamel off a cup.'

" 'If it comes to calling names,' said Jerry, 'you ain't the only pebble on the beach. Whatever you might think, I tell you you ain't. You're the round turn and two-half hitches of a figure of fun as makes the angels weep. That's what you are. And you're the right-hand strand, and the left-hand strand, and the centre strand, and the core, and the serving, and the marling, of a three-stranded, left-handed, poorly worked junk of a half-begun and never finished odds and ends of a Port Mahon soldier. You look like a Portuguese drummer. You've a whelky red nose that shines like a port side-light. You've a face like a muddy field where they've been playing football in the rain. Your hair is an insult and a shame. I blush when I look at you. You give me a turn like the first day out to a first voyager. Kiss, will you? Kiss? Man, I tell you you'd paralyze a shark if you kissed him. Paralyze him, strike him cold. That's what a kiss of yours'd do.'

" 'You ought to 'a' been a parson,' said Joe, 'that's what you'd ought. There's many would 'a' paid you for talk like that. But for all your fine talk, and for all your dandy language, you'll not come the old soldier over me. No, nor ten of you. You talk of kissing, when there's a handsome young man, the likes of me, around. Neither you nor ten of you. To hear you talk one'd think you was a Emperor or a Admiral. One would think you was a Bishop or a King. One might mistake you for a General or a Member of Parliament. You might. Straight, you might. A General or a Bishop or a King. And what are you? What are you? I ask you plain. What are you?—I'll tell you what you are.

" 'You're him as hired himself out as a scarecrow, acos no one'd take you as a fo'c'sle hand. You're him as give the colic to a weather-cock. You're him as turned old Mother Bomby's beer. You're him as drowned the duck and stole the monkey. You're him as got the medal give him for having a face that made the bull tame. You're——'

" 'Now don't you cast no more to me," said Jerry. 'For I won't take no lip from a twelve-a-shilling, cent-a-corner, the likes of you are. You're the clippings of old junk, what the Dagoes smoke in cigarettes. A swab, and a-wash-deck-broom, and the half pint of paint'd make a handsomer figger of a man than what you are. I've seen a coir whisk, what they grooms a mule with, as had a sweeter face than you got. So stand aside, before you're put aside. I'm the king of this here island. You can go chase yourself for another. Stand clear, I say, or I'll give you a jog'll make your bells ring.'

"Now, while they were argufying, young Jim, the young apprentice feller, he creeps up to the queen upon the throne. She was beautiful, she was, and she shone in the sun, and she looked straight ahead of her like a wax-work in a show. And in her hand she had a sack full of jewels, and at her feet she had a sack full of gold, and by her side was an empty throne ready for the king she married. But round her right hand there was a red snake, and round her left hand there was a blue snake, and the snakes hissed and twisted, and they showed their teeth full of poison. So Jim looked at the snakes, and he hit them a welt, right and left, and he kissed the lady.

"And immediately all the bells and the birds of the world burst out a-ringing and a-singing. The lady awoke from her sleep, and Jim's old clothes were changed to cloth of gold. And there he was, a king, on the throne besides the lady.

"But the red snake turned to a big red devil who took a-hold of Joe, and the blue snake turned to a big blue devil, who took a-hold of Jerry. And 'Come you here, you brawling pugs,' they said, 'come and shovel sand.' And Joe and Jerry took the spades that were given to them. And 'Dig, now,' said the devils. 'Heave round. Let's see you dig. Dig, you scarecrows. And tell us when you've dug to London.' "

WILLIAM SOMERSET MAUGHAM

WILLIAM SOMERSET MAUGHAM (English, 1874-   ). Popular novelist, playwright and story teller. Early life and study of medicine mirrored in semi-autobiographical novel, *Of Human Bondage* (considered his masterpiece). Others: *The Moon and Sixpence, Cakes and Ale*. Effective society plays: *The Circle, Our Betters*. In his stories (*The Trembling of a Leaf*, including the famous "Rain") he is romancer of the Far East par excellence.

THE PATTERN

PHILIP felt a shiver pass through his heart. He had never before lost a friend of his own age, for the death of Cronshaw, a man so much older than himself, had seemed to come in the normal course of things. The news gave him a peculiar shock. It reminded him of his own mortality, for like everyone else Philip, knowing perfectly that all men must die, had no intimate feeling that the same must apply to himself; and Hayward's death, though he had long ceased to have any warm feeling for him, affected him deeply. He remembered on a sudden all the good talks they had had, and it pained him to think that they would never talk with one another again; he remembered their first meeting and the pleasant months they had spent together in Heidelberg. Philip's heart sank as he thought of the lost years. He walked on mechanically not noticing where he went, and realised suddenly, with a movement of irritation, that instead of turning down the Haymarket he had sauntered along Shaftesbury Avenue. It bored him to retrace his steps; and besides, with that news, he did not want to read, he wanted to sit alone and think. He made up his mind to go to the British Museum. Solitude was now his only luxury. Since he had been at Lynn's he had often gone there and sat in front of the groups from the Parthenon; and, not deliberately thinking, had allowed their divine masses to rest his troubled soul. But this afternoon they had nothing to say to him, and after a few minutes, impatiently, he wandered out of the room. There were too many people, provincials with foolish faces, foreigners poring over guide-books; their hideousness besmirched the everlasting masterpieces, their restlessness troubled the god's immortal repose. He went into another room and here there was hardly anyone. Philip sat down wearily. His nerves were on edge. He could not get the people out of his mind. Sometimes at Lynn's they affected him in the same way, and he looked at them file past him with horror; they were so ugly and there was such meanness in their faces, it was terrifying; their features were distorted with paltry desires, and you felt they were strange to any ideas of beauty. They had furtive eyes and weak chins. There was no wickedness in them, but only pettiness and vulgarity. Their humour was a low facetiousness. Sometimes he found himself looking at them to see what animal they resembled, (he tried not to, for it quickly became an obsession,) and he saw in them all the sheep or the horse or the fox, or the goat. Human beings filled him with disgust.

But presently the influence of the place descended upon him. He felt quieter. He began to look absently at the tombstones with which the room was lined. They were the work of Athenian stone masons of the fourth and fifth centuries before Christ, and they were very simple, work of no great talent but with the exquisite spirit of Athens upon them; time had mellowed the marble to the colour of honey, so that unconsciously one thought of the bees of Hymettus, and softened their outlines. Some represented a nude figure, seated on a bench, some the departure of the dead from those who loved him, and some the dead clasping hands with one who remained behind. On all was the tragic word farewell; that and nothing more. Their simplicity was infinitely touching. Friend parted from friend, the son from his mother, and the restraint made the survivor's grief more poignant. It was so long, long ago, and century upon century had passed over that unhappiness; for two thousand years those who wept had been dust as those they wept for. Yet the woe was alive still, and it filled Philip's heart so that he felt compassion spring up in it, and he said:

'Poor things, poor things.'

And it came to him that the gaping sight-seers and the fat strangers with their guide-books, and all those mean, common people who thronged the shop, with their trivial desires and vulgar cares, were mortal and must die. They too loved and must part from those they loved, the son from his mother, the wife from her husband; and perhaps it was more tragic because their lives were ugly and sordid, and they knew nothing that gave beauty to the world. There was one stone which was very beautiful, a bas relief of two young men holding each other's hand; and the reticence of line, the simplicity, made one like to think that the sculptor here had been touched with a genuine emotion. It was an exquisite memorial to that than which the world offers but one thing more precious, to a friendship; and as Philip looked at it, he felt the tears come to his eyes. He thought of Hayward and his eager admiration for him when first they met, and how disillusion had come and then indifference, till nothing held them together but habit and old memories. It was one of the queer things of life that you could not imagine existence without him; then separation came, and everything went on in the same way, and the companion who had seemed essential proved unnecessary. Your life proceeded and you did not even miss him. Philip thought of those early days in Heidelberg when Hayward, capable of great things, had been full of enthusiasm for the future, and how, little by little, achieving nothing, he had resigned himself to failure. Now he was dead. His death had been as futile as his life. He died ingloriously, of a stupid disease, failing once more, even at the end, to accomplish anything. It was just the same now as if he had never lived.

Philip asked himself desperately what was the use of living at all. It all seemed inane. It was the same with Cronshaw: it was quite unimportant that he had lived; he was dead and forgotten, his book of poems sold in remainder by second-hand booksellers; his life seemed to have served nothing except to give a pushing journalist occasion to write an article in a review. And Philip cried out in his soul:

'What is the use of it?'

The effort was so incommensurate with the result. The bright hopes of youth had to be paid for at such a bitter price of disillusionment. Pain and disease and unhappiness weighed down the scale so heavily. What did it all mean? He thought of his own life, the high hopes with which he had entered upon it, the limitations which his body forced upon him, his friendlessness, and the lack of affection which had surrounded his youth. He did not know that he had ever done anything but what seemed best to do, and what a cropper he had come! Other men, with no more advantages than he, succeeded, and others again, with many more, failed. It seemed pure chance. The rain fell alike upon the just and upon the unjust, and for nothing was there a why and a wherefore.

Thinking of Cronshaw, Philip remembered the Persian rug which he had given him, telling him that it offered an answer to his question upon the meaning of life; and suddenly the answer occurred to him: he chuckled: now that he had it, it was like one of the puzzles which you worry over till you are shown the solution and then cannot imagine how it could ever have escaped you. The answer was obvious. Life had no meaning. On the earth, satellite of a star speeding through space, living things had arisen under the influence of conditions which were part of the planet's history; and as there had been a beginning of life upon it so, under the influence of other conditions, there would be an end: man, no more significant than other forms of life, had come not as the climax of creation but as a physical reaction to the environment. Philip remembered the story of the Eastern King who, desiring to know the history of man, was brought by a sage five hundred volumes; busy with affairs of state, he bade him go and condense it; in twenty years the sage returned and his history now was in no more than fifty volumes, but the King, too old then to read so many ponderous tomes, bade him go and shorten it once more; twenty years passed again and the sage, old and gray, brought a single book in which was the knowledge the King had sought; but the King lay on his deathbed, and he had no time to read even that; and then the sage gave him the history of man in a single line; it was this: he was born, he suffered, and he died. There was no meaning in life, and man by living served no end. It was immaterial whether he was born or not born, whether he lived or ceased to live. Life was insignificant and death without consequence. Philip exulted, as he had exulted in his boyhood when the weight of a belief in God was lifted from his shoulders: it seemed to him that the last burden of responsibility was taken from him; and for the first time he was utterly free. His insignificance was turned to power, and he felt himself suddenly equal with the cruel fate which had seemed to persecute him; for, if life was meaningless, the world was robbed of its cruelty. What he did or left undone did not matter. Failure was unimportant and success amounted to nothing. He was the most inconsiderable creature in that swarming mass of mankind which for a brief space occupied the surface of the earth; and he was almighty because he had wrenched from chaos the secret of its nothingness. Thoughts came tumbling over one another in Philip's eager fancy, and he took long breaths of joyous satisfaction. He felt inclined to leap and sing. He had not been so happy for months.

'Oh, life,' he cried in his heart, 'Oh life, where is thy sting?'

For the same uprush of fancy which had shown him with all the force of mathematical demonstration that life had no meaning, brought with it another idea; and that was why Cronshaw, he imagined, had given him the Persian rug. As the weaver elaborated his pattern for no end but the pleasure of his aesthetic sense, so might a man live his life, or if one was forced to believe that his actions were outside his choosing, so might a man look at his life, that it made a pattern. There was as little need to do this as there was use. It was merely something he did for his own pleasure. Out of the manifold events of his life, his deeds, his feelings, his thoughts, he might make a design, regular, elaborate, complicated, or beautiful; and though it might be no more than an illusion that he had the power of selection, though it might be no more than a fantastic legerdemain in which appearances were interwoven with moonbeams, that did not matter: it seemed, and so to him it was. In the vast warp of life, (a river arising from no spring and flowing endlessly to no sea,) with the background to his fancies that there was no meaning and that nothing was important, a man might get a personal satisfaction in selecting the various strands that worked out the pattern. There was one pattern, the most obvious, perfect, and beautiful, in which a man was born, grew to manhood, married, produced children, toiled for his bread, and died; but there were others intricate and wonderful, in which happiness did not enter and in which success was not attempted; and in them might be discovered a more troubling grace. Some lives, and Hayward's was among them, the blind indifference of chance cut off while the design was still imperfect; and then the solace was comfortable that it did not matter; other lives, such as Cronshaw's, offered a pattern which was difficult to follow: the point of view had to be shifted and old standards had to be altered before one could understand that such a life was its own justification. Philip thought that in throwing over the desire for happiness he was casting aside the last of his illusions. His life had seemed horrible when it was measured by something else. Happiness mattered as little as pain. They came in, both of them, as all the other details of his life came in, to the elaboration of the design. He seemed for an instant to stand above the accidents of his existence, and he felt that they could not affect him again as they had done before. Whatever happened to him now would be one more motive to add to the complexity of the pattern, and when the end approached he would rejoice in its completion. It would be a work of art, and it would be none the less beautiful because he alone knew of its existence, and with his death it would at once cease to be.

Philip was happy.

GUY DE MAUPASSANT

GUY DE MAUPASSANT (French, 1850-1893). The great realist of French literature. Strongly influenced by Flaubert, a personal friend. After success at 30, became one of most popular French writers. Ten years later he was hopelessly insane. Slick craftsmanship makes him father of modern commercial story. Most famous tale: *"Boule de Suif."* Novels: *Une Vie, Bel-Ami.*

THE NECKLACE

SHE was one of those pretty and charming girls who are sometimes, as if by a mistake of destiny, born in a family of clerks. She had no dowry, no expectations, no means of being known, understood, loved, wedded, by any rich and distinguished man; and she let herself be married to a little clerk at the Ministry of Public Instruction.

She dressed plainly because she could not dress well, but she was as unhappy as though she had really fallen from her proper station; since with women there is neither caste nor rank; and beauty, grace, and charm act instead of family and birth. Natural fineness, instinct for what is elegant, suppleness of wit, are the sole hierarchy, and make from women of the people the equals of the very greatest ladies.

She suffered ceaselessly, feeling herself born for all the delicacies and all the luxuries. She suffered from the poverty of her dwelling, from the wretched look of the walls, from the worn-out chairs, from the ugliness of the curtains. All those things, of which another woman of her rank would never even have been conscious, tortured her and made her angry. The sight of the little Breton peasant who did her humble housework aroused in her regrets which were despairing, and distracted dreams. She thought of the silent ante-chambers hung with Oriental tapestry, lit by tall bronze candelabra, and of the two great footmen in knee-breeches who sleep in the big armchairs, made drowsy by the heavy warmth of the hot-air stove. She thought of the long *salons* fitted up with ancient silk, of the delicate furniture carrying priceless curiosities, and of the coquettish perfumed boudoirs made for talks at five o'clock with intimate friends, with men famous and sought after, whom all women envy and whose attention they all desire.

When she sat down to dinner, before the round table covered with a table-cloth three days old, opposite her husband, who uncovered the soup tureen and declared with an enchanted air, "Ah, the good *pot-au-feu!* I don't know anything better than that," she thought of dainty dinners, of shining silverware, of tapestry which peopled the walls with ancient personages and with strange birds flying in the midst of a fairy forest; and she thought of delicious dishes served on marvelous plates, and of the whispered gallantries which you listen to with a sphinx-like smile, while you are eating the pink flesh of a trout or the wings of a quail.

She had no dresses, no jewels, nothing. And she loved nothing but that; she felt made for that. She would so have liked to please, to be envied, to be charming, to be sought after.

She had a friend, a former schoolmate at the convent, who was rich, and whom she did not like to go and see any more, because she suffered so much when she came back.

But, one evening, her husband returned home with a triumphant air, and holding a large envelope in his hand.

"There," said he, "here is something for you."

She tore the paper sharply, and drew out a printed card which bore these words:

"The Minister of Public Instruction and Mme. Georges Ramponneau request the honor of M. and Mme. Loisel's company at the palace of the Ministry on Monday evening, January 18th."

Instead of being delighted, as her husband hoped, she threw the invitation on the table with disdain, murmuring:

"What do you want me to do with that?"

"But, my dear, I thought you would be glad. You never go out, and this is such a fine opportunity. I had awful trouble to get it. Every one wants to go; it is very select, and they are not giving many invitations to clerks. The whole official world will be there."

She looked at him with an irritated eye, and she said, impatiently:

"And what do you want me to put on my back?"

He had not thought of that; he stammered:

"Why, the dress you go to the theater in. It looks very well, to me."

He stopped, distracted, seeing that his wife was crying. Two great tears descended slowly from the corners of her eyes towards the corners of her mouth. He stuttered:

"What's the matter? What's the matter?"

But, by a violent effort, she had conquered her grief, and she replied, with a calm voice, while she wiped her wet cheeks:

"Nothing. Only I have no dress, and therefore I can't go to this ball. Give your card to some colleague whose wife is better equipped than I."

He was in despair. He resumed:

"Come, let us see, Mathilde. How much would it cost, a suitable dress, which you could use on other occasions, something very simple?"

She reflected several seconds, making her calculations and wondering also what sum she could ask without drawing on herself an immediate refusal and a frightened exclamation from the economical clerk.

870

Finally, she replied, hesitatingly:

"I don't know exactly, but I think I could manage it with four hundred francs."

He had grown a little pale, because he was laying aside just that amount to buy a gun and treat himself to a little shooting next summer on the plain of Nanterre, with several friends who went to shoot larks down there, of a Sunday.

But he said:

"All right. I will give you four hundred francs. And try to have a pretty dress."

The day of the ball drew near, and Mme. Loisel seemed sad, uneasy, anxious. Her dress was ready, however. Her husband said to her one evening:

"What is the matter? Come, you've been so queer these last three days."

And she answered:

"It annoys me not to have a single jewel, not a single stone, nothing to put on. I shall look like distress. I should almost rather not go at all."

He resumed:

"You might wear natural flowers. It's very stylish at this time of the year. For ten francs you can get two or three magnificent roses."

She was not convinced.

"No; there's nothing more humiliating than to look poor among other women who are rich."

But her husband cried:

"How stupid you are! Go look up your friend Mme. Forestier, and ask her to lend you some jewels. You're quite thick enough with her to do that."

She uttered a cry of joy:

"It's true. I never thought of it."

The next day she went to her friend and told of her distress.

Mme. Forestier went to a wardrobe with a glass door, took out a large jewel-box, brought it back, opened it, and said to Mme. Loisel:

"Choose, my dear."

She saw first of all some bracelets, then a pearl necklace, then a Venetian cross, gold, and precious stones of admirable workmanship. She tried on the ornaments before the glass, hesitated, could not make up her mind to part with them, to give them back. She kept asking:

"Haven't you any more?"

"Why, yes. Look. I don't know what you like."

All of a sudden she discovered, in a black satin box, a superb necklace of diamonds; and her heart began to beat with an immoderate desire. Her hands trembled as she took it. She fastened it around her throat, outside her high-necked dress, and remained lost in ecstasy at the sight of herself.

Then she asked, hesitating, filled with anguish:

"Can you lend me that, only that?"

"Why, yes, certainly."

She sprang upon the neck of her friend, kissed her passionately, then fled with her treasure.

The day of the ball arrived. Mme. Loisel made a great success. She was prettier than them all, elegant, gracious, smiling, and crazy with joy. All the men looked at her, asked her name, endeavored to be introduced. All the attachés of the Cabinet wanted to waltz with her. She was remarked by the minister himself.

She danced with intoxication, with passion, made drunk by pleasure, forgetting all, in the triumph of her beauty, in the glory of her success, in a sort of cloud of happiness composed of all this homage, of all this admiration, of all these awakened desires, and of that sense of complete victory which is so sweet to woman's heart.

She went away about four o'clock in the morning. Her husband had been sleeping since midnight, in a little deserted ante-room, with three other gentlemen whose wives were having a very good time.

He threw over her shoulders the wraps which he had brought, modest wraps of common life, whose poverty contrasted with the elegance of the ball dress. She felt this and wanted to escape so as not to be remarked by the other women, who were enveloping themselves in costly furs.

Loisel held her back.

"Wait a bit. You will catch cold outside. I will go and call a cab."

But she did not listen to him, and rapidly descended the stairs. When they were in the street they did not find a carriage; and they began to look for one, shouting after the cabmen whom they saw passing by at a distance.

872

They went down towards the Seine, in despair, shivering with cold. At last they found on the quay one of those ancient noctambulant coupés which, exactly as if they were ashamed to show their misery during the day, are never seen round Paris until after nightfall.

It took them to their door in the Rue des Martyrs, and once more, sadly, they climbed up homeward. All was ended for her. And as to him, he reflected that he must be at the Ministry at ten o'clock.

She removed the wraps, which covered her shoulders, before the glass, so as once more to see herself in all her glory. But suddenly she uttered a cry. She had no longer the necklace around her neck!

Her husband, already half-undressed, demanded:

"What is the matter with you?"

She turned madly towards him:

"I have—I have—I've lost Mme. Forestier's necklace."

He stood up, distracted.

"What!—how?—Impossible!"

And they looked in the folds of her dress, in the folds of her cloak, in her pockets, everywhere. They did not find it.

He asked:

"You're sure you had it on when you left the ball?"

"Yes, I felt it in the vestibule of the palace."

"But if you had lost it in the street we should have heard it fall. It must be in the cab."

"Yes. Probably. Did you take his number?"

"No. And you, didn't you notice it?"

"No."

They looked, thunderstruck, at one another. At last Loisel put on his clothes.

"I shall go back on foot," said he, "over the whole route which we have taken, to see if I can't find it."

And he went out. She sat waiting on a chair in her ball dress, without strength to go to bed, overwhelmed, without fire, without a thought.

Her husband came back about seven o'clock. He had found nothing.

He went to Police Headquarters, to the newspaper offices, to offer a reward; he went to the cab companies—everywhere, in fact, whither he was urged by the least suspicion of hope.

873

She waited all day, in the same condition of mad fear before this terrible calamity.

Loisel returned at night with a hollow, pale face; he had discovered nothing.

"You must write to your friend," said he, "that you have broken the clasp of her necklace and that you are having it mended. That will give us time to turn round."

She wrote at his dictation.

At the end of a week they had lost all hope.

And Loisel, who had aged five years, declared:

"We must consider how to replace that ornament."

The next day they took the box which had contained it, and they went to the jeweler whose name was found within. He consulted his books.

"It was not I, madame, who sold that necklace; I must simply have furnished the case."

Then they went from jeweler to jeweler, searching for a necklace like the other, consulting their memories, sick both of them with chagrin and with anguish.

They found, in a shop at the Palais Royal, a string of diamonds which seemed to them exactly like the one they looked for. It was worth forty thousand francs. They could have it for thirty-six.

So they begged the jeweler not to sell it for three days yet. And they made a bargain that he should buy it back for thirty-four thousand francs, in case they found the other one before the end of February.

Loisel possessed eighteen thousand francs which his father had left him. He would borrow the rest.

He did borrow, asking a thousand francs of one, five hundred of another, five louis here, three louis there. He gave notes, took up ruinous obligations, dealt with usurers, and all the race of lenders. He compromised all the rest of his life, risked his signature without even knowing if he could meet it; and, frightened by the pains yet to come, by the black misery which was about to fall upon him, by the prospect of all the physical privations and of all the moral tortures which he was to suffer, he went to get the new necklace, putting down upon the merchant's counter thirty-six thousand francs.

When Mme. Loisel took back the necklace Mme. Forestier said to her, with a chilly manner:

"You should have returned it sooner, I might have needed it."

She did not open the case, as her friend had so much feared. If she had detected the substitution, what would she have thought, what would she have said? Would she not have taken Mme. Loisel for a thief?

Mme. Loisel now knew the horrible existence of the needy. She took her part, moreover, all on a sudden, with heroism. That dreadful debt must be paid. She would pay it. They dismissed their servant; they changed their lodgings; they rented a garret under the roof.

She came to know what heavy housework meant and the odious cares of the kitchen. She washed the dishes, using her rosy nails on the greasy pots and pans. She washed the dirty linen, the shirts, and the dish-cloths, which she dried upon a line; she carried the slops down to the street every morning, and carried up the water, stopping for breath at every landing. And, dressed like a woman of the people, she went to the fruiterer, the grocer, the butcher, her basket on her arm, bargaining, insulted, defending her miserable money sou by sou.

Each month they had to meet some notes, renew others, obtain more time.

Her husband worked in the evening making a fair copy of some tradesman's accounts, and late at night he often copied manuscript for five sous a page.

And this life lasted ten years.

At the end of ten years they had paid everything, everything, with the rates of usury, and the accumulations of the compound interest.

Mme. Loisel looked old now. She had become the woman of impoverished households—strong and hard and rough. With frowsy hair, skirts askew, and red hands, she talked loud while washing the floor with great swishes of water. But sometimes, when her husband was at the office, she sat down near the window, and she thought of that gay evening of long ago, of that ball where she had been so beautiful and so fêted.

What would have happened if she had not lost that necklace? Who knows? who knows? How life is strange and how changeful! How little a thing is needed for us to be lost or to be saved!

But, one Sunday, having gone to take a walk in the Champs Elysées to refresh herself from the labors of the week, she suddenly perceived a woman who was leading a child. It was Mme. Forestier, still young, still beautiful, still charming.

Mme. Loisel felt moved. Was she going to speak to her? Yes, certainly. And now that she had paid, she was going to tell her all about it. Why not?

She went up.

"Good-day, Jeanne."

The other, astonished to be familiarly addressed by this plain good-wife, did not recognize her at all, and stammered:

"But—madame!—I—do not know—— You must have mistaken."

"No. I am Mathilde Loisel."

Her friend uttered a cry.

"Oh, my poor Mathilde! How you are changed!"

"Yes, I have had days hard enough, since I have seen you, days wretched enough—and that because of you!"

"Of me! How so?"

"Do you remember that diamond necklace which you lent me to wear at the ministerial ball?"

"Yes. Well?"

"Well, I lost it."

"What do you mean? You brought it back."

"I brought you back another just like it. And for this we have been ten years paying. You can understand that it was not easy for us, us who had nothing. At last it is ended, and I am very glad."

Mme. Forestier had stopped.

"You say that you bought a necklace of diamonds to replace mine?"

"Yes. You never noticed it, then! They were very like."

And she smiled with a joy which was proud and naïve at once.

Mme. Forestier, strongly moved, took her two hands.

"Oh, my poor Mathilde! Why, my necklace was paste. It was worth at most five hundred francs!"

FRANCOIS MAURIAC

FRANÇOIS MAURIAC (French, 1885-   ). Devout and highly principled
Catholic essayist and novelist. Member of French Academy, Nobel Prize-
winner, 1952. A soldier in World War I, member of the Resistance in War II.
His novels (including *A Woman of the Pharisees, Knot of Vipers, The Dark
Angels*) deal primarily with violent passions, in which sinners ultimately
receive grace.

THE ETERNAL BOURGEOISE

A WOMAN who belonged to the highest society of Cortona, a very
pious woman, gave proof of so much devotion to Margaret that
the saint prayed for her benefactress incessantly. One day Christ
spoke to her about this soul. "My daughter," he told her, "tell
your confessor about the shortcomings of her for whom you pray
to Me so often. I shall tell you what they are one after the other
so that your confessor may be able to tell her about them to her
great gain." It is Christ Himself Who proposes this terrifyingly
minute examination of conscience to so many perfect people who,
every week, bring trifles to the confessional and glory in finding
no sin in themselves.

"Tell her that she who is so devoted to you out of love for Me
had, before her marriage, a heart of doubtful virtue. Let her confess
having desired too passionately the man who is now her husband
and of having sought him with immoderate desire. Let her confess
this false virtue in her looks, her words, her gestures. . . .

Let her confess that at the time when a misfortune occurred to
one of her parents, she gave false testimony and helped, as much
as was in her power to do so, to render the judge's sentence unjust,
and that she felt less grief for the degrading record which the
accused thereby incurred than for the money which she made him
lose.

Let her reveal her offense against Me when she betook herself
to the Palace of the Podestat to hear herself proclaimed the most
beautiful among her friends (already queens of beauty!).

Let her admit often having accused servants secretly to their
masters, hoping to win their friendship by an indiscreet zeal in
meddling in their affairs, a zeal which was only hypocrisy since
she had no real affection either for them or for anyone except her
husband and children whom she loved excessively.

Let her reveal her inordinate fondness for delicate foods.

Let her bewail her hardness of heart toward the poor.

Let her admit the use she has made of ill-gotten gains. Let her remember everything she has thus spent. How much money has she not spent in this way, money pilfered from her husband, money coming from frauds, money extorted by violence, money won at gambling. . . .

As the mother of a family, she was in charge of household expenses; let her remember how many useless purchases she made, how many superfluous things she bought with money that was wrongly acquired. . . . (What rich and pious woman ever asks herself questions about 'those things which make one shudder,' which Bourdaloue has denounced as being at the source of every great fortune?).

Let her admit the jealousy that she harbored against her parents who did not support her husband's quarrels, the proud domination she exercised in her husband's family, she who would never have allowed her sister-in-law to behave so in her own. Let her admit her greed in regard to her husband's wards whom she had to take care of because they were poor. Let her remember all the injuries she directed against persons of the household in season and out, and with what pride she adorned her body. . . .

Let her confess the bad things she said and the rash judgments she made concerning the neighbor whose qualities she scorned and disparaged, recalling the faults that she knew about and concealing the good and finding the means of accusing him of other faults of which he was not guilty.

Let her confess the harsh disclosures she made about those who were absent and her flatteries before those who were present.

Let her admit her thirst for honor and praise, her desire to seem richer than others, her jealousy at the idea that others might be superior to her in wealth and beauty, her distraction at church in the presence of other women.

In spite of what I have done for her, I have been unable to attach Myself to her, and if at times she has served Me, it has been out of fear, not out of love.

Although she is free of the vice of impurity, yet she has soiled the marriage bed. She has felt no repugnance at finding herself among those who offend Me in their flesh, she who is full of spiritual vices.

Let her admit how careful she has been to blame others, whether for their ill-gotten gains, their lands, the luxuriousness of their clothes and their perfumes, she who has sought the pleasures of good living and has given alms out of ostentation.

Let her confess her indiscretions concerning her servants, her rash judgments concerning the poor and how she scorned their pleadings, their tears, and their pleasures, their games, and their eating and drinking as well (this last trait is wonderful).

She denies herself nothing in what concerns the number and richness of her garments and does not worry herself at all about covering their nakedness nor appeasing their hunger.

Let her admit having usurped the name which befitted My Mother only when she had herself called Sovereign, she who ridiculed others when they assumed that name.

Although she has moved in the society of the most beautiful and best dressed persons, she has always thought herself superior to them.

Let her admit the frivolity which brings her to exaggerate her sufferings, always regarding them as greater than those of others, she who remains cold and indifferent before their misfortunes.

Let her confess her harshness in regard to her servants to whom she gave no rest after hard work, whether they were ill or not. Instead of the comforting which they needed they received only insults and abuse and were accused of gluttony and negligence. As for herself, their mistress treated herself with high consideration, spoke when she should have kept quiet, and kept quiet when she should have spoken. Let her confess having avoided deformed persons. . . . In spite of all these faults let her have confidence in My mercy. Let her not delay going to her confessor. Yet I say unto you, Margaret, My daughter, that this woman whom you recommend so urgently to My mercy will not fully agree to these favors."

HERMAN MELVILLE

HERMAN MELVILLE (American, 1819-1891). American fiction writer, whose major work, *Moby Dick*, was an utter failure when published—now justly considered one of world's masterpieces. Unable to support family as writer, worked for 20 years as New York Inspector of Customs. His South Sea stories (*Typee, Omoo, Mardi*) enjoyed limited popularity. Navy classic, *Billy Budd*, completed just before death, not published till 1924.

"THE WHALE WATCH" and *"THE CHASE"*
Chapter CXVII

THE four whales slain that evening had died wide apart; one, far to windward; one, less distant, to leeward; one ahead; one astern.

These last three were brought alongside ere nightfall; but the windward one could not be reached till morning; and the boat that had killed it lay by its side all night; and that boat was Ahab's.

The waif-pole was thrust upright into the dead whale's spout-hole and the lantern hanging from its top, cast a troubled flickering glare upon the black, glossy back, and far out upon the midnight waves, which gently chafed the whale's broad flank, like soft surf upon a beach.

Ahab and all his boat's crew seemed asleep but the Parsee; who crouching in the bow, sat watching the sharks, that spectrally played round the whale, and tapped the light cedar planks with their tails. A sound like the moaning in squadrons over Asphaltites of unforgiven ghosts of Gomorrah, ran shuddering through the air.

Started from his slumbers, Ahab, face to face, saw the Parsee; and hooped round by the gloom of the night they seemed the last men in a flooded world. "I have dreamed it again," said he.

"Of the hearses? Have I not said, old man, that neither hearse nor coffin can be thine?"

"And who are hearsed that die on the sea?"

"But I said, old man, that ere thou couldst die on this voyage, two hearses must verily be seen by thee on the sea; the first not made by mortal hands; and the visible wood of the last one must be grown in America."

"Aye, aye! a strange sight that, Parsee:—a hearse and its plumes floating over the ocean with the waves for the pall-bearers. Ha! Such a sight we shall not soon see."

"Believe it or not, thou canst not die till it be seen, old man."

"And what was that saying about thyself?"

"Though it come to the last, I shall still go before thee thy pilot."

"And when thou art so gone before—if that ever befall—then ere I can follow, thou must still appear to me, to pilot me still?— Was it not so? Well, then, did I believe all ye say, oh my pilot! I have here two pledges that I shall yet slay Moby-Dick and survive it."

"Take another pledge, old man," said the Parsee, as his eyes lighted up like fireflies in the gloom—"Hemp only can kill thee."

"The gallows, ye mean.—I am immortal then, on land and on sea," cried Ahab, with a laugh of derision:—"Immortal on land and on sea!"

Both were silent again, as one man. The gray dawn came on, and the slumbering crew arose from the boat's bottom, and ere noon the dead whale was brought to the ship.

Chapter CXXXIV

. . . "Great God! but for one single instant show thyself," cried Starbuck; "never, never wilt thou capture him, old man—In Jesus' name no more of this, that's worse than devil's madness. Two days chased; twice stove to splinters; thy very leg once more snatched from under thee; thy evil shadow gone—all good angels mobbing thee with warnings:—what more wouldst thou have?—Shall we keep chasing this murderous fish till he swamps the last man? Shall we be dragged by him to the bottom of the sea? Shall we be towed by him to the infernal world? Oh, oh,—Impiety and blasphemy to hunt him more!"

"Starbuck, of late I've felt strangely moved to thee; ever since that hour we both saw—thou know'st what, in one another's eyes. But in this matter of the whale, be the front of thy face to me as the palm of this hand—a lipless, unfeatured blank. Ahab is for ever Ahab, man. This whole act's immutably decreed. 'Twas rehearsed by thee and me a billion years before this ocean rolled. Fool! I am the Fates' lieutenant; I act under orders. Look thou, underling! that thou obeyest mine.—Stand round me, men. Ye see an old man cut down to the stump; leaning on a shivered lance; propped up on a lonely foot. 'Tis Ahab—his body's part; but Ahab's soul's a centipede, that moves upon a hundred legs. I feel strained, half-stranded, as ropes that tow dismasted frigates in a gale; and I may look so. But ere I break, ye'll hear me crack; and till ye hear *that*, know that Ahab's hawser tows his purpose yet. Believe ye, men, in the things called omens? Then laugh aloud, and cry encore! For ere they drown, drowning things will twice rise to the surface; then rise again, to sink for evermore. So with Moby-Dick —two days he's floated—to-morrow will be the third. Aye, men, he'll rise once more,—but only to spout his last! D'ye feel brave, men, brave?"

"As fearless fire," cried Stubb.

"And as mechanical," muttered Ahab. Then as the men went forward, he muttered on: "The things called omens! And yesterday I talked the same to Starbuck there, concerning my broken boat. Oh! how valiantly I seek to drive out of others' hearts what's clinched so fast in mine!—The Parsee—the Parsee!—gone, gone? and he was to go before:—but still was to be seen again ere I could perish—How's that?—There's a riddle now might baffle all the lawyers backed by the ghosts of the whole line of judges:—like a hawk's beak it pecks my brain. *I'll, I'll* solve it, though!"

When dusk descended, the whale was still in sight to leeward.

So once more the sail was shortened, and everything passed nearly as on the previous night; only, the sound of hammers, and the hum of the grindstone was heard till nearly daylight, as the men toiled by lanterns in the complete and careful rigging of the spare boats and sharpening their fresh weapons for the morrow. Meantime, of the broken keel of Ahab's wrecked craft the carpenter made him another leg; while still as on the night before, slouched Ahab stood fixed within his scuttle; his hid, heliotrope glance anticipatingly gone backward on its dial; sat due eastward for the earliest sun. . . .

Chapter CXXXV

. . . The boats had not gone very far, when by a signal from the mastheads—a downward pointed arm, Ahab knew that the whale had sounded; but intending to be near him at the next rising, he held on his way a little sideways from the vessel; the becharmed crew maintaining the profoundest silence, as the head-beat waves hammered and hammered against the opposing bow.

"Drive, drive in your nails, oh ye waves! to their uttermost heads drive them in! ye but strike a thing without a lid; and no coffin and no hearse can be mine:—and hemp only can kill me! Ha! ha!"

Suddenly the waters around them slowly swelled in broad circles; then quickly upheaved, as if sideways sliding from a submerged berg of ice, swiftly rising to the surface. A low rumbling sound was heard; a subterraneous hum; and then all held their breaths; as bedraggled with trailing ropes, and harpoons, and lances, a vast form shot lengthwise, but obliquely from the sea. Shrouded in a thin drooping veil of mist, it hovered for a moment in the rainbowed air; and then fell swamping back into the deep. Crushed thirty feet upwards, the waters flashed for an instant like heaps of fountains, then brokenly sank in a shower of flakes, leaving the circling surface creamed like new milk round the marble trunk of the whale.

"Give way!" cried Ahab to the oarsmen, and the boats darted forward to the attack; but maddened by yesterday's fresh irons that corroded in him, Moby Dick seemed combinedly possessed by all the angels that fell from heaven. The wide tiers of welded tendons overspreading his broad white forehead, beneath the transparent skin, looked knitted together; as head on, he came churning his tail among the boats; and once more flailed them apart; spilling out the irons and lances from the two mates' boats, and dashing in one side of the upper part of their bows, but leaving Ahab's almost without a scar.

While Daggoo and Queequeg were stopping the strained planks; and as the whale swimming out from them, turned, and showed one entire flank as he shot by them again; at that moment a quick cry went up. Lashed round and round to the fish's back; pinioned in the turns upon turns in which, during the past night, the whale had reeled the involutions of the lines around him, the half torn body of the Parsee was seen; his sable raiment frayed to shreds; his distended eyes turned full upon old Ahab.

The harpoon dropped from his hand.

"Befooled, befooled!"—drawing in a long lean breath—"Aye, Parsee! I see thee again.—Aye, and thou goest before; and this, *this* then is the hearse that thou didst promise. But I hold thee to the last letter of thy word. Where is the second hearse? Away, mates, to the ship! those boats are useless now; repair them if ye can in time, and return to me; if not, Ahab is enough to die—Down, men! the first thing that but offers to jump from this boat I stand in, that thing I harpoon. Ye are not other men, but my arms and my legs; and so obey me.—Where's the whale? gone down again?"

But he looked too nigh the boat; for as if bent upon escaping with the corpse he bore, and as if the particular place of the last encounter had been a stage in his leeward voyage, Moby-Dick was now again steadily swimming forward; and had almost passed the ship,—which thus far had been sailing in the contrary direction to him, though for the present her headway had been stopped. He seemed swimming with his utmost velocity, and now only intent upon pursuing his own straight path in the sea.

"Oh! Ahab," cried Starbuck, "not too late is it, even now, the third day, to desist. See! Moby-Dick seeks thee not. It is thou, thou, that madly seekest him!" . . .

From the ship's bows, nearly all the seamen now hung inactive; hammers, bits of plank, lances, and harpoons, mechanically retained in their hands, just as they had darted from their various employments; all their enchanted eyes intent upon the whale, which from side to side strangely vibrating his predestinating head, sent a broad band of overspreading semicircular foam before him as he rushed. Retribution, swift vengeance, eternal malice were in his whole aspect, and spite of all that mortal man could do, the solid white buttress of his forehead smote the ship's starboard bow, till men and timbers reeled. Some fell flat upon their faces. Like dislodged trucks, the heads of the harpooneers aloft shook on their bull-like necks. Through the breach, they heard the waters pour, as mountain torrents down a flume.

"The ship! The hearse!—the second hearse!" cried Ahab from the boat; "its wood could only be American!"

Diving beneath the settling ship, the whale ran quivering along its keel; but turning under water, swiftly shot to the surface again, far off the other bow, but within a few yards of Ahab's boat, where, for a time, he lay quiescent.

"I turn my body from the sun. What ho, Tashtego! let me hear thy hammer. Oh! ye three unsurrendered spires of mine; thou uncracked keel; the only god-bullied hull; thou firm deck, and haughty helm, and Pole-pointed prow,—death-glorious ship! must ye then perish, and without me? Am I cut off from the last fond pride of meanest shipwrecked captains? Oh, lonely death on lonely life! Oh, now I feel my topmost greatness lies in my topmost grief! Ho, ho! from all your furthest bounds, pour ye now in, ye bold billows of my whole foregone life, and top this one piled comber of my death! Towards thee I roll, thou all-destroying but unconquering whale; to the last I grapple with thee; from hell's heart I stab at thee; for hate's sake I spit my last breath at thee. Sink all coffins and hearses to one common pool! and since neither can be mine, let me then tow to pieces, while still chasing thee, though tied to thee, thou damned whale! *Thus* I give up the spear!"

The harpoon was darted; the stricken whale flew forward; with igniting velocity the line ran through the groove;—ran foul. Ahab stooped to clear it; he did clear it; but the flying turn caught him round the neck, and voicelessly as Turkish mutes bowstring their victim, he was shot out of the boat, ere the crew knew he was gone. Next instant, the heavy eye-splice in the rope's final end flew out of the stark-empty tub, knocked down an oarsman, and smiting the sea, disappeared in its depths.

For an instant, the tranced boat's crew stood still; then turned. "The ship? Great God, where is the ship?" Soon they through dim, bewildering mediums saw her sidelong fading phantom, as in the gaseous Fata Morgana; only the uppermost masts out of water;

884

while fixed by infatuation, or fidelity, or fate, to their once lofty perches, the pagan harpooneers still maintained their sinking lookouts on the sea. And now, concentric circles seized the lone boat itself, and all its crew, and each floating oar, and every lance-pole, and spinning, animate and inanimate, all round and round in one vortex, carried the smallest chip of the Pequod out of sight.

But as the last whelmings intermixingly poured themselves over the sunken head of the Indian at the mainmast, leaving a few inches of the erect spar yet visible, together with long streaming yards of the flag, which calmly undulated, with ironical coincidings, over the destroying billows they almost touched;—at that instant, a red arm and a hammer hovered backwardly uplifted in the open air, in the act of nailing the flag faster and yet faster to the subsiding spar. A sky-hawk that tauntingly had followed the main-truck downwards from its natural home among the stars, pecking at the flag, and incommoding Tashtego there; this bird now chanced to intercept its broad fluttering wings between the hammer and the wood; and simultaneously feeling that ethereal thrill, the submerged savage beneath, in his death-gasp, kept his hammer frozen there; and so the bird of heaven, with arch-angelic shrieks, and his imperial beak thrust upwards, and his whole captive form folded in the flag of Ahab, went down with his ship, which, like Satan, would not sink to hell till she had dragged a living part of heaven along with her, and helmeted herself with it.

Now small fowls flew screaming over the yet yawning gulf; a sullen white surf beat against its steep sides; then all collapsed, and the great shroud of the sea rolled on as it rolled five thousand years ago.

MENG HAO-JAN

MÊNG HAO-JAN (Chinese, 689-740). Political satirist and lyricist. Spent early days studying in the mountains. When he failed to pass official examination, decided to devote remaining life to literature. Satirical poems incurred Emperor's wrath. Friend and disciple of famous Buddhist poet, Wang Wei.

THE LOST ONE

The red gleam o'er the mountains
  Goes wavering from sight,
And the quiet moon enhances
  The loveliness of night.

I open wide my casement
   To breathe the rain-cooled air,
And mingle with the moonlight
   The dark waves of my hair.

The night wind tells me secrets
   Of lotus lilies blue;
And hour by hour the willows
   Shake down the chiming dew.

I fain would take the zither,
   By some stray fancy led;
But there are none to hear me,
   And who can charm the dead?

So all my day-dreams follow
   The bird that leaves the nest;
And in the night I gather
   The lost one to my breast.

A FRIEND EXPECTED

Over the chain of giant peaks
   The great red sun goes down,
And in the stealthy floods of night
   The distant valleys drown.

Yon moon that cleaves the gloomy pines
   Has freshness in her train;
Low wind, faint stream, and waterfall
   Haunt me with their refrain.

The tired woodman seeks his cot
   That twinkles up the hill;
And sleep has touched the wanderers
   That sang the twilight still.

To-night—ah! beauty of to-night
   I need my friend to praise,
So take the lute to lure him on
   Through the frgrant, dew-lit ways.

GEORGE MEREDITH

GEORGE MEREDITH (English, 1828-1909). Long ignored because of his halting style, later became revered as master of Victorian novel. Striking creator of human portraits in *The Egoist, Diana of the Crossways.* Elaborate analyst of psychological situations, in the light of what he called "the comic spirit." Best poem, *Modern Love,* is based on his own first marriage.

THE PUNISHMENT OF SHAHPESH, THE PERSIAN, ON KHIPIL, THE BUILDER

THEY relate that Shahpesh, the Persian, commanded the building of a palace, and Khipil was his builder. The work lingered from the first year of the reign of Shahpesh even to his fourth. One day Shahpesh went to the river-side where it stood, to inspect it. Khipil was sitting on a marble slab among the stones and blocks; round him stretched lazily the masons and stonecutters and slaves of burden; and they with the curve of humorous enjoyment on their lips, for he was reciting to them adventures, interspersed with anecdotes and recitations and poetic instances, as was his wont. They were like pleased flocks whom the shepherd hath led to a pasture freshened with brooks, there to feed indolently; he, the shepherd, in the midst.

Now, the King said to him, "O Khipil, show me my palace where it standeth, for I desire to gratify my sight with its fairness."

Khipil abased himself before Shahpesh, and answered, " 'Tis even here, O King of the age, where thou delightest the earth with thy foot and the ear of thy slave with sweetness. Surely a site of vantage, one that dominateth earth, air, and water, which is the builder's first and chief requisition for a noble palace, a palace to fill foreign kings and sultans with the distraction of envy; and it is, O Sovereign of the time, a site, this site I have chosen, to occupy the tongues of travellers and awaken the flights of poets!"

Shahpesh smiled and said, "The site is good! I laud the site! Likewise I laud the wisdom of Ebn Busrac, where he exclaims:

> "*Be sure, where Virtue faileth to appear,*
> *For her a gorgeous mansion men will rear;*
> *And day and night her praises will be heard,*
> *Where never yet she spake a single word.*"

Then said he, "O Khipil, my builder, there was once a farm-servant that, having neglected in the seed-time to sow, took to singing the richness of his soil when it was harvest, in proof of which he displayed the abundance of weeds that coloured the land everywhere. Discover to me now the completeness of my halls and apartments, I pray thee, O Khipil, and be the excellence of thy construction made visible to me!"

Quoth Khipil, "To hear is to obey."

He conducted Shahpesh among the unfinished saloons and imperfect courts and roofless rooms, and by half-erected obelisks, and columns pierced and chipped, of the palace of his building. And he was bewildered at the words spoken by Shahpesh; but now the King exalted him, and admired the perfection of his craft, the greatness of his labour, the speediness of his construction, his assiduity; feigning not to behold his negligence.

Presently they went up winding balusters to a marble terrace, and the King said, "Such is thy devotion and constancy in toil, O Khipil, that thou shalt walk before me here."

He then commanded Khipil to precede him, and Khipil was heightened with the honour. When Khipil had paraded a short space he stopped quickly, and said to Shahpesh, "Here is, as it chanceth, a gap, O King! and we can go no further this way."

Shahpesh said, "All is perfect, and it is my will thou delay not to advance."

Khipil cried, "The gap is wide, O mighty King, and manifest, and it is an incomplete part of thy palace."

Then said Shahpesh, "O Khipil, I see no distinction between one part and another; excellent are all parts in beauty and proportion, and there can be no part incomplete in this palace that occupieth the builder four years in its building: so advance, do my bidding."

Khipil yet hesitated, for the gap was of many strides, and at the bottom of the gap was a deep water, and he one that knew not the motion of swimming. But Shahpesh ordered his guard to point their arrows in the direction of Khipil, and Khipil stepped forward hurriedly, and fell in the gap, and was swallowed by the water below. When he rose the second time, succour reached him, and he was drawn to land trembling, his teeth chattering. And Shahpesh praised him, and said, "This is an apt contrivance for a bath, Khipil O my builder! well conceived; one that taketh by surprise; and it shall be thy reward daily when much talking hath fatigued thee."

888

Then he bade Khipil lead him to the hall of state. And when they were there Shahpesh said, "For a privilege, and as a mark of my approbation, I give thee permission to sit in the marble chair of yonder throne, even in my presence, O Khipil."

Khipil said, "Surely, O King, the chair is not yet executed."

And Shahpesh exclaimed, "If this be so, thou art but the length of thy measure on the ground, O talkative one!"

Khipil said, "Nay, 'tis not so, O King of splendours! blind that I am! yonder 's indeed the chair."

And Khipil feared the King, and went to the place where the chair should be, and bent his body in a sitting posture, eyeing the King, and made pretence to sit in the chair of Shahpesh, as in conspiracy to amuse his master.

Then said Shahpesh, "For a token that I approve thy execution of the chair, thou shalt be honoured by remaining seated in it up to the hour of noon; but move thou to the right or to the left, showing thy soul insensible of the honour done thee, transfixed thou shalt be with twenty arrows and five."

The King then left him with a guard of twenty-five of his body-guard; and they stood around him with bent bows, so that Khipil dared not move from his sitting posture. And the masons and the people crowded to see Khipil sitting on his master's chair, for it became rumoured about. When they beheld him sitting upon nothing, and he trembling to stir for fear of the loosening of the arrows, they laughed so that they rolled upon the floor of the hall, and the echoes of laughter were a thousand-fold. Surely the arrows of the guards swayed with the laughter that shook them.

Now, when the time had expired for his sitting in the chair, Shahpesh returned to him, and he was cramped, pitiable to see; and Shahpesh said, "Thou hast been exalted above men, O Khipil! for that thou didst execute for thy master has been found fitting for thee."

Then he bade Khipil lead the way to the noble gardens of dalliance and pleasure that he had planted and contrived. And Khipil went in that state described by the poet, when we go draggingly, with remonstrating members,

> Knowing a dreadful strengh behind,
> And a dark fate before.

They came to the gardens, and behold, these were full of weeds and nettles, the fountains dry, no tree to be seen—a desert. And Shahpesh cried, "This is indeed of admirable design, O Khipil! Feelest thou not the coolness of the fountains?—their refreshingness? Truly I am grateful to thee! And these flowers, pluck me now a handful, and tell me of their perfume."

Khipil plucked a handful of the nettles that were there in the place of flowers, and put his nose to them before Shahpesh, till his nose was reddened; and desire to rub it waxed in him, and possessed him, and became a passion, so that he could scarce refrain from rubbing it even in the King's presence. And the King encouraged him to sniff and enjoy their fragrance, repeating the poet's words:

> *Methinks I am a lover and a child,*
> *A little child and happy lover, both!*
> *When by the breath of flowers I am beguiled*
> *From sense of pain, and lulled in odorous sloth.*
> *So I adore them, that no mistress sweet*
> *Seems worthier of the love which they awake:*
> *In innocence and beauty more complete,*
> *Was never maiden cheek in morning lake.*
> *Oh, while I live, surround me with fresh flowers,*
> *Oh, when I die, then bury me in their bowers!*

And the King said, "What sayest thou, O my builder? that is a fair quotation, applicable to thy feelings, one that expresseth them?

Khipil answered, " 'Tis eloquent, O great King! comprehensiveness would be its portion, but that it alludeth not to the delight of chafing."

Then Shahpesh laughed, and cried, "Chafe not! it is an ill thing and a hideous! This nosegay, O Khipil, it is for thee to present to thy mistress. Truly she will receive thee well after its presentation! I will have it now sent in thy name, with word that thou followest quickly. And for thy nettled nose, surely if the whim seize thee that thou desirest its chafing, to thy neighbour is permitted what to thy hand is refused."

The King set a guard upon Khipil to see that his orders were executed, and appointed a time for him to return to the gardens.

At the hour indicated Khipil stood before Shahpesh again. He was pale, saddened; his tongue drooped like the tongue of a heavy bell, that when it soundeth giveth forth mournful sounds only: he had also the look of one battered with many beatings. So the King said, "How of the presentation of the flowers of thy culture, O Khipil?"

He answered, "Surely, O King, she received me with wrath, and I am shamed by her."

And the King said, "How of my clemency in the matter of the chafing?"

Khipil answered, "O King of splendours! I made petition to my neighbours whom I met, accosting them civilly and with imploring, for I ached to chafe, and it was the very raging thirst of desire to chafe that was mine, devouring eagerness for solace of chafing. And they chafed me, O King; yet not in those parts which throbbed for the chafing, but in those which abhorred it."

Then Shahpesh smiled and said, " 'Tis certain that the magnanimity of monarchs is as the rain that falleth, the sun that shineth: and in this spot it fertilizeth richness; in that encourageth rankness. So art thou but a weed, O Khipil! and my grace is thy chastisement."

Now, the King ceased not persecuting Khipil, under pretence of doing him honour and heaping favours on him. Three days and three nights was Khipil gasping without water, compelled to drink the drought of the fountain, as an honour at the hands of the King. And he was seven days and seven nights made to stand with stretched arms, as they were the branches of a tree, in each hand a pomegranate. And Shahpesh brough the people of his court to regard the wondrous pomegranate-shoot planted by Khipil, very wondrous, and a new sort, worthy the gardens of a King. So the wisdom of the King was applauded, and men wotted he knew how to punish offences in coin, by the punishment inflicted on Khipil the builder. Before that time his affairs had languished, and the currents of business instead of flowing had become stagnant pools. It was the fashion to do as did Khipil, and fancy the tongue a constructor rather than a commentator; and there is a doom upon that people and that man which runneth to seed in gabble, as the poet says in his wisdom:

If thou wouldst be famous, and rich in splendid fruits,
Leave to bloom the flower of things, and dig among the roots.

Truly after Khipil's punishment there were few in the dominions of Shahpesh who sought to win the honours bestowed by him on gabblers and idlers: as again the poet:

When to loquacious fools with patience rare
I listen, I have thoughts of Khipil's chair:
His bath, his nosegay, and his fount I see,—
Himself stretch'd out as a pomegranate-tree.

And that I am not Shahpesh I regret,
So to inmesh the babbler in his net.
Well is that wisdom worthy to be sung,
Which raised the Palace of the Wagging Tongue!

And whoso is punished after the fashion of Shahpesh, the Persian, on Khipil the Builder, is said to be one "in the Palace of the Wagging Tongue" to this time.

ADAM MICKIEWICZ

ADAM MICKIEWICZ (Polish, 1798-1855). Polish patriot, admired for his deep humanity and sentiment. Arrested for political activities, exiled to Russia. Died in Constantinople trying to raise Polish legion to fight for country's liberation. Playwright and poet. *Pan Tadeusz*, his masterwork, a tribute to the free Poland of his dreams.

ZEVILA

THE HISTORIES of many women of fair virtue and men of courage are recorded in the chronicles of Greece and Rome. So, too, would we find them in our own chronicles of Lithuania if some learned scribe had bent his efforts to the golden stylus and inscribed their stories in our annals; but since none have been moved to do so, I, myself, have resolved to set down here in homely words a short history from our ancient books.

About the year of Our Lord 1400, Prince Koryat, a great and powerful monarch, reigned over Novogrodek and Soinim and Leda. His only daughter, Zevila, (which is in our tongue, Diana), was a comely damsel and fair, but it was rumored that she dreaded the marriage vows, since she shook her head when princes and great barons from distant lands sent their ambassadors requesting her hand, saying she would rest a maid for the days of her life. Howbeit, the Princess Zevila had for a long time loved in her secret heart the Knight Poray, a man of her own country in whose prowess and military cunning her father, Prince Koryat, found good comfort and who, in the absence of the prince, was left in command of the kingdom. Poray was at no small pains to meet his lady in secret, so that they might together unbosom their sweet sentiments the one for the other.

It befell that Prince Koryat when he returned from the wars was sore aggrieved to see a change in his beloved daughter. Her sighs and tears, her ashen cheeks and trembling words when she greeted him, told him at once how matters stood.

"A bawd! My Zevila a bawd!" he cried. "So, thy debauch has led thee to assoil thy father's line. Be gone from my eyes and know that you and the man who brought you to this dishonor shall die a hard death together!"

So it was trumpeted throughout the city that he who would name Zevila's lover and prove the fellow's guilt should receive a rich reward. Yet with all the trumpeting, there was no man who knew about the secret amours of the princess or who would bear a tale to Koryat. Love of Zevila lay deep in the hearts of her subjects and serving folk, and furthermore, no breath of suspicion had fallen upon the Knight Poray who, although he discreetly bewailed his misfortune, showed to the court a jovial face.

When Prince Koryat found that all the trumpeting and inquests stirred no man to speak, he tried with mighty threats to force the secret from his daughter's lips. But no force prevailed upon her.

"My father," she said. "I do confess my own full share of guilt, so punish me, as I am not worthy to cry thee mercy for what I have done; but 'tis not for me to visit like ruin upon another. That would be an even greater offense against the gods."

On hearing this the prince put aside his threatening manner and fell to wheedling. Concealing his ire with silken speech he pledged himself in honeyed words to forgive her of her sin if only he might learn the name of her seducer.

Zevila spoke not, replying only with sobs and tears. Then the prince, waxing angry, commanded that his only daughter be put in chains and cast into a dungeon, from which she was to be led forth anon and put to death.

Now hath any writing man the words to relate the sound of the grief and lamenting that arose from the whole city! The people likened the Princess Zevila in their hearts unto a deity, and looked upon her as a tender mother who helped the poor and softened as much as she could the hard will of the prince. Wherefore, the people surged to the court, weeping bitterly and begging the prince to be merciful toward poor Zevila. But they gained nothing for their tears.

Now in those days, says the history, there was always strife between the men of Lithuania and the Russian *kniazes* or princes. One day the *kniaz* Ivan who wished to take Koryat's city, marched with great haste to spread his camps around the place. He attacked so swiftly that before the full tidings of his deeds were heard much blood had been spilled.

All this happened on the day before the Great Feast, the morning on which Princess Zevila was to die.

Seeing his plight, Prince Koryat prayed Poray to ride forth with a small company of knights and lay on the foe with guile, while the prince strengthened the walls of his city. Poray, not knowing how strong the foe was but never losing heart, rode forth and fell upon Ivan's men who, he found, were out of sorts and craven. He dealt them such a mighty blow that they ran back to their Cossack camp and would have met their doom had not night fallen to end their sorry plight.

Without tarrying Poray set his men about the enemy, encompassing them, then he, himself, rode back into the city to bring the glad tidings to Koryat. The people made merry and the prince rode forth with his train and was full of praise for his knight. He called Poray the defender of the city and bade him to the castle for a mighty feast.

Now when those two were alone Poray fell down at the feet of his prince, speaking many words.

"Forsooth, my lord, my prince," he said, "I have laid heavy defeat upon your foe and, the gods willing, we shall destroy them to the last one, for which I pray as my reward that you do not put to death your only daughter but, by your grace give her to me as wife. For such a reward I swear to repay you with my blood and all my prowess, in all ways I am able."

The prince was angered and spoke thus his displeasure!

"How now, Poray! Why do you make me rejoice and sadden my heart in the same breath. I rejoice in your noble service, but what you ask is not in my power. Our revered forefathers, the Lithuanian princes, have never given their daughters to wed with their subjects, and woe be unto him who follows not the customs of his ancestors. As for the man who, goaded by success and pride, seeketh beyond his station—I will not dwell on that! Still there is the fact that my wanton child has assoiled the honor of our princely house. I trust it was not you who led her astray and put this shame upon her, and yet, why your sudden heart for this trollop?"

Thus they discoursed, then parted, each seeming still in a friendly mind with the other; each having mastered his wrath at least long enough to conceal it. Poray, hurt by his lord's ingratitude and foreseeing evil for his fortune, let seeds of vengeance spring up in his soul. The prince, no less, was fearful that Poray, for the love if his mistress and his knightly fortune, might seize the capital for his own. Koryat brooded over his need to take the knight's life but he dared not do it at once, because such a deed would sit ill on the people who were now making a great noise and calling Poray their defender. And, furthermore, he himself was still in need of Poray's right hand to crush his enemy.

This, sayeth the chronicle, was on the eve of the Great Feast. In the morning the Princess Zevila was to die.

Meanwhile Ivan, the Russian *kniaz*, hard beaten and surrounded, sat fretting in his camp, waiting for the dawn of the day of his defeat, hopeless, not knowing what more he could do. Suddenly into his tent ran sentries with word that a man in black armor had ridden into the encampment and would have audience with him. Did Ivan wish to hear the man?

When the knight in black armor was fetched he spoke thus to Ivan, "*Kniaz* Ivan, I am Poray who has twice beaten your Russian men and who holds you surrounded. I come to deliver to you the city, the prince, and all his possessions and men-at-arms on one condition: you must swear with a mighty oath that you will not harm our folk with fire or sword and that you will grant me to wife the princess inprisoned in the city, as well as the full protection of your men-at-arms."

As the *kniaz* agreed, cocks crowed in the early light and it was the day of the Great Feast, the day on which the Princess Zevila was to die.

A great tumult arose throughout the whole city, the like of which no man hath the cunning to describe. Those of the townsfolk who were hot of blood and resisted forfeited their heads; their fellows, being struck by fear, yielded themselves to the foe.

Poray then broke open the prison and found—oh, the horror of it!—his beloved, pale as ashes, alone and forgotten on a bed of rags there in the dungeon hole. When she saw Poray she fell in a swoon.

They bore her forth into the light and did what they could, yet she lay as one dead. A great press of folk about her crowded around, crying and calling unto her, but she did not open her eyes.

For a long time she lay there, then between her lids she marveled to see the people pressing about her and among them the armed foe. Then Poray spoke to her, "Pray, quiet your fears, my sweet.

Those are Ivan's men-at-arms who avenge our hurt and will serve as our protectors."

Zevila, hearing this, almost swooned again, but suddenly she drew the sword of Poray and smote him fair in the breast with such might that the blade sank deep.

"Traitor," she cried, "is your homeland such a mean thing in your heart that you would sell it for the smoothness of a woman's flesh? Oh, man of no honor, is this the way you would repay me for my so great a love? And ye, vassals, why do you not spend your wrath and vengeance on Ivan's brigands there?"

So saying, Zevila struck out with the sword at the foemen nigh about; then all the people stirred as though a fire had touched them and each man of them fell upon the unsuspecting Russians with swords and whatever weapons he could find to hand. Many foemen were done to death indoors and in the streets and others were taken alive for captives. Zevila hastened to the place where Prince Koryat, her father, stood fettered to the barricade.

"My father," she cried, then fell down there dead at his feet.

They buried Zevila at the foot of the mountain called Mendoga, and there the people came to make a *kopiec* or memorial mound and planted trees about. And even unto this day the old folk, being thankful to Almighty God that He did not offer them up to disgrace and the scorn of their foe, tell the story of Zevila to their young.

EDNA ST. VINCENT MILLAY

EDNA ST. VINCENT MILLAY (American, 1882-1950). One of the great figures in modern American poetry. Became famous at 19, while still in college, for long poem, "Renascence." In New York, worked with Provincetown Players and Theatre Guild. Among many volumes of verse: *A Few Figs from Thistles, Wine from These Grapes, Fatal Interview.* Her sonnets have been called best since Shakespeare.

WHAT LIPS MY LIPS HAVE KISSED

What lips my lips have kissed, and where, and why,
I have forgotten, and what arms have lain
Under my head till morning; but the rain
Is full of ghosts tonight, that tap and sigh

Upon the glass and listen for reply;
And in my heart there stirs a quiet pain
For unremembered lads that not again
Will turn to me at midnight with a cry.
Thus in the winter stands the lonely tree,
Nor knows what birds have vanished one by one,
Yet knows its boughs more silent than before:
I cannot say what loves have come and gone;
I only know that summer sang in me
A little while, that in me sings no more.

ELEGY BEFORE DEATH

There will be rose and rhododendron
    When you are dead and under ground;
Still will be heard from white syringas
    Heavy with bees, a sunny sound.

Still will the tamaracks be raining
    After the rain has ceased, and still
Will there be robins in the stubble,
    Brown sheep upon the warm green hill.

Spring will not ail nor autumn falter;
    Nothing will know that you are gone,
Saving alone some sullen plough-land
    None but yourself set foot upon;

Saving the may-weed and the pig-weed
    Nothing will know that you are dead,—
These, and perhaps a useless wagon
    Standing beside some tumbled shed.

Oh, there will pass with your great passing
    Little of beauty not your own,—
Only the light from common water,
    Only the grace from simple stone.

JOHN MILTON

JOHN MILTON (English, 1608-1674). The noblest of England's poets. In youth wrote more lyric poems (*Lycidas, L'Allegro, Il Penseroso*). In middle years composed pamphlets on civil and religious liberty (*Areopagitica*) and sonnets. Late in life, blind and in retirement, wrote *Paradise Lost, Paradise Regained, Samson Agonistes*. His command of blank verse unrivaled in English.

IL PENSEROSO

Hence, vain, deluding Joys,
   The brood of Folly without father bred!
How little you bestéd,
   Or fill the fixéd mind with all your toys!
Dwell in some idle brain,
   And fancies fond with gaudy shapes possess,
As thick and numberless
   As the gay motes that people the sunbeams,
Or likest hovering dreams,
   The fickle pensioners of Morpheus' train.
But, hail! thou Goddess, sage and holy!
Hail, divinest Melancholy!
Whose saintly visage is too bright
To hit the sense of human sight,
And therefore to our weaker view,
O'erlaid with black, staid Wisdom's hue;
Black, but such as in esteem
Prince Memnon's sister might beseem,
Or that starred Ethiop queen that strove
To set her beauty's praise above
The Sea-nymphs, and their powers offended.
Yet thou art higher far descended;
Thee bright-haired Vesta long of yore
To solitary Saturn bore;
His daughter she; in Saturn's reign
Such mixture was not held a stain.
Oft in glimmering bowers and glades
He met her, and in secret shades
Of woody Ida's inmost grove,
Whilst yet there was no fear of Jove.

Come, pensive Nun, devout and pure,
Sober, steadfast, and demure,
All in a robe of darkest grain,
Flowing with majestic train,
And sable stole of cypress lawn
Over thy decent shoulders drawn.
Come; but keep thy wonted state
With even step, and musing gait,
And looks commercing with the skies
Thy rapt soul sitting in thine eyes;
There, held in holy passion still,
Forget thyself to marble, till
With a sad, leaden, downward cast
Thou fix them on the earth as fast.
And join with thee calm Peace and Quiet,
Spare Fast, that oft with gods doth diet,
And hears the Muses in a ring
Aye round about Jove's altar sing;
And add to these retiréd Leisure,
That in trim gardens takes his pleasure;
But, first and chiefest, with thee bring
Him that yon soars on golden wing,
Guiding the fiery-wheeléd throne,
The cherub Contemplation;
And the mute Silence hist along,
'Less Philomel will deign a song,
In her sweetest, saddest plight,
Smoothing the rugged brow of Night,
While Cynthia checks her dragon yoke
Gently o'er the accustomed oak.
Sweet bird, that shun'st the noise of folly,
Most musical, most melancholy!
Thee, chauntress, oft the woods among
I woo, to hear thy evensong;
And, missing thee, I walk unseen
On the dry, smooth-shaven green,
To behold the wandering moon
Riding near her highest noon,
Like one that had been led astray
Through the heaven's wide, pathless way,

And oft, as if her head she bowed,
Stooping through a fleecy cloud.
Oft, on a plat of rising ground,
I hear the far-off curfew sound,
Over some wide-watered shore,
Swinging slow with sullen roar;
Or, if the air will not permit,
Some still, removéd place will fit,
Where glowing embers through the room
Teach light to counterfeit a gloom,
Far from all resort of mirth,
Save the cricket on the hearth,
Or the bellman's drowsy charm
To bless the doors from nightly harm.
Or let my lamp, at midnight hour,
Be seen in some high, lonely tower
Where I may oft outwatch the Bear,
With thrice-great Hermes, or unsphere
The spirit of Plato, to unfold
What world or what vast regions hold
The immortal mind that hath forsook
Her mansion in this fleshly nook;
And of those demons that are found
In fire, air, flood, or underground,
Whose power hath a true consent
With planet or with element.
Sometime let gorgeous Tragedy
In sceptered pall come sweeping by,
Presenting Thebes, or Pelops' line,
Or the tale of Troy divine.
Or what—though rare—of later age
Ennobled hath the buskined stage.
But, O sad Virgin! that thy power
Might raise Musæus from his bower;
Or bid the soul of Orpheus sing
Such notes as, warbled to the string,
Drew iron tears down Pluto's cheek,
And made Hell grant what love did seek;
Or call up him that left half told
The story of Cambuscan bold,

Of Camball, and of Algarsife,
And who had Canace to wife,
That owned the virtuous ring and glass,
And of the wondrous horse of brass
On which the Tartar king did ride;
And if aught else great bards beside
In sage and solemn tunes have sung,
Of tourneys, and of trophies hung,
Of forests, and enchantments drear,
Where more is meant than meets the ear.
Thus, Night, oft see me in thy pale career,
Till civil-suited Morn appear,
Not tricked and frounced, as she was wont
With the Attic boy to hunt,
But kerchiefed in a comely cloud,
While rocking winds are piping loud,
Or ushered with a shower still,
When the gust hath blown his fill,
Ending on the rustling leaves,
With minute-drops from off the eaves.
And. when the sun begins to fling
His flaring beams, me, Goddess, bring
To archéd walks of twilight groves,
And shadows brown, that Silvan loves,
Of pine, or monumental oak,
Where the rude ax with heavéd stroke
Was never heard the nymphs to daunt,
Or fright them from their hallowed haunt.
There in close covert, by some brook,
Where no profaner eye may look,
Hide me from day's garish eye,
While the bee with honeyed thigh,
That at her flowery work doth sing,
And the waters murmuring,
With such dewy-feathered Sleep.
And let some strange, mysterious dream
Wave at his wings, in airy stream
Of lively portraiture displayed,
Softly on my eyelids laid;
And, as I wake, sweet music breathe
Above, about, or underneath,

Sent by some Spirit to mortals good,
Or the unseen Genius of the wood.
But let my due feet never fail
To walk the studious cloister's pale,
And love the high embowéd roof,
With antique pillars massy-proof,
And storied windows richly dight,
Casting a dim, religious light,
There let the pealing organ blow,
To the full-voiced choir below,
In service high and anthems clear,
As may with sweetness, through mine ear,
And may at last my weary age
Find out the peaceful hermitage
The hairy gown and mossy cell,
Where I may sit and rightly spell
Of every star that heaven doth shew,
And every herb that sips the dew,
Till old experience do attain
To something like prophetic strain.
These pleasures, Melancholy, give,
And I with thee will choose to live.

MOLIERE

MOLIÈRE (Jean-Baptiste Poquelin, French, 1622-1673). France's greatest comic poet. A complete man of the theater, passing his life as actor, playwright, manager. Company he founded is ancestor of present Théatre Française. His greatest works are comedies of character: *Le Tartuffe, Dom Juan, Le Misanthrope, Le Bourgeois Gentilhomme.* Unremitting satirist of sham and hypocrisy. Founded the comedy of manners in France.

FIRST LESSON IN PHILOSOPHY

Philosophy-Master. What have you a mind to learn?
Mr. Jourdain. Everything I can, for I have all the desire in the world to be a scholar, and it vexes me that my father and mother had not made me study all the sciences when I was young.

Master. That's a very reasonable feeling. *Nam sine doctrina vita est quasi mortis imago.* You understand that, and are acquainted with the Latin, of course?

M. Jour. Yes; but act as if I were not acquainted with it. Tell me what it means.

Master. It means that "without learning life is as it were an image of death."

M. Jour. That same Latin's in the right.

Master. Don't you know some principles, some rudiments of science?

M. Jour. Oh, yes! I can read and write. . . . But now I must confide a secret to you. I'm in love with a person of quality, and I should be glad if you would help me to write something to her in a short billet-doux, which I'll drop at her feet.

Master. Very well.

M. Jour. That will be gallant, won't it?

Master. Undoubtedly. Is it verse you wish to write to her?

M. Jour. No, no; none of your verse.

Master. You would only have prose?

M. Jour. No, I would neither have verse nor prose.

Master. It must be one or the other.

M. Jour. Why so?

Master. Because, sir, there's nothing to express oneself by but prose or verse.

M. Jour. Is there nothing, then, but verse or prose?

Master. No, sir; whatever is not prose is verse, and whatever is not verse is prose.

M. Jour. And when one talks what may that be, then?

Master. Prose.

M. Jour. How? When I say, "Nicole, bring me my slippers and give me my nightcap," is that prose?

Master. Yes, sir.

M. Jour. On my conscience, I have spoken prose above these forty years without knowing it; and I am hugely obliged to you for informing me of this.

M. Jour. (to his wife). I am ashamed of your ignorance. For example, do you know what it is you now speak?

Mme. Jour. Yes, I know that what I speak is right, and that you ought to think of living in another manner.

M. Jour. I don't talk of that. I ask you what the words are that you now speak?

Mme. Jour. They are words that have a good deal of sense in them, and your conduct is by no means such.

M. Jour. I don't talk of that, I tell you. I ask you what it is that I now speak to you, which I say this very moment?

Mme. Jour. Mere stuff.

M. Jour. Pshaw, no, it is not that. That which we both of us say, the language we speak this instant?

Mme. Jour. Well?

M. Jour. How is it called?

Mme. Jour. It's called just what you please to call it.

M. Jour. It's prose, you ignorant creature.

Mme. Jour. Prose?

M. Jour. Yes, prose. Whatever is prose is not verse, and whatever is not verse, is prose. Now, see what it is to study.

THOMAS MOORE

THOMAS MOORE (Irish, 1779-1852). Famous Irish versifier of most melodious rhythms. Student of law in London, government official in Bermuda, traveler in United States and Canada. Author of *Lalla Rookh* and *Life of Sheridan,* but chiefly remembered for his *Irish Melodies,* based on traditional Irish airs.

GO WHERE GLORY WAITS THEE

Go where glory waits thee;
But while fame elates thee,
  Oh still remember me!
When the praise thou meetest
To thine ear is sweetest,
  Oh then remember me!
Other arms may press thee,
Dearer friends caress thee,
All the joys that bless thee
  Sweeter far may be;
But when friends are nearest,
And when joys are dearest
  Oh then remember me!

When at eve thou rovest
By the star thou lovest,
   Oh then remember me!
Think, when home returning,
Bright we've seen it burning,
   Oh thus remember me!
Oft as summer closes,
When thine eye reposes
On its lingering roses,
   Once so loved by thee,
Think of her who wove them,
Her who made thee love them—
   Oh then remember me!

When around thee dying
Autumn leaves are lying,
   Oh then remember me!
And at night when gazing
On the gay hearth blazing,
   Oh still remember me!
Then should music, stealing
All the soul of feeling,
To thy heart appealing,
   Draw one tear from thee;
Then let memory bring thee
Strains I used to sing thee—
   Oh then remember me!

OFT, IN THE STILLY NIGHT

Oft, in the stilly night,
Ere Slumber's chain has bound me,
Fond Memory brings the light
   Of other days around me;
     The smiles, the tears,
     Of boyhood's years,
The words of love then spoken;
     The eyes that shone,
     Now dimm'd and gone,
   The cheerful hearts now broken!

Thus, in the stilly night,
　Ere Slumber's chain has bound me,
Sad Memory brings the light
　Of other days around me.

When I remember all
　The friends, so link'd together,
I've seen around me fall,
　Like leaves in wintry weather;
　　I feel like one,
　　Who treads alone
　Some banquet-hall deserted,
　　Whose lights are fled,
　　Whose garlands dead,
　And all but he departed!
Thus, in the stilly night,
　Ere Slumber's chain has bound me,
Sad Memory brings the light
　Of other days around me.

SWEET INNISFALLEN

Sweet Innisfallen, fare thee well,
May calm and sunshine long be thine!
How fair thou art let others tell—
　To *feel* how fair shall long be mine.

Sweet Innisfallen, long shall dwell
　In memory's dream that sunny smile,
Which o'er thee on that evening fell
　When first I saw thy fairy isle.

'Twas light, indeed, too blest for one,
　Who had to turn to paths of care—
Through crowded haunts again to run,
　And leave thee bright and silent there;

No more unto thy shores to come,
　But, on the world's rude ocean tost,
Dream of thee sometimes as a home
　Of sunshine he had seen and lost.

Far better in thy weeping hours
    To part from thee, as I do now,
When mist is o'er thy blooming bowers,
    Like sorrow's veil on beauty's brow.

For, though unrivall'd still thy grace,
    Thou dost not look, as then, too blest,
But thus in shadow, seem'd a place
    Where erring man might hope to rest—

Might hope to rest, and find in thee
    A gloom like Eden's, on the day
He left its shade, when every tree,
    Like thine, hung weeping o'er his way.

Weeping or smiling, lovely isle!
    And all the lovelier for thy tears—
For tho' but rare thy sunny smile,
    'Tis heaven's own glance when it appears.

Like feeling hearts, whose joys are few,
    But, when indeed they come, divine—
The brightest life the sun e'er threw
    Is lifeless to one gleam of thine!

LOVE'S YOUNG DREAM

Oh! the days are gone when Beauty bright
        My heart's chain wove!
When my dream of life, from morn till night,
        Was love, still love,
        New hope may bloom,
        And days may come
    Of milder, calmer beam,
But there's nothing half so sweet in life
        As Love's young dream!
Oh! there's nothing half so sweet in life
        As Love's young dream!

Though the bard to purer fame may soar,
    When wild youth's past;
Though he win the wise, who frowned before,
    To smile at last;
    He'll never meet
    A joy so sweet,
  In all his noon of fame,
As when first he sang to woman's ear
    His soul-felt flame,
And, at every close, she blushed to hear
    The one loved name!

Oh! that hallowed form is ne'er forgot
    Which first love traced;
Still it lingering haunts the greenest spot
    On memory's waste!
    'Twas odor fled
    As soon as shed;
  'Twas morning's wingéd dream;
'Twas a light that ne'er can shine again
    On life's dull stream!
Oh! 'twas light that ne'er can shine again
    On life's dull stream.

COME, YE DISCONSOLATE

Come, ye disconsolate, where'er you languish;
  Come, at God's altar fervently kneel;
Here bring your wounded hearts, here tell your anguish—
  "Earth has no sorrow that Heaven cannot heal."

Joy of the desolate, Light of the straying
  Hope, when all others die, fadeless and pure,
Here speaks the Comforter, in God's name saying,
  "Earth has no sorrow that Heaven cannot cure."

Go, ask the infidel what boon he brings us,
  What charm for aching hearts *he* can reveal
Sweet as that heavenly promise Hope sings us,
  "Earth has no sorrow that God cannot heal."

BELIEVE ME, IF ALL THOSE ENDEARING
YOUNG CHARMS

Believe me, if all those endearing young charms
    Which I gaze on so fondly to-day
Were to change by to-morrow, and fleet in my arms,
    Like fairy-gifts fading away,
Thou wouldst still be adored, as this moment thou **art,**
    Let thy loveliness fade as it will;
And around the dear ruin each wish of my heart
    Would entwine itself verdantly still.

It is not while beauty and youth are thine own,
    And thy cheeks unprofaned by a tear,
That the fervor and faith of a soul can be known
    To which time will but make thee more dear;
No, the heart that as truly loved never forgets,
    But as truly loves on to the close,
As the sunflower turns on his god when he sets
    The same look which she turned when he rose.

THE TURF SHALL BE MY FRAGRANT
SHRINE

The turf shall be my fragrant shrine;
My temple, Lord ! that arch of thine;
My censer's breath the mountain airs,
And silent thoughts my only prayers.

My choir shall be the monlight waves,
When murmuring homeward to their caves,
Or when the stillness of the sea,
Even more than music, breathes of Thee!

I'll seek, by day, some glade unknown,
All light and silence, like thy throne!
And the pale stars shall be, at night,
The only eyes that watch my rite.

Thy heaven, on which 'tis bliss to look,
Shall be my pure and shining book,
Where I shall read, in words of flame,
The glories of thy wondrous name.

I'll read thy anger in the rack
That clouds awhile the day-beam's track;
Thy mercy in the azure hue
Of sunny brightness breaking through!

There's nothing bright above, below,
From flowers that bloom to stars that glow,
But in its light my soul can see
Some feature of thy Deity!

There's nothing dark below, above,
But in its gloom I trace thy love,
And meekly wait that moment when
Thy touch shall turn all bright again!

MORI OGAI

MORI OGAI (Japanese, 1860-1922). Classical stylist, noted as both original writer and translator. As an army doctor, went to Germany to study army hygiene. Later translated many German classics into Japanese. Also author of over 60 novels and short stories. Major influence in modern Japanese literature.

THE PIER

THE pier is long—long—

The rails of four railroads cut straight and obliquely the beams of the iron bridge on which the long and short cross-beams are like the bars of the xylophone on which children play. Through the cracks of the cross-beams, that almost catch the heels of shoes and wooden clogs, here and there the black waves are shown, reflected on the white flashes of sunshine.

The sky has cleared into a deep blue. On the inside of the train where she was sitting with her husband starting today, she did not think the wind was blowing.

When leaving the jinriksha, in which she rode from the station of Yokohama, and standing on this pier, she found that the wind of the fifth of March was still blowing as if to bite the skin, fluttering the skirts of the Azuma coat.

It is the Azuma coat in silver gray, which she loosely wears on her body, that carries the child of her husband, who is starting to-day, this day which is not far from the month of confinement.

She came with her hair in Sokuhatsu. Her boa is of white ostrich. Holding the light green umbrella with tassels, she walks along, surrounded by four or five maidservants.

The pier is long—long——

The big ships are anchoring on the right and the left of the pier. Some are painted in black, some in white.

The anchored ships are making a fence for the wind. Every time she leaves the place where there are ships, a gust of wind blows and flutters the skirts of her Azuma coat.

Two years ago, immediately after he was graduated from the university of literature, the count, her husband, had married her. It was during the previous year that she gave birth to her first child, a princess like a jewel. At the end of the year her husband became a Master of Ceremonies at the Court. And, now, he is starting to London, charged with his official duty.

In his newly made gray overcoat, flinging the cane with crooked handle, her husband is walking rapidly along the pier. The viscount, who is going with him, and whose height is taller by a head than his, also walks rapidly beside him, clad in a suit of similar color.

The French ship, on which her husband is about to go abroad, is anchoring at the extreme end of the right side of the pier.

A stool, like that which is used to repair the wires of a trolley, is stationed on the pier, and from it a gangplank is laid across to the bulwark.

While walking slowly, she sees her husband and the viscount, his companion, crossing the gangplank and entering the ship.

The group of people looking after them are standing, here and there, on the pier. Almost all of them are those who came to bid adieu to her husband and the viscount. Perhaps there are no other passengers on this ship about to sail who are so important and are looked at by so many people.

Some of them are going to the foot of the stool on which the gangplank is laid, and stop there to wait for their companions.

Some of them are standing at the place, a bit before the stool, where the blocks and ropes are laid down.

Among these people there must be some who are intimately known to her husband, and some who know him but slightly. But, standing under this clear sky, they all seem dejected; or is it only her fancy?

The pier is long—long——

Following slowly after them, unconsciously she looks off to her right where there were many round windows on the side of the ship. The faces and chests of women are seen from one of those round windows. Three of them are from thirty to forty years of age; all with white aprons on their chests. They must be the waitresses of the ship. Supposing them to be the waitresses who wait on the passengers of the ship, on which her husband is on board, she feels envious of even those humble women.

There is also a woman at the bulwark, looking down on the pier, who wears a big bonnet with white cloth and carries a small leather bag in her hand. Two big eyes, as if painted with shadows, are shining on her wrinkled face above the large nose, like a hook. She looks like a Jewess. She also must be a traveler who is going on this ship. She is also envious of her.

The pier is long—long——

At last she arrives at the foot of the gangplank. Cautiously she carries her body, which has the second infant of her husband under the Azuma coat, and descends on the deck of the big, black-painted ship. She hands the umbrella to a maidservant.

Led by the people who have come to say farewell and were already on board, she goes back along the bulwark toward the prow. There are rooms for passengers at the end of the way, the numbers of which increase from twenty-seven to twenty-nine.

The viscount is standing at the entrance and addresses her.

"This is the room, madam."

Peeping into the room she finds two beds, under which the familiar packages and trunks are deposited. Her husband is standing before one of the beds.

"Look it through, madam. It is like this."

This is the room; she must look through it carefully. During the long, long voyage of her husband, this is the room where her dreams must come and go.

A man, who looks like the captain, comes, and, addressing her

912

husband in French, guides him to the saloon of the ship. She follows her husband and the viscount and enters the room.

This is a spacious and beautiful saloon. Several tables are arranged, each bearing a flower basket. . . . Gradually the people who came to say farewell gather into the room.

By the order of this man, who looks like the captain, a waiter brings forth many cups in the shape of morning-glories, and, pouring champagne into them, he distributes them among the people. Another waiter brings cakes, like those which are brought with ice cream, piled on a plate in the form of the well crib, and distributes them among the people.

The people who received the cups go after another, and stand before her husband and the viscount, wishing them a happy voyage, and drink from the cups.

Sitting on a small chair beside the table, she is waiting for the time when the congratulations are at an end. During his busy moments, now and then, her husband lifts his eyes to her.

However, there is no more to be said to her before many people. Also, there is no more to be said to him, before many people.

The bell rings. Having bidden farewell to her husband and to the viscount the people are going out, one after another. She also follows them, saluting her husband and the viscount.

Again crossing the dangerous gangplank, she descends to the pier. She receives the light green umbrella from the hand of her maid-servant, and raises it.

Her husband and the viscount are standing on the bulwark, looking in her direction. She is looking up at them from under her umbrella. She feels that her eyes, as she looks up, are growing gradually larger and larger.

Again the bell rings. A few French sailors begin to untie the rope from the gangplank. A Japanese laborer in Hanten is standing on the stool like that which is used in repairing the trolley, preparing to draw down the gangplank. Hanging on the rope of the wheel, pulled by the man in Hanten, the gangplank at last leaves the bulwark.

The noon-gun of the city of Yokohama resounds. With this as a signal, the ship, from the hold of which for some time a noise has been issuing, silently begins to move.

The elderly Europeans, who seem to be a married couple, are standing at the bulwark. They are talking about something of a jolly nature with a white-haired old man who is standing on the pier, with one of his feet placed on an apparatus to roll the ropes, which looks like a big bobbin. They do not seem to regret the parting.

It looks as if the ship is moving. It looks as if the pier is moving. There seems to be the distance of a Pallaraxe between the place where her husband and the viscount are standing and the place where she is standing. She feels her eyes growing larger and larger.

Some of the people who are looking after them are running to the end of the pier. She cannot do such an immodest thing. Suddenly something white waves at the bulwark. It was a handkerchief waved by the hand of a woman who wears a big bonnet decorated with a white cloth. A tall man stands at the end of the pier, in red waistcoat and tan shoes. A white handkerchief waves also from the hand of this man. This also must be a parting in human life.

These two persons set the fashion, and the handkerchiefs are waved here and there. White things are waving also from the people who are looking after the group surrounding the count. She also grasps the batiste handkerchief which she has brought in her sleeve, but she cannot do such an immodest thing.

When the ship seemed to have left the pier, it turned its prow a bit to the right. The place where her husband and the viscount were standing has disappeared at last.

Still she can see a boy about fifteen or sixteen, standing at the stern, in a blue, cold-looking garment like a blouse. What mother is waiting for him in France? Or has he no parents? What is he looking at, standing by the rail at the stern?

Slowly she turned her feet and walked among the maidservants surrounding her.

The pier is long—long——

At the place where the black-painted ship was anchored, until a short time ago, the water is glittering like the scales of fish, as the small ripples are reflecting the pale sunshine.

EDUARD MORIKE

EDUARD MÖRIKE (German, 1804-1875). German poet and novelist, creative in both the classical and the folk manner. His private life was not happy —career as vicar and marriage were unsuccessful. Famous novella: *Mozart on His Trip to Prague.* Best poems are extremely simple, remarkable imitations of folk songs.

BEAUTY ROHTRAUT

What is the name of King Ringang's daughter?
   Rohtraut, Beauty Rohtraut!
And what does she do the livelong day,
Since she dare not knit and spin alway?
O hunting and fishing is ever her play!
And, heigh! that her huntsman I might be!
I'd hunt and fish right merrily!
     Be silent, heart!

And it chanced that, after this some time,
   Rohtraut, Beauty Rohtraut!
The boy in the Castle has gained access,
And a horse he has got and a huntsman's dress,
To hunt and to fish with the merry Princess;
And, O! that a king's son I might be!
Beauty Rohtraut I love so tenderly.
     Hush! hush! my heart.

Under a gray old oak they sat,
   Beauty, Beauty Rohtraut!
She laughs: "Why look you so slyly at me?
If you have heart enough, come, kiss me."
Cried the breathless boy, "Kiss thee?"
But he thinks kind fortune has favored my youth;
And thrice he has kissed Beauty Rohtraut's mouth.
     Down! down! mad heart.

Then slowly and silently they rode home,—
   Rohtraut, Beauty Rohtraut!
The boy was lost in his delight:

"And, wert thou Empress this very night,
I would not heed or feel the blight;
Ye thousand leaves of the wild wood wist
How Beauty Rohtraut's mouth I kiss'd.
        Hush! hush! wild heart."

AN ERROR CHANCED

An error chanced in the moonlight garden
Of a once inviolate love.
Shuddering I came on an outworn deceit,
And with sorrowing look, yet cruel,
Bade I the slender
Enchanting maiden
Leave me and wander far.
Alas! her lofty forehead
Was bowed, for she loved me well;
Yet did she go in silence
Into the dim gray
World outside.

Sick since then,
Wounded and woeful heart!
Never shall it be whole.

Meseems that, spun of the air, a thread of magic
Binds her yet to me, an unrestful bond;
It draws, it draws me faint with love toward her.
Might it yet be some day that on my threshold
I should find her, as erst, in the morning twilight,
Her traveler's bundle beside her,
And her eye true-heartedly looking up to me,
Saying, "See, I've come back,
Back once more from the lonely world!"

A SONG FOR TWO IN THE NIGHT

She: How soft the night wind strokes the meadow grasses
And, breathing music, through the woodland passes!

916

Now that the upstart day is dumb,
One hears from the still earth a whispering throng
Of forces animate, with murmured song
Joining the zephyrs' well-attunèd hum.

He: I catch the tone from wondrous voices brimming,
Which sensuous on the warm wind drifts to me,
While, streaked with misty light uncertainly,
The very heavens in the glow are swimming.

She: The air like woven fabric seems to wave,
Then more transparent and more lustrous groweth;
Meantime a muted melody outgoeth
From happy fairies in their purple cave.
To sphere-wrought harmony
Sing they, and busily
The thread upon their silver spindles floweth.

He: Oh lovely night! how effortless and free
O'er samite black—though green by day—thou movest!
And to the whirring music that thou lovest
Thy foot advances imperceptibly.
Thus hour by hour thy step doth measure—
In trancèd self-forgetful pleasure
Thou'rt rapt; creation's soul is rapt with thee!

EARLY AWAY

The morning frost shines gray
    Along the misty field
Beneath the pallid way
    Of early dawn revealed.

Amid the glow one sees
    The day-star disappear;
Yet o'er the western trees
    The moon is shining clear.

So, too, I send my glance
    On distant scenes to dwell;
I see in torturing trance
    The night of our farewell.

917

Blue eyes, a lake of bliss,
  Swim dark before my sight,
Thy breath, I feel, thy kiss;
  I hear thy whispering light.

My cheek upon thy breast
  The streaming tears bedew,
Till, purple-black, is cast
  A veil across my view.

The sun comes out; he glows,
  And straight my dreams depart,
While from the cliffs he throws
  A chill across my heart.

THE FORSAKEN MAIDEN

Early when cocks do crow
  Ere the stars dwindle,
Down to the hearth I go,
  Fire must I kindle.

Fair leap the flames on high,
  Sparks they whirl drunken;
I watch them listlessly
  In sorrow sunken.

Sudden it comes to me,
  Youth so fair seeming,
That all the night of thee
  I have been dreaming.

Tears then on tears do run
  For my false lover;
Thus has the day begun—
  Would it were over!

WEYLA'S SONG

Thou art Orplede, my land
Remotely gleaming;
The mist arises from thy sun-bright strand
To where the faces of the gods are beaming.

918

Primeval rivers spring renewed
Thy silver girdle weaving, child!
Before the godhead bow subdued
Kings, thy worshipers and watchers mild.

SECLUSION

Let, oh world, ah let me be!
Tempt me not with gifts of pleasure.
Leave alone this heart to treasure
All its joy, its misery.

What my grief I can not say,
'Tis a strange, a wistful sorrow;
Yet through tears at every morrow
I behold the light of day.

When my weary soul finds rest
Oft a beam of rapture brightens
All the gloom of cloud, and lightens
This oppression in my breast.

Let, oh world, ah, let me be!
Tempt me not with gifts of pleasure.
Leave alone this heart to treasure
All its joy, its misery.

THE SOLDIER'S BETROTHED

Oh dear, if the king only knew
How brave is my sweetheart, how true!
He would give his heart's blood for the king,
But for me he would do the same thing.

My love has no ribbon or star,
No cross such as gentlemen wear,
A gen'ral he'll never become;
If only they'd leave him at home!

919

For stars there are three shining bright
O'er the Church of St. Mary each night;
We are bound by a rose-woven band,
And a house-cross is always at hand.

THE OLD WEATHERCOCK: AN IDYLL

At Cleversulzbach in the Underland
A hundred and thirteen years did I stand
Up on the tower in wind and rain,
An ornament and a weathervane.
Through night and tempest gazing down,
Like a good old cock I watched the town.

THINK OF IT, MY SOUL!

Somewhere a pine is green,
Just where who knoweth,
And in a garth unseen
A rose-tree bloweth.
These are ordained for thee—
Think, oh, soul, fixedly—
Over thy grave to be;
Swift the time floweth.

Two black steeds on the down
Briskly are faring,
Or on their way to town
Canter uncaring.
These may with heavy tread
Slowly convey the dead
E'en ere the shoes be shed
They now are wearing.

ERINNA TO SAPPHO

"Many the paths to Hades," an ancient proverb
Tells us, "and one of them thou thyself shalt follow,
Doubt not!" My sweetest Sappho, who can doubt it?
Tells not each day the old tale?

Yet the foreboding word in a youthful bosom
Rankles not, as a fisher bred by the seashore,
Deafened by use, perceives the breaker's thunder no more.
—Strangely, however, today my heart misgave me. Attend:
Sunny the glow of morn-tide, pouring
Through the trees of my well-walled garden,
Roused the slugabed (so of late thou calledst Erinna)
Early up from her sultry couch.
Full was my soul of quiet, although my blood beat
Quick with uncertain waves o'er the thin cheek's pallor.
Then, as I loosed the plaits of my shining tresses,
Parting with nard-moist comb above my forehead
The veil of hair—in the glass my own glance met me.
Eyes, strange eyes, I said, what will ye?
Spirit of me, that within there dwelled securely as yet,
Occultly wed to my living senses—
Demon-like, half smiling thy solemn message,
Thou dost nod to me, Death presaging!
—Ha! all at once like lightning a thrill went through me,
Or as a deadly arrow with sable feathers
Whizzing had grazed my temples,
So that, with hands pressed over my face, a long time
Dumb-struck I sat, while my thought reeled at the frightful
     abyss.

Tearless at first I pondered,
Weighing the terror of Death;
Till I bethought me of thee, my Sappho,
And of my comrades all,
And of the muses' lore,
When straightway the tears ran fast.

But there on the table gleamed a beautiful hair-net, thy gift,
Costly handwork of Byssos, spangled with golden bees.
This, when next in the flowery festal season
We shall worship the glorious child of Demeter,
This will I offer to her for thy and my sake,
So may she favor us both (for she much availeth),
That no mourning lock thou untimely sever
From thy beloved head for thy poor Erinna.

MULTATULI

MULTATULI (Eduard Douwes Dekker), (Dutch, 1820-1887). One of the most powerful novelists of Holland. At 18 left for Dutch East Indies, became bitter foe of colonialism. Fame rests on two novels: *Max Havelaar* and *Woutertje Pieterse*. Exerted considerable influence on succeeding generation of Dutch writers.

THE STORY OF SAÏDJAH

SAÏDJAH's father had a buffalo, which he used for plowing his field. When this buffalo was taken away from him by the district chief at Parang-Koodjang he was very dejected, and spoke no word for many a day. For plowing time was come, and he feared that if the rice-field was not worked in time, the opportunity to sow would be lost, and lastly, that there would be no paddy to cut, and none to keep in the store-room of the house. I have here to tell readers who know Java, but not Bantam, that in that Residency there is personal landed property, which is not the case elsewhere. Saïdjah's father, then, was very uneasy. He feared that his wife would have no rice, nor Saïdjah himself, who was still a child, nor his little brothers and sisters. And the district chief, too, would denounce him to the Assistant Resident if he was behindhand in the payment of his taxes, for this is punished by the law. Saïdjah's father then took a poniard, which he had inherited from his father. It was not very handsome, but there were silver bands round the sheath, and at the end a silver plate. He sold it to a Chinaman in the capital, and came home with twenty-four guilders, with which he bought another buffalo.

Saïdjah, who was then about seven, soon made friends with the new buffalo. I purposely say "made friends," for it was indeed touching to see how the buffalo was attached to the little boy who watched over and fed him. Of this attachment I shall soon give an example. The large strong animal bends its heavy head to the right, to the left, or downwards, just as the pressure of the child's finger directs. Such a friendship the little Saïdjah had soon been able to make with the newcomer; and it seemed as if the encouraging voice of the child gave more strength to the heavy shoulders of the animal, when it tore open the stiff clay and traced its way in deep sharp furrows. The buffalo turned willingly, on reaching the end of the field, not losing an inch of ground when plowing backwards the new furrow, which was ever near the old, as if the *sawah* was a garden ground raked by a giant. Quite near were the *sawahs* of the father of Adinda (the child who was to marry Saïdjah), and when the little brothers of Adinda came to the limit of their fields, as the father of Saïdjah was there with his plow, the children called out merrily to each other, and each praised the strength and docility of his buffalo. But I believe that Saïdjah's buffalo was the best of all, perhaps because its master knew better how to speak to the animal, for buffaloes are very responsive to kind words.

Saïdjah was nine and Adinda six, when this buffalo was taken from Saïdjah's father by the chief. Saïdjah's father, who was very poor, thereupon sold to the Chinaman two silver curtain-hooks—inheritances from his wife's parents—for eighteen guilders, and with that money he bought a new buffalo. Saïdjah was very dejected, for he knew from Adinda's little brothers that the other buffalo had been driven to the capital, and he had asked his father if he had not seen the animal when he was there to sell the curtain-hooks. To this question his father refused to give an answer, and therefore the lad feared that his buffalo had been slaughtered, like the others which the chief had taken from the people. And Saïdjah wept much when he thought of the poor buffalo, which he had known for so long, and could eat nothing for days. It must be remembered that he was only a child.

The new buffalo soon got acquainted with the boy and obtained in the heart of Saïdjah the same place as his predecessor—alas, too soon, for the wax impressions of the heart are soon smoothed to make room for other writing. However this may be, the new buffalo was not so strong as the former: true, the old yoke was too large for his neck, but the poor animal was willing, like the other, and though Saïdjah could boast no more of the strength of his buffalo when he met Adinda's brothers at the boundaries, yet maintained that none surpassed his in willingness, and if the furrow was not so straight as before, or if lumps of earth had been turned but not cut, he willingly made this right as well as he could by means of his spade. Moreover, no buffalo had any such star on his forehead as this one had. The village priest himself said that there was good luck in the course of the hair-whorls on its shoulders.

Once when they were in the field, Saïdjah called in vain to his buffalo to make haste. The animal did not move. Saïdjah grew angry at this unusual refractoriness, and could not refrain from scolding. He called him a s——. Anyone who has been in India will understand me, and he who has not is the gainer if I spare him the explanation.

Saïdjah did not mean anything bad. He only used the word because he had often heard it used by others when they were dissatisfied with their buffaloes. But it was useless: his buffalo did not move. He shook his head as if to throw off the yoke, he blew and trembled, there was anguish in his blue eye, and the upper lip was curled, baring the gums.

"Fly, fly!" Adinda's brothers cried, "Fly, Saïdjah, there's a tiger!" And they all unyoked their buffaloes, and throwing themselves on their broad backs, galloped away through *sawahs*, irrigation trenches, mud, brushwood, forest and jungle, along fields and roads, but when they tore panting and dripping with perspiration into the village of Badoer, Saïdjah was not with them. For when he had freed his buffalo from the yoke and mounted him as the others had done in order to escape, an unexpected jump made him lose his seat and fall to the ground. The tiger was very close. . . . The buffalo, driven on by his own speed alone, and not of his own will, had gone further than Saïdjah, and scarcely had it conquered the momentum when it returned and, placing its big body, supported by its feet like a roof over the child, turned its horned head toward the tiger, which bounded forward—but for the last time. The buffalo caught him on his horns, and only lost some flesh, which the tiger took out of his neck. The tiger lay there with his belly torn open. Saïdjah was saved. Certainly there had been luck in the star on the buffalo's head.

When this buffalo had been taken away from Saïdjah's father and slaughtered, Saïdjah was just twelve, and Adinda was wearing *sarongs* and making figures on them. She had already learned to express thoughts in melancholy drawings on her tissue, for she had seen Saïdjah's sadness. And Saïdjah's father was also sad, but his mother still more so. For she had cured the wound in the neck of the faithful animal which had brought her child home unhurt. As often as she saw this wound, she thought how far the gashes of the tiger might have gone into the tender body of her child; and every time she put fresh dressings on the wound, she caressed the buffalo and spoke kindly to him, that the faithful animal might know how grateful a mother can be. Afterwards she hoped that the buffalo understood her, for he must have known why she wept when he was taken away, and that it was not Saïdjah's mother who caused him to be slaughtered. Some days afterward, Saïdjah's father fled out of the country, for he was afraid of being punished for not paying his taxes, and he had no other heirlooms to sell with which to buy another buffalo. His parents had left him but few things. However, he went on for some years after the loss of his last buffalo by working with hired animals: but that is a very unremunerative labor, and moreover sad for one who has had buffaloes of his own.

Saïdjah's mother died of grief, and his father, in a moment of dejection, left Bantam to find work in the Buitenzorg district. But he was punished with stripes because he had left Lebak without a passport, and brought back by the police to Badoer. There he was put in prison, because he was supposed to be mad, which I can well believe, and it was feared he would run amok in a moment of frenzy. But he was not long in prison, for he died soon after. What became of Saïdjah's brothers and sisters I do not know. The house they lived in at Badoer was empty for some time, and then fell down, for it was only built of bamboo covered with cane. A little dust and dirt covered the spot where there had been so much suffering. There are many such places in Lebak.

Saïdjah was already fifteen when his father set out for Buitenzorg, and he did not accompany him thither, because he had other plans in mind. He had been told that there were gentlemen in Batavia who drove in carriages, and that it would be easy to get work as a carriage boy, for which young lads are used, so as not to disturb the equilibrium of the two-wheeled carriage by too much motion. He would, they said, earn much that way if he behaved himself—perhaps in three years he would be able to save enough to buy two buffaloes. This was a pleasant prospect. With the proud gait of one who had conceived a grand idea, he entered Adinda's house one day after his father had gone away, and communicated his plans to her.

"Think of it," said he. "When I come back we shall be old enough to marry, and have enough to buy two buffaloes!"

"I will gladly marry you, Saïdjah, when you come back. I will spin and weave *sarongs* and *slendangs,* and be very diligent all the while."

"Oh, I believe you, Adinda, but—if I find you already married?"

"Saïdjah, you know very well I will marry nobody but you. My father promised me to your father."

"And you yourself—?"

"When I come back, I will call from afar off."

"Who will hear it, if we are stamping rice in the village?"

"That is true, but, Adinda—oh, yes, this is better: wait for me in the wood, under the Ketapan, where you gave me the Melatti flowers."

"But, Saïdjah, how am I to know when I am to go to the Ketapan?"

Saïdjah considered a moment and said: "Count the moons. I shall stay away three times twelve moons, not counting this moon. See, Adinda, at every new moon cut a notch in your rice block on the floor. When you have cut three times twelve lines, I will be under the Ketapan the next day. Do you promise to be there?"

"Yes, Saïdjah. I will be there, under the Ketapan, near the djatis, when you come back."

Thereupon Saïdjah tore a piece off his much-worn blue turban and gave it to Adinda to keep as a pledge, and then left her and Badoer. He walked many days, passing through Rankas-Belong, not yet capital of Lebak, through Warong-Goonoong, the home of the Assistant Resident, and the next day he came to Pamarangand, which lies in a garden. The day after, he came to Serang, and was astonished at the magnificence and size of the place, and the number of tiled stone houses. He had never before seen the like. He remained there a day, because he was tired, but in the coolness of the night he went his way, and the following day arrived at Tangerang. There he bathed in the river and rested at the home of an acquaintance of his father's who showed him how to make straw hats like those from Manila. He remained a day in order to learn the art, because he thought he might be able to turn it to use later on, if by chance he should fail to find other work in Batavia. The following day toward evening he thanked his host and departed. As soon as it was dark, and no one could see him, he took out the Melatti leaves Adinda had given him, for he was sad, thinking that he would not see her for so long. Neither on the first nor the second day had he realized how lonely he was, because he was captivated by the grand idea of earning money enough to buy two buffaloes, whereas his father had never had more than one, and was too excited over the prospect of seeing Adinda again to grieve over his departure. He had left her in anxious hope. The prospect of seeing her again so occupied his heart that on leaving Badoer and passing the tree, he felt something akin to joy, as if the thirty-six moons were already past. It had seemed that he had only to turn round to see Adinda waiting for him. But the further he went, the more did he realize the length of the period before him. There was something in his soul that made

926

him walk more slowly—he felt an affliction in his knees, and though it was not dejection that overcame him it was a mournful sadness. He thought of returning, but what would Adinda think of his want of courage?

Therefore he walked on, though not so fast as on the first day. He had the Melatti in his hand and often pressed them to his breast. He had aged much during the past few days, and could not understand how he had been able to live so calmly before, when Adinda was so near that he could see her as often as he liked. Now he could not recapture that calmness. Nor did he understand why, after having taken his leave, he had not gone back once again to see her. He recalled how recently he had quarreled with her about a cord she had made for her brother's kite, which had broken because there was some defect in her work. This made him lose a bet he had with the Tjipoeroet children. "How was it possible," he thought, "to have been angry over that with Adinda?" If there was a defect in the cord, and if the bet *was* lost, ought he to have been so rude and called her names? What, he wondered, if he died at Batavia without having asked her forgiveness? Would it not make him seem a wicked man? When it was learned that he had died in a distant place, would not everyone at Badoer say, "It is well Saïdjah has died—he spoke insolently to Adinda!"

Thus his thoughts ran, uttered at first involuntarily and softly, soon in a quiet monologue, and finally in a melancholy song.

He arrived at Batavia, and asked a certain gentleman to take him into his service, which the gentleman did, because Saïdjah spoke no Malay—an advantage there, for servants who do not understand that language are not so corrupt as the others, who have been longer in touch with the Europeans. But Saïdjah soon learned Malay, though he behaved well, for he always remembered the two buffaloes he was going to buy. He grew tall and strong, because he ate every day—not always the case at Badoer. In the stable he was liked, and would certainly not have been rejected if he had asked the hand of the coachman's daughter. His master liked him so much that he soon promoted him to be a house servant, increased his wages, and continually made him presents, to show how pleased he was. Saïdjah's mistress had read Sue's novel, so popular for a short while, and always thought of Prince Djalma when she saw Saïdjah, and the young girls, too, understood better than before why the Javanese painter, Radeen Saleh, had been so successful at Paris. But they thought Saïdjah ungrateful when after almost a three years he asked for his dismissal and a certificate of good behavior. This could not be refused, and Saïdjah went on his journey with a joyful heart.

He counted the treasures he was carrying home. In a roll of bamboo he had his passport and certificate. In a case fastened to a leather girdle something heavy swung against his shoulder, but he enjoyed the feel of that, and no wonder! What would Adinda say? It contained thirty piastres—enough to buy three buffaloes! Nor was that all: on his back was a silver-covered sheath with his poniard. The hilt was indeed a fine one, for he had wound it round with a silk wrapper. And he had still more treasures! In the folds of his loin-cloth he kept a belt of silver links with gold clasps. True, the belt was short, but then Adinda was slender! Suspended by a cord round his neck, and under his clothes, he wore a silken bag in which were the withered Melatti leaves.

Is it to be wondered at that he stopped no longer at Sangerang than to visit the acquaintances who made such fine straw hats? That he said so little to the girls on his way who asked him whence he came and where he was going—the usual salutations; that he no longer thought Serang so beautiful (he who had learned to know Batavia); that he no longer hid himself behind the enclosure as he did three years before when he saw the Resident go riding out (he who had seen the much grander Lord at Buitenzorg, grandfather of Solo); that he paid little attention to the tales of those who went part of the way with him and gave news of Bantam-Kidool—is no wonder. No, he had sublime visions in his mind's eye. He looked for the Ketapan tree in the clouds when he was still far from Badoer. He caught at the air as if to embrace the form that was to meet him under the tree. He pictured to himself the face of Adinda, her head, her shoulders, saw the heavy chignon, black and glossy, confined in a net, hanging down her back; her large eyes glistening in dark reflection, the nostrils raised so proudly as a child (was it possible?), when he had vexed her; and the corner of her lips, when she smiled; and finally, her breasts, now doubtless swelling under her shawl. He could imagine her saying to him, "Welcome, Saïdjah! I have thought of you as I was spinning and weaving and stamping the rice on the floor which shows three times twelve lines cut by my hand. And I am under the Ketapan the first day of the new moon. Welcome, Saïdjah! I will be your wife."

928

That was the music that resounded in his ears and prevented him from listening to all the news that was told him on the road.

At last he saw Ketapan, or rather a large, dark spot with many stars above it. That must be the Ljati wood, near the tree where he should again see Adinda next morning, after sunrise. He sought in the dark and felt many trunks, finding at last a rough spot on the south side of a tree, and thrust his finger into a hole which Si-Panteh had cut with his knife to exorcise the Evil Spirit that had caused his mother's toothache, a short time before the birth of Panteh's little brother. That was the Ketapan he sought.

Yes, this was indeed the spot where he had looked upon Adinda for the first time with a different eye. She had become different from his other comrades. There she had given him the leaves. He sat down at the foot of the tree and looked at the stars, and when he saw a shooting-star he took it as a welcome of his return to Badoer, and wondered whether Adinda were now asleep, whether she had correctly cut the number of moons on the wood? How terrible if she had missed a moon, as if thirty-six were not quite enough! Had she, he wondered, made him some nice *sarongs* and *slendangs?* Who would now be living in her father's house? Then he thought of his childhood, and his mother, and how the buffalo had saved him from the tiger, of what would have become of Adinda if the buffalo had not been so faithful. He watched the sinking of the stars, and as each disappeared, he calculated how much nearer he was to Adinda. For she would certainly come at the first beam—at daybreak she would be there. Why had she not come the day before?

He was hurt that she had not anticipated the supreme moment that had lighted his soul for three years with indescribable brightness; unjust as he was in his selfishness, it seemed to him that Adinda ought to have been waiting for him. He complained unjustly, for the sun had not yet risen. But the stars were growing pale, and strange colors floated over the mountain tops, which appeared darker as they contrasted sharply with places elsewhere illuminated. Here and there something glowed in the east—arrows of gold and fire darted along the horizon, but disappeared again and seemed to fall down behind the impenetrable curtain which hid the day. It grew lighter and lighter around him: he now saw the landscape and could already distinguish a part of the wood behind which Badoer lay. There Adinda slept.

No, surely, she did not sleep! How could she? Did she not know that Saïdjah would be waiting for her. She had not slept the whole night certainly; the village night police had knocked at her door to ask why her lamp burned so long, and with a sweet laugh she had replied that she had vowed to weave a *slendang* which must be ready before the first day of the new moon. Or perhaps she had passed the night in darkness, sitting on the rice floor, counting with eager fingers the thirty-six lines. Or possibly amused herself by pretending that she miscalculated, and had counted the lines all over again each time, enjoying the delicious assurance that the thirty-six moons had come and gone since her Saïdjah had left her.

Now that it was becoming light, she would be busying herself with useless little things, glancing from time to time over the wide horizon, looking for the sun, the lazy sluggard!

There was a line of bluish red, touching the clouds and making their edges light. The arrows of fire shot higher and higher, and ran over the dark ground, illuminating wide spaces of the earth, meeting, crossing, unrolling, running, and at last uniting in vast patches of fire, painting the azure earth in pigments of shining gold. There was red, blue, and purple, yellow gold. God in Heaven—it was at last daybreak!—Adinda!

Saïdjah had never learned to pray, and it would have been a pity to teach him: a more devout prayer and a more fervent expression of gratitude than his would have been impossible. He would no go to Badoer: actually to see her again was not so wonderful as to await her coming. He sat down at the foot of the Ketapan, and his eyes wandered over the landscape. Nature smiled at him, and seemed to welcome him like a mother. Saïdjah was overjoyed at seeing so many spots that reminded him of his earlier life. Though his eyes and thoughts wandered, his longings always reverted to the path which leads from Badoer to the Ketapan tree. His senses were wholly alive to Adinda. He saw the abyss to the left, where the earth was yellow, the spot where once a young buffalo had sunk down to the depths: they had all descended there with strong rattan cords, and Adinda's father had been the bravest of the rescue party. How Adinda had clapped her hands! Farther along, over there on the other side by the clump of cocoa-trees, whose leaves waved over the village, Si-Penah had fallen from a tree and been killed. How his mother had wailed—because, she said, Si-Penah was still such a little one—as if her grief had been less if he were larger! True, he *was* small, smaller and more fragile than Adinda.

There was no one on the little road leading from Badoer to the tree.

—By and by she would come. It was still very early.

Saïdjah saw a squirrel spring playfully up the trunk of a cocoanut tree and run untiringly to and fro. He forced himself to stand and regard the animal, for this calmed his thoughts, which had been working hard since early morning. His thoughts then ran into song.

There was still no one on the little road. . . .

He caught sight of a butterfly disporting joyously in the increasing warmth. . . .

Still, there was no one on the little road. The sun climbed higher into the heavens, and it grew warm. . . .

Still, no one appeared on the little road. . . . No one.

She must have fallen asleep toward morning, weary with watching during the night, during many nights. She had not slept for weeks. That was it! Ought he to get up and go to Badoer? That would look as though he doubted her coming. . . . That man over there was too far away, and Saïdjah did not wish to speak to anyone about Adinda. He would see her alone. Surely, surely, she would come soon!

He would wait. . . .

But what if she were ill—dead?

Like a wounded stag he flew along the pathway toward the village. He saw nothing and heard nothing. Normally he would have heard, for there were men standing in the road at the entrance to the village, who cried out, "Saïdjah! Saïdjah!"

Was it his eagerness, or what, that prevented his finding Adinda's house? He had already run to the end of the village, and as if mad, he turned back, beating his head in despair to think that he had passed her house. But he soon found himself back at the entrance of the village, and—was it a dream? Again he had missed the house. Once more he flew back and suddenly stood still, and took his head in both hands to press out the madness that stunned him.

"Drunk, drunk!" he exclaimed. "I am drunk!"

The women of Badoer came out of their houses and saw with sorrow poor Saïdjah standing there, for they knew that he had been looking for Adinda's house, and that the house was no longer there. . . .

When the chief of Parang-Koodjang had taken away the buffaloes belonging to Adinda's father, Adinda's mother had died of grief,

931

and her baby sister soon after, for there was no one to suckle her. Adinda's father, fearing punishment for failing to pay his land taxes, had fled the district, taking with him Adinda and her brothers. He had heard how Saïdjah's father had been punished at Buitenzorg with stripes, because he had left Badoer without a passport. He had therefore not gone to Buitenzorg, nor to the Preangan, nor to Bantam, but to Tjilangkahan, bordering upon the sea. There he had hidden in the woods, awaiting the arrival of Pa-Ento, Pa-Lontah, Si-Penah, Pa-Ansive, Abdoel Isma, and others who had been robbed of their buffaloes by the chief of Parang-Koodjang, all of whom feared punishment for failure to pay their taxes. There, during the night, they had taken possession of a fishing-boat, and gone to sea. They steered toward the west, as far as Java Head. There they turned northward, until they came in sight of Prince's Island, and sailed round the east coast, going thence to the Lampoons. That at least was what people whispered to one another in Lebak whenever there was any question about buffaloes or land-taxes.

But Saïdjah could scarcely understand what they had told him. There was a buzzing in his ears, as if a gong were sounding in his head. He felt the blood throbbing convulsively in his temples; it seemed as though his head would burst under the pressure. He said nothing, and looked about stupified, not seeing anything. At last he laughed horribly. An old woman led him to her cottage. She would take care of the piteous fool. His laugh gradually became less horrible, but he still spoke no word. During the night the inmates of the hut were frightened by the sound of his voice. He sang out monotonously: "I don't know where I shall die!"

Some of the natives collected a little money in order to offer a sacrifice to the crocodile of the Tji-Udjiung, in order to cure Saïdjah, whom they thought insane. But he was not insane, for on a certain night when the moon was extraordinarily clear, he rose from his couch and quietly left the hut, and sought out the place where Adinda's house had stood. It was not easy to find it, for many houses had fallen down. But he recognized the spot by looking at the rays of moonlight that filtered down through the trees, as sailors measure their positions by lighthouses and mountain-tops.

That was the spot. There had Adinda lived!

Stumbling over half-decayed bamboos and pieces of fallen roof, he made his way to the sanctuary which he sought. He found some few remains of the enclosure still standing erect. There had been

Adinda's room, and there was the bamboo pin on which she had hung her dress when she was retiring at night. The walls of the room were turned to dust. He took up a handful of it, pressed it to his lips, and breathed hard. . . .

The next day he asked the old woman who had taken him in, where the rice-floor was, that stood in Adinda's house. The woman was glad at last to hear him speak, and ran through the village to look for the remains of the floor. She pointed out to Saïdjah the proprietor, and Saidjah followed in silence. He came to the rice-floor. On it he counted thirty-two lines. . . .

He gave the old woman piastres enough to buy a buffalo, and left Badoer. At Tjilangkahan he bought a fishing-boat, and after sailing for two days, reached the Lampoon Islands, where the insurgents had arisen against the Dutch rule. He joined a troop of Badoer men, not so much with the idea of fighting as of finding Adinda, for he was naturally tender-hearted, and more disposed to sorrow than to bitterness.

One day after the insurgents had suffered a defeat, he wandered through a village that had just been taken by the Dutch army, and was therefore in flames. Saïdjah knew that the defeated troop was composed largely of Badoer men. He wandered like a ghost among the houses that had not yet been burned. In one of them he found the dead body of Adinda's father with a bayonet wound in the breast. Near him lay the bodies of Adinda's three brothers, still boys—children, in fact.

Not far off lay the body of Adinda, naked and horribly mutilated. A small piece of blue linen had penetrated into the gaping wound in the breast, which seemed to have made an end to a long struggle.

Saïdjah went off to meet some Dutch soldiers who were driving the surviving insurgents at the point of the bayonet into the fire of the burning houses. He went out to meet the broad bayonets, and pressed forward with all his might, until the steel was buried up to the hilt in his breast.

Not long after there was much rejoicing at Batavia for the new victory, which so added to the laurels of the Dutch-Indian army. And the Government wrote that tranquillity had been restored in the Lampoons. The King of Holland, enlightened by his statesmen, again rewarded so much heroism with many orders of knighthood.

LADY MURASAKI

LADY MURASAKI (Japanese, *ca.* 978-1031). Realistic court diarist, novelist and poet. Lived most of life connected with Emperor's court at Kyoto, and last years in the entourage of Empress Akiko. Chief work, *The Tale of Genji*, is most impressive of Japanese novels—54 sections, translated into 6 English volumes by Arthur Waley. Her *Diary* also a classic.

THE FESTIVAL OF RED LEAVES

THERE was an elderly lady-of-the-bedchamber who, though she was an excellent creature in every other way and was very much liked and respected, was an outrageous flirt. It astonished Genji that despite her advancing years she showed no sign of reforming her reckless and fantastic behaviour. Curious to see how she would take it, he one day came up and began joking with her. She appeared to be quite unconscious of the disparity between their ages and at once counted him as an admirer. Slightly alarmed, he nevertheless found her company rather agreeable and often talked with her. But, chiefly because he was frightened of being laughed at if anyone found out, he refused to become her lover, and this she very much resented. One day she was dressing the Emperor's hair. When this was over His Majesty sent for his valets and went with them into another room. Genji and the elderly lady were left alone together. She was fuller than ever of languishing airs and poses, and her costume was to the last degree stylish and elaborate. 'Poor creature,' he thought, 'how little difference it all makes!' and he was passing her on his way out of the room when suddenly the temptation to give a tug at her dress became irresistible. She glanced swiftly round, eyeing him above the rim of a marvellously painted summer-fan. The eyelids beneath which she ogled at him were blackened and sunken; wisps of hair projected untidily around her forehead. There was something singularly inappropriate about this gawdy, coquettish fan. Handing her his own instead, he took it from her and examined it. On paper coated with a red so thick and lustrous that you could see yourself reflected in it a forest of tall trees was painted in gold. At the side of this design, in a hand which though out-of-date was not lacking in distinction was written the poem about the Forest of Oaraki. He made no doubt that the owner of the fan had written it in allusion to her own advancing years and was expecting him to make a gallant reply. Turning over in his mind how best to divert the extravagant ardour of this strange creature, he could, to his own amusement, think only of another poem about the same forest; but to this it would have been ill-bred to allude He was feeling very uncomfortable lest someone should come in and see them together. She however was quite at her ease and seeing that he remained silent she recited with many arch looks the poem: 'Come to me in the forest and I will cut pasture for your horse, though it be but the under leaf whose season is past.' 'Should I seek your woodland,' he answered, 'my fair name would be gone, for down its glades at all times the pattering of hoofs is heard,' and he tried to get away; but she held him back saying: 'How odious you are! That is not what I mean at all. No one has ever insulted me like this before,' and she burst into tears. 'Let us talk about it some other time,' said Genji; 'I did not mean . . .' and freeing himself from her grasp he rushed out of the room, leaving her in great dudgeon. She felt indeed after this repulse prodigiously old and tottering. All this was seen by His Majesty who, his toilet long ago completed, had watched the ill-assorted pair with great amusement from behind his Imperial screen. 'I am always being told,' he said, 'that the boy takes no interest in the members of my household. But I cannot say that he seems to me unduly shy,' and he laughed. For a moment she was slightly embarrassed; but she felt that any relationship with Genji, even if it consisted of being rebuffed by him in public, was distinctly a feather for her cap, and she made no attempt to defend herself against the Emperor's raillery. The story soon went round of the Court. It astonished no one more than To no Chujo who, though he knew that Genji was given to odd experiments, could not believe that his friend was really launched upon the fantastic courtship which rumour was attributing to him. There seemed no better way of discovering whether it was conceivably possible to regard the lady in such a light than to make love to her himself.

The attentions of so distinguished a suitor went a long way towards consoling her for her late discomfiture. Her new intrigue was of course carried on with absolute secrecy and Genji knew nothing about it. When he next met her she seemed to be very cross with him, and feeling sorry for her because she was so old he made up his mind that he must try to console her. But for a long while he was completely occupied by tiresome business of one kind and another. At last one very dismal evening when he was strolling in the neighborhood of the Ummeiden he heard this lady playing most agreeably on her lute. She was so good a performer that she was often called upon to play with the professional male musicians in the Imperial orchestra. It happened that at this moment she was somewhat downcast and discontented, and in such a mood she played with even greater feeling and verve. She was singing the 'Melon-grower's Song'; admirably, he thought, despite its inappropriateness to her age. So must the voice of the mysterious lady at O-Chou have sounded in Po Chü-i's ears when he heard her singing on her boat at night; and he stood listening. At the end of her song the player sighed heavily as though quite worn out by the passionate vehemence of her serenade. Genji approached softly humming the 'Azumaya': 'Here in the portico of the eastern house rain splashes on me while I wait. Come, my beloved, open the door and let me in.' Immediately, indeed with an unseemly haste, she answered as does the lady in the song, 'Open the door and come in,' adding the verse: 'In the wide shelter of that portico no man yet was ever splashed with rain,' and again she sighed so portentously that although he did not at all suppose that he alone was the cause of this demonstration, he felt it in any case to be somewhat exaggerated and answered with the poem: 'Your sighs show clearly that, despite the song, you are an-other's bride, and I for my part have no mind to haunt the loggias of your eastern house.' He would gladly have passed on, but he felt that this would be too unkind, and seeing that someone else was coming towards her room, he stepped inside and began talking lightly of indifferent subjects, in a style which though it was in reality some-what forced she found very entertaining.

It was intolerable, thought To no Chujo, that Genji should be praised as a quiet and serious young man and should constantly re-buke him for his frivolity, while all the time he was carrying on a multiplicity of interesting intrigues which out of mere churlishness he kept entirely hidden from all his friends. For a long while Chujo had been waiting for an opportunity to expose this sanctimonious imposture and when he saw Genji enter the gentlewoman's apartment you may be sure he was delighted. To scare him a little at such a moment would be an excellent way to punish him for his unfriend-liness. He slackened his pace and watched. The wind sighed in the trees. It was getting very late. Surely Genji would soon begin to doze? And indeed he did now look as though he had fallen asleep. Chujo stole on tiptoe into the room; but Genji who was only half-dreaming instantly heard him, and not knowing that Chujo had fol-lowed him, got it into his head that it was a certain Commissioner of Works who years ago had been supposed to be an admirer of the lady. The idea of being discovered in such a situation by this important old gentleman filled him with horror. Furious with his companion for having exposed him to the chance of such a predicament: 'This is too bad,' he whispered, 'I am going home. What possessed you to let me in on a night when you knew that someone else was coming?' He had only time to snatch up his cloak and hide behind a long folding-screen before Chujo entered the room and going straight up to the screen began in a businesslike manner to fold it up. Though she was no longer young, the lady did not lose her head in this alarming crisis. Being a woman of fashion, she had on more than one occasion found herself in an equally agitating position, and now despite her astonishment, after considering for a moment what had best be done with the intruder, she seized him by the back of his coat and with a practised though trembling hand pulled him away from the screen. Genji had still no idea that it was Chujo. He had half a mind to show himself, but quickly remembered that he was oddly and inadequately clad, with his headdress all awry. He felt that if he ran for it he would cut much too strange a figure as he left the room, and for a moment he hesitated. Wondering how much longer Genji would take to recognize him, Chujo did not say a word but putting on the most ferocious air imaginable, drew his sword from the scabbard. Whereupon the lady crying 'Gentlemen! Gentlemen!' flung herself between them in an attitude of romantic supplication. They could hardly refrain from bursting into laughter. It was only by day when very carefully painted and bedizened that she still retained a certain superficial air of youth and charm. But now this woman of fifty-seven or eight, disturbed by a sudden brawl in the midst of her amours, created the most astonishing spectacle as she knelt at the feet of two young men in their 'teens beseeching them not to die for her. Chujo however refrained from showing the slightest sign of amusement and continued to look as alarming and ferocious as he could. But he was now in full view and Genji realized in a moment that Chujo had all the while known who he was and had been amusing himself at his expense. Much relieved at this discovery, he grabbed at the scabbard from which Chujo had drawn the sword and held it fast lest his friend should attempt to escape and then, despite his annoyance at having been followed, burst into an uncontrollable fit of laughter. 'Are you in your right mind?' said Genji at last. 'This is really a very poor sort of joke. Do you mind letting me get into my cloak?' Whereupon Chujo snatched the cloak from him and would not give it back. 'Very well then,' said Genji; 'if you are to have my cloak I must have yours,' and so saying he pulled open the clasp of Chujo's belt and began tugging his cloak from his shoulders. Chujo resisted and a long tussle followed in which the cloak was torn to shreds. 'Should you now get it in exchange for yours, this tattered cloak will but reveal the secrets it is meant to hide,' recited To no Chujo; to which Genji replied with an acrostic poem in which he complained that Chujo with whom he shared so many secrets should have found it necessary to spy upon him in this fashion. But neither was really angry with the other and setting their disordered costumes to rights they both took their departure.

SANEATSU MUSHAKOJI

SANEATSU MUSHAKOJI (Japanese, 1885-   ). Modern Japanese dramatist, noted for unconventional ideological plots. Embarked on impressive literary career after leaving school. Influenced by European dramatists: Ibsen, Maeterlinck, Tolstoy. Authored several novels, books of essays, and many plays. Plays known in translation: *A Family Affair, The Sister.*

A FAMILY AFFAIR

ACT III

A living room in the Yamada home, luxuriously furnished in Western style. Shuzo *is alone, seated in a rocking-chair. He is smoking a cigar and reading a newspaper. There is a knock at the door.*

Shuzo.   Come in.

(*Enter* Hiroko, *his wife.*)

Hiroko.   What is it you wish?

(*She seats herself on a chair near him.*)

Shuzo (*still reading the paper*).   I want to talk over something with you.

Hiroko: Is it something very important?

Shuzo: Not especially so. It is about Jiro, your son.

Hiroko: About Jiro! Oh! that frightens me.

Shuzo: Why should you be frightened? (*Puts down the newspaper.*)

Hiroko: He is capable of doing such alarming things.

Shuzo: Oh, he is not so rash as all that.

Hiroko: No; he isn't exactly rash, but if he made up his mind to do a certain thing, he would do it even at the expense of his life.

Shuzo: You are right. But he is a very interesting boy. He will be a great man some day, if he doesn't get switched off on the wrong track.

Hiroko: And he has no regard whatever for his home and family.

Shuzo: That is true. Heaven knows he pays no attention to me. He thinks I am old and stupid, and that I want everything my own way.

Hiroko: Now, I doubt if he thinks that.

Shuzo: Oh, yes, he does. He has a stronger will than I have, and he has more brains, too. He is a deep one. We get on his nerves, and he pities us.

Hiroko: Do you think so?

Shuzo: Certainly. Now I am a self-made man and had to fight my way up in the world, but Jiro has always been taken care of, and has led an easy life. That is why I cannot understand how he comes to be so strong-willed.

Hiroko: Somehow he has changed a great deal since his brother Taro went abroad.

Shuzo: He has seemed to me very gloomy lately, and very obstinate.

Hiroko: Don't you think he will get over that when Taro comes back.

Shuzo: No; I don't think he will. He will dominate Taro. Taro has strong passions, but his will is weaker than Jiro's. I doubt if Taro is capable of anything more dangerous than falling prey to women.

Hiroko: You class women as a danger, do you?

Shuzo: I was only joking. At any rate, Taro will be all right. He isn't foolish.

Hiroko: I don't like that kind of joking.

Shuzo: Well, what I want to tell you about Jiro has to do with Fuji.

Hiroko: With Fuji? Surely not!

Shuzo: You think not? Then listen. To-day the father of Fuji, our former maid, came to see me, and told me that Fuji had refused to marry the man her family had chosen for her. I think Jiro is behind this. I heard, also, that about two weeks ago, Jiro went to Fuji's house to see her.

Hiroko: Did her father tell you that?

Shuzo: No; he didn't tell me that. You know what I think? That he and Jiro are working together—that they have framed up against me. I tried to catch the old fellow by remarking that we appreciated the hospitable way in which he had received Jiro at his house. He said, "Not at all. We were surprised to have him drop in so unexpectedly." So much for that. I am certain, too, that about two weeks ago, when I was discussing Fuji's marriage with you, Jiro was listening on the sly. I thought so at the time, and that is why I asked you the next day where Jiro had gone. But you are so stupid you had no idea where he was.

Hiroko: And you are too clever for anything, of course.

Shuzo: I'm keeping a sharp eye on Jiro because I am more interested in his future than I am in Taro's.

Hiroko: Taro is more dependable.

Shuzo: Maybe so. And I admit that if Jiro should succeed me as head of the family, things might all go to smash. But to finish my story. When I asked Ota, the man I sent to arrange Fuji's marriage, how her family took to the idea, he reported that they showed neither surprise nor interest. That means Jiro had been there first. Later on I remarked in Jiro's presence that Fuji had refused the marriage proposal, and I knew he was laughing up his sleeve at me, but I didn't want to have a scene with him just then, so I ignored it. The disobedient rascal! And I thought he promised you he wouldn't go to see Fuji.

Hiroko: So he did promise.

Shuzo: You are sure?

Hiroko: Certainly. He gave me his promise not to see her, on condition that I keep my promise to him.

Shuzo: That's interesting. I am going to cross-examine him, and I want you here as a witness. But remember that you are to be on the side of the prosecution, not the defence. He's a tough customer. He knows already that we are on his trail.

Hiroko: That doesn't seem very likely.

Shuzo: But he knows that Fuji's father has been here to see me.

(*A knock at the door.*)

Who is it?

Jiro (outside): Jiro.

Shuzo: Come in.

940

(Jiro *enters calmly and sits on a chair near his mother.*)

Jiro What is it you want?

Shuzo: Don't you know what I want?

Jiro: Well, I think perhaps I do.

Shuzo: What makes you think so.

Jiro: Something I heard from Fuji's father. Besides, you are so sharp that I have to be sharp, too.

Shuzo: I have a number of things to say to you. But first of all, why did you interfere with Fuji's marriage?

Jiro: I didn't go that far. I merely went to see her father.

Shuzo: To get him to interfere, eh?

Jiro: Perhaps—though I have absolute confidence in Fuji. The point is, I knew that if her father tried to dictate to her, it would only cause trouble, so I went to win him over to her side.

Shuzo: That's a strange line of talk. What do you mean when you say you have absolute confidence in her?

Jiro: Oh, you are not clever enough to understand that. Fuji is deeply in love with someone who is also in love with her. I knew that she would refuse this arranged marriage, and I wanted to make the refusal as easy for her as possible.

Shuzo: Who is it that is in love with her?

Jiro: I can't tell you that.

Shuzo: It is not likely that it is you, is it? (*Smiles.*) If it should be, you would both have to commit suicide.

Jiro: Do you really think it is I? And do you really care as much as that about the family name, and the laws of conventionality?

Hiroko: Jiro! What are you saying? How dare you! Say that again!

Jiro: I can repeat it as often as you like. Would you drive apart two who are so deeply in love? Of course I can't tell whether or not they would actually commit suicide. That is a matter of secondary importance, anyway. But you are really so afraid of conventional laws that you would drive them apart?

Hiroko: Do you mean that you are not afraid of the criticism of society?

Jiro: Not at all. I am afraid of it. But I am much more afraid of ruining human life.

Hiroko: What an unnatural child you are. You were born to disgrace your parents.

Jiro: No, mother. I think I was not born for that purpose, though I admit I do not know why I was born. But certainly not for anything as easy as disgracing my parents. My task is more difficult than that.

Hiroko: Jiro, be still! You are going too far.

Jiro: Mother!

Hiroko: I am shocked at you!

Jiro: Mother!

Hiroko: I am not your mother, and you are not my child. Go ahead—say what you please!

Shuzo (to Hiroko): Be quiet! Jiro didn't say that he wanted to marry Fuji. (*To* Jiro): You don't know how sacred the family name is, nor how important public opinion is, and you don't frighten me by all that wild talk. I haven't the slightest use for the sort of man that kills himself for the sake of a woman. Now see here, Jiro. Isn't it true that when we discharged Fuji, you promised your mother that you would have no correspondence with her?

Jiro: Yes, that is true. That is why I have had no correspondence with her.

Shuzo: You are sure you haven't?

Jiro: Absolutely. Some day, two or three years from now, the man who will then be her husband will prove my innocence.

Shuzo: You had no correspondence. All right. But you also promised your mother that you would not go to see Fuji, either.

Jiro: Yes, I promised that.

Shuzo: But you did see her after all, didn't you?

Jiro: Yes, I saw her.

Shuzo: Ah! And why?

Jiro: Well, I went to her home, and she was there, and I couldn't help meeting her. But I didn't go there with that purpose. I did not break the spirit of my promise to mother. If you still think I did, please forgive me.

Shuzo: I may forgive that. But you don't mind, do you, if Fuji becomes a geisha girl?

Jiro: Father! You are not going to punish Fuji because of my actions! I had to make those promises to mother in order to convince her of my innocence. I ought never to have made them!

Shuzo: You are ready to accept your punishment?

Jiro: If it is what I deserve.

Shuzo: Well then . . . you will never be Fuji's husband!

Jiro: Oh! Why, I wouldn't be if you wanted me to. In the first place, Fuji doesn't want to marry me.

942

Hiroko: She doesn't? You are not telling us that to clear yourself?

Jiro: Mother, you are so suspicious!

Shuzo: You are sure she doesn't want to marry you?

Jiro: Of course I am.

Shuzo: Absolutely certain?

Jiro: Absolutely.

Shuzo: You have given me your word as a man.

Jiro: And you mistrust me like a woman.

Shuzo: You have been acting very strangely.

Jiro: How?

Shuzo: First, you made a special trip to Fuji's house. Next, you concealed from us the name of the man who is in love with her. Finally, you got angry when I said you would be getting mixed up in a double-suicide.

Jiro: The first charge I think I have already explained to you. The second is made necessary by the fact that I have not the man's permission to reveal his identity. To the last accusation I will say that I got angry thinking how cruel you are, and how differently I should look at things if I were in your position. I pitied you, father and mother, for being so stupid as to worry over such a matter.

Shuzo: Do you still imagine that we will allow you to marry Fuji?

Jiro: No. I never suspected you of being that liberal. But if I were in love with Fuji so desperately that I contemplated suicide, then I think you would allow me to marry her, because it would be better for you to make your son happy than to let him kill himself after a scandal.

Hiroko: You are trying to make fools of us.

Jiro: Yes; I am.

Hiroko: You have no respect for your parents.

Jiro: I have always gone on the assumption that parents love their children.

Hiroko: No child talks back to his parents as you do.

Jiro: Perhaps not. But why worry over that?

Hiroko: Father, why don't you do something to him? He makes me angry!

Jiro: And you make me angry.

Shuzo: Jiro, you are amusing yourself at our expense just because you are clever. You are forgetting the beneficence of your parents.

Jiro: The beneficence of parents! That should mean giving the child happiness. When a child grows up he doesn't love his parents any longer—he wants to run away from them. That is true in my case, but you are still trying to impose your beneficence on me, and it won't work.

Hiroko: A queer sort of child you are!

Jiro: Father! Mother! You don't understand what you are talking about. You know nothing of a young man's heart. These times are different from those of your own youth. And besides, a young tree doesn't want to stay in the shade of an old tree. A young tree wants the sunlight. It wants to brave the winds. Old people think life is made for suffering; young people think it is made for enjoyment. To enjoy to the fullest one's own life! to find one's own happiness—are not those words beautiful?

Shuzo: But, Jiro, you must not forget self-sacrifice.

Jiro: I am not forgetting self-sacrifice. I would gladly sacrifice myself by my own will, but not by the will of others. If I were the man you suspected me of being, I am certain I should leave this house and run away with the girl. I would willingly disgrace my parents and become an outcast from society.

Hiroko: How dare you say such a thing?

Shuzo (to Hiroko): Be still. Jiro doesn't know what he is saying. But I believe him when he says he is not the man in question. (*To* Jiro): Now that I am convinced you are not he, you may go. I have nothing more to say to you.

(*Jiro opens the door and goes out. Shutzo and Hiroko look after him. There is a silence. Then——*)

Hiroko: Such trouble! What are we going to do?

Shuzo: After all, Jiro is our younger son. Maybe we will let him marry her. Anyway, don't worry about it.

Hiroko: Jiro is a very queer boy. I can't understand him.

Shuzo: Say!

Hiroko: Well?

Shuzo: I have thought of something—something terrible!

Hiroko: What is it?

Shuzo: The man may be—Taro!

Hiroko: Surely not!

Shuzo: Perhaps not. But why, otherwise, should Jiro talk so strangely? Taro stopped writing just about the time we sent him word of Fuji's dismissal. Before that he had written two or three times a week. In fact, I couldn't understand why he should write

944

so often, but I supposed it was merely because the two boys were so fond of each other. Now I realise more than ever how peculiar it was. And Jiro swore he would never correspond with Fuji, and that he would never marry her. I don't think he was lying.

Hiroko: Oh, if it is true, it is terrible!

Shuzo: Quite right. What shall we do?

Hiroko: Do you think they will commit suicide if we separate them?

Shuzo: I don't think Taro is as foolish as that.

Hiroko: Then do you think it will ruin his health?

Shuzo: I don't think so.

Hiroko: But he will hate us.

Shuzo: Yes; I suppose he will. And Jiro will hate us, too.

Hiroko: Still, if we were to let Taro marry her, it would mean the disgrace of our house.

Shuzo: That is just it. We would be ashamed for the rest of our lives. (*He glances at the door and speaks in a lower tone.*) Jiro may be listening to us.

Hiroko: No, surely not!

Shuzo: You can't trust him.

Jiro (*outside the door*): No; you can't trust him. (*He opens the door and appears.*) You were right when you guessed that Taro is the man; but you were wrong about their relationship. You have no idea how deeply they are in love.

Shuzo: Never mind about that. I shall write to Taro and tell him that we know all about his affair with Fuji, and that we are very sorry, but we cannot countenance it.

Jiro: If you write him that, I shall write him this: "Father and mother are very happy over the affair, and everything has been settled much easier than you expected." I swear I will do this. The thing has come to light through my carelessness, and I am responsible for its solution. Both of them trusted me, and I considered myself worthy of their trust. I shall therefore help them get married.

Shuzo: If you do what you threaten, I will drive you out of this house.

Jiro: I am ready to be driven out. I am ready to stand on my own feet. I knew that when I told Taro and Fuji not to worry about me. When I cried a while ago, it was merely because I pitied you both so much.

(*There is an astonished silence on the part of the parents
for a few moments, then—*)

Hiroko: What kind of a child is this!

Shuzo: Even I am astonished!

Jiro: Death would be nothing to me. (*Tears start from his eyes.*)

Shuzo: I wish I could turn you out, but I haven't the courage. It is harder for a parent to lose his child than for a child to lose his parent. Jiro, haven't you someone you want to marry?

Jiro: I? Not yet.

Shuzo: Then I shall find someone for you.

Jiro: All right.

Shuzo: You are in love with Fuji, aren't you?

Jiro: I can't answer that.

Shuzo: Jiro, I will consent to anything you wish. You may write whatever you like to Taro. It will make him happy. And even if I lose the whole world, I won't lose you. I love you.

Jiro: Thank you, father. Taro and Fuji will be so happy! And mother, don't you worry. If you do lose the respect of society, you will gain our love. Please forgive me everything I said to you before.

Shuzo: Jiro, you are not thinking about dying?

Jiro: Far from it. I have something else to do.

(*He bows and goes out quietly.*)

Shuzo (*to Hiroko*): Don't worry any more. All your children have come back to you. I feel that I, too, am coming back to you. Year after next we shall see our first grandchild.

(Hiroko *looks up at* Shuzo. *They smile at each other.*)

CURTAIN.

MU'TAMID

MU'TAMID (Arabic, 1040-1095). A member of the Abbasid Dynasty, who became King of Seville when Moslem Spain was broken into petty states. Later lost his kingdom and was exiled to Morocco. Of some importance as a poet.

THE PHILOSOPHER PENITENT

Then must I lose my all of joy to thee,
　Thou plunderer, Time, and thief of my delight,
And in my cup of sadness shall there be
No lingering lees of my felicity?

946

True, I have been of late no little while
    A stranger to the lute-string and the cup;
Sweet looks, and tremulous eyes, and subtle smile
Have tempted not, nor crafty fingers' guile.

And now behold, my head is waxen grey,
    Yet not with plentitude of years; and lo,
My limbs are lean, my flesh consumed away,
Yet not with waste and ravage of decay,

But because I have sinned, and mocked the wise,
    And fouled the fountain of my hopes. Alas,
My spring of youth is muddied and there rise
No waters but the salt tears of these eyes.

But I will chide my sorrow, I will speak
    Thus to my weeping, saying: "Hence, my tears!
And, O sad heart, strew not upon my cheek
These symbols of the coward and the weak."

For if the shaft of Destiny hath quit
    The bow of Fate, whose hand shall be so skilled
To pluck the flying arrow back? Whose wit
Shall by a hair's breadth change the course of it?

Not ours, not ours, who spend our little time
    Tracing a broken couplet on the sand,
Till, wearied of the pleasant pantomime,
Death, the great poet, adds the lacking rhyme.

TEARS OF THE WORLD

Weep for me, friend, for now that I am hence,
    Lo, in Time's dust the footprints of my pride!
Lament, strong lions of my great defence,
    Shed tears, my young gazelles and dewy-eyed!
Look ye, the cold stars even in the height
Weep, and the clouds lift not their mournful night.

947

Weep, Wahîd, weep, and Zahi with the towers,
Weep ye for him that shall not come again.
All waters of the earth, all dew and showers
Have tears for Mu'tamid, and the summer rain
That once strewed pearls upon him, is become
A sea-wave full of sand and sound and foam.

N

SAROJINI NAIDU

SAROJINI NAIDU (Indian, 1879-1949). Gifted English language lyricist of Indian themes. One of first Indians to achieve mastery of English verse. A woman who married out of her caste, and later became President of the Indian National Congress. Principal volumes: *The Golden Threshold, The Bird of Time, The Broken Wing.*

SUMMER WOODS

O I am tired of painted roofs and soft and silken floors,
And long for wind-blown canopies of crimson *gulmohurs!*

O I am tired of strife and song and festivals and fame,
And long to fly where cassia-woods are breaking into flame.

Love, come with me where koels call from flowering glade and glen,
Far from the toil and weariness, the praise and prayers of men.

O let us fling all care away, and lie alone and dream
'Neath tangled boughs of tamarind and *molsari* and *neem!*

And bind our brows with jasmine sprays and play on carven flutes,
To wake the slumbering serpent-kings among the banyan roots,

And roam at fall of eventide along the river's brink,
And bathe in water-lily pools where golden panthers drink!

You and I together, Love, in the deep blossoming woods
Engirt with low-voiced silences and gleaming solitudes,

Companions of the lustrous dawn, gay comrades of the night,
Like Krishna and like Radhika, encompassed with delight.

NATSUME SOSEKI

NATSUME SOSEKI (Japanese, 1867-1916). Writer of bizarre and fantastic tales. Essayist, critic and poet. Studied in England and taught English in Japan. First enormously successful novel: *I Am a Cat*. Later works: *Young Master, Kusamakura*. His style, marked by wit and urbanity, influenced the contemporary Japanese novel.

OUR CAT'S GRAVE

AFTER we removed to Waseda our cat began to grow lean and lank. She did not seem to want to join the children in frisking about at all. When the sun shone, she would go to sleep on the verandah. Stretching her front legs out straight, she would put her square chin down on them, and, fixing her eyes on the plants in the garden, would not move for hours. No matter how noisily the children might play about her, she did not seem to be at all disturbed.

As to the children, they practically refused to associate with their old friend whom they treated like a stranger, as much as to say, "This kitten isn't friendly enough for a playmate."

Not only the children but also our maid-servant cared little for Puss: she took the trouble to put the three meals for the poor animal in a corner of the kitchen but would do nothing else.

The three meals, however, were usually made away with by a big and thievish tabby-cat of the neighbourhood before our cat had touched them. She did not even appear to get angry at this, and never quarreled. She slept quietly all the time.

But her manner of sleeping was without freedom or ease. She did not lie comfortably and enjoy the pleasant sunshine. It seemed she could not afford to move but this is not sufficient to describe her state. In other words she found life exceedingly dull and she knew that she could not shake off this feeling without moving, but to move would make her feel more lonely. She seemed to have decided to lie still and put up with her surroundings.

Her eyes were ever upon the plants in the garden, but she was probably entirely unconscious of the shapes of the leaves and of their stalks. She lay with her vacant bluish-yellow eyes riveted upon some spot.

Just as the children, her former playmates, did not seem to recognize her existence, she herself did not seem to recognize the very existence of the world around her.

Sometimes, however, she would go out, like one who had business to attend to. On these occasions she was invariably driven home by the same tom-cat of the neighbourhood, and, terror-stricken, she would spring upon the verandah, break her way through one of the closed paper doors and rush to the hearthside.

It was only at these times that the family were reminded of her existence and that she seemed to feel any satisfaction in realizing that she was still alive.

After several repetitions of this experience, the hair on her tail grew thinner little by little. At first the hair dropped out in several spots leaving small hole-like patches. These patches grew larger till her whole tail was bare. Later on it hung down like a piece of rope.

Utterly tired of all things, she began to lick the affected parts. "My dear, I'm afraid there must be something wrong with the cat," said I to my wife.

"Perhaps so;" said she quite indifferently, "perhaps it's due to her advanced age." So after this I too left the wretched animal in her pitiable plight.

Then after a few days I noticed that the poor cat was throwing up everything she ate. Moving the forepart of her neck with a wavy motion she gave a mournful sound which was something between a sneeze and a hiccup. Pitiable as she looked, I could not help her. So every time I found her in this awkward situation, I thought I would drive her out.

Otherwise she would go on spoiling the mats and cushions without compunction. Most of the *hattan* silk cusions used for visitors had already been spoiled by her.

"This won't do," I said to my wife. "She has some kind of stomach trouble, I suppose. Dissolve some *hotan* in water and give it to the poor beast."

But she did not deign to answer. A few days later, I asked her if she had given the cat any *hotan* and she replied: "Why, my dear, I've tried in vain to make her take the medicine, but she would not open her mouth. As you see, even when we give her fishbones, she vomits." She added explanatorily.

"All right, then you had not better give her any," said I crossly, returning to my book.

No sooner had the cat got rid of her nausea than she slept quietly. Lately she had shrunk into herself in an uncomfortable way and appeared to feel that she had no place to go except the verandah upon which she slept.

Some changes were visible in the expression of her eyes. First they looked as if they were fixed on some distant object brought suddenly into the near field of her vision and there was something calm about her eyes even in the midst of her wretchedness. But then they began to move in a strange way. The fire of her eyes, however, sank lower and lower like sheet lightning after a summer sunset.

However, I left her just as she was. My wife also did not seem to care for the poor creature. The children had long ceased to think of their former pet, of course.

One evening she was lying on her stomach at the foot of one of the children's beds, when, all at once she gave a deep growl such as she used to do when some one tried to seize her fish.

I was the only one who thought it very strange at the time. The children were sound asleep. Their mother was busy sewing.

After a while the cat uttered another growl. At last my wife dropped her work. "What's the matter with the cat?" I cried. "It would be terrible if the cat should bite our children during the night."

"Nonsense!" said she, resuming her sewing on the sleeves of an undershirt. The cat growled again at intervals.

The next day, the poor creature lay down on the edge of the hearth and mewed all day long. That seemed somewhat repulsive to us when we went there for the tea kettle or to make tea. But when it was evening my wife as well as myself forgot all about the cat. That night the cat died. The next morning when the maid-servant went to the backyard shed to fetch some firewood, it was already lying stiff on an old kitchen stove.

My wife took the trouble of going there to see the body of the poor creature. Thereupon, her former indifference was gone and she suddenly began making a great fuss about it. She sent for our rickshaman, and getting him to buy an oblong grave-post, she asked me to write something on it. I wrote: "In Memory of A Cat" on its front and "*Konoshitani, Inazuma okoru yoi aran*," on its back. The rickshaman wanted to know if he might bury the cat as it was, and the maid-servant added that she could not think of cremating it.

The children also began to make much of the cat again suddenly. They planted two glass bottles, one on each side of the grave-post, and filled them with twigs of blossoming *hagi*. They filled a cup with water and placed it before the grave. The flowers and the water were changed every day. In the evening on the third day, my three-year-old daughter—I was watching her through a window of my study —walked up to the grave all alone, and after gazing at the plain-wood grave-post for a while, put out her toy dipper, scooped up water from the cup which was offered to the cat, and drank it. That was not the only time she did so. The water strewn with the fallen petals of *hagi* flowers often served to cure the thirst of little Aiko in the evening quiet.

On each death-anniversary of the cat, my wife has made it a rule to offer a small slice of salted salmon and a bowl of rice with dried bonito shavings on it before the grave. She has never forgotten to do so even until now. Only she seems to have come recently to place them on top of the wardrobe in her sitting room instead of walking out into the garden with them.

NIZAMI

NIZAMI (Persian, 1140-1203). First great romantic poet of Persia. Spent 30 years composing his *Khamsa* (*Five Treasures*), of which best-known is *Khosru and Shireen*. Dedicated poems to various rulers, but avoided court life. Also composed religious and moral poems. Works exhibit extravagant imagination, are highly ornamented.

FERHAD THE SCULPTOR

The first epic of Nizami was "Khosru and Shireen," which relates the love story of the King of Persia and the beautiful Princess Shireen. Ferhad was an eminent sculptor whose passionate love for the same maiden gave the monarch vexation. To remove him from his court the king required him to hew a channel for a river through the lofty mountain of Beysitoun, and to decorate it with sculpture. He promised also that if Ferhad should accomplish this stupendous task, he should receive as his bride the object of his love. The enamored artist accepted the work on this condition. It is related that as he struck the rock, he constantly invoked the name of Shireen.

On lofty Beysitoun the lingering sun
Looks down on ceaseless labors, long begun;

The mountain trembles to the echoing sound
Of falling rocks that from her sides rebound.
Each day, all respite, all repose, denied,
Without a pause the thundering strokes are plied;
The mist of night around the summit coils,
But still Ferhad, the lover-artist, toils.
And still, the flashes of his axe between,
He sighs to every wind, "Alas, Shireen!"
A hundred arms are weak one block to move
Of thousands moulded by the hand of love
Into fantastic shapes and forms of grace,
That crowd each nook of that majestic place.
The piles give way, the rocky peaks divide,
The stream comes gushing on, a foaming tide,—
A mighty work for ages to remain,
The token of his passion and his pain.
As flows the milky flood from Allah's throne,
Rushes the torrent from the yielding stone.
And, sculptured there, amazed, stern Khosru stands,
And frowning sees obeyed his harsh commands:
While she, the fair beloved, with being rife,
Awakes from glowing marble into life.
O hapless youth? O toil repaid by woe!
A king thy rival, and the world thy foe.
Will she wealth, splendor, pomp, for thee resign,
And only genius, truth, and passion thine?
Around the pair, lo! chiselled courtiers wait,
And slaves and pages grouped in solemn state;
From columns imaged wreaths their garlands throw,
And fretted roofs with stars appear to glow:
Fresh leaves and blossoms seem around to spring,
And feathered throngs their loves seem murmuring.
The hands of Peris might have wrought those stems
Where dew-drops hang their fragile diadems,
And strings of pearl and sharp-cut diamonds shine,
New from the wave, or recent from the mine.
"Alas, Shireen!" at every stroke he cries,—
At every stroke fresh miracles arise.
"For thee my life one ceaseless toil has been;
Inspire my soul anew,—alas, Shireen!"

One evening Jesus lingered in the market-place,
Teaching the people parables of truth and grace,
When in the square remote a crowd was seen to rise,
And stop with loathing gestures and abhorring cries.

The Master and his meek disciples went to see
What cause for this commotion and disgust could be,
And found a poor dead dog beside the gutter laid;
Revolting sight! at which each face its hate betrayed.

One held his nose, one shut his eyes, one turned away;
And all among themselves began aloud to say,—
"Destested creature! he pollutes the earth and air!"
"His eyes are blear!" "His ears are foul!" "His ribs are bare!"

"In his torn hide there's not a decent shoe-string left!"
"No doubt the execrable cur was hung for theft!"
Then Jesus spake, and dropped on him this saving wreath,—
"Even pearls are dark before the whiteness of his teeth!"

The pelting crowd grew silent and ashamed, like one
Rebuked by sight of wisdom higher than his own;
And one exclaimed, "No creature so accursed can be,
But some good thing in him a loving eye will see."

NOVALIS

NOVALIS (Friedrich von Hardenberg, German 1772-1801). One of most original writers of German Romantic School. Catholic medievalist, imbued with mystical and mythological inspirations. Created the "blue flower," favorite romantic symbol. Died young of tuberculosis. Most significant work: an unfinished novel, *Heinrich von Ofterdingen*. Free-verse poem: *Hymns to the Night*.

THE POET'S DAUGHTER

THE journey was now ended. It was toward evening when our travelers arrived, safe and in good spirits, in the world-renowned city of Augsburg, and rode through the lofty streets to the house of old

Schwaning. . . . They found the house illuminated, and a merry music reached their ears. "What will you wager," said the merchants, "that your grandfather is giving a merry entertainment? We come as if called. How surprised he will be at the uninvited guests! Little does he dream that the true festival is now to begin." . . .

Among the guests, Heinrich had noticed a man who appeared to be the person that he had seen often at his side, in that book. His noble aspect distinguished him before all the rest. A cheerful earnestness was the spirit of his countenance. An open, beautifully arched brow; great, black, piercing and firm eyes; a roguish trait about the merry mouth, and altogether clear and manly proportions made it significant and attractive. He was strongly built, his movements were easy and full of expression, and where he stood, it seemed as if he would stand forever. Heinrich asked his grandfather about him. "I am glad," said the old man, "that you have remarked him at once. It is my excellent friend Klingsohr, the poet. Of his acquaintance and friendship you may be prouder than of the emperor's. But how stands it with your heart? He has a beautiful daughter; perhaps she will supplant the father in your regards. I shall be surprised if you have not observed her." Heinrich blushed. "I was absent, dear grandfather. The company was numerous, and I noticed only your friend." "It is very easy to see," replied Schwaning, "that you are from the North. We will soon find means to thaw you here. You shall soon learn to look out for pretty eyes."

The old Schwaning led Heinrich to Klingsohr, and told him how Heinrich had observed him at once, and felt a very lively desire to be acquainted with him. Heinrich was diffident. Klingsohr spoke to him in a very friendly manner of his country and his journey. There was something so confidential in his voice, that Heinrich soon took heart and conversed with him freely. After some time Schwaning returned, and brought with him the beautiful Mathilde. "Have compassion on my shy grandson, and pardon him for seeing your father before he did you. Your gleaming eyes will awaken his slumbering youth. In his country the spring is late."

Heinrich and Mathilde colored. They looked at each other with wondering eyes. She asked him with gentle, scarce audible words: "Did he like to dance?" Just as he was affirming this question a merry dancing-music struck up. Silently he offered her his hand, she gave hers, and they mingled in the ranks of the waltzing pairs. Schwaning and Klingsohr looked on. The mother and the merchant rejoiced in Heinrich's activity, and in his beautiful partner. . . .

Heinrich wished the dance never to end. With intense satisfaction his eye rested on the roses of his partner. Her innocent eye shunned him not. She seemed the spirit of her father in the loveliest disguise. Out of her large, calm eyes, spoke eternal youth. On a light, heaven-blue ground reposed the mild glory of the dusky stars. Around them brow and nose sloped gracefully. A lily inclined toward the rising sun was her face; and from the slender white neck, blue veins meandered in tempting curves around the delicate cheeks. Her voice was like a far-away echo, and the small brown curly head seemed to hover over the light form.

The music banished reserve and roused every inclination to cheerful sport. Baskets of flowers in full splendor breathed forth odors on the table, and the wine crept about among the dishes and the flowers, shook his golden wings, and wove curtains of bright tapestry between the guests and the world. Heinrich now, for the first time, understood what a feast was. A thousand gay spirits seemed to him to dance about the table, and in still sympathy with gay men, to live by their joys and to intoxicate themselves with their delights. The joy of life stood like a sounding tree full of golden fruits before him. Evil did not show itself, and it seemed to him impossible that ever human inclination should have turned from this tree to the dangerous fruit of knowledge, to the tree of conflict. He now understood wine and food. He found their savor surpassingly delicious. They were seasoned for him by a heavenly oil, and sparkled from the cup the glory of earthly life. . . .

It was deep in the night when the company separated. The first and only feast of my life, said Heinrich to himself when he was alone.

He went to the window. The choir of the stars stood in the dark sky, and in the east a white sheen announced the coming day. With full transport Heinrich exclaimed: "You, ye everlasting stars, ye silent pilgrims, you I invoke as witnesses of my sacred oath! For Mathilde I will live, and eternal truth shall bind my heart to hers. For me too the morn of an everlasting day is breaking. The night is past. I kindle myself, a never-dying sacrifice to the rising sun!"

Heinrich was heated, and it was late, toward morning, when he fell asleep. The thoughts of his soul ran together into wondrous dreams. A deep blue river shimmered from the green plain. On the smooth surface swam a boat. Mathilde sat and rowed. She was decked with garlands, sang a simple song, and looked toward him with a sweet sorrow. His bosom was oppressed, he knew not why. The sky was bright, and peaceful the flood. Her heavenly coun-

957

tenance mirrored itself in the waves. Suddenly the boat began to spin round. He called to her, alarmed. She smiled, and laid the oar in the boat, which continued incessantly to whirl. An overwhelming anxiety seized him. He plunged into the stream, but could make no progress, the water bore him. She beckoned, she appeared desirous to say something. Already the boat shipped water, but she smiled with an ineffable inwardness, and looked cheerfully into the whirlpool. All at once it drew her down. A gentle breath streaked across the waves, which flowed as calm and as shining as before. The terrific agony deprived him of consciousness. His heart beat no more. He did not come to himself until he found himself on dry ground. He might have swam far, it was a strange country. He knew not what had befallen him; his mind was gone;— thoughtless he wandered farther into land. He felt himself dreadfully exhausted. A little fountain trickled from a hill, it sounded like clear bells. With his hand he scooped a few drops, and wetted his parched lips. Like an anxious dream the terrible event lay behind him. He walked on and on; flowers and trees spoke to him. He felt himself so well, so at home. Then he heard again that simple song. He pursued the sound. Suddenly some one held him back by his garment. "Dear Heinrich!" called a well-known voice. He looked round, and Mathilda clasped him in her arms. "Why didst thou run from me, dear heart?" said she, drawing a long breath, "I could scarce overtake thee." Heinrich wept. He pressed her to his bosom.—"Where is the river?" he exclaimed with tears. "Seest thou not its blue waves above us?" He looked up, and the blue river was flowing gently above their heads. "Where are we, dear Mathilda?" "With our parents." "Shall we remain together?" "Forever," she replied, while she pressed her lips to his, and so clasped him that she could not be separated from him again. She whispered a strange mysterious word into his mouth, which vibrated through his whole being. He wished to repeat it, when his grandfather called and he awoke. He would have given his life to remember that word.

O

EUGENE O'NEILL

EUGENE O'NEILL (American, 1888-1953). Dramatist of the tragic sense of life, often judged America's most important playwright. Experiences as young seaman recorded in early *Plays of the Sea*. After period in tuberculosis sanatorium, studied in Harvard's "47 Workshop" and joined Provincetown Players. Styles range from naturalism of *Beyond the Horizon*, to expressionism of *The Emperor Jones*, to symbolism of *The Great God Brown*, to special techniques of *Strange Interlude* and *Mourning Becomes Electra*. Nobel Prize, 1936.

THE GREAT GOD BROWN

SCENE. Cybel's parlor. An automatic, nickel-in-the-slot player-piano is at center, rear. On its right is a dirty gilt second-hand sofa. At the left is a bald-spotted crimson plush chair. The backdrop for the rear wall is cheap wall-paper of a dull yellow-brown, resembling a blurred impression of a fallow field in early spring. There is a cheap alarm clock on top of the piano. Beside it her mask is lying.

DION is seated on his back, fast asleep on the sofa, His mask has fallen down on his chest. His pale face is singularly pure, spiritual and sad.

The player-piano is groggily banging out a sentimental medley of "Mother—Mammy" tunes.

CYBEL is seated on the stool in front of the piano. She is a strong, calm, sensual, blonde girl of twenty or so, her complexion fresh and healthy, her figure full-breasted and wide-hipped, her movements slow and solidly languorous like an animal's, her large eyes dreamy with the reflected stirring of profound instincts. She chews gum like a sacred cow forgetting time with an eternal cud. Her eyes are fixed, incuriously, on DION's pale face.

Cybel (*as the tune runs out, glances at the clock, which indicates midnight, then goes slowly to to Dion and puts her hand gently on his forehead*). Wake up!

Dion (*stirs, sighs and murmurs dreamily*). "And He laid His hands on them and healed them." (*Then with a start he opens his eyes and, half sitting up, stares at her bewilderedly*) What—where —who are you? (*He reaches for his mask and claps it on defensively*).

Cybel (*placidly*). Only another female. You was camping on my steps, sound asleep. I didn't want to run any risk getting into more trouble with the cops pinching you there and blaming me, so I took you to sleep it off.

Dion (*mockingly*). Blessed are the pitiful, Sister! I'm broke— but you will be rewarded in Heaven!

Cybel (*calmly*). I wasn't wasting my pity. Why should I? You were happy, weren't you?

Dion (*approvingly*). Excellent! You're not a moralist, I see.

Cybel (*going on*). And you look like a good boy, too—when you're asleep. Say you better beat it home to bed or you'll be locked out.

Dion (*mockingly*). Now you're becoming maternal, Miss Earth. Is that the only answer—to pin my soul into every vacant diaper? (*She stares down at his mask, her face growing hard. He laughs*) But please don't stop stroking my aching brow. Your hand is cool mud poultice on the sting of thought!

Cybel (*calmly*). Stop acting. I hate ham fats. (*She looks at him as if waiting for him to remove his mask—then turns her back indifferently and goes to the piano*) Well, if you simply got to be a regular devil like all the other visiting sports, I s'pose I got to play with you. (*She takes her mask and puts it on—then turns. The mask is the rouged and eye-blackened countenance of the hardened prostitute. In a coarse, harsh voice*) Kindly state your dishonorable intentions, if any! I can't sit up all night keeping company! Let's have some music! (*She puts a plug in the machine. The same sentimental medley begins to play. The two masks stare at each other. She laughs*) Shoot! I'm all set! It's your play, Kid Lucifer!

Dion (*slowly removes hs mask She stops the music with a jerk. His face is gentle and sad—humbly*). I'm sorry. It has always been such an agony for me to be touched!

Cybel (*taking off her mask—sympathetically as she comes back and sits down on her stool*). Poor kid! I've never had one, but I can guess. They hug and kiss you and take you on their laps and pinch you and want to see you getting dressed and undressed—as if they owned you—I bet you I'd never let them treat one of mine that way!

Dion (*turning to her*). You're lost in blind alleys, too. (*Suddenly holding out his hand to her*) But you're strong. Let's be friends.

Cybel (*with a strange sternness, searches his face*). And never nothing more?

Dion (*with a strange smile*). Let's say, never anything less (*She takes his hand. There is a ring at the outside door bell. They stare at each other. There is another ring*).

Cybel (*puts on her mask, Dion does likewise. Mockingly*). When you got to love to live it's hard to love living. I better join the A.F. of. L. and soap-box for the eight-hour night! Got a nickel, baby? Play a tune. (*She goes out. Dion puts a nickel in. The same sentimental tune starts. Cybel returns, followed by Billy Brown. His face is rigidly composed, but his superior disgust for Dion can be seen. Dion jerks off the music and he and Billy look at each other for a moment, Cybel watching the both—then, bored, she yawns*) He's hunting for you. Put out the lights when you go. I'm going to sleep. (*She starts to go—then, as if reminded of something—to Dion*) Life's all right, if you let it alone. (*Then mechanically flashing a trade smile at Billy*) Now you know the way, Handsome, call again! (*She goes*).

Brown (*after an awkward pause*). Hello, Dion! I've been looking all over town for you. This place was the very last chance. . . . (*Another pause—embarrassedly*) Let's take a walk.

Dion (*mockingly*). I've given up exercise. They claim it lengthens your life.

Brown (*persuasively*). Come on, Dion, be a good fellow. You're certainly not staying here——

Dion. Billy would like to think me taken in *flagrante delicto*, eh?

Brown. Don't be a damn fool! listen to me! I've been looking you up for purely selfish reasons. I need your help.

Dion (*astonished*). What?

Brown. I've a proposition to make that I hope you'll consider favorably out of old friendship. To be frank, Dion, I need you to lend me a hand down at the office.

Dion (*with a harsh laugh*). So it's the job, is it? Then my poor wife did a-begging go!

Brown (*repelled—sharply*).   On the contrary, I had to beg her
to beg you to take it. (*More angrily*) Look here, Dion! I won't
listen to you talk that way about Margaret! And you wouldn't if
you weren't drunk! (*Suddenly shaking him*) What in hell has come
over you, anyway! You didn't use to be like this! What the devil
are you going to do with yourself—sink into the gutter and drag
Margaret with you? If you'd heard her defend you, lie about you,
tell me how hard you were working. what beautiful things you
were painting, how you stayed at home and idolized the children!
—when everyone knows you've been out every night sousing and
gambling away the last of your estate. . . . (*He stops, ashamed,
controlling himself*).

Dion (*wearily*).   She was lying about her husband, not me, you
fool! But it's no use explaining. (*Then, in a sudden, excitable
passion*) What do you want? I agree to anything—except the humiliation of yelling secrets at the deaf!

Brown (*trying a bullying tone—roughly*).   Bunk! Don't try to
crawl out! There's no excuse and you know it. (*Then as Dion
doesn't reply—penitently*) But I know I shouldn't talk this way
old man! It's only because we're such old pals—and I hate to see
you wasting yourself—you who had more brains than any of us!
But, damn it, I suppose you're too much of a rotten cynic to believe
I mean what I've just said!

Dion (*touched*).   I know Billy was always Dion Anthony's
friend.

Brown.   You're damn right I am—and I'd proved it long ago
if you'd given me half a chance. After all, I couldn't keep chasing
after you and be snubbed every time. A man has some pride!

Dion (*bitterly mocking*).   Dead wrong! Never more! None whatever! It's immoral! Blessed are the poor in spirit, Brother! When
shall I report?

Brown (*eagerly*).   Then you'll take the—you'll help me?

Dion (*wearily bitter*).   I'll take the job. One must do something
to pass away the time, while one is waiting—for one's next incarnation.

Brown (*jokingly*).   I'd say it was a bit early to be worrying
Humorist had given me weak eyes, so now I'll have to foreswear
about that. (*Trying to get Dion started*) Come along, now. It's
pretty late.

Dion (*shakes his hand off his shoulder and walks away from him
—after a pause*).   Is my father's chair still there?

Brown (*turns away—embarrassed*). I— don't really remember, Dion—I'll look it up.

Dion (*taking off his mask slowly*). I'd like to sit where he spun what I have spent. What aliens we were to each other! When he lay dead, his face looked so familiar that I wondered where I had met that man before. Only at the second of my conception. After that, we grew hostile with concealed shame. And my mother? I remember a sweet strange girl, with affectionate, bewildered eyes as if God had locked her in dark closet without any explanation. I was the sole doll our ogre, her husband, allowed her and she played mother and child with me for many years in that house until at last through two tears I watched her die with the shy pride of one who has lengthened her dress and put up her hair. And I felt like a forsaken toy and cried to be buried with her, because her hands alone had caressed without clawing. She lived long and aged greatly in the two days before they closed her coffin. The last time I looked, her purity had forgotten me, she was stainless and imperishable, and I knew my sobs were ugly and meaningless to her virginity; so I shrank away, back into life, with naked nerves jumping like fleas, and in due course of nature another girl called me her boy in the moon and married me and became three mothers in one person, while I got paint on my paws in an endeavor to see God! (*He laughs wildly—claps on his mask*) But that Ancient Humorist had given me weak eyes, so now I'll have to forswear my quest for Him and go in for the Omnipresent Successful Serious One, the Great God Mr. Brown, instead! (*He makes him a sweeping, mocking bow*).

Brown (*repelled but cajolingly*). Shut up, you nut! You're still drunk. Come on! Let's start! (*He grabs Dion by the arm and switches off the light*).

Dion. (*from the darkness—mockingly*). I am thy shorn, bald, nude sheep! Lead on, Almighty Brown, thou Kindly Light!

Curtain

JIRO OSARAGI

OSARAGI JIRO (Japanese, 1897-   ). Eminent Japanese novelist and historical writer. Majored in political science and French law and literature. Taught language and history, then worked in Foreign Office. Author of 6 major novels and innumerable short stories. In his fiction, a concise psychological observant.

From
HOMECOMING

SAEKO said good-night and went up to her apartment on the second floor. She undressed, put on a chemise, and sat down at her dressing-table to take the pins out of her hair.

The door opened suddenly and Nobu's reflection in the mirror startled Saeko.

"I'd like to talk to you a minute," he announced from the doorway. "I didn't want Otane around. I thought it might be embarrassing."

"I'll put something on. Wait in the next room."

"Pardon me for bursting in, but, after all, I'm—"

"Never mind that. Please do as I say."

There was only a thin piece of silk around her body. Saeko felt ashamed suddenly and blushed. Nobu had looked away, but stood there waiting. She walked over to the bed and wrapped a light kimono around her. She spoke as she was picking out an obi. "Can't this wait until tomorrow morning?"

"No. It would be better to talk about it now," he insisted. "It concerns Otane. I want to send her away. . . . I want to throw off this whole slovenly existence I'm leading now. That's what I want to talk over with you."

"I hardly see that it's any of my business. But aren't you being rather hard on Otane? She's served you faithfully all these years."

"But her life never meant anything anyway. What about me? Do I have to go on dragging the sins of my youth with me the rest of my life? They become a pretty heavy load at my age. I realized I was wrong at the time, but my friends all acted that way, and I was young, so I just slipped into it. . . ."

"If you can talk so selfishly about it, it's plain you still haven't repented what you did. Of course, it takes a human being to repent." Saeko finished tying her obi and turned around toward him. "Let's go into the next room. This place is a mess."

"Saeko!" He looked into her face, his eyes intense. "That's not nice of you. This is your room, isn't it? I'm your husband. How can you order me out? . . . I'm sorry from the bottom of my heart. You don't understand how I've suffered these six years. I've tried to tell you, but you just wouldn't listen."

"You're breaking your promise now. We made an agreement, and you can't change it when it pleases you. And be kind enough to leave that door open."

"You're cold, Saeko—to stay angry so long about a trifle."

"I'm not in the least angry. I have nothing to be angry about."

"You say that, and torture me like this?"

"Torture you, indeed!"

"Saeko, I didn't want to say it, but a woman is a woman."

"Are you trying to get me really angry? Are you trying to make me say what I'd rather not say?"

"Don't get angry! Don't get angry! That's all I ask."

The color of fear on his elegant face provoked Saeko to speak. "You who crushed the feelings of my youth, you come here now and speak this way? And think of Otane, if you will. She's not like me. That poor creature's been trained to accept this kind of life and think herself lucky to have it. She's given herself to you entirely, with utter faith—and you want to get rid of her now she no longer suits your convenience. It would be an abominable thing to do."

"But—if you gave her a decent sum of money, she'd be glad to go back to her parents."

Saeko burst out laughing. "I shall most certainly do nothing of the kind. I refuse, definitely. I find it a very amusing idea. Who's buying what?"

"All right. I can manage to scrape that much together myself."

"Tell me—when you've sent Otane away, with whom do you intend to go on living in this house?"

Nobu paled. He understood well enough what she meant, but was too choked with humiliation to speak.

"Aren't you being cruel? Otane's a good, simple woman. What a shock it'll be for her! And have you thought what things are like outside now that you're pushing her into the streets?"

"That's why I'm giving her the money."

"Has she agreed to this? Or is it all your own idea? When I first found out about you and her, the only reason I felt I could forgive you was that at least you loved her. But if you slighted my feelings out of pure whim, if you tell me now that everything you've been saying is a lie—aren't you making it all the harder for me to bear as a woman? I've left it all up to you. I've stayed out of your way."

"But you were all wrong about it. You're completely mistaken about what happened between us."

"I know nothing about it and don't want to! The man is responsible in such cases. Otane and I felt embarrassed toward each other as women, and you and she were shy of discussing the matter because you both knew that what you were doing was wrong. Well, good night now. Think it over. If this is what you intend to do, it's absurd to complain about needing more money."

Nobu's eyes flashed, and he shouted: "Saeko! You're in love with someone!"

"What?"

"You are! You must be!"

"I'll leave it to your imagination. Of course, I don't know what may happen in the future, but surely you can see how improbable it is that I'm in love now. I go in for things the whole way. If I were really in love with someone else, I wouldn't be at all in the mood to go on feeding a purely nominal husband and his Number Two. You can be sure of that, can't you?"

Nobu said nothing, but he put his arms around her shoulders and pulled her toward him. They were strong arms, the arms of an oarsman, but Saeko pressed her two hands against his chest and bent her body back bow-like to ward him off.

"Saeko, it's you I've always loved. Really, from my heart—"

"Take your hands off me. I'll call Otane. The plain truth is you're saying that because you want money."

"Saeko! Don't say things like that!"

"Never mind. I know you and your blood and your background Things have gone badly for you, haven't they? But stop this dis gusting, unmanly display. Instead of these attentions, give me Otane's consolation money. Then we can separate for good. I hadn't thought of it until you mentioned it, but there is a man I could fall in love with. I want to go to him."

The strength ebbed out of Nobu's arms. He stood stiff and spiritless. His face sagged, pale and ugly, with his mouth open. Saeko took her chance, walked out the door, and called Otane's name in her ordinary tone.

"Forgive me, Saeko, forgive me. You shouldn't torture me so cruelly." Nobu was whining like a beaten puppy. "If you're satisfied, let's leave things as they are. I'll try to bear it. . . . But don't get angry. Please don't get angry."

Saeko was listening to the stillness of the house. Otane wasn't coming.

"Just try to act like a man," she said irritably. "But I seem to be more manly than you, don't I? Good night!"

Nobu was slow to move. Saeko had reached the point where she could have loosened her sash and lain down on the bed right in front of him. She could have undressed, indifferent to his presence. She had always taken good care of herself, and her body was still young. It always gave her confidence to look at it in a full-length mirror. The man's slowness was irritating her beyond endurance. She felt there was nothing too cruel for her to do. Nobu apologized one last time and finally went out. She didn't even bother to lock the door behind him.

"Aah!" She sighed out all the feeling she'd been holding in, and sprawled her thinly covered body on the bed, throwing out her arms and legs. She could feel the dark stillness of the peony garden outside her window. The waves broke at intervals on the pebbled shore, but the sudden sounds only made the night more quiet.

Her eyes were shut. She could hear her troubled blood. Her mind was calm. It had come out of the incident indifferent. But she was becoming conscious of the weight of her extended body.

Her heartbeat quickened suddenly. She had moved her arms and legs deliberately, and then realized that her new position was the same as the one she had taken automatically that night in Singapore after parting from Kyogo Moriya. She thought about it, comparing the two positions in detail as though reviewing a school lesson. She lay still, her eyes closed, and the sense of fulfillment she had had that night seeped into her body and lured her mind into a trance. She was like a sponge growing heavy as it takes in water. At the height of fullness, she bit her lip and moaned low.

He was so much older than she, and he could make her feel this way! Her inner eyes stared at this fact in growing surprise, while the inhuman loneliness of the way she was living now shadowed her heart. She had nothing in the world to fear now. But what would become of her if she went on as she was? Kyogo Moriya hated her, there could be no doubt. She thought of these things, and something like a tremor of fear ran up and down her almost naked body.

She sighed, sat up, and turned off the lamp beside her bed.

OVID

OVID (Latin, 43 B.C.-19 A.D.). Urbane and sophisticated Latin poet. Of equestrian family, traveled widely before devoting self to fashionable life of Rome. Early exiled for wantonness in writings. Remains one of most influential and graceful poets of antiquity. Major works: *Amores, Heroides, Ars Amatoria, Metamorphoses, Epistulae ex Ponto.*

SAPPHO TO PHAON

Say, lovely youth, that doth my heart command,
Can Phaon's eyes forget his Sappho's hand?
Must then her name the wretched writer prove,
To thy remembrance lost, as to thy love?
Ask not the cause that I new members choose,
The lute neglected, and the Lyric Muse.
Love taught my tears in sadder notes to flow,
And tuned my heart to elegies of woe.
I burn, I burn, as when through ripened corn
By driving winds the spreading flames are borne.
Phaon to Etna's scorching fields retires,
While I consume with more than Etna's fires!
No more my soul a charm in music finds,
Music has charms alone for peaceful minds:
Soft scenes of solitude no more can please,
Love enters there, and I'm my own disease.
No more the Lesbian dames my passion move,
Once the dear objects of my guilty love;
All other loves are lost in only thine,
Ah, youth ungrateful to a flame like mine!
Whom would not all those blooming charms surprise,
Those heavenly looks, and dear deluding eyes?
The harp and bow would you like Phœbus bear,
A brighter Phœbus Phaon might appear;
Would you with ivy wreathe your flowing hair,
Not Bacchus' self with Phaon could compare:
Yet Phœbus loved, and Bacchus felt the flame,
One Daphne warmed, and one the Cretan dame;
Nymphs that in verse no more could rival me,
Than e'en those gods contend in charms with thee. . . .

Brown as I am, an Ethiopian dame
Inspired young Perseus with a generous flame;
Turtles and doves of different hues unite,
And glossy jet is paired with shining white.
If to no charms thou wilt thy heart resign,
But such as merit, such as equal thine,
By none, alas! by none thou canst be moved:
Phaon alone by Phaon must be loved!
Yet once thy Sappho could thy cares employ;
Once in her arms you centered all your joy:
No time the dear remembrance can remove,
For, oh! how vast a memory has love!
My music, then you could not ever hear,
And all my words were music to your ear.
You stopped with kisses my enchanting tongue,
And found my kisses sweeter than my song.
In all I pleased, but most in what was best;
And the last joy was dearer than the rest.
Then with each word, each glance, each motion fired,
You still enjoyed, and yet you still desired,
Till all dissolving in the trance we lay,
And in tumultuous raptures died away. . . .

O scarce a youth, yet scarce a tender boy!
O useful time for lovers to employ!
Pride of thy age and glory of thy race,
Come to these arms, and melt in this embrace!
The vows you never will return, receive;
And take at least the love you will not give.
See, while I write, my words are lost in tears!
The less my sense, the more my love appears.
Sure 'twas not much to bid one kind adieu;
(At least to feign was never hard to you!)
"Farewell, my Lesbian love," you might have said;
Or coldly thus, "Farewell, oh Lesbian maid!"
No tear did you, no parting kiss receive,
Nor knew I then how much I was to grieve.
No lover's gift your Sappho could confer,
And wrongs and woes were all you left with her.
No charge I gave you, and no charge could give,
But this, "Be mindful of your loves, and live."

Now by the Nine, those powers adored by me,
And Love, the god that ever waits on thee,
When first I heard (from whom I hardly knew)
That you were fled, and all my joys with you,
Like some sad statue, speechless, pale I stood,
Grief chilled my breast, and stopped my freezing blood;
No sigh to rise, no tear had power to flow,
Fixed in a stupid lethargy of woe:
But when its way the impetuous passion found,
I rend my tresses, and my breast I wound;
I rave, then weep; I curse, and then complain;
Now fiercer pangs distract the mournful dame
Whose firstborn infant feeds the funeral flame. . . .
Stung with my love, and furious with despair,
All torn my garments, and my bosom bare,
My woes, thy crimes, I to the world proclaim:
Such inconsistent things are love and shame!
'Tis thou art all my care and my delight,
My daily longing, and my dream by night.
O night, more pleasing than the brightest day,
When fancy gives what absence takes away,
And dressed in all its visionary charms,
Restores my fair deserter to my arms! . . .
But when with day, the sweet delusions fly,
And all things wake to life and joy, but I;
As if once more forsaken, I complain,
And close my eyes to dream of you again.

P

YITSKHOK LEYBUSH PERETZ

YITSKHOK LEYBUSH PERETZ (Polish-Hebrew, 1852-1915). The classic of
modern Yiddish literature. Born in Poland, exposed early to ideological conflict between traditionalism and modernism. After 10 years of law practice,
became leader of new trend in Yiddish literature. Works include poetry,
socially oriented stories, and symbolic dramas (*The Golden Chain, At Night
in the Old Market Place*).

IF NOT HIGHER

EARLY every Friday morning, at the time of the Penitential Prayers,
the Rabbi of Nemirov would vanish.

He was nowhere to be seen—neither in the synagogue nor in the
two Houses of Study nor at a *minyan*. And he was certainly not at
home. His door stood open; whoever wished could go in and out;
no one would steal from the rabbi. But not a living creature was
within.

Where could the rabbi be? Where should he be? In heaven, no
doubt. A rabbi has plenty of business to take care of just before the
Days of Awe. Jews, God bless them, need livelihood, peace, health,
and good matches. They want to be pious and good, but our sins are
so great, and Satan of the thousand eyes watches the whole earth
from one end to the other. What he sees he reports; he denounces,
informs. Who can help us if not the rabbi!

That's what the people thought.

But once a Litvak came, and he laughed. You know the Litvaks.
They think little of the Holy Books but stuff themselves with Talmud
and law. So this Litvak points to a passage in the *Gemarah*—it
sticks in your eyes—where it is written that even Moses, our Teacher, did not ascend to heaven during his lifetime but remained suspended two and a half feet below. Go argue with a Litvak!

So where can the rabbi be?

"That's not my business," said the Litvak, shrugging. Yet all the while—what a Litvak can do!—he is scheming to find out.

That same night, right after the evening prayers, the Litvak steals into the rabbi's room, slides under the rabbi's bed, and waits. He'll watch all night and discover where the rabbi vanishes and what he does during the Penitential Prayers.

Someone else might have got drowsy and fallen asleep, but a Litvak is never at a loss; he recites a whole tractate of the Talmud by heart.

At dawn he hears the call to prayers.

The rabbi has already been awake for a long time. The Litvak has heard him groaning for a whole hour.

Whoever has heard the Rabbi of Nemirov groan knows how much sorrow for all Israel, how much suffering, lies in each groan. A man's heart might break, hearing it. But a Litvak is made of iron; he listens and remains where he is. The rabbi, long life to him, lies on the bed, and the Litvak under the bed.

Then the Litvak hears the beds in the house begin to creak: he hears people jumping out of their beds, mumbling a few Jewish words, pouring water on their fingernails, banging doors. Everyone has left. It is again quiet and dark; a bit of light from the moon shines through the shutters.

(Afterward the Litvak admitted that when he found himself alone with the rabbi a great fear took hold of him. Goose pimples spread across his skin, and the roots of his earlocks pricked him like needles. A trifle: to be alone with the rabbi at the time of the Penitential Prayers! But a Litvak is stubborn. So he quivered like a fish in water and remained where he was.)

Finally the rabbi, long life to him, arises. First he does what befits a Jew. Then he goes to the clothes closet and takes out a bundle of peasant clothes: linen trousers, high boots, a coat, a big felt hat, and a long wide leather belt studded with brass nails. The rabbi gets dressed. From his coat pocket dangles the end of a heavy peasant rope.

The rabbi goes out, and the Litvak follows him.

On the way the rabbi stops in the kitchen, bends down, takes an ax from under the bed, puts it in his belt, and leaves the house. The Litvak trembles but continues to follow.

The hushed dread of the Days of Awe hangs over the dark streets.

Every once in a while a cry rises from some *minyan* reciting the Penitential Prayers, or from a sickbed. The rabbi hugs the sides of the streets, keeping to the shade of the houses. He glides from house to house, and the Litvak after him. The Litvak hears the sound of his heartbeats mingling with the sound of the rabbi's heavy steps. But he keeps on going and follows the rabbi to the outskirts of the town.

A small wood stands behind the town.

The rabbi, long life to him, enters the wood. He takes thirty or forty steps and stops by a small tree. The Litvak, overcome with amazement, watches the rabbi take the ax out of his belt and strike the tree. He hears the tree creak and fall. The rabbi chops the tree into logs and the logs into sticks. Then he makes a bundle of the wood and ties it with the rope in his pocket. He puts the bundle of wood on his back, shoves the ax back into his belt, and returns to the town.

He stops at a back street beside a small broken-down shack and knocks at the window.

"Who is there?" asks a frightened voice. The Litvak recognizes it as the voice of a sick Jewish woman.

"I," answers the rabbi in the accent of a peasant.

"Who is I?"

Again the rabbi answers in Russian. "Vassil."

"Who is Vassil, and what do you want?"

"I have wood to sell, very cheap." And, not waiting for the woman's reply, he goes into the house.

The Litvak steals in after him. In the gray light of early morning he sees a poor room with broken, miserable furnishings. A sick woman, wrapped in rags, lies on the bed. She complains bitterly, "Buy? How can I buy? Where will a poor widow get money?"

"I'll lend it to you," answers the supposed Vassil. "It's only six cents."

"And how will I ever pay you back?" said the poor woman, groaning.

"Foolish one," says the rabbi reproachfully. "See, you are a poor sick Jew, and I am ready to trust you with a little wood. I am sure you'll pay. While you, you have such a great and mighty God and you don't trust him for six cents."

"And who will kindle the fire?" said the widow. "Have I the strength to get up? My son is at work."

"I'll kindle the fire," answers the rabbi.

As the rabbi put the wood into the oven he recited, in a groan, the first portion of the Penitential Prayers.

As he kindled the fire and the wood burned brightly, he recited, a bit more joyously, the second portion of the Penitential Prayers. When the fire was set he recited the third portion, and then he shut the stove.

The Litvak who saw all this became a disciple of the rabbi.

And ever after, when another disciple tells how the Rabbi of Nemirov ascends to heaven at the time of the Penitential Prayers, the Litvak does not laugh. He only adds quietly, "If not higher."

BENITO PEREZ GALDOS

BENITO PÉREZ GALDOS (Spanish, 1843-1920). Prolific Spanish novelist, often compared with Dickens and Tolstoy. An observing narrator of real life with depth and sympathy. Many of his books motivated by liberal ideas—e.g., *Gloria*, an indictment of religious and racial prejudice, and *Misericordia*, a study of the Madrid underworld. Left some 80 novels, 24 plays and 15 volumes of miscellaneous writings.

MADAMA ESTHER

ESTHER Spinoza, the wife of Moses Morton, a very wealthy Jewish merchant of Hamburg, who had afterwards settled in London, was, like her husband, descended from a family of Spanish Jews; but the Morton family had got itself involved with German and Dutch alliances, while that of Spinoza had kept itself unmixed, and its pedigree could be clearly traced as far back as to Daniel Spinoza, a Jew of Cordova, banned by the edict of proscription of 1492. Esther Spinoza was a Spaniard by blood, though not by birth; Spanish too in her serious character, her deeply-seated and strongly-controlled vehemence, her strict sense of duty—while the melancholy light of her black eyes, her tall figure, and her graceful gait were those of a true Spaniard. Spanish too was her mother-tongue that she had spoken like a native, from her cradle. It is a well-known fact that all the Hebrew families descended from the Spanish exiles have clung to that language, though for lack of replanting on its native soil it has often degenerated greatly; and the Spaniard who, even at the present day, visits Constantinople, Belgrade, Jerusalem, Venice, Rome or Cairo—all of them places whither some of the miserable dust was blown that the storm swept from Spain—may hear among the Jews an archaic form of Castilian which rings in his ears as a melancholy and sweet surprise, as if it were an echo from the dead past of his native land—a sigh from the grave after four centuries of oblivion. The Spanish Jews, most of them very abject, have clung to the language of their oppressors and read the rabbinical books in that tongue; their love for the country that has been so ruthless a step-mother is as fervent as their devotion to that ancient eastern home which they have never recovered, and they weep for her as hundreds of years ago they wept by the waters of Babylon. The feeling is less strong, no doubt, among the wealthier Hebrews. The Spinozas loved the memory of the second country they had lost, but Esther hated the land with all her heart, excepting the language which she kept up diligently and took care to teach to her children.

She did not profess her own faith with any fervor of enthusiasm; still, she was loyal to it with a steady and dutiful feeling which was not so much devotion as respect for the creed of her ancestors and attachment to the name and history of an unhappy and persecuted race. This indeed amounted to a passion, a fanaticism, which might have reproduced in her the grand characteristics of Deborah the "Mother in Israel," of Jael who transfixed the foe with a nail of the tragical Judith and gentler heroine Esther. The spirit of her race filled her and inspired her, but she had not the same devotion to its formulas and rites; and though she fulfilled its precepts with her children and servants, she did so because she thought it well to perpetuate this potent bond of union—a sort of ideal father-land—on whose sacred ground a hapless nation, bereft of soil, might meet. Esther was a model of the domestic virtues which are universal among the higher class of Hebrew women, and which need neither cause surprise nor give rise to invidious reflections. There is no need to analyze them, nor to wonder whether, as many have thought, the secret of them lies in superior culture or in intrinsic natural morality. She was a good wife and a tender mother, and those who said she was worthy to have been a Christian did her no more than justice.

Esther and her husband were enormously wealthy; it might be said of them that the Lord had prospered the work of their hands.

They lived in perfect harmony, surrounded by every luxury that art could produce. Their houses almost revived the fabulous glories of the palace of Haroun-al-Raschid. They were respected by all and the guests even of Kings; and having acquired a financial position which almost gave them the importance of a political power, they had extricated Nations from difficulties. They had no native soil, but the proudest rulers had sued to them; titles, honors, respect, consideration, position and adulation—all that potentates enjoy or covet, was theirs. They stood like divinities, before whom every minister of finance was ready to burn incense; and the Pope himself, as secular sovereign, gave them titles and crosses and never called them *Deicides,* but on the contrary, "potent seignors." Esther Spinoza having visited Rome, a Cardinal constituted himself her guide through the collections, and another presented her with mosaics, cameos and carnelians, while a third sold her a marble crucifix for a thousand *livres,* and for five hundred a Spanish manuscript of the Talmud, on vellum, of the XIIIth century.

They had no kingdom but they reigned everywhere, for the dominion of Mammon is a wide one; "the earth is *his,*" we may say, "and the fulness thereof," and the home of the north and the south winds. No one had ever thought of asking any member of this illustrious family in the exalted position they occupied, whether they too had said: *"Crucify Him and release unto us Barrabas."*

In spite of her fifty years, Madama Esther was still extremely handsome, as among Spanish women of rank is not uncommon; it may be accounted for by the finely-tempered balance of certain natures, combined with easy circumstances and the inestimable advantage of a life free from anxiety, menial toil and no more suffering or sorrow than is enough to prove that perfect happiness is but a myth. She indulged in few arts of the toilet, and those she used were not to conceal her years, but merely to make them look beautiful, as though she were proud of her bright and fresh maturity, the true homage of age to youth. In looking at her it became easy to understand the lasting spring of the women of whom we are told in the Bible that they lived a hundred and twenty years and more, as though it were nothing.

SAINT-JOHN PERSE

SAINT-JOHN PERSE (Alexis Saint-Léger Léger, French, 1887-   ). Elegant
poet and diplomat. Born in Guadeloupe, went to Paris for education. Entered
the Foreign Service, working closely with Briand. Came to America when
Nazis took France. Painter of rich and unusual images, especially admired
by poets and intellectuals. Most famous work, *Anabasis*, has been translated
by T. S. Eliot.

SNOWS

AND then came the snows, the first snows of absence, falling upon
the great woven cloths of dreams and reality; and with every
affliction remitted to men of memory, there came the freshness of
clean sheets on our temples. And it was in the morning, under the
grey salt of dawn, a little before the sixth hour, as in a haven of
fortune, an asylum of grace and mercy where the swarm of the
great odes of silence could be scattered.

And all the night, unknown to us, beneath that canopy of feather,
bearing its noble imprint and cure of souls, the high towns of
pumice-stone perforated by luminous insects had not ceased to grow
and excel, in the oblivion of their weight. And they alone knew
something about it whose memory is uncertain whose story aberrant.
The share that the mind took in these conspicuous things, we do
not know.

No one surprised, no one knew the first laying of that silky hour
on the loftiest brow of stone, the first touch of that agile and very
futile thing, the sweep as it were of eyelashes. On the bronze revet-
ments and the out-thrusts of chromium-plated steel, on the rubble
of heavy porcelain, on the coarse-glass tiles, on the black-marble
spindle and on the white-metal spur, no one surprised, no one
tarnished it,

This mist of a breath at its birth, like the first fright of a blade
unsheathed . . . it was snowing and we shall tell the wonder of it:
dawn silent in its plumes, like a great fabulous owl a prey to the
winds of the spirit, puffed out its white dahlia body. On all sides
a miracle and a fête. May grace alight on this terrace-slope where
the Architect showed to us one recent summer the eggs of a night-jar.

ALEXANDER PETOFI

ALEXANDER PETŐFI (Hungarian, 1822-1849). Most widely known Hungarian poet. Fighter for Hungarian independence in the 1840's. Majority of his compositions are simple lyrics, modeled on folk poetry. Notable for vivid imagination, fiery patriotism.

LONGING FOR DEATH

Give me a coffin and a grave,
   And let the grave be deep and low;
And bury with me all I feel,
   All passions strong, all thoughts of woe.

O, mind and heart, twice cursed, e'er have
   You been the bane of my whole life!
Why torture me with burning scourge?
   Why should not end now all this strife?

Why should this feverish brain inspire
   To rise above the stars on high?
When angry Fate hath it ordained
   That crawl upon the earth should I.

Why have I not fair heavenly wings,
   If my aims soar to heaven's dome?
To carry me into heights where
   Immortality is at home!

And if to me this world is void
   Of joy, why have I, then, a breast?
Created that of human joys
   It be the home, the shelt'ring nest!

Or if there be a heart which flames
   And burns in passion's deep abyss,
Why, then, this icy look on me,
   Thou God of happiness and bliss?

978

Give me a coffin and a grave,
    And let the grave be deep and low;
And bury with me all I feel,
    All passions strong, all thoughts of woe.

IF GOD

If God Almighty thus did speak to me:
"My son, I grant permission unto thee
To have thy Death as thou thyself shalt say;"
Thus unto my Creator I would pray:

"Let it be autumn, when the zephyrs sway
The sere leaves wherewith mellow sunbeams play;
And let me hear once more the sad, sweet song
Of errant birds, that will be missed ere long.

"And unperceived, as winter's chilling breath
Waiting o'er autumn bearing subtle Death
Thus let Death come; most welcome will He be
If I observe Him when he's close to me.

"Like to the birds, again I will outpour
A mellower tune than e'er I sang before,
A song which moves the heart, makes dim the eyes
And mounts up swelling to the very skies.

"And, as my swan song draweth to its end,
My sweetheart fair and true may o'er me bend;
Thus would I die, caressing her fair face,
Kissing the one on earth who holds most grace.

"But if the Lord this boon should disallow,
With spring of war let Him the land endow;
When the rose-blooms that color earth again
Are blood-red roses in the breasts of men."

FRANCESCO PETRARCA

FRANCESCO PETRARCA (Italian, 1304-1374). Latin and Italian Poet
Laureate. Precursor of the Renaissance, has been called "the first modern
man of letters." Now best remembered for his Italian lyrics, *Le Rime*, addressed to his beloved, Laura. These remained models of style for centuries.
Also wrote Latin epic, *Africa*, and many letters and philosophic treatises in
the classic Latin manner.

SONNETS TO LAURA

All ye who list, in wildly warbled strain,
    Those sighs with which my youthful heart was fed,
    Erewhile fond passion's maze I wont to tread,
Erewhile I lived estrang'd to manlier pain;
For all those vain desires, and griefs as vain,
    Those tears, those plaints, by am'rous fancy bred,
    If ye by love's strong power have e'er been led,
Pity, nay, haply pardon, I may gain.
Oft on my check the conscious crimson glows,
    And sad reflection tells—ungrateful thought!—
How jeering crowds have mock'd my love-lorn woes:
But folly's fruits are penitence and shame,
    With this just maxim, I've too dearly bought,
That man's applause is but a transient dream.

Poor, solitary bird, that pour'st thy lay,
    Or haply mournest the sweet season gone,
As chilly night and winter hurry on,
And daylight fades, and summer flies away!
If, as the cares that swell thy little throat,
    Thou knew'st alike the woes that wound my rest,
    Oh, thou wouldst house thee in this kindred breast,
And mix with mine thy melancholy note!
Yet little know I ours are kindred ills:
    She still may live the object of thy song:
Not so for me stern Death or Heaven wills!
    But the sad season, and less grateful hour,
And of past joy and sorrow thoughts that throng,
    Prompt my full heart this idle lay to pour.

Alone and pensive, the deserted strand
    I wander o'er with slow and measured pace,

And shun with eager eye the lightest trace
Of human foot imprinted on the sand.
I find, alas! no other resting-place
    From the keen eye of man; for, in the show
    Of joys gone by, it reads upon my face
The traces of the flame that burns below.
And thus, at length, each leafy mount and plain,
    Each wandering stream and shady forest, know,
What others know not, all my life of pain.
    And e'en as through the wildest tracts I go,
Love whispers in my ear his tender strain,
Which I with trembling lip repeat to him again.

Swift current, that from rocky Alpine vein,
    Gathering the tribute to thy waters free,
    Mov'st joyous onward night and day with me,
Where nature leads thee, me love's tyrant chain!
Roll freely on; nor toil nor rest restrain
    Thine arrowy course; but ere thou yieldest in
The tribute of thy waters to the main,
    Seek out heaven's purest sky, earth's deepest green;
There wilt thou find the bright and living beam
    That o'er thy left bank sheds its heavenly rays:
If unto her too slow my footsteps seem,—
    While by her feet thy lingering current strays,
Forming to words the murmurs of its stream,—
    Say that the weary flesh the willing soul delays.

In what ideal world or part of heaven
    Did Nature find the model of that face
    And form, so fraught with loveliness and grace,
In which to our creation she has given
Her prime proof of creative power above?
What fountain nymph or goddess ever let
    Such lovely tresses float of gold refined
    Upon the breeze, or in a single mind
Where have so many virtues ever met,
E'en though those charms have slain my bosom's weal?
    He knows not love, who has not seen her eyes
    Turn when she sweetly speaks, or smiles, or sighs,
Or how the power of love can hurt or heal.

Creatures there be, of sight so keen and high,
　That even on the sun they bend their gaze;
　Others, who, dazzled by too fierce a blaze,
Issue not forth till evening veils the sky;
Others, who, with insane desire, would try
　The bliss which dwells within the fire's bright rays,
　But, in their sport, find that its fervor slays.
Alas! of this last heedless band am I:
　Since strength I boast not, to support the light
Of that fair form, nor in obscure sojourn
　Am skilled to fence me, nor enshrouding night.
Wherefore, with eyes which ever weep and mourn,
　My fate compels me still to court her sight,
Conscious I follow flames which shine to burn.

Waved to the winds were those long locks of gold
　Which in a thousand burnished ringlets flowed,
　And the sweet light beyond all measure glowed
Of those fair eyes which I no more behold,
Nor (so it seemed) that face aught harsh or cold
　To me (if true or false, I know not) showed;
　Me, in whose breast the amorous lure abode,
If flames consumed, what marvel to unfold?
That step of hers was of no mortal guise,
　But of angelic nature; and her tongue
Had other utterance than of human sounds.
A living sun, a spirit of the skies,
I saw her. Now, perhaps, not so. But wounds
　Heal not, for that the bow is since unstrung.

PILPAY

PILPAY (Sanskrit, dates unknown). Legendary fabulist, known through an
ancient Sanskrit collection called *Panchatantra*. Translated into Pahlavi about
550, thereafter into Arabic. Versions also exist in Mongol, Malay and Afghan
languages.

THE MAN AND THE ADDER

A MAN mounted upon a Camel once rode into a thicket, and went
to rest himself in that part of it from whence a caravan was just

departed, and where the people having left a fire, some sparks of it, being driven by the wind, had set a bush, wherein lay an Adder, all in a flame. The fire environed the Adder in such a manner that he knew not how to escape, and was just giving himself over to destruction, when he perceived the Man already mentioned, and with a thousand mournful conjurations begged of him to save his life. The Man, on this, being naturally compassionate, said to himself, "It is true these creatures are enemies to mankind; however, good actions are of great value, even of the very greatest when done to our enemies; and whoever sows the seed of good works, shall reap the fruit of blessings." After he had made this reflection, he took a sack, and tying it to the end of his lance, reached it over the flame to the Adder, who flung himself into it; and when he was safe in, the traveler pulled back the bag, and gave the Adder leave to come forth, telling him he might go about his business; but hoped he would have the gratitude to make him a promise, never to do any more harm to men, since a man had done him so great a piece of service.

To this the ungrateful creature answered, "You much mistake both yourself and me: think not that I intend to be gone so calmly; no, my design is first to leave thee a parting blessing, and throw my venom upon thee and thy Camel."

"Monster of ingratitude!" replied the Traveler, "desist a moment at least, and tell me whether it be lawful to recompense good with evil."

"No," replied the Adder, "it certainly is not; but in acting in that manner I shall do no more than what yourselves do every day; that is to say, retaliate good deeds with wicked actions, and requite benefits with ingratitude."

"You cannot prove this slanderous and wicked aspersion," replied the Traveler: "nay, I will venture to say that if you can show me any one other creature in the world that is of your opinion, I will consent to whatever punishment you think fit to inflict on me for the faults of my fellow-creatures."

"I agree to this willingly," answered the Adder; and at the same time spying a Cow, "Let us propound our question," said he, "to this creature before us, and we shall see what answer she will make." The Man consented; and so both of them accosting the Cow, the Adder put the question to her, how a good turn was to be requited. "By its contrary," replied the Cow, "if you mean according to the custom of men; and this I know by sad experience. I belong," said she, "to a man, to whom I have long been several ways extremely beneficial: I have been used to bring him a calf every year, and to supply his house with milk, butter, and cheese; but now I am grown old, and no longer in a condition to serve him as formerly I did, he has put me in this pasture to fat me, with a design to sell me to a butcher, who is to cut my throat, and he and his friends are to eat my flesh: and is not this requiting good with evil?"

On this, the Adder, taking upon him to speak, said to the Man, "What say you now? are not your own customs a sufficient warrant for me to treat you as I intend to do?"

The Traveler, not a little confounded at this ill-timed story, was cunning enough, however, to answer, "This is a particular case only, and give me leave to say, one witness is not sufficient to convince me; therefore pray let me have another."

"With all my heart," replied the Adder; "let us address ourselves to this Tree that stands here before us." The Tree, having heard the subject of their dispute, gave his opinion in the following words: "Among men, benefits are never requited but with ungrateful actions. I protect travelers from the heat of the sun, and yield them fruit to eat, and a delightful liquor to drink; nevertheless, forgetting the delight and benefit of my shade, they barbarously cut down my branches to make sticks, and handles for hatchets, and saw my body to make planks and rafters. Is not this requiting good with evil?"

The Adder, on this, looking upon the Traveler, asked if he was satisfied. But he was in such a confusion that he knew not what to answer. However, in hopes to free himself from the danger that threatened him, he said to the Adder, "I desire only one favor more; let us be judged by the next beast we meet; give me but that satisfaction, it is all I crave: you know life is sweet; suffer me therefore to beg for the means of continuing it." While they were thus parlaying together, a Fox passing by was stopped by the Adder, who conjured him to put an end to their controversy.

The Fox, upon this, desiring to know the subject of their dispute, said the Traveler, "I have done this Adder a signal piece of service, and he would fain persuade me that, for my reward, he ought to do me a mischief." "If he means to act by you as you men do by others, he speaks nothing but what is true," replied the Fox; "but, that I may be better able to judge between you, let me understand what service it is that you have done him."

The Traveler was very glad of this opportunity of speaking for himself, and recounted the whole affair to him: he told him after what manner he had rescued him out of the flames with that little sack, which he showed him.

"How!" said the Fox, laughing outright, "would you pretend to make me believe that so large an Adder as this could get into such a little sack? It is impossible!" Both the Man and the Adder, on this, assured him of the truth of that part of the story; but the Fox positively refused to believe it. At length said he, "Words will never convince me of this monstrous improbability; but if the Adder will go into it again, to convince me of the truth of what you say, I shall then be able to judge of the rest of this affair."

"That I will do most willingly," replied the Adder; and, at the same time, put himself into the sack.

Then said the Fox to the Traveler, "Now you are the master of your enemy's life: and, I believe, you need not be long in resolving what treatment such a monster of ingratitude deserves of you." With that the Traveler tied up the mouth of the sack, and, with a great stone, never left off beating it till he had pounded the Adder to death; and, by that means, put an end to his fears and the dispute at once.

PINDAR

PINDAR (Greek, 518-438 B.C.). Sublime poetic eulogist, most accomplished writer of Greek choral lyrics. His major surviving works are celebration odes, written for aristocratic families and dedicated to the victors of the Panhellenic Games. Characterized by brilliant imagery and use of myths to point a moral.

JASON

(From the Fourth Pythian Ode. In honor of Arcesilaus, King of Cyrene, victor in chariot race, 466 B.C.

In time a noble stranger came,
A youth of glorious port; his manly frame
The country tunic clasped; two spears he bore.
Above, to fence the shivering rain,
A skin of spotted pard he threw.
Adown his youthful neck amain
His hair in glittering ringlets flew.

('Twas then in thronging crowds the people pressed,
 What time the busy forum filled),
 Then first he proved his manly breast,
And stood amid the throng by timorous fears unchilled.

 Who might he be? thus each in wonder cried;
 Is he Apollo? Is he Mars,
 So awful from the brazen cars,
 So fair to win bright Venus for his bride?
 In Naxus sure men said
 Otus and Ephialte were dead;
 And earth-born Tityus' giant form
 The winged shaft of Dian slew,
 What time in dread avenging storm
 From her unconquered bow it flew,
 A warning dread that men should fear,
Nor aim audacious love beyond their mortal sphere.

 So each to the other babbled;—but in haste
 High on his mule-drawn chariot Pelias came,
 Eager, and full of fear: in stealthy shame
A frightened glance upon the ground he cast,
 That glance the single sandal spied,
 The left foot bare! with easy grace
 As bent his inward dread to hide,
 "Tell, friend," he cried, "thy dwelling place;
 What nameless mother sent her darling here,
 The darling of her doting age?
 Speak nor let glozing falsehood sear
Thy birth, whate'er it be, nor lies thy soul engage."

 Then frank and brave the gentle youth replied,
 " From Chiron's cave I come, his nurseling I,
 Where Philyra my innocent infancy
And Chariclo, the Centaur's child, did guide.
 Twice ten the years I count, yet ne'er
 Hath word of falsehood stained my tongue,
 Nor deed of ill, nor ribald jeer.
 I come to claim mine own from wrong.
 Home to mine own I come, my father's heir.
 That crown usurped by lawless might,

Which erst old Æolus did wear,
He and his sons. From Jove, I claim my father's right.

For yielding to vile greed of power, men say,
    The promptings of a felon breast,
    Pelias my sire hath dispossessed,
And torn his long descended crown away.
      So when I first drew breath,
    Lest ruffian hands should do me death,
    My parents in the king's despite,
    Feigning an infant's early doom,
    Drest up with tears a funeral rite,
    And laid a puppet in the tomb.
    But me to Chiron's loving care,
All wrapt in princely robe, at dead of night, they bare.

Such is my tale;—no more the occasion needs;
    Then deign, kind citizens, to show me plain
    The dwelling whence my sires in lawful reign
Issued, all princely drawn by milk-white steeds.
      For Æson's son, no stranger I
    Come welcome to my home and free.
    Ask ye my name? The Centaur high
    Who bred me, bade me Jason be."
He spoke: but him his father's heart had known;
    Down his cheeks rolled the happy tears,
    To see his long-lost stripling grown
A prince of noble youths, the fairest of his peers.

Soon flock his brethren at the wondrous tale.
    Pheres from Hypereia's neighbor spring,
    Admetus eke, and brave Melampus bring,
And Amythaon from Messenia's vale,
      Cousinly greeting. He the while
    Spread bounteous forth the genial feast,
    And with kind word and courteous smile
    Received each new arriving guest.
High was the lordly cheer. and loud and long;
    Flew swiftly by each mirthful hour;
    Echoed five days and nights the song,
Five days and nights they culled joy's holiest, brightest flower.

987

But when the sixth day dawned, his tale of wrong
    To his assembled kinsman bold,
     In manly phrase the Chieftain told;
  Approving murmurs broke from all the throng.
       Forth from the council-tent
      Amid his peers the hero went
    Straightway the robber king to seek.
      They passed within the portal high.
    He heard and with a smiling cheek
     Wore a deceitful courtesy.
     Then, in sage words of peaceful flow
And counsel calm, the hero thus addressed his foe:

" Son of Poseidon! oft the blinded heart
    Of man in folly seeks for crafty gain,
    Nor heeds the after-reckoning of grim pain,
To choose the juster and the wiser part.
     Yet were it well that I and you,
      With peaceful words and counsel sage,
     Should weave a web both wise and true,
      And turn to peace our mutual rage.
I speak of what thou know'st. A single womb.
     Cretheus and bold Salmoneus bore.
     From these in third descent we come;
But Fate shrinks back ashamed when kinsmen join in **war.**

It must not be that we with sword and steel
    Our great forefather's heritage should share.
    Freely the flocks and herds,—my father's heir,
Yea, and the fruitful lands to thee I deal.
     Long hast thou these unduly held.
      Keep them, and swell thy robber store.
     It doth not yearn my soul to yield
      All these to thee; do thou restore
The royal sceptre and the righteous throne,
     Where Cretheus' son, my sire, erewhile
     With princely justice ruled his own.
These, without sterner force or trick of fraudful **guile,**

Restore, lest thence worse evil should ensue."
　　　Briefly, as best his grief to hide,
　　　In accents calm the king replied:
" That which thy words invite me, will I do,
　　　　But now mine age is old;
　　　Thy blood is young, thy heart is bold;
　　　Thou may'st the infernal wrath allay:
　For murdered Phrixus bids us come
　　　Where lives Æetes far away,
　And call his exiled spirit home,
　　　And fetch the fleece of golden sheen,
On which he soared erewhile to 'scape the vengeful Queen.

For so a wondrous vision of my sleep
　　　Enjoined; without delay my way I took,
　　　Lest aught of vain or false my soul should mock,
　To seek the God of Delphi's holy steep.
　　　He bade me brook no slow delay,
　　　But man a bark with instant speed
　　　The sacred vision to obey.
　　　Do thou perform the holy deed;
　And by great Jove, our common sire, I swear,
　　　Sceptre and throne to yield thee free."
　　　Their mutual faith they promised fair,
That strong and sure to both should their high compact be.

OLYMPIA

*(Eighth Olympian Ode. To Alcimedon of Ægina, victor in wrestling,
460 B.C.)*

Olympia! mother of the old-crowned games!
　　　Great spring of Truth divine!
　　Where seers around the holy shrine,
　　With augury of sacred flames,
Essay the mind of Jove, the Thunder-King,
　　　If aught of hope he bring
To heroes straining for the glorious wreath,
Which bids the aching heart in triumph breathe.

(And oft success attends on pious prayers)
O holy Pisan grove,
Receive our revel-pomp in love!
For glorious is his praise who shares
The grace which thy victorious garlands shed!
Yet many a path men tread,
And various are the roads of sweet success,
When the good Gods the toils of mortals bless.

DAVID PINSKI

DAVID PINSKI (Russian-Hebrew, 1872-   ). Foremost dramatist in Yiddish. Born in Ukraine, studied in Vienna. Under influence of I. L. Peretz in Warsaw, attached self to Jewish Socialist Movement. Came to U.S.A. in 1899, emigrated to Israel in 1950. Wrote historical romances, realistic novels of Jewish life, and plays: *The Treasure, King David and His Wives, The Final Balance.*

AND THEN HE WEPT

BEREL the carrier, poor but cheerful, lived in a cellar. Its two small windows below the cobbled pavement of the courtyard were gray and muddy, scarcely admitting the sunbeams that sometimes reached them. Dampness leaked from the walls, mold glittered and sparkled in the corners.

A table stood near the wall, between the two windows. Two of the legs were its own, the others proxies—sticks of wood, which often disappeared when there was nothing else with which to heat the stove. At such times the table was shoved against the wall and remained standing, Berel said, "with God's help."

There were three white chairs as well, all without backs. As soon as a back toppled, Berel intended to hammer it into place again. but meanwhile the two sticks supporting the table had been burned up and no other firewood remained. So Berel would pull a solemn face and hand down a truly philosophical decision: one can sit on a chair even though it has no back, but potatoes must be cooked. And he would intone in a Passover voice, most impressively, while the chairback entered the oven along with other scraps that Berel and his children had scavenged.

Two beds completed the furnishings. Rags, which Berel persisted in calling pillows and blankets, covered them, and under and near them stood boxes filled with more rags. Berel announced proudly that these were shirts, tablecloths—all sorts of household riches.

Did all this worry Berel? He laughed.

"What more do I need? Not a thing. As long as there's life . . ."

He had four children; two slept with him in one bed, two with the mother in the second bed. But he had no fear of more children. "Children," he said, "are a delight, a joy. Of course, they need a lot, but what's the difference? As long as I can come home and there's someone to play with, to make myself foolish with. What a pleasure! What a gang I have!"

Only his wife Bas-Sheve caused Berel dissatisfaction. He couldn't bear her moaning, her wailing and complaining.

"Eh," Berel said, shrugging, "my wife isn't fit for anything—always crying. She wants so much—what is there that she doesn't want? You'd think she had a contract with God, and He had promised to provide for her."

The tears had barely come to her eyes when Berel began to pose in front of her, his right hand against his cheek, his left hand supporting the right, his face twisted into woe and his head rocking back and forth. Bas-Sheve didn't find the imitation amusing. She grew angry. "All you do is laugh!"

"But I'm crying. Can't you see?" mocked Berel in his weepy voice.

"I wish we were crying for you, you great provider!" Her piece recited, she turned her back sharply. Berel wasn't insulted. Curses couldn't bother him. It almost seemed that without her curses life would be dull.

Only when she began to curse herself did Berel really become angry. "Almighty God," she cried out once when there was nothing to eat and a child was ill into the bargain (not at all a rare coincidence in Berel's house), "Almighty God, rescue me from this dark and bitter life!" Her voice trembled; she meant it in earnest. At that moment she had no fear of death, and Berel felt it. His ribs seemed to crack with anguish. Outraged, furious, he began to scream, "May your tongue wither!"

Bas-Sheve, reduced to silence, wept instead, while Berel cast angry glances at her. "What good does crying do? That's all I want to know. You fool!"

As far as Berel was concerned, a human being should never cry unless, God forbid, someone died. But once . . .

Once of an evening Berel played so hard with the children,

wrestled and cavorted and carried on so lustily, that he plummeted onto his bed—and the bed exploded into bits.

He rose from the ruins, laughing. "Hoorah! Just wait, children. We'll deliver a funeral oration over the bed," Crouching like the humpbacked village orator, Berel made as if to speak. Bas-Sheve, clutching her head, broke into a wail. "It's too much—I can't stand any more. It's the last straw. I'll kill myself."

"Shh, let me say the eulogy." Berel tried to calm her, to draw her into the game. But she kept on moaning, "God in heaven, how can I be rid of this miserable life? At least we owned two beds, and now we don't even have that."

Berel grew angry. "Cow! What shall I do with you? Come on, cry some more. So the bed's smashed! You cow! Come on, moo-oo. Why aren't you bellowing?"

"May I bellow for the loss of your head!" She threw herself at him. "If only I could get rid of you I'd see daylight! Whenever you lift a finger it turns out a misfortune. Murderer, you're my private Angel of Death."

Berel's good humor was restored by the familiar accusations. "Come on, tell the truth—why all this uproar? Why upset the universe? What's a broken bed—a catastrophe? Has the sky collapsed? Listen. Think what might have happened to one of us, and instead it's happened to the bed!"

He remonstrated. She wept.

Blotting the tears with her apron, she thought of the future. No new shoes for the children. The first few pennies that came into the house would have to go for a new bed . . . though perhaps the old one could still be fixed. Meanwhile she and the two girls would sleep on the floor, and he—that foul hunk of disaster—he'd sleep in the remaining bed.

When Berel finished she answered tartly and with tears, "Sure, you have lots of beds, don't you? Go, crawl on the floor in the mud and the damp, and you'll learn how to laugh—may this be your last laugh!" Bas-Sheve glared at him.

Berel laughed. "What a joke! Berel, that great gentleman, has to sleep on the floor. Come on, kids, drag down the mattress," he told the boys.

"Not while I'm alive will I let you sleep on the floor!" She leaped up and shielded the mattress with her body.

Berel was astonished. "What's wrong? Are you crazy?"

992

"When you're dead, then you can lie on the ground. Not now."

Berel grew stern. "Bas-Sheve, this is no time for foolishness. Let me get some sleep." He reached for the mattress.

She pushed his head away and pointed to the bed. "Lie down, and may you never get up."

"I don't sleep in women's beds," he joked. "Come on, let me get some sleep." He grabbed the mattress.

"I said no and I meant it," screamed Bas-Sheve, clutching the mattress with both hands.

"So I'll lie down without a mattress!" Berel laughed and took off his coat.

Bas-Sheve rushed at him with her nails. Her cheeks flushed, her eyes burned. Berel grew excited. It was his young Bas-Sheve again! Warmth flooded his heart, a smile flowed across his face. "Ah, my pretty wife," he called and wanted to embrace her. But she thrust him off, her hatred absolute. "Get away from me quietly. If you don't I'll break your head."

She turned her back and began to prepare the bed for him. In that instant he grabbed the mattress, spun it onto the floor near the stove, and threw himself on top of it.

"Come on, boys," he ordered, "let's get to sleep."

Bas-Sheve cried out in fury, "Get on that bed!"

"Tomorrow."

"Stop ordering me around—may you wither and rot."

He laughed.

"Get into that bed! Do you hear what I say?"

"Ho-hum."

Frenzied, she began to kick the one remaining bed with her feet.

"There—take that! There!"

Berel and the children jumped up in horror while she kept kicking with all her strength.

Berel tried to control her, to soothe her. He caught and held her tightly. "Have you gone mad?"

She tore herself away. Her heart contracted, her head blazed. She wanted to smash, smash, smash . . . But he held her too strongly. She tried to bite him.

"Bas-Sheve! Look, Bas Sheve," he stammered, twisting away from her teeth. He managed to lower her to a chair. Slowly Bas-Sheve calmed herself and began to weep. The children formed a chorus, wailing with fright.

Berel felt lost. He stood before Bas-Sheve and didn't take his sorrowful eyes off her. "Bas-Shevenke, little Bas-Sheve, stop, please stop!"

His voice twitched. "Bas-Shevenke," he pleaded gently, softly. His heart warmed with a marvelous tenderness, his throat seemed to choke and thicken. And that time Berel wept too.

LUIGI PIRANDELLO

LUIGI PIRANDELLO (Italian, 1867-1936). Leading modern dramatist of Italy. Began career as naturalistic novelist and story writer. Turned to theater in middle age. Developed highly individual technique, to explore metaphysical problems—especially the question of personal identity. Most famous plays: *Right You Are If You Think You Are, Six Characters in Search of an Author.* Nobel Prize, 1934.

HORSE IN THE MOON

IN SEPTEMBER, upon that high and arid clayey plain, jutting perilously over the African sea, the melancholy countryside still lay parched from the merciless summer sun; it was still shaggy with blackened stubble, while a sprinkling of almond trees and a few aged olive trunks were to be seen here and there. Nevertheless, it had been decided that the bridal pair should spend at least the first few days of their honeymoon in this place, to oblige the bridegroom.

The wedding feast, which was held in a room of the deserted villa, was far from being a festive occasion for the invited guests. None of those present was able to overcome the embarrassment, or rather the feeling of dismay inspired in him by the aspect and bearing of that fleshy youth, barely twenty years of age, with purplish face and with the little darting black eyes, which were preternaturally bright, like a madman's. The latter no longer heard what was being said around him; he did not eat, and he did not drink, but became, from moment to moment, redder and more purple of countenance.

Everyone knew that he had been madly in love with the one who now sat beside him as his bride, and that he had done perfectly mad things on her account, even to the point of attempting to kill himself. He was very rich, the sole heir to the Bernardi fortune, while she, after all, was only the daughter of an infantry colonel who had come there the year before, with the regiment from Sicily.

But in spite of this, the colonel, who had been warned against the inhabitants of the island, had been reluctant about giving his consent to this match, for the reason that he had not wanted to leave his daughter there among people that were little better than savages.

The dismay which the bridegroom's aspect and actions inspired in the guests increased when the latter came to contrast him with his extremely young bride. She was really but a child, fresh, vivacious, and aloof; it seemed that she always shook off every unpleasant thought with a liveliness that was, at once, charming, ingenuous and roguish. Roguish as that of a little tomboy who as yet knows nothing of the world. A half-orphan, she had grown up without a mother's care; and indeed, it was all too evident that she was going into matrimony without any preparation whatsoever. Everyone smiled, but everyone felt a chill, when, at the end of the meal, she turned to the bridegroom and exclaimed:

"For goodness' sake, Nino, why do you make those tiny eyes? Let me—no, they burn! Why do your hands burn like that? Feel, Papa, feel how hot his hands are—Do you suppose he has a fever?"

The colonel, on pins and needles, did what he could to speed up the departure of the countryside guests. He wanted to put an end to a spectacle that impressed him as being indecent. They all piled into a half-dozen carriages. The one in which the colonel rode proceeded slowly down the lane and lagged a little behind, for the reason that the bridal couple, one on one side and one on the other, holding hands with the mother and father, had wanted to follow a short distance on foot, down to where the highway which led to the distant city began. At that point, the colonel leaned down and kissed his daughter on the head; he coughed and muttered: "Goodby, Nino."

"Goodby, Ida," said the bridegroom's mother with a laugh; and the carriage rattled away at a good pace, in order to overtake the others.

The two stood there for a moment gazing after it. But it was really only Ida who gazed; for Nino saw nothing, was conscious of nothing; his eyes were fastened upon his bride as she stood there, alone with him at last—his, all his—But what was this? Was she weeping?

"Daddy—" said Ida, as she waved her handkerchief in farewell. "There, do you see? He, too—"

"No, Ida—Ida dear—" and stammering, almost sobbing, trembling violently, Nino made an effort to embrace her.

"No, let me alone, please."

"I just wanted to dry your eyes—"

"Thanks, my dear; I'll dry them myself."

Nino stood there awkwardly. His face, as he looked at her, was pitiful to behold, and his mouth was half-open. Ida finished drying her eyes.

"But what's the matter?" she asked him. "You're trembling all over—No, no, Nino, for heaven's sake, no; don't stand there like that! You make me laugh. And if I once start laughing—you'll see—I'll never stop! Wait a minute; I'll wake you up."

She put her hands on his temples and blew in his eyes. At the touch of those fingers, at the breath from those lips, he felt his legs giving way beneath him; he was about to sink down on one knee, but she held him up and burst into a loud laugh:

"Upon the highway? Are you crazy? Come on, let's go! Look at that little hill over there! We shall be able to see the carriages still. Let's go look!"

And she impetuously dragged him away by one arm.

From all the countryside roundabout, where so many weeds and grasses, so many things dispersed by the hand of time lay withered, there mounted into the heat-ridden air something like a dense and ancient drought, mingling with the warm, heavy odor of the manure that lay fermenting in little piles upon the fallow fields, and with the sharper fragrance of sage and wildmint. Of that dense drought, those warm and heavy odors, that piercing fragrance, he alone was aware. She, as she ran, could hear how gaily the wood-larks sang up to the sun, from behind the thick hedges and from between the rugged yellowish tufts of burnt-over stubble; she could hear, too, in that impressive silence, the prophetic crow of cocks from distant barnyards; and she felt herself wrapped, every now and then, in the cool, keen breath that came up from the neighboring sea, to stir the few tired and yellowed leaves that were left on the almond trees, and the close-clustering, sharp-pointed, ashen-hued olive leaves.

It did not take them long to reach the hilltop; but he was so exhausted from running that he could no longer stand; he wanted to sit down, and tried to make her sit down also, there on the ground beside him, with his arm about her waist. But Ida put him off with "Let me have a look first."

She was beginning to feel restless inside, but she did not care to show it. Irritated by a certain strange and curious stubbornness on his part, she could not, she would not stand still, but longed to keep on fleeing, still farther away; she wanted to shake him up, to distract him, to distract herself as well, so long as the day lasted.

Down there, on the other side of the hill, there stretched away a devastated plain, a sea of stubble, amid which one could make out occasionally the black and meandering traces of wood-ashes that had been sprinkled there; now and again, too, the crude yellow gleam was broken by a few clumps of caper or of licorice. Away over there, as if on the other shore of that vast yellow sea, the roofs of a hamlet rose from the tall dark poplars.

And now Ida suggested to her husband that they go over there, all the way over to that hamlet. How long would it take? An hour or less. It was not more than five o'clock. Back home, in the villa, the servants must still be busy clearing away the things. They would be home before evening.

Nino made a feeble attempt at opposition, but she took him by the hands and dragged him to his feet; in a moment, she was running down the side of the hill and was off through the sea of stubble, as light and quick as a young doe. He was not fast enough to keep up with her, but, redder-faced than ever and seemingly stunned by it all, ran after her, pantingly and perspiringly, and kept calling to her to wait and give him her hand.

"Give me your hand, at least! At least, give me your hand!" he shouted.

All of a sudden, she uttered a cry and stopped short. A flock of cawing ravens had just flown up from in front of her, stretched out upon the earth, was a dead horse. Dead? No, no, it wasn't dead; it had its eyes open. Heavens, what eyes! What eyes! A skeleton, that was what it was. And those ribs! And those flanks!

Nino came up fuming and fretting:

"Come on, let's go—let's go back—at once!"

"It's alive, look!" cried Ida, shivering from compassion. "Lift its head—heavens, what eyes! Look, Nino!'

"Yes, yes," said he, panting still. "They've just put it out here —Leave it alone; let's go! What a sight! Don't you smell?"

"And those ravens!" she exclaimed with a shudder. "Are those ravens going to eat it alive?"

"But Ida, for heaven's sake!" he implored her, clasping his hands.

"Nino, that will do!" she cried. It was more than she could endure to see him so stupid and so contrite. "Answer me: what if they eat it alive?"

"What do I know about whether or not they'll eat it? They'll wait—"

"Until it dies here, of hunger, of thirst?" Her face was all drawn with horror and pity. "Just because it's old? Because it can't work any more? Ah, poor beast! What a shame! What a shame! Haven't you any heart, standing there like that?"

"Excuse me," he said, losing his temper, "but you feel so much sympathy for an animal—"

"And oughtn't I to?"

"But you don't feel any for me!"

"And are you an animal? Are you dying of hunger and thirst as you sit there in the stubble? You feel—Oh, look at the ravens, Nino, look, up there, circling around—Oh, what a horrible, shameful, monstrous thing!—Look—Oh, the poor beast—try to lift him up! Come, Nino, get up; maybe he can still walk—Nino, get up, help me—shake yourself out of it!"

"But what do you expect me to do?" he burst out, exasperatedly. "Do you expect me to drag him back? Put him on my shoulders? What's a horse more or less? How do you think he is going to walk? Can't you see he's half-dead?"

"And if we brought him something to eat?"

"And to drink, too?"

"Oh, Nino, you're wicked!" And the tears stood in Ida's eyes.

Overcoming her shudders, she bent over very gently to caress the horse's head. The animal, with a great effort had managed to get to its knees; and even in its last degrading agony, it showed the traces of a noble beauty in head and neck.

Nino, owing possibly to the blood that was pounding in his veins, possibly owing to the bitterness and contempt she had manifested, or to the perspiration that was trickling from him, now suddenly felt his breath failing him; he grew giddy, his teeth began chattering, and he was conscious of a weird trembling all over his body. He instinctively turned up his coat collar, and with his hands in his pockets, went over and huddled down in gloomy despair upon a rock some distance away.

The sun had already set, and from the distant highway could be heard the occasional sound of horses' bells.

Why were his teeth chattering like that? For his forehead was burning up, the blood in his veins stung him, and there was a roaring in his ears. It seemed to him that he could hear so many far-away bells. All that anxiety, that spasm of expectation, her

998

coldness and caprice, that last foot-race, and that horse there, that cursed horse—Oh, God! was it a dream? A nightmare within a dream? Did he have a fever? Or perhaps, a worse illness? Ah! How dark it was, God—how dark! And now, his sight was clouding over. And he could not speak, he could not cry out. He tried to call "Ida, Ida!" but he could not get the words out of his parched throat.

Where was Ida? What was she doing?

She had gone off to the distant hamlet, to seek aid for that horse; she did not stop to think that the peasants had brought the animal there to die.

He remained there, alone upon the rock, a prey to those growing tremors; and as he sat there, huddled to himself like a great owl upon a perch, he suddenly beheld a sight that seemed—Ah, yes—he could see it plainly enough now—an atrocious sight, like a vision from another world. The moon. A huge moon, coming slowly up from behind that sea of stubble. And black against that enormous. vapory copper disk, the headstrong head of that horse, waiting still with its neck stretched out—it had, perhaps, been waiting like that always, darkly etched upon that copper disk, while from far up in the sky could be heard the caw of circling ravens.

When Ida, angry and disillusioned, came groping her way back over the plain, calling "Nino, Nino!" the moon had already risen; the horse had dropped down as if dead; and Nino—where was Nino? Oh, there he was over there; he was on the ground, too.

Had he fallen asleep there?

She ran up to him, and found him with a death-rattle in his throat. His face, also, was on the ground; it was almost black, and his eyes, nearly closed, were puffed and bloodshot.

"Oh, God!"

She looked about her, as if in a swoon. She opened her hands which held a few dried beans that she had brought from the hamlet over there to feed to the horse. She looked at the moon, then at the horse, and then at the man lying on the ground as if dead. She felt faint, assailed as she was by the sudden suspicion that everything she saw was unreal. Terrified, she fled back to the villa calling in a loud voice for her father, her father—to come and take her away. Oh, God! away from that man with the rattle in his throat—that rattle, the meaning of which she did not understand! away from under that mad moon, away from under those cawing ravens in the sky—away, away, away—

PO CHU-I

PO CHÜ-I (Chinese, 772-846). One of China's greatest statesmen. Many of his poems are occasional, others written to protest social evils. Most famous, *Song of Everlasting Remorse* and *Lute Song*, are long narratives in ballad form. Also composed verse to folk tunes. Had great influence on his contemporaries.

IN YUNG-YANG

I was a child in Yung-yang,
A little child I waved farewell.
After long years again I dwell
In world-forgotten Yung-yang.
Yet I recall my play-time,
And in my dreams I see
The little ghosts of May-time
Waving farewell to me.

My father's house in Yung-yang
Has fallen upon evil days.
No kinsmen o'er the crooked ways
Hail me as once in Yung-yang.

No longer stands the old Moot-hall;
Gone is the market from the town;
The very hills have tumbled down
And stoned the valleys in their fall.

Only the waters of the Ch'in and Wei
Roll green and changeless as in days gone by.

Yet I recall my play-time,
And in my dreams I see
The little ghosts of May-time
Waving farewell to me.

RAIN AT DAWN

At dawn the crickets shrill, then cease their 'plain,
The dying candle flickers through my eaves;
Though windows bar the wild dust and the rain,
I hear the drip, drip, dripping on the broad banana leaves.

SHE WHO MUST PART FROM HER SONS

The First Wife Speaks:

Sons say farewell to their mother, mother farewell to her sons;
The bright day loses its brightness at the sobs of such little ones.
He is the great Commander who conquered the West Frontier;
Last year he won the battle; the Emperor holds him dear.
Two million silver pieces were his in a shining shower—
And he went to Lo-yang and wedded this woman fair as a flower!

When the new life comes to the castle, the old wife goes from the
    door;
But my babies, my lotus blossoms, she hated them even more.
To take a new wife to your bosom and send the old wife away
Is bad enough, but the worst thing is that my babes must stay,
Stay in your house without me: one is learning to walk,
And the other just sits up swaying, a gurgle his only talk.
The boy baby cries, and the toddler weeps and clings to my dress
With a faint foreboding of evil that would vanish at my caress.
Just that you two may make merry, you turn from your former wife.
The mother of little children, and shut her out, in her life.
It isn't even so happy as the crow's or the blackbird's fate;
Their young do not leave the mother; mate does not leave his mate.
Or the plum trees abloom in the garden, haven of bird and bee;
Though their blossoms fall to the greensward, their fruit still clings
    to the tree.

New wife, new wife to my husband, hear but this word from me:
Still in Lo-yang, our native city, there are many as fair as we.
May our General win one more victory, one more great gift
    from the throne!
Then a newer wife yet will enter, and you shall go forth—alone.

CHAO CHUN IN TARTARY

When the Han envoy turns his horses homeward,
    Pray him to bear this message back for me:
"The Lady Chao Chun asks but this one question—
    'When will they send the gold to set me free?'

1001

And if the Emperor inquire about me,
  Whether my face has grown less fair or more,
Say not that I have lost my beauty grieving!
Say not that I'm less lovely than before!

EDGAR ALLAN POE

EDGAR ALLAN POE (American, 1809-1849). Erratic, intemperate genius, whose influence has been world-wide—particularly in France. A journalist in Philadelphia and New York. His life a ceaseless struggle with poverty and alcoholism. Originated the modern detective story ("The Murders in the Rue Morgue"), wrote remarkable tales of terror ("Fall of the House of Usher") and America's most quoted poem ("The Raven").

THE MASQUE OF THE RED DEATH

THE "Red Death" had long devastated the country. No pestilence had ever been so fatal, or so hideous. Blood was its Avatar and its seal—the redness and the horror of blood. There were sharp pains, and sudden dizziness, and then profuse bleeding at the pores, with dissolution. The scarlet stains upon the body and especially upon the face of the victim, were the pest ban which shut him out from the aid and from the sympathy of his fellowmen. And the whole seizure, progress and termination of the disease, were the incidents of half an hour.

But the Prince Prospero was happy and dauntless and sagacious. When his dominions were half depopulated, he summoned to his presence a thousand hale and lighthearted friends from among the knights and dames of his court, and with these retired to the deep seclusion of one of his castellated abbeys. This was an extensive and magnificent structure, the creation of the prince's own eccentric yet august taste. A strong and lofty wall girdled it in. This wall had gates of iron. The courtiers, having entered, brought furnaces and massy hammers and welded the bolts. They resolved to leave means neither of ingress or egress to the sudden impulses of despair or of frenzy from within. The abbey was amply provisioned. With such precautions the courtiers might bid defiance to contagion. The external world could take care of itself. In the meantime it was folly to grieve, or to think. The prince had provided all the appliances of pleasure. There were buffoons, there were improvisatori, there were ballet-dancers, there were musicians, there was Beauty, there was wine. All these and security were within. Without was the "Red Death."

It was toward the close of the fifth or sixth month of his seclusion, and while the pestilence raged most furiously abroad, that the Prince Prospero entertained his thousand friends at a masked ball of the most unusual magnificence.

It was a voluptuous scene, that masquerade. But first let me tell of the rooms in which it was held. There were seven—an imperial suite. In many palaces, however, such suites form a long and straight vista, while the folding doors slide back nearly to the walls on either hand, so that the view of the whole extent is scarcely impeded. Here the case was very different; as might have been expected from the duke's love of the *bizarre*. The apartments were so irregularly disposed that the vision embraced but little more then one at a time. There was a sharp turn at every twenty or thirty yards, and at each turn a novel effect. To the right and left, in the middle of each wall, a tall and narrow Gothic window looked out upon a closed corridor which pursued the windings of the suite. These windows were of stained glass whose color varied in accordance with the prevailing hue of the decorations of the chamber into which it opened. That at the eastern extremity was hung, for example, in blue—and vividly blue were its windows. The second chamber was purple in its ornaments and tapestries, and here the panes were purple. The third was green throughout, and so were the casements. The fourth was furnished and lighted with orange —the fifth with white—the sixth with violet. The seventh apartment was closely shrouded in black velvet tapestries that hung all over the ceiling and down the walls, falling in heavy folds upon a carpet of the same material and hue. But in this chamber only, the color of the windows failed to correspond with the decorations. The panes here were scarlet—a deep blood color. Now in no one of the seven apartments was there any lamp or candelabrum, amid the profusion of golden ornaments that lay scattered to and fro or depended from the roof. There was no light of any kind emanating from lamp or candle within the suite of chambers. But in the corridors that followed the suite, there stood, opposite to each window, a heavy tripod, bearing a brazier of fire that projected its rays through the tinted glass and so glaringly illumined the room. And thus were produced a multitude of gaudy and fantastic appearances. But in the western or black chamber the effect of the fire-light that streamed upon the dark hangings through the blood-tinted panes, was ghastly in the extreme, and produced so wild a look upon the countenances of those who entered, that there were few of the company bold enough to set foot within its precincts at all.

It was in this apartment, also, that there stood against the western wall, a gigantic clock of ebony. Its pendulum swung to and fro with a dull, heavy, monotonous clang; and when the minute-hand made the circuit of the face, and the hour was to be stricken, there came from the brazen lungs of the clock a sound which was clear and loud and deep and exceedingly musical, but of so peculiar a note and emphasis that, at each lapse of an hour, the musicians of the orchestra were constrained to pause, momentarily, in their performance, to hearken to the sound; and thus the waltzers perforce ceased their evolutions; and there was a brief disconcert of the whole gay company; and, while the chimes of the clock yet rang, it was observed that the giddiest grew pale, and the more aged and sedate passed their hands over their brows as if in confused revery or meditation. But when the echoes had fully ceased, a light laughter at once pervaded the assembly; the musicians looked at each other and smiled as if at their own nervousness and folly, and made whispering vows, each to the other, that the next chiming of the clock should produce in them no similar emotion; and then, after the lapse of sixty minutes (which embrace three thousand and six hundred seconds of the Time that flies), there came yet another chiming of the clock, and then were the same disconcert and tremulousness and meditation as before.

But, in spite of these things, it was a gay and magnificent revel. The tastes of the duke were peculiar. He had a fine eye for colors and effects. He disregarded the *decora* of mere fashion. His plans were bold and fiery, and his conceptions glowed with barbaric lustre. There are some who would have thought him mad. His followers felt that he was not. It was necessary to hear and see and touch him to be *sure* that he was not.

He had directed, in great part, the movable embellishments of the seven chambers, upon occasion of this great *fête;* and it was his own guiding taste which had given character to the masqueraders. Be sure they were grotesque. There were much glare and glitter and piquancy and phantasm—much of what has been since seen in "Hernani." There were arabesque figures with unsuited limbs and appointments. There were delirious fancies such as the madman

1004

fashions. There was much of the beautiful, much of the wanton, much of the *bizarre*, something of the terrible, and not a little of that which might have excited disgust. To and fro in the seven chambers there stalked, in fact, a multitude of dreams. And these —the dreams—writhed in and about, taking hue from the rooms, and causing the wild music of the orchestra to seem as the echo of their steps. And, anon, there strikes the ebony clock which stands in the hall of the velvet. And then, for a moment, all is still, and all is silent save the voice of the clock. The dreams are stiff-frozen as they stand. But the echoes of the chime die away—they have endured but an instant—and a light, half-subdued laughter floats after them as they depart. And now again the music swells, and the dreams live, and writhe to and fro more merrily than ever, taking hue from the many tinted windows through which stream the rays from the tripods. But to the chamber which lies most west-wardly of the seven, there are now none of the maskers who venture, for the night is waning away; and there flows a ruddier light through the blood-colored panes; and the blackness of the sable drapery appalls; and to him whose foot falls upon the sable carpet, there comes from the near clock of ebony a muffled peal more solemnly emphatic than any which reaches *their* ears who indulge in the more remote gayeties of the other apartments.

But these other apartments were densely crowded, and in them beat feverishly the heart of life. And the revel went whirlingly on, until at length there commenced the sounding of midnight upon the clock. And then the music ceased, as I have told; and the evolutions of the waltzers were quieted; and there was an uneasy cessation of all things as before. But now there were twelve strokes to be sounded by the bell of the clock; and thus it happened, perhaps, that before the last echoes of the last chime had utterly sunk into silence, there were many individuals in the crowd who had found leisure to become aware of the presence of a masked figure which had arrested the attention of no single individual before. And the rumor of this new presence having spread itself whispering around, there arose at length from the whole company, a buzz, or murmur, expressive of disapprobation and surprise—then, finally, of terror, of horror, and of disgust.

In an assembly of phantasms such as I have painted, it may well be supposed that no ordinary appearance could have excited such sensation. In truth the masquerade license of the night was nearly unlimited; but the figure in question had out-Heroded Herod, and gone beyond the bounds of even the prince's indefinite decorum. There are chords in the hearts of the most reckless which cannot be touched without emotion. Even with the utterly lost, to whom life and death are equally jests, there are matters of which no jest can be made. The whole company, indeed, seemed now deeply to feel that in the costume and bearing of the stranger neither wit nor propriety existed. The figure was tall and gaunt, and shrouded from head to foot in the habiliments of the grave. The mask which concealed the visage was made so nearly to resemble the countenance of a stiffened corpse that the closest scrutiny must have had difficulty in detecting the cheat. And yet all this might have been endured, if not approved, by the mad revellers around. But the mummer had gone so far as to assume the type of the Red Death. His vesture was dabbled in *blood*—and his broad brow, with all the features of the face, was besprinkled with the scarlet horror.

When the eyes of Prince Prospero fell upon this spectral image (which with a slow and solemn movement, as if more fully to sustain its *rôle*, stalked to and fro among the waltzers) he was seen to be convulsed, in the first moment, with a strong shudder either of terror or distaste; but, in the next, his brow reddened with rage.

"Who dares?" he demanded hoarsely of the courtiers who stood near him—"who dares insult us with this blasphemous mockery? Seize him and unmask him—that we may know whom we have to hang at sunrise, from the battlements!"

It was in the eastern or blue chamber in which stood the Prince Prospero as he uttered these words. They rang throughout the seven rooms loudly and clearly—for the prince was a bold and robust man, and the music had become hushed at the waving of his hand.

It was in the blue room where stood the prince, with a group of pale courtiers by his side. At first, as he spoke, there was a slight rushing movement of this group in the direction of the intruder, who at the moment was also near at hand, and now, with deliberate and stately step, made closer approach to the speaker. But from a certain nameless awe with which the mad assumptions of the mummer had inspired the whole party, there were found none who put forth hand to seize him; so that, unimpeded, he passed within a yard of the prince's person; and, while the vast assembly, as if with one impulse, shrank from the centres of the room to the walls, he made his way uninterruptedly, but with the same solemn and measured step which had distinguished him from the first, through the blue chamber to the purple—through the purple to the green—through the green to the orange—through this again to the white—and even thence to the violet, ere a decided movement had been made to arrest him. It was then, however, that the Prince Prospero, maddening with rage and the shame of his own momentary cowardice, rushed hurriedly through the six chambers, while none followed him on account of a deadly terror that had seized upon all. He bore aloft a drawn dagger, and had approached, in rapid impetuosity, to within three or four feet of the retreating figure, when the latter, having attained the extremity of the velvet apartment, turned suddenly and confronted his pursuer. There was a sharp cry—and the dagger dropped gleaming upon the sable carpet, upon which, instantly afterwards, fell prostrate in death the Prince Prospero. Then, summoning the wild courage of despair, a throng of the revellers at once threw themselves into the black apartment, and, seizing the mummer, whose tall figure stood erect and motionless within the shadow of the ebony clock, gasped in unutterable horror at finding the grave-cerements and corpse-like mask which they handled with so violent a rudeness, untenanted by any tangible form.

And now was acknowledged the presence of the Red Death. He had come like a thief in the night. And one by one dropped the revellers in the blood-bedewed halls of their revel, and died each in the despairing posture of his fall. And the life of the ebony clock went out with that of the last of the gay. And the flames of the tripods expired. And Darkness and Decay and the Red Death held illimitable dominion over all.

ALEXANDER POPE

ALEXANDER POPE (English, 1688-1744). Foremost literary figure of the 18th century Classicists. A dwarfed cripple, 4½ feet tall. Famous for his translation of Homer, *An Essay on Criticism* and the poem, "The Rape of the Lock." Gave English verse a technical finish it had never previously possessed. Hence, in an age of formal standards, was acknowledged Europe's greatest poet during his lifetime.

AN ESSAY ON MAN

Hope humbly then; with trembling pinions soar;
Wait the great teacher Death, and God adore.

What future bliss, he gives not thee to know,
But gives that hope to be thy blessing now;
Hope springs eternal in the human breast—
Man never is, but always to be blessed
The soul, uneasy and confined from home,
Rests and expatiates in a life to come.
Lo, the poor Indian! whose untutored mind
Sees God in clouds, or hears him in the wind;
His soul proud science never taught to stray
Far as the solar walk, or milky way,
Yet simple nature to his hope has given,
Behind the cloud-topped hill, an humbler heaven.

Know then thyself, presume not God to scan,
The proper study of mankind is man.
Placed on this isthmus of a middle state,
A being darkly wise, and rudely great:
With too much knowledge for the sceptic side,
With too much weakness for the stoic's pride,
He hangs between; in doubt to act, or rest;
In doubt to deem himself a god, or beast;
In doubt his mind or body to prefer;
Born but to die, and reasoning but to err;
Alike in ignorance, his reason such,
Whether he thinks too little or too much:
Chaos of thought and passion, all confused;
Still by himself abused or disabused;
Created half to rise and half to fall;
Great lord of all things, yet a prey to all;
Sole judge of truth, in endless error hurled:
The glory, jest, and riddle of the world!

Whate'er the passion—knowledge, fame, or pelf,
Not one will change his neighbor with himself.
The learned is happy nature to explore,
The fool is happy that he knows no more;
The rich is happy in the plenty given,
The poor contents him with the care of Heaven.
See the blind beggar dance, the cripple sing,
The sot a hero, lunatic a king;
The starving chemist in his golden views
Supremely blest, the poet in his muse.

See some strange comfort every state attend,
And pride bestowed on all, a common friend;
See some fit of passion every age supply,
Hope travels through nor quits us when we die.
  Behold the child, by nature's kindly law,
Pleased with a rattle, tickled with a straw:
Some livelier plaything gives his youth delight,
A little louder, but as empty quite:
Scarfs, garters, gold, amuse his riper stage,
And beads and prayer-books are the toys of age:
Pleased with this bauble still, as that before;
Till tired he sleeps, and life's poor play is o'er.

Honor and shame from no condition rise:
Act well your part, there all the honor lies.
Fortune in men has some small difference made,
One flaunts in rags, one flutters in brocade;
The cobbler aproned, and the parson gowned,
The friar hooded, and the monarch crowned.
"What differ more (you cry) than crown and cowl!"
I'll tell you, friend! a wise man and a fool.
You'll find, if once the monarch acts the monk,
Or, cobbler-like, the parson will be drunk,
Worth makes the man, and want of it the fellow;
The rest is all but leather or prunella.

MARCEL PROUST

MARCEL PROUST (French, 1871-1922). Creator of the most fabulous single
work in modern literature: *Remembrance of Things Past*. He spent many
years in a dark, cork-lined chamber writing this 7-volume novel; then published it at his own expense. Ostensibly a meticulous recreation of the author's
early life and later social excursions, it is actually a kind of metaphysical
exploration of concepts like Time, Memory, Art and Reality.

THE DEATH OF BERGOTTE

I LEARNED that a death had occurred during the day which distressed
me greatly, that of Bergotte. It was known that he had been ill for
a long time past. Not, of course, with the illness from which he had

suffered originally and which was natural. Nature hardly seems capable of giving us any but quite short illnesses. But medicine has annexed to itself the art of prolonging them. Remedies, the respite that they procure, the relapses that a temporary cessation of them provokes, compose a sham illness to which the patient grows so accustomed that he ends by making it permanent, just as children continue to give way to fits of coughing long after they have been cured of the whooping cough. Then remedies begin to have less effect, the doses are increased, they cease to do any good, but they have begun to do harm thanks to that lasting indisposition. Nature would not have offered them so long a tenure. It is a great miracle that medicine can almost equal nature in forcing a man to remain in bed, to continue on pain of death the use of some drug. From that moment the illness artificially grafted has taken root, has become a secondary but a genuine illness, with this difference only that natural illnesses are cured, but never those which medicine creates, for it knows not the secret of their cure.

For years past Bergotte had ceased to go out of doors. Anyhow, he had never cared for society, or had cared for it for a day only, to despise it as he despised everything else and in the same fashion, which was his own, namely to despise a thing not because it was beyond his reach but as soon as he had reached it. He lived so simply that nobody suspected how rich he was, and anyone who had known would still have been mistaken, for he would have thought him a miser, whereas no one was ever more generous. He was generous above all towards women—girls, one ought rather to say—who were ashamed to receive so much in return for so little. He excused himself in his own eyes because he knew that he could never produce such good work as in an atmosphere of amorous feelings. Love is too strong a word, pleasure that is at all deeply rooted in the flesh is helpful to literary work because it cancels all other pleasures, for instance the pleasures of society, those which are the same for everyone. And even if this love leads to disillusionment, it does at least stir, even by so doing, the surface of the soul which otherwise would be in danger of becoming stagnant. Desire is therefore not without its value to the writer in detaching him first of all from his fellow men and from conforming to their standards, and afterwards in restoring some degree of movement to a spiritual machine which, after, a certain age, tends to become paralysed. We do not succeed in being happy but we make observation of the reasons which prevent us from being happy and which would have remained invisible to us but for these loopholes opened by disappointment. Dreams are not to be converted into reality, that we know; we would not form any, perhaps, were it not for desire, and it is useful to us to form them in order to see them fail and to be instructed by their failure. And so Bergotte said to himself· 'I am spending more than a multimillionaire would spend upon girls, but the pleasures or disappointments that they give me make me write a book which brings me money." Economically, this argument was absurd, but no doubt he found some charm in thus transmitting gold into caresses and caresses into gold. We saw, at the time of my grandmother's death, how a weary old age loves repose. Now in society, there is nothing but conversation. It may be stupid, but it has the faculty of suppressing women who are nothing more than questions and answers. Removed from society, women become once more what is so reposeful to a weary old man, an object of contemplation. In any case, it was no longer a question of anything of this sort. I have said that Bergotte never went out of doors, and when he got out of bed for an hour in his room, he would be smothered in shawls, plaids, all the things with which a person covers himself before exposing himself to intense cold or getting into a railway train. He would apologise to the few friends whom he allowed to penetrate to his sanctuary, and, pointing to his tartan plaids, his travelling-rugs, would say merrily: "After all, my dear fellow, life, as Anaxagoras has said, is a journey." Thus he went on growing steadily colder, a tiny planet that offered a prophetic image of the greater, when gradually heat will withdraw from the earth, then life itself. Then the resurrection will have to come to an end, for if, among future generations, the works of men are to shine, there must first of all be men. If certain kinds of animals hold out longer against the invading chill, when there are no longer any men, and if we suppose Bergotte's fame to have lasted so long, suddenly it will be extinguished for all time. It will not be the last animals that will read him, for it is scarcely probable that, like the Apostles on the Day of Pentecost, they will be able to understand the speech of the various races of mankind without having learned it.

In the months that preceded his death, Bergotte suffered from insomnia, and what was worse, whenever he did fall asleep, from nightmares which, if he awoke, made him reluctant to go to sleep again. He had long been a lover of dreams, even of bad dreams, because thanks to them and to the contradiction they present to the reality which we have before us in our waking state, they give us, at the moment of waking if not before, the profound sensation of having slept. But Bergotte's nightmares were not like that. When he spoke of nightmares, he used in the past to mean unpleasant things that passed through his brain. Latterly, it was as though proceeding from somewhere outside himself that he would see a hand armed with a damp cloth which, passed over his face by an evil woman, kept scrubbing him awake, an intolerable itching in his thighs, the rage—because Bergotte had murmured in his sleep that he was driving badly—of a raving lunatic of a cabman who flung himself upon the writer, biting and gnawing his fingers. Finally, as soon as in his sleep it had grown sufficiently dark, nature arranged a sort of undress rehearsal of the apoplectic stroke that was to carry him off: Bergotte arrived in a carriage beneath the porch of Swann's new house, and tried to alight. A stunning giddiness glued him to his seat, the porter came forward to help him out of the carriage, he remained seated, unable to rise, to straighten his legs. He tried to pull himself up with the help of the stone pillar that was by his side, but did not find sufficient support in it to enable him to stand.

He consulted doctors who, flattered at being called in by him, saw in his virtue as an incessant worker (it was twenty years since he had written anything), in his overstrain, the cause of his ailments. They advised him not to read thrilling stories (he never read anything), to benefit more by the sunshine, which was "indispensable to life" (he had owed a few years of comparative health only to his rigorous seclusion indoors), to take nourishment (which made him thinner, and nourished nothing but his nightmares). One of his doctors was blessed with the spirit of contradiction, and whenever Bergotte consulted him in the absence of the others, and, in order not to offend him, suggested to him as his own ideas what the others had advised, this doctor, thinking that Bergotte was seeking to have prescribed for him something that he himself liked, at once forbade it, and often for reasons invented so hurriedly to meet the case that in face of the material objections which Bergotte raised, this argumentative doctor was obliged in the same sentence to contradict himself, but, for fresh reasons, repeated the original prohibition. Bergotte returned to one of the first of these doctors, a man who prided himself on his cleverness, especially in the presence of one of the leading men of letters, and who, if Bergotte insinuated: "I seem to remember, though, that

Dr. X—— told me—long ago, of course—that that might congest my kidneys and brain . . ." would smile sardonically, raise his fingers and enounce: "I said use, I did not say abuse. Naturally every remedy, if one takes it in excess, becomes a two-edged sword." There is in the human body a certain instinct for what is beneficial to us, as there is in the heart for what is our moral duty, an instinct which no authorisation by a Doctor of Medicine or Divinity can replace. We know that cold baths are bad for us, we like them, we can always find a doctor to recommend them, not to prevent them from doing us harm. From each of these doctors Bergotte took something which, in his own wisdom, he had forbidden himself for years past. After a few weeks, his old troubles had reappeared, the new had become worse. Maddened by an unintermittent pain, to which was added insomnia broken only by brief spells of night-mare, Bergotte called in no more doctors and tried with success, but to excess, different narcotics, hopefully reading the prospectus that accompanied each of them, a prospectus which proclaimed the necessity of sleep but hinted that all the preparations which induce it (except that contained in the bottle round which the prospectus was wrapped, which never produced any toxic effect) were toxic, and therefore made the remedy worse than the disease. Bergotte tried them all. Some were of a different family from those to which we are accustomed, preparations for instance of amyl and ethyl. When we absorb a new drug, entirely different in composition, it is always with a delicious expectancy of the unknown. Our heart beats as at a first assignation. To what unknown forms of sleep, of dreams, is the newcomer going to lead us? He is inside us now, he has the control of our thoughts. In what fashion are we going to fall asleep? And, once we are asleep, by what strange paths, up to what peaks, into what unfathomed gulfs is he going to lead us? With what new grouping of sensations are we to become acquainted on this journey? Will it bring us to the end of illness? To blissful happiness? To death? Bergotte's death had come to him overnight, when he had thus entrusted himself to one of these friends (a friend? or an enemy, rather?) who proved too strong for him. The circumstances of his death were as follows. An attack of uraemia, by no means serious, had led to his being ordered to rest. But one of the critics having written somewhere that in *Vermeer's Street in Delft* (lent by the Gallery at The Hague for an exhibition of Dutch painting), a picture which he adored and imagined that he knew by heart, a little patch of yellow wall (which he could not remember)

1013

was so well painted that it was, if one looked at it by itself, like some priceless specimen of Chinese art, of a beauty that was sufficient in itself. Bergotte ate a few potatoes, left the house, and went to the exhibition. At the first few steps that he had to climb he was overcome by giddiness. He passed in front of several pictures and was struck by the stiffness and futility of so artificial a school, nothing of which equalled the fresh air and sunshine of a Venetian palazzo, or of an ordinary house by the sea. At last he came to the Vermeer which he remembered as more striking, more different from anything else that he knew, but in which, thanks to the critic's article, he remarked for the first time some small figures in blue, that the ground was pink, and finally the precious substance of the tiny patch of yellow wall. His giddiness increased; he fixed his eyes, like a child upon a yellow butterfly which it is trying to catch, upon the precious little patch of wall. "That is how I ought to have written," he said. "My last books are too dry, I ought to have gone over them with several coats of paint, made my language exquisite in itself, like this little patch of yellow wall." Meanwhile he was not unconscious of the gravity of his condition. In a celestial balance there appeared to him, upon one of its scales, his own life, while the other contained the little patch of wall so beautifully painted in yellow. He felt that he had rashly surrendered the former for the latter. "All the same," he said to himself, "I have no wish to provide the 'feature' of this exhibition for the evening papers."

He repeated to himself: "Little patch of yellow wall, with a sloping roof, little patch of yellow wall." While doing so he sank down upon a circular divan; and then at once he ceased to think that his life was in jeopardy and, reverting to his natural optimism, told himself: "It is just an ordinary indigestion from those potatoes; they weren't properly cooked; it is nothing." A fresh attack beat him down; he rolled from the divan to the floor, as visitors and attendants came hurrying to his assistance. He was dead. Permanently dead? Who shall say? Certainly our experiments in spiritualism prove no more than the dogmas of religion that the soul survives death. All that we can say is that everything is arranged in this life as though we entered it carrying the burden of obligations contracted in a former life; there is no reason inherent in the conditions of life on this earth that can make us consider ourselves obliged to do good, to be fastidious, to be polite even, nor make the talented artist consider himself obliged to begin over again a score of times a piece of work the admiration aroused by which will matter little to his body devoured by worms, like the patch of yellow wall painted with so much knowledge and skill by an artist who must for ever remain unknown and is barely identified under the name Vermeer. All these obligations which have not their sanction in our present life seem to belong to a different world, founded upon kindness, scrupulosity, self-sacrifice, a world entirely different from this, which we leave in order to be born into this world, before perhaps returning to the other to live once again beneath the sway of those unknown laws which we have obeyed because we bore their precepts in our hearts, knowing not whose hand had traced them there—those laws to which every profound work of the intellect brings us nearer and which are invisible only—and still!—to fools. So that the idea that Bergotte was not wholly and permanently dead is by no means improbable.

They buried him, but all through the night of mourning, in the lighted windows, his books arranged three by three kept watch like angels with outspread wings and seemed, for him who was no more, the symbol of his resurrection.

ALEXANDER SERGEYEVICH PUSHKIN

ALEXANDER SERGEYEVICH PUSHKIN (Russian, 1799-1837). The first great figure in Russian literature, and fountainhead of much of its later glory. *Evgeny Onegin, Pique Dame* (both turned into operas by Tchaikovsky), *Boris Godunov* (similarly treated by Moussorgsky), *Ruslan and Ludmila,* and *Fairy Tales* are major works. Partly of African ancestry, exiled for a time because of his liberalism. Later joined the Czar's entourage, killed in duel. Great champion of Russian genius.

OUTLIVED DESIRE

Outlived desire now departs,
   My dreams I cannot love again;
I reap the fruit of empty hearts,
   The fruit of pain.

The tempest of a cruel fate
   My fair and flowery garlands rend;
Unhappy and alone I wait:
   When comes the end?

So, stricken by the early cold,
   The whistling, bitter gales of grief,
Still the autumnal branches hold
   One shuddering leaf.

THE PRISONER

In a damp cell behind bars sit I;
Outside an eagle, young and born to fly,
The sad companion of my prisoned day
Flutters his wing and pecks his bleeding prey.

Then pecks no more, but through the window stares
As though we thought the same thing unawares,
As though with look and cry his heart would say:
'Brother, the time is come to fly away.

We are free birds together, free and proud;
Fly where the mountains whiten through the cloud
To that sea country blue beneath the sky
Where only walks the wind, the wind and I'.

THE COACH OF LIFE

The swaying coach, for all its load,
   Runs lightly as it rocks;
Grey Time goes driving down the road,
   Nor ever leaves the box.

We jump into the coach at dawn,
   Alert and fresh and free,
And holding broken bones in scorn,
   'Go on' shout we.

By midday all is changed about,
   Our morning hearts are cool;
We fear the steep descents, and shout:
   'Go slow, you fool!'

By dusk we're used to jolt and din,
   And when the light is gone
We sleep before we reach the inn,
   As Time drives on.

THE PROPHET

I dragged my steps across a desert bare,
   My spirit parched with heat;
And lo, a seraph with six wings was there;
   He stood where two roads meet.

Soft as the coming of a dream at night,
   His fingers touched my head;
He raised the lids of my prophetic sight,
   An eagle's, wide with dread.

He touched my ears. They filled with sound and song:
   I heard the heaven's motion,
The flight of angels, and the reptile throng
   That moves beneath the ocean.

I heard the soundless growth of plant and tree:
   Then, stooping to my face,
With his right hand he tore my tongue from me.
   Vain, sinful tongue and base.

A serpent's fiery fang he thrust instead
   Through my faint lips apart;
He slit my breast, and with a sword stained red
   Hewed out my quaking heart.

A coal of living fire his fingers placed
   Deep in my gaping side.
Dead as I lay upon the desert waste,
   I heard God's Voice that cried:

'Arise, O prophet, having seen and heard;
   Strong in my Spirit, span
The universal earth, and make my word
   Burn in the heart of man'.

THE POET

When the poet by Apollo
For his service is not claimed,
In a life inane and hollow
He is sunken, he is maimed.
Then his soul, as cold as clay,
Sleeps unvisited by Song:
He frequents the wordly throng,
Insignificant as they.
But let once Apollo's word
Fall upon his listening ear,
His awakened soul is stirred
Like an eagle soaring clear.
Wild and sad, he turns away
From the pleasures of the town,
Scorning man and man's renown
And the idols of a day.
Full of voices, in the throes
Of confusion forth he goes,
Lonely, to the forest trees
And the shores of barren seas.

THE UPAS TREE

Across the desert dry as bone,
   Stark sentinel of burning sands,
In the wide universe alone
   The deadly Upas stands.

Born in a day of wrath it rose
   Out of the waste, whose nature sent
Deep through its roots and sombre boughs
   Poison for nourishment.

In noonday heat from out its bark
   The beads of oozing venom come,
And with the cooler breath of dark
   Set in a shining gum.

1018

No bird among its boughs may fly,
  Beneath its shade no tiger stray:
The whirlwind when it ventures nigh
  Infected storms away.

The wandering showers of the plain,
  Caught on its branches interlaced,
In drops of dark unwholesome rain
  Sink in the thirsty waste.

Yet once a man, with cold command,
  Dared send a man to seek the tree.
All night across the dreadful sand
  He went obediently.

He brought the deathly gum at dawn
  With leaves by poison withered brown,
And from his forehead pale and drawn
  Coldly the sweat ran down.

Before his master as he went
  His steps grew weak and faltering,
And the poor slave died in the tent
  Of the remorseless King.

The venom taken from his hand
  The King's obedient arrows fed,
And they through every neighbouring land
  Death and disaster sped.

THE DON

Through open fields, across the plain
  I see him yonder, streaming on!
From all your distant sons, again
  I greet you, shining Don.

O quiet Don, each river knows
  That you their famous brother are;
Araxes greets you as he flows,
  And Oxus from afar.

By cruel foes no longer chased
  The horses of the Don draw nigh,
Already scent there home, and taste
  The streams of Arpachai.

Then watch, O holy Don, for there
  They come, brave Cossacks, born your own!
Once more the sparkling wine prepare
  From vineyards you have grown.

R

FRANCOIS RABELAIS

FRANÇOIS RABELAIS (French, *ca.* 1490-1553). A monk who later became a physician and scholar. *Gargantua and Pantagruel*, his sprawling comic allegory, was written over period of 20 years to entertain patients and patrons. Today the symbol of the burlesque and ribald, it nonetheless carried a message: that man is basically good and only needs new kind of education to call forth that goodness.

THE LOST HATCHET

THERE once lived a poor honest country fellow of Gravot, Tom Wellhung by name, a wood cleaver by trade, who in that low drudgery made shift so to pick up a sorry livelihood. It happened that he lost his hatchet. Now, tell me, who ever had more cause to be vexed than poor Tom? Alas, his whole estate and life depended on his hatchet; by his hatchet he earned many a fair penny of the best woodmongers or log merchants, among whom he went a jobbing; for want of his hatchet he was like to starve; and had Death but met him six days after without a hatchet, the grim fiend would have mowed him down in the twinkling of a bedstaff. In this sad case he began to be in a heavy taking, and called upon Jupiter with most eloquent prayers (for, you know, Necessity was the mother of Eloquence). With the whites of his eyes turned up towards heaven, down on his marrowbones, his arms reared high, his fingers stretched wide, and his head bare, the poor wretch without ceasing was roaring out by way of Litany at every repetition of his supplications, "My hatchet, Lord Jupiter, my hatchet, my hatchet, only my hatchet, O Jupiter, or money to buy another, and nothing else; alas, my poor hatchet!"

Jupiter happened then to be holding a grand council about certain urgent affairs, and old Gammer Cybele was just giving her opinion,

1021

or, if you had rather have it so, it was young Phœbus the Beau; but, in short, Tom's outcry and lamentations were so loud that they were heard with no small amazement at the council board by the whole consistory of the gods. "What a devil have we below," quoth Jupiter, "that howls so horridly? By the mud of Styx, haven't we had all along, and haven't we here still, enough to do to set to rights a world of puzzling business of consequence? . . . Let us, however, dispatch this howling fellow below: you, Mercury, go see who it is, and know what he wants." Mercury looked out at heaven's trapdoor, through which, as I am told, they hear what's said here below; by the way, one might well enough mistake it for the scuttle of a ship; though Icaromenippus said it was like the mouth of a well. The light-heeled deity saw it was honest Tom, who asked for his lost hatchet; and accordingly he made his report to the Synod. "Marry," said Jupiter, "we are finely holped up, as if we had now nothing else to do here but to restore lost hatchets. Well, he must then have it for all this, for so 'tis written in the Book of Fate (do you hear?), as well as if it was worth the whole duchy of Milan. The truth is, the fellow's hatchet is as much to him as a kingdom to a king. Come, come, let no more words be scattered about it; let him have his hatchet again. Run down immediately, and cast at the poor fellow's feet three hatchets,—his own, another of gold, and a third of massy silver, all of one size: then, having left it to his will to take his choice, if he take his own, and be satisfied with it, give him t'other two. If he take another, chop his head off with his own; and henceforth serve me all those losers of hatchets after that manner." Having said this, Jupiter, with an awkward turn of his head, like a jackanapes swallowing of pills, made so dreadful a phiz that all the vast Olympus quaked again. Heaven's foot messenger, thanks to his low-crowned, narrow-brimmed hat, and plume of feathers, heelpieces, and running stick with pigeon wings, flings himself out at heaven's wicket, through the empty deserts of the air, and in a trice nimbly alights on the earth, and throws at friend Tom's feet the three hatchets, saying to him, "Thou hast bawled long enough to be a-dry; thy prayers and requests are granted by Jupiter: see which of these three is thy hatchet, and take it away with thee."

Wellhung lifts up the golden hatchet, peeps upon it, and finds it very heavy, then, staring at **Mercury**, cries, "Godszouks, this is none of mine; I won't ha' 't!" The same he did with the silver one, and said, " 'Tis not this, either: you may e'en take them again."

At last he takes up his own hatchet, examines the end of the helve, and finds his mark there; then, ravished with joy, like a fox that meets some straggling poultry, and sneering from the top of his nose, he cried, "By the mass, this is my hatchet! Master god, if you will leave it me, I will sacrifice to you a very good and huge pot of milk, brimful, covered with fine strawberries, next Ides (*i.e.* the 15th) of March."

"Honest fellow," said Mercury, "I leave it thee; take it; and because thou hast wished and chosen moderately, in point of hatchet, by Jupiter's command I give thee these two others. Thou hast now wherewith to make thyself rich; be honest." Honest Tom gave Mercury a whole cart load of thanks, and revered the most great Jupiter. His old hatchet he fastens close to his leathern girdle, and girds it about his breech like Martin of Cambray; the two others, being more heavy, he lays on his shoulder. Thus he plods on, trudging over the fields, keeping a good countenance among his neighbors and fellow-parishioners with one merry saying or other after Patelin's way. The next day, having put on a clean white jacket, he takes on his back the two precious hatchets, and comes to Chinon, the famous city, noble city, ancient city, yea, the first city of the world, according to the judgment and assertion of the most learned Massoreths. In Chinon he turned his silver hatchet into fine testons, crown pieces, and other white cash; his golden hatchet into fine angels, curious ducats, substantial ridders, spankers, and rose nobles. Then with them he purchases a good number of farms, barns, houses, outhouses, thatch houses, stables, meadows, orchards, fields, vineyards, woods, arable lands, pastures, ponds, mills, gardens, nurseries, oxen, cows, sheep, goats, swine, hogs, asses, horses, hens, cocks, capons, chickens, geese, ganders, ducks, drakes and a world of other necessaries, and in a short time became the richest man in all the country. His brother bumpkins, and the yeomen and other country-puts thereabouts, perceiving his good fortune were not a little amazed, insomuch that their pity of poor Tom was soon changed into an envy of his so great and unexpected rise; and, as they could not for their souls devise how this came about, they made it their business to pry up and down, and lay their heads together, to inquire, seek, and inform themselves by what means, in what place, on what day, what hour, how, why, and wherefore, he had come by this great treasure.

At last, hearing it was by losing his hatchet, "Ha! ha!" said they, "was there no more to do but lose a hatchet, to make us rich?"

With this they all fairly lost their hatchets out of hand. The devil a one that had a hatchet left; he was not his mother's son that did not lose his hatchet. No more was wood felled or cleared in that country, through want of hatchets. Nay, the Æsopian apologue even saith that certain petty country gents of the lower class, who had sold Wellhung their little mill and little field to have wherewithal to make a figure at the next muster, having been told that this treasure was come to him by that means only, sold the only badge of their gentility, their swords, to purchase hatchets to go to lose them, as the silly clodpates did, in hopes to gain store of chink by that loss.

You would have truly sworn they had been a parcel of your petty spiritual usurers, Rome-bound, selling their all, and borrowing of others to buy store of mandates, a pennyworth of a new-made pope.

Now they cried out and brayed, and prayed and bawled, and lamented and invoked Jupiter: "My hatchet! my hatchet! Jupiter, my hatchet!" on this side, "My hatchet!" on that side, "My hatchet! Ho, ho, ho, ho, Jupiter, my hatchet!" The air round about rang again with the cries and howlings of these rascally losers of hatchets.

Mercury was nimble in bringing them hatchets,—to each offering that which he had lost, as also another of gold and a third of silver.

Everywhere he still was for that of gold, giving thanks in abundance to the great giver, Jupiter; but, in the very nick of time that they bowed and stooped to take it from the ground, whip in a trice Mercury lopped off their heads, as Jupiter had commanded; and of heads thus cut off the number was just equal to that of the lost hatchets.

You see how it is now; you see how it goes with those who in the simplicity of their hearts wish and desire with moderation. Take warning by this, all you greedy, fresh-water shirks, who scorn to wish for anything under ten thousand pounds; and do not, for the future, run on impudently, as I have sometimes heard you wishing, "Would to God I had now one hundred and seventy-eight millions of gold! oh, how I should tickle it off!" The deuce on you, what more might a king, an emperor, or a pope wish for? For that reason, indeed, you see that after you have made such hopeful wishes all the good that comes to you of it is the itch or scab, and not a cross in your breeches to scare the devil that tempts you to make these wishes; no more than those two mumpers, one of whom only wished to have in good old gold as much as hath been spent, bought, and sold in Paris, since its first foundations were laid, to

1024

this hour, all of it valued at the price, sale, and rate of the dearest
year in all that space of time. Do you think the fellow was bashful?
had he eaten sour plums unpeeled? were his teeth on edge, I pray
you? The other wished Our Lady's church brimful of steel needles,
from the floor to the top of the roof, and to have as many ducats
as might be crammed into as many bags as might be sewed with
each and every one of those needles, till they were all either broke
at the point or eye. This is to wish with a vengeance! What think
you of it? What did they get by it, in your opinion? Why, at night
both my gentlemen had kibed heels, a tetter in the chin, a churchyard cough in the lungs, a catarrh in the throat, a swingeing boil
at the rump, and the devil of one musty crust of a brown George
the poor dogs had to scour their grinders with. Wish, therefore, for
mediocrity, and it shall be given unto you, and over and above yet;
that is to say, provided you bestir yourselves manfully and do your
best in the mean time.

JEAN BAPTISTE RACINE

JEAN BAPTISTE RACINE (French, 1639-1699). Classical tragedian who
brought French drama to its highest peak. Adhered to the Greek unities and
concentrated on psychological conflict between characters. Used mainly Latin
and Greek themes in his 11 plays. Best: *Andromaque, Bérénice, Phèdre,
Athalie*. Emotional range of his poetry unsurpassed in French.

ORESTES AND HERMIONE

Hermione. What have I done? Where am I? Where is Pyrrhus?
Ye gods! what mean these horrors? I'm undone!
My soul is on the rack! I cannot bear it!
Why do I wander like some guilty ghost?
What brought me to this place? What keeps me here?
The court of Pyrrhus has no room for me!
Do I still doubt if I should love or hate him?
Hard-hearted man! how unconcerned he left me!
Did he once sigh? bestow one pitying look?
Once shed a tear? or speak one soft, kind word?
Did he so much as feign one moment's sorrow,
To calm my griefs, and mitigate his falsehood?
Why am I still thus anxious for his life?
Why do I start at his impending fate?

1025

Shall he, then, live? Shall the base traitor live
To laugh at my distress? No, let him perish!
Be quick, Orestes! Execute my orders!
Alas! my orders! O preposterous guilt!
Can I decree the death of him I love?
Was it for this my soul delighted in him?
Was it for this I left my father's court?
Have I, then, crossed so many realms and seas
To murder Pyrrhus?—

(Cleone enters.)

O Cleone, help me!
What have I done? Is Pyrrhus yet alive?
What say'st thou? Answer me: where is the king?
 Cleone. Madam, I saw the cruel prince set forward,
Triumphant in his looks, and full of joy.
Still as he walked, his ravished eyes were fixed
On the fair captive; while through shouting crowds
She passed along with a dejected air,
And seemed to mourn her Hector to the last.
 Herm. Insulting tyrant! I shall burst with rage!
But say, Cleone, didst thou mark him well?
Was his brow smooth? Say did there not appear
Some shade of grief, some little cloud of sorrow?
Did he not stop? Did he not once look back?
Didst thou approach him? Was he not confounded?
Did he not——Oh, be quick, and tell me all!
 Cle. Madam, the tumult of his joy admits
No thought but love. Unguarded he marches on,
'Midst a promiscuous throng of friends and foes.
His cares all turn upon Astyanax,
Whom he has lodged within the citadel,
Defended by the strength of all his guards.
 Herm. Enough! he dies! the traitor! Where's Orestes?
 Cle. Madam, I fear——
 Herm. Is he still resolute? Is he still determined?
 Cle. Madam, I fear——
 Herm. How! Is Orestes false? Does he betray me, too?
 Cle. A thousand doubts
Perplex his soul, and wound him with remorse:
His virtue and his love prevail by turns.
He told me Pyrrhus should not fall ignobly,—

Pyrrhus, the warlike son of great Achilles.
He dreads the censure of the Grecian states,—
Of all mankind, and fears to stain his honor.

    Herm.   Poor timorous wretch! 'Tis false! He basely fears
To cope with dangers, and encounter death;
'Tis that he fears! Am I bright Helen's daughter?
To vindicate her wrongs all Greece conspired;
For her, confederate nations fought, and kings were slain,
Troy was o'erthrown, and a whole empire fell:
My eyes want force to raise a lover's arm
Against a tyrant that has dared to wrong me!

    Cle.   Madam, like Helen, trust your cause to Greece.

    Herm.   No! I'll avenge myself: I'll to the temple;
I'll overturn the altar, stab the priest;
I'll hurl destruction like a whirlwind round me!
They must not wed! they must not live! they shall not!
Let me begone! I have no time to lose!
Stand off! hold me not! I am all distraction!
O Pyrrhus, tyrant! traitor! thou shalt bleed!

                    (Orestes enters.)

    Orestes.   Madam, 'tis done; your orders are obeyed:
The tyrant lies expiring at the altar.

    Herm.   Is Pyrrhus slain?

    Or.   Even now he gasps in death.
Our Greeks, all undistinguished in the crowd,
Flocked to the temple and dispersed themselves
On every side the altar. I was there:
Pyrrhus observed me with a haughty eye,
And, proud to triumph over Greece in me,
From his own brows he took the diadem,
And bound it on the temples of his captive:
"Receive," said he, "my crown! receive my faith!
Mine and my people's sovereign reign, forever!
From this blessed hour, a father to your son,
I'll scourge his foes: henceforth be he styled
The Trojan king: I swear it at the altar,
And call the gods to ratify my vows!"
His subjects with loud acclamations shook
The spacious dome. Our Greeks, enraged, cried out,
"Revenge! revenge!" broke through the thronging press,
And rushed tumultuous on the unguarded king:

Their eager fury left no work for me.
Pyrrhus awhile opposed their clashing swords,
And dealt his fatal blows on every side
With manly fierceness; till, oppressed by numbers,
Streaming with blood, all over gashed with wounds,
He reeled, he groaned, and at the altar fell.
Haste, Madam, let us fly! Haste to our ships!
They lie unmoored,—our friends attend us there.

    Herm. What have they done?

    Or. Madam, forgive their rage!
I own your vengeance had been more complete
Had Pyrrhus fallen by me, and had he known
Hermione chastised him by my arm.

    Herm. Peace, monster, peace! Go, tell thy horrid tale
To savages, and howl it in the deserts!
Wouldst thou impute to me thy barbarous guilt?
Me wouldst thou make the accomplice of thy crimes?
Hence to thy Greeks, and boast thy foul exploits!
My soul abhors them! I disclaim the deed!
Begone! I know thee not, thou fell barbarian!
What had he done? What could provoke thy madness
To assassinate so great, so brave a man?
Who set thee on?

    Or. Oh, grant me patience, Heaven!
With your own lips did you not curse the tyrant,
Pronounce his death, and urge me to destroy him?

    Herm. What if, transported by my boundless passion,
I could not bear to see him wed another.—
Were you to obey a jealous woman's frenzy?
You should have div'd into my inmost thoughts:
My heart, though full of rage, was free from malice;
And all my anger was excess of love.
Why did you take me at my word? You saw
The struggles of my soul; you heard me rave:
You should have questioned me a thousand times,
Yet still have doubted, and still questioned on.
Before you ventured on a life so precious.

    Or. Hear me but speak: Heaven knows, against my will— —

    Herm. Why did you not return? why not consult me
A second time? and, undetermined still,
Again return, and still find new delays?

What had your rash, officious Greeks—dire bloodhounds!
To do with my revenge? What drew you hither?
To bring on me the vengeful woes that haunt you?
Are these the fruits of your detested love?
Your fatal embassy, your hateful presence,
Drove Pyrrhus to my rival, and destroys
Both him and me. He might have loved me still,
Had you ne'er interposed. Avaunt! Begone!
And leave me in Epirus. I renounce
My friends, my country, Greece, and all mankind:
But, chiefly, I renounce thee, monster! thee!

       (Exit.)

 Or. Am I awake? Where am I? Soft, my soul!
Be not too rash.——Was that Hermione?
Why should her anger thunder against me?
Was not this blood shed all by her command?
I am, indeed, a most outrageous monster!
A ruffian, murderer. a base assassin!
And all to please a false, ungrateful woman.
Henceforward let the laws of nations cease;
And let the pale that severs right and wrong,
Things sacred and profane. be broken down:
Gods in their temples. kings upon their thrones,
Are not in safety while Orestes lives.
Oh, never more shall my torn mind be healed,
Nor taste the gentle comforts of repose;
A dreadful band of gloomy cares surround me,
And lay strong siege to my distracted soul!

JEAN PAUL RICHTER

JEAN PAUL RICHTER (German, 1763-1825). Sentimental interpreter of
everyday life. After early poverty, was supported by numerous patronesses.
Settled in Weimar and Bayreuth. Extravagantly popular during his lifetime,
his novels are seldom read today. Most famous: *Titan, 'Teens, The Life of
Quintus Fixlein.*

THE NEW-YEAR'S NIGHT OF AN UNHAPPY MAN

AN old man stood on the new-year's midnight at the window. and
gazed with a look of long despair, upwards to the immovable ever-

blooming heaven, and down upon the still, pure, white earth, on which no one was then so joyless and sleepless as he. For his grave stood near him; it was covered over only with the snow of age, not with the green of youth; and he brought nothing with him out of the whole rich life, nothing with him, but errors, sins and disease, a wasted body, a desolated soul, the breast full of poison, an old age full of remorse. The beautiful days of his youth turned round to-day, as spectres, and drew him back again to that bright morning on which his father first placed him at the cross-road of life, which, on the right hand, leads by the sun-path of Virtue into a wide peaceful land full of light and of harvests, and full of angels, and which, on the left hand, descends into the mole-ways of Vice, into a black cavern full of down-dropping poison, full of aiming serpents, and of gloomy, sultry vapours.

Ah! the serpents hung about his breast, and the drops of poison on his tongue.—And he knew, now, where he was!

Frantic, and with unspeakable grief, he called upwards to Heaven: "Oh! give me back my youth again!—O, Father! place me once more at the cross-path of life, that I may choose otherwise than I did."

But his father and his youth had long since passed away.

He saw fiery exhalations dancing on the marshes, and extinguishing themselves in the churchyard, and he said: "These are the days of my folly!"—He saw a star fly from heaven, and, in falling, glimmer and dissolve upon the earth. "That am I!" said his bleeding heart, and the serpent-teeth of remorse dug therein further in its wounds.

His flaming fancy showed him sleepwalkers slinking away on the house-tops; and a windmill raised up its arms threateningly to destroy him; and a mask that remained behind in the empty charnel-house, assumed by degrees his own features.

In the midst of this paroxysm, suddenly the music for the new-year flowed down from the steeple, like distant church-anthems. He became more gently moved.—He looked round on the horizon and upon the wide world, and thought on the friends of his youth, who, better and more happy than he, were now instructors of the earth, fathers of happy children, and blest men—and he exclaimed: "Oh! I also might have slumbered, like you, this new-year's night with dry eyes, had I chosen it—Ah! I might have been happy, beloved parents! had I fulfilled your new-year's wishes and instructions."

In feverish recollection of the period of his youth, it appeared

1030

to him as if the mask with his features raised itself up in the charnel-house—at length, through the superstition, which, on the new-year's night, beholds spirits and futurity, it grew to a living youth in the position of the beautiful boy of the Capitol, pulling out a thorn; and his former blooming figure was bitterly placed as a phantasma before him.

He could behold it no longer—he covered his eyes.—A thousand, hot, draining tears streamed into the snow.—He, now, only softly sighed, inconsolably and unconsciously: "Only come again, youth! come again!"

And it came again, for he had only dreamed so fearfully on the new-year's night.—He was still a youth.—His errors alone had been no dream; but he thanked God, that, still young, he could turn round in the foul ways of Vice, and fall back on the sun-path which conducts into the pure land of harvests.

Turn with him, youthful reader, if thou standest on his path of error: This frightful dream will, in future, become thy judge; but shouldst thou one day call out, full of anguish: "Come again, beautiful youth!"—it would not come again.

RAINER MARIA RILKE

RAINER MARIA RILKE (German, 1875-1926). Highly disciplined and dedicated German poet. Extensive traveler and love correspondent. Painter and translator. Born Catholic, became mystic. Bulk of his work concerned with the ultimate themes of nature, love, death. Most widely known works: *The Journal of My Other Self, Sonnets to Orpheus, Duinese Elegies, Stories of God.*

O SELDOM

O seldom into the breathless
Restless rustle of life,
Reaches one of the crowning, deathless
Hours that consecrate strife;
Hour that accidentally seest,
That imprisons thy hand with fingers gentle:
    Come and be the only
    Guest at my lonely feast.

HOW GLORIOUS THE CHRYSANTHEMUMS

How glorious the chrysanthemums that day!
I almost shuddered at their splendour white . . .
And then you came to take my soul away
Deep in the night . . .

Such fear had I, and you came dear and wary,
Just when a dream had flashed you on my sight.
You came—and like a song from lips of fairy,
Rang out the night . . .

PRAYER OF THE MAIDENS TO MARY

I

O see how narrow are our days,
    How full of fear our bed;
We reach out awkward arms always
    To gather the roses red.

Thou must be mild to us, Mary,
    Out of Thy blood we blow;
And what a pain is yearning
    Thou alone canst know;

For Thou hast known this maiden's woe
    In Thine own soul's desire:
It feels as cold as Christmas snow,
    And yet is all on fire . . .

AFTER THE PRAYER

II

But I feel how my heart is glowing
    Warmer and warmer in my breast,
And every evening poorer growing,
    Nor any night can bring me rest.

1032

I tear at the white silken tissue,
And my shy dreams cry out to Thee:
    Let me be sorrow of Thy sorrow,
        O let us both
By the same wonder wounded be.

THY GREAT TOWNS, LORD

Thy great towns, Lord, are lost to shame,
    Things merged in misery and maddened;
The greatest is like flight from flame,—
    Comfort is none for them to be gladdened,
Their life is shorter than their name.

Therein dwell men from kennelled door to door,
    Starved into meagre shape and timid gesture,
Like herded lambkins shepherded before:
    Thine earth breathes sweet outside in springtide vesture,
But they are not and know of it no more.

And children there grow up on blind staircases,
    And up and down the self-same shadows wind,
And know not of the outside sunny spaces,
    Where flowers bloom fair for happy hands to bind,
And must be children, children of a kind.

And budding girls are to the unknown turning,
    And wishing back the peace of childhood eves;
They find not that for which their hearts are burning,
    And close again their open-trembling leaves.
And have in black back-garrets all untended
    The days of disappointed motherhood,

The listless whimpering of long nights unended,
    And cold years with no courage in the blood.
And all in darkness stand the beds for dying
    To which they like a beggar woman fade,
Till by the slow consumption of their sighing
    They at the last are on the death-bed laid.

1033

Behold how all is opened: we are so;
    For we are but such blessedness in space.
What in a beast was blood and dark, did grow
    To be a soul in us, and cries apace

For thee, as a soul ever. Thou indeed
    Takest it only up into thy face
As it were landscape: gently and with no greed.
    And so we think, for whom its pulses race

It is not thou. And yet, art thou not he
    To whom we lost ourselves till naught remained?
And shall we ever in any other be?

With us infinity fades like a mist.
    But thou, O mouth, so that it be explained,
Be! O thou teller unto us, exist.

ABISHAG

I

She lay, and serving-men her lithe arms took,
And bound them round the withering old man,
And on him through the long sweet hours she lay,
A little fearful of his many years.

And many times she turned amidst his beard
Her face, as often as the night-owl screeched,
And all that was the night around them reached
Its feelers manifold of longing fears.

As they had been the sisters of the child
The stars trembled, and fragrance searched the room,
The curtain stirring sounded with a sign
Which drew her gentle glances after it.

But she clung close upon the dim old man,
And, by the night of nights not overtaken,
Upon the cooling of the King she lay
Maidenly, and lightly as a soul.

1034

The King sate thinking out the empty day
Of deeds accomplished and untasted joys,
And of his favorite bitch that he had bred—
But with the evening Abishag was arched
Above him. His dishevelled life lay bare,
Abandoned as diffamèd coasts, beneath
The quiet constellation of her breasts.

But many times, as one in women skilled,
He through his eye-brows recognized the mouth
Unmoved, unkissed; and saw: the comet green
Of her desires reached not to where he lay.
He shivered. And he listened like a hound,
And sought himself in his remaining blood.

LOVE-SONG

By what device shall I my soul prevent
From touching thine? My soul how shall I lift
To other things above thee? Great
Indeed is my desire to have it pent
In something lost in some still spot, and let it mate
With darkness which thy gladness shall not rift,
And which shall not with thy own deeps vibrate.

But all that touches us,
Takes us together, thee and me, as does
A fiddle-bow one voice prolong
Out of two chords. Upon what instrument
Then are we stretched? What master's face is o'er us bent?
O sweet song.

THE ELOPEMENT

Often as a child she had escaped
Her women to behold beneath the skies,
Because inside they are so otherwise,
The wind weave when the evening first is draped;

And yet no night of tempest ever had
Into such fragments torn the giant park
As it was now torn into by her bad

Conscience, since down the silken ladder's fall
He took and bore her onward through the dark

Until the carriage was all.
And the black vehicle she smelt,
And round it chase in hiding,
And danger.
And he was faced with cold, she felt,
And the blackness and the coldness in her gliding,
She crept into the collar of her cloak.
And felt her hair, as if it were not riding,
And she, strange, heard how a stranger
Spoke:
Iambytheeabiding.

ESTHER

The serving-women combed her seven days through
The ashes of her torment and her sorrow
Out of her hair the sediment and deposit,
And bore it out and dried it in the sun,
Spice that they did not feed it with was none
Another day and this one; but then was it

The time when she, now being all anointed
Even as a corpse is, at no hour appointed
Should enter in the open palace grim
In order at the way's end to behold
The face of him concerning whom we are told
That any one must die who looks on him.

As though the ruby of her crown were dull
Before, she felt it flash ere he was seen
And filled herself already with his mien
Like to a vessel, till she grew so full

1036

That she flowed over with the monarch's might
Or ever on her face the third hall gleamed,
That ran green over her with the malachite
Of its four walls. But she had never dreamed
With all her gems so long a way to wend her,
And they grew heavier with the King's great splendour
And with her terror cold. She, wandering,
Went on till, when she saw him there recline,
Towering upon a throne of tourmaline,
Before her, looking verily like a thing:

The right handmaiden took her fainting, and
Upreared her in the reach of the monarch's hand.
He touched her with his sceptre's point, and she
Conceived it without senses, inwardly.

JEAN ARTHUR RIMBAUD

JEAN ARTHUR RIMBAUD (French, 1854-1891). Brilliant poetic genius,
who at 19 deliberately ceased writing. Ran away from home as adolescent.
After year of literary life in Paris, set off on walking tour with Verlaine. Was
shot by him, but recovered. After much travel, settled in Ethiopa as a slave-
trader. His aesthetic theories had marked influence on modern literature.
Major works: *Les Illuminations, Une Saison en Enfer*

DRUNKEN BOAT

As I descended the impassable streams
I felt myself no longer held by the drag-poles:
Clamorous Redskins had taken my crew for targets,
First having nailed them naked to the flagpoles.

But I was unconcerned for any crew,
Porters of Flemish grain or English cotton.
And when my haulers had done with their hurly-burly
The streams let me pass on as though forgotten.

Amidst the furious chopping of the tides
Last winter, muffled as a midnight scurvy,
I ran! and peninsulas that slip their bonds
Have never been more gloriously topsy-turvy.

The tempest blessed my maritime alarms.
Lighter than a cork I danced upon the waves,
Ten nights, nor missed the silly eyes of lanterns,
On the eternal rolling of those graves.

Sweeter than the juice of held fruit to a child
The green water would my broken cockle whelm,
And streaks of bluish wines and of disgorgements
Washed me and bore off grappling-irons and helm.

And thenceforth I was deluged in the poem
Of the sea infused with meteors latescent
Devouring the green azure where, wan flotation,
A pensive drowned man is at times quiescent.

Or, of a sudden tinting the bluishness, swirls
And soft rhythms under the rutilant day,
Stronger than alcohol, larger than your lyres,
The bitter red vortices of love stew away!

I know the heavens lightning-rived, the waterspout,
Surfs, and the currents; I know the evening sky,
The dawn exalted as a poplar light with doves;
And I have sometimes seen what man thinks he may descry.

I have seen the low sun stained with mystic terrors,
Lighting long violet coagulations;
Like olden actors in an antique drama
The waves roll off their compass-agitations.

I have dreamed through green nights of dazzling snows,
Of a kiss that, welling in the eyes of the sea, over long stirs,
The circulation of unheard-of saps,
And the yellow and blue alarm of phosphorous songsters.

I have followed, months through, like the noise of hysterical stables,
The shore-battering blows of the billows' barrages,
Without thinking that over the short-winded ocean
Their luminous feet might force forward the snouts of the barges.

I have come, understand! on incredible Floridas
Where flowers blend with panther-eyes, and the skin
Of men with rainbows taut as a bridle,
Under ocean horizons, where sea-green hordes rush in.

I have seen swamps ferment, enormous fish-traps
Where in the rushes Leviathan rotting sleeps;
Downpourings of waters in the midst of calm,
And the distances whirled to the cataract deeps,

Glaciers, suns of silver, pearl floods, skies of embers,
Hideous jetsam in deep gulfs of gloom,
Where giant serpents eaten of grubbing maggots
Fall from the gnarled trees with black perfume.

I'd have liked to show children these ocean doradoes,
The great gold fish, the fish that sings;
Foam-wreaths of flowers have blessed my far-sea driftings
And at times ineffable winds have lent me wings.

At times, weary martyr of the zones and poles,
The ocean, whose sobbing softly cradles me,
Lifts me its flowers of dark with yellow air-holes;
And I have stayed there as a woman on her knee,

Peninsula tossing to my sides the quarrels
And the guano of chattering birds with pallid eyes;
And I floated on, while across my slender lines
Drowned men came drifting down to sleep sidewise.

Then I, lost boat beneath the leafy bays,
Hurled by tornadoes to the birdless ether,
I whose sea-drunk carcass no Monitor
Nor packet of the Guilds would have fished for beneath her,

1039

Free, fumid, risen with violet mists,
I who bored through the ruddy sky's diadem
Like a wall that was decked, to the poet's taste,
With sun-touched lichen and azure phlegm,

I who ran spotted with electric lunes,
Mad plank, with hippocampi at the gunwales,
When July was battering with bludgeon blows
The ultramarine skies with their flaming funnels,

I who trembled, sensing at fifty leagues
The rut of Behemoth, the loud Maelstrom's frets,
Eternal spinner of blue fixities—
I long for Europe's ancient parapets.

I have seen starry archipelagoes, and isles
Whose frenzied skies are clear above the rower;
Is it in those deep nights you in your exile sleep,
Mid millions of golden birds, O future Overthrower?

True, I have wept too long. Dawn breaks the heart.
All moons are hateful, every sun is gall.
Tart love has swollen me with dizzying torpors.
Oh, that my keel were darting! Oh, that I fled the squall!

If I want water of Europe, it is the black
Cold puddle where, as evening gathers nigh,
A squatting plaintive youngster will release
A boat as fragile as a butterfly.

I can no longer, bathed in your languor, waves,
Take the backwash of freighters as they bowse,
Nor breast the pride of colours and salutes,
Nor sail beneath the horrid eyes of scows!

EDWIN ARLINGTON ROBINSON

EDWIN ARLINGTON ROBINSON (American, 1869-1935). Reflective poetic traditionalist, who achieved individual style through precision and simplicity. Worked at odd jobs until President Theodore Roosevelt's recognition got him job in New York Custom House. *The Children of the Night* contains famous character portraits of Richard Cory, Miniver Cheevy, Luke Havergal, *et al.* *The Man Against the Sky* brought national fame. Also: *Merlin, Lancelot, Tristram.*

STAFFORD'S CABIN

Once there was a cabin here, and once there was a man;
And something happened here before my memory began.
Time has made the two of them the fuel of one flame
And all we have of them is now a legend and a name.

All I have to say is what an old man said to me,
And that would seem to be as much as there will ever be.
"Fifty years ago it was we found it where it sat."
And forty years ago it was old Archibald said that.

"An apple tree that's yet alive saw something, I suppose,
Of what it was that happened there, and what no mortal knows
Some one on the mountain heard far off a master shriek,
And then there was a light that showed the way for men to seek.

"We found it in the morning with an iron bar behind,
And there were chains around it; but no search could ever find,
Either in the ashes that were left, or anywhere,
A sign to tell of who or what had been with Stafford there.

"Stafford was a likely man with ideas of his own—
Though I could never like the kind that likes to live alone;
And when you met, you found his eyes were always on your shoes,
As if they did the talking when he asked you for the news.

"That's all, my son. Were I to talk for a half a hundred years
I'd never clear away from there the cloud that never clears.
We buried what was left of it,—the bar, too, and the chains;
And only for the apple tree there's nothing that remains."

Forty years ago it was I heard the old man say,
"That's all, my son." And here again I find the place today,
Deserted and told only by the tree that knows the most,
And overgrown with goldenrod as if there were no ghost.

NEW ENGLAND

Here where the wind is always north-north-east
And children learn to walk on frozen toes,
Wonder begets an envy of all those
Who boil elsewhere with such a lyric yeast
Of love that you will hear them at a feast
Where demons would appeal for some repose,
Still clamoring where the chalice overflows
And crying wildest who have drunk the least.

Passion is here a soilure of the wits,
We're told, and Love a cross for them to bear;
Joy shivers in the corner where she knits
And Conscience always has the rocking-chair,
Cheerful as when she tortured into fits
The first cat that was ever killed by Care.

ROMAIN ROLLAND

ROMAIN ROLLAND (French, 1866-1944). Renowned novelist and playwright.
Leading pacifist at beginning of present century. In later years turned Stalinist
fellow traveler. Author of biographies of Beethoven, Michelangelo, Tolstoy and
others. Winner of Nobel Prize in 1915 for *Jean-Christophe,* heroic novel modeled
roughly on life of Beethoven.

THE TRAP

THE first questions that enter my childish mind:
   "Where did I come from? and where am I confined?——"
   I was born into a comfortable middle-class family, surrounded
by loving relatives, in a pleasant part of the country whose joyous
flavor I later tasted and celebrated through the voice of my *Colas.*
   How does it happen that, from the moment of my birth, the first
feeling—the strongest, most persistent of my early childhood—

should be—dim, haunting, sometimes rebellious, sometimes resigned: "I am a prisoner!"

Francis the First, on entering the tottering nave of my old Saint Martin of Clamecy, said (so the legend runs): "There's a fine trap!"—I was in "the Trap."

At the beginning, a visual impression: the first horizon presented to my childish view—a rather large paved court, with a garden in the middle, surrounded on three sides by three walls of the house that to me seemed very high. On the fourth side, the street and the houses opposite, separated by a canal. Although this quadrangle was terraced above the water, it seemed to the child, confined to his room on the ground floor, like a ditch in the zoological gardens at the foot of four walls.

A significant impression: children's diseases and a delicate constitution. Although I come of healthy parents and robust ancestry— (The Rollands and the Courots, tall, bony, without physical defects, and endowed with boundless nervous energy that keeps them up and about until their last day, have all lived to a ripe old age; my maternal grandparents lived merrily on past their eightieth year; at the very moment of this writing my eighty-eight-year-old father is happily watering his garden)—I, made of the same lime and sand that, in spite of everything, have resisted fatigue and the trials of a busy existence, have borne, all my life, the painful consequences of a childhood accident: the carelessness of a young servant who, forgetting me in the winter-cold when I was less than a year old, brought me close to death and bequeathed to me for life a bronchial weakness and shortness of breath. Over and over again one can find in my works, spurting up, involuntarily, like an interrupted flight, the "respiratory" expressions: "stifling," "open windows," "fresh air," "the breath of the heroes . . ."—the bird that flutters its wings, or crouches, feverish, in the cage of the wounded breast.

Finally, moral impressions, powerful and penetrating: the thought of death that enveloped the first ten years of my life. Death had entered the family circle; it had struck down at my side a little sister, younger than I, of whom I shall speak later; and her shadow continued to inhabit the house. An excitable mother, whose grief was never allayed, feverishly nursed the memory of the departed child. And I, who had seen her disappear in a few days, and whom the constant sight of this mother, brooding over her solitary thought, also bound, despite the heedlessness of my age that sought an escape —I was all the more readily exposed to the idea that was going about, since, until I was ten or twelve years old, my own life was threatened. Frequent colds, bronchitis, sore throats, persistent nose-bleeds took away my zest for life; and in my little bed I would keep repeating:

"I don't want to die!"

while my mother, in tears, would answer, hugging me to her:

"No, my little boy. The good God will not want to take you away from me, too!"

This only half convinced me, for what did I know about God, except that, from my first steps, he had taken advantage of his power. And my most lucid thought in regard to him was, without my realizing it, that of the Gardener for his Lord:

"The good man said: Those are the moves of a prince . . . .
In appealing to kings, you make great fools of yourselves.
You must never let them enter your lands. . . ."

In the threefold prison of the old house, my weak chest, and the ill-omened circle of death, the earliest consciousness of my childhood grew up under the anxious surveillance of my mother's affection. Fragile plant, sister to the wistaria and the petunias blooming in the court and along the walls, whose breath from short-lived lips mingled with the dank odor of the stagnant canal; like them, rooted to the ground, yet aspiring to the light, the little prisoner, only half-awakened, kept groping blindly and instinctively in the air for invisible roads of escape.

The closest at hand: the murky canal, flowing along the terrace-wall over which I hung. Muddy and green, without a ripple, it bore up the deep, heavy boats that the bargemen forced along by the sheer forward thrust of their thin bodies. I could hear the grinding of the cables along the railing at the edge. A turn-bridge creaked and began to move slowly. From the cabin of the boat whose sky-light was decorated with a pot of geraniums, mounted a thin blue spiral of smoke. Seated before the door in silence, a woman was knitting; from time to time she glanced indifferently in my direction. The boat passed. . . . And I, leaning over the wall, saw the wall and myself passing. We were leaving the boat behind us; it was we who were going away. Now we are far out in the open: without a jar, without a motion. So slowly we slipped along that it seemed as though we should glide, like the night-sky, into eternity, without a change. And then we found each other again, the wall and I,

1044

still dreaming in the same place. The boat had gone. Would it ever reach its destination? Another was coming up after it. It looked just the same. . . .

Then I imagined another route, free and without locks: the air. A child often lifts his face toward the sky, toward the wandering clouds and the twittering swallows, toward the great white clouds, like whimsical monuments formed by the childish eye. (That is his first sculpture; the child uses the air as his clay.) It is needless to speak of the rest: the threatening clouds, the rumbling storms of Central France with their crashing thunder. It is in them that the enemy returns—the Master with his beetling eyebrows closes the shutters of the sky on the frail prisoner. Then come the hands of deliverance, the fingers of the sorceress that open my window on the plains of the air. . . . And now come the bells, the bells of Saint Martin! They sound in the first pages of my *Jean-Christophe*. Their music is engraved on my unawakened heart. They pealed forth from the open tower of the old cathedral above my house. But it was not the church that these ecclesiastical songsters called forth in me. Later I shall tell of my encounters with the God of the church. They were cold, ceremonious and distant. In spite of my honest efforts, I never succeeded in getting in touch with him. God alone knows whether I sought him. But the God who knows it is not the same God. The God who heard me—the God whom I created so that he would listen to me, and in whom I have confided all my life—was in the hovering song-birds, the bells, and in the air. Not the Lord of Saint Martin's hidden in his retreat above the sculptured arches. But the God Liberty—At that time, to be sure, I had no knowledge of the span of his wings, but I heard them flutter in the airy heights. Nor was I even sure that they were more real than the white clouds. They ever remained for me a nostalgic dream that let me glance at space for a moment before taking their flight and letting the trap-door fall again over the cave of my life. . . . Much, much later (I shall tell how), I climbed, I pushed upward, I forced the trap with my forehead and, freed at last, I found traces of the bells once more. But all through childhood I groped about in a sealed cave—the great, beautiful cave of Burgundy, like a crypt full of wine-casks set in rows, and covered with cobwebs. Everyone else was at ease there, except one, and I heard them laugh as one laughs in my country. I did not look down upon the laughter and the drinking—But oh! for a taste of the sun outside! Was there really a sun? (If only I had the answer!) Or even the night?—And since none of those strong men tried to leave, I conscious of my weakness, crouched in my corner, beaten.

At sixteen or seventeen years of age, when I read *Hamlet*, with what resonance these fraternal words echoed under the vault of my cave:

"*. . . what have you, my good friends, deserved at the hands of Fortune, that she sends you to prison hither?*"

"*Prison, my lord?*"

"*Denmark's a prison.*"

"*Then is the world one.*"

"*A goodly one, in which there are many confines, wards and dungeons. . . .*"

It is true that, a few lines further on, a magic word fills me with infinite hope:

"*O God. I could be bounded in a nut-shell and count myself a king of infinite space. . . .*"

That is the story of my life.

PIERRE DE RONSARD

PIERRE DE RONSARD (French, 1524-1585). Most eminent of Renaissance poets. Plans for diplomatic career frustrated by deafness at 18. Became leader of group of poets called La Pléiade. Received rich honors from French kings during lifetime, was neglected after death. Has since taken place among great French lyricists. Best work: the sonnets in three sets of *Amours*.

THE ROSE

See, Mignonne! hath not the Rose,
That this morning did unclose
   Her purple mantle to the light,
Lost, before the day be dead,
The glory of her raiment red,
   Her color, bright as yours is bright?

Ah, Mignonne! in how few hours
The petals of her purple flowers
   All have faded, fallen, died!
Sad Nature! mother ruinous!
That seest thy fair child perish thus
   'Twixt matin song and eventide.

Hear me, Darling! speaking sooth:
Gather the fleet flower of your youth!
    Take ye your pleasure at the best!
Be merry ere your beauty flit!
For length of days will tarnish it.
    Like roses that were loveliest.

WELCOME TO SPRING

God shield ye, heralds of the spring,
Ye faithful swallows fleet of wing,
    Hoops, cuckoos, nightingales,
Turtles and every wilder bird,
That make your hundred chirpings heard
    Through the green woods and dales.

God shield ye, Easter daisies all,
Fair roses, buds and blossoms small;
    And ye, whom erst the gore
Of Ajax and Narciss did print,
Ye wild thyme, anise, balm, and mint
    I welcome ye once more.

God shield ye, bright embroidered train
Of butterflies, that, on the plain,
    Of each sweet herblet sip;
And ye new swarm of bees that go
Where the pink flowers and yellow grow
    To kiss them with your lip.

A hundred thousand times I call—
A hearty welcome on ye all:

    This season how I love!
This merry din on every shore,
For winds and storms, whose sullen roar
    Forbade my steps to rove.

1047

OF HIS LADY'S OLD AGE

When you are very old, at evening
  You'll sit and spin beside the fire, and say,
    Humming my songs, "Ah well, ah well-a-day!
When I was young, of me did Ronsard sing."
None of your maidens that doth hear the thing,
  Albeit with her weary task foredone,
    But wakens at my name, and calls you one
Blest, to be held in long remembering.

I shall be low beneath the earth, and laid
On sleep, a phantom in the myrtle shade,
  While you beside the fire, a grandame gray,
My love, your pride, remember and regret;
Ah, love me, love! we may be happy yet,
  And gather roses, while 'tis called to-day.

EDMOND ROSTAND

EDMOND ROSTAND (French, 1868-1918). Colorful virtuoso of the drama,
whose name is chiefly associated with florid heroic masterpiece, *Cyrano de
Bergerac.* Other works: *L'Aiglon, Chantecler, La dernière nuit de Don Juan.*
His work the final flower of the romantic theater of Victor Hugo.

TO SARAH

In these drab days, alone there never cloys
Your pallid grace, descending a wide stair,
Wreathing a frontlet, holding a lily, sword in air:
Queen of Fair Gestures, Princess of Poise.
In these tame times your flames are mutinous!
You speak verse. You die of love. You are ever fresh.
You hold forth arms of dream, then arms of flesh,
And when Phèdre appears, we are all incestuous.

Avid of suffering, you deepen with the years;
We have seen flowing—for they flow!—your tears:

All the dew of our soul on your cheek lingers.
But you know, Sarah, that at times there stray—
And furtively you feel them as you play—
The lips of Shakespeare on your jeweled fingers.

CYRANO TO HIS CHIDING FRIENDS

Do what?
Seek a potent protector, slink under a patron,
And like the low ivy, both early and late run
Round a trunk-prop and, licking the bark,
Climb by a ruse instead of rising stark?
No, thanks! Like everyone, set dearly down
Lines to a financier? Change into a clown
In the base hope of seeing, on the lips of a minister,
A smile spread, at last, that may not be sinister?
No, thanks! Dine daily on a bitter pill?
Have a belly worn with walking? A skin still
Quicker to catch the dirt upon the knees?
Execute daily dorsal suppleties?
No, thanks! With one hand pet a goat until it preens,
And with the other confiscate its greens?
Donor of senna that rhubarb be neared,
Always burn incense in somebody's beard?
No, thanks! From one lap leap to the lap beyond,
To become a big man in a small pond,
To navigate with madrigal-propellers
And the sighs of old maids as my sail-swellers?
No, thanks! At the publishing house of kindly Blanks
Pay to have my verses done? No, thanks!
Be named high-priest by the council of buffoons
That meets before the bars of old saloons?
No, thanks! Work that my name shall go
High with one sonnet, and write no more? No,
Thanks! Discover talent only in loons,
Be terrorized by threats of vague lampoons,
And endlessly to say "Just let me be
Among the personals in the *Mercury!*"
No, thanks! Calculate? Have fears—and show 'em?
And rather make a visit than poem?

Draw up petitions, be presented . . . everything! ! !
No, thanks! No, thanks! No, thanks! No, thanks! But—sing,
Dream, laugh, go by, be alone, be free,
With a vibrant voice, and a steady eye to see,
And when I please, to set my hat awry,
At a yea or a nay take arms—or versify!
To work, unheeding wealth or glory's tune,
Toward the journey I'm thinking of making to the moon!
Never to write a line save from the heart,
Modestly to say to myself from the very start:
"Be satisfied with flowers, fruits, even leaves,
If it is your own garden that achieves!"
Then if fame and fortune send a soft appeaser,
Not to be obliged to render aught unto Cæsar,
But clear in your own eyes make your merit shine:
In short, disdaining the parasitic vine,
Even if you haven't to the oak's crest grown,
Not to soar high, perhaps, but rise alone!

JALAL UD-DIN RUMI

JALAL UD-DIN RUMI (Persian, 1207-1273). Most eminent mystic poet and
Dervish of Persia. A devotee of Sufism, regarded by contemporaries as a
spiritual guide. Founded the order of Mowlavies ("Whirling Dervishes").
His greatest work: *Masnavi*, a poem in 6 books, containing stories, fables.
and moral precepts.

THE MERCHANT AND THE PARROT

There was once a merchant, who had a parrot,
A parrot fair to view, confined in a cage;
And when the merchant prepared for a journey,
He resolved to bend his way towards Hindustan.
Every servant and maiden in his generosity
He asked, what present he should bring them home,
And each one named what he severally wished,
And to each one the good master promised his desire.

Then he said to the parrot, "And what gift wishest thou,
That I should bring to thee from Hindustan?"
The parrot replied, "When thou seest the parrots there,
Oh, bid them know of my condition.
Tell them, 'A parrot, who longs for your company,
Through Heaven's decree is confined in my cage.
He sends you his salutation, and demands his right,
And seeks from you help and counsel.
He says, "Is it right that I in my longings
Should pine and die in this prison through separation?
Is it right that I should be here fast in this cage,
While you dance at will on the grass and the trees?
Is this the fidelity of friends,
I here in a prison, and you in a grove?
Oh remember, I pray you, that bower of ours,
And our morning-draughts in the olden time;
Oh remember all our ancient friendships,
And all the festive days of our intercourse!" ' "
The merchant received its message,
The salutation which he was to bear to its fellows;
And when he came to the borders of Hindustan,
He beheld a number of parrots in the desert.
He stayed his horse, and he lifted his voice,
And he repeated his message, and deposited his trust;
And one of those parrots suddenly fluttered.
And fell to the ground, and presently died.
Bitterly did the merchant repent his words;
"I have slain," he cried, "a living creature.
Perchance this parrot and my little bird were close of kin,
Their bodies perchance were two and their souls one.
Why did I this? why gave I the message?
I have consumed a helpless victim by my foolish words!
My tongue is as flint, and my lips as steel;
And the words that burst from them are sparks of fire.
Strike not together in thy folly the flint and steel.
Whether for the sake of kind words or vain boasting;
The world around is as a cotton-field by night;
In the midst of cotton, how shall the spark do no harm?"
   The merchant at length completed his traffic,
And he returned right glad to his home once more.
To every servant he brought a present,

To every maiden he gave a token;
And the parrot said, "Where is my present?
Tell all that thou hast said and seen!"
He answered, "I repeated thy complaints
To that company of parrots, thy old companions,
And one of those birds, when it inhaled the breath of thy sorrow,
Broke its heart, and fluttered, and died."
And when the parrot heard what its fellow had done,
It too fluttered, and fell down, and died.
When the merchant beheld it thus fall,
Up he sprang, and dashed his cap to the ground.
"Oh, alas!" he cried, "my sweet and pleasant parrot,
Companion of my bosom and sharer of my secrets!
Oh alas! alas! and again alas!
That so bright a moon is hidden under a cloud!"
After this, he threw its body out of the cage;
And lo! the little bird flew to a lofty bough.
The merchant stood amazed at what it had done;
Utterly bewildered he pondered its mystery.
It answered, "Yon parrot taught me by its action:
'Escape,' it told me, 'from speech and articulate voice,
Since it was thy voice that brought thee into prison;'
And to prove its own words itself did die."
    It then gave the merchant some words of wise counsel,
And at last bade him a long farewell.
"Farewell, my master, thou hast done me a kindness,
Thou hast freed me from the bond of this tyranny.
Farewell, my master, I fly towards home;
Thou shalt one day be free like me!"

THE DESTINY OF MAN

Seeks thy spirit to be gifted
    With a deathless life?
Let it seek to be uplifted
    O'er earth's storm and strife.

Spurn its joys—its ties dissever;
    Hopes and fears divest;
Thus aspire to live forever—
    Be forever blest!

Faith and doubt leave far behind thee;
    Cease to love or hate;
Let not Time's illusions blind thee;
    Thou shalt Time outdate.

Merge thine individual being
    In the Eternal's love;
All this sensuous nature fleeing
    For pure bliss above.

Earth receives the seed and guards it;
    Trustfully it dies;
Then, what teeming life rewards it
    For self-sacrifice!

With green leaf and clustering blossom
    Clad, and golden fruit,
See it from earth's cheerless bosom
    Ever sunward shoot!

Thus, when self-abased, Man's spirit
    From each earthly tie
Rises disenthralled t' inherit
    Immortality!

S

SA'DI

SA'DI (Persian, 1184-1291). One of the most versatile figures in Persian literature: poet, philosopher, teacher, Sufi. Great traveler and a soldier against the Christians during the Crusades. His *Gulistan (Rose Garden)*, in prose and verse, is most widely read Persian classic.

THE GULISTAN

Purgatory May Be Paradise

A KING was embarked along with a Persian slave on board a ship. The boy had never been at sea, nor experienced the inconvenience of a ship. He set up a weeping and wailing, and all his limbs were in a state of trepidation; and, however much they soothed him, he was not to be pacified. The king's pleasure-party was disconcerted by him; but they had no help. On board that ship there was a physician. He said to the king: "If you will order it, I can manage to silence him." The king replied: "It will be an act of great favor." The physician so directed that they threw the boy into the sea, and after he had plunged repeatedly, they seized him by the hair of the head and drew him close to the ship, when he clung with both hands by the rudder, and, scrambling upon the deck, slunk into a corner and sat down quiet. The king, pleased with what he saw, said: "What art is there in this?" The physician replied: "Originally he had not experienced the danger of being drowned, and undervalued the safety of being in a ship; in like manner as a person is aware of the preciousness of health when he is overtaken with the the calamity of sickness. *A barley loaf of bread has, O epicure, no relish for thee. That is my mistress who appears so ugly to thy eye. —To the houris, or nymphs of paradise, purgatory would be a hell: ask the inmates of hell whether purgatory is not paradise.—There is a distinction between the man that folds his mistress in his arms and him whose two eyes are fixed on the door expecting her.*"

The Wrestler

A person had become a master in the art of wrestling; he knew three hundred and sixty sleights in this art, and could exhibit a fresh trick for every day throughout the year. Perhaps owing to a liking that a corner of his heart took for the handsome person of one of his scholars, he taught him three hundred and fifty-nine of those feats, but he was putting off the last one, and under some pretence deferring it.

In short, the youth became such a proficient in the art and talent of wrestling that none of his contemporaries had ability to cope with him, till he at length had one day boasted before the reigning sovereign, saying: "To any superiority my master possesses over me, he is beholden to my reverence of his seniority, and in virtue of his tutorage; otherwise I am not inferior in power, and am his equal in skill." This want of respect displeased the king. He ordered a wrestling match to be held, and a spacious field to be fenced in for the occasion. The ministers of state, nobles of the court, and gallant men of the realm were assembled, and the ceremonials of the combat marshalled. Like a huge and lusty elephant, the youth rushed into the ring with such a crash that had a brazen mountain opposed him he would have moved it from its base. The master being aware that the youth was his superior in strength, engaged him in that strange feat of which he had kept him ignorant. The youth was unacquainted with its guard. Advancing, nevertheless, the master seized him with both hands, and, lifting him bodily from the ground, raised him above his head and flung him on the earth. The crowd set up a shout. The king ordered them to give the master an honorary dress and handsome largess, and the youth he addressed with reproach and asperity, saying: "You played the traitor with your own patron, and failed in your presumption of opposing him." He replied: "O sire! my master did not overcome my by strength and ability, but one cunning trick in the art of wrestling was left which he was reserved in teaching me, and by that little feat had today the upper hand of me." The master said: "I reserved myself for such a day as this. As the wise have told us, put not so much into a friend's power that, if hostilely disposed, he can do you an injury. Have you not heard what that man said who was treacherously dealt with by his own pupil: *'Either in fact there was no good faith in this world, or nobody has perhaps practised it in our days. No person learned the art of archery from me who did not in the end make me his butt.'*"

1055

From Slavery to Slavery

Having taken offence with the society of my friends at Damascus, I retired into the wilderness of the Holy Land, or Jerusalem, and sought the company of brutes till such time as I was made a prisoner by the Franks, and employed by them, along with some Jews, in digging earth in the ditches of Tripoli. At length one of the chiefs of Aleppo, between whom and me an intimacy had of old subsisted, happening to pass that way, recognized me, and said: "How is this? and how came you to be thus occupied?" I replied: "What can I say? *I was flying from mankind into the forests and mountains, for my resource was in God and in none else. Fancy to thyself what my condition must now be, when forced to associate with a tribe scarcely human?—To be linked in a chain with a company of acquaintance were pleasanter than to walk in a garden with strangers.*"

He took pity on my situation; and, having for ten dinars redeemed me from captivity with the Franks, carried me along with him to Aleppo. Here he had a daughter, and her he gave me in marriage, with a dower of a hundred dinars. Soon after this damsel turned out a termagant and vixen, and discovered such a perverse spirit and virulent tongue as quite unhinged all my domestic comfort. *A scolding wife in the dwelling of a peaceable man is his hell even in this world. Protect and guard us against a wicked inmate. Save us, O Lord, and preserve us from the fiery, or hell, torture.*

Having on one occasion given a liberty to the tongue of reproach, she was saying: "Are you not the fellow whom my father redeemed from the captivity of the Franks for ten dinars?" I replied: "Yes, I am that same he delivered from captivity for ten dinars, and enslaved me with you for a hundred!" *I have heard that a reverend and mighty man released a sheep from the paws and jaws of a wolf. That same night he was sticking a knife into its throat, when the spirit of the sheep reproached him, saying: "Thou didst deliver me from the clutches of a wolf, when I at length saw that thou didst prove a wolf to me thyself."*

WEALTH

He that owns wealth, in mountain, wold, or waste,
Plays master—pitches tent at his own taste;
Whilst he who lacks that which the world commends
Must pace a stranger, e'en in his own lands.

1056

PRIEST SAIGYO

PRIEST SAIGYO (Japanese, 1118-1190). *Tanka* nature poet. At 23 gave up
the life of a courtier to become an itinerant priest, his wife becoming a nun.
His poetry admired for its lucidity and simplicity. Principal collection:
Sankashū.

FORSAKEN

Why should I bitter be,
    Although he cold has grown?
There was a time when he to me
    And I to him were quite unknown.

THE AUTUMN MOON

I envy much the autumn moon,
    Which, journeying without delay,
Can follow, in the western sky,
    My friend who travels far away.

THE OLD CHERRY-TREE

Particularly will I gaze
    Upon the agéd cherry tree;
It and its flowers are pitiful.
    How many more springs can it see?

FLOWERS AND THE MOON

Suppose no clouds ever covered the moon
    And cherry flowers did not fall,
Why, then, I think in such a world,
    No sorrow should I know at all!

THE MOON

All things are ever changing
    In this transitory world,
But yet the moon is shining
    With the same light as of old.

1057

SPRING AND AUTUMN

In spring when we see flowers,
  Would that there were no night!
In autumn when we see the moon,
  That there were no light!

GEORGE SAND

GEORGE SAND (Amandine Aurore Lucie Dupin, Baroness Dudevant, French, 1804-1876). Scandalous libertine and liberal. A remarkable woman who flouted the conventions of her time to leave husband, become novelist, and have series of notorious amours (including De Musset and Chopin). Her rather facile works favored the sociological theme. An ardent feminist—her best stories depict rebellious women: *Consuelo, Lélia, Elle et Lui.*

THE PLOUGHMAN AND HIS CHILD

I WAS walking on the border of a field which some peasants were carefully preparing for the approaching seed-time. The area was vast; the landscape was vast also, and enclosed with great lines of verdure, somewhat reddened by the approach of autumn, that broad field of vigorous brown, where recent rains had left, in some furrows, lines of water which the sun made glitter like fine threads of silver. The day had been clear and warm, and the earth, freshly opened by the cutting of the ploughshares, exhaled a light vapor. In the upper part of the field, an old man gravely held his plough of antique form, drawn by two oxen, with pale yellow skins—real patriarchs of the meadow—large in stature, rather thin, with long turned-down horns, old laborers whom long habit had made "brothers," as they are called by our country people, and who, when separated from each other, refuse to work with a new companion, and let themselves die of sorrow. The old husbandman worked slowly, in silence, without useless efforts; his docile team did not hurry any more than he; but, owing to the continuity of a labor without distraction, and the appliance of tried and well-sustained strength, his furrow was as soon turned as that of his son, who was ploughing at a short distance from him, with four oxen not so stout, in a vein of stronger and more stony soil.

But that which afterwards attracted my attention was really a beautiful spectacle—a noble subject for a painter. At the other ex-

1058

tremity of the arable field, a good-looking young man was driving a magnificent team: four pairs of young animals of a dark color, a mixture of black and bay with streaks of fire, with those short and frizzly heads which still savor of the wild bull, those large savage eyes, those sudden motions, that nervous and jerking labor which still is irritated by the yoke and the goad, and only obeys with a start of anger the recently imposed authority. They were what are called newly-yoked steers. The man who governed them had to clear a corner formerly devoted to pasturage, and filled with century-old stumps, the task of an athlete, for which his energy, his youth, and eight almost unbroken animals were barely sufficient.

A child six or seven years old, beautiful as an angel, with his shoulders covered, over his blouse, by a lamb-skin, which made him resemble the little Saint John the Baptist of the painters of the Restoration, walked in a furrow parallel to the plough, and touched the flank of the oxen with a long and light stick pointed with a slightly sharpened goad. The proud animals quivered under the small hand of the child, and made their yokes and the thongs bound over their foreheads creak, while they gave violent shocks to the plough handles. When a root stopped the ploughshare, the husbandman shouted with a powerful voice, calling each beast by his name, but rather to calm than excite; for the oxen, irritated by this sudden resistance, leaped, dug up the ground with their broad forked feet, and would have cast themselves out of the track, carrying the plough across the field, if, with his voice and goad, the young man had not restrained the four nearest him, while the child governed the other four. He also, shouted, the poor little fellow, with a voice he wished to make terrible, but which remained as gentle as his angelic face. It was all beautiful in strength or in grace, the landscape, the man, the child, the bulls under the yoke; and in spite of this powerful struggle in which the earth was overcome, there was a feeling of gentleness and deep calm which rested upon all things. When the obstacle was surmounted, and the team had resumed its equal and solemn step, the husbandman, whose feigned violence was only an exercise of vigor, and an expenditure of activity, immediately recovered the serenity of simple souls, and cast a look of paternal satisfaction on his child, who turned to smile on him.

Then the manly voice of this young father of a family struck up the melancholy and solemn strain which the ancient tradition of the country transmits, not to all ploughmen indiscriminately, but to those most consummate in the art of exciting and sustaining the ardor of

1059

the oxen at work. This chant, the origin of which was perhaps considered sacred, and to which mysterious influences must formerly have been attributed, is still reputed, at this day, to possess the virtue of keeping up the courage of the animals, of appeasing their dissatisfaction, and of charming the ennui of their long task. It is not enough to know how to drive them well while tracing a perfectly straight furrow, to lighten their labor by raising or depressing the point of the ploughshare opportunely in the soil: no one is a perfect ploughman if he does not know how to sing to the oxen, and this is a science apart, which requires taste and peculiar adaptation. This chant is, to say the truth, only a kind of recitative, interrupted and resumed at will. Its irregular form and its false intonations, speaking according to the rules of musical art, render it untranslatable. But it is none the less a beautiful chant, and so appropriate to the nature of the labor which it accompanies, to the gait of the oxen, to the calmness of those rural scenes, to the simplicity of the men who sing it, that no genius, a stranger to the labors of the soil, could have invented it, and no singer other than a "finished ploughman" of that country could repeat it. At those epochs of the year when there is no other labor and no other movement in the country than that of ploughing, this chant, so simple and so powerful, rises like the voice of a breeze, to which its peculiar toning gives it a kind of resemblance. The final note of each phrase, continued and trilled with an incredible length and power of breath, ascends a quarter of a note with systematic dissonance. This is wild, but the charm of it is invincible, and when you become accustomed to hear it, you cannot conceive how any song could be sung at those hours and in those places without disturbing their harmony.

It was then that, on seeing this beautiful pair, the man and the child, accomplish under such poetical conditions, and with so much gracefulness united with strength, a labor full of grandeur and solemnity, I felt a deep pity mingled with an involuntary respect. "Happy the husbandman!" Yes, doubtless, I should be happy in his place, if my arm, suddenly become strong, and my chest, become powerful, could thus fertilize and sing nature, without my eyes ceasing to see and my brain to comprehend the harmony of colors and of sounds, the fineness of tones, and the gracefulness of outlines—in one word, the mysterious beauty of things! and especially without my heart ceasing to be in relation with the divine feeling which presided over the immortal and sublime creation!

CARL SANDBURG

CARL SANDBURG (American, 1878-   ). The folk singer of America. Of
Swedish immigrant parentage, became a great rover over the U.S. His poems
of the prairies and early days of industrialism are already classics (*Chicago
Poems, Smoke and Steel*). His militant sympathy for working classes dominates
The People, Yes. Most impressive accomplishment: a monumental biography
of Lincoln.

THE PEOPLE, YES

The people will live on.
The learning and blundering people will live on.
They will be tricked and sold and again sold
And go back to the nourishing earth for rootholds,
The people so peculiar in renewal and comeback,
You can't laugh off their capacity to take it.
The mammoth rests between his cyclonic dramas.

The people so often sleepy, weary, enigmatic,
is a vast huddle with many units saying:
"I earn my living.
I make enough to get by
and it takes all my time.
If I had more time
I could do more for myself
and maybe for others.
I could read and study
and talk things over
and find out about things.
It takes time.
I wish I had the time."

The people is a tragic and comic two-face:
hero and hoodlum: phantom and gorilla twisting to moan with a gargoyle mouth: "They
buy and sell me . . . it's game . . .
sometime I'll break loose . . ."

Once having marched
Over the margins of animal necessity,
Over the grim line of sheer subsistence
　　Then man came
To the deeper rituals of his bones,
To the lights lighter than any bones,
To the time for thinking things over,
To the dance, the song, the story,
Or the hours given over to dreaming,
　　Once having so marched.
Between the finite limitations of the five senses
and the endless yearnings of man for the beyond
the people hold to the humdrum bidding of work and food
while reaching out when it comes their way
for lights beyond the prison of the five senses,
for keepsakes lasting beyond any hunger or death.
　　This reaching is alive.
The panderers and liars have violated and smutted it.
　　Yet this reaching is alive yet
　　for lights and keepsakes.

　　　The people know the salt of the sea
　　　and the strength of the winds
　　　lashing the corners of the earth.
　　　The people take the earth
　　　as a tomb of rest and a cradle of hope.
　　　Who else speaks for the Family of Man?
　　　They are in tune and step
　　　with constellations of universal law.

　　The people is a polychrome,
　　a spectrum and a prism
　　held in a moving monolith,
　　a console organ of changing themes,
　　a clavilux of color poems
　　wherein the sea offers fog
　　and the fog moves off in rain
　　and the labrador sunset shortens
　　to a nocturne of clear stars
　　serene over the shot spray
　　of northern lights.

The steel mill sky is alive.
The fire breaks white and zigzag
shot on a gun-metal gloaming.
Man is a long time coming.
    Man will yet win.
Brother may yet line up with brother:

This old anvil laughs at many broken hammers.
    There are men who can't be bought.
    The fireborn are at home in fire.
    The stars make no noise.
    You can't hinder the wind from blowing.
    Time is a great teacher.
    Who can live without hope?

In the darkness with a great bundle of grief
    the people march.
In the night, and overhead a shovel of stars for
    keeps, the people march:
                "Where to? what next?"

GEORGE SANTAYANA

GEORGE SANTAYANA (Spanish-American, 1863-1952). America's philosopher-poet. Though born in Spain, he was educated in Boston and taught at
Harvard for 20-odd years. Primarily a philosopher and aesthetician, he began
by writing verse. Later composed a popular novel: *The Last Puritan.* Most
important philosophic works: *The Life of Reason* and *The Realms of Being.*
Autobiography: *Persons and Places.*

SOLIPSISM

I could believe that I am here alone,
    And all the world my dream;
The passion of the scene is all my own,
    And things that seem but seem.

Perchance an exhalation of my sorrow
    Hath raised this vaporous show,
For whence but from my soul should all things borrow
    So deep a tinge of woe?

I keep the secret doubt within my breast
    To be the gods' defence,
To ease the heart by too much ruth oppressed
    And drive the horror hence.

O sorrow that the patient brute should cower
    And die, not having sinned!
O pity that the wild and fragile flower
    Should shiver in the wind!

Then were I dreaming dreams I know not of,
    For that is part of me
That feels the piercing pang of grief and love
    And doubts eternally.

But whether all to me the vision come
    Or break in many beams,
The pageant ever shifts, and being's sum
    Is but the sum of dreams.

MY HEART REBELS AGAINST MY GENERATION

My heart rebels against my generation,
That talks of freedom and is slave to riches,
And, toiling 'neath each day's ignoble burden,
    Boasts of the morrow.

No space for noonday rest or midnight watches,
No purest joy of breathing under heaven!
Wretched themselves, they heap, to make them happy,
    Many possessions.

But thou, O silent Mother, wise, immortal,
To whom our toil is laughter,—take, divine one,
This vanity away, and to thy lover
    Give what is needful:—

A staunch heart, nobly calm, averse to evil,
The windy sky for breath, the sea, the mountain,
A well-born, gentle friend, his spirit's brother,
    Ever beside him.

What would you gain, ye seekers, with your striving,
Or what vast Babel raise you on your shoulders?
You multiply distress, and your children
    Surely will curse you.

O leave them rather friendlier gods, and fairer
Orchards and temples, and a freer bosom!
What better comfort have we, or what other
    Profit in living,

Than to feed, sobered by the truth of Nature,
Awhile upon her bounty and her beauty,
And hand her torch of gladness to the ages
    Following after?

She hath not made us, like her other children,
Merely for peopling of her spacious kingdoms,
Beasts of the wild, or insects of the summer,
    Breeding and dying,

But also that we might, half knowing, worship
The deathless beauty of her guiding vision,
And learn to love, in all things mortal, only
    What is eternal.

I WOULD I MIGHT FORGET THAT I AM I

I would I might forget that I am I,
And break the heavy chain that binds me fast,
Whose links about myself my deeds have cast.
What in the body's tomb doth buried lie
Is boundless; 'tis the spirit of the sky,
Lord of the future, guardian of the past,
And soon must forth, to know his own at last.
In his large life to live, I fain would die.
Happy the dumb beast, hungering for food,
But calling not his suffering his own;
Blessed the angel, gazing on all good,
But knowing not he sits upon a throne;
Wretched the mortal, pondering his mood,
And doomed to know his aching heart alone.

AS IN THE MIDST OF BATTLE THERE IS ROOM

As in the midst of battle there is room
For thoughts of love, and in foul sin for mirth;
As gossips whisper of a trinket's worth
Spied by the death-bed's flickering candle-gloom;
As in the crevices of Cæsar's tomb
The sweet herbs flourish on a little earth:
So in this great disaster of our birth
We can be happy, and forget our doom.
For morning, with a ray of tendered joy
Gilding the iron heaven, hides the truth,
And evening gently woos us to employ
Our grief in idle catches. Such is youth;
Till from that summer's trance we wake, to find
Despair before us, vanity behind.

SAPPHO

SAPPHO (Greek, *ca.* 650 B.C.). Historiographically maligned gentle poetess
of ancient Greece. Born on the island of Lesbos of noble family. Headed band
of feminine worshipers of Aphrodite. Her simple emotional style has been
imitated for centuries.

HYMN TO APHRODITE
(*Translation by Henry T. Wharton*)

Immortal Aphrodite of the broidered throne (*Poikilóthron,* sometimes printed *Poikilóphron,* various-minded), daughter of Zeus,
weaver of wiles, I pray thee break not my spirit with anguish and
distress, O Queen. But come hither, if ever before thou didst hear
my voice afar and listen, and, leaving thy father's golden house,
camest with chariot yoked, and fair, fleet sparrows drew thee, flapping fast their wings around the dark earth, from heaven through
mid sky. Quickly arrived they; and thou, blessed one, smiling with
immortal countenance, didst ask, What now is befallen me, and
why now I call, and what I in my weak heart most desire to see?
"What beauty now wouldst thou draw to love thee? Who wrongs

1066

thee, Sappho? For even if she flies, she shall soon follow; and if she rejects gifts, shall yet live; if she loves not, shall soon love, however loth." Come, I pray thee, now too, and release me from cruel cares; and all that my heart desires to accomplish, accomplish thou, and be thyself my ally.

(Translation of J. H. Merivale)

Immortal Venus, throned above
In radiant beauty, child of Jove,
O skilled in every art of love
     And artful snare;
Dread power, to whom I bend the knee,
Release my soul and set it free
From bonds of piercing agony
     And gloomy care.
Yet come thyself, if e'er, benign,
Thy listening ears thou didst incline
To my rude lay, the starry shine
     Of Jove's court leaving.
In chariot yoked with coursers fair,
Thine own immortal birds, that bear
Thee swift to earth, the middle air
     With bright wings cleaving.
Soon they were sped—and thou, most blest,
In thine own smiles ambrosial dressed,
Didst ask what griefs my mind oppressed—
     What meant my song—
What end my frenzied thoughts pursue—
For what loved youth I spread anew
My amorous nets—"Who, Sappho, who
     Hath done thee wrong?
What though he fly, he'll soon return;
Still press thy gifts, though now he spurn;
Heed not his coldness—soon he'll burn,
     E'en though thou chide."
And saidst thou this, dread goddess? Oh,
Come then once more to ease my woe;
Grant all, and thy great self bestow,
     My shield and guide!

1067

Glittering-throned, undying Aphrodite,
Wile-weaving daughter of high Zeus, I pray thee,
Tame not my soul with heavy woe, dread mistress,
      Nay, nor with anguish!
But hither come, if ever erst of old time
Thou didst incline, and listenedst to my crying,
And from thy father's palace down descending,
      Camest with golden
Chariot yoked: the fair swift-flying sparrows
Over dark earth with multitudinous fluttering,
Pinion on pinion, through middle ether
      Down from heaven hurried.
Quickly they came like light, and thou, blest lady,
Smiling with clear undying eyes didst ask me
What was the woe that troubled me, and wherefore
      I had cried to thee:
What thing I longed for to appease my frantic
Soul; and whom now must I persuade, thou askedst,
Whom must entangle to thy love, and who now,
      Sappho, hath wronged thee?
Yea, for if now he shun, he soon shall chase thee;
Yea, if he take not gifts he soon shall give them;
Yea, if he love not, soon shall he begin to
      Love thee, unwilling.
Come to me now too, and from tyrannous sorrow
Free me, and all things that my soul desires to
Have done, do for me, queen, and let thyself too
      Be my great ally!

(Translation of Francis T. Palgrave)

Golden-throned beyond the sky,
Jove-born immortality:
Hear and heal a suppliant's pain;
Let not love be love in vain!

Come, as once to Love's imploring
Accents of a maid's adoring,

Wafted 'neath the golden dome,
Bore thee from thy father's home;

When far off thy coming glowed,
Whirling down th' ethereal road,
On thy dove-drawn progress glancing,
'Mid the light of wings advancing;

And at once the radiant hue
Of immortal smiles I knew;
Heard the voice of reassurance
Ask the tale of love's endurance:

Why such prayer? And who for thee,
Sappho, should be touched by me;
Passion-charmed in frenzy strong,
Who hath wrought my Sappho wrong?

"Soon for flight pursuit wilt find
Proffered gifts for gifts declined;
Soon, through long resistance earned,
Love refused be love returned."

To thy suppliant so returning,
Consummate a maiden's yearning,
Love, from deep despair set free,
Championing to Victory!

JEAN-PAUL SARTRE

JEAN-PAUL SARTRE (French, 1905-   ). The philosopher of postwar opportunism. Leader of French School of Existentialism, and author of its bible: *L'Être et le Néant*. Active during war in the Resistance, afterward editor of his own journal. Successful plays: *Les Mouches, Huis-Clos, Les Mains Sales*. Widely known novel: 4-volume *Les Chemins de la Liberté*.

THE WALL

THEY pushed us into a big white room and I began to blink because the light hurt my eyes. Then I saw a table and four men behind the table, civilians, looking over the papers. They had bunched another group of prisoners in the back and we had to cross the whole room to join them. There were several I knew and some others who must have been foreigners. The two in front of me were blond with round skulls; they looked alike. I supposed they were French. The smaller one kept hitching up his pants; nerves.

It lasted about three hours; I was dizzy and my head was empty; but the room was well heated and I found that pleasant enough: for the past 24 hours we hadn't stopped shivering. The guards brought the prisoners up to the table, one after the other. The four men asked each one his name and occupation. Most of the time they didn't go any further—or they would simply ask a question here and there: "Did you have anything to do with the sabotage of munitions?" Or "Where were you the morning of the 9th and what were you doing?" They didn't listen to the answers or at least didn't seem to. They were quiet for a moment and then looking straight in front of them began to write.

It was my turn.

"Your name is Pablo Ibbieta?"

"Yes."

The man looked at the papers and asked me, "Where's Ramon Gris?"

"I don't know."

"You hid him in your house from the 6th to the 19th."

"No."

They wrote for a minute and then the guards took me out. In the corridor Tom and Juan were waiting between two guards. We started walking. Tom asked one of the guards, "So?"

"So what?" the guard said.

"Was that the cross-examination or the sentence?"

"Sentence," the guard said.

"What are they going to do with us?"

The guard answered dryly. "Sentence will be read in your cell."

As a matter of fact, our cell was one of the hospital cellars. It was terrifically cold there because of these drafts. We shivered all night and it wasn't much better during the day.

There was a bench in the cellar and four mats. When they took us back we sat and waited in silence. After a long moment, Tom said, "We're screwed."

"I think so too," I said, "but I don't think they'll do anything to the kid."

"They don't have a thing against him," said Tom. "He's the brother of a militiaman and that's all."

Around eight o'clock in the evening a major came in with two *falangistas*. He had a sheet of paper in his hand. He asked the guard, "What are the names of those three?"

"Steinbock, Ibbieta and Mirbal," the guard said.

The major put on his eyeglasses and scanned the list: "Steinbock ... Steinbock ... Oh yes ... You are sentenced to death. You will be shot tomorrow morning." He went on looking. "The other two as well."

"That's not possible," Juan said. "Not me."

The major looked at him amazed. "What's your name?"

"Juan Mirbal," he said.

"Well, your name is there," said the major. "You're sentenced."

"I didn't do anything," Juan said.

The major shrugged his shoulders. "A Belgian doctor is coming shortly. He is authorized to spend the night with you." He made a military salute and left.

"What did I tell you," Tom said. "We get it."

"Yes," I said, "it's a rotten deal for the kid."

I said that to be decent but I didn't like the kid. His face was too thin and fear and suffering had disfigured it, twisting all his features. Three days before he was a smart sort of kid, not too bad; but now he looked like an old fairy and I thought how he'd never be young again, even if they were to let him go. It wouldn't have been too hard to have a little pity for him but pity disgusts me, or rather it horrifies me.

It was almost dark, a dim glow filtered through the airholes and the pile of coal and made a big stain beneath the spot of sky; I could already see a star through the hole in the ceiling: the night would be pure and icy.

The door opened and two guards came in, followed by a blond man in a tan uniform. He saluted us. "I am the doctor," he said. "I have authorization to help you in these trying hours."

He had an agreeable and distinguished voice. I said, "What do you want here?"

"I am at your disposal. I shall do all I can to make your last moments less difficult."

"What did you come here for? You aren't here on an errand of mercy. Besides, I know you. I saw you with the fascists in the barracks yard the day I was arrested."

I was going to continue, but something surprising suddenly happened to me; the presence of this doctor no longer interested me. Generally when I'm on somebody I don't let go. But the desire to talk left me completely; I shrugged and turned my eyes away. A little later I raised my head; he was watching me curiously. The guards were sitting on a mat. Pedro, the tall thin one, was twiddling his thumbs, the other shook his head from time to time to keep from falling asleep.

I looked at my two friends. Tom had hidden his face in his hands. I could only see the fat white nape of his neck. Little Juan was the worst, his mouth was open and his nostrils trembled. The doctor went to him and put his hand on his shoulder to comfort him: but his eyes stayed cold. Then I saw the Belgian's hand drop stealthily along Juan's arm, down to the wrist. Juan paid no attention. The Belgian took his wrist between three fingers, distractedly, the same time drawing back a little and turning his back to me. But I leaned backward and saw him take a watch from his pocket and look at it for a moment, never letting go of the wrist. After a minute he let the hand fall inert and went and leaned his back against the wall, then, as if he suddenly remembered something very important which had to be jotted down on the spot, he took a notebook from his pocket and wrote a few lines. "Bastard," I thought angrily, "let him come and take my pulse. I'll shove my fist in his rotten face."

He didn't come but I felt him watching me. I raised my head and returned his look. Impersonally, he said to me, "Doesn't it seem cold to you here?" He looked cold, he was blue.

"I'm not cold," I told him.

He never took his hard eyes off me. Suddenly I understood and my hands went to my face: I was drenched in sweat. In this cellar, in the midst of winter, in the midst of drafts, I was sweating. I ran my hands through my hair, gummed together with perspiration; at the same time I saw my shirt was damp and sticking to my skin: I had been dripping for an hour and hadn't felt it. But that swine of a Belgian hadn't missed a thing; he had seen the drops rolling down my cheeks and thought: this is the manifestation of an almost pathological state of terror; and he had felt normal and proud of being alive because he was cold. I wanted to stand up and smash his face but no sooner had I made the slightest gesture than my rage and shame were wiped out; I fell back on the bench with indifference.

Suddenly Juan spoke. "You're a doctor?"

"Yes," the Belgian said.

"Does it hurt ... very long?"

"Huh? When ...? Oh, no," the Belgian said paternally. "Not at all. It's over quickly." He acted as though he were calming a cash customer.

"But I ... they told me ... sometimes they had to fire twice."

"Sometimes," the Belgian said, nodding. "It may happen that the first volley reaches no vital organs."

"Then they had to reload their rifles and aim all over again?" He thought for a moment and then added hoarsely, "That takes time!"

He had a terrible fear of suffering, it was all he thought about: it was his age. I never thought much about it and it wasn't fear of suffering that made me sweat.

Tom began speaking in a low voice. He had to talk, without that he wouldn't have been able to recognize himself in his own mind.

"Do you understand?" he said. " I don't understand."

I began to speak in a low voice too. I watched the Belgian. "Why? What's the matter?"

"Something is going to happen to us that I can't understand."

There was a strange smell about Tom. It seemed to me I was more sensitive than usual to odors. I grinned. "You'll understand in a while."

"It isn't clear," he said obstinately. "I want to be brave but first I have to know ... Listen, they're going to take us into the courtyard. Good. They're going to stand up in front of us. How many?"

"I don't know. Five or eight. Not more."

"All right. There'll be eight. Someone'll holler 'aim!' and I'll see eight rifles looking at me. I'll think how I'd like to get inside the wall, I'll push against it with my back ... with every ounce of strength I have, but the wall will stay, like in a nightmare. I can imagine all that. If you only knew how well I can imagine it."

"All right, all right!" I said, "I can imagine it too."

"It must hurt like hell. You know, they aim at the eyes and the mouth to disfigure you," he added mechanically. "I can feel the wounds already; I've had pains in my head and in my neck for the past hour. Not real pains. Worse. This is what I'm going to feel tomorrow morning. And then what?"

I well understood what he meant but I didn't want to act as if I did. I had pains too, pains in my body like a crowd of tiny scars. I couldn't get used to it. But I was like him, I attached no importance to it. "After," I said, "you'll be pushing up daisies."

He kept on chewing his words, with something like distraction.

1073

He certainly talked to keep himself from thinking. Naturally, I agreed with him, I could have said everything he said: it isn't *natural* to die. And since I was going to die, nothing seemed natural to me. Only it didn't please me to think the same things as Tom. And I knew that, all through the night, every five minutes, we would keep on thinking things at the same time. I looked at him sideways and for the first time he seemed strange to me: he wore death on his face. My pride was wounded: for the past 24 hours I had lived next to Tom, I had listened to him, I had spoken to him and I knew we had nothing in common. And now we looked as much alike as twin brothers, simply because we were going to die together. Tom took my hand without looking at me . . .

I felt relaxed and over-excited at the same time. I didn't want to think any more about what would happen at dawn, at death. It made no sense. I only found words or emptiness. But as soon as I tried to think of anything else I saw rifle barrels pointing at me. Perhaps I lived through my execution twenty times; once I even thought it was for good: I must have slept a minute. They were dragging me to the wall and I was struggling; I was asking for mercy. If I had wanted to, I think I could have slept a while; I had been awake for 48 hours. I was at the end of my rope. But I didn't want to lose two hours of life: they would come to wake me up at dawn, I would follow them, stupefied with sleep and I would have croaked without so much as an "Oof!"; I didn't want that, I didn't want to die like an animal, I wanted to understand. Then I was afraid of having nightmares. I got up, walked back and forth, and, to change my ideas, I began to think about my past life. A crowd of memories came back to me pell-mell. There were good and bad ones—or at least I called them that *before*. There were faces and incidents. I saw the face of a little *novillero* who was gored in Valencia during the *Feria*, the face of one of my uncles, the face of Ramon Gris. I remembered my whole life: how I was out of work for three months in 1926, how I almost starved to death. I remembered a night I spent on a bench in Granada: I hadn't eaten for three days. I was angry, I didn't want to die. That made me smile. How madly I ran after happiness, after women, after liberty. Why? I wanted to free Spain, I admired Pi y Margall, I joined the anarchist movement, I spoke in public meetings: I took everything as seriously as if I were immortal.

At that moment I felt that I had my whole life in front of me and I thought, "It's a damned lie." It was worth nothing because it was finished. I wondered how I'd been able to walk, to laugh with the girls: I wouldn't have moved so much as my little finger if I had only imagined I would die like this. My life was in front of me, shut, closed, like a bag and yet everything inside of it was unfinished. For an instant I tried to judge it. I wanted to tell myself, this is a beautiful life. But I couldn't pass judgment on it; it was only a sketch; I had spent my time counterfeiting eternity, I had understood nothing. I missed nothing: there were so many things I could have missed, the taste of *manzanilla* or the baths I took in summer in a little creek near Cadiz; but death had disenchanted everything.

In the state I was in, if somebody had come and told me I could go home quietly, that they would leave me my life whole, it would have left me cold: several hours or several years of waiting is all the same when you have lost the illusion of being eternal. I clung to nothing, in a way I was calm. But it was a horrible calm—because of my body; my body, I saw with its eyes, I heard with its ears, but it was no longer me; it sweated and trembled by itself and I didn't recognize it any more. I had to touch it and look at it to find out what was happening, as if it were the body of someone else. At times I could still feel it, I felt sinkings, and fallings, as when you're in a plane taking a nosedive, or I felt my heart beating. But that didn't reassure me. Everything that came from my body was all cockeyed. Most of the time it was quiet and I felt no more than a sort of weight, a filthy presence against me; I had the impression of being tied to an enormous vermin.

The Belgian took out his watch, looked at it. He said, "It is three-thirty."

Bastard! He must have done it on purpose. Tom jumped; we hadn't noticed time was running out; night surrounded us like a shapeless, somber mass, I couldn't even remember that it had begun.

Little Juan began to cry. He wrung his hands, pleaded, "I don't want to die. I don't want to die."

He ran across the whole cellar waving his arms in the air then fell sobbing on one of the mats. He wept: I could clearly see he was pitying himself; he wasn't thinking about death. For one second, one single second, I wanted to weep myself, to weep with pity for myself. But the opposite happened: I glanced at the kid, I saw his thin sobbing shoulders and I felt inhuman: I could pity neither the others nor myself. I said to myself, "I want to die cleanly."

Tom had gotten up, he placed himself just under the round opening and began to watch for daylight. I was determined to die cleanly and I only thought of that. But ever since the doctor told us the time, I felt time flying, flowing away drop by drop.

It was still dark when I heard Tom's voice: "Do you hear them?" Men were marching in the courtyard.

"Yes."

"What the hell are they doing? They can't shoot in the dark."

After a while we heard no more. I said to Tom, "It's day."

Pedro got up, yawning, and came to blow out the lamp. He said to his buddy, "Cold as hell."

The cellar was all grey. We heard shots in the distance.

"It's starting," I told Tom. "They must do it in the court in the rear."

Tom asked the doctor for a cigarette. I didn't want one; I didn't want cigarettes or alcohol. From that moment on they didn't stop firing.

"Do you realize what's happening," Tom said.

He wanted to add something but kept quiet, watching the door. The door opened and a lieutenant came in with four soldiers. Tom dropped his cigarette.

"Steinbock?"

Tom didn't answer. Pedro pointed him out.

"Juan Mirbal?"

"On the mat."

"Get up," the lieutenant said.

Juan did not move. Two soldiers took him under the arms and set him on his feet. But he fell as soon as they released him.

The soldiers hesitated.

"He's not the first sick one," said the lieutenant. "You two carry him; they'll fix it up down there."

He turned to Tom. "Let's go."

Tom went out between two soldiers. Two others followed, carrying the kid by the armpits. He hadn't fainted; his eyes were wide open and tears ran down his cheeks. When I wanted to go out the lieutenant stopped me.

"You Ibbieta?"

"Yes."

"You wait here; they'll come for you later."

They left. The Belgian and the two jailers left too, I was alone. I did not understand what was happening to me but I would have liked it better if they had gotten it over with right away. I heard shots at almost regular intervals; I shook with each one of them. I wanted to scream and tear out my hair. But I gritted my teeth and pushed my hands in my pockets because I wanted to stay clean.

After an hour they came to get me and led me to the first floor, to a small room that smelt of cigars and where the heat was stifling. There were two officers sitting smoking in the armchairs, papers on their knees.

"You're Ibbieta?"

"Yes."

"Where is Ramon Gris?"

"I don't know."

The one questioning me was short and fat. His eyes were hard behind his glasses. He said to me, "Come here."

I went to him. He got up and took my arms, staring at me with a look that should have pushed me into the earth. At the same time he pinched my biceps with all his might. It wasn't to hurt me, it was only a game: he wanted to dominate me. He also thought he had to blow his stinking breath square in my face. We stayed for a moment like that, and I almost felt like laughing. It takes a lot to intimidate a man who is going to die; it didn't work. He pushed me back violently and sat down again. He said, "It's his life against yours. You can have yours if you tell us where he is."

These men dolled up with their riding crops and boots were still going to die. A little later than I, but not too much. They busied themselves looking for names in their crumpled papers, they ran after other men to imprison or suppress them; they had opinions on the future of Spain and on other subjects. Their little activities seemed shocking and burlesqued to me; I couldn't put myself in their place, I thought they were insane. The little man was still looking at me, whipping his boots with the riding crop. All his gestures were calculated to give him the look of a live and ferocious beast.

"So? You understand?"

"I don't know where Gris is," I answered. "I thought he was in Madrid."

The other officer raised his pale hand indolently. This indolence was also calculated. I saw through all their little schemes and I was stupefied to find there were men who amused themselves that way.

"You have a quarter of an hour to think it over," he said slowly.

"Take him to the laundry, bring him back in fifteen minutes. If he still refuses he will be executed on the spot."

They knew what they were doing: I had passed the night in waiting; then they had made me wait an hour in the cellar while they shot Tom and Juan and now they were locking me up in the laundry; they must have prepared their game the night before. They told themselves that nerves eventually wear out and they hoped to get me that way.

They were badly mistaken. In the laundry I sat on a stool because I felt very weak and I began to think. But not about their proposition. Of course I knew where Gris was; he was hiding with his cousins, four kilometers from the city. I also knew that I would not reveal his hiding place unless they tortured me (but they didn't seem to be thinking about that). All that was perfectly regulated, definite and in no way interested me. Only I would have liked to understand the reasons for my conduct. I would rather die than give up Gris. Why? I didn't like Ramon Gris any more. My friendship for him had died a little while before dawn at the same time as my desire to live. Undoubtedly I thought highly of him: he was tough. But it was not for this reason that I consented to die in his place; his life had no more value than mine; no life had value. They were going to slap a man up against a wall and shoot at him t'll he died, whether it was I or Gris or somebody else made no difference. I knew he was more useful than I to the cause of Spain but I thought to hell with Spain and anarchy; nothing was important. Yet I was there, I could save my skin and give up Gris and I refused to do it. I found that somehow comic; it was obstinacy. I thought, "I must be stubborn!" And a droll sort of gaiety spread over me.

They came for me and brought me back to the two officers. A rat ran out from under my feet and that amused me. I turned to one of the *falangistas* and said, "Did you see the rat?"

He didn't answer. He was very sober, he took himself seriously. I wanted to laugh but I held myself back because I was afraid that once I got started I wouldn't be able to stop.

"Well," said the fat officer, "have you thought about it?"

I looked at them with curiosity, as insects of a very rare species. I told them, "I know where he is. He is hidden in the cemetery. In a vault or in the gravediggers' shack."

It was a farce. I wanted to see them stand up, buckle their belts and give orders busily.

1078

They jumped to their feet. "Let's go. Molés, go get fifteen men from Lieutenant Lopez. You," the fat man said, "I'll let you off if you're telling the truth, but it'll cost you plenty if you're making monkeys out of us."

They left in a great clatter and I waited peacefully under the guard of *falangistas*. From time to time I smiled, thinking about the spectacle they would make. I felt stunned and malicious. I imagined them lifting up tombstones, opening the doors of the vaults one by one. I represented this situation to myself as if I had been someone else: this prisoner obstinately playing the hero, these grim *falangistas* with their moustaches and their men in uniform running among the graves; it was irresistibly funny. After half an hour the little fat man came back alone. I thought he had come to give the orders to execute me. The others must have stayed in the cemetery.

The officer looked at me. He didn't look at all sheepish. "Take him into the big courtyard with the others," he said. "After the military operations a regular court will decide what happens to him."

"Then they're not . . . not going to shoot me? . . ."

"Not now, anyway. What happens afterwards is none of my business."

I still didn't understand. I asked, "But why . . . ?"

He shrugged his shoulders without answering and the soldiers took me away. In the big courtyard there were about a hundred prisoners, women, children and a few old men. I began walking around the central grass-plot, I was stupefied. At noon they let us eat in the mess hall. Two or three people questioned me. I must have known them, but I didn't answer: I didn't even know where I was.

Around evening they pushed about ten new prisoners into the court. I recognized Garcia, the baker. He said, "What damned luck you have! I didn't think I'd see you alive."

"They sentenced me to death," I said, "and then they changed their minds. I don't know why."

"They arrested me at two o'clock," Garcia said.

"Why?" Garcia had nothing to do with politics.

"I don't know," he said. "They arrest everybody who doesn't think the way they do. He lowered his voice. "They got Gris."

I began to tremble. "When?"

"This morning. He messed it up. He left his cousin's on Tuesday because they had an argument. There were plenty of people to

1079

hide him but he didn't want to owe anything to anybody. He said,
'I'd go and hide in Ibbieta's place, but they got him, so I'll go hide
in the cemetery.' "

"In the cemetery?"

"Yes. What a fool. Of course they went by there this morning,
that was sure to happen. They found him in the gravediggers' shack.
He shot at them and they got him."

"In the cemetery!"

Everything began to spin and I found myself sitting on the
ground: I laughed so hard I cried.

FRIEDRICH VON SCHILLER

FRIEDRICH VON SCHILLER (German, 1759-1805). Germany's greatest
dramatist. After years of antagonism, a great friend of Goethe's. His life was
a triumph of creative will over disease. His 9 great plays, technically of the
first order, are deeply imbued with pathos for moral freedom. Prominent among
them: *Don Carlos, Wallenstein's Camp, Mary Stuart, William Tell.*

WILLIAM TELL AND THE TYRANT

Scene—*The hollow way at Küssnacht*

Tell (*among the rocks overhanging the pass*).   Here through the
  hollow way he'll pass; there is
No other road to Küssnacht. Here I'll do it! . . .
The opportunity is good: the bushes
Of alder there will hide me; from that point
My arrow hits him; the strait pass prevents
Pursuit. Now, Gessler, balance thy account
With Heaven! Thou must be gone; thy sand is run! . . .
Remote and harmless I have lived; my bow
Ne'er bent save on the wild beast of the forest;
My thoughts were free of murder. Thou hast scared me
From my peace; to fell asp-poison hast thou
Changed the milk of kindly temper in me;
Thou hast accustomed me to horrors. Gessler!
The archer who could aim at his boy's head
Can send an arrow to his enemy's heart. . . .

1080

Poor little boys! My kind, true wife! I will
Protect them from thee. Viceroy! when I drew
That bowstring and my hand was quivering,
And with devilish joy thou mad'st me point it
At the child, and I in fainting anguish
Entreated thee in vain; then, with a grim,
Irrevocable oath, deep in my soul,
I vowed to God in Heaven that the next aim
I took should be thy heart. The vow I made
In that despairing moment's agony,
Became a holy debt—and I will pay it.

(Various characters gradually appear upon the scene, among
them Stüssi, Frau Armgart, and the members of a wedding procession, who come up the pass; at length Gessler [the Austrian
Landvogt or Viceroy], and Rudolph der Harras approach, riding
up the pass, while Tell disappears among the rocks.)

Gessler. Say what you like, I am the Kaiser's servant,
And must think of pleasing him. He sent me,
Not to caress these hinds, to soothe or nurse them.
Obedience is the word! The point at issue is,
Shall Boor or Kaiser here be lord o' th' lands?
  Armgart. Now is the moment! Now for my petition.
  Gess. This Hat at Altdorf, mark you, I set up,
Not for the joke's sake, or to try the hearts
O' th' people—these I know of old—but that
They might be taught to bend their necks to me,
Which are too straight and stiff; and in the way
Where they are hourly passing I have planted
This offence, so that their eyes may fall on't,
And remind them of their lord, whom they forgot.
  Rudolph. But the people have some rights—
  Gess. Which now
Is not a time for settling or admitting.
Mighty things are on the anvil. The House
Of Hapsburg must wax powerful; what the Father
Gloriously began, the Son must forward.
This people is a stone of stumbling, which
One way or t' other must be put aside.
  Arm. Mercy, gracious Viceroy! Justice! Justice!

Gess.   Why do you plague me here and stop my way
I' th' open road? Off! Let me pass!

Arm.   My husband
Is in prison; these orphans cry for bread.
Have pity, good your grace, have pity on us!

Rud.   Who or what are you, then? Who is your husband?

Arm.   A poor wild-hay-man of the Rigiberg,
Whose trade is, on the brow of the abyss,
To mow the common grass from craggy shelves
And nooks to which the cattle dare not climb.

Rud.   By Heaven, a wild and miserable life!
Do now! do let this poor drudge free, I pray you!—
Whatever be his crime, that horrid trade
Is punishment enough. You shall have justice;
In the castle there make your petition;
This is not the place.

Arm.   No, no! I stir not
From this spot till you give up my husband!
'Tis the sixth month he has lain i' th' dungeon,
Waiting for the sentence of some judge in vain.

Gess.   Woman! Would'st lay thy hands on me? Begone!

Arm.   Justice Viceroy! thou art judge o' th' land here,
I' th' Kaiser's stead and God's. Perform thy duty!
As thou expectest justice from above,
Show it to us.

Gess.   Off! take the mutinous rabble from my sight.

Arm.   No, no! I now have nothing
More to lose. Thou shalt not move a step, Lord,
Till thou hast done me right. Ay, knit thy brows,
And roll thy eyes as sternly as thou wilt;
We are so wretched, wretched now we care not
Aught more for thy anger.

Gess.   Woman, make way!
Or else my horse shall crush thee.

Arm.   Let it! there!
Here am I with my children. Let the orphans
Be trodden underneath thy horse's hoofs!
'Tis not the worst that thou hast done.

Rud.   Woman, art mad?

Arm.   'Tis long that thou has trodden
The Kaiser's people under foot. Too long!

1082

Oh, I am but a woman! Were I a man
I should find something else to do
Than lie here crying in the dust.

    Gess.   Where are my servants?
Quick! take her hence! I may forget myself,
And do the thing I shall repent.

    Rud.   My lord,
The servants cannot pass; the place above
Is crowded with a bridal company.

    Gess.   I've been too mild a ruler to this people;
They are not tamed as they should be; their tongues
Are still at liberty. This shall be altered!
I will break that stubborn humor. Freedom,
With its pert vauntings, shall no more be heard of.
I will enforce a new law in these lands;
There shall not—

    (An arrow pierces him; he presses his hand on his heart, and
slides from his horse into the arms of Rudolph, who has dismounted.)

    Rud.   Lord Viceroy—God! What is it? whence came it?

    Gess.   'Tis Tell's arrow.

    Tell (*from a rock above*).   Thou hast found the archer;
Seek no other. Free are the cottages,
Secure is innocence from thee; thou wilt
Torment the land no more.

ARTHUR SCHNITZLER

ARTHUR SCHNITZLER (Austrian, 1862-1931). Impressionist playwright and
novelist. Physician and literary interpreter of Vienna's *"belle epoche."* His
sophisticated, pessimistic plays have been accused of immorality and decadence, but they brilliantly preserve the flavor of an era. Among them: *Anatol,
Reigen, Professor Bernhardi.*

FLOWERS

I WANDERED about the streets the whole afternoon, while the snow
fell slowly, in large flakes—and now I am at home, my lamp is
burning, my cigar is lighted and my books lie close by; in fact, I
have everything that affords true comfort. Yet all is in vain; I can
think of but one thing.

But had she not been dead for a long time as far as I was concerned?—yes, dead; or, as I thought with the childish pathos of the deceived, "worse than dead?" And now that I know that she is not "worse than dead," but simply dead, like the many others who lie out there, under the ground, forever—in spring, in the hot summer, and when the snow falls, as today—without any hope of ever returning—since that time I know that she did not die a moment sooner for me than she did for the rest of the world. Sorrow?—no. It is only the general horror that we all feel when something that once belonged to us, and whose entire being is still clear in our minds, sinks into the grave.

It was very sad when I discovered that she was deceiving me; —but there was so much else with it!—the fury and sudden hatred, and the horror of existence, and—ah, yes—the wounded vanity; —the sorrow only came later! But then there was the consolation that she also must be suffering.—I have them all yet, I can reread them at any time, those dozens of letters which sob, pray, and beseech forgiveness!—And I can still see her before me, in her dark dress and small straw hat, standing at the street corner in the twilight as I stepped out of the gate—looking after me.—And I still think of the last meeting when she stood in front of me with her large, beautiful eyes, set in that round, childlike face that now had become pale and wan.—I did not give her my hand when she left me;—when she left me for the last time.—And I watched her go down the street from my window and then she disappeared —forever. Now she can never return. . . .

My knowing it at all is due to an accident. I could have been unaware of it for weeks and months. I happened to meet her uncle one morning. I had not seen him for at least a year, as he does not come to Vienna very often. In fact, I had only met him two or three times before this. Our first meeting was three years ago at a bowling party. She and her mother were there also.—And then the following summer: I was in the Prater with a few friends. Her uncle was sitting at the next table with some gentlemen. They were all gay, and he drank to my health. And before he left he came up to me and told me confidentially that his niece was madly in love with me!—And in my half-giddiness it seemed very foolish and queer that the old gentleman should tell such a thing here, midst the music of the cymbals and violins—to me, who knew it so well, and on whose lips still clung the impression of her last kiss. And now, this morning! I almost walked past him. I asked for his niece, more out of politeness than interest. I knew nothing more about her; her letters had stopped coming a long time ago; only flowers she sent me, regularly. Recollections of our happiest days! Once a month they came; no card: just silent, humble flowers.—And when I asked the old gentleman he was all astonishment. "You don't know that the poor girl died a week ago?" It was a terrible shock! —Then he told me more. And her illness? "Melancholia—anæmia. —The doctors themselves were not quite sure."

I remained a long while on the spot where the old gentleman had left me;—I was enervated, as if I had just gone through some great trouble.—And now it seems to me as if today marks the termination of a part of my life. Why—why? It was simply something external. I had no more feeling for her; in fact, I seldom thought of her any more. But now that I have written this all down I feel better; I am more composed—I am beginning to appreciate the coziness of my home.—It is foolish and tormenting to think of it any more.—There are certainly others today who have a great deal more to mourn about than I.

I have taken a walk. It is a serene winter's day. The sky looks so grey, so cold, so far away.—And I am very calm. The old gentleman whom I met yesterday—it seems as if it had been weeks ago. And when I think of her I can see her in a peculiarly sharp and finished outline; only one thing is lacking: the anger which always associated itself with my thoughts of her. The real appreciation that she is no more on earth, that she is lying in a coffin, that she has been buried, I have not—I feel no sorrow. The world seemed calmer to me today. I once knew for just one moment that there is neither happiness nor sorrow; no, there are only the grimaces of joy and sadness; we laugh and we weep and we invite our soul to be present. I could sit down now and read deep, serious books, and should soon be able to penetrate into all of their learning. Or, I could stand in front of old pictures, which heretofore have meant nothing to me, and now appreciate their true beauty.—And when I think of certain dear friends who have died, my heart does not feel as sad as it used to—death has become something friendly; it stalks among us but does not want to harm us.

Snow, high, white snow on all the streets. Little Gretel came to me and suggested that we ought to take a sleigh ride. And we drove out into the country, over the smooth road, the sleigh bells ringing and the blue-grey sky above us. Gretel rested against my shoulder and looked out upon the long road with happy eyes. We came to an inn that we knew well from the summer. The oven was all aglow, and it was so hot that we had to move the table away, as Gretel's left ear and cheek became fire red. I had to kiss the paler cheek. Afterwards, the return home in the twilight! Gretel sat very close to me and held both of my hands in hers.—Then she said: "At last I have you again." She had thus, without racking her brain, struck the right note to make me happy. But perhaps it was the biting clear air that unchained my thoughts, for I feel freer and more contented than I have in the last few days.

A short while ago again, as I lay dozing on my couch, a strange thought came to my mind. I appeared hard and cold to myself. As one who, without tears, in fact, without any emotion, stands at the grave in which he has buried a dear one. As one who has grown so hard that he cannot reconcile the horror of death.—Yes, irreconcilable, that is it.

Gone, quite gone! Life, happiness, and a little love drives all that foolishness away. I go again among people. I like them; they are harmless, they chatter about all sorts of jolly things. And Gretel is a dear, kind creature; and she is prettiest when she stands at my window and the sunbeams shine on her golden hair.

Something strange happened today.—It is the day on which she always sent me flowers. And the flowers came again as—as if nothing had changed. They came with the first mail, in a long, narrow white box. It was quite early, and I was still sleepy. And only when I was actually opening the box did I gain full consciousness. Then I almost had a shock. And there lay, daintily tied with a golden string, violets and pinks.—They lay as in a coffin. And as I took the flowers in my hand a shudder went through my heart. —But I understand how it is that they came again today. When she felt her illness, perchance even when she felt death approaching, she gave her usual order to the florist so that I would not miss her attention. Certainly, that is the explanation; as something quite natural, as something touching perhaps.—And still as I held them in my hands, these flowers, and they seemed to nod and tremble, then, in spite of reason and will power, I looked upon them as something ghostly, as if they had come from her, as if they were her greeting—as if she wanted always, even now that she was dead, to tell me of her love—of her tardy faithfulness. Ah, we do not understand death, we will never understand it; and a person is dead only after all that have known him have also passed away. To-day I grasped the flowers differently than usual, as if I might injure them were I to hold them too tight—as if their souls might begin to sob softly. And as they now stand in front of me on my desk, in a narrow, light-green vase, they seem to nod their heads in mournful gratitude. The full pain of a useless yearning spreads over me from them, and I believe that they could tell me something if we could only understand the language of *all* living things—not only of the things that talk.

I do not want to let myself be fooled. They are only flowers. They are a message from the past. They are no call, surely no call from the grave. They are simply flowers, and some florist tied them together mechanically, put a bit of cotton around them, then laid them in the white box, and mailed it.—And now that they are here, why do I think about them?

I spend many hours in the open air and take long, lonely walks. When I am among people I do not feel compatible with them. And I noticed it when the sweet, blonde girl sits in my room, chattering away about all sorts of things—I don't know about what. When she is gone, in a moment it is as if she were miles away from me, as if the flood of people had engulfed her and left no traces behind. I should hardly be surprised if she did not come again.

The flowers are in the tall, green vase; their stems are in the water and their scent fills the room. They still retain their odour —in spite of the fact that I have had them a week and that they are already fading. And I believe all sorts of nonsense that I used to laugh at: I believe in the possibility of conversing with things in nature—I believe that one can communicate with clouds and springs; and I am waiting for these flowers to begin to talk. But no, I feel sure that they are always speaking—even now—they are forever crying out; and I can almost understand them.

How glad I am that the winter is over! Already the breath of spring throbs in the air. I am not living any differently than before, still I sometimes feel as if the boundaries of my existence are expanding. Yesterday seems far off, and the happenings of a few days past are like vague dreams. It is still the same when Gretel leaves me, especially when I have not seen her for several days; then our friendship appears like an affair of the past ages. She always comes, from afar, from so far away!—But when she begins to chatter it is like olden times again, and I then have a clear consciousness of the present. And then her words are almost too loud and the colours seem too harsh. Yet as soon as she leaves me all is gone; there are no after-pictures or gradual, fading recollections.—And then I am alone with my flowers. They are now quite faded, quite faded. They have no more perfume. Gretel had not noticed them at all; but today she saw them and it seemed as if she wanted to question me, but then she suddenly appeared to have a secret horror for them;—she stopped speaking altogether and soon left me.

The petals are slowly falling off. I never touch them; anyway, if I did they would crumble. It makes me very sad to see them faded. I do not know why I have not the courage to make an end of all this nonsense. The faded flowers make me ill. I cannot stand them and I rush out. Once in the street, I feel that I have to hurry back to them, to care for them. And then I find them in the same green vase where I left them, tired and sad. Last evening I wept before them, as one weeps at a grave. Yet I never gave a thought to the sender of them. Perhaps I am wrong, yet it seems as if Gretel feels that there is something strange in my room. She does not laugh any more. She does not speak so loud, with that clear, lively voice to which I am accustomed. And I do not receive her as I used to. Then there is the fear that she will question me; and I realise what torture those questions would be.

She frequently brings her sewing, and if I am still at my books she sits quietly at the table and sews or crochets; and she waits patiently until I have finished and put my books away and come up to her and take her sewing out of her hands. Then I remove the green shade from the lamp so that a mellow light floods the room. I do not like dark corners.

Spring! My window is wide open. Late last evening Gretel and I looked out on to the street. The air was warm and balmy. And when I looked at the corner, where the street lamp spreads a weak light, I suddenly saw a shadow. I saw it and I did not—I know that I did not see it—I closed my eyes and I could suddenly see through my eyelids. There stood the miserable creature, in the pale lamp light, and I saw her face very clearly, as if the yellow sunshine were on it, and I saw in the pale, emaciated face those wounded eyes. Then I walked slowly away from the window and sat down at my desk; the candle spluttered in the breeze. And I remained motionless, for I knew that the poor creature was standing at the corner, waiting; and if I had dared to touch the faded flowers I would have taken them out of the vase and brought them to her. Thus I thought, and sincerely thought; yet I knew all the while that it was foolish. Now Gretel also left the window and came over to the back of my chair

1088

where she remained a moment to touch my hair with her lips. Then she went and left me alone.

I stared at the flowers. There are hardly any more. Mostly bare stems, dry and pitiful. They make me ill and drive me mad. And it must be evident; otherwise Gretel would have asked me; but she feels it, too. Now she had fled as if there were ghosts in my room.

Ghosts!—They are, they are!—Dead things playing with life! And if faded flowers smell mouldy it is only the remembrance of the time when they were in bloom. And the dead return as long as we do not forget them. What difference does it make if they cannot speak now;—I hear them! She does not appear any more, yet I can see her! And the spring outside, and the sunshine on my rug. and the perfume of the lilacs in the park, and the people who pass below and do not interest me, are they life? If I pull down the curtains, the sun is dead. I do not care to know about all these people, and they are dead. I close my window, and the perfume of the lilacs is gone and spring is dead. I am more powerful than the sun, the people, and the spring. But more powerful than I is remembrance, for that comes when it wills and from it there is no escape. And these dry stems are more powerful than the perfume of the lilacs and the spring.

I was pondering over these pages when Gretel entered. She had never come so early. I was surprised, astonished. She remained a moment on the threshold, and I gazed at her without greeting her. Then she smiled and approached me. In her hand she carried a bouquet of fresh flowers. Then, without speaking, she laid them on my desk. In the next moment, she seized the withered stems in the green vase. It seemed as if someone had grasped my heart;—but I could not utter a sound. And when I wanted to rise and take her by the arm, she smiled at me. Holding the faded flowers high above her, she hurried to the window and threw them out into the street. I felt I wanted to throw myself after them; but Gretel stood at the sill, facing me. And on her head was the sunshine, the bright sunshine. And the aroma of lilacs came in through the window. And I looked at the empty, green vase on my desk;—I am not sure, yet I think I felt freer,—yes, freer. Then Gretel approached me, picked up her bouquet, and held in front of my face cool, white lilacs. Such a healthy, fresh perfume—so soft, so cool; I wanted to bury my face in them. Laughing, white, beautiful flowers—and I felt that the spectre was gone. Gretel stood behind me and ran her hands through my hair. "You silly boy," she said. Did she know what she had done? I grasped her hands and kissed her.

In the evening we went out into the open, into the spring. We have just returned! I have lighted my candle. We took a long walk, and Gretel is so tired that she has fallen asleep in the chair. She is very beautiful when she smiles thus in her sleep.

Before me, in the narrow, green vase are the lilacs. Down on the street—no, no, they are not there any longer. Already the wind has blown them away with the rest of the dust.

SIR WALTER SCOTT

SIR WALTER SCOTT (Scottish, 1771-1832). Prolific as well as imaginative practitioner of the historical romance and sentimental novel. Based adventure stories on sound research, heavily influencing French and other period novelists. Most famous of these: *Ivanhoe, Quentin Durward, The Talisman.* His long narrative poems still effective: *The Lay of the Last Minstrel, Lady of the Lake.*

THE NUBIAN

RICHARD surveyed the Nubian in silence as he stood before him, his looks bent upon the ground, his arms folded on his bosom, with the appearance of a black marble statue of the most exquisite workmanship waiting life from the touch of a Prometheus. The king of England, who, as it was emphatically said of his successor, Henry the Eighth, loved to look upon a man, was well pleased with the thews, sinews, and symmetry of him whom he now surveyed and questioned him in the lingua Franca, "Art thou a pagan?"

The slave shook his head, and raising his finger to his brow crossed himself in token of his Christianity, then resumed his posture of motionless humility.

"A Nubian Christian, doubtless," said Richard, "and mutilated of the organ of speech by these heathen dogs?"

The mute again slowly shook his head, in token of negative, pointed with his forefinger to heaven, and then laid it upon his own lips.

"I understand thee," said Richard; "thou doest suffer under the infliction of God, not by the cruelty of man. Canst thou clean an armor and belt, and buckle it in time of need?"

The mute nodded, and stepping toward the coat of mail, which hung with the shield and helmet of the chivalrous monarch, upon the pillar of the tent, he handled it with such nicety of address, as sufficiently to show that he fully understood the business of the armor bearer.

"Thou art an apt, and wilt doubtless be a useful, knave. Thou shalt wait in my chamber, and on my person," said the king, "to show how much I value the gift of the royal Soldan. If thou hast no tongue, it follows thou canst carry no tales, neither provoke me to be sudden by an unfit reply."

The Nubian again prostrated himself till his brow touched the earth, then stood erect, at some paces distant, as waiting for his new master's commands.

"Nay, thou shalt commence thy office presently," said Richard, "for I see a speck of rust darkening on that shield; and when I shake it in the face of Saladin, it should be bright and unsullied as the Soldan's honor and mine own."

A horn was winded without, and presently Sir Henry Neville entered with a packet of dispatches. "From England, my lord," he said, as he delivered it. "From England,—our own England" repeated Richard, in a tone of melancholy enthusiasm. "Alas! they little think how hard their sovereign has been beset by sickness and sorrow, faint friends, and forward enemies." Then, opening the dispatches, he said hastily, "Ha! this comes from no peaceful land: they too have their feuds. Neville, begone; I must peruse these tidings alone, and at leisure."

Neville withdrew accordingly, and Richard was soon absorbed in the melancholy details which had been conveyed to him from England, concerning the factions that were tearing to pieces his native dominions,—the disunion of his brothers, John and Geoffrey, and the quarrels of both with the High Justiciary Longchamp, Bishop of Ely; the oppressions practiced by the nobles upon the peasantry, and rebellion of the latter against their masters, which had produced everywhere scenes of discord, and in some instances the effusion of blood. Details of incidents mortifying to his pride, and derogatory from his authority, were intermingled with the earnest advice of his wisest and most attached counselors, that he should presently return to England, as his presence offered the only hope of saving the kingdom from all the horrors of civil discord, of which France and Scotland were likely to avail themselves.

Filled with the most painful anxiety, Richard read, and again read, the ill-omened letters, compared the intelligence with some of them contained with the same facts as differently stated in others, and soon became totally insensible to whatever was passing around him although seated, for the sake of coolness, close to the entrance of his tent, and having the curtains withdrawn, so that he could see and be seen by the guards and others who were stationed without.

Deeper in the shadow of the pavilion, and busied with the task his new master had imposed, sat the Nubian slave, with his back rather turned toward the king. He had finished adjusting the hauberk and brigandine, and was now busily employed on a broad pavise, or buckler, of unusual size, and covered with steel plating, which Richard often used in reconnoitering, or actually storming, fortified places, as a more effectual protection against missile weapons than the narrow triangular shield used on horseback.

This pavise bore neither the royal lions of England, nor any other device, to attract the observation of the defenders of the walls against which it was advanced. The care, therefore, of the armorer was addressed to causing its surface to shine as bright crystal, in which he seemed to be peculiarly successful. Beyond the Nubian, and scarcely visible from without, lay the large dog, which might be termed his brother slave, and which, as if he felt awed by being transferred to a royal owner, was couched close to the side of the mute, with his head and ears on the ground, and his limbs and tail drawn close around and under him.

While the monarch and his new attendant were thus occupied, another actor crept upon the scene, and mingled among the group of English yeomen, about a score of whom, respecting the unusually pensive posture and close occupation of their sovereign, were, contrary to their wont, keeping a silent guard in front of his tent. It was not, however, more vigilant than usual. Some were playing at games of hazard with small pebbles, other spoke together in whispers of the approaching day of battle, and several lay asleep, their bulky limbs folded in their green mantles.

Amid these careless warders glided the puny form of a little old Turk, poorly dressed like a marabout or santon of the desert,—a sort of enthusiast, who sometimes ventured into the camp of the Crusaders, though treated always with contumely, and often with violence. Indeed, the luxury and profligate indulgence of the Christian leaders had occasioned a motley concourse in their tents, of musicians, Jewish merchants, Copts, Turks, and all the varied refuse of the Eastern nations; so that the caftan and turban—though to drive both from the Holy Land was the professed object of the expedition

—were nevertheless neither an uncommon nor an alarming sight in the camp of the Crusaders. When, however, the little insignificant figure we have described approached so nigh as to receive some interruption from the warders, he dashed his dusky green turban from his head, showed that his beard and eyebrows were shaved like those of a professed buffoon, and that the expression of his fantastic and writhen features, as well as of his little black eyes, which glittered like jet, was that of a crazed imagination.

"Dance, marabout," cried the soldiers, acquainted with the manners of these wandering enthusiasts,—"dance, or we will scourge thee with our bowstrings, till thou spin as never top did under schoolboy's lash." Thus shouted the reckless warders, as much delighted at having a subject to tease as a child when he catches a butterfly, or a schoolboy upon discovering a bird's nest.

The marabout, as if happy to do their behests, bounded from the earth, and spun his giddy round before them with singular agility, which when contrasted with his slight and wasted figure and diminutive appearance, made him resemble a withered leaf twirled round and round at the pleasure of the winter's breeze. His single lock of hair streamed upwards from his bald and shaven head, as if some genie upheld him by it; and indeed it seemed as if supernatural art were necessary to the execution of the wild whirling dance, in which scarce the tiptoe of the performer was seen to touch the ground.

Amid the vagaries of his performance, he flew here and there, from one spot to another, still approaching, however, though almost imperceptibly, to the entrance of the royal tent; so that, when at length he sunk exhausted on the earth, after two or three bounds still higher than those which he had yet executed, he was not above thirty yards from the king's person.

For the space of a quarter of an hour, or longer, after the incident related, all remained perfectly quiet in the front of the royal habitation. The king read and mused in the entrance of his pavilion; behind, and with his back turned to the same entrance, the Nubian slave still burnished the ample pavise; in front of all, at an hundred paces distant, the yeomen of the guard stood, sat, or lay extended on the grass, attentive to their own sports, but pursuing them in silence; while on the esplanade betwixt them and the front of the tent lay, scarcely to be distinguished from a bundle of rags, the senseless form of the marabout.

But the Nubian had the advantage of a mirror, from the brilliant reflection which the surface of the highly polished shield now afforded, by means of which he beheld, to his alarm and surprise, that the marabout raised his head gently from the ground, so as to survey all around him, moving with a well-adjusted precaution, which seemed entirely inconsistent with a state of inebriety. He couched his head instantly, as if satisfied he was unobserved, and began, with the slightest possible appearance of voluntary effort, to drag himself, as if by chance, ever nearer and nearer to the king, but stopping and remaining fixed at intervals, like the spider, which, moving towards her object, collapses into apparent lifelessness when she thinks she is the subject of observation. This species of movement appeared suspicious to the Ethiopian, who, on his part, prepared himself as quietly as possible to interfere the instant that interference should seem to be necessary.

The merchant meanwhile glided on gradually and imperceptibly, serpent-like, or rather snail-like, till he was about ten yards' distance from Richard's person, when, starting on his feet, he sprang forward with the bound of a tiger, stood at the king's back in less than an instant, and brandished aloft the cangiar, or poniard, which he had hidden in his sleeve.

Not the presence of his whole army could have saved their heroic monarch; but the motions of the Nubian had been as well calculated as those of the enthusiast, and, ere the latter could strike, the former caught his uplifted arm. Turning his fanatical wrath upon what thus unexpectedly interposed betwixt him and his object, the Charegite, for such was the seeming marabout, dealt the Nubian a blow with the dagger, which, however, only grazed his arm, while the far superior strength of the Ethiopian easily dashed him to the ground.

Aware of what had passed, Richard had now arisen, and with little more of surprise, anger, or interest of any kind in his countenance than an ordinary man would show in brushing up the stool on which he had been sitting, and exclaiming only "Ha, dog!" dashed almost to pieces the skull of the assassin, who uttered twice, once in a loud and once in a broken tone, the words "Allah ackbar!" —God is victorious.—and expired at the king's feet.

"Ye are careful warders," said Richard to his archers, in a tone of scornful reproach, as, aroused by the bustle of what had passed, in terror and tumult they now rushed into his tent; "watchful sentinels ye are, to leave me to do such hangman's work with my own hand. Be silent, all of you, and cease your senseless clamor!

Saw ye never a dead Turk before? Here, cast that carrion out of the camp, strike the head from the trunk, and stick it on a lance, taking care to turn the face to Mecca, that he may the easier tell the foul impostor, on whose inspiration he came hither, how he has sped on his errand.—For thee, my swart and silent friend," he added, turning to the Ethiopian. "But how's this? thou art wounded, and with a poisoned weapon, I warrant me; for by force of stab so weak an animal as that could scarce hope to do more than raise the lion's hide. Suck the poison from the wound, one of you; the venom is harmless on the lips, though fatal when it mingles with the blood."

The yeomen looked on each other confusedly and with hesitation, the apprehension of so strange a danger prevailing with those who feared no other.

"How now, sirrah?" continued the king; "are you dainty-lipped, or do you fear death, that you dally thus?"

"Not the death of a man," said Long Allan, to whom the king looked as he spoke; "but methinks I would not die like a poisoned rat for the sake of a black chattel there, that is bought and sold in market like a Martlemas ox."

"His Grace speaks to men of sucking poison," muttered another yeoman, "as if he said, 'Go to, swallow a gooseberry!'"

"Nay," said Richard, "I never bade a man do that which I would do not myself."

And without further ceremony, and in spite of the general expostulations of those around, and the respectful opposition of the Nubian himself, the king of England applied his lips to the wound of the black slave, treating with ridicule all remonstrances, and overpowering all resistance. He had no sooner intermitted his singular occupation, than the Nubian started from him, and casting a scarf over his arm, intimated by gestures, as firm in purpose as they were respectful in manner, his determination not to permit the monarch to renew so degrading an employment. Long Allan also interposed, saying that if it were necessary to prevent the king engaging again in a treatment of this kind, his own lips, tongue, and teeth were at the service of the negro (as he called the Ethiopian), and that he would eat him up bodily, rather than King Richard's mouth again should approach him.

Neville, who entered with other officers, added his remonstrances.

"Nay, nay, make not a needless halloo about a hart that the hounds have lost, or a danger when it is over," said the king. "The

1095

wound will be a trifle, for the blood is scarce drawn,—an angry
cat had dealt a deeper scratch,—and, for me, I have but to take a
dram of orvietan by way of precaution, though it is needless."

Thus spoke Richard, a little ashamed, perhaps, of his own condescension, though sanctioned both by humanity and gratitude.
But when Neville continued to make remonstrances on the peril to
his royal person, the king imposed silence on him.

"Peace, I prithee; make no more of it. I did it but to show these
ignorant prejudiced knaves how they might help each other when
these cowardly caitiffs come against us with sarbacanes and poisoned shafts."

SE'AMI

SE'AMI (Japanese, 1363-1443). Chief representative of the *Nō* play, created
by self and father. Author of nearly half the *Nō* plays still performed. Most
famous: *Takasago*. Was also praised as an actor and dramatic critic.

SOTOBA KOMACHI

Characters:
First Priest
Second Priest
Chorus
Komachi, as herself
and as her former
lover

Both Priests:
The mountains are not high on which we hide
The mountains are not high on which we hide
The lonely deepness of our hearts.
First Priest:
I am a priest from the Koya Hills
Coming down now to make my way to the city.
Second Priest:
The Buddha that was is gone away.
The Buddha to be has not yet come to the world.
Both Priests:
At birth we woke to dream in this world between
What then shall we say is real?
By chance we took the forms of men

1096

From a thousand possibilities.
We stumbled on the treasure of the holy law
The seed of all salvation
And then with thoughtful hearts we put our bodies
In these thin and ink-black robes,
We knew of lives before this birth
We knew of lives before this birth
And knew we owed no love to those who to this life
Engendered us.
We recognize no parents.
No children cared for us.
We walked a thousand miles and the way seemed short.
In the fields we lay down
And slept the night in the hills
Which now became our proper dwelling place
Our proper home.

Komachi:
'Like a root-cut reed
Should the tide entice
I would come
I would come I know but no wave asks
No stream invites this grief.'

How sad that once I was proud
Long ago
Proud and graceful
Golden birds in my raven hair
When I walked like willows nodding, charming
As the breeze in spring.
The voice of the nightingale
The petals of the wood rose wide stretched
Holding dew
At the hour before their breathless fall:
I was lovlier than these.
Now
I am foul in the eyes of the humblest creatures
To whom my shame is shown.
Unwelcome months and days pile over me
The wreck of a hundred years
In the city to avoid the eyes of men
Lest they should say "Can it be she?"

In the evening
West with the moon I steal past the palace,
Past the towers
Where no guard will question in the mountains
In the shadows of the trees
None challenge so wretched a pilgrim as this
To Love's Tomb
The autumn hills
The River Katsura
Boats in the moonlight rowed by whom?
I cannot see. . . .
But rowed by whom!

Oh, too, too, painful. . . .
Here on this withered stump of tree
Let me sit and collect my senses.

First Priest:
Come on. The sun is down. We must hurry on our way. But look! that old beggar woman sitting there on a sacred stupa. We should warn her to come away.

Second Priest:
Yes, of course.

First Priest:
Excuse me, old lady, but don't you know that's a stupa there you're sitting on? the holy image of the Buddha's incarnation. You'd better come away and rest some other place.

Komachi:
The holy image of the Buddha you say? But I saw no words or carvings on it. I took it for a tree stump only.

First Priest:
'Withered stumps
Are known as pine or cherry still
On the loneliest mountain.'

Komachi:
I, too, am a fallen tree.
But still the flowers of my heart
Might make some offering to the Buddha.
But this you call the Buddha's body. Why?

First Priest:
The stupa represents the body of Kongosatta Buddha, the Diamond

Lord, when he assumed the temporary form of each of his manifestations.

Komachi:
In what forms then is he manifested?

First Priest:
In Earth and Water and Wind and Fire and Space.

Komachi:
The same five elements as man. What was the difference then?

First Priest:
The form was the same but not the power.

Komachi:
And what is a stupa's power?

First Priest:
"He that has once looked upon a stupa shall for all eternity avoid the three worst catastrophes."

Komachi:
"One sudden thought can strike illumination."
Is that not just as good?

Second Priest:
If you've had such an illumination, why are you lingering here in this world of illusion?

Komachi:
Though my body lingers, my heart has left it long ago.

First Priest:
Unless you had no heart at all you wouldn't have failed to feel the presence of a stupa.

Komachi:
It was because I felt it that I came perhaps.

Second Priest:
In that case you shouldn't have spread yourself out on it without so much as a word of prayer.

Komachi:
It was on the ground already. . . .

First Priest:
Just the same it was an act of discord.

Komachi:
"Even from discord salvation springs."

Second Priest:
From the evil of Daiba

Komachi:
Or the love of Kannon.
First Priest:
From the folly of Handoku
Komachi:
Or the wisdom of
Monju.
First Priest:
What we call evil
Komachi:
Is also good.
First Priest:
Illusion
Komachi:
Is Salvation.
Second Priest:
"Salvation
Komachi:
Cannot be watered like trees."
First Priest:
"The brightest mirror
Komachi:
Is not on the wall."
Chorus:
Nothing is separate.
Nothing persists.
Of Buddha and man there is no distinction,
At most a seeming difference planned
For the humble, ill-instructed men
He has vowed from the first to save.
"Even from discord salvation springs."
So said Komachi. And the priests:
"Surely this beggar is someone beyond us."
Then bending their heads to the ground
Three times did they do her homage
The difficult priests
The difficult priests
Who thought to correct her.
First Priest:
Who are you then? Give us your name; we will pray for your soul.

Komachi:

For all my shame I will tell you. Pray for the wreck of Komachi, the daughter of Yoshizane of Ono, Lord of Dewa.

Both Priests:

How sad to think that you were she.
Exquisite Komachi
The brightest flower long ago
Her dark brows arched
Her face bright powdered always
When cedar-scented halls could scarce contain
Her damask robes.

Komachi:

I made verses in our speech
And in the speech of the foreign Court.

Chorus:

When she passed the banquet cup
Reflected moonlight lay on her sleeve.
How was ever such lovliness lost?
When did she change?
Her hair a tangle of frosted grass
Where the black curls lay on her neck
And the color lost from the twin arched peaks
Of her brow.

Komachi:

'Oh shameful in the dawning light
These silted seaweed locks that of a hundred years
Now lack but one.'

Chorus:

What do you have in the bag at your waist?

Komachi:

Death today or hunger tomorrow.
Only some beans I've put in my bag.

Chorus:

And in the bundle on you back?

Komachi:

A soiled and dusty robe.

Chorus:

And in the basket on your arm?

Komachi:

Sagittaries black and white.

Chorus:
Tattered coat
Komachi:
Broken hat
Chorus:
Can scarcely hide her face.
Komachi:
Think of the frost and the snow and the rain.
I've not even sleeves enough to dry my tears.
But I wander begging things from men
That come and go along the road.
When begging fails
An awful madness seizes me
And my voice is no longer the same. . . .
       Hey! Give me something, you priests!
First Priest:
What do you want?
Komachi:
To go to Komachi!
First Priest:
What are you saying? You *are* Komachi!
Komachi:
No. Komachi was beautiful.
Many letters came, many messages
Thick as rain from a summer sky
But she made no answer, even once,
Even an empty word.
Age is her retribution now.
Oh, I love her!
I love her!
First Priest:
You love her! What spirit has possessed you to make you say such
things?
Komachi:
Many loved her
But among them all
It was Shosho who loved her deepest
Shii no Shosho, the Captain.
Chorus:
The wheel turns back.

I live again a cycle of unhappiness
Riding with the wheels
That came and went again each night.
The sun.
What time is it now?
Dusk.
The moon will be my friend on the road
And though the watchmen stand at the pass
They shall not bar my way.

Komachi: (*re-costumed as her lover*)
My wide white skirts hitched up

Chorus:
My wide white skirts hitched up
My tall black hat pulled down
And my sleeves thrown over my head
Hidden from the eyes of men on the road
In the moonlight
In the darkness coming, coming
When the night rains fell
When the night winds blew the leaves like rain
When the snow lay deep

Komachi:
And the melting drops fell
One by one from the rafters

Chorus:
I came and went, came and went
One night, two nights, three,
Ten (and this was the Harvest Night).
And did not see her.
Faithful as a cock that marks each dawn
I came and carved my mark upon the pillar.
I was to come a hundred nights,
I lacked but one. . . .
Oh, dizziness . . . pain. . . .

Chorus:
He was grieved at the pain in his breast
When the last night came and he died
Shii no Shosho, the Captain.

Komachi:
It was his unsatisfied love possessed me so

1103

His anger that turned my wits.
In the face of this I will pray
For life in the worlds to come
The sands of goodness I will pile
Into a towering hill.
Before the golden, gentle Buddha I will lay
Poems as my flowers
Entering in the way
Entering in the way

SEI SHONAGON

SEI SHONAGON (Japanese, *ca.* 966-1013). Early Japanese poetical court diarist. The daughter of a poet. Served as lady-in-waiting to the Empress. Her private sketchbook or diary later became celebrated literary work. It is made up of epigrammatic, anecdotal pictures of court life.

A CUCKOO PICNIC

SINCE the 1st May it had been raining or cloudy every day, and we were bored to death. I suggested that we should go and hear the cuckoo, and everyone was wildly excited at once and agreed, saying: "I too! I too!" Someone said: "Far away near Kamo River is a bridge. It is not called Tanabata's Bridge, but something like it and more difficult. However, near there the cuckoo sings nearly every day."

"No, no! It's only a cicada," said another. Anyway, we decided to go out there, and asked the officer on duty to order the carriage to the veranda.

"It would certainly be allowed, as it is raining," we said, and when the carriage came from the north guard-room it arrived at our veranda and four of us got in and started from the northern gate. The others said, enviously: "What a pity we can't order another carriage and go together."

But the Empress said "No," so we paid no attention to this.

On our way past the racecourse we saw crowds of noisy people.

"What can be going on?" we asked.

"They are practising archery on horseback. Pray stop and see," the man who runs beside the carriage answered. He stopped the carriage, but we could see nothing of the General of the Left, who they said had arrived, and only a few sixth-grade people were strolling about.

"It isn't worth watching. Let us get on quickly," we agreed.

And on we went. This road is quite interesting about the time of Kamo festival.

"By and by we shall come to the house of the Empress's uncle," we said, and we got out of the carriage there.

Lord Akinobu Ason's house is built in the simplest way and very rustic—paper screens with pictures of horses, and others woven of strips of bamboo and fine grass-woven blinds, and so on. One could see they kept up the old customs, and the house itself had little spaciousness. Just as we were looking about us with interest the cuckoos burst into song with such zest as to be absolutely noisy. We were dreadfully sorry the Empress could not hear them, and also for those of us who had wanted to come and could not.

"Now you are in the country, you must see our country ways," said Akinobu Ason, and accordingly rice plants were brought and some cleanly dressed young women showed us how the stripping of the grain is done and how it is put into a kind of revolving machine. Two of them kept it turning while they marked time with a song. It was very curious, and we laughed so much that we quite forgot the cuckoo and the poems to be written about her.

Then in came food on the beautiful old tables one sees in Chinese pictures, but that did not interest any of us, and he said: "I know this is very countrified stuff, but the only way is to keep on attacking the host until he provides something you really like. If you have no appetite it is not like our usual City visitors."

So he cheered us on, saying: "These bracken fronds I picked myself."

"But surely you don't expect us to sit round the tables like common people," I remonstrated and at once he had the refreshment taken from the little tables.

"Why, no! one sees all of you are accustomed to the strictest etiquette in the August Presence," he said, and so served us separately.

While we were making merry we heard the driver calling: "It's going to rain," and out we all hurried and into the carriage.

"But I want to get my poem done before we start," I cried.

"No, No! On the way back!" someone said.

We picked any amount of lovely deutzia along the road and stuck

1105

the sprays into the blinds and the sides of the carriage, and thatched the roofs with great boughs of it, until it looked exactly as if the carriage were covered with white damask. Our men, much interested, helped us, sticking the sprays into every crevice of the wickerwork, crying, "More, more. A bit just here!" thoroughly enjoying themselves.

In we all got, hoping to meet someone who would notice our display. But no one turned up. There were only dull priests and a few servants on the road. Such a pity! Presently we arrived at the East Ward and said to each other: "It will never do if we meet no one and not the least notice is taken of our gorgeously decorated carriage!"

So we stopped forthwith in front of the palace in that ward and asked for the Lord Chamberlain sending word by the messenger: "Is the Lord Chamberlain at home? We are just returning from a cuckoo picnic."

Back came the messenger.

"His Lordship says: 'I will come out at once.' Do please wait."

It seems he was putting on his ceremonial trousers in a hurry. So we thought there was no need to wait and whipping up set off for the Eastern Gate. And there he followed us, rushing down the road and tying his trousers as he ran. Behind him rushed his followers and valets. We urged the driver on, faster! faster! and when we arrived at the gate he overtook us, perfectly breathless. It was then he noticed the splendour of our carriage and said: "What in the world—! Are there common mortals in such a carriage? Do get out and let me see!"

And he and his followers laughed with delight over the joke.

"But your poems—your poems! I want to hear them now!" he begged.

"Now? Certainly not! Her Majesty will hear them first!" I said demurely.

The rain began to pelt while we were talking, and he said: "Why in the world has this gate no roof when every other gate is weatherproof? And to-day of all days, when we want shelter. And how am I to get home? I rushed out after you regardless of consequences, and what am I to do?"

We all chorused: "Come into the Palace!"

"And may I ask how I am to go there in a soft-crowned cap?"

"Send home for what you want," we suggested.

Down came the rain, and our men began pulling us with all

speed. Off went the Lord Chamberlain, and under an umbrella. Slowly and reluctantly he trudged along, turning to look back with a spray of deutzia in his hand. It was very amusing.

In the Palace her Majesty asked for the story of our adventures, and we told the tale of the Lord Chamberlain and Ichijo Street. Everyone laughed, even the sulky stay-at-homes. But then came the question: "And where are the poems?"

Of course, it had to come out that we had made none. The Empress said at once; "Oh what a pity! All the officers will have heard of the picnic, and with what face can we say no poems came of such an adventure? You had much better have done it while the cuckoo was singing and you were considering it seriously. But set to work even now, for if not your visit will be wasted!"

Really, we had been idiots. And while we were regretting all this and consulting over poems, in comes a short poem from the Lord Chamberlain written on fine white flower-paper and fastened to the deutzia spray he had taken.

> "The cuckoo's cry. Had I known you
> were fled to seek it
> I should have bid you carry my whole
> heart's greeting today."

I thought the messenger might be waiting, so I sent someone hurrying for my writing-box, but the Empress said: "No—be quick. Use mine!"

And she did me the honor to slip in some paper. So I said to Saisho: "Be quick. Your turn, please."

"No, yours, please!" said she. And in the midst of our polite wrangling the sky grew black and the rain came down in sheets and the thunder roared so terrifically that we were frightened into rushing away to shut all the blinds and the outside doors in a perfect panic. And poetry was forgotten.

The thunder lasted so long that as it stopped darkness came on. And still we would have struggled with the poems but that many of the officers and other visitors came up to inquire for the Empress's health after the storm, and of course we had to meet them and do the honors, so again the poems went to the wall as far as I was concerned, and the other ladies did not trouble about it, for they declared the Lord Chamberlain's poem was addressed to me, and it was my business to answer. I was not in the mood for it, much as I regretted it.

I really wish no one knew anything about the picnic," I said, and the Empress retorted· "You could certainly patch up a poem among you. It is only that you don't care to."

I think she was a little cross. It was strange altogether.

"But we missed our chance, and now the mood has evaporated," I said.

"You mean your interest has evaporated," she said.

And there we left it.

Two days passed and we were discussing the cuckoo picnic. Saish ɪ said: "But how did you like the bracken-shoots which our host said he had picked himself?"

The Empress, listening, said with a laugh: "I think your refreshments were the only things you remembered." And she scribbled the end of a verse on a piece of paper:

"The longing for the bracken haunts her memory still."

"Do be poetical and finish it!" she said.

It was really rather amusing, and I took my brush and wrote.

"And drowns the cuckoo's note we sallied out to hear."

"Candid enough!" said the laughing Empress. "But why did.ı't you remember the cuckoo as affectionately?"

I felt a little out of countenance.

"I don't know why," I said, "but I have a kind of feeling I shall compose no more short poems. I always am uncomfortable when the subject comes up and your Majesty commands me to set to work. Besides, how am I to do it when I am so stupid as to have no knowledge of metre and evolve a winter poem in spring and a spring one in autumn, and in plum-blossom time descant upon chrysanthemums? You see, my ancestor was a well-known poet, so that mine really ought to be better than others, and, if they were, one might really plume oneself when people said, 'This short poem absolutely fitted the occasion. But then, of course, she had the advantage of a poetical heritage.' But if one has no special aptitude and yet thinks oneself clever, and so composes at large, it really is a little hard on the ancestor!"

The Empress laughed and answered: "Well, well! Do as you please. I shall not insist on your poetising any more!"

So I was feeling easier in my mind.

But while all this was in my head the Empress's brother was eagerly preparing to hold the All Night Waking. As it grew late a competition for short poems was announced, and all the ladies asked to compete. Great excitement! I was there and talking to the Empress about something else, when the Prince came up to me and said: "Why, is it possible you are not going to write us a poem? Do, I beseech you!"

I answered: "I have been honored by permission to do exactly as I please, and so I am not going to write. I have not one idea to rattle on another."

"But how extraordinary! Do you really mean to say you have permission to be dumb? Did her Majesty give it? I don't so much mind about other times, but to-night of all times you cannot refuse!"

He was as eager as possible and I as decided! While they were criticising the other poems the Empress wrote me a tiny note. I opened it at once and found this:

"Even though a descendant of the famous Motosuke,
Why—why not join in the battle of the poems to-night?"

I was really obliged to laugh. It was so very amusing, and the Prince called out: "But what is it? What is it?"

[I wrote:]

"If I had not the reputation of my heritage to consider,
Would I not gaily join in the battle of poems to-night?"

And I said to the Empress: "If I had not this incubus of reputation to keep up, I would turn out thousands of poems on the spot."

MENDELE MOCHER SFORIM

MENDELE MOCHER SFORIM (Shalom Jacob Abramowitsch, Lithuanian-Hebrew, 1836-1917). Yiddish folklorist, sometimes called the grandfather of Yiddish literature. Earlier works, written in Hebrew, helped revive that language as a literary medium. He then transformed Yiddish from a colloquial tongue to an exact literary form. Introduced the novel of social criticism. Novels: *Dos Kleine Menshele, Die Takse, Die Klyatsche.*

THE NAG

THIS is Mendele the book peddler speaking. Glory be to the Creator! For, after His creation of all this enormous universe, He took counsel with His host of heavenly angels and did create a universe in-little—by which you may take to mean man, who is justly called *olam katan* (a microcosm), since man, if you look at him closely, combines in himself all species of creatures and creations. You will find in him all possible wild beasts, as well as all the different breeds of cattle. You will find in him the lizard, the leech, the Spanish fly, the Prussian cockroach, and, to top it all off, a devil and a werewolf, a clown, a Jew-baiter, and many another uncanny foe of man and scourge of God. You will see, as well, among these universes-in-little all sorts of amazing sights. Here's a tomcat, for instance, playing with a baby mouse; here's a polecat making its way into a hencoop and sinking its teeth into the necks of the poor little fowl; here's a monkey mimicking and mocking everyone in sight; here's a dog standing up on its hind legs and wagging its tail for anybody who throws it a crust; here's a spider leading a fly astray, enmeshing it, strangling it, and sucking all the juices out of it; here are midges, overtaking a passer-by and humming all sorts of secrets in his ears; here are thousands of things no less amazing.

However, that's not at all what I'm leading up to.

Glory to the Holy Name (I have said), Who contemplates in silence all that is going on in this universe-in-little and still does not give it the quietus, and puts off His wrath, and tolerates transgressions, and evinces not a little mercy toward man the imperfect. In short, I was about to tell you, at this point, of a certain great favor bestowed upon me right after He had, at first, chastised me just a little.

My little nag, kind masters, is no more. My faithful horse, who passed all the days of her life in righteous toil, who served me faithfully and truly, who could have given pointers in topography to the natives of all the tiny hamlets and crossroads settlements, who was a remarkable connoisseur of little wayside inns, who had, in my company, crisscrossed almost all the pales of Israel, who was personally known to almost all of our orthodox communities— my poor nag departed this life one fine day, as a matter of fact it was on Lag Baomer, in the town of Glupsk [Foolstown]. It is painful to give the reason; poverty, however, is no disgrace; the poor little thing simply passed away from starvation. Her daily fodder consisted of chopped straw, and only on rare occasions would there fall to her lot a few dry crusts of bread that I had bought from beggars who wandered about with sacks over their shoulders. Ah, woe to the horse that falls into the hands of a peddler of Jewish books!

A wanderer, she wanders without end and in all probability labors more than her fellow creatures who draw wares more choice than ours and yet she is supposed to exist on practically nothing. A Jewish bookman lives all his life on virtually the same footing, and, one might say, he himself, with his wife and children, dies from hunger ten times a day. . . .

However, that's still not what I'm leading up to.

The Lord (I have said) sent me a visitation. I was left without a horse, had nothing with which to buy another, and yet I had to get to the fairs in time. As you can see, I was up against it.

And there I was, sitting all by myself in the House of Prayer, in low spirits, when suddenly a friend of mine walked in, headed straight for me, and asked:

"Reb Mendele, would you like to buy a nag, maybe?"

"I'd buy it with pleasure," I answered with a sigh, "but where would I get the money?"

"Bah!" said he. "That's no trouble at all. You won't have to pay a copper of spot cash. It's quite possible they'll lend you a little something besides. Never fear, they know you're an honest man."

"In that case," I said, "I am most willing to buy your nag right now, without any further beating around the bush. Well, let's go, if you please—we'll have a look at her."

"Why, there's no need of putting yourself out, actually. I have the nag right here with me. . . ."

"What do you mean, you have it here with you?" I voiced my astonishment.

"Why, right here—inside my coat," my friend smiled.

"Are you laughing at me or what?" I asked in vexation. "Look for someone else to make fun of—I don't find your little jokes at all entertaining right now."

"God forbid! I'm not joking at all," said my friend, and took from under his coat a whole stack of papers. "You see, Reb Mendele, all this belongs to a certain gentleman, a good friend of mine—you'll find his name right here on his stories. And it is one of these tales that bears the title, *The Nag*. The man who wrote it is, at present— and may this never be said of you!— he is . . . well, how am I to put it to you? He has bees in his bonnet, as the saying goes, but just the same, we who are his good friends would very much like to see his stories in print, as is fit and proper. To whom else were we to turn in this matter but to you, Reb Mendele, who enjoys such

1111

well-earned prestige in our region? We are asking you to go through these stories quite thoroughly and put them in shape. We rely upon you in this. You can go right ahead and print *The Nag*. We'll talk over the terms later, and I can assure you that you won't be out anything. If you need some money right now, why, we won't quibble over a small amount. Well, now, do you want to do it, Reb Mendele?"

"Do I? What a question, really! I want to with all my heart," I answered, and almost launched into a dance, so overjoyed was I.

I attended to my affairs and, full of zeal, tackled *The Nag*. I spared no labor and did my work properly.

And now, gentlemen, just a word or two concerning *The Nag*.

The Nag is written in a high-flown manner, after the fashion in which the ancients wrote. Each man will understand it in his own way and in keeping with his common sense. For honest folk who don't go grabbing at the stars in the sky, it will be simply a fairy tale. Those who look deeper may find in it a reflection of all of us who are sinners. Take me, now—I have seen in the nag all our little Jewish souls and have grasped the secret of why they exist in this world. I'm ready to wager that, in turning the pages of this book, many of us—each according to his nature—will exclaim vehemently: "Why, this aimed at our Nusen Reb Heikes"—"—at our Zalman Yukele Reb Moteles"—"—at Hershke Reb Abeles." Still others will declare: "He has discovered the secret of our poorbox collections, of our benevolent city fathers and all our lovely ways," and so on and on.

That's the sort of problem I posed to the Rabbinical judiciary in the town of Glupsk and to all the bigwigs in the vicinity. "As you know," I told them, "at the time I put out *The Tax*, I promised the public a sequel. It was more than a promise. It was a vow. Tell me, my dear sirs, what's the proper, lawful thing to do now? I am publishing *The Nag*. May I consider that I have fulfilled my promise concerning a sequel to *The Tax*?"

Well, they certainly pondered, and then pondered some more. They scratched and scratched behind their ears and, at last, came to a decision. "Yes, Reb Mendele," they answered, "after due deliberation, we do hereby release you from your vow. Let *The Nag* be considered the equivalent of your having kept your word, as if you had turned out the second part of *The Tax* and everything appertaining thereto. The thing isn't so bad, really, and, after all, you've appealed to almost every taste."

How many thanks, then, should I render to the All Highest!
Had I acquired *The Nag* just so, without any deposit toward the
purchase of a horse, it would have been well. Had I acquired it
with a small deposit, but it did not serve as a substitute for the
second part of *The Tax*, and had the Rabbinical judiciary not absolved me of my vow without scratching behind their ears, that,
too, would have been well. And even if they had scratched, but had
given no reason for doing so, even then everything would have
been well.

And therefore I should render thanks to the All Highest over
and over again, because *The Nag* did have something of *The Tax*
about it, and because the Rabbinical judiciary had released me from
my vow, and because they did scratch themselves most horrendously
as they gave me absolution, and because I know why they scratched
themselves and understand that *The Nag* is worth scratching oneself
behind the ear about . . . by way of redemption for all our transgressions.

That, gentlemen, is precisely what I wanted to say right out in
my brief foreword. Whatever I have in mind is on the tip of my
tongue.

> Humbly,
> *Mendele the Book Peddler*

Written the first day of the month
of Elul, in a cart laden with books,
on the road between the town of Glupsk
and Teterevka (Grouseville).

WILLIAM SHAKESPEARE

WILLIAM SHAKESPEARE (English, 1564-1616). The Bard of England,
against whose works all English poetry and drama are measured. Little known
of his life, except that he was an actor and playwright. His understanding of
humanity unsurpassed, his dramatic and lyric poetry the finest flower of
Elizabethan Age. Used every form of his time: The great tragedies: *Hamlet,
Othello, Macbeth, King Lear.* Comedies: *Twelfth Night, A Midsummer Night's
Dream.* Historicals: *Henry IV* and *V.* Romantic drama: *The Tempest.*

Speech by John of Gaunt from *King Richard the Second*

This royal throne of kings, this scepter'd isle,
This earth of majesty, this seat of Mars,

1113

This other Eden, demi-paradise,
This fortress built by Nature for herself
Against infection and the hand of war,
This happy breed of men, this little world,
This precious stone set in the silver sea,
Which serves it in the office of a wall,
Or as a moat defensive to a house,
Against the envy of less happier lands,
This blessed plot, this earth, this realm, this England,
This nurse, this teeming womb of royal kings,
Fear'd by their breed and famous by their birth,
Renowned for their deeds as far from home,—
For Christian service and true chivalry,—
As is the sepulchre in stubborn Jewry
Of the world's ransom, blessed Mary's Son:
This land of such dear souls, this dear, dear land,
Dear for her reputation through the world,
Is now leas'd out,—I die pronouncing it,—
Like to a tenement, or pelting farm:
England, bound in with the triumphant sea,
Whose rocky shore beats back the envious siege
Of watery Neptune, is now bound in with shame,
With inky blots, and rotten parchment bonds:
That England, that was wont to conquer others,
Hath made a shameful conquest of itself.

Speech by Prince Henry over the body of Hotspur from
King Henry the Fourth, Part I

... Fare thee well, great heart!
Ill-weaved ambition, how much art thou shrunk!
When that this body did contain a spirit,
A kingdom for it was too small a bound;
But now two paces of the vilest earth
Is room enough: this earth that bears thee dead
Bears not alive so stout a gentleman.
If thou wert sensible of courtesy,
I should not make so dear a show of zeal:
But let my favours hide thy mangled face;
And, even in thy behalf, I'll thank myself
For doing these fair rites of tenderness.

Adieu, and take thy praise with thee to heaven!
Thy ignomy sleep with thee in the grave,
But not remember'd in thy epitaph!

Speech by Berowne from *Love's Labour's Lost*

Why, all delights are vain; but that most vain,
Which, with pain purchased, doth inherit pain:
As, painfully to pore upon a book
To seek the light of truth; while truth the while
Doth falsely blind the eyesight of his look:
Light, seeking light, doth light of light beguile:
So, ere you find where light in darkness lies,
Your light grows dark by losing of your eyes.
Study me how to please the eye indeed,
By fixing it upon a fairer eye;
Who dazzling so, that eye shall be his heed,
And give him light that it was blinded by.
Study is like the heaven's glorious sun,
That will not be deep-search'd with saucy looks:
Small have continual plodders ever won,
Save base authority from others' books.
These earthly godfathers of heaven's lights,
That give a name to every fixèd star,
Have no more profit of their shining nights
Than those that walk and wot not what they are.
Too much to know, is to know naught but fame;
And every godfather can give a name.

Speech by the Archbishop of Canterbury from *King Henry the Fifth*

Therefore doth heaven divide
The state of man in divers functions,
Setting endeavour in continual motion;
To which is fixèd, as an aim or butt,
Obedience: for so work the honey-bees,
Creatures that by a rule in nature teach
The act of order to a peopled kingdom.
They have a king and officers of sorts;
Where some, like magistrates, correct at home,
Others, like merchants, venture trade abroad,
Others, like soldiers, armed in their stings,

1115

Make boot upon the summer's velvet buds;
Make pillage they with merry march bring home
To the tent-royal of their emperor:
Who, busied in his majesty, surveys
The singing masons building roofs of gold,
The civil citizens kneading up the honey,
The poor mechanic porters crowding in
Their heavy burdens at his narrow gate,
The sad-ey'd justice, with his surly hum,
Delivering o'er to executors pale
The lazy yawning drone. I this infer
That many things, having all reference
To one consent, may work contrariously;
As many arrows, loosèd several ways,
Fly to one mark; as many ways meet in one town;
As many fresh streams meet in one salt sea;
As many lines close in the dial's centre;
So may a thousand actions, once afoot,
End in one purpose, and be all well borne
Without defeat.

Speech by Titania from *A Midsummer Night's Dream*

These are the forgeries of jealousy:
And never, since the middle summer's spring,
Met we on hill, in dale, forest, or mead,
By pavèd fountain or by rushy brook,
Or in the beached margent of the sea,
To dance our ringlets to the whistling wind,
But with thy brawls thou hast disturb'd our sport.
Therefore the winds, piping to us in vain,
As in revenge, have suck'd up from the sea
Contagious fogs; which falling in the land,
Hath every pelting river made so proud,
That they have overborne their continents:
The ox hath therefore stretch'd his yoke in vain,
The ploughman lost his sweat; and the green corn
Hath rotted ere his youth attain'd a beard:
The fold stands empty in the drownèd field,
And crows are fatted with the murrion flock;
The nine-men's-morris is fill'd up with mud;

1116

And the quaint mazes in the wanton green,
For lack of tread, are undistinguishable:
The human mortals want their winter here;
No night is now with hymn or carol blest:—
Therefore the moon, the governess of floods,
Pale in her anger, washes all the air,
That rheumatic diseases do abound:
And thorough this distemperature we see
The seasons alter: hoary-headed frosts
Fall in the fresh lap of the crimson rose;
And on old Hiems' thin and icy crown
An odorous chaplet of sweet summer buds
Is, as in mockery, set: the spring, the summer,
The childing autumn, angry winter, change
Their wonted liveries; and the mazèd world,
By their increase, now knows not which is which:
And this same progeny of evil comes
From our debate, from our dissension;
We are their parents and original.

Speech by Jaques from *As You Like It*

All the world's a stage,
And all the men and women merely players;
They have their exits and their entrances;
And one man in his time plays many parts,
His acts being seven ages. At first the infant,
Mewling and puking in the nurse's arms.
And then the whining school-boy with his satchel,
And shining morning face, creeping like snail,
Unwillingly to school. And then the lover,
Sighing like furnace, with a woful ballad,
Made to his mistress' eyebrow. Then a soldier,
Full of strange oaths, and bearded like the pard,
Jealous in honour, sudden and quick in quarrel,
Seeking the bubble reputation
Even in the cannon's mouth. And then the justice,
In fair round belly with good capon lin'd,
With eyes severe, and beard of formal cut,
Full of wise saws and modern instances;

1117

And so he plays his part. The sixth age shifts
Into the lean and slipper'd pantaloon,
With spectacles on nose and pouch on side,
His youthful hose well sav'd, a world too wide
For his shrunk shank; and his big manly voice,
Turning again toward childish treble, pipes
And whistles in his sound. Last scene of all,
That ends this strange eventful history,
Is second childishness and mere oblivion,
Sans teeth, sans eyes, sans taste, sans everything.

Clown's Songs from *Twelfth Night*

I

O mistress mine! where are you roaming?
O! stay and hear; your true love's coming,
   That can sing both high and low.
Trip no further, pretty sweeting;
Journeys end in lovers meeting,
   Every wise man's son doth know.

What is love? 'tis not hereafter;
Present mirth hath present laughter;
   What's to come is still unsure.
In delay there lies no plenty;
Then come kiss me, sweet-and-twenty,
   Youth's a stuff will not endure.

IV

Come away, come away, death,
   And in sad cypress let me be laid.
Fly away, fly away, breath;
   I am slain by a fair cruel maid.
My shroud of white, stuck all with yew,
     O! prepare it.
My part of death, no one so true
     Did share it.

Not a flower, not a flower sweet,
  On my black coffin let there be strown;
Not a friend, not a friend greet
  My poor corse, where my bones shall be thrown.
A thousand thousand sighs to save,
    Lay me, O! where
Sad true lover never find my grave,
    To weep there.

Soliloquy by Ophelia from *Hamlet*

O, what a noble mind is here o'erthrown!
The courtier's, soldier's, scholar's eye, tongue, sword;
Th' expectancy and rose of the fair state,
The glass of fashion and the mould of form,
The observ'd of all observers,—quite, quite down!
And I, of ladies most deject and wretched,
That suckt the honey of his music vows,
Now see that noble and most sovereign reason,
Like sweet bells jangled, out of tune and harsh;
That unmatcht form and feature of blown youth
Blasted with ecstasy: O, woe is me
To have seen what I have seen, see what I see!

Speech by King Lear from *King Lear*

You see me here, you gods, a poor old man,
As full of grief as age; wretched in both!
If it be you that stir these daughters' hearts
Against their father, fool me not so much
To bear it tamely; touch me with noble anger,
And let not women's weapons, water-drops,
Stain my man's cheeks! No, you unnatural hags,
I will have such revenges on you both
That all the world shall—I will do such things,—
What they are yet I know not,—but they shall be
The terrors of the earth. You think I'll weep;
No, I'll not weep:
I have full cause of weeping, but this heart
Shall break into a hundred thousand flaws
Or ere I'll weep. O fool! I shall go mad.

Speech by Coriolanus from *Coriolanus*

You common cry of curs! whose breath I hate
As reek o' the rotten fens, whose loves I prize
As the dead carcases of unburied men
That do corrupt my air, I banish you;
And here remain with your uncertainty!
Let every feeble rumour shake your hearts!
Your enemies, with nodding of their plumes,
Fan you into despair! Have the power still
To banish your defenders; till at length
Your ignorance,—which finds not, till it feels,—
Making but reservation of yourselves,—
Still your own foes,—deliver you as most
Abated captives to some nation
That won you without blows! Despising,
For you, the city, thus I turn my back:
There is a world elsewhere.

Speech by Prince Henry from *King John*

O vanity of sickness! fierce extremes
In their continuance will not feel themselves.
Death, having prey'd upon the outward parts,
Leaves them invisible; and his siege is now
Against the mind, the which he pricks and wounds
With many legions of strange fantasies,
Which, in their throng and press to that last hold,
Confound themselves. 'Tis strange that death should sing.
I am the cygnet to this pale faint swan,
Who chants a doleful hymn to his own death,
And from the organ-pipe of frailty sings
His soul and body to their lasting rest.

Speech by King Henry from *King Henry the Sixth, Part III*

This battle fares like to the morning's war,
When dying clouds contend with growing light,
What time the shepherd, blowing of his nails,

Can neither call it perfect day nor night.
Now sways it this way, like a mighty sea
Forc'd by the tide to combat with the wind;
Now sways it that way, like the self-same sea
Forc'd to retire by fury of the wind:
Sometime the flood prevails, and then the wind;
Now one the better, then another best;
Both tugging to be victors, breast to breast,
Yet neither conqueror nor conqueréd:
So is the equal poise of this fell war.
Here on this molehill will I sit me down.
To whom God will, there be the victory!
For Margaret my queen, and Clifford too,
Have chid me from the battle; swearing both
They prosper best of all when I am thence.
Would I were dead! if God's good will were so;
For what is in this world but grief and woe?
O God! methinks it were a happy life,
To be no better than a homely swain;
To sit upon a hill, as I do now,
To carve out dials quaintly, point by point,
Thereby to see the minutes how they run,
How many make the hour full complete;
How many hours bring about the day;
How many days will finish up the year;
How many years a mortal man may live.
When this is known, then to divide the times:
So many hours must I tend my flock;
So many hours must I take my rest;
So many hours must I contemplate;
So many hours must I sport myself;
So many days my ewes have been with young;
So many weeks ere the poor fools will ean;
So many years ere I shall shear the fleece:
So minutes, hours, days, months, and years,
Pass'd over to the end they were created,
Would bring white hairs unto a quiet grave.
Ah! what a life were this! how sweet! how lovely!
Gives not the hawthorn bush a sweeter shade
To shepherds looking on their silly sheep,
Than doth a rich embroider'd canopy

To kings, that fear their subjects' treachery?
O, yes! it doth; a thousand-fold it doth.
And to conclude, the shepherd's homely curds,
His cold thin drink out of his leather bottle,
His wonted sleep under a fresh tree's shade,
All which secure and sweetly he enjoys,
Is far beyond a prince's delicates,
His viands sparkling in a golden cup,
His body couchéd in a curious bed,
When care, mistrust, and treason wait on him.

"Blow, Winds" from *King Lear*

Blow, winds, and crack your cheeks! rage! blow!
You cataracts and hurricanoes, spout
Till you have drenched our steeples, drowned the cocks!
You sulphurous and thought-executing fires,
Vaunt-couriers to oak-cleaving thunderbolts,
Singe my white head! And thou, all-shaking thunder,
Smite flat the thick rotundity o' the world!
Crack nature's molds, all germins spill at once
That make ingrateful man! . . .
Rumble thy bellyful! Spit, fire! spout, rain!
Nor rain, wind, thunder, fire, are my daughters:
I tax not you, you elements, with unkindness;
I never gave you kingdom, called you children,
You owe me no subscription: then let fall
Your horrible pleasure; here I stand, your slave,
A poor, infirm, weak and despised old man:
But yet I call you servile ministers,
That have with two pernicious daughters joined
Your high-engendered battles 'gainst a head
So old and white as this. O! O! 'tis foul!

Portrait of Brutus from *Julius Caesar*

This was the noblest Roman of them all:
All the conspirators, save only he,
Did that they did in envy of great Cæsar;

He only, in a general honest thought
And common good to all, made one of them.
His life was gentle, and the elements
So mixed in him that Nature might stand up
And say to all the world "This was a man!"

Portrait of Caesar from *Julius Caesar*

Why, man, he doth bestride the narrow world
Like a Colossus, and we petty men
Walk under his huge legs and peep about
To find ourselves dishonorable graves.
Men at some time are masters of their fates:
The fault, dear Brutus, is not in our stars,
But in ourselves, that we are underlings.
Brutus, and Cæsar: what should be in that Cæsar?
Why should that name be sounded more than yours?
Write them together, yours is as fair a name;
Sound them, it doth become the mouth as well;
Weigh them, it is as heavy; conjure with 'em,
Brutus will start a spirit as soon as Cæsar.
Now, in the names of all the gods at once,
Upon what meat doth this our Cæsar feed,
That he is grown so great? Age, thou art shamed!
Rome, thou hast lost the breed of noble bloods!
When went there by an age, since the great flood,
But it was famed with more than with one man?
When could they say till now that talked of Rome
That her wide walls encompassed but one man?
Now is it Rome indeed, and room enough,
When there is in it but one only man.

"Fear" from *Julius Caesar*

Cowards die many times before their death;
The valiant never taste of death but once.
Of all the wonders that I yet have heard,
It seems to me most strange that men should fear;
Seeing that death, a necessary end,
Will come when it will come.

Friends, Romans, countrymen, lend me your ears;
I come to bury Cæsar, not to praise him.
The evil that men do lives after them;
The good is oft interred with their bones;
So let it be with Cæsar. The noble Brutus
Hath told you Cæsar was ambitious:
If it were so, it was a grievous fault,
And grievously hath Cæsar answered it.
Here, under leave of Brutus and the rest—
For Brutus is an honorable man;
So are they all, all honorable men—
Come I to speak in Cæsar's funeral.
He was my friend, faithful and just to me:
But Brutus says he was ambitious;
And Brutus is an honorable man.
He hath brought many captives home to Rome,
Whose ransoms did the general coffers fill:
Did this in Cæsar seem ambitious?
When that the poor have cried, Cæsar hath wept:
Ambition should be made of sterner stuff:
Yet Brutus says he was ambitious;
And Brutus is an honorable man.
You all did see that on the Lupercal
I thrice presented him a kingly crown,
Which he did thrice refuse: was this ambition?
Yet Brutus says he was ambitious;
And, sure, he is an honorable man.
I speak not to disprove what Brutus spoke,
But here I am to speak what I do know.
You all did love him once, not without cause:
What cause withholds you then to mourn for him?
O judgment! thou art fled to brutish beasts,
And men have lost their reason. Bear with me;
My heart is in the cóffin there with Cæsar,
And I must pause till it come back to me.

If you have tears, prepare to shed them now.
You all do know this mantle: I remember
The first time ever Cæsar put it on;
'Twas on a summer's evening, in his tent,

That day he overcame the Nervii:
Look, in this place ran Cassius' dagger through:
See what a rent the envious Casca made:
Through this the well-beloved Brutus stabbed;
And as he plucked his cursed steel away,
Mark how the blood of Cæsar followed it,
As rushing out of doors, to be resolved
If Brutus so unkindly knocked, or no:
For Brutus, as you know, was Cæsar's angel:
Judge, O you gods, how dearly Cæsar loved him!
This was the most unkindest cut of all;
For when the noble Cæsar saw him stab,
Ingratitude, more strong than traitors' arms,
Quite vanquished him: then burst his mighty heart;
And, in his mantle muffling up his face,
Even at the base of Pompey's statue,
Which all the while ran blood, great Cæsar fell.
O, what a fall was there, my countrymen!
Then I, and you, and all of us fell down,
Whilst bloody treason flourished over us.

"I Have Lived Long Enough" from *Macbeth*

I have lived long enough: my way of life
Is fallen into the sere, the yellow leaf,
And that which should accompany old age,
As honor, love, obedience, troops of friends,
I must not look to have; but, in their stead,
Curses, not loud but deep, mouth-honor, breath,
Which the poor heart would fain deny, and dare not.

Canst thou not minister to a mind diseased,
Pluck from the memory a rooted sorrow,
Raze out the written troubles of the brain,
And with some sweet oblivious antidote
Cleanse the stuffed bosom of that perilous stuff
Which weighs upon the heart?

"Tomorrow, and Tomorrow, and Tomorrow" from *Macbeth*

Tomorrow, and tomorrow, and tomorrow,
Creeps in this petty pace from day to day,

1125

To the last syllable of recorded time;
And all our yesterdays have lighted fools
The way to dusty death. Out, out, brief candle!
Life's but a walking shadow, a poor player
That struts and frets his hour upon the stage
And then is heard no more: it is a tale
Told by an idiot, full of sound and fury,
Signifying nothing.

"This Above All" from *Hamlet*

And these few precepts in thy memory
See thou character. Give thy thoughts no tongue,
Nor any unproportioned thought his act.
Be thou familiar, but by no means vulgar.
Those friends thou hast, and their adoption tried,
Grapple them to thy soul with hoops of steel,
But do not dull thy palm with entertainment
Of each new-hatched unfledged comrade. Beware
Of entrance to a quarrel; but being in,
Bear't, that the opposed may beware of thee.
Give every man thy ear, but few thy voice:
Take each man's censure, but reserve thy judgment.
Costly thy habit as thy purse can buy,
But not expressed in fancy; rich, not gaudy:
For the apparel oft proclaims the man;
And they in France of the best rank and station
Are most select and generous in that.
Neither a borrower nor a lender be:
For loan oft loses both itself and friend,
And borrowing dulls the edge of husbandry.
This above all: to thine own self be true,
And it must follow, as the night the day,
Thou canst not then be false to any man.

"Frailty, Thy Name Is Woman" from *Hamlet*

O, that this too too solid flesh would melt,
Thaw and resolve itself into a dew!
Or that the Everlasting had not fix'd
His canon 'gainst self-slaughter! O God! O God!

How weary, stale, flat and unprofitable
Seem to me all the uses of this world!
Fie on't! oh fie! 'tis an unweeded garden,
That grows to seed; things rank and gross in nature
Possess it merely. That it should come to this!
But two months dead! nay, not so much, not two:
So excellent a king; that was, to this,
Hyperion to a satyr: so loving to my mother,
That he might not beteem the winds of heaven
Visit her face too roughly. Heaven and earth!
Must I remember? why, she would hang on him,
As if increase of appetite had grown
By what it fed on: and yet, within a month—
Let me not think on't—Frailty, thy name is woman!—
A little month, or ere those shoes were old
With which she follow'd my poor father's body,
Like Niobe, all tears:—why she, even she—
O God! a beast that wants discourse of reason
Would have mourned longer—married with my uncle,
My father's brother, but no more like my father
Than I to Hercules: within a month;
Ere yet the salt of most unrighteous tears
Had left the flushing in her galled eyes,
She married. O, most wicked speed, to post
With such dexterity to incestuous sheets!
It is not, nor it cannot come to good:
But break, my heart, for I must hold my tongue!

"To Be, Or Not To Be" from *Hamlet*

To be, or not to be: that is the question:
Whether 'tis nobler in the mind to suffer
The slings and arrows of outrageous fortune,
Or to take arms against a sea of troubles,
And by opposing end them. To die: to sleep;
No more; and by a sleep to say we end
The heart-ache, and the thousand natural shocks
That flesh is heir to. 'Tis a consummation
Devoutly to be wish'd. To die, to sleep;
To sleep? Perchance to dream! aye, there's the rub;

1127

For in that sleep of death what dreams may come,
When we have shuffled off this mortal coil,
Must give us pause: there's the respect
That makes calamity of so long life;
For who would bear the whips and scorns of time,
The oppressor's wrong, the proud man's contumely,
The pangs of despised love, the law's delay,
The insolence of office, and the spurns
That patient merit of the unworthy takes,
When he himself might his quietus make
With a bare bodkin? who would fardels bear,
To grunt and sweat under a weary life,
But that the dread of something after death,
The undiscovered country from whose bourn
No traveler returns, puzzles the will,
And makes us rather bear those ills we have
Than fly to others that we know not of?
Thus conscience does make cowards of us all,
And thus the native hue of resolution
Is sicklied o'er with the pale cast of thought,
And enterprises of great pitch and moment
With this regard their currents turn awry
And lose the name of action.

GEORGE BERNARD SHAW

GEORGE BERNARD SHAW (Irish, 1856-1950). Leading English dramatist, novelist and critic. Wit and reformer as well. First worked as music critic and founded Socialist Fabian Society. Propagandistic prefaces to his plays are sometimes more brilliant than the plays. Disciple of Ibsen, but created own witty drama of ideas. Most-praised works: *St. Joan, Pygmalion, Major Barbara, Candida, Caesar and Cleopatra, Man and Superman.*

THE MIRACULOUS REVENGE

I ARRIVED in Dublin on the evening of the 5th of August, and drove to the residence of my uncle, the Cardinal Archbishop. He is, like most of my family, deficient in feeling, and consequently cold to me personally. He lives in a dingy house, with a side-long view of the portico of his cathedral from the front windows, and of a monster national school from the back. My uncle maintains no retinue. The people believe that he is waited upon by angels. When I knocked at the door, an old woman, his only servant, opened it, and informed me that her master was then officiating in the cathedral, and that he had directed her to prepare dinner for me in his absence. An unpleasant smell of salt fish made me ask her what the dinner consisted of. She assured me that she had cooked all that could be permitted in His Holiness's house on a Friday. On my asking her further why on a Friday, she replied that Friday was a fast day. I bade her tell His Holiness that I had hoped to have the pleasure of calling on him shortly, and drove to a hotel in Sackville Street, where I engaged apartments and dined.

After dinner I resumed my eternal search—I know not for what; it drives me to and fro like another Cain. I sought in the streets without success. I went to the theatre. The music was execrable, the scenery poor. I had seen the play a month before in London, with the same beautiful artist in the chief part. Two years had passed since, seeing her for the first time, I had hoped that she, perhaps, might be the long-sought mystery. It had proved otherwise. On this night I looked at her and listened to her for the sake of that bygone hope, and applauded her generously when the curtain fell. But I went out lonely still. When I had supped at a restaurant, I returned to my hotel, and tried to read. In vain. The sound of feet in the corridors as the other occupants of the hotel went to bed distracted my attention from my book. Suddenly it occurred to me that I had never quite understood my uncle's character. He, father to a great flock of poor and ignorant Irish; an austere and saintly man, to whom livers of hopeless lives daily appealed for help heavenward; who was reputed never to have sent away a troubled peasant without relieving him of his burden by sharing it; whose knees were worn less by the altar steps than by the tears and embraces of the guilty and wretched: he had refused to humour my light extravagances, or to find time to talk with me of books, flowers, and music. Had I not been mad to expect it? Now that I needed sympathy myself, I did him justice. I desired to be with a true-hearted man, and to mingle my tears with his.

I looked at my watch. It was nearly an hour past midnight. In the corridor the lights were out, except one jet at the end. I threw a cloak upon my shoulders, put on a Spanish hat, and left my apartment, listening to the echoes of my measured steps retreating through the deserted passages. A strange sight arrested me on the landing of the grand staircase. Through an open door I saw the moonlight shining through the windows of a saloon in which some entertainment had recently taken place. I looked at my watch again. It was but one o'clock; and yet the guests had departed. I entered the room, my boots ringing loudly on the waxed boards. On a chair lay a child's clock and a broken toy. The entertainment had been a children's party. I stood for a time looking at the shadow of my cloaked figure upon the floor, and at the disordered decorations, ghostly in the white light. Then I saw that there was a grand piano, still open, in the middle of the room. My fingers throbbed as I sat down before it, and expressed all that I felt in a grand hymn which seemed to thrill the cold stillness of the shadows into a deep hum of approbation, and to people the radiance of the moon with angels. Soon there was a stir without too, as if the rapture was spreading abroad. I took up the chant triumphantly with my voice, and the empty saloon resounded as though to the thunder of an orchestra.

"Hallo, sir!" "Confound you, sir—" "Do you suppose that this—" "What the deuce—?"

I turned, and silence followed. Six men, partially dressed, and with dishevelled hair, stood regarding me angrily. They all carried candles. One of them had a bootjack, which he held like a truncheon. Another, the foremost, had a pistol. The night porter was behind trembling.

"Sir," said the man with the revolver, coarsely, "may I ask whether you are mad, that you disturb people at this hour with such an unearthly noise?"

"Is it possible that you dislike it?" I replied, courteously.

"Dislike it!" said he, stamping with rage. "Why—damn everything—do you suppose we were enjoying it?"

"Take care. He's mad," whispered the man with the bootjack.

I began to laugh. Evidently they did think me mad. Unaccustomed to my habits, and ignorant of music as they probably were, the mistake, however absurd, was not unnatural. I rose. They came closer to one another; and the night porter ran away.

"Gentlemen," I said, "I am sorry for you. Had you lain still and listened, we should all have been the better and happier. But what you have done, you cannot undo. Kindly inform the night porter that I am gone to visit my uncle, the Cardinal Archbishop. Adieu!"

I strode past them, and left them whispering among themselves.

1130

Some minutes later I knocked at the door of the Cardinal's house. Presently a window on the first floor was opened; and the moonbeams fell on a grey head, with a black cap that seemed ashy pale against the unfathomable gloom of the shadow beneath the stone sill.

"Who are you?"

"I am Zeno Legge."

"What do you want at this hour?"

The question wounded me. "My dear uncle," I exclaimed, "I know you do not intend it, but you make me feel unwelcome. Come down and let me in, I beg."

"Go to your hotel," he said sternly. "I will see you in the morning. Goodnight" He disappeared and closed the window.

I felt that if I let this rebuff pass, I should not feel kindly towards my uncle in the morning, nor, indeed, at any future time. I therefore plied the knocker with my right hand, and kept the bell ringing with my left until I heard the doorchain rattle within. The Cardinal's expression was grave nearly to moroseness as he confronted me on the threshold.

"Uncle," I cried, grasping his hand, "do not reproach me. Your door is never shut against the wretched. I am wretched. Let us sit up all night and talk"

"You may thank my position and not my charity for your admission, Zeno," he said. "For the sake of the neighbours, I had rather you played the fool in my study than upon my doorstep at this hour. Walk upstairs quietly, if you please. My housekeeper is a hard-working woman: the little sleep she allows herself must not be disturbed."

"You have a noble heart, uncle. I shall creep like a mouse."

"This is my study," he said, as we entered an ill-furnished den on the second floor. "The only refreshment I can offer you, if you desire any, is a bunch of raisins. The doctors have forbidden you to touch stimulants, I believe."

"By heaven—!" He raised his finger. "Pardon me: I was wrong to swear. But I had totally forgotten the doctors. At dinner I had a bottle of *Grave*."

"Humph! You have no business to be travelling alone. Your mother promised me that Bushy should come over here with you."

"Pshaw! Bushy is not a man of feeling. Besides, he is a coward. He refused to come with me because I purchased a revolver."

"He should have taken the revolver from you, and kept to his post."

1131

"Why will you persist in treating me like a child, uncle? I am very impressionable, I grant you; but I have gone round the world alone, and do not need to be dry-nursed through a tour in Ireland."

"What do you intend to do during your stay here?"

I had no plans; and instead of answering I shrugged my shoulders and looked around the apartment. There was a statuette of the Virgin upon my uncle's desk. I looked at its face, as he was wont to look in the midst of his labours, I saw there eternal peace. The air became luminous with an infinite network of the jewelled rings of Paradise descending in roseate clouds upon us.

"Uncle," I said, bursting into the sweetest tears I had ever shed, "my wanderings are over. I will enter the Church, if you will help me. Let us read together the third part of *Faust*; for I understand it at last."

"Hush, man," he said, half rising with an expression of alarm, "Control yourself."

"Do not let my tears mislead you. I am calm and strong. Quick, let us have Goethe:

> *Das Unbeschreibliche,*
> *Hier ist gethan;*
> *Das Ewig-Weibliche,*
> *Zieht uns hinan."*

"Come, come. Dry your eyes and be quiet. I have no library here."

"But I have—in my portmanteau at the hotel," I said, rising. "Let me go for it, I will return in fifteen minutes."

"The devil is in you, I believe. Cannot—"

I interrupted him with a shout of laughter. "Cardinal," I said noisily, "you have become profane; and a profane priest is always the best of good fellows. Let us have some wine; and I will sing you a German beer song."

"Heaven forgive me if I do you wrong," he said; "but I believe God has laid the expiation of some sin on your unhappy head. Will you favor me with your attention for a while? I have something to say to you, and I have also to get some sleep before my hour for rising, which is half-past five."

"My usual hour for retiring—when I retire at all. But proceed. My fault is not inattention, but over-susceptibility."

"Well, then, I want you to go to Wicklow. My reasons—"

"No matter what they may be," said I, rising again. "It is enough that you desire me to go. I shall start forthwith."

"Zeno! will you sit down and listen to me?"

I sank upon my chair reluctantly. "Ardor is a crime in your eyes, even when it is shown in your service," I said. "May I turn down the light?"

"Why?"

"To bring on my sombre mood, in which I am able to listen with tireless patience."

"I will turn it down myself. Will that do?"

I thanked him, and composed myself to listen in the shadow. My eyes, I felt, glittered. I was like Poe's raven.

"Now for my reasons for sending you to Wicklow. First, for your own sake. If you stay in town, or in any place where excitement can be obtained by any means, you will be in Swift's Hospital in a week. You must live in the country, under the eye of one upon whom I can depend. And you must have something to do to keep you out of mischief, and away from your music and painting and poetry, which, Sir John Richards writes to me, are dangerous for you in your present morbid state. Second, because I can entrust you with a task which, in the hands of a sensible man, might bring discredit on the Church. In short, I want you to investigate a miracle."

He looked attentively at me. I sat like a statue.

"You understand me?" he said.

"Nevermore," I replied, hoarsely. "Pardon me," I added, amused at the trick my imagination had played me, "I understand you perfectly. Proceed."

"I hope you do. Well, four miles distant from the town of Wicklow is a village called Four Mile Water. The resident priest is Father Hickey. You have heard of the miracles at Knock?"

I winked.

"I did not ask you what you think of them, but whether you have heard of them. I see you have. I need not tell you that even a miracle may do more harm than good to the Church in the country, unless it can be proved so thoroughly that her powerful and jealous enemies are silenced by the testimony of followers of their heresy. Therefore, when I saw in a Wexford newspaper last week a description of a strange manifestation of the Divine Power which was said to have taken place at Four Mile Water, I was troubled in my mind about it. So I wrote to Father Hickey, bidding him give me an

1133

account of the matter if it were true, and, if not, to denounce from the altar the author of the report, and to contradict it in the paper at once. This is his reply. He says—well, the first part is about Church matters: I need not trouble you with it. He goes on to say—"

"One moment. Is that his own handwriting? It does not look like a man's."

"He suffers from rheumatism in the fingers of his right hand, and his niece, who is an orphan, and lives with him, acts as his amanuensis. Well—"

"Stay. What is her name?"

"Her name? Kate Hickey."

"How old is she?"

"Tush, man, she is only a little girl. If she were old enough to concern you, I should not send you into her way. Have you any more questions to ask about her?"

"None. I can fancy her in a white veil at the rite of confirmation, a type of faith and innocence. Enough of her. What says the Reverend Hickey of the apparitions?"

"They are not apparitions. I will read you what he says. Ahem!

'In reply to your inquiries concerning the late miraculous event in this parish, I have to inform you that I can vouch for its truth, and that I can be confirmed not only by the inhabitants of the place, who are all Catholics, but by every person acquainted with the former situation of the graveyard referred to, including the Protestant Archdeacon of Baltinglas, who spends six weeks annually in the neighbourhood. The newspaper account is incomplete and inaccurate. The following are the facts: About four years ago, a man named Wolfe Tone Fitzgerald settled in this village as a farrier. His antecedents did not transpire, and he had no family. He lived by himself, was very careless of his person; and when in his cups, as he often was, regarded the honor neither of God nor man in his conversation. Indeed it it were not speaking ill of the dead, one might say that he was a dirty, drunken, blasphemous blackguard. Worse again, he was, I fear, an atheist, for he never attended Mass, and gave his Holiness worse language even than he gave the Queen. I should have mentioned that he was a bitter rebel, and boasted that his grandfather had been out in '98, and his father with Smith O'Brien. At last he went by the name of Brimstone Billy, and was held up in the village as the type of all wickedness.

'You are aware that our graveyard, situated on the north side of the water, is famous throughout the country as the burial place of the nuns of St. Ursula, the hermit of Four Mile Water, and many other holy people. No Protestant has ever ventured to enforce his legal right of interment there, though two have died in the parish within my own recollection. Three weeks ago, this Ftzgerald died in a fit brought on by drink, and a great hullabaloo was raised in the village when it became known that he would be buried in the graveyard. The body had to be watched to prevent its being stolen and buried at the cross-roads. My people were greatly disappointed when they were told I could do nothing to stop the burial, particularly as I of course refused to read any service on the occasion. However, I bade them not interfere; and the interment was effected on the 14th of July, late in the evening, and long after the legal hour. There was no disturbance. Next morning, the graveyard was found moved to the south side of the water, with the one newly-filled grave left behind on the north side; and thus they both remain. The departed saints would not lie with the reprobate. I can testify to it on the oath of a Christian priest; and if this will not satisfy those outside the Church, everyone, as I said before, who remembers where the graveyard was two months ago, can confirm me.

'I respectfully suggest that a thorough investigation into the truth of this miracle be proposed to a committee of Protestant gentlemen. They shall not be asked to accept a single fact on hearsay from my people. The ordnance maps show where the graveyard was; and anyone can see for himself where it is. I need not tell your Eminence what a rebuke this would be to those enemies of the holy Church that have sought to put a stain on her by discrediting the late wonderful manifestations at Knock Chapel. If they come to Four Mile Water, they need cross-examine no one. They will be asked to believe nothing but their own senses.

'Awaiting your Eminence's counsel to guide me further in the matter,

'*I am, etc.*'

"Well, Zeno," said my uncle, "what do you think of Father Hickey now?"

"Uncle, do not ask me. Beneath this roof I desire to believe everything. The Reverend Hickey has appealed strongly to my love of legend. Let us admire the poetry of his narrative and ignore the balance of probability between a Christian priest telling a lie on his oath and a graveyard swimming across a river in the middle of the night and forgetting to return."

"Tom Hickey is not telling a lie, sir. You may take my word for that. But he may be mistaken."

"Such a mistake amounts to insanity. It is true that I myself, awaking suddenly in the depth of night, have found myself convinced that the position of my bed had been reversed. But on opening my eyes the illusion ceased. I fear Mr. Hickey is mad. Your best course is this. Send down to Four Mile Water a perfectly sane investigator; an acute observer; one whose perceptive faculties, at once healthy and subtle, are absolutely unclouded by religious prejudice. In a word, send me. I will report to you the true state of affairs in a few days, and you can then make arrangements for transferring Hickey from the altar to the asylum."

"Yes, I had intended to send you. You are wonderfully sharp and you would make a capital detective if you could only keep your mind to one point. But your chief qualification for this business is that you are too crazy to excite the suspicions of those whom you may have to watch. For the affair may be a trick. If so, I hope and believe that Hickey has no hand in it. Still, it is my duty to take every precaution."

"Cardinal; may I ask whether traces of insanity have ever appeared in our family?"

"Except in you and in my grandmother, no. She was a Pole; and you resemble her personally. Why do you ask?"

"Because it has often occurred to me that you are, perhaps, a little cracked. Excuse my candour, but a man who has devoted his life to the pursuit of a red hat, who accuses everyone else besides himself of being mad, and who is disposed to listen seriously to a tale of a peripatetic graveyard, can hardly be quite sane. Depend upon it, uncle, you want rest and change. The blood of your Polish grandmother is in your veins."

"I hope I may not be committing a sin in sending a ribald on the Church's affairs," he replied, fervently. "However, we must use the instruments put into our hands. Is it agreed that you go?"

"Had you not delayed me with this story, which I might as well have learned on the spot, I should have been there already."

"There is no occasion for impatience, Zeno. I must first send to Hickey to find a place for you. I shall tell him that you are going

1136

to recover your health, as, in fact, you are. And, Zeno, in Heaven's name be discreet. Try to act like a man of sense. Do not dispute with Hickey on matters of religion. Since you are my nephew, you had better not disgrace me."

"I shall become an ardent Catholic, and do you infinite credit, uncle."

"I wish you would, although you would hardly be an acquisition to the Church. And now I must turn you out. It is nearly three o'clock, and I need some sleep. Do you know your way back to your hotel?"

"I need not stir. I can sleep in this chair. Go to bed, and never mind me."

"I shall not close my eyes until you are safely out of the house. Come, rouse yourself, and say goodnight."

The following is a copy of my first report to the Cardinal:

Four Mile Water, County Wicklow,
10th August

My Dear Uncle,

The miracle is genuine. I have affected perfect credulity in order to throw the Hickeys and the countryfolk off their guard with me. I have listened to their method of convincing sceptical strangers. I have examined the ordnance maps, and cross-examined the neighbouring Protestant gentle folk. I have spent a day upon the ground on each side of the water, and have visited it at midnight. I have considered the upheaval theories, subsidence theories, volcanic theories, and tidal wave theories which the provincial *savants* have suggested. They are all untenable. There is only one scoffer in the district, an Orangeman; and he admits the removal of the cemetery, but says it was dug up and transplanted in the night by a body of men under the command of Father Tom. This also is out of the question. The interment of Brimstone Billy was the first which had taken place for four years; and his is the only grave which bears a trace of recent digging. It is alone on the north bank, and the inhabitants shun it after nightfall. As each passer-by during the day throws a stone upon it, it will soon be marked by a large cairn. The graveyard, with a ruined stone chapel still standing in its midst, is on the south side. You may send down a committee to investigate the matter as soon as you please. There can be no doubt as to the miracle having actually taken place, as recorded by Hickey. As for me, I have grown so accustomed to it that if the county Wicklow were to waltz off with me to Middlesex, I should be quite impatient of any expressions of surprise from my friends in London.

Is not the above a businesslike statement? Away then, with this stale miracle. If you would see for yourself a miracle which can never pall, a vision of youth and health to be crowned with garlands for ever, come down and see Kate Hickey, whom you suppose to be a little girl. Illusion, my lord Cardinal, illusion! She is seventeen, with a bloom and a brogue that would lay your asceticism in ashes at a flash. To her I am an object of wonder, a strange man bred in wicked cities. She is courted by six feet of farming material, chopped off a spare length of coarse humanity by the Almighty, and flung into Wicklow to plough the fields. His name is Phil Langan; and he hates me. I have to consort with him for the sake of Father Tom, whom I entertain vastly by stories of your wild oats at Salamanca. I exhausted all my authentic anecdotes the first day; and now I invent gallant escapades with Spanish donnas, in which you figure as a youth of unstable morals. This delights Father Tom infinitely. I feel that I have done you a service by thus casting on the cold sacerdotal abstraction which formerly represented you in Kate's imagination a ray of vivifying passion.

What a country this is! A Hesperidean garden: such skies! Adieu, uncle.

Zeno Legge.

Behold me, then, at Four Mile Water, in love. I had been in love frequently; but not oftener than once a year had I encountered a woman who affected me as seriously as Kate Hickey. She was so shrewd, and yet so flippant! When I spoke of art she yawned. When I deplored the sordidness of the world she laughed, and called me "poor fellow!" When I told her what a treasure of beauty and freshness she had she ridiculed me. When I reproached her with brutality she became angry, and sneered at me for being what she called a fine gentleman. One sunny afternoon we were standing at the gate of her uncle's house, she looking down the dusty road for the detestable Langan, I watching the spotless azure sky, when she said:

"How soon are you going back to London?"

"I am not going back to London, Miss Hickey. I am not yet tired of Four Mile Water."

1138

"I'm sure Four Mile Water ought to be proud of your approbation."

"You disapprove of my liking it, then? Or is it that you grudge me the happiness I have found here? I think Irish ladies grudge a man a moment's peace."

"I wonder you have ever prevailed on yourself to associate with Irish ladies, since they are so far beneath you."

"Did I say they were beneath me, Miss Hickey? I feel that I have made a deep impression on you."

"Indeed! Yes, you're quite right. I assure you I can't sleep at night for thinking of you, Mr. Legge. It's the best a Christian can do, seeing you think so mighty little of yourself."

"You are triply wrong, Miss Hickey: wrong to be sarcastic with me, wrong to pretend that there is anything unreasonable in my belief that you think of me sometimes, and wrong to discourage the candour with which I always avow that I think constantly of myself."

"Then you had better not speak to me, since I have no manners."

"Again! Did I say you had no manners? The warmest expressions of regard from my mouth seem to reach your ears transformed into insults. Were I to repeat the Litany of the Blessed Virgin, you would retort as though I had been reproaching you. This is because you hate me. You never misunderstand Langan, whom you love."

"I don't know what London manners are, Mr. Legge; but in Ireland gentlemen are expected to mind their own business. How dare you say I love Mr. Langan?"

"Then you do not love him?"

"It is nothing to you whether I love him or not."

"Nothing to me that you hate me and love another?"

"I did not say that I hated you. You are not so very clever yourself at understanding what people say, though you make such fuss because they don't understand you." Here, as she glanced down the road again, she suddenly looked glad.

"Aha!" I said.

"What do you mean by 'Aha!'?"

"No matter. I will now show you what a man's sympathy is. As yon perceived just then, Langan—who is too tall for his age, by-the-bye—is coming to pay you a visit. Well, instead of staying with you, as a jealous woman would, I will withdraw."

"I don't care whether you go or stay, I'm sure. I wonder what you would give to be as fine a man as Mr. Langan."

1139

"All I possess: I swear it! But solely because you admire tall men more than broad views. Mr. Langan may be defined geometrically as length without breadth; altitude without position; a line on the landscape, not a point in it."

"How very clever you are!"

"You do not understand me, I see. Here comes your lover, stepping over the wall like a camel. And here go I, out through the gate like a Christian. Good afternoon, Mr. Langan. I am going because Miss Hickey has something to say to you about me which she would rather not say in my presence. You will excuse me?"

"Oh, I'll excuse you," said he boorishly. I smiled, and went out. Before I was quite out of hearing, Kate whispered vehemently to him, "I *hate* that fellow."

I smiled again; but I had scarcely done so when my spirits fell. I walked hastily away with a coarse threatening sound in my ears like that of the clarionets whose sustained low notes darken the woodland in "Der Freischütz." I found myself presently at the graveyard. It was a barren place, enclosed by a mud wall with a gate to admit funerals, and numerous gaps to admit the peasantry, who made short cuts across it as they went to and fro between Four Mile Water and the market town The graves were mounds overgrown with grass; there was no keeper; nor were there flowers, railings or any of the conventionalities that make an English graveyard repulsive. A great thornbush, near what was called the grave of the holy sisters, was covered with scraps of cloth and flannel, attached by peasant women who had prayed before it. There were three kneeling there as I entered, for the reputation of the place had been revived of late by the miracle, and a ferry had been established close by, to conduct visitors over the route taken by the graveyard. From where I stood I could see on the opposite bank the heap of stones, perceptibly increased since my last visit, marking the deserted grave of Brimstone Billy. I strained my eyes broodingly at it for some minutes, and then descended the river bank and entered the boat.

"Good evenin' t'your honour," said the ferryman, and set to work to draw the boat hand-over-hand by a rope stretched across the water.

"Good evening. Is your business beginning to fall off yet?"

"Faith, it never was as good as it might ha' been. The people that comes from the south side can see Billy's grave—Lord have mercy on him—across the wather; and they think bad of payin' a

1140

penny to put a stone over him. It's them that lives tow'rst Dublin that makes the journey. Your honour is the third I've brought from south to north this blessed day."

"When do most people come? In the afternoon, I suppose?"

"All hours, sur, except afther dusk. There isn't a sowl in the counthry ud come within sight of that grave wanst the sun goes down."

"And you! Do you stay here all night by yourself?"

"The holy heavens forbid! Is it me stay here all night? No, your honour; I tether the boat at siven o'hlyock, and lave Brimstone Billy—God forgimme!—to take care of it t'll mornin."

"It will be stolen some night, I'm afraid."

"Arra, who'd dar come next or near it, let alone stale it? Faith, I'd think twice before lookin at it meself in the dark. God bless your honour, and gran'che long life."

I had given him sixpence. I went to the reprobate's grave and stood at the foot of it, looking at the sky, gorgeous with the descent of the sun. To my English eyes, accustomed to giant trees, broad lawns, and stately mansions, the landscape was wild and inhospitable. The ferryman was already tugging at the rope on his way back (I had told him I did not intend to return that way), and presently I saw him make the painter fast o the south bank; put on his coat; and trudge homeward. I turned towards the grave at my feet. Those who had interred Brimstone Billy, working hastily at an unlawful hour, and in fear of molestation by the people, had hardly dug a grave. They had scooped out earth enough to hide their burden, and no more. A stray goat had kicked away a corner of the mound and exposed the coffin. It occurred to me, as I took some of the stones from the cairn, and heaped them so as to repair the breach, that had the miracle been the work of a body of men, they would have moved the one grave instead of the many. Even from a supernatural point of view, it seemed strange that the sinner should have banished the elect, when, by their superior numbers, they might so much more easily have banished him.

It was almost dark when I left the spot, After a walk of half a mile, I recrossed the water by a bridge, and returned to the farmhouse in which I lodged. Here, finding that I had had enough of solitude, I only stayed to take a cup of tea. Then I went to Father Hickey's cottage.

Kate was alone when I entered. She looked up quickly as I

opened the door, and turned away disappointed when she recognized me.

"Be generous for once," I said. "I have walked about aimlessly for hours in order to avoid spoiling the beautiful afternoon for you by my presence. When the sun was up I withdrew my shadow from your path. Now that darkness has fallen, shed some light on mine. May I stay half an hour?"

"You may stay as long as you like, of course. My uncle will soon be home. He is clever enough to talk to you."

"What! More sarcasms! Come, Miss Hickey, help me to spend a pleasant evening. It will only cost you a smile. I am somewhat cast down. Four Mile Water is a paradise; but without you, it would be a little lonely."

"It must be very lonely for you. I wonder why you came here."

"Because I heard that the women here were all Zerlinas like you, and the men Masettos, like Mr. Phil—where are you going to?"

"Let me pass, Mr. Legge. I had intended never speaking to you again after the way you went on about Mr. Langan today; and I wouldn't either, only my uncle made me promise not to take any notice of you, because you were—no matter; but I won't listen to you any more on the subject."

"Do not go. I swear never to mention his name again. I beg your pardon for what I said: you shall have no further cause for complaint. Will you forgive me?"

She sat down, evidently disappointed by my submission. I took a chair, and placed myself near her. She tapped the floor impatiently with her foot. I saw that there was not a movement I could make, not a look, not a tone of my voice, which did not irritate her.

"You were remarking," I said, "that your uncle desired you to take no notice of me because—"

She closed her lips, and did not answer.

"I fear I have offended you again by my curiosity. But indeed, I had no idea that he had forbidden you to tell me the reason."

"He did not forbid me. Since you are so determined to find out—"

"No, excuse me. I do not wish to know, I am sorry I asked."

"Indeed! Perhaps you would be sorrier still to be told. I only made a secret of it out of consideration for you."

"Then your uncle has spoken ill of me behind my back. If that be so, there is no such thing as a true man in Ireland. I would not have believed it on the word of any woman alive save yourself."

1142

"I never said my uncle was a backbiter. Just to show you what he thinks of you, I will tell you whether you want to know it or not, that he bid me not mind you because you were only a poor mad creature, sent down here by your family to be out of harm's way."

"Oh, Miss Hickey!"

"There now! You have got it out of me; and I wish I had bit my tongue out first. I sometimes think—that I mayn't sin!—that you have a bad angel in you."

"I am glad you told me this," I said gently. "Do not reproach yourself for having done so, I beg. Your uncle has been misled by what he has heard of my family, who are all more or less insane. Far from being mad, I am actually the only rational man named Legge in the three kingdoms. I will prove this to you, and at the the same time keep your indiscretion in countenance, by telling you something I ought not to tell you. It is this. I am not here as an invalid or a chance tourist. I am here to investigate the miracle. The Cardinal, a shrewd if somewhat erratic man, selected mine from all the long heads at his disposal to come down here, and find out the truth of Father Hickey's story. Would he have entrusted such a task to a madman, think you?"

"The truth of—who dared to doubt my uncle's word? And so you are a spy, a dirty informer."

I started. The adjective she had used, though probably the commonest expression of contempt in Ireland, is revolting to an Englishman.

"Miss Hickey," I said, "there is in me, as you have said, a bad angel. Do not shock my good angel—who is a person of taste—quite away from my heart, lest the other be left undisputed monarch of it. Hark! The chapel bell is ringing the angelus. Can you, with that sound softening the darkness of the village night, cherish a feeling of spite against one who admires you?"

"You come between me and my prayers," she said hysterically, and began to sob. She had scarcely done so, when I heard voices without. Then Langan and the priest entered.

"Oh Phil," she cried, running to him, "take me away from him: I can't bear—" I turned towards him, and showed him my dog-tooth in a false smile. He felled me at one stroke, as he might have felled a poplar tree.

"Murdher!" exclaimed the priest. "What are you doin, Phil?"

"He is an informer," sobbed Kate. "He came down here to spy

1143

on you, uncle, and to try and show that the blessed miracle was a make-up. I knew it long before he told me, by his insulting ways. He wanted to make love to me."

I rose with difficulty from beneath the table, where I had lain motionless for a moment.

"Sir," I said, "I am somewhat dazed by the recent action of Mr. Langan, whom I beg, the next time he converts himself into a fulling-mill, to do so at the expense of a man more nearly his equal in strength than I. What your niece has told you is partly true. I am indeed the Cardinal's spy; and I have already reported to him that the miracle is a genuine one. A committee of gentlemen will wait on you tomorrow to verify it, at my suggestion. I have thought that the proof might be regarded by them as more complete if you were taken by surprise. Miss Hickey, that I admire all that is admirable in you is but to say that I have a sense of the beautiful. To say that I love you would be mere profanity. Mr. Langan, I have in my pocket a loaded pistol, which I carry from a silly English prejudice against you countrymen. Had I been the Hercules of the ploughtail, and you in my place, I should have been a dead man now. Do not redden; you are safe as far as I am concerned."

"Let me tell you before you leave my house for good," said Father Hickey, who seemed to have become unreasonably angry, "that you should never have crossed my threshold if I had known you were a spy; no, not if your uncle were his Holiness the Pope himself."

Here a frightful thing happened to me. I felt giddy, and put my hand to my head. Three warm drops trickled over it. Instantly I became murderous. My mouth filled with blood, my eyes were blinded with it; I seemed to drown in it. My hand went involuntarily to the pistol. It is my habit to obey my impulses instantaneously. Fortunately the impulse to kill vanished before a sudden perception of how I might miraculously humble the mad vanity in which these foolish people had turned upon me. The blood receded from my ears; and I again heard and saw distinctly.

"And let *me* tell you," Langan was saying, "that if you think yourself handier with cold lead than you are with your fists, I'll exchange shots with you, and welcome, whenever you please. Father Tom's credit is the same to me as my own, and if you say a word against it, you lie."

"His credit is in my hands," I said. "I am the Cardinal's witness. Do you defy me?"

"There is the door," said the priest, holding it open before me.

"Until you can undo the visible work of God's hand your testimony can do no harm to me."

"Father Hickey," I replied, "before the sun rises again upon Four Mile Water, I will undo the visible work of God's hand, and bring the pointing finger of the scoffer upon your altar."

I bowed to Kate, and walked out. It was so dark that I could not at first see the garden-gate. Before I found it, I heard through the window Father Hickey's voice, saying. "I wouldn't for ten pound that this had happened, Phil. He's as mad as a March hare. The Cardinal told me so."

I returned to my lodging, and took a cold bath to cleanse the blood from my neck and shoulder. The effect of the blow I had received was so severe, that even after the bath and a light meal I felt giddy and languid. There was an alarum-clock on the mantel-piece. I wound it; set the alarum for half-past twelve; muffled it so that it should not disturb the people in the adjoining room; and went to bed, where I slept soundly for an hour and a quarter. Then the alarum woke me, and I sprang up before I was thoroughly awake. Had I hesitated, the desire to relapse into perfect sleep would have overpowered me. Although the muscles of my neck were painfully stiff, and my hands unsteady from my nervous disturbance, produced by the interruption of my first slumber, I dressed myself resolutely, and, after taking a draught of cold water, stole out of the house. It was exceedingly dark and I had some difficulty in finding the cow-house, whence I borrowed a spade, and a truck with wheels, ordinarily used for moving sacks of potatoes. These I carried in my hands until I was beyond earshot of the house, when I put the spade on the truck, and wheeled it along the road to the cemetery. When I approached the water, knowing that no one would dare to come thereabout at such an hour, I made greater haste, no longer concerning myself about the rattling of the wheels. Looking across to the opposite bank, I could see a phosphorescent glow, marking the lonely grave of Brimstone Billy. This helped me to find the ferry station, where, after wandering a little and stumbling often, I found the boat, and embarked with my implements. Guided by the rope, I crossed the water without difficulty; landed; made fast the boat; dragged the truck up the bank; and sat down to rest on the cairn of the grave. For nearly a quarter of an hour I sat watching the patches of jack-o'-lantern fire, and collecting my strength for the work before me. Then the distant bell of the chapel clock tolled one. I rose, took the spade, and in about ten minutes uncovered the coffin, which

1145

smelt horribly. Keeping to windward of it, and using the spade as a lever, I contrived with great labor to place it on the truck. I wheeled it without accident to the landing-place, where, by placing the shafts of the truck upon the stern of the boat and lifting the foot by main strength, I succeeded in embarking my load after twenty minutes' toil, during which I got covered with clay and perspiration, and several times all but upset the boat. At the southern bank I had less difficulty in getting truck and coffin ashore, and dragging them up to the graveyard.

It was now past two o'clock, and the dawn had begun, so that I had no further trouble from want of light. I wheeled the coffin to a patch of loamy soil which I had noticed in the afternoon near the grave of the holy sisters. I had warmed to my work; my neck no longer pained me; and I began to dig vigorously, soon making a shallow trench, deep enough to hide the coffin with the addition of a mound. The chill pearl-coloured morning had by this time quite dissipated the darkness. I could see, and was myself visible, for miles around. This alarmed me, and made me impatient to finish my task. Nevertheless, I was forced to rest for a moment before placing the coffin in the trench. I wiped my brow and wrists, and again looked about me. The tomb of the holy women, a massive slab supported by four stone spheres, was grey and wet with dew. Near it was the thornbush covered with rags, the newest of which were growing gaudy in the radiance which was stretching up from the coast on the east. It was time to finish my work. I seized the truck; laid it alongside the grave; and gradually prized the coffin off with the spade until it rolled over into the trench with a hollow sound like a drunken remonstrance from the sleeper within. I shovelled the earth round and over it, working as fast as possible. In less than a quarter of an hour it was buried. Ten minutes more sufficed to make the mound symmetrical, and to clear the traces of my work from the adjacent sward. Then I flung down the spade: threw up my arms; and vented a sigh of relief and triumph. But I recoiled as I saw that I was standing on a barren common, covered with furze. No product of man's handiwork was near me except my truck and spade and the grave of Brimstone Billy, now as lonely as before. I turned towards the water. On the opposite bank was the cemetery, with the tomb of the holy women, the thornbush with its rags stirring in the morning breeze, and the broken mud wall. The ruined chapel was there too, not a stone shaken from its crumbling walls, not a sign to show that it and its precinct were less rooted in their place than the eternal hills around.

I looked down at the grave with a pang of compassion for the unfortunate Wolfe Tone Fitzgerald, with whom the blessed would not rest. I was even astonished, though I had worked expressly to this end. But the birds were astir, and the cocks crowing. My landlord was an early riser. I put the spade on the truck again, and hastened back to the farm, where I replaced them in the cow-house. Then I stole into the house, and took a clean pair of boots, an overcoat, and a silk hat. These, with a change of linen, were sufficient to make my appearance respectable. I went out again, bathed in the Four Mile Water, took a last look at the cemetery, and walked to Wicklow, whence I travelled by the first train to Dublin.

Some months later, at Cairo, I received a packet of Irish newspapers and a leading article, cut from the *Times*, on the subject of the miracle. Father Hickey had suffered the meed of his inhospitable conduct. The committee, arriving at Four Mile Water the day after I left, had found the graveyard exactly where it had formerly stood. Father Hickey, taken by surprise, had attempted to defend himself by a confused statement, which led the committee to declare finally that the miracle was a gross imposture. The *Times*, commenting on this after adducing a number of examples of priestly craft, remarked, "We are glad to learn that the Rev. Mr. Hickey has been permanently relieved of his duties as the parish priest of Four Mile Water by his ecclesiastical superior. It is less gratifying to have to record that it has been found possible to obtain two hundred signatures to a memorial embodying the absurd defense offered to the committee, and expressing unabated confidence in the integrity of Mr. Hickey."

PERCY BYSSHE SHELLEY

PERCY BYSSHE SHELLY (English, 1792-1822). One of major Romantic poets. Lived and wrote in the light of Greek classicism. Expelled from Oxford for pamphlet on atheism. Eloped with Mary Wollstonecraft (author of *Frankenstein*). Drowned in Italy. Many of his long works are didactic and philosophical. Better-loved are such shorter lyrics as "Adonais," "Ode to the West Wind," "To Night," etc.

LOVE

When the lamp is shattered,
  The light in the dust lies dead—
When the cloud is scattered,
  The rainbow's glory is shed.
When the lute is broken,
  Sweet tones are remembered not;
When the lips have spoken,
  Loved accents are soon forgot.

As music and splendour
  Survive not the lamp and the lute,
The heart's echoes render
  No song when the spirit is mute—
No song but sad dirges,
  Like the wind through a ruined cell,
Or the mournful surges
  That ring the dead seaman's knell.

When hearts have once mingled,
  Love first leaves the well-built nest;
The weak one is singled
  To endure what it once possest.
O Love! who bewailest
  The frailty of all things here,
Why choose you the frailest
  For your cradle, your home, and your bier?

Its passions will rock thee
  As the storms rock the ravens on high;
Bright reason will mock thee
  Like the sun from a wintry sky.

From thy nest every rafter
    Will rot, and thine eagle home
Leave thee naked to laughter,
    When leaves fall and cold winds come.

INVOCATION

Rarely, rarely, comest thou,
    Spirit of Delight!
Wherefore hast thou left me now
    Many a day and night?
Many a weary night and day
'Tis since thou art fled away.

How shall ever one like me
    Win thee back again?
With the joyous and the free
    Thou wilt scoff at pain.
Spirit false! thou hast forgot
All but those who need thee not.

As a lizard with the shade
    Of a trembling leaf,
Thou with sorrow art dismay'd;
    Even the sighs of grief
Reproach thee, that thou art not near,
And reproach thou wilt not hear.

Let me set my mournful ditty
    To a merry measure;
Thou wilt never come for pity,
    Thou wilt come for pleasure;
Pity then will cut away
Those cruel wings, and thou wilt stay.

I love all that thou lovest,
    Spirit of Delight!
The fresh Earth in new leaves drest
    And the starry night;
Autumn evening, and the morn
When the golden mists are born.

I love snow and all the forms
   Of the radiant frost;
I love waves, and winds, and storms,
   Everything almost
Which is Nature's, and may be
Untainted by man's misery.

I love tranquil solitude,
   And such society
As is quiet, wise, and good;
   Between thee and me
What diff'rence? but thou dost possess
The things I seek, not love them less.
I love Love—though he has wings,
   And like light can flee,
But above all other things,
   Spirit, I love thee—
Thou art love and life! O come!
Make once more my heart thy home!

DEJECTION

  The sun is warm, the sky is clear,
    The waves are dancing fast and bright,
Blue isles and snowy mountains wear
    The purple noon's transparent might:
    The breath of the moist earth is light
Around its unexpanded buds;
    Like many a voice of one delight—
The winds, the birds, the ocean-floods—
The City's voice itself is soft like Solitude's.

  I see the Deep's untrampled floor
    With green and purple seaweeds strown;
I see the waves upon the shore,
    Like light dissolved in star-showers, thrown:
    I sit upon the sands alone;
The lightning of the noontide ocean
    Is flashing round me, and a tone
Arises from its measured motion—
How sweet! did any heart now share in my emotion.

Alas! I have nor hope nor health,
    Nor peace within nor calm around,
Nor that content, surpassing wealth,
    The sage in meditation found,
    And walked with inward glory crowned—
Nor fame, nor power, nor love, nor leisure;
    Others I see whom these surround—
Smiling they live, and call life pleasure;
To me that cup has been dealt in another measure.

Yet now despair itself is mild
    Even as the winds and waters are;
I could lie down like a tired child,
    And weep away the life of care
    Which I have borne, and yet must bear,
Till death like sleep might steal on me,
    And I might feel in the warm air
My cheek grow cold, and hear the sea
Breathe o'er my dying brain its last monotony.

ODE TO THE WEST WIND

O wild West Wind, thou breath of Autumn's being,
Thou, from whose unseen presence the leaves dead
Are driven, like ghosts from an enchanter fleeing,
Yellow, and black, and pale, and hectic red,
Pestilence-stricken multitudes: O thou
Who chariotest to their dark wintry bed
The wingèd seeds, where they lie cold and low,
Each like a corpse within its grave, until
Thine azure sister of the Spring shall blow
Her clarion o'er the dreaming earth, and fill
(Driving sweet buds like flocks to feed in air)
With living hues and odours plain and hill:
Wild Spirit, which art moving everywhere;
Destroyer and Preserver; hear, oh, hear!

Thou on whose stream, mid the steep sky's commotion,
Loose clouds like earth's decaying leaves are shed,
Shook from the tangled boughs of Heaven and Ocean,
Angels of rain and lightning: there are spread

1151

On the blue surface of thine airy surge,
Like the bright hair uplifted from the head
Of some fierce Maenad, even from the dim verge
Of the horizon to the zenith's height,
The locks of the approaching storm. Thou dirge
Of the dying year, to which this closing night
Will be the dome of a vast sepulchre,
Vaulted with all thy congregated might
Of vapours, from whose solid atmosphere
Black rain, and fire, and hail, will burst: oh, hear!

Thou who didst waken from his summer dreams
The blue Mediterranean, where he lay,
Lull'd by the coil of his crystalline streams,
Beside a pumice isle in Baiae's bay,
And saw in sleep old palaces and towers
Quivering within the wave's intenser day,
All overgrown with azure moss and flowers
So sweet, the sense faints picturing them! Thou
For whose path the Atlantic's level powers
Cleave themselves into chasms, while far below
The sea-blooms and the oozy woods which wear
The sapless foliage of the ocean, know
Thy voice, and suddenly grow grey with fear,
And tremble and despoil themselves: oh, hear!

If I were a dead leaf thou mightest bear;
If I were a swift cloud to fly with thee;
A wave to pant beneath thy power, and share
The impulse of thy strength, only less free
Than thou, O uncontrollable! If even
I were as in my boyhood, and could be
The comrade of thy wanderings over Heaven,
As then, when to outstrip thy skyey speed
Scarce seemed a vision, I would ne'er have striven
As thus with thee in prayer in my sore need.
Oh, lift me as a wave, a leaf, a cloud!
I fall upon the thorns of life! I bleed!
A heavy weight of hours has chained and bowed
One too like thee: tameless, and swift, and proud.

Make me thy lyre, even as the forest is:
What if my leaves are falling like its own!
The tumult of thy mighty harmonies
Will take from both a deep, autumnal tone,
Sweet though in sadness. Be thou, Spirit fierce,
My spirit! Be thou me, impetuous one!
Drive my dead thoughts over the universe
Like withered leaves to quicken a new birth!
And, by the incantation of this verse,
Scatter, as from an unextinguished hearth
Ashes and sparks, my words among mankind!
Be through my lips to unawakened earth
The trumpet of a prophecy! O Wind,
If Winter comes, can Spring be far behind?

TO NIGHT

Swiftly walk o'er the western wave,
    Spirit of Night!
Out of the misty eastern cave,
Where, all the long and lone daylight,
Thou wovest dreams of joy and fear,
Which make thee terrible and dear—
    Swift be thy flight!

Wrap thy form in a mantle gray,
    Star-inwrought!
Blind with thine hair the eyes of day;
Kiss her until she be wearied out,
Then wander o'er city, and sea, and land,
Touching all with thine opiate wand—
    Come, long-sought!

When I arose and saw the dawn,
    I sighed for thee;
When light rode high, and the dew was gone,
And noon lay heavy on flower and tree,
And the weary day turned to his rest,
Lingering like an unloved guest,
    I sighed for thee.

1153

Thy brother Death came, and cried,
  Wouldst thou me?
Thy sweet child Sleep, the filmy-eyed,
Murmured like a noontide bee,
Shall I nestle near thy side?
Wouldst thou me?—And I replied,
  No, not thee!

Death will come when thou art dead,
  Soon, too soon—
Sleep will come when thou art fled;
Of neither would I ask the boon
I ask of thee, beloved Night—
Swift be thine approaching flight,
  Come soon, soon!

SHEN TS'UNG-WEN

SHÉN TS'UNG-WÉN (Chinese, 1902-   ). Prolific Chinese novelist and
critic. Had military rather than conventional academic background. Edited
Ta-kung pao literary supplement. Author of some 60 novels, volumes of stories
and other works.

UNDER COVER OF DARKNESS

THE bamboo raft, nimbly manned by the two men, glided quietly
downstream. The raftsmen had passed unseen through the river
patrols, and were now only two miles from their destination, but
suddenly the raft ran aground on a wild bank overgrown with rushes
and reeds, and while the raft remained still and unmoving, they
heard the murmuring of the water and the rustling of the wind
through the reeds.

Lu-Yi, an officer of the signal corps of the guerrilla troops, began
to blame the younger man, hoarsely. "What's the matter?" he asked.
"Are you possessed by devils? You think it's funny, don't you?
But if we are stranded here, they will soon find us out, and we shall
be shot to pieces by their guns."

The boy who had been crouching on the raft stood up slowly,
but still he made no sound. There was a faint shimmering light on

the dark surface of the river, and in the water there lay the reflection of two men standing on a raft, a reflection which was upsidedown. Silently the boy walked to the other end of the raft.

"Well, we have run aground. I guess we have caught in something!" It was the voice of a very young boy.

He went up to the older man, and still leaning against the oar which he held in one hand, he took over the bamboo pole and tried to push it hither and thither in the marshy water. They were at a bend in the river where the water was shallow, but from the murmur of the water it was clear that the river ran swift round the bend; and there was no reason why the rafts should remain still, unless something had caught hold of the bamboo raft from underneath.

Their spirits were tried. Lu-Yi began to grumble again, impatiently. "There's two miles to go," he said. "It's a desperately dangerous area. There might be enemy patrols at any moment. . . ."

The boy seemed to have no feeling for fear or sorrow. He silently listened to the older man, and then untied the automatic pistol and bullet-case from his belt, rolled up his trousers, and gently slid into the water. He found a foothold and stooped down to push the raft with both hands. They heard the long, low squeak of the bamboos, but the raft did not move, and seemed, indeed, to be constrained by unseen hands.

Lu-Yi was still impatient. "Be careful," he murmured. "I know you are strong. but be careful. Better take off your clothes and feel with your hands underneath the bamboos. There seem to be devils and ghosts there. . . ."

"Yes," the boy answered, with a little giggle. "Devils and ghosts. But let me try. . . ."

He began to move slowly in the water, stretching his hands under the bamboos. Touching the ropes and knots which joined the raft together, he stooped down, his arms and shoulders buried under the cold water, and his chin kissing the rippling surface of the river Meanwhile his feet sank in mud to the knees, and it took an effort to pull them up again. He was still feeling among the knots and ropes when he felt something hard and round striking against his fingers. He realized then that it was a millstone entangled among ropes and clothes. He reached out his hands and felt the coldwetness of a human body. "A body!" he shouted out in mingled alarm and delight, for now at last he knew what was obstructing the raft. "A body!" he exclaimed. "It's the funniest thing. . . ."

"Well, what is it?"

He did not answer. He ran his fingers over the body and touched the hair, the face, and then the arms. It was bound to the millstone with heavy ropes, which had somewhat curled round the bamboos.

"Even with a millstone round its neck, this body prevents us from moving," the boy laughed silently.

"Then take it away," the other commanded, and he was more impatient than ever when he heard the crowing of the first cocks in the distance. "The body of a good-for-nothing," he added contemptuously. "No good when he was alive, and no good when he was dead," he murmured softly.

The boy was still wading round the raft, trying to disentangle the rope. Lu-Yi drew his knife from his belt and tapped it against the side of the raft. "Boy, come here," he said. "Take the knife and cut the rope in two. If the devil doesn't loosen his hold, cut his hand off. Hurry up! We're in terrible danger, and we have to get to the army."

The boy amused by the expression "loosen his hold," wondered at his companion's impatience.

There was a muffled noise of a knife stirring up the water, and the raft began to turn a little. A little while later he went to the stern of the raft and put his shoulder against it. He began to push hard, but he only succeeded in lifting the raft a little above the level of the water. The raft kept turning, but did not move forward. It was difficult to manage the knife under water, and perhaps in the end they would have to take the raft to pieces and then join the bamboos up again. But there was no time. Besides, less than a mile downstream, they knew there was a pontoon bridge held by the enemy. Lu-Yi could no longer restrain his impatience. He began to curse the boy for his lightheartedness and slowness, and promised to write a report on his negligence, inefficiency, and lack of responsibility. The boy remained calm, unmoved.

"Well, then, we had better walk instead of wasting our time on the river," he said, in a perfectly matter-of-fact voice. "Otherwise we won't get there before dawn."

"There are traps laid for us all over the hills and valley," the other answered. "The devils are ready with their ropes and millstones there. If we walk those two miles, it's likely we'll have millstones round our necks before dawn."

"Fears can't stop us," the boy replied. "There's no other way."

At last the older man was convinced. They carried the two bullet-cases and the rest of their equipment on to the embankment, groping and stumbling in the dark. Then they sat among the tall reeds and whispered about the routes they would take. They had no idea of the ponds and marshes and streams which lay in their way, and the villages and guard stations through which they would have to pass. In the black sky not a single star lay visible. Each one had brought a shirt torch, but in the enveloping darkness they seemed to see eyes glaring at them, and they knew that the slightest light shown by them would call for a bullet from the enemy. And if the enemy knew that they were passing along the river, the lives of all those who followed them on the bamboo rafts would be endangered.

After a while they decided not to take the road over the hills, but to follow the path which lay along the edge of the river. The flood water had receded during the past few days, and now the path was dry. Besides, there was always the chance that they would come across a sampan or canoe left somewhere along the bank.

The small path wound through bushy reeds. The earth was muddy and slippery underfoot, and there was a strange smell, a smell which grew inexplicably stronger as they went forward.

"Mind your steps! There's probably another body somewhere around. Don't fall over it."

"I forgot to feel the pockets of the fellow under the raft. Probably he was one of our comrades."

"Who else could it be?"

"Now I remember. The message of number seventy-four was stitched into the back of his trousers, the message of thirteen was hidden in a cigarette, and. . . ."

"Rubbish! Don't talk. We are still under close watch. Look out, because we don't want to have two more corpses in the place."

Lu-Yi was embarrassed by the strange smell, and thought the corpse could hardly be more than five yeards away from them. He held his torch in his hand, and made as though he was going to flick on the light. but the boy prevented him. They pricked up their ears and listened intently. They heard the approaching splash of rhythmic oars. They were about five feet away from the river. but thick bushes of reeds screened them from sight. They were both aware of the critical situation they were in, for it was evident that the approaching boat was patrolling the river to prevent the guerrillas from using it as a means of communication. If the patrol boat had reached the bend in the river and discovered the raft and their footprints, they would be followed immediately. and God

1157

knows what would happen then. Fortunately, they were already on land. . . .

At that moment, frightened by the steps of the two wanderers or by the splashing of the oars in the river, a waterfowl rose, flapped its wings, and flew up into the dark sky. And then, after describing aimless and purposeless evolutions, it darted towards the opposite bank of the river. They heard whispers among the oarsmen; probably they had already suspected the presence of strangers among the reeds. But the boat, instead of pursuing them, followed in the direction of the waterfowl, and they heard the leisurely pad of oars as the boat went towards the other bank.

The two wanderers lay on the bank with their pistols pointed in the direction of the boat. They were calm and determined, but when they heard the boat moving into the distance, they held out their hands silently at the same moment and clasped one another's hands with excitement and relief. Then they went on.

They could still smell the corpse, which was evidently lying somewhere to their left, away from the path. Suddenly Lu-Yi felt a hand snatching at his sleve.

"Devil take you! What do you want?" he groaned.

"I think it is comrade seventy-four. Let me go and feel his body. A minute, or half a minute. . . ."

Without waiting for an answer from the older man, who was clearly displeased by the suggestion, the boy bent down and ran swiftly towards the place in the bushes where the heavy foetid smell came from. He was back half a minute later.

"It's him all right," the boy said. "And it smells like him. He was a daring and dauntless fellow when alive, and now, even in corruption, his smell is terrific."

"What have you got?"

"A handful of maggots."

"Are you sure it is him?"

Yes, I tore off his collar. The papers are there. I knew it right away."

"Nice fellows—both of you!"

They strode along the path in silence. They were soon out of the bushes, but new dangers seemed to be lying in wait for them. Soon they came to a hillside, where the path diverged, one road leading down towards the ford, and the other winding strangely among the battlemented rocks. A few lights were shining above the ford: evidently the place was well guarded. They gazed into one another's faces and neither could decide which pass was more dangerous or easier to get through.

Each minute gained gave them more hope, but they had no time to lose. They knew that the path to the ford was more familiar to them, and, if necessary, they could wade or swim across the river. They made a dash for the river. The boy saw that a fire was going out, and was probably unattended, but the older man held him back.

"Don't go near the fire, boy!"

"Don't worry. The fire must have been left behind by the patrols who boarded the boat. Probably they left it intentionally, to make us think they were there."

Once more the boy won the older man's consent. Crawling on all fours, they made their way towards the dying embers. They passed the fire unharmed, and found themselves before a long smooth road which wound along the edge of the hills and the river. They were light hearted now, and all the danger forgotten, until some minutes later the boy thought he heard the clop-clop of a horse's hooves along the road. Lu-Yi listened. He too, heard the sound and imagined that the enemy was approaching, followed perhaps by a wolfhound trained to smell out strangers at night. They decided to hide in the woods which bordered the hill, and blindly they crawled among the shadows of rocks and trees. Later, they heard the sound of hoof-beats along the road at the place where they had been, and they even imagined they could see the sparks from under the horse's feet and the white, thick vapour coming from the horse's mouth, and the sleek shadow of its back.

On his way down the slope, Lu-Yi twisted his ankle, but he knew that he would have to go as fast as possible if they were to avoid the guard station.

The sound of cocks crowing was wafted down the river. They decided, then, to bury their automatics among the reeds and swim downstream. If they could once pass the pontoon bridge, they would find themselves in safe territory less than a quarter of a mile away. But Lu-Yi knew that with his twisted ankle, it would be impossible for him to swim. They could go over the hills, but the tracks there were unknown to them, and hardly visible even in broad daylight. Moreover, beyond the hills lay precipitous slopes looking down over a ravine, and it would be easy for the enemy patrols to pick them out.

Knowing that the position was hopeless, Lu-Yi broke out into angry remonstrances.

"Boy, it's a trick played by devils. I know I am going to die here, and become a mess of worms. Next time you pass this way, better feel my collar as well. I can't walk. My right leg hurts abominably, and I am sure I can't swim. You go downstream, and I'll go to the hills—and give me your pistol."

"No, if you are hurt, I'll go with you. We'll go up the hill and die together if we have to."

"Why should we die together, my dear little devil," Lu-Yi answered, in a tone of annoyance. "Give me your pistol, and make your own way downstream."

The boy was silent. The older man repeated his command.

"I'll do as you say," the boy answered at last in a low voice. He unslung his belt, and all the time he was wondering how anyone could climb up hills and down valleys with only one game leg. He hesitated before handing the pistol over. They had gone on many dangerous errands together, and they had worked well together, and now Lu-Yi had to take the most dangerous road of all. He hardly dared to leave his companion. Lu-Yi saw this, and tried to console him.

"Boy, don't worry about me. With two pistols I shall kill many before I am killed. I prefer climbing to swimming, and in any case your journey will be hard. There may be barbed wire rising from the bottom of the river near the pontoon bridge. You may have to climb over the bridge—that's dangerous. I think I shall find my way easily enough over the hill, and when I find you I shall give you your pistol back. We'll meet again, my dear little devil."

Both knew that he was lying. Hardly had Lu-Yi finished speaking when he stepped forward and helped the boy untie his pistol belt, and the bandolier of bullets which fell down from his shoulders. Then he patted the boy on the arm and asked him to jump into the water before he himself went uphill. The kindly dogmatism of the older man, the deep friendship which existed between them, and the strict discipline which existed among the guerrilla troops, all these exhorted the boy to slide down the embankment and into the water without another word.

The stream murmured quietly and coldly, and the boy threw himself in the water, imitating the cry of a wildfowl to show that he was already on his way, and meanwhile the older man, as a sign of final greeting, threw a pebble which landed a little way from the boy's foot. Thus, for the last time, they bade each other farewell and went on their ways.

1160

The boy exerted all the strength of his young limbs, and cautiously moved downstream. He saw fires burning at each end of the pontoon bridge, and each fire cast a dazzling shadow on the water. The bridge was formed of a number of sampans and fishing boats fastened together with iron thews; there was a sentry at each end, and there were also three or four soldiers patrolling the bridge. With his face showing only a little above water, the boy attempted to surrender to the force of the water, hoping to slide under the bridge without making the slightest sound. Suddenly he heard a whistling sound from the hilltop, and a moment later there was the sound of shooting. He knew then that the whereabouts of his friend had been discovered, but what puzzled him was that there was no answering fire from his friend. The bridge was only two yards away from him, shining in the light of the flares. He dived swiftly. There were no obstacles rising from the bottom of the river. Three yards past the bridge he came to the surface, and at that very moment he heard the automatic pistol shooting seven times in rapid succession Soon afterwards he heard four successive pistol shots, and for the moment there were no more sounds.

Later he heard three rifle shots, then there was silence, followed by a solitary pistol shot. Immediately afterwards he heard a shrill scream from someone on the bridge. A torchlight swept over the bridge, and all around. Once more the boy dived, and when he came to the surface again all was silent in the boundless darkness except for the interminable murmur of the water beneath his body. The black night air permeating all the space overhead seemed to press down on the river and penetrate through his skin and into his veins. He knew that the safety zone lay less than a quarter of a mile away.

He saw a camp fire blazing through the darkness, and the recognition of the friendly light and the illusory warmth which came from the fire gave him new strength.

"Password!"

"Nine ... ty, with both feet wrapped in cloth."

"Why only one? Where's your companion?"

"Ask the ghost of your ancestor."

"Is he lost then?"

There was no reply. Only a splashing sound was heard when the boy climbed up the river bank.

SHIH NAI-AN

SHIH NAI-AN (Chinese, ca. 1290-1365). Traditional author of *All Men Are Brothers*, one of four or five masterpieces of Chinese fiction. Written in the fourteenth century, improved and embellished during two succeeding centuries, receiving its final form. The novel is based on a cycle of stories about a band of outlaws.

"DEATH OF THE TIGERS"

LET it here be told only how Li K'uei feared lest Li Ta lead men out to pursue him. Carrying his mother on his back he turned towards the wilds of the mountain into the small lonely paths where no men were. After a while had passed, he saw that the sky was dark with night, and he carried his mother into a valley. Now his old mother's two eyes were dim and she did not know if it were morning or night. But Li K'uei knew this valley, and it was called the I Valley. On the other side only were there any homes. And the mother and son, taking advantage of the light of the new moon, went slowly step by step up the valley, and the mother said as she was on her son's back, "My son, if you could fetch a mouthful of water for me to drink it would be well."

And again Li K'uel said, "I am suffering more than I can bear, too."

Now Li K'uei saw that step by step he had come to the edge of pine trees and to a place where there was a great green stone. There he put his mother down and he thrust his sword into the earth beside her and he commanded her, saying, "Be patient and sit awhile and I will go and seek water for you to drink."

Now Li K'uei had heard the gurgling sound of water and he sought a path thither and when he had climbed over several foothills he came to the side of a brook and he dipped up water in his hands and he drank several mouthfuls. And to himself he thought, "How can I fetch this water to give my mother to drink?"

He stood up and looked east and he looked west. In the far distance upon the point of the mountain he saw a temple. He said, "Ha, it is well!"

And grasping vines and branches he climbed up the mountain side and went to the front of the temple. When he pushed the gate open and looked in he saw it was a temple to The Dragon God of Sze Chou. In front of the god was a stone urn for incense. Li-K'uei

1162

put his hand out to seize this. Now this urn was fastened upon a stone altar beneath and Li K'uei pulled at it awhile, but how could he pull it up? Then his anger rose and he jerked the altar and urn and all and he pulled them up and carried them to the stone terrace in front of the terrace and threw them down and knocked off the urn from the altar. He took the urn then and went again to the brook and he soaked it clean in the brook and he pulled some wild grass and he washed the urn clean. Then he dipped up half the urn full of water and, bearing it in both hands, he went along his old path, and stumbling along he came again to the valley.

But when he had come to the stone by the pine trees he did not see his mother. There was only the sword thrust into the ground. Then Li K'uei called, "Mother, drink some water!"

But there was no sound anywhere. When he had called and there was no answer, Li K'uei's heart was filled with fear and he put down the urn and staring about he looked in all four directions. He did not see his mother, but when he had gone not more than thirty-odd paces he saw a pool of blood upon the grass. When he saw this his flesh began to tremble. Following the flow of the blood he went to seek, and he sought to the mouth of a great cave. There he saw two tiger cubs gnawing upon a human leg. Li K'uei could not check his shivering and he said, "I returned from the mountain lair especially to seek out my old mother, and I carried her on my back through a thousand pains and bitternesses, and I did but bring her here for you to eat! As for that leg which that cursed tiger has dragged hither, if it is not my mother's then whose is it?"

When the fire of his anger rose in his heart he ceased his shivering and his red and yellow whiskers stood erect. He lifted up the sword in his hand; he stabbed at those two tiger cubs. Now the two cubs were terrified and with their teeth bared and their claws outspread they charged to attack Li K'uei, but Li K'uei lifted his hand and stabbed one to death. Then the other one turned and hastened into the cave, and Li K'uei pursued it into the cave and stabbed it to death also.

Now when Li K'uei had rushed into the tigers' den, as he stood crouching there and staring about him, he saw the mother tiger standing looking into the den, her teeth bared and her claws outspread. And Li K'uei cried, "Truly it was you, you wicked wild beast, who ate my mother!"

And he put down his sword and he took his dagger out from his person. Now that mother tiger reached the mouth of the cave and she thrust her tail into the den and whirled it about, and was about to sit down upon her haunches in the den. But Li K'uei could see very clearly there in the den and he reached his dagger to the point below the tigress's tail and with all his strength he thrust forward, and he thrust it straight into the beast's anus. Yet he used his strength too heavily and he had thrust the very handle of the dagger through to the tigress's belly and the tigress gave a great growl and with the dagger in her vitals she rushed out of the cave and leaped to a point on the mountain beyond. Then Li K'uei took his sword and he hastened out of the cave. The tigress, suffering the pain, leaped down the mountain. Li K'uei was just about to hasten after her when he saw a great wind come out of the trees beside him, and the leaves fall from the trees like rain, and to himself he thought, "Clouds come with the dragon, wind with the tiger."

Now the place where this wind rose was beneath the light of the new moon. There came forth a deep growl and all of a sudden there leaped out a slant-eyed, white-browed tiger. That great beast charged at Li K'uei with its whole strength. But Li K'uei was not fearful nor agitated. He took advantage of the force of the beast's attack and he lifted his sword in his hand and thrust it straight into the tiger's throat.

As for the tiger, he did not attack with his hind feet nor strike with his tail, for he tried to save himself his pain, and moreover, Li K'uei had pierced his windpipe. The tiger retreated not more than five or seven paces when Li K'uei heard a sound as though the half of a great mountain fell. Straightway then did the tiger die there beside the rock.

In this short time did Li K'uei kill the two tigers and their cubs. Then he went once more into the den with his knife and looked about, lest there be yet another tiger. But there was none. And Li K'uei was weary by now also, and he went to The Temple To The Dragon God, and he slept there until dawn.

On the morning of the next day Li K'uei went to collect his mother's two legs and such of her bones as had not yet been devoured, and he took a cloth and wrapped them up. He went behind The Temple To The Dragon God and he dug a hole and buried them, and there he did weep mightily for a while. Yet he was hungry and thirsty too, and at last he tied up his bundle again and took his sword and seeking a path he slowly crossed the valley.

1164

HENRYK SIENKIEWICZ

HENRYK SIENKIEWICZ (Polish, 1846-1916). Vivid historical novelist of Poland. Traveled in America and Africa. Won Nobel Prize, 1905. Beloved in native country for patriotic trilogy based on Polish history. Known the world over for *Quo Vadis*, novel of the Roman Empire. Other novels translated: *With Fire and Sword, The Deluge.*

THE LIGHTHOUSE KEEPER OF ASPINWALL

ON a time it happened that the lighthouse keeper in Aspinwall, not far from Panama, disappeared without a trace. Since he disappeared during a storm, it was supposed that the ill-fated man went to the very edge of the small, rocky island on which the lighthouse stood, and was swept out by a wave. This supposition seemed the more likely, as his boat was not found next day in its rocky niche. The place of lighthouse keeper had become vacant. It was necessary to fill this place at the earliest moment possible, since the lighthouse had no small significance for the local movement as well as for vessels going from New York to Panama. Mosquito Bay abounds in sandbars and banks. Among these, navigation, even in the day-time, is difficult; but at night, especially with the fogs which are so frequent on those waters warmed by the sun of the tropics, it is nearly impossible. The only guide at that time for the numerous vessels is the lighthouse.

The task of finding a new keeper fell to the United States consul living in Panama, and this task was no small one: first, because it was absolutely necessary to find a man within twelve hours; second, the man must be unusually conscientious—it was not possible, of course, to take the first comer at random; finally, there was an utter lack of candidates. Life on a tower is uncommonly difficult, and by no means enticing to people of the South, who love idleness and the freedom of vagrant life. That lighthouse keeper is almost a prisoner. He cannot leave his rocky island except on Sundays. A boat from Aspinwall brings him provisions and water once a day, and returns immediately; on the whole island, one acre in area, there is no inhabitant. The keeper lives in the lighthouse; he keeps it in order. During the day he gives signals by displaying flags of various colors to indicate changes of the barometer; in the evening he lights the lantern. This would be no great labor were it not that to reach the lantern at the summit of the tower he must pass over more than four hundred steep and very high steps; sometimes he must make this journey repeatedly during the day. In general, it is the life of a monk, and indeed more than that—the life of a hermit. It was not wonderful, therefore, that Mr. Isaac Falconbridge was in no small anxiety as to where he should find a permanent successor to the recent keeper; and it is easy to understand his joy when a successor announced himself most unexpectedly on that very day. He was a man already old. seventy years or more, but fresh, erect with the movements and bearing of a soldier. His hair was perfectly white, his face as dark as that of a Creole; but, judging from his blue eyes, he did not belong to the people of the South. His face was somewhat downcast and sad, but honest. At the first glance he pleased Falconbridge. It remained only to examine him. Therefore the following conversation began:

"Where are you from?"

"I am a Pole."

"Where have you worked up to this time?"

"In one place and another."

"A lighthouse keeper should like to stay in one place."

"I need rest."

"Have you served? Have you testimonials of honorable government service?"

The old man drew from his bosom a piece of faded silk, resembling a strip of an old flag, unwound it, and said:

"Here are the testimonials. I received this cross in 1830. This second one is Spanish from the Carlist War; the third is the French legion; the fourth I received in Hungary. Afterward I fought in the States against the South; there they do not give crosses."

Falconbridge took the paper and began to read.

"H'm! Skavinski? Is that your name? H'm! Two flags captured in a bayonet attack. You were a gallant soldier."

"I am able to be a conscientious lighthouse keeper."

"It is necessary to ascend the tower a number of times daily. Have you sound legs?"

"I crossed the plains on foot." (The immense steppes between the East and California are called "the plains.")

"Do you know sea service?"

"I served three years on a whaler."

"You have tried various occupations."

"The only one I have not known is quiet."

"Why is that?"

1166

The old man shrugged his shoulders. "Such is my fate."

"Still you seem to me too old for a lighthouse keeper."

"Sir," exclaimed the candidate suddenly in a voice of emotion, "I am greatly wearied, knocked about. I have passed through much, as you see. This place is one of those which I have wished for most ardently. I am old, I need rest. I need to say to myself, 'Here you will remain; this is your port.' Ah, sir, this depends now on you alone. Another time perhaps such a place will not offer itself. What luck that I was in Panama! I entreat you—as God is dear to me, I am like a ship which if it misses the harbor will be lost. If you wish to make an old man happy—I swear to you that I am honest, but—I have enough of wandering."

The blue eyes of the old man expressed such earnest entreaty that Falconbridge, who had a good, simple heart, was touched.

"Well," said he, "I take you. You are lighthouse keeper."

The old man's face gleamed with inexpressible joy.

"I thank you."

"Can you go to the tower to-day?"

"I can."

"Then good-bye. Another word—for any failure in service you will be dismissed."

"All right."

That same evening, when the sun had descended on the other side of the isthmus, and a day of sunshine was followed by a night without twilight, the new keeper was in his place evidently, for the lighthouse was casting its bright rays on the water as usual. The night was perfectly calm, silent, genuinely tropical, filled with a transparent haze, forming around the moon a great colored rainbow with soft, unbroken edges; the sea was moving only because the tide raised it. Skavinski on the balcony seemed from far below like a small black point. He tried to collect his thoughts and take in his new position; but his mind was too much under pressure to move with regularity. He felt somewhat as a hunted beast feels when at last it has found refuge from pursuit on some inaccessible rock or in a cave. There had come to him, finally, an hour of quiet; the feeling of safety filled his soul with a certain unspeakable bliss. Now on that rock he can simply laugh at his previous wanderings, his misfortunes and failures. He was in truth like a ship whose masts, ropes, and sails had been broken and rent by a tempest, and cast from the clouds to the bottom of the sea—a ship on which the tempest had hurled waves and spat foam, but which still wound its

1167

way to the harbor. The pictures of that storm passed quickly through his mind as he compared it with the calm future now beginning. A part of his wonderful adventures he had related to Falconbridge; he had not mentioned, however, thousands of other incidents. It had been his misfortune that as often as he pitched his tent and fixed his fireplace to settle down permanently, some wind tore out the stakes of his tent, whirled away the fire, and bore him on toward destruction. Looking now from the balcony of the tower at the illuminated waves, he remembered everything through which he had passed. He had campaigned in the four parts of the world, and in wandering had tried almost every occupation. Labor-loving and honest, more than once he had earned money, and had always lost it in spite of every provision and the utmost caution. He had been a gold miner in Australia, a diamond-digger in Africa, a rifleman in public service in the East Indies. He established a ranch in California —the drought ruined him; he tried trading with wild tribes in the interior of Brazil—his raft was wrecked on the Amazon; he himself alone, weaponless, and nearly naked, wandered in the forest for many weeks living on wild fruits, exposed every moment to death from the jaws of wild beasts. He established a forge in Helena, Arkansas, and that was burned in a great fire which consumed the whole town. Next he fell into the hands of Indians in the Rocky Mountains, and only through a miracle was he saved by Canadian trappers. Then he served as a sailor on a vessel running between Bahia and Bordeaux, and as harpooner on a whaling-ship; both vessels were wrecked. He had a cigar factory in Havana, and was robbed by his partner while he himself was lying sick with the vomito. At last he came to Aspinwall, and there was to be the end of his failures—for what could reach him on that rocky island? Neither water nor fire nor men. But from men Skavinski had not suffered much; he had met good men oftener than bad ones.

But it seemed to him that all the four elements were persecuting him. Those who knew him said that he had no luck, and with that they explained everything. He himself became something of a mono-maniac. He believed that some mighty and vengeful hand was pursuing him everywhere, on all lands and waters. He did not like, however, to speak of this; only at times, when someone asked him whose hand that could be, he pointed mysteriously to the Polar Star, and said, "It comes from that place." In reality his failures were so continuous that they were wonderful, and might easily drive a nail into the head, especially of the man who had experienced them. But

Skavinski had the patience of an Indian, and that great calm power of resistance which comes from truth of heart. In his time he had received in Hungary a number of bayonet-thrusts because he would not grasp at a stirrup which was shown as means of salvation to him, and cry for quarter. In like manner he did not bend to misfortune. He crept up against the mountain as industriously as an ant. Pushed down a hundred times, he began his journey calmly for the hundred and first time. He was in his way a most peculiar original. This old soldier, tempered. God knows in how many fires, hardened in suffering, hammered and forged, had the heart of a child. In the time of the epidemic in Cuba, the vomito attacked him because he had given to the sick all his quinine, of which he had a considerable supply, and left not a grain for himself.

There had been in him also this wonderful quality—that after so many disappointments he was ever full of confidence, and did not lose hope that all would be well yet. In winter he grew lively, and predicted great events. He waited for these events with impatience, and lived with the thought of them whole summers. But the winters passed one after another, and Skavinski lived only to this—that they whitened his head. At last he grew old, began to lose energy; his endurance was becoming more and more like resignation, his former calmness was tending toward supersensitiveness, and that tempered soldier was degenerating into a man ready to shed tears for any cause. Besides this, from time to time he was weighed down by a terrible homesickness which was roused by any circumstance—the sight of swallows, gray birds like sparrows, snow on the mountains, or melancholy music like that heard on a time. It mastered the old man thoroughly, and swallowed all other desires and hopes. This ceaseless wanderer could not imagine anything more precious, than a quiet corner in which to rest, and wait in silence for the end. Perhaps specially because some whim of fate had so hurried him over all seas and lands that he could hardly catch his breath, did he imagine that the highest human happiness was his due; but he was so accustomed to disappointments that he thought of rest as people in general think of something which is beyond reach. He did not dare to hope for it. Meanwhile, unexpectedly, in the course of twelve hours he had gained a position which was as if chosen for him out of all the world. We are not to wonder, then, that when he lighted his lantern in the evening he became as it were dazed—that he asked himself if that was reality, and he did not dare to answer that it was. But at the same time reality convinced him with

1169

incontrovertible proofs; hence hours one after another passed while he was on the balcony. He gazed, and convinced himself. It might seem that he was looking at the sea for the first time in his life. The lens of the lantern cast into the darkness an enormous triangle of light, beyond which the eye of the old man was lost in the black distance completely, in the distance mysterious and awful. But that distance seemed to run toward the light. The long waves following one another rolled out from the darkness, and went bellowing towards the base of the island; and then their foaming backs were visible, shining rose-coloured in the light of the lantern. The incoming tide swelled more and more, and covered the sandy bars. The mysterious speech of the ocean came with a fullness more powerful and louder, at one time like the thunder of cannon, at another like the distant dull sound of the voices of people. At moments it was quiet; then to the ears of the old man came some great sigh, then a kind of sobbing, and again threatening outbursts. At last the wind bore away the haze, but brought black, broken clouds, which hid the moon. From the west it began to blow more and more; the waves sprang with rage against the rock of the lighthouse, licking with foam the foundation walls. In the distance a storm was beginning to bellow. On the dark, disturbed expanse certain green lanterns gleamed from the masts of ships. These green points rose high and then sank; now they swayed to the right, and now to the left. Skavinski descended to his room. The storm began to howl. Outside, people on those ships were struggling with night, with darkness, with waves but inside the tower it was calm and still. Even the sounds of the storm hardly came through the thick walls, and only the measured tick-tack of the clock lulled the wearied old man to his slumber.

Hours, days, and weeks began to pass. Sailors assert that sometimes when the sea is greatly roused, something from out of the midst of night and darkness calls them by name. If the infinity of the sea may call out thus, perhaps when a man is growing old, calls come to him, too, from another infinity still darker and more deeply mysterious; and the more he is wearied by life the dearer are those calls to him. But to hear them quiet is needed. Besides old age loves to put itself aside, as if with a foreboding of the grave. The lighthouse had become for Skavinski such a half grave. Nothing is more monotonous than life on a beacon-tower. If young people consent to take up this service they leave it after a time. Lighthouse keepers are generally men not young, gloomy, and confined to

1170

themselves. If by chance one of them leaves his lighthouse and goes among men, he walks in the midst of them like a person roused from deep slumber. On the tower there is a lack of minute impressions which in ordinary life teach men to adapt themselves to everything. All that a lighthouse keeper comes in contact with is gigantic and devoid of definitely outlined forms. The sky is one whole, the water another; and between those two infinities the soul of man is in loneliness. That is a life in which thought is continual meditation, and out of that meditation nothing rouses the keeper, not even his work. Day is like day as two beads in a rosary, unless changes of weather form the only variety. But Skavinski felt more happiness than ever in life before. He rose with the dawn, took his breakfast, polished the lens, and then sitting in the balcony gazed into the distance of the water; and his eyes were never sated with the pictures which he saw before him. On the enormous turquoise ground of the ocean were to be seen generally flocks of swollen sails gleaming in the rays of the sun so brightly, that the eyes were blinking before the excess of light. Sometimes the ships, favored by the so-called trade winds, went in an extended line one after another, like a chain of sea-mews or albatrosses. The red casks indicating the channel swayed on the light wave with gentle movement. Among the sails appeared every afternoon grayish feather-like plumes of smoke. That was a steamer from New York which brought passengers and goods to Aspinwall, drawing behind it a frothy path of foam. On the other side of the balcony Skavinski saw, as if on his palm, Aspinwall and its busy harbor, and in it a forest of masts, boats, and craft; a little farther, white houses and the towers of the town. From the height of his tower the small houses were like the nests of sea-mews, the boats were like beetles, and the people moved around like small points on the white stone boulevard. From early morning a light eastern breeze brought a confused hum of human life, above which predominated the whistle of steamers. In the afternoon six o'clock came; the movements in the harbor began to cease; the mews hid themselves in the rents of the cliffs; the waves grew feeble and became in some sort lazy; and then on the land, on the sea, and on the tower came a time of stillness unbroken by anything. The yellow sands from which the waves had fallen back glittered like golden stripes on the width of the waters; the body of the tower was outlined definitely in blue. Floods of sunbeams were poured from the the sky on the water and the sands and the cliff. At that time a certain lassitude full of sweetness seized the old man. He felt that the rest which he was enjoying was excellent; and when he thought that it would be continuous nothing was lacking to him.

Skavinski was intoxicated with his own happiness; and since a man adapts himself easily to improved conditions, he gained faith and confidence by degrees; for he thought that if men built houses for invalids, why should not God gather up at last His own invalids? Time passed, and confirmed him in this conviction. The old man grew accustomed to his tower, to the lantern, to the rock, to the sand-bars, to solitude. He grew accustomed also to the sea-mews which hatched in the crevices of the rock, and in the evening held meetings on the roof of the lighthouse. Skavinski threw them generally the remnants of his food; and soon they grew tame, and afterward when he fed them, a real storm of white wings encircled him, and the old man went among the birds like a shepherd among sheep. When the tide ebbed he went to the low sandbanks, on which he collected savory periwinkles and beautiful pearl shells of the nautilus, which receding waves had left on the sand. In the night by the moonlight and the tower he went to catch fish, which frequented the windings of the cliff in myriads. At last he was in love with his rocks and his treeless little island, grown over only with small thick plants exuding sticky resin. The distant views repaid him for the poverty of the island, however. During afternoon hours, when the air became very clear he could see the whole isthmus covered with the richest vegetation. It seemed to Skavinski at such times that he saw one gigantic garden—bunches of cocoa, and enormous musa, combined as it were in luxurious tufted bouquets, right there behind the houses of Aspinwall. Farther on, between Aspinwall and Panama, was a great forest over which every morning and evening hung a reddish haze of exhalations—a real tropical forest with its feet in stagnant water, interlaced with lianas and filled with the sound of one sea of gigantic orchids, palms, milk-trees, iron-trees, gum-trees.

Through his field-glass the old man could see not only trees and the broad leaves of bananas, but even legions of monkeys and great marabous and flocks of parrots, rising at times like a rainbow cloud over the forest. Skavinski knew such forests well, for after being wrecked on the Amazon he had wandered whole weeks among similar arches and thickets. He had seen how many dangers and deaths lie concealed under those wonderful and smiling exteriors. During the nights which he had spent in them he heard close at hand the sepulchral voices of howling monkeys and the roaring of

1172

the jaguars; he saw gigantic serpents coiled like lianas on trees; he knew those slumbering forest lakes full of torpedo-fish and swarming with crocodiles; he knew under what a yoke man lives in those unexplored wildernesses in which are single leaves that exceed a man's size ten times—wildernesses swarming with blood-drinking mosquitoes, tree-leeches, and gigantic poisonous spiders. He had experienced that forest life himself, had witnessed it, had passed through it; therefore it gave him the greater enjoyment to look from his height and gaze on those *matos*, admire their beauty, and be guarded from their treacherousness. His tower preserved him from every evil. He left it only for a few hours on Sunday. He put on then his blue keeper's coat with silver buttons, and hung his crosses on his breast. His milk-white head was raised with a certain pride when he heard at the door, while entering the church, the Creoles say among themselves, "We have an honorable lighthouse keeper and not a heretic, though he is a Yankee." But he returned straightway after Mass to his island, and returned happy, for he had still no faith in the mainland. On Sunday also he read the Spanish newspaper which he bought in the town, or the *New York Herald*, which he borrowed from Falconbridge; and he sought in it European news eagerly. The poor old heart on that lighthouse tower, and in another hemisphere, was beating yet for its birthplace. At times too, when the boat brought his daily supplies and water to the island, he went down from the tower to talk with Johnson, the guard. But after a while he seemed to grow shy. He ceased to go to the town, to read the papers and to go down to talk politics with Johnson. Whole weeks passed in this way, so that no one saw him and he saw no one. The only signs that the old man was living were the disappearance of the provisions left on shore, and the light of the lantern kindled every evening with the same regularity with which the sun rose in the morning from the waters of those regions. Evidently, the old man had become indifferent to the world. Homesickness was not the cause, but just this—that even homesickness had passed into resignation. The whole world began now and ended for Skavinski on his island. He had grown accustomed to the thought that he would not leave the tower till his death, and he simply forgot that there was anything else besides it. Moreover, he had become a mystic; his mild blue eyes began to stare like the eyes of a child, and were as if fixed on something at a distance. In presence of a surrounding uncommonly simple and great, the old man was losing the feeling of personality; he was ceasing to exist as an individual,

was becoming merged more and more in that which inclosed in.
He did not understand anything beyond his environment; he felt
only unconsciously. At last it seems to him that the heavens, the
water, his rock, the tower, the golden sand-banks, and the swollen
sails, the sea-mews, the ebb and flow of the tide—all form a mighty
unity, one enormous mysterious soul; that he is sinking in that
mystery, and feels that soul which lives and lulls itself. He sinks and
is rocked, forgets himself; and in that narrowing of his own individual existence, in that half-waking, half-sleeping, he has discovered a rest so great that it nearly resembles half-death.

But the awakening came.

On a certain day, when the boat brought water and a supply of
provisions, Skavinski came down an hour later from the tower, and
saw that besides the usual cargo there was an additional package.
On the outside of this package were postage stamps of the United
States, and the address: "Skavinski, Esq.," was written on coarse
canvas.

The old man, with aroused curiosity, cut the canvas, and saw
books; he took one in his hand, looked at it, and put it back;
thereupon his hands began to tremble greatly. He covered his eyes
as if he did not believe them; it seemed to him as if he were dreaming. The book was Polish—what did that mean? Who could have
sent the book? Clearly, it did not occur to him at the first moment
that in the beginning of his lighthouse career he had read in the
Herald, borrowed from the consul, of the formation of a Polish
society in New York, and had sent at once to that society half his
month's salary, for which he had, moreover, no use on the tower.
The society had sent him the books with thanks. The books came in
the natural way; but at the first moment the old man could not
seize those thoughts. Polish books in Aspinwall, on his tower, amid
his solitude—that was for him something uncommon, a certain
breath from past times, a kind of miracle. Now it seemed to him,
as to those sailors in the night, that something was calling him by
name with a voice greatly beloved and nearly forgotten. He sat
for a while with closed eyes, and was almost certain that, when
he opened them, the dream would be gone.

The package, cut open, lay before him, shone upon clearly by
the afternoon sun, and on it was an open book. When the old man
stretched his hand toward it again, he heard in the stillness the
beating of his own heart. He looked; it was poetry. On the outside
stood printed in great letters the title, underneath the name of the

author. The name was not strange to Skavinski; he saw that it belonged to the great poet, whose production he had read in 1830 in Paris. Afterward, when campaigning in Algiers and Spain, he had heard from his countrymen of the growing fame of the great seer; but he was so accustomed to the musket at that time that he took no book in hand. In 1849, he went to America, and in the adventurous life which he led he hardly ever met a Pole, and never a Polish book. With the greater eagerness, therefore, and with a livelier beating of the heart, did he turn to the title-page. It seemed to him then that on his lonely rock some solemnity is about to take place. Indeed it was a moment of great calm and silence. The clocks of Aspinwall were striking five in the afternoon. Not a cloud darkened the clear sky; only a few sea-mews were sailing through the air. The ocean was as if cradled to sleep. The waves on the shore stammered quietly, spreading softly on the sand. In the distance the white houses of Aspinwall, and the wonderful groups of palm, were smiling. In truth, there was something there solemn, calm, and full of dignity. Suddenly, in the midst of that calm of Nature, was heard the trembling voice of the old man, who read aloud as if to understand himself better:

"Thou art like health, O my birth-land Litva!
How much we should prize thee he only can know who has
    lost thee.
Thy beauty in perfect adornment this day
I see and describe, because I am yearning for thee."

His voice failed Skavinski. The letters began to dance before his eyes; something broke in his breast, and went like a wave from his heart higher and higher, choking his voice and pressing his throat. A moment more he controlled himself, and read further:

"O Holy Lady, who guardest bright Chenstohova,
Who shinest in Ostrobrama and preservest
The castle town Novgrodek with its trusty people,
As Thou didst give me back to health in childhood,
When by my weeping mother placed beneath Thy care
I raised my lifeless eyelids upward,
And straightway walked unto Thy holy threshold,
To thank God for the life restored me,—
So by wonder now restore us to the bosom of our birthplace."

The swollen wave broke through the restraint of his will. The old man sobbed, and threw himself on the ground; his milk-white hair was mingled with the sand of the sea. Forty years had passed since he had seen his country, and God knows how many since he heard his native speech; and now that speech had come to him itself—it had sailed to him over the ocean, and found him in solitude on another hemisphere—it so loved, so dear, so beautiful! In the sobbing which shook him there was no pain—only a suddenly aroused immense love, in the presence of which other things are as nothing. With that great weeping he had simply implored forgiveness of that beloved one, set aside because he had grown so old, had become so accustomed to his solitary rock, and had so forgotten it that in him even longing had begun to disappear. But now it returned as if by a miracle; therefore the heart leaped in him.

Moments vanished one after another; he lay there continually. The mews flew over the lighthouse, crying as if alarmed for their old friend. The hour in which he fed them with the remnants of his food had come; therefore, some of them flew down from the light-house to him; then more and more came, and began to pick and shake their wings over his head. The sound of the wings roused him. He had wept his fill, and had now a certain calm and brightness; but his eyes were as if inspired. He gave unwittingly all his provisions to the birds, which rushed at him with an uproar, and he himself took the book again. The sun had gone already behind the gardens and the forest of Panama, and was going slowly beyond the isthmus to the other ocean; but the Atlantic was full of light yet; in the open air there was still perfect vision; therefore, he read further:

"Now bear my longing soul to those forest slopes, to those green meadows."

At last the dusk obliterates the letters on the white paper—the dusk short as a twinkle. The old man rested his head on the rock, and closed his eyes. Then "She who defends bright Chenstohova" took his soul and transported it to "those fields colored by various grain." On the sky were burning yet those long stripes, red and golden, and on those brightnesses he was flying to beloved regions. The pine-woods were sounding in his ears; the streams of his native place were murmuring. He saw everything as it was; everything asked him, "Dost remember?" He remembers! He sees broad fields;

1176

between the fields, wood and villages. It is night now. At this hour
his lantern usually illuminates the darkness of the sea; but now he
is in his native village. His old head has dropped on his breast, and
he is dreaming. Pictures are passing before his eyes quickly, and a
little disorderly. He does not see the house in which he was born,
for war had destroyed it; he does not see his father and mother,
for they died when he was a child; but still the village is as if he
had left it yesterday—the line of cottages with lights in the windows,
the mound, the mill, the two ponds opposite each other, and thundering all night with a chorus of frogs. Once he had been on guard
in that village all night; now that past stood before him at once in a
series of views. He is an Uhlan again, and he stands there on guard;
at a distance is the public-house; he looks with swimming eyes.
There is thundering and singing and shouting amid the silence of
the night, with voices of fiddles and bass-viols "U-ha! U-ha!" Then
the Uhlans knock out fire with their horseshoes, and it is wearisome
for him there on his horse. The hours drag on slowly; at last the
lights are quenched: now as far as the eye reaches there is mist,
and mist impenetrable; now the fog rises, evidently from the fields,
and embraces the whole world with a whitish cloud. You would say,
a complete ocean. But that is fields; soon the land-rail will be heard
in the darkness, and the bitterns will call from the reeds. The night
is calm and cool—in truth, a Polish night! In the distance the pine-
wood is sounding without wind, like the roll of the sea. Soon dawn
will whiten the east. In fact, the cocks are beginning to crow behind
the hedges. One answers to another from cottage to cottage; the
storks are screaming somewhere on high. The Uhlan feels well and
bright. Someone had spoken of a battle tomorrow. Hei! that will
go on, like all the others, with shouting, with flutterings of flaglets.
The young blood is playing like a trumpet, though the night cools
it. But it is dawning. Already night is growing pale; out of the
shadows come forests, the thicket, a row of cottages, the mill, the
poplars. The well is squeaking like a metal banner on a tower. What
a beloved land, beautiful in the rosy gleams of the morning! Oh,
the one land, the one land!

Quiet! the watchful picket hears that someone is approaching. Of
course, they are coming to relieve the guard.

Suddenly some voice is heard above Skavinski:

"Here, old man! Get up! What's the matter?"

The old man opens his eyes, and looks with wonder at the person
standing before him. The remnants of the dream-visions struggle in

1177

his head with reality. At last the visions pale and vanish. Before him stands Johnson, the harbor guide.

"What's this?" asked Johnson; "are you sick?"

"No."

"You didn't light the lantern. You must leave your place. A vessel from St. Geromo was wrecked on the bar. It is lucky that no one was drowned, or you would go to trial. Get into the boat with me; you'll hear the rest at the Consulate."

The old man grew pale; in fact he had not lighted the lantern that night.

A few days later, Skavinski was seen on the deck of a steamer, which was going from Aspinwall to New York. The poor man had lost his place. There opened before him new roads of wandering; the wind had torn that leaf away again to whirl it over lands and seas, to sport with it till satisfied. The old man had failed greatly during those few days, and was bent over; only his eyes were gleaming. On his new road of life he held at his breast his book, which from time to time he pressed with his hand as if in fear that that too might go from him.

SOLOMON

SOLOMON (Hebrew, 10th Century, B.C.). Kingly poet and philosopher. Most powerful ruler of the Hebrew monarchy. Organizer, builder and reformer. The exceptionally lyrical, erotic "Song of Songs," attributed to him, has been endlessly disputed and interpreted by scholars—the commonest and most ingenious interpretation being that it is an allegory.

"THE SONG OF SOLOMON"

IV

BEHOLD, thou art fair. my love; behold, thou art fair; thou hast doves' eyes within thy locks: thy hair is as a flock of goats, that appear from mount Gilead.

Thy teeth are like a flock of sheep that are even shorn, which came up from the washing; whereof every one bear twins, and none is barren among them.

Thy lips are like a thread of scarlet, and thy speech is comely; thy temples are like a piece of a pomegranate within thy locks.

Thy neck is like the tower of David builded for an armoury, whereon there hang a thousand bucklers, all shields of mighty men.

Thy two breast are like two young roes that are twins which feed among the lilies.

Until the day break, and the shadows flee away, I will get me to the mountain of myrrh, and to the hill of frankincense.

Thou art all fair, my love; there is no spot in thee.

Come with me from Lebanon, my spouse, with me from Lebanon: look from the top of Amana, from the top of Shenir and Hermon, from the lions' dens, from the mountains of the leopards.

Thou hast ravished my heart, my sister, my spouse; thou hast ravished my heart with one of thine eyes, with one chain of thy neck.

How fair is thy love, my sister, my spouse! How much better is thy love than wine! and the smell of thine ointments than all spices!

Thy lips, O my spouse, drop as the honeycomb: honey and milk are under thy tongue; and the smell of thy garments is like the smell of Lebanon.

A garden inclosed is my sister, my spouse; a spring shut up, a fountain sealed.

Thy plants are an orchard of pomegranates, with pleasant fruits; camphire, with spikenard,

Spikenard and saffron; calamus and cinnamon, with all trees of frankincense: myrrh and aloes, with all the chief spices:

A fountain of gardens, a well of living waters, and streams from Lebanon.

Awake, O north wind; and come, thou south; blow upon my garden, that the spices thereof may flow out. Let my beloved come into his garden, and eat his pleasant fruits.

V

I AM come into my garden, my sister, my spouse: I have gathered my myrrh with my spice; I have eaten my honeycomb with my honey; I have drunk my wine with my milk: eat, O friends; drink, yea, drink abundantly, O beloved.

I sleep, but my heart waketh: it is the voice of my beloved that knocketh, saying, Open to me, my sister, my love, my dove, my undefiled: for my head is filled with dew, and my locks with the drops of the night.

I have put off my coat; how shall I put it on? I have washed my feet; how shall I defile them?

My beloved put in his hand by the hole of the door, and my bowels were moved for him.

I rose up to open to my beloved; and my hands dropped with myrrh, and my fingers with sweet smelling myrrh, upon the handles of the lock.

I opened to my beloved; but my beloved had withdrawn himself, and was gone: my soul failed when he spake: I sought him, but I could not find him; I called him, but he gave me no answer.

The watchmen that went about the city found me, they smote me, they wounded me; the keepers of the walls took away my veil from me.

I charge you, O daughters of Jerusalem, if ye find my beloved, that ye tell him, that I am sick of love.

What is thy beloved more than another beloved, O thou fairest among women? What is thy beloved more than another beloved, that thou dost so charge us?

My beloved is white and ruddy, the chiefest among ten thousand.

His head is as the most fine gold, his locks are bushy, and black as a raven.

His eyes are as the eyes of doves by the rivers of waters, washed with milk, and fitly set.

His cheeks are as a bed of spices, as sweet flowers: his lips like lilies, dropping sweet smelling myrrh.

His hands are as gold rings set with the beryl: his belly is as bright ivory overlaid with sapphires.

His legs are as pillars of marble, set upon sockets of fine gold: his countenance is as Lebanon, excellent as the cedars.

His mouth is most sweet; yea, he is altogether lovely. This is my beloved, and this is my friend, O daughters of Jerusalem.

SOMADEVA

SOMADEVA (Sanskrit, 11th Century). Legendary Kashmir Brahmin. Little known of his life. His celebrated collection of stories, *The Ocean of the Streams of Story*, is based on a still earlier collection.

DEVASMITA

THERE is a city in the world famous under the name of Támraliptá, and in that city there was a very rich merchant named Dhanadatta.

And he, being childless, assembled many Bráhmans and said to them with due respect, "Take such steps as will procure me a son soon." Then those Bráhmans said to him: "This is not at all difficult, for Bráhmans can accomplish all things in this world by means of ceremonies in accordance with the Scriptures. To give you an instance, there was in old times a king who had no sons, and he had a hundred and five wives in his harem. And by means of a sacrifice to procure a son, there was born to him a son named Jantu, who was like the rising of the new moon to the eyes of his wives. Once on a time an ant bit the boy on the thigh as he was crawling about on his knees, so that he was very unhappy and sobbed loudly. Thereupon the whole harem was full of confused lamentation, and the king himself shrieked out 'My son! my son;' like a common man. The boy was soon comforted, the ant having been removed, and the king blamed the misfortune of his only having one son as the cause of all his grief. And he asked the Bráhmans in his affliction if there was any expedient by which he might obtain a large number of children. They answered, 'O king, there is one expedient open to you; you must slay this son and offer up all his flesh in the fire. By smelling the smell of that sacrifice all thy wives will obtain sons.' When he heard that, the king had the whole ceremony performed as they directed; and he obtained as many sons as he had wives. So we can obtain a son for you also by a burnt-offering." When they had said this to Dhanadatta, the Bráhmans, after a sacrificial fee had been promised them, performed a sacrifice: then a son was born to that merchant. That son was called Guhasena, and he gradually grew up to man's estate. Then his father Dhanadatta began to look out for a wife for him.

Then his father went with that son of his to another country, on the pretence of traffic, but really to get a daughter-in-law. There he asked an excellent merchant of the name of Dharmagupta to give him his daughter named Devasmitá for his son Guhasena. But Dharmagupta, who was tenderly attached to his daughter, did not approve of that connection, reflecting that the city of Támraliptá was very far off. But when Devasmitá beheld that Guhasena, her mind was immediately attracted by his virtues, and she was set on abandoning her relations, and so she made an assignation with him by means of a confidante, and went away from that country at night with her beloved and his father. When they reached Támraliptá they were married, and the minds of the young couple were firmly knit together by the bond of mutual love. Then Guhasena's father died, and he himself was urged by his relations to go to the country of Katáha for the purpose of trafficking; but his wife Devasmitá was too jealous to approve of that expedition, fearing exceedingly that he would be attracted by some other lady. Then, as his wife did not approve of it, and his relations kept inciting him to it, Guhasena, whose mind was firmly set on doing his duty, was bewildered. Then he went and performed a vow in the temple of the god, observing a rigid fast, trusting that the god would show him some way out of his difficulty. And his wife Devasmitá also performed a vow with him; then Siva was pleased to appear to that couple in a dream; and giving them two red lotuses the god said to them, "Take each of you one of these lotuses in your hand. And if either of you shall be unfaithful during your separation, the lotus in the hand of the other shall fade, but not otherwise." After hearing this, the two woke up, and each beheld in the hand of the other a red lotus, and it seemed as if they had got one another's hearts. Then Guhasena set out, lotus in hand. but Devasmitá remained in the house with her eyes fixed upon her flower. Guhasena for his part quickly reached the country of Katáha, and began to buy and sell jewels there. And four young merchants in that country, seeing that that unfading lotus was ever in his hand. were greatly astonished. Accordingly they got him to their house by an artifice, and made him drink a great deal of wine, and then asked him the history of the lotus, and he being intoxicated told them the whole story. Then those four young merchants, knowing that Guhasena would take a long time to complete his sales and purchases of jewels and other wares, planned together, like rascals as they were, the seduction of his wife out of curiosity, and eager to accomplish it set out quickly for Támraliptá without their departure being noticed. There they cast about for some instrument, and at last had recourse to a female ascetic of the name of Yogakaramdiká, who lived in a sanctuary of Buddha; and they said to her in an affectionate manner, "Reverend madam, if our object is accomplished by your help, we will give you much wealth." She answered them: "No doubt you young men desire some woman in this city, so tell me all about it, I will procure you the object of your desire. What woman do you desire? I will quickly procure her for you." When they heard that they said, "Procure us an interview with the wife of the merchant Guhasena named Devasmitá." When she heard that, the ascetic undertook to manage that business for them. and she gave those young merchants her own house to reside in. Then she gratified the ser-

1182

vants at Guhasena's house with gifts of sweetmeats and other things, and afterwards entered it with her pupil. Then, as she approached the private rooms of Devasmitá, a hound, that was fastened there with a chain, would not let her come near, but opposed her entrance in the most determined way. Then Devasmitá seeing her, of her own accord sent a maid, and had her brought in, thinking to herself, "What can this person be come for?" After she had entered, the wicked ascetic gave Devasmitá her blessing, and treating the virtuous woman with affected respect, said to her, "I have always had a desire to see you, but to-day I saw you in a dream, therefore I have come to visit you with impatient eagerness; and my mind is afflicted at beholding you separated from your husband, for beauty and youth are wasted when one is deprived of the society of one's beloved." With this and many other speches of the same kind she tried to gain the confidence of the virtuous woman in a short interview, and then taking leave of her she returned to her own house. On the second day she took with her a piece of meat full of pepper dust, and went again to the house of Devasmitá, and there she gave that piece of meat to the hound at the door, and the hound gobbled it up, pepper and all. Then owing to the pepper dust, the tears flowed in profusion from the animal's eyes, and her nose began to run. And the cunning ascetic immediately went into the apartment of Devasmitá, who received her hospitably, and began to cry. When Devasmitá asked why she shed tears, she said with affected reluctance: "My friend, look at this hound weeping outside here. This creature recognised me to-day as having been its companion in a former birth, and began to weep; for that reason my tears gushed through pity." When she heard that, and saw that hound outside apparently weeping, Devasmitá thought for a moment to herself, "What can be the meaning of this wonderful sight?" Then the ascetic said to her, "My daughter, in a former birth, I and that hound were the two wives of a certain Bráhman. And our husband frequently went about to other countries on embassies by order of the king. Now while he was away from home, I lived at my good will and pleasure, and so did not cheat the elements, of which I was composed, and my senses, of their lawful enjoyment. For considerate treatment of the elements and senses is held to be the highest duty. Therefore I have been born in this birth with a recollection of my former existence. But she, in her former life, through ignorance, confined all her attention to the preservation of her character, therefore, she has been degraded and born again as one of the canine race, however, she too remem-

1183

bers her former birth." The wise Devasmitá said to herself, "This is a novel conception of duty; no doubt this woman has laid a treacherous snare for me"; and so she said to her, "Reverend lady, for this long time I have been ignorant of this duty, so procure me an interview with some charming man." Then the ascetic said, "There are residing here some young merchants that have come from another country, so I will bring them to you." When she had said this, the ascetic returned home delighted, and Devasmitá of her own accord said to her maids: "No doubt those scoundrelly young merchants, whoever they may be, have seen that unfading lotus in the hand of my husband, and have on some occasion or other, when he was drinking wine, asked him out of curiosity to tell the whole story of it, and have now come here from that island to deceive me, and this wicked ascetic is employed by them. So bring quickly some wine mixed with Datura, and when you have brought it, have a dog's foot of iron made as quickly as possible." When Devasmitá had given these orders, the maids executed them faithfully, and one of the maids, by her orders, dressed herself up to resemble her mistress. The ascetic for her part chose out of the party of four merchants (each of whom in his eagerness said—"Let me go first"—) one individual, and brought him with her. And concealing him in the dress of her pupil, she introduced him in the evening into the house of Devasmitá, and coming out, disappeared. Then that maid, who was disguised as Devasmitá, courteously persuaded the young merchant to drink some of that wine drugged with Datura. That liquor, like his own immodesty, robbed him of his senses, and then the maids took away his clothes and other equipments and left him stark naked; then they branded him on the forehead with the mark of a dog's foot. and during the night took him and pushed him into a ditch full of filth. Then he recovered consciousness in the last watch of the night, and found himself plunged in a ditch, as it were the hell *Avíchi* assigned to him by his sins. Then he got up and washed himself and went to the house of the female ascetic, in a state of misery, feeling with his fingers the mark on his forehead. And when he got there, he told his friends that he had been robbed on the way, in order that he might not be the only person made ridiculous. And the next morning he sat with a cloth wrapped round his branded forehead, giving as an excuse that he had a headache from keeping awake so long, and drinking too much. In the same way the next young merchant was maltreated, when he got to the house of Devasmitá, and when he returned home stripped, he said,

1184

"I put on my ornaments there, and as I was coming out I was plundered by robbers." In the morning he also, on the plea of a headache, put a wrapper on to cover his branded forehead.

In the same way all the four young merchants suffered in turn branding and other humiliating treatment, though they concealed the fact. And they went away from the place, without revealing to the female Buddhist ascetic the ill-treatment they had experienced, hoping that she would suffer in a similar way. On the next day the ascetic went with her disciple to the house of Devasmitá, much delighted at having accomplished what she undertook to do. Then Devasmitá received hr courteously, and made her drink wine drugged with Datura, offered as a sign of gratitude. When she and her disciple were intoxicated with it, that chaste wife cut off their ears and noses, and flung them also into a filthy pool. And being distressed by the thought that perhaps these young merchants might go and slay her husband, she told the whole circumstance to her mother-in-law. Then her mother-in-law said to her, "My daughter, you have acted nobly, but possibly some misfortune may happen to my son in consequence of what you have done."

So the wise Devasmitá forthwith put on the dress of a merchant. Then she embarked on a ship, on the pretence of a mercantile expedition, and came to the country of Katáha where her husband was. And when she arrived there, she saw that husband of hers, Guhasena, in the midst of a circle of merchants, like consolation in external bodily form. He seeing her afar off in the dress of a man, as it were, drank her in with his eyes, and thought to himself, "Who may this merchant be that looks so like my beloved wife?" So Devasmitá went and represented to the king that she had a petition to make, and asked him to assemble all his subjects. Then the king full of curiosity assembled all the citizens, and said to that lady disguised as a merchant, "What is your petition?" Then Devasmitá said, "There are residing here in your midst four slaves of mine who have escaped, let the king make them over to me." Then the king said to her, "All the citizens are present here, so look at everyone in order to recognise him, and take those slaves of yours." Then she seized upon the four young merchants, whom she had before treated in such a humiliating way in her house, and who had wrappers bound round their heads. Then the merchants, who were there. flew in a passion, and said to her, "These are the sons of distinguished merchants, how then can they be your slaves?" Then she answered them, "If you do not believe what I say, examine their foreheads which I marked with a dog's foot." They consented, and removing the head-wrappers of these four, they all beheld the dog's foot on their foreheads. Then all the merchants were abashed, and the king, being astonished, himself asked Devasmitá what all this meant. She told the whole story, and all the people burst out laughing, and the king said to the lady, "They are your slaves by the best of titles." Then the other merchants paid a large sum of money to the chaste wife, to redeem those four from slavery, and a fine to the king's treasury. Devasmitá received that money, and recovered her husband, and being honoured by all good men, returned then to her own city Támraliptá, and she was never after ·a ⁻s separated from her beloved.

SOPHOCLES

SOPHOCLES (Greek, 496-406 B.C.). Early master of the drama, next to Aeschylus in time and rank. Is said to have introduced third actor into the drama, and made each play a unit instead of part of a trilogy. Of his 123 plays, 7 survive. Among them: *Antigone, Electra, Ajax, Oedipus Tyrannus.* Notable for humanizing his characters and for skillful play construction.

ANTIGONE

Antigone, the daughter of Œdipus, having buried her father, returns to Thebes. Eteocles and Polynices, her brothers, having fallen by each other's hand, the kingdom devolves on Creon, their uncle. The tragedy of Antigone begins with Creon's edict forbidding the rites of burial to Polynices, as a traitor, and threatening with death any one who should dare to bury him. In violation of the decree, Antigone sprinkles dust and pours libations over the body of her brother, but is arrested and condemned to be immured in a cave. Tiresias, the seer, warns Creon that the offended people will rage, that his cities shall be polluted and his palace filled with woe. Creon relents and gives orders for the burial of Polynices, and goes himself to free Antigone. He is too late; she has killed herself, and her lover, Creon's son Hæmon, lies slain by her side. In the meantime, Eurydice, the queen, has stabbed herself before the altar. As the play closes, Creon is in utter misery.

ANTIGONE BEFORE KING CREON

Guards bring in Antigone

Guard. I come, although I swore the contrary,
Bringing this maiden, whom in act we found
Decking the grave.
And now, O king, take her, and as thou wilt,
Judge and convict her.
    Creon. How and where was it that ye seized and brought her?
    Guard. She was in act of burying. Thou knowest all.
    Creon. Dost know and rightly speak the tale thou tell'st?
    Guard. I saw her burying that self-same corpse
Thou bad'st us not to bury. Speak I clear?
    Creon. How was she seen, and taken in the act?
    Guard. The matter passed as follows:—When we came,
With all those dreadful threats of thine upon us,
Sweeping away the dust which, lightly spread,
Covered the corpse, and laying stripped and bare
The tainted carcase, on the hill we sat
To windward, shunning the infected air,
Each stirring up his fellow with strong words,
If any shirked his duty. This went on
Some time, until the glowing orb of day
Stood in mid heaven, and the scorching heat
Fell on us. Then a sudden whirlwind rose,
A scourge from heaven, raising squalls on earth,
And filled the plain, the leafage stripping bare
Of all the forest, and the air's vast space
Was thick and troubled, and we closed our eyes,
Until the plague the Gods had sent was past;
And when it ceased, a weary time being gone,
The girl is seen, and with a bitter cry,
Shrill as a bird's, when it beholds its nest
All emptied of its infant brood, she wails;
Thus she, when she beholds the corpse all stripped,
Groaned loud with many moanings, and she called
Fierce curses down on those who did the deed.
And in her hand she brings some fine, dry dust,
And from a vase of bronze, well wrought, upraised,
She pours the three libations o'er the dead.

And we, beholding, give her chase forthwith,
And run her down, naught terrified at us.
And then we charged her with the former deed,
As well as this. And nothing she denied.
But this to me both bitter is and sweet,
For to escape one's-self from ill is sweet,
But to bring friends to trouble, this is hard
And painful. Yet my nature bids me count
Above all these things safety for myself.

   Creon (to Antigone). Thou, then — yes, thou, who bend'st thy face to earth—
Confessest thou, or dost deny the deed?
   Antig. I own I did it, and will not deny.
   Creon (to Guard). Go thou thy way, where'er thy will may choose,
Freed from a weighty charge.

(Exit Guard.)

(To Antigone). And now for thee.
Say in few words, not lengthening out thy speech,
Knew'st thou the edicts which forbade these things?
   Antig. I knew them. Could I fail? Full clear were they.
   Creon. And thou didst dare to disobey these laws?
   Antig. Yes, for it was not Zeus who gave them forth,
Nor Justice, dwelling with the Gods below,
Who traced these laws for all the sons of men;
Nor did I deem thy edicts strong enough,
That thou, a mortal man, shouldst over-pass
The unwritten laws of God that know not change.
They are not of to-day nor yesterday,
But live for ever, nor can man assign
When first they sprang to being. Not through fear
Of any man's resolve was I prepared
Before the Gods to bear the penalty
Of sinning against these. That I should die
I knew, (how should I not?) though thy decree
Had never spoken. And, before my time
If I shall die, I reckon this a gain;
For whoso lives, as I, in many woes,
How can it be but he shall gain by death?

And so for me to bear this doom of thine
Has nothing painful. But, if I had left
My mother's son unburied on his death,
In that I should have suffered; but in this
I suffer not. And should I seem to thee
To do a foolish deed, 'tis simply this,—
I bear the charge of folly from a fool. . . . .
And yet how could I higher glory gain
Than placing my true brother in his tomb?
There is not one of these but would confess
It pleases them, did fear not seal their lips.
The tyrant's might in much besides excels,
And it may do and say whate'er it will.

    Creon.   Of all the race of Cadmos thou alonⱼ
Look'st thus upon the deed.

    Antig.   They see it too
As I do, but their tongue is tied for thee.

    Creon.   Art not ashamed against their thoughts to think?

    Antig.   There is naught base in honoring our own blood.

    Creon.   And was he not thy kin who fought against him?

    Antig.   Yea, brother, of one father and one mother.

    Creon.   Why then give honor which dishonors him?

    Antig.   The dead below will not repeat thy words.

    Creon.   Yes, if thou give like honor to the godless.

    Antig.   It was his brother, not his slave, that died.

    Creon.   Wasting this land, while *he* died fighting for it.

    Antig.   Yet Hades still craves equal rites for all.

    Creon.   The good craves not the portion of the bad.

    Antig.   Who knows if this be holy deemed below?

    Creon.   Not even when he dies can foe be friend.

    Antig.   My nature leads to sharing love, not hate.

    Creon.   Go then below; and if thou must have love,
Love them. While I live, women shall not rule.

ANTIGONE AND ISMENE

Ismene, sister of Antigone, had in fear of the king's decree refused to join her in performing the burial rites for her brother Polynices. But when Antigone is arrested, Ismene is willing and eager to share her fate.

Enter Ismene, led in by Attendants

1189

Chorus. And, lo! Ismene at the gate
Comes shedding tears of sisterly regard,
And o'er her brow a gathering cloud
    Mars the deep roseate blush,
    Bedewing her fair cheek.
Creon (to Ismene). And thou who, creeping as a viper creeps
Didst drain my life in secret, and I knew not
That I was rearing two accursed ones,
Subverters of my throne,—come, tell me, then,
Wilt thou confess thou tookst thy part in this,
Or wilt thou swear thou didst not know of it?
    Ism. I did the deed, if she did go; with her
I share the guilt, and bear an equal blame.
    Antig. Nay, justice will not suffer this, for thou
Didst not consent, nor did I let thee join.
    Ism. Nay, in thy troubles, I am not ashamed
in the same boat with thee to share thy fate.
    Antig. Who did it, Hades knows, and those below:
I do not love a friend who loves in words.
    Ism. Do not, my sister, put me to such shame,
As not to let me join in death with thee,
And so to pay due reverence to the dead.
    Antig. Share not my death, nor make thine own this deed
Thou hadst no hand in. My death shall suffice.
    Ism. What life to me is sweet, bereaved of thee?
    Antig. Save thou thyself. I grudge not thy escape.
    Ism. Ah, woe is me! and must I miss thy fate?
    Antig. Thou mad'st thy choice to live, and I to die.
    Ism. 'Twas not because I failed to speak my thoughts.
    Antig. To these didst thou, to those did I seem wise.
    Ism. And yet the offence is equal in us both.
    Antig. Take courage. Thou dost live. My soul long since
Hath died to render service to the dead.
    Creon. Of these two girls the one goes mad but now,
The other ever since her life began.
    Ism. E'en so, O king; no mind that ever lived
Stands firm in evil days, but goes astray.
    Creon. Thine did, when, with the vile, vile deeds thou chosest.
    Ism. How could I live without her presence here?
    Creon. Speak not of presence. She is here no more.
    Ism. And wilt thou slay thy son's betrothed bride?

Creon. Full many a field there is which he may plough.
Ism. None like that plighted troth 'twixt him and her.
Creon. Wives that are vile I love not for my sons.
Ism. Ah, dearest Hæmon, how thy father shames thee!
Creon. Thou with that marriage dost but vex my soul.
Chor. And wilt thou rob thy son of her he loved?
Creon. 'Tis Death, not I, shall break the marriage off.
Chor. Her doom is fixed, it seems, then. She must die.
Creon. Fixed, yes, by me and thee. No more delay,
Lead them within, ye slaves. These must be kept
Henceforth as women, suffered not to roam;
For even boldest natures shrink in fear
When they see Hades overshadowing life.

KING ŒDIPUS

The terrible story of Œipus had a strong fascination for the Greeks, as illustrating the conflict of moral laws and the supremacy of destiny. Laius, King of Thebes, learned from the oracle of Apollo, at Delphi, that he was destined to perish by the hand of his own son. He ordered his wife Jocasta, therefore, to destroy the infant. She gave it to a herdsman, who left it, tied with thongs, on Mount Cithæron. But a shepherd of Corinth found the babe and delivered it to King Polybus, who adopted it as his own child, and called it Œdipus (Swollen-foot). When grown up, Œdipus is told by the oracle that he would slay his father and marry his mother. On his return to Corinth he met Laius in a narrow pass and, in a dispute about the road, slew him. Passing to Thebes, he destroyed the Sphinx, a monster which had been inflicting damage on the city. Œdipus was, therefore, raised to the throne and the widowed Jocasta receives him as her husband. A pestilence arises, and the oracle declares that it cannot be abated until the murder of Laius is avenged. On investigation the appalling secret is discovered, whereupon Jocasta commits suicide, and Œdipus tears out his own eyes and goes into exile.

Jocasta. Princes of Thebes, we deemed it meet to seek
The temples of the gods, and in our hands
These votive wreaths, this odorous incense bear.
The soul of Œdipus on a wild sea
Of anxious care is tossed;—nor, as becomes

The prudent, weighs by former oracles
This late response, but lends a willing ear
To all who speak of terrors. Since my voice
Avails no more, Lycæan king, to thee
I fly, for thou art nearest to our need,
And come in prayer a suppliant to thy shrine,
That thou mayst grant us thine auspicious aid;
Since all now tremble, when we thus behold
Our very pilot shuddering and appalled.

Enter Corinthian

 Corinthian. Can ye inform me, strangers, where your king,
Great Œdipus, his regal state maintains;
Or, if ye know, where I may find the monarch?
 Chorus. These are th' imperial halls—he is within—
This is his wife, the mother of his children.
 Cor. Blest may she be, and ever with the blest
Hold glad communion; to her royal lord
A most accomplished consort.
 Joc. Equal joy
Attend thee, stranger,—thy kind greeting claims
This due return of courtesy. But say,
Whence cam'st thou to our Thebes, and what thy tidings?
 Cor. Joy to thy house, O lady! and thy lord.
 Joc. What joy?—and from what region art thou come?
 Cor. From Corinth At my words thou wilt rejoice:
Why shouldst thou not—yet fond regrets will rise.
 Joc. What dost thou mean, and whence this two-fold influence?
 Cor. The assembled States of Isthmus, rumor tells,
Will choose thy lord to mount the vacant throne.
 Joc. How vacant? Reigns not Polybus in Corinth?
 Cor. No more!—His only kingdom is the tomb.
 Joc. Haste, haste, attendant, and convey with speed
These tidings to your lord. Vain oracles!
Where are your bodings now? My Œdipus,
Fearing to slay this man, forsook his country;
Now Fate, and not his hand, hath laid him low.

Enter Œdipus

 Œdipus. Why, my beloved Jocasta, has thou sent
To bid my presence hither?

1192

Joc.   Hear this man—
Attend his tidings, and observe the end
Of these most true and reverend oracles.
    Œd.   Who is this stranger—with what message charged?
    Joc.   He is from Corinth, thence despatched to tell thee
That Polybus, thy father, is no more.
    Œd.   What sayest thou, stranger? Be thyself the speaker.
    Cor.   Then, in plain terms, the king is dead and gone.
    Œd.   Died he by treason, or the chance of sickness?
    Cor.   Slight ills dismiss the aged to their rest.
    Œd.   Then by disease, it seems, the monarch died.
    Cor.   And bowed beneath a withering weight of years.
    Œd.   Ha! is it thus? Then, lady, who would heed
The Pythian shrine oracular, or birds
Clanging in air, by whose vain auspices
I was fore-doomed the murderer of my father?
In the still silence of the tomb he sleeps.
While I am here—the fatal sword untouched,
Unless he languished for his absent child,
And I was thus the author of his doom.
Now in the grave he lies, and with him rest
Those vain predictions, worthy of our scorn.
    Joc.   Did I not tell thee this before?
    Œd.   Thou didst,
But terror urged me onward.
    Joc.   Banish now
This vain solicitude.
    Œd.   Should I not fear
The dark pollution of my mother's bed?
    Joc.   Oh, why should mortals fear, when fortune's sway
Rules all, and wariest foresight naught avails?
Best to live on unheeding, as thou may'st.
    Œd.   Phœbus foretold that I should wed my mother,
And shed with impious hand a father's blood.
For this I fled my own Corinthian towers
To seek a distant home—that home was blest;
Though still I languished to embrace my parents,
    Cor.   This fear then urged thee to renounce thy country?
    Œd.   Old man, I would not be a father's murderer.
    Cor.   Then wherefore, since thy welfare I regard,
Should I forbear to rid thee of this terror?

Œd. Do so, and rich shall be thy recompense.

Cor. This hope impell'd me here, that when our State
Hails thee her monarch, I might win thy favor.

Œd. Ne'er will I seek the authors of my birth.

Cor. 'Tis plain, my son, thou know'st not what thou doest!

Œd. How! how! old man, by heaven, unfold thy meaning.

Cor. If this preclude thee from returning home—

Œd. I fear lest Phœbus saw, alas! too clearly!

Cor. If thou dost dread pollution from thy parents—

Œd. That restless dread for ever haunts my soul.

Cor. Know, then, thy terrors all are causeless here.

Œd. How so? if of these parents I was born?

Cor. But Polybus is not allied to thee.

Œd. How say'st thou? was not Polybus my father?

Cor. No more than I—our claims are equal here.

Œd. Had he who gave me life no nearer claim
Than thou, a stranger?

Cor. Nor to him or me
Ow'st thou thy birth.

Œd. Then wherefore did he grant
A son's beloved name?

Cor. He from my hand
Received thee as a gift.

Œd. With such fond love
How could he cherish thus an alien child?

Cor. His former childless state to this impelled him.

Œd. Gav'st thou a purchased slave, or thy own child?

Cor. I found thee in Cithæron's shadowy glades.

Œd. Why didst thou traverse those remoter vales?

Cor. It was my charge to tend the mountain herds.

Œd. Wert thou a herdsman, and engaged for hire?

Cor. I was, my son, but thy preserver too.

Œd. From what affliction didst thou then preserve me?

Cor. This let thy scarr'd and swollen feet attest.

Œd. Ha! why dost thou revive a woe long passed?

Cor. I loosed thy bound and perforated feet.

Œd. Such foul reproach mine infancy endured.

Cor. From this event arose the name thou bear'st.

Œd. Thou didst receive me then from other hands,
Nor find me as by chance?

Cor. No; to my hand
Another herdsman gave thee.

Œd. Who was he?
Canst thou inform me this?

Cor. He was, I believe,
A slave of Laius.

Œd. What! of him who erst
Ruled o'er this land?

Cor. The same;—this man to him
Discharged an herdsman's office.

Œd. Lives he yet
That I may see him?

Cor. Ye, his countrymen,
Are best prepared this question to resolve.

Œd. Is there, of you who now attend our presence,
One who would know the herdsman he describes,
Familiar erst or here, or in the field?
Speak—for the time demands a prompt disclosure.

Ch. He is, I deem, no other than the man
Whom thou before didst summon from the fields.
This none can know more than the Queen.

Œd. Think'st thou, O Queen, the man whose presence late
We bade, is he of whom this stranger speaks?

Joc. Who—spake of whom?—Regard him not, nor dwell,
With vain remembrance, on unmeaning words!

Œd. Nay, Heaven forfend, when traces of my birth
Are thus unfolding, I should cease to follow.

Joc. Nay, by the Gods I charge thee! search no more,
If life be precious still. Be it enough
That I am most afflicted.

Œd. Cheer thee, lady,
Though my descent were proved e'en trebly servile,
No stain of infamy would light on thee.

Joc. Ah yield, I do conjure thee—seek no more.

Œd. I will not yield, till all be clearly known.

Joc. 'Tis for thy peace I warn thee—yet be wise.

Œd. That very wisdom wounds my peace most deeply.

Joc. Unhappy—never may'st thou know thy birth.

Œd. Will none conduct this shepherd to our presence?
Leave her to triumph in her lordly race.

1195

Joc. Woe! woe! unhappy! henceforth by that name
Alone can I address thee, and by that
Alone for ever.

Œd. I will on
To trace my birth, though it be most obscure.
Pride swells her thus, for in a woman's breast
Pride reigns despotic, and she thinks foul scorn
Of my ignoble birth. I deem myself
The child of Fortune, in whose favoring smile
I shall not be dishonored. She alone
Hath been my fostering parent; from low state
My kindred mouths have raised me into greatness.
Sprung from such lineage, none I heed beside,
Nor blush reluctant to explore my birth.

Enter Herdsman

Œd. Approach, old man! look on me, and reply
To my demand. Wert thou the slave of Laius?

Herd. I was his slave—bred in his house—not purchased.
My better part of life was passed in tending
The monarch's flocks.

Œd. What regions wert thou then
Wont to frequent?

Herd. Cithæron and the meads
Adjacent.

Cor. Then answer, dost thou recollect the babe
Thou gav'st me there, as mine own child to cherish?

Herd. What wouldst thou? Whither do thy questions tend?

Cor. This is that child, my friend, who stands before thee.

Herd. A curse light on thee! wilt thou not be silent?

Œd. Reprove him not, old man, for thine own words,
Far more than his, demand a stern reprover.

Herd. I did:—Oh, had that moment been my last!

Œd. This shall be, if thou wilt not speak the truth.

Herd. And if I speak it, I am trebly lost.

Œd. This man, it seems, still struggles to elude us.

Herd. No, I confessed long since I gave the child.

Œd. And whence received? thine own, or from another?

Herd. No, not mine own; I from another's hand
Bare him.

Œd. And from what Theban, from what roof?

Herd. Oh, by the gods! my lord, inquire no further.

Œd. If I repeat th' inquiry, thou art lost.

Herd. The palace of King Laius gave him birth.

Œd. Sprung from a slave, or of the royal stock?

Herd. The child was called the son of Laius; here
The royal consort can inform thee better.

Œd. Didst thou from her receive him?

Herd. Yea, O king!—

Œd. And for what purpose?

Herd. That I might destroy him—

Œd. What—the unnatural mother!

Herd. She was awed
By woe-denouncing oracles.

Œd. What woe?

Herd. That he should prove the murderer of his parents.

Œd. Why, then, to this old man thy charge consign?

Herd. From pity, O my lord, I deemed that he
To his own land would bear the child afar.
He saved him to despair. If thou art he
Of whom he spake, how dark a doom is thine!

Œd. Woe! woe! 'tis all too fatally unveiled.
Thou Light! Oh. may I now behold thy beams
For the last time! Unhallowed was my birth;
In closest ties united, where such ties
Were most unnatural;—with that blood defiled,
From whose pollution most the heart recoils.

CARL SPITTELER

CARL SPITTELER (Swiss, 1845-1924). Swiss poet and essayist. A rebellious
neo-classicist, whose position in German literature is still in dispute. Though
he wrote both realistic and romantic works, his major career was spent on a
modern Greek epic, *Olympian Spring*. A lonely and unusual figure. Nobel
Prize-winner, 1919.

THEME

Bell, my silver tonguéd bell,
Oh, thy secret prithee tell:

Dwellst where bats and night-owls roam,
Lonely in thy moldered home;
Tell me, whence thy solemn ring?
And who taught thee, pray, to sing?

When in gloomy shaft I lay,
Night of hell I saw alway.
In this tower high and free
Through the whirling winds I see
Human sorrow graced by soul.
And thou wonderst why I toll?

"HERACLES PASSING TO EARTH"

But now the king the host of heralds did invite.
"The harpers bring, the singing maids, into my sight,
That Heracles unto the lovely sounds of mirth,
With courage fortified, may tread his way to earth!"
Before the gate there rose the buzz of strings subdued,
And laughter from the throat, as if a bird had cooed,
Betrayed the sportive singing-maidens' coming nigh.
Spake Zeus to Heracles: "It hurts to say good-by!"
And leads him to the court and fountain. At the brink
A little, and the rest he gives his son with cheer:
"Drink heartily!" he says, "this spring is true and clear!"
Then, with his hands upon the youthful shoulders: "Man!
Now let there happen what there will and come what can:
Into a royal font baptismal thou hast dipped,
And from the dripping fountain-flood of truth hast sipped.
That thou hast drunk with Zeus out of one glass today
The might of thousand rascals cannot wrench away.
In some dark hour shouldst thou in want of comfort be.
Look up, remember then: thou hast a bond with me
What I could do for thee is done. The retinue
That is to follow on thy way, come let us view."

With playing of the strings and bursts of song about,
Now from the house the king doth with his son step out.
Hark: cracks of whips and jingling! Plumes and pinions bold!
A chariot train of princely Titans now behold.
"I welcome ye!" spake Zeus. "What do ye bring me now?"
"We came the son of Zeus with talents to endow."
"Then thanks! For thus I know the way of kinsmen dear."
And now round Heracles the princes formed a sphere:
Nobility from Artemis and from Apollo
Comes valor, thought so keen that no mistake can follow
From Pallas—Hermes now his glance with kindness fills,
And Aphrodite mirth into his hearts instils.
Zeus spake and bound about the bosom of his son
The scroll of fate: "Now that thou really must be gone,
Receive my counsel: keep a stubborn head!
And be no simple fool—no rascal dread!"
The escorts then round Heracles with song and play
All turned into the fields to journey far away.
Ahead into the sky rang high the travel-song,
And golden grain looked down the hillsides all along.
No working-man, when Heracles did come in sight,
But sent to him some little words of kindness bright.
"Fare well on earth and prosper in the human land!"
And every lad ran toward him with outstreched hand.
A maiden laughs with eyes and mouth and checks—in zest
A bunch of flowers now she fastens to his breast.
And other human souls that came across his ways
At him with wonder in their dreamy eyes would gaze:
"Who cometh there whose steps sound victory so loud?
This hero's stature is of upright stock and proud!"
A maiden of the human beings one, but fairer
By far than all the other maidens be and rarer,
Drew near to him, her locks as if in slumber swaying,
And made him halt, upon his breast her finger laying.
Then pensively she bowed her forehead, sighing: "Oh,
Where is the street that we on earth do not yet know

1199

—Oh, tell me this, thou great unknown, oh tell thou me—
That over mountains, sombre forests, leads to thee?
If 'twere a thousand miles through many nights and days,
I would with quick'ning pulse o'ertake thee on thy ways.
If sharpest thorns should give me wounds, I would not bind
My bleeding foot at all, until I thee should find.
Forsee: on earth I know not where thou shalt be with me."
So I will go and dwell where thou shalt be with me."
Thus, dreaming, sighed the maid. Her speech was done; at last
She passed along her way with glances backward cast.
And Heracles, with all about him loving, kind,
In ecstasy of soul began within his mind:
"On earth I see a mountain looming to remind me.
A vow I'll make in solemn worship that shall bind me:
Ye joyous fields of high Olympos, beauty-bright,
Thou sky that floatest o'er the clouds in lofty height,
Ye dear ones all, unto my vow oh witness bear:
Now for my work I live, not for myself, I swear,
With heart and hands, nor rest nor pleasure taking more,
To love the great and do what ne'er was done before.
Oh, ye my human brothers, human sisters dear,
Your friend I'll be, your help devoted and sincere.
And no reward, except upon accomplished deed,
A silent, knowing glance but from the best, I need.
Hail, earth! I gladly pay the tax of pain you ask,
With courage spirited I come to do my task."
Thus cried he. Harps resounded, choirs rejoiced in song,
And through the folds of golden fields they passed along.

SSU-K'UNG T'U

SSÜ-K'UNG T'U (Chinese, 837-908). Scholarly pedantic stylist. Like many another Chinese poet, gave up an official career to write in retirement. His work shows great erudition rather than originality. Most famous: a 24-stanza poem, Êrh-shih-ssu shih-p'in.

RETURN OF SPRING

A lovely maiden, roaming
   The wild dark valley through,
Culls from the shining waters
   Lilies and lotus blue.
With leaves the peach-trees are laden,
   The wind sighs through the haze,
And the willows wave their shadows
   Down the oriole-haunted ways.
As, passion-tranced, I follow,
   I hear the old refrain
Of Spring's eternal story,
   That was old and is young again.

THE COLOUR OF LIFE

Would that we might for ever stay
The rainbow glories of the world,
The blue of the unfathomed sea,
The rare azalea late unfurled,
The parrot of a greener spring,
The willows and the terrace line,
The stranger from the night-steeped hills,
The roselit brimming cup of wine.
Oh for a life that stretched afar,
Where no dead dust of books were rife,
Where spring sang clear from star to star;
Alas! what hope for such a life?

SET FREE

I revel in flowers without let,
An atom at random in space;
My soul dwells in regions ethereal,
And the world is my dreaming-place.

1201

As the tops of the ocean I tower,
As the winds of the air spreading wide,
I am 'stablished in might and dominion and power,
With the universe ranged at my side.

Before me the sun, moon, and stars,
Behind me the phœnix doth clang;
In the morning I lash my leviathans,
And I bathe my feet in Fusang.

FASCINATION

Fair is the pine grove and the mountain stream
That gathers to the valley far below,
The black-winged junks on the dim sea reach,
    adream,
The pale blue firmament o'er banks of snow.
And her, more fair, more supple smooth than jade,
Gleaming among the dark red woods I follow:
Now lingering, now as a bird afraid
Of pirate wings she seeks the haven hollow.
Vague, and beyond the daylight of recall,
Into the cloudland past my spirit flies,
As though before the gold of autumn's fall,
Before the glow of the moon-flooded skies.

TRANQUIL REPOSE

It dwells in the quiet silence,
    Unseen upon hill and plain,
'Tis lapped by the tideless harmonies,
    It soars with the lonely crane.

As the springtime breeze whose flutter
    The silken skirts hath blown,
As the wind-drawn note of the bamboo flute
    Whose charm we would make our own,—

Chance-met, it seems to surrender;
    Sought, and it lures us on;
Ever shifting in form and fantasy,
    It eludes us, and is gone.

JOHN ERNST STEINBECK

JOHN ERNST STEINBECK (1902-   ). Contemporary writer of powerful
sociological novels. Born in the California country celebrated in *Tortilla Flat*
and *Cannery Row.* Labored as newsman and bricklayer in New York. Best
works are infused with sympathy for the underprivileged. *Grapes of Wrath,*
epic of the dust bowl, has been compared with *Uncle Tom's Cabin.* Other
novels: *Of Mice and Men, The Pearl.*

OWNERS AND TENANTS

THE owners of the land had come onto the land, or more often a
spokesman for the owners came. They came in closed cars, and they
felt the dry earth with their fingers, and sometimes they drove big
earth augers into the ground for soil tests. The tenants from their
sun-beaten dooryards, watched uneasily when the closed cars drove
along the fields. And at last the owner men drove into the dooryards
and sat in their cars to talk out of the windows. The tenant men
stood beside the cars for a while, and then sqatted on their hams
and found sticks with which to mark the dust.

In the open doors the women stood looking out, and behind them
the children—corn-headed children, with wide eyes, one bare foot
on top of the other bare foot, and the toes working. The women
and the children watched their men talking to the owner men. They
were silent.

Some of the owner men were kind because they hated what they
had to do, and some of them were angry because they hated to be
cruel, and some of them were cold because they had long ago found
that one could not be an owner unless one were cold. And all of
them were caught in something larger than themselves. Some of
them hated the mathematics that drove them, and some were afraid,
and some worshiped the mathematics because it provided a refuge
from thought and from feeling. If a bank or a finance company
owned the land, the owner man said, The Bank—or the Company—
needs—wants—insists—must have— as though the Bank or the
Company were a monster, with thought and feeling, which had
ensnared them. These last would take no responsibility for the banks
or the companies because they were men and slaves, while the banks
were machines and masters all at the same time. Some of the owner
men were a little proud to be slaves to such cold and powerful masters. The owner men sat in the cars and explained. You know the
land is poor. You've scrabbled at it long enough, God knows.

The squatting tenant men nodded and wondered and drew figures in the dust, and yes, they knew, God knows. If the dust only wouldn't fly. If the top would only stay on the soil, it might not be so bad.

The owner men went on leading to their point: You know the land's getting poorer. You know what cotton does to the land; robs it, sucks all the blood out of it.

The squatters nodded—they knew, God knew. If they could only rotate the crops they might pump blood back into the land.

Well, it's too late. And the owner men explained the workings and thinkings of the monster that was stronger than they were. A man can hold land if he can just eat and pay taxes; he can do that.

Yes, he can do that until his crops fail one day and he has to borrow money from the bank.

But—you see, a bank or a company can't do that, because those creatures don't breathe air, don't eat side-meat. They breathe profits; they eat the interest on money. If they don't get it, they die the way you die without air, without side-meat. It is a sad thing, but it is so. It is just so.

The squatting men raised their eyes to understand. Can't we just hang on? Maybe the next year will be a good year. God knows how much cotton next year. And with all the wars—God knows what price cotton will bring. Don't they make explosives out of cotton? And uniforms? Get enough wars and cotton'll hit the ceiling. Next year, maybe. They looked up questioningly.

We can't depend on it. The bank—the monster has to have profits all the time. It can't wait. It'll die. No, taxes go on. When the monster stops growing, it dies. It can't stay one size.

Soft fingers began to tap the sill of the car window, and hard fingers tightened on the restless drawing sticks. In the doorways of the sun-beaten tenant houses, women sighed and shifted feet so that the one that had been down was now on top, and the toes working. Dogs came sniffing near the owner cars and wetted on all four tires one after another. And the chickens lay in the sunny dust and fluffed their feathers to get the cleansing dust down to the skin. In the little sties the pigs grunted inquiringly over the muddy remnants of the slops.

The squatting men looked down again. What do you want us to do? We can't take less share of the crop—we're half starved now. The kids are hungry all the times. We got no clothes, torn an' ragged. If all the neighbors weren't the same, we'd be ashamed to go to meeting.

And at last the owner men came to the point. The tenant system won't work any more. One man on a tractor can take the place of twelve or fourteen families. Pay him a wage and take all the crop. We have to do it. We don't like to do it. But the monster's sick. Something's happened to the monster.

But you'll kill the land with cotton.

We know. We've got to take cotton quick before the land dies. Then we'll sell the land. Lots of families in the East would like to own a piece of land.

The tenant men looked up alarmed. But what'll happen to us? How'll we eat?

You'll have to get off the land. The plows'll go through the door-yard.

And now the squatting men stood up angrily. Grampa took up the land, and he had to kill the Indians and drive them away. And Pa was born here, and he killed weeds and snakes. Then a bad year came and he had to borrow a little money. An' we was born here. There in the door—our children born here. And Pa had to borrow money. The bank owned the land then, but we stayed and we got a little bit of what we raised.

We know that—all that. It's not us, it's the bank. A bank isn't like a man. Or an owner with fifty thousand acres, he isn't like a man either. That's the monster.

Sure, cried the tenant men, but it's our land. We measured it and broke it up. We were born on it, and we got killed on it, died on it. Even if it's no good, it's still ours. That's what makes it ours—being born on it, working it, dying on it. That makes ownership, not a paper with numbers on it.

We're sorry. It's not us. It's the monster. The bank isn't like a man.

Yes, but the bank is only made of men.

No, you're wrong there—quite wrong there. The bank is something else than men. It happens that every man in a bank hates what the bank does, and yet the bank does it. The bank is something more than men, I tell you. It's the monster. Men made it, but they can't control it.

The tenants cried: Grampa killed Indians, Pa killed snakes for the land. Maybe we can kill banks—they're worse than Indians and snakes. Maybe we got to fight to keep our land, like Pa and Grampa did.

And now the owner men grew angry. You'll have to go.

But it's ours, the tenant men cried. We—

1205

No. The bank, the monster owns it. You'll have to go.

We'll get our guns, like Grandpa when the Indians came. What then?

Well—first the sheriff, and then the troops. You'll be stealing if you try to stay, you'll be murderers if you kill to stay. The monster isn't men, but it can make men do what it wants.

But if we go, where'll we go? How'll we go? We got no money.

We're sorry, said the owner men. The bank, the fifty-thousand-acre owner can't be responsible. You're on land that isn't yours. Once over the line maybe you can pick cotton in the fall. Maybe you can go on relief. Why don't you go on West to California? There's work there and it never gets cold. Why, you can reach out anywhere and pick an orange. Why, there's always some kind of crop to work in. Why don't you go there? And the owner men started their cars and rolled away.

The tenant men squatted down on their hams again to mark the dust with a stick, to figure, to wonder. Their sun-burned faces were dark, and their sun-whipped eyes were light. The women moved cautiously out of the door-ways towards their men, and the children crept behind the women, cautiously, ready to run. The bigger boys squatted beside their fathers, because that made them men. After a time the women asked, What did he want?

And the men looked up for a second, and the smolder of pain was in their eyes. We got to get off. A tractor and a superintendent. Like factories.

Where'll we go? the women asked.

We don't know. We don't know.

And the women went quickly, quietly back into the houses and herded the children ahead of them. They knew that a man so hurt and so perplexed may turn in anger, even on people he loves. They left the men alone to figure and wonder in the dust.

After a time perhaps the tenant man looked about—at the pump put in ten years ago, with a goose-neck handle and iron flowers on the spout, at the chopping block where a thousand chickens had been killed, at the hand plow lying in the shed, and the patent crib hanging in the rafters over it.

The children crowded about the women in the houses. What are we going to do, Ma? Where are we going to go?

The women said: We don't know, yet. Go out and play. But don't go near your father. He might whale you if you go near him. And

, women went on with the work, but all the time they watched the men squatting in the dust—perplexed and figuring.

The tractors came over the roads and into the fields, great crawlers moving like insects, having the incredible strength of insects. They crawled over the ground, laying the track and rolling on it and picking it up. Diesel tractors, puttering while they stood idle; they thundered when they moved, and then settled down to a droning roar. Snub-nosed monsters, raising the dust and sticking their snouts into it, straight down the country, through fences, through dooryards, in and out of gullies in straight lines. They did not run on the ground, but on their own roadbeds. They ignored hills and gulches, water courses, fences, houses.

The man sitting in the iron seat did not look like a man; gloved, goggled, rubber dust mask over the nose and mouth, he was a part of the monster, a robot in the seat. The thunder of the cylinders sounded through the country, became one with the air and the earth, so that earth and air muttered in sympathetic vibration. The driver could not control it—straight across the country it went, cutting through a dozen farms and straight back. A twitch at the controls could swerve the cat, but the driver's hands could not twitch because the monster that built the tractor, the monster that sent the tractor out, had somehow got into the driver's hands, into his brain and muscle, had goggled him and muzzled him—goggled his mind, muzzled his speech, goggled his perception, muzzled his protest. He could not see the land as it was, he could not smell the land as it smelled; his feet did not stamp the clods or feel the warmth and power of the earth. He sat in an iron seat and stepped on iron pedals. He could not cheer or beat or curse or encourage the extension of his power, and because of this he could not cheer or whip or curse or encourage himself. He did not know or own or trust or beseech the land. If a seed dropped did not germinate, it was nothing. If the young trusting plant withered in drought or drowned in a flood of rain, it was no more to the driver than to the tractor.

He loved the land no more than the bank loved the land. He could admire the tractor—its machined surfaces, its surge of power, the roar of its detonating cylinders; but it was not his tractor. Behind the tractor rolled the shining disks, cutting the earth with blades—not plowing but surgery, pushing the cut earth to the right where the second row of disks cut it and pushed it to the left; slicing blades shining, polished by the cut earth. And pulled behind the disks, the harrows combing with iron teeth so that the little clods broke up and the earth lay smooth. Behind the harrows, the long seeders—twelve curved iron penes erected in the foundry, orgasms set by gears, raping methodically, raping without passion. The driver sat in his iron seat and he was proud of the straight lines he did not will, proud of the tractor he did not own or love, proud of the power he could not control. And when that crop grew, and was harvested, no man had crumbled a hot clod in his fingers and let the earth sift through his fingertips. No man had touched the seed, or lusted for the growth. Men ate what they had not raised, had no connection with the bread. The land bore under iron, and under iron gradually died; for it was not loved or hated, it had no prayers or curses.

At noon the tractor driver stopped sometimes near a tenant house and opened his lunch; sandwiches wrapped in waxed paper, white bread, pickle, cheese, Spam, a piece of pie branded like an engine part. He ate without relish. And tenants not yet moved away came out to see him, looked curiously while the goggles were taken off, and the rubber dusk mask, leaving white circles around the eyes and a large white circle around nose and mouth. The exhaust of the tractor putted on, for fuel is so cheap it is more efficient to leave the engine running than to heat the Diesel nose for a new start. Curious children crowded close, ragged children who ate their fried dough as they watched. They watch hungrily the unwrapping of the sandwiches, and their hunger-sharpened noses smelled the pickle, cheese, and Spam. They didn't speak to the driver. They watched his hand as it carried food to his mouth. They did not watch him chewing; their eyes followed the hand that held the sandwich. After a while the tenant who could not leave the place came out and squatted in the shade beside the tractor.

"Why, you're Joe Davis's boy!"

"Sure," the driver said.

"Well, what are you doing this kind of work for—against your own people?"

"Three dollars a day. I got damn sick of creeping for my dinner —and not getting it. I got a wife and kids. We got to eat. Three dollars a day, and it comes every day."

"That's right," the tenant said. "But for your three dollars a day fifteen or twenty families can't eat at all. Nearly a hundred people have to go out and wander on the roads for your three dollars a day. Is that right?"

And the driver said, "Can't think of that. Got to think of my own kids. Three dollars a day, and it comes every day. Times are changing, mister, don't you know? Can't make a living on the land unless you've got two, five, ten thousand acres and a tractor. Crop land isn't for little guys like us any more. You don't kick up a howl because you can't make Fords, or because you're not the telephone company. Well, crops are like that now. Nothing to do about it. You try to get three dollars a day someplace. That's the only way."

The tenant pondered. "Funny thing how it is. If a man owns a little property, the property is him, it's part of him, and it's like him. If he owns property only so he can walk on it and handle it and be sad when it isn't doing well, and feel fine when the rain falls on it, the property is him, and someway he's bigger because he owns it. Even if he isn't successful he's big with his property. That is so."

And the tenant pondered more. "But let a man get property he doesn't see, or can't take time to get his fingers in, or can't be there to walk on it—why, then the property is the man. He can't do what he wants, he can't think what he wants. The property is the man, stronger than he is. And he is small, not big. Only his possessions are big—and he's the servant of his property. That is so, too."

The driver munched the branded pie and threw the crust away. "Times are changed, don't you know? Thinking about stuff like that don't feed the kids. Get your three dollars a day, feed your kids. You got no call to worry about anybody's kids but your own. You get a reputation for talking like that, and you'll never get three dollars a day. Big shots won't give you three dollars a day if you worry about anything but your three dollars a day."

"Nearly a hundred people on the road for your three dollars. Where will we go?"

"And that reminds me," the driver said, "you'd better get out soon. I'm going through the dooryard after dinner."

"You filled in the well this morning."

"I know. Had to keep the line straight. But I'm going through the dooryard after dinner. Got to keep the lines straight. And—well, you know Joe Davis, my old man, so I'll tell you this. I got orders wherever there's a family not moved out—if I have an

1209

accident—you know, get too close and cave the house in a little—well, I might get a couple of dollars. And my youngest kid never had no shoes yet."

"I built it with my hands. Straightened old nails to put the sheathing on. Rafters are wired to the stringers with baling wire. It's mine. I built it. You bump it down—I'll be in the window with a rifle. You even come too close and I'll pot you like a rabbit."

"It's not me. There's nothing I can do. I'll lose my job if I don't do it. And look—suppose you kill me? They'll just hang you, but long before you're hung there'll be another guy on the tractor, and he'll bump the house down. You're not killing the right guy."

"That's so," the tenant said. "Who gave you orders? I'll go after him. He's the one to kill."

"You're wrong. He got his orders from the bank. The bank told him, 'Clear those people out or it's your job!'"

"Well, there's a president of the bank. There's a board of directors. I'll fill up the magazine of the rifle and go into the bank."

The driver said, "Fellow was telling me the bank gets orders from the East. The orders were, 'Make the land show profit or we'll close you up.'"

"But where does it stop? Who can we shoot? I don't aim to starve to death before I kill the man that's starving me."

"I don't know. Maybe there's nobody to shoot. Maybe the thing isn't men at all. Maybe, like you said, the property's doing it. Anyway I told you my orders."

"I got to figure," the tenant said. "We all got to figure. There's some way to stop this. It's not like lightning or earthquakes. We've got a bad thing made by men, and by God that's something we can change." The tenant sat in his doorway, and the driver thundered his engine and started off, tracks falling and curving, harrows combing, and the phalli of the seeder slipping into the ground. Across the dooryard the tractor cut, and the hard, foot-beaten ground was seeded field, and the tractor cut through again; the uncut space was ten feet wide. And back he came. The iron guard bit into the house-corner, crumbled the wall, and wrenched the little house from its foundation so that it fell sideways, crushed like a bug. And the driver was goggled and a rubber mask covered his nose and mouth. The tractor cut a straight line on, and the air and the ground vibrated with its thunder. The tenant man stared after it, his rifle in his hand. His wife was beside him, and the quiet children behind. And all of them stared after the tractor.

STENDHAL

STENDHAL (Marie-Henri Beyle, French, 1783-1842). Forerunner of the modern novel. Rejecting provincial life, became soldier under Bonaparte, later a French consul. As a novelist, possessed acute psychological insight, a disenchanted viewpoint. In his two masterpieces, *Le Rouge et le Noir* and *La Chartreuse de Parme*, the "Stendhal hero" is always at odds with his world.

THE CHARTREUSE OF PARMA

I.—Fabrice del Dongo

"THREE members of your family," said Count Mosca to the Duchess of Sanseverina, "have been Archbishops of Parma. Could a better career be open to your nephew Fabrice?"

The Duchess disliked the notion; and indeed Fabrice del Dongo seemed a person but little fitted for an ecclesiastical career. His ambitions were military; his hero was Napoleon. The great escapade of his life had been a secret journey into France to fight at Waterloo. His father, the Marquis del Dongo, was loyal to the Austrian masters of Lombardy; and during Fabrice's absence his elder brother Arcanio had laid an information against him as a conspirator against Austrian rule. Consequently Fabrice, on his return, found himself exposed to the risk of ten years in an Austrian prison. By his own address and by the good offices of his aunt, the Countess Pietravera, Fabrice was able to escape from Milanese territory.

Immediately afterwards the Countess wedded the aged and wealthy Duke of Sanseverina, and transferred her beauty and unbounded social talents from Milan to the court of Prince Ranuce Ernest IV., absolute ruler of Parma. The Duke had his ambitions gratified by an appointment as Ambassador to a distant country; the Duchess, left behind at Parma, was able to devote herself to the interests of Count Mosca, the Prince's chief Minister, and to counteract the intrigues of the celebrated Marchioness Raversi, head of the party that sought to overthrow him.

The welfare of her beloved nephew was the most cherished of all the Duchess's aims, and she succeeded in inspiring Count Mosca with an equal enthusiasm for the prosperity of that errant youth. But she hesitated over the project of making him an Archbishop.

"You must understand," explained the Count, "that I do not intend to make Fabrice an exemplary priest of the conventional kind.

No, he will above all remain a great noble; he may continue to be absolutely ignorant if he so pleases, and will become a Bishop and an Archbishop just the same—provided, of course, that I succeed in retaining the Prince's confidence."

Ultimately the Duchess agreed, and undertook to persuade Fabrice to enter the Church. The persuasion was not easy; but at length Fabrice, having been convinced that the clerical yoke would bear but lightly upon him, consented to the step, and as a preliminary spent three years in a theological college at Naples.

When at the end of three years Fabrice, now a Monsignore, returned to Parma, matters there were at a crisis; the Raversi party were gaining ground, and Count Mosca was in danger. Nor did the Prince's interview with the young cleric improve matters. Ranuce Ernest IV. had two ruling passions—an ambition to become ruler of united Italy, and a fear of revolution. Count Mosca, the diplomatist, was the only man who could further his hopes in one direction; his fears in the other were carefully kept alive by Rassi, the fiscal-general—to such an extent that each night the Prince looked under his bed to see if by chance a liberal were lurking there. Rassi was a man of low origin, who kept his place partly by submitting good-humouredly to the abuse and even the kicks of his master, and partly by rousing that master's alarms and afterwards allaying them by hanging or imprisoning liberals, with the ready assistance of a carefully corrupted judicial bench.

Towards this nervous Prince, Fabrice bore himself with an aristocratic assurance, and a promptness and coolness in conversation that made a bad impression. His political notions were correct enough, according to the Prince's standard; but plainly, he was a man of spirit, and the Prince did not like men of spirit; they were all cousins-germane of Voltaire and Rousseau. He deemed Fabrice, in short, a potential if not an actual liberal, and therefore dangerous.

Nevertheless Count Mosca carried the day against his rivals— a triumph due less to his own efforts than to those of the Duchess, to whose charms as the court's chief ornament the Prince was far from insusceptible. The Count's success was Fabrice's; that youth found himself established as co-adjutor to the Archbishop of Parma, with a reversion to the Archbishopric on the demise of its worthy occupant.

On Fabrice's return from Naples, the Duchess had found him developed from a boy into a young man, and the handsomest young man in Italy; her affection for him became sisterly; she was nearly in love with him. She had no cause for jealousy, for Fabrice, although prone to flirtation, had no affairs of the heart. The word love, as yet, had no meaning for him.

II.—Giletti

One of our hero's flirtations had consequences with a very pronounced bearing on his after career. During a surreptitious visit to the theatre he became captivated with the actress, Marietta Valserra. Stolen visits of two minutes' duration to Marietta's lodging on the fourth floor of an old house behind the theatre were an agreeable variation of the monotony of Fabrice's clerical duties, and of his visits among the most important and least entertaining families in Parma. But the trifling little intrigue came to the ears of Count Mosca, with the result that the travelling company to which Marietta belonged received its passports and was requested to move on.

In the affair, moreover, Fabrice had a rival. Giletti was the low comedian of the company, and the ugliest member of it; he assumed proprietorship over Marietta, who, although she did not love him, was at any rate horribly afraid of him. Giletti several times threatened to kill Fabrice; whereby Fabrice was not disturbed.

Count Mosca was passionately archæological, and this taste he shared with Fabrice, who had cultivated the hobby at Naples. It so happened that the two were engaged in excavations near the bridge over the Po where the main road passes into Austrian territory at Castel-Maggiore. Early one morning Fabrice, after surveying the work that was going on in the trenches, strolled away with a gun, intent upon lark-shooting. A wounded bird dropped on the road, and as Fabrice followed it he encountered a battered old carriage driving towards the frontier. In it were Giletti, Marietta and an old woman who passed as Marietta's mother.

Giletti leapt to the conclusion that Fabrice had come there, gun in hand, to insult him, and possibly to carry off Marietta. He leapt out of the carriage.

"Brigand!" he yelled, "we are only a league from the frontier—now I can finish you!"

Fabrice saw a pistol levelled at him at a distance of three feet; he knocked it aside with the butt of his gun, and it went off harmlessly. Giletti then clutched the gun; the two men wrestled for it, and it exploded close to Giletti's ear. Staggered for an instant, he quickly recovered himself; drawing from its sheath a "property" sword, he fell once more upon Fabrice.

"Look out! he will kill you," came an agitated whisper from Marietta; "take this!"

A sort of hunting knife was flung out of the carriage door. Fabrice picked it up, and was nearly stunned forthwith by a blow from the handle of the "property" sword. Happily Giletti was too near to use his sword-point. Pulling himself together, Fabrice gave his enemy a gash on the thigh. Giletti, swearing furiously, injured Fabrice on the cheek. Blood poured down our hero's face. The thought, "I am disfigured for life!" flashed through his mind. Enraged at the idea, he thrust the hunting knife at Giletti's breast with all his force. Giletti fell and lay motionless.

"He is dead!" said Fabrice to himself. Then, turning to the coach, he asked, "Have you a looking-glass?"

His eyes and teeth were undamaged; he was not permanently disfigured. Hastily, then, he turned to thoughts of escape. Marietta gave him Giletti's passport; obviously his first business was to get across the frontier. And yet the Austrian frontier was no safe one for him to cross. Were he recognised, he might expect ten years in an Imperial fortress. But this was the less immediate danger, and he determined to risk it.

With considerable trepidation he walked across the bridge, and presented Giletti's passport to the Austrian gendarme.

The gendarme looked at it, and rose, "You must wait, monsieur; there is a difficulty," he said, and left the room. Fabrice was profoundly uncomfortable; he was nearly for bolting, when he heard the gendarme say to another, "I am done up with the heat; just go and put your visa on a passport in there when you have finished your pipe; I'm going for some coffee."

This gendarme, in fact, knew Giletti, and was quite well aware that the man before him was not the actor. But, for all he could tell, Giletti had lent the passport for reasons of his own. The easiest way out of the difficulty was to get another gendarme to see to the visa. This man affixed it as a matter of course, and Fabrice escaped danger number one.

The rest was very easy, thanks to Ludovico, an old servant of the Duchess, whom Fabrice met at an eating-house where he had turned in for some very necessary refreshment. With the aid of this excellent fellow Fabrice had his wounds attended to, and was safely smuggled out of Austrian territory into Bologna.

The party opposed to Count Mosca hastened to take advantage of Fabrice's offence. He was represented as a murderer; the workmen in the trenches who had seen the affray, and knew that Fabrice had acted in self-defence, were either bribed or got out of the way. Rassi accused Fabrice of being a liberal; and since the Prince was ill-disposed towards the young man, not all the endeavours of Count Mosca could save him from a sentence of twenty years' imprisonment, should he be so impudent as to venture upon the territory of Parma.

Just before the sentence was presented to the Prince for final confirmation, the Prince learned that the Dutchess of Sanseverina sought an audience with him. He rubbed his hands; the greatest beauty of his court had come to beg mercy for her nephew; there would be tears and frantic appeals. For a quarter of an hour the Prince gloated over the prospect; then he ordered that the Duchess be admitted.

She entered—in travelling costume; never had she looked more charming, never more cheerful. "I trust your Serene Highness will pardon my unorthodox costume," she said, smiling archly; "but as I am about to leave Parma for a very long time, I have felt it my duty to come and thank you ere I go for all the kindnesses you have deigned to confer upon me."

The Prince was astonished and profoundly chagrined. "Why are you going?" he asked, as calmly as he could.

"I have had the project for some time," she replied, "and a little insult paid to Monsignor del Dongo has hastened it."

The Prince was beside himself. What would his court be without the Duchess? At all costs he much check her flight.

At this moment Count Mosca, pale with anxiety, begged admittance. He had just heard of the Duchess's intention to leave Parma.

"Let me speak as a friend to friends," said the Prince, collecting himself; "what can I do, Madame, to arrest your hasty resolution?"

"If your highness were to write a gracious letter revoking the unjust sentence upon Fabrice del Dongo, I might re-consider my decision; and, let me add, if the Marchioness Raversi were advised by you to retire to the country early to-morrow morning for the benefit of her health—"

"Was there ever such a woman?" cried the Prince, stamping up and down the room.

But he agreed. At his orders Count Mosca sat down and wrote the letter required. The Prince objected to the phrase "unjust sentence," and Count Mosca, courtier-like, abstained from using it. The Prince did not mind the banishment of the Marchioness Raversi; he liked exiling people.

At seven o'clock next morning the Prince summoned Rassi, and dictated to him another letter. The sentence of twenty years, upon the criminal del Dongo was to be reduced by the Prince's clemency, at the supplication of the Duchess Sanseverina, to twelve years; and the police were instructed to do their utmost to arrest the offender.

The only difficulty was that of tempting Fabrice into the territory of Parma. A hint to the Marchioness Raversi and her associates removed the obstacle. A forged letter, purporting to be from the Duchess, reached Fabrice at Bologna, telling him that there would be little danger in his meeting her at Castelnovo, within the frontier. Fabrice repaired joyfully to Castelnovo. That night he lay a prisoner in the citadel of Parma; while the Duchess, alone in her room with locked door, sobbed her heart out and raved helplessly against the treachery of princes.

"So long as her nephew is in the citadel," said the Prince to himself, "the Duchess will be in Parma."

The citadel of Parma is a colossal building with a flat roof 180 feet above the level of the ground. On this roof are erected two structures: one, the governor's residence; the other, the Farnese tower, a prison specially erected for a recalcitrant prince of earlier days. In this tower Fabrice, as a prisoner of importance, was confined; and as he looked from the window on the evening of his arrival and beheld the superb panorama of the distant Alps, he reflected pleasantly that he might have found a worse dungeon.

On the next morning his attention was absorbed by something nearer at hand. His window overlooked one belonging to the governor's palace; in this window were many bird cages, and at eleven o'clock a maiden came to feed the birds. Fabrice recognised her as Clelia Conti, the governor's daughter. He succeeding in attracting her attention; she blushed and withdrew. But next day she came again at the same hour. On the third day, however, a heavy wooden shutter was clapped upon the window. Nothing daunted, Fabrice proceeded patiently to cut a peep-hole in the shutter by aid of the main-spring of his watch. When he had succeeded in removing a square piece of the wood, he looked with delight upon Clelia gazing at his window with eyes of profound pity, unconscious that she was observed.

Gradually he broke down the maiden's reserve. She discovered the secret of the peep-hole; she consented to communicate with him; finally the two conversed by a system of signals. Fabrice even dared to tell Clelia that he loved her—and truly he was in love, **for** the first time in his life. The worst of it was that these declarations were apt to bring the conversation to an end; so Fabrice was sparing of them.

Clelia, meanwhile, was in sore perplexity. Her father, General Fabio Conti the governor, was a political opponent of Count Mosca, and had ambitions of office. These ambitions might be forwarded, he deemed, by the successful marriage of his daughter. He did not desire that she should remain a lovely recluse, feeding birds at the top of the citadel. Accordingly he had presented to her an ultimatum; either she must marry the Marquis Crescenzi, the wealthiest noble-man of Parma, who sought her hand, or she must retire to a convent.

The signalled conversation with Fabrice, therefore, could not last long. And yet she had beyond doubt fallen deeply in love with Fabrice. She knew he was her father's prisoner, and belonged to the party hostile to her father; she was ashamed, as a daughter, of her love for him. But she admired him, and pitied him; she was well aware that he was a victim of political intrigue, for why should a nobleman of Fabrice's standing be thus punished for killing a mere actor? The stolen interviews with the captive were as dear to her as to him; and so dear were they to him that, after months of imprisonment he declared that he had never been so happy in his life.

IV.—The Escape

One night, as Fabrice looked through his peep-hole, he became aware of a light flashing from the town. Obviously some attempt was being made at signalling. He observed the flashes, counting them in relation to the order of the letters in the alphabet—one for A, two for B, and so on. He discovered that the message was from the Duchess, and was directed to himself. He replied, on the same system, by passing his lantern in front of the peep-hole. The answer from the distance was important; arrangements were being made for his escape. But he did not want to escape.

Next day he told Clelia of his message, and of his unwillingness to leave the prison. She gave no answer, but burst into tears. How could she tell him that she herself must presently leave—for marriage or a convent?

Next day, Fabrice, by his goaler's connivance, received a long letter from Clelia. She urged him to escape, declaring that at any time the Prince might order his execution, and in addition that he was in danger of death by poison. Straightway he sought an interview with Clelia, with whom he had not hitherto conversed save by signals from their windows. The goaler arranged that they should meet when Fabrice was being conducted from his cell to the roof of the Farnese tower, where he was occasionally allowed to take exercise.

"I can speak but few words to you," she said trembling, with tears in her eyes. "Swear that you will obey the Duchess, and escape when she wishes and as she wishes."

"And condemn myself to live far away from her whom I love?"

"Swear it! for my sake, swear it!" she implored him.

"Well then, I swear it!"

The preparations were quickly advanced. Three knotted ropes were smuggled with Clelia's aid into Fabrice's cell—one for descending the 35 feet between his window and the roof of the citadel; another for descending the tremendous wall of 180 feet between the roof and the ramparts; a third for the 30 feet between the top of the ramparts and the ground.

A feast-day, when the garrison of the citadel would presumably be drunk, was chosen for the attempt. Fabrice spent the time of waiting in cutting a hole in his shutter large enough to enable him to get through. Fortunately, on the night of the feast-day a thick fog arose and enveloped the citadel. The Duchess had seen to it that the garrison was plentifully supplied with wine.

Fabrice attached one of the shorter ropes to his bed, and struggled through the shutter—an ungainly figure, for round his body were wound the immense ropes necessary for the long descent. Once on the roof-platform he made his way along the parapet until he came to a new stove which he had been told marked the best spot for lowering the rope. He could hear the soldiers talking near at hand, but the fog made him invisible. Unrolling his rope, and fastening his rope to the parapet by threading it through a water-duct, he flung it over; then, with a prayer and a thought of Clelia, he began to descend.

At first he went down mechanically, as if doing the feat for a wager. About half-way down his arms seemed to lose their strength; he nearly let go—he might have fallen had he not supported himself by clinging to the vegetation on the wall. From time to time he felt horrible pain between the shoulders. Birds hustled against him now and then; he feared at the first contact with them that pursuers were coming down the rope after him. But he reached the rampart undamaged save for bleeding hands.

He was quite exhausted; for a few minutes he slept. On waking and realising the situation, he attached his third rope to a cannon, and hurried down to the ground. Two men seized him just as he fainted at the foot.

A few hours afterwards a carriage crossed the frontier with Ludovico on the box, and within it the Duchess watching over the sleeping Fabrice. The journey did not end until they had reached Locarno on Lake Maggiore.

V.—Clelia's Vow

To Locarno soon afterwards came the news that Ranuce Ernest IV. was dead. Fabrice could now safely return, for the young Ranuce Ernest V. was believed to be entirely under the influence of Count Mosca, and was an honest youth without the tyrannical instincts of his father. Nevertheless the Duchess returned first, to make certain of Fabrice's security. She employed her whole influence to hasten forward the wedding of Clelia with the Marquis Crescenzi; she was jealous of the ascendancy the girl had gained over her beloved nephew.

Fabrice, on reaching Parma, was well received by the young Prince. Witnesses, he was told, had been found who could prove that he had killed Giletti in self defence. He would spend a few days in a purely nominal confinement in the city goal, and then would be tried by impartial judges and released.

Imagine the consternation of the Duchess when she learnt that Fabrice, having to go to prison, had deliberately given himself up at the citadel!

She saw the danger clearly. Fabrice was in the hands of Count Mosca's political opponents, among whom General Conti was still a leading spirit. They would not suffer him to escape this time. Fabrice would be poisoned.

1219

Clelia, too, knew that this would be his fate. When she saw him once again at the old window, happily signalling to her, she was smitten with panic terror. Her alarm was realised when she learnt of a plot between Rassi and her father to poison the prisoner.

On the second day of his confinement Fabrice was about to eat his dinner when Clelia, in desperate agitation, forced her way into his cell.

"Have you tasted it?" she cried, grasping his arm.

Fabrice guessed the state of affairs with delight. He seized her in his arms and kissed her.

"Help me to die," he said.

"Oh, my beloved," she answered, "let me die with you."

"Let me not spoil our happiness with a lie," said he as he embraced her. "I have not yet tasted."

For an instant Clelia looked at him in anger; then she fell into his arms.

At that instant there came a sound of men hurrying. There entered the Prince's aide-de-camp, with order to remove Fabrice from the citadel and to seize the poisoned food. The Duchess had heard of the plot, and had persuaded the Prince to take instant action.

Clelia, when her father was in danger of death on account of the plot, vowed before the Virgin Mary never again to look upon the face of Fabrice. Her father escaped with a sentence of banishment; and Clelia, to the profound satisfaction of the Duchess, was wedded to the Marquis Crescenzi. The Duchess was now a widow, Count Mosca a widower. Their long friendship, after Fabrice's acquittal, was cemented by marriage.

The loss of Clelia left Fabrice inconsolable. He shunned society; he lived a life of religious retirement, and gained a reputation for piety that even inspired the jealousy of his good friend the Archbishop.

At length Fabrice emerged from his solitude; he came forth as a preacher, and his success was unequalled. All Parma, gentle and simple, flocked to hear the famous devotee—slender, ill-clad, so handsome and yet so profoundly melancholy. And ere he began each sermon, Fabrice looked earnestly round his congregation to see if Clelia was there.

But Clelia, adhering to her vow, stayed away. It was not until she was told that a certain Anetta Marini was in love with the preacher, and that gossip asserted that the preacher was smitten with Anetta Marini, that she changed her mind.

One evening, as Fabrice stood in the pulpit, he saw Clelia before him. Her eyes were filled with tears; he looked so pale, so thin, so worn. But never had he preached as he preached that night.

After the sermon he received a note asking him to be at a small garden door of the Crescenzi Palace at midnight on the next night. Eagerly he obeyed; when he reached the door, a voice called him to enter. The darkness was intense; he could see nothing.

"I have asked you to come here," said the voice, "to say that I still love you. But I have vowed to the Virgin never to see your face; that is why I receive you in this darkness. And let me beg you—never preach before Anetta Marini."

"My angel," replied the enraptured Fabrice, "I shall never preach again before anyone; it was only in the hope of seeing you that I preached at all."

During the following three years the two often met in darkness. But twice, by accident, Clelia broke her vow by looking on Fabrice's face. Her conscience preyed upon her; she wore away and died.

A few days afterwards Fabrice resigned his reversion to the Archbishopric, and retired to the Chartreuse of Parma. He ended his days in the monastery only a year afterwards.

WALLACE STEVENS

WALLACE STEVENS (American, 1879-1955). Poet of enchanting imagery. Educated for the law, spent most of life with an insurance company. Was slow winning recognition—first from other poets, finally from reading public. Now acknowledged one of important American poets. Books of verse: *Harmonium, Ideas of Order, Parts of a World.*

DOMINATION OF BLACK

At night, by the fire,
The colors of the bushes
And of the fallen leaves,
Repeating themselves,
Turned in the room,

Like the leaves themselves
Turning in the wind.
Yes: but the color of the heavy hemlocks
Came striding.
And I remembered the cry of the peacocks.

The colors of their tails
Were like the leaves themselves
Turning in the wind.
In the twilight wind.
They swept over the room,
Just as they flew from the boughs of the hemlocks
Down to the ground.
I heard them cry—the peacocks.
Was it a cry against the twilight
Or against the leaves themselves
Turning in the wind.
Turning as the flames
Turned in the fire,
Turning as the tails of the peacocks
Turned in the loud fire,
Loud as the hemlocks
Full of the cry of the peacocks,
Or was it a cry against the hemlocks.

Out of the window,
I saw how the planets gathered
Like the leaves themselves
Turning in the wind.
I saw how the night came,
Came striding like the color of the heavy hemlocks.
I felt afraid.
And I remembered the cry of the peacocks.

AN EXTRACT

from Addresses to the Academy of Fine Ideas

On an early Sunday in April, a feeble day,
He felt curious about the winter hills
And wondered about the water in the lake.

It had been cold since December. Snow fell first,
At New Year and, from then until April, lay
On everything. Now it had melted, leaving
The gray grass like a pallet, closely pressed;
And dirt. The wind blew in the empty place.
The winter wind blew in an empty place—
There was that difference between the and an,
The difference between himself and no man,
No man that heard a wind in an empty place.
It was time to be himself again, to see
If the place, in spite of its witheredness, was still
Within the difference. He felt curious
Whether the water was black and lashed about
Or whether the ice still covered the lake. There was still
Snow under the trees and on the northern rocks,
The dead rocks, not the green rocks, the live rocks. If,
When he looked, the water ran up the air or grew white
Against the edge of the ice, the abstraction would
Be broken and winter would be broken and done,
And being would be being himself again,
Being, becoming seeing and feeling and self,
Black water breaking into reality.

ANECDOTE OF THE JAR

I placed a jar in Tennessee,
And round it was, upon a hill.
It made the slovenly wilderness
Surround that hill.

The wilderness rose up to it,
And sprawled around, no longer wild.
The jar was round upon the ground
And tall and of a port in air.

It took dominion everywhere.
The jar was gray and bare.
It did not give of bird or bush,
Like nothing else in Tennessee.

ROBERT LOUIS STEVENSON

ROBERT LOUIS STEVENSON (Scottish, 1850-1894). Writer of essays and novels in the Scott-Dumas manner. A sickly traveler, who died in the South Seas. Affectionately venerated by his generation. Most popular work: adventure novel, *Treasure Island*. First-rate tales of supernatural: *Dr. Jekyll and Mr. Hyde* and *Thrawn Janet*.

THRAWN JANET

THE Reverend Murdoch Soulis was long minister of the moorland parish of Balweary, in the vale of Dule. A severe, bleak-faced old man, dreadful to his hearers, he dwelt in the last years of his life without relative or servant or any human company, in the small and lonely manse under the Hanging Shaw. In spite of the iron composure of his features, his eye was wild, seared, and uncertain; and when he dwelt, in private admonitions, on the future of the impenitent, it seemed as if his eye pierced through the storms of time to the terrors of eternity. Many young persons, coming to prepare themselves against the season of the Holy Communion, were dreadfully affected by his talk. He had a sermon on 1st Peter, v and 8th, "The devil as a roaring lion," on the Sunday after every seventeenth of August, and he was accustomed to surpass himself upon that text both by the appalling nature of the matter and the terror of his bearing in the pulpit. The children were frightened into fits, and the old looked more than usually oracular, and were, all that day, full of those hints that Hamlet deprecated. The manse itself, where it stood by the water of Dule among some thick trees, with the Shaw overhanging it on the one side, and on the other many cold, moorish hilltops rising toward the sky, had begun, at a very early period of Mr. Soulis's ministry, to be avoided in the dusk hours by all who valued themselves upon their prudence; and guidmen sitting at the clachan alehouse shook their heads together at the thought of passing late by that uncanny neighborhood. There was one spot, to be more particular, which was regarded with special awe. The manse stood between the high road and the water of Dule, with a gable to each; its back was toward the kirktown of Balweary, nearly half a mile away; in front of it, a bare garden, hedged with thorn, occupied the land between the river and the road. The house was two stories high, with two large rooms on each. It opened not directly on the garden, but on a causewayed path, or passage, giving on the road on the one hand, and closed on the other by the tall willows and elders that bordered on the stream. And it was this strip of causeway that enjoyed among the young parishioners of Balweary so infamous a reputation. The minister walked there often after dark, sometimes groaning aloud in the instancy of his unspoken prayers; and when he was from home, and the manse door was locked, the more daring schoolboys ventured, with beating hearts, to "follow my leader" across that legendary spot.

This atmosphere of terror, surrounding, as it did, a man of God of spotless character and orthodoxy, was a common cause of wonder and subject of inquiry among the few strangers who were led by chance or business into that unknown, outlying country. But many even of the people of the parish were ignorant of the strange events which had marked the first year of Mr. Soulis's ministrations; and among those who were better informed, some were naturally reticent, and others shy of that particular topic. Now and again, only, one of the older folk would warm into courage over his third tumbler, and recount the cause of the minister's strange looks and solitary life.

Fifty years syne, when Mr. Soulis cam' first into Ba'weary, he was still a young man—a callant, the folk said—fu' o' book learnin' and grand at the exposition, but, as was natural in sae young man, wi' nae leevin' experience in religion. The younger sort were greatly taken wi' his gifts and his gab; but auld, concerned, serious men and women were moved even to prayer for the young man, whom they took to be a self-deceiver, and the parish that was like to be sae ill-supplied. It was before the days o' the moderates—weary fa' them; but ill things are like guid—they baith come bit by bit, a pickle at a time; and there were folk even then that said the Lord had left the college professors to their ain devices, an' the lads that went to study wi' them wad hae done mair and better sittin' in a peat-bog, like their forebears of the persecution, wi' a Bible under their oxter and a speerit o' prayer in their heart. There was nae doubt, onyway, but that Mr. Soulis had been ower lang at the college. He was careful and troubled for mony things besides the ae thing needful. He had a feck o' books wi' him—mair than had ever been seen before in a' that presbytery; and a sair wark the carrier had wi' them, for they were a' like to have smoored in the Deil's Hag between this and Kilmackerlie. They were books o' divinity, to be sure, or so they ca'd them; but the serious were o' opinion there was little service for sae mony, when the hail o' God's Word would gang in the neuk of a plaid. Then he wad sit half the day and half the nicht forbye, which was scant decent—writin', nae less; and first, they were feared he wad read his sermons; and syne it proved he was writin' a book himsel', which was surely no fittin' for ane of his years an' sma' experience.

Onyway it behooved him to get an auld, decent wife to keep the manse for him an' see to his bit denners; and he was recommended to an auld limmer—Janet M'Clour, they ca'd her—and sae far left to himsel' as to be ower persuaded. There was mony advised him to the contrar, for Janet was mair than suspeckit by the best folk in Ba'weary. Lang or that, she had had a wean to a dragoon; she hadnae come forrit for maybe thretty year; and bairns had seen her mumblin' to hersel' up on Key's Loan in the gloamin', whilk was an unco time an' place for a God-fearin' woman. Howsoever, it was the laird himsel' that had first tauld the minister o' Janet; and in thae days he wad have gane a far gate to pleesure the laird. When folk tauld him that Janet was sib to the deil, it was a' superstition by his way of it; an' when they cast up the Bible to him an' the witch of Endor, he wad threep it doun their thrapples that thir days were a' gane by, and the deil was mercifully restrained.

Weel, when it got about the clachan that Janet M'Clour was to be servant at the manse, the folk were fair mad wi' her an' him thegether; and some o' the guidwives had nae better to dae than get round her door cheeks and chairge her wi' a' that was ken'd again her, frae the sodger's bairn to John Tamson's twa kye. She was nae great speaker; folk usually let her gang her ain gate, an' she let them gang theirs, wi' neither Fair-guid-een nor Fair-guid-day; but when she buckled to she had a tongue to deave the miller. Up she got, an' there wasnae an auld story in Ba'weary but she gart somebody lowp for it that day; they couldnae say ae thing but she could say twa to it; till, at the hinder end, the guidwives up and claught haud of her, and clawed the coats aff her back, and pu'd her doun the clachan to the water o' Dule, to see if she were a witch or no, soum or droun. The carline skirled till ye could hear her at the Hangin' Shaw, and she focht like ten; there was mony a guidwife bure the mark of her neist day, an' mony a lang day after; and just in the hettest o' the collieshangie, wha suld come up (for his sins) but the new minister.

"Women," said he (and he had a grand voice), "I charge you in the Lord's name to let her go."

1226

Janet ran to him—she was fair wud wi' terror—an' clang to him an' prayed him, for Christ's sake, save her frae the cummers; an' they, for their pairt, tauld him a' that was ken't, and maybe mair.

"Woman," says he to Janet, "is this true?"

"As the Lord sees me," says she, "as the Lord made me, no a word o't. Forbye the bairn," says she, 'I've been a decent woman a' my days."

"Will you,' says Mr. Soulis, "in the name of God, and before me, His unworthy minister, renounce the devil and his works?"

Well, it wad appear that when he askit that, she gave a girn that fairly frichtit them that saw her, an' they could hear her teeth play dirl thegether in her chafts; but there was naething for it but the ae way or the ither; an' Janet lifted up her hand and renounced the deil before them a'.

"And now," said Mr. Soulis to the guidwives, "home with ye, one and all, and pray to God for His forgiveness."

And he gied Janet his arm, though she had little on her but a sark, and took her up the clachan to her ain door like a leddy of the land; an' her skreighin' and laughin' as was a scandal to be heard.

There were mony grave folk lang ower their prayers that nicht; but when the morn cam' there was sic a fear fell upon a' Ba'weary that the bairns hid theirsels, and even the men-folk stood and keekit frae their doors. For there was Janet comin' doun the clachan—her or her likeness, nane could tell—wi' her neck thrawn, and her heid on ae side, like a body that has been hangit, and a girn on her face like an unstreakit corp. By an' by they got used wi' it, and even speered at her to ken what was wrang; but frae that day forth she couldnae speak like a Christian woman, but slavered and played click wi' her teeth like a pair o' shears; and frae that day forth the name o' God cam' never on her lips. Whiles she wad try to say it, but it michtnae be. Them that kenned best said least; but they never gied that Thing the name o' Janet M'Clour; for the auld Janet, by their way o't, was in muckle hell that day. But the minister was neither to haud nor to bind; he preached about naething but the folks' cruelty that had gi'en her a stroke of the palsy; he skelpt the bairns that meddled her; and he had her up to the manse that same nicht and dwalled there a' his lane wi' her under the Hangin' Shaw.

Weel, time gaed by: and the idler sort commenced to think mair lichtly o' that black business. The minister was weel thocht o'; he was aye late at the writing, folk wad see his can'le doun by the Dule water after twal' at e'en; and he seemed pleased wi' himsel' and upsitten as at first though a' body could see that he was dwining. As for Janet she cam' an' she gaed; if she didnae speak muckle afore, it was reason she should speak less then; she meddled naebody; but she was an eldritch thing to see, an' nane wad hae mistrysted wi' her for Ba'weary glebe. About the end o' July there cam' a spell o' weather, the like o't never was in that countryside; it was lown an' het an' heartless; the herds couldnae win up the Black Hill, the bairns were ower weariet to play; an' yet it was gousty too, wi' claps o' het wund that rumm'led in the glens, and bits o' shouers that slockened naething. We aye thocht it but to thun'er on the morn; but the morn cam', and the morn's morning, and it was aye the same uncanny weather, sair on folks and bestial. Of a' that were the waur, nane suffered like Mr. Soulis; he could neither sleep nor eat, he tauld his elders; an' when he wasnae writin' at his weary book, he wad be stravaguin' ower a' the countryside like a man possessed, when a' body else was blythe to keep caller ben the house.

Abune Hangin' Shaw, in the bield o' the Black Hill, there's a bit inclosed grund wi' an iron yett; and it seems in the auld days, that was the kirkyaird o' Ba'weary, and consecrated by the Papists before the blessed licht shone upon the kingdom. It was a great howff o' Mr. Soulis's, onyway; there he would sit an' consider his sermons; and indeed it's a bieldy bit. Weel, as he cam' ower the wast end o' the Black Hill, ae day, he saw first twa, an' syne fower, an' syne seeven corbie craws fleein' round an' round abune the auld kirkyard. They flew laigh and heavy, an' squawked to ither as they gaed; and it was clear to Mr. Soulis that something had put them frae ordinar. He wasnae easy fleyed, an' gaed straucht up to the wa's; an' what suld he find there but a man, or the appearance of a man, sittin' in the inside upon a grave. He was of a great stature, an' black as hell, and his een were singular to see. Mr. Soulis had heard tell o' black men, mony's the time; but there was something unco about this black man that daunted him. Het as he was, he took a kind o' cauld grue in the marrow o' his banes; but up he spak for a' that; an' says he: "My friend, are you a stranger in this place?" The black man answered never a word; he got upon his feet, an' begude to hirstle to the wa' on the far side; but he aye lookit at the minister; an' the minister stood an' lookit back, till a' in a meenute the black man was over the wa' an' rinnin' for

1228

he bield o' the trees. Mr. Soulis, he hardly kenned why, ran after
him; but he was sair forjaskit wi' his walk an' the het, unhalesome
weather; and rin as he likit, he got nae mair than a glisk o' the
black man amang the birks, till he won doun to the foot o' the
hillside, an' there he saw him ance mair, gaun, hap, step, an' lowp,
ower Dule water to the manse.

Mr. Soulis wasnae weel pleased that this fearsome gangrel suld
mak' sae free wi' Ba'weary manse; an' he ran the harder, an', wet
shoon, ower the burn, an' up the walk; but the deil a black man
was there to see. He stepped out upon the road, but there was
naebody there; he gaed a' ower the gairden, but na, nae black man.
At the hinder end, and a bit feared as was but natural, he lifted
the hasp and into the manse; and there was Janet M'Clour before
his een, wi' her thrawn craig, and nane sae pleased to see him. And
he aye minded sinsyne, when first he set his een upon her, he had
the same cauld and deidly grue.

"Janet," says he, "have you seen a black man?"

"A black man?" quo' she. "Save us a'! Ye're no wise, minister.
There's nae black man in a' Ba'weary."

But she didnae speak plain, ye maun understand; but yam-
yammered, like a powney wi' the bit in its moo.

"Weel," says he, "Janet, if there was nae black man, I have
spoken with the Accuser of the Brethren."

And he sat down like ane wi' a fever, an' his teeth chittered in
his heid.

"Hoots," says she, "think shame to yoursel', minister"; an' gied
him a drap brandy that she keept aye by her.

Syne Mr. Soulis gaed into his study amang a' his books. It's a
lang, laigh, mirk chalmer, perishin' cauld in winter, an' no very
dry even in the tap o' the simmer, for the manse stands near the
burn. Sae doun he sat, and thocht of a' that had come an' gane
since he was in Ba'weary, an' his hame, an' the days when he was
a bairn an' ran daffin' on the braes; and that black man aye ran
in his heid like the owercome of a sang. Aye the mair he thocht,
the mair he thocht o' the black man. He tried the prayer, an' the
words wouldnae come to him; an' he tried, they say, to write at
his book, but he couldnae mak' nae mair o' that. There was whiles
he thocht the black man was at his oxter, an' the swat stood upon
him cauld as well-water; and there was other whiles, when he cam'
to himsel' like a christened bairn and minded naething.

The upshot was that he gaed to the window an' stood glowrin' at

1229

Dule water. The trees are unco thick, an' the water lies deep an' black under the manse; an' there was Janet washin' the cla'es wi' her coats kilted. She had her back to the minister, an' he, for his pairt, hardly kenned what he was lookin' at. Syne she turned round an' shawed her face; Mr. Soulis had the same cauld grue as twice that day afore, an' it was borne in upon him what folk said, that Janet was deid lang syne, an' this was a bogle in her clay cauld flesh. He drew back a pickle and he scanned her narrowly. She was tramp-trampin' in the cla'es, croonin' to hersel'; and eh! Gude guide us, but it was a fearsome face. Whiles she sang louder, but there was nae man born o' woman that could tell the words o' her sang; an' whiles she lookit side-lang doun, but there was naething there for her to look at. There gaed a scunner through the flesh upon his banes; and that was Heeven's advertisement. But Mr. Soulis just blamed himsel', he said, to think sae ill of a puir, auld afflicted wife that hadnae a freend forby himsel'; and he put up a bit prayer for him and her, an' drank a little caller water—for his heart rose again the meat—an' gaed up to his naked bed in the gloaming.

That was a nicht that has never been forgotten in Ba'weary, the nicht o' the seeventeenth of August, seeventeen hun'er and twal'. It had been het afore, as I hae said, but that nicht it was hetter than ever. The sun gaed doun amang unco-lookin' clouds; it fell as mirk as the pit; no a star, no a breath o' wund; ye couldnae see your han' before your face, and even the auld folk cuist the covers frae their beds and lay pechin' for their breath. Wi' a' that he had upon his mind, it was gey and unlikely Mr. Soulis wad get muckle sleep. He lay an' he tummled; the gude, caller bed that he got into brunt his very banes; whiles he slept, and whiles he waukened; whiles he heard the time o' nicht, and whiles a tyke yowlin' up the muir, as if somebody was deid; whiles he thocht he heard bogles claverin' in his lug, an' whiles he saw spunkies in the room. He behooved, he judged, to be sick; an' sick he was—little he jaloosed the sickness.

At the hinder end, he got a clearness in his mind, sat up in his sark on the bedside, and fell thinkin' ance mair o' the black man an' Janet. He couldnae well tell how—maybe it was the cauld to his feet—but it cam' in upon him wi' a spat that there was some connection between their twa, an' that either or baith o' them were bogles. And just at that moment, in Janet's room which was neist to his, there cam' a stramp o' feet as if men were wars'lin', an' then a loud bang; an' then a wund gaed reishling round the fower quarters of the house; an' then a' was aince mair as seelent as the grave.

Mr. Soulis was feared for neither man nor deevil. He got his tinder box, an' lighted a can'le, an' made three steps o't ower to Janet's door. It was on the hasp, an' he pushed it open, an' keeked bauldly in. It was a big room, as big as the minister's ain, an' plenished wi' grand, auld, solid gear, for he had naething else. There was a fower-posted bed wi' auld tapestry; and a braw cabinet of aik, that was fu' o' the minister's divinity books, an' put there to be out o' the gate; an' a wheen duds o' Janet's lying here and there about the floor. But nae Janet could Mr. Soulis see; nor ony sign of a contention. In he gaed (an' there's few that wad ha'e followed him) an' lookit a' round, an' listened. But there was naethin' to be heard, neither inside the manse nor in a' Ba'weary parish, an' naethin' to be seen but the muckle shadows turnin' round the can'le. An' then a' at aince, the minister's heart played dunt an' stood stock-still; an' a cauld wund blew amang the hairs o' his heid. Whaten a weary sicht was that for the puir man's een! For there was Janet hangin' frae a nail beside the auld aik cabinet: her heid aye lay on her shouther, her een were steeked, the tongue projekit frae her mouth, and her heels were twa feet clar abune the floor.

"God forgive us all!" thocht Mr. Soulis; "poor Janet's dead."

He cam' a step nearer to the corp; an' then his heart fair whammled in his inside. For by what cantrip it wad ill-beseem a man to judge, she was hingin' fae a single nail an' by a single wursted thread for darnin' hose.

It's an awfu' thing to be your lane at nicht wi' siccan prodigies o' darkness; but Mr. Soulis was strong in the Lord. He turned an' gaed his ways oot o' that room, and lockit the door ahint him; and step by step, doon the stairs, as heavy as leed; and set doon the can'le on the table at the stairfoot. He couldnae pray, he couldnae think, he was dreepin' wi' caul' swat, an' naething could he hear but the dunt-dunt-duntin' o' his ain heart. He micht maybe have stood there an hour, or maybe twa, he minded sae little; when a' o' a sudden he heard a laigh, uncanny steer upstairs; a foot gaed to an' fro in the cha'mer whaur the corp was hingin'; syne the door was opened, though he minded weel that he had lockit it; an' syne there was a step upon th landin', an' it seemed to him as if the corp was lookin' ower the rail and doun upon him whaur he stood.

He took up the can'le again (for he couldnae want the licht) and,

as saftly as ever he could, gaed straucht out o' the manse an' to the
far end o' the causeway. It was aye pitmirk; the flame o' the can'le,
when he set it on the grund, brunt steedy and clear as in a room;
naething moved, but the Dule water seepin' and sabbin' doon the
glen, an' yon unhaly footstep that cam' ploddin' doun the stairs
inside the manse. He kenned the foot ower weel, for it was Janet's;
and at ilka step that cam' a wee thing nearer, the cauld got deeper
in his vitals. He commended his soul to Him that made an' keepit
him; "and O Lord," said he, "give me strength this night to war
against the powers of evil."

By this time the foot was comin' through the passage for the
door; he could hear a hand skirt alang the wa', as if the fearsome
thing was feelin' for its way. The saughs tossed an' maned thegether,
a lang sigh cam' ower the hills, the flame o' the can'le was blawn
aboot; an' there stood the corp of Thrawn Janet, wi' her grogram
goun an' her black mutch, wi' the heid aye upon the shouther, an'
the girn still upon the face o't—leevin', ye wad hae said—deid, as
Mr. Soulis weel kenned—upon the threshold o' the manse.

It's a strange thing that the saul of man should be that thirled
into his perishable body; but the minister saw, an' his heart didnae
break.

She didnae stand there lang; she began to move again an' cam'
slowly toward Mr. Soulis whaur he stood under the saughs. A' the
life o' his body, a' the strength o' his speerit, were glowerin' frae
his een. It seemed she was gaun to speak, but wanted words, an'
made a sign wi' the left hand. There cam' a clap o' wund, like a
cat's fuff; oot gaed the can'le, the saughs skrieghed like folk; an'
Mr. Soulis kenned that, live or die, this was the end o't.

"Witch, beldam, devil!" he cried, "I charge you, by the power of
God, begone—if you be dead, to the grave—if you be damned, to
hell."

An' at that moment the Lord's ain hand out o' the Heevens struck
the Horror whaur it stood; the auld, deid, desecrated corp o' the
witchwife, sae lang keepit frae the grave and hirsled round by deils,
lowed up like a brunstane spunk and fell in ashes to the grund; the
thunder followed, peal on dirling peal, the rairing rain upon the
back o' that; and Mr. Soulis lowped through the garden hedge, and
ran, wi' skelloch upon skellock, for the clachan.

That same mornin', John Christie saw the Black Man pass the
Muckle Cairn as it was chappin' six; before eicht, he gaed by the
change-house at Knockdow; an' no lang after, Sandy M'Lellan saw

him gaun linkin' doun the braes frae Kilmackerlie. There's little
doubt it was him that dwalled sae lang in Janet's body; but he
was awa' at last; and sinsyne the deil has never fashed us in
Ba'weary.

But it was a sair dispensation for the minister; lang, lang he
lay ravin' in his bed; and frae that hour to this, he was the man
ye ken the day.

THEODOR STORM

THEODOR STORM (German, 1817-1888). Lawyer and judge, who was exiled
to Prussia for 10 years for his sympathies in the Schleswig-Holstein dispute
with Denmark. Devoted his evenings to creating a literature of romantic mood-
pictures. Of his stories, "Immensee" is a universal favorite.

VERONIKA

I. At the Mill

IT WAS at the beginning of April on the day before Palm Sunday.
The mild rays of the late afternoon sun shone on the young grass at
the side of the path which led down gradually along a mountain
slope. At this moment one of the most respected jurists of the city,
a man of middle age, with calm but distinctive features, was walking
leisurely, exchanging only an occasional word with the clerk at his
side. Their destination was a water-mill not far off whose owner,
troubled by age and illness, wished to make over his property to
his son.

A few paces behind followed another couple; beside a young man
with fresh, intelligent features walked a beautiful, still very youthful
woman. He spoke to her, but she did not seem to hear. Her dark eyes
gazing straight ahead, she walked silently, as though unaware of anyone at her side.

As the mill became visible in the valley below, the counsellor
turned his head. "Well cousin," he called, "you write a passable
hand; how would you like to learn a little about making contracts?"

But the cousin waved his hand in protest. "Go on!" he said and
looked questioningly at his companion. "Meanwhile I'll have a con-
versation-lesson with your wife!"

"Well, at least don't teach him too much, Veronika!"

The young woman only inclined her head as in assent. Behind them, from the towers of the city, the sound of the evening chime came spreading over the country-side. Her hand, which had just stroked back the black hair beneath her white satin hat, glided down over her breast and, making the sign of the cross, she began softly to recite the Angelus. The glance of the young man who, like his relative, belonged to a protestant family, followed the uniform movement of her lips with an expression of impatience.

Several months ago he had come to the city as an architect to work on the addition to a church and since then had been an almost daily guest in the house of the counsellor. He had entered immediately into a lively and friendly association with the wife of his cousin. The two were drawn together through the youth which they had in common as well as through his accomplishment in drawing, which she also practiced with enthusiasm and skill. Now she had found him a friend and teacher at the same time. Soon, however, as he sat beside her evenings, it was not so much the drawing lying before her upon which his eyes rested, as it was her small, busy hand; and she who had been wont to cast aside her pencil at any given moment, now drew silently and obediently without looking up, as though caught in his gaze. It may be that they hardly realized themselves, that, every evening when saying "Good night," their hands remained together a little longer and their fingers were clasped a little tighter. The counsellor, whose thoughts were usually with his business, thought still less about it; he was glad that his wife had found stimulation and understanding for her favorite occupation, which he himself was unable to give her. Only once, just after the young architect had left their house, the dreamy expression in her eyes had surprised him. "Vroni," he said, holding her back by the hand as she tried to pass. "It's true then, isn't it, what your sisters say." "What is, Franz?" "Of course," he said, "now I see it myself, you have spiritual eyes." She blushed and submitted without speaking as he drew her closer and kissed her.

Today, in the fine weather, she and Rudolf had been invited by the counsellor to accompany him on his official errand to the near-by mill.

Since yesterday's social gathering, when she had displayed, at the request of her husband, a drawing which had been completed under his eyes, everything had become different between them. Rudolf felt it only too well; he recalled how it had come about that he had

1234

opposed the excessive praise of the others with such sharp and passionate criticism.

Veronika had long ended her prayer, but he waited in vain for her to turn her eyes toward him.

"You are angry with me, Veronika," he said at last. The young woman nodded slightly, but her lips remained firmly closed.

He looked at her. Obstinacy still lay upon her brow.

"I should think," he said, "you might know how it could happen! Or don't you know, Veronika?"

"I know only," she said, "that you have hurt me. And," she added, "that you wanted to hurt me."

He remained silent for a while. "Did you not notice," he asked hesitantly, "the knowing eye of the old man who stood opposite you?"

She turned her head and glanced up at him fleetingly.

"I had to do it myself, Veronika. Forgive me! I can't bear to have you criticized by others."

It seemed as though a veil drew over her eyes, and long black lashes sank upon her cheeks; but she did not answer.

A short time later they had reached the mill. The counsellor was led into the house by the miller's son; Rudolf and Veronika entered the garden lying at the side, and continued to walk silently up the long incline; it was almost as though they were angry with each other, as though they had to stop for want of breath when they tried to speak an occasional word.

When they had wandered through the garden, they passed over a narrow foot-bridge into the lower door of the mill-building, which stood by a swift stream at the edge of the garden. Through the clattering of the works and the roar of the falling water which drowned every sound coming from outside, a strange sense of separation reigned in the almost dusky room. Veronika had walked over to the door which led to the mill-race and gazed down into the thrashing wheels upon which the water glistened in the evening sun. Rudolf did not follow; he stood within, beside the big cogwheel, his gloomy eyes unswervingly upon her. Finally she turned her head. She spoke, he saw how her lips moved, but he did not understand her words.

"I don't understand!" he said and shook his head.

As he was about to go to her, she had already stepped back into the inner room. In passing she came so close to the wheel beside which he stood, that the teeth almost touched her hair. She did not see it, since she was still blinded by the evening sun; but she felt her hands seized and herself drawn quickly to the side. As she looked up, her eyes met his. They remained silent; a sudden unmindfulness dropped like a shadow over them. At their heads thundered the mill works; from outside came the monotonous rushing of the water, plunging over the wheels into the depths. Gradually, however, the young man's lips began to move, and, protected by the deafening noise, in which his voice was lost, he whispered intoxicated, maddening words. Her ears could not discern them, but she read their meaning from his lips, from the impassioned pallor of his face. She threw her head back and closed her eyes; only her mouth smiled and betrayed life. Thus she stood holding her face toward him helplessly, her hands obliviously in his.

Then suddenly the roaring ceased; the mill stood still. They heard the mill-hands walking above, and outside, the dripping water fell from the wheels, tinkling into the pond. The lips of the young man became dumb, and when Veronika withdrew from him, he did not try to hold her back. Not until she had gone out through the door into the open, did he seem to regain his speech. He called her name and extended his arms to her, pleadingly. But she shook her head, without turning to look at him, and walked slowly through the garden to the dwelling.

As she went in through the door which had been left partly open, she saw opposite her the old miller, with folded hands lying in his bed. Over it a wooden crucifix was attached, from which hung a rosary. A young woman with a child in her arm had just come over to the bedside and was bending over the covers. "He only needs air," she said. "He enjoys his food well enough."

"Who is your doctor?" asked the counsellor, who was standing close by, holding a document in his hand.

"Doctor?" she repeated, " We have no doctor."

"You're doing wrong there!"

The young woman let out an embarrassed laugh. "It's old age," she said, as she wiped her chubby boy's little nose with her apron, "The doctor couldn't help that."

Veronika listened breathlessly to this conversation. The old man began to cough and put his hand to his eyes.

"Is this your will, Martin, as it is written here?" the counsellor now asked. But the sick man seemed not to hear him.

"Father." said the young woman, "Is that right as the counsellor has just read it?"

"Of course," said the sick man, "Everything is all right."

"And you have considered everything well?" asked the counsellor.

The old man nodded. "Yes, yes," he said, "I have worked hard; but the boy shouldn't have it too bad. . . ."

The son, who until now had been sitting in the corner smoking, entered into the conversation. "Of course, the old man's part has to be considered too," he said, and cleared his throat several times, "The old man will live away a neat sum yet."

The counsellor cast his gray eyes down upon the coarse peasant. "Is that your son, Weismann?" he asked, pointing at the child playing at the bed side. "Send him out, if you expect to do any more talking!"

The man was silent; but his eyes met those of the counsellor with an almost threatening expression.

The old man stroked his hard hand over the cover. And said quietly, "It won't be so very long, Jakob!—But," he added, turning to the counsellor, "in keeping with the village customs, he will have to bury me; that will cost something, too."

The young lady disappeared without a sound, just as she had come, from the open door in which she had been standing during these proceedings.

Outside she saw Rudolf on the other side of the garden in conversation with the mill-hand, but she turned away and followed a footpath, which led below the mill down to the stream. Her eyes strayed unconsciously into the distance; she did not notice how dusk was sinking upon the mountains ahead of her, nor how, gradually, even while she was strolling up and down, the moon was rising behind them and pouring its light over the silent valley. Life in its naked poverty confronted her as she had never before seen it; an endless, arid way,—at the end, death. She felt as though she had been living in a dream until now, and as if she were now wandering in a reality without solace, in which she did not know how to find her way.

It was late when the voice of her husband called her back to the mill where he awaited her at the door. On the way home she walked silently at his side, without feeling his understanding eyes upon her. "You have been frightened, Veronika!" he said and laid his hand upon her cheek. "But," he added, "these people live according to different standards; they are harsh, not only towards their kin, but also towards themselves."

She looked up at her husband's calm face for a moment; then she cast her eyes upon the ground and walked humbly at his side.

Just as silently Rudolf walked at the side of the old clerk. His eyes hung upon the hand of the woman, illuminated by the moonlight, which had only a short time ago rested so weakly in his own. He hoped that he would be able to hold it once more, if only for a moment when saying good night.—But it was to be otherwise; for, as they approached the city, he noticed the small hands, one after the other, slip into a pair of dark gloves which, as he well knew, Veronika usually carried only for the sake of completing her costume.

Finally they had reached the house; but before he was quite aware of it in his dejection, he felt the hasty touch of her covered fingers upon his own. With a distinctly spoken "Good night" Veronika had opened the door and had disappeared into the darkness of the hall ahead of her husband.

II. Palm Sunday

The morning of Palm Sunday had arrived. The streets of the city were thronged with country-folk from the neighboring villages. Here and there in the sunshine in front of the house-doors stood the children of protestant inhabitants, gazing down toward the open door of the Catholic Church. This was the day of the great Easter procession. —Now the bells were ringing, and the procession became visible under the Gothic arch, and surged out into the street. At the head the orphan boys with black crosses in their hands, behind them in white veiled hoods, the Sisters of Mercy, then the various public schools and finally the whole endless train of country and city folk, of men, women, of children, and old people, all singing, praying, dressed in their best clothes, men and boys bare-headed, their caps in their hands. Overhead at measured intervals, carried upon shoulders, the colossal religious pictures: Christ at Calvary, Christ jeered by the soldiers, in the center, high above everything, the tremendous cross, finally the Holy Sepulchre.

The ladies of the city did not customarily participate in the public festivities.

Veronika sat half dressed in her bedroom at a small dressing table. Before her lay open a small, gilt-edge Testament, such as the Catholic Church permits its members. She seemed to have forgotten herself over her reading, for her long black hair hung loose over her white night-gown, while her hand, holding a tortoise-shell comb lay idly in her lap.

As the din of the approaching procession reached her ears she raised her head and listened. Ever more distinctly came the dull

1238

sound of steps, the singing, monotonous murmuring of prayers. "Holy Mary, Mother of Mercy!," it came from outside, and from the rear of the procession resounded a subdued: "Pray for us poor sinners, now, and in the hour of death."

Veronika recited the familiar words softly. She had pushed back her chair; with her arms at her sides, she stood in the back of the room, her eyes steadfastly directed toward the window. New people came and went continuously, new voices spoke, one picture after the other was carried by. Then suddenly a heart-rending tone penetrated the air. The *castrum doloris* approached, accompanied by the sound of trumpets, surrounded by people, followed by the acolytes and the highest priests in festive vestment. The ribbons fluttered, the black crepe of the canopy rippled in the air; underneath it in a garden of flowers lay the image of the Crucified One. The metallic peal of the trumpets was like a summons to the Day of Judgment.

Veronika was still standing motionless; her knees trembled; beneath the accentuated black eyebrows her eyes lay as if extinguished in the pale countenance.

When the procession had passed, she sank to the floor beside the chair upon which she had been sitting, and covering her face with both hands, she cried, with the words in Luke: "Father, I have sinned against Heaven, and I am not worthy of being called your child!"

III. In the Confessional

The counsellor belonged to that ever increasing community of those who saw in the appearance of Christianity not so much a miracle, but rather the natural result of the spiritual development of humanity. He himself, therefore, did not go to any church; nevertheless, he permitted his wife to retain the habits of her youth and parental home, perhaps in the expectation of her gradual, independent liberation from them.

Since their wedding two years before Veronika had gone to confession and communion only at Easter-time, which had now begun again. He was already acquainted with the way in which she went about in the house on the preceding days, quiet and apparently indifferent; therefore, it had not struck him that the enthusiastically undertaken drawing lessons had ceased ever since that evening walk. But the time passed, the May sun began to beam warmly into the room, and Veronika put off her confession again. At last it could escape him no longer that her cheeks became paler from day to day, that little shadows became visible under her eyes, left there by sleepless nights. Thus he found her one morning upon entering the bedroom unnoticed, standing at the window lost in thought.

"Vroni," he said, putting his arm around her, "Won't you try holding up your little head again?"

She shuddered, as if he had surprised unguarded thoughts in her, but she sought to control herself. "Go, Franz!," she said, taking his hand tenderly and leading him back to the door.

Then, soon after he had left her alone, she dressed and departed from the house, prayer-book in hand.

A short time later she entered St. Lambert's. Meanwhile the morning was advancing. Outside the windows of the vast hall the leaf-covered branches of the Linden trees cast their shadows; in the choir, upon the doors of the reliquary, a broken sunray fell through the stained glass panes. In the confessionals in the nave of the church here and there people sat or kneeled before opened prayer-books, preparing for confessions. There was no sound but the whispering from the confessionals, now and then a deep breath, the rustling of a dress, or a soft footfall upon the flagstones. Soon Veronika, too, was kneeling in one of the confessionals, not far from the picture of the Holy Mother, who looked down upon her, smiling compassionately. Her completely black costume made the transparent pallor of her face still more striking. The priest, a robust middle-aged man, leaned his head against the screen which separated him from his penitent.

Veronika began the introductory formula in a half whisper: "Forgive me, Father, for I have sinned," and with wavering voice she continued: "I confess to Almighty God and to you, Father, . . ." Her words became slower and slower, less and less understandable; then she stopped.

The dark eye of the priest was calm and directed upon her with an expession almost of fatigue, since he had been hearing confessions for hours. "Turn ye to the Lord!" he said mildly. "Sin is death; but repentance is life."

She tried to collect her thoughts. And again, as so often since that hour, her inward ear heard the turbulent roar of the mill; and again she stood before him in the mysterious twilight—her hands caught in his, closing her eyes under the stress of the overwhelming emotion, transfixed in mortification, not daring to escape, and even less, to remain.—Her lips moved, but she could not get it out; she tried in vain.

The Priest remained silent for a moment. "Courage! my daughter!" he then said, raising his head with the rich black hair. "Think of the words of the Lord: 'Receive ye the Holy Spirit; those whom ye free from sin, their sins shall be forgiven!'"

She glanced up. The flushed countenance, the powerful bull-neck of the man in vestments was close before her eyes. She began once more; but an unconquerable resentment came over her, a reluctance, as before something unchaste, worse than that which she had come here to confess. She was frightened. Was not this revolt in her a temptation of the deadly sin from which she wanted to be released? She bowed her head in silent conflict upon the prayer-book lying before her. Meanwhile, the expression of fatigue had vanished from the face of the priest. He began to speak, earnestly and forcibly, and then with all the magic of persuasion; softly, yet sonorously the tone of his voice came to her ears. At any other time she would have sunk to the dust, enraptured; but this time the newly awakened emotion was stronger than all the power of rhetoric and all the habit of her youth. Her hand fumbled at her veil which was thrown back over her hat.

"Forgive me, father," she stammered. Then, silently shaking her head, she drew the veil down without having received the sign of the cross, stood up, and went hastily down the aisle. Her clothes rustled past the church benches; she gathered them in her hand; it seemed to her as though unseen hands were reaching out to keep her there.

Outside, beneath the high doorway she stood still, breathing deeply. She was troubled in spirit; she had rejected the redeeming hand which had led her since childhood; she knew no other which she might grasp now. Then, as she stood undecided on the sunny square, she heard the voice of a child beside her, and a small brown hand offered her a bouquet of primroses for sale. It was indeed spring outside in the world. As though she had not known it, like a messenger it came to her heart.

She bent down to the child and bought his flowers; then, the bouquet in her hand, she walked down the street towards the city gate. The sun glittered on the stones; from the open window of a house a canary sent forth its loud song. She walked slowly on and soon reached the last houses. From there a foot-path led off to the side up toward the hills which bounded the city. Veronika breathed more freely; her eyes rested upon the green of the fields which bordered the path; now and then the air stirred and brought the gentle fragrance of the cowslips growing at the foot of the mountain. Farther

1241

on, where, at the border of the fields the forest began, the path rose steeper, and physical effort became necessary although Veronika had been used to mountain climbing since her early youth. Now and then she stopped and gazed from the shadows of the firs into the sunny valley which sank deeper and deeper below her.

When she had reached the summit she sat on the ground among the wild thyme which had spun itself over the mountain at this spot. As she breathed the spicy air of the forest her eye swept over toward the blue mountan-chain which lay on the horizon like a haze. Behind her, at short intervals, the spring wind was blowing through the tops of the pines. Now and then the call of a blackbird sounded out of the depths of the forest, or above her the cry of a bird of prey which floated invisible in the immeasurable vastness of space.

Veronika removed her hat and supported her head with her hand.

Thus in solitude and quiet a period of time passed. Nothing approached her but the pure breezes which touched her brow and the calls of the birds which reached her ear from the distance. At times a bright glow flushed her cheeks and her eyes became large and shining.

Now the bells sounded up from the city. She raised her head and listened. They rang shrilly and hastily. "Requiescat!," she said softly, for she had recognized the little bell from St. Lambert's tower which informed the community that beneath one of its roofs the grim messenger of the Lord had entered.

At the foot of the mountains lay the cemetery. She could see the stone cross towering over the grave of her father who, but a few years before, had passed away in her arms as a priest intoned his prayers. And farther on, there, where the water glistened, was that ugly barren patch of earth which she had so often entered as a child, full of shy curiosity, where, according to the commandment of the church, those who had not received the sacrament of the altar were buried beside those who had taken their own lives. This would now be her resting place, too, since Easter confessions were at an end for her.

An expression of pain crept about her mouth and then disappeared.

She stood up, a decision firm and clear in her soul.

A moment longer she looked down upon the city and let her eyes wander over the sunlit roofs as if in search of something. Then she turned and walked through the pines down the mountain the way she had come. Soon she was in the green of the fields again. She seemed to hurry, walking erect with firm steps.

Thus she reached her house. From the maid she learned that her husband was in his room. As she opened the door and saw him sitting calmly at his desk she remained hesitantly on the threshold.

"Franz," she called softly.

He laid his pen aside.

"Is it you, Vroni?," he said, turning to her. "You're late! Was your list of transgressions so long?"

"Don't joke!" she said pleadingly as she stepped up to him and took his hand. "I did not confess."

He looked up at her, surprised. She, however, knelt before him and pressed her lips upon his hand.

"Franz," she said, "I have hurt you!"

"Me, Veronika?" he asked, and took her face softly between his hands.

"And now you have come to confess to your husband?"

"No, Franz," she replied, "Not to confess, but to confide in you, in you alone,—and you,—help me, and if you can,—forgive me!"

For a moment he gazed at her earnestly, then he raised her with both arms and laid her head upon his breast. "Then speak, Veronika!"

She did not stir, but her mouth began to speak and, as his eyes hung upon her lips, she felt how his arms tightened about her.

TO A DECEASED

But this is more than I can bear,
That still the laughing sun is bright,
As in the days when you were there,
That clocks are striking, unaware,
And mark the change of day and night—

That we, as twilight dims the air,
Assemble when the day is done,
And that the place where stood your chair
Already many others share,
And that you seem thus missed by none;

When meanwhile from the gate below
The narrow strips of moonlight spare
Into your vault down deeply go
And with a ghostly pallid glow
Are stealing o'er your coffin there.

1243

THE CITY

The shore is gray, the sea is gray,
And there the city stands;
The mists upon the houses weigh
And through the calm, the ocean gray
Roars dully on the strands.

There are no rustling woods, there fly
No birds at all in May,
The wild goose with its callous cry
Along on autumn nights soars by,
The wind-blown grasses sway.

And yet my whole heart clings to thee,
Gray city by the sea;
And e'er the spell of youth for me
Doth smiling rest on thee, on thee
Gray city by the sea.

THE HEATH

It is so quiet here. There lies
The heath in noon's warm sunshine gold.
A gleam of light, all rosy, flies
And hovers round the mounds of old.
The herbs are blooming; fragrance fair
Now fills the bluish summer air.

The beetles rush through bush and trees,
In little golden coats of mail;
And on the heather-bells the bees
Alight on all its branches frail.
From out the grass there starts a throng
Of larks and fills the air with song.

A lonely house, half-crumbled, low:
The farmer, in the doorway bent,
Stands watching in the sunlight's glow
The busy bees in sweet content.
And on a stone near by his boy
Is carving pipes from reeds with joy.

Scarce trembling through the peace of noon
The town-clock strikes—from far, it seems.
The old man's eye-lids droop right soon,
And of his honey crops he dreams.—
The sounds that tell our time of stress
Have not yet reached this loneliness.

CONSOLATION

Let come to me whatever may,
While you are with me it is day.

Though in the world I wander far,
My home is ever—where you are.

Your face is all in all to me,
The future's frown I do not see.

HARRIET BEECHER STOWE

HARRIET BEECHER STOWE (American, 1811-1896). Author of a book that
changed the face of a country. Daughter and wife of clergymen. Wrote her
novels and stories while raising six children. *Uncle Tom's Cabin*, hardly a
great work of art, nonetheless had powerful influence in turning the country's
attention toward evils of slavery. It has been translated into nearly every
written language.

TOPSY

ONE morning, while Miss Ophelia was busy in some of her domestic
cares, St. Clare's voice was heard, calling her at the foot of the stairs.

"Come down here, cousin; I've something to show you."

"What is it?" said Miss Ophelia, coming down, with her sewing
in her hand.

"I've made a purchase for your department—see here," said St.
Clare; and, with the word, he pulled along a little negro girl, about
eight or nine years of age.

She was one of the blackest of her race; and her round, shining
eyes, glittering as glass beads, moved with quick and restless glances
over everything in the room. Her mouth, half open with astonish-

ment at the wonders of the new Mas'r's parlor, displayed a white and brilliant set of teeth. Her woolly hair was braided in sundry little tails, which stuck out in every direction. The expression of her face was an odd mixture of shrewdness and cunning, over which was oddly drawn, like a kind of veil, an expression of the most doleful gravity and solemnity. She was dressed in a single filthy, ragged garment, made of bagging; and stood with her hands demurely folded before her. Altogether, there was something odd and goblin-like about her appearance,—something, as Miss Ophelia afterwards said, "so heathenish," as to inspire that good lady with utter dismay; and, turning to St. Clare, she said:

"Augustine, what in the world have you brought that thing here for?"

"For you to educate, to be sure, and train in the way she should go. I thought she was rather a funny specimen in the Jim Crow line. Here, Topsy," he added, giving a whistle, as a man would call the attention of a dog, "give us a song, now, and show us some of your dancing."

The black, glassy eyes glittered with a kind of wicked drollery, and the thing struck up, in a clear shrill voice, an old negro melody, to which she kept time with her hands and feet, spinning round, clapping her hands, knocking her knees together, in a wild, fantastic sort of time, and producing in her throat all those odd guttural sounds which distinguish the native music of her race; and finally, turning a somerset or two, and giving a prolonged closing note as odd and unearthly as that of a steam-whistle, she came suddenly down on the carpet, and stood with her hands folded, and a most sanctimonious expression of meekness and solemnity over her face, only broken by the cunning glances which she shot askance from the corners of her eyes.

Miss Ophelia stood silent, perfectly paralyzed with amazement.

St. Clare, like a mischievous fellow as he was, appeared to enjoy her astonishment; and, addressing the child again, said:

"Topsy, this is your new mistress. I'm going to give you up to her; see, now, that you behave yourself."

"Yes, Mas'r," said Topsy, with sanctimonious gravity, her wicked eyes twinkling as she spoke.

"You're going to be good, Topsy, you understand," said St. Clare.

"Oh, yes, Mas'r," said Topsy, with another twinkle, her hands still devoutly folded.

"Now, Augustine, what upon earth is this for?" said Miss Ophelia.

"Your house is so full of these little plagues, now, that a body can't set down their foot without treading on 'em. I get up in the morning, and find one asleep behind the door, and see one black head poking out from under the table, one lying on the door-mat,—and they are mopping and mowing and grinning between all the railings, and tumbling over the kitchen floor! What on earth did you want to bring this one for?"

"For you to educate,—didn't I tell you? You're always preaching about educating. I thought I would make you a present of a fresh-caught specimen, and let you try your hand on her, and bring her up in the way she should go."

"*I* don't want her. I am sure;—I have more to do with 'em now than I want to."

"That's you Christians, all over!—you'll get up a society, and get some poor missionary to spend all his days among just such heathen. But let me see one of you that would take one into your house with you, and take the labor of their conversion on yourselves! No; when it comes to that, they are dirty and disagreeable, and it's too much care, and so on."

"Augustine, you know I didn't think of it in that light," said Miss Ophelia, evidently softening. "Well, it might be a real missionary work," said she, looking rather more favorably on the child.

St. Clare had touched the right string. Miss Ophelia's conscientiousness was ever on the alert. "But," she added, "I really didn't see the need of buying this one;—there are enough now, in your house, to take all my time and skill."

"Well, then, cousin," said St. Clare, drawing her aside, "I ought to beg your pardon for my good-for-nothing speeches. You are so good, after all, that there's no sense in them. Why, the fact is, this concern belonged to a couple of drunken creatures that keep a low restaurant that I have to pass by every day, and I was tired of hearing her screaming, and them beating and swearing at her. She looked bright and funny, too, as if something might be made of her,—so I bought her, and I'll give her to you. Try, now, and give her a good orthodox New England bringing up, and see what it'll make of her. You know I haven't any gift that way; but I'd like you to try."

"Well, I'll do what I can," said Miss Ophelia; and she approached her new subject very much as a person might be supposed to approach a black spider, supposing them to have benevolent designs toward it.

1247

"She's dreadfully dirty, and half naked," she said.

"Well, take her down stairs, and make some of them clean and clothe her up."

Miss Ophelia carried her to the kitchen regions.

"Don't see what Mas'r St. Clare wants of 'nother nigger!" said Dinah, surveying the new arrival with no friendly air. "Won't have her round under *my* feet, *I* know!"

"Pah!" said Rosa and Jane, with supreme disgust; "let her keep out of our way! What in the world Mas'r wanted another of these low niggers for, I can't see!"

"You go 'long! No more nigger dan you be, Miss Rosa," said Dinah, who felt this last remark a reflection on herself. "You seem to tink yourself white folks. You an't nerry one, black *nor* white. I'd like to be one or turrer."

Miss Ophelia saw that there was nobody in the camp that would undertake to oversee the cleansing and dressing of the new arrival; and so she was forced to do it herself, with some very ungracious and reluctant assistance from Jane.

When she saw, on the back and shoulders of the child, great welts and calloused spots, ineffaceable marks of the system under which she had grown up thus far, her heart became pitiful within her.

"See there!" said Jane, pointing to the marks, "don't that show she's a limb? We'll have fine works with her, I reckon. I hate these nigger young uns! so disgusting! I wonder that Mas'r would buy her!"

The "young un" alluded to heard all these comments with the subdued and doleful air which seemed habitual to her, only scanning, with a keen and furtive glance of her flickering eyes, the ornaments which Jane wore in her ears. When arrayed at last in a suit of decent and whole clothing, her hair cropped short to her head, Miss Ophelia, with some satisfaction, said she looked more Christianlike than she did, and in her own mind began to mature some plans for her instruction.

Sitting down before her, she began to question her. "How old are you, Topsy?"

"Dunno, Missis," said the image, with a grin that showed all her teeth.

"Don't know how old you are? Didn't anybody ever tell you? Who was your mother?"

1248

"Never had none!" said the child, with another grin.

"Never had any mother? What do you mean? Where were you born?"

"Never was born!" persisted Topsy, with another grin, that looked so goblin-like, that, if Miss Ophelia had been at all nervous, she might have fancied that she had got hold of some sooty gnome from the land of Diablerie; but Miss Ophelia was not nervous, but plain and business-like, and she said, with some sternness:

"You mustn't answer me in that way, child; I'm not playing with you. Tell me where you were born, and who your father and mother were."

"Never was born," reiterated the creature, more emphatically; "never had no father nor mother, nor nothin'. I was raised by a speculator, with lots of others. Old Aunt Sue used to take car on us."

The child was evidently sincere; and Jane, breaking into a short laugh, said:

"Laws, Missis, there's heaps of 'em. Speculators buys 'em up cheap, when they's little, and get's 'em raised for market."

"How long have you lived with your master and mistress?"

"Dunno, Missis."

"Is it a year, or more, or less?"

"Dunno, Missis."

"Laws, Missis, those low negroes,—they can't tell; they don't know anything about time," said Jane; "they don't know what a year is; they don't know their own ages."

"Have you ever heard anything about God, Topsy?"

The child looked bewildered, but grinned as usual.

"Do you know who made you?"

"'Nobody, as I knows on," said the child, with a short laugh.

The idea appeared to amuse her considerably; for her eyes twinkled, and she added:

"I spect I grow'd. Don't think nobody never made me."

"Do you know how to sew?" said Miss Ophelia, who thought she would turn her inquiries to something more tangible.

"No, Missis."

"What can you do?—what did you do for your master and mistress?"

"Fetch water, and wash dishes, and rub knives, and wait on folks."

"Were they good to you?"

"Spect they was," said the child, scanning Miss Ophelia cunningly.

1249

Miss Ophelia rose from this encouraging colloquy; St. Clare was leaning over the back of her chair.

"You find virgin soil there, cousin; put in your own ideas,—you won't find many to pull up."

AUGUST STRINDBERG

AUGUST STRINDBERG (Swedish, 1849-1912). One of the leading literary rebels of Europe at turn of the century. Unhappy teacher, actor, newspaperman. Prolific dramatist, novelist, critic. Lifelong conflict with women reflected in his naturalistic plays—*The Father* and *Miss Julia*—and novels like *Confessions of a Fool*. Tendency to emotional instability apparent in all his work, but experiments in dramatic form had lasting influence.

A FUNERAL

THE cooper sat with the barber in the inn at Engsung and played a harmless game of lansquenet for a barrel of beer. It was one o'clock in the afternoon of a snowy November day. The tavern was quite empty, for most people were still at work. The flames burned brightly in the clay fire-place which stood on four wooden feet in a corner, and looked like a coffin; the fir twigs on the ground smelt pleasantly; the well-panelled walls kept out all draughts and looked warm: the bull-finch in his cage twittered now and then, and looked out of the window, but he had to put his head on one side to see if it was fine. But it was snowing outside. The innkeeper sat behind his counter and reckoned up chalk-strokes on a black slate; now and then he interjected a humorous remark or a bright idea which seemed to please the other two.

Then the great bell in the church began to toll with a dull and heavy sound, in keeping with the November day.

"What the devil is that cursed ringing for?" said the cooper, who felt too comfortable in life to enjoy being reminded of death.

"Another funeral," answered the innkeeper. "There is never anything else."

"Why the deuce do people want to have such a fuss made about them after they are dead," said the barber. "Trump that, Master Cooper!"

1250

"So I did," said the cooper, and pocketed the trick in his leather apron.

Down the sloping road which led to the Nicholai Gate, a funeral procession wended its way. There was a simple, roughly planed coffin, thinly coated with black paint so that the knots in the wood showed through. A single wreath of whortleberries lay on the coffin lid. The undertaker's men who carried the bier looked indifferent and almost humiliated because they were carrying a bier without a cover and fringes.

Behind the coffin walked three women—the dead man's mother and her two daughters; they looked crushed with grief. When the funeral reached the gate of the churchyard, the priest met it and shook hands with the mourners; then the service began in the presence of some old women and apprentices who had joined the procession.

"I see now—it is the clerk, Hans Schönschreiber," said the innkeeper, who had gone to the window, from which he could overlook the churchyard.

"And none of his fellow-clerks follow him to the grave," said the cooper. "A bad lot, these clerks.

"I know the poor fellow," said the barber. "He lived like a church mouse and died of hunger."

"And a little of pride," added the innkeeper.

"Not so little though," the cooper corrected him. "I knew his father; he was a clerk too. See now! these fellows who go in for reading and writing die before their time. They go without dinner and beg if necessary in order to look fine gentlemen; and yet a clerk is only a servant and can never be his own master for only the King is his own master in this life."

"And why should it be more gentleman-like to write?" asked the barber. "Isn't it perhaps just as difficult to cut a courtier's hair and to make him look smart, or to let someone's blood when he is in danger of his life?"

"I would like to see the clerk who would take less than ten years to make a big beer barrel," said the cooper. "Why, one knows the fellows require two years to draw up their petitions and such-like."

"And what is the good of it all?" asked the innkeeper. "Can I scribble such letters as they do, but don't I keep my accounts right? See here I draw a crucifix on the slate—that means the sexton; here I scribble the figure of a barrel—that stands for the cooper; then in

1251

a twinkling, however many strokes I have to make, I know exactly how many each has drunk."

"Yes, but no one else except yourself can read it, Mr. Innkeeper," objected a young man who had hitherto sat silent in a corner.

"That is the best of it," answered the innkeeper, "that no one can poke his nose into my accounts, and therefore I am just as good a clerk as anyone."

The cooper and the barber grinned approval.

"I knew the dead man's father," resumed the innkeeper. "He was a clerk too! And when he died I had to rub out many chalk-strokes which made up his account, for he wanted to be a fine gentleman, you see. All the inheritance he left to the son, who now lies with his nose pointing upwards, was a mother and two sisters. The young fellow wanted to be a tradesman in order to get food for four mouths, but his mother would not consent; she said it was a shame to step downward when one was above. And heavens, how the poor young fellow had to write! I know exactly what went on. The three women lived in one room and he in a rat-hole. All he could scrape together he had to give them; and when he came from work to eat his dinner, they deafened him with complaints. There was no butter on the bread, no sugar on the cakes; the elder sister wanted to have a new dress, and the younger a new mantle. Then he had to write through the whole night, and how he wrote! At last when his breast-bone stuck out like a hook and his face was as yellow as a leather strap, one day he felt tired; he came to me and borrowed a bottle of brandy. He was melancholy but also angry, for the elder sister had said she wanted a velvet jacket such as she had seen in the German shop, and his mother said ladies of their class could not do with less. The young fellow worked and slaved, but not with the same zest as formerly. And fancy! when he came here and took a glass to ease his chest, his conscience reproached him so much that he really believed he was stealing. And he had other troubles, the poor young fellow. A wooer came after the younger sister—a pewterer from Peter Apollo Street. But the sister said 'No!' and so did the mother, for he was only a pewterer. Had he been a clerk, she would have said 'Yes' and persuaded him that she loved him, and it is likely that she would really have done so, for such is love!"

All laughed except the young man, who struck in, "Well, innkeeper, but he loved her, although she was so poor and he was well off; that proves that love can be sincere, doesn't it?"

"Pooh!" said the innkeeper, who did not wish to be interrupted.

'But something else happened, and that finished him. He went and fell in love. His mother and sister had not counted on that, but it was the law of nature. And when he came and said that he thought of marrying, do you know what they said?—'Have you the means to?' And the youth, who was a little simple, considered and discovered that he had not means to establish a new family since he had one already, and so he did not marry; but he got engaged. And then there was a lot of trouble! His mother would not receive his fiancée, because her father could not write, and especially because she herself had been a dressmaker. It was still worse when the young man went in the evenings to her, and would not stay at home. A fine to-do there was! But still he went on working for his mother and sisters, and I know that in the evening he sat and wrote by his fiancée's side, while she sewed, only to save time and to be able to be near her. But his mother and sisters believed evil of the pair, and showed it too. It was one Sunday about dinner-time; he told me himself the young fellow, when he came here to get something for his chest, for now he coughed terribly. He had gone out with his fiancée to Brunkeberg, and as they were coming home over the North Bridge, whom did they meet but his mother and sisters? His fiancée wanted to turn back, but he held her arm firmly and drew her forward. But his mother remained standing by the bridge railings and looked into the water; the elder sister spat before her, and did the same, but the younger—she was a beauty! She stood still and stared at the young woman's woollen mantle and laughed, for she had one of English cloth—and just because of that, her brother's fiancée had to wear wool. Fancy the impudent hussy!'"

"That was simply want of sense in the child," said the young man.

"Want of sense!" exclaimed the cooper indignantly. "Want of sense!" But he could not say any more.

The innkeeper took no notice of the interruption and continued: "It was a Christmas Eve, the last Christmas Eve on which he was alive. He came to me as usual to get something for his chest, which was very bad. 'A Merry Christmas, Hans!' I said. I sat where I am sitting now, and he sat just where you are sitting, young sir. 'Are you bad?' I asked. 'Yes,' he answered, 'and your slate is full.' 'It doesn't matter,' I answered, 'we can write down the rest in the great book up there. A glass of hot *Schnapps* does one good on Christmas Eve.' He was coughing terribly, and so he took a drink. Then his tongue was loosened. He said how miserable and forlorn he felt this evening. He had just left his home. The Christmas table was laid.

1253

His mother and sisters were soft and mild, as one usually is on such an evening. They said nothing, they did not reproach him, but when he took his coat and was about to go out, his mother wept and said it was the first Christmas Eve that her son was absent. But do you think that she had so much heart as to say 'Go to her, bring her here, and let us be at peace like friends.' No! she only thought of herself, and so he went with an aching heart. Poor fellow! But hear what followed. Then he came to his fiancée. She was glad and happy to have him, and now she saw that he loved her better than anything else on earth. But the young man, whose heart was torn in two, was not so cheerful as she wished him to be, and then she was vexed with him, a little only of course. Then they talked about marriage, but he could not agree with her. No, he had duties towards his father's widow. But she quoted the priest who had said a man should leave father and mother and remain with his wife. He asked whether he had not left his mother and home this evening with a bleeding heart in order to be with her. She replied that she had already noticed, when he came, that he was depressed because he was going to spend the evening with her. He answered it was not that which depressed him, but his having to leave his old mother on Christmas Eve. Then she objected that he could not deny he had been depressed when he came to her—and so they went on arguing, you can imagine how!"

The cooper nodded intelligently.

"Well, it was a pleasant Christmas for him. Enough! The young fellow was torn in two, piece by piece; he never married. But now he lies at rest, if the coffin nails hold; but it was a sad business for him, poor devil, even if he was a fool. And God bless his soul! Hans Schönschreiber, if you have no greater list of debts than you had with me, they are easily settled!"

So saying, the innkeeper took his black slate from the counter, and with his elbow rubbed out a whole row of chalk-strokes which had been made under a hieroglyph which looked like a pen in an inkpot.

"See," said the barber, who had been looking through the window to hide his red eyes, "see, there she is!"

Outside in the churchyard the funeral service was at an end; the priest had pressed the hands of the mourners and was about to go; the sexton plied his spade in order to fill up the grave again, as a woman dressed in black pressed through the crowd, fell on her knees by the edge of the grave, and offered a silent prayer. Then she let fall a wreath of white roses into the grave, and a faint sobbing and whispering was audible as the rose leaves fell apart on the black coffin lid. Then she stood up to go, erect and proud, but did not at first notice in the crowd that her dead lover's mother was regarding her with wild and angry looks as though she saw her worst enemy, who had robbed her of her dearest. Then they stood for a moment opposite one another, revengeful and ready for battle; but suddenly their features assumed a milder expression, their pale faces twitched, and they fell in each other's arms and wept. They held each other in a long, convulsive embrace, and then departed side by side.

The innkeeper wept like a child without attempting to hide his emotion, the barber pressed his face against the window, and the cooper took the cards out of his pocket as though to arrange them; but the young man, his head propped in his hands, had placed himself against the wall in order to have a support, for he wept so that his whole body shook and his legs trembled.

The innkeeper first broke the silence. "Who will now help the poor family? The pewterer would be accepted now, were he to make another proposal."

"How do you know that, innkeeper?" asked the young man, much moved, as he stepped into the centre of the room.

"Well, I heard it yesterday when I was up there helping at the preparations for the funeral. But the pewterer will not have her now, as she would not have him then."

"Yes he will, innkeeper!" said the young man. "He will have her though she were ever so selfish and bad-tempered, poor, and wretched, for such is love!"

So saying, he left the astonished innkeeper and his friends.

"Deuce take me—that was he himself!" said the barber.

"Things do not always end so happily," remarked the cooper.

"How about the clerk?" objected the barber.

"No, they did not end well with him, but with the others, you know. They had, as it were, more right to live than he, the young one; for they were alive first, and he who first comes to the mill, grinds his corn first."

"The young fellow was stupid, that was the whole trouble," said the barber.

"Yes, yes," concluded the inkeeper. "He certainly was stupid, but it was fine of him anyhow."

In that they were all agreed.

SUDRAKA

SUDRAKA (Sanskrit, 1st or 2nd century B.C.). Legendary Hindu Prince and
Sanskrit dramatist, to whom the drama *Mricchakatikā* (*The Clay Cart*) is at-
tributed. Even this is dubious, since play probably dates from fifth century
A.D. Nothing known of his life.

THE CLAY CART

The first scene represents a court in front of Caru-datta's house.
His friend Maitreya—who, although a Brahman, acts the part of
a sort of jovial companion, and displays a disposition of mixed
shrewdness and simplicity—laments Caru-datta's fallen fortunes,
caused by his too great liberality. Caru-datta replies thus.—

Caru-datta.   Think not, my friend, I mourn departed wealth.
One thing alone torments me.—that my guests
Desert my beggared house, like to the bees
That swarm around the elephant, when dews
Exhale from his broad front; but quickly leave
His dried-up temples when they yield no sweets.
   Maitreya.   The sons of slaves! These guests you speak of are
always ready to make a morning meal off a man's property.
   Caru-datta.   It is most true, but I bestow no thought
On my lost property,—as fate decrees
Wealth comes and goes; but this is torture to me,—
That friendships I thought firm hang all relaxed
And loose, when poverty sticks closest to me.
From poverty 'tis but a step to shame—
From shame to loss of manly self-respect;
Then comes disdainful scorn, then dark despair
O'erwhelms the mind with melancholy thoughts,
Then reason goes, and last of all comes ruin.
Oh! poverty is source of every ill.
   Maitreya.   Ah well, cheer up! Let's have no more of these woe-
begone memories. What's lost can't be recovered.
   Caru-datta.   Good! I will grieve no more. Go you, my friend,
And offer this oblation, just prepared,
Unto the gods, and mothers of us all.
   Maitreya.   Not I.

Caru-datta.   And why not, pray?

Maitreya.   Why, what's the use, when the gods you have worshiped have done nothing for you?

Caru-datta.   Friend, speak not thus, for worship is the duty
Of every family; the gods are honored
By offerings, and gratified by acts
Of penance and restraint in thought and word.
Therefore, delay not to present the oblation.

Maitreya.   I don't intend to go; send some one else.

Caru-datta.   Stay quiet then for a little, till I have finished
My religious meditations and prayer.

They are supposed here to retire, and a voice is heard behind the scenes:—

Stop! Vasanta-sena, stop!

The heroine of the play now appears in front of Caru-datta's house, pursued by the king's worthless but wealthy brother-in-law, called Sàmsthanaka, who is an embodiment of everything vicious and mean, in exact contrast to Caru-datta.

Samsthanaka.   Stop! Vasanta-sena, stop! Why do you run away? Don't be alarmed. I am not going to kill you. My poor heart is on fire with love, like a piece of meat placed on a heap of burning coals.

Vasanta-sena.   Noble sir, I am only a weak woman.

Samsthanaka.   That is just why I don't intend murdering you.

Vasanta-sena.   Why then do you pursue me? Do you seek my jewels?

Samsthanaka.   No, I only seek to gain your affections.

At this point the frightened Vasanta-sena discovers that she is close to Caru-datta's house. He is not only loved by her, but greatly respected as a man of honor; and under cover of the evening darkness, now supposed to have supervened, she slips into the courtyard of his house by a side door, and hides herself. A companion who is with the king's brother now counsels him to desist from following her, by remarking:—

An elephant is bound by a chain,
A horse is curbed by a bridle and rein;
But a woman is only held by her heart—
If you can't hold that, you had better depart.

1257

Samsthanaka, however, forces his way into Caru-datta's house; and there finding Caru-datta's friend and companion Maitreya, thus addresses him:—

Take this message to Caru-datta.—Vasanta-sena loves you, and has taken refuge in your house. If you will deliver her up, you shall be rewarded by my everlasting friendship; if not, I shall remain your enemy till death. Give this message, so that I may hear you from the neighboring terrace; refuse to say exactly what I have told you, and I will crush your head as I would a wood apple beneath a door.

He then leaves the stage.

Maitreya accordingly delivers the message. Soon afterwards the heroine Vasanta-sena ventures into the presence of Caru-datta, asks pardon for intruding into his house, requests him to take charge of a golden casket containing her ornam~ as a deposit left in trust, and solicits his friend's escort back   r own house.

Maitreya is too much alarmed to accom   ay her, so Caru-datta himself escorts Vasanta-sena home.

So far is an epitome of the first act.

At the commencement of the secc   a gambler is introduced running away from the keeper of a _   .ing house, named Mathura and another gambler to whom the first gambler has lost money who are both pursuing him.

First Gambler. The master of the tables and the gamester are at my heels: how can I escape them? Here is an empty temple: I will enter it walking backwards, and pretend to be its idol.

Mathura. Ho there! stop, thief! A gambler has lost ten suvarnas, and is running off without paying. Stop him, stop him!

Second Gambler. He has run as far as this point; but here the track is lost.

Marthura. Ah! I see,—the footsteps are reversed: the rogue has walked backwards into this temple which has no image in it.

They enter and make signs to each other on discovering the object of their search, who pretends to be an idol fixed on a pedestal.

Second Gambler. Is this a wooden image, I wonder?

Mathura. No, no, it must be made of stone, I think. (*So saying*

1258

they shake and pinch him.) Never mind, sit we down here, and play out our game. (*They commence playing.*)

First Gambler (*still acting the image, but looking on and with difficulty restraining his wish to join in the game. Aside*). The rattling of dice is as tantalizing to a penniless man as the sound of drums to a dethroned monarch; verily it is sweet as the note of a nightingale.

Second Gambler. The throw is mine, the throw is mine!

Mathura. No, it is mine, I say.

First Gambler (*forgetting himself and jumping off his pedestal*). No, I tell you it is mine.

Second Gambler. We've caught him!

Mathura. Yes, rascal, you're caught at last: hand over the suvarnas.

First Gambler. Worthy sir, I'll pay them in good time.

Mathura. Hand them over this very minute, I say. (*They beat him.*)

First Gambler (*aside to Second Gambler*). I'll pay you half if you will forgive me the rest.

Second Gambler. Agreed.

First Gambler (*aside to Mathura*). I'll give you security for half if you will let me off the other half.

Mathura. Agreed.

First Gambler. Then good morning to you, sirs; I'm off.

Mathura. Hullo! stop there, where are you going so fast? Hand over the money.

First Gambler. See here, my good sirs, one has taken security for half, and the other has let me off another half. Isn't it clear I have nothing to pay?

Mathura. No, no, my fine fellow: my name is Mathura, and I'm not such a fool as you take me for. Don't suppose I'm going to be cheated out of my ten suvarnas in this way. Hand them over, you scoundrel.

Upon that they set to work beating the unfortunate gambler, whose cries for help bring to his rescue another gamster who happens to be passing. A general scuffle now takes place, and in the midst of the confusion the first gambler escapes. In his flight he comes to the house of Vasanta-sena, and finding the door open, rushes in. Vasanta-sena inquires who he is and what he wants. He then recites his story, and makes known to her that having been once in the service of Caru-datta, and having been discharged by him on account of his reduced circumstances, he has been driven to seek a livelihood by gambling. The mention of Caru-datta at once secures Vasanta-sena's aid; and the pursuers having now tracked their fugitive to the door of her house, she sends them out a jeweled bracelet, which satisfies their demands, and they retire. The gambler expresses the deepest gratitude, hopes in return to be of use to Vasanta-sena at some future time, and announces his intention of abandoning his disreputable mode of life and becoming a Buddhist mendicant.

The third act opens with a scene inside Caru-datta's house. The time is supposed to be night. Caru-datta and Maitreya are absent at a concert. A servant is preparing their sleeping couches, and commences talking to himself thus:—

A good master who is kind to his servants, even though he be poor, is their delight; while a harsh fellow, who is always finding fault and has nothing but his money to be proud of, is a perpetual torment from morning to night. Well, well! one can't alter nature; an ox can't be kept out of a field of corn, and a man once addicted to gambling can't be induced to leave off. My good master has gone to a concert. I must await his return; so I may as well take a nap in the hall.

Meanwhile Caru-datta and Maitreya come back, and the servant delivers Vasanta-sena's golden casket, saying that it is his turn to take charge of it by night. They now lie down.

Maitreya. Are you sleepy?
Caru-datta. Yes:
I feel inconstant sleep, with shadowy form
Viewless and wayward, creep across my brow
And weigh my eyelids down; her soft approach
Is like Decay's advance, which stronger grows
Till it has mastered all our faculties,
And life is lost in blank unconsciousness.

The whole household is soon buried in slumber, when a thief named Sarvilaka is seen to approach. His soliloquy, while he proceeds to accomplish his design of breaking into the house, is curious, as showing that an Indian burglar's mode of operation in ancient

1260

imes differed very little from that now in fashion. Moreover, it appears that the whole practice of housebreaking was carried on by professional artists according to certain fixed rules and principles, which a master of the science, named Yogacarya, had embodied in a kind of "Thieves' Manual" for the better training of his disciples. It is evident, too, that the fraternity of thieves, burglars, and rogues had a special presiding Deity and Patron in India, much in the same way as in ancient Greece and Rome.

It may be noted also, as still more curious, that the particular burglar here introduced is represented as a Brahman, that he is made to speak the learned language, Sanskrit, and to display acquaintance with Sanskrit literature; while all the subordinate characters in Indian dramas, including women of rank, are represented as speaking one or other of the provincial dialects called Prakrit. Here is part of the burglar's soliloquy:—

I advance creeping stealthily along the ground, like a snake wiggling out of its worn-out skin, making a path for my operations by the sheer force of my scientific craft, and artfully constructing an opening just big enough to admit my body with ease.

This friendly night which covers all the stars
With a thick coat of darkness, acts the part
Of a kind mother, shrouding me, her son,
Whose valor is displayed in night assaults
Upon my neighbors, and whose only dread
Is to be pounced upon by royal watchmen.

Good! I have made a hole in the garden wall, and am now in the midst of the premises. Now for an attack on the four walls of the house itself.

Men call this occupation mean, which thrives
By triumphing o'er sleeping enemies.
This, they say, is not chivalry but burglary:
But better far reproach with independence,
Than cringing service without liberty;
And did not Aswatthaman long ago
O'erpower in night attack his slumbering foe?

Where shall I make my breach? Ah! here's a rat hole—this is the very thing we disciples of the god Skanda hail as the best guide

1261

to our operations, and the best omen of success. Here then I must begin my excavation, that is clear; but how shall I proceed? The golden-speared god has taught four methods of making a breach:—namely,—pulling out baked bricks, cutting through unbaked ones; soaking a mud wall with water, and boring through one made of wood. This wall is evidently of baked bricks, so they must be pulled out. Now for the shape of the hole. It must be carved according to some orthodox pattern: shall it be like a lotus blossom, the sun, a crescent, a lake, a triangle, or a jar? I must do it cleverly, so that to-morrow morning people may look at my handiwork with wonder, and say to each other, "None but a skilled artist could have done this!" The jar shape looks best in a wall of baked bricks. Be it so: now, then, to work! Reverence to the golden-speared god Karttikeya, the giver of all boons! Reverence to Yogacarya, whose chief disciple I am, and who was so pleased with his pupil that he gave me a magical pigment, which, when spread over my body, prevents any police officer from catching sight of me and any weapons from harming my limbs. Ah! what a pity! I have forgotten my measuring line. Never mind, I can use my Brahmanical cord,—a most serviceable implement to all Brahmans, especially to men of my profession. It serves to measure a wall, or to throw round ornaments which have to be drawn from their places, or to lift the latch of a door, or to bind up one's finger when bitten by insects or snakes. And now, to commence measuring. Good! the hole is exactly the right size; only one brick remains! Ah! botheration! I am bitten by a snake: I must bind up my finger and apply the antidote that's the only cure. Now I am all right again. Let me first peep in. What! A light gleams somewhere! Never mind! the breach being perfect, I must creep in. Reverence to Karttikeya! How now! two men asleep! Are they really asleep, or only shamming? If they are shamming, they won't bear the glimmer of this lamp when passed over their faces;—they are fast asleep, I believe,—their breathing is regular, their eyes are firmly closed, their joints are all relaxed, and their limbs protrude beyond the bed. What have we here? Here are tabors, a lute, flutes, and books; why, I must have broken into the house of a dancing master; I took it for the mansion of a man of rank.

He helps himself to the casket, and proceeds to make good his escape.

The noise he makes in going out rouses its inmates, and they

liscover that the house has been robbed. Caru-datta is greatly
shocked at the loss of Vasanta-sena's casket, which had been
deposited with him in trust. He has only one valuable thing left,
—a necklace or string of jewels, forming part of the private property
of his wife. This he sends by Maitreya to Vasanta-sena as a substitute for the casket.

SUN HSI-CHEN

SUN HSI-CHEN (Chinese, 1906-   ). Novelist popular among Chinese youth.
Admired for his stories of rural life. Most widely known books: *Beaten Gold,
Woman of the Night,* and a war trilogy: *The Field of War, War,* and
After War.

AH AO

THROUGHOUT the day, from early dawn Ah Ao had remained hidden
under a bed in the small dark room, her head bent, her body still,
scarcely daring to breathe.

At the foot of the Purple-Red Mountain, down which spilled a
dense growth of fragrant pines and other trees, a small stream ran
into the open cornfields, and beside it stood a row of seven houses,
most of them old and dilapidated. This place was known as Tao
Village, although none of the inhabitants was named Tao. In four of
the seven houses lived the family Chen, the house on the western end
was a family temple reserved for the spirits, while in the center of
the row stood a comparatively new and handsome residence (some
eighteen years old) which was owned by Chin the Rich.

It was in the seventh house, poorest of all, consisting of five little
rooms, where the Wang family dwelt, that Ah Ao lay hidden. Half
of this house was in fact mortgaged to Chin the Rich who, two years
before, when old Wang died, had lent his widow forty thousand cash
to pay for the funeral feast and obsequies. Consequently she now
lived with her son, Small One Brother, and her daughter, Ah Ao, in
only the nether part of the little hut, which did not belong to Chin
the Rich. In the room next to the kitchen—or rather in one corner of
the kitchen itself, since the bed was separated from it only by a few
thin planks—Ah Ao, in secret dread, trembled and stifled her lungs
all day.

Some grindstones and empty bamboo baskets leaned against the
wall of the kitchen, which was just now very noisy. There were four

square wooden tables, with long benches ranged on each side, and these, with their occupants, completely choked up the little room Altogether one could count more than thirty men, including not only the male population of Tao Village but also guests from the neighboring villages of Yu and Red Wall. They sat drinking and feasting in exuberant mood. Most of them wore blue or white cotton shirts and trousers and were in their bare feet. Chin the Rich, Wu the Merchant, who could read and write, and the Hairy-Headed Village Elder, respected for his age, wore long gowns, however, made of linen. Only on rare occasions did these long-gown men visit such a lowly establishment, and it was plain that they were now quite aware of the extraordinary dignity their appearance lent to the feast.

The food seemed simple enough, with but four big bowls of meat, fish, turnips and soup, spread on each table, but they were refilled again and again, and each time emptied almost as soon as replenished. Later on, besides, the women of the village would have to be fed. Everybody gorged, helping himself to great hunks of meat and full bowls of wine without any pretense at etiquette; their presence at the feast was not in the interest of good will, but a punitive measure against the mother of a shameless daughter. Never mind the financial burden to Widow Wang! It was the only way of justice.

The fact was that only by mortgaging the other half of her house had the unhappy woman managed to get together the money to finance this strange banquet. A sentimental person might have observed that what the guests clipped between the blades of chopsticks was actually Widow Wang's flesh and blood; for the feast meant utter ruin to her. By this sacrifice, however, she was saving the life of her daughter, who was, no one could deny it, guilty of that crime. Now, although a crime of such a nature necessarily required two to commit it, the unwritten but powerful law of custom nevertheless made her alone responsible, and gave any villager the right to attack, insult, abuse or kill her, as he saw fit. By what other means, then, could the child's life be saved, than through this, an expensive banquet in honor of the offended villagers, with the especial aim of winning mercy from Chin the Rich, Wu the Merchant and the Hairy-Headed Village Elder? Even though it meant her own death in the end, still the widow would have gone through with it.

Two days before, in the afternoon, she had sent her son to Chin. He had bowed, begged mercy and requested the loan of thirty thousand cash, pledging the rest of the Wang House as security. Then with this money the boy had, again at his mother's instruction, gone

1264

to the market where he bought thirty pounds of meat, more than twenty pounds of fish, fully a bushel of turnips and some other ingredients of the feast. Since early in the morning of the previous day she had busied herself with cleaning and making ready this food. preparing rice wine and attending to other duties, so that she had not once had a moment to rest.

With the arrival of the guests she had become even busier. All alone, she worked ceaselessly, serving everybody, keeping all the bowls filled with food, pouring forth the warm wine that was like emptying the vessels of her own body, but all the same managing to smile and give the appearance of enjoying her duties immensely.

"Brother Lucky Root," shouted one coarse fellow, "don't hesitate! This isn't an occasion for ceremony, but a free feed. See, you don't have to give anything in return; so eat up! Fill yourself to the brim!"

"You are quite right," agreed Lucky Root. "Why be slow about it, eh? Let's eat; for such opportunities as this are rare indeed. As a matter of fact this girl now, Ah Ao; shameless, but still rather good-looking. How many girls around compare with her? Actually—?"

"The more girls like Ah Ao the more free feasts," yelled a third. "Personally I hope we'll have others."

"Ai-ya, Old Fa! Always boasting. You, the hungry devil with women! But don't forget the facts in this case; the girl right under your noses chooses instead a fellow from a neighboring village, not you!"

"Old Fa, ha, ha!"

"Ho, what an—Old Fa!"

The Widow Wang did not appear to understand these remarks, but bent her attention on the tasks of service and of maintaining the smile on her face. She did not once frown. But Ah Ao heard and trembled and crawled still farther toward the wall. She did not know whether the feeling she experienced was humiliation or terror or indignation or merely a heavy sadness, but something like a great stone seemed to be crushing her down, and her heart burned as if pierced by a shaft of red-hot iron. A few days ago she had boldly resigned herself to whatever fate might bring, but now she wanted only to crawl, crawl, crawl.

The Hairy-Headed Elder at last came to the issue. "To be precise," he began slowly, "this is perhaps after all not so serious a matter. It is natural for a grown girl to want marriage, isn't it so? But to make love—to a young man—in secret, you know, and without anybody's knowledge—without the usual formalities—who can excuse it?"

"Exactly!" exclaimed Wu the Merchant. "Widow Wang, this is something that can come to a mother only as punishment for her own sins in the past. Such a daughter, just consider, is not only a disgrace to your own family name but to the whole Tao Village as well. You very well know that according to age-old custom this crime merits nothing less than death. Recall, now, the case of the Chao girl—it happened three or four years ago in Stone Gate Village—who was beaten to death for the very same offense. Do you remember, she was buried without even a coffin? Nobody could call it cruelty, but only justice; for she had violated the laws of right conduct. Moreover, the worst of it is that even after their death such girls continue to dishonor the good name of the community. Ending life does not end their sin—no, indeed, and, as everyone knows, death doesn't begin to make up for it!"

"What you have just said is undeniably true. Death doesn't cover up the crime at all. But, on the other hand, it's not altogether the girl's fault. The mother is to blame also—a certain laxness, a waning of discipline. Again, in this case it may be that the mother was not herself very virtuous in some previous incarnation. Widow Wang, let me advise you to take care—in this life you had better be more strict."

The Village Elder was the donor of this speech, which oddly did not seem to anger the Widow, but on the contrary encouraged her to speak. She moved forward timidly, her hands pulling nervously on the edge of her worn dress. She spoke, in a very low voice, and smiled painfully:

"Yes, Honored Elder—that is correct. If she did wrong it was really my fault. I don't know what unpardonable sin I have back of me in some previous existence, but it must be as you say. And this terrible crime of my daughter, you're quite right, death would only be the punishment deserved. Still—" she broke suddenly into tears. "But I can't speak, I haven't 'face' to say—only I ask—*mercy!* Spare her life at least."

This was a reckless demand, an extraordinary request indeed, and were it not that the villagers were at that moment eating her food she would never have escaped ridicule by them. They believed in enforcing justice and morality to the letter, and ordinarily would stand no nonsense. Yet it seemed generally understood that because they had appeared, and had eaten, and had enjoyed themselves, and had some of them even come on their own invitation, they would not be altogether adamant. But their decision rested upon the opinions voiced

1266

by Chin the Rich, Wu the Merchant and the Hairy-Headed. Everybody remained silent until Chin finally gave the verdict.

"Wu has, I agree, spoken very wisely, and very much to the point. 'Death doesn't begin to cover up the crime.' Precisely! Then, perhaps, or so it seems to me, little is to be gained by taking her life now. The guilt has been admitted, and the Widow Wang, asking mercy, has begged us also to give 'face' to her late husband. She wants us to spare her daughter's life, and everything considered that is perhaps possible, but at the same time we cannot permit such an altogether immoral woman to continue to besmirch the village good name. She must leave at once!"

The Elder shared this view. "What is done is done; though totally without honor, still it's no use, now, to kill her. Better, as you say, expel her—move her out immediately."

These two having rendered a judgment, the rest of the guests, who considered themselves a kind of "jury," reined in their tongues. The decision was unanimously approved. The pale, weary face of the Widow Wang broke out suddenly into a genuine smile; she bowed low to the three wise men and obsequiously thanked the members of the self-appointed jury. But, back in the darkness, the hidden Ah Ao heard and yet curiously did not feel happy at all at this reprieve. She understood well enough that life had been miraculously restored to her, but although the prospect of death had been terrifying she was after all too young to have a deep fear of it, whereas to be banished from the village, to leave and never again to see her mother, to bid farewell to her brother, to plunge into an unknown, uncertain future —that was something which she knew to be worse than death. Grief shook her body, seemed to break, to shatter it, so that it was no longer whole, but a heap of something that mysteriously still trembled with life.

It had happened two months before, in early April, on a day filled with an ineffable softness, an unbearable languor and gladness that made men dreamy-eyed, drowsy and as if drunk with some wonderful wine.

Ah Ao, on her way home in the afternoon from the near-by Yu Village, thought that she had never known such a glorious day. There was a new warmth in her body, a strange vigor in her as if she had just begun to live. The fields bordering the road were touched from a withered yellow into a lush new green, the trees were coming to life, and in their budding limbs birds had appeared and were joyously

1267

chattering. The whole world, as far as she could see, was young, fresh, growing, awakened, expectant. She felt in harmony with all that she saw, and expectant too. Of what? She did not know, but somehow she found herself walking more slowly. Her face burned as from some inner fire, and she became all at once conscious of her body, vibrant and warm against the fabric of her garments.

"Ah Ao—" a voice called from somewhere.

Surprised and a little afraid, she stopped, looked around, peered over the fields into the clustered pines and through the rocky pass, but saw no one. Above her head a pair of eagles circled. She blushed, rubbed her burning face and walked on.

"Ah Ao—" someone cried again, but this time much nearer. She stopped, more puzzled, but saw no one, and started to go on, when once more she heard the same voice, now quite close, speak out, "Ah Ao, it's me!" Turning round quickly, she saw, protruding from the bushes and greenery, a head. Then slowly a young man in a long linen gown gave her a full-length view of himself, including his handsome red-buttoned cap. He was perhaps twenty years old, not a bad-looking fellow, and he wore on his face a pleased look. Ah Ao recognized him. He was the son of Li, a shop-owner in the neighboring village. His name, she knew as Ah Hsian.

"*Ai-ya!* so it's you," said Ah Ao. "You frightened me almost to death. Where did you come from?" Nevertheless, she seemed not altogether dissatisfied that he had appeared.

"I?" he demanded. "I? I just happened to be coming from town, saw you in the distance and hid myself to have some fun with you."

"You impudent rascal!" she shouted gaily, raising her hand as if to slap him. "Frightening a person to death!"

"I apologize, Ah Ao, with all my heart. The truth is I have something very important to tell you."

"For example?"

But the youth suddenly became weak or timid. He kept murmuring "I—I—I—" Then he seized her hand.

"What is this?" Ah Ao started back quickly, but for some reason her legs refused to move. Her body quivered, as from some shock, and again she felt her flesh warm beneath her garments. All the strength seemed to run out of her. He put his arms around her, pulled her toward him, and then led her into the forest. She could not summon up any resistance, her mind did not seem to work as usual, she was hardly conscious that they moved at all, and she did not utter a

1268

sound. She only knew that within she felt intolerably buoyant and enlarged.

They sat down under the leafy arm of a tree, her head resting upon his shoulder. Her eyes closed and she breathed rapidly. She felt his hand close softly over her breast, over her beating heart. She felt his lips upon hers, and suddenly she knew a bodily glow that she had never felt before.

"Caw-w-w," a magpie circling overhead, startled her, and for a moment recalled to her that the world existed. She trembled. "Ah Hsian! No, no! Don't, please! Mother will beat me to death!"

"Don't, you must not worry. Trust me, believe in me; everything will be wonderful, like this always."

His voice shook too, and some strange vibrancy of it, some summons which she had never heard before, and which would not be denied, completely overpowered her. He caressed her arms, her face, her throat. She ceased to resist.

"What is the matter with you, Ah Ao?" Widow Wang asked her daughter when, very much agitated, she returned home late that afternoon. "Fever?" She touched her forehead, which was covered with a short fringe of hair. "Have you caught a cold?"

"Nothing at all. I—I simply don't feel very well—" Ah Ao murmured, half to herself. She went to the bed and lay down and for a long time she did not stir. She knew very well the risks, the danger, the fate opening up ahead of her, but just as well she knew that she would meet Ah Hsian again, whenever he asked, yes, even tomorrow!

She expected something dreadful to happen; she prepared herself for it. In the future, after each interval with him, she waited dully for the exposure of their crime, and each time was rather surprised when no one came to denounce her. Nevertheless, she resigned herslf to ultimate discovery, but found comfort in the thought that her lover would come to her defense, take punishment as pronounced; and she imagined herself, in his moment of disgrace, going proudly to his side, sharing whatever fate imposed upon him. And what she constantly feared did happen at last, but its consequences were nothing like what she had romantically foreseen. It was just three days before the Widow Wang offered the villagers such a splendid banquet.

Behind Purple-Red Mountain there was a small hill, the name of which had long been forgotten. Halfway up its flank, nearly buried in the foliage, was a temple to the mountain god. The surrounding forests were owned by one of the great landlords, and few ventured to trespass through the leafy lanes. The place was pervaded by a ghostly stillness, but it was gentle shelter for young lovers.

On this day Lao Teh, the Spotted Face, a woodcutter, had stealthily crept into the forest to steal wood. He had gathered a load and was prepared to leave just as the setting sun splashed ruddily against the wall behind the mountain temple. The sight invited him, and he sat down on the threshold of the enclosure, sighed, lighted his pipe and gazed at the sky.

But was that not a sound? Thrusting the pipe into his girdle, he seized his ax and stood ready to combat with any wild animal that might rush forth. He waited for several minutes, tense and excited. He thought of running away but reconsidered, remembering that "an offensive is the best defensive." Picking up a stone as big as a goose egg, he threw it with all his strength into the thickest part of the forest.

To his astonishment it was not a wild beast but a man that burst from the trees. He did not stop or even look in Lao Teh's direction, but vanished like a devil. Lao Teh nevertheless saw enough of him to recognize Ah Hsian. Somewhat perplexed, he advanced toward the spot whence he had emerged.

Then, in a moment he came upon Ah Ao, languidly spread out, with her dress loosened, her dark hair starred with bits of green leaves, and altogether wearing a look of abandon. The spectacle somehow aroused in Lao Teh, the Spotted Face, an intense fury. He stared with wide-open eyes, and then he bent down and severely struck her.

"Ha! Ah Ao! The devil! You've done a fine thing!" She did not speak, but lifted up eyes that implored and eloquently begged pity. "Scandalous and shameless one! To come here in secret and lie with him!"

Later on, this scene and the subsequent abuse flung upon her by the infuriated Lao Teh remained rather obscure in Ah Ao's mind. She could not remember how, under his guidance, she returned home in disgrace, nor how news of her love spread throughout the village in a few minutes. Only afterward all the eyes she looked into were full of wrath, cold-gleaming eyes of hate. Even her mother gazed at her with anger and bitterness, yet deeper, deep down in those eyes, was a look of poignant sadness that troubled her heart. But the blows of bamboo sticks, the beatings that came in rapid succession, the curses hurled at her, not one of these caused her any pain, nor any shame, nor even the least regret.

She had expected all this, and now it had come. It was no accident, but had all along been in the certainty of fate, and she was prepared for everything that happened. The single unforeseen development that dismayed and depressed her was that her lover suffered none of the consequences and did not appear to be in the least interested in her any longer.

Even before the men guests had finished sipping the last of their wine, the women began to come for their share, and during all this time Ah Ao continued to press closely against the wall, hovering in her hiding place, hungry and shivering, not because it was cold, not because she felt any longer the fear of death, but from some nameless malady that had seized her inmost being. The women ate no more lightly than their menfolk, and like the men they dropped cynical, sardonic remarks meant to stab mother and daughter cruelly.

The air seemed charged with heightened drama when Mrs. Li, the fat mother of Ah Hsian, unexpectedly appeared at the feast. She had come, it was soon apparent, not to apologize for the part her son had taken in the affair, but on the contrary to curse the Widow Wang for permitting her daughter to induce him to commit adultery. At sight of the unhappy mother, she pointed fixedly at her and began loudly to revile her: "Miserable woman! Where there is such a daughter, there is such a mother also! And you have the 'face' to come to meet me? Actually? My son is pure, chaste, good; he has made the genuflections before the image of Confucius; he has understood well the teachings of the great sage. Yet you, shameless mother and immoral daughter, attempt to seduce and ruin him! I am resolved to die with you this instant!"

And, saying this, she did indeed rush toward the Widow Wang and appeared to be determined to dash her brains out against her. Other woman guests grouped round them, forming a little circle, not without experiencing an inner satisfaction at the scene, and comforting and soothing the wrath of the offended Mrs. Li. The fat woman in fact so far forgot her original intention that she partook heartily of the feast and in the end contented herself with muttering now and then, "She abused my son, seduced him—from now on he will be unable to raise his head above others!"

When the last guest had gone, the old woman stepped slowly into the little dark enclosure, carrying an oil lamp in her hand. She called to Ah Ao to come out and eat, and the girl dragged herself forth, but she had scarcely strength enough to stand erect. A moment ago she had thought herself famished; now she could not swallow a morsel.

Midnight. Widow Wang was not yet in bed. She moved about in the little room, picking up articles from here and there, busily arranging them in the baggage which Ah Ao must take with her when she left at tomorrow's dawn. Finally she fastened the bag.

Spring nights are brief; in a very short time the cocks began to crow. The widow awoke her son and daughter, lighted a lantern, gave them their morning food and then accompanied Ah Ao almost at once to the barrow which stood beside the door.

"Understand, daughter, it's not I who wants to desert you—you have spoiled yourself—" But the stooped figure shook with sudden tears. She seemed to brace herself against the air, and continued, managing to smile very gently: "Just be careful, Ah Ao. From now on stand firmly on your own feet, and I shall have no more cause for worry. As for me, daughter, well just think that I am dead, no longer in this world. If we can't meet here again, then perhaps after death; anyway, let's hope!"

She sat beside Ah Ao on the barrow pushed by her son until they reached the great oak, at the main road, half a mile from her home. She alighted there, bade a last farewell to her daughter and stood watching the receding lantern till, like the last flutter of life in a great void of death, its dim spark crept into utter darkness.

SU TUNG-P'O

SU TUNG-P'O (Su Shih, 1036-1101). Statesman and poet, highly revered by Chinese literary public. Also a great calligrapher and painter. Great number of his poems survive, as well as many brilliant prose essays. Collected works: *Tung-p'o ch'uan-chi*.

AUTUMN SUN

A DESCENDANT of Yüeh Wang, a worthy gentleman, dwells in a village without soil and croons verses without words. He once told Tung-p'o, the retired Scholar, that his mind was as pure as the rays of the Autumn Sun, his emotions as peaceful as its tranquillity. 'I love virtue,' he said, 'and am determined to bring it to perfection with the persistence of the Autumn Sun. I dislike all crops, and, in my dislike, desire to chastise them even as the Autumn Sun strikes that group of trees. So I am anxious to write some verses upon it. What does the master think?'

The retired Scholar with a smile answered, 'How can a gentleman like yourself appreciate the Autumn Sun? Born into a luxurious mansion, when older you roamed through the Emperor's Courts.— Out of doors you were sheltered by a large umbrella, at home you were waited upon behind curtain and veil. You could stand the hot weather up to the point of warmth and the winter to the point of coolness—that's all! What then can you know about the Autumn Sun?

'Now, a man like myself really appreciates it. When the summer floods become excessive, when the clouds become vapour and the rains fall, when the thunder rolls and the lightning flashes, rivers and lakes merge together and the god of the soil is in danger of drowning, then do boats sail on the city walls, the fish and the dragon enter the house, mildew covers the utensils, frogs and earth-worms crawl about the tables. At night, one must move five times to avoid the damp; in daytime, one must dry the clothes in the sun for three changes. But still there is nothing in all this to worry about!

'Now, in San-Wu there is a plot of ploughed land. The ripened grain becomes covered with fungi, the matured rice curls up into the mud. Drains and dykes overflow into one other, walls are ruined with holes and collapse into the mud. One's eyes glisten with tears as the smoke from the fuel in boiler and cauldron fills the room. All around, the neighborhood is silent. The crane cries in the doorway; the wife rises in the night and heaves a deep sigh, when she reckons up the number of foodless days, and wonders whether the clothing will last to the end of the year.

'Suddenly the cauldron sends out sparks in myriad confusion, and the lamp-wick hangs down in double blossom. Clear blows the west wind; the drums and bells resound. The slaves joyously tell me that this is the sign of no more rain. So I rise early to divine it, and I find that Hesperus, the evening star, is placid and no longer flashes as it bathes in the Valley of Sunshine and rises over Fu-Sang. Ere one has winked, the whole prospect has changed with wingéd flight to the crossbeams of the house. In that moment I feel as though I am awakening from a drunken slumber, like a dumb man who can speak, a paralytic who can rise and walk, or as though I am returning to my ancestral village and get my first glimpse of the elders! Have you, Sir, also tasted joy like this?' 'That's fine!' he answered, 'Although I cannot say that I have personally experienced this, yet I can well appreciate it.'

'The Sun,' continued the retired Scholar, 'moves through the Southern and the Northern Heavens in different ways. Its fierce and fiery heat is not the result of tyranny, nor is its soothing warmth due to tenderness, for the warmth of to-day is the heat of yesterday. Why then consider Summer as Tun and Winter as Ts'ui? We little men are easily vexed or glad, so that the dread of summer or the love of winter is just the same to us as the numbers 3 and 4 to a crowd of monkeys!

'From now onwards, understand this and be not in doubt. Live without plastering the door; go out without putting on a labourer's hat; and do not complain of the summer heat if you would not forget the virtues of the Autumn Sun.'

Whereat my nobleman clapped his hands and laughed as he wrote this down.

JONATHAN SWIFT

JONATHAN SWIFT (Irish, 1667-1745). Creator of one of world's most brutal and morbid satires on mankind, *Gulliver's Travels*, that later generations used as a children's book. Other famous satire, *The Tale of a Tub*, castigates Christianity. A masterful prose stylist, whose life was embittered by political setbacks. His ambiguous relations with two women, "Stella" and "Vanessa," have intrigued scholars, but remain unsolved.

THE EMPEROR OF LILLIPUT

THE Emperor is taller by almost the breadth of my nail than any of his court, which alone is sufficient to strike an awe into the beholders. His features are strong and masculine, with an Austrian lip, and arched nose; his complexion olive, his countenance erect, his body and limbs well-proportioned, all his movements graceful, and his deportment majestic. He was then past his prime, being twenty-eight years and three-quarters old, of which he had reigned seven in great felicity, and generally victorious. For the better convenience of beholding him, I lay on my side, so that my face was parallel to his, and he stood but three yards off. However, I have had him since many times in my hand, and therefore cannot be mistaken in my description. His dress was very plain and simple, and the fashion of it between the Asiatic and the European; but he had on his head a light helmet of gold, adorned with jewels, and a plume on the crest.

He held his sword drawn in his hand, to defend himself if I should happen to break loose. It was almost three inches long; the hilt and scabbard were gold, enriched with diamonds. His voice was shrill, but very clear and articulate; and I could distinctly hear it when I stood up. His Imperial Majesty spoke often to me, and I returned answers; but neither of us could understand a syllable.

THOUGHTS AND APHORISMS

AN old miser kept a tame jackdaw, that used to steal pieces of money, and hide them in a hole, which the cat observing, asked, "Why he would hoard up those round shining things that he could make no use of?"

"Why," said the jackdaw, "my master has a whole chestful, and makes no more use of them than I."

If the men of wit and genius would resolve never to complain in their works of critics and detractors, the next age would not know that they ever had any.

I never wonder to see men wicked, but I often wonder to see them not ashamed.

Imaginary evils soon become real ones, by indulging our reflections on them; as he, who in a melancholy fancy sees something like a face on the wall or the wainscot, can, by two or three touches with lead pencil, make it look visible, and agreeing with what he fancied.

Men of great parts are often unfortunate in the management of public business, because they art apt to go out of the common road by the quickness of their imagination. This I once said to my Lord Bolingbroke, and desired he would observe, that the clerks in his office used a sort of ivory knife with a blunt edge to divide a sheet of paper, which never failed to cut it even, only requiring a steady hand; whereas if they should make use of a sharp penknife, the sharpness would make it often go out of the crease, and disfigure the paper.

"He who does not provide for his own house," St. Paul says, "is worse than an infidel!" And I think he who provides only for his own house is just equal with an infidel.

When I am reading a book, whether wise or silly, it seems to me to be alive, and talking to me.

I never yet knew a wag (as the term is) who was not a dunce.

A person reading to me a dull poem of his own making, I prevailed on him to scratch out six lines together; in turning over the leaf, the ink being wet, it marked as many lines on the other side; whereof the poet complaining, I bid him be easy, for it would be better if those were out too.

We have just enough religion to make us hate, but not enough to make us love one another.

When we desire or solicit anything, our minds run wholly on the good side or circumstances of it; when it is obtained, our minds run wholly on the bad ones.

The latter part of a wise man's life is taken up in curing the follies, prejudices, and false opinions he had contracted in the former.

Would a writer know how to behave himself with relation to posterity, let him consider in old books what he finds that he is glad to know, and what omissions he most laments.

It is grown a word of course for writers to say, "the critical age," as divines say, "this sinful age."

It is pleasant to observe how free the present age is in laying taxes on the next: "Future ages shall talk of this: this shall be famous to all posterity;" whereas their time and thoughts will be taken up about present things, as ours are now.

I never heard a finer piece of satire against lawyers, than that of astrologers, when they pretend by rules of art to tell when a suit will end, and whether to the advantage of the plaintiff or defendant; thus making the matter depend entirely upon the influence of the stars, without the least regard to the merits of the cause.

I have known some men possessed of good qualities, which were very serviceable to others, but useless to themselves; like a sun-dial on the front of a house, to inform the neighbors and passengers, but not the owner within.

If a man would register all his opinions upon love, politics, religion, learning, &c., beginning from his youth, and so go on to old age, what a bundle of inconsistencies and contradictions would appear at last!

The stoical scheme of supplying our wants by lopping off our desires, is like cutting off our feet when we want shoes.

The reason why so few marriages are happy, is because young ladies spend their time in making nets, not in making cages.

The power of fortune is confessed only by the miserable; for the happy impute all their success to prudence or merit.

Ambition often puts men upon doing the meanest offices; so climbing is performed in the same posture with creeping.

Although men are accused for not knowing their own weakness, yet perhaps as few know their own strength. It is in men as in soils, where sometimes there is a vein of gold which the owner knows not of.

An idle reason lessens the weight of the good ones you gave before.

Arbitrary power is the natural object of temptation to a prince; as wine or women to a young fellow, or a bribe to a judge, or avarice to old age, or vanity to a woman.

The humor of exploding many things under the name of trifles, fopperies and only imaginary goods, is a very false proof either of wisdom or magnanimity, and a great check to virtuous actions. For instance, with regard to fame; there is in most people a reluctance and unwillingness to be forgotten. We observe, even among the vulgar, how fond they are to have an inscription over their grave. It requires but little philosophy to discover and observe that there is no intrinsic value in all this; however, if it be founded in our nature, as an incitement to virtue, it ought not to be ridiculed.

Complaint is the largest tribute Heaven receives, and the sincerest part of our devotion.

The common fluency of speech in many men, and most women, is owing to a scarcity of matter, and a scarcity of words; for whoever is a master of language, and hath a mind full of ideas, will be apt in speaking to hesitate upon the choice of both; whereas common speakers have only one set of ideas, and one set of words to clothe them in; and these are always ready at the mouth; so people come faster out of church when it is almost empty, than when a crowd is at the door.

To be vain is rather a mark of humility than pride. Vain men delight in telling what honors have been done them, what great company they have kept, and the like, by which they plainly confess that these honors were more than their due, and such as their friends would not believe if they had not been told: whereas a man truly proud thinks the greatest honors below his merit, and consequently scorns to boast. I therefore deliver it as a maxim, that whoever desires the character of a proud man ought to conceal his vanity.

I have known several persons of great fame for wisdom in public affairs and councils governed by foolish servants.

I have known great ministers, distinguished for wit and learning, who preferred none but dunces.

I have known men of great valor cowards to their wives.

I have known men of the greatest cunning perpetually cheated.

Dignity, high station, or great riches, are in some sort necessary to old men, in order to keep the younger at a distance, who are otherwise too apt to insult them upon the score of their age.

Every man desires to live long, but no man would be old.

Love of flattery, in most men, proceeds from the mean opinion they have of themselves; in women, from the contrary.

Kings are commonly said to have long hands; I wish they had as long ears.

Princes, in their infancy, childhood and youth, are said to discover prodigious parts and wit, to speak things that surprise and astonish: strange, so many hopeful princes, so many shameful kings! If they happen to die young, they would have been prodigies of wisdom and virtue: if they live, they are often prodigies, indeed, but of another sort.

Apollo was held the god of physic and sender of diseases. Both were originally the same trade, and still continue.

"That was excellently observed," said I, when I read a passage in an author where his opinion agrees with mine: when we differ, there I pronounce him to be mistaken.

Very few men, properly speaking, live at present; but are providing to live another time.

As universal a practice as lying is, and as easy a one as it seems, I do not remember to have heard three good lies in all my conversation, even from those who were most celebrated in that faculty.

ALGERNON CHARLES SWINBURNE

ALGERNON CHARLES SWINBURNE (English, 1837-1909). Poet of late Victorian Era, who shocked his contemporaries by personal life (dipsomaniac) and literary output (earlier works, *Poems and Ballads*, seemed sex-obsessed). Other famous works: *Atalanta in Calydon* and *Songs Before Sunrise*. Master of verbal music and the singing line.

WHEN THE HOUNDS OF SPRING

When the hounds of spring are on winter's traces,
  The mother of months in meadow or plain
Fills the shadows and windy places
  With lisp of leaves and ripple of rain;

And the brown bright nightingale amorous
Is half assuaged for Itylus,
For the Thracian ships and the foreign faces,
    The tongueless vigil, and all the pain.

Come with bows bent, and with emptying of quivers,
    Maiden most perfect, lady of light,
With a noise of winds and many rivers,
    With a clamor of waters, and with might;
Bind on thy sandals, O thou most fleet,
Over the splendor and speed of thy feet;
For the faint east quickens, the wan west shivers,
    Round the feet of the day and the feet of the night.

Where shall we find her, how shall we sing to her,
    Fold our hands round her knees, and cling?
O that man's heart were as fire and could spring to her,
    Fire, or the strength of the streams that spring!
For the stars and the winds are unto her
As raiment, as songs of the harp-player;
For the risen stars and the fallen cling to her,
    And the southwest-wind and the west-wind sing.

For winter's rains and ruins are over,
    And all the season of snows and sins;
The days dividing lover and lover,
    The light that loses, the night that wins;
And time remembered is grief forgotten,
And frosts are slain and flowers begotten,
And in green underwood and cover
    Blossom by blossom the spring begins.

The full streams feed on flower of rushes,
    Ripe grasses trammel a traveling foot,
The faint fresh flame of the young year flushes
    From leaf to flower and flower to fruit;
And fruit and leaf are as gold and fire,
And the oat is heard above the lyre,
And the hoofed heel of a satyr crushes
    The chesnut-husk at the chestnut-root.

And Pan by noon and Bacchus by night,
    Fleeter of foot than the fleet-foot kid,
Follows with dancing and fills with delight
    The Maenad and the Bassarid;
And soft as lips that laugh and hide
The laughing leaves of the trees divide,
And screen from seeing and leave in sight
    The god pursuing the maiden hid.

The ivy falls with the Bacchanal's hair
    Over her eyebrows hiding her eyes;
The wild vine slipping down leaves bare
    Her bright breast shortening into sighs;
The wild vine slips with the weight of its leaves,
But the berried ivy catches and cleaves
To the limbs that glitter, the feet that scare
    The wolf that follows, the fawn that flies.

MAN

Before the beginning of years,
    There came to the making of man
Time, with a gift of tears;
    Grief, with a glass that ran;
Pleasure, with pain for leaven;
    Summer, with flowers that fell;
Remembrance fallen from heaven,
    And madness risen from hell;
Strength without hands to smite;
    Love that endures for a breath;
Night, the shadow of light,
    And life, the shadow of death.
And the high gods took in hand
    Fire, and the falling of tears,
And a measure of sliding sand
    From under the feet of the years;
And froth and drift of the sea;
    And dust of the laboring earth;
And bodies of things to be
    In the houses of death and of birth;

And wrought with weeping and laughter,
  And fashioned with loathing and love,
With life before and after
  And death beneath and above,
For a day and a night and a morrow,
  That his strength might endure for a span
With travail and heavy sorrow,
  The holy spirit of man.

From the winds of the north and the south
  They gathered as unto strife;
They breathed upon his mouth,
  They filled his body with life;
Eyesight and speech they wrought
  For the veils of the soul therein,
A time for labor and thought,
They gave him light in his ways,
  And love, and a space for delight,
And beauty and length of days,
  And night, and sleep in the night.
His speech is a burning fire;
  With his lips he travaileth;
In his heart is a blind desire,
  In his eyes foreknowledge of death;
He weaves, and is clothed with derision;
  Sows, and he shall not reap;
His life is a watch or a vision
  Between a sleep and a sleep.

THE GARDEN OF PROSERPINE

Here, where the world is quiet;
  Here, where all trouble seems
Dead winds' and spent waves' riot
  In doubtful dreams of dreams;
I watch the green field growing
For reaping folk and sowing,
For harvest-time and moving,
  A sleepy world of streams.

I am tired of tears and laughter,
  And men that laugh and weep;
Of what may come hereafter
  For men that sow to reap:
I am weary of days and hours,
Blown buds of barren flowers,
Desires and dreams and powers
  And everything but sleep.

Here life has death for neighbor,
  And far from eye or ear
Wan waves and wet winds labor,
  Weak ships and spirits steer;
They drive adrift, and whither
They wot not who make thither;
But no such winds blow hither,
And no such things grow here.

No growth of moor or coppice,
  No heather-flower or vine,
But bloomless buds of poppies,
  Green grapes of Proserpine,
Pale beds of blowing rushes,
Where no leaf blooms or blushes
Save this whereout she crushes
  For dead men deadly wine.

Pale, without name or number,
  In fruitless fields of corn,
They bow themselves and slumber
  All night till light is born;
And like a soul belated,
In hell and heaven unmated,
By cloud and mist abated
  Comes out of darkness morn.

Though one were strong as seven,
  He too with death shall dwell,
Nor wake with wings in heaven,
  Nor weep for pains in hell;

Though one were fair as roses,
His beauty clouds and closes;
And well though love reposes,
    In the end it is not well.

Pale, beyond porch and portal,
    Crowned with calm leaves, she stands
Who gathers all things mortal
    With cold immortal hands;
Her languid lips are sweeter
Than love's who fears to greet her,
To men that mix and meet her
    From many times and lands.

She waits for each and other,
    She waits for all men born;
Forgets the earth her mother,
    The life of fruits and corn;
And spring and seed and swallow
Take wing for her and follow
Where summer song rings hollow
    And flowers are put to scorn.

There go the loves that wither,
    The old loves with wearier wings;
And all dead years draw thither,
    And all disastrous things;
Dead dreams of days forsaken,
Blind buds that snows have shaken,
Wild leaves that winds have taken,
    Red strays of ruined springs.

We are not sure of sorrow;
    And joy was never sure;
Today will die tomorrow;
    Time stoops to no man's lure;
And love, grown faint and fretful,
With lips but half regretful
Sighs, and with eyes forgetful
    Weeps that no loves endure.

From too much love of living,
　From hope and fear set free,
We thank with brief thanksgiving
　Whatever gods may be
That no life lives for ever;
That dead men rise up never;
That even the weariest river
　Winds somewhere safe at sea.

Then star nor sun shall waken,
　Nor any change of light:
Nor sound of waters shaken,
　Nor any sound or sight:
Nor wintry leaves nor vernal,
Nor days nor things diurnal;
Only the sleep eternal
　In an eternal night.

T

RABINDRANATH TAGORE

RABINDRANATH TAGORE (Indian, 1861-1941). Foremost Bengali **poet**. Member of famous family of artists, musicians and reformers. When translated, won immediate favor in the West. Outstanding works: *Chitrā* (*Beauty*), *Gitanjali* (*Handful of Songs*), and *Gorā*, a novel after Kipling.

TO NATURE

1

Thou tanglest my heart in a hundred nooses of love,
What is this thy play?
It is but a little feeble life—
Why so many bonds to bind it?
At every turn and every moment
Thou winnest my love with thy wiles,
But hast none to give, thou stealer of hearts!
I wander about in search of thy heart,
      O cruel Nature;
So many flowers, such light, such songs and scents,
      But where is love?
Hidden in the wealth of thy beauty thou laughest
      While we weep.

2

Day and night in the deserted playfield
      Thou playest in jest;
We wot not whom thou lovest or slightest;
He to whom thou art kind and loving in the morning,
The evening finds him lying neglected in the dust.

Still I love thee and cannot forget,
                    Thou enchantress!
Thy loveless embrace awakes in the heart
                    A thousand songs;
In happiness and grief and misery I live in the sunlight,
Nor crave the frozen stillness of the endless night.

3

Half open, half-veiled, thy face
                    Is the abode of mystery;
To the heart it brings the ache of love
                    Mingled with fear;
Thy ever-new phases pass understanding,
And the heart is filled with laughter and tears.
Stretching forth my heart and soul I rush towards thee,
                    But thou eludest my grasp;
I see the slight, sweet, mocking smile
                    On thy sun-red lips;
If I wish to flee thou spreadest thy nets for my feet,—
What arts, what strength. fleet-footed, quick of tongue!

4

Thou knowest not thy own limits,
                    Thine own mystery;
So in the blind night when the seven worlds
                    Are steeped in slumber,
Curious and silent-footed thou standest in the sky
Lighting million torches of star-rays.

5

In another place thou sittest ever lone
                    With a vow of eternal silence,
All around is the hard, treeless. dreary
                    Solitude of the desert;
Eon after eon rise overhead the sun and the moon,
They look and they pass without a word.

6

Again, thou rompest and playest like a girl
       With hair and garments flying in the wind,
With laughter overflowing as a fountain,
       Without a trace of shame;
Thy heart cannot hold its own measure,—
Words and songs without end.

7

Yet again with wrath-lit frenzied eyes,
       Slaying in a moment,
Thou strikest the breast of hapless Earth
       With incessant curses of fire;
Sometimes in the dusk moved by a noble grief
A pale shadow as of pity falls on thy face.

8

It is thus thou hast conquered
       Innumerable hearts;
For ages and ages thy countenance
       Has been fresh and sweet;
Disguised in many forms thou art near all,
Yet hast thou given thyself to none.

9

The more am I baffled the more I remember
       The great opulence of thy beauty;
So grows my love as increases my pain,
       As I laugh and cry;
The farther thou goest the heavier is my soul trammelled,
The less I understand thee the more I love thee.

JUNICHIRO TANIZAKI

JUNICHIRO TANIZAKI (Japanese, 1886-   ). One of Japan's most distinguished modern novelists. Started his career under Western influence of Baudelaire, Wilde and Poe. After earthquake of 1923, turned to classical Japanese literature and wrote most important novels, including *Some Prefer Nettles*. Recently engaged in new translation of *The Tale of Genji*.

From *SOME PREFER NETTLES*

O-HISA, his father-in-law's mistress, drove a moth from the clear-lacquer table, the breeze from her fan cool through Kaname's light kimono. The clean smell of spring mushrooms rose faintly from the soup. It was pitch-dark now in the garden, and the croaking of the rain-frogs had risen to a clamor.

"I'd like to learn the Tokyo style of singing myself."

"You'll be scolded for dangerous thoughts. And I'm afraid I'll have to join the scolding—you've no idea how much better the Osaka style is for you."

"I don't object to it so much. But the teacher is rather a problem."

"Let me see—you go to someone in Osaka, don't you?"

"That's right. But I was thinking more of the teacher here." Kaname laughed.

"He's unbearable. Lecture, lecture, lecture."

"All old people are that way." Kaname laughed again. "That reminds me. I noticed the bran bag. You still use it?"

"That's right. Your father-in-law uses soap himself, but he won't let me. He says women mustn't ruin their skin with soap."

"And the nightingale dung?"

"I go on with that too. But it hasn't made my skin a bit whiter."

Kaname was finishing off the meal with his second decanter of saké, and O-hisa had brought in a dish of loquats when the telephone rang. She ran to answer it, leaving a half-peeled loquat in an antique glass saucer.

"Yes . . . yes . . . I see. I'll tell him." Kaname could see her in the hall nodding into the telephone. In a minute or two she was back. "Misako will stay here too, he says. They'll be home before long."

"Really? And she said she wouldn't. . . . It seems an awfully long time since I last spent the night here."

"It has been a long time."

More than that, though, it seemed a long time since he and his wife, Misako, had slept alone together. There had of course been those two or three nights—their first alone in he did not know how many years—when little Hiroshi was in Tokyo with Takanatsu; but they had been able then to lie down side by side and go off to sleep as unconcernedly as two strangers at an inn, so deadened had their marital nerves become. He suspected that tonight, however, her father hoped for great changes to come from throwing them together. This benevolent scheming was a little disconcerting, but not enough so that Kaname felt pressed to try for an escape. He was sure that the time had passed when one night could make a difference.

"Hasn't it grown heavy?" said Kaname. "Not a breath of air." He looked out to the veranda. The incense, on the point of going out, sent a column of smoke straight and unwavering into the air. The breeze in the garden had died, and with it the breeze from O-hisa's fan, motionless in her lap and as though forgotten.

"It's clouding over. I wonder if it will rain."

"It might well. I almost hope it will."

Above the motionless leaves a star here and there broke through the clouds. For a moment he thought he could hear, as with a sixth sense, Misako's voice fighting back the old man; and he knew that almost unconsciously he had come to a point where he could support his wife's decision with an even stronger one of his own.

"What time do you suppose it is?"

"Eight thirty, possibly."

"Only eight thirty. Isn't it quiet, though?"

"It's still early, but you may want to go to bed. They should be back before long."

"I suppose it seemed from what he said over the telephone that the conversation was not going very well?" Kaname was secretly more interested in having O-hisa's views than the old man's.

"Shall I bring you something to read?"

"Thank you. What sort of things do you read?"

"He brings home old wood-block books and tells me I should read them. But I can't get interested in the dusty old things."

"You'd rather read a woman's magazine?"

"He says if I have time for that sort of trash I should be practising my calligraphy."

"What copybook does he have you on?"

"There are a couple. *O-ie* method."

"Well, let me look at one of your dusty books."

1289

"How about a travel guide?"

"That should do, I suppose."

"Let's go out to the cottage, then. I have everything ready."

O-hisa led the way along a covered passage to the garden cottage. As she slid back the paper-paneled door to the rear of the tearoom, Kaname caught the rustling of a mosquito net in the darkness beyond. A cool breath of air came through the open door.

"The wind seems to have come up again."

"And all of a sudden it's a little chilly," Kaname answered.

"We'll have a shower before long."

The mosquito net rustled again, this time not from the wind. O-hisa felt her way inside and, groping for the lamp; at Kaname's pillow, turned the switch.

"Shall I get you a larger bulb?"

"This will do nicely. The print's always big in old books."

"Suppose I leave the shutters open. You won't want it too hot."

"I wish you would. I can close them later."

Kaname crawled under the net himself when O-hisa had gone. The room was not a large one, and the linen mosquito netting cut it off smaller yet, so that the two mattresses were almost touching. It was a novel arrangement for Kaname and Misako. At home these summer nights they hung up as large a mosquito net as possible and slept, one at each end, with Hiroshi between them. Kaname rolled over on his stomach, a little bored, and lighted a cigarette. He tried to make out the picture in the alcove beyond the light-green netting. Something in modest, neutral colors, a landscape it seemed to be, wider than it was high. With the light inside the net, however, the rest of the room lay in deep shadow, and he could make out neither the details nor the artist's signature. Below it in a bowl was what he took to be a blue and white porcelain burner. There was a faint smell of incense through the room—he noticed it for the first time. Plum blossom, he judged. For an instant he thought he saw O-hisa's face, faint and white, in a shadowy corner beside the bed. He started up, but quickly caught himself. It was the puppet the old man had brought back from Awaji, a lady puppet in a modest dotted kimono.

A gust of wind came through the open window and the shower began. Kaname could hear large drops falling against the leaves. He raised himself on an elbow and stared out into the wooden depths of the garden. A small green frog, a refugee from the rain, clung halfway up the fluttering side of the net, its belly reflecting the light from the bed lamp.

"It's finally begun."

The door slid open, and this time, half a dozen old-style Japanese books in arm, it was no puppet that sat faintly white in the shadows beyond the netting.

T'AO CH'IEN

T'AO CH'IEN (Chinese, 372-427). Profoundly influential rustic poet of China. After brief official career, retired to live rural life. His prose poem, *Kuei-ch'ü-lai tz'u (Returning to Live on the Farm)*, and shorter lyric poems are known to all Chinese school children. Simplicity of his life and work earned him reputation as "the most harmonious product of Chinese culture."

RETURNING TO LIVE ON THE FARM

Six Poems

When I was young, I was not fitted for a worldly rhythm.
By nature I loved the mountains and the hills.
I fell into the net of the world by mistake,
And I have stayed there for thirty years.
A bird in the cage longs for the old forest,
And a fish in the pond thinks of his former pool.
I cultivated rough land in the south,
And, keeping to simple ways, I returned to the field and garden.
I have over ten *mu* of land
And a thatched house of eight or nine rooms.
Birch and willow shade the back eaves;
Peach and plum spread their branches in the front courtyard.
Villages lie in the distance.
Smoke rises like mist from faraway fields.
Dogs bark in hidden lanes,
And roosters crow.
There is no worldly hubbub.
There is space, and I have leisure.
For a long time I was in a cage,
But now I am back with nature.

1291

In the country there is little of human affairs.
The lane has but few wheel tracks,
And white sun shines on the closed door.
In the empty room I have no thoughts of the world.
Often, strolling along the winding roads
And wearing cotton garments, we visit each other.
When we meet, we do not gossip,
But simply talk about how the hemp and mulberry have shot up.
Daily the hemp and mulberry grow taller,
And our fields each day are extended.
Frequently we fear that a frost will come
And kill the plants as if they were weeds.

I plant beans at the foot of the southern hill.
Grass flourishes, but the beans rarely sprout.
In the early morning I go out to weed,
And in the moonlight I return, carrying my hoe.
The path is narrow, and as the shrubs and grasses are tall,
Evening dew moistens my clothes.
These wet clothes are not worth worrying about.
I only hope that my dream will not leave me.

I have been away from the pleasure of the hills and streams,
From the rushing sound of the wild trees.
Wearing a raincoat, I go with my nephews and children
To walk in the meadows
And stroll on the hills and dikes.
This seems to be a spot where once someone lived;
There are the remains of a well and an oven,
And mulberry and bamboo wither among the other trees.
I ask a wood-gatherer
What kind of man lived here.
He replies
That all have died,
And that they saw the shift of power at court.
These words are not empty.
Man's life is like a shifting illusion;
At the end we shall return to emptiness.

Depressed and alone, I take my staff and return,
Passing along the zigzag, rough, and thorny roads.

The stream of the mountain is clear and shallow;
Coming upon it I wash my feet.
I strain my fresh wine
And, having a chicken, invite my close neighbors.
The sunset enters my gate.
The glow of firewood takes the place of a bright candle.
When I am happy I regret that the evening is too short,
And in no time it is dawn!

I plant sprouts on the eastern hill,
And they grow lushly in the field.
Although I am tired of carrying the hoe,
This muddy wine comforts me.
The sun sets, and I return with a cart of firewood.
The road is dim, the light already dusky.
Returning farmers watch the chimney smoke.
A child, waiting behind the crack of the door under the eaves,
Asks what I have been doing.
For a hundred years I have been on the road,
And now I only wish that the mulberry and hemp were ripe.
In the month of the silkworm we can weave,
And my simple heart wants just this!
I clear three paths and watch for my friends.

TORQUATO TASSO

TORQUATO TASSO (Italian, 1544-1595). Classicist of the idyllic pastoral
and ardent religiosity. Most celebrated works: *Rinaldo*, epic poem; *Aminta*,
pastoral play; *Jerusalem Delivered*, Counter-Reformation epic of the Crusades.
In later years his mind was clouded as result of excessive religious scruples.

THE GOLDEN AGE

O lovely age of gold!
Not that the rivers rolled
With milk. or that the woods wept honey-dew;
Not that the ready ground
Produced without a wound,
Or the mild serpent had no tooth that slew:

1293

Not that a cloudless blue
    Forever was in sight,
Or that the heaven, which burns
And now is cold by turns,
Looked out in glad and everlasting light;
No, nor that even the insolent ships from far
Brought war to no new lands, nor riches worse than war.

    But solely that that vain
    And breath-invented pain,
That idol of mistake, that worshiped cheat,
    That Honor—since so called
    By vulgar minds appalled,—
Played not the tyrant with our nature yet.
    It had not come to fret
    The sweet and happy fold
    Of gentle human kind;
    Nor did its hard law bind
Souls nursed in freedom; but that law of gold,
That glad and golden law, all free. all fitted.
Which Nature's own hand wrote—what pleases is permitted.

    Then among streams and flowers.
    The little winged Powers
Went singing carols without torch or bow;
    The nymphs and shepherds sat
    Mingling with innocent chat
Sports and low whispers, and with whispers low,
    Kisses that would not go.
    The maid, her childhood o'er,
    Kept not her bloom uneyed,
    Which now a veil must hide,
Nor the crisp apples which her bosom bore;
And oftentimes, in river or in lake,
The lover and his love their merry bath would take.

    'Twas thou, thou, Honor, first
    That didst deny our thirst
Its drink, and on the fount thy covering set;
    Thou badst kind eyes withdraw
    Into constrainèd awe,

And keep the secret for their tears to wet;
    Thou gatherdst in a net
      The tresses from the air,
    And mad'st the sports and plays
    Turn all to sullen ways,
And put'st on speech a rein—in steps a care.
Thy work it is—thou shade that wilt not move—
That what was once the gift, is now the theft, of love.

    Our sorrows and our pains,
    These are thy noble gains.
But oh, thou Love's and Nature's masterer,
    Thou conqueror of the crowned,
    What dost thou on this ground,
Too small a circle for thy mighty sphere?
    Go, and make slumber dear
      To the renowned and high;
    We here, a lowly race,
    Can live without thy grace,
After the use of mild antiquity.
    Go, let us love—since years
No truce allow, and life soon disappears.
Go let us love: the daylight dies, is born;
    But unto us the light
Dies once for all, and sleep brings on eternal night.

ALFRED LORD TENNYSON

ALFRED LORD TENNYSON (English. 1808-1892). Poet of English national life. Artful, subtle, often morbid. In disciplined sensibility and concern for traditional morality, represents peak of Victorian literature. Most popular work: *Idylls of the King*, based on Arthurian legends. Most moving: *In Memoriam*, elegy on his friend Arthur Hallam. Succeeded Wordsworth as Poet Laureate.

CHORIC SONG FROM THE LOTOS-EATERS

I

There is sweet music here that softer falls
Than petals from blown roses on the grass,
Or night-dews on still waters between walls
Of shadowy granite, in a gleaming pass;

1295

Music that gentlier on the spirit lies,
Than tired eyelids upon tired eyes;
Music that brings sweet sleep down from the blissful skies.
Here are cool mosses deep,
And through the moss the ivies creep,
And in the stream the long-leaved flowers weep,
And from the craggy ledge the poppy hangs in sleep.

II

Why are we weighed upon with heaviness,
And utterly consumed with sharp distress,
While all things else have rest from weariness?
All things have rest; why should we toil alone,
We only toil, who are the first of things,
And make perpetual moan,
Still from one sorrow to another thrown;
Nor ever fold our wings,
And cease from wanderings,
Nor steep our brows in slumber's holy balm;
Nor harken what the inner spirit sings,
"There is no joy but calm!"—
Why should we only toil, the roof and crown of things?

III

Lo! in the middle of the wood,
The folded leaf is wooed from out the bud
With winds upon the branch, and there
Grows green and broad, and takes no care,
Sun-steeped at noon, and in the moon
Nightly dew-fed; and turning yellow
Falls, and floats adown the air.
Lo! sweetened with the summer light,
The full-juiced apple, waxing over-mellow,
Drops in a silent autumn night.
All its allotted length of days
The flower ripens in its place,
Ripens and fades, and falls, and hath no toil,
Fast-rooted in the fruitful soil.

IV

Hateful is the dark-blue sky,
Vaulted o'er the dark-blue sea.
Death is the end of life; ah, why
Should life all labor be?
Let us alone. Time driveth onward fast,
And in a little while our lips are dumb.
Let us alone. What is it that will last?
All things are taken from us, and become
Portions and parcels of the dreadful past.
Let us alone. What pleasure can we have
To war with evil? Is there any peace
In ever climbing up the climbing wave?
All things have rest, and ripen toward the grave
In silence—ripen, fall, and cease.
Give us long rest or death, dark death, or dreamful ease.

V

How sweet it were, hearing the downward stream,
With half-shut eyes ever to seem
Falling asleep in a half-dream!
To dream and dream, like yonder amber light,
Which will not leave the myrrh-bush on the height;
To hear each other's whispered speech;
Eating the Lotos day by day,
To watch the crisping ripples on the beach,
And tender curving lines of creamy spray;
To lend our hearts and spirits wholly
To the influence of mild-minded melancholy;
To muse and brood and live again in memory,
With those old faces of our infancy
Heaped over with a mound of grass,
Two handfuls of white dust, shut in an urn of brass!

VI

Dear is the memory of our wedded lives,
And dear the last embraces of our wives

And their warm tears; but all hath suffered change;
For surely now our household hearths are cold,
Our sons inherit us, our looks are strange,
And we should come like ghosts to trouble joy.
Or else the island princes over-bold
Have eat our substance, and the minstrel sings
Before them of the ten years' war in Troy,
And our great deeds, as half-forgotten things.
Is there confusion in the little isle?
Let what is broken so remain.
The gods are hard to reconcile;
'Tis hard to settle order once again.
There *is* confusion worse than death,
Trouble on trouble, pain on pain,
Long labor unto aged breath,
Sore task to hearts worn out by many wars
And eyes grown dim with gazing on the pilot stars.

VII

But, propped on beds of amaranth and moly,
How sweet—while warm airs lull us, blowing lowly—
With half-dropped eyelid still,
Beneath a heaven dark and holy,
To watch the long bright river drawing slowly
His waters from the purple hill—
To hear the dewy echoes calling
From cave to cave through the thick-twined vine—
To watch the emerald-colored water falling
Through many a woven acanthus-wreath divine!
Only to hear and see the far-off sparkling brine,
Only to hear were sweet, stretched out beneath the pine.

VIII

The Lotos blooms below the barren peak,
The Lotos blows by every winding creek;
All day the wind breathes low with mellower tone;
Through every hollow cave and alley lone
Round and round the spicy downs the yellow Lotos-dust is blown.

We have had enough of action, and of motion we,
Rolled to starboard, rolled to larboard, when the surge was seething
  free,
Where the wallowing monster spouted his foam-fountains in the sea.
Let us swear an oath, and keep it with an equal mind,
In the hollow Lotos-land to live and lie reclined
On the hills like gods together, careless of mankind.
For they lie beside their nectar, and the bolts are hurled
Far below them in the valleys, and the clouds are lightly curled
Round their golden houses, girdled with the gleaming world;
Where they smile in secret, looking over wasted lands,
Blight and famine, plague and earthquake, roaring deeps and fiery
  sands,
Clanging fights, and flaming towns, and sinking ships, and praying
  hands.
But they smile, they find a music centered in a doleful song
Steaming up, a lamentation and an ancient tale of wrong,
Like a tale of little meaning though the words are strong;
Chanted from an ill-used race of men that cleave the soil,
Sow the seed, and reap the harvest with enduring toil,
Storing yearly little dues of wheat, and wine and oil;
Till they perish and they suffer—some, 'tis whispered—down in
  hell
Suffer endless anguish, others in Elysian valleys dwell,
Resting weary limbs at last on beds of asphodel.
Surely, surely, slumber is more sweet than toil, the shore
Than labor in the deep mid-ocean, wind and wave and oar;
Oh, rest ye, brother mariners, we will not wander more.

WILLIAM MAKEPEACE THACKERAY

WILLIAM MAKEPEACE THACKERAY (English, 1811-1863). Voluminous
novelist of Victorian Period. Well born, wrote unceasingly after losing fortune.
A keen satirist of social snobbery, using unaffected conversational, sometimes
sermonizing, style. *Vanity Fair*, one of the masterpieces of the English novel,
Becky Sharp one of its celebrated heroines. Other novels: *Pendennis, The
Virginians, Henry Esmond, The Newcomes.*

VANITY FAIR

ONE gusty, raw day at the end of April—the rain whipping the
pavement of that ancient street where the old Slaughter's Coffee-

house was once situated—George Osborne came into the coffee-room, looking very haggard and pale, although dressed rather smartly in a blue coat and brass buttons, and a neat buff waistcoat of the fashion of those days. Here was his friend Captain Dobbin, in blue and brass too, having abandoned the military frock and French-gray trousers, which were the usual coverings of his lanky person.

Dobbin had been in the coffee-room for an hour or more. He had tried all the papers, but could not read them. He had looked at the clock many scores of times; and at the street, where the rain was pattering down, and the people, as they clinked by in pattens, left long reflections on the shining stone; he tattooed at the table; he bit his nails most completely, and nearly to the quick (he was accustomed to ornament his great big hands in this way); he balanced the tea-spoon on the milkjug; upset it, etc., etc.; and in fact showed those signs of disquietude, and practised those desperate attempts at amuse-ment, which men are accustomed to employ when very anxious and expectant, and perturbed in mind.

Some of his comrades, gentlemen who used the room, joked him about the splendour of his costume and his agitation of manner. One asked him if he was going to be married. Dobbin laughed and said he would send his acquaintance (Major Wagstaff of the Engineers) a piece of cake when that event took place. At length Captain Osborne made his appearance, very smartly dressed, but very pale and agi-tated, as we have said. He wiped his pale face with a large yellow bandana pocket-handkerchief that was prodigiously scented. He shook hands with Dobbin, looked at the clock, and told John, the waiter, to bring him some curaçoa. Of this cordial he swallowed off a couple of glasses with nervous eagerness. His friend asked with some inter-est about his health.

"Couldn't get a wink of sleep till daylight, Dob," said he. "Infernal headache and fever. Got up at nine, and went down to the Hummums for a bath. I say, Dob, I feel just as I did on the morning I went out with Rocket at Quebec."

"So do I," William responded. "I was a deuce deal more nervous than you were, that morning. You made a famous breakfast, I re-member. Eat something now."

"You're a good old fellow, Will. I'll drink your health, old boy, and farewell to—"

"No, no; two glasses are enough," Dobbin interrupted him. "Here, take away the *liqueurs*, John. Have some cayenne-pepper with your fowl. Make haste, though, for it is time we were there."

It was about half an hour from twelve when this brief meeting and colloquy took place between the two captains. A coach, into which Captain Osborne's servant put his master's desk and dressing-case, had been in waiting for some time; and into this the two gentlemen hurried under an umbrella, and the valet mounted on the box, cursing the rain and the dampness of the coachman who was steaming beside him. "We shall find a better trap than this at the carriage door," says he; "that's a comfort." And the carriage drove on, taking the road down Piccadilly, where Apsley House and St. George's Hospital wore red jackets still; where there were oil lamps; where Achilles was not yet born; nor the Pimlico arch raised; nor the hideous equestrian monster which pervades it and the neighborhood—and so they drove down by Brompton to a certain chapel near the Fulham road there.

A chariot was in waiting with four horses; likewise a coach of the kind called glass coaches. Only a very few idlers were collected, on account of the dismal rain.

"Hang it!" said George, "I said only a pair."

"My master would have four," said Mr. Joseph Sedley's servant, who was in waiting; and he and Mr. Osborne's man agreed, as they followed George and William into the church, that it was a "reg'lar shabby turnhout; and with scarce so much as a breakfast or a wedding faviour."

"Here you are," said our old friend, Jos Sedley, coming forward. "You're five minutes late, George my boy. What a day, eh? Demmy, it's like the commencement of the rainy season in Bengal. But you'll find my carriage is water-tight. Come along, my mother and Emmy are in the vestry."

Jos Sedley was splendid. He was fatter than ever. His shirt-collars were higher; his face was redder; his shirt-frill flaunted gorgeously out of his variegated waistcoat. Varnished boots were not invented as yet; but the Hessians on his beautiful legs shone so, that they must have been the identical pair in which the gentleman in the old picture used to shave himself; and on his light green coat there bloomed a fine wedding favour, like a great white spreading magnolia.

In a word, George had thrown the great cast. He was going to be married. Hence his pallor and nervousness—his sleepless night and agitation in the morning. I have heard people who have gone through the same thing own to the same emotion. After three or four ceremonies, you get accustomed to it, no doubt; but the first dip, everybody allows, is awful.

The bride was dressed in a brown silk pelisse (as Captain Dobbin

1301

has since informed me), and wore a straw bonnet with a pink ribbon; over the bonnet she had a veil of white Chantilly lace, a gift from Mr. Joseph Sedley, her brother. Captain Dobbin himself had asked leave to present her with a gold chain and watch, which she sported on this occasion; and her mother gave her her diamond brooch—almost the only trinket which was left to the old lady. As the service went on, Mrs. Sedley sat and whimpered a great deal in a pew, consoled by the Irish maid-servant and Mrs. Clapp from the lodgings. Old Sedley would not be present. Jos acted for his father, giving away the bride, whilst Captain Dobbin stepped up as groomsman to his friend George.

There was nobody in the church besides the officiating persons and the small marriage party and their attendants. The two valets sat aloof superciliously. The rain came rattling down on the windows. In the intervals of the service you heard it, and the sobbing of old Mrs. Sedley in the pew. The parson's tones echoed sadly through the empty walls. Osborne's "I will" was sounded in very deep bass. Emmy's response came fluttering up to her lips from her heart, but was scarcely heard by anybody except Captain Dobbin.

When the service was completed, Jos Sedley came forward and kissed his sister, the bride, for the first time for many months—George's look of gloom had gone, and he seemed quite proud and radiant. "It's your turn, William," says he, putting his hand fondly upon Dobbin's shoulder; and Dobbin went up and touched Amelia on the cheek.

Then they went into the vestry and signed the register. "God bless you, old Dobbin," George said, grasping him by the hand, with something very like moisture glistening in his eyes. William replied only by nodding his head. His heart was too full to say much.

"Write directly, and come down as soon as you can, you know," Osborne said. After Mrs. Sedley had taken an hysterical adieu of her daughter, the pair went off to the carriage. "Get out of the way, you little devils," George cried to a small crowd of damp urchins, that were hanging about the chapel door. The rain drove into the bride and bridegroom's faces as they passed to the chariot. The postillion's favours draggled on their dripping jackets. The few children made a dismal cheer as the carriage, splashing mud, drove away.

William Dobbin stood in the church porch, looking at it, a quiet figure. The small crew of spectators jeered him. He was not thinking about them or their laughter.

"Come home and have some tiffin, Dobbin," a voice cried behind him, as a pudgy hand was laid on his shoulder, and the honest fellow's reverie was interrupted. But the captain had no heart to go a feasting with Jos Sedley. He put the weeping old lady and her attendants into the carriage along with Jos, and left them without further words passing. This carriage, too, drove away, and the urchins gave another sarcastical cheer.

"Here, you little beggars," Dobbin said, giving some sixpences amongst them, and then went off by himself through the rain. It was all over. They were married, and happy, he prayed God. Never since he was a boy, had he felt so miserable and so lonely. He longed with a heart-sick yearning for the first few days to be over, that he might see her again.

JOHANN LUDWIG TIECK

JOHANN LUDWIG TIECK (1773-1853). One of the leaders of the German Romantic School. Experimented in every literary form, was most successful with short stories and *novellen*. Influenced not only German writers, but such men as Gogol, Coleridge, Scott, Longfellow, Hawthorne. Best work: *Puss-in-Boots*, satirical fairy tales.

THE FRIENDS

IT WAS a beautiful spring morning, when Lewis Wandel went out to visit a sick friend, in a village some miles distant from his dwelling. This friend had written to him to say that he was lying dangerously ill, and would gladly see him and speak to him once more.

The cheerful sunshine now sparkled in the bright green bushes; the birds twittered and leapt to and fro on the branches; the larks sang merrily above the thin fleeting clouds; sweet scents rose from the fresh meadows, and the fruit-trees of the garden were white and gay in blossom.

Lewis's eye roamed intoxicate around him; his soul seemed to expand; but he thought of his invalid friend, and he bent forward in silent dejection. Nature had decked herself all in vain, so serenely and so brightly; his fancy could only picture to him the sick bed and his suffering brother.

"How song is sounding from every bough!" cried he; "the notes of the birds mingle in sweet unison with the whisper of the leaves;

and yet in the distance, through all the charm of the concert, come the sighs of the sick one."

Whilst he thus communed, a troop of gaily-clad peasant girls issued from the village; they all gave him a friendly salutation, and told him that they were on their merry way to a wedding; that work was over for that day, and had to give place to festivity. He listened to their tale, and still their merriment rang in the distance on his ear; still he caught the sound of their songs, and became more and more sorrowful. In the wood he took his seat on a dismantled tree, drew the oft-read letter from his pocket, and ran through it once more:—

"My very dear friend,—I cannot tell why you have so utterly forgotten me, that I receive no news from you. I am not surprised that men forsake me; but it heartily pains me to think that you too care nothing about me. I am dangerously ill; a fever that saps my strength: if you delay visiting me any longer, I cannot promise you that you will see me again. All nature revives, and feels fresh and strong; I alone sink lower in languor; the returning warmth cannot animate me; I see not the green fields, nothing but the tree that rustles before my window, and sings death-songs to my thoughts; my bosom is pent, my breathing is hard; and often I think the walls of my room will press closer together and crush me. The rest of you in the world are holding the most beautiful festival of life, whilst I must languish in the dwelling of sickness. Gladly would I dispense with spring, if I could but see your dear face once more: but you that are in health never earnestly think what it really is to be ill, and how dear to us then, in our helplessness, the visit of a friend is: you do not know how to prize those precious minutes of consolation, because the whole world receives you in the warmth and the fervour of its friendship. Ah! if you did but know, as I do, how terrible is death, and how still more terrible it is to be ill,—O Lewis, how would you hasten then to behold once more this frail form, that you have hitherto called your friend, and that by and by will be so ruthlessly dismembered! If I were well, I would haste to meet you, or fancy that you may perhaps be ill at this moment. If I never see you again—farewell."

What a painful impression did the suffering depicted in this letter make upon Lewis's heart, amid the liveliness of Nature, as she lay in brilliancy before him! He melted into tears, and rested his head on his hand.—"Carol now, ye foresters," thought he; "for ye know no

1304

lamentation; ye lead a buoyant poetic existence, and for this are those swift pinions granted you; oh, how happy are ye, that ye need not mourn; warm summer calls you, and ye wish for nothing more; ye dance forth to meet it, and when winter is advancing, ye are gone! O light-winged merry forest-life, how do I envy thee! Why are so many heavy cares burdened upon poor man's heart? Why may he not love without purchasing his love by wailing—his happiness by misery? Life purls on like a fleeting rivulet beneath his feet, and quenches not his thirst, his fervid longing."

He became more and more absorbed in thought, and at last he rose and pursued his way through the thick forest. "If I could but help him," cried he; "if Nature could but supply me with a means of saving him; but as it is, I feel nothing but my own impotency, and the pain of losing my friend. In my childhood I used to believe in enchantment and its supernatural aids; would I now could hope in them as happily as then!"

He quickened his steps; and involuntarily all the remembrances of the earliest years of his childhood crowded back upon him: he followed those forms of loveliness, and was soon entangled in such a labyrinth as not to notice the objects that surrounded him. He had forgotten that it was spring—that his friend was ill: he hearkened to the wondrous melodies, which came borne, as if from distant shores, upon his ear: all that was most strange united itself to what was most ordinary: his whole soul was transmuted. From the far vista of memory, from the abyss of the past, all those forms were summoned forth that ever had enraptured or tormented him: all those dubious phantoms were aroused, that flutter formlessly about us, and gather in dizzy hum around our heads. Puppets, the toys of childhood, and spectres, danced along before him, and so mantled over the green turf, that he could not see a single flower at his feet. First love encircled him with its twilight morning gleam, and let down its sparkling rainbow over the mead: his earliest sorrows glided past him in review, and threatened to greet him in the same guise at the end of his pilgrimage. Lewis sought to arrest all these changeful feelings, and to retain a consciousness of self amid the magic of enjoyment,—but in vain. Like enigmatic books, with figures grotesquely gay, that open for a moment and in a moment are closed, so unstably and fleetingly all floated before his soul.

The wood opened, and in the open country on one side lay some old ruins, encompassed with watch-towers and ramparts. Lewis was astonished at having advanced so quickly amid his dreams. He emerged from his melancholy, as he did from the shades of the wood; for often the pictures within us are but the reflection of outward objects. Now rose on him, like the morning sun, the memory of his first poetical enjoyments, of his earliest appreciations of that luscious harmony which many a human ear never inhales.

"How incomprehensibly," said he, "did those things commingle then, which seemed to me eternally parted by such vast chasms; my most undefined presentiments assumed a form and outline, and gleamed on me in the shape of a thousand subordinate phantoms, which till then I had never descried! So names were found me for things that I had long wished to speak of: I became recipient of earth's fairest treasures, which my yearning heart had so long sought for in vain: and how much have I to thank thee for since then, divine power of fancy and of poetry! How hast thou smoothed for me the path of life, that erst appeared so rough and perplexed! Ever hast thou revealed to me new sources of enjoyment and happiness, so that no arid desert presents itself to me now: every stream of sweet voluptuous inspiration hath wound its way through my earth-born heart: I have become intoxicate with bliss, and have communed with beings of heaven."

The sun sank below the horizon, and Lewis was astonished that it was already evening. He was insensible of fatigue, and was still far from the point which he had wished to reach before night: he stood still, without being able to understand how the crimson of evening could be so early mantling the clouds; how the shadows of everything were so long, while the nightingale warbled her song of wail in the thicket. He looked around him: the old ruins lay far in the background, clad in blushing splendour; and he doubted whether he had not strayed from the direct and well-known road.

Now he remembered a phantasy of his early childhood, that till that moment had never recurred to him: it was a female form of awe, that glided before him over the lonely fields: she never looked round, yet he was compelled, against his will, to follow her, and to be drawn on into unknown scenes, without in the least being able to extricate himself from her power. A slight thrill of fear came over him, and yet he found it impossible to obtain a more distinct recollection of that figure, or to usher back his mind into the frame, in which this image had first appeared to him. He sought to individualise all these singular sensations, when, looking round by chance, he really found himself on a spot which, often as he had been that way, he had never seen before.

"Am I spell-bound?" cried he; "or have my dreams and fancies crazed me? Is it the wonderful effect of solitude that makes me irrecognisable to myself; or do spirits and genii hover round me and hold my senses in thrall? Sooth, if I cannot enfranchise myself from myself, I will await that woman-phantom that floated before me in every lonely place in my childhood."

He endeavoured to rid himself of every kind of phantasy, in order to get into the right road again; but his recollections became more and more perplexed; the flowers at his feet grew larger, the red glow of evening more brilliant, and wondrously shaped clouds hung drooping on the earth, like the curtains of some mystic scene that was soon to unfold itself. A ringing murmur arose from the high grass, and the blades bowed to one another, as if in friendly converse; while a light warm spring rain dropped pattering amongst them, as if to wake every slumbering harmony in wood, and bush, and flower. Now all was rife with song and sound; a thousand sweet voices held promiscuous parley; song entwined itself in song, and tone in tone; while in the waning crimson of eve lay countless blue butterflies rocking, with its radiance sparkling from their wavy wings. Lewis fancied himself in a dream, when the heavy dark-red clouds suddenly rose again, and a vast prospect opened on him in unfathomable distance. In the sunshine lay a gorgeous plain, sparkling with verdant forests and dewy underwood. In its centre glittered a palace of a myriad hues, as if composed all of undulating rainbows and gold and jewels: a passing stream reflected its various brilliancy, and a soft crimson æther environed this hall of enchantment; strange birds, he had never seen before, flew about, sportively flapping each other with their red and green wings: larger nightingales warbled their clear notes to the echoing landscape: lambent flames shot through the green grass, flickering here and there, and then darting in coils round the mansion. Lewis drew nearer, and heard ravishing voices sing the following words:—

Traveller from earth below,
Wend thee not farther,
In our hall's magic glow
Bide with us rather.
Hast thou with longing scann'd
Joy's distant morrow,
Cast away sorrow,
And enter the wish'd-for land.

Without further scruple, Lewis stepped to the shining threshold, and lingering but a moment ere he set his foot on the polished stone, he entered. The gates closed after him.

"Hitherward! hitherward!" cried invisible lips, as from the inmost recesses of the palace; and with loudly throbbing heart he followed the voices. All his cares, all his olden remembrances were cast away: his inmost bosom rang with the songs that outwardly encompassed him: his every regret was stilled: his every conscious and unconscious wish was satisfied. The summoning voices grew so loud, that the whole building re-echoed them, and still he could not find their origin, though he long seemed to have been standing in the central hall of the palace.

At length a ruddy-cheeked boy stepped up to him, and saluted the stranger guest: he led him through magnificent chambers, full of splendour and melody, and at last entered the garden, where Lewis, as he said, was expected. Entranced he followed his guide, and the most delicious fragrance from a thousand flowers floated forth to meet him. Broad shady walks received them. Lewis's dizzy gaze could scarcely gain the tops of the high immemorial trees: bright-coloured birds sat perched upon the branches: children were playing on guitars in the shade, and they and the birds sang to the music. Fountains shot up, with the clear red of morning, sparkling upon them: the flowers were as high as shrubs, and parted spontaneously as the wanderer pressed through them. He had never before felt the hallowed sensations that then enkindled in him; never had such pure heavenly enjoyment been revealed to him: he was over-happy.

But bells of silver sound rang through the trees, and their tops were bowed: the birds and children with the guitars were hushed: the rose-buds unfolded: and the boy now conducted the stranger into the midst of a brilliant assembly.

Lovely dames of lofty form were seated on beautiful banks of turf, in earnest conference. They were above the usual height of the human race, and their more than earthly beauty had at the same time something of awe in it, from which the heart shrunk back in alarm. Lewis dared not interrupt their conversation: it seemed as if he were among the god-like forms of Homer's song, where every thought must be excluded that formed the converse of mortals. Odd little spirits stood round, as ready ministers, waiting attentively for the wink of the moment that should summon them from their posture of quietude: they fixed their glances on the stranger, and then looked jeeringly and significantly at each other. At last the beautiful women ceased speaking, and beckoned Lewis to approach; he was still standing with an embarrassed air, and drew near to them with trembling.

"Be not alarmed," said the fairest of them all; "you are welcome to us here, and we have long been expecting you: long have you wished to be in our abode,—are you satisfied now?"

"Oh, how unspeakably happy I am!" exclaimed Lewis; "all my dearest dreams have met with their fulfilment, all my most daring wishes are gratified now: yes, I am, I live among them. How it has happened so, I cannot comprehend: sufficient for me, that it is so. Why should I raise a new wail over this enigma, ere my olden lamentations are scarcely at an end?"

"Is this life," asked the lady, "very different from your former one?"

"My former life," said Lewis, "I can scarcely remember. But has, then, this golden state of existence fallen to my lot? this beautiful state, after which my every sense and prescience so ardently aspired; to which every wish wandered, that I could conceive in fancy, or realise in my inmost thought; though its image, veiled in mist, seemed ever strange in me—and is it, then, mine at last? have I, then, achieved this new existence, and does it hold me in its embrace? Oh, pardon me, I know not what I say in my delirium of ecstasy, and might well weigh my words more carefully in such an assemblage."

The lady sighed; and in a moment every minister was in motion; there was a stirring among the trees, everywhere a running to and fro, and speedily a banquet was placed before Lewis of fair fruits and fragrant wines. He sat down again, and music rose anew on the air. Rows of beautiful boys and girls sped round him, intertwined in the dance, while uncouth little cobolds lent life to the scene, and excited loud laughter by their ludicrous gambols. Lewis noted every sound and every gesture: he seemed newly-born since his initiation into this joyous existence. "Why," thought he, "are those hopes and reveries of ours so often laughed at, that pass into fulfilment sooner than ever had been expected? Where, then, is that border-mark between truth and error which mortals are ever ready with such temerity to set up? Oh, I ought in my former life to have wandered oftener from the way, and then perhaps I should have ripened all the earlier for this happy transmutation."

The dance died away; the sun sank to rest; the august dames arose; Lewis too left his seat, and accompanied them on their walk through the quiet garden. The nightingales were complaining in a softened tone, and a wondrous moon rose above the horizon. The blossoms

1309

opened to its silver radiance, and every leaf kindled in its gleam; the wide avenues became of a glow, casting shadows of a singular green; red clouds slumbered on the green grass of the fields: the fountains turned to gold, and played high in the clear air of heaven.

"Now you will wish to sleep," said the loveliest of the ladies, and shewed the enraptured wanderer a shadowy bower, strewed with soft turf and yielding cushions. Then they left him, and he was alone.

He sat down and watched the magic twilight glimmering through the thickly-woven foliage. "How strange is this!" said he to himself; "perhaps I am now only asleep, and I may dream that I am sleeping a second time, and may have a dream in my dream; and so it may go on for ever, and no human power ever be able to awake me. No! unbeliever that I am! it is beautiful reality that animates me now, and my former state perhaps was but the dream of gloom." He lay down, and light breezes played round him. Perfume was wafted on the air, and little birds sang lulling songs. In his dreams he fancied the garden all around him changed: the tall trees withered away; the golden moon fallen from the sky, leaving a dismal gap behind her; instead of the watery jet from the fountains, little genii gushed out, caracolling over each in the air, and assuming the strangest attitudes. Notes of woe supplanted the sweetness of song, and every trace of that happy abode had vanished. Lewis awoke amid impressions of fear, and chid himself for still feeding his fancy in the perverse manner of the habitants of earth, who mingle all received images in rude disorder, and present them again in this garb in a dream. A lovely morning broke over the scene, and the ladies saluted him again. He spoke to them more intrepidly, and was to-day more inclined to cheerfulness, as the surrounding world had less power to astonish him. He contemplated the garden of the palace, and fed upon the magnificence and the wonders that he met there. Thus he lived many days happily, in the belief that his felicity was incapable of increase.

But sometimes the crowing of a cock seemed to sound in the vicinity; and then the whole edifice would tremble, and his compainions turn pale: this generally happened of an evening, and soon afterwards they retired to rest. Then often there would come a thought of earth into Lewis's soul; then he would often lean out of the windows of the glittering palace to arrest and fix these fleeting remembrances, and to get a glimpse of the high road again, which, as he thought, must pass that way. In this sort of mood, he was one afternoon alone, musing within himself why it was just as impossible for him to recall a distinct remembrance of the world, as formerly it had been to feel a presage of this poetic place of sojourn,—when all at once a post-horn seemed to sound in the distance, and the rattle of carriage-wheels to make themselves heard. "How strangely," said he to himself, "does a faint gleam, a slight reminiscence of earth, break upon my delight—rendering me melancholy and dejected! Then, do I lack anything here? Is my happiness still incomplete?"

The beautiful women returned. "What do you wish for?" said they, in a tone of concern; "you seem sad."

"You will laugh." replied Lewis; "yet grant me one favour more. In that other life I had a friend, whom I now but faintly remember: he is ill, I think; restore him by your skill."

"Your wish is already gratified," said they.

"But," said Lewis, "vouchsafe me two questions."

"Speak!"

"Does no gleam of love fall on this wondrous world? Does no friendship perambulate these bowers? I thought the morning blush of spring-love would be eternal here, which in that other life is too prone to be extinguished, and which men afterwards speak of as of a fable. To confess to you the truth, I feel an unspeakable yearning after those sensations."

"Then you long for earth again?"

"Oh, never!" cried Lewis; "for in that cold earth I used to sigh for friendship and for love, and they came not near me. The longing for those feelings had to supply the place of those feelings themselves; and for that reason I turned my aspirations hitherward, and hoped here to find every thing in the most beautiful harmony."

"Fool!" said the venerable woman: "so on earth you sighed for earth, and knew not what you did in wishing to be here; you have overshot your desires, and substituted phantasies for the sensations of mortals."

"Then who are ye?" cried Lewis, astounded.

"We are the old fairies," said she, "of whom you surely must have heard long ago. If you ardently long for earth, you will return thither again. Our kingdom flourishes when mortals are shrouded in night; but their day is *our* night. Our sway is of ancient date, and will long endure. It abides invisibly among men—to your eye alone has it been revealed." She turned away, and Lewis remembered that it was the same form which had resistlessly dragged him after it in his youth, and of which he felt a secret dread. He followed now also, crying, "No, I will not go back to earth! I will stay here!" "So then," said he to himself, "I divined this lofty being even in my childhood! And so the solution of many a riddle, which we are too idle to investigate, may be within ourselves."

He went on much further than usual, till the fairy garden was soon left far behind him. He stood on a romantic mountain-range, where the ivy climbed in wild tresses up the rocks; cliff was piled on cliff, and awe and grandeur seemed to hold universal sway. Then there came a wandering stranger to him, who accosted him kindly, and addressed him thus:—"Glad I am after all, to see you again."

"I know you not," said Lewis.

"That may well be," replied the other; "but once you thought you knew me well. I am your late sick friend."

"Impossible! you are quite a stranger to me!"

"Only," said the stranger, "because to-day you see me for the first time in my true form: till now you only found in me a reflection of yourself. You are right too in remaining here; for there is no love, no friendship—not here, I mean, where all illusion vanishes."

Lewis sat down and wept.

"What ails you?" said the stranger.

"That it is you—you who were the friend of my youth: is not that mournful enough? Oh, come back with me to our dear, dear earth, where we shall know each other once more under illusive forms—where there exists the superstition of friendship! What am I doing here?"

"What will that avail?" answered the stranger. "You will want to be back again; earth is not bright enough for you: the flowers are too small for you, the song too suppressed. Colour there, cannot emerge so brilliantly from the shade; flowers there are of small comfort, and so prone to fade; the little birds think of their death, and sing in modest constraint: but here every thing is on a scale of grandeur."

"Oh, I will be contented!" cried Lewis, as the tears gushed profusely from his eyes. "Do but come back with me, and be my friend once more; let us leave this desert, this glittery misery!"

Thus saying, he opened his eyes, for some one was shaking him roughly. Over him leant the friendly but pale face of his once sick friend. "But are you dead?" cried Lewis.

"Recovered am I, wicked sleeper," he replied. "Is it thus you visit your sick friend? Come along with me; my carriage is waiting there, and a thunder-storm is rising."

Lewis rose: in his sleep he had glided off the trunk of the tree; his friend's letter lay open beside him. "So am I really on the earth again?" he exclaimed with joy; "really? and is this no new dream?"

"You will not escape from the earth," answered his friend with a smile; and both were locked in heart-felt embraces.

"How happy I am," said Lewis, "that I have you once more, that I feel as I used to do, and that you are well again!"

"Suddenly," replied his friend, "I felt ill; and as suddenly I was well again. So I wished to go to you, and do away with the alarm that my letter must have caused you; and here, half-way, I find you asleep."

"I do not deserve your love at all," said Lewis.

"Why?"

"Because I just now doubted of your friendship."

"But only in sleep."

"It would be strange enough though," said Lewis, "if there really were such things as fairies."

"There are such, of a certainty," replied the other; "but it is all a fable, that their whole pleasure is to make men happy. They plant those wishes in our bosoms which we ourselves do not know of; those over-wrought pretensions—that super-human covetousness of super-human gifts; so that in our desponding delirium we afterwards despise the beautiful earth with all its glorious stores."

Lewis answered with a pressure of the hand.

LEO TOLSTOY

LEO TOLSTOY (Russian, 1828-1910). The sage among the master Russian novelists. An aristocrat who, after a spiritual conversion, altered his life in effort to become a later-day saint. Moral conflict forms basis of all his writing. Two of his novels belong among the greatest: *Anna Karenina* and *War and Peace*, world's most ambitious war story. Also notable are his plays and short stories.

WHERE LOVE IS

IN A certain town there lived a shoemaker named Martin Avdeitch. He lived in a basement room which possessed but one window. This window looked onto the street, and through it a glimpse could be caught of the passers-by. It is true that only their legs could be seen, but that did not matter, as Martin could recognize people by their boots alone. He had lived here for a long time, and so had many acquaintances. There were very few pairs of boots in the neighborhood which had not passed through his hands at least once, if not twice. Some he had resoled, others he had fitted with side-pieces, others, again, he had resewn where they were split, or provided with new toe-caps. Yes, he often saw his handiwork through that window. He was given plenty of custom, for his work lasted well, his materials were good, his prices moderate, and his word to be depended on. If he could do a job by a given time it should be done; but if not, he would warn you beforehand rather than disappoint you. Everyone knew Avdeitch, and no one ever transferred his custom from him. He had always been an upright man, but with the approach of old age he had begun more than ever to think of his soul, and to draw nearer to God.

His wife had died while he was still an apprentice, leaving behind her a little boy of three. This was their only child, indeed, for the two elder ones had died previously. At first Martin thought of placing the little fellow with a sister of his in the country, but changed his mind, thinking: "My Kapitoshka would not like to grow up in a strange family, so I will keep him by me." Then Avdeitch finished his apprenticeship, and went to live in lodgings with his little boy. But God had not seen fit to give Avdeitch happiness in his children. The little boy was just growing up and beginning to help his father and to be a pleasure to him, when he fell ill, was put to bed, and died after a week's fever.

Martin buried the little fellow and was inconsolable. Indeed, he was so inconsolable that he began to murmur against God. His life seemed so empty that more than once he prayed for death and reproached the Almighty for taking away his only beloved son instead of himself, the old man. At last he ceased altogether to go to church.

Then one day there came to see him an ancient peasant-pilgrim—one who was now in the eighth year of his pilgrimage. To him Avdeitch talked, and then went on to complain of his great sorrow.

"I no longer wish to be a God-fearing man," he said. "I only wish to die. That is all I ask of God. I am a lonely, hopeless man."

"You should not speak like that, Martin," replied the old pilgrim. "It is not for us to judge the acts of God. We must rely, not upon our own understanding, but upon the Divine wisdom. God saw fit that your son should die and that you should live. Therefore it must be better so. If you despair, it is because you have wished to live too much for your own pleasure."

"For what, then, should I live?" asked Martin.

"For God alone," replied the old man. "It is He who gave you life, and therefore it is He for whom you should live. When you come to live for Him you will cease to grieve, and your trials will become easy to bear."

Martin was silent. Then he spoke again.

"But how am I to live for God?" he asked.

"Christ has shown us the way," answered the old man. "Can you read? If so, buy a Testament and study it. You will learn there how to live for God. Yes, it is all shown you there."

These words sank into Avdeitch's soul. He went out the same day, bought a large-print copy of the New Testament, and set himself to read it.

At the beginning Avdeitch had meant only to read on festival days, but when he once began his reading he found it so comforting to the soul that he came never to let a day pass without doing so. On the second occasion he became so engrossed that all the kerosene was burnt away in the lamp before he could tear himself away from the book.

Thus he came to read it every evening, and, the more he read, the more clearly did he understand what God required of him, and in what way he could live for God; so that his heart grew ever lighter and lighter. Once upon a time, whenever he had lain down to sleep, he had been used to moan and sigh as he thought of his little Kapioshka; but now he only said—"Glory to Thee, O Lord! Glory to Thee! Thy will be done!"

From that time onwards Avdeitch's life became completely changed. Once he had been used to go out on festival days and drink tea in a tavern, and had not denied himself even an occasional glass of *vodka*. This he had done in the company of a boon companion, and, although no drunkard, would frequently leave the tavern in an excited state and talk much nonsense as he shouted and disputed with this friend of his. But now he had turned his back on all this, and his life had become quiet and joyous. Early in the morning he would sit down to his work, and labour through his appointed hours. Then he would take the lamp down from a shelf, light it, and sit down to read. And the more he read, the more he understood, and the clearer and happier he grew at heart.

It happened once the Martin had been reading late. He had been reading those verses in the sixth chapter of the Gospel of St. Luke which run:

1315

"And unto him that smiteth thee on the one cheek offer also the other; and him that taketh away thy cloak forbid not to take thy coat also. Give to every man that asketh of thee; and of him that taketh thy goods ask them not again. And as ye would that men should do to you, do ye also to them likewise."

Then, further on, he had read those verses where the Lord says:

"And why call ye Me, Lord, Lord, and do not the things which I say? Whosoever cometh to Me and heareth my sayings, and doeth them, I will show you to whom he is like: He is like a man which built an house, and digged deep, and laid the foundation on a rock: and when the flood arose, the storm beat vehemently upon that house, and could not shake it: for it was founded upon a rock. But he that heareth and doeth not, is like a man that without a foundation built an house upon the earth; against which the stream did beat vehemently, and immediately it fell; and the ruin of that house was great."

Avdeitch read these words, and felt greatly cheered in soul. He took off his spectacles, laid them on the book, leaned his elbows upon the table, and gave himself up to meditation. He set himself to measure his own life by those words, and thought to himself:

"Is my house founded upon a rock or upon sand? It is well if it be upon a rock. Yet it seems so easy to me as I sit here alone. I may so easily come to think that I have done all that the Lord has commanded me, and grow careless and—sin again. Yet I will keep on striving, for it is goodly so to do. Help Thou me, O Lord."

Thus he kept on meditating, though conscious that it was time for bed; yet he was loathe to tear himself away from the book. He began to read the seventh chapter of St. Luke, and read on about the centurion, the widow's son, and the answer given to John's disciples; until in time he came to the passage where the rich Pharisee invited Jesus to his house, and the woman washed the Lord's feet with her tears and He justified her. So he came to the forty-fourth verse and read:

"And He turned to the woman, and said unto Simon, Seest thou this woman? I entered into thine house, and thou gavest Me no water for My feet: but she hath washed My feet with tears, and wiped them with the hairs of her head. Thou gavest Me no kiss: but this woman since the time I came in hath not ceased to kiss My feet. My head with oil thou didst anoint: but this woman hath anointed My feet with ointment."

He read these verses and thought:

" 'Thou gavest Me no water for My feet' . . . 'Thou gavest Me no

1316

kiss' . . . 'My head with oil thou didst not anoint' . . . "—and once again he took off his spectacles, laid them on the book, and became lost in meditation.

"I am even as that Pharisee," he thought to himself. "I drink tea and think only of my deeds. Yes, I think only of having plenty to eat and drink, of being warm and clean—but never of entertaining a guest. And Simon too was mindful only of himself, although the guest who had come to visit him was—who? Why, even the Lord Himself! If, then, He should come to visit *me*, should I receive Him any better?"—and, leaning forward upon his elbows, he was asleep almost before he was aware of it.

"Martin!" someone seemed to breathe in his ear.

He started from his sleep.

"Who is there?" he said. He turned and looked toward the door, but could see no one. Again he bent forward over the table. Then suddenly he heard the words:

"Martin, Martin! Look thou into the street to-morrow, for I am coming to visit thee."

Martin roused himself, got up from the chair, and rubbed his eyes. He did not know whether it was dreaming or awake that he had heard these words, but he turned out the lamp and went to bed.

The next morning Avdeitch rose before daylight and said his prayers. Then he made up the stove, got ready some cabbage soup and porridge, lighted the samovar, slung his leather apron about him, and sat down to his work in the window. He sat and worked hard, yet all the time his thoughts were centered upon the night before. He was of two minds about the vision. At one moment he would think that it must have been his fancy, while the next moment he would find himself convinced that he had really heard the voice. "Yes, it must have been so," he concluded.

As Martin sat thus by the window he kept looking out of it as much as working. Whenever a pair of boots passed with which he was acquainted he would bend down to glance upwards through the window and see their owner's face as well. The doorkeeper passed in new felt boots, and then a water-carrier. Next, an old soldier, a veteran of Nicholas' army, in old, patched boots, and carrying a shovel in his hands, halted close by the window. Avdeitch knew him by his boots. His name was Stepanitch, and he was kept by a neighbouring tradesman out of charity, his duties being to help the doorkeeper. He began to clear away the snow from in front of

1317

Avdeitch's window, while the shoemaker looked at him and then resumed his work.

"I think I must be getting into my dotage," thought Avdeitch with a smile. "Just because Stepanitch begins clearing away the snow I at once jump to the conclusion that Christ is about to visit me. Yes, I am growing foolish now, old greybeard that I am."

Yet he had hardly made a dozen stitches before he was craning his neck again to look out of the window. He could see that Stepanitch had placed his shovel against the wall, and was resting and trying to warm himself a little.

"He is evidently an old man now and broken," thought Avdeitch to himself. "He is not strong enough to clear away snow. Would he like some tea, I wonder? That reminds me that the samovar must be ready now."

He made fast his awl in his work and got up. Placing the samovar on the table, he brewed the tea, and then tapped with his finger on the window-pane. Stepanitch turned round and approached. Avdeitch beckoned to him, and then went to open the door.

"Come in and warm yourself," he said. "You must be frozen."

"Christ requite you!" answered Stepanitch. "Yes, my bones are almost cracking."

He came in, shook the snow off himself, and, though tottering on his feet, took pains to wipe them carefully, that he might not dirty the floor.

"Nay, do not trouble about that," said Avdeitch. "I will wipe your boots myself. It is part of my business in this trade. Come you here and sit down, and we will empty this tea-pot together."

He poured out two tumblerfuls, and offered one to his guest; after which he emptied his own into the saucer, and blew upon it to cool it. Stepanitch drank his tumblerful, turned the glass upside down, placed his crust upon it, and thanked his host kindly. But it was plain that he wanted another one.

"You must drink some more," said Avdeitch, and refilled his guest's tumbler and his own. Yet, in spite of himself, he had no sooner drunk his tea than he found himself looking out into the street again.

"Are you expecting anyone?" asked his guest.

"Am—am I expecting anyone? Well, to tell the truth, yes. That is to say, I am, and I am not. The fact is that some words have got fixed in my memory. Whether it was a vision or not I cannot tell, but at all events, my old friend, I was reading in the Gospels last night about Our Little Father Christ, and how He walked this earth and suffered. You have heard of Him, have you not?"

"Yes, yes, I have heard of Him," answered Stepanitch; "but we are ignorant folk and do not know our letters."

"Well, I was reading of how He walked this earth, and how He went to visit a Pharisee, and yet received no welcome from him at the door. All this I read last night, my friend, and then fell to thinking about it—to thinking how some day I too might fail to pay Our Little Father Christ due honour. 'Suppose,' I thought to myself, 'He came to me or to anyone like me? Should we, like the great lord Simon, not know how to receive Him and not go out to meet Him?' Thus I thought, and fell asleep where I sat. Then as I sat sleeping there I heard someone call my name; and as I raised myself the voice went on (as though it were the voice of someone whispering in my ear): 'Watch thou for me to-morrow, for I am coming to visit thee.' It said that twice. And so those words have got into my head, and, foolish though I know it to be, I keep expecting *Him*—the Little Father—every moment."

Stepanitch nodded and said nothing, but emptied his glass and laid it aside. Nevertheless Avdeitch took and refilled it.

"Drink it up; it will do you good," he said. "Do you know," he went on, "I often call to mind how, when Our Little Father walked this earth, there was never a man, however humble, whom He despised, and how it was chiefly among the common people that He dwelt. It was always with *them* that He walked; it was from among *them*—from among such men as you and I—from among sinners and working folk—that He chose His disciples. 'Whosoever,' He said, 'shall exalt himself, the same shall be abased; and whosoever shall abase himself, the same shall be exalted.' 'You,' He said again, 'call me Lord; yet will I wash you feet.' 'Whosoever,' He said, 'would be chief among you, let him be the servant of all. Because,' He said, 'blessed are the lowly, the peacemakers, the merciful, and the charitable.'"

Stepanitch had forgotten all his tea. He was an old man, and his tears came easily. He sat and listened, with the tears rolling down his cheeks.

"Oh, but you must drink your tea," said Avdeitch; yet Stepanitch only crossed himself and said the thanksgiving, after which he pushed his glass away and rose.

"I thank you, Martin Avdeitch," he said. "You have taken me in, and fed both soul and body."

"Nay, but I beg of you to come again," replied Avdeitch. "I am only too glad of a guest."

So Stepanitch departed, while Martin poured out the last of the tea and drank it. Then he cleaned the crockery, and sat down again to his work by the window—to the stitching of a back-piece. He stitched away, yet kept on looking through the window—looking for Christ, as it were—and ever thinking of Christ and His works. Indeed, Christ's many sayings were never absent from Avdeitch's mind.

Two soldiers passed the window, the one in military boots, and the other in civilian. Next, there came a neighbouring householder in polished goloshes; then a baker with a basket. All of them passed on. Presently a woman in woollen stockings and rough country shoes approached the window, and halted near the buttress outside it. Avdeitch peered up at her from under the lintel of his window, and could see that she was a plain-looking, poorly-dressed woman and had a child in her arms. It was in order to muffle the child up more closely—little though she had to do it with!—that she had stopped near the buttress and was now standing there with her back to the wind. Her clothing was ragged and fit only for summer, and even from behind his window-panes Avdeitch could hear the child crying miserably and its mother vainly trying to soothe it. Avdeitch rose, went to the door, climbed the steps, and cried out: "My good woman, my good woman!"

She heard him and turned round.

"Why need you stand there in the cold with your baby?" he went on. "Come into my room, where it is warm, and where you will be able to wrap the baby up more comfortably than you can here. Yes, come in with you."

The woman was surprised to see an old man in a leather apron and with spectacles upon his nose calling out to her, yet she followed him down the steps, and they entered his room. The old man led her to the bedstead.

"Sit you down here, my good woman," he said. "You will be near the stove, and can warm yourself and feed your baby."

"Ah, but I have no milk left in my breast," she replied. "I have had nothing to eat this morning." Nevertheless she put the child to suck.

Avdeitch nodded his head approvingly, went to the table for some bread and a basin, and opened the stove door. From the stove he took and poured some soup into the basin, and drew out also

1320

a bowl of porridge. The latter, however, was not yet boiling, so he set out only the soup, after first laying the table with a cloth.

"Sit down and eat, my good woman," he said, "while I hold your baby. I have had little ones of my own, and know how to nurse them."

The woman crossed herself and sat down, while Avdeitch seated himself upon the bedstead with the baby. He smacked his lips at it once or twice, but made a poor show of it, for he had no teeth left. Consequently the baby went on crying. Then he bethought him of his finger, which he wriggled to and fro towards the baby's mouth and back again—without, however, actually touching the little one's lips, since the finger was blackened with work and sticky with shoemaker's wax. The baby contemplated the finger and grew quiet—then actually smiled. Avdeitch was delighted. Meanwhile the woman had been eating the meal, and now she told him, unasked, who she was and whither she was going.

"I am a soldier's wife," she said, "but my husband was sent to a distant station eight months ago, and I have heard nothing of him since. At first I got a place as cook, but when the baby came they said they could not do with it and dismissed me. That was three months ago, and I have got nothing since, and have spent all my savings. I tried to get taken as a wet nurse but no one would have me, for they said I was too thin. I have just been to see a tradesman's wife where our grandmother is in service. She had promised to take me on, and I quite thought that she would, but when I arrived to-day she told me to come again next week. She lives a long way from here, and I am quite worn out and have tired my baby for nothing. Thank Heaven, however, my landlady is good to me, and gives me shelter for Christ's sake. Otherwise I should not have known how to bear it all."

Avdeitch sighed and said: "But have you nothing warm to wear?"

"Ah, sir," replied the woman, "although it is the time for warm clothes I had to pawn my last shawl yesterday for two *grivenki*."

Then the woman returned to the bedstead to take her baby, while Avdeitch rose and went to a cupboard. There he rummaged about, and presently returned with an old jacket.

"Here," he said. "It is a poor old thing, but it will serve to cover you."

The woman looked at the jacket, and then at the old man. Then she took the jacket and burst into tears. Avdeitch turned away, and went creeping under the bedstead, whence he extracted a box and

1321

pretended to rummage about in it for a few moments; after which he sat down again before the woman.

Then the woman said to him: "I thank you in Christ's name, good grandfather. Surely it was He Himself who sent me to your window. Otherwise I should have seen my baby perish with the cold. When I first came out the day was warm, but now it has begun to freeze. But He, Our Little Father, had placed you in your window, that you might see me in my bitter plight and have compassion upon me."

Avdeitch smiled and said: "He did indeed place me there: yet, my poor woman, it was for a special purpose that I was looking out."

Then he told his guest, the soldier's wife, of his vision, and how he had heard a voice foretelling that to-day the Lord Himself would come to visit him.

"That may very well be," said the woman as she rose, took the jacket, and wrapped her baby in it. Then she saluted him once more and thanked him.

"Also, take this in Christ's name," said Avdeitch, and gave her a two-*grivenka* piece with which to buy herself a shawl. The woman crossed herself, and he likewise. Then he led her to the door and dismissed her.

When she had gone Avdeitch ate a little soup, washed up the crockery again, and resumed his work. All the time, though, he kept his eye upon the window, and as soon as ever a shadow fell across it he would look up to see who was passing. Acquaintances of his came past, and people whom he did not know, yet never anyone very particular.

Then suddenly he saw something. Opposite his window there had stopped an old pedlar-woman, with a basket of apples. Only a few of the apples, however, remained, so that it was clear that she was almost sold out. Over her shoulder was slung a sack of shavings, which she must have gathered near some new building as she was going home. Apparently, her shoulder had begun to ache under their weight, and she therefore wished to shift them to the other one. To do this, she balanced her basket of apples on the top of a post, lowered the sack to the pavement, and began shaking up its contents. As she was doing this, a boy in a ragged cap appeared from somewhere, seized an apple from the basket, and tried to make off. But the old woman, who had been on her guard, managed to turn and seize the boy by the sleeve, and although he struggled and tried to break away, she clung to him with both hands, snatched his cap off, and finally grasped him by the hair. Thereupon the youngster began to shout and abuse his captor. Avdeitch did not stop to make fast his awl, but threw his work down upon the floor, ran to the door, and went stumbling up the steps—losing his spectacles as he did so. Out into the street he ran, where the old woman was still clutching the boy by the hair and threatening to take him to the police, while the boy, for his part, was struggling in the endeavour to free himself.

"I never took it," he was saying. "What are you beating me for? Let me go."

Avdeitch tried to part them as he took the boy by the hand and said:

"Let him go, my good woman. Pardon him for Christ's sake."

"Yes, I will pardon him," she retorted, "but not until he has tasted a new birch-rod. I mean to take the young rascal to the police."

But Avdeitch still interceded for him.

"Let him go, my good woman," he said. "He will never do it again. Let him go for Christ's sake."

The old woman released the boy, who was for making off at once had not Avdeitch stopped him.

"You must beg the old woman's pardon," he said, "and never do such a thing again. I saw you take the apple."

The boy burst out crying, and begged the old woman's pardon as Avdeitch commanded.

"There, there," said Avdeitch. "Now I will give you one. Here you are,"—and he took an apple from the basket and handed it to the boy. "I will pay you for it, my good woman," he added.

"Yes, but you spoil the young rascal by doing that," she objected. "He ought to have received a reward that would have made him glad to stand for a week."

"Ah, my good dame, my good dame," exclaimed Avdeitch. "That may be *our* way of rewarding, but it is not God's. If this boy ought to have been whipped for taking the apple, ought not we also to receive something for our sins?"

The old woman was silent. Then Avdeitch related to her the parable of the master who absolved his servant from the great debt which he owed him, whereupon the servant departed and took his own debtor by the throat. The old woman listened, and also the boy.

"God has commanded us to pardon one another," went on Avdeitch, "or *He* will not pardon us. We ought to pardon all men, and especially the thoughtless."

The old woman shook her head and sighed.

"Yes, that may be so," she said, "but these young rascals are so spoilt already!"

"Then it is for us, their elders, to teach them better," he replied.

"That is what I say myself at times," rejoined the old woman. "I had seven of them once at home, but have only one daughter now." And she went on to tell Avdeitch where she and her daughter lived, and how they lived, and how many grandchildren she had.

"I have only such strength as you see," she said, "yet I work hard, for my heart goes out to my grandchildren—the bonny little things that they are! No children could run to meet me as they do. Aksintka, for instance, will go to no one else. 'Grandmother,' she cries, 'dear grandmother, you are tired' "—and the old woman became thoroughly softened. "Everyone knows what boys are," she added presently, referring to the culprit. "May God go with him!"

She was raising the sack to her shoulders again when the boy darted forward and said:

"Nay, let me carry it, grandmother. It will be all on my way home."

The old woman nodded assent, gave up the sack to the boy, and went away with him down the street. She had quite forgotten to ask Avdeitch for the money for the apple. He stood looking after them, and observing how they were talking together as they went.

Having seen them go, he returned to his room, finding his spectacles—unbroken—on the steps as he descended them. Once more he took up his awl and fell to work, but had done little before he found it difficult to distinguish the stitches, and the lamplighter had passed on his rounds. "I too must light up," he thought to himself. So he trimmed the lamp, hung it up, and resumed his work. He finished one boot completely, and then turned it over to look at it. It was all good work. Then he laid aside his tools, swept up the cuttings, rounded off the stitches and loose ends, and cleaned his awl. Next he lifted the lamp down, placed it on the table, and took his Testament from the shelf. He had intended opening the book at the place which he had marked last night with a strip of leather, but it opened itself at another instead. The instant it did so, his vision of last night came back to his memory, and, as instantly, he thought he heard a movement behind him as of someone moving towards him. He looked round and saw in the shadow of a dark corner what appeared to be figures—figures of persons standing there, yet could not distinguish them clearly. Then the voice whispered in his ear:

"Martin, Martin, dost thou not know Me?"

"Who art Thou?" said Avdeitch.

"Even I!" whispered the voice again. "Lo, it is I!"—and there stepped from the dark corner Stepanitch. He smiled, and then, like the fading of a little cloud, was gone.

"It is I!" whispered the voice again—and there stepped from the same corner the woman with her baby. She smiled, and the baby smiled, and they were gone.

"And it is I!" whispered the voice again—and there stepped forth the old woman and the boy with the apple. They smiled, and were gone.

Joy filled the soul of Martin Avdeitch as he crossed himself, put on his spectacles, and set himself to read the Testament at the place where it had opened. At the top of the page he read:

"For I was an hungred, and ye gave Me meat: I was thirsty, and ye gave Me drink: I was a stranger, and ye took Me in."

And further down the page he read:

"Inasmuch as ye have done it unto one of the least of these my brethren ye have done it unto Me."

Then Avdeitch understood that the vision had come true, and that his Saviour had in very truth visited him that day, and that he had received Him.

ANTHONY TROLLOPE

ANTHONY TROLLOPE (English, 1815-1882). Novelist recreator of the average in life and conduct. Spent early years as Irish civil servant. Famous for his methodical way of writing—1,000 words an hour—and frank admission that he did it for money. Author of over 40 novels, most famous being the 6 Barsetshire stories, including *The Warden* and *Barchester Towers*.

HE KNEW HE WAS RIGHT

THE Glascock marriage was a great affair in Florence; so much so that there were not a few who regarded it as a strengthening of peaceful relations between the United States and the United Kingdom, and who thought that the Alabama claims and the question of naturalisation might now be settled with comparative ease. An English lord was about to marry the niece of an American Minister to a foreign court. The bridegroom was not, indeed, quite a lord as yet, but it was known to all men that he must be a lord in a very short time, and the bride was treated with more than usual bridal honours because she belonged to a legation. She was not, indeed, an ambassador's daughter, but the niece of a daughterless ambassador, and therefore almost as good as a daughter. The wives and daughters of other ambassadors, and the other ambassadors themselves, of course, came to the wedding; and as the palace in which Mr. Spalding had apartments stood alone, in a garden, with a separate carriage entrance, it seemed for all wedding purposes as though the whole palace were his own.

The English Minister came, and his wife,—although she had never quite given over turning up her nose at the American bride whom Mr. Glascock had chosen for himself. It was such a pity, she said, that such a man as Mr. Glascock should marry a young woman from Providence, Rhode Island. Who in England would know anything of Providence, Rhode Island? And it was so expedient, in her estimation, that a man of family should strengthen himself by marrying a woman of family. It was so necessary, she declared, that a man when marrying should remember that his child would have two grandfathers, and would be called upon to account for four great-grandfathers. Nevertheless Mr. Glascock was —Mr. Glascock; and, let him marry whom he would, his wife would be the future Lady Peterborough. Remembering this, the English Minister's wife gave up the point, when the thing was really settled, and benignly promised to come to the breakfast with all the secretaries and attachés belonging to the legation, and all the wives and daughters thereof. What may a man not do, and do with éclat, if he be heir to a peer and have plenty of money in his pocket?

Mr. and Mrs. Spalding were covered with glory on the occasion; and perhaps they did not bear their glory as meekly as they should have done. Mrs. Spalding laid herself open to some ridicule from the English Minister's wife because of her inability to understand with absolute clearness the condition of her niece's husband in respect to his late and future seat in Parliament, to the fact of his being a commoner and a nobleman at the same time, and to certain information which was conveyed to her, surely in a most unnecessary manner, that if Mr. Glascock were to die before his father her

1326

niece would never become Lady Peterborough, although her niece's son, if she had one, would be the future lord. No doubt she blundered, as was most natural; and then the British Minister's wife made the most of the blunders; and when once Mrs. Spalding ventured to speak of Caroline as her ladyship, not to the British Minister's wife, but to the sister of one of the secretaries, a story was made out of it almost as false as it was ill-natured. Poor Caroline was spoken of as her ladyship backwards and forwards among the ladies of the legation in a manner which might have vexed her had she known anything about it; but, nevertheless, all the ladies prepared their best flounces to go to the wedding. The time soon would come when she would in truth be a "ladyship," and she might be of social use to any one of the ladies in question.

. . . Everybody who was anybody in Florence was to be present. There were only to be four bridesmaids, Caroline herself having strongly objected to a greater number. As Wallach Petrie had fled at the first note of preparation for these trivial and unpalatable festivities, another American young lady was found; and the sister of the English secretary of legation, who had so maliciously spread that report about her "ladyship," gladly agreed to be the fourth.

It was generally admitted among the various legations in Florence that there had not been such a wedding in the City of Flowers since it had become the capital of Italia. Mr. Glascock and Miss Spalding were married in the chapel of the legation,—a legation chapel on the ground floor having been extemporised for the occasion. This greatly enhanced the pleasantness of the thing, and saved the necessity of matrons and bridesmaids packing themselves and their finery into close fusty carriages. A portion of the guests attended in the chapel, and the remainder, when the ceremony was over, were found strolling about the shady garden.

The whole affair of the breakfast was very splendid and lasted some hours. In the midst of the festivities the bride and bridegroom were whisked away with a pair of gray horses to the railway station, and before the last toast of the day had been proposed by the Belgian Councillor of Legation, they were half-way up the Apennines on their road to Bologna.

Mr. Spalding behaved himself like a man on this occasion Nothing was spared in the way of expense, and when he made that celebrated speech, in which he declared that the republican

1327

virtue of the New World had linked itself in a happy alliance with the aristocratic splendour of the Old, and went on with a simile about the lion and the lamb, everybody accepted it with good humour in spite of its being a little too long for the occasion.

"It has gone off very well, mamma, has it not?" said Nora, as she returned home with her mother to her lodgings.

"Yes, my dear; much, I fancy, as these things generally do."

"I thought it was so nice. And she looked very well. And he was so pleasant, and so much like a gentleman,—not noisy, you know, and yet not too serious."

"I dare say, my love."

"It is easy enough, mamma, for a girl to be married, for she has nothing to do but wear her clothes and look as pretty as she can. And if she cries and has a red nose it is forgiven her. But a man has so difficult a part to play. If he tries to carry himself as though it were not a special occasion, he looks like a fool that way; and if he is very special, he looks like a fool the other way. I thought Mr. Glascock did it very well."

TU FU

TU FU (Chinese, 712-770). Once called the God of Verse. Friend of Li Po. Became a courtier; was exiled by Emperor Su Tsung because of his outspoken demeanor. For a time traveled as a homeless wanderer. Did some painting. A certain sadness overshadows his poetry.

TO A LOST LADY

Be still!
Tell me no more of spring,
No more of flowers.
Bring mourning boughs
And black weeds stricken by blight.

Be still!
Let the glad sun
Dip down behind the mountains,
While I put on grief's robe
And lie
Among the leaves she loved—
For it is night.

THE HOME IN THE HEART

Fire wrecked the house where I was born
   And stripped the rafters bare:
I put to sea in my gilded barque,
   But I could not shake despair.

I took my flute and played to the moon,
   But she hid behind a cloud,
For my song was sad, the music faint;
   Only my heart beat loud.

I turned me to the mountain,
   But I found no solace there,
For childhood joys seemed vanished,
   With my home into thin blue air.

I longed for death—but then the moon
   Shone mirrored in the sea,
And I caught one glimpse of a maiden's face
   As her boat was passing me.

Were it her wish, I'd rout despair
   And bear a true man's part:
I'd build another dwelling—
   And this one, in her heart!

ON THE RIVER CHOU

Beneath the wide cloud-ridden sky
My boat is gliding swiftly by.

I watch the quiet water; soon
The drifting clouds have hid the moon.

As I lean back within my boat,
Upon the sky I seem to float.

And as I drift, I like to dream
That my heart is the quiet stream,

The River Chou so still and fair—
And my beloved is mirrored there.

1329

THE POET DREAMS

Now the sad rains are falling. Let us say now: the sky weeps because
its fine weather is all gone. Boredom piles up on us like heavy
rain-clouds: where is our gaiety and wit? Let us sit indoors.

Now is the time for poetry that remembers summer. Let it be put
down gently on white paper like full-blown petals falling from
exquisite trees. And let my lips drink from this cup of summer
wine each time my brush is dipped into the ink. Thus will I keep
my fancy from floating off like clouds or smoke: for time past
escapes from us, my love, quicker than a flight of birds.

IVAN SERGEYEVICH TURGENEV

IVAN SERGEYEVICH TURGENEV (Russian, 1818-1883). The most con-
sciously artistic and "Western" of the great Russian novelists. Admired particularly by stylists like Henry James. Interested in politics of his day. Considerably responsible through his novels for abolition of serfdom in Russia.
Major works: (novels) *Fathers and Sons, Virgin Soil,* and (play) *A Month
in the Country.*

THE NIHILIST

"WHERE is your new friend?" he asked Arkadi.

"He has gone out already. He generally gets up very early and
makes some excursion. But I must tell you, once for all, that you
need not take any notice of him; he does not care for conventionalities."

"Yes, so I perceive."

Paul Petrovitch began slowly to spread butter on his bread.

"Will he remain here any length of time?"

"That depends. He will go from here to his father's."

"And where does his father live?"

"In our district; eighty versts from here. He has a little estate
there. He used to be the regimental doctor."

"Ta-ta, ta-ta! I have been continually asking myself, where could
I have heard that name before? Bazarof, Bazarof! Nicholas, do

you not remember that in our father's division there was a Dr. Bazarof?"

"I seem to remember something of the sort."

"Yes, it is right enough. So this doctor is his father—hm!"

Paul Petrovitch twisted his moustache.

"Well, and what is Mr. Bazarof junior?" asked he slowly.

"What is Bazarof?" Arkadi smiled. "Shall I tell you, uncle, what he really is?"

"Do me that favor, my dear nephew."

"He is a Nihilist."

"What?" asked Nicholas Petrovitch.

As for Paul Petrovitch, he suddenly raised the knife, on whose point was a little piece of butter, and remained motionless.

"He is a Nihilist," repeated Arkadi.

"Nihilist!" said Nicholas Petrovitch. "The word comes from the Latin *nihil*, nothing. as far as I can tell, and therefore designates a person who acknowledges nothing."

"Or rather, who respects nothing," said Paul Petrovitch, who recommenced buttering his bread.

"Or rather, who regards everything from a critical point of view," remarked Arkadi.

"Does not that come to the same thing?" asked Paul Petrovitch.

"No, by no means. A Nihilist is a man who bows to no authority, who accepts no principles on faith alone, however high may be the regard in which this principle is held in human opinion."

"And do you consider that right?" asked Paul Petrovitch.

"That depends on the point of view, uncle; some think it right, while others consider it quite wrong."

"Indeed. Well, I see it is not *our* point of view. We of the old school are of opinion that without principles, that are received on faith alone, as you express it, the world could not exist. But *vous avez changé tout cela*. Well, may God give you good health and the rank of general; as for us, we will be content with admiring you, you—what do you call yourselves?"

"Nihilists," said Arkadi, accenting each syllable.

"Yes. We used to have Hegelists, now we have Nihilists. We shall see how you manage to exist in the nothing, the vacuum, as under an air-pump. And now, brother Nicholas, be so good as to ring; I should like to drink my cocoa."

The combat took place the same evening at tea. Paul had come down into the drawing-room in a state of irritation, and ready for the fight. He only awaited an opportunity to throw himself on the enemy; but he had long to wait. Bazarof never spoke much before the "two old fellows," as he called the two brothers; besides, he did not feel very well this evening, and swallowed one cup of tea after another in silence. Paul was devoured by impatience: at length he found the opportunity he had been seeking.

The conversation turned on one of the neighboring landholders.

"He is a simpleton, a bad aristocrat," said Bazarof, who had known him at St. Petersburg.

"Permit me to ask you," said Paul, with trembling lips, "whether the words 'simpleton' and 'aristocrat' are in your opinion synonymous?"

"I said 'bad aristocrat,'" replied Bazarof carelessly, sipping his tea.

"That is true; But I assume that you rank aristocrats and bad aristocrats in the same category. I think it right to inform you that such is not my opinion. I venture to say that I am generally considered a liberal man and lover of progress; but it is just on that account that I respect the aristocrats, the true aristocrats. Consider, my dear sir"—Bazarof fixed his eyes on Paul—"my dear sir," continued he, with dignity, "consider the English nobility: they do not give up one iota of their rights, and yet they respect the rights of others just as much; they demand what is due to them, and yet they are always careful to render their due to others. It is the nobility that has given England its liberty, and that is its strongest support."

"That is an old song we have often heard," replied Bazarof; "but what do you mean by it?"

"I mean to prove by it, my dear sir, that without the consciousness of one's own dignity, without self-respect—and all these sentiments prevail among the aristocracy—there can be no solid foundation for the commonwealth, for the edifice of the State. The individual, the personality, my dear sir—that is the essential; a man's personality must stand firm as a rock, for everything rests on this basis. I know quite well that you think my manners, my dress, even my habit of cleanliness, absurd; but all this springs from self-respect, from a feeling of duty—yes, yes, sir, from a feeling of duty. I live in an out-of-the-way corner of the province; but I do not neglect my person on that account—in my own person I respect the man."

"Excuse me, Paul Petrovitch," replied Bazarof; "you say that you respect yourself, and you sit there with your arms crossed. What advantage can that be to the commonwealth? If you did not respect yourself you would not act differently."

Paul Petrovitch turned pale.

"That is quite another matter," replied he. "I have no intention of telling you why I stay with my arms crossed, as you are pleased to call it. I merely wished to tell you that aristocracy depends upon principle; and it is only immoral or worthless men who can live nowadays without principles. I said so to Arkadi the day after his arrival; and I am merely repeating it to you today. Is it not the case, Nicholas Petrovitch?"

Nicholas Petrovitch nodded assent.

"Aristocracy, liberalism, principles, progress," repeated Bazarof—"all words quite foreign to our language, and perfectly useless. A true Russian need not use them."

"What does he need, then, in your opinion? According to you, we are outside the limits of humanity, outside its laws. That is going rather too far; the logic of history requires—"

"What do you need that logic for? We can do very well without it."

"How?"

"I will give an example. I fancy that you do not need the aid of logic in carrying a piece of bread to your mouth when you are hungry. What is the use of all these abstractions?"

Paul lifted up his hands.

"I no longer understand you," said he. "You insult the Russian people. I do not understand how it is possible not to acknowledge principles—rules! What have you, then, to guide you through life?"

"I have told you before, uncle," interposed Arkadi, "that we do not acknowledge any authorities,"

"We act according as anything seems useful to us," added Bazarof; "to-day it seems to us useful to deny, and we do deny."

"Everything?"

"Absolutely everything."

"What? Not only art, poetry, but even—I hesitate to say it."

"Everything," repeated Bazarof, with most indomitable calm.

Paul looked at him fixedly. He had not expected this answer. Arkadi blushed with pleasure.

"Excuse me," said Nicholas, "you deny everything, or, to speak more correctly, you destroy everything; but you must also rebuild."

"That does not concern us. First of all, we must clear the ground."

"The present state of the people requires it," added Arkadi seriously. "We must fulfill this duty; we have no right to abandon ourselves to the satisfaction of our personal vanity."

This last speech did not please Bazarof. It smacked of philosophy,

1333

that is, of romanticism; for he gave this name even to philosophy. But he did not think this a fitting moment to contradict his young pupil.

"No, no!" exclaimed Paul, with sudden emotion. "I will not believe that you gentlemen have a right idea of the Russian people, and that you express its real wants, its surest wishes. No, the Russian people is not what you represent it. It has a reverent respect for tradition; it is patriarchal; it cannot live without faith."

"I shall not attempt to contradict you," replied Bazarof. "I am even ready to admit that this once you are right."

"But if I am right?"

"That proves nothing whatever."

"Nothing whatever," repeated Arkadi, with the assurance of an experienced chess-player, who, having foreseen a move that his opponent considers dangerous, does not seem in the least disconcerted by it.

"How can you say that proves nothing?" said Paul, stupefied. "Do you then separate yourself from your people?"

"And what if I did? The people believe that when it thunders, the prophet Elijah is riding over the heavens in his chariot. Well, must I share its opinion in this matter? You think you will confound me by telling me that the people is Russian. Well, am I not Russian, too?"

"No; after all that you have just said, you are not. I will no longer acknowledge you to be Russian."

"My grandfather followed the plough," replied Bazarof, with lofty pride. "Ask any one of your peasants which of us two—you or me—he is readiest to acknowledge as his fellow-citizen. You cannot even talk to him."

"And you, who can talk to him, you despise him."

"Why not, if he deserves it? You condemn the tendency of my ideas; but how do you know that it is accidental, that it is not rather determined by the universal spirit of the people whom you defend so well?"

"Come, the Nihilists are very useful."

"Whether they are or not is not for us to decide. Do not you also think that you are good for something?"

"Gentlemen, gentlemen, no personalities," exclaimed Nicholas, rising.

Paul smiled, and placing his hand on his brother's shoulder, forced him to sit down again.

"Set your mind at rest," said he; "I shall not forget myself, if only because of that feeling of dignity of which this gentleman speaks so scornfully. Excuse me," continued he, once more addressing Bazarof; "you probably think that your mode of looking at things is a new one; that is a mistake on your part. The materialism you profess has been held in honor more than once, and has always proved itself insufficient."

"Another foreign word!" replied Bazarof. He was beginning to become bitter, and the complexion of his face was assuming an unpleasant yellow. "In the first place, let me tell you that we do not preach; that is not one of our habits."

"What do you do, then?"

"I will tell you. We have begun by calling attention to the extortionate officials, the need of roads, the absence of trade, the manner of executing justice."

"Yes, yes; you are informers, *divulgators*, that is the name given to you, if I am not much mistaken. I agree with you in many of your criticisms; but—"

"Then we soon discovered that it was not enough to talk about the wounds to which we are succumbing, that all this only tended to platitudes and dogmatism. We perceived that our advanced men, our *divulgators*, were worth nothing whatever; that we were taking up our time with follies, such as art for art's sake, creative power which does not know itself, the parliamentary system, the need of lawyers, and a thousand other foolish tales; while we were overwhelmed by the grossest superstition; while all our joint-stock companies were becoming bankrupt. All this is only because there is a dearth of honest men; while even the liberation of the serfs, with which Government is much occupied, will produce no good effects, because our peasants are themselves ready to steal, so that they may go and drink poisonous drugs in the taverns."

"Good," replied Paul, "very good. You have discovered all that, and all the same you are determined to undertake nothing serious?"

"Yes, we are determined!" repeated Bazarof, somewhat sharply. Suddenly he began to reproach himself for having said so much before this gentleman.

"And you confine yourself to abuse?"

"We abuse, if necessary."

"And that is what is called Nihilism?"

"That is what is called Nihilism!" repeated Bazarof, this time in a particularly irritating tone.

Paul winced a little.

"Good!" said he, with forced calm and constrained manner. "The mission of Nihilism is to remedy all things, and you are our saviours and our heroes. Excellent! But why do you abuse the others so much, and call them chatterboxes? Do you not chatter as much as the rest?"

"Come, if there is anything we have to reproach ourselves with, it is certainly not this," muttered Bazarof between his teeth.

"What! can you say that you act, or even prepare for action?"

Bazarof remained silent. Paul trembled, but he restrained his anger.

"Then act, destroy," continued he; "but how dare you destroy without ever knowing why you destroy?"

"We destroy because we are a force," said Arkadi, gravely.

Paul looked at his nephew and smiled.

"Yes, force is responsible to no one," continued Arkadi, drawing himself up.

"Wretched man," exclaimed Paul Petrovitch, no longer able to contain himself, "if you would but consider what you assert of Russia alone, with your absurd phrases! No, it would require an angel's patience to endure that force! The Mongol and the savage Kalmuk have force, too. But how can this force help us? What ought to be dear to us is civilization; yes, yes, my dear sirs, the fruits of civilization. And do not tell me that these fruits are worthless; the merest dauber of signboards, the most wretched fiddler, who, for five kopecks an evening, plays polkas and mazurkas, are more useful than you, because they are representatives of civilization, and not of the Mongolian brute force! You consider yourselves advanced, and your proper place would be in a Kalmuk kibitka. Force! Consider one moment, you strong gentlemen, that at most there are only a few dozen of you, while the others may be counted by millions, and that they will not allow you to tread under foot their most sacred traditions; no, they will tear you to pieces."

"If they tear us to pieces, we must put up with it," replied Bazarof. "But you are quite out in your reckoning. We are not so few as you suppose."

"What! You seriously believe that you will be able to bring the whole people into your ranks?"

"Do you not know that a kopeck candle is enough to set the whole city of Moscow on fire?" answered Bazarof.

"Excellent! First, almost Satanic pride, and then irony, which reveals your bad taste. This is how youth is carried away; this is how the inexperienced hearts of these boys are seduced. Look! there is one of them by your side; he almost worships you." Arkadi turned away, frowning. "And this contagion has already spread. I have been told that at Rome our painters no longer set foot into the Vatican; they call Raphael a bungler, because, as they say, he is considered an authority—and those who say this are themselves incapacity personified; their imagination cannot soar beyond the 'Girl at the Well;' however they may try, they cannot attain anything better! And how ugly is this 'Girl at the Well!' I suppose you have the highest opinion of these fellows, have you not?"

"As far as I am concerned," replied Bazarof, "I would not give twopence for Raphael, and I do not suppose that the others are worth much more."

"Bravo, bravo! Do you hear, Arkadi? That is how young people should express themselves now! O, I can quite understand why they follow in your footsteps! Formerly they used to feel the need of learning something. As they did not wish to be considered ignorant, they were forced to work. But now they need only say, 'There is nothing but folly and rubbish in the world;' and there is an end to everything. The students may well rejoice. Formerly they were only foolish boys —behold them suddenly transformed into Nihilists!"

"It appears to me that you are forgetting the sentiment of personal dignity, on which you laid so much stress just now," remarked Bazarof phlegmatically, while Arkadi's face flushed with indignation, and his eyes flashed. "Our dispute has led us too far. I think we should do well to stop here. Yet," added he, rising, "I should agree with you if you could name to me a single institution of our social. civil, or family life, which does not deserve to be swept away without mercy."

"I could name a million such," exclaimed Paul Petrovitch, "a million! Take, for instance, the commune."

A cold smile passed over Bazarof's lips.

"As for the commune," said he, "you had better talk to your brother about that. I suppose he must know by this time what to think of the commune, the solidarity of the peasants, their temperance, and similar jokes."

"And the family, the family, such as we still find it among our peasants!" exclaimed Paul Petrovitch.

"In my opinion that is another question that you would do well not to examine too closely. Come, take my advice, Paul Petrovitch, and take two days to consider the matter. Nothing else will occur to you just at present; consider all our institutions one after another, and contemplate them carefully. Meantime Arkadi and I will—"

"Turn everything to ridicule," interrupted Paul Petrovitch.

"No; dissect frogs. Come, Arkadi. Good afternoon, gentlemen."

The two friends went out. The brothers remained alone together, and for some time could only look at each other in silence.

"So that is the youth of to-day," began Paul Petrovitch at length; "those are our successors!"

MARK TWAIN

MARK TWAIN (Samuel Langhorne Clemens, American, 1835-1910). Humane and gentle satirist, whose last works reveal strain of disillusioned pessimism. Adventures of childhood on the Mississippi appear in the beloved boys' stories, *Adventures of Tom Sawyer* and *Adventures of Huckleberry Finn* (considered by some the great American novel). Later satirical novel: *A Connecticut Yankee at King Arthur's Court.*

THE CELEBRATED JUMPING FROG
OF CALAVERAS COUNTY

In compliance with the request of a friend of mine, who wrote me from the East, I called on good-natured, garrulous old Simon Wheeler, and inquired after my friend's friend, Leonidas W. Smiley, as requested to do, and I hereunto append the result. I have a lurking suspicion that *Leonidas W.* Smiley is a myth; that my friend never knew such a personage; and that he only conjectured that if I asked old Wheeler about him, it would remind him of his infamous *Jim* Smiley, and he would go to work and bore me to death with some exasperating reminiscence of him as long as and as tedious as it should be useless to me. If that was the design, it succeeded.

I found Simon Wheeler dozing comfortably by the barroom stove of the dilapidated tavern in the decayed mining camp of Angel's, and I noticed that he was fat and bald-headed, and had an expression of winning gentleness and simplicity upon his tranquil countenance. He roused up and gave me good-day. I told him a friend of mine had commissioned me to make some inquiries about a cherished companion of his boyhood named *Leonidas W.* Smiley—*Reverend Leonidas W.* Smiley, a young minister of the Gospel, who he had heard was at one time a resident of Angel's Camp. I added that if Mr. Wheeler could tell me anything about this Reverend Leonidas W. Smiley I would feel under many obligations to him.

Simon Wheeler backed me into a corner and blockaded me there with his chair, and then sat down and reeled off the monotonous narrative which follows this paragraph. He never smiled, he never frowned, he never changed his voice from the gentle-flowing key to which he tuned his initial sentence, he never betrayed the slightest suspicion of enthusiasm; but all through the interminable narrative there ran a vein of impressive earnestness and sincerity which showed me plainly that, so far from his imagining that there was anything ridiculous or funny about his story, he regarded it as a really important matter, and admired its two heroes as men of transcendent genius in *finesse.* I let him go on his own way, and never interrupted him once.

Reverend Leonidas W. H'm, Reverend Le—well, there was a feller here once by the name of *Jim* Smiley, in the winter of '49—or maybe it was the spring of '50—I don't recollect exactly, somehow, though what makes me think it was one or the other is because I remember the big flume warn't finished when he first came to the camp; but anyway, he was the curiousest man about always betting on anything that turned up you ever see, if he could get anybody to bet on the other side; and if he couldn't he'd change sides. Anyway what suited the other man would suit *him*—anyway just so's he got a bet, *he* was satisfied. But still he was lucky, uncommon lucky; he most always come out winner. He was always ready and laying for a chance; there couldn't be no solit'ry thing mentioned but that feller'd offer to bet on it, and take ary side you please, as I was just telling you. If there was a horse-race, you'd find him flush or you'd find him busted at the end of it; if there was a dog-fight, he'd bet on it; if there was a cat-fight, he'd bet on it; if there was a chicken-fight, he'd bet on it; why if there was two birds setting on a fence, he would bet you which one would fly first; or if there was a camp-meeting he would be there reg'lar to bet on Parson Walker which he judged to be the best exhorter about here, and so he was, too, and a good man. If he even see a straddle-bug start to go anywhere, he would bet how long it would take him to get to—to wherever he was going to, and if you took him up, he would foller that straddle-bug to Mexico but what he would find out where he was bound for and how long he was on the road. Lots of the boys here has seen that Smiley and can tell you about him. Why, it never made no difference to *him* —he'd bet on *anything*—the dangdest feller. Parson Walker's wife laid very sick once, for a good while, and it seemed as if they warn't going to save her; but one morning he come in, and Smiley up and asked him how she was, and he said she was considerable better—thank the Lord for His inf'nite mercy—and coming on so smart that with the blessing of Prov'dence she'd get well yet; and Smiley, before he thought, says, "Well, I'll resk two-and-a-half she don't anyway."

Thish-yer Smiley had a mare—the boys called her the fifteen-minute nag, but that was only in fun, you know, because of course, for all she was slow and always had the asthma, or the distemper, or the consumption, or something of that kind. They used to give her two or three hundred yards' start, and then pass her under way; but always at the fag end of the race she'd get excited and desparate like, and come cavorting and straddling up, and scattering her legs around limber, sometimes in the air and sometimes out to one side among the fences, and kicking up m-o-r-e dust and raising m-o-r-e racket with her coughing and sneezing and blowing her nose—and *always* fetch up at the stand just about a neck ahead, as near as you cipher it down.

And he had a little small bull-pup, that to look at him you'd think he warn't worth a cent but to set around and look ornery and lay for a chance to steal something. But as soon as money was up on him he was a different dog; his under-jaw'd begin to stick out like the fo'-castle of a steamboat, and his teeth would uncover and shine like the furnaces. And a dog might tackle him and bully-rag him, and bite him, and throw him over his shoulder two or three times, and Andrew Jackson—which was the name of the pup—Andrew Jackson would never let on but what *he* was satisfied, and hadn't expected nothing else—and the bets being doubled and doubled on the other side all the time, till the money was all up; and then all of a sudden he would grab that other dog just by the j'int of his hind leg and freeze to it—not chaw, you understand, but only just grip and hang on till they throwed up the sponge, if it was a year. Smiley always come out winner on that pup, till he harnessed a dog once that didn't have no hind legs, because they'd been sawed off in a circular saw, and when the thing had gone along far enough, and the money was all up, and he came to make a snatch for his pet holt, he see in a minute how he'd been imposed on, and how the other dog had him in the door, so to speak, and he 'peared surprised, and then he looked sorter dis-couraged-like, and didn't try no more to win the fight, and so he got shucked out bad. He gave Smiley a look, as much as to say his heart was broke, and it was *his* fault for putting up a dog that hadn't no hind legs for him to take holt of, which was his main dependence in a fight, and then he limped off a piece and laid down and died. It was a good pup, was that Andrew Jackson, and would have made a name for hisself if he'd lived, for the stuff was in him and he had genius—I know it, because he hadn't no opportunities to speak of, and it don't stand to reason that a dog could make such a fight as he could under them circumstances if he hadn't no talent. It always makes me feel sorry when I think of that last fight of his'n, and the way it turned out.

Well, thish-yer Smiley had rat-terriers, and chicken cocks, and tom-cats, and all them kind of things till you couldn't rest, and you couldn't fetch nothing for him to bet on but he'd match you. He ketched a frog one day, and took him home, and said he cal'lated to educate him; and so he never done nothing for three months but set in his back yord and learn that frog to jump. And you bet you he *did* learn him, too. He'd give him a little punch behind, and the next minute you'd see that frog whirling in the air like a doughnut—see him turn one summerset, or maybe a couple, if he got a good start, and come down flat-footed and all right like a cat. He got him up so in the matter of ketching flies, and kep' him in practice so constant, that he'd nail a fly every time as fur as he could see him. Smiley said all a frog wanted was education and he could do 'most anything— and I believe him. Why, I've seen him set Dan'l Webster down here on this floor—Dan'l Webster was the name of the frog—and sing out, "Flies, Dan'l, flies!" and quicker'n you could wink he'd spring straight up and snake a fly off'n the counter there, and flop ag'in as solid as a gob of mud, and fall to scratching the side of his head with his hind foot as indifferent as if he hadn't no idea he'd been doin' any more'n any frog might do. You never see a frog so modest and straightfor'- ard as he was, for all he was so gifted. And when it come to fair and square jumping on a dead level, he could get over more ground at one straddle than any animal of his breed you ever see. Jumping on a dead level was his strong suit, you understand; and when it come to that, Smiley would ante up money on him as long as he had a red. Smiley was monstrous proud of his frog, and well he might be, for fellers that had traveled and been everywhere all said he laid over any frog that ever *they* see.

Well, Smiley kep' the beast in a little lattice box, and he used to fetch him down-town sometimes and lay for a bet. One day a feller— a stranger in the camp, he was—come acrost him with his box, and says:

"What might it be that you've got in the box?"

And Smiley says, sorter indifferent like, "It might be a parrot, or it might be a canary, maybe, but it ain't—it's only just a frog."

And the feller took it, and looked at it careful, and turned it round this way and that, and says, "H'm—so 'tis. Well, what's *he* good for?"

"Well," Smiley says, easy and careless, "he's good enough for *one* thing, I should judge—he can outjump any frog in Calaveras County."

The feller took the box again, and took another long, particular look, and give it back to Smiley, and says, very deliberate, "Well," he says, "I don't see no p'ints about that frog that's any better'n any other frog."

"Maybe you don't," Smiley says. "Maybe you understand frogs and maybe you don't understand 'em; maybe you've had experience, and maybe you ain't only a amature, as it were. Anyways, I've got *my* opinion, and I'll resk forty dollars that he can outjump any frog in Calaveras County."

And the feller studied a minute, and then says, kinder sad like, "Well, I'm only a stranger here, and I ain't got no frog; but if I had a frog I'd bet you."

And then Smiley says, "That's all right—that's all right—if you'll hold my box a minute I'll go and get you a frog." And so the feller took the box, and put up his forty dollars along with Smiley's, and set down to wait.

So he set there a good while thinking and thinking to himself, and then he got the frog out and pried his mouth open and took a teaspoon and filled him full of quail shot—filled him pretty near up to his chin—and set him on the floor. Smiley he went to the swamp and slopped around in the mud for a long time, and finally he ketched a frog, and fetched him in, and give him to this feller, and says:

"Now, if you're ready, set him alongside of Dan'l, with his forepaws just even with Dan'l's, and I'll give the word." Then he says, "One—two—three—*git!*" and him and the feller touched up the frogs from behind, and the new frog hopped off lively, but Dan'l give a heave, and hysted up his shoulders—so—like a Frenchman, but it warn't no use—he couldn't budge; he was planted as solid as a church, and he couldn't no more stir than if he was anchored out. Smiley was a good deal surprised, and he was disgusted, too, but he didn't have no idea what the matter was, of course.

The feller took the money and started away; and when he was going out at the door, he sorter jerked his thumb over his shoulder—so—at Dan'l, and says again, very deliberate, "Well," he says, "*I* don't see no p'ints about that frog that's any better'n any other frog."

Smiley he stood scratching his head and looking down at Dan'l a long time, and at last he says, "I do wonder what in the nation that frog throw'd off for—I wonder if there ain't something the matter with him—he 'pears to look mighty baggy, somehow." And he ketched Dan'l by the nap of the neck and hefted him, and says, "Why, blame my cats, if he don't weigh five pound!" and turned him upside down and he belched out a double handful of shot. And then he see how it was, and he was the maddest man—he set the frog down and took out after that feller, but he never ketched him. And——

[Here Simon Wheeler heard his name called from the front yard, and got up to see what was wanted.] And turning to me as he moved away, he said: "Jest set where you are, stranger, and rest easy—I ain't going to be gone a second."

But by your leave, I did not think that a continuation of the history of the enterprising vagabond *Jim* Smiley would be likely to afford me much information concerning the Reverend *Leonidas W.* Smiley, and so I started away.

At the door I met the sociable Wheeler returning, and he button-holed me and recommenced:

"Well, thish-yer Smiley had a yaller, one-eyed cow that didn't have no tail, only just a short stump like a bannanner, and——"

However, lacking both time and inclination, I did not wait to hear about the afflicted cow, but took my leave.

U

MIGUEL DE UNAMUNO

MIGUEL DE UNAMUNO (Spanish, 1864-1936). Unique philosopher and powerful personality of modern Spain. A professor of Greek, exiled for his lofty spirit and writings. He attempted to synthesize the many aspects of present-day culture. Admired poem: *El Cristo de Vélazquez*. Novels: *Niebla, Tres novelas ejemplares.* Internationally famous philosophic work: *Del sentimiento trágico de la vida.*

THREE GENERATIONS

SCENE: the dining room of a village inn in my native Basque country; actors: grandfather, son, and grandson; audience: myself, profoundly moved. Three generations of the same family had met there to eat together. The old man, an honorable independent workman, was plain and uneducated, speaking Castilian only with difficulty; his son, a mature man, who in his youth had gone to America where he had made a fortune, married and raised a family, was returning to his native soil to visit his aged father and introduce the grandson; and the grandson, still very young, was a good looking boy, very neat, very finical, and very well groomed, whose careful training was apparent in every move of his knife and fork.

Between frequent draughts of wine, the grandfather was evidencing his joy at the sight of such an elegant grandson, repeating dotingly again and again in his meagre Castilian, "I thought I was going to die without ever seeing you." The father, between the grandfather and his son, between his memories and his hopes, was thinking of God knows what, and the youngster was eating politely and coldly, looking impatiently at his grandfather from time to time as if bored.

That scene was full of meaning, not because of what its actors said, but rather what they left unsaid.

That pretty youth did not seem to be interested in anything and was paying no attention to his father's father. They were separated by an abyss. I doubt that he had ever stopped to consider that he owed his good fortune, his education, and everything that was serving as a base for his egoism to the simple, noble, honorable spirit that the old man transmitted to his son, the stalwart toiler who had made a fortune.

Immediately I was reminded that a few years ago I had heard a poor man confess sadly and bitterly that, having amassed a fortune, married and raised a family also in America, he was disdained by his children. "They scorn me," he said tearfully, "they scorn me because I don't speak correctly and because I don't know the things they have learned from the teachers I hired." Later I had the opportunity of meeting one of his sons and I can assure you that he knew less than his father. He could talk about bookish things, jabber a little French and even less English, sigh for Paris, and find fault with his father's people.

You should have heard him constantly comparing our country and the one in which he was born. There was no limit to the superficiality of his comparisons. To him everything revolved around paved streets, water-closets, street cars, restaurants, and theatres. To him civilization meant urbanization and conveniences and, in addition, a certain show of good manners. The real essence of culture was completely unknown to him. He possessed not one grain of poetic feeling or sensibility. He told me that he was not interested in old stones.

Only this lack of sensibility, this want of poetic feeling, or—let us state it clearly—this cold-heartedness can explain certain things. Many an American of Spanish parents comes to Europe without enough piety, or curiosity even, to visit his parents' fatherland; Paris calls him. In his father's town, perhaps a tiny village hidden in the mountains, there are no asphalt boulevards or electric trollies; above all, there is no *Moulin Rouge* or *chez Maxim*. Not all can feel the deep penetrating poetry of one of those little villages.

How beautiful, how deeply pious and poetical is the account by that great poet, Zorrilla de San Martín, of his visit to his father's people in the mountains behind Santander! Zorrilla de San Martín is a poet, a true poet, a noble delicate spirit, guarding the treasure of our secular culture.

I am not known as a flatterer of my country; I could more correctly be called a bitter critic of its defects. I have never hidden our weaknesses, but when I happen to meet one of those pretty youths who find fault with everything around here, I find myself turning against them and the superiorities of the lands that they have come to boast about. Because they both fail to see our real ills and to comprehend the best features of their own countries.

One of my neighbors in Salamanca, where I now live and write, once went to Bilbao, my native city, and in front of the city hall, a massive, showy, poorly designed building, he stopped and exclaimed, "I wish we had something like this in Salamanca." A native of Salamanca, who has never been near the beautiful old cathedral of this city except to show it to some visitor, said this.

At the end of each year I receive many letters spontaneously from my unknown American readers. The vast majority of them are written in a kindly, amiable tone, urging me to keep on with my work, or, if they do censure me for something, they do it discreetly, honestly, and respectfully. But there are also some, although very few, mostly anonymous, written in a sly, under-handed manner, saying injurious things about me, or more correctly, about my country, its men, and its ways. What nonsense comes from the pens of those artful nitwits. Not long ago I received a letter whose author, after using the term Galician in its derogatory sense—an act which belittles the user more than anyone else—asked me if certain Spanish family names, such as *Iglesias* and *de la Iglesia* originate in foundling asylums, or if they are given to children found in their vicinity.

If I were a spiteful, ill-natured individual, I would have answered that these names and many more had their origin in such asylums, and among them the names of some saints, including the name of San Martín, so justly famous in Argentina.

In my Basque country there has been developing for some time, because of the material prosperity of the region, a most blameworthy feeling of disdain toward those who come there from other parts of Spain to earn a living, working there and increasing the general prosperity of the country. They call them *maquis* and say that they have come there to kill their hunger. That is right, but they also kill the hunger of those that are making sport of them. It is a line of reasoning like that of the factory owner who seriously asserts that he is feeding two or three hundred workers, when it is they who are feeding him and giving him something more in addition.

That poorly disguised hostility toward the immigrant or stranger is a phenomenon that arises when the partner in production becomes a competitor in consumption, when the planting and the reaping are ended and it is time to divide the harvest. It is then that the descendants of the first inhabitants resort to trickery and seek to obtain special privileges as if they had created the fertility of the soil. Is it any merit of mine that my native mountains are filled with rich iron mines?

It is all right for those poor laborers to drag out their lives extracting ore from the depths of the mountains or doing any other work that adds to the wealth of the region; it is all right for them to work. But, as soon as they show any interest in political or social affairs, they are reminded that they came there to work, they are ridiculed for being industrious.

On one occasion an Argentine friend, whose name I had given to an emigrant, wrote me an interesting letter saying, among other things, "Do not encourage ambitious people to come here; we need hands and capital, but not talent. There are too many scholars here in America. In some countries, having nothing else to do, they plan revolutions." I understood immediately what my friend was saying and, by reading between the lines, I understood many things that he did not say. I recalled the bitter tale of a friend and countryman of mine who was a doctor. He suffered a great deal overseas precisely because he was a competent doctor. His learned colleagues outdid themselves to help him . . . suffer.

What have I been led to say by the sight of that family represented by three generations? I can see them yet: the old man striving to use a fork and not his hands as he would have done at home, the youth daintily cutting his meat and peeling his peaches with studied elegance, and between them, the rude man who had made a fortune. I do not know whether he was ashamed to have such a father or such a son or proud of one or the other or of both of them. How well groomed the boy was! How artistic was his head on the outside! I do not know what it was like on the inside but most surely it was furnished with the latest fads from Parisian books.

The mature man, the maker of fortunes, seemed to me to be only the connecting link between his father and his son. And I set about comparing the strong plain old man with the delicate disdainful youth. And, of the two, the old man seemed to be the younger, hardly more than a child. He was probably more than seventy but his was the illusion and the enthusiasm, while the youth seemed to have been born bored and carrying the weight of the greatest disillusionment on his artistic head.

Why was that reunion held in a place as public as the dining room of an inn? Why were those three not before the grandfather's hearth, in the house where the father was born? Perhaps it was on a mountain top whither one had to climb along a stony path, possibly muddy in spots. The youth's delicate feet were only accustomed to smooth macadam and his shining boots had never been spattered by mud. Surely that house did not have even the inn's primitive conveniences. I imagine that in the opinion of the pretty boy with well combed locks it was not a dwelling of a civilized country. For I am almost certain that I know what concept of civilization that scornful, finical upstart had. It was ridiculous and extremely superficial.

No people can progress far until it has lost that concept of civilization which looks upon it mainly as conveniences and facilities for material well-being. Hygiene is important and comfort is more so; but we must agree that among a people that is hygienically careless, the life of the spirit can be far more carefully guarded than among people that is daily sprinkled with antiseptics. Hygiene itself is indispensable but it should not become a monomania or superstition.

The maxim says: *mens sana in corpore sano,* a sound mind in a sound body, and not *corpus sanum in mente sana;* let us put first things first. Of the two extremes, and they are both abominable, I prefer Job on the dung-heap to a spruce young gentleman whose principle occupation is bathing and perfuming himself.

It is evident that not all the grandsons of our rude, homespun mountain folk feel like the pretty youth I have described; besides, I am glad to believe most of them pride themselves on their ancestry, and if they do not visit their ancestral homes, it is because they cannot and not through laziness. I know all that very well, but I would not like to fail to add my protest against those vain superficial striplings who come here and disdain everything they cannot comprehend, those who judge a people by its manners and who seem to think that the most important agents of civilization are the janitor, the cook, the tailor, and the dancer.

V

PAUL VALERY

PAUL VALÉRY (French, 1871-1945). Poet of philosophical abstractions. Influenced early by Mallarmé. First works were prose: *Introduction à la méthode de Léonard de Vinci* and *La Soirée avec Monsieur Teste*. Most famous poem: *"La Jeune parque." Charmes:* poems on love and death. Skeptical, disillusioned, he advocated refined discipline of the mind.

NARCISSUS

A Fragment

. . . Perhaps you expected a face that was free from tears,
You calms, you always decked with leaves and flowers,
And haunted depths of the incorruptible,
O nymphs! . . . But yielding to the enchanted slopes
That were my irretrievable roadway to you,
Permit this fair reflection of man's disorder.
Happy your blended forms, you deep and level waters!
I am alone. . . . If the gods, the waves, and the echoes
And so many sighs allow! I am alone!
But still I am he who comes unto himself
When he comes near the banks this growth adorns.

On the peaks the light has halted its pure plunder,
The voice of the fountains turns to talk of dusk,
Calm concord hearkens, wherein I hear hope.
I hear the night grass grow in the holy shadows,
And the perfidious moon now elevates her mirror
Even to the secrets of the dying pool.

And I! My body cast upon these reeds,
I languish, Sapphire, in my mournful beauty!
I must henceforth adore the magic waters
Where I have forgotten the olden smile and the rose.
Let me bewail your pure and fatal glory,
Fountain so softly closed around by me,
Where my eyes draw forth from the lethal azure
Those same dark eyes of their astounded soul!
What loss within oneself so calm a place affords!
The soul, even unto destruction, seeks a god
Demanding of the wave, the lonely wave
That gleams inviting soft advent of swan . . .
Never have thirsty flocks bemired these waters!
Others who have wandered here have found repose,
And in the dark earth a clear, opening tomb;
But it is not calm, alas! that I shall find,
When the opaque delight where the splendor sleeps
Yields to my body the horror of widening leafage
And, driving back the shade and the frightening thickness,
I see! I fall! and come from this tyrant body
Peacefully to share the eternal charms!
There, nude between the arms that spring from the forest,
A tender gleam of daylight doubtfully plays;
And there the glimmer of day becomes a bridegroom,
Pure in the place where the sad water lures me,
Delightful spirit, desirable and cold!
I behold in the water my flesh of moon and the dawn-dew,
Obedient form opposed to my desires!
There are the pure stirrings of my silver arms!
My lingering hands in the adorable gold grow weary
Of seeking the captive whom the leaves entwine,
And I cry to echo the names of the hidden gods!

But how fair his mouth in that mute blasphemy!
O likeness! . . . Yet more perfect than myself,
Immortal ephemeron, clear before my eyes,
Pale limbs of pearl and softly silken hair,
Must the shadow darken us who scarce have loved,
Must the night already part us, O Narcissus,
And press between us the blade that halves a fruit!

What is it?
           My plaint is baneful? . . .
                              The mere stir
Of the breath I set upon your lips, my double,
Has coursed a tremor on your limpid wave? . . .
You tremble! But these words I, kneeling, breathe
Are still no more than a hesitant soul between us,
Between that clear brow and my spent memory . . .
I am so near you I can drink you in,
O countenance? . . . My thirst is a naked slave . . .

Till this rapt hour I did not know myself,
Nor how to cherish, how attain my soul? . . .
But watching you, dear slave, obey the least
Of the shadows sadly retreating in my heart,
And on my brow a secret fire and storm,
Watching, O marvel! watching my murmurous mouth
Betray . . . snare on the water a flower of fancy,
And mad events that sparkle in the eye!
I have found a treasure of impotence and pride!
May no sweet virgin whom the satyr stalks,
None! Swift in flight, deft in unfeeling fall,
No nymph, no maiden, ever lure me on
As you within the waters, my illimitable soul!

THE SYLPH

Seen not nor known
I am the scent shed
Living and dead
In the wind blown

Seen not nor known
Genius or chance?
Hardly seed sown
When the flowers dance!

Nor read nor possessed!
What errors shown
For swift renowns—

Seen not nor known,
The glimpse of a breast
Between two gowns!

LOST WINE

One day I cast into the sea
(But I no longer remember under what skies)
As an offering unto Nonentity
A little wine of a sort I prize.

Who, O liquor, wished you to part?
Perhaps you were an omen I could not divine:
Perhaps concerned with my heart,
Thinking of blood, and pouring wine?
I watched the sea resume,
After a rosy spume,
Its usual transparency. . . .

Lost the wine, drunk the waves!
I saw leaping from sea-caves
Figures of greatest profundity.

VALMIKI

VALMIKI (Indian, *ca.* 4th century B. C.). Legendary author of a poem of
24,000 verses on the exploits of Rama *(Rāmāyana)*. In Hindu literature this
work compares with the Greek *Odyssey*, and exists in several versions.

NÁRAD

Om

To sainted Nárad, prince of those
Whose lore in words of wisdom flows,
Whose constant care and chief delight
Were Scripture and ascetic rite,
The good Válmíki, first and best
Of hermit saints, these words addressed:—

"In all this world, I pray thee, who
Is virtuous, heroic, true?
Firm in his vows, of grateful mind,
To every creature good and kind?
Bounteous, and holy, just, and wise,
Alone most fair to all men's eyes?
Devoid of envy, firm, and sage,
Whose tranquil soul ne'er yields to rage?
Whom, when his warrior wrath is high,
Do Gods embattled fear and fly?
Whose noble might and gentle skill
The triple world can guard from ill?
Who is the best of princes, he
Who loves his people's good to see?
The store of bliss, the living mine
Where brightest joys and virtues shine?
Queen Fortune's best and dearest friend,
Whose steps her choicest gifts attend?
Who may with Sun and Moon compare,
With Indra, Vishnu, Fire, and Air?
Grant, Saint divine, the boon I ask,
For thee, I ween, an easy task,
To whom the power is given to know
If such a man breathe here below."

Then Nárad, clear before whose eye
The present, past, and future lie,
Made ready answer: "Hermit, where
Are graces found so high and rare?
Yet listen, and my tongue shall tell
In whom alone these virtues dwell.
From old Ikshváku's line he came,
Known to the world by Ráma's name:—
With soul subdued, a chief of might,
In Scripture versed, in glory bright.
His steps in virtue's paths are bent,
Obedient, pure, and eloquent.
In each emprise he wins success,
And dying foes his power confess.
Tall and broad-shouldered, strong of limb,
Fortune has set her mark on him.

Graced with a conch-shell's triple line,
His throat displays the auspicious sign.
High destiny is clear impressed
On massive jaw and ample chest.
His mighty shafts he truly aims,
And foemen in the battle tames.
Deep in the muscle, scarcely shown,
Embedded lies his collar-bone.
His lordly steps are firm and free,
His strong arms reach below his knee;
All fairest graces join to deck
His head, his brow, his stately neck,
And limbs in fair proportion set:—
The manliest form e'er fashioned yet.
Graced with each high imperial mark,
His skin is soft and lustrous dark.
Large are his eyes that sweetly shine
With majesty almost divine.
His plighted word he ne'er forgets;
On erring sense a watch he sets.
By nature wise, his teacher's skill
Has trained him to subdue his will.
Good, resolute and pure, and strong,
He guards mankind from scathe and wrong,
And lends his aid, and ne'er in vain,
The cause of justice to maintain.
Well has he studied o'er and o'er
The Vedas and their kindred lore.
Well skilled is he the bow to draw,
Well trained in arts and versed in law;
High-souled and meet for happy fate,
Most tender and compassionate;
The noblest of all lordly givers,
Whom good men follow, as the rivers
Follow the King of Floods, the sea:—
So liberal, so just is he.
The joy of Queen Kausalyá's heart,
In every virtue he has part;
Firm as Himálaya's snowy steep,
Unfathomed like the mighty deep;

The peer of Vishnu's power and might,
And lovely as the Lord of Night;
Patient as Earth, but, roused to ire,
Fierce as the world-destroying fire;
In bounty like the Lord of Gold,
And Justice' self in human mould.
With him, his best and eldest son,
By all his princely virtues won
King Dasaratha willed to share
His kingdom as the Regent Heir.
But when Kaikeyí, youngest queen,
With eyes of envious hate had seen
The solemn pomp and regal state
Prepared the prince to consecrate,
She bade the hapless king bestow
Two gifts he promised long ago,
That Ráma to the woods should flee,
And that her child the heir should be.

By chains of duty firmly tied,
The wretched King perforce complied.
Ráma, to please Kaikeyí went
Obedient forth, to banishment.
Then Lakshman's truth was nobly shown,
Then were his love and courage known,
When for his brother's sake he dared
All perils, and his exile shared.
And Sítá, Ráma's darling wife,
Loved even as he loved his life,
Whom happy marks combined to bless,
A miracle of loveliness,
Of Janak's royal lineage sprung,
Most excellent of women, clung
To her dear lord, like Rohiní
Rejoicing with the Moon to be.
The King and People, sad of mood,
The hero's car awhile pursued.
But when Prince Ráma lighted down
At Sringavera's pleasant town,

Where Gangá's holy waters flow,
He bade his driver turn and go.
Guha, Nishádas' King, he met,
And on the farther bank was set.
Then on from wood to wood they strayed,
O'er many a stream, through constant shade,
As Bharadvája bade them, till
They came to Chitrakúta's hill.
And Ráma there, with Lakshman's aid,
A pleasant little cottage made,
And spent his days with Sítá, dressed
In coat of bark and deerskin vest.
And Chitrakúta grew to be
As bright with those illustrious three
As Meru's sacred peaks that shine
With glory, when the Gods recline
Beneath them: Siva's self between
The Lord of Gold and Beauty's Queen.

The aged King for Ráma pined,
And for the skies the earth resigned.
Bharat, his son, refused to reign,
Though urged by all the twice-born train.
Forth to the woods he fared to meet
His brother, fell before his feet,
And cried "Thy claim all men allow:—
O come, our lord and King be thou."
But Ráma nobly chose to be
Observant of his sire's decree.
He placed his sandals in his hand,
A pledge that he would rule the land:—
And bade his brother turn again.
Then Bharat, finding prayer was vain,
The sandals took and went away;
Nor in Ayodhyá would he stay,
But turned to Nandigráma, where
He ruled the realm with watchful care,
Still longing eagerly to learn
Tidings of Ráma's safe return.

Then lest the people should repeat
Their visit to his calm retreat,
Away from Chitrakúta's hill
Fared Ráma, ever onward till
Beneath the shady trees he stood
Of Dandaká's primeval wood.
Virádha, giant fiend, he slew,
And then Agastya's friendship knew.
Counselled by him he gained the sword
And bow of Indra, heavenly lord:—
A pair of quivers too, that bore
Of arrows an exhaustless store.
While there he dwelt in greenwood shade,
The trembling hermits sought his aid,
And bade him with his sword and bow
Destroy the fiends who worked them woe:—
To come like Indra strong and brave,
A guardian God to help and save.
And Ráma's falchion left its trace
Deep cut on Súrpanakhá's face:—
A hideous giantess who came
Burning for him with lawless flame.
Their sister's cries the giants heard,
And vengeance in each bosom stirred;
The monster of the triple head,
And Dúshan to the contest sped.
But they and myriad fiends beside
Beneath the might of Ráma died.

When Rávan, dreaded warrior, knew
The slaughter of his giant crew—
Rávan, the King, whose name of fear
Earth, hell, and heaven all shook to hear—
He bade the fiend Márícha aid
The vengeful plot his fury laid.
In vain the wise Márícha tried
To turn him from his course aside:—
Not Rávan's self, he said, might hope
With Ráma and his strength to cope.

1357

Impelled by fate and blind with rage
He came to Ráma's hermitage.
There, by Márícha's magic art,
He wiled the princely youths apart,
The vulture slew, and bore away
The wife of Ráma as his prey.
The son of Raghu came and found
Jatáyu slain upon the ground.
He rushed within his leafy cot;
He sought his wife, but found her not.
Then, then the hero's senses failed;
In mad despair he wept and wailed.
Upon the pile that bird he laid,
And still in quest of Sítá strayed.
A hideous giant then he saw,
Kabandha named, a shape of awe.

The monstrous fiend he smote and slew,
And in the flame the body threw;
When straight from out the funeral flame
In lovely form Kabandha came,
And bade him seek in his distress
A wise and holy hermitess.
By counsel of this saintly dame
To Pampá's pleasant flood he came,
And there the steadfast friendship won
Of Hanumán the Wind-God's son.
Counselled by him he told his grief
To great Sugríva, Vánar chief,
Who, knowing all the tale, before
The sacred flame alliance swore.
Sugríva to his new-found friend
Told his own story to the end:—
His hate of Báli for the wrong
And insult he had borne so long.
And Ráma lent a willing ear
And promised to allay his fear.
Sugríva warned him of the might
Of Báli, matchless in the fight,
And, credence for his tale to gain,
Showed the huge fiend by Báli slain.

1358

The prostrate corse of mountain size
Seemed nothing in the hero's eyes;
He lightly kicked it, as it lay,
And cast it twenty leagues away.
To prove his might his arrows through
Seven palms in line, uninjured, flew.
He cleft a mighty hill apart,
And down to hell he hurled his dart.
Then high Sugríva's spirit rose,
Assured of conquest o'er his foes.
With his new champion by his side
To vast Kishkindhá's cave he hied.
Then, summoned by his awful shout,
King Báli came in fury out,
First comforted his trembling wife,
Then sought Sugriva in the strife.
One shaft from Ráma's deadly bow
The monarch in the dust laid low.
Then Ráma bade Sugríva reign
In place of royal Báli slain.
Then speedy envoys hurried forth
Eastward and westward, south and north,
Commanded by the grateful King
Tidings of Ráma's spouse to bring.
Then by Sampáti's counsel led,
Brave Hanumán, who mocked at dread,
Sprang at one wild tremendous leap
Two hundred leagues, across the deep.
To Lanká's town he urged his way,
Where Rávan held his royal sway.
There pensive 'neath Asoka boughs
He found poor Sítá, Ráma's spouse.
He gave the hapless girl a ring,
A token from her lord and King.
A pledge from her fair hand he bore;
Then battered down the garden door.
Five captains of the host he slew,
Seven sons of councillors o'erthrew;
Crushed youthful Aksha on the field,
Then to his captors chose to yield.

Soon from their bonds his limbs were free,
But honoring the high decree
Which Brahmá had pronounced of yore,
He calmly all their insults bore.
The town he burnt with hostile flame,
And spoke again with Ráma's dame,
Then swiftly back to Ráma flew
With tidings of the interview.

Then with Sugríva for his guide,
Came Ráma to the ocean side.
He smote the sea with shafts as bright
As sunbeams in their summer height,
And quick appeared the River's King
Obedient to the summoning.
A bridge was thrown by Nala o'er
The narrow sea from shore to shore.
They crossed to Lanká's golden town,
Where Ráma's hand smote Rávan down.
Vibhíshan there was left to reign
Over his brother's wide domain.
To meet her husband Sítá came;
But Ráma, stung with ire and shame,
With bitter words his wife addressed
Before the crowd that round her pressed.
But Sítá, touched with noble ire,
Gave her fair body to the fire.
Then straight the God of Wind appeared,
And words from heaven her honor cleared.
And Ráma clasped his wife again,
Uninjured, pure from spot and stain,
Obedient to the Lord of Fire
And the high mandate of his sire.
Led by the Lord who rules the sky,
The Gods and heavenly saints drew nigh,
And honored him with worthy meed,
Rejoicing in each glorious deed.
His task achieved, his foe removed,
He triumphed, by the Gods approved.
By grace of Heaven he raised to life
The chieftains slain in mortal strife;

Then in the magic chariot through
The clouds to Nandigráma flew.
Met by his faithful brothers there,
He loosed his votive coil of hair;
Thence fair Ayodhyá's town he gained,
And o'er his father's kingdom reigned.
Disease or famine ne'er oppressed
His happy people, richly blest
With all the joys of ample wealth,
Of sweet content and perfect health.
No widow mourned her well-loved mate,
No sire his son's untimely fate.
They feared not storm or robber's hand,
No fire or flood laid waste the land:
The Golden Age seemed come again
To bless the days of Ráma's reign.
From him the great and glorious King,
Shall many a princely scion spring.
And he shall rule, beloved by men,
Ten thousand years and hundreds ten,
And when his life on earth is past
To Brahmá's world shall go at last.

Whoe'er this noble poem reads
That tells the tale of Ráma's deeds,
Good as the Scriptures, he shall be
From every sin and blemish free.
Whoever reads the saving strain,
With all his kin the heavens shall gain.
Bráhmans who read shall gather hence
The highest praise for eloquence.
The warrior, o'er the land shall reign,
The merchant, luck in trade obtain;
And Súdras, listening, ne'er shall fail
To reap advantage from the tale.

GIOVANNI VERGA

GIOVANNI VERGA (Italian, 1840-1922). One of Italy's leading realistic fiction writers. Immortalized in his novels the peasants of Sicily. Spent a time in the fashionable world of Florence, but returned to Sicily to do best work: *Vita dei Campi* (stories), *Mastro Don Gesualdo* (novel). Author of *Cavalleria Rusticana*, basis of Mascagni's popular opera.

GRAMIGNA'S MISTRESS

THIS is no more than the sketch of a story, but it has the merit of being very short, and of being historical—a human document, as they say nowadays; and as such will perhaps be interesting to those who study the great book of the heart. I will tell it just as I heard it myself among the fields and country lanes; almost with the same simple and picturesque words as are used in the popular narrative.

Some years ago, down in the district of the Simeto, they were hunting a brigand; one Gramigna, if I mistake not,—and that is as ill a name as the weed that bears it,—who had filled the whole countryside with the terror of his renown.

Police, soldiery, and mounted militia had pursued him for two months, and had never succeeded in fastening their claws upon him; he was alone, but he was as good as ten others, and the evil weed threatened to take root.

To make matters worse, it was nearly harvest time, the hay already lay scattered upon the meadows, and the ears of corn bowed their heads, as if nodding consent to the reapers, who were ready with sickle in hand; and yet not a single farmer dared show his nose beyond his garden hedge, for fear of finding Gramigna lying among the furrows, his carbine between his knees, ready to blow out the brains of the first man who should offer to meddle with him.

Hence the complaints were universal. So the prefect summoned before him all these gentlemen of the police, the "*carabinieri*," and the soldiery, and said a few words to them of a kind that made them prick up their ears. The next day there was a general earthquake: patrols, troops, vedettes in every ditch and behind every wall—they drove him before them like a wild beast, through a whole province, by day and by night, on foot, on horseback, and by the telegraph. Still Gramigna slipped through their hands, and answered them with volleys of shot when they trod too closely on his heels. In the fields, in the villages, at the farms, beneath the boughs that overshadow the tavern doors, in every place of meeting, people talked of nothing but him, Gramigna, and that furious chase, that desperate flight.

The *carabinieri's* horses dropped down from sheer weariness, the worn-out soldiers flung themselves to rest upon the ground in every stable, the patrols fell asleep as they walked. Only he, Gramigna, was never weary, never slept, but still fled on, clambering up precipices, creeping among the corn, crawling on all fours through the thickets of prickly pear, scrambling like a wolf along the dry torrent-beds. The principal topic of conversation among the gossips at the village doors was the consuming thirst that the hunted creature must be enduring, down there on the vast, arid plain, beneath the June sun. The idlers stood agape at the very thought.

Peppa, one of the handsomest girls of Licodia, was at this time about to be married to Master Finu, surnamed the "Tallow-candle," who owned sunny lands and had a bay mule in his stable, and was a fine young fellow, "beautiful as the sun," who could carry the banner of St. Margaret as straight as a pillar, without bending his back. Peppa's mother wept for joy at the good luck that had befallen her daughter, and spent her time in turning over the bride's outfit as it lay in its trunk—"all of white stuff, in fours," like that of a queen, and golden earrings that hung down to the shoulders, and gold rings for all the ten fingers; she had as much gold as St. Margaret herself, and was to be married just about St. Margaret's Day, which fell in June, after the hay was cut. Every evening, "Tallow-candle," as he returned from the fields, would leave his mule at Peppa's door and come in to tell her that the crops were a joy to behold, if only Gramigna did not set fire to them, that the corn-bin behind the bed would not be large enough to hold all the grain that harvest, and that it seemed to him a thousand years till the time should come when he might take his bride home behind him on the bay mule.

But one fine day Peppa said to him, "Let your mule be—for I will not marry you."

Poor "Tallow-candle" stood aghast, and the old woman began tearing her hair when she heard her daughter give up the best match in the village.

"I love Gramigna," the girl said to her, "and I will marry no one else."

"Ah me!" the mother went crying about the house, her gray hair flying in the wind like a witch's—"Ah me! that demon has got even in here and bewitched my daughter!"

"No," Peppa would reply, and her eye was fixed and as hard as steel, "no, he has not been here."

"Where have you seen him, then?"

"I have not seen him, I have heard of him. But listen—I feel him, here, burning me."

The affair made a stir in the village, though they tried to hush it up. The gossips who had envied Peppa the prosperous crops, the bay mule, and the fine young fellow who carried St. Margaret's banner without bending his back, now went about telling all manner of ugly tales—how Gramigna came to visit her by night in the kitchen, and how he had been seen hiding under the bed.

The poor mother had a lamp lighted "for the souls in purgatory," and the priest even came to the house and laid his stole upon Peppa's heart, so as to drive out that devil of a Gramigna, who had taken possession of it. Still she persisted in saying that she did not even know the fellow by sight, but that she saw him at night in her dreams; and she rose every morning with parched lips, almost as though she too had suffered the burning thirst that he must be enduring.

Then the old woman shut her up in the house, that she might no longer hear them talk of Gramigna, and stopped up the very cracks in the door with pictures of the saints. But Peppa listened from behind the sacred images to what the people in the street were saying, and grew red and pale, as though the devil were blowing all the flames of hell across her face. At last she heard them say that Gramigna had been brought to bay, among the prickly-pear thickets of Palagonia.

"He kept up a two hours' fire," they said, "and there is one *carabiniere* killed, and three soldiers and more are wounded. But they sent such a hail of shot upon him, that this time they found a pool of blood where he had stood."

Then Peppa made the sign of the cross at her old woman's bedside, and fled through the window.

Gramigna was among the prickly pears of Palagonia, for they had not been able to dislodge him from such a rabbit-warren. Wounded and blood-stained, pale from a two days' fast, burnt with fever, he stood there, his carbine leveled.

When he saw her coming towards him, fearless and firm, through the thickets of prickly pear, in the dim light of the dawn, he debated for a moment whether he should pull the trigger.

"What do you want?" he asked; "what have you come here for?"

1364

"I have come to be with you," she replied, looking at him fixedly "Are you Gramigna?"

"Yes, I am Gramigna. If you have come here after those twenty ounces of the reward, you have mistaken your reckoning."

"No, I have come to stay by you," she replied.

"Get you gone," said he; "you cannot stay here, and I will have no one with me. If you have come after money, you have made a mistake, I tell you; I have nothing—see; it is two days since I have even had a bit of bread."

"I cannot go home again now," she said; "the road is full of soldiers."

"Go! What do I care for that? Every one for himself!"

As she was turning away, like a dog driven off by kicks, he called after her:—

"Look here, go and get me a flask of water from the torrent down there; if you want to stay with me, you must risk your skin."

She went without a word; and when Gramigna heard the fusillade, he laughed out, saying to himself, "That was meant for me!"

But when he saw her return in a little while, pale and bleeding, with the flask on her arm, first he tore it from her, and drank so long and deep a draught that his very breath failed him, and then —"Did you escape it?" he asked; "how did you manage?"

"The soldiers were on the opposite bank, and on this side the bushes were thick."

"But they put a bullet into you? Your clothes are stained with blood."

"Yes."

"Where are you wounded?"

"In the shoulder."

"That's no matter—you can still walk."

So he suffered her to stay with him. She followed him, barefooted, all torn and feverish from her wound; she would go hunting after a flask of water or a crust of bread for him, and when she returned empty-handed, amid the volleys of shot, her lover, devoured by hunger and thirst, would beat her. At last, one night when the moon shone brightly through the thickets of prickly pear, Gramigna said, "They are coming," and made her stand with her back against a rock at the bottom of a cleft; then he fled in the opposite direction.

The shots echoed nearer and nearer among the bushes, and the darkness was lighted up by sudden bursts of flame. All at once

1365

Peppa heard a trampling close by, and Gramigna reappeared, dragging himself along, with one leg broken, so that he had to prop himself against the shoots of the prickly pear to reload his carbine.

"It is over," he said; "now they will take me."

And what froze her blood more than all was the glitter in his eye, that made him look like a madman. Then, when he fell like a log upon the dead branches, the soldiers were upon him, all at once.

Next day they dragged him on a cart through the streets of the village, mangled and bleeding. The crowd that pressed round to gaze at him, laughed when they saw how small and pale and ugly he was, like a clown. It was for him that Peppa had left Master Finu, the "Tallow-candle"!

Poor "Tallow-candle" went away and hid himself, as though it were his part to be ashamed.

And Peppa was led along between the soldiers, handcuffed, as if she too had been a thief—she, who had as much gold as St. Margaret.

Her poor mother had to sell all the "white stuff" of the bridal outfit, and the golden earrings, and the rings for the ten fingers, to pay lawyers for her daughter, and get her home again once more, poor, sickly, and shame-faced—ugly, too, now, like Gramigna, and with Gramigna's child upon her bosom. Yet when she was restored to her at the end of the trial, the old woman recited the "Ave Maria" there in the bare and fast-darkening barrack-room, among all the *carabinieri*; it was as though they had given her back a treasure —to her, the poor old woman who had nothing else in the world, and she wept like a fountain for joy.

But Peppa seemed to have no more tears left, and she spoke never a word; nor did the village folk ever see her again, though the two women had to work with their hands for their daily bread. People said that Peppa had learnt her trade, there in the wood, and that she went out thieving by night. In reality, she sat crouching in the corner of the kitchen, like a wild beast, and only left it when her old woman was dead of hard work, and she had to sell the house.

"Do you see now!" the "Tallow-candle" said to her, for he loved her still. "I could crush your head between two stones for all the harm you have done to yourself and others."

"It is true," Peppa answered, "I know it. It was the will of God."

When the house and her few remaining goods and chattels were sold, she left the village by night, as she had come—without turning back to give one look at the roof beneath which she had slept so long—and went away with her boy to do the will of God in the city, near the prison where Gramigna was shut up.

She could only see the dark shutters upon the great, silent face of the building, and when she stood looking at it, trying to make out where he might be, the sentries drove her away. At last they told her that for some time back he had no longer been there—that they had taken him away over the sea, handcuffed, and with his wallet about his neck.

She said nothing. She never left the place, because she did not know where to go, and no one was expecting her anywhere. She made shift to live, doing jobs for the soldiers and the jailers, as if she herself were a part of that great, dark silent building; and for the *carabinieri*, who had taken Gramigna from her, there among the prickly-pear thickets, and had broken his leg with gun-shots, she felt a sort of respectful tenderness—an animal admiration for strength.

On holidays, when she saw them with their plumes and their glittering epaulettes, stiff and straight in their gala uniforms, she devoured them with her eyes; and she was always about the barracks, sweeping out the halls and polishing the boots, so that they nick-named her "the dust-clout of the *carabinieri*."

Only when, at nightfall, she saw them load their guns and go out, two by two, with their trousers turned up, and revolvers slung across their chests, or when they mounted their horses, under the great lantern that gleamed upon the muzzles of the carbines, and she heard the trampling of the horses' hoofs and the clink of the scabbards die away in the darkness, then she would turn pale and shiver as she closed the stable doors. And when her little one played with the rest in the great square before the prison running in and out among the soldiers' legs, and the other children would call after him, "The son of Gramigna!—the son of Gramigna!" then she would fly into a rage and pursue them, pelting them with stones.

EMILE VERHAEREN

ÉMILE VERHAEREN (Belgian, 1855-1916). Poet Laureate of Belgium. Apostle of industrial progress. Frequent visitor in England. Early work realistic and violent—later poetry symbolic free verse. Has been compared with Whitman. Major works: *Les Rythmes Souverains, Les Flamandes, Les Heures Claires.*

THE MILL

Slowly in the depths of the night the windmill turns.
Under a somber, melancholy sky
It turns and turns, and its wind-burnt canvas moans
A sad and worn and heavy lullaby.

Since the dawn its arms, like arms in supplication,
Have stretched out and have fallen, and they will
Fall on and on across the darkened air
And weary nature slumbering now and still.

A cheerless winter night broods over the hamlet,
The weary clouds are restless overhead;
And along the thickets that gather up their shadows,
The pathways point a horizon that is dead.

Under a rim of earth, a few beechen shanties
Wretchedly huddle in a miserable round;
A brass lamp that is hanging from the ceiling
Speckles with light the window and the ground.

And across the wide field, and the slumbering void
They hold—puny hovels—with the blinking eyes
Of their broken panes with the ragged curtain,
The old mill that turns and, weary, turns, and dies.

THE POOR

There are poor souls
Where tears are starred
And pale as stones
In a graveyard.

There are poor backs
Weighed down with ills
Like the roofs of hovels
In the hills.

There are poor hands
Like leaves the wind wore,
Like yellow, dying leaves
By the door.

There are poor eyes
Humble and kind and warm,
Sadder than the eyes of beasts
Beneath the storm.

There are poor folk
With movements forbearing and worn,
On whom misery battens—
Wherever men are born.

PIOUS EVENINGS

To farthest off the sun at setting sheds
The haircloth of its silence and its calm;
On Byzantine backgrounds carefully it spreads
All things as clearly as a quiet psalm.

The downpour slashed the air with blades of hail
And now the heavens shine like a sanctuary;
It is the hour when the western fires fail,
When the day's gold and the twilight's silver vary.

Nothing stirs on the horizon, unless it be
An infinite giant march of oaks in the gloom,
Stretching beyond the farms one just can see,
Along the fallow fields and the corners of broom.

1369

The trees move on—as mortuary friars
Pass by, and twilight weighs upon their bands,
As the long troop of penitents aspires
On pilgrimage to ancient holy lands.

And as the road leads upward to the sky,
Where the setting sun far peony petals strews,
To see those long bare trees, to see those monks pass by,
You'd say they were setting out tonight, by twos,

Toward their God who fills the heavens with sprinkled gold;
And the stars, gleaming high ahead of them,
Are each the light of a candle that they hold
Of which we cannot see the towering stem.

PAUL VERLAINE

PAUL VERLAINE (French, 1844-1896). Chief figure in the French Symbolist
Movement. Poetic descendant of Baudelaire. Began career as middle-class
clerk. Left wife to go vagabonding with Rimbaud. Died in misery and poverty.
Major volumes: *Fêtes galantes, Romances sans paroles, La Bonne chanson.*
His life and legend almost as influential as his actual work.

MYSTIC TWILIGHT

Memory with the twilight
Flushes and trembles on the horizon
Of hope that soars with a high light,
Recoils, collects, and flies on
Like a mysterious valley up
Which many a flaunting flower—
Tulip, lily, buttercup—
Thrusts forth in a bower
Where the poison-perfume stilly—
Buttercup, tulip, and lily—
In a ghostly, weird, and wry light
With my reason, soul and senses strewn,
Blends in an unbounded swoon
Memory with the twilight.

STREETS

Let us dance!

Surpassingly I loved her eyes,
Clearer than the starry skies;
I loved their swift surprise.

Let us dance!

She had such wild ways, truly
A sweetheart most unruly;
And she took life so coolly.

Let us dance!

But beyond these memories start
The kisses her flower-lips dart. . . .
Since she is dead to my heart.

Let us dance!

I recall, still I recall
Pensive hours at evenfall:
And they are best of all.
Let us dance!

MY FAMILIAR DREAM

I often have the queer and radiant dream
Of an unknown woman I love, and who loves me,
Who never will be wholly as before, nor seem
Quite other; who loves, and probes my mystery.

She understands me; my translucent heart—
Only for her, alas!—quite plain appears,
Only for her; and the dampness that will start
On my brow, she alone can dry it with her tears.

Is she blonde, brunette, or red-haired? I do not know.
Her name? I remember it is resonant and sweet
As those of lovers life has beaten low.

Her look is as the look in a statue's head,
And for her voice, where calm and sorrow meet,
She has the tone of loved ones who are dead.

WOMAN AND CAT

She was playing with her cat;
They were enraptured who saw
The white hand and the white paw
In their evening frolic-pat.

It hid—O innocent gazer!—
Under black silken veils
Murderous agate nails
Clear and sharp as a razor.

She too was compact of sweets,
Withholding her steely claws;
But the devil's eye has no beam . . .

And in her boudoir, when the dark meets
Her airy laughter, and withdraws,—
Four points of phosphorus gleam.

THE SONG OF THE INGÉNUES

We are the ingénues—
Blue eyes, long hair, sweet looks—
Who live with rainbow dews
In seldom read books.

We set forth intertwined,
And the day no purer seems
Than the depths of our mind
And our azure dreams;

And we romp through the fields,
Where our happy calls rise
Till day to dusk yields—
Chasing butterflies.

And a shepherdess' bonnet
Screens our face from strong light,
And our gown—lace upon it—
Is immaculate white.

Cavaliers of romances
Who capture the skies
Shower their glances,
Greetings, and sighs,

But in vain their romantic
Stir, their fine flirts—
Before the gigantic
Guardian, our skirts.

And our free laughter falls
At the imagination
Of these cling-to-the-walls—
Though at times a sensation

Stirs the frock that covers
Our heart that preens
To know we're the future lovers
Of libertines.

YOUNGLINGS

High heels in a struggle with a long skirt,
As the wind roused or as the land lay,
Twinkled a glimpse above, if we were alert—
Intercepted!—and we loved that gulls' play.

Sometimes the sting of an insect bolder
Than we, sought a fair neck to scrutinize,
And there was the sudden lightning of a shoulder
And that feast overwhelmed our young fools' eyes.

Twilight came, an uncertain autumnal glow:
The fair ones, clinging dreamily to our arms,
Spoke words that were so specious and so low
That our souls forever hold their eager qualms.

1373

CAVITRI

Mahabharatta

To save her husband, Cavitri's deep vow bids
Her stand, while three days and three nights unroll,
Erect, nor move limbs, body, nor eyelids—
Rigid, Vyaca tells us, as a pole.

Neither your cruel rays, Curya, nor the swoon
Chandra spreads over the summits of the moon
Can weaken, as your mighty spheres revolve,
That glorious woman's flesh nor her resolve. . . .

Should forgetfulness with black, bleak treachery
Or lean-faced envy toward me incline,
Impassive as Cavitri may I be,
And in my soul as lofty a design.

WHAT HAVE YOU DONE?

The sky, above the roof,
   Is so blue and so calm!
The tree above the roof
   Cradles its palm.

The bell, in the sky we watch,
   Quietly rings;
A bird on the tree we watch,
   Mournfully sings.

Lord, O Lord, life is here
   Gently fluttering down.
That peaceful stir we hear
   Comes from the town.

—What have you done, you there
   Endlessly weeping; in sooth,
What have you done, you there,
   With your youth?

1374

AUTUMN SONG

The heavy thrall
Of the sobbing call
Of the fall
Weighs, nor departs,
Like my heart's
Pall.

Overcome
And dumb,
As the hours creep
I see the haze
Of olden days
And weep.

And I go away
The wind's prey,
In barren, brief
Whirl hither and yon
Like a wan
Dead leaf.

JULES VERNE

JULES VERNE (French, 1828-1905). The father of science fiction. Began
career as opera librettist till he discovered gift for imagining adventures of the
future. His works are still read with entertainment, especially *Twenty Thousand Leagues Under the Sea* and *Around the World in Eighty Days.*

THE BOTTOM OF THE SEA

AND now, how can I retrace the impression left upon me by that
walk under the waters? Words are impotent to relate such wonders!
Captain Nemo walked in front, his companions followed some steps
behind. Conseil and I remained near each other, as if an exchange
of words had been possible through our metallic cases. I no longer
felt the weight of my clothing, or my shoes, of my reservoir of air,

or of my thick helmet, in the midst of which my head rattled like an almond in its shell.

The light, which lit the soil thirty feet below the surface of the ocean, astonished me by its power. The solar rays shone through the watery mass easily and dissipated all color, and I clearly distinguished objects at a distance of a hundred and fifty yards. Beyond that the tints darkened into fine gradations of ultra-marine, and faded into vague obscurity. Truly this water which surrounded me was but another air denser than the terrestrial atmosphere, but almost as transparent. Above me was the calm surface of the sea. We were walking on fine, even sand, not wrinkled, as on a flat shore, which retains the impression of the billows. This dazzling carpet, really a reflector, repelled the rays of the sun with wonderful intensity, which accounted for the vibration which penetrated every atom of liquid. Shall I be believed when I say that, at the depth of thirty feet, I could see as if I was in broad daylight?

For a quarter of an hour I trod on this sand sown with the impalpable dust of shells. The hull of the "Nautilus," resembling a long shoal, disappeared by degrees; but its lantern, when darkness should overtake us in the waters, would help to guide us on board by its distinct rays. Soon forms of objects outlined in the distance were discernible. I recognized magnificent rocks, hung with a tapestry of zoophytes of the most beautiful kind, and I was at first struck by the peculiar effect of this medium.

It was then ten in the morning, the rays of the sun struck the surface of the waves at rather an oblique angle, and at the touch of their light, decomposed by refraction as through a prism, flowers, rocks, plants, shells, and polypi were shaded at the edges by the seven solar colors. It was marvelous, a feast for the eyes, this complication of colored tints, a perfect kaleidoscope of green, yellow, orange, violet, indigo, and blue; in one word, the whole palette of an enthusiastic colorist! Why could I not communicate to Conseil the lively sensations which were mounting to my brain, and rival him in expressions of admiration? For aught I knew, Captain Nemo and his companion might be able to exchange thoughts by means of signs previously agreed upon. So for want of better, I talked to myself; I declaimed in the copper box which covered my head, thereby expending more air in vain words than was, perhaps, expedient.

Various kinds of isis, clusters of pure tuft-coral, prickly fungi, and anemones, formed a brilliant garden of flowers, enameled with porplutæ, decked with their collarettes of blue tentacles, sea-stars studding the sandy bottom, together with asterophytons like fine lace embroidered by the hands of naiads; whose festoons were waved by the gentle undulations caused by our walk. It was a real grief to me to crush under my feet the brilliant specimens of molluscs which strewed the ground by thousands, of hammerheads, donaciæ (veritable bounding shells), of staircases, and red helmet-shells, angel-wings, and many others produced by this inexhaustible ocean. But we were bound to walk, so we went on, whilst above our heads waved shoals of physalides, leaving their tentacles to float in their train, medusæ whose umbrellas of opal or rose-pink, escaloped with a band of blue, sheltered us from the rays of the sun and fiery pelagiæ which, in the darkness, would have strewn our path with phosphorescent light.

All these wonders I saw in the space of a quarter of a mile, scarcely stopping, and following Captain Nemo, who beckoned me on by signs. Soon the nature of the soil changed; to the sandy plain succeeded an extent of slimy mud, which the Americans call "ooze," composed of equal parts of silicious and calcareous shells. We then traveled over a plain of sea-weed of wild and luxuriant vegetation. This sward was of close texture, and soft to the feet, and rivalled the softest carpet woven by the hand of man. But whilst verdure was spread at our feet, it did not abandon our heads. A light network of marine plants, of that inexhaustible family of sea-weeds of which more than two thousand kinds are known, grew on the surface of the water. I saw long ribbons of fucus floating, some globular, others tuberous, laurenciæ and cladostephi of most delicate foliage, and some rhodomeniæ palmatæ, resembling the fan of a cactus. I noticed that the green plants kept nearer the top of the sea whilst the red were at a greater depth, leaving to the black or brown hydrophytes the care of forming gardens and parterres in the remote beds of the ocean.

We had quitted the "Nautilus" about an hour and a half. It was near noon; I knew by the perpendicularity of the sun's rays, which were no longer refracted. The magical colors disappeared by degrees, and the shades of emerald and sapphire were effaced. We walked with a regular step, which rang upon the ground with astonishing intensity; the slightest noise was transmitted with a quickness to which the ear is unaccustomed on the earth; indeed, water is a better conductor of sound than air, in the ratio of four to one. At this period the earth sloped downward; the light took a uniform tint. We were at a depth of a hundred and five yards and twenty inches, undergoing a pressure of six atmospheres.

At this depth I could still see the rays of the sun, though feebly; to their intense brilliancy had succeeded a reddish twilight, the lowest state between day and night; and we could still see well enough.

FRANCOIS VILLON

FRANÇOIS VILLON (French, *ca.* 1431-1465?). One of the brightest stars of medieval France. Wrecked by debauchery, jail and torture, he was sentenced to death, then banished. His total work: *Le Petit Testament, Le Grand Testament* and some 40 shorter poems. He crystallized vivid perceptions of life's pleasures and ironies.

BALLAD OF OLD-TIME LADIES

Tell me where, in what land of shade,
    Bides fair Flora of Rome, and where
Are Thais and Archipiade,
    Cousins-german of beauty rare,
    And Echo, more than mortal fair,
That, when one calls by river-flow
    Or marish, answers out of the air?
But what is become of last year's snow?

Where did the learn'd Helosa vade,
    For whose sake Abelard might not spare
(Such dole for love on him was laid)
    Manhood to lose and a cowl to wear?
    And where is the queen who willed whilere
That Buridan, tied in a sack, should go
    Floating down Seine from the turret-stair?
But what is become of last year's snow?

Blanche, too, the lily-white queen, that made
    Sweet music as if she a siren were;
Broad-foot Bertha; and Joan the maid,

The good Lorrainer, the English bare
  Captive to Rouen and burned her there;
Beatrix, Eremburge, Alys,—lo!
  Where are they, Virgin debonair?
  But what is become of last year's snow?

ENVOI

Prince, you may question how they fare
  This week, or liefer this year, I trow:
Still shall the answer this burden bear,
  But what is become of last year's snow?

BALLAD OF OLD-TIME LORDS

Where is Calixtus, third of the name,
  That died in the purple whiles ago,
Four years since he to the tiar came?
  And the King of Aragon, Alfonso?
  The Duke of Bourbon. sweet of show,
And the Duke Arthur of Brittaine?
  And Charles the Seventh, the Good? Heigho!
But where is the doughty Charlemaine?

Likewise the King of Scots, whose shame
  Was the half of his face (or folks say so),
Vermeil as amethyst held to the flame,
  From chin to forehead all of a glow?
  The King of Cyprus, of friend and foe
Renowned; and the gentle King of Spain,
  Whose name, God 'ield me, I do not know?
But where is the doughty Charlemaine?

Of many more might I ask the same,
  Who are but dust that the breezes blow;
But I desist, for none may claim
  To stand against Death, that lays all low,
  Yet one more question before I go:
Where is Lancelot, King of Behaine?
  And where are his valiant ancestors, trow?
But where is the doughty Charlemaine?

ENVOI

Where is Du Guesclin, the Breton prow?
  Where Auvergne's Dauphin, and where again
The late good duke of Alençon? Lo!
  But where is the doughty Charlemaine?

VILLON'S EPITAPH

The following is the epitaph, in ballad form, that Villon made
for himself and his companions, expecting no better than to be
hanged in their company.

Brothers, that after us on life remain,
  Harden your hearts against us not as stone;
For, if to pity us poor wights you're fain,
  God shall the rather grant you benison.
You see us six, the gibbet here upon:
As for the flesh that we too well have fed,
'Tis all devoured and rotted, shred by shred.
  Let none make merry of our piteous case,
Whose crumbling bones the life long since hath fled:
  The rather pray, God grant us of His grace!

Yea, we conjure you, look not with disdain,
  Brothers, on us, though we to death were done
By justice. Well, you know the saving grain
  Of sense springs not in every mother's son:
  Commend us, therefore, now we're dead and gone,
To Christ, the Son of Mary's maidenhead,
That He leave not His grace on us to shed
  And save us from the nether torture-place.
Let no one harry us: forsooth we're sped:
  The rather pray, God grant us of His grace!

We are whiles scoured and sodden of the rain
  And whiles burnt up and blackened of the sun:
Corbies and pyets have our eyes outa'en
  And plucked our beard and hair out, one by one.
  Whether by night or day; rest have we none:

1380

Now here, now there, as the wind shifts its stead.
We swing and creak and rattle overhead,
  No thimble dinted like our bird-pecked face.
Brothers, have heed and shun the life we led:
  The rather pray, God grant us of his grace!

ENVOI

Prince Jesus, over all empoweréd,
Let us not fall into the Place of Dread,
  But all our reckoning with the Fiend efface.
Folk, mock us not that are forspent and dead:
  The rather pray, God grant us of His grace!

VIRGIL

VIRGIL (Latin, 70-19 B.C.). Didactic poet, heavily imitative of the Greeks. The *Aeneid*, glorifying the birth of Rome, derives from Homer's epics, but remains most imposing work of Latin literature. His patriotism manifest in the *Georgics*, his love of the rural in the early *Eclogues*.

ECLOGUE IV: "THE MESSIAH"

Sicilian Muse, begin a loftier strain!
Tho' lowly shrubs, and trees that shade the plain,
Delight not all; Sicilian Muse, prepare
To make the vocal woods deserve a consul's care.
The last great age, foretold by sacred rhymes,
Renews its finished course: Saturnian times
Roll round again; and mighty years, begun
From their first orb, in radiant circles run.
The base degenerate iron offspring ends;
A golden progeny from heaven descends.
O chaste Lucina, speed the mother's pains,
And haste the glorious birth! thy own Apollo reigns!
The lovely boy, with his auspicious face,
Shall Pallio's consulship and triumph grace;
Majestic months set out with him to their appointed race.

1381

The father banished virtue shall restore,
And crimes shall threat the guilty world no more.
The son shall lead the life of gods, and be
By gods and heroes seen, and gods and heroes see.
The jarring nations he in peace shall bind,
And with paternal virtues rule mankind.
Unbidden Earth shall wreathing ivy bring,
And fragrant herbs (the promises of spring),
As her first offerings to her infant king.
The goats with strutting dugs shall homeward speed,
And lowing herds secure from lions feed.
His cradle shall with rising flowers be crowned:
The serpent's brood shall die; the sacred ground
Shall weeds and poisonous plants refuse to bear;
Each common bush shall Syrian roses wear.
But when heroic verse his youth shall raise,
And form it to hereditary praise,
Unlabored harvests shall the fields adorn,
And clustered grapes shall blush on every thorn;
The knotted oaks shall showers of honey weep,
And thro' the matted grass the liquid gold shall creep.
Yet of old fraud some footsteps shall remain:
The merchant still shall plow the deep for gain;
Great cities shall with walls be compassed round,
And sharpened shares shall vex the fruitful ground;
Another Tiphys shall new seas explore;
Another Argo land the chiefs upon the Iberian shore;
Another Helen other wars create,
And great Achilles urge the Trojan fate.
But when to ripened manhood he shall grow,
The greedy sailor shall the seas forego;
No keel shall cut the waves for foreign ware,
For every soil shall every product bear.
The laboring hind his oxen shall disjoin;
No plow shall hurt the glebe, no pruning hook the vine;
Nor wool shall in dissembled colors shine.
But the luxurious father of the fold,
With native purple, or unborrowed gold,
Beneath his pompous fleece shall proudly sweat;
And under Tyrian robes the lamb shall bleat.

The Fates, when they this happy web have spun,
Shall bless the sacred clew, and bid it smoothly run.
Mature in years, to ready honors move,
O of celestial seed! O foster son of Jove!
See, laboring Nature calls thee to sustain
The nodding frame of heaven, and earth, and main!
See to their base restored, earth, seas, and air;
And joyful ages, from behind, in crowding ranks appear.
To sing thy praise, would Heaven my breath prolong,
Infusing spirits worthy such a song,
Not Thracian Orpheus should transcend my lays,
Nor Linus crowned with never-fading bays;
Tho' each his heavenly parent should inspire;
The Muse instruct the voice, and Phœbus tune the lyre.
Should Pan contend in verse, and thou my theme,
Arcadian judges should their god condemn.
Begin, auspicious boy, to cast about
Thy infant eyes, and, with a smile, thy mother single out:
Thy mother well deserves that short delight,
The nauseous qualms of ten long months and travel to requite.
Then smile: the frowning infant's doom is read;
No god shall crown the board, nor goddess bless the bed.

WALTHER VON DER VOGELWEIDE

WALTHER VON DER VOGELWEIDE (Austrian, *ca.* 1170-1230). Didactic
wandering court singer of Middle Ages. His accomplishments include political,
religious and love songs. Championed German independence of papal claims,
though his political allegiance shifted with his patrons, as was custom of
the times.

MOURNINGS

To me is barred the door of joy and ease,
There stand I as an orphan, lone, forlorn,
And nothing boots me that I frequent knock.
Strange that on every hand the show'r should fall,

And not one cheering drop should reach to me!
On all around the gen'rous Austrian's gifts,
Gladd'ning the land, like genial rain descend:
A fair and gay adorned mead is he,
Whereon are gathered of the sweetest flowers:
Would that his rich and ever gen'rous hand
Might stoop to pluck one little leaf for me,
So might I fitly praise a scene so fair!

Fain (could it be) would I a home obtain,
And warm me by a hearth-side of my own.
Then, then, I'd sing about the sweet birds' strain,
And fields and flowers, as I have whilome done;
And paint in song the lily and the rose
That dwell upon *her* cheek who smiles on me.
But lone I stray—no home its comfort shows:
Ah, luckless man! still doomed a *guest* to be!

A mournful one am I, above whose head
A day of perfect bliss hath never past;
Whatever joys my soul have ravished,
Soon was the radiance of those joys o'ercast.
And none can show me that substantial pleasure
Which will not pass away like bloom from flowers;
Therefore, no more my heart such joys shall treasure,
Nor pine for fading sweets and fleeting hours.

Ah! where are hours departed fled?
    Is life a dream, or true indeed?
Did all my heart hath fashioned
    From fancy's visitings proceed?
Yes! I have slept; and now unknown
    To me the things best known before:
The land, the people, once mine own,
    Where are they?—they are here no more:
My boyhood's friends, all aged, worn,
    Despoiled the woods, the fields, of home,
Only the stream flows on forlorn;
    (Alas! that e'er such change should come!)

1384

And he who knew me once so well
    Salutes me now as one estranged:
The very earth to me can tell
    Of naught but things perverted, changed:
And when I muse on other days,
    That passed me as the dashing oars
The surface of the ocean raise,
    Ceaseless my heart its fate deplores.

MAY AND HIS LADY

When from the sod the flow'rets spring,
    And smile to meet the sun's bright ray,
When birds their sweetest carols sing
    In all the morning pride of May,
What lovelier than the prospect there?
Can earth boast anything more fair?
To me it seems an almost heaven,
So beauteous to my eyes that vision bright is given.

But when a lady, chaste and fair,
    Noble, and clad in rich attire,
Walks through the throng with gracious air,
    As sun that bids the stars retire,—
Then, where are all thy boastings, May?
What hast thou beautiful and gay
Compared with that supreme delight?
We leave thy loveliest flowers, and watch that lady bright.

Wouldst thou believe me,—come and place
    Before thee all this pride of May;
Then look but on my lady's face,
    And, which is best and brightest? say:
For me, how soon (if choice were mine)
This would I take, and that resign!
And say, "Though sweet thy beauties, May!
I'd rather forfeit all than lose my lady gay."

"Lady," I said, "this garland wear!
   For thou wilt wear it gracefully:
And on thy brow 'twill sit so fair,
   And thou wilt dance so light and free;
Had I a thousand gems, on thee,
   Fair one! their brilliant light should shine:
Would'st thou such gift accept from me,—
   Oh, doubt me not,—it should be thine.

"Lady, so beautiful thou art,
   That I on thee the wreath bestow,
'Tis the best gift I can impart;
   But whiter, rosier flow'rs, I know,
Upon the distant plain they're springing,
   Where beauteously their heads they rear,
And birds their sweetest songs are singing:
   Come! let us go and pluck them there."

She took the beauteous wreath I chose,
   And like a child at praises glowing,
Her cheeks blushed crimson as the rose,
   When by the snow-white lily growing:
But all from those bright eyes eclipse
   Received; and then, my toil to pay,
Kind, precious words fell from her lips:
   What more than this I shall not say.

W

WANG WEI

WANG WEI (Chinese, ca. 700-760). Leading Sung landscape painter. Also devout Buddhist as well as successful politician. Su Shih said of him: "There is painting in his poetry and poetry in his painting." Noted for his four-line *chueh-chu* poems.

BEST HAPPINESS OF ALL

I am old and I am bored. I was never very wise and my mind has not ever walked much further than my feet. Only my forest, my forest . . . I go back and back to wander there.

The blue fingers of the moon play on my old lute there. The wind scatters the clouds there and comes down to flutter my robe.

You ask me what is the best happiness of all? In the forest it is sweet to hear a girl singing on the path, after she has stopped to ask her way, and thanked you with a smile.

THE PEACH GARDEN

The fisherman's boat is carried away along the water hugging
   the spring hills;
By two banks the peach blossom marks the limits of an ancient
   ferry;
The fisherman sits gazing at the pink blossoms regardless of the
   distance,
Drifting to the end of a green mountain stream, careless of where
   he goes.

1387

A narrow passage in the mountains leads by secret detours to the beginning of an open bay,

There the hills open out on a vast expanse of flat land:

He approaches it and it is a village of 1000 homes scattered amid flowers and bamboo.

The stranger begins to distinguish the speech of the Han dynasty.

Those who dwelt there had not changed the fashion of their clothes since the days of Ch'in.

These village dwellers lived together at the source of the Wu Ling River;

They had fled away from the world to live the lives of peasants.

The moon is bright underneath the pines,

Shining on their quiet windows;

The sun rises; dogs bark and chickens crow.

The inhabitants are startled to hear a man has come from the world of men,

And vie with each other in hospitality.

They compete to invite him into their houses and ask him whence he has come.

When morning comes they sweep away the fallen flowers and open the village gates.

When night falls fishermen and woodcutters come home by way of the stream.

Once upon a time these people, seeking a place of refuge, left their fellow men.

They sought to obtain immortality and they did not go back.

In among the ravines and gorges what could they know of the affairs of the world?

All they could see of the world were distant clouds and hills.

Their visitor did not suspect this was a holy place, unknown to mortal men;

His earthly heart had not extinguished earthly desires and he thought of his native home.

Once out of the cave he does not mind that he is separated from it by hills and water.

(When once again) he leaves his family to go on the same long journey,

He says to himself, I have been there before, I cannot miss the way.

How should he know that the mountains and ravines had all changed?

He can only remember that on the former occasion he plunged deep into the green hills

Where mountain rivulets meandered to and fro, leading him to
    misty woods.
(Again) the spring is here and everywhere peach flowers stain
    the water,
But he cannot trace the way to the land of immortality.
Where shall he hunt for it now?

ON A DARK AUTUMN IN A HILL HUT

On the empty hill new rain has fallen;
Out of the dusk comes the autumn.
The bright moon shines forth between the pines,
Above the rocks flows the clear stream,
Babel in the bamboos proclaims the washing girls are returning
    home,
The lotus swing beneath the fisherman's boat,
The fragrance of spring sighs and expires,
How can we detain it before it goes?

JAKOB WASSERMANN

JAKOB WASSERMANN (German, 1873-1934). Problem novelist, whose complex plots and unusual characters gave his stories universal appeal. A wanderer
in his youth, finally settled in Austria. Not identified with any literary school.
His most successful novel: *The World's Illusion*. Others: *The Maurizius Case,
Doctor Kerkhoven*.

THE BEAST

IN one of the former capitals of central Germany great labour riots,
which the citizens still recall with horror, broke out in the wake
of the revolution. Thousands of striking labourers gathered in mobs
and marched, on that misty February morning, towards the busy
streets of the inner city. The jeering rabble, usually idle all the
time, joined them, and the deploying police was soon no longer
able to cope with the threatening throng. The iron shutters rattled
down over the displays in the shop-windows; cafés and restaurants
were locked in panicky haste; house doors were slammed to, and
curious and terrified faces appeared at the windows when the wild
shouting and whistling of the approaching masses became audible.

These broke their way like an unstemmed flood; stones were hurled at the houses and smashed the windows. Here and there a shot was fired. The constabulary force saw itself reduced to take measures of defense and prepared to resist the mob with sabres and clubs. Turmoil and bitterness grew with each passing moment. The shouts and yells sounded more and more horrible. Bare arms and grimly threatening fists were stretched forth; eyes burned with rapacious and vindictive hatred. Women goaded on the men; ragged children filled the air with ear-splitting screams; and the slightest provocation, perhaps an irritating word, and murder and plundering would have been inevitable.

At that moment, there drove across a public square which the most advanced of the throng had just reached, a rather huge wagon resembling a furniture van, but which instead of side-walls had loose brown canvas hangings, and these showed the coat-of-arms of the royal family which had till recently ruled over the country. The sight of the hated emblems whipped the anger of the rioters into fury. In an instant the wagon was surrounded; the efforts of the police to break through the human ring were futile. The driver had pulled up the two horses, which, on being reined in so abruptly, trembled violently. A man jumped from the running-board at the rear of the wagon, unslung a rifle from his shoulder and cocked the trigger. This was the signal for the attack. A well-aimed blow knocked him down; thirty or forty arms reached for the cloth decorated with the escutcheon. The coachman's vehement, threatening gesticulation remained unnoticed; a word which he hurled at them was drowned in the turmoil and the protecting cover fell away in shreds from the frame-work. No sooner had this happened, when all, even the boldest of them, were seized with the utmost horror. The whistling, screaming, howling subsided as if by command, and they who beheld the sight, subdued by their horror-stricken silence those in the rear who, only dimly conscious of something ominous, stared with frightened, reluctant glances at the necks in front of them.

On the wagon was a Nubian lion from the royal zoological gardens. Owing to the high cost of feeding and maintaining him and also because of a certain aversion against such playthings of their erstwhile lords, the new government had decided to sell the beast to a foreign country. And thus, on that very morning the lion had been sent to the railroad station to be forwarded to his new destination.

As the canvas-wall slipped down from the frame, the lion roused himself and then surveyed the thousands of people, so steadily, with an expression of awe-inspiring majesty, until no sound could be heard from them, not a breath was audible. In his flashing eyes was reflected the picture of an alien world. But what was the nature of that world out there? A world as hard and cold as stone, a world with no heaven or horizon, one of mysterious sounds and offensive odours. Did he have an inkling of the wild passions which burst forth from despair and misery, he, who knew neither despair nor misery, and of passions only the elemental, natural ones of his superior kind? Did he actually take in those disturbed, ugly faces before him, or was it only a partial aspect or some impression of a detail that reached him: grinning teeth, distorted forehead, protruding chin; the violent wrath in the glance, the soulless glance of Megæra, the sullen sneer of the emaciated?

But those out there felt, with almost religious awe, something entirely unknown to him. In the dirty holes where they lived and brooded their evil; where their sick ones were lying and their children were born, and where they gave way to gloomy thoughts over the injustice which was their heritage of an evil order. On all their ways and journeys and in all the dreams of their servile imaginations they never had a vision which reminded them so much of what lay beyond their world, of the greatness and might of Nature. An undefinable horror took possession of their gloom-enveloped souls. They trembled, their muscles became limp, and they bowed their heads and cast down their eyes; their closely knitted ranks broke and gaps opened here and there. This enabled the policemen to arrest several dangerous ringleaders, and for the time being the rebellion was nipped in the bud.

FRANZ WERFEL

FRANZ WERFEL (Austrian, 1890-1945). Novelist, playwright and poet, who found success in America where he fled from Nazi Germany. His main theme: humanity and divine providence. His widely popular novels include: *Verdi*, *The Forty Days of Musa Dagh* and *The Song of Bernadette*. Play: *Jacobowsky and the Colonel*. Admired in Germany for his early lyric poetry.

THEOLOGOUMENA

WHAT argument is there against the notion that man is the center of creation? Are there any more complex and more differentiated orgnisms than he? The stars, for example?

I turned to a modern astronomer for an answer to this question. He informed me that the stars are suns similar to our own sun, many of them thousands of times larger and many of them thousands of times smaller. These tremendous, white-hot, gaseous spheres, he told me, are the only form in which matter occurs in that indescribable void that we call the universe. Though astro-physics determines the weight of the stars and their temperatures, the nature of sidereal matter has nothing to do with what we on earth call matter, least of all with the highly organized matter out of which the bodies of living, terrestrial creatures are constructed. Atoms, I was informed, cannot sustain themselves under the enormous pressure prevailing in sidereal spheres and increasing at a high ratio towards their center; consequently, they disintegrate into their hypothethical components, into protons and electrons that travel as waves and rays out into universal space.

"The stars which compose the comparatively sparse population of the universe," concluded the astronomer, "are, accordingly, nothing but inconceivably rarefied condensations of certain chemical elements (hydrogen, oxygen, nitrogen, carbon, and, to name a few of the less common ones, argon and crypton), spherical in form, a raging whirl of exploded atoms engaged in a mysteriously eruptive vital activity."

"Vital activity?" I repeated questioningly. "Does that mean you believe that the stars might be living bodies, mentally alive bodies, personalities, so to speak. which is, after all, the same thing? The latter-day gnostics held the view that stars are the heavenly hosts in material form and that their glowing, eruptive, vital activity represents nothing but the great hymn of praise, the 'Holy, Holy, Holy' with which the angels eternally celebrate the Creator."

At these words, the modern scientist gave me a startled look; then his lips tightened, whether with annoyance or irony I do not know. "Intelligence," he corrected me, "is a phenomenon which is developed only by the most highly differentiated matter in animal and human form, and for the one and only purpose of self-defense and self-assertion for survival . . . The stars, on the other hand, consist of inorganic matter in its most primal and simple form."

"Then organic matter," I interrupted, "highly differentiated, organic matter only exists on the planets? What about the planets, professor?"

"They are extremely rare and exceptional cases in the universe," answered the scientist, "if the prevalent hypothesis is correct. According to this hypothesis, planets and families of planets originate when two stars or suns approach too close to each other in their orbits so that the gravitation of the larger star attracts the smaller one so overpoweringly that part of its matter is torn out of its body, assumes shape and begins to rotate about the larger star in the congealing form of one or more planets."

"Could there be masculine and feminine stars?" I interrupted the astronomer. Again I received a look of disapproval as he continued, "As far as inorganic matter is concerned, it can be charged with either positive or negative electricity, nothing more. Sexual differences and characteristics which serve for the propagation of a species exist only in the more differentiated organic matter, beginning with certain plants."

"Thank you, professor. Forget my stupid question . . . But there's one more thing. If I understand you correctly, it's against the traffic regulations of the universe for the orbits of stars to approach each other too closely."

"Quite right," he responded. "This approach of the stars' orbits and the tearing off of planetary systems thus brought about, are, as our research assumes, among the most unusual catastrophes in the universe, far more unusual, for example, than the explosion of stars (which is in itself quite a rare event) and the formation of nova that is associated with it and that we can observe in our telescopes now and then. The planets, my dear fellow, are a catastrophic anomaly in the realm of matter. And of all the planets, a planet with the earth's conditions of life seems to be the most anomalous of anomalies."

"How can that be, my dear professor?" said I abruptly. "Can it be that the highly differentiated organic matter of which we spoke cannot sustain its life upon the other planets that revolve about our sun?"

"In all probability, no," he answered rather glumly. "On one of them, for example, the atmosphere is too dense, on another it is too rarefied, on a third there isn't any at all, on a fourth the temperature is much too high, on a fifth it is much too low."

"Just a moment, professor. Two stars disturb the harmony by coming too close to each other. The result is that sun-like matter is torn off, catapulted outward and finally cools down slowly. That is, it becomes rock and water, sand and mud, this exiled matter that owes its existence to an infraction, a clumsy violation of law. Is that correct, professor?"

"Approximately, my friend," he grumbled, "if we subtract your mythologically moralizing commentary."

"And out of this exiled, out of this banished, out of this deeply humiliated matter," I continued to question, "does the germ of life spring forth until, in a comparatively short time, it has developed into the human soul that is capable of ecstatically comprehending God?"

"Here you are leaving the paths of science," declared the astronomer, disgusted.

"If, as you say, the earth is already an anomaly, my dear professor, what then is humanity?"

"An anomaly raised to the twelfth power," he laughed contemptuously . . .

When I left the learned man, I realized that science had not lessened my faith but had unintentionally strengthened it. If the earth really is the most anomalous of all anomalies, then for that reason alone it revolves in the innermost center of the universe, a center that can only be a *product of the mind;* for indeed, within the universe, all space and time dimensions are meaningless. And if humanity is really the great exceptional case, as modern theory seems disposed to profess, how easy should it be for everyone to believe that this humanity is the crown and the goal of creation, and that God Himself had decided from the very beginning not to become *Sirius, Aldebaran* or *Cassiopeia* in order to incorporate Himself into a created thing and to have experience of it, but to become something far more rare, greater and more precious, a man.

WALT WHITMAN

WALT WHITMAN (American, 1819-1892). Prophetic singer of odes to democratic Americanism. The U. S.'s most universally praised poet. Served as journalist in New York, became army nurse during Civil War. First edition of
Leaves of Grass was received with hostility, accused of immorality. His own
criticism of America contained in prose work, *Democratic Vistas.* Style, modeled
on Old Testament, extravagantly admired by poets, but has not been successfully
imitated.

From *SONG OF MYSELF*

X

The runaway slave came to my house and stopt outside,
I heard his motions crackling the twigs of the woodpile,
Through the swung half-door of the kitchen I saw him limpsy and
weak,
And went where he sat on a log and led him in and assured him,
And brought water and fill'd a tub for his sweated body and bruis'd
feet,

And gave him a room that enter'd from my own, and gave him
some coarse clean clothes,
And remember perfectly well his revolving eyes and his awkwardness,
And remember putting plasters on the galls of his neck and ankles;
He staid with me a week before he was recuperated and pass'd
north,
I had him sit next to me at table, my fire-lock lean'd in the corner.

XXIV

Walt Whitman, a kosmos, of Manhattan the son,
Turbulent, fleshy, sensual, eating, drinking and breeding,
No sentimentalist, no stander above men and women or apart from
them,
No more modest than immodest.

Unscrew the locks from the doors!
Unscrew the doors themselves from their jambs!

Whoever degrades another degrades me,
And whatever is done or said returns at last to me.

Through me the afflatus surging and surging, through me the current
and index.

I speak the pass-word primeval, I give the sign of democracy,
By God! I will accept nothing which all cannot have their counterpart
of on the same terms.

XXXIII

I understand the large hearts of heroes,
The courage of present times and all times,
How the skipper saw the crowded and rudderless wreck of the
steam-ship, and Death chasing it up and down the storm,
How he knuckled tight and gave not an inch, and was faithful of
days and faithful of nights,
And chalk'd in large letters on a board, *Be of good cheer, we will
not desert you;*
How he follow'd with them and tack'd with them three days and
would not give it up,
How he saved the drifting company at last,
How the lank loose-gown'd women look'd when boated from the
side of their prepared graves,
How the silent old-faced infants and the lifted sick, and the sharp-
lipp'd unshaven men;
All this I swallow, it tastes good. I like it well, it becomes mine,
I am the man, I suffer'd, I was there.
The disdain and calmness of martyrs,
The mother of old, condemn'd for a witch, burnt with dry wood,
her children gazing on,
The hounded slave that flags in the race, leans by the fence, blowing,
cover'd with sweat.
The twinges that sting like needles his legs and neck, the murderous
buckshot and the bullets,
All these I feel or am.

I am the hounded slave, I wince at the bite of the dogs,
Hell and despair are upon me, crack and again crack the marksmen,

I clutch the rails of the fence, my gore dribs, thinn'd with the ooze
    of my skin,
I fall on the weeds and stones,
The riders spur their unwilling horses, haul close,
Taunt my dizzy ears and beat me violently over the head with
    whip-stocks.

Agonies are one of my changes of garments,
I do not ask the wounded person how he feels, I myself become
    the wounded person,
My hurts turn livid upon me as I lean on a cane and observe.

O CAPTAIN! MY CAPTAIN!

O Captain! my Captain! our fearful trip is done,
The ship has weathered every rack, the prize we sought is won,
The port is near, the bells I hear, the people all exulting,
While follow eyes the steady keel, the vessel grim and daring;
    But O heart! heart! heart!
        O the bleeding drops of red,
            Where on the deck my Captain lies,
                Fallen cold and dead.

O Captain! my Captain! rise up and hear the bells;
Rise up—for you the flag is flung—for you the bugle trills,
For you bouquets and ribboned wreaths—for you the shores acrowd-
    ing,
For you they call, the swaying mass, their eager faces turning;
    Here Captain! dear father!
        This arm beneath your head!
            It is some dream that on the deck
                You've fallen cold and dead.

My Captain does not answer, his lips are pale and still,
My father does not feel my arm, he has no pulse nor will,
The ship is anchored safe and sound, its voyage closed and done,
From fearful trip the victor ship comes in with object won;
    Exult O shores, and ring O bells!
        But I, with mournful tread,
            Walk the deck my Captain lies,
                Fallen cold and dead.

From *TO A FOIL'D EUROPEAN REVOLUTIONAIRE*

(No songs of loyalty alone are these,
   But songs of insurrection also;
For I am the sworn poet of every dauntless rebel, the world over,
And he going with me leaves peace and routine behind him,
And stakes his life, to be lost at any moment.)

When liberty goes out of a place, it is not the first to go, nor the
     second or third to go,
It waits for all the rest to go—it is the last.

When there are no more memories of heroes and martyrs,
And when all life, and all the souls of men and women are discharged
     from any part of the earth,
Then only shall liberty, or the idea of liberty, be discharged from
     that part of the earth,
And the infidel come into full possession.

From *AS A STRONG BIRD ON PINIONS FREE*

Beautiful World of new, superber Birth, that rises to my eyes,
Like a limitless golden cloud, filling the western sky. . . .
Thou Wonder World, yet undefined, unform'd—neither do I define
     thee;
How can I pierce the impenetrable blank of the future?
I feel thy ominous greatness, evil as well as good;
I watch thee, advancing, absorbing the present, transcending the
     past;
I see thy light lighting and thy shadow shadowing, as if the entire
     globe;
But I do not undertake to define thee—hardly to comprehend thee;
I but thee name—thee prophesy—as now!

From *SONG OF THE OPEN ROAD*

XI

Listen! I will be honest with you,
I do not offer the old smooth prizes, but offer rough new prizes,

These are the days that must happen to you:
You shall not heap up what is call'd riches,
You shall scatter with lavish hand all that you earn or achieve,
You but arrive at the city to which you were destin'd, you hardly settle yourself to satisfaction, before you are call'd by an irresistible call to depart,
You shall be treated to the ironical smiles and mockings of those who remain behind you,
What beckonings of love you receive you shall only answer with passionate kisses of parting,
You shall not allow the hold of those who spread their reach'd hands toward you.

XII

Allons! after the great Companions, and to belong to them!
They too are on the road—they are the swift and majestic men —they are the greatest women,
Enjoyers of calms of seas and storms of seas,
Sailors of many a ship, walkers of many a mile of land,
Habitués of many distant countries, habitués of far-distant dwellings,
Trusters of men and women, observers of cities, solitary toilers,
Pausers and contemplators of tufts, blossoms, shells of the shore,
Dancers at wedding-dances, kissers of brides, tender helpers of children, bearers of children,
Soldiers of revolts, standers by gaping graves, lowerers-down of coffins,
Journeyers over consecutive seasons, over the years, the curious years each emerging from that which preceded it,
Journeyers as with companions, namely their own diverse phases,
Forth-steppers from the latent unrealized baby-days,
Journeyers gayly with their own youth, journeyers with their bearded and well-grain'd manhood,
Journeyers with their womanhood, ample, unsurpass'd, content,
Journeyers with their own sublime old age of manhood or womanhood,
Old age, calm, expanded, broad with the haughty breadth of the universe,
Old age, flowing free with the delicious near-by freedom of death.

I HEAR AMERICA SINGING

I hear America singing, the varied carols I hear,
Those of mechanics, each one singing his as it should be blithe and strong,
The carpenter singing his as he measures his plank or beam,
The mason singing his as he makes ready for work, or leaves off work,
The boatman singing what belongs to him in his boat, the deck-hand singing on the steamboat deck,
The shoemaker singing as he sits on his bench, the hatter singing as he stands,
The wood-cutter's song, the plowboy's on his way in the morning, or at noon intermission or at sundown,
The delicious singing of the mother, or of the young wife at work, or of the girl sewing or washing,
Each singing what belongs to him or her and to none else,
The day what belongs to the day—at night the party of young fellows, robust, friendly,
Singing with open mouths their strong melodious songs.

FOR YOU, O DEMOCRACY

Come, I will make the continent indissoluble,
I will make the most splendid race the sun ever shone upon,
I will make divine magnetic lands,
    With the love of comrades,
        With the life-long love of comrades.

I will plant companionship thick as trees along all the rivers of America, and along the shores of the great lakes, and all over the prairies,
I will make inseparable cities with their arms about each other's necks,
    By the love of comrades,
        By the manly love of comrades.

For you these from me, O Democracy, to serve you *ma femme!*
For you, for you I am trilling these songs.

1400

JOHN GREENLEAF WHITTIER

JOHN GREENLEAF WHITTIER (American, 1807-1892). Antislavery balladist. His New England Quaker background painted in narrative poem, *Snowbound*. Became widely known as pamphleteer and editor of various abolitionist papers. Now more often remembered as a writer of popular ballads and nature poet.

THE SLAVE-SHIPS

> "That fatal, that perfidious bark,
> Built i' the eclipse, and rigged with curses dark."
> —*Milton's Lycidas.*

"All ready!" cried the captain;
   "Ay, ay!" the seamen said;
"Heave up the worthless lubbers,—
   The dying and the dead."
Up from the slave-ship's prison
   Fierce, bearded heads were thrust:
"Now let the sharks look to it,—
   Toss up the dead ones first!"

Corpse after corpse came up,—
   Death had been busy there;
Where every blow is mercy,
   Why should the spoiler spare?
Corpse after corpse they cast
   Sullenly from the ship,
Yet bloody with the traces
   Of fetter-link and whip.

Gloomily stood the captain,
   With his arms upon his breast,
With his cold brow sternly knotted,
   And his iron lip compressed.
"Are all the dead dogs over?"
   Growled through that matted lip,—
"The blind ones are no better,
   Let's lighten the good ship."

Hark! from the ship's dark bosom,
    The very sounds of hell!
The ringing clank of iron,—
    The maniac's short, sharp yell!—
The hoarse, low curse, throat-stilled,—
    The starving infant's moan,—
The horror of a breaking heart
    Poured through a mother's groan.

Up from that loathsome prison
    The stricken blind ones came:
Below, had all been darkness,—
    Above, was still the same.
Yet the holy breath of heaven
    Was sweetly breathing there,
And the heated brow of fever
    Cooled in the soft sea air.

"Overboard with them, shipmates!"
    Cutlass and dirk were plied;
Fettered and blind, one after one,
    Plunged down the vessel's side.
The saber smote above,—
    Beneath, the lean shark lay,
Waiting with wide and bloody jaw
    His quick and human prey.

God of the earth! what cries
    Rang upward unto thee?
Voices of agony and blood,
    From ship-deck and from sea.
The last dull plunge was heard,—
    The last wave caught its stain,—
And the unsated shark looked up
    For human hearts in vain.

Red glowed the western waters,—
    The setting sun was there,
Scattering alike on wave and cloud
    His fiery mesh of hair.

Amidst a group in blindness,
    A solitary eye
Gazed, from the burdened slaver's deck,
    Into that burning sky.

"A storm," spoke out the gazer,
    "Is gathering and at hand,—
Curse on 't—I'd give my other eye
    For one firm rood of land."
And then he laughed,—but only
    His echoed laugh replied,—
For the blinded and the suffering
    Alone were at his side.

Night settled on the waters,
    And on a stormy heaven,
While fiercely on that lone ship's track
    The thunder-gust was driven.
"A sail!—thank God, a sail!"
    And as the helmsman spoke,
Up through the stormy murmur
    A shout of gladness broke.

Down came the stranger vessel,
    Unheeding on her way,
So near, that on the slaver's deck
    Fell off her driven spray.
"Ho! for the love of mercy,—
    We're perishing and blind!"
A wail of utter agony
    Came back upon the wind:

"Help *us!* for we are stricken
    With blindness every one;
Ten days we've floated fearfully,
    Unnoting star or sun.
Our ship's the slaver Leon,—
    We've but a score on board,—
Our slaves are all gone over,—
    Help,—for the love of God!"

On livid brows of agony
    The broad red lightning shone,—
But the roar of wind and thunder
    Stifled the answering groan
Wailed from the broken waters
    A last despairing cry,
As, kindling in the stormy light,
    The stranger ship went by.

In the sunny Guadaloupe
    A dark-hulled vessel lay,—
With a crew who noted never
    The nightfall or the day
The blossom of the orange,
    Was white by every stream,
And tropic leaf, and flower, and bird
    Were in the warm sunbeam.

And the sky was bright as ever,
    And the moonlight slept as well,
On the palm-trees by the hillside,
    And the streamlet of the dell:
And the glances of the Creole
    Were still as archly deep,
And her smiles as full as ever
    Of passion and of sleep.

But vain were bird and blossom,
    The green earth and the sky,
And the smile of human faces,
    To the slaver's darkened eye;
At the breaking of the morning,
    At the star-lit evening time,
O'er a world of light and beauty
    Fell the blackness of his crime.

CHRISTOPH MARTIN WIELAND

CHRISTOPH MARTIN WIELAND (German, 1733-1813). Translator of Shakespeare. Strongly influenced High German literary style. Edited and published first modern literary review in German. His novel, *Der goldene Spiegel*, brought appointment as tutor to Weimar princes, where he lived most of his life. Most famous work: *Oberon*, a verse romance.

SIR HUON ENTERS THE SULTAN'S PALACE

Now through the outward court swift speeds the knight;
   Within the second from his steed descends;
   Along the third his pace majestic bends:
Where'er he enters, dazzled by his sight,
   The guards make way,—his gait, his dress, his air,
   A nuptial guest of highest rank declare.
Now he advances towards an ebon gate,
Where with drawn swords twelve Moors gigantic wait,
   And piecemeal hack the wretch who steps unbidden there.

But the bold gesture and imperial mien
   Of Huon as he opes the lofty door,
   Drive back the swords that crossed his path before,
And at his entrance flamed with lightning sheen.
   At once, with rushing noise, the valves unfold:
   High throbs the bosom of our hero bold,
When, locked behind him, harsh the portals bray:
Through gardens decked with columns leads the way,
   Where towered a gate incased with plates of massy gold.

There a large fore-court held a various race
   Of slaves, hapless race, sad harem slaves,
   Who die of thirst 'mid joy's o'erflowing waves!
And when a man, whom emir honors grace,
   Swells in his state before their hollow eye,
   Breathless they bend, with looks that seem to die,
Beneath the weight of servitude oppresed;
Bow down, with folded arms across the breast,
   Nor dare look up to mark the pomp that glitters by.

Already cymbals, drums and fifes resound;
  With song and string the festive palace clangs;
  The Sultan's head already heaving hangs,
While vinous vapors float his brain around:
  Already mirth in freer current flows,
  And the gay bridegroom, wild with rapture, glows.
Then, as the bride, in horror turned away,
Casts on the ground her looks that never stray,
  Huon along the hall with noble freedom goes.

Now to the table he advances nigh,
  And with uplifted brow in wild amaze
  The admiring guests upon the stranger gaze:
Fair Rezia, tranced, with fascinated eye
  Still views her dream, and ever downward bends:
  The Sultan, busy with the bowl, suspends
All other thoughts: Prince Bakeban alone,
Warned by no vision, towards the guest unknown,
  All fearless of his fate, his length of neck extends.

Soon as Sir Huon's scornful eyes retrace
  The man of yesterday, that he, the same
  Who lately dared the Christian God defame,
Sits at the left, high-plumed in bridal grace,
  And bows the neck as conscious of his guilt:
  Swift as the light he grasps the sabre's hilt;
Off at the instant flies the heathen's head;
And, o'er the Caliph and the banquet shed,
  Up spirts his boiling blood, by dreadful vengeance spilt!

As the dread visage of Medusa fell,
  Swift flashing on the sight, with instant view
  Deprives of life the wild-revolted crew;
While reeks the tower with blood, while tumults swell,
  And murderous frenzy, fierce and fiercer grown,
  Glares in each eye, and maddens every tone,—
At once, when Perseus shakes the viper hair,
Each dagger stiffens as it hangs in air,
  And every murderer stands transformed to living stone!

1406

Thus, at the view of this audacious feat,
  The jocund blood that warmed each merry guest
  Suspends its frozen course in every breast:
Like ghosts, in heaps, all-shivering from their seat
  They start, and grasp their swords and mark their prey;
  But, shrunk by fear, their vigor dies away:
Each in its sheath their swords remain at rest:
With powerless fury in his look expressed,
  Mute sunk the caliph back, and stared in wild dismay.

The uproar which confounds the nuptial hall
  Forces the dreamer from her golden trance:
  Round her she gazes with astonished glance,
While yells of frantic rage her soul appal:
  But, as she turns her face towards Huon's side,
  How throbs his bosom, when he sees his bride!—
"'Tis she,—'tis she herself!" he wildly calls:
Down drops the bloody steel; the turban falls;
  And Rezia knows her knight, as float his ringlets wide.

"'Tis he!" she wild exclaims: yet virgin shame
  Stops in her rosy mouth the imperfect sound:
  How throbs her heart; what thrillings strange confound,
When, with impatient speed, the stranger came,
  And, love-emboldened, with presumptuous arms
  Clasped, in the sight of all, her angel charms!
And, Oh, how fiery red, how deadly pale
Her cheek, as love and maiden fear assail,
  The while he kissed her lip that glowed with sweet alarms!

Twice had his lip already kissed the maid:—
  "Where shall the bridal ring, Oh, where be found?"
  Lo! by good fortune, as he gazes round,
The elfin ring shines suddenly displayed,
  Won from the giant of the iron tower:
  Now, all-unconscious of its magic power,
This ring, so seeming base, the impatient knight
Slips on her finger, pledge of nuptial rite:—
  "With this, O bride beloved! I wed thee from this hour!"

Then, for the third time, at these words, again
  The bridegroom kissed the soft reluctant fair:
  The Sultan storms and stamps in wild despair:—
"Thou sufferest, then,—inexpiable stain!
  This Christian dog to shame thy nuptial day?—
  Seize, seize him, slaves!—ye die, the least delay!
Haste! drop by drop, from every throbbing vein,
By lengthened agonies his life-blood drain,—
  Thus shall the pangs of hell his monstrous guilt repay."

At once, in flames, before Sir Huon's eyes,
  A thousand weapons glitter at the word;
  And, ere our hero snatches up his sword,
On every side the death-storms fiercely rise:
  On every side he turns his brandished blade:
  By love and anguish wild, at once the maid
Around him wreathes her arm, his shield her breast,
Seizes his sword, by her alone repressed:—
  "Back! daring slaves!" she cries, "I, I the hero aid!

"Back!—to that breast,—here, here the passage lies!—
  No other way than through the midst of mine!"—
  And she, who lately seemed Love's bride divine,
Now flames a Gorgon with Medusa's eyes!
  And ever, as the emirs near inclose,
  She dares with fearless breast their swords oppose:—
"Spare him, my father! spare him! and, O thou,
Destined by fate to claim my nuptial vow,
  Spare him!—in both your lives the blood of Rezia flows!"

The Sultan's frenzy rages uncontrolled:
  Fierce on Sir Huon storm the murderous train;
  Yet still his glittering falchion flames in vain,
While Rezia's gentle hand retains its hold:
  Her agonizing shrieks his bosom rend.
  And what remains the princes to defend?
What but the horn can rescue her from death?—
Soft through the ivory flows his gentle breath,
  And from its spiry folds sweet fairy tones ascend.

Soon as its magic sounds, the powerless steel
  Falls without struggle from the lifted hand:
  In rash vertigo turned, the emir band
Wind arm in arm and spin the giddy reel:
  Throughout the hall tumultuous echoes ring;
  All, old and young, each heel has Hermes' wing:
No choice is left them by the fairy tone:
Pleased and astonished, Rezia stands alone
  By Huon's side unmoved, while all around them spring.

The whole divan, one swimming circle, glides
  Swift without stop: the old bashaws click time:
  As if on polished ice, in trance sublime,
The iman hoar with some spruce courtier slides:
  Nor rank nor age from capering refrain:
  Nor can the king his royal foot restrain;
He, too, must reel amid the frolic row,
Grasp the grand vizier by his beard of snow,
  And teach the aged man once more to bound amain.

The dancing melodies, ne'er heard before,
  From every crowded antechamber round,
  First draw the eunuchs forth with airy bound;
The women next, and slaves that guard the door
  Alike the merry madness seizes all.
  The harem's captives, at the magic call,
Trip gaily to the tune and whirl the dance:
In party-colored shirts the gardeners prance.
  Rush 'mid the youthful nymphs and mingle in the ball.

Entranced, with fearful joy, while doubt alarms,
  Fair Rezia stands almost deprived of breath:—
  "What wonder at the time when instant death
Hangs o'er us, that a dance the god disarms!
  A dance thus rescues from extreme distress!"
  "Some friendly genius deigns our union bless,"
Sir Huon says. Meanwhile amid the throng
With eager step darts Sherasmin along,
  And towards them Fatma hastes unnoticed through the press.

"Haste!" Sherasmin exclaims; "not now the hour
   To pry with curious leisure on the dance,—
   All is prepared,—the steeds impatient prance,—
While raves the castle, while unbarred the tower,
   And every gate wide open, why delay?
   By luck I met Dame Fatma on the way,
Close-packed, like beast of burden, for the flight."
"Peace! 'tis not yet the time," replies the knight;
   "A dreadful task impends,—for that must Huon stay."

Pale Rezia shudders at the dreadful sound,
   And looks with longing eye, that seems to say,
   "Why, on the brink of ruin, why delay?
Oh, hasten! let our footsteps fly the ground,
   Ere bursts the transient charm that binds their brain.
   And rage and vengeance repossess the train!"
Huon, who reads the language of her eyes,
With looks of answering love alone replies,
   Clasps to his heart her hand, nor dares the deed explain.

And now the fairy tones to soft repose
   Melt in the air: each head swims giddy round,
   And every limb o'ertired forgets to bound;
Wet every thread, and every pore o'erflows.
   The breath half-stopped scarce heaves with struggling pain;
   The drowsy blood slow creeps through every vein;
Involuntary joy, like torture, thrills:
The king, as from a bath, in streams distills,
   And pants upon his couch, amid the exhausted train.

Stiff, without motion, scarce with sense endued,
   Down, one by one, the o'erwearied dancers fall,
   Where swelling bolsters heave around the wall:
Emirs and lowly slaves, in contrast rude,
   Mix with the harem goddesses, as chance
   Tangles the mazes of the frantic dance:
At once together by a whirlwind blown,
On the same bed, in ill-paired union thrown,
   The groom and favorite lie confused in breathless trance.

OSCAR WILDE

OSCAR WILDE (English, 1854-1900). Cultivated literary eccentric and social satirist. One of leaders of Aesthetic Movement in 90's. Exotic stylist, particularly in play *Salome*, novel *The Picture of Dorian Gray*, and fairy tales. His drawing room comedies the best since Sheridan: *Lady Windermere's Fan, The Importance of Being Earnest, An Ideal Husband.* His last years darkened by aberrational ignominy.

THE SELFISH GIANT

EVERY afternoon, as they were coming from school, the children used to go and play in the Giant's garden.

It was a large lovely garden, with soft green grass. Here and there over the grass stood beautiful flowers like stars, and there were twelve peach-trees that in the Spring-time broke out into delicate blossoms of pink and pearl, and in the autumn bore rich fruit. The birds sat on the trees and sang so sweetly that the children used to stop their games in order to listen to them. "How happy we are here!" they cried to each other.

One day the Giant came back. He had been to visit his friend the Cornish ogre, and had stayed with him for seven years. After the seven years were over he had said all that he had to say, for his conversation was limited, and he determined to return to his own castle. When he arrived he saw the children playing in the garden.

"What are you doing there?" he cried in a very gruff voice, and the children ran away.

"My own garden is my own garden," said the Giant; "anyone can understand that, and I will allow nobody to play in it but myself." So he built a high wall all round it, and put up a notice-board.

TRESPASSERS
WILL BE
PROSECUTED

He was a very selfish Giant.

The poor children had now nowhere to play. They tried to play on the road, but the road was very dusty and full of hard stones, and they did not like it. They used to wander round the high wall when their lessons were over, and talk about the beautiful garden inside. "How happy we were there," they said to each other.

Then the Spring came, and all over the country there were little blossoms and little birds. Only in the garden of the Selfish Giant it was still winter. The birds did not care to sing in it, as there were no children, and the trees forgot to blossom. Once a beautiful flower put its head out from the grass, but when it saw the notice-board it was so sorry for the children that it slipped back into the ground again, and went off to sleep. The only people who were pleased were the Snow and the Frost. "Spring has forgotten this garden," they cried, "so we will live here all the year round." The Snow covered up the grass with her great white cloak, and the Frost painted all the trees silver. Then they invited the North Wind to stay with them, and he came. He was wrapped in furs, and he roared all day about the garden, and blew the chimney-pots down. "This is a delightful spot," he said; "we must ask the Hail on a visit." So the Hail came. Every day for three hours he rattled on the roof of the castle till he broke most of the slates, and then he ran round and round the garden as fast as he could go. He was dressed in gray, and his breath was like ice.

"I can not understand why the Spring is so late in coming," said the Selfish Giant, as he sat at the window and looked out at his cold white garden; "I hope there will be a change in the weather."

But the Spring never came, nor the Summer. The Autumn gave golden fruit to every garden, but to the Giant's garden she gave none. "He is too selfish," she said. So it was always Winter there, and the North Wind, and the Hail, and the Frost, and the Snow danced about through the trees.

One morning the Giant was lying awake in bed when he heard some lovely music. It sounded so sweet to his ears that he thought it must be the King's musicians passing by. It was really only a little linnet singing outside his window, but it was so long since he had heard a bird sing in his garden that it seemed to him to be the most beautiful music in the world. Then the Hail stopped dancing over his head, and the North Wind ceased roaring, and a delicious perfume came to him through the open casement. "I believe the Spring has come at last," said the Giant; and he jumped out of bed and looked out.

What did he see?

He saw a most wonderful sight. Through a little hole in the wall the children had crept in, and they were sitting in the branches of

1412

the trees. In every tree that he could see there was a little child. And the trees were so glad to have the children back again that they had covered themselves with blossoms, and were waving their arms gently above the children's heads. The birds were flying about and twittering with delight, and the flowers were looking up through the green grass and laughing. It was a lovely scene, only in one corner it was still winter. It was the farthest corner of the garden, and in it was standing a little boy. He was so small that he could not reach up to the branches of the tree, and he was wandering all round it, crying bitterly. The poor tree was still quite covered with frost and snow, and the North Wind was blowing and roaring above it. "Climb up, little boy," said the Tree, and it bent its branches down as low as it could; but the boy was too tiny.

And the Giant's heart melted as he looked out. "How selfish I have been!" he said; "now I know why the Spring would not come here. I will put that poor little boy on the top of the tree, and then I will knock down the wall, and my garden shall be the children's playground for ever and ever." He was really very sorry for what he had done.

So he crept downstairs and opened the front door quite softly, and went out into the garden. But when the children saw him they were so frightened that they all ran away, and the garden became winter again. Only the little boy did not run, for his eyes were so full of tears that he did not see the Giant coming. And the Giant stole up behind him and took him gently in his hand, and put him up into the tree. And the tree broke at once into blossoms, and the birds came and sang on it, and the little boy stretched out his two arms and flung them round the Giant's neck, and kissed him. And the other children, when they saw that the Giant was not wicked any longer, came running back, and with them came the Spring. "It is your garden now, little children," said the Giant, and he took a great axe and knocked down the wall. And when the people were going to market at twelve o'clock they found the Giant playing with the children in the most beautiful garden they had ever seen.

All day long they played, and in the evening they came to the Giant to bid him good-bye.

"But where is your little companion?" he said: "the boy I put into the tree." The Giant loved him the best because he had kissed him.

"We don't know," answered the children; "he has gone away."

"You must tell him to be sure and come here to-morrow," said the Giant. But the children said that they did not know where he lived, and had never seen him before; and the Giant felt very sad.

Every afternoon, when school was over, the children came and played with the Giant. But the little boy whom the Giant loved was never seen again. The Giant was very kind to all the children, yet he longed for his first little friend, and often spoke of him. "How I would like to see him!" he used to say.

Years went over, and the Giant grew very old and feeble. He could not play about any more, so he sat in a huge armchair, and watched the children at their games, and admired his garden. "I have many beautiful flowers," he said; "but the children are the most beautiful flowers of all."

One winter morning he looked out of his window as he was dressing. He did not hate the Winter now, for he knew that it was merely the Spring asleep, and that the flowers were resting.

Suddenly he rubbed his eyes in wonder, and looked and looked. It certainly was a marvelous sight. In the farthest corner of the garden was a tree quite covered with lovely white blossoms. Its branches were all golden, and silver fruit hung down from them, and underneath it stood the little boy he had loved.

Downstairs ran the Giant in great joy, and out into the garden. He hastened across the grass, and came near to the child. And when he came quite close his face grew red with anger, and he said, "Who hath dared to wound thee?" For on the palms of the child's hands were the prints of two nails, and the prints of two nails were on the little feet.

"Who hath dared to wound thee?" cried the Giant; "tell me, that I may take my big sword and slay him."

"Nay!" answered the child; "but these are the wounds of Love."

"Who art thou?" said the Giant, and a strange awe fell on him, and he knelt before the little child.

And the child smiled on the Giant, and said to him, "You let me play once in your garden, to-day you shall come with me to my garden, which is Paradise."

And when the children ran in that afternoon, they found the Giant lying dead under the tree, all covered with white blossoms.

WILLIAM WORDSWORTH

WILLIAM WORDSWORTH (English, 1770-1850). Grand poet of the common-place. One of founders (with friend Coleridge) of the English Romantic Movement. Preface to their joint work, *Lyrical Ballads*, became famous manifesto. He glorified the Lake District and its simple inhabitants. More ambitious work: *The Prelude, The Excursion.* Later poetry less inspired. Ended days as Poet Laureate.

INTIMATIONS OF IMMORTALITY

I

There was a time when meadow, grove and stream,
 The earth, and every common sight,
  To me did seem
  Apparelled in celestial light,
 The glory and the freshness of a dream.
 It is not now as it hath been of yore;—
  Turn wheresoe'er I may,
   By night or day,
The things which I have seen I now can see no more.

II

  The rainbow comes and goes,
  And lovely is the rose;
  The moon doth with delight
Look round her when the heavens are bare;
  Waters on a starry night
  Are beautiful and fair;
 The sunshine is a glorious birth;—
 But yet I know, where'er I go,
That there hath passed away a glory from the earth.

III

Now, while the birds thus sing a joyous song.
 And while the young lambs bound
  As to the tabor's sound,

To me alone there came a thought of grief;
A timely utterance gave that thought relief;
    And I again am strong.
The cataracts blow their trumpets from the steep—
No more shall grief of mine the season wrong:
I hear the echoes through the mountains throng;
The winds come to me from the fields of sleep;
    And all the earth is gay.
       Land and sea
   Give themselves up to jollity;
      And with the heart of May
    Doth every beast keep holiday:—
     Thou child of joy,
Shout round me, let me hear thy shouts, thou happy shepherd-boy!

IV

Ye blessèd creatures, I have heard the call
  Ye to each other make; I see
The heavens laugh with you in your jubilee;
   My heart is at your festival,
    My head hath its coronal,
The fullness of your bliss I feel—I feel it all.
   Oh, evil day! if I were sullen,
   While Earth herself is adorning,
    This sweet May morning;
   And the children are culling,
    On every side,
  In a thousand valleys far and wide,
  Fresh flowers; while the sun shines warm,
And the babe leaps up on his mother's arm:—
   I hear, I hear, with joy I hear!
  —But there's a tree, of many one,
A single field which I have looked upon—
Both of them speak of something that is gone:
    The pansy at my feet
    Doth the same tale repeat:
Whither is fled the visionary gleam?
Where is it now, the glory and the dream?

Our birth is but a sleep and a forgetting:
The soul that rises with us, our life's star,
    Hath had elsewhere its setting,
        And cometh from afar;
    Not in entire forgetfulness,
    And not in utter nakedness,
But trailing clouds of glory do we come
        From God, who is our home:
Heaven lies about us in our infancy!
Shades of the prison-house begin to close
        Upon the growing boy;
But he beholds the light, and whence it flows,
        He sees it in his joy;
The youth, who daily farther from the east
    Must travel, still is Nature's priest,
        And by the vision splendid
        Is on his way attended;
At length the man perceives it die away,
And fade into the light of common day.

VI

Earth fills her lap with pleasures of her own;
Yearnings she hath in her own natural kind,
And, even with something of a mother's mind,
        And no unworthy aim,
        The homely nurse doth all she can
To make her foster-child, her inmate man,
    Forget the glories he hath known,
And that imperial palace whence he came.

VII

Behold the child among his new-born blisses,
A six-years' darling of a pigmy size!
See, where 'mid work of his own hand he lies,
Fretted by sallies of his mother's kisses,

With light upon him from his father's eyes!
See, at his feet, some little plan or chart,
Some fragment from his dream of human life,
Shaped by himself with newly-learnéd art;
    A wedding or a festival,
    A mourning or a funeral;
      And this hath now his heart,
      And unto this he frames his song:
      Then will he fit his tongue
To dialogues of business, love, or strife;
    But it will not be long
    Ere this be thrown aside,
    And with new joy and pride
The little actor cons another part;
Filling from time to time his "humorous stage"
With all the persons, down to palsied age,
That Life brings with her in her equipage;
    As if his whole vocation
    Were endless imitation.

VIII

Thou, whose exterior semblance dost belie
    Thy soul's immensity;
Thou best philosopher, who yet dost keep
Thy heritage; thou eye among the blind,
That, deaf and silent, readest the eternal deep,
Haunted forever by the eternal mind,—
    Mighty Prophet! Seer blessed!
    On whom those truths do rest,
Which we are toiling all our lives to find;
In darkness lost, the darkness of the grave;
Thou, over whom thy immortality
Broods like the day, a master o'er a slave,
A presence which is not to be put by;
Thou little child, yet glorious in the might
Of heaven-born freedom, on thy being's height,
Why with such earnest pains dost thou provoke
The years to bring the inevitable yoke,

1418

Thus blindly with thy blessedness at strife?
Full soon thy soul shall have her earthly freight,
And custom lie upon thee with a weight,
Heavy as frost, and deep almost as life!

IX

    O joy! that in our embers
    Is something that does live,
    That nature yet remembers
    What was so fugitive!
The thought of our past years in me doth breed
Perpetual benedictions: not indeed
For that which is most worthy to be blessed;
Delight and liberty, the simple creed
Of childhood, whether busy or at rest,
With new-fledged hope still fluttering in his breast,—
    Not for these I raise
  The song of thanks and praise;
  But for those obstinate questionings
  Of sense and outward things,
  Fallings from us, vanishings;
  Blank misgivings of a creature
Moving about in worlds not realized,
High instincts, before which our mortal nature
Did tremble, like a guilty thing surprised:
  But for those first affections,
  Those shadowy recollections,
  Which, be they what they may,
Are yet the fountain light of all our day,
Are yet a master light of all our seeing;
  Uphold us, cherish, and have power to make
Our noisy years seem moments in the being
Of the eternal silence: truths that wake
    To perish never;
Which neither listlessness, nor mad endeavor,
    Nor man, nor boy,
Nor all that is at enmity with joy,
Can utterly abolish or destroy!

Hence, in a season of calm weather,
          Though inland far we be,
Our souls have sight of that immortal sea
          Which brought us hither;
          Can in a moment travel thither,
And see the children sport upon the shore,
And hear the mighty waters rolling evermore.

                    X

Then sing, ye birds—sing, sing a joyous song!
          And let the young lambs bound
          As to the tabor's sound!
     We, in thought, will join your throng,
          Ye that pipe and ye that play,
          Ye that through your hearts to-day
          Feel the gladness of the May!
What though the radiance which was once so bright
Be now forever taken from my sight,—
          Though nothing can bring back the hour
Of splendor in the grass, of glory in the flower;
          We will grieve not, rather find
          Strength in what remains behind;
          In the primal sympathy,
          Which, having been, must ever be
          In the soothing thoughts that spring
          Out of human suffering;
          In the faith that looks through death,
In years that bring the philosophic mind.

                    XI

And oh, ye fountains, meadows, hills, and groves,
Forbode not any severing of our loves!
Yet in my heart of hearts I feel your might;
I only have relinquished one delight,
To live beneath your more habitual sway.
I love the brooks, which down their channels fret,
Even more than when I tripped lightly as they;
The innocent brightness of a new-born day
          Is lovely yet;

The clouds that gather round the setting sun
Do take a sober coloring from an eye
That hath kept watch o'er man's mortality:
Another race hath been and other palms are won.
Thanks to the human heart by which we live;
Thanks to its tenderness, its joys, and fears,
To me the meanest flower that blows can give
Thoughts that do often lie too deep for tears.

Y

YAMANOE NO OKURA

YAMANOE NO OKURA (Japanese, 659-733). Moralist and philosopher. One of the best poets from the *Manyōshū* anthology. Notable for his sympathy for the suffering poor and for children. Pursued a diplomatic career.

AN ELEGY ON THE IMPERMANENCE OF HUMAN LIFE

We are helpless before time
Which ever speeds away.
And pains of a hundred kinds
Pursue us one after another.
Maidens joy in girlish pleasures,
With ship-borne gems on their wrists,
And hand in hand with their friends;
But the bloom of maidenhood,
As it cannot be stopped,
Too swiftly steals away.
When do their ample tresses
Black as a mud-snail's bowels
Turn white with the frost of age?
Whence come those wrinkles
Which furrow their rosy cheeks?
The lusty young men, warrior-like,
Bearing their sword-blades at their waists,
In their hands the hunting bows,
And mounting their bay horses,
With saddles dressed with twill,
Ride about in triumph;

But can their prime of youth
Favour them for ever?
Few are the nights they keep,
When, sliding back the plank doors,
They reach their beloved ones
And sleep, arms intertwined,
Before, with staffs at their waists,
They totter along the road,
Laughed at here, and hated there.
This is the way of the world;
And, cling as I may to life,
I know no help!

Envoy

Although I wish I were thus,
Like the rocks that stay for ever,
In this world of humanity
I cannot keep old age away.

A DIALOGUE ON POVERTY

On the night when the rain beats,
Driven by the wind,
On the night when the snow-flakes mingle
With the sleety rain,
I feel so helplessly cold.
I nibble at a lump of salt,
Sip the hot, oft-diluted dregs of saké;
And coughing, snuffling,
And stroking my scanty beard,
I say in my pride,
'There's none worthy, save I!'
But I shiver still with cold.
I pull up my hempen bed-clothes,
Wear what few sleeveless clothes I have,
But cold and bitter is the night!
As for those poorer than myself,
Their parents must be cold and hungry,
Their wives and children beg and cry.
Then, how do you struggle through life?

Wide as they call the heaven and earth,
For me they have shrunk quite small;
Bright though they call the sun and moon,
They never shine for me.
Is it the same with all men,
Or for me alone?
By rare chance I was born a man
And no meaner than my fellows,
But, wearing unwadded sleeveless clothes
In tatters, like weeds waving in the sea,
Hanging from my shoulders,
And under the sunken roof,
Within the leaning walls,
Here I lie on straw
Spread on bare earth,
With my parents at my pillow,
My wife and children at my feet,
All huddled in grief and tears.
No fire sends up smoke
At the cooking-place,
And in the cauldron
A spider spins its web.
With not a grain to cook,
We moan like the 'night-thrush.'
Then, 'to cut,' as the saying is,
'The ends of what is already too short,'
The village headman comes,
With rod in hand, to our sleeping-place,
Growling for his dues.
Must it be so hopeless—
The way of this world?

Envoy

Nothing but pain and shame in this world of men,
But I cannot fly away,
Wanting the wings of a bird.

SUFFERING FROM OLD AGE AND PROLONGED ILLNESS, AND THINKING OF HIS CHILDREN

So long as lasts the span of life,
We wish for peace and comfort
With no evil and no mourning,
But life is hard and painful.
As the common saying has it,
Bitter salt is poured into the smarting wound,
Or the burdened horse is packed with an upper load,
Illness shakes my old body with pain.
All day long I breathe in grief
And sigh throughout the night.
For long years my illness lingers,
I grieve and groan month after month,
And though I would rather die,
I cannot, and leave my children
Noisy like the flies of May.
Whenever I watch them
My heart burns within.
And tossed this way and that,
I weep aloud.

Envoys

I find no solace in my heart;
Like the bird flying behind the clouds
I weep aloud.

Helpless and in pain,
I would run out and vanish,
But the thought of my children holds me.

No children to wear them in wealthy homes,
They are thrown away as waste,
Those silks and quilted clothes!

With no sackcloth for my children to wear,
Must I thus grieve,
For ever at a loss!

Though vanishing like a bubble,
I live, praying that my life will be long
Like a rope of a thousand fathoms.

Humble as I am,
Like an arm-band of coarse twill,
How I crave a thousand years of life!

WILLIAM BUTLER YEATS

WILLIAM BUTLER YEATS (Irish, 1865-1939). Greatest Irish poet. Leader of the Irish Renaissance in literature, co-founder with Lady Gregory of the Abbey Theatre. Nobel Prize, 1923. Wrote romantic and mythological lyrics, highly personal poems, plays and critical essays. Among them: *The Wind Among the Reeds, Responsibilities, The Tower, A Full Moon in March, Stories of Red Hanrahan.*

AN IRISH AIRMAN FORESEES HIS DEATH

I know that I shall meet my fate
Somewhere among the clouds above;
Those that I fight I do not hate,
Those that I guard I do not love;
My country is Kiltartan Cross,
My countrymen Kiltartan's poor,
No likely end could bring them loss
Or leave them happier than before.
Nor law, nor duty bade me fight,
Nor public men, nor cheering crowds,
A lonely impulse of delight
Drove to this tumult in the clouds;
I balanced all, brought all to mind,
The years to come seemed waste of breath,
A waste of breath the years behind
In balance with this life, this death.

AN APPOINTMENT

Being out of heart with government,
I took a broken root to fling
Where the proud, wayward squirrel went,
Taking delight that he could spring;

And he, with that low whinnying sound
That is like laughter, sprang again
And so to the other tree at a bound.
Nor the tame will, nor timid brain,
Bred that fierce tooth and cleanly limb
And threw him up to laugh on the bough;
No government appointed him.

THE ROSE TREE

'O words are lightly spoken,'
Said Pearse to Connolly,
'Maybe a breath of politic words
Has withered our Rose Tree;
Or maybe but a wind that blows
Across the bitter sea.'

'It needs to be but watered,'
James Connolly replied,
'To make the green come out again
And spread on every side,
And shake the blossom from the bud
To be the garden's pride.'

'But where can we draw water,'
Said Pearse to Connolly,
'When all the wells are parched away?
O plain as plain can be
There's nothing but our own red blood
Can make a right Rose Tree.'

COME GATHER ROUND ME, PARNELLITES

Come gather round me, Parnellites,
And praise our chosen man;
Stand upright on your legs awhile,
Stand upright while you can,
For soon we lie where he is laid,
And he is underground;
Come fill up all those glasses
And pass the bottle round.

1427

And here's a cogent reason,
And I have many more,
He fought the mind of England
And saved the Irish poor,
Whatever good a farmer's got
He brought it all to pass;
And here's another reason,
That Parnell loved a lass.

And here's a final reason,
He was of such a kind
Every man that sings a song
Keeps Parnell in his mind.
For Parnell was a proud man,
No prouder trod the ground,
And a proud man's a lovely man,
So pass the bottle round.

The Bishops and the Party
That tragic story made,
A husband that had sold his wife
And after that betrayed;
But stories that live longest
Are sung above the glass,
And Parnell loved his country,
And Parnell loved his lass.

Z

EMILE ZOLA

ÉMILE ZOLA (French, 1840-1902). Founder of the Naturalistic School of
French literature. Tried to apply new scientific concepts to literature. Remembered, also, for his dedicated defense of Dreyfus, *J'Accuse*. Like Balzac,
he wanted to embrace all French society in his novels. Most nearly successful:
Germinal, L'Assommoir, La Débâcle. Most widely read: *Nana*.

A FIGHT WITH FLAILS

WHEN the relatives, invited to a baptism and supper, had gone to
look over the farm, Buteau, dissatisfied at losing the afternoon, took
off his jacket and began to thresh, in the paved corner of the courtyard; for he needed a sack of wheat. But he soon wearied of
threshing alone, he wanted, to warm him up, the double cadence
of the flails, tapping in measure; and he called Françoise, who often
aided him in this work, her arms as hard as those of a lad:—"Eh,
Françoise, will you come?"

His wife, who was preparing a ragoût of veal with carrots, and
who had alrady put on an old dress, was forced to follow him. She
took a flail, her own. With both hands she made it whirl above her
head, bringing it down upon the wheat, which it struck with a sharp
blow. Buteau, opposite her, did the same, and soon nothing was seen
but the bits of flying wood. The grain leaped, fell like hail, beneath
the panting toc-toc of the two threshers.

At a quarter to seven o'clock, as the night was coming on,
Fouan and the Delhommes presented themselves.

"We must finish," Buteau cried to them, without stopping. "Fire
away, Françoise!"

She did not pause, tapped harder, in the excitement of the work
and the noise. And it was thus that Jean, who arrived in his turn,
with the permission to dine out, found them. Françoise, on seeing

him, stopped short, troubled. Buteau, having wheeled about, stood for an instant motionless with surprise and anger. "What are you doing here?"

But Lise cried out, with her gay air: "Eh! true, I have not told you. I saw him this morning, and asked him to come."

The inflamed face of her husband became so terrible, that she added, wishing to excuse herself: "I have an idea, Père Fouan, that he has a request to make of you."

"What request?" said the old man.

Jean colored, and stammered, greatly vexed that the matter should be broached in this way, so quickly, before everybody. But Buteau interrupted him violently, the smiling glance that his wife had cast upon Françoise had sufficed to enlighten him: "Are you making game of us? She is not for you, you scoundrel!"

This brutal reception restored Jean his courage. He turned his back, and addressed the old man: "This is the story, Père Fouan, it's very simple. As you are Françoise's guardian, it is necessary for me to address myself to you to get her, is it not? If she will take me, I will take her. It is marriage that I ask."

Francoise, who was still holding her flail, dropped it, trembling with fright. She ought, however, to have expected this; but never could she have thought that Jean would dare to demand her thus, immediately. Why had he not talked with her about it first? She was overwhelmed, she could not have said if she trembled with hope or with fear. And, all of a quiver, she stood between the two men.

Buteau did not give Fouan time to answer. He resumed, with a growing fury:—"Eh? you have gall! An old fellow of thirty-three marry a girl of eighteen! Only fifteen years difference! Is it not laughable?"

Jean commenced to get angry. "What difference does it make to you, if I want her and she wants me?" And he turned towards Françoise, that she might give her decision. But she remained frightened, stiffened, and seeming not to understand the case. She could not say No; she did not say Yes, however. Buteau, besides, was looking at her as if he would kill her, to force back the Yes in her throat. If she married, he would lose her land. The sudden thought of this result put the climax to his rage.

"See here, father, see here, Delhomme, it's not right to give this girl to that old villain, who is not even of the district, who comes from nobody knows where, after having dragged his ugly mug in all directions! A failure of a joiner who has turned farmer, because, very sure, he has some dirty business to hide!"

"And afterwards? If I want her and she wants me!" repeated Jean, who had controlled himself. "Come, Françoise, speak."

"But it's true!" cried Lise, carried away by the desire of marrying off her sister, in order to disembarrass herself of her, "what have you to say, if they come to an understanding? She has no need of your consent; it's very considerate in her not to send you about your business with a flea in your ear. You exhaust our patience!"

Then Buteau saw that the marriage would be decided upon, if the young girl spoke. At that instant La Grande (the old aunt) entered the court-yard, followed by the Charleses, who had returned with Éloide. And he summoned them with a gesture, without knowing yet what he would say. Then his face puffed out, he bawled, shaking his fist at his wife and sister-in-law:

"Name of God! I'll break the heads of both of them, the jades!"

The Charleses caught his words, open-mouthed, with consternation. Madam Charles threw herself forward, as if to cover with her body Éloide, who was listening; then, pushing her towards the kitchen garden, she herself cried out, very loudly: "Go look at the salads; go look at the cabbages! Oh! the fine cabbages!"

Buteau continued, violently abusing the two women, upon whom he heaped all sorts of epithets. Lise, astonished at this sudden fit, shrugging her shoulders, repeating: "He is crazy! he is crazy!"

"Tell him it's none of his business!" cried Jean to Françoise.

"Very sure it's none of his business!" said the young girl, with a tranquil air.

"Ah! it's none of my business, eh?" resumed Buteau. "Well, I'm going to make you both march, jades that you are!"

This mad audacity paralyzed, bewildered Jean. The others, the Delhommes, Fouan, La Grande, held aloof. They did not seem surprised; they thought, evidently, that Buteau had a right to do as he pleased in his own house. Then Buteau felt himself victorious in his undisputed strength of possession. He turned towards Jean. "And now for you, scoundrel, who came here to turn my house upside down! Get out of here on the instant! Eh! you refuse. Wait, wait!"

He picked up his flail, he whirled it about his head, and Jean had only the time to seize the other flail, Françoise's, to defend himself. Cries burst forth, they strove to throw themselves between them; but the two men were so terrible that they drew back. The long handles of the flails carried the blows for several yards; they swept the court-yard. The two adversaries stood alone, in the centre, at a distance from each other, enlarging the circle of their flails. They uttered not a word, their teeth set. Only the sharp blows of the pieces of wood were heard at each stroke.

Buteau had launched forth the first blow, and Jean, yet stooping, would have had his head broken, if he had not leaped backwards. Instantly, with a sudden stiffening of the muscles, he arose, he raised, he brought down the flail, like a thresher beating the grain. But already the other was striking also, the two flail ends met, bent back upon their leather straps, in the mad flight of wounded birds. Three times the same clash was reproduced. They saw only those bits of wood whirl and hiss in the air at the extremity of the handles, always ready to fall and split the skulls which they menaced.

Delhomme and Fouan, however, had rushed forward, when the women cried out. Jean had just rolled in the straw, treacherously stricken by Buteau, who, with a blow like a whip stroke, along the ground, fortunately deadened, had hit him on the legs. He sprang to his feet, he brandished his flail in a rage that the pain increased. The end described a large circle, fell to the right, when the other expected it to the left. A few lines nearer, and the brains would have been beaten out. Only the ear was grazed. The blow, passing obliquely, fell with all its force upon the arm, which was broken clean. The bone cracked with the sound of breaking glass.

"Ah! the murderer!" howled Buteau, "he has killed me!"

Jean, haggard, his eyes red with blood, dropped his weapon. Then, for a moment, he stared at them all, as if stupefied by what had happened there, so rapidly; and he went away, limping, with a gesture of furious despair.

When he had turned the corner of the house, towards the plain, he saw La Trouille, who had witnessed the fight, over the garden hedge. She was still laughing at it, having come there to skulk around the baptismal repast, to which neither her father nor herself had been invited. Mahomet would split his sides with merriment over the little family fête, over his brother's broken arm! She squirmed as if she had been tickled, almost ready to fall over, so much was she amused at it all.

"Ah! Caporal, what a hit!" cried she. "The bone went crack! It wasn't the least bit funny!"

He did not answer, slackening his step with an over-whelmed

air. And she followed him, whistling to her geese, which she had brought to have a pretext for stationing herself and listening behind the walls. Jean, mechanically, returned towards the threshing machine, which was yet at work amid the fading light. He thought that it was all over, that he could never see the Buteaus again, that they would never give him Françoise. How stupid it was! Ten minutes had sufficed; a quarrel which he had not sought, a blow so unfortunate, just at the moment when matters were progressing favorably! And now there was an end to it all! The roaring of the machine, in the depths of the twilight, prolonged itself like a great cry of distress.

ARNOLD ZWEIG

ARNOLD ZWEIG (German, 1887-   ). Militant pacifist. His most famous novel, *The Case of Sergeant Grischa,* came out of painful World War I experiences. Emigrated to Israel, a refugee from Nazi Germany. There wrote extensively on Zionism. Best stories: in *Playthings of Time.* Essays: *Juden auf der deutschen Bühne.*

THE APPARITION

TELL me a story!—that's easy to say. These mountains bring back almost too vivid memories of blessed, happy days when I was as carefree as a colt and of those others when I was preparing myself for the task (or was it preparing itself for me?) that, for the time being, I hold in abeyance yet dare not interrupt. But as my eyes trouble me and I cannot, just now, enjoy the flights of fancy of others in the delightful pursuit of reading, I must, for better or worse, pass my leisure time in telling stories.

It happened during the coldest part of winter in the eastern Carpathians. This is a country of mountains that rise abruptly from the plains, and of heavy-coated browsing sheep; little hamlets, villages, and farms dot the plain, divided from each other by tongues of woodland slipping down the mountainside, and by fields wrested, ages ago, from the stark Slovak soil. This region lies far away—fully four hundred years! Miracles, saints, and demons still remain familiar phenomena there while fear, superstitious fear, is felt—and perhaps rightly so—only towards government officials, newspapers, machinery, the telephone, and the radio.

The inhabitants are without exception religious. The Jews believe in the Jewish lore, the Slovaks in the Christian, literally and reverently, and they carry on the customs their fathers have handed down to them in writing and by word of mouth. They are also very poor in that region, the Slovakian peasants a little less so, the Jews a little more, and these two are dependent upon each other, inevitably and by turns, as in the good fable of the lion and the mouse.

In this state of poverty and intense cold, Rifke Leah left her cottage early one winter's evening and went into the woods where the snow lay deep and undisturbed. Rifke Leah carried a short spade and, arriving at a familiar spot near the edge of the wood which seemed shielded from prying eyes, she busily began to shovel away the snow and to break up the ice beneath to cleanse herself. She shivered as she cowered and washed herself in the crystal-clear, crystal-cold water which came down from the mountains under a crust of ice and which, suddenly freed of its coverlet, steamed as it came in contact with the warmer air—but she shivered chiefly because she feared someone might pass by and surprise her.

It was early evening, the moon was still low and yellow, but bright wintry stars were shining through the bare branches. . . . Then, as she had divined, she suddenly heard—a short distance away—the voices of some peasants taking a short-cut through the woods from the village tavern to their homes. Merciful God—men! They have been drinking, they are singing—good-natured men but ready for pranks when in liquor. She represses her cry of alarm, throws her skirt over her head so that no one recognizes her, and dashes, or rather glides, silently homeward through the snow under the light of the pale golden moon—a mysterious figure, swathed in white. Rifke Leah succeeds in eluding them; trembling, with beating heart, she makes a detour around the tavern and reaches her cottage a few minutes later.

Meanwhile the three peasants stood mutely beside the dark water, which had miraculously thawed in the midst of the snow and which was still steaming. What had they witnessed? A lovely, white form had floated away amid the trees; it must have been the Holy Mother of God come to assure the village of a better harvest. In their greatest need came heavenly kindness—take off your hats: a miracle has happened here in the midst of the snowy desolation of the forest. Indeed, the vapours were still rising like incense before their eyes! They corroborate each other—they have seen the Holy Mother of God, white and lovely, float away amid the trees.

1434

The next morning and especially on the following Sunday they eagerly told of the miracle whose scene they had hastily marked by sticking branches into the snow around the pool of water. They had not neglected to cross themselves, kneel down, and thank the Mother of God for her visit.

The women and many people in distress made their way to the spot, which was frozen over again and covered with snow. One of the faithful hung a picture of the miraculous visitor and her Divine Child on the nearest tree, paper flowers from the church came next, then a little shed was built to protect the picture from the rain. Devout peasants and townsfolk, in ever-increasing numbers, made pilgrimages thither. The priests, hearing of it and being simple folk like the others, saw no reason to doubt a miracle that had already brought joy, solace, and cure from small ailments to so many of the faithful.

Spring came early that year; warm sunlight flooded the fields which peasants—cheered by the promise of the Queen of Heaven —were confidently tilling with their teams. The Jews had also, in due course, heard of the forest shrine. Oddly enough, Rifke Leah and her husband were the first to know its exact site. "Benjamin always was wide awake," the Jews said, and followed his lead. When the warm weather set in, he and his wife sold bread, wafers, biscuits, lemonade, and candles to the pilgrims.

The following autumn, after an abundant harvest, the foundations of a chapel commemorating the blessed visit of the Mother of God were laid. Before the winter began, the Bishop of Kosice came for the dedication. Not without heavy misgivings had he listened to the remarks of the local clergy, remarks which at first seemed harmless enough but which gradually came to reflect an urgent desire of the people. Many paths led to salvation and none should be disregarded, nor was this the time to ignore spiritual needs because of mental snobbishness. A miracle must have occurred; people believed it and it was working.

He visualized the brown, weatherbeaten faces of the peasants, their eyes opened wide in wonder; if he questioned and cross-questioned them as to what they had actually seen, they would insist it had been the Mother of God floating away through the wintry forest—nothing else. They had found the warm, dewy pool sending vapours into the night—nothing else. Let sceptics jeer, make insinuations, offer explanations of all sorts—he, the bishop, would be unworthy of shepherding these souls, if, through fear of fostering a delusion, he refused to bestow upon the scene of the apparition the dignity of official as well as spiritual consecration. He came; he stood before them simply and gravely, chanting praises in Latin and asking God's blessing upon the land and the simple faith of these country people.

For Kosice, far off in the east of Europe, is also some hundreds of years behind the times. It isn't so long ago that bloody battles were fought there with gipsies who had made savoury meals of human flesh. The Jews of that region, when they are among themselves, say to each other that it is only fair that their trade, especially that with pilgrims, has so greatly improved.

Benjamin, Rifke Leah's husband, occasionally drinks a glass too much. That is why he happened to be so communicative to an eminent scholar and politician who came there a year later from the capital city of Prague to tell the Jews how and why they should vote. It was he—he clung to the ancient traditions of his land and people with tender mockery—who sometimes told this story, not to sneer at the incident but to characterize these distant people and places, where even today the Middle Ages are alive in human hearts. He possessed a sympathetic understanding of the sincerity and simple piety as well as of the humour and gentle roguishness of this tale. That is why I have retold it—at leisure, beneath green trees, surrounded by green mountains, facing the blue heavens, which we strange creatures so frequently fashion into figments of our own childish desires so that our dreams, fears, and hopes may be as much a part of them as the fleecy clouds and may pass as they do.

ACKNOWLEDGMENTS

Aeschylus: "The Complaint of Prometheus," from *Prometheus Bound*, translated by Elizabeth Barrett Browning; "A Prayer to Artemis," from *The Suppliants*, translated by Miss Swanwick; "The Vision of Cassandra," from *Agamemnon*, translated by Edward Fitzgerald.

Ryunosuke Akutagawa: "Rashomon," from *Rashomon and Other Stories*, translated by Takashi Kojima, reprinted by permission of Liveright Publishing Corp., New York.

Sholem Aleikhem: "The Passover Guest," from *Yiddish Tales*, translated by Helena Frank, reprinted by permission of the Jewish Publication Society of America.

Vittorio Alfieri: "David Soothes Saul's Madness" and "The Death of Saul," from *Saul*.

Hans Christian Andersen: "The Lovers," reprinted from *The Universal Anthology*, edited by Richard Garnett, Merrill & Baker, New York. (Copyright, 1899, by Richard Garnett.)

Leonid Nikolayevic Andreyev: "Valia," translated by Lizzie B. Gorin, reprinted from *Greatest Short Stories*, P. F. Collier & Son, New York.

Guillaume Apollinaire: Poems from *Modern French Poetry*, compiled and translated by Joseph T. Shipley, reprinted by permission of Greenberg, New York.

Ludovico Ariosto: "Alcina the Enchantress," from *Orlando Furioso*, translated by W. S. Rose, reprinted from *The Universal Anthology*, edited by Richard Garnett, Merrill & Baker, New York. (Copyright, 1899, by Richard Garnett.)

Aristophanes: "Grand Chorus of Birds," from *The Birds*, translated by A. C. Swinburne.

Sholem Asch: "A Jewish Child," from *Yiddish Tales*, translated by Helena Frank, reprinted by permission of the Jewish Publication Society of America.

Attar (Farid ud-Din) : "The Bird Parliament," translated by Edward Fitzgerald.

Sri Aurobindo: Poems from *Poems, Past and Present*, reprinted by permission of the Sri Aurobindo Ashram Press, Pondicherry, India.

Mary Austin: "Papago Wedding," reprinted from *One Smoke Stories*, by permission of Houghton Mifflin, Boston.

Isaak Babel: "The Birth of a King," from *Benya Krik the Gangster and Other Stories*, translated by Elisaveta Fen, reprinted by permission of Schocken Books, Inc., New York.

1437

James Matthew Barrie: "Courtships," from *Auld Licht Idylls*, reprinted by permission of Charles Scribner's Sons, New York.

Bashō: Poems from *An Anthology of Haiku Ancient and Modern*, translated by Asataro Miyamori, reprinted by permission of Taisei-Do Shobo Co., Kobe, Japan.

Charles Baudelaire: Poems from *Modern French Poetry*, translated by Joseph T. Shipley, reprinted by permission of Greenberg, New York.

Stephen Vincent Benét: "Freedom's a Hard-Bought Thing," from *Selected Works of Stephen Vincent Benét*, published by Rinehart & Co., New York; reprinted by permission of Brandt & Brandt, agents for the estate of Stephen Vincent Benét. (Copyright, 1940, by Stephen Vincent Benét.)

Pierre Jean de Béranger: Poems from *The Universal Anthology*, edited by Richard Garnett, tr. by William Young, Merrill & Baker, New York. Copyright, 1899, by Richard Garnett.)

Bhartrihari: Poems, translated by Arthur W. Ryder, from *1001 Poems of Mankind*, edited by Henry W. Wells, Tupper & Love, Atlanta.

Bhāsa: "True Love" from *Svapnavāsavadatta*, and "Serenity" from *Pratimā Nātakam*, from *Sanskrit Literature*, by K. Chandrasekharan and Brahmasri V. H. Subrahmanya Sastri, reprinted by permission of The P.E.N. All-India Centre, Bombay.

Bhavabhūti: "The Rescue of Malātī," from *Malātī Mādhava*; "The Story of the Ramayana," from *Uttara Rāmacharita*; from *Sanskrit Literature* by K. Chandrasekharan and Brahmasri V. H. Subrahmanya Sastri, reprinted by permission of The P.E.N. All-India Centre, Bombay.

Hayyim Nahman Bialik: Poems translated by Leo Auerbach and Joseph T. Shipley, reprinted from *The Guardian*, Philadelphia, Nov., 1924; courtesy *New Palestine*.

Bilhana: "An Indian Love-Lament," from *Saurīsuratapanchāsikā*, translated by Sir Edwin Arnold.

Björmstjerne Björnson: "The Father," from *The Bridal March*, translated by R. B. Anderson.

Karl Georg Büchner: *Woyzeck*, translated by and reprinted by permission of Theodore Hoffman.

Ivan Bunin: "Sunstroke," translated by Helen Matheson, from *Great Russian Short Stories*, edited by Stephen Graham, reprinted by permission of Ernest Benn Limited, London.

John Bunyan: "The Golden City," from *The Pilgrim's Progress*.

Robert Burns: "The Twa Dogs," from *Burns into English, Renderings of Select Dialect Poems of Robert Burns* by William Kean Seymour, Philosophical Library, New York.

Pedro Calderón de la Barca: "Segismund's Dream," from *La vida es sueño (Life Is a Dream)*, translated by Edward Fitzgerald.

Karel Capek: "The Island," translated by Sarka B. Hrbkova, from *Great Stories of All Nations*, edited by Lieber and Williams, Copyright 1927 by Brentano's, Inc.; reprinted by permission of Coward-McCann, Inc., New York.

Giosué Carducci: Poems from *Italian Lyrists of To-day*, translated by G. A. Greene, Macmillan Co., New York.

Miguel de Cervantes y Saavedra: "Sancho Panza in His Island," from *Don Quixote*, reprinted from *Half Hours with the Best Authors* by Charles Knight, C. Arthur Pearson, Ltd., London.

Adalbert von Chamisso: *Peter Schlemihl, the Shadowless Man*, from *The World's Greatest Books*, edited by Lord Northcliffe, S. S. McClure, McKinlay, Stone, and Mackenzie. (Copyright, 1910, S. S. McClure Co.)

François-René de Chateaubriand: "Chactas Relates the Death of Atala," from *Atala*.

Bankim Chandra Chatteree: "The Bride's Arrival," from *Devi Choudhurani*, Part III, reprinted from *Bengali Literature* by Annadasankar and Lila Ray, by permission of The P.E.N. All-India Centre, Bombay.

Geoffrey Chaucer: "The Pardoner's Tale" from *The Canterbury Tales*, retold in prose by Lieber and Williams, from *Great Stories of All Nations*, edited by Lieber and Williams. (Copyright, 1927, by Brentano's.)

Anton Chekhov: "The Slanderer," translated by Herman Bernstein, reprinted from *Greatest Short Stories*, by permission of P. F. Collier & Son, New York.

Chikamatsu Monzaemon: "Adventures of the Hakata Damsel," translated by Asataro Miyamori, revised by Robert Nichols, from *Masterpieces of Chikamatsu, the Japanese Shakespeare*, reprinted by permission of Routledge & Kegan Paul, Ltd., London.

Ch'u Yuan: Poems from *Li Sao and Other Poems of Ch'u Yuan*, translated by Yang Hsien-yi and Gladys Yang, reprinted by permission of the Foreign Language Press, Peking.

Confucius: Poems from the *Shih Ching*, translated by Williams Jennings, reprinted from *The Universal Anthology*, edited by Richard Garnett, Merrill & Baker, New York. (Copyright, 1899, by Richard Garnett.)

Joseph Conrad: "The Lagoon," from *Tales of Unrest*, reprinted by permission of the trustees of the Joseph Conrad Estate, Messrs. J. M. Dent & Sons, Ltd., London. (Copyright, 1908, 1920, Doubleday, Page and Company.)

James Fenimore Cooper: "The Ariel on the Shoals," from *The Pilot*.

Stephen Crane: "The Bride Comes to Yellow Sky," reprinted from *Stephen Crane: An Omnibus*, edited by R. W. Stallman, by permission of Alfred A. Knopf, Inc., New York. (Copyright, 1925, by William H. Crane and, 1952, by Alfred A. Knopf, Inc.)

Dandin: "The Courtesan's Mother," from *Dasakumāracharita*, reprinted from *Sanskrit Literature* by K. Chandrasekharan and Brahmasri V. H. Subrahmanya Sastri, by permission of The P.E.N. All-India Centre, Bombay.

Gabriele D'Annunzio: "Four Sonnets," translated by G. A. Greene, reprinted by permission of Macmillan Co., New York.

Dante Alighieri: Selection from *The Divine Comedy*, translated by "Mr. Carey," reprinted from *Half Hours with the Best Authors* by Charles Knight, C. Arthur Pearson, Ltd., London, 1899.

Alphonse Daudet: "The Death of the Dauphin," translated by Stuart Merrill. (Copyright, 1890.)

David: "Psalms" from the Book of Psalms, King James Version of The Holy Bible.

Richard Dehmel: Poems from *Contemporary German Poetry*, selected and translated by Jethro Bithell. (Walter Scott Publishing Company, 1909.)

1439

Grazia Deledda: "The Open Door," from *Chiaroscuro* (Fratelli Treves, Milan), translated by E. M. Baker, from *Great Italian Short Stories*, edited by Decio Pettoello, Ernest Benn, Ltd., London, 1930.

Charles Dickens: "The Convict in the Marshes," from *Great Expectations*.

Emily Dickinson: Poems from *The Poems of Emily Dickinson*, edited by Martha Dickinson Bianchi, reprinted by permission of Little, Brown, & Co., Boston.

Feodor Mikhaylovich Dostoyevsky: "The Murderer's Confession to Sonia," from *Crime and Punishment*.

John Dryden: "Zegri and Abencerrage" from *The Conquest of Granada by the Spaniards*.

Joseph von Eichendorff: Poems from *Leaves from the Life of a Good-for-Nothing*, translated by Mrs. A. L. Wister. "The Broken Ring," translated by C. G. Leland, and "Morning Prayer," translated by Alfred Baskerville, reprinted from *Representative German Poems*, Henry Holt & Co., New York.

Mihail Eminescu: Poems from *Poems of Mihail Eminescu*, translated from the Rumanian and rendered into the original metres by E. Sylvia Pankhurst and I. O. Stefanovici, reprinted by permission of Routledge & Kegan Paul, Ltd., London.

Euripides: "Medea's Wrongs" and "Medea's Last Words to Her Children," from *Medea*.

Abraham Ibn Ezra: Poems translated by Emma Lazarus, reprinted from *A Golden Treasury of Jewish Literature*, edited by Leo W. Schwarz, Rinehart & Co., New York, reprinted by permission of Leo W. Schwarz. (Copyright, 1937, by Leo W. Schwarz.)

William Faulkner: "A Rose for Emily," reprinted by permission of Random House, Inc., New York. (Copyright, 1931, by William Faulkner.)

Firdausi: "Rustam and Akwan Dev," from *Shah-nàmah*, translated by E. H. Palmer, reprinted from *The Universal Anthology*, edited by Richard Garnett, Merrill & Baker, New York. (Copyright, 1899, by Richard Garnett.)

Gustave Flaubert: "Salammbô and Her Lover," from *Salammbô*.

Anatole France: Poems from *Modern French Poetry*, compiled and translated by Joseph T. Shipley, reprinted by permission of Greenberg, New York.

Ferdinand Freiligrath: "The Lion's Ride," translated by C. T. Brooks, and "The Specter Caravan," translated by J. C. Mangan, reprinted from *The German Classics, Masterpieces of German Literature*, edited by Kuno Francke, The German Publication Society, New York.

Robert Frost: Poems from *Complete Poems of Robert Frost*, reprinted by permission of Henry Holt & Co., New York. (Copyright, 1930, 1949, by Henry Holt & Co.,'Inc., copyright 1936, 1948, by Robert Frost.)

Fuzulî: Poems, reprinted from *Turkish Literature*, P. F. Collier & Son, New York.

Solomon Ibn Gabirol: Poems translated by Emma Lazarus, from *A Golden Treasury of Jewish Literature*, edited by Leo W. Schwarz, Rinehart & Co., New York, reprinted by permission of Leo W. Schwarz. (Copyright, 1937, by Leo W. Schwarz.)

John Galsworthy: "Quality," from *The Inn of Tranquillity*, reprinted by permission of Charles Scribner's Sons, New York.

Vsevolod Garshin: "The Signal," reprinted from *Best Russian Short Stories*, edited by Thomas Seltzer, reprinted by permission of Random House, Inc., New York.

Théophile Gautier: "The Mummy's Foot," from *One of Cleopatra's Nights*, translated by Lafcadio Hearn, Brentano's, New York. (Copyright, 1890.)

Khalil Gibran: "Behind the Garment," from *The Secrets of the Heart*, translated by Anthony Rizcallah Ferris, edited by Martin L. Wolf, Philosophical Library, New York, 1947.

André Gide: "My Mother," from *Autumn Leaves*, translated by Elsie Pell, Philosophical Library, New York, 1950.

Jean Giraudoux: "May on Lake Asquam," from *Campaigns and Intervals*, translated by Elizabeth S. Sargeant, reprinted by permission of Houghton Mifflin Co., Boston.

Johann Wolfgang von Goethe: *Faust*, translated by Sir Theodore Martin.

Nikolai Gogol: "St. John's Eve," from *Evenings on a Farm Near Dikanka*, reprinted from *Taras Bulba, and Other Tales*, Everyman's Library, by permission of E. P. Dutton & Co., New York.

Oliver Goldsmith: "The Disabled Soldier," from *Citizen of the World*, originally titled "Letter CXVIII."

Ivan Alexandrovich Goncharov: Selections from *Oblomof*, reprinted from *The Universal Anthology*, edited by Richard Garnett, Merrill & Baker, New York. (Copyright, 1899, by Richard Garnett.)

Maxim Gorky: "One Autumn Night," reprinted from *Best Russian Short Stories*, edited by Thomas Seltzer, reprinted by permission of Random House, New York.

Judah Halevi: Poems, translated by Emma Lazarus, reprinted from *A Golden Treasury of Jewish Literature*, edited by Leo W. Schwarz, Rinehart & Co., New York, reprinted by permission of Leo W. Schwarz. (Copyright, 1937, by Leo W. Schwarz.)

Knut Hamsun: "The Call of Life," translated by Anders Orbeck, from *Norway's Best Stories*, edited by Hanna Astrup Larsen, W. W. Norton & Co., New York. Reprinted by permission of the American-Scandinavian Foundation.

Thomas Hardy: "Squire Petrick's Lady," from *A Group of Noble Dames*, reprinted by permission of Harper & Brothers, New York. (Copyright, 1891.

Bret Harte: "The Outcasts of Poker Flat," reprinted from *The Luck of Roaring Camp*, by permission of Houghton Mifflin & Co., Boston. (Copyright, 1872.)

Gerhart Hauptmann: Selection from *The Weavers*, translated by Mary Morison, reprinted from *The Universal Anthology*, edited by Richard Garnett, Merrill & Baker, New York. (Copyright, 1899, by Richard Garnett.)

Nathaniel Hawthorne: "The Ambitious Guest," reprinted by permission of Houghton Mifflin Co., New York.

Johann Peter Hebel: "Kannitverstan," translated by Paul Pratt, reprinted by permission of Alfred A. Knopf, Inc., New York.

Heinrich Heine: Poems, translated by Sir Theodore Martin, and selections from *Memoirs*, translated by Gilbert Cannon.

Ernest Hemingway: "Ten Indians," from *Men Without Women*, reprinted by permission of Charles Scribner's Sons, New York. Copyright 1927 by Charles Scribner's Sons, 1955 by Ernest Hemingway.

O. Henry: "The Whirligig of Life," from *Whirligigs*, copyright, 1903, 1931, Doubleday, Doran & Co., New York.

Johann Gottfried von Herder: "Sir Olaf," translated by Elizabeth Craigmyle, "Esthonian Bridal Song," translated by W. Taylor, reprinted from *An Anthology of World Poetry*, edited by Mark Van Doren, Reynal & Hitchcock, New York. (Copyright, 1936.)

Hermann Hesse: Poems, translated by Margarete Münsterberg, reprinted from *The German Classics*, edited by Kuno Francke, The German Publication Society, New York.

Hitomaro Kakinomoto: Poems from *The Manyōshū*. Published for the Nippon Gakujutsu Shinkōkai by the Iwanami Shoten, Tokyo, 1940. "The Mountain Top" and "My Love Who Loves Me Not," translated by Mabel Lorenz Ives, from *Poems for Enjoyment*, ed. Elias Lieberman, Harper & Bros., New York.

Friedrich Hölderlin: Poems, translated by Charles Wharton Stork, reprinted from *The German Classics*, edited by Kuno Francke, The German Publication Society, New York.

Homer: Selection from *The Iliad*, translated by John Gibson Lockhart.

Horace: "Ode 1," translated by Charles Stuart Calverly, "Epode 2," translated by Sir Theodore Martin, reprinted from *The Universal Anthology*, edited by Richard Garnett, Merrill & Baker, New York. (Copyright, 1899, by Richard Garnett.)

Ricarda Huch: "Midnight," translated by Margarete Münsterberg, reprinted from *The German Classics*, edited by Kuno Francke, The German Publication Society, New York.

Victor Hugo: Selections from *Les Misérables*.

Henrik Ibsen: Scenes from *Peer Gynt*, translated by Horace Maynard Finney, published by Philosophical Library, New York.

Muhammad Iqbal: "Community," translated by A. J. Arberry, reprinted from *Mysteries of Selflessness*, by permission of John Murray, Ltd., London.

Jens Peter Jacobsen: "The Plague at Bergamo," reprinted from *Short Story Classics*, P. F. Collier & Son, New York, 1927.

Henry James: Selections from *Confidence*, reprinted by permission of Houghton, Mifflin & Co., Boston.

Jami: "Zulaikha," translated by R. T. H. Griffith, reprinted from *The Universal Anthology*, edited by Richard Garnett, Merrill & Baker, New York. (Copyright, 1899, by Richard Garnett.)

Jataka: "The Strider over Battle-Fields," from *Virtue Is Its Own Reward*, translated by H. C. Warren, reprinted from *Buddhism in Translations* by H. C. Warren, by permission of the Harvard University Press, Cambridge.

Jayadeva: "Hymn to Vishnu," from the *Gītā Govinda*, translated by Sir Edwin Arnold, reprinted from *An Anthology of World Poetry*, edited by Mark Van Doren, Reynal & Hitchcock, New York.

Juan Ramon Jiménez: "Fortunate Being" and "The Best That I Have," from *Ten Centuries of Spanish Poetry*, edited by Eleanor L. Turnbull, Johns Hopkins Press, Baltimore, reprinted by permission of the author. "Elegies," "The Diary of a Newly-Married Man," and "Stone and Heaven," translated by Thomas McGreevy, from *The European Caravan*, edited by Putnam, Darnton, Reavey & Bronowsky; Brewer, Warren & Putnam, New York; reprinted by permission of the author.

Maurus Jókai: Selections from *Timar's Two Worlds*, translated by Mrs. Hegan Kennard, published by Messrs. Blackwood, London.

James Joyce: "Araby," from *Dubliners*, included in *The Portable James Joyce*, copyright 1946, 1947, by The Viking Press, Inc., reprinted by permission of The Viking Press, New York.

Franz Kafka: "A Country Doctor," from *The Penal Colony*, translated by Willa and Edwin Muir, reprinted by permission of Schocken Books, Inc., New York.

Nagai Kafu: "The Bill-Collecting," translated by Torao Taketomo, reprinted from *Paulownia*, by permission of Dodd, Mead & Co., New York.

Kagawa Kageki: Poems from *Masterpieces of Japanese Poetry Ancient and Modern*, translated by Miyamori Asatarō, reprinted by permission of the Maruzen Co., Tokyo.

Kālidāsa: "The City of Ujjain," from *The Cloud Messenger*, translated by A. W. Ryder, reprinted from *A Garland of Indian Poetry*, edited by H. G. Rawlinson, by permission of the Royal Indian Society, London.

Gottfried Keller: "A Legend of the Dance," translated by Martin Wyness. reprinted from *Seven Legends*, Gowans & Gray, Glasgow. (Copyright, 1911.)

Omar Khayyam: Poems from the *Rubaiyat*, translated by Edward Fitzgerald.

Kan Kikuchi: "The Madman on the Roof," translated by Yozan T. Iwasaki and Glenn Hughes, reprinted from *Three Modern Japanese Plays* by permission of Appleton-Century-Crofts, Inc., New York. (Copyright, 1923, Stewart Kidd Co.)

Rudyard Kipling: "False Dawn," from *Plain Tales from the Hills*, reprinted by permission of Doubleday & Co., New York.

Joseph Kiss: "Jehovah," translated by William N. Lowe, reprinted from *Magyar Poetry*, Amerikai Magyar Nepszava, New York. (Copyright, 1908.)

Heinrich von Kleist: "The Beggar-Woman of Locarno," translated by E. N. Bennett, reprinted from *Selected German Short Stories* (*World's Classics*), by permission of Oxford University Press, London.

Vladimir Korolenko: "The Old Bell-Ringer," translated by Maxim Lieber, reprinted from "Great Short Stories of the World" edited by Clark and Lieber, Robert M. McBride Co., 1925. Reprinted by permission of the translator.

Zygmunt Krasinski: "A Legend," translated by Sarka Hrbkova, reprinted from *Great Stories of All Nations*, edited by Lieber and Williams. (Copyright. 1927, by Brentano's.)

Selma Lagerlöf: "The Eclipse," translated by Velma Swanston Howard, reprinted from the *American-Scandinavian Review* (December, 1922).

Lao Shê: "The Last Train," from *Contemporary Chinese Short Stories*, edited and translated by Yuan Chia-Hua and Robert Payne, reprinted by per-

Maurice Maeterlinck: "The Life of the Dead," from *The Great Beyond*, translated by Marta K. Neufeld & Renee Spodheim, Philosophical Library, New York, 1947.

Stéphane Mallarmé: "The Afternoon of a Faun," reprinted from *Modern French Poetry*, compiled and translated by Joseph T. Shipley, reprinted by permission of Greenberg Publishers, New York.

Thomas Mann: "A Weary Hour," translated by H. T. Lowe-Porter, from *Stories of Three Decades*, reprinted by permission of Alfred A. Knopf, Inc., New York. Copyright 1936 by Alfred A. Knopf, Inc.

Alessandro Manzoni: "The Interrupted Wedding," from *The Betrothed*.

John Masefield: "The Western Islands," from *A Mainsail Haul*, reprinted by permission of The Macmillan Co., New York. (Copyright, 1913.)

William Somerset Maugham: "The Pattern," from *Of Human Bondage*, reprinted by permission of Doubleday & Co., New York.

Guy de Maupassant: "The Necklace," translated by Jonathan Sturges, reprinted from *The Odd Number* by permission of Harper & Brothers, New York.

François Mauriac: "The Eternal Bourgeoise," from *Saint Margaret of Cortona*, translated by Bernard Frechtman, Philosophical Library, New York.

Mêng Hao-jan: Poems from *A Lute of Jade*, Wisdom of the East Series, edited by J. L. Cranmer-Byng, reprinted by permission of John Murray, Ltd., London.

George Meredith: "The Punishment of Shahpesh, the Persian, on Khipil, the Builder," from *The Shaving of Shagpat*. (Copyright, 1898, by Charles Scribner's Sons.)

Adam Mickiewicz: "Zevila," translated by Lola Gay-Tifft, from *The Blue Flower*, edited by Hermann Kesten, reprinted by permission of Roy Publishers, New York.

Edna St. Vincent Millay: "Elegy Before Death," from *Second April and Other Poems*, published by Harper & Brothers (copyright, 1920, 1948, by Edna St. Vincent Millay); "What Lips My Lips Have Kissed," from *The Harp-Weaver and Other Poems*; published by Harper & Bros. (copyright, 1920, 1948, by Edna St. Vincent Millay), reprinted by permission of Brandt & Brandt, agents for the estate of Edna St. Vincent Millay.

Molière: "First Lesson in Philosophy," from *The Bourgeois Gentleman*.

Mori Ogai: "The Pier," translated by Torao Taketomo, from *Paulownia*, reprinted by permission of Dodd Mead & Co., New York. (Copyright, 1918.)

Eduard Mörike: "Beauty Rohtraut," translated by George Meredith, reprinted by permission of Charles Scribner's Sons. Other poems, translated by Charles Wharton Stork, from *The German Classics, Masterpieces of German Literature*, edited by Kuno Francke, reprinted by permission of the German Publication Society, New York.

Multatuli: "The Story of Saïdjah," from *Max Havelaar*, translated by Alphonse Nahuys, reprinted by permission of Maatschappij der Nederlandse Letterkunde, Leiden, Holland.

Lady Murasaki: "The Festival of Red Leaves," from *The Tale of Genji*, translated by Arthur Waley, reprinted by permission of Houghton Mifflin Co., Boston.

Alexander Sergeyevich Pushkin: Poems, from *Poems from the Russian*, translated by Frances Cornford and Esther Polianowski Salaman, reprinted by permission of Faber & Faber Ltd., London.

François Rabelais: "The Lost Hatchet," from *Gargantua and Pantagruel*. (Copyright, 1899.)

Jean Baptiste Racine: "Orestes and Hermione," from *Andromaque*.

Jean Paul Richter: "The New-Year's Night of an Unhappy Man," from *The Death of an Angel*, translated by A. Kenney, Black and Armstrong, London, 1839.

Rainer Maria Rilke: Poems, from *Contemporary German Poetry*, translated by Jethro Bithell, Walter Scott Publishing Company, New York, 1909.

Jean Arthur Rimbaud: Poems, from *Modern French Poetry*, translated by Joseph T. Shipley, reprinted by permission of Greenberg, New York.

Edwin Arlington Robinson: Poems, from *Collected Poems*, reprinted by permission of The Macmillan Company, New York.

Romain Rolland: "The Trap," from *Journey Within*, translated by Elsie Pell, Philosophical Library, New York.

Pierre de Ronsard: "The Rose" and "Of His Lady's Old Age," translated by Andrew Lang; "Welcome to Spring," translated by H. F. Carey, reprinted from *The Universal Anthology* edited by Richard Garnett, Merrill & Baker, New York. (Copyright, 1899, by Richard Garnett.)

Edmond Rostand: Poems, from *Modern French Poetry*, translated by Joseph T. Shipley, reprinted by permission of Greenberg, New York.

Sa'di: "The Gulistan," translated by Sir Edwin Arnold, reprinted by permission of Harper & Brothers, New York.

Priest Saigyō: Poems, from *Masterpieces of Japanese Poetry, Ancient and Modern*, translated by Miyamori Asataro, reprinted by permission of Tasei-Do Shobo Co., Kobe, Japan.

George Sand: "The Ploughman and His Child," from *The Devil's Pool*. (Copyright, 1900.)

Carl Sandburg: Selection from *The People, Yes*, reprinted by permission of Harcourt, Brace & Co., New York. (Copyright, 1936.)

George Santayana: From *Poems*, copyright 1923 by Charles Scribner's Sons, 1951 by George Santayana. Reprinted by permission of the publishers.

Sappho: "Hymn to Aphrodite," translations by Henry T. Wharton, J. H. Merivale, J. A. Symonds, and Francis T. Palgrave; reprinted from *The Universal Anthology*, edited by Richard Garnett, Merrill & Baker, New York. (Copyright, 1899, by Richard Garnett.)

Jean-Paul Sartre: "The Wall," from *The Wall and Other Stories*, translated by Lloyd Alexander, reprinted by permission of New Directions, Norfolk.

Friedrich von Schiller: "William Tell and the Tyrant," from *William Tell*. (Copyright, 1900.)

Arthur Schnitzler: "Flowers," reprinted from *Great Stories of all Nations*, edited by Lieber and Williams, Coward-McCann Inc., New York, 1927.

Sir Walter Scott: "The Nubian," from *The Talisman*.

Se'ami: "Sotoba Komachi," translated by Sam Houston Brock, reprinted by permission of the *New Mexico Quarterly*, Albuquerque.

Sei Shōnagon: "A Cuckoo Picnic" and "The Aritōshi Shrine," from *The Sketch Book of the Lady Sei Shonagon*, translated by Nobuko Kobayashi, reprinted by permission of John Murray, Ltd., London.

Mendele Mocher Sforim: Selection from *The Nag,* translated by Moshe Spiegel, reprinted by permission of the Beechhurst Press, New York.

George Bernard Shaw: "The Miraculous Revenge," from *Short Stories, Scraps, and Shavings,* reprinted from *44 Irish Short Stories,* edited by Devin A. Garrity by permission of Devin-Adair Co., New York.

Shên Ts'ung-wên: "Under Cover of Darkness," from *Contemporary Chinese Short Stories,* edited and translated by Yuan Chia-Hua and Robert Payne, reprinted by permission of Noel Carrington, Transatlantic Arts Co., Ltd., London.

Shih Nai-an: "Death of the Tigers," from *All Men Are Brothers,* translated by Pearl S. Buck, reprinted by permission of the John Day Company, New York. (Copyright, 1937, by Pearl S. Buck.)

Henryk Sienkiewicz: "The Lighthouse Keeper of Aspinwall," from *Yanko the Musician,* translated by Jeremiah Curtin, Little, Brown & Co., Boston. (Copyright, 1893.)

Solomon: Selection from "The Song of Solomon," from the King James Version of the Bible.

Somadeva: "Devasmita," from the *Katha-sarit-sagara,* reprinted from *Great Stories of All Nations,* edited by Lieber and Williams, Coward-McCann Inc., New York. (Copyright, 1927, by Brentano's.)

Sophocles: Selections from *Antigone* and *Oedipus Tyrannus.* (Copyright, 1900.)

Carl Spitteler: "Theme" and "Heracles' Passing to Earth" from "Olympian Spring," translated by Margarete Münsterberg, from *The German Classics, Masterpieces of German Literature,* edited by Kuno Francke, reprinted by permission of the German Publication Society, New York.

Ssü-k'ung T'u: Poems, from *A Lute of Jade,* translated by L. Cranmer-Byng, reprinted by permission of John Murray, Ltd., London.

John Steinbeck: "Owners and Tenants," from *The Grapes of Wrath,* reprinted by permission of The Viking Press, Inc., New York. (Copyright, 1939, by John Steinbeck.)

Stendhal: Selections from *Chartreuse of Parma,* from *The World's Greatest Books,* edited by Lord Northcliffe, and S. S. McClure, McKinlay, Stone and Mackenzie. (Copyright, 1910, by S. S. McClure Co.)

Wallace Stevens: "Domination of Black" and "Anecdote of the Jar," from *Harmonium;* "An Extract," from *Parts of a World;* reprinted by permission of Alfred A. Knopf, Inc., New York.

Robert Louis Stevenson: "Thrawn Janet," from *The Merry Men.*

Theodor Storm: "Veronika," translated by Charles H. Stubing from Storm's *Sämtliche Schriften* (Braunschweig: G. Westermann, 1868). "To a Deceased," "The City," and "The Heath," translated by Margarete Münsterberg, and "Consolation," translated by Charles Wharton Stork, reprinted from *The German Classics of the Nineteenth and Twentieth Centuries,* edited by Kuno Francke and William Guild Howard, German Publication Society, New York.

Harriet Beecher Stowe: "Topsy," from *Uncle Tom's Cabin.*

August Strindberg: "A Funeral," reprinted from *The German Lieutenant and other Stories,* by permission of T. Werner Laurie, Ltd., London.

Sūdraka: "The Clay Cart," translated by Sir Monier Monier-Williams, reprinted from *The Universal Anthology*, edited by Richard Garnett, Merrill & Baker, New York. (Copyright, 1899, by Richard Garnett.)

Sun Hsi-chen: "Ah Ao," translated by Edgar Snow, from *Living China*, reprinted by permission of the translator.

Su Tung-p'o: "Autumn Sun," from *Selections from the Works of Su Tung-p'o*, translated by Cyril Drummond Le Gros Clark, reprinted by permission of Jonathan Cape Ltd., London.

Jonathan Swift: "The Emperor of Lilliput," from *Gulliver's Travels.*

Algernon Charles Swinburne: "When the Hounds of Spring," and "Man," from *Atalanta in Calydon.*

Rabindranath Tagore: "To Nature," from *Sheaves, Poems and Songs by Rabindranath Tagore*, translated by Nagendranath Gupta, Philosophical Library, New York.

Junichirō Tanizaki: Selection from *Some Prefer Nettles*, translated by Edward G. Seidensticker, reprinted by permission of Alfred A. Knopf, Inc., New York.

T'ao Ch'ien: "Returning to Live on the Farm," from *The Poems of T'ao Ch'ien*, translated by Lily Pao-hu Chang and Marjorie Sinclair, reprinted by permission of the University of Hawaii Press, Honolulu.

Torquato Tasso: "The Golden Age," from *Aminta*, reprinted from *The Universal Anthology*, edited by Richard Garnett, Merrill & Baker, New York. (Copyright, 1899, by Richard Garnett.)

Johann Ludwig Tieck: "The Friends," from *Tales from Phantasus*, James Burns, London, 1845.

Leo Tolstoy: "Where Love Is," from *Master and Man and Other Parables and Tales*, reprinted by permission of E. P. Dutton & Co., New York. (Translated, 1885.)

Tu Fu: "The Poet Dreams" translated by Peter Rudolph from translation of Judith Gautier; from *Chinese Love Poems*, Peter Pauper Press, Mt. Vernon, N. Y. Other poems from *Chinese Love Poems* translated by Mabel Lorenz Ives; published by B. L. Hutchinson, Upper Montclair, N. J.

Ivan Sergeyevich Turgenev: "The Nihilist," from *Fathers and Sons.* (Copyright, 1900.)

Mark Twain: "The Celebrated Jumping Frog of Calaveras County." (Copyright, American Publishing Co.)

Miguel de Unamuno: "Three Generations," from *Perplexities and Paradoxes*, translated by Stuart Gross, Philosophical Library, New York.

Paul Valéry: Poems, from *Modern French Poetry*, compiled and translated by Joseph T. Shipley, reprinted by permission of Greenberg, New York.

Vālmīki: "Nārad," from *Selections from the Rāmāyana*, from *Hindu Literature*, P. F. Collier & Son, New York. (Copyright, 1900, by The Colonial Press.)

Giovanni Verga: "Gramigna's Mistress.' (Copyright, 1900.)

Emile Verhaeren: Poems, from *Modern French Poetry*, compiled and translated by Joseph T. Shipley, reprinted by permission of Greenberg, New York.

Paul Verlaine: Poems, from *Modern French Poetry*, compiled and translated by Joseph T. Shipley, reprinted by permission of Greenberg, New York.

1449

Jules Verne: "The Bottom of the Sea," from *Twenty Thousand Leagues Under the Sea.* (Copyright, 1900.)

François Villon: Poems. (Copyright, 1900.)

Virgil: "Eclogue IV: 'The Messiah'," translated by John Dryden.

Wang Wei: "Best Happiness of All," translated by Peter Randolph, from *Chinese Love Poems,* Peter Pauper Press, Mt. Vernon, reprinted by permission of Peter Bulem and Edna Beilenson. "On a Dark Autumn In a Hill Hut" and "The Peach Garden," translated by Soame Jenyns, from *Selections from the Three Hundred Poems of the T'ang Dynasty,* reprinted by permission of John Murray, Ltd., London.

Jakob Wassermann: "The Beast," from *Der Geist des Pilgers,* reprinted by permission of the estate of Jakob Wassermann.

Franz Werfel: "Theologoumena," from *Between Heaven and Earth,* translated by Maxim Newmark, Philosophical Library, New York.

Christoph Martin Wieland: "Sir Huon Enters the Sultan's Palace," from *Oberon.* (Copyright, 1900.)

Oscar Wilde: "The Selfish Giant," from *The Happy Prince and Other Tales,* London, 1885.

Yamanoe No Okura: Pcems, from *The Manyōshū,* published for the Nippon Gakujutsu Shinkōkai by the Iwanami Shoten, 1940, reprinted by permission of the Iwanami Shoten, Tokyo.

William Butler Yeats: "An Irish Airman Foresees His Death," "An Appointment" and "The Rose Tree," from *Collected Poems of W. B. Yeats;* "Come Gather Round Me, Parnellites," from *Last Poems and Plays:* reprinted by permission of The Macmillan Co., New York.

Émile Zola: "A Fight with Flails," from *La Terre.* (Copyright, 1900.)

Arnold Zweig: "The Apparition," from *Playthings of Time,* translated by Emma D. Ashton, reprinted by permission of The Viking Press, Inc., New York. (Copyright, 1935, by The Viking Press, Inc.)